Garage Sale & Flea Market

Annual

TENTH EDITION
CASHING IN ON TODAY'S LUCRATIVE COLLECTIBLES MARKET

COLLECTOR BOOKS

A Division of Schroeder Publishing Co., Inc.

Front cover:

Kelloggs Crackle doll, MIB, $55.00; Pop and Snap, loose, each $24.00.
Holt Howard letter opener, Kozy Kitten, $45.00 – 60.00. Chinese tin,
#MF330, Cadillac sedan, current, 11x4x3", $15.00 – 35.00. Head vace, Alice
in Wonderland, Enesco, 1950s, $450.00. Depression glass, pink Manhattan
footed tumbler, 5¼", $22.00. Red Wing vase, #1356, 7½", 1940s, $32.00–
42.00. Skipper, bendable legs, 1965, MIB, $350.00 – 400.00.

Cover design by Beth Summers
Book design by Karen Smith and Beth Ray

COLLECTOR BOOKS
P.O. Box 3009
Paducah, Kentucky 42002-3009
www.collectorbooks.com

Copyright © 2002 Schroeder Publishing Co.

The current values in this book should be used only as a guide. They are not intended to set prices, which vary from one section of the country to another. Auction prices as well as dealer prices vary greatly and are affected by condition as well as demand. Neither the editors nor the publisher assumes responsibility for any losses that might be incurred as a result of consulting this guide.

Searching For A Publisher?

We are always looking for people knowledgeable within their fields. If you feel that there is a real need for a book on your collectible subject and have a large comprehensive collection, contact Collector Books.

A Word From the Editor

The lives of all Americans have been changed since the tragedies of September 11. We can only shake our heads in disbelief that such schemes could come from the minds of human beings. Clearly and without comparison the greatest losses were and are being suffered by the family and friends of the thousands of victims whose lives have been taken from them, directly or indirectly, by the actions of these despicable terrorists. I know you all join with me in praying that God will continue to sustain these brave Americans who have to deal with their grief on a day-to-day basis.

Most of us are now CNN 'junkies.' Two or three times a day we tune in, hoping only to see what has now become the routine — White House briefings with the media asking the same questions over and over, anthrax warnings, or reports on daily bombing runs. What we dread is 'breaking news.' The economy is suffering, all the way from the giant industries of transportation and finance down to the smallest private business. Thousands have lost their jobs, many have lost their homes, and fortunes that were won on the stock market have all but disappeared. Very importantly, we have lost our sense of security. But we are a resilient society, and Americans have banded together to fight back, to regain what we have lost, and we will. We have seen recessions before and know that they have always been followed by economic prosperity, and so will this one.

Even before the September 11 tragedy, we in the antiques and collectibles arena had recognized that changes were occurring. EBay had become the primary Internet auction, every day offering a staggering volume of items for sale. The balance of supply and demand was affected. There were no 'pickers'; everyone had become a dealer. Many were willing to turn a quick profit — buying at weekend garage sales and selling to the high bidder a few days later, often oblivious and uncaring in regard to established values. Some items did well to bring 75% of what they once did. But buyers were happy, so were sellers. As one of our advisors so aptly put it: (the Internet) 'illustrates the forces at work which bring to the entire globe a giant worldwide flea market economy...the collectible landscape has changed forever.'

'Sounds gloomy,' you say? Not at all. As devastating as we perceive forest fires, soon the burned-out region begins to flourish. Out of the ashes comes regrowth, fertilized by the potash that remains there. The market is self-perpetuating as well. The high prices of a few years ago discouraged new collectors and kept show attendance in check. As prices on many items soften, younger collectors are finding they can afford to become interested, and a new generation emerges on the scene. Thus the viability of the antiques and collectibles market is guaranteed.

We are encouraged these days by government spokespersons to adapt to the 'new normalcy.' New awareness and caution, having to comply with more restrictions and security procedures, and needing to become more patient to do all this. What we really yearn for is the 'old normalcy.' Obviously, that is no more, and may never be again. But we can hang on to our identities and to the things we fill our free time with that define our individuality. Without that, there is no normalcy.

On the garage sale level, we found this an especially competitive summer. College students and newlyweds have learned they can literally furnish their homes and apartments on a shoestring. And shop-a-holics can still get their 'fix' without wrecking the family budget. So we veteran garage salers have to get up and out pretty early in the morning if we're going to bring home any treasures. Still we managed to find good saleable merchandise that will bring a good margin of profit when we sell it on the next level, perhaps at the flea market — if not there, then eBay. (We didn't 'do' the fall flea market this year. If you read last year's edition, you may remember that we had a particularly good summer, realizing a profit of more than $5,000.00. Since we celebrated our 35th wedding anniversary this past August, we used the money we made to put toward our dream trip — not Hawaii, not a Caribbean cruise, but a caribou hunt in Newfoundland! It was great, but timing didn't permit us to do the flea market as well.) I did sell some of our more exiting buys on eBay as we found them: a forest green and milk glass Anchor Hocking relish tray mint in the box realized $80.00 (we paid $3.00); a Fiesta Kitchen Kraft spoon in cobalt went for around $90.00 (it cost us $1.00); a Paul Revere handled plate brought a little over $100.00 (our price: 75¢); a partial set of ironstone dinnerware sold for ten times our purchase price of $15.00; and we sold a wonderful Marshall Studio tile-top coffee table for $200.00, giving us a profit of $75.00 on that item. Other goodies we've yet to sell include a Hull vase, a Rogers Brothers silver-plated tea service in the First Love pattern, a beautiful Fenton cranberry Coin Spot water set, a service of Noritake china, some pewter, hammered aluminum, a few Star Wars items, some character collectibles, and many other nice odds and ends.

Though the market has been forever altered and revamped, structure is still a necessary factor in its existence. For the person who wants to be a successful collector or dealer, having an understanding of the marketplace is not an option. Knowing what any given item went for on eBay last week is not enough. Whether you regard it as a hobby or a serious money-making opportunity, you must become knowledgeable to succeed. Use this book to make it work for you. It will serve as a tool to educate you toward becoming a wise garage sale and flea market shopper.

As usual, this year's edition touches on several new categories. If you're into garage sale shopping, you know that competition is fierce. You'll have a definite advantage over the average shopper if you'll first take the time to become familiar with new areas of activity. The key is knowledge. We'll suggest references for in-depth study, all written by by today's leading experts. We're going to zero in on items from the 1940s on, since that's where the market's activity is strongest today. We'll list clubs and newsletters related to many specific areas; we recommend all of them very highly. There is much knowledge to be gleaned by working through clubs with collectors whose interests are similar to yours. Tradepapers are listed as well; they contain a wealth of timely information. If you're not already subscribing, see about getting sample copies. A quick search of the web will offer up several connections to your subject.

An exclusive feature of this book is the section called Special Interests. It contains the addresses of authors, collectors, and dealers sorted by specific collectible categories. Not only are these people potential buyers, but under most circumstances, they'll be willing to help you with questions that remain after you've made a honest attempt at your own research. Just remember if you do write one of our people, you will have to include an SASE

if you want a response. And if you call, please consider the differences in time zones. But first, please, read the text. Then go to your library; you should be able to find most of the books we reference. Check them out for study — they're all wonderful. Buy the ones you find particularly helpful or interesting; good books soon pay for themselves many times over.

If you'd like to collect some nice pieces to decorate your home, as more and more people are doing, or if you're interested in becoming a dealer but find there's no room in the budget for extra spending, we'll show you how to earn extra money by holding your own garage sale. And we'll give you some timely pointers on how to set up at your first flea market.

Remember that our prices in no way reflect what you will be paying at garage sales. Our values are well established and generally accepted by seasoned collectors and authorities; they have been checked over before publication by people well versed in their particular fields.

How to Hold Your Own Garage Sale

Just as we promised we would, here are our suggestions for holding your own garage sale. If you're toying with the idea of getting involved in the business of buying and selling antiques and collectibles but find yourself short of any extra cash to back your venture, this is the way we always recommend you get started. Everyone has items they no longer use; get rid of them! Use them to your advantage. Here's how.

Get Organized. Gather up your merchandise. Though there's not a lot of money in selling clothing, this is the perfect time to unload things you're not using. Kids' clothing does best, since it's usually outgrown before it's worn out, and there's a lot of budget-minded parents who realize this and think it makes good sense to invest as little as possible in their own children's wardrobes. Everything should of course be clean and relatively unwrinkled to sell at all, and try to get the better items on hangers.

Leave no stone unturned. Clean out the attic, the basement, the garage — then your parent's attic, basement, and garage. If you're really into it, bake cookies, make some crafts. Divide your house plants; pot the starts in attractive little containers — ladies love 'em. Discarded and outgrown toys sell well. Framed prints and silk flower arrangements you no longer use, recipe books and paperbacks, tapes, records, and that kitchen appliance that's more trouble to store than it's worth can be turned into cash to get you off and running!

After you've gathered up your merchandise, you'll need to price it. Realistically, clothing will bring at the most about 15% to 25% of what you had to pay for it, if it's still in excellent, ready-to-wear shape and basically still in style. There are tons of used clothing out there, and no one is going to buy much of anything with buttons missing or otherwise showing signs of wear. If you have good brand-name clothing that has been worn very little, you would probably do better by taking it to a resale or consignment shop. They normally price things at about one-third of retail, with their cut being 30% of that. Not much difference money-wise, but the garage-sale shopper that passes up that $150.00 suit you're asking $25.00 for will probably give $50.00 for it at the consignment shop, simply because like department stores, many have dressing rooms with mirrors so you can try things on and check them for fit before you buy. Even at $25.00, the suit is no bargain if it doesn't fit when you get it home.

Remember that garage-sale buyers expect to find low prices. Depending on how long you plan on staying open, you'll have one day, possibly two to move everything. If you start out too high, you'll probably be stuck with a lot of leftover merchandise, most of which you've already decided is worthless to you. The majority of your better buyers will hit early on; make prices attractive to them and you'll do all right. If you come up with some 'low-end' collectibles — fast-food toys, character glasses, played-with action figures, etc. — don't expect to get much out of them at a garage sale. Your competition down the block may underprice you. But if you have a few things you think have good resale potential, offer them at about half of 'book' price. If they don't sell at your garage sale, take them to a flea market or a consignment shop. You'll probably find they sell better on that level, since people expect to find prices higher there than at garage sales.

You can use pressure-sensitive labels or masking tape for price tags on many items. But *please* do not use either of these on things where damage is likely to occur when they are removed. For instance (as one reader pointed out), on boxes containing toys, board games, puzzles, etc.; on record labels or album covers; or on ceramics or glass with gold trim or unfired, painted decoration. Unless a friend or a neighbor is going in on the sale with you, price tags won't have to be removed; the profit will all be yours. Of course, you'll have to keep tabs if others are involved. You can use a sheet of paper divided into columns, one for each of you, and write the amount of each sale down under the appropriate person's name, or remove the tags and restick them on a piece of poster board, one for each seller. I've even seen people use straight pins to attach small paper price tags which they remove and separate into plastic butter tubs. When several go together to have a sale, the extra help is nice, but don't let things get out of hand. Your sale can get *too* big. Things become too congested, and it's hard to display so much merchandise to good advantage.

Advertise. Place your ad in your local paper or on your town's cable TV information channel. It's important to make your ad interesting and upbeat. Though most sales usually start early on Friday or Saturday mornings, some people are now holding their sales in the early evening, and they seem to be having good crowds. This gives people with day jobs an opportunity to attend. You *might* want to hold your sale for two days, but you'll do 90% of your selling during the first two or three hours, and a two-day sale can really drag on. Make signs — smaller ones for street corners near your home to help direct passers-by, and a large one for your yard. You might even want to make another saying 'Clothing ½-Price after 12:00.' (It'll cut way down on leftovers that you'll otherwise have to dispose of yourself.) Be sure that you use a wide-tipped felt marker and print in letters big enough that the signs can be read from the street. Put the smaller signs up a few days in advance unless you're expecting rain. (If you are, you might want to include a rain date in your advertising unless your sale will be held under roof.) Make sure you have a lot of boxes and bags and plenty of change. If you price your items in increments of 25¢, you won't need anything but a few rolls of quarters, maybe ten or fifteen ones, and a few five-dollar bills. Then on the day of the sale, put the large sign up in a prominent place out front with some balloons to attract the crowd. Take a deep breath, brace yourself, and raise the garage door!

What to Do With What's Left. After the sale, pack up any good collectibles that didn't sell. Think about that consignment shop or setting up at a flea market. (We'll talk about that later on.) Sort out the better items of clothing for Goodwill or a similar charity, unless your city has someone who will take your leftovers and sell them on consignment. This is a fairly new concept, but some of the larger cities have such 'bargain centers.'

Learning to Become a Successful Bargain Hunter

Let me assure you, anyone who takes the time to become an informed, experienced bargain hunter will be successful. There is enough good merchandise out there to make it well worthwhile, at all levels. Once you learn what to look for, what has good resale potential, and what price these items will probably bring for you, you'll be equipped and ready for any hunting trip. You'll be the one to find treasures. They are out there!

Garage sales are absolutely wonderful for finding bargains. But you'll have to get up early! Even non-collectors can spot quality merchandise, and at those low garage sale prices (low unless of course held by an owner who's done his homework) those items will be the first to move.

In order for you to be a successful garage sale shopper, you have to learn how to get yourself organized. It's important to conserve your time. The sales you hit during the first early-morning hour will prove to be the best nine times out of ten, so you must have a plan before you ever leave home. Plot your course. Your local paper will have a section on garage sale ads, and local cable TV channels may also carry garage sale advertising. Most people hold their sales on the weekend, but some may start earlier in the week, so be sure to turn to the 'Garage Sales' ads daily. Write them down and try to organize them by areas — northwest, northeast, etc. At first, you'll probably need your city map, but you'll be surprised at how quickly the streets will become familiar to you. Upper middle-class neighborhoods generally have the best sales and the best merchandise, so concentrate on those areas, though sales in older areas may offer older items. (Here's where you have to interpret those sale ads.) When you've decided where you want to start, go early! If the ad says 8:00, be there at 7:00. This may seem rude and pushy, but if you can bring yourself to do it, it will pay off. And chances are when you get there an hour early, you'll not be their first customer. If they're obviously not ready for business, just politely inquire if you may look. If you're charming and their nerves aren't completely frayed from trying to get things ready, chances are they won't mind.

Competition can be fierce during those important early-morning hours. Learn to scan the tables quickly, then move to the area that looks the most promising. Don't be afraid to ask for a better price if you feel it's too high, but most people have already priced garage sale merchandise so that it will sell. Keep a notebook to jot down items you didn't buy the first time around but think you might be interested in if the price were reduced later on. After going through dozens of sales (I've done as many as thirty or so in one morning), you won't remember where you saw what! Often by noon, at least by mid-afternoon, veteran garage sale buyers are finished with their rounds and attendance becomes very thin. Owners are usually much more receptive to the idea of lowering their prices, so it may pay you to make a second pass. In fact, some people find it advantageous to go to the better sales on the last day as well as the first. They'll make an offer for everything that's left, and since most of the time the owner is about ready to *pay* someone to take it at that point, they can usually name their price. Although most of the collectibles will normally be gone at this point, there are nearly always some useable household items and several pieces of good, serviceable clothing left. The household items will sell at flea markets or consignment shops, and if there are worthwhile clothing items, take them to a resale boutique. They'll either charge the 30% commission fee or buy the items outright for about half of the amount they feel they can ask, a new practice some resale shops are beginning to follow. Because they want only clothing that is in style, in season, and like new, their prices may be a little higher than others shops, so half of that asking price is a good deal.

Tag sales are common in the larger cities. They are normally held in lieu of an auction, when estates are being dispersed, or when families are moving. Sometimes only a few buyers are admitted at one time, and as one leaves another is allowed to take his place. So just as is true with garage sales, the early bird gets the goodies. Really serious shoppers begin to arrive as much as an hour or two before the scheduled opening time. I know of one who will spend the night in his van and camp on the 'doorstep' if he thinks the sale is especially promising. And he can tell you fantastic success stories! But since it's customary to have tag sale items appraised before values are set, be prepared to pay higher prices. That's not to say, though, that you won't find bargains here. If you think an item is overpriced, leave a bid. Just don't forget to follow through on it, since if it doesn't sell at their asking price, they may end up holding it for you. It's a good idea to check back on the last day of the sale. Often the prices on unsold items may have been drastically reduced.

Auctions can go either way. Depending on the crowd and what items are for sale, you can sometimes spend all day and never be able to buy anything anywhere near 'book' price. Better items often go high. On the other hand, there are often 'sleepers' that can be bought cheaply enough to resell at a good profit. Toys, dolls, Hummels, Royal Doultons, banks, cut glass, and other 'high-profile' collectibles usually sell well, but white ironstone, dinnerware sets from the '20s through the '50s, silver-plated hollow ware, books, records, and linens, for instance, often pass relatively unnoticed by the majority of the buyers.

If there is a consignment auction house in your area, check it out. These are usually operated by local auctioneers, and the sales they hold in-house often involve low-income estates. You won't find something every time, so try to investigate the merchandise ahead of schedule to see if it's going to be worth your time to attend. Competition is probably less at one of these than any of the other types of sales we've mentioned, and wonderful

buys have been made from time to time.

Flea markets are often wonderful places to find bargains. I don't like the small ones — not that I don't find anything there, but I've learned to move through them so fast (to get ahead of the crowd), I don't get my 'fix'; I just leave wanting more. If you've never been to a large flea market, you don't know what you're missing. Even if you're not a born-again collector, I guarantee you will love it. And they're excellent places to study the market. You'll be able to see where the buying activity is; you can check and compare prices, talk with dealers and collectors, and do hands-on inspections. I've found that if I first study a particular subject by reading a book or a magazine article, this type of exposure to that collectible really 'locks in' what I have learned.

Because there are many types of flea market dealers, there are plenty of bargains. The casual, once-in-a-while dealer may not always keep up with changing market values. Some of them simply price their items by what they themselves had to pay for it. Just as being early at garage sales is important, here it's a must. If you've ever been in line waiting for a flea market to open, you know that cars are often backed up for several blocks, and people will be standing in line waiting to be admitted hours before the gate opens. Browsers? Window shoppers? Not likely. Competition! So if you're going to have a chance at all, you'd better be in line yourself. Take a partner and split up on the first pass so that you can cover the grounds more quickly. It's a common sight to see the serious buyers conversing with their partners via walkie-talkies, and if you like to discuss possible purchases with each other before you actually buy, this is a good way to do it.

Learn to bargain with dealers. Their prices are usually negotiable, and most will come down by 10% to 20%. Be polite and fair, and you can expect the same treatment in return. Unpriced items are harder to deal for. I have no problem offering to give $8.00 if an item is marked $10.00, but it's difficult for me to have to ask the price and then make a counter offer. So I'll just say 'This isn't marked. Will you take...?' I'm not an aggressive barterer, so this works for me.

There are so many reproductions on the flea market level (and at malls and co-ops), that you need to be suspicious of anything that looks too new! Some fields of collecting have been especially hard hit. Whenever a collectible becomes so much in demand that prices are high, reproductions are bound to make an appearance. For instance, Black Americana, Nippon, Roseville, banks, toys of all types, teddy bears, lamps, glassware, doorstops, cookie jars, prints, advertising items, and many other fields have been especially vulnerable. Learn to check for telltale signs — paint that is too bright, joints that don't fit, variations in sizes or colors, creases in paper that you can see but not feel, and so on. Remember that zip codes have been used only since 1963, and this can sometimes help you date an item in question. Check glassware for areas of wavy irregularities often seen in new glass. A publication we would highly recommend to you is called *Antique and Collector Reproduction News*, a monthly report of 'Fakes, Frauds, and Facts.' To subscribe, call 1-800-227-5531. You can find them on the web at repronews.com. Rates are very reasonable compared to the money you may save by learning to recognize reproductions.

Antique malls and co-ops should be visited on a regular basis. Many mall dealers restock day after day, and traffic and buying competition is usually fierce. As a rule, you won't often find great bargains here; what you do save on is time. And if time is what you're short of, you'll be able to see a lot of good merchandise under one roof, on display by people who've already done the leg work and invested *their* time, hence the higher prices. But there are always underpriced items as well, and if you've taken the time to do your homework, you'll be able to spot them right away.

Unless the dealer who rents the booth happens to be there, though, mall and co-op prices are usually firm. But often times they'll run sales — '20% off everything in booth #101.' If you have a dealer's license, and you really should get one, most will give you a courtesy 10% discount on items over $10.00, unless you want to pay with a credit card.

Antique shows are exciting to visit, but obviously if a dealer is paying several hundred dollars to set up for a three-day show, he's going to be asking top price to offset expenses. So even though bargains will be few, the merchandise is usually superior, and you may be able to find that special item you've been looking for.

Mail order buying is not only very easy, but most of the time economical as well. Many people will place an ad in 'For Sale' sections of tradepapers. Some will describe and price their merchandise in their ad, while others offer lists of items they have in exchange for a SASE (stamped, self-addressed envelope). You're out no gas or food expenses, their overhead is minimal so their prices are usually very reasonable, so it works out great for both buyer and seller. I've made a lot of good buys this way, and I've always been fairly and honestly dealt with. You may want to send a money order or cashier's check to save time, otherwise (especially on transactions involving larger sums of money) the seller might want to wait until your personal check clears.

Goodwill stores and re-sale shops are usually listed in the telephone book. When you travel, it will pay you to check them out. If there's one in your area, visit it often. You never know what may turn up there.

Internet shopping is, of course, the big thing today. There are set-price antique malls and online auctions. The great thing is the fact that there will be a higher concentration of your specific collectible interest available to you at the click of a mouse than you will ever find under one roof anywhere else. It's collectibles heaven. I've been able to buy items I didn't even know existed right from my own swivel chair. I haven't found things to be any more expensive than they would be from the other sources we've mentioned; in fact, I feel that some of my purchases have been real bargains. In every collecting category, there will always be those extremely rare and desirable pieces where the sky is the limit, and when such an item comes up for bid, I've seen some astronomical prices realized, but this has always been true, well before online shopping.

What's Hot on Today's Market

Last year we told you that the market was changing, and by now, of course, it has become obvious to us all that it certainly has, and we have yet to see the outcome. The Internet is generally termed the villain in this metamorphoses. The balance of supply and demand has been thrown out of kilter, as we say here in the Midwest. With the click of a mouse, we can access thousands of items in minutes. Don't like the price? Wait on one less expensive, it will come along. Many Internet sellers are weekend shoppers simply looking for a quick turnover. They know how the game works and don't expect to get book price. The slow-down of the economy is another culprit. Hardest hit is middle-class America, primarily those who buy the types of collectibles we deal with in this publication. Purse strings have been drawn a little tighter. Many of us are concentrating more on necessary expenses and trying to conserve. We tend to indulge our whims a little less often. Demand is down, the supply is not, and as a result, prices in some areas have softened. In most cases, except for top-of-the-line examples, sales of products from the past twenty years have come to a screeching halt. Conversely, though, quality, vintage merchandise continues to hold its own, with selling prices often showing increases. Rarities and high-end items always sell well, since there are so few of them around to meet the demands of well-to-do collectors who always have money to spend. We're still caught mid-way in this chain of events, but change is a natural evolution of our lives, and we always emerge on the other side wiser, more savvy, and in control. We will this time. So for now, we'll do our best to let you know what items are strongest in each area mentioned below.

Toys. Good toys are consistently 'hot.' Good robots and space toys from the '50s and '60s can command prices ranging from several hundred to several thousand dollars. Mr. Atomic by Yonezawa for Linemar can easily bring in excess of $15,000.00 mint in the box. Sales for toy soldiers made by companies such as Barclay, Britains, Manoil, and Grey Iron are strong. Rock 'n Roll/TV show/character memorabilia continues to sell well. GI Joe collectibles haven't faltered; the original figures range from $300.00 up to $800.00 and more. GI Joe dealers tell us collector interest is still high. Vintage Barbie dolls very often realize prices exceeding $500.00 at McMaster's. In fact, don't be surprised to hear that a #1 Barbie still mint and in the original box may go as high as $6,500.00! (Some of the newer Barbie dolls have cooled down because collectors are finding themselves overwhelmed with an over abundance of dolls who vary only in the color of their hair.) Older pressed-steel and cast-iron toys have recently seen record-breaking final bids at auction. An Arcade Yellow Cab Baggage Express Truck by Arcade in very good condition brought $12,000.00 at a recent Bertoia auction, and good Buddy L toys chalked up hammer prices of $2,000.00 up to more than $6,000.00. The Beanie Baby market is flailing to an extent but still has a devoted following, and high-end prices though down are still amazing.

Pottery and Porcelain. As always, good American pottery is a solid investment. Roseville seems to have been virtually unscathed by all the Chinese reproductions that have flooded the market for the past several years, and prices continue to climb. Rookwood will always be solid; even production Rookwood prices are amazing. For a large and unique piece by a well-known artist, you may find it necessary to pay as much as you might for a new car (or even a home)! Dealers report an increased interest in Hull pottery, and the updated 2001 value guide shows substantial increases in many items. Good McCoy continues to be hot, and Royal Haeger generates enthusiasm from an ever-increasing circle of its own devotees. California studio potters have been on top for several years and continue to be today, among them Kay Finch, Florence Ceramics, Brayton Laguna, and many others whose output may not have been quite as extensive: Brad Keeler, Will-George, Dorothy Kindell, Cleminson, Max Weil, Hedi Schoop, Sascha Brastoff, Howard Pierce, and Matthew Adams, for instance. Each possess diverse characteristics of their own that endear them to collectors. Don't overlook Red Wing, Camark, Cowan, Muncie, Van Briggle, Shawnee, and Abingdon. Aside from the vases and pots obviously made for the florist trade, any piece of marked American pottery (and unmarked, if you can identify its maker) are worth picking up at garage sale prices.

Most novelties and figurines of mid-twentieth century manufacture have dropped off a little in value, simply because they are so plentiful on the Internet (for instance, Ceramic Arts Studios, Rosemeade, Josef, Royal Copley, Kreiss, and Lefton). Rare Holt Howard pixies continue on upward, as do many items in that market, but at the same time, some Holt Howard prices have declined. Head vases, salt and pepper shakers, wall pockets, string holders, reamers, and clothes sprinkler bottles continue to be popular. While common examples have softened to an extent, the better examples never have.

In dinnerware, the prime focus right now is on designer lines from the '50s — Hall by Zeisel, Homer Laughlin by Schreckengost, Russel Wright, Franciscan Starburst, and many others in that mid-century high-style genre.

Restaurant china is attracting a lot of attention, and there's two volumes of in-depth information available on the subject. Good pieces of vintage Fiesta are still strong, as eBay sales will attest, and besides the old colors, watch for items in lilac — they're often as desirable as the old line. Several lines of Johnson Brothers dinnerware have become very collectible. Chintz patterns continue to be very desirable, Lipper's Blue Danube sells well, so does Blue Garland by Johann Haviland. Lefton's Holly lines are always good. The Moss Rose pattern, also made in Japan, has emerged as a very popular collectible line, and it's fairly plentiful right now.

Glassware. Gene Florence's Fire-King and Kitchen Glassware books continue to promote the on-going popularity of Jade-ite, just as his *Elegant Glassware* book has promoted the sales of quality glassware. Dealers tell us that Fostoria, Heisey, and Cambridge sales remain strong. Colored glass, especially red and forest green, sells well. Crackle glass is well worth looking for, and you'll sometimes be able to pick up some nice Fenton items well underpriced — never pass them by. Westmoreland's mid-century carnival glass, milk glass, and giftware items are appreciating at a very nice pace. L.G. Wright's figural items are worth picking up, and the late carnival glass by Indiana surprised us this year by attracting a new round of collector interest. Good Depression glass will still find a ready market. There's absolutely no interest in generic stemware, no matter how lovely, so don't be tempted to buy it up, unless you plan to use it yourself.

Jewelry. Good costume jewelry by well known designers continues to sell for amazing sums, but Marcia 'Sparkles' Brown's book on unsigned jewelry has caused collectors to take a second look at what Sparkles calls the 'orphans.' ('Learn to judge quality,' she urges collectors.) The Bakelite market is still strong, and any nice piece has excellent sales potential, though the average price may be somewhat lower than last year, due to the influence of Internet auctions and 'week-end dealers.'

Furniture. Good pine furniture is strong, especially in the east and south. Arts and Crafts style furniture is considered very trendy now; watch for pieces still in their original finish. Signed examples can be very pricey, especially Gustaf Stickley's. But L.&J.G. and Stickley Bros. furniture is good as well; also watch for Roycroft, Limbert, Lifetime, and Old Hickory. Even unsigned examples in this style when well made and in good condition are well worth your attention. Fifties Modern pieces such as the boomerang tables and the cube chairs are still very good; chairs made of molded fiberglass or with a leather sling seat or an aluminum or wire-work frame typify this genre. Originality is critical. Heywood-Wakefield furniture has a devoted following. And don't overlook the rugs, clocks, lighting fixtures, and other accessories from that era; good examples by noted designers often sell for several hundred dollars each.

Advertising. This is diverse field, with many subsections — for instance: automobilia, breweriana, soda-pop, tobacciana, gas station, character icons, and fast food. In automobilia, neon signs and clocks are high-dollar items, but even old license plates in good condition can command three-digit sales. Breweriana buffs look for items like neon signs, clocks, back-bar figures, thermometers, and trays, often using them to decorated their rec rooms. Coca-Cola items are always good, since there are thousands of collectors for them, and by no means are they all after vintage items. A large percentage of the Coca-Cola items sold today was made after 1950. Pepsi-Cola is running a close second, and Hires, 7-Up, and Orange Crush are coming on as well. Character icons such as Poppin' Fresh, Borden's Elsie, Mr. Peanut, the Campbell Kids, Joe Camel, Aunt Jemima, and Reddy Kilowatt each have their own fan clubs, and we find that items with their likenesses generally sell very quickly.

Dolls. Our doll advisors tell us that virtually all kinds of dolls remain strong, and values continue to increase. One reason they give for the market's strength is the fact that doll people are well organized. Clubs, newsletters, conventions, interaction of all sorts abounds in the doll world. Classic, antique dolls are seldom found at the garage sale/flea market level, but certainly you may find mid-century dolls. Even though they may be in a 'well loved' condition, many can be re-dressed, rewigged, and cleaned up, with plenty of margin for profit. Also watch for Mattel talkers (Chatty Cathy among them), Dawn and Ideal dolls, Holly Hobbie, Strawberry Shortcake, celebrity dolls, and Little Kiddles.

Other Collectibles. Souvenir spoons, certainly fishing lures, compacts and lipstick cases, perfume bottles, old buttons, cookbooks, children's books, cat and dog collectibles, Halloween, and Christmas items are always good. Kitchen gadgets, anodized aluminum, Kromex canister sets, and pyrex bowls with assorted fired-on decorations are very popular right now as well. Vintage clothing, hats, and accessories are 'in.' Denims continue to bring unbelievable prices, especially the double XX jeans and those with the big 'E' on the red tab of the back pocket. But also watch for small 'e' jeans made from the late 1960s until 1970 and the 'red line' styles of the 1980s. The handmade Enid Collins bags and purses from the 1960s command good prices; check out any jeweled purse for the Collins name.

But remember, the most important factor to consider when buying any of these items for resale is condition. If they show more than just a little wear or are damaged more than a minimal amount, don't waste you're time on them at any price. Today's collectors are more discerning than ever, thanks again to the Internet and the preponderance of supply over demand. Condition is all important.

How to Evaluate Your Holdings

When viewed in its entirety, granted, the antiques and collectibles market can be overwhelming. But in each line of glassware, any type of pottery or toys, or any other field I could mention, there are examples that are more desirable than others, and these are the ones you need to be able to recognize. If you're a novice, it will probably be best at first to choose a few areas that you find most interesting and learn just what particular examples or types of items are most in demand within that field. Concentrate on the top 25%. This is where you'll do 75% of your business. Do your homework. Quality sells. Obviously no one can be an expert in everything, but gradually you can begin to broaden your knowledge. As an added feature of our guide, information on clubs and newsletters, always a wonderful source of up-to-date information on any subject, is contained in each category when available. (Advisors' names are listed as well. We highly recommend that you exhaust all other resources before you contact them with your inquiries. Their role is simply to check over our data before we go to press to make sure it is as accurate as we and they can possibly make it for you; they do not agree to answer readers' questions, though some may. If you do write, you must send them an SASE. If you call, please take the time zones into consideration. Some of our advisors are professionals and may charge an appraisal fee, so be sure to ask. Please, do *not* be offended if they do not respond to your contacts, they are under no obligation to do so.)

There are many fields other than those we've already mentioned that are strong and have been for a long time. It's impossible to list them all. But we've left very little out of this book; at least we've tried to represent each category to some extent and where at all possible to refer you to a source of further information. It's up to you to read, observe the market, and become acquainted with it to the point that you feel confident enough to become a part of today's antiques and collectibles industry.

The thousands of current values found in this book will increase your awareness of today's wonderful world of buying, selling, and collecting antiques and collectibles. Use it to educate yourself to the point that you'll be the one with the foresight to know what and how to buy as well as where and how to turn those sleepers into cold, hard cash.

In addition to this one, there are several other very fine price guides on the market. One of the best is *Schroeder's Antiques Price Guide*; another is *The Flea Market Trader*. Both are published by Collector Books. *The Antique Trader Antiques and Collectibles Price Guide*, *Warman's Antiques and Their Prices*, and *Kovel's Antiques and Collectibles Price List* are others. You may want to invest in a copy of each. Where you decide to sell will have a direct bearing on how you price your merchandise, and nothing will affect an item's worth more than condition.

If you're not familiar with using a price guide, here's a few tips that may help you. When convenient and reasonable, antiques will be sorted by manufacturer. This is especially true of pottery and most glassware. If you don't find the item you're looking for under manufacturer, look under a broader heading, for instance, cat collectibles, napkin dolls, cookie jars, etc. And don't forget to use the index. Most guides of this type have very comprehensive indexes — a real boon to the novice collector. If you don't find the exact item you're trying to price, look for something similar. For instance, if it's a McCoy rabbit planter you're researching, go through the McCoy section and see what price range other animal planters are in. (There are exceptions, however, and if an item is especially rare and desirable, this will not apply. Here's where you need a comprehensive McCoy book.) Or if you have a frame-tray puzzle with Snow White and the Seven Dwarfs, see what other Disney frame-trays are priced at. Just be careful not to compare apples to oranges. Dates are important as well. You can judge the value of a 7" Roseville Magnolia vase that's not listed in any of your guides; just look at the price given for one a little larger or smaller and adjust it up or down. Pricing collectibles is certainly not a science; the bottom line is simply where the buyer and the seller finally agree to do business. Circumstances dictate sale price, and we can only make suggestions, which we base on current sales, market observations, and the expert opinions of our advisors.

Once you've found book price, decide how much less you can take for it. Book price represents a high average retail. A collectible will often change hands many times, and obviously it will not always be sold at book price. How quickly do you want to realize a profit? Will you be patient enough to hold out for top dollar, or would you rather price your merchandise lower so it will turn over more quickly? Just as there are both types of dealers, there are two types of collectors. Many are bargain hunters. They shop around — do the legwork themselves. On the other hand, there are those who are willing to pay whatever the asking price is to avoid spending precious time searching out pieces they especially want, but they represent the minority. You'll often see tradepaper ads listing good merchandise (from that top 25% we mentioned before) at prices well above book value. This is a good example of a dealer who knows that his merchandise is good enough to entice the buyer who is able to pay a little more and doesn't mind waiting for him (or her) to come along, and that's his prerogative.

Don't neglect to access the condition of the item you want to sell. This is especially important in online and mail-order selling. Most people, especially inexperienced buyers and sellers, have a tendency to overlook some flaws and to overrate merchandise. Mint condition means that an item is complete and undamaged — in effect, just as it looked the day it was made. Glassware, china, and pottery may often be found today in mint condition. Check for signs of wear, though, since even wear will downgrade value. Remember that when a buyer doesn't have the option of seeing for himself, your written description is all he has to go by. Save yourself the hassle of costly and time-consuming returns by making sure the condition of your merchandise is accurately and completely described. Unless a toy is still in its original box and has never been played with, you seldom see one in mint condition. Paper collectibles are almost never found without some deterioration or damage. Most price guides will list values that apply to glass and ceramics that are mint (unless another condition is specifically indicated within some descriptions). Other items are usually evaluated on the assumption that they are in the best as-found condition common to that area of collecting, for instance magazines are simply never found in mint condition. Grade your merchandise as though you were the buyer, not the seller. You'll be building a reputation that will go a long way toward contributing to your success. If it's glassware or pottery you're assessing, an item in less than excellent condition will be mighty hard to sell at any price. Just as a guideline (a basis to begin your evaluation, though other things will factor in), use a scale of one to five with good being a one, excellent being a three, and mint being a five. As an example, a beer tray worth $250.00 in mint condition would then be worth $150.00 if excellent and $50.00 if only good. Remember, the first rule of buying (for resale or investment) is 'Don't put your money in damaged goods.' And the second rule should be be, 'If you do sell damaged items, indicate 'as is' on the price tag, and don't price the item as though it were mint.' The Golden Rule applies just as well to us as antique dealers as it does to any other interaction. Some shops and co-ops have poor lighting, and damage can be easily missed by a perspective buyer — your honesty will be greatly appreciated. If you include identification on your tags as well, be sure it's accurate. If you're not positive, say so. Better yet, let the buyer decide.

Deciding Where to Best Sell Your Merchandise

Personal transactions are just one of many options. Overhead and expenses will vary with each and must be factored into your final pricing. If you have some especially nice items and can contact a collector willing to pay top dollar, that's obviously the best of the lot. Or you may decide to sell to a dealer who may be willing to pay you only half of book. Either way, your expenses won't amount to much more than a little gas or a phone call.

Internet auctions may be your preferred venue. Look at completed auctions for sales results of similar items to decide. Factor in the cost of photography (sales of items with no photograph suffer), image hosting, and listing fees. Remember that the cost of boxes and bubble wrap must also be considered, not to mention the time spent actually listing the item, answering e-mail questions, contacting the buyer with the winning bid, leaving feedback, etc.

Internet selling works. In fact, I know some dealers who have quit doing shows and simply work out of their home. No more unpacking, travel expenses, or inconvenience of any kind to endure. You may sell through a set-price online mall or an auction. If you choose the auction (eBay is the most widely used right now), you can put a 'reserve' on everything you sell, a safeguard that protects the seller and prevents an item from going at an unreasonably low figure should there be few bidders.

Classified Ads are another way to get a good price for your more valuable merchandise without investing much money or time. Place a 'For Sale' ad or run a mail bid in one of the collector magazines or newsletters, several of which are listed in the back of this book. Many people have had excellent results this way. One of the best to reach collectors in general is *The Antique Trader Weekly* (P.O. Box 1050, Dubuque, Iowa 52004). It covers virtually every type of antiques and collectibles and has a large circulation. If you have glassware, china, or pottery from the Depression era, you should have good results through *The Depression Glass Daze* (Box 57, Otisville, Michigan 48463). If you have several items and the cost of listing them all is prohibitive, simply place an ad saying (for instance) 'Several pieces of Royal Copley (or whatever) for sale, send SASE for list.' Be sure to give your correct address and phone number.

When you're making out your list or talking with a prospective buyer by phone, try to draw a picture with words. Describe any damage in full; it's much better than having a disgruntled customer to deal with later, and you'll be on your way to establishing yourself as a reputable dealer. Sometimes it's wise to send out photographs. Seeing the item exactly as it is will often help the prospective buyer make up his or her mind. Send a SASE along and ask that your photos be returned to you, so that you can send them out again, if need be. A less expensive alternative is to have your item photocopied. This works great for many smaller items, not just flat shapes but things with some dimension

as well. It's wonderful for hard-to-describe dinnerware patterns or for showing their trademarks.

If you've made that 'buy of a lifetime' or an item you've hung onto for a few years has turned out to be a scarce, highly sought collectible, you have two good options: eBay and mail bids. Either way, you should be able to get top dollar for your prize. You'll want to start your online auction with a high but reasonable reserve. Should the item fail to meet reserve, relist it with one that is lower than the original. The final bid the first time around will give you a good idea of where it may go the second time.

If you do a mail bid, this is how you'll want your ad to read: 'Mail Bid. Popeye cookie jar by American Bisque, slight wear (or 'mint' — briefly indicate condition), closing 6/31/95, right to refuse' (standard self-protection clause meaning you will refuse ridiculously low bids), and give your phone number. Don't commit the sale to any bidder until after the closing date, since some may wait until the last minute to try to place the winning bid.

Be sure to let your buyer know what form of payment you prefer. Some dealers will not ship merchandise until personal checks have cleared. This delay may make the buyer a bit unhappy. So you may want to request a money order or a cashier's check. Nowadays there are several hassle-free ways to make transactions online, for instance, through Pay Pal or Billpoint.

Be very careful about how you pack your merchandise for shipment. Breakables need to be well protected. There are several things you can use. Plastic bubble wrap is excellent and adds very little weight to your packages. Or use scraps of foam rubber such as carpet padding (check with a carpet-laying service or confiscate some from family and friends who are getting new carpet installed). I've received items wrapped in pieces of egg-crate type mattress pads (watch for these at garage sales). If there is a computer business near you, check their dumpsters for discarded foam wrapping and other protective packaging. It's best not to let newspaper come in direct contact with your merchandise, since the newsprint may stain certain surfaces. After you've wrapped them well, you'll need boxes. Find smaller boxes (one or several, whatever best fits your needs) that you can fit into a larger one with several inches of space between them. First pack your well-wrapped items snugly into the smaller box, using crushed newspaper to keep them from shifting. Place it into the larger box, using more crushed paper underneath and along the sides, so that it will not move during transit. Remember, if it arrives broken, it's still your merchandise, even though you have received payment. You may want to insure the shipment; check with your carrier. Some have automatic insurance up to a specified amount.

After you've mailed your box, it's good to follow it up with a phone call or an e-mail after a few days. Make sure it arrived in good condition and that your customer is pleased with the merchandise. Most people who sell by mail or the Internet allow a 10-day return privilege, providing their original price tag is still intact. For this purpose, you can simply initial a gummed label or use one of those pre-printed return address labels that most of us have around the house.

For very large or heavy items such as furniture or slot machines, ask your buyer for his preferred method of shipment. If the distance involved is not too great, he may even want to pick it up himself.

Flea market selling can either be a lot of fun, or it can turn out to be one of the worst experiences of your life. Obviously you will have to deal with whatever weather conditions prevail, so be sure to listen to weather reports so that you can dress accordingly. You'll see some inventive shelters you might want to copy. Even a simple patio umbrella will offer respite from the blazing sun or a sudden downpour. I've recently been seeing stands catering just to the needs of the flea market dealer — how's that for being enterprising! Not only do they carry specific items the dealers might want, but they've even had framework and tarpaulins, and they'll erect shelters right on the spot!

Be sure to have plastic table covering in case of rain and some large clips to hold it down if there's much wind. The type of clip you'll need depends on how your table is made, so be sure to try them out before you actually get caught in a storm. Glass can blow over, paper items can be ruined, and very quickly your career as a flea market dealer may be cut short for lack of merchandise!

Price your things, allowing yourself a little bargaining room. Unless you want to collect tax separately on each sale (for this you'd need a lot of small change), mentally calculate the amount and add this on as well. Sell the item 'tax included.' Everybody does.

Take snacks, drinks, paper bags, plenty of change, and somebody who can relieve you occasionally. Collectors are some of the nicest people around. I guarantee that you'll enjoy this chance to meet and talk them, and often you can make valuable contacts that may help you locate items you're especially looking for yourself.

Auction houses are listed in the back of this book. If you have an item you feel might be worth selling at auction, be sure to contact one of them. Many have appraisal services; some are free while others charge a fee, dependent on number of items and time spent. We suggest you first make a telephone inquiry before you send in a formal request.

In Summation

In times of recession, perhaps particularly in times of upheaval, by instinct we struggle to regain a sense of stability and normalcy. We can find comfort from our past. Though we've been through bad times before — world wars, atomic bombs, the Great Depression, and presidential assassinations — we have survived, and more than that, we have always grown both in unity and accomplishment. Who we are is the outgrowth of where we once were compounded by the grit, ingenuity, and determination it took to get us to 'now.' Our heritage is strength.

How better to connect with our past than through antiques and collectibles. Even when our family was young and money was a usually a scarce commodity in our household, we were collectors. We had to be, it's who we are. As Americans, we're getting back to business, and though it may take a little time, there is a strong, unquenchable spirit alive in the antiques/collectibles industry as well. It will survive.

Abbreviations

dia – diameter	**NM – near mint**
ea – each	**oz – ounce**
EX – excellent	**pc – piece**
G – good condition	**pr – pair**
gal – gallon	**pt – pint**
L – long, length	**qt – quart**
lg – large	**sm – small**
M – mint condition	**sq – square**
med – medium	**VG – very good**
MIB – mint in (original) box	**W – wide**
MIP – mint in package	**w/ – with**
MOC – mint on card	**(+) – has been reproduced**

Abingdon

You may find smaller pieces of Abingdon around, but it's not common to find many larger items. This company operated in Abingdon, Illinois, from 1934 until 1950, making not only nice vases and figural pieces but some kitchen items as well. Their cookie jars are very well done and popular with collectors. They sometimes used floral decals and gold to decorate their wares, and a highly decorated item is worth a minimum of 25% more than the same shape with no decoration. Some of their glazes also add extra value. If you find a piece in black, bronze, or red, you can add 25% to those as well. Note that if you talk by phone about Abingdon to a collector, be sure to mention the mold number on the base.

For more information we recommend *Abingdon Pottery Artware, 1934–50, Stepchild of the Great Depression,* by Joe Paradis (Schiffer).

See also Cookie Jars.

Advisor: Louise Dumont (See Directory, Abingdon)

Club: Abingdon Pottery Collectors Club
Elaine Westover, Membership and Treasurer
210 Knox Hwy. 5, Abingdon, IL 61410; 309-462-3267

Ashtray, Abingdon, #306, 8x3".....................................**$60.00**
Ashtray, octagonal, #551, 7" sq....................................**$24.00**
Bookend, dolphin, #444, 5¾", ea.................................**$45.00**
Bookends, sea gulls, #305, 6", pr...............................**$155.00**
Bowl, La Fleur, #154, 8" dia...**$14.00**
Bowl, Rhythm, #419, 5" dia..**$42.00**
Bowl, scroll handles, scalloped, #478, 11½" L............**$30.00**
Bowl, Tulip, #642...**$60.00**
Box, Butterfly, #607D, 4¾" dia....................................**$90.00**
Box, Geranium, #543D, 3½"..**$80.00**
Candle holders, Fern Leaf, #427, 5½", pr **$55.00**

Chang Jar, #310, copper brown, with lid, 11", $150.00.

Compote, fluted, #638, 4"..**$35.00**
Cornucopia, double; #482, 11" L **$28.00**

Dish, Hibiscus, #527, 10" dia **$40.00**
Dish, Shell, #500, 15" L...**$32.00**
Figurine, Fruit Girl, #3904, 10"...................................**$280.00**
Figurine, goose sitting, #571, 5"...................................**$40.00**
Figurine, kangaroo, #605D, 7".....................................**$200.00**
Flowerpot, La Fleur, #152, 6" **$18.00**
Grease jar, Daisy, #679, 4½" **$40.00**
Jar, elephant, #606, 9¾" **$215.00**
Jardiniere, La Fleur, #P6, 5" dia **$25.00**
Lamp base, Fluted, #258, 23½".....................................**$110.00**
Nut dish, Daisy, #385, 3½" dia **$28.00**
Pitcher, Fern Leaf, #430, 8" **$130.00**
Planter, Apple Blossom, #415, 11".................................**$45.00**
Planter, Daffodil, 5¼"..**$80.00**
Planter, dog, #670, 4"..**$45.00**
Planter, donkey, #669, 7½" **$80.00**
Planter, gazelle, #704, 4¾"...**$50.00**
Plaque, wall mask, #376M, 7½".....................................**$210.00**
Plate, Bamboo, #715D, 10½" dia..................................**$180.00**
Plate, salad; Daisy, #387, 7½".......................................**$22.00**
Plate, snack; Apple Blossom, 6 compartment, #115, 11½".**$55.00**
Range set, Daisy, #690D, 3-pc **$80.00**
Teapot, Daisy, #683, 6¼" **$70.00**
Tile, geisha girl, #400, 5" sq...**$90.00**
Urn, Regency, #539, 7" **$30.00**

Vase, Draped, #557, 10½", $45.00.

Vase, Dutch boy or girl, #469/#470, 8", ea **$75.00**
Vase, Echo, #352, 4" **$28.00**
Vase, Geranium, #389, 7" **$60.00**
Vase, Han, #312, 6"...**$25.00**
Vase, Hollyhock, #496, 7½" **$35.00**
Vase, pillow; #577, 7" **$22.00**
Vase, sea horse, #596D, 8" **$65.00**
Vase, sq w/wheel handles, #466, 8".............................**$50.00**
Wall pocket, butterfly, #601D, 8½" **$115.00**
Wall pocket, Dutch boy or girl, #489/#490, 10", ea..**$130.00**
Wall pocket, Morning-Glory, #377, 7½".......................**$40.00**
Window box, Sunburst, #448, 9" L................................**$45.00**

Adams, Matthew

In the 1950s a trading post located in Alaska contacted Sascha Brastoff to design a line of decorative ceramics with depictions of Eskimos, Alaskan scenes, or with animals indigenous to that area. These items were intended to target the tourist trade.

Brastoff selected Matthew Adams as the designer. These earlier examples have the Sascha B mark on the front, and the pattern number often appears on the back.

After the Alaska series became successful, Matthew Adams left Brastoff's studio and opened his own. Pieces made in his studio are all signed Matthew Adams in script on the front. Some carry the word Alaska as well. The location of his studio or studios are unknown at the present time, but collectors report finding examples that carry a 'Made in Alaska' paper label.

Advisor: Marty Webster (See Directory, Adams, Matthew)

Jar, cabin on stilts, 7", $75.00.

Ashtray, elk on green, ovoid, 8x9"...............................$45.00
Ashtray, Eskimo w/baby on back, green w/gold streaks, #148, 9x9"..$110.00
Ashtray, polar bear, gold trim, teardrop shape, 6x6" ..$42.00
Ashtray, walrus, boomerang, free-form, 5¾x11¾"......$65.00
Bowl, cabin on stilts, free-form, 9½x8"........................$35.00
Bowl, cabin on stilts, oval, 6x11" $45.00
Bowl, Eskimo girls (2) wearing brown coats w/white fur trim on green w/gold trim, #190.................................$105.00
Bowl, Eskimo leaving his igloo, rim dips at sides, #111, oval, 5⅞x6"..$50.00
Bowl, igloo, blue on white & green, sides extend to form handles, 6x7"...$30.00
Cigarette lighter, table; cabin on stilts on green w/gold trim, tapered, 5x5" $50.00
Cigarette lighter & holder, cabin on stilts, brown w/gold trim, 2-pc...$65.00
Creamer, polar bear, 4¾" $43.00
Creamer & sugar bowl, seals, brown on white..........$80.00

Plate, dog sled & igloo in night scene, gold trim, #162, 7⅝" $60.00
Plate, Eskimo child in parka, #162, 7½" $50.00
Plate, igloo in Northern Lights, gold trim, 7½" dia $36.00
Platter, cabin on stilts on blue w/gold trim, 12" dia ...$45.00
Salt & pepper shakers, igloos, gold trim, 3¾", pr.......$60.00
Salt & pepper shakers, seals, brown, green & white w/gold trim, NM, pr $115.00
Vase, Northern Lights & mountains, 7", EX $75.00
Vase, walrus on green w/gold trim, 4½x 5" dia..........$45.00
Water set, walrus, pitcher, 11½"; +6 mugs, 4½"; gold trim, EX $255.00

Advertising Character Collectibles

The advertising field holds a special fascination for many of today's collectors. It's vast and varied, so its appeal is universal; but the characters of the ad world are its stars right now. Nearly every fast-food restaurant and manufacturer of a consumer product has a character logo. Keep your eyes open on your garage sale outings; it's not at all uncommon to find the cloth and plush dolls, plastic banks and mugs, bendies, etc., such as we've listed here. There are several books on the market that are geared specifically toward these types of collectibles. One is *Advertising Character Collectibles* by Warren Dotz, published by Collector Books. Others you'll enjoy reading are *Collectible Aunt Jemima* by Jean Williams Turner (Schiffer); *Cereal Boxes and Prizes, The 1960s* (Flake World Publishing), by Scott Bruce; and *Hake's Guide to Advertising Collectibles* by Ted Hake (Wallace-Homestead). *Schroeder's Collectible Toys, Antique to Modern,* is another source. (It's also published by Collector Books.)

See also Advertising Watches; Breweriana; Bubble Bath Containers; Cereal Boxes and Premiums; Character Clocks and Watches; Character and Promotional Drinking Glasses; Coca-Cola Collectibles; Fast-Food Collectibles; Novelty Radios; Novelty Telephones; Pez Candy Containers; Pin-Back Buttons; Salt and Pepper Shakers; Soda Pop Memorabilia.

Aunt Jemima

One of the most widely recognized ad characters of them all, Aunt Jemima has decorated bags and boxes of pancake flour for more than ninety years. In fact, the original milling company carried her name, but by 1926 it had become part of the Quaker Oats Company. She and Uncle Mose were produced in plastic by the F&F Mold and Die Works in the 1950s, and the salt and pepper shakers, syrup pitchers, cookie jars, etc., they made are perhaps the most sought-after of the hundreds of items available today. (Watch for reproductions.) Age is a big worth-assessing factor for memorabilia such as we've listed below, of course, but so is condition. Watch for very chipped or worn paint on the F&F products, and avoid buying soiled cloth dolls.

Advisor: Judy Posner (See Directory, Advertising)

Baking Mix Set, features Junior Flako & Aunt Jemima products w/pans & utensils, early 1960s, complete, MIB **$150.00**

Candle holders, Premium Nursery Rhyme, 16 characters in 4 colors, F&F Mold & Die Co, 1950s, 3", EX.........**$100.00**

Clipboard, Aunt Jemima Butter Lite, yellow w/5 images of Aunt Jemima down side, for grocery store use, unused, M **$75.00**

Clock, Buckwheat Pancakes, plastic with cardboard face, electric, copyright 1956, 7" x 7½", EX, from $75.00 to $100.00. (These clocks are fantasy items made in the 1990s with color copy inserts, they were sold in original boxes; buyer beware!)

Clock, Seal in the Freshness Forever, waffle encased in plastic on trapezoidal base, present-day image, 1989-90, 7", EX...**$85.00**

Coloring book, Hooray! It's Aunt Jemima Day, by Anne Sellers Leaf, 1950s, unused, EX..............................**$75.00**

Cookie jar, F&F Mold and Die Works, 12", M/NM from $550.00 to $600.00.

Creamer, Uncle Mose, F&F Mold & Die Co, EX..........**$80.00**

Doll, Breakfast Bear, blue plush, in chef's hat, apron & bandana, Aunt Jemima premium, 13", M..................**$175.00**

Dolls, Aunt Jemima & Uncle Mose, stuffed oilcloth, 1940s-50s, 11" & 12", EX, ea **$100.00**

Dolls, Diana & Wade, stuffed oilcloth, 1950, 9", EX, pr..**$75.00**

Hat, paper, Aunt Jemima Breakfast Club/Eat a Better Breakfast..., red & black lettering & head image on white, 1953, EX+...**$50.00**

Magazine ad, Aunt Jemima Cornbread, full color, McCall's, October 1958, 14x10½", EX **$15.00**

Measuring cup, beige plastic ¼-cup size w/Aunt Jemima embossed on handle, 1980s, EX, from $40 to......**$45.00**

Pancake mold, rabbit, horse, swan & squirrel, metal w/wood handle, 1950s, 8½" dia **$130.00**

Pin-back button, Aunt Jemima Breakfast Club/Eat a Better Breakfast, bust image in center, 4" dia, NM...........**$4.00**

Place mat, paper, The Story of Aunt Jemima, from Aunt Jemima's Kitchen Restaurants, 1950s, 10x14", EX.**$35.00**

Plate, paper; white w/Aunt Jemima bust & gold trim, 1950s, 9¼" dia, EX **$35.00**

Pot holder, red graphics on white, 1970s, M...............**$35.00**

Recipe booklet, Cake Mix Miracles, 1940s premium, 27 pages, EX..**$45.00**

Recipe booklet, Pancakes Unlimited, 1958, 31 pages, scarce, NM+ **$55.00**

Recipe box, hard red plastic w/Aunt Jemima image, EX.**$225.00**

String holder, bust, black face w/white head scarf, chalkware, original paint, 1950s, 7¾", EX...................**$400.00**

Syrup pitcher, thick ceramic w/Aunt Jemima in red lettering, 1988 premium, NM...**$30.00**

Table card, diecut cardboard, Folks...It's a Treat To Eat Out Often..., dated 1953, 3x4¾", unused, M................**$55.00**

Tin, shows products on multicolored nostalgic background, Quaker limited edition, dated 1983, 6", EX..........**$25.00**

Big Boy

Bob's Big Boy, home of the nationally famous Big Boy, the original double-deck hamburger, was founded by Robert C. 'Bob' Wian in Glendale, California, in 1938. He'd just graduated from high school, and he had a dream. With the $300.00 realized from the sale of the car he so treasured, he bought a run-down building and enough basic equipment to open his business. Through much hard work and ingenuity, Bob turned his little restaurant into a multimillion-dollar empire. Not only does he have the double-deck two-patty burger to his credit, but car hops and drive-in restaurants were his creation as well.

With business beginning to flourish, Bob felt he needed a symbol — something that people would recognize. One day in walked a chubby lad of six, his sagging trousers held up by reluctant suspenders. Bob took one look at him and named him Big Boy, and that was it! It was a natural name for his double-deck hamburger — descriptive, catchy, and easy to remember. An artist worked out the drawings, and Bob's Pantry was renamed Boy's Big Boy.

The enterprise grew fast, and Bob added location after location. In 1969 when he sold out to the Marriott Corporation, he had 185 restaurants in California, with franchises such as Elias Big Boy, Frisch's Big Boy, and Shoney's Big Boy in other states. The Big Boy burger and logo was recognized by virtually every man, woman, and child in America, and Bob retired knowing he had made a significant contribution to millions of people everywhere.

Since Big Boy has been in business for over sixty years, you'll find many items and numerous variations. Some, such as the large statues, china, and some menus, have been reproduced. If you're in doubt, consult an experienced collector for help. Many items of jewelry, clothing, and kids promotions were put out over the years, too numerous to itemize separately. Values range from $5.00 up to $1,000.00.

Advisor: Steve Soelberg (See Directory, Advertising)

Bank, Big Boy figure, soft molded vinyl with removable head, 1973, 9", from $20.00 to $30.00.

Ashtray, glass w/red painted Big Boy logo, 3¾" dia, EX ..**$15.00**
Bank, ceramic figure holding hamburger **$500.00**
Bank, plastic figure in red & white checked overalls, 1973, 9" **$20.00**
Bank, vinyl figure w/ or w/out hamburger, M, ea......**$25.00**
Box, lunch/pencil; red plastic......................................**$25.00**
Comic book, Adventures of Big Boy, #1 ....**$250.00**
Comic book, Adventures of Big Boy, #2-#5, ea........**$100.00**
Comic book, Adventures of Big Boy, #6-#10, ea **$50.00**
Comic book, Adventures of Big Boy, #11-#100, ea **$25.00**
Comic book, Adventures of Big Boy, #101-#250, ea ..**$10.00**
Counter display, papier-mache figure w/hamburger, 1960s **$750.00**
Cup, robin's-egg blue w/Bob serving burger, maroon interior, Walker China, 3"..**$50.00**
Decal, Big Boy for President, M **$5.00**
Doll, complete w/hamburger & shoes, Dakin, M **$150.00**
Figure, pewter, Big Boy Collection Series...Limited Edition, 1 of 500, 1936, 3½", EX..**$50.00**
Figure, PVC, Bob on yellow surfboard w/blue wave underneath, 1990, 3" **$10.00**
Food bag, Frisch's Big Boy Burger, 1950s, M.............**$25.00**
Gameboard, Big Boy, complete w/game pcs, M **$200.00**
Handbook, employee, 1956...**$100.00**

Key chain, flat silver-tone figure, M **$25.00**
Matchbook cover, Home of the Famous Big Boy Double Decker, diecut hamburger images front & back on blue, EX...**$12.00**
Menu, Bob's original #1 location.................................**$350.00**
Night light, plug-in-socket type, plastic, MIB **$70.00**
Ornament, Happy Holidays **$20.00**
Pen, Parker, MIB...**$20.00**
Pennant, felt, Big Boy Club, 2 versions, 1950s, ea **$50.00**
Plate, dinner; Elias Brothers...**$50.00**
Playing cards, red, unopened, M..................................**$40.00**
Radio, transistor; soda can shape, M **$1,000.00**
Salt & pepper shakers, ceramic Big Boy figure & figural hamburger, marked Special 1995 Ltd Edition, EX, pr .**$20.00**
Tumbler, tall w/turquoise logo, 1956, M......................**$50.00**
Watch, man's gold quartz, Windert, MIB...................**$150.00**
Yo-yo, wood, blue or red, 1956, M..............................**$50.00**

Campbell Kids

The introduction of the world's first canned soup was announced in 1897. Later improvements in the manufacturing process created an evolutionary condensed soup. The Campbell's® Soup Company is now the primary beneficiary of this early entrepreneurial achievement. Easily identified by their red and white advertising, the company has been built on a tradition of skillful product marketing through five generations of consumers. Now a household name for all ages, Campbell's Soups have grown to dominate 80% of the canned soup market.

The first Campbell's licensed advertising products were character collectibles offered in 1910 — composition dolls with heads made from a combination of glue and sawdust. They were made by the E.I. Horsman Company and sold for $1.00 each. They were the result of a gifted illustrator, their creator, Grace Drayton, who in 1904 gave life to the chubby-faced cherub 'Campbell's Kids.'

In 1994 the Campbell's Soup Kids celebrated their 90th birthday. They have been revised a number of times to maintain a likeness to modern-day children. Over the years hundreds of licensees have been commissioned to produce collectibles and novelty items with the Campbell's logo in a red and white theme.

Licensed advertising reached a peak from 1954 through 1956 with thirty-four licensed manufacturers. Unusual items included baby carriages, toy vacuums, games, and apparel. Many of the more valuable Campbell's advertising collectibles were made during this period. In 1956 a Campbell's Kid doll was produced from latex rubber. Called 'Magic Skin,' it proved to be the most popular mail-in premium ever produced. Campbell's received more than 560,000 requests for this special girl chef doll.

For more information, we recommend *Campbell's Soup Collectibles, A Price and Identification Guide,* by David and Micki Young (Krause Publications). The book may be ordered through The Soup Collector Club.

Advisor: David Young (See Directory, Advertising)

Club: The Soup Collector Club
414 Country Lane Ct.
Wauconda, IL 60084, fax/phone: 847-487-4917;
e-mail: soupclub@yahoo.com

Website: www.soupcollector.com or Club site:
clubs.yahoo.com/clubs/campbellssoupcollectorclub

**Menu board, self-framed tin litho,
23½" x 17½", EX, $145.00.** (Photo
courtesy Buffalo Bay)

Bank, ceramic Campbell Boy figure in chef's garb, 1970s, 8",
  EX...**$45.00**
Bank, chicken noodle soup can, Kids graphics w/poem on
  side, 4¾"...**$20.00**
Bank, metal pail w/lid & plastic handle, 6 different Kids
  graphics, Shackman, 1980, 2½", M........................**$30.00**
Book, The Campbell Kids at Home, Rand McNally Elf Book,
  1954, M...**$48.00**
Calendar, 1974 linen hanger, M'm! M'm! Good!, Campbell
  Boy as chef, Norcross, 27x16", M.........................**$15.00**
Clock, 2 Kids holding wooden spoons in pot (clock center),
  w/sm plastic shelf & oven mitts, 1987, 9x13".......**$25.00**
Coin purse, red w/girl's face, chain for handle, 3".....**$24.00**
Coloring book, A Story of Soup, shows Kids in prehistoric
  dress, 1977, EX...**$26.00**
Comic book, Captain America & The Campbell Kids, promo-
  tional, Marvel, 1980, M...................................**$24.00**
Container, plastic soap dispenser w/plastic pump on top,
  MRS Imports, 1991, 4x3¼", MIP.........................**$8.00**
Cookie jar, ceramic, white w/Kids graphics, Westwood, 1991,
  MIB...**$35.00**
Cup, ceramic, Salute America, Kids as Uncle Sam & Liberty,
  1986, M...**$21.00**
Cup, plastic, M'm! M'm! Good!, Kids graphics, w/lid,
  microwavable, 1992, M....................................**$5.00**
Cup, plastic, molded Kid head w/yellow hair, 1976, NM..**$12.00**
Decal, Boy chef w/spoon raised in front of barbecue,
  Meyercord, 1954, 5x6x5", M................................**$8.00**
Dinnerware, child's set, stoneware plate, bowl, cup & saucer,
  Kids graphics, 1992, MIB...................................**$12.00**

Dinnerware, tumbler, bowl & spoon, Kids graphics, Zak
  Designs, 1995, MIP.......................................**$20.00**
Dish, Kid scene, Buffalo pottery, 7½" dia..................**$65.00**
Doll, boy or girl, vinyl w/cloth clothes, 1970s soup-label pre-
  miums, unmarked, 10", ea from $30 to.................**$45.00**
Doll, Colonial boy or girl (Paul Revere & Betsy Ross repli-
  cas), 1976 premiums, 10", M, ea from $45 to.......**$65.00**
Doll, girl, rubber & vinyl w/cloth outfit, Ideal, 1955, 8", EX,
  minimum value...**$125.00**
Doll, Pirate, porcelain, comes in lg soup can box, Home
  Shopper, 1995, 10", EX...................................**$80.00**
Fork & spoon set, Kids graphics on handle, Westwood, 1992,
  MIB...**$8.00**
Hot pad/oven mitt, graphics of Kid chef holding loaf of
  bread, 1992, M..**$8.00**
Kaleidoscope, vegetable soup-can shape, Steven Mfg, 1981,
  5", EX...**$40.00**
Paperweight, etched glass, 1978, M.........................**$45.00**
Place mats, 2 Kids stirring soup w/wooden spoons, set of 4,
  EX...**$50.00**
Plate, Campbell Soup Company, Camden Plant, 1869-1990, 2
  Kids stand in front of building, 7½" dia, EX........**$42.00**
Plate, Chicken Noodle Soup, 2 Kids & teddy bear sitting on table,
  trimmed in 23k gold, Danbury Mint, 1994, 8"............**$35.00**
Plate, Vegetable Beef Soup, 2 Kids in kitchen, Danbury Mint,
  1994, 8" dia, MIB...**$35.00**
Play-Kit, w/yo-yo, top, paddle ball & trick book, Duncan,
  1963, MIP...**$40.00**
Salt & pepper shakers, ceramic, Kid as dancing chef on sides,
  Westwood, 1991, MIB, pr.................................**$10.00**
Salt & pepper shakers, painted metal, can shape, pepper is a
  grinder, 6", pr...**$75.00**
Salt & pepper shakers, plastic figures, w/stoppers, F&F Mold
  & Die Co, 1950s, 4¼", EXIB, pr........................**$40.00**
Spoons, 1 w/boy & 1 w/girl as terminals, International Silver
  Co, 1960s, M (mailing envelope).......................**$65.00**

Spoons, 6", $30.00 each. (Photo
courtesy David Young)

String holder, Kid's head w/hole in mouth for string, chalkware, 6¾", EX **$225.00**

Tea set, child size, Kids graphics, Chilton, 1993, MIB ..**$20.00**

Thimble, china, Campbell Girl at stove, banded top & bottom, Franklin Mint, 1980, ¾", M **$15.00**

Vanity set, comb, brush & mirror, yellow plastic, 1985, MOC..**$35.00**

Cap'n Crunch

Cap'n Crunch was the creation of Jay Ward, whom you will no doubt remember was also the creator of the Rocky and Bullwinkle show. The Cap'n hails from the '60s and was one of the first heroes of the presweetened cereal crowd. Jean LaFoote was the villain always scheming to steal the Cap'n's cereal.

Wiggle figures, yellow or blue plastic, Quaker Oats, 1969, 2¾" to 3¼", EX, $50.00 each. (Photo courtesy Scott Bruce)

Bank, figural, painted plastic, 1973, VG **$65.00**

Bank, Treasure Chest, blue plastic, 1984, NM **$5.00**

Beanie, Tiger Shark Meanie, in original printed bag, M, from $16 to...**$20.00**

Big Slick Gyro Car, blue plastic, 1972, MIP **$15.00**

Binoculars, blue plastic, 1972, MIP **$15.00**

Boson whistle, blue & white w/Cap'n & Sea Dog, 1960s, EX..**$10.00**

Cap'n Crunch Cruiser, plastic, 1987, EX......................**$10.00**

Cap'n Rescue Kit, paper, 1986, MIP **$10.00**

Coloring book, Whitman, 1968, VG **$20.00**

Comic book, Center of the Earth, 1987, 8-page, EX ...**$10.00**

Doll, Cap'n Crunch, plush, Quaker Oats Co, 1990, 18"..**$20.00**

Figure, Cap'n Crunch, blue plastic, 1986, 1½", VG.......**$5.00**

Figure, Smog Master, silver plastic robot, 1986, 1½", NM..**$5.00**

Figure, Soggie, nearly clear plastic, 1986, 1½", EX.......**$5.00**

Frisbee, blue plastic w/Cap'n in center, MIP, 1970s, EX.**$50.00**

Handkerchief, white w/4 colorful scenes, 8x8", EX....**$50.00**

Kaleidoscope, cardboard, 1960s, 7", EX.......................**$35.00**

Membership kit, Quaker Oats, 1965, M (EX mailer), from $200 to...**$300.00**

Puzzle, 8 figures, wooden, Fisher-Price, 8½x12" **$38.00**

Ring, plastic figure, NM...**$100.00**

Sea Cycle, wind-up, moves through water, mail-in premium, General Mills, 1970s, MIB **$20.00**

Treasure chest, tan w/Cap'n Crunch & skull & crossbones, 5 gold coins, shovel, lock & treasure map inside, EX **$75.00**

Tumbler, plastic, Ship Shape, 1963, 6", NM..................**$25.00**

Charlie Tuna

Poor Charlie, never quite good enough for the Star-Kist folks to can, though he yearns for them to catch him; but since the early 1970s he's done a terrific job working for them as the company logo. A dapper blue-fin tuna in glasses and a beret, he's appeared in magazines, done TV commercials, modeled for items as diverse as lamps and banks, but still they deny him his dream. 'Sorry, Charlie.'

Alarm clock, image of Charlie & Sorry Charlie sign on round face, 2 bells, footed, 1969, 4" dia, M.....................**$65.00**

Bank, ceramic figure, 10", from $50 to **$65.00**

Bathroom scale, painted metal, 1970s, NM, from $65 to ..**$75.00**

Camera, figural, light blue & white, red mouth & hat, wrist strap, 1971 premium, EX.......................................**$60.00**

Cigarette case, clear gloss enamel over picture of Charlie, holds 10, 3x4" **$48.00**

Dispenser, scotch tape; Sorry Charlie scene on both sides, black & ivory Bakelite, battery-operated, 1974, 6x4x3"...**$60.00**

Doll, vinyl, 2-tone blue w/pink hat & glass, marked Star-Kist Foods, 7"...**$65.00**

Figure, arms (fins) open, side-glance eyes, soft vinyl, 1973 Star-Kist Foods Inc., 7", $35.00.

Figure, painted vinyl, fins (arms) open, side-glance eyes, 1973, 7", MIB...**$200.00**

Food mixer, clear plastic w/decal of Charlie, crank turns metal rods, marked Hoan #226, 1970s, 3½x5" dia **$20.00**

Key ring, raised design on gold-tone disk, M **$10.00**

Lamp, painted plaster figure of Charlie, EX **$75.00**

Mug, thermal, marked Thermo Serve, 1977, from $5.00 to $7.00.

Patch, Charlie embroidered on green background w/yellow coral & orange starfish, Sorry Charlie sign, 1975, 3", NM **$12.00**
Pendant, Charlie on anchor, M **$10.00**
Telephone, figural, eyes light up when phone rings, 1987 premium **$50.00**
Tumbler, Tell 'Em Charlie Sent You, shows Charlie & girl tuna, 3½" **$6.50**
Watch, employee giveaway, shows Charlie w/fishhook & says Sorry Charlie, 1971, EX **$60.00**

Colonel Sanders

There's nothing fictional about the Colonel — he was a very real guy, who built an empire on the strength of his fried chicken recipe with 'eleven herbs and spices.' In the 1930s the Colonel operated a small cafe in Corbin, Kentucky. As the years went by, he developed a chain of restaurants which he sold in the mid-'60s. But even after the sale, the new company continued to use the image of the handsome southern gentlemen as their logo. The Colonel died in 1980.

Bank, white plastic, black bow tie, holding chicken bucket, ca 1970s, 10", EX, $40.00.

Ad sign, 2-sided diecut metal figure of the Colonel w/can pointed up, pipe in center to mount on base, 55½", VG **$375.00**
Bank, plastic figure, dated 1977, 7½" **$12.50**
Bank, plastic figure, Run Starling Plastics LTD, 1965, 13", NM, from $30 to **$40.00**
Bank, plastic figure w/arm around restaurant building & holding bucket of chicken, white w/red & black trim, 6", EX **$125.00**
Coin, Visit the Colonel at Mardis Gras, M **$10.00**
Coloring book, Favorite Chicken Stories, 1960s, EX ...**$25.00**
Hand puppet, white w/Colonel in white suit, plastic, 1960s, EX **$20.00**
Magazine ad, features the Colonel, 1967, 10x13" **$8.00**
Mask, multicolored plastic, 1960s, M **$38.00**
Nodder, bisque, Charlsprod Japan, 1960s, 7½", M, from $100 to **$125.00**
Nodder, papier-mache, Tops Enterprises, 1960s, 7½", MIB **$150.00**
Pin, Colonel's head, metal, EX **$6.50**
Playset, Let's Play at Kentucky Fried Chicken, Child Guidance, 1970s, EXIB **$140.00**
Poker chip, plastic, w/portrait, 1960s, M **$17.50**
Postcard, Colonel's original motel, linen, EX **$8.00**
Print block, Kentucky Fried Chicken smiling face, metal mounted on wood, 1960s, 2⅜x1½", EX **$10.00**
Record, Christmas Eve w/Colonel Sanders, cover features the Colonal in Santa cap, RCA, 1967, EX+ **$40.00**
Salt & pepper shakers, Colonel & Mrs Harland Sanders (busts), marked Marquardt Corp, 1972, 3½", pr from $85 to **$95.00**
Salt & pepper shakers, plastic Colonel figures, Starling Plastics Ltd, 1965, 4¼", pr **$35.00**
Tea set, plastic, 1970s, MIB **$110.00**
Tie tac, gold-tone molded head w/diamond chip, M .**$65.00**
Wind-up toy figure, walks w/moving arms & nodding head, 3¼", NM **$15.00**

Elsie the Cow and Family

She's the most widely recognized cow in the world; everyone knows Elsie, Borden's mascot. Since the mid-1930s, she's been seen on booklets and posters; modeled for mugs, creamers, dolls, etc.; and appeared on TV, in magazines, and at grocery stores to promote their products. Her husband is Elmer (who once sold Elmer's Glue for the same company) and her twins are best known as Beulah and Beauregard, though they've been renamed in recent years (now they're Bea and Beaumister). Elsie was retired in the 1960s, but due to public demand was soon reinstated to her rightful position and continues today to promote the company's dairy products.

Advisor: Lee Garmon (See Directory, Advertising)

Bag, Borden's Dog Food, shows Elsie's face & running dog, red, blue & tan, M **$50.00**

Bank, plastic Beauregard figure, red, Irwin, 1950s, 5", EX **$65.00**

Banner, You Can Make the Difference, Elsie's head & The Borden Difference, red, white & blue silk, 72x30", EX **$85.00**

Book, Elsie's Things To Do, 1945, 24 pages, unused, EX **$40.00**

Bottle, milk; Borden's & Elsie's picture in red on clear glass, 1-qt, EX..**$55.00**

Box, pill; gold-tone metal w/Elsie photo, 3-compartment, hinged lid, 2" dia **$35.00**

Christmas card, Season's Greetings From Borden's & Your Milkman, image of Beauregard in wreath, 1940s, 5x5½", EX..**$35.00**

Cigarette lighter, applied Elsie face, 1950s, EX...........**$55.00**

Clock, Borden's Milk & Ice Cream Sold Here, round w/glass front, decal of Elsie in center, 21", VG **$150.00**

Comic book, Free w/Your Purchase of a Bottle of Elmer's Glue, shows Elsie & Elmer demonstrating use for glue, 1950s, EX..**$75.00**

Compact, gold-tone metal w/Elsie's logo & 1857–Second 100 Years..**$75.00**

Cookie jar, barrel shape w/figural Elsie head on lid, embossed Elsie & Handle With Care, 13", from $400 to **$500.00**

Cottage cheese container, Awarded First Prize at the New York State Fair 1958, wax w/tin lid, 8-oz, EX **$18.00**

Creamer & sugar bowl, Elsie & Elmer, marked McCoy USA..**$80.00**

Creamer and sugar bowl, Elsie and Beauregard, plastic, marked F&F, M, $125.00 for the pair.

Creamer & sugar bowl, molded plastic heads, marked TBC The Borden Co, Made in USA, 3½", from $45 to.**$55.00**

Cup, sundae; clear glass w/Elsie portrait, 6" **$10.00**

Display, Elsie's face w/daisy necklace in lg daisy petals, bright colors, 14" dia **$45.00**

Doll, Elsie, plush body w/rubber head & felt hooves, cloth ribbon around neck, moos when shaken, 1950s, 14", EX..**$125.00**

Hand puppet, Elsie's baby, vinyl w/cloth body, EX...**$75.00**

Lamp, Elsie w/Beauregard sitting in chair, from $350 to...**$375.00**

Letter opener, red plastic w/round image of Elsie flashing to Borden's Milk 23 Ways Guarded, EX **$70.00**

Menu, Elsie in apron w/cup on cover, opens to listings, 1950s..**$20.00**

Mug, Beulah portrait, gold trim, 1940s **$65.00**

Mug, white w/picture in center, Universal-Cambridge, from $35 to..**$40.00**

Needle book, image of Elsie in yellow daisy on red background, 5¼", VG..**$35.00**

Night light, Elsie's head..**$35.00**

Place mat, paper, Elsie Says for Over 125 Years Folks Have Known..., 5 color scenes w/geometric border, 11x17", M..**$25.00**

Postcard, Elsie & Beauregard in Person, from tour, vintage, EX..**$18.00**

Postcard, Elsie the Cow & Her Brand New Twins, color, 1957, EX..**$9.00**

Push-button puppet, Mespo, 6", EX..**$80.00**

Recipe book, Elsie's Hostess Recipe Book/...Sour Cream/Cottage Cheese/Lite-Line Yogurt, shows Elsie in apron, 1970s, M..**$25.00**

Salt & pepper shaker, bust, white w/yellow ribbon at neck, 1-pc, from $100 to..**$125.00**

Salt & pepper shakers, ceramic figures of Beulah & Beauregard seated, Japan, 3½", EX, pr.................**$75.00**

Salt & pepper shakers, half-figures, names at bottom, pr from $150 to..**$175.00**

Sign, diecut Elsie head, 16x20"..**$125.00**

Sweater, Elsie image woven into fabric, 100% orlon arcylic, vintage premium item, lg, EX..**$50.00**

Tab button, tin litho image of Elsie in yellow daisy on blue background, vintage, 1½", VG..**$15.00**

Tablecloth, cotton, printed scene w/Elsie & family at outdoor barbecue, 1940s, 36x56", NM..**$145.00**

Toy truck, Borden's Fresh Milk, metal w/plastic trim, yellow & white w/daisy decal, Buddy L, 1960s, 11", VG+ **$125.00**

Tray, Borden's Ice Cream w/Elsie's picture, maroon, green & yellow, 10½x15", EX **$230.00**

Tumbler, clear glass w/image of Elmer in tiny car & Beulah w/checkered flag, 1930s, 4¾", M **$55.00**

Tumbler, clear glass w/image of Elsie in daisy & name below, 6", M..**$25.00**

Tumbler, clear glass w/images of Elsie, Elmer & Beauregard in 1776 garb, red, white & blue, M....................**$22.00**

Gerber Baby

Since the late 1920s, the Gerber company has used the smiling face of a baby to promote their line of prepared strained baby food. Several dolls and rubber squeeze toys have been made over the years. Even if you're a novice collector, they'll be easy to spot. Some of the earlier dolls hold a can of product in their hand. Look for the Gerber mark on later dolls. For further information see *A Collector's Guide to the Gerber Baby* by Joan Stryker Grubaugh, Ed.D.

Bank, Gerber Baby Food Commemorative, 1928 label, 1978..**$10.00**

Bank, Orange Juice, repro of early label, printed top..**$13.00**

Beach towel, white velour w/classic image & Gerber name, 1988, 62x32" **$15.00**

Bottle, blue plastic, kitten or penguin shape, 1970s...**$10.00**

Cafeteria tray, 1950s...**$40.00**

Can, Chopped Vegetables & Beef w/Rice, 1931-39, 3x2" dia, EX..**$15.00**

Clock, hexagonal wooden frame, time & temperature, 1970s, 1½"..**$40.00**

Cup, silver metal w/penny-size baby head mounted on side, 1990 ....**$55.00**

Decal, stick-on, classic round image, blue & white, 1970s...**$3.00**

Doll, Black drink & wet, w/accessories, Atlanta Novelty Co for JC Penney, 1981, 12", NRFB.........................**$100.00**

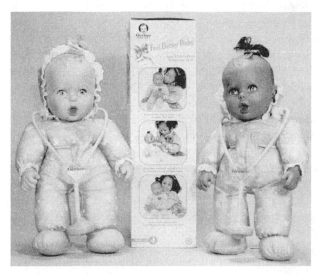

Doll, Feel Better Baby, 1994, either style, $25.00. (Photo courtesy Joan Stryker Grubaugh)

Doll, foam-filled, red dress, blanket & pink tub, Atlanta Novelty, 1985, 12".......................................**$30.00**

Doll, premium (last issue), Atlanta Novelty, 1985, 12", MIB, from $60 to..**$75.00**

Doll, premium (2nd), movable head & limbs, drinks & wets, w/accessories, Sun Rubber, 1955-59 ....**$140.00**

Doll, rag-type, I'm a Gerber Kid, various outfits & hair coloring, Atlanta Novlety, 1981-84, 11½", ea **$20.00**

Doll, squeak vinyl boy or girl, I'm a Gerber Kid, 1980s, 8", ea **$20.00**

License plate, metal, baby & Gerber, 1981 ....**$14.00**

Mug, clear glass w/blue Safety Around the Clock, dancing clock image on 1 side & baby image on reverse, 1980s, 5½"..**$18.00**

Patch, cloth oval w/Fifty Years of Caring under image flanked by 1928/1978, blue on white w/blue border.........**$10.00**

Pendant, pewter, 1979...**$25.00**

Postcard, Fremont Canning Co or Gerber Products Co, color, 1930s, from $8 to.......................................**$10.00**

Recipe book, Recipes for Toddlers, 1952.................**$5.00**

Spoon, baby on handle, silver-plated, marked Winthrop, 5½", EX..**$15.00**

Tote bag, plastic, classic image, name & phrase, dark blue on white, w/handle, early 1990s **$3.00**

Toy phone, Talk-Back, Arrow Products, 1969.............**$35.00**

Waist (Sports) pouch, black nylon w/Gerber in white, integral waistband, 1990s **$10.00**

Swiss Bells, 1969, $35.00. (Photo courtesy Joan Stryker Grubaugh)

Green Giant

The Jolly Green Giant has been a well-known ad fixture since the 1950s (some research indicates an earlier date); he was originally devised to represent a strain of European peas much larger than the average size peas Americans had been accustomed to. At any rate, when Minnesota Valley Canning changed its name to Green Giant, he was their obvious choice. Rather a terse individual himself, by 1974 he was joined by Little Green Sprout, with the lively eyes and more talkative personality.

In addition to a variety of toys and other memorabilia already on the market, in 1988 Benjamin Medwin put out a line of Little Green Sprout items. These are listed below.

Advisor: Lil West (See Directory, Advertising)

Ad, Jolly Green Giant, paper, color, 1950, 13x10", EX .**$10.00**

Bank, Little Sprout, ceramic, 6", Japan, M **$40.00**

Bank, Little Sprout, composition, plays Valley of the Green Giant, 8½" **$50.00**

Brush holder, Little Sprout, w/4 brushes, Benjamin Medwin, MIB **$40.00**

Clock, Little Sprout holding round dial on front of base, talking alarm, 1986, 10½", EX.................................**$25.00**

Cookie jar, Little Sprout, Benjamin Medwin, 1990-92, MIB **$65.00**

Dinnerware set, plate, cup, knife & fork, 1991, MIB..**$10.00**

Doll, Green Giant, cloth, 1966, 16", M (in original mailer), from $25 to..**$35.00**

Doll, Green Giant, vinyl, 1970s, 9", EX......................**$85.00**

Doll, Little Sprout, plush w/felt hat & clothes, 1970, from $20 to **$30.00**

Doll, Little Sprout, stuffed cloth, 1974, 10½", NM.......**$15.00**

Doll, Little Sprout, talker, MIP **$55.00**

Doll, Little Sprout, vinyl, 1970s-90s, 6½", EX, from $10 to **$20.00**

Fabric, Green Giant & Little Sprout, 48x45" **$20.00**

Farm Factory, w/Little Sprout finger puppet & all accessories, MIB **$20.00**

Flashlight, Little Sprout, MIB.................................**$45.00**

Jump rope, Little Sprout, MIB.................................**$20.00**

Kite, plastic, mail-in premium, late 1960s, 42x48", unused, M...**$30.00**

Lamp, Little Sprout holding balloons, touch-on, 1985-86, 14½", M, from $35 to...**$45.00**

Lapel pin, Green Giant.......................................**$7.00**

Magnet, Little Sprout, Benjamin Medwin, 1988, 2-pc, MIB..**$10.00**

Napkin holder, Little Sprout, Benjamin Medwin, MIB ..**$10.00**

Pencil sharpener, Niblets Corn can shape, 1960s, 5x3" dia, MIB **$25.00**

Planter, Little Sprout, Benjamin Medwin, 1988, MIB...**$35.00**

Puzzles, 1981, $15.00 each. (Photo courtesy Lil West)

Salt & pepper shakers, Little Sprout, Benjamin Medwin, 1990-92, MIB, pr **$25.00**

Scouring pad holder w/pad, Little Sprout, Benjamin Medwin, 1988, MIP...**$15.00**

Sleeping bag, yellow w/green characters, 31x64", M (w/original plastic bag)...**$35.00**

Spoon rest, Little Sprout, Benjamin Medwin, 1988, MIB..**$30.00**

Telephone, Little Sprout, Made in Hong Kong, Pillsbury Co., 1984, MIB, $100.00. (Photo courtesy Lil West)

Toy truck, Green Giant Corn tractor-trailer, Nylint, 21", VG **$55.00**

Toy truck, Green Giant Peas stake truck, Tonka, 1953, EX **$300.00**

Wastebasket, Green Giant Niblets Whole Kernel Golden Corn label on metal oval form, 1970s..................**$45.00**

Joe Camel

Joe Camel, the ultimate 'cool character,' was only on the scene for a few years as a comic character. The all-around Renaissance beast, he dated beautiful women, drove fast motorcycles and cars, lazed on the beach, played pool, hung around with his pals (the Hard Pack), and dressed formally for dinner and the theatre. He was 'done in' by the anti-cigarette lobby because he smoked. Now reduced to a real camel, his comic strip human persona is avidly collected by both women and men. Prices have been steadily rising as more and more people come to appreciate him as the great icon he is.

Advisors: C.J. Russell and Pamela E. Apkarian-Russell (See Directory, Halloween)

Alarm clock, pyramid shape, battery-operated, RJRTC, 1993, 5x5x4", EX **$30.00**

Apron, Max & Ray's barbecue **$30.00**

Ashtray, cobalt glass, 57 Chevy, license plate on front & back, M...**$25.00**

Ashtray, plastic, Camel Lights, oblong w/image of Joe playing pool, MIB (marked Camel Pool Table Ashtray) **$25.00**

Calendar, 1992, Year in Pictures, MIP **$20.00**

Poker chips, in casino tin, $65.00. (Photo courtesy C.J. Russell and Pamela E. Apkarian-Russell)

Compact mirror, white plastic w/Joe & the Gang before lg Camels sign w/city buildings either side, 3½x2½"..**$20.00**

Dart board & cabinet, Joe's Place on front, wooden, 19x21½x3", NM..**$125.00**

Diecast model dragster, 1/64 scale, w/case, MIB........**$50.00**

Diecast model NASCAR race car, Jimmy Spencer #23, 1995, 1/64 scale, MIB **$25.00**

Jacket, yellow, MIP **$12.00**

Light, Joe as pool player, 8½x21", EX........................**$30.00**

Lighter, Joe's 75th anniversary, Zippo, MIB.................**$25.00**

Mirror, Joe on Harley motorcycle, thumbs up & in leather jacket & hat, 8x10"..**$35.00**

Mouse pad, various designs, ea...................................**$10.00**

Mug, Joe, Hard Pack & pals playing cards in bar, 6¾"..**$20.00**

Plate, Joe playing billiards, marked RJRTC, MIB.........**$40.00**

Salt & pepper shakers, ceramic figures as Max & Ray, pr..**$25.00**

Salt & pepper shakers, plastic figures, 1993 RJRTC on bottom, 4", EX, pr...**$20.00**

Stein, ceramic, Joe in Alpine outfit playing accordion..**$125.00**

Vest, Joe's Fish & Game Club logo on right front top pocket, khali...**$20.00**

Wheel cover, multicolor image of Joe in jeep on blue, 1993...**$40.00**

M & M Candy Men

Toppers for M&M packaging first appeared about 1988; since then other M&M items have been introduced that portray the clever antics of these colorful characters. Toppers have been issued for seasonal holidays as well as Olympic events.

Advisors: Bill and Pat Poe (See Directory, Fast-Food Collectibles)

Cookie jar, produced by Haeger, 1982, marked M&M Mars, from $175.00 to $225.00. (Photo courtesy Joyce and Fred Roerig)

Banner, beach scene, plastic, 1995, 26x30" **$12.00**

Banner, Holiday Express, Christmas scene w/train, plastic, 1996, 26x30"...**$12.00**

Bean Bag toys, M&M shape, red, green, blue or yellow, 6", ea from $5 to **$10.00**

Bean bag toys, peanut shape, golfer or witch, 6", ea from $10 to...**$20.00**

Book, Plain & Peanut & the Missing Christmas Present, 1993, NM...**$6.00**

Calculator, yellow w/different color M&M keys, MIB, from $10 to..**$20.00**

Chair, blue w/candies graphic on front, glass holders on armrests, inflatable vinyl, 26" **$40.00**

Clock, cuckoo; Red comes out of top & Yellow swings on chime string, NMIB...**$45.00**

Coin holder, set of 6 containers full of mini M&Ms, 1996, per set...**$10.00**

Cookie cutter, plain shape, standing w/arms up, red plastic, 3" **$4.00**

Dispenser, spaceship w/M symbol, press button to dispense candy, battery-op, red, yellow or blue, MOC, ea...**$8.00**

Dispenser, 1991, peanut, brown, sm, from $2 to **$5.00**

Dispenser, 1991, peanut, orange, green or yellow, sm, ea **$5.00**

Dispenser, 1991, plain, brown, sm, from $5 to **$10.00**

Dispenser, 1991, plain, holding bouquet of flowers, yellow, sm, from $2 to...**$5.00**

Dispenser, 1991, plain, red, lg, from $10 to **$15.00**

Dispenser, 1992, peanut, red, lg..................................**$20.00**

Dispenser, 1995, peanut football player, yellow, lg....**$20.00**

Dispenser, 1997, peanut shape, basketball player **$15.00**

Display, Red standing w/hands at waist, inflatable, w/hanger & repair kit, 30", MIB..................................**$22.50**

Doll, bear, Brown in yellow shirt w/brown letters, plush, 15"...**$23.50**

Egg cup, Yellow w/arms in back holding basket w/egg cup inside, Mars, 1993, EX **$28.00**

Figure, peanut w/bendable arms & legs, blue or yellow, 7", ea from $15 to..**$20.00**

Figure, plain M&M w/bendable arms & legs, red, 5½" .**$20.00**

Figurine, Red as Santa in sleigh w/Yellow as reindeer pulling it, marked FTP, 2 pcs, 5x10" on white base, EX ..**$30.00**

Figurine, Red holding torch, on white base, 1988, EX...**$40.00**

Jack-o-lantern, Yellow as pumpkin, marked Mars 1999, 11x9", MIB...**$20.00**

Jar, utility; Red & Yellow carry wisks, Green measuring cups & Orange a rolling pin, ceramic, 1996, 5x4½" dia, MIB.**$25.00**

Magnet, red plain M&M or yellow peanut, plush, 2", ea..**$8.00**

Planter, Green on swing w/Red standing behind w/flowers in hand, R&G carved in tree, ceramic, 6½x5½"..**$20.00**

Poster, Yellow w/bags of candy & Red pointing w/caption: Hey You, Don't Forget Your M&Ms, 17x22", M....**$30.00**

Shower radio & toothbrush holder, Yellow in mask, snorkel & flippers, Official M&M, battery-operated, MIB..**$30.00**

Topper, Christmas, peanut w/bag of toys on shoulder, green, round base, 1997..**$3.50**

Topper, Christmas, plain M&M going down chimney w/bag of toys, green, round base, 1992 ....**$3.50**

Topper, Christmas, plain M&M on ice skates wearing green, round base, 1989..**$3.50**

Topper, Easter, peanut w/paint brush & chick in egg, turquoise, pink, lavender or lime green, round base, 1994, ea ..**$4.00**

Topper, Valentine's Day, peanut w/bow & arrow, brown, heart w/arrow on round base, 1992....................**$7.00**

Topper, Valentine's Day, plain M&M postman holding pink valentine, red, round base **$4.00**

Utensil holder, 1 in chef's hat holding rolling pin, 3 others hold spoon or wisk, Mars, 1996, NM **$5.00**

Wristwatch, plain M&M skate boarder as second hand, in plastic case w/cardboard sleeve, 1994 ....**$50.00**

Wristwatch, plain M&M's face, in padded sleeve, 1993 ..**$45.00**

Michelin Man (Bibendum or Mr. Bib)

Perhaps one of the oldest character logos around today, Mr. Bib actually originated in the late 1800s, inspired by a stack of tires that one of the company founders thought suggested the figure of a man. Over the years his image has changed considerably, but the Michelin Tire Man continues today to represent his company in many countries around the world.

Ashtray, ceramic, Mr Bib seated on rim, single rest ...**$55.00**
Ashtray, molded cream plastic Mr Bib on black base, 1940s, 6x3¾" dia, from $75 to..**$90.00**
Car air freshener, waving figure sitting in tire, Japanese promo, M...**$30.00**
Clock, hexagonal w/image of Mr Bib running above Michelin X, white plastic frame w/metal back, 14x16", EX..**$135.00**
Costume, nylon & metal figure w/yellow sash lettered Michelin, eyes outlined w/black goggles, EX.....**$900.00**
Cuff links, gold-tone w/white Mr Bib on blue background, ⅞" dia, pr **$50.00**
Cup, plastic, Mr Bib on side, EX **$5.00**
Desk ornament/pen holder, ceramic Mr Bib figure, made for 100-year birthday, rare **$50.00**
Dice game, white plastic container w/3-D Mr Bib holds 8 dice w/black letters & blue Mr Bib figures, 3½x2½", M **$85.00**
Doll, Mr Bib standing, holding baby & wearing blue bib w/Michelin in embossed lettering, 7"..................**$125.00**
Figure, ceramic, Mr Bib w/hands at waist, green glaze, 1950s, made in Holland, 12½" **$500.00**
Figure, plastic, adjusts to fit on top of truck cab, 1970s-80s, 18", EX...**$140.00**
Figure, plastic, on motorcycle, EX..............................**$110.00**
Figure, plastic, white, lettering on banner, 12", NM, from $50 to..**$75.00**
Key chain, running figure, 1½", EX **$15.00**
Nodder, attaches to dashboard, 2 styles, ea **$18.00**
Playing cards, Mr Bib courts, wide non-standard, VG ..**$18.00**
Puzzle, forms figure of Mr Bib on motorcycle, MIP ...**$55.00**
Radio, Mr Bib figure, made in Italy/distributed in France, 5x6½", from $250 to...**$300.00**
Ramp walker, wind-up, MIB...**$25.00**
Sign, porcelain, pointed bottom, Michelin lettered above Mr Bib w/tire, 31½x27", NM......................................**$300.00**

Signs, diecut porcelain: Mr. Bib on bicycle, red, two-sided, 18" x 15", NM, $450.00; Mr. Bib running beside tire, blue, 18" x 15", NM, $275.00.

Snow dome, Mr Bib in mountains, European issue, MIB .**$50.00**
Standee, diecut cardboard figure wearing sash w/hand up as if to say Stop & other hand pointing, easel back, 72", EX..**$90.00**
Watch fob, Mr Bib on front, Earth Moving Tires, 1½x1¾", EX..**$20.00**
Yo-yo, Mr Bib in black outline on white, EX..............**$10.00**

Mr. Peanut

The trademark character for the Planters Peanuts Company, Mr. Peanut, has been around since 1916. His appearance has changed a little from the original version, becoming more stylized in 1961. Today he's still a common sight on Planters' advertising and product containers.

Mr. Peanut has been modeled as banks, salt and pepper shakers, whistles, and many other novelty items. His image has decorated T-shirts, beach towels, playing cards, sports equipment, etc.

Today Mr. Peanut has his own 'fan club,' Peanut Pals, the collectors' organization for those who especially enjoy the Planters Peanuts area of advertising.

Advisors: Judith and Robert Walthall (See Directory, Advertising)

Club: Peanut Pals
Judith Walthall, Founder
P.O. Box 4465, Huntsville, AL 35815; 256-881-9198. Website: www.peanutpals.org. Dues: Primary member, $20 per year; Associate member (16 years old and over), $10 per year; Under 16 years old, $3 per year. Annual directory and convention news sent to members. For membership, write to PO Box 652, St. Clairsville, OH 43950. Sample newsletter: $2.

Backpack sack, heavy white cloth w/image of Mr Peanut, premium, 1974, 14" sq, EX, from $12 to...............**$15.00**
Ballpoint pen, Bic, white & blue w/blue image of Mr Peanut, premium, 1988, 6", EX, from $3 to.........................**$4.00**
Ballpoint pen, Planters Snacks/Cheez Curls/Corn Chips/Pretzels lettered on barrel, Mr Peanut image on top, 1983, EX...**$10.00**
Bowl, display; clear plastic w/logo decal, mid-1960s, 7½x9" dia, EX..**$35.00**
Coin, XIII Olympic Winter Games, Lake Placid, Mr Peanut w/Olympic logo on 1 side, logo on other, 1980, 2" dia, EX..**$10.00**
Coloring book, America...Ecology..., 1972, M...............**$8.00**
Coloring book, 12 Months, 1972, M............................**$8.00**
Cushion, white vinyl w/I Am a Bingo Nut lettered in blue by Mr Peanut image, handled, fantasy item, 1980s, 14", NM **$5.00**
Display rack, 2-tiered w/slanted front, blue plastic w/3 for 99¢ & Planters lettered on marquee, 1980s, NM ..**$25.00**
Doilies, white plastic w/logo in center, set of 4, 1959, 4½" dia, MIP (sealed)..**$25.00**

Magnet, white metal w/colorful image of Mr Peanut, by Andy Rooney, 1994, 3x1¼", NM..................**$3.00**

Mask, cardboard, Planters Mr Peanut lettered on wrap-around hat attached to smiling peanut face w/monocle, 12x16", EX..................**$375.00**

Mechanical pencil, blue & yellow w/Mr Peanut figure atop, 1970-90, M..................**$10.00**

Mug, clear glass w/Planters Fresh Roast Peanuts & Mr Peanut logo, Anchor Hocking, 1991, M..................**$25.00**

Mug, light blue plastic, 1960s, EX..................**$10.00**

Music box, Planters Peanuts & Snacks on side of wooden delivery truck, plays America the Beautiful, Price Bros, 8x5", EX..................**$40.00**

Night light, white sq w/'Mister Peanut' & character, EX..................**$25.00**

Nut bag, cellophane, coupon on back for Mr Peanut Mechanical Pencil & Bank, 1945s, 7x4", VG, from $5 to..................**$10.00**

Nut dish, 3-compartment w/Mr Peanut figure in center, plastic, 4-color, 1950s, 4½x5" dia, EX..................**$50.00**

Oil & vinegar set, ceramic figures of Mr Peanut in classic pose, late 1950s, 7", EX+, pr, from $150 to........**$200.00**

Peanut-butter maker, Picam, plastic, w/knife, scoop, catch pan & recipes, 1970, 12", MIB from $35 to..........**$40.00**

Peanut-butter maker, plastic, 1967, marked Emenee, 12¼", MIB, $65.00. (Photo courtesy B.J. Summers)

Picnic jug, Planters Corn Chips, insulated plastic w/swing handle, Mr Peanut logo, 1983..................**$25.00**

Pin, 75th Anniversary (1906-1981), gold-tone metal w/enamel detail, Planters name diecut across top, 1", EX........**$15.00**

Pitcher & tumbler set, yellow plastic w/blue Planters Peanuts lettered above blue image of Mr Peanut, 4 tumblers, 1980..................**$25.00**

Plate, pewter, 75th Anniversay logo, Wilton Armatale, 1981, 6" dia, EX..................**$45.00**

Recipe book, Soup to Nuts, 1978s, unused, M, from $8 to..................**$10.00**

Roadster, plastic peanut shape w/Mr Peanut driving, 1950s, NM..................**$500.00**

Spoon, gold-tone w/sq-framed embossed image of Mr Peanut at top, 1978, M..................**$15.00**

Store display, plastic, 1979, 12" x 7½", $40.00. (Photo courtesy B.J. Summers)

Straw, plastic w/figure of Mr Peanut on end, premium, 8", EX, from $3 to..................**$5.00**

Tennis ball, image of Mr Peanut, Dunlop, 1980s, EX...**$5.00**

Tote bag, blue canvas w/yellow, white & black image of Mr Peanut & Planters Peanuts, 1980s, 19x12", unused, M..................**$15.00**

Tray, Planters/Temptation Beyond Endurance, Mr Peanut image on blue sq w/flat rim, 1989, 14", NM........**$30.00**

Old Crow

Old Crow collectors have learned to date this character by the cut of his vest and the tilt of his head along with other characteristics of his stance and attire. Advertising Kentucky whiskey, he appears as an elegant gent in his tuxedo and top hat.

Advisor: Geneva Addy (See Directory, Dolls)

Ashtray, black glass, 1¼x3½", EX..................**$30.00**

Bottle, bright red vest, gold cane, American, 12½"....**$75.00**

Bottle, light red vest, yellow cane, Royal Doulton, 12½"..**$175.00**

Bottle topper, ceramic figure, sm..................**$35.00**

Bottle topper, plastic figure..................**$35.00**

Figure, brass w/We Pour It brass plaque on black base, 13", EX..................**$75.00**

Figure, chalkware, no cane or glasses, 14"..................**$45.00**

Figure, composition, flaked paint, 9"..................**$100.00**

Figure, composition, flaked paint, 30", G-..................**$400.00**

Figure, 5" crow in brass birdcage..................**$65.00**

Jigger, plastic..................**$18.00**

Key chain, figural..................**$10.00**

Lamp, plastic lantern w/brass paint, Advertising Novelty Co, 13½"..................**$75.00**

Lamp, porcelain, red vest w/gold buttons, 1960s, 14", from $175 to..................**$200.00**

Pitcher, glass w/metal ring & handle, 5"..................**$25.00**

Playing cards, Two Crows You See Good Luck to Thee, 2 decks, 1967, EX..................**$40.00**

Roly-Poly, plastic, leaded rocker, 9"..................**$95.00**

Stand for bottle, 3 crows (9", 7" & 5") on 9" plastic base..................**$95.00**

Stand for bottle, 9" crow in birdcage (on side)...........**$75.00**
Stand-up, cardboard, 8"...**$30.00**
Stir stick, black plastic figure, Perfection Plastics, 1950s, 6½"...**$10.00**
Thermometer, Taste the Greatness of Historic Old Crow, red, white & black, 13½", EX....................................**$200.00**
Tumbler, bourbon; clear w/black crow & lettering, 5" ..**$12.50**
Tumbler, clear w/crow stem, Libbey..........................**$35.00**

Poppin' Fresh (Pillsbury Doughboy) and Family

Who could be more lovable than the chubby blue-eyed Doughboy with the infectious giggle introduced by the Pillsbury Company in 1965. Wearing nothing but a neck scarf and a chef's hat, he single-handedly promoted the company's famous biscuits in a tube until about 1969. It was then that the company changed his name to 'Poppin' Fresh' and soon after presented him with a sweet-faced, bonnet-attired mate named Poppie. Before long, they had created a whole family for him. Many premiums such as dolls, salt and pepper shakers, and cookie jars have been produced over the years. In 1988 the Benjamin Medwin Co. made several items for Pillsbury; all of these white ceramic Doughboy items are listed below. Also offered in 1988, the Poppin' Fresh Line featured the plump little fellow holding a plate of cookies; trim colors were mauve pink and blue. The Funfetti line was produced in 1992, again featuring Poppin' Fresh, this time alongside a cupcake topped with Funfetti icing (at that time a fairly new Pillsbury product), and again the producer was Benjamin Medwin.

Advisor: Lil West (See Directory, Advertising)

Club: The Lovin' Connection
2343 10000 Rd.
Oswego, KS 67356; 316-795-2842

Address book, spiral-bound, Poppin' Fresh on front, EX ..**$6.00**
Bank, Poppin' Fresh, ceramic, Doughboy White Ceramic Line, Benjamin Medwin, 1988, MIB......................**$30.00**
Bank, Poppin' Fresh, ceramic, 1980s mail-in premium, M ..**$35.00**
Bowl, bread; embossed image, Doughboy White Ceramic Line, Benjamin Medwin, 1988, rare, 16", MIB, from $150 to...**$200.00**
Bowls, mixing; embossed image, Doughboy White Ceramic Line, Benjamin Medwin/Portugal, 1988, scarce, set of 3, MIB **$95.00**
Bulletin board/chalkboard, Poppin' Fresh Line, 1988, very hard to find **$85.00**
Canisters, ceramic w/embossed image, Doughboy White Ceramic Line, Benjamin Medwin, 1988, set of 4, MIB, from $95 to...**$135.00**
Canisters, glass, marked Goodies w/image of Poppin' Fresh, glass or wooden knob, Anchor Hocking (unmarked), 1991, ea **$35.00**
Canisters, metal, mauve & blue on white, Poppin' Fresh Line, Benjamin Medwin, 1988, set of 4......................**$100.00**

Cookie jar, Doughboy White Ceramic Line, Benjamin Medwin, 1988, MIB..**$50.00**
Cookie jar, Funfetti Line, Benjamin Medwin, 1991, from $55 to..**$65.00**
Cookie jar, Poppin' Fresh figure, ceramic, Cookies embossed across chest, 1973, 11", EX...........................**$75.00**
Creamer & sugar bowl w/spoon, Doughboy White Ceramic Line, 1988, MIB **$35.00**
Decals, set of 18, MIP...**$10.00**
Display figure, Poppin' Fresh, styrofoam, 1980s, 2-pc, 50", EX, from $200 to..**$225.00**
Doll, Poppin' Fresh, bean bag, 2 styles, M, ea from $10 to..**$20.00**
Doll, Poppin' Fresh, stuffed cloth, pull-string talker, Mattel, 16", NM..**$100.00**
Doll, Poppin' Fresh, stuffed cloth, 1970s, 14", VG......**$15.00**
Doll, Poppin' Fresh, stuffed cloth, 1972, 11", EX, from $15 to..**$20.00**
Doll, Poppin' Fresh, stuffed plush, 1982, M, from $40 to..**$50.00**
Figure, Grandmommer, vinyl, 1974, 5", M, from $75 to **$95.00**
Figure, Grandpopper, vinyl, 1974, 5¼", M, from $75 to **$95.00**
Figure, Poppie Fresh, vinyl, 1972, 6", NM **$15.00**
Figure, Poppin' Fresh, cold-cast porcelain, set of 4 in various poses, 5", MIB **$60.00**
Figure, Poppin' Fresh, vinyl, 1971, 7", NM **$15.00**
Figure, Poppin' Fresh & Poppie, vinyl, on stands as set, M, pr from $35 to...**$40.00**
Finger puppet, Biscuit (cat) or Flapjack (dog), vinyl, 1974, ea **$35.00**
Finger puppet, Bun Bun (girl), Popper (boy), Poppin' Fresh or Poppie, vinyl, 1974, ea **$25.00**
Finger Puppets, Poppin' Fresh & Pals, set of 3, rare, MIB...**$235.00**
Jack-in-the-box, can shape, Poppin' Fresh Biscuits on side, Poppin' pops out end, 5", EX.............................**$75.00**

Jar, snap-on lid, Anchor Hocking, three sizes, 1½-liter, 2-litre, and 3-liter (smallest harder to find), from $20.00 to $25.00 each. (Photo courtesy Lil West)

Jewelry box & jewelry, Poppin' Fresh, pewter, w/pin, necklace & earrings, EX...**$20.00**
Key chain, Poppin' Fresh figure, soft vinyl, MOC.........**$6.00**

Lotion/soap dispenser, embossed image, Doughboy White Ceramic Line, Benjamin Medwin, 1988, MIB........**$22.00**

Magnets, Poppin' Fresh & Poppie, Doughboy White Ceramic Line, Benjamin Medwin, 1988, 2-pc set, MIB.......**$20.00**

Magnets, Poppin' Fresh & Poppie, plastic, 1970s premium, 2-pc set, MIP **$35.00**

Memo pad, diecut Poppin' Fresh in upper left corner, 40 sheets, 7x4", EX..**$8.00**

Mug, ceramic, features Poppin' Fresh, 1985, 5", VG...**$15.00**

Mug, plastic figure, 1979, 4½", from $10 to **$15.00**

Napkin holder, Doughboy White Ceramic Line, Benjamin Medwin, 1988, MIB..**$25.00**

Napkin holder, Funfetti Line, Benjamin Medwin, 1992, MIB **$20.00**

Pencil, blue & white, M...**$20.00**

Plant holder, Doughboy White Ceramic Line, Benjamin Medwin, 1988, MIB..**$25.00**

Playhouse, vinyl, w/4 finger puppets (Poppin' Fresh, Poppie, Popper & Bun Bun), 1974, rare, complete, from $250 to **$300.00**

Pop-up can, Poppin' Fresh, blue version, EX **$300.00**

Pop-up can, Poppin' Fresh, orange version, M........**$200.00**

Potpourri burner, Doughboy White Ceramic Line, Benjamin Medwin, 1988, rare, 3-pc, M **$50.00**

Radio, Poppin' Fresh, plastic, w/headphones, 1985, 6½", MIB **$85.00**

Salt & pepper shakers, ceramic, Poppin' Fresh, Doughboy White Ceramic Line, Benjamin Medwin, range size, 1988, MIB, pr..**$20.00**

Salt & pepper shakers, ceramic, Poppin' Fresh, white w/blue details painted over glaze, 1969, 3½", EX, pr.......**$25.00**

Salt & pepper shakers, ceramic, Poppin' Fresh w/cupcake, Funfetti Line, 1992, MIB, pr **$35.00**

Salt & pepper shakers, plastic, Poppin' Fresh & Poppie, white w/blue details, range size, dated 1988, pr...........**$35.00**

School box, Poppin' Fresh, w/pencils, eraser, etc, EX..**$100.00**

Scouring pad holder w/pad, Doughboy White Ceramic Line, Benjamin Medwin, 1988, M **$20.00**

Soap dish, Poppie, Doughboy White Ceramic Line, Benjamin Medwin, 1988, M **$20.00**

Spoon holder, Funfetti Line, Benjamin Medwin, recent issue but dated 1988, MIB **$15.00**

Spoon rest, Poppin' Fresh & Poppie, Doughboy White Ceramic Line, Benjamin Medwin, recent issue but dated 1988, MIB **$15.00**

Standee, Poppin' Fresh, promotional, 1985, from $20 to..**$30.00**

Timer, plastic, digital, 1992, M **$10.00**

Tool holder w/tools, Doughboy White Ceramic Line, Benjamin Medwin, 1988..**$20.00**

Tool holder w/tools, Funfetti Line, Benjamin Medwin, 1992, MIB **$20.00**

Towel holder, Poppie, Doughboy White Ceramic Line, Benjamin Medwin, 1988, M **$25.00**

Towel holder, Poppin' Fresh, Doughboy White Ceramic Line, Benjamin Medwin, 1988, M, from $25 to.............**$30.00**

Towels, Poppin' Fresh Line, Cannon, 1988, 4-pc set, MIP...**$30.00**

Toy truck, battery-operated, Nylint, 1989, MIB.........**$100.00**

Trivet, Poppin' Fresh Line, 1988, M............................**$25.00**

Wristwatch, gold-tone case, M......................................**$50.00**

Reddy Kilowatt

Reddy was developed during the late 1920s and became very well known during the 1950s. His job was to promote electric power companies all over the United States, which he did with aplomb! Reddy memorabilia is highly collectible today, with the small-head plastic figures sometimes selling for $200.00 or more. On Reddy's 65th birthday (1992), a special 'one-time-only' line of commemoratives was issued. This line consisted of approximately thirty different items issued in crystal, gold, pewter, silver, etc. All items were limited editions and quite costly. Because of high collector demand, new merchandise is flooding the market. Watch for items such as a round mirror, a small hand-held game with movable sqs, a ring-toss game, etc., marked 'Made in China.'

Advisor: Lee Garmon (See Directory, Advertising)

Ashtray, clear glass w/red pryo head image of Reddy, 3½" sq **$18.00**

Book, Safety First, Pennsylvania Power & Light Co, 254 pages, 1957, EX..**$15.00**

Booklet, Canning & Other Methods of Home Preservation of the Victory Corps, 1940s, 26 pages, 1940s, VG+..**$35.00**

Booklet, Our Favorite Cakes, black & red litho, 18 pages, 1940s, EX **$25.00**

Booklet, Wartime Menus & Recipes, red, white & blue w/Reddy Victory logo on cover, 1940s, EX+........**$40.00**

Bottle cap, Your Electric Servant, Florida Power Corporation, $10.00. (Photo courtesy Lee Garmon)

Charm, brass Reddy figure, c 1954, USA, M (on original card w/poem)..**$25.00**

Cookie cutter, Reddy's face, red plastic, 1950s, 3" dia, EX..**$25.00**

Cuff links, MIB...**$65.00**

Egg separator, yellow plastic w/Reddy's face & Do It Electrically **$15.00**

Figure, lg head, red & white plastic on black outlet switch-plate base, MCMLXI, 6", from $150 to **$175.00**

Napkins, package of 8, 1970, MIP............................**$32.00**

Night light, Panelescent Sylvania, 3" dia, from $35 to ..**$40.00**

Patch, red Reddy in center on white, w/Reddy Kilowatt, Your Electric Servant in white on blue border, 3" dia, EX..**$25.00**
Pencil holder, gold-tone aluminum, M........................**$42.00**
Pencil sharpener, 1950s, 1" dia, EX...........................**$15.00**
Penknife, 2-blade, Zippo, EX....................................**$50.00**
Pot holder, MIP...**$30.00**
Shot glasses, clear glass w/Reddy decals in red & black, Libbey logo on bottom, set of 4, MIB.................**$180.00**
Slide-tile puzzle, white w/red & blue graphics, reproduction, 3x3½"..**$10.00**
Tie clip, metal figure on wire clip, 1950s, from $20 to **$30.00**
Trivet, Your Servant of the Century, octagonal, 6x6", EX..**$20.00**

Figure, 1950s, 6", small head, $200.00 (large-head version, $100.00). (Photo courtesy Lee Garmon)

Smokey Bear

The year 1994 was the 50th anniversary of Smokey Bear, the fire-prevention spokesbear for the State Foresters, Ad Council, and US Forest Service. After ruling out other mascots (including Bambi), by 1944 it had been decided that a bear was best suited for the job, and Smokey was born. When a little cub was rescued from a fire in a New Mexico national forest in 1950, Smokey's role intensified. Over the years his appearance has evolved from one a little more menacing to the lovable bear we know today.

The original act to protect the Smokey Bear image was enacted in 1974. The character name in the 'Smokey Bear Act' is Smokey Bear. Until the early 1960s, when his name appeared on items such as sheet music and Little Golden Books, it was 'Smokey *the* Bear.' Generally, from that time on, he became known as simply Smokey Bear.

Advisor: Glen Brady (See Directory, Advertising)

Ashtray, metal bucket shape, Smokey Says Use Your Ashtray, for car use, from $20 to **$25.00**
Badge, Junior Forest Rager, tin w/embossed letters **$8.00**

Bank, ceramic, Norcrest, marked A-478, 8", from $275.00 to $300.00. (Photo courtesy Jim and Beverly Mangus)

Bank, stands w/shovel & hand waving, Save With Smokey, Prevent Forest Fires on base, plastic, 8", EX **$25.00**
Blotter, I Will Be Careful, 1955, unused, EX.................**$8.00**
Book, True Story of..., Big Golden Book, 1973, G **$18.00**
Bowl, ceramic seated Smokey w/bucket, unmarked Norcrest, from $125 to...**$150.00**
Candy jar, ceramic, figure of Smokey holding shovel, Norcrest, from $400 to **$425.00**
Cigarette lighter, chrome, Smokey Says..., Japan, 2¼", M...**$65.00**
Cigarette snuffer, Smokey bust, Hollywood Accessories, MIP...**$30.00**
Cookie jar, Smokey's head, unmarked Norcrest, from $625 to...**$675.00**
Hand puppet, painted vinyl head w/cloth body, Ideal, 1960s, EX+...**$40.00**
Handkerchief, picnic scenes, 8", EX...........................**$25.00**
Junior Forest Ranger Kit, complete w/many items, US Department of Agriculture, 1956-57, EX+.............**$65.00**
Magic slate, Watkins-Strathmore, diecut cardboard, 1969, EX...**$85.00**
Mug, Only You Can..., official, M................................**$25.00**
Nodder, plastic, Smokey holding shovel, 1960s, EX+..**$175.00**
Ruler, Smokey's Friends Don't Play w/Matches.............**$8.00**
Salt & pepper shakers, ceramic figures of Smokey w/water bucket or shovel, 1960s, 3½", NM+, pr from $60 to...........**$75.00**
Sign, cardboard litho, Use Care in Burning Brush & Trash!, fall scene/Smokey's head, US Forest Service, 1956, 17x14", EX..**$40.00**
Stand-up, diecut Smokey holds chart detailing Forest Fire Danger Today, used at Forest Ranger Stations, 7½" .**$35.00**
Sugar shaker, ceramic w/various Smokey decals, vintage, Japan, 4¾", EX..**$70.00**
Tab button, head image of Smokey framed in yellow w/lettering, 2", EX...**$15.00**
Tray, Smokey w/shovel, trees & sign that says Prevent Forest Fires, Norcrest, NMIB **$100.00**

Snap!, Crackle!, and Pop!

Rice Krispies, the talking cereal, was first marketed by Kellogg's in 1928. Capitalizing on the sounds the cereal made in milk, the company chose elves named 'Snap,' 'Crackle,' and 'Pop' as their logos a few years later. The first of the Rice Krispie dolls were introduced in 1948. These were 12" tall, printed on fabric for the consumer to sew and stuff. The same dolls in a 16" size were offered in 1954. Premiums and memorabilia of many types followed over the years; all are very collectible.

Binoculars, paper & plastic, 1980s, MIP.......................**$10.00**
Canteen, yellow, white & red plastic, 1973, NM.........**$25.00**
Dolls, stamped cloth, set of 3, 1948, NM+ **$160.00**
Dolls, stuffed cloth w/vinyl heads, Rushton, 18", EX, ea ..**$30.00**
Dolls, vinyl, MIB (box marked Kellogg's Rice Krispies Doll) **$55.00**
Drawing template, yellow plastic, 1970, 3x5", NM **$15.00**
Hand puppets, cloth bodies w/soft plastic heads, felt hands, set of 3, 1950s, 8½", VG+........................**$75.00**
Joke machine, 4 in series, 1987, MIP, ea......................**$3.00**
Key chain, metal, paper & plastic, 1980s, EX.............**$10.00**
Parade drum, shows trio w/Toucan Sam, 4x9" dia, EX ..**$5.00**
Patch, glow-in-the-dark iron-on cloth, 1974, 2", MIP ..**$15.00**
Ring, soft rubbers face makes different expressions w/spinning dial, brass band, 1950s, EX **$175.00**
Salt & pepper shakers, ceramic, Snap! & Pop! figures, Japan, 1950s, 2½", EX, pr **$85.00**
Squeeze toy, plastic, 1978, EX....................................**$35.00**
Sticker, glow-in-the-dark paper, 1971, M **$10.00**
Trade card, Kellogg's Magic Color Card, 1933, VG+...**$25.00**

Tony the Tiger

Kellogg's introduced Tony the Tiger in 1953, and since then he's appeared on every box of their Frosted Flakes. In his deep, rich voice, he's convinced us all that they are indeed 'Gr-r-r-reat'!

Baseball, Tony's face & paw-print signature, regulation, M (still in plastic)..**$5.00**
Bowl & mug set, plastic bowl w/tiger stripes, mug w/Tony's face on side & feet as base, cereal premium, 1964, M **$35.00**
Bowling set, NMIB **$150.00**
Can, shaped like Kellogg's Racing Car w/Tony driving, 7⅜x3¼", M **$5.00**
Container/cookie jar, plastic head, Kellogg's, 1968, EX, from $75 to..**$95.00**
Cookie jar, painted plastic head figure, 1968, 8x7", VG+..**$85.00**
Figure, Bean Bag Bunch, w/tag, Kellogg's, MIP **$9.00**
Figure, plush, mail-in premium, 1997, 8".....................**$8.00**
Figure, squeeze vinyl, Product People, 1970s, 9", NM+ ..**$100.00**
Figure, stuffed cloth, 1973, 14", EX **$40.00**
Frisbee, plastic, 1989, MIP...**$2.00**
Hat, plush w/paper tiger face & plush tail, mail-in premium, 1970s, child size, EX...............................**$28.00**
Hat, white paper w/graphics, given on plant tour in Battlecreek MI, Kellogg's, 1968, M **$25.00**
Padlock, colored plastic, 1987, MIP..............................**$5.00**

Page marker/paper clip, plastic, 1979, NM....................**$3.00**
Patch, glow-in-the-dark, 1965, 4", NM **$25.00**
Pen, Tony's Secret Message, 1980s, M...........................**$3.00**
Place mat, vinyl, characters on both sides, 1981, EX..**$10.00**
Poster, Meet Tony on Tour, paper, 1989, 18x14", NM...**$5.00**

Radio, battery operated, Kellogg's, 1980, 7", MIB, $40.00.

Recipe book, 1990, 8 pages, 5½x8½", VG **$5.00**
Reflector, Tony's Safe Biking Booster, plastic & paper, 1981, M **$2.00**
Spoon, silver-plated, Tony figural terminal, marked C Kelly 1965, EX...**$15.00**
Tony's Mystery Drawing Disk, paper, 1980, MIP..........**$3.00**
Transfer sheet, Tony, Toucan Sam, Poppy & Dig 'Em, 1980s, MIP..**$10.00**
Valentine card, set of 30, 1984, MIB..........................**$10.00**

Miscellaneous

Alka-Seltzer, bank, Speedy figure, painted soft vinyl, early 1960s, 5¾", EX...**$200.00**
Alka-Seltzer, charm, image of Speedy marching next to fizzing glass, background flickers, metal frame, 1¼" sq, EX+...**$60.00**
Alka-Seltzer, thermometer, dial type w/glass front, head image of Speedy holding up a glass, 12¼" dia, EX **$325.00**
Alpo, jar, ceramic figure of Dan the Dog, gray & white w/black collar, 8", EX..**$65.00**
Betty Crocker, doll, stuffed cloth, Kenner, 1974, 13", VG **$20.00**
Buster Brown Shoes, doll, Buster Brown, stuffed cloth, 1974, 14", NM..**$40.00**
Chips Ahoy, figure, rubber, Nabisco, 1990s, 5", M......**$20.00**
Chiquita Bananas, doll, Chiquita Banana Girl, stuffed cloth, mail-in premium, 1974, NM, minimum value.......**$40.00**
Donald Duck Chocolate Syrup, can, image of Donald on yellow, ca 1950, 15-oz, 4½", EX+.............................**$120.00**

Dunkin' Donuts, doll, Dunkin' Munchkin, stuffed cloth, 15", EX, from $15 to..**$20.00**

Dutch Boy National Lead Co, paperweight, embossed image of Dutch Boy character, made of lead or solder, 3½" dia, EX..**$40.00**

Dutch Boy Paints, puppet, Dutch Boy, soft vinyl head w/cloth body, white shirt w/blue overalls, 1960s, EX **$28.00**

Eskimo Pie, doll, Eskimo Pie Boy, stuffed cloth, Chase Bag Co, 1974, 15", EX, from $15 to **$20.00**

Esso, bank, plastic, 6½", $110.00. (Photo courtesy B.J. Summers)

Heinz, drinking glasses, fountain shape w/Tomato Man image & inscription, 1950s, 5", M, set of 3 ....**$65.00**

Hush Puppies, store display, hound dog figure on base w/embossed lettering, 1960s-70s, 17", VG+........**$100.00**

Jack Frost, doll, Jack Frost, stuffed cloth, 17", M **$50.00**

Jell-O, hand puppet, Sweet Tooth Sam, green vinyl head w/1 long fang & black top hat, EX+............................**$85.00**

Kayo Chocolate Drink, window decal, image of Kayo (Moon Mullins' pal) pointing to lg bottle, 4x3", unused, NM **$30.00**

Keebler, bank, Ernie the Keebler Elf, ceramic, lg, NM .**$60.00**

Keebler, bank, Ernie the Keebler Elf, ceramic, sm, NM..**$25.00**

Kool-Aid, bank, Kool-Aid Man pitcher on yellow base, plastic, 7", NM..**$60.00**

Lysol, doll, Lysol Kid, stuffed cloth w/yellow hair, Trudy Corp, 1986, NM, minimum value..........................**$30.00**

Magic Chef, bank, Baker Man, vinyl, 1990s, 7", EX....**$20.00**

Magic Chef, display figure, Baker Man standing on base lettered For Easier Better Cooking, composition, 28", VG+..**$100.00**

Margon Corp, nodder head for Margon Rolling Eyes for Dolls, vinyl doll head on metal base, eyes move, 1940s, EX...**$85.00**

Mr Bubble, figure, Mr Bubble Tub Pal, pink vinyl, Airwick Industries, 1990, 8", NM **$25.00**

Mr Softee, school book cover, blue on brown w/images of Mr Softee logo, truck & product packaging, unused, 1950s-60s, M..**$18.00**

Nestlé Quik, figure, Quik Bunny, bendable, 6", EX ...**$10.00**

Nestlé Quik, mug, Farfel litho image on white ceramic, 3½", 1950s, NM..**$45.00**

Northern Toilet Paper, doll, stuffed cloth w/vinyl head, rooted hair, several variations, 1980s, NM, ea from $25 to **$35.00**

Oscar Mayer, ring, Little Oscar, red & yellow plastic, 1970s, EX..**$5.00**

Poll Parrot Shoes, figures, Bride & Groom, celluloid, Sonsco, 4", EX...**$65.00**

Poll Parrot Shoes, ring, brass w/embossed parrot, 1950s, EX...**$65.00**

Purina Foods, tumbler, green plastic w/Beautena cow advertising, 4¾", EX...**$18.00**

Raid, figure, Raid Bug, plush, 5 different styles, 1980s, M, ea from $50 to..**$125.00**

Ralston Wheat Chex, toy figure, Magic Pup, plastic w/cloth ears, painted trim, w/hot dog magnet, premium, 1950s, 3", EX...**$65.00**

Red Goose Shoes, Tuck-A-Tub Theatre Play Kit, premium, 1950s, complete, unused, NM................................**$50.00**

Spiller's Flour, scale, Flour Fred figure, multi-pc w/3 weighted figures, spoons & platforms, 1979, 12¾", EX **$225.00**

Spiller's Flour, sprinkler bottle, Flour Fred figure, hard plastic, 7", EX...**$110.00**

Sunshine Animal Crackers, figure, elephant, stuffed cloth, 1930s, EX, minimum value....................................**$85.00**

Teddy Snow Crop, hand puppet, polar bear, white plush cloth w/rubber face & red cloth chest label, Clinton Foods, 8", NM **$50.00**

Wilkins Coffee, hand puppet, Wonkins (Jim Henson ad character), painted rubber, 1958, 7", VG+ **$100.00**

9-Lives, bowl, Morris: Frankly I Deserve..., 1977, Star Kist, $18.00. (Photo courtesy June Moon)

Advertising Tins

In her book *Modern Collectible Tins* (Collector Books), Linda McPherson declares these colorful, very attractive tin containers an official new area of collecting. There are so many of these 'new' tins around, though (she warns), that you'll probably want to narrow your choices down to either a specific type of product or company to avoid being inundated with them! She says the best of the lot are usually those offered as mail-in premiums and suggests we avoid buying tins with paper labels and plastic lids. Besides the esthetics factor, condition and age also help determine price. The values suggested below represent what you might pay in an antique store for tins in mint condition. But what makes this sort of collecting so much fun is that you'll find them much cheaper at garage sales, Goodwill stores, and flea markets. Other books available include *Encyclopedia of Advertising Tins, Vol. II,* by David Zimmerman, and three volumes of *Antique Tins* by Fred Dodge. (All are published by Collector Books.)

Advisor: Linda McPherson (See Directory, Advertising)

Andes, heart shape, name on red, 6"............................**$4.00**
Andes Happy Easter Creme de Menthe Mints, egg shape, 6x4"..**$7.00**
Archway Gingersnaps, tall box w/peaked lid, One Pound/Good Eatin', red, white & yellow on light brown, 8¼"...**$10.00**
Armour Pure Lard, pail w/bail handle, green & white, 4 lbs, 6"..**$18.00**
Azalea Brand (Nuts & Nut Candies), green & red on cream, 3x8" dia...**$5.00**
Barnum's Animals (Crackers), pail w/plastic handle, caged animals on red, 1991, 6".......................................**$16.00**
Bazooka Bubble Gum, round w/bail handle, red, white & blue, 1991, 5½x7"...**$10.00**
Beatrix Potter/Peter Rabbit Cookies, round, graphics on white, 5½x7½"..**$8.00**
Big Mac, hamburger shape, came w/McDonaldland character-shaped gummies, 1996, 4¼x3½".................**$10.00**
Brach's Jelly Beans, tall round, Happy Birthday Bugs, Bugs & friends on light blue, 6¼", 1989 ....**$5.00**
Butterfinger, oval, blue on yellow, 2½x3½x5½".........**$10.00**
Cadbury's Chocolate Covered Biscuits, oblong box, hinged lid, white, 1989, 3½x8¾x3¾"..................................**$8.00**
Campbell's Tomato Soup, round, slip lid, 3¾x3¼".......**$6.00**
Campfire Marshmallows, tall round, white, 8" **$20.00**
Carnation Hot Cocoa Mix, oblong box, 1st edition, Wishing You a Very Warm Winter, red & green, 1995, 8" L.**$8.00**
Celestial Seasonings Cinnamon Rose Tea oblong box, cowboy riding off into sunset w/girl in foreground, 1983, 4¾" L **$8.00**
Chase & Sanborn Coffee, tall round, For All Coffee Makers/Founded 1882, blue, 1993, 5"....................**$7.00**
Chiclets, round, green w/portrait on lid, 3½x5¾" **$20.00**
Chocolat Poulain, brown w/portrait on hinged lid, 4x5½"...**$14.00**
Chupa Chups Fruit Lollipops, oblong crate shape w/graphics, 5x10½x6¼"..**$16.00**
Chupa Chups Soda Pops, pop-can shape, yellow on red, 6¼"...**$12.00**
Dove Chocolate, egg shape, design on purple or roses on blue, 3x5", ea **$7.00**
Fleer Double Bubble, octagonal, America's Original Bubble Gum!, blue, 6"..**$9.00**

Grandma's Original Amaretto Cake, tall octagonal, graphics on brown, 10¾" **$7.00**
Hallmark Crown Chocolatier, scalloped round, floral & ribbon design on white, 1993, 2½x5¾"......................**$5.00**
Heaton's Swiss Cream Caramels, oblong octagonal, woman on phone, 4¼x5½x3¾"......................................**$7.00**

Hershey's Carousel, peaked top with carousel horses on sides, 1996, 5½" x 4½", from $6.00 to $8.00. (Photo courtesy Linda McPherson)

Hershey's Chocolate & Cocoa, flat round, brown, 2¾x7¼"..**$10.00**
Hershey's Fun Tin, tall round, confetti & candy bar graphics on pink w/brown lid, 1991, 6½x8" **$8.00**
Hershey's Krackel, oblong w/rounded corners, red, 1¼x7¾x4¼"...**$14.00**
Hershey's Milk Chocolate, barn shape w/peaked roof, Amish graphics, 4¾x3¾x3"......................................**$10.00**
Honey Nut Cheerios, tall box, 5½"...............................**$7.00**
Jelly Belly, oblong w/rounded corners, hinged lid, 20 Assorted Flavors, jelly bean graphics, ¾x2½x3¾" .**$5.00**
Kellogg's Frosted Flakes, tall box, Tony the Tiger saying 'They're Gr-r-reat!' on dark blue, 1984, 6½".........**$18.00**
King Leo Stick Candy, round, red & white on blue, 24-oz or 32-oz size, ea...**$5.00**
Life Savers, tall round, any Christmas graphic, 1990-95, 5½", ea..**$5.00**
Log Cabin Syrup, cabin shape, 100th Anniversary, plastic cap, 1987, 3¾x4¾"...**$20.00**
M&M's Peanut, diner shape, Christmas Village series #4, 1996, 8¾" L..**$8.00**
Mickey & Co (Assorted Hard Candies), oval, Mickey & Minnie graphics, red, 9½" L....................................**$14.00**
Mickey Mouse Cookies, lunch-box shape w/handle, 6x7½", 1996 ....**$16.00**
Moores Coffee Merchants & Blenders, box w/truck graphics, 3x4x4¾" **$7.00**
National Biscuit Shredded Wheat, oblong box, special edition of 1939 box, red on white, 1987, 6¼x8x4¼" **$23.00**
Nestle Crunch, candy-bar shape w/torn wrapper graphics, 10¼" L..**$14.00**

Oreo Cookies, Cheinco, 7½x5½" diameter, from $15.00 to $20.00. (Photo courtesy Linda McPherson)

Reese's (Peanut Butter Cups), tall round, Holiday Classics series #2, bear in Christmas stocking on green, 1990, 6¾" **$6.00**

Riesen Chocolate Chews, box, brown, 4½x4¼" sq.......**$7.00**

Russel Stover Butter Mints, flat round, ribbon-wrapped mints graphics, 2x6½" **$6.00**

Russell Stover Looney Tunes Surprise Tin, tall box, Bugs Bunny on yellow & green, 1997, 4" **$5.00**

Ry Krisp Crackers, tall box, food graphics on white, 1980, 9" **$14.00**

Salerno, tall box, 50 Years/Golden Goodness, children's portraits on red, 10¼" **$18.00**

Stauffer's Animal Crackers, tall round, red & yellow stripes w/blue, 7¼" **$16.00**

Uneeda Bakers Butter Wafers, tall round, 6½x6" **$25.00**

Advertising Watches

The concept of the advertising watch is strictly twentieth century. Some were produced through the 1960s, but it wasn't until the early 1970s that watches were increasingly used for advertising. Now, many themes, subjects, and types are available. Collectible ad watches include mechanical/battery-operated pocket watches, mechanical/battery-operated wristwatches, digital/analog (with hands) watches, dress/sports watches, company logo/character watches, corporate/in-house watches, catalog/store retail watches, and give-away/premium watches.

Condition, originality, cleanliness, scarcity, completeness, cross-collectibility, and buyer demand all affect value. The more recently issued the watch, the better its condition must be. Original mint packaging (including any paperwork) can triple value. Look for original watch offers and order forms on old packaging and magazines; they are desirable for documentation and are collectible in their own right. Look through 'parts boxes'; an old, nonworking ad pocket or wristwatch, even without a strap, may have value. A higher degree of wear is acceptable on an older watch.

A popular character/event will add value. Currently, demand is good for some '70s characters such as Mr. Peanut and Charlie the Tuna, the '80s – '90s M&M watches, and the '90s Pillsbury Doughboy. Demand for a watch that features a forgotten or less popular character may be limited, even if it is an older one, and value could be affected.

Great numbers of watches exist for Coca-Cola, Pepsi, various automobiles, and Camel and other tobacco products. These are usually of most interest to collectors who specialize in those fields. A 'reverse attitude' may exist — the more watches produced for a theme or character, the less desirable it is to the typical ad watch collector.

Copyright dates can lead to confusion about the age of a watch. The date may refer to the publishing date of the character or logo, not the year the watch was made. Date watches by style and features. Generally analog watches are more collectible than digital. A watch need not be working; most are not of high quality. Examine watches displayed in glass cases at outdoor shows for signs of moisture buildup and sun fading. Remove dead batteries only if you can do so without damaging the watch or packaging.

Common watches that currently have little value are the 1984 Ronald McDonald House Coca-Cola carded watches, the 1995 Kodak Lion King, Life Cereals Mask and Where's Waldo watches, and all the Burger King, McDonald's, and Taco Bell watches for various movies.

Advisor: Sharon Iranpour (See Directory, Advertising Watches)

Newsletter: *The Premium Watch Watch©*
Sharon Iranpour, Editor
24 San Rafael Dr.
Rochester, NY 14618-3702; 716-381-9467 or
Fax: 716-383-9248; e-mail: watcher1@rochester.rr.com

Pre-1970s

Many mechanical pocket and wristwatches are known; most appeal to 'masculine' interests and professions such as automobiles and related products. As early as the 1920s, Chevrolet gave wristwatches to top-performing salesmen; the watch case was in the shape of a car radiator front. Many commemorative watches were issued for special events like world's fairs.

Buster Brown Pocket Watch, 1960s, VG **$75.00**

Chevrolet Salesman's Award Wristwatch, 1927, EX...**$400.00**

FS Fertilizer Pocket Watch, G **$35.00**

Mr Peanut Wristwatch, yellow face w/date window, 1967, VG **$50.00**

Mr Peanut Wristwatch, yellow face 1966, VG.............**$50.00**

New York World's Fair Ingraham Pocket Watch, 1939, VG **$500.00**

Red Goose Shoes Wristwatch, 1960s, G....................**$130.00**

Reddy Kilowatt Pocket Watch, 1930s, VG **$250.00**

Rexall Ingersoll Pocket Watch, 1909, EX **$150.00**

Shell Oil Girard-Perregaux Pocket Watch, 1940s, VG ..**$350.00**

St Louis World's Fair Ingersoll Pocket Watch, 1904, EX ..**$200.00**

Toppie Elephant, 1950s, G..............................**$100.00**
Twinkie the Brown Shoe Elf, 1920s, G....................**$100.00**
Westinghouse Refrigerator Pocket Watch, MIB...........**$75.00**

The 1970s

The most common were mechanicals with a heavy metal case, often marked Swiss Made. Some had wide straps with snaps or straps with holes. Mechanical digital watches and revolving disks appeared. As a general rule, special packaging had not been created. Wristwatches from the '70s are appearing at Internet auction sites and at shows in greater frequency due to growing interest. They are generally valued from $75.00 to $300.00 in very good to mint condition. Watches listed in this section are all mechanical wristwatches.

Big Boy, watch hands are arms, 1970, EX..................**$75.00**
Buster Brown, red costume, 1970s, VG.....................**$75.00**
Charlie Tuna, faces left, 1971, VG.............................**$50.00**
Charlie Tuna, faces right, 1973, VG..........................**$50.00**
Count Chocula, Booberry & Frankenberry, Lafayette Watch
    Co, MIB **$300.00**
Ernie the Keebler Elf, 1970s, G **$50.00**
Goodyear Tires, revolving disk, 1970s, G...................**$50.00**
Goofy Grape, 1976, G **$200.00**
Mr Peanut, blue face, mechanical, digital, 1975, EX...**$50.00**
Punchy, red strap, mechanical, digital, 1970s, VG **$50.00**
Raid Bug Spray, revolving disk, 1970s, EX...............**$150.00**
Ritz Crackers, 1971, MIB **$200.00**
Ronald McDonald, 1970s, MIB **$50.00**
Scrubbing Bubbles, 1970s, VG....................................**$50.00**
Tony the Tiger, 1976, MIB **$200.00**

The 1980s

Digital and analog battery-operated watches became the norm; mechanicals all but disappeared early in the decade. Watches became slim and lightweight with plastic commonly used for both the case and the strap. Electronic hands (visible only when the battery is good), clam shell, and pop-up digital watches appeared; revolving disks were frequently used. Toward the end of the decade, printing on straps began. Specially designed packaging became more commonplace. Hanger cards added design to otherwise plain digital watches. These are most desirable in excellent, unopened condition. Watches from the 1980s are generally valued from $10.00 to $50.00 in mint condition. Watches listed in this section are battery operated unless noted otherwise.

Bart Simpson, by Butterfinger Candy, M **$20.00**
Brach's Peppermint, 1980s, MIB..................................**$15.00**
Campbell Kids, mechanical windup, 4 different, 1982 (w/slip
    cover), ea..**$75.00**
Captain Midnight, by Ovaltine, 1988, M **$40.00**
Charlie the Tuna, 25th Anniversary, 1986, MIB..........**$25.00**
Cherry 7-Up, 1980s, M..**$15.00**
Kellogg's Atlantis Do & Learn Set, 1983, MIB **$25.00**

Kellogg's Watch Set by Atlantis, 1982, digital, features molded faces of Toucan Sam, Tony Tiger, Dig 'em, and Poppy, $30.00. (Photo courtesy June Moon)

Kraft Cheese & Macaroni Club, 1980s, M **$10.00**
M&Ms, various, 1980s, M **$25.00**
Max Headroom, by Coca-Cola, 1987, man's/lady's, M .**$10.00**
Swiss Miss, mechanical wind-up, 1981, EX **$50.00**
Welch's Grape Juice, 1989, M **$20.00**

The 1990s

Case and strap design became innovative. New features were holograms on the watch face, revolving subdials, 'talking' features, water watches (liquid within case/straps), stopwatches and timers, game watches, giga pets, and clip-on clocks. Classic and retro styling became popular. Very well designed packaging including special boxes and printed tins became more common as did printed plastic straps. Clear printed resin straps (Swatch type) and diecut rubber straps emerged. Companies created their own retail catalogs and websites to sell logo merchandise. Licensing agreements produced many tie-ins with movies, TV, and sports events. Most plastic watches currently sell in the $5.00 to $15.00 range; there is little market for the most common. Quality, hard-to-find gold- and silver-tone watches rarely sell beyond $25.00 at the present.

Quaker Chewy Granola Wildlife, $5.00; Mars Snickers Candy Bar Anniversary, with revolving subdial, $35.00; Campbell Kids 125th Anniversary, $50.00; Pillsbury Doughboy Talking Watch, $15.00. (Photo courtesy Sharon Iranpour)

Dunkin' Donuts, 1999, M.............................**$10.00**
Eggo Waffles Eggosaurus, 1990, M............................**$15.00**
Kool Aid Hologram, 1991, M............................**$15.00**
Kraft Superbowl XXX, watch in goal post box, 1996, MIB............................**$20.00**
Mr. Magoo, by Nutrasweet, 1995, M............................**$30.00**
Oreo Cookie Watch, 1998, M............................**$50.00**

Quisp, 1997 – 98, MIB, $20.00. (Photo courtesy Sharon Iranpour)

The 2000s

At the turn of the twenty-first century, millennium ad watches were eagerly sought by collectors; it is unlikely any more will be made. Fewer premiums are being offered new on specially marked packages or on store forms. More offers and retail watches are appearing on Internet websites. Online auction sites, primarily eBay, make it easier to find older watches, newer regional pieces, and corporate in-house watches from special projects or events.

Airline Memorabilia

Even before the Wright brothers' historic flight prior to the turn of the century, people have been fascinated with flying. What better way to enjoy the evolution and history of this amazing transportation industry than to collect its memorabilia. Today just about any item ever used or made for a commercial (non-military) airline is collectible, especially dishes, glasswares, silver serving pieces and flatware, wings and badges worn by the crew, playing cards, and junior wings given to passengers. Advertising items such as timetables and large travel agency plane models are also widely collected. The earlier, the better! Anything pre-war is good; items from before the 1930s are rare and often very valuable. See also Restaurant China.

Advisor: Dick Wallin (See Directory, Airline)

Cup & saucer, TWA, white w/red stripe & gold logo.**$20.00**

Bank, 1932 Stearman, Shell graphics, 24k gold-plated, Gearbox, 1,500 made, movable propeller, MIB .**$180.00**
Bowl, Delta, white w/blue outer rings & logo, marked Delta Airlines, Mayer China **$25.00**
Bumper sticker, TWA McDonnel Douglas, Have a Super Day w/jumbo jet, w/backing, 3x9", EX............................**$10.00**
Casserole, entree; American Airlines, white w/black trim & impressed logo, Pfaltzgraff, 1980s, 7½" dia, EX ...**$10.00**

Dinnerware, American Airlines 'Arlite' China by Syracuse China Co., very lightweight, 1940s, cup, $25.00; plate, $100.00. (Photo courtesy Dick Wallin)

Envelope, ticket; Braniff Airlines, red, white & blue w/logo, sketch of stewardess & routes Braniff flew, 1942, EX............**$20.00**
Knife, dinner; United Airlines, silver-plated on stainless steel, United & logo etching, ca 1961-74, EX................**$10.00**
Pennant, Newark Airport, red w/white plane in clouds & lettering, felt, 25", VG............................**$30.00**
Pin, Junior Hostess, TWA, enameled TWA w/gold-tone wing............................**$15.00**
Pin-back button, Whittelsey Avian, First England to Australia Plane, full-color biplane, ¾" dia............................**$15.00**
Plate, dinner; Air France, porcelain, divided, made by Raynaud, Limoges, 1960s, EX............................**$15.00**
Plate, PanAm, Walker China, blue stripe & winged globe logo, 8", EX............................**$500.00**
Playing Cards, TAT, 1929 combined rail/air cross-country trip in 48 hours, in slipcase box, EX............................**$2.00**
Playing cards, United Airlines, blue w/name & logo, M (sealed box)............................**$5.00**
Program, Air Tour; Pacific Northwest States, lists events & ads, 7 pages, 1930, 6x9", VG+............................**$40.00**
Salt & pepper shakers, British Airways, white w/navy stripe, Royal Doulton, 2x1½" dia, pr............................**$15.00**
Ticket jacket envelope, PanAm w/Boeing 314 Flying Boat, 1930s, EX............................**$25.00**

Akro Agate

The Akro Agate Company operated in West Virginia from 1914 until 1951, and in addition to their famous marbles they made children's dishes as well as many types of novelties — flowerpots, powder jars with Scottie dogs on top, candlesticks, and ashtrays, for instance — in many colors and patterns. Though some of their glassware was made in solid colors, their most popular products were made of the same swirled colors as their marbles. Though many pieces are not marked, you will find some that are marked with their distinctive logo: a crow flying through the letter 'A' holding an Aggie in its beak and one in each claw. Some novelty items may instead carry one of these trademarks: 'JV Co, Inc,' 'Braun & Corwin,' 'NYC Vogue Merc Co USA,' 'Hamilton Match Co,' and 'Mexicali Pickwick Cosmetic Corp.'

Color is a very important worth-assessing factor. Some pieces may be common in one color but rare in others. Occasionally an item will have exceptionally good colors, and this would make it more valuable than an example with only average color. When buying either marbles or children's tea sets in original boxes, be sure the box contains its original contents. For more information we recommend *The Complete Line of the Akro Agate Co.* by our advisors, Roger and Claudia Hardy.

Advisors: Roger and Claudia Hardy (See Directory, Akro Agate)

Club: Akro Agate Collectors Club
Clarksburg Crow newsletter
Claudia and Roger Hardy
10 Bailey St., Clarksburg, WV 26301-2524; 304-624-4523

Ashtray, Akro Agate Ware embossed **$250.00**
Ashtray, card suit in center, rare, 4" dia or 4" sq, from $250 to **$300.00**
Ashtray, Coca-Cola embossed, rare, from $2,000 to ..**$2,500.00**
Ashtray, early, 5" sq, from $50 to **$90.00**
Ashtray, ellipsoid, from $15 to **$25.00**
Ashtray, Goodrich Tire, from $50 to **$60.00**

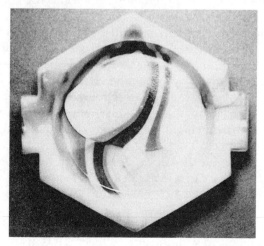

Ashtray, hexagonal, marbleized colors, 4½", from $20.00 to $30.00. (Photo courtesy Albert Morin)

Ashtray, Hotel Lincoln or Hotel Edison, from $65 to...**$150.00**

Ashtray, leaf shape, from $5 to...................................**$10.00**
Ashtray, rectangular, w/oxblood, 3¾", from $50 to..**$150.00**
Ashtray, rectangular, 3¾", from $8 to.........................**$15.00**
Ashtray, shell shape, from $5 to **$10.00**
Ashtray, star shape, rare, 6", from $175 to **$300.00**
Ashtray, w/oxblood, 2⅞" sq, from $25 to **$45.00**
Ashtray, 2⅞" sq, from $5 to **$10.00**
Basket, 1-handle, from $250 to **$400.00**

Basket, two-handled, from $30.00 to $40.00.

Bell, common colors, from $90 to.............................**$125.00**
Bowl, #320, from $20 to..**$35.00**
Bowl, footed, 8" dia, from $250 to.............................**$400.00**
Bowl, tab handle, from $45 to.....................................**$50.00**
Candlestick, single, 4¼", ea from $100 to **$150.00**
Flowerpot, #1308-#1311, from $150 to.....................**$225.00**
Flowerpot, Banded Dart, 2½"-5½", from $45 to **$90.00**

Flowerpot, Graduated Dart, 2" to 5¼", from $10.00 to $50.00.

Flowerpot, Grand Daddy, #308, 6⅜", from $200 to..**$300.00**
Flowerpot, Rib Top, 1¾"-4", from $5 to.......................**$35.00**
Flowerpot, Stacked Disc, 2½"-5½", from $10 to **$50.00**
Mexicali jar, w/hat lid, from $40 to **$50.00**

Planter, #650, scarce, 11¼", from $250 to.................**$350.00**
Planter, #653, rectangular, 8", from $20 to...................**$40.00**
Planter, iris, from $8 to...**$12.00**
Powder jar, ivy, from $45 to **$60.00**
Puff box, apple, orange, from $275 to.....................**$300.00**
Puff box, Colonial Lady, common colors, from $75 to..**$125.00**

Puff box, Colonial Lady, pumpkin (rare color), $1,200.00. (Photo courtesy Albert Morin)

Puff box, Scottie dog, common colors, from $75 to.**$125.00**
Thumbpot, mini-flowerpot, from $20 to **$45.00**
Thumbpot, mini-flowerpot, w/oxblood, from $75 to .**$100.00**
Urn, beaded top, from $5 to...**$15.00**
Vase, #306, Graduated Dart, 5", from $45 to **$60.00**
Vase, #311, from $125 to...**$150.00**
Vase, #312, 8¾", from $90 to **$125.00**
Vase, #316, rectangular, 4½", from $40 to **$55.00**
Vase, #316, 6¼", from $125 to **$175.00**
Vase, hand, 3¼", from $15 to **$30.00**
Vase, iris, from $8 to...**$12.00**
Vase, ribs & flutes, 3"-5½", from $8 to........................**$45.00**

Children's Dishes

Concentric Ring, teapot, lg, white, 2¾" **$20.00**
Concentric Ring, teapot, sm, 2⅜" **$65.00**
Interior Panel, cup, lg, yellow, 1½".............................**$45.00**
Interior Panel, cup, sm, orange, 1⅜" **$25.00**
Miss America, cup, white **$48.00**
Miss America, plate, colors other than white, 4½", from $40
 to...**$225.00**
Miss America, plate, white, 4½" **$28.00**
Miss America, teapot, white, from $150 to **$170.00**
Octagonal, cup, lg, closed handle...............................**$15.00**
Octagonal, cup, lg, open handle **$30.00**
Octagonal, plate, lg, closed handle **$8.00**
Octagonal, teapot, lg, open handle..............................**$18.00**
Raised Daisy, cup **$40.00**
Raised Daisy, sugar bowl..**$35.00**
Raised Daisy, teapot **$75.00**
Stacked Disc, cup..**$7.00**
Stacked Disc, teapot **$18.00**

Stacked Disc & Interior Panel, cup **$35.00**
Stacked Disc & Interior Panel, teapot **$65.00**
Stippled Band, cup, sm...**$18.00**
Stippled Band, plate, sm...**$10.00**
Stippled Band, sugar bowl, sm.....................................**$85.00**

Marbles

Corkscrew, 2-color, ⅝", from $2 to **$5.00**
Corkscrew, 3-color, ⅝", from $10 to............................**$15.00**
Corkscrew, 4-color, ⅝", from $30 to............................**$50.00**
Corkscrew, 5-color, ⅝", from $100 to.........................**$250.00**
Golden onyx, ⅝", from $75 to **$100.00**
Green oxblood, ⅝", from $100 to...............................**$150.00**
Lemonade, ⅝"...**$15.00**
Lemonade & oxblood, ⅝", from $45 to **$60.00**
Limeade, ⅝", from $20 to...**$25.00**
Popeye, ⅝"...**$30.00**
Red & Royal Blue, ⅝", from $45 to **$60.00**
Sparkler, ⅝"...**$40.00**
#0, Cardinal Reds, box of 25 ....**$450.00**
#0, Carnelians, box of 25, from $550 to **$600.00**
#0, Moonies, box of 25, from $1,500 to **$1,800.00**
#00, Chinese Checkers, box of 60................................**$50.00**
#40, Click Game, boxed set..**$800.00**
#116, Popeye, boxed set, from $900 to..................**$1,000.00**
#150, tin box, complete w/bag, from $350 to **$400.00**
#200, tin box, complete w/bag, from $550 to **$600.00**
#250, complete w/bag, from $300 to **$350.00**
#300, complete w/bag, from $500 to **$600.00**

Aluminum

The aluminum items which have become today's collectibles range from early brite-cut giftware and old kitchen wares to furniture and hammered aluminum cooking pans. But the most collectible, right now, at least, is the giftware of the 1930s through the 1950s.

There were probably several hundred makers of aluminum accessories and giftware with each developing their preferred method of manufacturing. Some pieces were cast; other products were hammered with patterns created by either an intaglio method or repousse. Machine embossing was utilized by some makers; many used faux hammering, and lightweight items were often decorated with pressed designs.

As early as the 1940s, collectors began to seek out aluminum, sometimes to add to the few pieces received as wedding gifts. By the late 1970s and early 1980s, aluminum giftware was found in abundance at almost any flea market, and prices of $1.00 or less were normal. As more shoppers became enthralled with the appearance of this lustrous metal and its patterns, prices began to rise and have not yet peaked for the products of some companies. A few highly prized pieces have brought prices of $400 or $500 and occasionally even more.

One of the first to manufacture this type of ware was Wendell August Forge, when during the late 1920s they expanded their line of decorative wrought iron and began to use aluminum, making small items as gifts for their customers. Very soon they were involved in a growing industry estimated at one point to be comprised of several hundred companies, among them Arthur Armour, the Continental Silver Company, Everlast, Buenilum, Rodney Kent, and Palmer-Smith. Few of the many original companies survived the WWII scarcity of aluminum.

During the '60s, anodized (colored) aluminum became very popular. It's being bought up today by the younger generations who are attracted to its neon colors and clean lines. Watch for items with strong color and little if any sign of wear — very important factors to consider when assessing value. Because it was prone to scratching and denting, mint condition examples are few and far between.

Prices differ greatly from one region to another, sometimes without regard to quality or condition, so be sure to examine each item carefully before you buy. There are two good books on the subject: *Hammered Aluminum, Hand Wrought Collectibles,* by Dannie Woodard; and *Collectible Aluminum, An Identification and Value Guide,* by Everett Grist (Collector Books).

See also Kitchen.

Condiment server, removable bowls, Everlast, 11", from $60.00 to $80.00.

Ashtray, Bruce Fox, sq w/horse head, 5½" **$40.00**
Ashtray, Everlast, bowl shape w/allover bamboo pattern, single rest, 5" dia **$15.00**
Bar tray, Arthur Armour, water lily pattern, self-handled, 8x17" **$45.00**
Bar tray, Wendell August Forge, wild rose pattern, 15x9"..**$40.00**
Basket, Federal Silver Co, sailing ship, serrated ruffled rim, knotted handle, 9" dia **$25.00**
Bookends, Bruce Cox, leaping fish figures, 7x3x5", pr..**$185.00**
Bowl, Everlast, fruit pattern on hammered background, 12½" dia **$18.00**
Bowl, Kensington, plain-spun w/smooth flared rim, 3½x11" dia **$5.00**

Bracelet, unmarked, C-type band w/leaf design.........**$15.00**
Bread tray, Continental, wild rose, 13x6" **$15.00**
Bread tray, Rodney Kent, tulip pattern on hammered background, scalloped rim, flower & ribbon handles, oval, 8x13" **$25.00**
Buffet server/bun warmer, II Farberware, smooth finish w/serrated rim, S-shaped legs w/tulip design, dome lid, 9" dia..**$20.00**
Cake stand, Wilson Metal, band-of-shields decoration, serrated edge, 8x12" **$15.00**
Candle holders, Melkraft, flower form, pr **$10.00**
Candlesticks, Buenilum, curved handle projects to point on other side of plain cup w/beaded rim, rectangular base, pr...**$25.00**
Candy dish, Neocraft by Everlast, 2 gold anodized butterfly bowls w/center loop handle, 12" **$15.00**
Casserole, Arthur Armour, dogwood & butterfly pattern, lid w/movable ring finial fits glass insert, flat bottom, 10" dia **$50.00**
Celery dish, Farberware, raspberries, leaves & flowers in center, 13½x7" **$12.00**
Cigarette box, Wendell August Forge, bittersweet pattern, hinged lid, 1½x3x5"...**$75.00**
Coaster set, Everlast, 5-petal flower pattern, serrated rim, 8-pc set w/box..**$25.00**
Coaster set, Rodney Kent, shaped like tulip blossoms, basket holder w/open-work ribbon handle, set of 4.......**$35.00**
Compote, Continental, wild rose pattern on bowl w/serrated rim, stem foot, 5x5" dia **$20.00**
Creamer & sugar bowl, unmarked, hammered pattern w/fluted rims, no lids, rounded handles.........................**$5.00**
Crumb brush & tray, grapevine pattern, Lucite brush handle, plastic bristles...**$35.00**
Dresser dish, Farberware, single rose pattern on lid w/black wooden finial, glass dish w/beaded rim & 2 handles.**$10.00**
Gravy boat, Continental, chrysanthemum pattern, serrated rim, side handle, underplate, 3x6" dia **$25.00**
Ice bucket, Everlast, hammered pattern w/barbell handles, w/tongs, no lid, 5x10" dia.....................................**$15.00**
Ice bucket, Everlast, intaglio handles, 7x3" **$25.00**
Napkin holder, Everlast, hammered trefoil shape w/rose pattern..**$20.00**
Nut bowl, Wilson, flower & leaf pattern, serrated ruffled rim, nutcracker & 6 picks in center, low base, 4x7" dia..**$10.00**
Pitcher, Continental, acorn & leaf pattern, coiled handle, applied ice lip, 8"..**$20.00**
Pitcher, Rodney Kent, tulip pattern w/serrated rim, applied ice lip, ear-shaped handle, 9" **$35.00**
Serving tray, Continental, deer & geese, 12x16" **$60.00**
Serving tray, Continental, rose pattern on hammered background, applied leaf handles, 17" dia **$10.00**
Serving tray, Everlast, bamboo pattern on hammered background, bamboo handles, 12x16".........................**$15.00**
Serving tray, Rodney Kent, tulip pattern on hammered background, flower & ribbon handles, 14x20"............**$35.00**
Tidbit tray, unmarked, rose pattern, fluted rims, 3-tiered, 11x10" dia **$5.00**

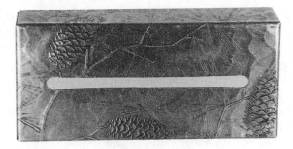

Tissue box, Wendell August Forge, 5" x 10", from $75.00 to $85.00.

Trivet, Everlast, pine cone pattern, oval, 11x8".......... **$15.00**

Umbrella stand/vase, Wendell August Forge, larkspur pattern, 22".. **$285.00**

Vase, Continental, chrysanthemum pattern, serrated rim, 10".. **$85.00**

Anodized (Colored)

Range set, lime green, drippings jar, salt and pepper shakers, from $35.00 to $45.00 for the set.

Ashtrays, crown-like shape, cigarettes held in notches, Parkit Safe, 3x1", set of 4, MIB.. **$24.00**

Bowl, 6", Bascal, set of 8, EX **$26.00**

Cake salver, hot pink w/black handle on cover, Regal, 13" plate, EX **$30.00**

Candle holders, leaf-&-grape embossed pattern in bowl-like bottom, Kraft, 4½", EX, pr **$20.00**

Coasters, set of 8, M **$25.00**

Coffee maker, blue w/ivory Bakelite handles, West Bend Flav-O-Matic, complete & working, EX................. **$25.00**

Creamer & sugar bowl on tray, gold w/black Bakelite handles, Neocraft, EX **$40.00**

Cups, 4½", set of 6 in black rack, 16x8", w/white handles & rubber ball feet, Anohue, EX+.............................. **$25.00**

Cups, 5½", M, set of 6... **$30.00**

Dessert bowls, w/glass inserts, 3½", set of 8", M........ **$50.00**

Ice bucket, red apple shape, 7", NM........................... **$25.00**

Measuring scoops, ½-cup, ⅓-cup & ¼-cup, NM, set of 3.. **$20.00**

Napkin rings, narrow, set of 8, MIB............................ **$28.00**

Napkin rings, wide, in original plastic box, set of 4, M.. **$50.00**

Percolator, blue w/white Bakelite handle, 1950s, M unused **$45.00**

Pitcher, gold, w/ice lip, no mark, NM......................... **$28.00**

Pitcher, green, w/8 5" tumblers, Colorcraft, Indianapolis Indiana, NM... **$60.00**

Popcorn set, 11" bowl & 4 5" individuals, M **$30.00**

Refrigerator boxes, 5¼x4⅜", NM, from $40 to........... **$50.00**

Rolling pin, w/stand, EX... **$30.00**

Salad set, Bascal, lg bowl & 8 footed individuals, EX+ .. **$50.00**

Shot glasses, 1¾", 6 in holder w/handle, Germany, MIB, from $25 to.. **$35.00**

Shot glasses, 6 on tray, NM.. **$30.00**

Soda/seltzer bottle, bright blue, Soda King, 11½", MIB.. **$65.00**

Spoons, iced tea; 8", NM, set of 6............................... **$25.00**

Straw/stirrer, set of 12, M, from $25 to **$30.00**

Teapot, gold w/red plastic knob on lid, rattan-wrapped handle, Japan, 6½", EX... **$35.00**

Tree ornaments, Christmas bells, 2x2", set of 5 .... **$18.00**

Tree ornaments, twisted icicles, 15 in box, NM.......... **$25.00**

Tumblers, 5", set of 6, M... **$25.00**

Tumblers, 5", set of 8 in chrome carrying rack, Perma Hues, M.. **$45.00**

Tumblers, 5" w/matching 9" straws, set of 6, NM....... **$45.00**

Tumblers, 5½", horizontal embossed rings, West Bend, set of 8, M... **$35.00**

Anchor Hocking/Fire-King

From the 1930s until the 1970s, Anchor Hocking (Lancaster, Ohio) produced a wide and varied assortment of glassware including kitchen, restaurant ware, and tableware for the home. Fire-King was their trade name for glassware capable of withstanding high oven temperatures without breakage. So confident were they in the durability of this glassware that they guaranteed it for two years against breakage caused by heat.

Many colors were produced over the years. Blues are always popular with collectors, and Anchor Hocking made two, Turquoise Blue and Azurite (light sky blue). They also made pink, Forest Green, Ruby Red, gold-trimmed lines, and some with fired-on colors. Jade-ite was a soft opaque green glass that was very popular from the 1940s until well into the 1960s. (See the Jade-ite category for more information.) During the late '60s they made Soreno in Avocado Green to tie in with home-decorating trends.

Bubble (made from the '30s through the '60s) was produced in just about every color Anchor Hocking ever made. It is especially collectible in Ruby Red. You may also hear this pattern referred to as Provencial or Bullseye.

Alice was a mid-'40s to '50s line. It was made in Jade-ite as well as white that was sometimes trimmed with blue or red. Cups and saucers were given away in boxes of Mother's Oats, but plates had to be purchased (so they're scarce today).

In the early '50s they produced a 'laurel leaf' design in peach and 'Gray Laurel' lustres (the gray is scarce), followed later in the decade and into the '60s with several lines of white glass decorated with decals — Honeysuckle, Fleurette, Primrose, and Game Bird, to name only a few.

One of their most expensive lines of dinnerware today is Philbe in Sapphire Blue, clear glass with a blue tint. It was made during the late 1930s. Values range from about $50.00 for a 6" plate to $1,500.00 for the cookie jar.

Early American Prescut was made from about 1960 through the mid-1970s. Few homes were without at least a piece or two. It was standard dime-store fare, inexpensive and accessible. It looks wonderful for serving a special buffet, and you'll find it often on your garage sale rounds, at prices that are a fraction of 'book.'

If you'd like to learn more about this type of very collectible glassware, we recommend *Anchor Hocking's Fire-King and More, Second Edition,* by Gene Florence (Collector Books).

See also Jade-ite.

Newsletter: *The '50s Flea!!!*
April and Larry Tvorak
Warren Center, PA 18851; Subscription: $5 per year for one yearly postwar glass newsletter; includes free 30-work classified ad

Alice, cup & saucer, white w/blue trim **$14.00**
Alice, plate, white, 9½" **$20.00**
Alice, plate, white w/blue trim.....................................**$30.00**
Anniversary Rose, bowl, dessert; white w/decals, 4⅝".**$8.00**
Anniversary Rose, creamer, white w/decals **$10.00**
Anniversary Rose, mug, white w/decals, 8-oz............**$20.00**
Blue Mosaic, cup, white w/decals, 7½" **$4.00**
Blue Mosaic, soup plate, white w/decals, 6⅝"............**$14.00**
Blue Mosaic, sugar bowl, white w/decals **$8.00**
Bubble, bowl, berry; Forest Green, 8⅜"......................**$14.00**
Bubble, candlesticks, crystal iridescent, pr **$16.00**
Bubble, pitcher, Royal Ruby, ice lip, 64-oz **$60.00**
Bubble, stem, goblet; Royal Ruby, 9-oz......................**$12.50**
Bubble, stem, juice; Forest Green, 4-oz.......................**$15.00**
Bubble, tumbler, lemonade; crystal iridescent, 16-oz, 5⅞" **$14.00**
Charm/Sq, bowl, dessert; Forest Green, 4¾"..............**$8.00**
Charm/Sq, cup & saucer, Ruby......................................**$8.50**
Charm/Sq, platter, Azur-ite or white, 11x8"................**$25.00**
Charm/Sq, sugar bowl, Ivory...**$20.00**
Classic/Rachael, bowl, crystal, deep, 5¼"...................**$6.00**
Classic/Rachael, plate, white, 14½".............................**$22.50**
Early American Prescut, ashtray, 5" **$10.00**
Early American Prescut, bowl, #767, 7¼"....................**$6.00**
Early American Prescut, bowl, console, #797, 9" **$15.00**
Early American Prescut, bowl, gondola, #752, 9⅜" **$4.00**
Early American Prescut, bowl, smooth rim, 3726, 4¼"..**$20.00**
Early American Prescut, bowl, 3-toed, #768, 6¾" **$4.50**
Early American Prescut, cake plate, footed, #706, 13½"..**$32.00**
Early American Prescut, candlestick, double; #784, 7x5⅝" **$32.00**
Early American Prescut, coaster, #700/702...................**$2.00**
Early American Prescut, lazy susan, #700/713, 9-pc...**$45.00**

Early American Prescut, pitcher, #791, 60-oz..............**$15.00**
Early American Prescut, plate, serving; #790, 13½" **$12.50**
Early American Prescut, plate, snack; #780, 10".........**$10.00**
Early American Prescut, relish, divided, tab handles, #770, 10"...**$7.00**
Early American Prescut, salt & pepper shakers, plastic lids, #725, pr..**$5.00**
Early American Prescut, sugar bowl, #753, w/lid..........**$4.00**
Early American Prescut, syrup, #707, 12-oz................**$20.00**
Early American Prescut, tumbler, #731, 10-oz **$4.00**
Early American Prescut, vase, #742, 10" **$12.50**
Fishscale, bowl, cereal; Ivory w/red, deep, 5½".........**$18.00**
Fishscale, bowl, vegetable; Ivory, 8¾"........................**$30.00**
Fishscale, plate, salad; Ivory w/red, 7⅜" **$15.00**
Fleurette, egg plate, white w/decals...........................**$150.00**
Fleurette, soup plate, white w/decals, 6⅝" **$12.00**
Fleurette, sugar bowl, white w/decals, w/lid **$10.00**
Forest Green, ashtray, hexagonal, 5¾".........................**$8.00**
Forest Green, comport, 6½"..**$35.00**

Forest Green, relish set, Waffle pattern base, from $75.00 to $85.00.

Forest Green, stem, cocktail; 3½-oz.............................**$10.00**
Forest Green, tumbler, iced tea; 13-oz **$7.50**
Forget Me Not, bowl, cereal; white w/decals, 5"........**$12.00**
Forget Me Not, casserole, white w/decals, oval, w/lid, 1½-qt..**$24.00**
Forget Me Not, loaf pan, white w/decals **$25.00**
Game Bird, bowl, vegetable; white w/decal, 8¼" **$60.00**
Game Bird, mug, white w/decal, 8-oz..........................**$8.00**
Game Bird, sugar bowl, white w/decal, w/lid............**$25.00**
Harvest, bowl, vegetable; white w/decal, 8¼"............**$15.00**
Harvest, cup, white w/decal, 7½" **$4.00**
Harvest, platter, white w/decal, 9x12" **$15.00**
Homestead, bowl, dessert; white w/decal, 4⅝" **$5.00**
Homestead, plate, salad; white w/decal, 7⅜" **$15.00**
Homestead, sugar bowl, white w/decal, w/lid **$10.00**
Honeysuckle, plate, dinner; white w/decal, 9⅛" **$6.00**
Honeysuckle, soup plate, white w/decal, 6⅝" **$9.00**
Honeysuckle, tumbler, water; white w/decal, 9-oz.....**$15.00**
Jane Ray, bowl, vegetable; white, 8¼".........................**$25.00**
Jane Ray, cup, demitasse; white **$20.00**

Jane Ray, plate, dinner; Ivory, 9⅛" $45.00
Jane Ray, saucer, white...$2.00
Laurel, bowl, dessert; gray, 4⅞" $7.00
Laurel, bowl, vegetable; Ivory or white, 8¼" $40.00
Laurel, plate, salad; gray, 7⅜"..$8.00
Laurel, saucer, Ivory or white, 5¾" $3.50
Laurel/Peach Lustre, creamer, footed $4.00
Laurel/Peach Lustre, cup, 8-oz......................................$3.50
Laurel/Peach Lustre, plate, serving; 11" $14.00
Laurel/Peach Lustre, soup plate, 7⅝".........................$10.00
Philbe, bowl, cereal; pink or green, 5½"......................$45.00
Philbe, creamer, blue, footed, 3¼"..............................$150.00
Philbe, plate, luncheon; crystal, 8" $37.50
Philbe, platter, crystal, closed handles, 12".................$30.00
Philbe, tumbler, iced tea; pink or green, footed, 15-oz,
    6½"...$85.00
Primrose, cake pan, white w/decal, 8" dia.................$12.00
Primrose, casserole, white w/decal, knob finial on lid, 1-
    qt...$12.00
Primrose, cup, snack; white w/decal, 5-oz....................$3.00
Primrose, plate, dinner; white w/decal, 9⅛" $7.00
Royal Ruby, bowl, popcorn; 5¼" $13.00
Royal Ruby, creamer, flat $12.00
Royal Ruby, goblet, ball stem......................................$11.00
Royal Ruby, punch bowl..$40.00
Royal Ruby, tumbler, water; 9-oz..................................$6.50
Sheaves of Wheat, cup & saucer, crystal $7.00
Sheaves of Wheat, plate, dinner; crystal, 9" $20.00
Sheaves of Wheat, tumbler, juice; crystal, 6-oz $12.00
Sheaves of Wheat, tumbler, water; crystal, 9-oz..........$15.00
Soreno, ashtray, Avocado or milk white, 6¼" $3.50
Soreno, butter dish, Avocado or milk white, ¼-lb........$6.00
Soreno, pitcher; water; aquamarine, 64-oz $18.00
Soreno, plate, snack; crystal, w/indent $3.00
Soreno, tumbler, juice; Honey Gold, 6-oz $2.50
Soreno, vase, Avocado or milk white, 9½".....................$7.00
Swirl, bowl, cereal; Ivory or white, 5⅞" $24.00
Swirl, bowl, flanged soup; Azur-ite, 9¼" $175.00
Swirl, creamer, Ivory or white, flat..............................$10.00
Swirl, custard cup, white w/gold trim............................$4.00
Swirl, plate, dinner; Azur-ite, 9⅛" $10.00
Swirl, plate, salad; Sunrise, 7⅜" $8.00
Swirl, soup plate, Rose-ite, 7⅝"..................................$150.00
Swirl, sugar bowl, pink, flat, tab handles, w/lid $15.00
Three Bands, bowl, fruit/dessert; Ivory, 4⅞" $100.00
Three Bands, cup & saucer, lustre..................................$4.00
Three Bands, plate, dinner; Burgundy, 9⅛" $300.00
Three Bands, plate, dinner; Ivory, 9⅛" $25.00
Turquoise Blue, bowl, berry; 4½" $10.00
Turquoise Blue, bowl, vegetable; 8" $22.00
Turquoise Blue, mug, 8-oz..$10.00
Turquoise Blue, plate, 10"..$30.00
Vienna Lace, bowl, dessert; 4⅝".....................................$5.00
Vienna Lace, cup & saucer, 8-oz $4.00
Vienna Lace, platter, white w/decal, 9x12"..................$17.00
Wheat, casserole, white w/decal, au-gratin lid, oval, 1½-
    qt $14.00

Wheat, mug, white w/decal..$50.00
Wheat, plate, white w/decal, 10"....................................$6.00
Wheat, soup plate, white w/decal, 6⅝".........................$8.00

Angels

Angels, Birthday

Not at all hard to find and still reasonably priced, birthday angels are fun to assemble into 12-month sets, and since there are many different series to look for, collecting them can be challenging as well as enjoyable. Generally speaking, angels are priced by the following factors: 1) company — look for Lefton, Napco, Norcrest, and Enesco marks or labels (unmarked or unknown sets are of less value); 2) application of flowers, bows, gold trim, etc. (the more detail, the more valuable); 3) use of rhinestones, which will also increase the price); 4) age; and 5) quality of the workmanship involved, detail, and accuracy of painting.

#1194, angel of the month series, white hair, 5", ea from $18
    to..$20.00
#1294, angel of the month, white hair, 5", ea from $18 to...$20.00
#1300, boy angels, wearing suit, white hair, 6", ea from $22
    to..$25.00
#1600 Pal Angel, month series of both boy & girl, 4", ea from
    $10 to..$15.00
Arnart, Kewpies, in choir robes, w/rhinestones, 4½", ea from
    $12 to..$15.00
Enesco, angels on round base w/flower of the month, gold
    trim, ea from $15 to...$18.00

High Mountain Quality, colored hair, 7", from $30.00 to $32.00 each. (Photo courtesy James Atkinson)

Kelvin, C-230, holding flower of the month, 4½", ea from $15
    to..$20.00
Kelvin, C-250, holding flower of the month, 4½", ea from $15
    to..$20.00
Lefton, #0130, Kewpie, 4½", ea from $35 to...............$40.00
Lefton, #0489, holding basket of flowers, 4", ea from $25
    to..$30.00

Lefton, #0556, boy of the month, 5½", ea from $25 to....**$30.00**

Lefton, #0574, day of the week series (like #8281 but not as ornate), ea from $25 to **$28.00**

Lefton, #0627, day of the week series, 3½", ea from $28 to **$32.00**

Lefton, #0985, flower of the month, 5", ea from $28 to..........**$32.00**

Lefton, #1323, angel of the month, bisque, ea from $18 to ..**$22.00**

Lefton, #1411, angel of the month, 4", ea from $28 to............**$32.00**

Lefton, #1987, angel of the month, ea from $30 to **$35.00**

Lefton, #2600, birthstone on skirt, 3¼", ea from $25 to...**$30.00**

Lefton, #3332, bisque, w/basket of flowers, 4", ea from $25 to...**$30.00**

Lefton, #5146, birthstone in skirt, 4½", ea from $22 to...**$28.00**

Lefton, #6224, applied flower/birthstone on skirt, 4½", ea from $18 to...**$25.00**

Lefton, #6883, sq frame, day of the week & months, 3¼x4", ea from $28 to...**$32.00**

Lefton, #6949, day of the week series in oval frame, 5", ea from $28 to...**$32.00**

Lefton, #6985, musical, sm, ea from $40 to **$45.00**

Lefton, #8281, day of the week series, applied roses, ea from $30 to..**$35.00**

Lefton, AR-1987, w/ponytail, 4", ea from $18 to **$22.00**

Lefton, 1987J, w/rhinestones, 4½", ea from $25 to.....**$30.00**

Napco, boy angel of the month March, St. Patrick's Day theme, gold trim, 4¾", from $20.00 to $25.00; girl angel of the month November, #A-1398, 4½", from $20.00 to $25.00.

Napco, A1360-1372, angel of the month, ea from $20 to ...**$25.00**

Napco, A1917-1929, boy angel of the month, ea from $20 to...**$25.00**

Napco, A4307, angel of the month, sm, ea from $22 to **$25.00**

Napco, C1361-1373, angel of the month, ea from $20 to...**$25.00**

Napco, C1921-1933, boy angel of the month, ea from $20 to...**$25.00**

Napco, S1291, day of the week 'Belle,' ea from $22 to **$25.00**

Napco, S1307, bell of the month, ea from $22 to.......**$25.00**

Napco, S1361-1372, angel of the month, ea from $20 to...**$25.00**

Napco, S1392, oval frame angel of the month, ea from $25 to...**$30.00**

Napco, S401-413, angel of the month, ea from $20 to ...**$25.00**

Napco, S429, day of the week angel (also available as planters), ea from $25 to......................................**$30.00**

Norcrest, F-120, angel of the month, 4½", ea from $18 to...**$22.00**

Norcrest, F-15, angel of the month, on round base w/raised pattern on dress, 4", ea from $18 to **$22.00**

Norcrest, F-167, bell of the month, 2¾", ea from $8 to.....**$12.00**

Norcrest, F-210, day of the week angel, 4½", ea from $18 to...**$22.00**

Norcrest, F-23, day of the week angel, 4½", ea from $18 to...**$22.00**

Norcrest, F-340, angel of the month, 5", ea from $20 to...**$25.00**

Norcrest, F-535, angel of the month, 4½", ea from $20 to...**$25.00**

Relco, 4¼", ea from $15 to **$18.00**

Relco, 6", ea from $18 to **$22.00**

SR, angel of the month, w/birthstone & 'trait' of the month (i.e. April - innocence), ea from $20 to **$25.00**

TMJ, angel of the month, w/flower, ea from $20 to...**$25.00**

Ucagco, white hair, 5¾", from $12 to **$15.00**

Wales, wearing long white gloves, white hair, Made in Japan, 6⅜", ea from $25 to...**$28.00**

Angels, Zodiac

These china figurines were made and imported by the same companies as the birthday angels. Not as many companies made the Zodiac series, though, which makes them harder to find. Because they're older and were apparently never as popular as the month pieces, they were not made or distributed as long as the birthday angels. Examples tend to be more individualized due to each sign having a specific characteristic associated with it.

Japan, wearing pastel dress w/applied pink rose on head, standing on cloud base w/stars, 4½", ea from $15 to.........**$20.00**

Japan, wearing pastel dress w/rhinestones on gold stars, applied pink rose on head, 4", ea from $20 to....**$25.00**

Josef, holds tablet w/sign written & framed in gold, 1960-1962, ea from $30 to...**$40.00**

Josef, no wings, sign written in cursive on dress, 4", ea from $30 to...**$40.00**

Lefton, K8650, applied flowers & gold stars, 4" when standing (1946-1953), ea from $40 to **$45.00**

Napco, A2646, wearing gold crown, applied 'coconut' gold trim on dress hem, 5", ea from $25 to **$30.00**

Napco, S1259, 'Your lucky star guardian angel' planter series, 4", ea from $30 to...**$35.00**

Napco, S980, 'Your lucky star guardian angel,' 4", ea from $22 to...**$28.00**

Semco, gold wings, applied roses & pleated ruffle on front edge of dress, 5", ea from $20 to **$25.00**

Ashtrays

Ashtrays, especially for cigarettes, did not become widely used in the United States much before the turn of the century. The first examples were simply receptacles made to hold ashes for pipes, cigars, and cigarettes. Later, rests were incorporated into the design. Ashtrays were made in a variety of materials. Some were purely functional, while others advertised or entertained, and some stopped just short of being works of art. They were made to accommodate smokers in homes, businesses, or wherever they might be. Today their prices range from a few dollars to hundreds. Since today so many people buy and sell on eBay and other Internet auction auction sites, there is much more exposure to ashtray collecting. Also these auction prices must be considered when determining the value of an item. Many of the very fine ashtrays from the turn of the century do not command the same price as they did in the early 1990s unless the maker's name is widely known. And now, in the twenty-first century, many of the old ashtrays are actually antiques. This may contribute to the continued fluctuation of prices in this still new collectibles field. For further information see *Collector's Guide to Ashtrays, Second Edition, Identification and Values,* by Nancy Wanvig.

See also specific glass companies and potteries; Japan Ceramics; Disney; Tire Ashtrays; World's Fairs.

Advisor: Nancy Wanvig (See Directory, Ashtrays)

Advertising, Canadian Club, The Best in the House, blue & white plastic, 5⅜" sq.................................**$7.00**
Advertising, Carling Black Label, bronze metal w/chrome strip, Hey Mabel, oval, 5¼" W...............................**$16.00**
Advertising, Child's Cash Shoe Store, tan stoneware, black picture & letters in center, 5⅜" sq.......................**$26.00**

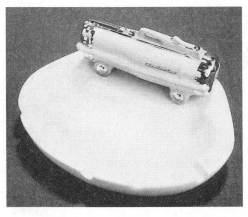

Advertising, Electrolux 'Sales Award — October 1961,' ceramic, 6½", $50.00. (Photo courtesy Nancy Wanvig)

Advertising, Financial Analysts Federation, blue name & logo in center, Chicago, 1963, 5¼" dia..........................**$7.00**
Advertising, General Electric, 75th Anniversary 1878-1953, cigar & cigarette rests, 5½" dia.............................**$22.00**
Advertising, Knights of Columbus, chrome, painted red, white & blue symbol, 1950s, 5⅝"........................**$12.00**
Advertising, Mohammed Temple, cast bronze, raised symbols in center, 1934, 5¼" dia.............................**$25.00**
Advertising, Monsanto, name on rise, You Get What You Pay For..., ceramic triangle, 5½" sides.......................**$12.00**
Advertising, National Scout Jamboree, ceramic, 1977, 5½" dia **$9.00**

Advertising, Registered Polled Herefords, clear glass w/white decal on back, 4⅛" sq..............................**$6.00**
Advertising, Schlitz, tan ceramic, brown logo & picture, 5¾"....................................**$25.00**
Advertising, Skol Lager, yellow glass, name in red & picture of 2 beer mugs on rise, 6" dia.............................**$11.50**
Advertising, Statler Hotel, green ceramic, match holder center, name in relief near edge, 5⅛" dia **$15.00**
Advertising, University of Virginia, tan ceramic, brown picture in center, 4½" dia..............................**$8.00**
Advertisng, Westinghouse, ceramic, trademark W, heavy, many rests, 7" W....................................**$35.00**
Art Deco, black panther beside tray w/some gold trim, pottery, 3" H **$17.00**
Art Deco, bronze nude on chrome base, 2⅜"............**$70.00**
Art Deco, bronze seal on marble base, 2 rests, 7" W.**$53.00**
Art Deco, chrome rectangle w/2 rests, rubber pad on bottom, 3¾" W....................................**$14.00**
Art Deco, stylized fish, chrome, rests between tail & body, 5⅝" dia **$24.00**

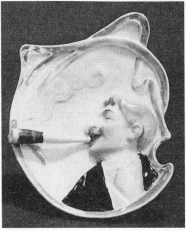

Art Nouveau, man with cigarette (which becomes rest) in relief, numbered, 6¼", $68.00. (Photo courtesy Nancy Wanvig)

Brass, Aladdin's lamp shape w/animals & birds embossed on cup, crudely made, old, 2¾"..............................**$11.00**
Bronze, elephant head w/white tusk, sand casting, 6¼" L **$50.00**
Cloisonne, green inside, copper cells, multicolored flowers, China, 3⅞" dia **$24.00**
Glass, Adam, pink, Jeannette, 4½" sq.........................**$30.00**
Glass, black amethyst, elephant figure in center, Greensburg Glass Works, 1930s, 6" dia **$42.00**
Glass, cobalt blue w/4 rows of Hobnails, Fenton, 1970s+, 6¼"..............................**$15.00**
Glass, cut crystal, heavy, 4 rests, 5½" **$20.00**
Glass, emerald green, 4 coins in center, Fostoria, 7¾" ..**$48.00**
Glass, Forest Green, hexagonal, Anchor Hocking, 5¾" ...**$9.00**
Glass, Williamsburg pressed pattern, amber, Federal, 4" dia **$7.00**
Japan, green basketweave w/flowers, Marutomoware, 4½" dia **$10.00**
Japan, Hummel type, Music Maker, boy w/accordion, Napco mark, 5½"..............................**$25.00**
Majolica, accordion player figural, w/cigar holder, match holder & striker, unmarked, very old, 6½".........**$350.00**

Marble, dark gray & tan, Art Deco styling, heavy, 6" sq...**$35.00**

Metal, chrome fretwork frame w/cobalt glass insert, Hong Kong, 4" dia...**$25.00**

Novelty, bedpan, For Old Butts & Ashes, gold edging, 1 snufferette, 5" L..**$11.00**

Novelty, big-mouth cat, bisque, glass eyes, holes in nose, Japan, 5" W **$40.00**

Novelty, big-mouth hobo w/top hat, fur hair, cigar in mouth, holes in nose, ceramic, Japan, 4" L.............**$40.00**

Novelty, Black face on bowl of pipe tray, ceramic, 2" .**$15.00**

Novelty, Cardinal Games, ceramic glove shape, also ad for Griesedieck Bros Beer, McCoy, 5" W....................**$48.00**

Novelty, drum major, lusterware, 1 rest, 3¼" H.........**$23.00**

Novelty, drunk at lamppost, ceramic, 5⅛" H.............**$14.00**

Novelty, elf's face, green hat, brown eyes, holes in ears, ceramic, 4½" L **$25.00**

Novelty, frog figural, orange ceramic, ash dump, 4⅝" H **$25.00**

Novelty, house w/brown chimney, 2 vents in chimney, 2 rests, ceramic, unmarked, 3¾"..............................**$15.00**

Novelty, King of Clubs, Kreiss & Co, 7" H **$25.00**

Novelty, Old Ironsides, This Material Was Taken From the US Frigate Constitution, bronze, 6¼" W **$35.00**

Novelty, Remember Pearl Harbor, heavy glass, 3¾" dia...**$40.00**

Novelty, Sailboat, clear glass w/blue plastic sail, 1 rest, 6" L **$14.00**

Novelty, Soeul Japan Olympics, metal, mascot in center, 1983, 5¼" dia **$15.00**

Novelty, top hat, black glass, 2 rests, 2⅛" H.............**$10.00**

Novelty, turtle, solid brass, 2 rests, 4" L....................**$9.00**

Pewter, dog figural handle, American, old, 3¾" H **$28.00**

Rosenthal, white porcelain w/raised decor on outside, 1950s, 4¼"..**$20.00**

Victorian, man crossing pond on logs (rest), with match holder and striker, 5", $145.00. (Photo courtesy Nancy Wanvig)

Autographs

'Philography' is an extremely popular hobby, one that is very diversified. Autographs of sports figures, movie stars, entertainers, and politicians from our lifetime may bring sev-eral hundred dollars, depending on rarity and application, while John Adams's simple signature on a document from 1800, for instance, might bring thousands. A signature on a card or cut from a letter or document is the least valuable type of autograph. A handwritten letter is generally the most valuable, since in addition to the signature you get the message as well. Depending upon what it reveals about the personality who penned it, content can be very important and can make a major difference in value.

Many times a polite request accompanied by an SASE to a famous person will result in receipt of a signed photo or a short handwritten note that might in several years be worth a tidy sum!

Obviously as new collectors enter the field, the law of supply and demand will drive the prices for autographs upward, especially when the personality is deceased. There are forgeries around, so before you decide to invest in expensive autographs, get to know your dealers.

Over the years many celebrities in all fields have periodically employed secretaries to sign their letters and photos. They have also sent out photos with preprinted or rubber stamped signatures as time doesn't always permit them to personally respond to fan mail. With today's advanced printing, even many long-time collectors have been fooled with a mechanically produced signature.

Advisors: Don and Anne Kier (See Directory, Autographs)

Newspaper: *Autograph Times*
2303 N 44th St., #225, Phoenix, AZ 85008; 602-947-3112 or fax: 602-947-8363

Adamson, Joy; signature on white 3x5" card **$69.00**

Anderson; Loni; signature on black & white glossy photo (sexy pose), 8x10" **$30.00**

Andrews, Julie; signature on color glossy as Mary Poppins w/umbrella, 8x10"..**$80.00**

Bacon, Kevin; signature on color glossy from Footloose, dancing night scene, 8x10" **$30.00**

Basinger, Kim; signature on color glossy in low-cut white gown from Batman movie, 8x10"........................**$40.00**

Baum, Vicki; signature (ink) on white 3x5" card, dated 1958..**$39.00**

Bergen, Edgar; signature (fountain pen ink) on light pink album page, his own name & 'Charlie,' M...........**$65.00**

Bertinelli, Valerie; signature on black & white glossy photo, early, 8x10"...**$25.00**

Brynner, Yul; signed (boldly) black & white glossy photo (as King of Siam), 8x10"..................................**$135.00**

Burton, Richard; signature (dark ink) on 3x5" card, dated 1954, rare..**$125.00**

Calhoun, Rory; signature (dark ink) on pink album page ..**$28.00**

Carey, MacDonald; signed black & white glossy portrait photo, 1960s, 8x10" **$25.00**

Carter, Jimmy; signature on thank-you card given to television station management......................................**$75.00**

Carter, Lynda; signature on black & white glossy photo as Wonder Woman, 8x10".......................................**$30.00**

Chevalier, Maurice; signature (pencil) on white 3x5" card, ca 1959 ......**$45.00**

Coburn, Charles; signature (dark green ink) on inscribed vintage album page, EX **$40.00**

Compton, Joyce; letter, handwritten, reflective content, 5-page, dated 1987......**$50.00**

Connery, Sean; signature on color photo as James Bond, white jacket & black bow tie, holding gun, 8x10" **$125.00**

Conway, Tim; signature on color glossy photo as member of McHale's Navy, 8x10" **$25.00**

Craig, Yvonne; signature on black & white glossy photo as Batgirl, 8x10" **$25.00**

D'Angelo, Beverly; signature on color glossy photo, red hair, 8x10" **$28.00**

Day, Doris; signature on black & white glossy, 1950s era, 8x10" **$50.00**

Dempsey, Jack; signature (dark ink) on album page .**$75.00**

Derek, Bo; signature on color glossy photo in skimpy swimsuit from movie 10, 8x10" **$35.00**

DeWolfe, Billy; signature on album page, ca 1950s, 5x6"..**$28.00**

Douglas, Kirk; signature on color glossy photo, wearing A's baseball jacket & holding bat, 8x10" **$50.00**

Dreiser, Theodore; signature & address clipped from envelope......**$55.00**

Drysdale, Don; signature on black & white postcard-size lithograph, printed by Meadow Gold......**$35.00**

Duvall, Robert; signature on colored glossy photo, recent, 8x10" **$40.00**

Earnhardt, Dale; signed & inscribed color lithographed photo, biographical info on back, signed in 1992, 8x10" **$125.00**

Eden, Barbara; signature on color photo as Jeannie, 8x10" **$35.00**

Foster, Jodie; signature on color photo from Anna & the King, 8x10" **$60.00**

Fullerton, Gordon; signature (felt pen) on NASA color lithograph (dressed in space suit), 8x10" **$59.00**

Funicello, Annette; full signature on black & white glossy photo as mousketeer, 8x10" **$60.00**

Garner, James; signature on color photo as Maverick, 8x10" **$30.00**

Gilbert, Melissa; signature on glossy photo as Laura Ingalls, 8x10" **$30.00**

Gooding, Cuba; signature on color glossy as character from Jerry Maguire, 8x10" **$30.00**

Gorshin, Frank; signature on glossy photo as Riddler, 8x10" **$30.00**

Greene, Lorne; inscribed sepia-tone photo as Ben Cartright standing beside horse, 1960s, 8x10"......**$145.00**

Guest, Edgar; signature (ink) on white 3x5" paper, dated 1938 ......**$18.00**

Harriman, W Averell; signature (black ink) on white 3x5" card **$38.00**

Heston, Charlton; signature on glossy photo from Ben Hur, 8x10" **$45.00**

Hoover, Herbert; signature (ink) on sm sheet of Waldorf-Astoria stationery, original envelope postmarked 1956 ......**$125.00**

Javits, Jacob; signature on black & white photo, NY Senator, 8x10" **$20.00**

Johnson, Luci; signature on typed letter on White House stationery, dated 1965 ......**$65.00**

Klemperer, Werner; signature on colored glossy photo as Colonel Klink, 8x10" **$40.00**

Knotts, Don; signature on colored photo as Barney Fife, 8x10" **$35.00**

Kudrow, Lisa; signature on color glossy photo, 8x10"....**$40.00**

Landon, Alf; signature on typed letter on personal stationery, 1-page, 1966......**$39.00**

Lee, Brenda; signed & inscribed black & white glossy photo, 1960s, 8x10"......**$20.00**

Leigh, Janet; signature on black & white glossy photo, sexy pose, 8x10"......**$30.00**

Lewis, Jerry; signed & inscribed black & white glossy photo as the Nutty Professor, 8x10" **$50.00**

Lindsay, John V; signature (ink) on sm Sardi's card, dated 1966 (while NY mayor)......**$39.00**

Lodge, Henry Cabot Jr; signature on typed letter on embossed US Embassy stationery from West Germany, 1968 ......**$44.00**

Lolobrigida, Gina; signature on black & white glossy photo, sexy pose, 8x10" **$50.00**

Lombardo, Guy; signed and inscribed black & white glossy photo, 8x10" **$75.00**

Loren, Sophia; signature on black & white glossy photo, wet blouse, 8x10" **$40.00**

Louise, Tina; signature on color photo as Ginger, 2-pc swimsuit, 8x10" **$25.00**

Lovelace, Linda; signature on black & white glossy photo, in bikini, 8x10" **$40.00**

MacRae, Gordon; signature on white 3x5" card......**$44.00**

Manke, John; signature (black ink) on card, ca 1970s..**$20.00**

Mantle, Mickey; signature (blue ink) on light pink album page **$85.00**

March, Hal; signed & inscribed black & white glossy photo, ca 1950-60s, 8x10" **$45.00**

Marshall, Herbet; signature on sepia-toned photo, standing w/cigarette, ca 1935, 8x10", EX **$35.00**

Martin, Pamela Sue; signature on colored glossy photo as Nancy Drew, sexy pose, 8x10" **$25.00**

McDivitt, James A; signature (ink) on cover postmarked June 7, 1965 (commemorating Gemini 4 flight), 5¢ Kennedy stamp **$35.00**

McDowell, Roddy; signature (ink) on black & white 3x5" card, ...**$18.00**

Meriwether, Lee; signature on colored glossy photo as Catwoman, 8x10" **$20.00**

Mitchum, Robert; signature (red ink) on album page, dated 1948 ......**$30.00**

Montgomery, Robert; signature (ink) on white 3x5" card, typed date 1969 at top **$25.00**

Morris, Chester; signature on blank white 3x5" card, dated 1965 on top border......**$20.00**

Nelson, Ozzie; signature (pencil) on light pink album page (signature of Horace Heidt in pencil on back) **$49.00**

Newman, Paul; signature (bold, ink) on white 3x5" card, dated 1968 .... **$85.00**

Nixon, Richard M; signature (ink, bold, w/short inscription) on his book: Six Crises, 1st edition, 1962, w/dust jacket **$275.00**

Olivier, Lawrence; signature on postcard-size black & white photo, as character from Clash of Titans, 1979, EX+ .**$50.00**

Parks, Bert; signature (ball-point pen, bold, clear) on white 3x5" card, dated 1961 .... **$18.00**

Pauling, Linus; signature on typed letter, mentions vitamin C, dated 1985 .... **$65.00**

Paulsen, Pat; signature on white 3x5" card, dated 1968 ..**$10.00**

Peppard, George; signature (ink) on white 3x5" card, dated 1967 .... **$15.00**

Pike, Bishop James A; signature (dark ink) on 3x5" card, 1960s **$70.00**

Previn, Andre; signed & inscribed black & white photo, in tuxedo, dated 1968 .... **$40.00**

Remick, Lee; signature (ink) on 3x5" card, dated 1963 ..**$20.00**

Reynolds, Debbie; signature on color glossy photo, formal attire, ca 1970s, 8x10" **$25.00**

Ripley, Robert; signature (bold) on black & white glossy photo, borderless, 7½x9½", EX **$145.00**

Rockefeller, Nelson; signature (dark, bold) on 3x5" card, dated 1970 .... **$30.00**

Rogers, Ginger; signature (green fountain pen) on light album page, personally dated by her (1943) **$45.00**

Rogers, Roy; signed & inscribed black & white glossy photo, playing guitar, 8x10" **$85.00**

Romero, Cesar; inscribed & signed black & white glossy photo, later years, 7½x9½" **$35.00**

Russo, Rene; signature on color glossy photo, 8x10" .**$40.00**

Rutherford, Ann; signature on sepia-tone semimatt photo ca 1940s, VG+ **$50.00**

Savalas, Telly; signature (ink) on white 3x5" card, dated 1968 .... **$20.00**

Selleck, Tom; signature on color glossy photo as Magnum PI, no shirt, 8x10" **$20.00**

Seymour, Jane; signature on color glossy photo, recent, 8x10" **$40.00**

Skelton, Red; signature (dark ink) on white 3x5" card, dated 1964 .... **$29.00**

Somers, Suzanne; signature on color glossy photo as Chrissy, 8x10" **$40.00**

Starr, Kay; signed & incribed black & white glossy photo, feather boa, ca 1967, 8x10" **$25.00**

Stone, Sharon; signature on color glossy photo, sexy pose, 8x10" **$45.00**

Strasberg, Susan; signature (ink) on white 3x5" card, dated 1961 .... **$39.00**

Taylor, Rod; signature on colored photo from The Time Machine, 8x10" **$28.00**

Thomas, Danny; inscribed signature (ink) on white 3x5" card, dated 1969 .... **$20.00**

Thomas, Lowell; signature on white 3x5" card **$25.00**

Thompson, Lea; signature on color photo, dated 2001, 8x10" **$25.00**

Udall, Morris; signature (black ink) on 1976 Presidential Candidate cachet, postmarked 1975, 3½x6" **$39.00**

Vanderbilt, Amy; signature (blue ball-point pen, bold) on black & white glossy photo, 1950s, 8x10" **$39.00**

Villechaize, Herve; signature (ink) on back of 3½x8" postcard, w/2 4x6" candid snapshots posing w/fans ..**$45.00**

Walker, Clint; signature on black & white glossy photo as Cheyenne, 8x10" **$40.00**

Walston, Ray; signature (dark ink) on white 3x5" card, dated 1964 .... **$18.00**

Ward, Burt; signature on color glossy photo as Robin, 8x10" **$30.00**

Ward, Sela; signature on color glossy photo, sexy pose, 8x10" **$28.00**

Weaver, Dennis; signature on black & white glossy photo as Chester Good, 8x10" **$20.00**

Welch, Raquel; signature on black & white glossy photo, in 2-pc swimsuit, 8x10" **$40.00**

Wells, Dawn; signature on black & white glossy photo as Mary Ann, 8x10" **$25.00**

Yorty, Sam; signature (red ink) on LBJ cachet, black LBJ graphics, 3½x6" **$30.00**

Moore, Clayton; on lobby card, $95.00. (Photo courtesy Don and Anne Kier)

Schwarzenegger, Arnold; on 8" x 10" black and white photo as Commando, $45.00. (Photo courtesy Don and Anne Kier)

Automobilia

Automobilia remains a specialized field, attracting antique collectors and old car buffs alike. It is a field that encompasses auto-related advertising and accessories like hood ornaments, gear shift and steering wheel knobs, sales brochures, and catalogs. Memorabilia from the high-performance, sporty automobiles of the sixties is very popular with baby boomers. Unusual items have been setting auction records as the market for automobilia heats up. Note: Badges vary according to gold content — 10k or sterling silver examples are higher than average. Dealership booklets (Ford, Chevy, etc.) generally run about $2.00 to $3.00 per page, and because many reproductions are available, very few owner's manuals sell for more than $10.00. Also it should be mentioned here that there are many reproduction clocks and signs out there. Any 'Guard' badges with round Ford logos are fake. Buyers beware.

See also License Plates; Tire Ashtrays.

Advisor: Leonard Needham (See Directory, Automobilia)

Ashtray, Ford, shield logo in red & white on clear glass, sq, NM **$20.00**

Banner, Blue Coal Treatment/Salute to Quality!/Protect Your Car Now, shows doorman helping lady from car, 35x93", EX+ **$100.00**

Booklet, Lincoln V-8 Engine, 1950, 12 pages, EX **$10.00**

Booklet, Pennsylvania Turnpike, 1953, 16 pages, EX.**$12.00**

Brochure, 1969 Corvette Stingray, color photos & specifics, 18x11", EX **$30.00**

Calendar, Federal Trucks, 1942, Pilot of the Fleet, girl in short skirt w/trucks in background, 34x16", EX+ **$60.00**

Calendar, PIE, tin w/cardboard backing, image of truck bursting through map above month & number holder, 19x12½", VG+ **$130.00**

Calendar, Your Ford Dealer, 1949, shows detailed drawn portrait of General Douglas McArthur, incomplete pad, 26x16", VG..**$20.00**

Catalog, Patrician Series #400 of the 1955 Packard, shows full line, 16 pages, orignial jacket, NM **$225.00**

Catalog, Pep Boys Auto & Radio Supplies — Tires/World's Fairest Prices, Summer/Fall, 1940, comic images of Boys, EX...**$65.00**

Catalog, showroom; 1952 Chevrolet, w/paints chips & upholstery samples, 31 pages, EX.................................**$225.00**

Clock, Chevrolet Time, neon, screwed-in dealer panel above logo, blue on white, metal frame, Lackner, 20" dia, EX..**$850.00**

Clock, Edsel Division of Ford Motor Co, light-up, round w/chrome frame, glass front, green on white, Pam, G+ **$700.00**

Clock, Oldsmobile Service, neon, round metal frame w/white tubing, emblem in center, 21" dia, EX **$600.00**

Display, wood w/1960 Buick pictured on glass front, hinged lid, lights-up, VG+ **$50.00**

Emblem, trunk; Pierce Arrow, nickel-plated w/inlaid design, 1930s, 2½" dia, EX...**$380.00**

Figure, Chrysler's Mr Fleet, vinyl, all-white version, 1970s, 10", VG, from $150 to **$250.00**

Gearshift knob, simulated onyx w/brass St Christopher medallion in center, EX...**$25.00**

Hood ornament, chrome nude figure w/knees bent & arms stretched back, windblown hair, 5", VG **$50.00**

Horn, Spartan SOS Deluxe, 6-volt, 16" L, EX **$60.00**

Hubcaps, 1959 Buick Electra or Electra 225, set of 4, EX...**$250.00**

Key chain/flashlight, Buick, tan & black, image of eagle in flight, EX..**$18.00**

Key holder, Dodge, enameled logo on leather, EX **$15.00**

Kit, Jaguar Drivers' Club, includes license plate attachment, decal, and plastic license holder, EXIB, $50.00. (Photo courtesy Collector's Auction Service)

License plate attachment, Member Buick Safety Legion, die-cut tin circle & bow-tie emblem, blue & white, 4¾x3", EX+ **$175.00**

License plate attachment, Pull With the USA or Pull Out, red, white & blue image of flag, tin, 3x10", EX+.........**$40.00**

Mask, See the New 1940 Chevrolet lettered on hat of winking moon-faced man, diecut cardboard, 12", EX+.........**$65.00**

Owner's manual, 1979 Eldorado, EX............................**$8.00**

Paperweight, Packard, embossed brass emblem, Ask the Man Who Owns One above image of touring car, 3½", EX+ **$325.00**

Pennant, Elgin Nat Road Races/Aug 29-30-1913, white on red w/blue image of early racer, 11½x29½", VG+ ...**$350.00**

Pocket mirror, Mack/Leading Gasoline Truck of America..., pictures early Bell Telephone truck, celluloid, 2½" dia, EX **$350.00**

Postcard, 1952 Oldsmobile 88 4-door sedan, photo image, EX...**$7.00**

Poster, 1946 Ford/Smart New Interior/The Smartest Ford Car Ever Built!, shows 3 interior scenes, 36x46", VG...**$80.00**

Radiator cap, whippet dog figure, 4" L, EX..............**$130.00**

Ruler, Chevrolet, celluloid, 1930s, 6", M **$28.00**

Shoe horn, 1979 Chevrolet Theme Line, bow-tie logo, plastic, EX...**$8.00**

Sign, Berry Bros Automobile Color Varnishes/Refinish Your Car the Berry Way, wood, resembles wrestling belt, 33" L, VG..**$285.00**

Sign, Buick Quick Service, tin, white and black on red, white, and blue bands, 16" x 26", EX, $250.00.

Sign, Cadillac, porcelain circle w/V-&-crown emblem on dark blue, white line border, 18", EX $475.00

Sign, Chevrolet, metal diecut bow-tie emblem w/white name on blue, white border, 7x20½", EX.....................$450.00

Sign, Dodge/Plymouth, neon, white on blue emblem w/bottom stepped & slightly V-shaped, 28x60", VG+ $1,500.00

Sign, Ford, porcelain V-shape w/Genuine Parts on curved panel atop oval Ford emblem, 8 below, blue & white, 2-sided, EX..$2,000.00

Sign, Garage, metal w/holes over lettering for lighting, white on black w/white line border, 2-sided, 7x61", VG+/EX...$900.00

Sign, GMC Trucks, porcelain, winged emblem & Trucks in white on 2-tone green, curved bottom corners, 2-sided, 48" L, EX..$520.00

Sign, Marrow Trucking lettered on grille-shaped emblem, red, black, white & gray, 16x24", EX+ $190.00

Sign, Motorola/Car Radio/Authorized Service, red, white & blue on white porcelain, 2-sided, 20x29", NM/EX+ $350.00

Sign, Oldsmobile Service, porcelain circle w/lettering around symbolic emblem, 2-sided, 60" dia, VG+/EX......$400.00

Sign, Overland Motor Car, tin chalkboard-look appearing to have wooden frame w/red rope border, We Use an..., 10x14", EX...$170.00

Sign, Pyrene Kills Auto Fires, diecut cardboard image of woman w/child watching man put out engine fire, 2-pc, 33, VG..$750.00

Sign, Southern Cowley Automobile Club/Danger Sound Klaxon, painted wood w/wood frame, red, white & black, 19x25", EX..$325.00

Sign, The Gray Line/Sight Seeing Everywhere, porcelain, red, white & blue globe graphics, 20 " dia, EX $130.00

Sign, tin, Camaro/Parts Service, image of 1969 red Camaro on blue, inverted corners, 12x18", EX+ $15.00

Sign, 66 (highway route), white diecut aluminum shield w/reflector dots outlining black numbers & border, 30x35", NM...$725.00

Taxi topper, red Taxi etched on milk glass tube w/amber light globes screwed into red end mounts, 12" L, NM..$100.00

Thermometer, Authorized United Motors Service, wood, arched top, sq bottom, orange & blue on white, 15x4", VG...$120.00

Thermometer, Lincoln Cab Co/Call a Lincoln, wood, arched top w/sq bottom, 15x4", VG................................$80.00

Tire cover & tire, Grandy & Hoge, leather w/stenciled dealer advertising, 4.75-19 5.00-19 4-ply tire, EX+......$25.00

Tray, stainless steel w/Ford & V-8 logo embossed in corner, from plant cafeteria, 12x18", EX $75.00

Visor mirror, decorative brown & tan plastic case w/a place to write service record, EX......................................$15.00

Windshield scraper, Pontiac, 1957 ....$6.00

Wrench, Ford 5-Z-152, script logo, EX........................$10.00

Autumn Leaf Dinnerware

A familiar dinnerware pattern to just about all of us, Autumn Leaf was designed by Hall China for the Jewel Tea Company who offered it to their customers as premiums. In fact, some people erroneously refer to the pattern as 'Jewel Tea.' First made in 1933, it continued in production until 1978. Pieces with this date in the backstamp are from the overstock that was in the company's warehouse when production was suspended. There are matching tumblers and stemware all made by the Libbey Glass Company, and a set of enameled cookware that came out in 1979. You'll find blankets, tablecloths, metal canisters, clocks, playing cards, and many other items designed around the Autumn Leaf pattern. All are collectible.

Since 1984 the Hall company has been making special items for the National Autumn Leaf Collectors Club. These pieces are designated as such by the 'Club' marking that is accompanied by the date of issue. Limited edition items (also by Hall) are being sold by China Specialties, a company in Ohio; but once you become familiar with the old pieces, these are easy to identify, since the molds have been redesigned or were not previously used for Autumn Leaf production.

For further study, we recommend *The Collector's Encyclopedia of Hall China* by Margaret and Kenn Whitmyer. For information on company products, see Jewel Tea.

Advisor: Gwynneth M. Harrison (See Directory, Autumn Leaf)

Club: National Autumn Leaf Collectors' Club
Gwynneth Harrison
P.O. Box 1, Mira Loma, CA 91752-0001; 909-685-5434
e-mail: morgan99@pe.net

Newsletter: *Autumn Leaf*
Bill Swanson, Editor
807 Roaring Springs Dr.
Allen, TX 75002-2112; 972-727-5527
e-mail: bescome@home.com

Baker, French; 1966-76, 2-pt, from $150 to $175.00

Baker, French; 3-pt, 1936-76, from $18 to $20.00

Baker, souffle; 1966-76, 4⅛", from $10 to $12.00

Baker, souffle; 1978, 4½", from $75 to.......................$80.00

Bean pot, 2-handle, 1960-76, from $225 to $250.00

Blanket, vellux, Autumn Leaf color, 1979-??, full size, from $150 to...$175.00

Book, Autumn Leaf Story, from $40 to **$60.00**
Bottle, Jim Beam, w/stand, from $115 to **$130.00**
Bowl, cereal; 1938-76, 6", from $8 to.........................**$12.00**
Bowl, cream soup; 1950-76, from $30 to....................**$40.00**
Bowl, milk white, Royal Glasbake, 4-pc set, from $400
   to **$500.00**
Bowl, mixing; 'new metal,' 1980-??, 3-pc set, from $250
   to **$275.00**
Bowl, mixing; 1933-76, 3-pc set, from $65 to **$85.00**
Bowl, refrigerator; 1980-??, set of 3+ plastic lids, from $250
   to **$275.00**
Bowl, salad; 1937-76, 9", from $15 to **$20.00**
Bowl, soup; Melmac, from $15 to **$20.00**
Bowl, vegetable; oval, Melmac, from $40 to **$50.00**
Bowl, vegetable; oval, w/lid, 1940-76, from $50 to **$75.00**
Bread box, metal, 1937-41, from $500 to **$800.00**
Butter dish, regular, ruffled top, 1961-76, ¼-lb, from $175
   to **$250.00**
Cake baker, Heatflow clear glass, Mary Dunbar, from $65
   to **$85.00**
Cake plate, 1937-76, from $20 to **$28.00**
Cake safe, metal, side motif, 1950-53, from $25 to.....**$50.00**
Cake safe, metal, top motif, 1935-41, from $25 to......**$50.00**
Calendar, 1940s & newer, from $100 to....................**$200.00**
Can, cleanser; from $750 to.....................................**$1,200.00**
Candlestick, metal, Douglas, pr from $70 to.............**$100.00**
Canister, Autumn Leaf color, patterned white plastic lid,
   Douglas, from $8 to..**$10.00**
Canister, brown & gold, 1960-62, from $20 to **$30.00**
Canisters, sq, 1959-??, 4-pc set, from $295 to **$350.00**
Casserole, round, w/lid, 1935-76, 2-qt, from $30 to ...**$45.00**
Catalog, Jewel, hard-bound cover, from $150 to **$300.00**
Catalog, Jewel, paper, from $5 to...............................**$20.00**
Clock, electric; #11D831, 1956-69, from $400 to.......**$550.00**
Coaster, metal, 3⅛", from $5 to **$8.00**
Coffee dispenser, 1941, from $200 to **$400.00**
Coffeepot, all china, 1942-45, 4-pc, from $275 to.....**$350.00**
Coffeepot, electric percolator, 1957-69, from $350
   to **$450.00**
Coffeepot, Rayed, 1937-49, 9-cup, from $30 to..........**$45.00**
Condiment/marmalade set, 1938-39, 3-pc, from $100
   to **$125.00**
Cookbook, Mary Dunbar, from $15 to........................**$30.00**
Cooker, waterless; metal, Mary Dunbar, from $50 to .**$75.00**
Cookie jar, Big Ear, Zeisel, 1957-69, from $250 to....**$275.00**
Cover, mixer; plastic, Mary Dunbar, 1950-61, from $35
   to **$50.00**
Cover, toaster; plastic, Mary Dunbar, 1950-51, from $30
   to **$50.00**
Creamer & sugar bowl, Ruffled D, 1940s style, 1940-76, from
   $25 to..**$45.00**
Cup, St Denis, 1942-76, from $35 to **$50.00**
Cup & saucer, Melmac, from $15 to............................**$20.00**
Custard cup, Radiance, 1936-76, from $6 to...............**$10.00**
Dripper, coffeepot; metal, 8- or 9-cup, from $20 to ...**$25.00**
Dutch oven, metal & porcelain, w/lid, 1979-??, 5-qt, from
   $125 to..**$175.00**

Flatware, stainless steel, 1960-68, ea place pc, from $25
   to **$30.00**
Fork, pickle; Jewel Tea from $40 to............................**$75.00**
Goblet, gold & frost on clear, footed, 1960-61, 10-oz, from
   $60 to..**$65.00**
Gravy boat w/underplate (pickle dish), 1942-76, from $40
   to **$55.00**
Hot pad, round, metal back, 1937-??, 7¼", from $15 to..**$20.00**

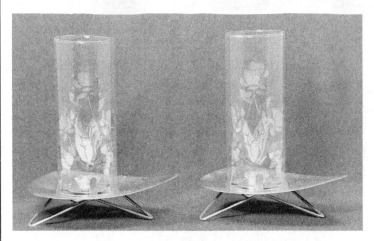

**Hurricane lamps, made by Douglas, 1960 – 62, $500.00
for the pair.**

Jug, ball; #3, 1938-76, from $35 to **$40.00**
Jug, utility; Rayed, 1937-76, from $20 to....................**$25.00**
Mug, conic, 1966-76, from $90 to..............................**$150.00**
Mug, Irish coffee; 1966-76, from $90 to....................**$150.00**
Napkin, muslin, 16" sq, from $30 to **$50.00**
Newsletter, Jewel News, from $10 to **$20.00**
Pan, sauce; w/warmer base, Douglas, 1960-62.........**$500.00**
Pan, sauce; wood handle, w/lid, 1½-qt, from $100 to....**$150.00**
Pickle dish, 1942-76, 9", from $20 to **$25.00**
Pie baker, 1937-76, from $20 to..................................**$35.00**
Plate, 1938-76, 6", from $5 to..**$8.00**
Plate, 1938-76, 7¼", from $5 to **$10.00**
Plate, 1938-76, 8", from $12 to....................................**$18.00**
Plate, 1938-76, 9", from $8 to **$12.00**
Plate, 1938-76, 10", from $12 to..................................**$18.00**
Platter, oval, Melmac, 14", from $40 to **$50.00**
Platter, oval, 1938-76, 11½", from $20 to **$25.00**
Playing cards, 75th Anniversary, 1974, from $25 to....**$50.00**
Range set: salt & pepper shakers & grease jar w/lid, 1936-76,
   from $50 to..**$60.00**
Salt & pepper shakers, range; left & right handles, 1936-76,
   pr from $20 to...**$30.00**
Saucer, regular, Ruffled D, 1936-76, from $1 to **$3.00**
Saucer, St Denis, 1974-76, from $6 to **$8.00**
Scales, Jewel Family, from $100 to............................**$200.00**
Shelf liner, plastic, 1956-57, from $125 to.................**$130.00**
Sherbet, gold & frost on clear, Libbey, 1960-61, 6½-oz, from
   $60 to..**$75.00**
Sifter, metal, from $300 to...**$400.00**
Stacking tea set, 4-pc, 1951-76, from $100 to...........**$125.00**
Sweeper, Little Jewel, from $175 to...........................**$210.00**

Tablecloth, plastic, 1950-53, 54x72", from $120 to....**$150.00**

Teapot, Donut, Club Piece, 1993, from $100.00 to $125.00.

Teapot, Nautilus, Club pc, from $85 to......................**$110.00**
Teapot, Newport, 1978, from $200 to........................**$250.00**
Teapot, Rayed, long spout, 1935, from $75 to............**$95.00**
Teapot, Rayed, long spout, 1978 sales award, from $800 to...**$1,600.00**
Teapot, Yew York, Club pc, 1984, from $650 to.......**$700.00**
Toy, Circus train, 1950, from $900 to **$1,200.00**
Toy, Jewel truck, green, 1970, from $350 to **$425.00**
Trash can, red, 1951, from $325 to **$400.00**
Tray, metal, oval, 18¾", from $75 to........................**$100.00**
Tray, tidbit; 1954-69, 3-tier, from $80 to **$100.00**
Tray, tidbit; 2-tier, 1954-69, from $80 to **$100.00**
Tray, wood & glass, from $125 to.............................**$140.00**
Tumbler, Brockway, 1975-76, 9-oz, from $30 to **$45.00**
Tumbler, gold & frost on clear, Libbey, 1960-61, 10- or 15-oz, ea from $50 to...**$65.00**
Tumbler, iced tea; frosted, Libbey, 1949-49, 5½", from $15 to.**$20.00**
Tumbler, juice; frosted, Libbey, 1950-53, 3¾", from $25 to....**$32.00**
Vase, bud; decal, regular, 1940, from $225 to **$275.00**
Vase, bud; 1994 Club gift, from $40 to **$60.00**
Warmer, oval, 1955-60, from $150 to **$200.00**
Warmer, round, 1956-60, from $125 to **$160.00**

Avon

You'll find Avon bottles everywhere you go! But it's not just the bottles that are collectible — so are items of jewelry, awards, magazine ads, catalogs, and product samples. Of course, the better items are the older ones (they've been called Avon since 1939 — California Perfume Company before that), and if you can find them mint in the box, all the better.

For more information we recommend *Hastin's Avon Collector's Price Guide* by Bud Hastin.

See also Cape Cod.

Bell, dinner; 24% lead crystal w/hummingbird & floral etching..**$30.00**
Bottle, after shave; Cadillac, gold, 7¼", MIB.............**$130.00**
Brooch, dragonfly, peach & ivory enameled wings w/clear rhinestone tail & eyes, pink body, marked KJL, 1½x3"......**$50.00**

Brooch, owl (solid perfume), green stone eyes, 1968 – 69, MIB, $25.00; Tortoise (solid perfume), gold metal with rhinestone eyes and a green stone 'shell,' 1971 – 75, MIB, $25.00. (Photo courtesy Monsen and Baer)

Cake server, stainless steel w/hummingbird etching, porcelain handle, marked 18/10 Stainless, China, 10", MIB..**$30.00**
Catalog, makeup, gift sets, lotions, creams & etc, 169-page, 1950s, 7x10½", VG...**$35.00**
Chess set, all pcs full, w/rare Avon Club board, M (individual M boxes) **$130.00**
Compact, Gay Look, w/attached lipstick, MIB..........**$105.00**
Doll, Barbie, Spring Petals, 2nd in series, 1996, M (VG+ box) **$40.00**
Figurine, bald eagle, 7¾" **$30.00**
Figurine, Fred Astaire, 3rd in series, 1984 ....**$55.00**
Figurine, Mrs PFE Albee, 1982, miniature, EX..........**$110.00**
Glass, brandy; hummingbird & flowers etching, 24% lead crystal, rare, MIB...**$200.00**
Key chain, 1964-65 Mustang, 1 side shows front, other shows back, metal **$60.00**
Little Chilly, Light-Up Snow Kid, battery-operated, 1993, NM..**$80.00**
Necklace, Heart of My Heart, faux pearls, 18½", +matching earrings, MIB...**$55.00**
Pin, corsage; pink rose w/gold-tone heart & silk flowers, mesh ribbon & faux pearls, 3", MIB....................**$45.00**
Pin, tropical bird, rhinestone eye & wings w/enameled blue body & purple head, 2½", MIB **$30.00**
Print, Albee Avon Ladies of the Past, signed DW Sheffler, framed under glass, 28x33"..................................**$70.00**
Spice canisters, house shape, w/rack, 10¾x14" **$70.00**
Stein, Classic Cars, handcrafted in Brazil, marked #178330, 1979, MIB **$45.00**
Vase, Seasons Greetings on bottom, clear glass w/vertical ribbing, Presidents Club, 1977, 6" **$30.00**
Vehicle, 1963 Buick Riviera, pewter, 1984, 4", on wooden base, MIB...**$45.00**

Barbie Doll and Her Friends

The Barbie doll was first introduced in 1959, and soon Mattel found themselves producing not only dolls but tiny garments, fashion accessories, houses, cars, horses, books, and games as well. Today's Barbie doll collectors want them all.

Though the early Barbie dolls are very hard to find, there are many of her successors still around. The trend today is toward Barbie exclusives — Holiday Barbie dolls and Bob Mackie dolls are all very 'hot' items. So are special-event Barbie dolls.

When buying the older dolls, you'll need to do a lot of studying and comparisons to learn to distinguish one Barbie from another, but this is the key to making sound buys and good investments. Remember, though, collectors are sticklers concerning condition; compared to a doll mint in box, they'll often give an additional 20% if that box has never been opened (or as collectors say 'never removed from box,' indicated in our lines by 'NRFB')! As a general rule, a mint-in-the-box doll is worth from 50% to 100% more than one mint, no box. The same doll, played with and in only good condition, is worth half as much (or less than that). If you want a good source for study, refer to one of these fine books: *A Decade of Barbie Dolls and Collectibles, 1981 – 1991,* by Beth Summers; *The Wonder of Barbie* and *The World of Barbie Dolls* by Paris and Susan Manos; *Barbie Doll Fashion, Vol I and Vol II*, by Sarah Sink Eames; *Barbie Exclusives, Books I and II,* by Margo Rana; *The Barbie Doll Boom, 1986 – 1995,* and *Collector's Encyclopedia of Barbie Doll Exclusives and More* by J. Michael Augustyniak; *The Barbie Doll Years, 4th Edition,* by Patrick C. Olds; *The Story of Barbie* by Kitturah Westenhouser; *Collector's Guide to Barbie Doll Vinyl Cases* by Connie Craig Kaplan; and *Schroeder's Collectible Toys, Antique to Modern.* (All are published by Collector Books.)

Dolls

Barbie, Live Action on Stage, 1970, NMIB, $250.00. (Photo courtesy McMasters Doll Auctions)

Allan, 1963, painted red hair, straight legs, MIB **$125.00**
Barbie, #1, 1958-59, blond or brunette hair, MIB, from $5,000 to...**$6,000.00**
Barbie, #2, 1959, blond or brunette hair, MIB, from $5,000 to...**$6,000.00**
Barbie, #3, 1960, blond hair (extra long), original swimsuit, NM **$1,100.00**
Barbie, #3, 1960, blond or brunette hair, original swimsuit, NM **$950.00**
Barbie, #4, 1960, blond or brunette hair, original swimsuit, M, from $450 to...**$500.00**

Barbie, #5, 1961, blond hair, MIB **$650.00**
Barbie, #5, 1961, red hair, original swimsuit, NM **$375.00**
Barbie, #6, blond hair, original swimsuit, EX............**$250.00**
Barbie, #6, brunette hair, MIB **$600.00**
Barbie, American Beauty Queen, 1991, NRFB **$35.00**
Barbie, American Girl, 1964, blond, brown or brunette hair, NRFB **$1,500.00**
Barbie, Angel of Joy, 1998, Timeless Sentiments, NRFB ...**$55.00**
Barbie, Army, 1989, American Beauty Collection, NRFB ..**$40.00**
Barbie, Beauty Secrets, 1980, Pretty Reflections, MIB.**$85.00**
Barbie, Bubble Cut, 1962, blond or brunette, NRFB, ea ..**$400.00**
Barbie, Bubble Cut w/side part, 1962-64, red hair, original swimsuit, NM **$500.00**
Barbie, Canadian, 1988, Dolls of the World, NRFB.....**$60.00**
Barbie, Circus Star, 1995, FAO Schwarz, MIB.............**$95.00**
Barbie, Cute 'N Cool, 1991, Target, MIB....................**$30.00**
Barbie, Diamond Dazzle, 1997, Bob Mackie, NRFB.**$135.00**
Barbie, Dorothy (Wizard of Oz), 1994, Hollywood Legends Series, NRFB..**$350.00**
Barbie, Dream Date, 1983, MIB..................................**$45.00**
Barbie, Egyptian Queen, 1994, Great Eras, NRFB.....**$125.00**
Barbie, Emerald Elegance, 1994, Toys R Us, MIB.......**$35.00**
Barbie, Fancy Frills, 1992, NRFB **$40.00**
Barbie, Flower Seller (My Fair Lady), 1995, Hollywood Legend Series, NRFB..**$70.00**
Barbie, Free Moving, 1974, NRFB **$165.00**
Barbie, Gift Giving, 1986, NRFB...............................**$35.00**
Barbie, Great Shape, 1984, MIB.................................**$25.00**
Barbie, Hair Fair, 1967, NRFB..................................**$250.00**
Barbie, Hawaiian Superstar, 1977, MIB.....................**$110.00**
Barbie, Holiday, 1988, NRFB, minimum value.......**$1,000.00**
Barbie, Holiday, 1989, NRFB....................................**$250.00**
Barbie, Holiday, 1990, NRFB....................................**$250.00**
Barbie, Holiday, 1991, NRFB....................................**$250.00**
Barbie, Holiday, 1992, NRFB....................................**$150.00**
Barbie, Holiday, 1993, NRFB....................................**$200.00**
Barbie, Holiday, 1994, NRFB....................................**$175.00**
Barbie, Holiday, 1995, NRFB......................................**$75.00**
Barbie, Holiday, 1996, NRFB......................................**$50.00**
Barbie, Holiday, 1997, NRFB......................................**$35.00**
Barbie, International Travel, 1995, Wessco, MIB.........**$50.00**
Barbie, Jewel Essence, 1996, Bob Mackie, NRFB **$150.00**
Barbie, Korean, 1988, Dolls of the World, NRFB........**$60.00**
Barbie, Little Bo Peep, 1996, Children's Collector Series, NRFB...**$115.00**
Barbie, Live Action, 1971, blond hair, NRFB.............**$165.00**
Barbie, Malibu, 1978, MIB...**$55.00**
Barbie, Music Lovin', 1986, NRFB **$50.00**
Barbie, New Living, 1969, blond hair, NRFB.............**$200.00**
Barbie, Norwegian, 1996, Dolls of the World, NRFB..**$75.00**
Barbie, Olympic Skating Star, 1987, NRFB.................**$50.00**
Barbie, Paint & Dazzle, 1993, NRFB **$25.00**
Barbie, Party Lace, 1989, NRFB **$35.00**
Barbie, Pink & Pretty, 1982, MIB...............................**$60.00**
Barbie, Quick Curl Miss America, 1972, original outfit, EX ..**$75.00**
Barbie, Radiant in Red, 1992, Toys R Us, MIB...........**$50.00**
Barbie, Show 'N Ride, 1988, Toys R Us, NRFB...........**$40.00**

Barbie, Spanish Speaking, brunette hair, 1968, NMIB, $300.00. (Photo courtesy McMasters Doll Auctions)

Kelley, Yellowstone, 1973, NRFB $175.00
Ken, Air Force, 1994, Stars & Stripes, NRFB...............$30.00
Ken, California Dream, 1988, NRFB $30.00
Ken, Gold Medal Skier, 1975, NRFB $100.00
Ken, Hawaiian, 1979, MIB $45.00
Ken, Live Action, 1971, NRFB...................................$100.00
Ken, Rhett Butler, 1994, Hollywood Legends Series, NRFB $75.00
Ken, Tin Man, 1995, Hollywood Legends Series, NRFB .$60.00
Ken, Totally Hair, 1991, NRFB $50.00
Midge, Cool Times, 1989, NRFB.................................$30.00
Midge, Ski Fun, 1992, NRFB $30.00
Nikki, Animal Lovin', 1989, NRFB $30.00
PJ, Fashion Photo, 1978, MIB $95.00
PJ, Sunsational Malibu, 1982, MIB..............................$40.00

Barbie, Star Dream, 1987, NRFB..............................$50.00
Barbie, Style Magic (Black), 1988, NRFB $30.00
Barbie, Swirl Ponytail, 1964, platinum hair, NRFB.$1,300.00
Barbie, Tango, 1991, Bob Mackie, NRFB..................$500.00
Barbie, Twist 'N Turn, 1971, brunette hair, NRFB.....$500.00
Barbie, Uptown Chick, 1994, Classique Collection, NRFB ..$75.00
Barbie, Walk Lively, 1972, blond hair, NRFB............$200.00

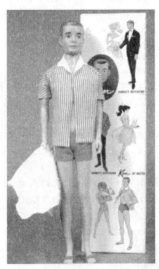

Ricky, painted red hair, 1964, MIB, $110.00. (Photo courtesy McMasters Doll Auctions)

Barbie, Walmart 25th Anniversary, Pink Jubilee, 1987, $55.00. (Photo courtesy Margo Rana)

Ricky, 1965, original outfit & shoes, NM $75.00
Scott, Skipper's Boyfriend, 1980, MIB.........................$55.00
Skipper, Deluxe Quick Curl, 1975, NRFB $125.00
Skipper, Homecoming Queen, 1989, NRFB.................$35.00
Skipper, Music Lovin', 1985, NRFB.............................$65.00
Skipper, Super Teen, 1980, NRFB................................$35.00
Skipper, 30th Anniversary, 1994, porcelain, NRFB....$165.00
Skooter, 1965, blond hair, bendable legs, MIB..........$225.00
Stacy, Twist 'N Turn, 1968, red hair, original swimsuit, NM..$350.00
Teresa, California Dream, 1988, MIB..........................$30.00
Tutti, Night Night Sleep Tight, 1966, NRFB...............$275.00
Whitney, Nurse, 1987, NRFB......................................$80.00

Accessories

Case, Barbie, Francie, Casey & Tutti, hard plastic, EX, from $50 to...$75.00
Case, Barbie & Stacey, vinyl, 1967, NM, from $65 to .$75.00
Case, Barbie Goes Travelin', vinyl, rare, NM............$100.00
Case, Barbie pictured in 4 different outfits, red vinyl, 1961, EX, from $30 to...$40.00
Case, Barbie wearing All That Jazz surrounded by flowers, vinyl, 1967, from $30 to $40.00

Barbie, Winter Fantasy, 1990, FAO Schwarz, NRFB..$200.00
Cara, Free Movin', 1975, NRFB.................................$125.00
Casey, Twist 'N Turn, 1968, blond or brunette hair, NRFB, ea $350.00
Chris, 1974, auburn hair, original outfit & shoes, EX..$75.00
Christie, Golden Dream, 1980, MIB............................$50.00
Christie, Pretty Reflections, 1979, NRFB.....................$85.00
Christie, Super Star, 1977, MIB $95.00
Francie, Busy, 1972, NRFB...$425.00
Francie, 30th Anniversary, 1996, NRFB......................$65.00
Ginger, Growing Up, 1977, MIB.................................$95.00
Jamie, New & Wonderful Walking, blond hair, original outfit, EX $225.00

Case, Barbie, 1962 hat box, black with blond Barbie, NM, from $50.00 to $65.00. (Photo courtesy Connie Craig Kaplan)

Case, Midge wearing Movie Date, blue vinyl, 1963, rare, NM, from $100 to...**$125.00**

Case, Tuttie Play Case, various scenes on blue or pink vinyl, EX, from $30 to.....................................**$40.00**

Furniture, Action Sewing Center, 1972, MIB...............**$50.00**

Furniture, Barbie Beauty Boutique, 1976, MIB...........**$40.00**

Furniture, Barbie Cafe, JC Penney Exclusive, 1993, MIB...**$45.00**

Furniture, Barbie Cookin' Fun Kitchen, MIB...............**$50.00**

Furniture, Barbie Dream Armoire, 1980, NRFB...........**$35.00**

Furniture, Barbie Dream Bath Chest & Commode, 1980, light pink, MIB...**$25.00**

Furniture, Barbie Dream Bed & Nightstand, 1984, pink, MIB...**$25.00**

Furniture, Barbie Dream Glow Vanity, 1986, MIB **$20.00**

Furniture, Barbie Dream Luxury Bathtub, 1984, pink, MIB **$20.00**

Furniture, Barbie Fashion Wraps Boutique, 1989, MIB..**$35.00**

Furniture, Cool Tops Skipper T-Shirt Shop, 1989, complete, MIB **$25.00**

Furniture, Living Pretty Cooking Center, 1988, MIB ...**$25.00**

Furniture, Magical Mansion, 1989, MIB **$125.00**

Furniture, Skipper's Suzy Goose Jeweled Bed, 1965, rare, MIB, minimum value, $150.00.

Furniture, Susy Goose Canopy Bed, 1962, MIB........**$150.00**

Furniture, Town & Country Market, 1971, MIB.........**$135.00**

Outfit, Barbie, All About Plaid, #3433, 1971-72, complete, M..**$200.00**

Outfit, Barbie, Dream-Ins, #1867, 1969, NRFB.........**$125.00**

Outfit, Barbie, Evening Elegance, #1414, 1980, NRFB..**$20.00**

Outfit, Barbie, Fancy-Dancy, #1858, NRFB...............**$200.00**

Outfit, Barbie, Fashion Classics, K-Mart, 1986, several different, MIP, ea..**$15.00**

Outfit, Barbie, Garden Party, #1606, 1964, NRFB **$200.00**

Outfit, Barbie, In Blooms, #3424, 1971, NRFB **$90.00**

Outfit, Barbie, Lace Caper, #1791, 1970, NRFB.........**$125.00**

Outfit, Barbie, Rain or Shine, #2788, 1979, NRFB.......**$20.00**

Outfit, Barbie, Tangerine Scene, #1451, 1970, NRFB..**$75.00**

Outfit, Barbie, Wedding of the Year, #5743, 1982, NRFB, $20.00.

Outfit, Barbie, Wild Things, #3439, 1971-72, complete, M...**$200.00**

Outfit, Francie, Clam Diggers, #1258, 1966, NRFB....**$185.00**

Outfit, Francie, Midi Bouquet, #3446, 1971, NRFB ...**$125.00**

Outfit, Francie, Simply Super, #3277, 1972, complete, M..**$175.00**

Outfit, Francie, Two for the Ball, #1232, MOC **$225.00**

Outfit, Francie & Casey, Snooze News, #1226, 1969, complete, M **$150.00**

Outfit, Ken, Bold Gold, #1436, 1970, NRFB **$75.00**

Outfit, Ken, Casual All-Stars, #1436, 1970, NRFB.......**$50.00**

Outfit, Ken, Denims for Fun, #3376, 1972, complete, M..**$75.00**

Outfit, Ken, Hiking Holiday, #1412, 1965, NRFB......**$250.00**

Outfit, Ken, Play It Cool, #1433, 1970, NRFB............**$100.00**

Outfit, Ken, Sea Scene, #1449, 1971, NRFB.................**$60.00**

Outfit, Ken, VIP Scene, #1473, 1971, NRFB................**$75.00**

Outfit, Ken & Brad, Beach Beat Fashion, 1972, MOC .**$125.00**

Outfit, Midge, Orange Blossom, #987, 1967, NRFB **$75.00**

Outfit, Ricky, Let's Explore, #1506, NRFB..................**$135.00**

Outfit, Skipper, All Over Felt, #3476, NRFB **$150.00**

Outfit, Skipper, Goin' Sleddin', #3475, 1971, NRFB **$75.00**

Outfit, Skipper, Ice Cream 'N Cake, #1970, 1969-70, MIB.**$200.00**

Outfit, Skipper, Jeepers Creepers, #1966, 1969, NRFB..**$125.00**

Outfit, Skipper, Little Miss Midi, #3468, 1971, NRFB...**$70.00**

Outfit, Skipper, Popover, #1943, NRFB.....................**$175.00**

Outfit, Skipper, Rolla-Scoot, #1940, 1967, NRFB.......**$150.00**

Outfit, Skipper, Velvet Blush, #1737, 1970, NRFB.....**$100.00**

Outfit, Tuttie, Birthday Beauties, #3617, 1968, NRFB..**$165.00**

Vehicle, ATC Cycle, Sears Exclusive, 1972, MIB.........**$65.00**

Vehicle, Barbie and Ken's Sand Buggy, 1970, EX/NM, $125.00. (Photo courtesy Patrick C. Olds)

Vehicle, Barbie & the Rockers Hot Rockin' Van, 1987, MIB......................................**$60.00**
Vehicle, Barbie Travelin' Trailer, MIB..........................**$40.00**
Vehicle, Beach Bus, 1974, MIB......................................**$45.00**
Vehicle, California Dream Beach Taxi, 1988, MIB **$35.00**
Vehicle, Ken's Classy Corvette, 1976, yellow, MIB......**$75.00**
Vehicle, Ken's Dream 'Vette, 1981, dark blue, MIB ..**$100.00**
Vehicle, Starlight Motorhome, 1994, MIB....................**$45.00**
Vehicle, Western Star Traveler Motorhome, 1982, MIB ..**$50.00**

Gift Sets

Barbie and Her Horse Dancer, sold in Canada, MIB, $75.00. (Photo courtesy Paris and Susan Manos)

Birthday Fun at McDonald's, 1994, NRFB....................**$75.00**
Dance Magic Barbie & Ken, 1990, NRFB....................**$50.00**
Golden Dreams Glamorous Nights, 1980, NRFB.......**$100.00**
Happy Birthday Barbie, 1985, NRFB..........................**$50.00**
Loving You Barbie, 1984, MIB....................................**$75.00**
Malibu Barbie Fashion Combo, 1978, NRFB **$80.00**
Skipper Party Time, 1964, NRFB **$500.00**
Stacey & Butterfly Pony, 1993, NRFB.........................**$30.00**
Sun Sensation Barbie Spray & Play Fun, Wholesale Clubs, 1992, MIB **$60.00**
Superstar Barbie & Ken, 1978, MIB **$175.00**
Superstar Barbie Fashion Change-Abouts, 1978, NRFB .**$95.00**
Superstar Barbie in the Spotlight, 1977, MIB............**$125.00**

Travelin' Sisters, 1995, NRFB..**$70.00**
Wedding Party Midge, 1990, NRFB **$150.00**

Miscellaneous

Barbie & Ken Sew Magic Add-Ons, 1973-74, MIB......**$55.00**
Barbie Beautiful Hair Vanity Set, 1994, MIB..............**$10.00**
Barbie Electric Drawing Set, 1970, MIB.....................**$75.00**
Barbie Make-up Case, 1963, NM **$25.00**
Barbie Shrinky Dinks, 1979, MIB **$30.00**
Barbie Young Travelers Play Kit, Sears Exclusive, 1964, MIB..**$75.00**
Bicycle, Camp Barbie, 1985, 16", NM.........................**$85.00**
Book, World of Barbie, Random House, hardcover, EX ..**$15.00**
Booklet, World of Barbie Fashion, 1968, M................**$10.00**
Game, Barbie 35th Anniversary, Golden, 1994, MIB ..**$60.00**
Ornament, Holiday Barbie, Hallmark, 1993, 1st edition, MIB **$75.00**
Tea set, Barbie, china, 16-pc, Chilton Globe, 1989, NRFB ..**$30.00**

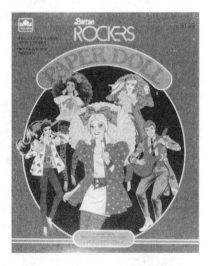

Paper Dolls, Barbie and the Rockers, #1528, 1986, Golden, M, $15.00. (Photo courtesy Lorraine Mieszala)

Barware

From the decade of the '90s, the cocktail shaker has emerged as a hot new collectible. These micro skyscrapers are now being saved for the enjoyment of future generations, much like the 1930s buildings saved from destruction by landmarks preservation committees of today.

Cocktail shakers — the words just conjure up visions of glamour and elegance. Seven hard shakes over your right shoulder and you can travel back in time, back to the glamor of Hollywood movie sets with Fred Astaire and Ginger Rogers and luxurious hotel lounges with gleaming chrome; back to the world of F. Scott Fitzgerald and *The Great Gatsby*; or watch *The Thin Man* movie showing William Powell instruct a bartender on the proper way to shake a martini — the reveries are endless.

An original American art form, cocktail shakers reflect the changing nature of various styles of art, design, and architecture of the era between WWI and WWII. We see the graceful lines of Art Nouveau in the early '20s being replaced by the rage for jagged geometric modern design. The geometric cubism of Picasso that influenced so many designers of the '20s was replaced with the craze for streamline design of '30s. Cocktail shakers of the early '30s were taking the shape of the new deity of American architecture, the skyscraper, thus giving the appearance of movement and speed in a slow economy.

Cocktail shakers served to penetrate the gloom of depression, ready to propel us into the future of prosperity like some Buck Rogers rocket ship — both perfect symbols of generative power, of our perpetration into better times ahead.

 Cocktail shakers and architecture took on the aerodynamically sleek industrial design of the automobile and airship. It was as Norman Bel Geddes said: 'a quest for speed.' All sharp edges and corners were rounded off. This trend was the theme of the day, as even the sharp notes of jazz turned into swing.

Cocktail shakers have all the classic qualifications of a premium collectible. They are easily found at auctions, antique and secondhand shops, flea markets, and sales. They can be had in all price ranges. They require little study to identify one manufacturer or period from another, and lastly they are not easily reproduced.

The sleek streamline cocktail shakers of modern design are valued by collectors of today. Those made by Revere, Chase, and Manning Bowman have taken the lead in this race. Also commanding high prices are those shakers of unusual design such as penguins, zeppelins, dumbbells, bowling pins, town crier bells, airplanes, even ladies' legs. They're all out there, waiting to be found, waiting to be recalled to life, to hear the clank of ice cubes, and to again become the symbol of elegance.

For more information we recommend *Vintage Bar Ware, An Identification and Value Guide,* by Stephen Visakay (Collector Books).

Advisor: Steve Visakay (See Directory, Barware)

Cocktail shaker, chromium-plated brass with Catalin trim, 11⅜", from $350.00 to $450.00. (Photo courtesy Stephen Visakay)

Canape tray, satin chromium over brass, 1935, 6¾x4⅝" .**$10.00**
Cocktail cup, Catalin w/chrome stem, marked NUDAWN USA, 6¾x3¼" dia **$27.50**

Cocktail cup, glass insert, marked Farber Bros, Pat, 4¼" ..**$11.00**
Cocktail glass, rooster figural, red enamel on clear, 1930s, 3¼"................................**$17.50**
Drink stirrer, female form, plastic, 1930s, 7"................**$5.00**
Ice bucket, black amethyst glass, from $60 to **$65.00**
Ice bucket, Decagon, amethyst glass, Cambridge, from $55 to................................**$65.00**
Ice bucket, Mt Vernon, red glass, Cambridge, from $95 to................................**$110.00**
Ice bucket, pink glass, oblong w/tub handles, Central Glass Co, from $75 to................................**$85.00**
Ice bucket, Plymouth, red glass, Fenton, from $85 to ..**$95.00**
Ice bucket, polar bear enameled on green frosted glass, Fostoria, from $45 to................................**$55.00**
Ice bucket, Ships, white on cobalt, Hazel Atlas, 4¼x5½"................................**$55.00**
Ice bucket, Swirl, blue glass, Fostoria, from $55 to....**$65.00**
Ice tub, Emerald Glo, metal holder, w/tongs, from $65 to................................**$70.00**
Mixer/blender/shaker, black porcelain & stainless steel, Oster................................**$110.00**
Roly-poly, Ships, white on blue, Hazel Atlas, 2½"......**$10.00**
Set, Sweet Ad-aline, comic inebriated men enameled on clear glass, chrome top, shaker +6 8-oz tumblers, from $75 to................................**$85.00**
Shaker, black glass, chrome lid, Paden #991, from $75 to................................**$80.00**
Shaker, cobalt glass barbell w/chrome top, from $125 to................................**$135.00**
Shaker, fighting cocks, silver on ruby glass, 1930s, 12"...**$500.00**
Shaker, Frosty Polar Bear, blue & white enameling on clear, 1930s-40s, 10"................................**$125.00**
Shaker, Gay '90s scene on clear glass, from $18 to....**$25.00**
Shaker, Manhattan, chrome over brass, Revere, 12¾" ..**$525.00**
Shaker, multicolor enamel stripes on clear glass, from $18 to................................**$25.00**
Shaker, orange Catalin trim, Krome Kraft, 1940s-60s, 12¾"................................**$50.00**
Shaker, Prelude, New Martinsville, 32-oz, from $150 to..**$185.00**
Shaker, pressed glass, cranberry flashed, silver-plated top, 1930s, 11"................................**$135.00**
Shaker, rooster, nickel-plate w/engraving & enameling, Meriden, Pat Jan 11, 1927 ....**$215.00**
Shaker, ruby glass, barbell shape, possibly New Martinsville, from $95 to................................**$110.00**
Shaker, ruby glass, footed, chrome lid, 11½"..........**$100.00**
Shaker, ruby glass, lady's boot shape, chrome lid & heel, from $500 to................................**$700.00**
Shaker, ruby glass, shouldered, chrome lid, Duncan & Miller, from $55 to................................**$60.00**
Shaker, spatter glass, 1930s, 7" **$110.00**
Shaker, Town Crier's bell, chrome w/walnut handle, 1937, 10⅜"................................**$60.00**
Soda siphon, chrome w/enameled top, Bel Geddes, marked, 10", from $100 to................................**$120.00**
Tray, metal & glass w/painted peacock, 1930s, 12¼x20" ..**$70.00**
Tumbler, glass, dice sealed in bottom, 4" **$6.00**

Bauer Pottery

Undoubtedly the most easily recognized product of the Bauer Pottery Company who operated from 1909 until 1962 in Los Angeles, California, was their colorful Ring dinnerware (made from 1932 until sometime in the early 1960s). They made other lines of dinnerware that are collectible as well, although by no means as easily found. Bauer also made a line of Gardenware vases and flowerpots for the florist trade.

In the lines of Ring and Plain ware, pricing depends to some extent on color. Use the low end of our range of values for light brown, Chinese yellow, orange-red, jade green, red-brown, olive green, light blue, turquoise, and gray; the high-end colors are delph blue, ivory, dusky burgundy, cobalt, chartreuse, papaya, and burgundy. Black is 50% higher than the high end; to evaluate white, double the high side. An in-depth study of colors and values may be found in *The Collector's Encyclopedia of California Pottery, Second Edition,* and *Collector's Encyclopedia of Bauer Pottery*, both by Jack Chipman.

Brusche Al Fresco, bowl, vegetable; Hemlock Green, divided, 9¼" **$30.00**
Brusche Al Fresco, sugar bowl, Hemlock Green, w/lid **$18.00**
Cal-Art Pottery, candlestick, triple; matt white **$50.00**
Cal-Art Pottery, vase, horn-of-plenty; matt blue, 6½" .**$45.00**
Contempo, bowl, soup/cereal; pink, deep, 5½" **$15.00**
Contempo, sugar bowl, gray, w/lid..............................**$20.00**
Florist/garden pottery, basket, hanging; orange-red, 8" ..**$225.00**
Florist/garden pottery, pot, stepped, diamond shape, minimum value **$150.00**
Hi-Fire, flower bowl, turquoise, deep, #211, 6" **$45.00**
Hi-Fire, vase, red-brown, #214, 7½"............................**$65.00**
La Linda, creamer, burgundy, old style........................**$15.00**
La Linda, platter, matt blue, oval, 10"..........................**$22.50**
Matt Carlton, bowl, green, ruffled rim, 3½x7"............**$85.00**
Matt Carlton, vase, carnation; jade green, 10" **$350.00**
Monterey, coffee server, w/lid, from $45 to **$65.00**
Monterey, fruit bowl, footed, 9", from $45 to **$65.00**
Monterey, saucer, from $6 to **$9.00**
Monterey Moderne, creamer, pink **$12.50**
Monterey Moderne, sugar bowl, chartreuse, 2-handled, w/lid **$20.00**

Monterey Moderne, teapot, six-cup, from $75.00 to $100.00. (Photo courtesy Jack Chipman)

Plain Ware, bean pot, 2-qt, from $75 to **$100.00**
Plain Ware, bowl, mixing; #4, 1½-gal, minimum value........**$200.00**
Plain Ware, coffee server, w/lid, from $65 to **$95.00**
Plain Ware, plate, salad; 8½", minimum value............**$45.00**
Ring Ware, baking dish, w/lid, 4", from $35 to **$50.00**
Ring Ware, bowl, lug soup; from $60 to......................**$75.00**
Ring Ware, chop plate, 14", from $125 to..................**$160.00**
Ring Ware, creamer, restyled, from $50 to...................**$75.00**
Ring Ware, cup & saucer, from $25 to **$65.00**
Ring Ware, teapot, 2-cup, from $85 to **$120.00**
Ring Ware, tumbler, 12-oz, from $50 to **$75.00**
Yellow Ware, mug, handmade, 3", minimum value....**$45.00**

Beanie Babies

Who can account for this latest flash in collecting that some liken to the rush for Cabbage Patch dolls we saw many years ago! The appeal of these stuffed creatures is disarming to both children and adults, and excited collectors are eager to scoop up each new-found treasure. There is much to be learned about Beanie Babies. For instance, there are different swing and tush tag styles, and these indicate year of issue:

#1, Swing tag: single heart-shaped tag; comes on Beanies with tush tags dated 1993.

#2, Swing tag: heart-shaped; folded, with information inside; narrow letters; comes on Beanies with tush tags dated 1993.

#3, Swing tag: heart-shaped; folded, with information inside; wider letters; comes on Beanies with tush tags dated 1993 and 1995.

#4, Swing tag: heart-shaped; folded, with information inside; wider lettering with no gold outline around the 'ty'; yellow star on front; first tag to include a poem and birth date; comes on Beanies with tush tags dated 1993, 1995, and 1996.

#5, Swing tag: heart-shaped; folded, with information inside; different font on front and inside; birth month spelled out, no style numbers, website listed; comes on Beanies with tush tags dated 1993, 1995, 1996, 1997, 1998, and 1999.

#6, Swing tag: features holographic star with '2000' across star; inside: Ty, Inc., Ty Canada, Ty Europe, and Ty Japan; birthdate, website address, and poem in smaller font than #5; new safety precaution on back, smaller font, and UPC; comes on Beanies with tush tags dated 2000.

Variations on #6 Swing tags: The twelve Zodiac Beanie Babies, released in September 2000, have all the characteristics of the sixth generation swing tag, with the exception of the word 'Zodiac' on the front of the swing tag, which replaces the star and 2000. The interiors of the three Holiday Beanie Babies' tags, released in October 2000, have blue backgrounds and white snowflakes.

#7, Swing tag: identical to #6 hang tag except 'Beanies' is written across the holographic star instead of '2000.' This tag appears in UK Beanie Babies (photo not available); comes on Beanies with tush tags dated 2000.

#8, Swing tag: shows a ¼" holographic star with the

#1 Swing tag

#2 Swing tag

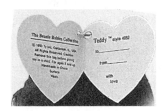

#3 Swing tag

#4 Swing tag

#5 Swing tag

#6 Swing tag

#6 Zodiac variation Swing tag

#6 Holiday variation Swing tag

#8 Swing tag

word 'Beanie' above and 'Baby' below in fine yellow print. Inside information identical to #6 swing tag; comes on Beanies with tush tags dated 2000 and 2001.

Prices are for toys with swing tags in mint or near-mint condition. For Beanies with a #1, #2, or #3 tag, add $30.00 to $50.00 to the prices suggested below. Style numbers are the last four digits in the UPC code located on the back of the Beanie's swing tag.

Key: R – Retired   BBOC – Beanie Babies Official Club

Advisor: Amy Hopper (See Directory, Beanie Babies)

#1 Bear, red w/#1 on chest, issued only to Ty sales reps, 253 made, R, minimum value **$5,000.00**

2001 Signature bear, #4375, from $7 to R **$10.00**

Addison, #4362, bear, given to fans at Chicago Cubs vs AZ Diamondbacks game at Wrigley Field, May 20, 2001, R, from $20 to **$25.00**

Ally, #4032, alligator, R **$40.00**

Almond, #4246, bear, R, from $5 to **$7.00**

Amber, #4243, tabby cat, gold, R, from $5 to **$7.00**

America, #4506, bear, issued in memory of those who lost their lives in the national catastrophe of September 11, 2001, all profits from the original purchase of this beanie go to the American Red Cross, from $7 to **$20.00**

Ants, #4195, anteater, R, from $5 to **$7.00**

Ariel, #4288, fundraising bear for the Elizabeth Glaser Pediatric AIDS Foundation, from $7 to **$10.00**

Aruba, #4314, angelfish, R, from $5 to..........................**$7.00**

Aurora, #4271, polar bear, R, from $7 to **$10.00**

August, #4371, birthday month bear, from $7 to **$10.00**

Baldy, #4074, eagle, R, from $7 to **$15.00**

Bananas, #4316, orangutan, R, from $5 to...................**$10.00**

Batty, #4035, bat, pink, R, from $5 to **$7.00**

Batty, #4035, bat, tie-dyed, R, from $5 to **$7.00**

BB, #4253, birthday bear, R, from $10 to **$15.00**

Beak, #4211, kiwi bird, R, from $10 to.......................**$15.00**

Beani, #4397, cat, gray, from $7 to **$10.00**

Bernie, #4109, St Bernard, R, from $5 to **$7.00**

Bessie, #4009, cow, brown, R, from $20 to **$35.00**

Billionaire Bear (1998), brown, new face, dollar sign on chest, issued only to Ty employees, R, minimum value **$900.00**

Billionaire II Bear (1999), purple, BB on chest, issued only to Ty employees, R, minimum value **$1,300.00**

Billionaire III Bear (2000), orange, issued only to Ty employees, R, minimum value **$1,100.00**

Billionaire IV Bear, 2001, issued only to Ty employees, minimum value **$1,000.00**

Blackie, #4011, bear, R, from $15 to **$30.00**

Blizzard, #4163, tiger, white, R, from $10 to **$15.00**

Bones, #4001, dog, brown, R, from $10 to.................**$20.00**

Bongo, #4067, monkey, 1st issue, brown, R, from $30 to .**$45.00**

Bongo, #4067, monkey, 2nd issue, brown w/tan tail, R, from $10 to...**$20.00**

Brigitte, #4374, pink poodle, from $7 to.....................**$10.00**

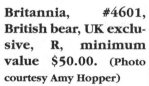
Britannia, #4601, British bear, UK exclusive, R, minimum value $50.00. (Photo courtesy Amy Hopper)

Bronty, #4085, brontosaurus, blue, R, minimum value ...**$415.00**

Brownie, #4010, bear, w/swing tag, R, minimum value ..**$2,000.00**

Bruno, #4183, terrier, R, from $5 to.................................**$7.00**

Bubbles, #4078, fish, yellow & black, R, minimum value ..**$45.00**

Buckingham, #4603, bear, UK exclusive, R, minimum value..**$65.00**

Bucky, #4016, beaver, R, from $10 to **$15.00**

Bumble, #4045, bee, R, minimum value...................**$275.00**

Bushy, #4285, lion, R, from $7 to..............................**$10.00**

Butch, #4227, bull terrier, R, from $5 to......................**$7.00**

Buzzie, #4354, bee, from $7 to...................................**$10.00**

Buzzy, #4308, buzzard, R, from $7 to **$10.00**

Canyon, #4212, cougar, R, from $5 to..........................**$7.00**

Cashew, #4292, bear, brown, R, from $7 to **$10.00**

Cassie, #4340, R, from $7 to **$10.00**

Caw, #4071, crow, R, from $225 to..........................**$300.00**

Celebrate, #4385, 15-year Ty anniversary bear, R, from $7 to...**$10.00**

Cheeks, #4250, baboon, R, from $5 to..........................**$7.00**

Cheery, #4359, sunshine bear, R, from $7 to..............**$10.00**

Cheezer, #4301, mouse, R, from $7 to **$10.00**

Chilly, #4012, polar bear, R, minimum value **$800.00**

China, #4315, panda bear, R, from $7 to **$10.00**

Chinook, #4604, bear, Canada exclusive, R, from $30 to **$50.00**

Chip, #4121, calico cat, R, from $5 to **$7.00**

Chipper, #4259, chipmunk, R, from $5 to....................**$7.00**

Chocolate, #4015, moose, R, from $10 to **$20.00**

Chops, #4019, lamb, R, from $60 to..........................**$75.00**

Cinders, #4295, bear, black, R, from $7 to...............**$10.00**

Classy, bear, #4373, 'The People's Beanie' (determined by voting on the Ty Internet website, April 2000), R, from $7 to **$10.00**

Claude, #4083, crab, tie-dyed, R, from $5 to..............**$10.00**

Clubby, bear, blue, BBOC exclusive, mail-order only, R, from $10 to..**$20.00**

Clubby II, bear, purple, BBOC exclusive, R, from $10 to ..**$15.00**

Clubby III, bear, brown, BBOC exclusive (mail-order or Internet order only), R, from $15 to.....................**$25.00**

Clubby IV, #4996, bear, BBOC exclusive, from $7 to .**$15.00**

Congo, #4160, gorilla, R, from $5.00 to $7.00. (Photo courtesy Amy Hopper)

Coral, #4079, fish, tie-dyed, R, minimum value...........**$60.00**

Courage, #4406, German shepherd, all profits from the original purchase of this Beanie go to the New York Police & Fire Widow's & Children's Benefit Fund due to the national tragedy on September 11, 2001, from $5 to **$20.00**

Creepers, #4376, skeleton, R, from $7 to....................**$10.00**

Crunch, #4130, shark, R, from $5 to..............................**$7.00**

Cubbie, #4010, bear, brown, R, from $20 to **$35.00**

Curly, #4052, bear, brown, R, from $10 to **$15.00**

Daisy, #4006, cow, black & white, R, from $10 to......**$15.00**

Darling, #4368, the fantasy dog, green, R, from $7 to ..**$10.00**

Dart, #4352, frog, R, from $7 to.................................**$10.00**

Dearest, #4350, bear, peach, R, from $7 to **$10.00**

December, #4387, birthday month bear, from $7 to ...**$10.00**

Derby, #4008, horse, 1st issue, fine yarn mane & tail, R, minimum value **$700.00**

Derby, #4008, horse, 2nd issue, coarse mane & tail, R, from $20 to...**$40.00**

Derby, #4008, horse, 3rd issue, white star on forehead, R, from $5 to..**$10.00**

Derby, #4008, horse, 4th issue, white star on forehead, fur mane & tail, R, from $5 to **$10.00**

Diddley, #4383, green dog, from $7 to.......................**$10.00**

Digger, #4027, crab, 1st issue, orange, R, minimum value ..**$300.00**

Digger, #4027, crab, 2nd issue, red, R, minimum value...**$70.00**

Dinky, #4341, dodo bird, from $7 to **$10.00**

Dizzy, #4365, dalmatian, three versions, R, from $7 to...**$10.00**

Doby, #4110, doberman, R, from $5 to **$10.00**

Doodle, #4171, tie-dyed rooster, R, from $15 to **$20.00**

Dotty, #4100, dalmatian, R, from $5 to **$10.00**

Early, #4190, robin, R, from $5 to **$10.00**

Ears, #4018, brown rabbit, R, from $10 ....**$20.00**

Echo, #4180, dolphin, R, from $10 to **$15.00**

Eggbert, #4232, baby chick, R, from $5 to **$10.00**

Eggs, #4337, Easter bear, pink, R, from $10 to...........**$15.00**

Employee Christmas Bear (1997), violet, new face, R, minimum value **$2,500.00**

Erin, #4186, green bear, R, from $10 to **$15.00**

Eucalyptus, #4240, koala, R, from $5 to **$10.00**

Ewey, #4219, lamb, R, from $5 to **$10.00**

Fetch, #4189, golden retriever, R, from $7 to **$10.00**

Fetcher, #4298, chocolate lab, R, from $7 to **$10.00**

Flash, #4021, dolphin, R, minimum value **$60.00**

Flashy, #4339, peacock, R, from $7 to........................**$10.00**

Fleece, #4125, white lamb w/cream face, R, from $5 to..**$15.00**

Fleecie, #4279, cream lamb w/purple neck ribbon, R, from $7 to **$10.00**

Flip, #4012, white cat, R, from $25 to **$35.00**

Flitter, #4255, pastel butterfly, R, from $5 to **$10.00**

Float, #4343, butterfly, R, from $7 to **$10.00**

Floppity, #4118, lavender bunny, R, from $10 to........**$15.00**

Flutter, #4043, tie-dyed butterfly, R, minimum value ..**$350.00**

Fortune, #4196, panda bear, R, from $5 to **$10.00**

Fraidy, #4379, cat, Halloween, R, from $7 to **$10.00**

Freckles, #4066, leopard, R, from $5 to **$10.00**

Frigid, #4270, king penguin, R, from $5 to..................**$10.00**

Frills, #4367, hornbill bird, R, from $7 to **$10.00**

Fuzz, #4237, bear, R, from $7 to.................................**$10.00**

Garcia, #4051, bear, tie-dyed, R, from $90 to............**$125.00**

Germania, #4236, German bear, UK exclusive, R, minimum value **$20.00**

Giganto, #4384, wooly mammoth, from $7 to **$10.00**

Gigi, #4191, poodle, black, R, from $5 to.....................**$7.00**

Glory, #4188, American bear w/stars, R, from $10 to.**$20.00**

Glow, #4283, lightning bug, R, from $5 to...................**$7.00**

Goatee, #4235, mountain goat, R, from $5 to **$10.00**

Gobbles, #4034, turkey, R, from $5 to **$10.00**

Goldie, #4023, goldfish, R, from $25 to **$40.00**

Goochy, #4230, jellyfish, R, from $5 to.......................**$10.00**

Grace, #4274, praying bunny, R, from $7 to **$10.00**

Gracie, #4126, swan, R, from $7 to **$10.00**

Groovy, #4256, bear, R, from $7 to **$15.00**

Grunt, #4092, razorback pig, red, R, minimum value.**$70.00**

Hairy, #4336, spider, R, from $7 to **$10.00**

Halo, #4208, angel bear, R, from $7 to **$10.00**

Halo II, #4269, angel bear, R, from $7 to **$10.00**

Happy, #4061, hippo, 1st issue, gray, R, minimum value..**$250.00**

Happy, #4061, hippo, 2nd issue, lavender, R, from $10 to **$15.00**

Haunt, #4377, black bear with pumpkin on chest, R, from $7 to..**$10.00**

Hero, #4351, bear, brown, w/necktie, R, from $10 to....**$15.00**

Hippie, #4218, rabbit, tie-dyed, R, from $10 to..........**$15.00**

Hippity, #4119, bunny, mint green, R, from $10 to **$15.00**

Hissy, #4185, snake, R, $5 to **$10.00**

Holiday Teddy (1997), #4200, R, from $15 to **$20.00**

Holiday Teddy (1998), #4204, R, from $25 to **$35.00**

Holiday Teddy (1999), #4257, R, from $10 to **$15.00**

Holiday Teddy (2000), #4332, R, from $10 to **$15.00**

Holiday Teddy (2001), #4395, from $7 to **$10.00**

Honks, #4258, goose, R, $5 to.....................................**$7.00**

Hoot, #4073, owl, R, from $15 to **$20.00**

Hope, #4213, praying bear, R, from $5 to **$10.00**

Hopper, #4342, rabbit, R, from $7 to **$10.00**

Hoppity, #4117, bunny, pink, R, from $10 to.............**$15.00**

Hornsly, #4345, triceratops, R, from $7 to **$10.00**

Howl, #4310, wolf, R, from $7 to **$10.00**

Huggy, #4306, bear, R, from $7 to **$10.00**

Humphrey, #4060, camel, R, minimum value **$900.00**

Iggy, #4038, iguana, all issues, R, from $5 to.............**$10.00**

Inch, #4044, worm, felt antenna, R, from $50 to **$80.00**

Inch, #4044, worm, yarn antenna, R, from $10 to **$15.00**

India, #4291, tiger, R, from $7 to **$10.00**

Inky, #4028, octopus, 1st issue, tan, no mouth, R, minimum value **$800.00**

Inky, #4028, octopus, 2nd issue, tan, w/mouth, R, minimum value **$325.00**

Inky, #4028, octopus, 3rd issue, pink, R, from $35 to..**$40.00**

Issy, #4404, bear, from $7 to.......................................$10.00

Issy, #4404, bear, Four Seasons Hotel exclusive, New York, minimum value **$180.00**

Jabber, #4197, parrot, R, from $5 to...........................**$7.00**

Jake, #4199, mallard duck, R, from $5 to....................**$7.00**

Jester, #4349, clown fish, from $7 to **$10.00**

Jinglepup, #4394, dog with Santa hat, from $7 to **$15.00**

Jolly, #4082, walrus, R, from $5 to **$10.00**

July, #4370, birthday month bear, R, from $7 to.........**$10.00**

Kaleidoscope, #4348, cat, R, from $7 to **$10.00**

Kirby, #4396, terrier, white, from $7 to......................**$10.00**

Kicks, #4229, soccer bear, R, from $7 to **$10.00**

Kiwi, #4070, toucan, R, minimum value **$60.00**

Knuckles, #4247, pig, R, from $5 to **$7.00**

Kooky, #4357, cat, R, from $7 to **$10.00**

Kuku, #4192, cockatoo, R, from $5 to **$7.00**

Lefty, #4057, donkey w/American flag, blue-gray, R, minimum value **$100.00**

Lefty 2000, #4290, donkey, red, white & blue, USA exclusive, R, from $7 to..**$10.00**

Legs, #4020, frog, R, from $25 to **$40.00**

Libearty, #4057, bear w/American flag, white, R, minimum value **$150.00**

Lips, #4254, fish, R, from $5 to..................................**$10.00**

Lizzy, #4033, lizard, 1st issue, tie-dyed, R, minimum value..**$300.00**

Lizzy, #4033, lizard, 2nd issue, blue, R, from $15 to.....**$25.00**

Loosy, #4206, goose, R, from $5 to **$7.00**

Lucky, #4040, ladybug, 1st issue, 7 spots, R, minimum value **$150.00**

Lucky, #4040, ladybug, 2nd issue, 21 spots, R, minimum value **$150.00**

Lucky, #4040, ladybug, 3rd issue, 11 spots, R, from $10 to...**$15.00**

Luke, #4214, black, Labrador puppy, R, from $5 to ...**$10.00**

M.C. Beanie, Ty Mastercard Beanie, available only through use of Ty Mastercard, minimum value...............**$100.00**

Mac, #4225, cardinal, R, from $5 to **$10.00**

Magic, #4088, dragon, R, from $20 to..................**$40.00**

Manny, #4081, manatee, R, minimum value.............**$70.00**

Maple, #4600, bear, Canada exclusive, R, minimum value **$65.00**

Mel, #4162, koala, R, from $5 to **$10.00**

Mellow, #4344, bear, tie-dyed, R, from $7 to **$10.00**

Midnight, #4355, black panther, from $7 to.................**$10.00**

Millennium, #4226, bear, R, from $10 to......................**$15.00**

Mistletoe, #4500, bear, red, from $7 to **$15.00**

Mooch, #4224, spider monkey, R, from $5 to **$7.00**

Morrie, #4282, eel, R, from $5 to....................................**$7.00**

Mr, #4363, groom bear, R, from $10 to **$15.00**

Mrs, #4364, bride bear, R, from $10 to.......................**$15.00**

Mystic, #4007, unicorn, 1st issue, soft fine mane & tail, R, minimum value **$200.00**

Mystic, #4007, unicorn, 2nd issue, coarse yarn mane & brown horn, R, from $10 to **$15.00**

Mystic, #4007, unicorn, 3rd issue, iridescent horn, R, from $7 to **$10.00**

Mystic, #4007, unicorn, 4th issue, iridescent horn, rainbow fur mane & tail, R, from $7 to **$10.00**

Nana, #4067, 1st issue of Bongo the monkey, R, minimum value **$2,300.00**

Nanook, #4104, husky dog, R, from $5 to..................**$10.00**

Nectar, #4361, hummingbird, R, from $7 to **$15.00**

Neon, #4239, sea horse, tie-dyed, R, from $5 to........**$10.00**

Nibbler, #4216, rabbit, cream, R, from $5 to **$10.00**

Nibbly, #4217, rabbit, brown, R, from $5 to.................**$10.00**

Niles, #4284, camel, R, from $7 to **$10.00**

Nip, #4003, cat, 1st issue, gold with white tummy, R, minimum value $300.00. Nip, #4003, cat, 3rd issue, gold with white paws, R, from $10.00 to $25.00. Nip, #4003, cat, 2nd issue, all gold, R, minimum value $400.00.

Nipponia, #4605, bear, Japan exclusive, R, minimum value **$60.00**

November, #4386, birthday month bear, from $7 to...**$10.00**

Nuts, #4114, squirrel, R, from $5 to **$10.00**

Oats, #4305, horse, R, from $7 to...............................**$10.00**

October, #4380, birthday month bear, from $7 to......**$10.00**

Osito, #4244, Mexican bear, USA exclusive, R, from $7 to **$10.00**

Patriot, #4360, bear, red, white & blue, R, from $10 to .**$15.00**

Patti, #4025, platypus, 1st issue, maroon, R, minimum value **$350.00**

Patti, #4025, platypus, 2nd issue, purple, R, from $10 to..**$20.00**

Paul, #4248, walrus, R, from $5 to **$10.00**

Peace, #4053, bear, tie-dyed, embroidered Peace sign, R, from $10 to **$20.00**

Peanut, #4062, elephant, light blue, R, from $5 to **$10.00**

Peanut, #4062, elephant, royal blue (manufacturing mistake), R, minimum value..**$2,000.00**

Pecan, #4251, bear, gold, R, from $5 to.....................**$7.00**

Peekaboo, #4303, turtle, R, from $7 to **$10.00**

Peking, #4013, panda bear, R, minimum value......**$1,100.00**

Pellet, #4313, hamster, R, from $7 to **$10.00**

Periwinkle, #4400, e-Beanie bear, blue, R, from $10 to .**$15.00**

Pierre, Ty Canada exclusive, minimum..................**$40.00**

Pinchers, #4026, lobster, R, from $10 to **$15.00**

Pinky, #4072, flamingo, R, from $7 to **$10.00**

Poopsie, #4381, bear, yellow, from $7 to **$10.00**

Poseidon, #4356, whale shark, R, from $7 to.............**$10.00**

Pouch, #4161, kangaroo, R, from $5 to **$10.00**

Pounce, #4122, cat, brown, R, from $5 to **$10.00**

Prance, #4123, cat, gray striped, R, $5 to...................**$10.00**

Prickles, #4220, hedgehog, R, from $5 to **$10.00**

Prince, #4312, bullfrog, R, from $7 to **$10.00**

Princess, #4300, bear, purple, commemorating Diana, Princess of Wales, PVC pellets, R, from $20 to **$35.00**

Princess, #4300, bear, purple, commemorating Diana, Princess of Wales, PE pellets, R, from $10 to **$15.00**

Propeller, #4366, fish, R, from $7 to..........................**$10.00**

Puffer, #4181, puffin, R, from $5 to **$7.00**

Pugsly, #4106, pug dog, R, from $5 to..........................**$7.00**

Pumkin', #4205, pumpkin, R, from $7 to.....................**$10.00**

Punchers, #4026, 1st issue of Pinchers the lobster, R, minimum value **$2,200.00**

Purr, #4346, kitten, R, from $7 to **$10.00**

Quackers, #4024, duck, 1st issue, no wings, R, minimum value..**$1,000.00**

Quackers, #4024, duck, 2nd issue, w/wings, R, from $7 to **$15.00**

Radar, #4091, bat, black, R, minimum value **$65.00**

Rainbow, #4037, chameleon, 4 versions, R, ea from $5 to.**$10.00**

Regal, #4358, King Charles spaniel, R, from $7 to......**$10.00**

Rescue, #4407, dalmatian, all profits from the original purchase of this Beanie go to the New York Police & Fire Widow's & Children's Benefit Fund due to the national tragedy on September 11, 2001, from $5 to.........**$20.00**

Rex, #4086, tyrannosaurus, R, minimum value.........**$350.00**

Righty, #4085, elephant w/American flag, gray, R, minimum value **$100.00**

Righty 2000, #4289, elephant, red, white & blue, USA exclusive, R, from $7 to **$10.00**

Ringo, #4014, raccoon, R, from $7 to.........................**$10.00**

Roam, #4209, buffalo, R, from $5 to **$10.00**

Roary, #4069, lion, R, from $5 to.............................**$10.00**

Rocket, #4202, blue jay, R, from $5 ....**$10.00**

Rover, #4101, dog, red, R, from $10 to.....................**$15.00**

Roxie, #4334, reindeer, black nose, R, from $7 to......**$10.00**

Roxie, #4334, reindeer, red nose, R, from $10 to........**$20.00**

Rufus, #4280, dog, R, from $7 to.............................**$10.00**

Runner, #4304, mustelidae, R, from $7 to.................**$10.00**

Sakura, #4602, Japanese bear, Japan exclusive, R, minimum value **$150.00**

Sammy, #4215, bear, tie-dyed, R, from $5 to.............**$10.00**

Santa, #4203, R, from $10 to.................................**$15.00**

Sarge, #4277, German shepherd, R, from $7 to **$10.00**

Scaly, #4263, lizard, R, from $5 to..........................**$10.00**

Scary, #4378, witch, R, from $7 to..........................**$10.00**

Scat, #4231, cat, R, from $5 to...............................**$10.00**

Schweetheart, #4252, orangutan, R, from $5 to..........**$10.00**

Scoop, #4107, pelican, R, from $5 to **$10.00**

Scorch, #4210, dragon, R, from $5 to **$10.00**

Scottie, #4102, Scottish terrier, R, from $7 to..............**$15.00**

Scurry, #4281, beetle, R, from $5 to **$7.00**

Seamore, #4029, seal, white, R, minimum value........**$60.00**

Seaweed, #4080, otter, R, from $7 to **$15.00**

September, #4372, birthday month bear, from $7 to ..**$10.00**

Sheets, #4620, ghost, R, from $7 to.........................**$10.00**

Siam, #4369, Siamese cat, from $7 to......................**$10.00**

Signature Bear (1999), #4228, R, from $7 to.............**$10.00**

Signature Bear (2000), #4266, R, from $10 to.............**$15.00**

Silver, #4242, tabby cat, gray, R, from $5 to.............**$10.00**

Slippery, #4222, seal, gray, R, from $5 to................**$10.00**

Slither, #4031, snake, R, minimum value.................**$800.00**

Slowpoke, #4261, sloth, R, from $5 to.....................**$10.00**

Sly, #4115, fox, 1st issue, all brown, R, minimum value..**$65.00**

Sly, #4115, fox, 2nd issue, brown w/white belly, R, from $10 to..**$15.00**

Smart, #4353, 2001 graduation owl, R, from $7 to......**$10.00**

Smooch, #4335, bear, R, from $10 to **$20.00**

Smoochy, #4039, frog, R, from $5 to **$10.00**

Sneaky, #4278, leopard, R, from $7 to **$10.00**

Sniffer, #4299, beagle, R, from $7 to **$10.00**

Snip, #4120, Siamese cat, R, from $5 to....................**$15.00**

Snort, #4002, bull, red w/cream feet, R, from $10 to .**$15.00**

Snowball, #4201, snowman, R, from $15 to **$20.00**

Snowgirl, #4333, snowgirl, R, from $10 to..................**$15.00**

Spangle, #4245, American bear, blue face, R, from $25 to **$30.00**

Spangle, #4245, American bear, pink face, R, from $10 to **$15.00**

Spangle, #4245, American bear, white face, R, from $10 to **$15.00**

Sparky, #4100, dalmatian, R, minimum value.............**$50.00**

Speckles, #4402, bear, e-Beanie exclusively through the Internet & Ty Trade on the official Ty website, from $10 to **$15.00**

Speedy, #4030, turtle, R, from $25 to.......................**$40.00**

Spike, #4060, rhinoceros, R, from $5 to......................**$7.00**

Spinner, #4036, spider, R, from $5 to **$7.00**

Splash, #4022, whale, R, minimum value **$45.00**

Spooky, #4090, ghost, orange neck ribbon, R, from $45 to **$50.00**

Spot, #4000, dog, 1st issue, no spot on back, R, minimum value **$1,000.00**

Spot, #4000, dog, 2nd issue, black spot on back, R, from $35 to **$40.00**

Springy, #4272, bunny, lavender, R, from $5 to...........**$7.00**

Spunky, #4184, cocker spaniel, R, from $5 to..............**$7.00**

Squealer, #4005, pig, R, from $7 to **$10.00**

Squirmy, #4302, worm, green, R, from $7 to **$10.00**

Starlett, #4382, white kitten, from $7 to.....................**$10.00**

Steg, #4087, stegosaurus, R, minimum value............**$400.00**

Stilts, #4221, stork, R, from $5 to...........................**$7.00**

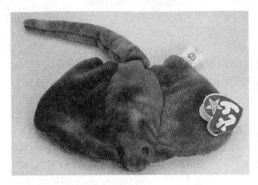

Sting, #4077, stingray, tie-dyed, R, minimum value $50.00.

Stinger, #4193, scorpion, R, from $5 to **$7.00**

Stinky, #4017, skunk, R, from $5 to **$10.00**

Stretch, #4182, ostrich, R, from $5 to **$7.00**

Stripes, #4065, 1st issue, gold tiger w/thin stripes, R, minimum value **$175.00**

Stripes, #4065, 2nd issue, tiger, caramel, wide stripes, R, from $10 to **$15.00**

Strut, #4171, rooster, R, from $7 to.............................**$10.00**

Sunny, e-Beanie bear, yellow-orange, R, from $10 to...**$15.00**

Swampy, #4273, alligator, R, from $7 to **$10.00**

Swirly, #4249, snail, R, from $5 to **$10.00**

Swoop, #4268, pterodactyl, R, from $7 to **$10.00**

Tabasco, #4002, bull, red feet, R, minimum value......**$60.00**

Tank, #4031, armadillo, 1st issue, no shell, 7 lines, R, minimum value **$160.00**

Tank, #4031, armadillo, 2nd issue, no shell, 9 lines, R, minimum value **$225.00**

Tank, #4031, armadillo, 3rd issue, w/shell, R, minimum value **$40.00**

Teddy, #4050, bear, brown, new face, R, from $30 to..**$50.00**

Teddy, #4050, bear, brown, old face, R, minimum value **$1,000.00**

Teddy, #4051, bear, teal, new face, R, minimum value **$850.00**

Teddy, #4051, bear, teal, old face, R, minimum value **$900.00**

Teddy, #4052, bear, cranberry, new face, R, minimum value **$850.00**

Teddy, #4052, bear, cranberry, old face, R, minimum value **$900.00**

Teddy, #4055, bear, violet, new face, R, minimum value $850.00

Teddy, #4055, bear, violet, old face, R, minimum value $900.00

Teddy, #4056, bear, magenta, new face, R, minimum value..$850.00

Teddy, #4056, bear, magenta, old face, R, minimum value..$900.00

Teddy, #4057, bear, jade, new face, R, minimum value...$850.00

Teddy, #4057, bear, jade, old face, R, minimum value.....$900.00

Thank You Bear, Ty retailer exclusive, R, from $225 to .$430.00

The Beginning, #4267, bear, white w/silver stars, R, from $10 to $20.00

The End, #4265, bear, black, R, from $10 to $20.00

Tiny, #4234, chihuahua, R, from $5 to........................$10.00

Tiptoe, #4241, mouse, R, from $5 to...........................$10.00

Tracker, #4198, basset hound, R, from $5 to..............$10.00

Tradee, #4403, bear, e-Beanie available only through Ty official website/store, from $10 to $15.00

Trap, #4042, mouse, R, minimum value $850.00

Tricks, #4311, dog, R, from $7 to $10.00

Trumpet, #4276, elephant, R, from $7 to....................$10.00

Tuffy, #4108, terrier, R, from $5 to............................$10.00

Tusk, #4076, walrus, R, minimum value $60.00

Twigs, #4068, giraffe, R, from $10 to $15.00

Ty 2K Bear, #4262, R, from $7 to $10.00

USA, #4287, bear, USA exclusive, R, from $7 to .$15.00

Unity, #4606, bear, blue, Ty Europe exclusive, R, from $20 to..$40.00

Valentina, #4233, bear, fuchsia w/white heart, R, from $7 to..$10.00

Valentino, #4058, bear, white w/red heart, R, from $10 to $15.00

Velvet, #4064, panther, R, from $10 to........................$20.00

Waddle, #4075, penguin, R, from $7.00 to $10.00.

Wallace, #4264, bear, green with red scarf, R, from $7 to $15.00

Waves, #4084, whale, R, from $5 to............................$15.00

Web, #4041, spider, black, R, minimum value $900.00

Weenie, #4013, dachshund, R, from $10 to $15.00

Whiskers, #4317, terrier, R, from $7 to......................$10.00

Whisper, #4187, deer, R, from $5 to...........................$10.00

Wiggly, #4275, octopus, R, from $7 to........................$10.00

Wise, #4194, 1998 graduation owl, R, from $7.00 to $10.00.

Wiser, #4238, 1999 graduation owl, R, from $7 to......$10.00

Wisest, #4286, 2000 graduation owl, R, from $7 to $10.00

Wrinkles, #4103, bulldog, R, from $5 to $10.00

Zero, #4207, penguin, w/Santa hat, R, from $10 to..........$15.00

Ziggy, #4063, zebra, R, from $10 to $20.00

Zip, #4004, cat, 1st issue, black w/white tummy, R, minimum value $500.00

Zip, #4004, cat, 2nd issue, all black, R, minimum value $650.00

Zip, #4004, 3rd issue, cat, black w/white paws, R, from $10 to $15.00

Zodaic Goat, #4329, R, from $7 to $10.00

Zodaic Horse, #4324, R, from $7 to $10.00

Zodiac Dog, #4326, R, from $7 to $10.00

Zodiac Dragon, #4322, R, from $7 to..........................$10.00

Zodiac Monkey, #4328, R, from $7 to..........................$10.00

Zodiac Ox, #4319, R, from $7 to $10.00

Zodiac Rabbit, #4321, R, from $7 to $10.00

Zodiac Rat, #4318, R, from $7 to $10.00

Zodiac Rooster, #4325, R, from $7 to........................$10.00

Zodiac Snake, #4323, R, from $7 to $10.00

Zodiac Tiger, #4320, R, from $7 to............................$10.00

Zodiac Pig, #4377, R, from $7 to $10.00

Beanie Buddies

This line is of special interest to Beanie Babies collectors, since these animals are larger versions of the Beanie Babies. Like Beanie Babies, Beanie Buddies are periodically retired, and the listings will indicate this. Again, production of these animals is ongoing, so these listings may not include all of those produced during the year 2001. The next edition of *Garage Sale & Flea Market Annual* will reflect any new products.

1997 Holiday Teddy, #9426, bear, from $10 to $20.00

1997 Holiday Teddy, #9053, bear, lg, from $30 to......$40.00

1997 Holiday Teddy, #9054, bear, X-lg, from $50 to ..**$60.00**

2001 Holiday Teddy, #9427, bear, from $10 to **$20.00**

Almond, #9425, bear, R, from $10 to **$15.00**

Amber, #9341, cat, R, from $10 to...........................**$20.00**

Ariel, #9409, bear, from $10 to **$15.00**

Baldy, #9408, eagle, R, from $10 to **$15.00**

Bananas, #9402, orangutan, R, from $10 to...............**$15.00**

Batty, #9378, bat, pink, from $10 to.........................**$15.00**

Batty, #9379, bat, black, from $100 to......................**$150.00**

BB, #9398, bear, from $10 to...................................**$15.00**

Beak, #9301, kiwi, R, from $10 to............................**$15.00**

Bones, #9377, dog, from $10 to **$15.00**

Bongo, #9312, monkey, R, from $10 to.....................**$15.00**

Britannia, #9601, bear, UK exclusive, R, from $50 to .**$90.00**

Bronty, #9353, brontosaurus, R, from $10 to..............**$15.00**

Bubbles, #9323, fish, R, from $10 to........................**$15.00**

Buckingham, #9607, bear, Ty UK exclusive, R, from $30 to..**$50.00**

Bushy, #9382, lion, R, from $10 to...........................**$15.00**

Cassie, #9405, collie, R, from $10 to **$15.00**

Celebrate, #9423, 15-year Ty anniversary bear, from $15 to..**$25.00**

Chilly, #9317, polar bear, R, from $10 to **$15.00**

Chip, #9318, calico cat, R, from $10 to......................**$15.00**

Chocolate, #9349, moose, R, from $10 to...................**$15.00**

Chops, #9394, lamb, R, from $10 to..........................**$15.00**

Clubby, #9990, bear, BBOC Gold member exclusive (mail-order only), R, from $15 to.....................................**$20.00**

Clubby II, #9991, bear, BBOC Platinum member exclusive (mail-order only), R, from $10 to........................**$20.00**

Clubby III, #9993, bear, BBOC member exclusive (mail-order only), R, from $15 to...**$20.00**

Clubby IV, bear, BBOC exclusive (mail or Internet order only), from $10 to...**$20.00**

Congo, #9361, gorilla, R, from $10 to **$15.00**

Coral, #9381, fish, tie-dyed, from $10 to....................**$15.00**

Digger, #9351, crab, orange, R, from $10 to...............**$15.00**

Digger, #9351, crab, tie-dyed, R, from $15 to.............**$30.00**

Dotty, #9051, dalmatian, lg, #9051, R, from $15 to.....**$35.00**

Dotty, #9052, dalmatian, X-lg, from $65 to.................**$70.00**

Dotty, #9364, dalmatian, R, from $10 to **$15.00**

Dragon, #9365, dragon, R, from $10 to **$15.00**

Ears, #9046, rabbit, lg, R, from $20 to.......................**$30.00**

Ears, #9047, rabbit, X-lg, R, from $30 to....................**$50.00**

Ears, #9388, rabbit, from $10 to...............................**$15.00**

Employee Bear, #9373, from $10 to **$15.00**

Erin, #9309, Irish bear, R, from $10 to **$15.00**

Eucalyptus, #9363, koala bear, R, from $10 to **$15.00**

Fetch, #9338, golden retriever, R, from $10 to **$20.00**

Flip, #9359, cat, white, R, from $10 to.......................**$15.00**

Flippity, #9358, bunny, R, from $10 to **$20.00**

Flitter, #9384, butterfly, from $10 to **$15.00**

Floppity, #9390, bunny, lilac, R, from $10 to **$20.00**

Fuzz, #9040, bear, lg, R, from $15 to........................**$30.00**

Fuzz, #9328, bear, R, from $10 to............................**$15.00**

Germania, #9063, bear, German exclusive, R, from $25 to..**$50.00**

Glory, #9410, bear, R, from $25 to............................**$40.00**

Gobbles, #9333, turkey, R, from $10 to.....................**$15.00**

Goochy, #9362, jellyfish, R, from $10 to....................**$15.00**

Grace, praying bunny, #9389, R, from $10 to **$15.00**

Groovy, #9345, bear, tie-dyed, R, from $10 to **$15.00**

Halo, #9337, angel bear, R, from $10 to **$15.00**

Halo II, #9386, angel bear, R, from $10 to **$15.00**

Happy, #9375, hippo, lavender, from $10 to...............**$15.00**

Hippie, #9038, bunny, X-lg, R, from $50 to **$100.00**

Hippie, #9039, bunny, lg, R, from $35 to..................**$55.00**

Hippie, #9357, bunny, R, from $10 to.......................**$15.00**

Hippity, #9324, bunny, mint green, R, from $10 to....**$15.00**

Hope, #9327, praying bear, R, from $10 to **$15.00**

Hornsly, #9407, triceratops, from $10 to....................**$15.00**

Humphrey, #9307, camel, R, from $10 to **$15.00**

Inch, #9331, worm, R, from $10 to **$15.00**

India, #9406, tiger, from $10 to **$15.00**

Inky, #9404, octopus, R, from $10 to **$15.00**

Jabber, #9326, parrot, R, from $10 to **$15.00**

Jake, #9304, mallard duck, R, from $10 to **$15.00**

Kicks, #9343, soccer bear, R, from $10 to..................**$15.00**

Lefty, #9370, donkey, gray, USA exclusive, R, from $10 to..**$15.00**

Libearty, #9342, bear, X-lg, USA exclusive, R, from $30 to..**$70.00**

Libearty, #9371, bear, lg, USA exclusive, R, from $20 to..**$30.00**

Libearty, #9371, bear, USA exclusive, R, from $10 to .**$15.00**

Lips, #9355, fish, R, from $10 to..............................**$15.00**

Lizzy, #9366, lizard, tie-dyed, R, from $10 to **$15.00**

Loosy, #9428, goose, from $10 to.............................**$15.00**

Lucky, #9354, ladybug, R, from $10 to **$15.00**

Luke, #9412, dog, from $10 to.................................**$15.00**

Maple, #9600, bear, Ty Canada exclusive, R, from $30 to .**$50.00**

Mellow, #9411, bear, from $10 to.............................**$20.00**

Millennium, #9325, bear, R, from $10 to....................**$15.00**

Mooch, #9416, spider monkey, R, from $10 to **$15.00**

Mystic, #9396, unicorn, from $10 to.........................**$15.00**

Nanook, #9350, husky, R, from $10 to **$15.00**

Neon, #9417, sea horse, R, from $10 to....................**$15.00**

Oats, #9393, horse, R, from $10 to...........................**$15.00**

Osito, #9344, Mexican bear, USA exclusive, R, from $10 to.**$15.00**

Patti, #9320, platypus, R, from $10 to **$15.00**

Peace, #9035, bear, jumbo, from $70 to **$100.00**

Peace, #9036, bear, X-lg, R, from $40 to....................**$70.00**

Peace, #9037, bear, lg, R, from $35 to **$45.00**

Peace, #9335, bear, pastel, R, from $10 to................**$15.00**

Peace, #9335, bear, R, from $10 to...........................**$15.00**

Peanut, #9300, elephant, light blue, R, from $15 to....**$30.00**

Peanut, #9300, elephant, royal blue, R, from $10 to...**$15.00**

Peking, #9310, panda, R, from $10 to **$15.00**

Periwinkle, #9415, bear, from $10 to **$20.00**

Pinchers, #9424, lobster, R, from $10 to **$15.00**

Pinky, #9316, flamingo, R, from $10 to.....................**$15.00**

Pouch, #9380, kangaroo, from $10 to.......................**$15.00**

Prince, #9401, frog, R, from $10 to **$15.00**

Princess, #9329, bear, R, from $10 to.......................**$20.00**

Pugsly, #9413, dog, R, from $10 to **$15.00**
Pumkin', #9332, pumpkin, R, from $10 to..................**$15.00**
Quackers, #9302, duck, no wings, R, from $175 to..**$200.00**
Quackers, #9302, duck, w/wings, R, from $10 to.......**$15.00**
Radar, #9422, bat, R, from $10 to **$20.00**
Rainbow, #9367, chameleon, from $10 to **$15.00**
Rex, #9368, tyrannosaurus, R, from $10 to **$20.00**
Righty, #9369, elephant, gray, USA exclusive, R, from $10
to..**$15.00**
Roam, #9378, buffalo, from $10 to **$15.00**
Rover, #9305, dog, R, from $10 to **$15.00**
Rufus, #9393, dog, R, from $10 to **$15.00**
Sakura, #9608, bear, Japanese exclusive, R, from $30 to .**$40.00**
Santa, #9385, R, from $10 to **$15.00**
Schweetheart, #9044, orangutan, X-lg, from $50 to **$60.00**
Schweetheart, #9045, orangutan, jumbo, R, from $85 to.**$150.00**
Schweetheart, #9343, orangutan, lg, from $30 to **$35.00**
Schweetheart, #9330, orangutan, R, from $10 to **$15.00**
Seal, #9419, seal, from $10 to **$15.00**
Signature Bear (2000), #9348, R, from $15 to.............**$30.00**
Silver, #9340, cat, R, from $10 to **$15.00**
Slither, #9339, snake, R, from $10 to.........................**$15.00**
Smoochy, #9315, frog, R, from $10 to **$15.00**
Sneaky, #9376, leopard, from $10 to **$15.00**
Snort, #9311, bull, R, from $10 to.............................**$15.00**
Snowball, #9429, snowman, from $10 to **$15.00**
Snowboy, #9342, R, from $10 to **$15.00**
Spangle, #9336, bear, R, from $15 to **$20.00**
Speedy, #9352, turtle, R, from $10 to **$15.00**
Spinner, #9334, spider, R, from $10 to **$15.00**
Spooky, #9421, ghost, R, from $10 to **$20.00**
Spunky, #9400, cocker spaniel, R, from $10 to **$15.00**
Squealer, #9313, pig, R, from $10 to **$15.00**
Steg, #9383, stegosaurus, R, from $10 to **$15.00**
Stretch, #9303, ostrich, R, from $10 to **$15.00**
Sunny, #9414, bear, from $10 to **$15.00**
Swoop, #9391, pterodactyl, from $10 to **$15.00**
Tangerine, #9418, bear, from $10 to **$20.00**
Teddy, #9306, bear, cranberry, R, from $10 to **$20.00**
Teddy, #9372, bear, teal, old face, from $10 to...........**$15.00**
The Beginning Bear, #9399, R, from $10 to **$15.00**
The Cardinal, #9395, cardinal, R, from $10 to **$15.00**
Tracker, #9319, basset hound, R, from $10 to **$15.00**
Trumpet, #9403, elephant, R, from $10 to **$15.00**
Twigs, #9308, giraffe, R, from $80 to **$100.00**
Ty 2K, #9346, bear, R, from $15 to **$20.00**
Unity, bear, Ty Europe exclusive, from $25 to............**$40.00**
Valentina, #9048, bear, lg, R, from $20 to..................**$30.00**
Valentina, #9049, bear, X-lg, R, from $35 to **$40.00**
Valentina, #9050, bear, jumbo, R, from $65 to **$100.00**
Valentina, #9397, bear, R, from $10 to **$15.00**
Valentino, #9347, bear, R, from $10 to **$15.00**
Waddle, #9314, penguin, R, from $10 to **$15.00**
Wallace, #9387, bear, R, from $10 to.........................**$15.00**
Weenie, #9356, dachshund, R, from $10 to **$15.00**
White Tiger, #9374, from $10 to **$15.00**
Zip, #9360, cat, R, from $10 to **$15.00**

McDonald's® Happy Meal Teenie Beanie Babies

The Teenie Beanie Babies debuted in April 1997 at McDonald's restaurants across the country. The result was the most successful Happy Meal promotion in the history of McDonald's. The toys were quickly snatched up by collectors, causing the promotion to last only one week instead of the planned five-week period. To date there have been four Teenie Beanie promotions, one annually in 1997, 1998, 1999, and 2000.

1997, Chocolate (moose), Patti (platypus), or Pinky (flamingo), ea from $12 to................**$15.00**
1997, Chops (lamb), from $15 to **$20.00**
1997, Goldie (goldfish), Seamore (seal), Snort (bull), or Speedy (turtle), ea from $5 to................**$9.00**
1997, Lizz (lizard) or Quacks (duck), ea from $5 to.....**$7.00**
1998, Bones (dog), Peanut (elephant), or Waddle (penguin), ea from $2 to................**$4.00**
1998, Bongo (monkey) or Doby (doberman), ea from $5 to................**$7.00**
1998, Happy (hippo), Inch (worm), Mel (koala), Pinchers (lobster), or Scoop (pelican), ea from $2 to..........**$4.00**
1998, Twigs (giraffe) or Zip (cat), ea from $2 to **$5.00**
1999, Antsy (anteater), Freckles (leopard), Smoochy (frog), Spunky (cocker spaniel), ea from $1 to................**$3.00**
1999, Claude (crab), Rocket (blue jay), Iggy (iguana), Strut (rooster), ea from $1 to................**$2.00**
1999, Nuts (squirrel), Stretchy (ostrich), 'Nook (husky), Chip (cat), ea from $1 to................**$2.00**
2000, At the Zoo: Tusk (walrus), Blizz (tiger), Schweetheart (orangutan), Spike (rhinoceros), ea from $2 to......**$4.00**
2000, Garden Bunch: Spinner (spider), Bumble (bee), Flitter (butterfly), Lucky (ladybug), ea from $2 to **$4.00**
2000, Under the Sea: Coral (fish), Sting (stingray), Goochy (jellyfish), Neon (sea horse), ea from $2 to...........**$4.00**

Special Edition Teenie Beanies and International Bears

These were offered at McDonald's as separate purchases, specially packaged for collectors, and not included in Happy Meals.

1999, Britannia (British bear), from $2 to **$4.00**
1999, Erin (Irish bear), from $2 to................**$4.00**
1999, Glory (American bear), from $4 to......................**$6.00**
1999, Maple (Canadian bear), from $2 to.....................**$4.00**
2000, Bronty, Rex or Steg, dinosaurs, ea from $3 to **$5.00**
2000, Bushy (lion), Springy (bunny), 'Mystery' items, ea from $2 to................**$4.00**
2000, Chilly (polar bear), Humphrey (camel), Peanut (royal blue elephant), The End (bear), ea from $3 to......**$5.00**
2000, Election/American Trio, Lefty (blue-gray donkey), Righty (gray elephant) or Libearty (bear), ea from $3 to................**$6.00**
2000, Germania (German bear), Osito (Mexican bear), Spangle (American bear), ea from $3 to................**$5.00**

2000, Millennium (bear), offered only 6/13/2000, benefit for Ronald McDonald House Charities, from $4 to......**$6.00**

Beatles Collectibles

Possibly triggered by John Lennon's death in 1980, Beatles fans (recognizing that their dreams of the band ever reuniting were gone along with him) began to collect vintage memorabilia of all types. Recently some of the original Beatles material has sold at auction with high-dollar results. Handwritten song lyrics, Lennon's autographed high school textbook, and even the legal agreement that was drafted at the time the group disbanded are among the one-of-a-kind multi-thousand dollar sales recorded.

Unless you plan on attending sales of this caliber, you'll be more apt to find the commercially produced memorabilia that literally flooded the market during the '60s and beyond when the Fab Four from Liverpool made their unprecedented impact on the entertainment world. A word about their 45 rpm records: they sold in such mass quantities that unless the record is a 'promotional' (made to send to radio stations or for jukebox distribution), they have very little value. Once a record has lost much of its original gloss due to wear and handling, becomes scratched, or has writing on the label, its value is minimal. Even in near-mint condition, $4.00 to $6.00 is plenty to pay for a 45 rpm (much less if it's worn), unless the original picture sleeve is present. (An exception is the white-labeled Swan recording of 'She Loves You/I'll Get You'). A Beatles' picture sleeve is usually valued at $30.00 to $40.00, except for the rare 'Can't Buy Me Love,' which is worth ten times that amount. (Beware of reproductions!) Albums of any top recording star or group from the '50s and '60s are becoming very collectible, and the Beatles' are among the most popular. Just be very critical of condition! An album must be in at least excellent condition to bring a decent price.

For more information we recommend *The Beatles, Second Edition,* by Barbara Crawford, Hollis Lamon, and Michael Stern (Collector Books).

See also Celebrity Dolls; Magazines; Movie Posters; Records; Sheet Music.

Advisor: Bojo/Bob Gottuso (See Directory, Character and Personality Collectibles)

Newsletter: *Beatlefan*
P.O. Box 33515, Decatur, GA 30033
Send SASE for information.

Bandage, The Beatles, Help! (in lg red letters) & Capitol on original wrapper, for release of 1965 LP, Curad, 3½", EX....................$35.00
Banner, Yeah! Yeah! Yeah! Beatles Stamps Are Here, paper, 3x20", EX....................**$50.00**
Beach towel, cartoon image of group in striped swim-suits, Yeah! Yeah! Yeah!, Cannon, 1960s, 55x34", unused, EX....................**$90.00**

Beanie Bears, Hey Jude, I Want To Hold Your Hand, Magical Mystery Tour, Sgt Pepper, by Apple, current, M, set of 4....................**$42.00**

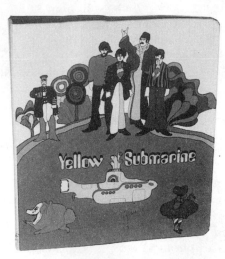

Binder, Yellow Submarine, three-ring, EX, $330.00. (Photo courtesy Bob Gottuso)

Book, Magical Mystery Tour, features 11 songs & many photos, Hansen Publishing, 1967, 40 pages, EX+.......**$40.00**
Book cover, black & white photos at edge, unused, EX....................**$18.00**
Bookmark, cardboard figure, Ringo from Yellow Submarine, 9", EX....................**$12.00**
Box, ceramic, Hard Days Night, multiple head shots, EX..**$35.00**
Bracelet, She Loves You in raised lettering on black & white photo disk w/heavy link chain, MOC....................**$160.00**
Bulletin board, Yellow Submarine, group photo, 17½x23", EX (in original wrapping)....................**$140.00**
Cake decorations, 4 plastic heads w/flat backs, EX....**$40.00**
Calendar card, 1964-65, Paladium doorway photo, 2¼x3½", NM....................**$20.00**
Candy dish, ceramic, photo decal & name in center, scalloped edge w/gold trim, 4½" dia, EX....................**$160.00**
Christmas ornament, Ringo in white suit, name on mirror display hanger, 1996, MIP....................**$32.00**
Clothes hanger, diecut cardboard cartoon image of Ringo w/plastic hook, Henderson-Hoggard Inc, 1968, NM+....................**$140.00**
Coasters, Yellow Submarine, set of 12 w/different images, EX (in package w/header card)....................**$200.00**
Coin, 'Commemorating the 1964 Visit to the United States' on 1 side w/faces & names on other, 1¼", VG+.......**$18.00**
Comb, plastic, Lido Toys, 14½", NM (beware of reproductions)....................**$225.00**
Concert booklet, black & white photos w/color photo cover, 1965, 12x12", EX....................**$30.00**
Cup, ceramic w/blue, gray & black decal, Broadhurst Bros, UK, EX....................**$125.00**
Decal, 4 dark brown mop tops over The Beatles in red, on 4x6½" card, unused, M....................**$80.00**
Diary, plastic cover w/color photo of band, Langman & Co/Scotland, 1965, 4x3", unused, NM+....................**$30.00**

Display, diecut cardboard 3-D stand-up w/waist-length group & sign reading The Beatles Yellow Submarine, 12x16", M...**$25.00**

Dolls, Sgt Pepper uniforms, w/original stands, Applause, 1988, 22", M, set of 4...**$150.00**

Door mat, color bust image of group on felt-like material w/rubber backing, 1970s, 18x26", VG+ **$210.00**

Figures, lead, Help!, figures set in snow scene from movie, M, set of 4 ....**$100.00**

Flasher rings, EX (Beware of reproductions), set of 4 ..**$80.00**

Frisbee, Rock 'N Roll Music LP promo, 1976, 9" dia, VG..**$35.00**

Greeting card, Enclosing a Little Something To Help You Get a Genuine Haircut, shows picture of bowl, 9x4", unused, NM **$45.00**

Hairbrush, Genco, 1964, MIP...**$40.00**

Handkerchief, w/colorful instruments & records w/faces & black & white song titles, NM **$90.00**

Harmonica, Hohner, 1964, MOC **$600.00**

Nodder dolls, plastic, Hong Kong, 4", M, set of 4 ......**$50.00**

Pennant, The Beatles, receding bust images above name, sq w/dowel rod, blue or black on white, 8½x10", VG+ **$160.00**

Poster, Anthology III, Their Music, Their Story, Their Video, 2-sided, M...**$10.00**

Press book, Help!, 13x18", VG+ **$60.00**

Press book, Let It Be, oversized trifold, unused **$90.00**

Ring, gold-tone metal w/group photo, EX **$45.00**

Scrapbook, photo cover, US version, 11x⅜x13½", unused, VG+...**$85.00**

Stationery, w/Apple name, address & Beatles information, Apple watermark, single sheet, EX **$24.00**

Stick pin, hand-painted diecut Yellow Submarine, 1", EX..**$35.00**

Ticket stub, A Hard Day's Night, diecut photo on blue card stock, from Baden PA, unused, 9x4" **$30.00**

Tote bag, plastic w/handle, original hang tag, Japan, 1966, 14x13", VG **$125.00**

Travel bag, white cloth w/blue photo head images surrounded by red lettering w/musical graphics, M.................**$200.00**

Tumbler, plastic w/color insert of group & lips at top under rim, original issue, VG...**$70.00**

Wallet, black & white group portrait on red vinyl w/facsimile signatures, Standard Plastic Products, 1964, EX......**$60.00**

Wallet, pink w/group photo, w/mirror & nail file, SPP, VG+...**$160.00**

Wallpaper, 4 different allover group images & names, 1962, 21" sq, EX+ **$65.00**

Beatnik Collectibles

The 'Beats,' later called 'Beatniks,' consisted of artists, writers, and others disillusioned with Establishment mores and values. The Beatniks were noncomformists, Bohemian free-thinkers who energetically expressed their disdain for society from 1950 to 1962. From a collector's point of view, the most highly regarded Beat authors are Allen Ginsberg, Lawrence Ferlinghetti, and Jack Kerouac. Books, records, posters, pamphlets, leaflets, and other items associated with them are very desirable. Although in their day they were characterized by the media as a 'Maynard G. Krebs' (of Dobie Gillis TV fame), today the contributions they made to American literature and the continuation of Bohemianism are recognized for their importance and significance in American culture.

Values are for examples in excellent to near-mint condition.

Advisor: Richard Synchef (See Directory, Beatnik and Hippie Collectibles)

Beatnik kit, w/beret, cigarette holder & beard, 1950s, 12x11" package **$75.00**

Book, Adept, The; Michael McClure, NY; Delacorte Press, 1971, McClure's 2nd Novel **$120.00**

Book, Third Mind, The; William Burroughs & Brian Gysin, NY; Viking, 1978...**$175.00**

Booklet, Berlin, Lawrence Ferlinghetti, Golden Mountain Press, 1961, 8-page, poetry.................................**$120.00**

Booklet, Burroughs, Wm; Prospectus for Naked Lunch, NY: Grove Press, 1962, 16-page.................................**$150.00**

Booklet, The Dead Star, William Burroughs, The Nova Broadcast Press, San Francisco, 1969, unusual format...**$225.00**

Handbill, poetry reading, Rexroth, Ginsberg, Ferlinghetti, Kandel, U of Santa Barbara Gym, April 8, 1970...**$550.00**

Magazine, City Lights, #3, Spring 1953, San Francisco: City Lights, early Ferlinghetti publication **$125.00**

Magazine, Life, September 21, 1959, Squaresville vs Beatsville **$55.00**

Magazine, Playboy, Beat Issue, July 1959, Ginsberg, Corso, Kerouac, etc...**$90.00**

Magazine, _Reflections From Chapel Hill_, Vol 1 #3, November 1, 1961, Chapel Hill, NC, early Ferlinghetti, $100.00. (Photo courtesy Richard Synchef)

Magazine, The Second Coming, March 1962, NY, Burrough's chapter from Nova Express, scarce **$175.00**

Paperback, Kerouac, Jack; Dharma Bums, Signet, 1959, 1st printing **$75.00**

Paperback, Planet News, 1961-67, Allen Ginsberg, City Lights Books, San Francisco, 1968, Pocket Poet Series #23..**$245.00**

Paperback, Wholly Communion, London, Lorimar Films, 1965, Ferlinghetti, others, movie tie-in **$80.00**

Pin-back buttons, celluloid: Love Is Happening, neon orange & blue, 1½", VG+ **$25.00**

Poster, poetry reading, Ginsberg, Ferlinghetti; McClure, etc, August 19, 1971, UC Berkley, 9x14".....**$265.00**

Record, Ferlinghetti, Fantasy Records, #7014, monaural LP, 1961, Ferlinghetti reading some of his most famous poems **$175.00**

Record, Lenny Bruce – American, monaural LP, Fantasy Records, #7011, red vinyl, 1961........................**$200.00**

Record, The Beatniks, 45 rpm movie promotional tie-in, 1960, scarce..**$175.00**

Beatrix Potter

Since 1902 when *The Tale of Peter Rabbit* was published by Fredrick Warne & Company, generations have enjoyed the adventures of Beatrix Potter's characters. Beswick issued ten characters in 1947 that included Peter Rabbit, Benjamin Bunny, Squirrel Nutkin, Jemima Puddleduck, Timmy Tiptoes, Tom Kitten, Mrs Tittlemouse, Mrs. Tiggywinkle, Little Pig Robinson, and Samuel Whiskers. The line grew until it included figures from other stories. Duchess (P1355) was issued in 1955 with two feet that were easily broken. Later issues featured the Duchess on a base and holding a pie. This was the first figure to be discontinued in 1967. Color variations on pieces indicate issue dates as do the different backstamps that were used. Backstamps have changed several times since the first figures were issued. There are three basic styles: Beswick brown, Beswick gold, and Royal Albert — with many variations on each of these.

Advisor: Nicki Budin (See Directory, Beatrix Potter)

And This Pig Had None, B6 ....**$55.00**
Aunt Pettitoes, B3 ....**$55.00**
Aunt Pettitoes, B6 ....**$75.00**
Benjamin Bunny, B3...**$55.00**
Benjamin Bunny, ears out, B3......................................**$195.00**

Benjamin Bunny, second version, 3A, $300.00.

Benjamin Bunny Sat on a Bank, B6.............................**$45.00**
Benjamin Bunny Sat on a Bank, head down, B3 ....**$55.00**
Benjamin Wakes Up, B6..**$75.00**
Chippy Hackee, B3..**$85.00**
Christmas Stocking, brown mice, red & white stocking, B6...**$250.00**
Cicily Parsley, blue dress, white apron, A3 ....**$95.00**
Cottontail, blue dress, brown chair, B3.......................**$45.00**
Cottontail, B6..**$45.00**
Cousin Ribby, cat in pink skirt & hat, green apron, blue shawl, yellow basket, B6................................**$50.00**
Cousin Ribby, cat in pink w/green apron & blue shawl, yellow basket, B3..**$55.00**
Diggory Diggory Delvet, gray mole, B3 ....**$75.00**
Flopsy Mopsy & Cottontail, brown & white bunnies w/mauve cloaks, on base, B2............................**$195.00**
Ginger, cat in light green w/white overtop.................**$500.00**
Hunca Munca, B3..**$65.00**
Hunca Munca, mouse w/cradle & babies, B2-gold ..**$175.00**
Hunca Munca, mouse w/cradle & babies, B3 ....**$65.00**
Hunca Munca Spills the Beads, mouse holding jar of rice, B6..**$125.00**
Hunca Munca Sweeping, mouse in dress w/broom, B3..**$25.00**
Jemima Puddleduck, gold, B2 ....**$160.00**
Jemima Puddleduck, light blue bonnet, pink shawl, B3..**$55.00**
Jemima Puddleduck Made a Feather Nest, B3 ....**$65.00**
Jemima Puddleduck Made a Feather Nest, B6 ....**$45.00**
John Joiner, brown dog in jacket, B6..........................**$55.00**
Johnny Townmouse, in jacket & waistcoat, B3 ....**$55.00**
Johnny Townmouse, in jacket & waistcoat, C3...........**$55.00**
Little Pig Robinson, in blue dress w/basket, B3..........**$75.00**
Little Pig Robinson, in blue dress w/basket, B6..........**$45.00**
Little Pig Robinson Spying, pig in chair w/spyglass, B6....**$150.00**
Miss Dormouse, mouse standing in doorway, B6.......**$85.00**
Miss Moppet, cat w/kerchief, B3 ....**$55.00**
Mr Alderman Ptolemy, B6...**$65.00**
Mr Benjamin Bunny, w/lilac pipe in, B3 ....**$60.00**
Mr Benjamin Bunny & Peter Rabbit, spanking, B3.....**$75.00**
Mr Drake Puddleduck, white duck in trousers, B3.....**$50.00**
Mr Jackson, brown frog, B3..**$55.00**
Mr Jackson, brown frog, B6..**$65.00**
Mr Jeremy Fisher, frog w/stripes, B3...........................**$65.00**
Mr Jeremy Fisher Digging, frog in coat & cravat digging, B4..**$195.00**
Mrs Flopsy Bunny, blue dress, pink purse, B3 ....**$65.00**
Mrs Tiggy Winkle, plaid blouse, white apron, B3 ......**$55.00**
Mrs Tittlemouse, skirt & blouse, C3 ....**$45.00**
No More Twists, brown & white mouse, B6................**$55.00**
Old Mr Bouncer, brown pants & coat, B6..................**$55.00**
Old Mr Bouncer, brown pants & coat, C3...................**$75.00**
Old Mr Brown, brown owl, B3 ....**$60.00**
Old Woman in Shoe, blue shoe, B3.............................**$45.00**
Old Woman in Shoe Knitting, yellow chair, B6 ....**$95.00**
Peter in the Gooseberry Net, bunny caught in green net, B6..**$75.00**
Peter Rabbit, dark blue jacket, 1st version, B3............**$65.00**
Peter Rabbit, light blue jacket, later version, B10 ....**$50.00**

Pickles, black dog w/jacket & apron holding a book, A3 .**$450.00**
Poorly Peter Rabbit, wrapped in blanket, B3 ....**$75.00**
Poorly Peter Rabbit, wrapped in blanket, B6 ....**$65.00**
Rebeccah Puddle-Duck, goose in coat & hat, B3 ....**$40.00**
Ribby, cat in white dress, apron & shawl, A3 ....**$75.00**
Ribby, cat in white dress, apron & shawl, B3 ....**$65.00**
Ribby & the Patty Pan, cat in dress & apron, B6........**$55.00**
Sally Henny Penny, rooster w/2 chicks, B3 ....**$75.00**
Samuel Whiskers, coat & hat, B3 ....**$45.00**
Samuel Whiskers, coat & pants, B6..........................**$45.00**
Simpkin, cat in green coat, B3 ....**$650.00**
Sir Isaac Newton, jacket & waistcoat, 3B **$450.00**
Tabitha Twitchit, cat in dress & apron, B3.................**$75.00**
Tabitha Twitchit, cat in dress & apron, B6.................**$40.00**
Tabitha Twitchit & Miss Moppet, Royal Albert mk, B6..**$150.00**
Thomasina Tittlemouse, furry mouse in brown & pink,
    B6..**$110.00**
Timmy Tiptoes, squirrel wearing jacket, B3 ....**$65.00**
Timmy Willie, brown mouse on lt green base, B3 .....**$45.00**
Timmy Willie, brown mouse on lt green base, B6 .....**$65.00**
Tom Kitten, dark blue outfit, 1st version, B3 ....**$85.00**
Tom Kitten, light blue outfit, B10...........................**$50.00**
Tom Kitten, light blue outfit, B4............................**$75.00**
Tom Thumb, mouse in chimney, B3..........................**$85.00**
Tom Thumb, mouse in chimney, B6..........................**$55.00**
Tommy Brock, lg patch on eyes, 2nd version, B3......**$65.00**

Beer Cans

In January of 1935 the Continental Can Co. approached a New Jersey brewery with the novel idea of selling beer in cans. After years of research, Continental had perfected a plastic coating for the inside of the can which prevented the beer from contacting and adversely reacting to metal. Consumers liked the idea and throw-away beer cans soon replaced returnable bottles as the most popular container in which to purchase beer.

The first beer can was a steel flat top which actually bore a picture of the newly invented 'can opener' and instructions on how to use it. Because most breweries were not equipped to fill a flat can, a 'cone top' was invented to facilitate passage through the bottle filler. By the 1950s the cone top was obsolete. Ten years later, can companies introduced a 'tab top' can which made the can opener unnecessary. Aluminum cans and cans ranging in size from six-ounce to one-gallon were popularized during the 1960s.

Beer can collecting reached its heyday during the 1970s. Thousands of collectors bought, drank, and saved cans throughout America. Unfortunately, the number of collectors receded, creating a huge supply of cans with minimal demand. There are many valuable beer cans today — however, they pre-date 1970. A post-1970 can worth more than a few dollars is rare.

Values are based on cans in conditions as stated. A can with flaws — rust, fading, or scratches — may still have value; however, it is generally much less than its excellent condition counterpart. Unless noted otherwise, all of the cans we list here are the 12-ounce size. The letters 'IRTP' in some of our descriptions stand for 'Internal Revenue Tax Paid.'

Newsletter: *Beer Cans and Brewery Collectibles*
Beer Can Collectors of America
747 Merus Ct., Fenton, MO 63026-2092
Fax/phone: 314-343-6486; e-mail: bcca@bcca.com
www.bcca.com Subscription: $30 per year for US residents; includes 6 issues and right to attend national CANvention©

Cone tops: Braumeister Pilsener, Independent Brg., Milwaukee, WI, VG, $50.00; Stegmaiers Gold Medal Beer, Stegmaiers Brg., Wilkes-Barre, PA, EX, $85.00; Goetz Country Club, M.K. Goetz Brg., St. Joseph, MO, EX+, $40.00.

Cone top, American Beer, American Brewing/Baltimore,
    1940s, VG **$70.00**
Cone top, Berghoff 1887 Beer, Berghoff Brewing/Ft Wayne,
    IRTP, EX...**$40.00**
Cone top, Beverwyck Famous Beer, Beverwyck
    Brewing/Albany, 1930s, EX+ **$110.00**
Cone top, Blatz Old Heidelberg Beer, Blatz
    Brewing/Milwaukee, IRTP, NM-..........................**$75.00**
Cone top, Burger Premium Quality, Burger Brewing,
    Cincinnati, 1950s, VG+ **$78.00**
Cone top Champagne Velvet Beer, Terre Haute Brewing,
    Terre Haute, EX+ **$35.00**
Cone top, Country Club Beer, MK Goetz Brewing/St Joseph,
    EX+ **$40.00**
Cone top, Dawson's Master Ale, Dawson's Brewing/New
    Bedford, IRTP, NM-...**$75.00**
Cone top, E&B Special Beer, E&B Brewing/Detroit, 1940s,
    EX+ **$40.00**
Cone top, Eastside Beer, Los Angeles Brewing/Los Angeles,
    IRTP, NM- **$55.00**
Cone top, Gibbons Beer, Lion Inc/Wilkes-Barre, 12-oz,
    EX...**$45.00**
Cone top, Gipps Amberlin Beer, Gipps Brewing/Peoria,
    EX+ **$30.00**
Cone top, Gold Star Beer, Hoff-Brau Brewing/Ft Wayne,
    IRTP, EX..**$55.00**
Cone top, Heileman's Beer, G Heileman Brewing/Lacrosse,
    Permis Dis #7-U-729, flat bottom, EX **$120.00**

Cone top, Kuebler Pilsner Beer, Kuebler Brewing/Easton, 1930s, G+ **$100.00**

Cone top, Oertels '92 Lager Beer, Oertels Brewing/Louisville, 1950s, VG **$40.00**

Cone top, Old German Beer, Queen City Brewing, Cumberland, EX **$30.00**

Cone top, Ortileb's Beer, HF Ortileb Brewing/Philadelphia, EX..**$40.00**

Cone top, Schlitz, Schlitz Brewing/Milwaukee, 1940s, EX **$50.00**

Cone top, Stoney's Pilsner Beer, Jones Brewing/Smithton, NM **$75.00**

Cone top, Wooden Shoe Lager Beer, Wooden Shoe Brewing/Minster, IRTP, NM..**$60.00**

Crowntainer, Altes Lager Beer, Tivoli Brewing/Detroit, IRTP, EX..**$45.00**

Crowntainer, Ebling Premium Beer, Ebling Brewing/New York, 1940s, EX..**$45.00**

Crowntainer, Fitzgerald's Burgomaster Beer, Fitzgerald Bros/Troy, enameled, 1940s, EX+..**$60.00**

Crowntainer, Gluek's Beer, Gluek Brewing/Minneapolis, 1940s, EX+..**$35.00**

Crowntainer, Neuweiller's Pilsner Beer, Neuweiller Brewing/Allentown, 1940s, EX+ **$30.00**

Crowntainer, Oertel's 92 Beer, Oertel Brewing/Louisville, IRTP, EX+..**$35.00**

Crowntainer, Old Shay Beer, Fort Pitt Brewing/Jeannette, 1940s, G+..**$70.00**

Flat top, Balboa Export Beer, Southern Brewing/Los Angeles, 1940s, VG **$65.00**

Flat top, Ballantine XXX Ale, Ballantine Brewing/Newark, NM **$25.00**

Flat top, Banner Extra Dry Premium Beer, Burkhardt Brewing/Akron, 1950s, EX+ **$20.00**

Flat top, Bull Dog Ale, Grace Bros/Santa Rosa, 1950s, EX+..**$20.00**

Flat top, Canadian Ace Bock Beer, Canadian Ace Brewing/Chicago, opened, NM+ **$50.00**

Flat top, Fergenspan Light Beer, C Fergenspan Brewing/Newark, IRTP, NM+..**$100.00**

Flat top, Fox Head Malt Liquor, Fox Head Brewing/Waukesha, EX..**$40.00**

Flat top, GEM Premium Beer, F&S Brewing/Shamokin, 12-oz, EX..**$20.00**

Flat top, Keglet Beer, Esslinger Inc/Philadelphia, EX+ ..**$45.00**

Flat top, Krueger Cream Ale, Kreuger Brewing/Newark, 1950s, VG **$50.00**

Flat top, O'Shanter Ale (Dry Hopped), American Brewing/Rochester, gray version, 1930s, NM **$150.00**

Flat top, Old German Brand Beer, Lebanon Valley/Lebanon, 1950s, NM+..**$40.00**

Flat top, Senate 250 Beer, Heurichs Brewing/Washington, 1950s, EX+..**$70.00**

Flat top, Steinbeck Lager Beer, Grace Bros Brewing/Santa Rosa, 1950s, EX..**$20.00**

Flat top, Topper Light Dry Beer, Rochester Brewing/Rochester, 1950s, VG+ **$30.00**

Pull tab, Bananza Premium Beer, Old Dutch Brewing/Allentown, 1970s, NM **$10.00**

Pull tab, Gibbons Season's Best, Lion Inc/Wilkes-Barre, 1960s, EX+..**$100.00**

Pull tab, Grand Union Beer, Eastern Brewing/Hammonton, NM..**$5.00**

Pull tab, Jax Draft Beer, Jackson Brewing/New Orleans, 1960s, EX+..**$15.00**

Pull tab, Ox-Bow Beer, Walter Brewing/Pueblo, 1970s, EX+..**$25.00**

Pull tab, Schmidt's Ale, Schmidt's Brewing/Philadelphia, 1960s, NM..**$15.00**

Pull tab, Waldbaums Premium Lager Beer, Eastern Brewing/Hammonton, 1970s, EX+ **$10.00**

Zip tab, Dawson Diamond Ale, Dawson's Brewing/New Bedford, bottom opened, 1956, NM+..**$25.00**

Bellaire, Marc

Marc Bellaire, originally Donald Edmund Fleischman, was born in Toledo, Ohio, in 1925. He studied at the Toledo Museum of Art under Ernest Spring while employed as a designer for the Libbey Glass Company. During World War II while serving in the Navy, he traveled extensively throughout the Pacific, resulting in his enriched sense of design and color.

Marc settled in California in the 1950s where his work attracted the attention of national buyers and agencies who persuaded him to create ceramic lines of his own, employing hand-decorated techniques throughout. As a result, he founded a studio in Culver City. There he produced high quality ceramics often decorated with ultra-modern figures or geometric patterns and executed with a distinctive flair. His most famous pattern was Mardi Gras, decorated with slim dancers on spattered or striped colors of black, blue, pink and white. Other major patterns were Jamaica, Balinese, Beachcomber, Friendly Island, Cave Painting, Hawaiian, Bird Isle, Oriental, Jungle Dancer, and Kashmir. (Kashmir usually has the name Ingle on the front and Bellaire on the back.)

It is to be noted that Marc was employed by Sascha Brastoff during the '50s. Many believe that he was hired for his creative imagination and style.

During the period 1951 – 1956, Marc was named one of the top ten artware designers by *Giftwares Magazine*. After 1956 he taught and lectured on art, design, and ceramic decorating techniques from coast to coast. Many of his pieces were one of a kind, and his work was commissioned throughout the United States.

During the 1970s he worked from his studio in Marin County, California. He eventually moved to Palm Springs where he set up his final studio/gallery. There he produced large pieces with a Southwestern style. Mr. Bellaire died in 1994.

Advisor: Marty Webster (See Directory, California Pottery)

Ashtray, Clown, multicolor on cream, 7"....................**$65.00**
Bowl, Beachcomber, low teardrop shape, 12" L.......**$100.00**

Bowl, dancing harlequins, footed, 7½" dia **$80.00**
Figurine, Jamaica man playing guitar.......................**$300.00**
Platter, Friendly Island, 10" **$135.00**
Tray, abstract guitarist in black w/white trim playing blue guitar, sq, 13¼" **$125.00**
Tray, Jungle Dancer, figure on black & green, 12" dia ..**$135.00**
Vase, abstract leaves on pink mottled background, 13¾" **$150.00**
Vase, Polynesian Woman, 9" **$100.00**

Bells

Bell collectors claim that bells rank second only to the wheel as being useful to mankind. Down through the ages bells have awakened people in the morning, called them to meals and prayers, and readied them to retire at night. We have heard them called rising bells, Angelus Bells (for deaths), noon bells, Town Crier bells (for important announcements), and curfew bells. Souvenir bells are often the first type collected, with interest spreading to other contemporaries, then on to old, more valuable bells. As far as limited edition bells are concerned, the fewer made per bell, the better. (For example a bell made in an edition of 25,000 will not appreciate as much as one from an edition of 5,000.)

For further information we recommend *World of Bells #5*, *Bell Tidings*, *Lure of Bells*, *Collectible Bells*, *More Bell Lore*, *Bells Now and Long Ago*, and *Legendary Bells*, all by Dorothy Malone Anthony.

Advisor: Dorothy Malone Anthony (See Directory, Bells)

Newsletter: *The Bell Tower*
The American Bell Association
P.O. Box 19443, Indianapolis, IN 46219

Porcelain, man, orange and blue in pink hat, Japan, 4¼", $25.00; lady, black hair, lavender coat, Japan, 4½", $25.00. (Photo courtesy Carole Bess White)

Brass, Colonial lady reading book figural, full skirt forms bell, fine old patina, 4x2" **$125.00**

Brass, elegant lady figural, much detail, skirt forms bell, 4½" **$155.00**
Brass, Elizabethan lady w/hands on hips figural, boot clapper..**$85.00**
Brass, girl w/umbrella figural, shoes are clappers, #6949 5¾" **$80.00**
Brass, lady in bonnet figural, 3x2" **$55.00**
Brass, monkey & octopus form handle, dragon on bell, Oriental w/artist signature, replaced clapper, 4¾" ..**$60.00**
Brass, school type, cast-iron clapper, turned wood handle, 7x4" **$60.00**
Brass, school type, original handle, EX patina, 12" ..**$150.00**
Brass, wall-mount style, recent reproduction, heavy, solid, 6x6½" dia **$40.00**
Brass cast-iron leaves & fruit w/cast-iron parrot handle, original paint (worn), 4⅞" **$50.00**
China, Beguiling Buttercup, Norman Rockwell, Gorham, 1979, 9x4" **$14.00**
China, butterflies w/gold on white, Royal Worcester .**$15.00**
China, Countryware, white w/molded overlapping petals, green Coalport crown mark, 4x2¼" **$17.50**
China, delicate flowers on white, Aynsley, 5½" **$22.50**
China, flowers on white, Coalport, Danbury Mint, 4" **$20.00**
China, Franciscan Desert Rose, Danbury Mint, 4¾" ...**$30.00**
China, green shamrocks on white, Royal Tara (Ireland), MIB **$25.00**
China, hand-painted flowers w/gold trim, porcelain clapper on metal wire, Hammersley & Co, 5¾" **$50.00**
China, lg open flower among greenery, artist signed w/gold at handle, attributed to Limoges (unmarked), 4x2⅞" **$40.00**
China, Meadow Sweet, bone china, Wedgwood, 4¼x2⅛" **$20.00**
China, violets & pansies on white bone china, Florence Collectables, Made in England, 4x2½" **$15.00**
Glass, amethyst w/etched flowers & leaves, crystal clapper, 4¾x2¼" **$30.00**
Glass, Bicentennial Liberty Bell, on wooden base, Seneca Glass, 4½" **$40.00**
Glass, blue, embossed leaves, faceted clapper, Viking ..**$25.00**
Glass, cobalt w/embossed ribs, blown, hand-signed Lundburg Studios, 4" **$35.00**
Glass, cobalt w/multicolor spatter handle, marked Ofnah Crystal Made in Czech Republic, 7" **$30.00**
Glass, cranberry, Mary Gregory-style boy, recent, 6"..**$35.00**
Glass, Daisy cutting, solid clapper on chain, Pairpoint, 6" **$250.00**
Glass, green w/Mary Gregory-style boy in landscape, recent, 5" **$30.00**
Glass, hand-painted roses on custard, souvenir Ely Minn w/gold, 6x3¼" **$100.00**
Glass, Harvard-cut band above 2 engraved flowers, cut handle, 5x2¾" **$375.00**
Glass, milk glass w/shield design, ruffled edge, 5¾x4¼"....**$45.00**
Glass, orange w/yellow curled handle, marked Ofnah Crystal Made in Czech Republic, 5" **$25.00**
Glass, ribbons of colors in clear, hand-blown, Italy sticker, 5" **$32.00**

Glass, ruby, Diamond Quilt, Viking, 5¾" $25.00

Glass, ruby w/engraved initial, red & white latticinio handle w/5 knobs, Pairpoint, 10¾x4⅞" $245.00

Glass, strawberry diamond & fan cuttings, glass clapper, 5½x2¾" $170.00

Glass, swirled brown, gold, pink & blue carnival colors, Pilgrim Glass sticker, 7"..$110.00

Glass, yellow & white wavy stripes, yellow & white latticinio handle w/6 knobs, Pairpoint, 10½x5½" $220.00

Porcelain, Cinderella figural, Happy Holidays 1999, Disney, 4" $25.00

Porcelain, farmer lady figural, flowers on skirt, gold trim, Czech, 5"...$30.00

Porcelain, hand-painted cherubs, lions & leopards, brass handle w/openwork, Capodimonte, 12¼x4"........$60.00

Porcelain, Mother's Day, Snoopy & Woodstock w/red roses, Schultz, Japan foil label, 1978.............................$32.50

Porcelain, Southern lady figural, marked Germany, #3557, 4¼" $55.00

Silver plate, Christmas caroler, Reed & Barton, 4¾" ...$15.00

Silver plate, Lincoln's Birthday commemorative, Reed & Barton, 4¾" $15.00

Silver plate, Mother's Day commemorative, mother w/new-born baby, Reed & Barton, 4¾" $15.00

Sterling silver, ancient warriors & fortress design, marked 925 & initialed MME, 3¾x2¾x2" $70.00

Sterling silver, Baloo figural handle, Disney limited edition $50.00

Sterling silver, llama figural handle, allover intricate engravings, marked 925, illegible hallmark, 3⅜".............$65.00

Sterling silver, simple sleek styling, eagle & lion touchmark of Reed & Barton, 4½" $65.00

Black Americana

There are many avenues one might pursue in the broad field of Black Americana and many reasons that might entice one to become a collector. For the more serious, there are documents such as bills of sale for slaves, broadsides, and other historical artifacts. But by and far, most collectors enjoy attractive advertising pieces, novelties and kitchenware items, toys and dolls, and Black celebrity memorabilia.

It's estimated that there are at least 50,000 collectors around the country today that specialize in this field. There are large auctions devoted entirely to the sale of Black Americana. The items they feature may be as common as a homemade pot holder or a magazine or as rare as a Lux Dixie Boy clock or a Mammy cookie jar that might go for several thousand dollars. In fact, many of the cookie jars have become so valuable that they're being reproduced; so are salt and pepper shakers, so beware.

For further study, we recommend *Black Collectibles Sold in America* by P.J. Gibbs.

See also Advertising, Aunt Jemima; Condiment Sets; Cookie Jars; Postcards; Salt and Pepper Shakers; Sheet Music; String Holders.

Advisor: Judy Posner (See Directory, Black Americana)

Ashtray, Dinah's Pancake & Chicken House, red graphics on clear glass, 1940s, 4¼" dia, EX $70.00

Ashtray, multicolored bobbin'-head boy on copper-colored tin bowl opposite double rest, marked Made in Japan, 4¼", EX $200.00

Book, color & fun; Sambo's Circus, by Bill Woggon, includes paper dolls, early 1960s, uncut, M $45.00

Book, coloring; Little Brown Koko, illustrated by Dorothy Wadstaff, 1941, 22 pages, unused, EX $125.00

Book, Little Black Sambo Magic Drawing Book, Platt & Munk #037A, artist-signed cover, 1946, 14 pages, EX ..$100.00

Book, Little Brown Koko, 1940, 1st edition, hardcover, 96 pages, EX...$90.00

Book, Story of the Mississippi, Harper, 1941, multicolored, hardcover, 40 pages, 10x11", EX $75.00

Book, Three Golliwogs Wiggie, Waggie & Wollie, by Enid Blyton, 1956, softcover, EX $50.00

Book & record set, Little Black Sambo, Music You Enjoy Inc, copyright 1941, 15 pages, EX $125.00

Book set, Charlotte Steiner's Story-Book Theatre, Little Black Sambo w/5 other story books, 1944, EX............$225.00

Box, Amos 'n Andy Candy, cardboard, Williamson Candy Co., 12" x 8½", G, $100.00. (Photo courtesy Collectors Auction Services)

Candy container, cardboard, porter pushing trunk, 1930s, EX+ $85.00

Canister, ceramic, head shape w/Coffee lettered on hair (lid) of tan-skinned girl w/glancing eyes, 5" $100.00

Card, birthday; Because You're 4 Today, golliwog, bear, toy soldier & clown, 4¾x4¼", M $30.00

Card, get-well; Hurry Honey & Get Well, Mammy at crystal ball, 1930s, EX...$22.00

Cigar lighter, cast-iron head of man looking up w/open mouth (insert cigar in mouth & push button to light), 6", VG $80.00

Clock, Smoking Sambo, sq w/image on paperboard face, wooden frame, 1930s, 15¼x15¼", VG+..............$200.00

Coffee container, Luzianne Mammy Instant Coffee, glass bottle w/label, tin lid, dated 1953, 4½", unused, M........$125.00

Cookbook, Aunt Jemima's Magical Recipes, Aunt Jemima on cover, 1954, 26 pages, EX $55.00

Decanter & shot cups, ceramic, boy on elephant, hand-painted, 4 plastic cups, Japan, ca 1949, 7".....................**$65.00**

Dinner bell, ceramic, Mammy figure, by Carolina, Laguna Beach, 1940s, EX **$65.00**

Display figure, smiling bakery chef standing w/arms open to hold sign or product, composition, 1937, 18", EX .**$325.00**

Doll, girl, hard plastic w/synthetic rooted hair, jointed at shoulders & hips, Beatrice Wright, ca 1967, 18", EX.......**$275.00**

Doll, girl, stuffed cloth w/painted eyes & mouth, stiff arms & legs, original sunsuit outfit, 1930-50, 6½", EX....**$100.00**

Doll, pickaninny, inflatable plastic w/flasher eyes, yellow skirt & hair bow, 10", EX **$35.00**

Egg timer, diecut wooden Mammy figure w/painted red dress & bandanna, white apron, 1930s, EX.................**$100.00**

Figure, cast metal, girl on potty, exaggerated features & open mouth, painted details, 4", EX **$250.00**

Figure, cast metal, man w/gigantic watermelon atop fence, painted details, Manoil, 1930s, 3" **$165.00**

Figure, celluloid, drummer standing wide-eyed in red jacket & blue pants, blue bow tie, 1930s, 9", EX..........**$110.00**

Fishing lure, Sam-Bo The Gloom Killer, painted plastic figure, 4½", EX (VG box)..**$55.00**

Game, Noddy's Ring Toss, England, 1960s, EXIB.....**$125.00**

Game, Snake Eyes, Selchow & Righter, 1941, NMIB ..**$100.00**

Handkerchief, golliwog, cotton, tan & brown on white, Made in Ireland label, 1940s, EX **$100.00**

Hat, paper, Sambo's Restaurant, colorful logo, Cellucap PA, 1960s, NM..**$85.00**

Humidor, hand-painted porcelain head form of smiling man in wooden lift-off hat, white collar, 7½", EX+......**$85.00**

Jack-in-the-box, Munchie Melon, Marx, 1960s, 8", NM ..**$150.00**

Matchcover, Club Plantation, Man Dat Sho Was Good!, black & white graphics w/red details, EX.......................**$40.00**

Menu, Club Plantation souvenir, naughty exaggerated ethnic female w/chain & lock on panties, 1940s, 6½x5", EX .**$70.00**

Menu, Sambo's Restaurant, 1967, 15", EX....................**$85.00**

Money clip, Coon Chicken Inn, brass color w/Black-face logo, 2½", unused, M **$10.00**

Mug, china, image of golliwog atop Santa's full sack of toys, gold trim, 4", EX **$75.00**

Mug, Uncle Ben's Rice 40th anniversary commemorative, 1943-83, M **$45.00**

Nodder, native figure, papier-mache, Woolworth, 1940s, 5", EX **$125.00**

Peanut vendor, Smilin' Sam the Salted Peanut Man, painted cast aluminum head, General Merchandise Co, 14", EX **$2,050.00**

Photo folder, Memories of Club Plantation, cover shows banjo player & cotton bale, 1940s, EX..................**$40.00**

Pincushion, cotton picker figure holding bale (cushion), velvet & cotton, 1920s, 4½", EX **$65.00**

Pitcher, earthenware, repeated images of Little Black Sambo, painted scalloped design on rim, 1930s, 3", EX.**$125.00**

Postcard, RCA Victor promotion w/Duke Ellington as Victor's Celebrated Jazz Composer-Pianist, 1940s, EX.......**$25.00**

Poster, Louis Satchmo Armstrong, L'Ambassadeur Du Jazz Bruxelles, red & black on white, 1958, 21x14", EX .**$125.00**

Print, Joe Lewis in Brown & Bigelow Tobacco Co boxing pose, ca 1935, 12x9½", VG **$30.00**

Record album, Delta Rhythm Boys, Dry Bones, 78 rpm, 4-record set, EX (w/cover).......................................**$65.00**

Salt dip server, ceramic, fisherman sitting & smoking pipe, 1940s, 5½", EX..**$225.00**

Sheet music, Blue Boogie, black & blue graphics, 1944, EX **$32.00**

Sign, Fairway Golf Balls, diecut cardboard image of Black boy on green w/flag pole watching ball go into hole, 48", EX **$550.00**

Sign, Golly It's Good!, diecut cardboard golliwog figure, J Robertson & Sons/England, 1950s-60s, 10", EX+..**$60.00**

Sign, Mil-Kay/The Vitamin Drink, cardboard, diecut filigree frame surrounds waiter holding up tray, 17x28", EX+ **$135.00**

Sign, Oxydol Soap, diecut cardboard bust image of Mammy holding up & pointing to product box, early, 10x8½", NM+ **$450.00**

Sign, Smoking Sambo, diecut paperboard figure on tin back w/felt-lined bottom stand, red, white & blue, 16", EX **$85.00**

Sign, Stephen's Hair Lotion, diecut cardboard, head image of native amid advertising & drum on post, 21x16", VG **$50.00**

Stacking Blocks, features Sambo & Tiger, 1940s, set of 5, EX **$125.00**

Tablecloth, Dinah's Shack, cloth, corner images of Dinah, name & steaming dishes, red, white & blue, 48x48", NM **$95.00**

Teapot, Gone With the Wind commemorative figural of Hattie McDaniel as Mammy, 50th anniversary, 1990, M **$125.00**

Tumbler, Old Folks at Home, Uncle Mose dancing before cabin, clear w/black & white fired-on decor, 1940s, 5", M **$35.00**

Wall caddy, diecut wood Mammy w/white ruffled collar, diecut utensils hold hooks, 1930s, 9½", EX........**$100.00**

Wall plaque, chalkware, woman w/fruit basket, 1940-50s, 7", EX **$100.00**

Whirligig, hand-painted aluminum folk art figure of man sawing log, 1940s, EX..**$24.00**

Wind-up toy, tin figure of boy w/hands lithoed in front & hands embossed at sides, dances in circles, 4½", EX+ **$120.00**

Black Cats

Kitchenware, bookends, vases, and many other items designed as black cats were made in Japan during the 1950s and exported to the United States where they were sold by various distributors who often specified certain characteristics they wanted in their own line of cats. Common to all these lines were the red clay used in their production and the medium used in their decoration — their features were applied over the glaze with cold (unfired) paint. The most collectible is a line marked (or labeled) Shafford. Shafford cats are plump and pleasant looking. They have green eyes with black pupils; white eyeliner, eyelashes, and whiskers; and red bow ties. The same design with yellow eyes was marketed by Royal, and another fairly easy-to-find 'breed' is a line by Wales with yellow eyes and gold whiskers. You'll find various other labels as well. Some collectors buy only Shafford, while others like them all.

When you evaluate your black cats, be critical of their paint. Even though no chips or cracks are present, if half of the paint is missing, you have a half-price item (if that). Collectors are very critical. These are readily available on Internet auctions, and unless pristine, they realize prices much lower than ours. Remember this when using the following values which are given for cats with near-mint to mint paint.

**Cruets, oil and vinegar, Shafford, 7½",
from $60.00 to $75.00 for the set.**

Ashtray, flat face, Shafford, hard-to-find size, 3¾"......**$50.00**

Ashtray, flat face, Shafford, 4¾" **$18.00**

Ashtray, head shape, not Shafford, several variations, ea from $12 to...**$15.00**

Ashtray, head shape w/open mouth, Shafford, 3", from $25 to...**$30.00**

Bank, seated cat w/coin slot in top of head, Shafford, from $225 to..**$275.00**

Bank, upright cat, Shafford-like features, marked Tommy, 2-part, from $150 to...**$175.00**

Cigarette lighter, Shafford, 5½"...................................**$175.00**

Cigarette lighter, sm cat stands on book by table lamp..**$65.00**

Condiment set, upright cats, yellow eyes, 2 bottles & pr of matching shakers in wireware stand, row arrangement **$95.00**

Condiment set, 2 joined heads, J & M bows w/spoons (intact), Shafford, 4"...**$95.00**

Condiment set, 2 joined heads, yellow eyes, not Shafford **$65.00**

Cookie jar, cat's head, fierce expression, yellow eyes, brown-black glaze, heavy red clay, rare, lg **$250.00**

Cookie jar, cat's head, Shafford, from $80 to **$100.00**

Creamer & sugar bowl, cat-head lids are salt & pepper shakers, yellow eyes variation, 5⅜"..............................**$50.00**

Creamer & sugar bowl, Shafford **$45.00**

Cruet, slender form, gold collar & tie, tail handle **$12.00**

Cruet, upright cat w/yellow eyes, open mouth, paw spout **$30.00**

Cruets, oil & vinegar; cojoined cats, Royal Sealy, 1-pc (or similar examples w/heavier yellow-eyed cats), 7¼"..**$40.00**

Decanter, long cat w/red fish in his mouth as stopper .**$75.00**

Decanter, upright cat holds bottle w/cork stopper, Shafford..**$50.00**

Decanter set, upright cat, yellow eyes, +6 plain wines .**$35.00**

Decanter set, upright cat, yellow eyes, +6 wines w/cat faces **$50.00**

Demitasse pot, tail handle, bow finial, Shafford, 7½"..**$165.00**

Desk caddy, pen forms tail, spring body holds letters, 6½" **$8.00**

Egg cup, cat face on bowl, pedestal foot, Shafford, from $95 to..**$125.00**

Grease jar, sm cat head, Shafford, scarce, from $95 to..**$110.00**

Ice bucket, cylindrical w/embossed yellow-eyed cat face, 2 sizes, ea **$75.00**

Measuring cups, 4 sizes on wooden wall-mount rack w/painted cat face, Shafford, rare, from $350 to...............**$400.00**

Mug, Shafford, cat handle w/head above rim, standard, 3½"..**$55.00**

Mug, Shafford, cat handle w/head below rim, scarce, 3½"..**$95.00**

Mug, Shafford, scarce, 4", from $70 to........................**$80.00**

Paperweight, cat's head on stepped chrome base, open mouth, yellow eyes, rare.......................................**$75.00**

Pincushion, cushion on cat's back, tongue measure ..**$25.00**

Pitcher, milk; seated upright cat, ear forms spout, tail handle, Shafford, 6" or 6½", ea...**$150.00**

Pitcher, squatting cat, pour through mouth, Shafford, rare, 5", 14½" circumference **$90.00**

Pitcher, squatting cat, pour through mouth, Shafford, scarce, 4½", 13" circumference...**$75.00**

Pitcher, squatting cat, pour through mouth, Shafford, very rare, 5½", 17" circumference...............................**$250.00**

Planter, cat & kitten in a hat, Shafford-like paint........**$30.00**

Planter, cat sits on knitted boot w/gold drawstring, Shafford-like paint, Elvin, 4¼x4½" **$30.00**

Planter, upright cat, Shafford-like paint, Napco label, 6"...**$20.00**

Pot holder caddy, 'teapot' cat, 3 hooks, Shafford, from $170 to...**$195.00**

Salad set, spoon & fork, funnel, 1-pc oil & vinegar cruet & salt & pepper shakers on wooden wall-mount rack, Royal Sealy..**$200.00**

Salt & pepper shakers, long crouching cat, shaker in ea end, Shafford, 10"..**$165.00**

Salt & pepper shakers, range size; upright cats, Shafford, scarce, 5", pr...**$65.00**

Salt & pepper shakers, round-bodied 'teapot' cat, Shafford, pr from $125 to..**$140.00**

Salt & pepper shakers, seated, blue eyes, Enesco label, 5¾", pr..**$15.00**

Salt & pepper shakers, upright cats, Shafford, 3¾" (watch for slightly smaller set as well), pr **$25.00**

Spice set, triangle, 3 rounded tiers of shakers, 8 in all, in wooden wall-mount triangular rack, very rare...**$450.00**

Spice set, 4 upright cat shakers hook onto bottom of wire-ware cat-face rack, Shafford, rare........................**$450.00**

Spice set, 6 sq shakers in wooden frame, Shafford..........**$175.00**

Spice set, 6 sq shakers in wooden frame, yellow eyes **$125.00**

Stacking tea set, mamma pot w/kitty creamer & sugar bowl, yellow eyes...**$85.00**

Stacking tea set, 3 cats w/red collar, w/gold ball, yellow eyes, 3-pc **$80.00**

Sugar bowl/planter, sitting cat, red bow w/gold bell, Shafford-like paint, Elvin, 4" **$25.00**

Teapot, bulbous body, head lid, green eyes, lg, Shafford, 7" **$75.00**

Teapot, bulbous body, head lid, green eyes, Shafford, med size, from $40 to **$45.00**

Teapot, bulbous body, head lid, green eyes, Shafford, sm, 4" - 4½" **$30.00**

Teapot, cat face w/double spout, Shafford, scarce, 5", from $200 to **$250.00**

Teapot, cat's face, yellow hat, blue & white eyes, pink ears, lg, from $40 to **$50.00**

Teapot, crouching cat, paw up to right ear is spout, green jeweled eyes, 8½" L...................................**$80.00**

Teapot, panther-like appearance, gold eyes, sm.........**$20.00**

Teapot, upright, slender cat (not ball-shaped), lift-off head, Shafford, rare, 8"...................................**$250.00**

Teapot, upright cat w/paw spout, yellow eyes & red bow, Wales, 8¼" **$60.00**

Teapot, yellow eyes, 1-cup **$30.00**

Teapot, yellow-eyed cat face embossed on front of standard bulbous teapot shape, wire bail **$60.00**

Thermometer, cat w/yellow eyes stands w/paw on round thermometer face **$30.00**

Toothpick holder, cat on vase atop book, Occupied Japan **$12.00**

Tray, flat face, wicker handle, Shafford, rare, lg.......**$185.00**

Utensil rack, flat-backed cat w/3 slots for utensils, cat only..**$125.00**

Wall pocket, flat-backed 'teapot' cat, Shafford..........**$125.00**

Wine, embossed cat's face, green eyes, Shafford, sm.**$75.00**

Blair Dinnerware

American dinnerware has been a popular field of collecting for several years, and the uniquely styled lines of Blair Ceramics are very appealing, though not often seen except in the Midwest (and it's there that prices are the strongest). Blair was located in Ozark, Missouri, manufacturing dinnerware only from the mid-'40s until the early '50s. Gay Plaid, recognized by its squared-off shapes and brush-stroke design (in lime, brown, and dark green on white), is the pattern you'll find most often. Several other lines were made as well. You'll be able to recognize all of them easily enough, since most pieces (except for the smaller items) are marked.

Bowl, fruit/cereal; Gay Plaid, 6½" sq, from $8 to **$10.00**

Bowl, onion soup; Gay Plaid, w/lid, rope handle......**$20.00**

Bowl, Rick-Rack **$12.00**

Casserole, Gay Plaid, rope handles............................**$37.00**

Coffeepot, Gay Plaid **$25.00**

Creamer, Bamboo, rope handle................................**$17.00**

Creamer, Gay Plaid, rope handle **$16.00**

Cup, Autumn Leaf, rope handle **$10.00**

Cup & saucer, Gay Plaid, closed handle....................**$17.00**

Cup & saucer, Gay Plaid, rope handle........................**$12.00**

Nut dish, Autumn Leaf...**$8.00**

Plate, dinner; Bamboo, square $14.00.

Plate, dinner; Gay Plaid...**$14.00**

Plate, luncheon; Bamboo, 8" sq................................**$8.00**

Plate, serving; Yellow Plaid, divided **$30.00**

Salt & pepper shakers, Gay Plaid, pr **$14.00**

Sugar bowl, Bamboo, w/lid, rope handle **$17.00**

Tumbler, Gay Plaid..**$14.00**

Blue Danube

A modern-day interpretation of the early Meissen Blue Onion pattern, Blue Danube is an extensive line of quality dinnerware that has been produced in Japan since the early 1950s and distributed by Lipper International of Wallingford, Connecticut. It is said that the original design was inspired by a pattern created during the Yuan Dynasty (1260 – 1368) in China. This variation is attributed to the German artist Kandleva. The flowers depicted in this blue-on-white dinnerware represent the ancient Chinese symbols of good fortune and happiness. The original design, with some variations, made its way to Eastern Europe where it has been produced for about two hundred years. It is regarded today as one of the world's most famous patterns.

At least one hundred twenty-five items have at one time or another been made available by the Lipper company, making it the most complete line of dinnerware now available in the United States. Collectors tend to pay higher prices for items with the earlier banner mark (1951 to 1976), and reticulated (openweave) pieces bring a premium. Unusual serving or decorative items generally command high prices as well. The more common items that are still being produced usually sell for less than retail on the secondary market.

The banner logo includes the words 'Reg US Pat Off' along with the pattern name. In 1976 the logo was redesigned and the pattern name within a rectangular box with an 'R' in circle to the right of it was adopted. Very similar lines of dinnerware have been produced by other companies, but these two marks are the indication of genuine Lipper Blue Danube. Among the copycats you may encounter are Mascot and Vienna Woods — there are probably others.

Advisor: Lori Simnionie (See the Directory under Blue Danube)

Baker, oval, 10", from $50 to **$55.00**
Bell, 6" **$25.00**
Biscuit jar, 9", from $50 to... **$60.00**
Bone dish/side salad; crescent shape, banner mark, 9", from $12 to.. **$15.00**
Bowl, cereal; banner mark, 6" **$12.00**
Bowl, cream soup; w/lid, from $30 to.......................... **$35.00**
Bowl, dessert; 5½", from $8 to **$10.00**
Bowl, divided vegetable; 11x7½" **$50.00**
Bowl, heart shape, 2¼x8½" **$65.00**
Bowl, lattice edge, 9", from $50 to............................... **$60.00**
Bowl, low pedestal skirted base, shaped rim, banner mark, 2x9x12", from $70 to **$80.00**
Bowl, soup; 8½" **$15.00**
Bowl, vegetable; oval, 10" L, from $30 to.................... **$40.00**
Bowl, vegetable; 3¼x10", from $45 to **$50.00**
Bowl, vegetable; 9", from $35 to **$40.00**
Bowl, wedding; w/lid, footed, sq, 8½x5", from $55 to **$65.00**
Box, white lacquerware, gold label w/rectangular logo, 2¼x4½"... **$30.00**
Butter dish, round, 8½"... **$85.00**

Cake breaker, $35.00; Trivet, 6" dia, $25.00.
(From the collection of Elaine France)

Cache pot, w/handles, 8x8"... **$45.00**
Cake pedestal, lattice edge, rectangular mark, 5x10" . **$75.00**
Cake pedestal, 4x10" **$55.00**
Cake server & knife, from $25 to **$30.00**
Candelabra, 5-light, 12x11" **$225.00**
Candlesticks, 6½", pr from $40 to............................... **$50.00**
Candy dish, w/lid, from $50 to.................................... **$60.00**
Casserole, individual; banner mark, 6" across handles ..**$35.00**
Casserole, 5½x10½" across handles **$65.00**
Chamber stick, Old Fashioned, 4x6" dia...................... **$25.00**
Cheese board, wooden, w/6" dia tile & glass dome, from $25 to **$35.00**
Chop plate, 12" dia.. **$40.00**
Coasters, set of 4, from $25 to **$35.00**
Coffee mug, 3⅛", set of 4 from $55 to **$60.00**
Coffeepot, embossed applied spout, ornate handle, 7½", from $60 to **$70.00**
Coffeepot, 6", from $40 to **$50.00**
Condiment bowl, 2½" deep, w/saucer, 6¾" **$25.00**
Cookie jar **$65.00**
Creamer, bulbous, 3½".. **$16.00**
Creamer, ovoid, 3½" **$15.00**
Creamer & sugar bowl, 'y' handles, bulbous, 4¾", 3½", from $35 to **$40.00**
Cup & saucer, 'y' handle, from $8 to **$10.00**
Cup & saucer, angle handle, scalloped rims, from $7 to ..**$9.00**
Cup & saucer, demitasse **$10.00**
Cup & saucer, farmer's; 4x5" (across handle), from $15 to... **$20.00**
Cup & saucer, Irish coffee; cylindrical cup, from $12 to..**$16.00**
Cutting board, 14x9½", +stainless steel knife **$45.00**
Dish, leaf shape, 5¾x4".. **$20.00**
Ginger jar, 5", from $35 to **$40.00**
Goblet, clear glass w/Blue Danube design, 7¼", set of 12, from $80 to... **$100.00**
Gravy boat, double spout, w/undertray, 3½x6", from $35 to **$40.00**
Gravy boat, 6⅜x9¾", from $65 to **$75.00**
Hurricane lamp, glass mushroom globe **$75.00**
Ice bucket, from $20 to.. **$30.00**
Ice cream scoop, cutting blade, no mark **$50.00**
Inkstand, 2 lidded inserts, shaped base, banner mark, 9" L **$300.00**
Mug, soup; 4 for **$65.00**
Mustard/mayonnaise, from $70 to **$75.00**
Napkin holders, set of 4, from $30 to **$35.00**
Napkins, Sunnyweave, set of 4, from $25 to............... **$30.00**
Pitcher, bulbous w/flared spout, fancy handle, 5¼", from $25 to **$30.00**
Pitcher, bulbous w/flared spout, fancy handle, 6¼"...**$40.00**
Pitcher, milk; 'y' handle, 5¼", from $25 to **$30.00**
Plate, bread & butter; 6¾"... **$6.00**
Plate, deviled eggs; from $80 to **$90.00**
Plate, lattice rim, 8".. **$15.00**
Plate, triangular, 9¾" L **$50.00**
Plate, 8¼", from $8 to **$11.00**
Plate, 10¼", from $10 to.. **$15.00**

Plate, 16", from $75 to..................................**$85.00**
Platter, 12x8½", from $35 to **$45.00**
Platter, 14x10", from $60 to........................**$65.00**
Salt & pepper shakers, dome top w/bud finial, bulbous bottom, 5", pr **$40.00**
Salt & pepper shakers, 5 holes in salt, 3 in pepper, 5", pr..**$25.00**
Salt box, wooden lid, 4¾x4¾" **$55.00**
Snack plate & cup **$25.00**
Soup ladle, from $35 to................................**$45.00**
Soup tureen, w/lid, from $135 to **$150.00**
Spooner, 4¾x4" **$50.00**
Sugar bowl, ovoid, w/lid, 5", from $20 to **$25.00**
Tablecloth, 50x70", +4 napkins **$95.00**
Tazza, attached pedestal foot, banner mark, 4½x15", from $85 to..**$95.00**
Tea tile/trivet, 6" **$25.00**
Teakettle, enamel, wooden handle, w/fold-down metal sides, 9x9½" **$25.00**
Teapot, 'y' handle, 6½", from $60 to............**$70.00**
Temple jar, 10½" **$60.00**
Tidbit tray, 2-tier **$35.00**
Tidbit tray, 3-tier **$40.00**
Tray, fluted shell shape w/rolled end, sm..................**$45.00**
Tray, rectangular, pierced handles, 14½"................**$105.00**
Undertray, for soup tureen **$45.00**
Vase, scalloped rim w/embossed decor, round foot, wide body, no mark, 6"..**$20.00**

Blue Garland

During the 1960s and 1970s, this dinnerware was offered as premiums through grocery stores. Its ornate handles, platinum trim, and the scalloped rims on the flat items and the bases of the hollowware pieces when combined with the 'Haviland' backstamp suggested to most supermarket shoppers that they were getting high quality dinnerware for very little. And indeed the line was of good quality, but the company that produced it had no connection at all to the famous Haviland company of Limoges, France, who produced fine china there for almost one hundred years. The mark is Johann Haviland, taken from the name of the founding company that later became Philip Rosenthal and Co. This was a German manufacturer who produced chinaware for export to the United States from the mid-1930s until well into the 1980s. Today's dinnerware collectors find the delicate wreath-like blue flowers and the lovely shapes very appealing.

Bell, from $50 to..**$60.00**
Beverage server (teapot/coffeepot), w/lid, 11", from $70 to..**$90.00**
Bowl, fruit; 5⅛", from $4.50 to **$6.00**
Bowl, oval, 10¾"..**$65.00**
Bowl, soup; 7⅝", from $9 to **$12.00**
Bowl, vegetable; 8½", from $35 to **$40.00**
Butter dish, ¼-lb, from $45 to **$55.00**
Candlesticks, 3½x4", pr from $75 to **$85.00**

Casserole/tureen, w/lid, 12", from $45 to **$55.00**
Chamber stick, metal candle cup & handle, 6" dia.....**$75.00**
Coaster/butter pat, 3¾" dia, from $10 to **$12.00**
Creamer, from $15 to....................................**$18.00**
Cup & saucer, flat, from $5 to **$8.00**
Cup & saucer, footed, from $10 to..............**$12.00**
Gravy boat, w/attached underplate, from $35 to........**$45.00**
Plate, bread & butter; 6¼", from $3 to........................**$4.00**
Plate, dinner; 10", from $8 to **$10.00**
Plate, salad; 7¾", from $7 to **$9.00**
Platter, 13", from $22 to..............................**$28.00**
Platter, 14½", from $30 to **$40.00**
Platter, 15½", from $35 to **$45.00**

Salt and pepper shakers, 4¼", from $35.00 to $40.00 for the pair.

Sugar bowl, w/lid, from $18 to **$22.00**
Teakettle, porcelain w/stainless steel lid....................**$25.00**
Tidbit tray, 1-tier **$45.00**
Tidbit tray, 2-tier **$50.00**
Tidbit tray, 3-tier **$75.00**

Blue Ridge Dinnerware

Blue Ridge has long been popular with collectors, and prices are already well established, but that's not to say there aren't a few good buys left around. There are! It was made by a company called Southern Potteries, who operated in Erwin, Tennessee, from sometime in the latter '30s until the mid-'50s. They made many hundreds of patterns, all hand decorated. Some collectors prefer to match up patterns, while others like to mix them together for a more eclectic table setting.

One of the patterns most popular with collectors (and one of the most costly) is called French Peasant. It's very much like Quimper with simple depictions of a little peasant man with his staff and a lady. But they also made many lovely floral patterns, and it's around these where most of the buying and selling activity is centered. You'll find roosters, plaids, and simple textured designs, and in addition to the dinnerware, some vases and novelty items as well.

Very few pieces of dinnerware are marked except for the 'china' or porcelain pieces which usually are. Watch for a similar type of ware often confused with Blue Ridge that is sometimes (though not always) marked Italy.

The values suggested below are for the better patterns. To evaluate the French Peasant line, double these figures; for the simple plaids and textures, deduct 25% to 50%, depending on their appeal.

If you'd like to learn more, we recommend *The Collector's Encyclopedia of Blue Ridge Dinnerware, Identification and Values, Vol. II* and *Blue Ridge Dinnerware* by Betty and Bill Newbound.

Advisors: Bill and Betty Newbound (See Directory, Dinnerware)

Newsletter: *National Blue Ridge Newsletter*
Norma Lilly
144 Highland Dr., Blountsville, TN 37617

Ashtray, individual	**$24.00**
Ashtray, railroad advertising, various made, ea from $60 to	**$75.00**
Ashtray w/rest (eared), from $25 to	**$30.00**
Basket, aluminum edge, 10", from $30 to	**$35.00**
Bonbon, Charm House, china, from $125 to	**$135.00**
Bonbon, divided, center handle, china, from $95 to	**$100.00**
Bonbon, flat shell, china, from $80 to	**$85.00**
Bowl, cereal; child's, from $85 to	**$95.00**
Bowl, cereal/soup; Premium, 6", from $20 to	**$25.00**
Bowl, hot cereal; from $14 to	**$17.00**
Bowl, mixing; lg, from $25 to	**$30.00**
Bowl, mixing; sm	**$20.00**
Bowl, Square Dancers, 11½", from $150 to	**$160.00**
Bowl, vegetable; round, 8", from $25 to	**$30.00**
Bowl, vegetable; w/lid, from $60 to	**$65.00**
Box, candy; china, 6" dia, from $135 to	**$150.00**
Box, Dancing Nudes, china, from $750 to	**$800.00**
Box, powder; round, from $150 to	**$175.00**
Box, Rose Step, pearlized, from $85 to	**$100.00**
Box, Seaside, w/ashtrays, from $200 to	**$250.00**
Box, Sherman Lily, from $700 to	**$750.00**
Butter dish, from $35 to	**$45.00**
Butter dish, Woodcrest	**$65.00**
Cake tray, Maple Leaf, china	**$75.00**
Carafe, w/lid, from $100 to	**$125.00**
Casserole, w/lid, from $50 to	**$55.00**
Celery dish, leaf shape, china, from $50 to	**$60.00**
Coffeepot, ovoid, from $150 to	**$175.00**
Creamer, Colonial, open, lg, from $18 to	**$20.00**
Creamer, demitasse; china, from $70 to	**$80.00**
Creamer, Fifties shape	**$15.00**
Creamer, pedestal foot, china, from $65 to	**$75.00**
Cup & saucer, demitasse; china, from $50 to	**$65.00**
Cup & saucer, demitasse; earthenware, from $40 to	**$45.00**
Cup & saucer, Holiday	**$65.00**
Cup & saucer, Jumbo, from $55 to	**$65.00**
Custard cup	**$18.00**
Demitasse pot, earthenware, from $110 to	**$120.00**

Dish, deviled egg; from $50 to	**$60.00**
Jug, batter; w/lid, from $75 to	**$85.00**
Jug, character; Pioneer Woman, from $575 to	**$600.00**
Lamp from pitcher, teapot, etc, from $60 to	**$75.00**
Lazy susan, complete, from $650 to	**$700.00**
Leftover, w/lid, lg, from $25 to	**$30.00**
Mug, child's, from $75 to	**$85.00**
Pitcher, Abby, earthenware, from $65 to	**$75.00**
Pitcher, Antique, china, 5", from $85 to	**$95.00**
Pitcher, Betsy, earthenware, from $120 to	**$125.00**
Pitcher, Chick, china, from $95 to	**$110.00**
Pitcher, Clara, china, from $90 to	**$95.00**

Pitcher, Fruit Basket, Alice shape, 6¼", from $150.00 to $175.00. (Photo courtesy Betty and Bill Newbound)

Pitcher, Helen, china, from $90 to	**$95.00**
Pitcher, Milady, china, from $150 to	**$190.00**
Pitcher, Rebecca, from $150 to	**$195.00**
Pitcher, Sculptured Fruit, china	**$95.00**
Pitcher, Spiral, china, 7", from $80 to	**$85.00**
Pitcher, Virginia, china, 4¼", from $150 to	**$190.00**
Plate, aluminum edge, 12", from $40 to	**$45.00**
Plate, artist signed, 10¼", from $575 to	**$625.00**
Plate, child's	**$125.00**
Plate, Christmas Tree, from $75 to	**$80.00**
Plate, dinner; Premium, 9¼", from $40 to	**$45.00**
Plate, dinner; 9¼", from $22 to	**$25.00**
Plate, dinner; 10½"	**$30.00**
Plate, divided; heavy	**$35.00**
Plate, Provincial Farm scenes, 6" sq, from $75 to	**$80.00**
Plate, Still Life, 8½", from $30 to	**$35.00**
Plate, 8" sq, from $15 to	**$20.00**
Platter, regular pattern, 15"	**$40.00**
Ramekin, w/lid, 5", from $25 to	**$30.00**
Relish, deep shell, china, from $80 to	**$85.00**
Relish, loop handle, china	**$85.00**
Relish, T-handle	**$75.00**
Salt & pepper shakers, Apple, 1¾", pr from $25 to	**$30.00**
Salt & pepper shakers, range; pr from $45 to	**$50.00**
Sconce, wall	**$90.00**
Sugar bowl, Charm House, china, from $75 to	**$85.00**
Sugar bowl, Colonial, eared, open, from $15 to	**$20.00**
Sugar bowl, Waffle, w/lid, from $20 to	**$25.00**
Tea set, child's play set, from $375 to	**$400.00**

Teapot, Ball shape, Premium, from $200 to **$225.00**
Teapot, Chevron handle **$170.00**
Teapot, Fine Panel, china, from $140 to **$150.00**
Teapot, Palisades, from $90 to **$100.00**
Teapot, Snub Nose, china **$190.00**
Tidbit tray, 2-tier **$30.00**
Toast, w/lid, Premium, from $200 to **$210.00**
Tray, demitasse; Colonial, 5½x7", from $120 to **$140.00**
Tray, demitasse; Skyline, 9½x7⅝", from $90 to **$95.00**
Tumbler, glass, from $12 to **$15.00**
Tumbler, juice; glass **$15.00**
Vase, boot form, 8" **$110.00**
Vase, handled, china, from $100 to **$110.00**

Blue Willow Dinnerware

Blue Willow dinnerware has been made since the 1700s, first by English potters, then Japanese, and finally American companies as well. Tinware, glassware, even paper 'go-withs' have been produced over the years — some fairly recently, due to on-going demand. It was originally copied from the early blue and white wares made in Nanking and Canton in China. Once in awhile you'll see some pieces in black, pink, red, or even multicolored.

Obviously the most expensive will be the early English wares, easily identified by their backstamps. You'll be most likely to find pieces made by Royal or Homer Laughlin, and even though comparatively recent, they're still collectible, and their prices are very affordable.

For further study we recommend *Blue Willow Identification and Value Guide* by Mary Frank Gaston.

See also Homer Laughlin; Royal China.

Advisor: Mary Frank Gaston

Newsletter: *American Willow Report*
Lisa Kay Henze, Editor
P.O. Box 900, Oakridge, OR 97463. Bimonthly newsletter, subscription: $15 per year, out of country add $5 per year

Newsletter: *The Willow Word*
Mary Berndt, Publisher
P.O. Box 13382, Arlington, TX 76094. Send SASE for information about subscriptions and the International Willow Collector's Convention.

Ashtray, fish figural w/open mouth, Japan, 5" L, from $25 to **$30.00**
Baking dish, oven proof, Japan, 2½x5", from $35 to **$40.00**
Biscuit jar, Two Temples II pattern, Traditional border, cane handle, English, from $175 to **$200.00**
Bottle, perfume; Mandarin pattern w/Dagger border, w/stopper, Copeland, 6", from $350 to **$400.00**
Bowl, reversed Traditional center pattern, unmarked Japan, 15", from $220 to **$240.00**

Bowl, salad; unmarked Japan, 3½x10", w/ceramic & wooden fork & spoon, from $120 to **$140.00**
Bowl, soup/cereal; Booths Variant pattern, Meakin, from $15 to **$20.00**
Bowl, soup/cereal; Shenango China, from $15 to **$20.00**

Bowl, vegetable; Japan, 10½", from $35.00 to $40.00.

Bowl, vegetable; Pictorial border pattern, porcelain, Royal Sometuke, from $70 to **$80.00**
Bowl, vegetable; stacking, Made in Japan, set of 4 w/lid, 9" dia, from $325 to **$375.00**
Candlesticks, unmarked, 6", pr **$42.50**
Coaster, Tennent's Pilsener Beer advertising, unmarked English, 4" dia, from $35 to **$45.00**
Coffeepot, graniteware, unmarked, 6", from $100 to ..**$120.00**
Creamer, hotel ware, Shenango China, 2½", from $30 to ..**$35.00**
Creamer, unmarked American, 2½", from $8 to **$12.00**
Cup & saucer, demitasse; Japan, 2½", 4½", from $14 to ...**$18.00**
Cup & saucer, Traditional pattern w/border, Allerton, from $25 to **$30.00**
Gravy boat, Shenango China, 6" L, from $45 to **$55.00**
Lamp, electric, made in style of oil lamp, Made in Japan, 4¼", from $45 to **$55.00**
Match safe, attached saucer, Shenango China, 2", from $75 to **$85.00**
Mug, USA mark, 3¾", from $8 to **$12.00**
Mustard pot, barrel shape, unmarked, 2½", from $65 to **$75.00**
Pitcher, Traditional pattern (simplified), Pictorial border pattern, unmarked, 8", from $60 to **$80.00**
Pitcher, Two Temples II pattern, Butterfly border, cylindrical, rope-style handle, unmarked, 9¾", from $150 to ..**$175.00**
Pitcher, Two Temples II reversed pattern, Butterfly border, Wedgwood & Co Ltd, 4¾", from $75 to **$90.00**
Plate, Booths Variant center w/Bow Knot border, gold trim, octagonal, Booths mark, 8¾", from $50 to **$60.00**
Plate, bread & butter; Traditional center w/border pattern, Allerton mark, from $15 to **$18.00**
Plate, cake/tea; Two Temples II center pattern, Butterfly border, handles, unmarked, 9", from $75 to **$100.00**
Plate, dinner; Booths pattern, Bow Knot border, gold trim, from $25 to **$35.00**
Plate, dinner; Traditional center & border, Shenango, from $15 to **$20.00**

Plate, luncheon; Traditional center, border pattern, Allerton, from $20 to.....................................**$30.00**

Platter, Canton pattern, Greenwood China, 7x10", from $55 to...**$65.00**

Platter, Traditional center pattern (simplified), Pictorial border, multicolored, Sebring Pottery Co, 13x17", from $50 to **$60.00**

Relish tray, 5 sections, Shenango China, 9½" dia, from $40 to...**$50.00**

Salt & pepper shakers, urn form w/handles, Japan, 3½", pr from $40 to...**$50.00**

Teakettle, Blue Willow Pantry Collection, Taiwan for Heritage Mint Ltd **$30.00**

Teapot, musical type, unmarked Japan, from $130 to ..**$150.00**

Teapot, w/stacking creamer, sugar bowl & lid, Japan, 2-cup, from $130 to...**$150.00**

Trivet, wrought-iron frame, Japan, from $35 to **$45.00**

Tumbler, clear glass, from 3" to 4", ea from $15 to **$18.00**

Tumbler, frosted glass, from 3 to 5¼", ea from $15 to ...**$25.00**

Tumbler, juice; ceramic, Japan, 3½", from $30 to.......**$35.00**

Bookends

You'll find bookends in various types of material and designs. The more inventive their modeling, the higher the price. Also consider the material. Cast-iron examples, especially if in original polychrome paint, are bringing very high prices right now. Brass and copper are good as well, though elements of design may override the factor of materials altogether. If they are signed by the designer or marked by the manufacturer, you can boost the price. Those with a decidedly Art Deco appearance are often good sellers. The consistent volume of common to moderately uncommon bookends that are selling online has given the impression that some are more easily available than once thought. Hence, some examples have not accrued in value. See *Collector's Guide to Bookends* by Louis Kuritzky (Collector Books) for more information.

Advisor: Louis Kuritzky (See Directory, Bookends)

Club: Bookend Collector Club
Louis Kuritzky
4510 NW 175h Pl.
Gainesville, FL 32605; 352-377-3193
Quarterly full-color newsletter: $25 per year

Anchor, gray metal, attributed to Dodge, ca 1947, 5¾" ..**$45.00**

Angelfish, clear glass, American Glass Co, 1940s, 8¼" ..**$135.00**

Atlas, painted chalk on polished stone base, JB Hirsch, 1940s, 7¾"..**$135.00**

Baby shoes, gray metal, Patent 1940, 5½"..................**$75.00**

Bear & Beehive, pewter, ca 1940, 8" **$100.00**

Bronco Rider, gray metal, Dodge, 1947, 5" **$75.00**

Cogwheel, brass, ca 1965, 3½"....................................**$150.00**

Crane, gray metal, ca 1946, 6¾"..................................**$75.00**

Dogwood, gray metal, PM Craftsman, ca 1965, 5¼"...**$40.00**

Flamingos, cast iron, unmarked Everstyle, 1948, 5¼"..**$125.00**

Galleon, gray metal, Made in Occupied Japan, 1946, 6¾"...**$75.00**

Horse on Arc, gray metal, Dodge, ca 1947, 5½".........**$60.00**

Lamp & Book, gray metal, Ronson, 1942, 5" **$100.00**

Lion on base, dark amber glass, Imperial Glass Co, 1978, 6"...**$125.00**

Looney Tunes, chalkware, Disney, 1994, 7"................**$85.00**

Lyre, clear glass, Fostoria, 1943-44, 7" **$150.00**

Mayo Tunnel, iron, Mine Equipment, Lancaster PA, 1940, 5"..**$75.00**

Oaken Door, wood w/metal ring, ca 1975..................**$15.00**

Pontiac emblem, aluminum, Bruce Fox, New Albany IN, 1983 ....**$50.00**

Rook (glancing to side), shiny white, #2274, 1945 ...**$600.00**

Sailfish, gray metal, PM Craftsman, ca 1965, 8"..........**$65.00**

Trout, gray metal, PM Craftsman, ca 1965, 4" **$50.00**

Tufts College, iron, ca 1970, 6½" **$60.00**

Whale, gray metal, PM Craftsman, ca 1965, 7½".........**$50.00**

Zion Park Sandstone, 1968 ....**$75.00**

Angelus Call to Prayer, gray metal, K&O, $125.00. (Photo courtesy Louis Kuritzky)

Books

Books have always fueled the mind's imagination. Before television lured us out of the library into the TV room, everyone enjoyed reading the latest novels. Western, horror, and science fiction themes are still popular to this day — especially those by such authors as Louis L'Amour, Steven King, and Ray Bradbury, to name but a few. Edgar Rice Burrough's Tarzan series and Frank L. Baum's Wizard of Oz books are regarded as classics among today's collectors. A first edition of a popular author's first book (especially if it's signed) is avidly sought after, so is a book that 'ties in' with a movie or television program.

Dick and Jane readers are fast becoming collectible. If you went to first grade sometime during the 1930s until the mid-1970s, you probably read about their adventures. These books were used all over the United States and in military base schools over the entire world. They were published here as well as in Canada, the Philippine Islands, Australia, and New Zealand; there were special editions for the Roman Catholic parochial schools and the Seventh Day Adventists', and even today they're in use in some Mennonite and Amish schools.

On the whole, ex-library copies and book club issues (unless they are limited editions) have very low resale values.

Besides the references in the subcategory narratives that follow, for further study we also recommend *Huxford's Old Book Value Guide* (Collector Books); *Collector's Guide to Children's Books, 1850 to 1950, Vols I, II,* and *III,* and *Boys' and Girls' Book Series* by Diane McClure Jones and Rosemary Jones; and *Whitman Juvenile Books* by David and Virginia Brown. All are published by Collector Books.

Magazine: *AB Bookman's Weekly*
P.O. Box AB, Clifton, NJ 07015; 201-772-0020 or fax: 201-772-9281. Sample copies: $10

Big Little Books

The Whitman Publishing Company started it all in 1933 when they published a book whose format was entirely different than any other's. It was very small, easily held in a child's hand, but over an inch in thickness. There was a cartoon-like drawing on the right-hand page, and the text was printed on the left. The idea was so well accepted that very soon other publishers — Saalfield, Van Wiseman, Lynn, World Syndicate, and Goldsmith — cashed in on the idea as well. The first Big Little Book hero was Dick Tracy, but soon every radio cowboy, cartoon character, lawman, and space explorer was immortalized in his own adventure series.

When it became apparent that the pre-teen of the '50s preferred the comic-book format, Big Little Books were finally phased out; but many were saved in boxes and stored in attics, so there's still a wonderful supply of them around. You need to watch condition carefully when you're buying or selling. For further information we recommend *Big Little Books, A Collector's Reference and Value Guide*, by Larry Jacobs (Collector Books).

Newsletter: *Big Little Times*
Big Little Book Collectors Club of America
Larry Lowery
P.O. Box 1242, Danville, CA 94526; 415-837-2086

Andy Panda & Tiny Tom, Whitman #1425, EX+ **$30.00**
Bambi, Whitman #1489, EX **$35.00**
Big Chief Wahoo & the Magic Lamp, Whitman #1483, NM..**$45.00**
Blondie & Baby Dumpling, Whitman #1415, EX **$20.00**
Bronc Peeler the Lone Cowboy, Whitman #1417, VG ..**$5.00**
Buck Jones in the Fighting Rangers, Whitman #1188, NM ...**$45.00**
Buck Rogers on the Moons of Saturn, Whitman #1143, EX...**$65.00**
Captain Easy Behind Enemy Lines, Whitman #1474, VG........**$5.00**
Chester Gump in the Pole to Pole Flight, Whitman #1402, EX..**$25.00**
Danger Trails in Africa, Whitman #1151, VG...............**$10.00**
Dick Tracy & the Boris Arson Gang, Whitman #1163, NM ..**$65.00**
Don Winslow & the Giant Girl Spy, Whitman #1408, EX **$20.00**

Donald Duck & the Green Serpent, Whitman #1432, EX.....**$40.00**
Ellery Queen the Adventure of the Last Man Club, Whitman #1406, EX+ **$45.00**
Flash Gordon & the Monsters of Mongo, #1166, EX+ ..**$90.00**
Flying the Fly Clipper w/Winsie Atkins, Whitman #1108, G..**$10.00**
G-Man on the Job, Whitman #1168, G..........................**$5.00**
Gene Autry Cowboy Detective, Whitman #1444, NM...**$40.00**
Hall of Fame of the Air, Whitman #1159, NM **$25.00**
Jackie Cooper in Gangster's Boy, Whitman #1402, EX **$25.00**
Jungle Jim & the Vampire Woman, Whitman #1139, G ...**$15.00**
Li'l Abner Among the Millionaires, Whitman #1401, VG.**$35.00**
Little Orphan Annie & the Big Train Robbery, Whitman #1140, EX...**$30.00**

***The Lone Ranger and the Vanishing Herd,* Whitman #1196, EX, $25.00. (Photo courtesy Larry Jacobs)**

Mickey Mouse & Pluto the Racer, Whitman #1128, NM .**$90.00**
Mickey Mouse Sails for Treasure, Whitman #750, EX..**$50.00**
Nancy & Sluggo, Whitman #1400, EX..........................**$45.00**
Og Son of Fire, Whitman #1115, G...............................**$10.00**
Perry Winkle & the Rinkydinks Get a House, Whitman #1487, EX...**$25.00**
Popeye & the Quest for the Rainbird, Whitman #1459, EX **$35.00**
Red Ryder & the Rimrock Killer, Whitman #1443, EX ..**$25.00**
Skyroads w/Hurricane Hawk, Whitman #1127, EX.....**$25.00**
Tarzan & the Ant Men, Whitman #1444, NM...............**$75.00**
Tim McCoy on the Tomahawk Trail, Whitman #1436, EX..**$30.00**
Uncle Wiggily's Adventures, Whitman #1405, EX.......**$20.00**

Children's Miscellaneous Books

Abu Kassim's Slippers, Nancy Green, WT Mars illustrations, pictorial boards, 1963 ....**$10.00**
Adventures of Rufus, Mary Brooks, pictorial boards, oversize, Locke, 1969, 60 pages **$15.00**
Andy & the Gopher, Audrey McKim, Ronni Solbert black & white illustrations, hardcover, 1st edition, Little Brown, 1959 ....**$25.00**
Angel & the Donkey, James Reeves, E Ardizzone illustrations, oblong hardcover, 1st American edition, McGraw-Hill, 1970 ....**$20.00**

Animals on the Ceiling, Richard Armour, Paul Galdone illustrations, 1st edition, McGraw-Hill, 1965 ....**$65.00**

Answers & More Answers, Mary Elting, hardcover, Grosset, 1961 ....**$10.00**

Ants to Zebra, Animal Verses for Children, Julian Fahy, sm oblong hardcover, 1st edition, Exposition Press, 1953 ....**$15.00**

Arturo & Mr Bang, Beatrice & Ferrin Fraser, hardcover, 1st edition, Bobbs-Merrill, 1963 ....**$20.00**

Assignment in Space, Blake Savage, hardcover, Whitman, 1950 ....**$10.00**

Bear Weather, Lillie D Chaffin, Helga Aichinger illustrations, oversize hardcover, 1st edition, Macmillan, 1969 .**$10.00**

Bill & Coo, Mazo DeLaRoche, Eileen A Soper illustrations, 1st edition, Macmillan, 1958 ....**$15.00**

Book of Clowns, Felix Sutton, James Schucker illustrations, hardcover, Grosset, 1953 ....**$20.00**

Bugles at the Border, Marry Gillett, Bruce Tucker, hardcover, 1st edition, Winston-Salem, 1968 ....**$10.00**

Caboose, Edith Thatcher Hurd, hardcover, 1st edition, Lothrop, 1951 ....**$20.00**

Cat in the Hat Comes Back, Dr Seuss, hardcover, later edition, Random House **$10.00**

The Chatterlings in Wordland, **Michael Lipman, 1935, Volland, Wise-Parslow revised edition, 96 pages, orange cover, color illustrations by the author, EX, $45.00.** (Photo courtesy Diane McClure Jones/Rosemary Jones)

Chimney-Top Lane, Gunnel Linde, Ilon Wikland illustrations, hardcover, 1st American edition, Harcourt, 1965, 160 pages..**$10.00**

Chipmunk on the Doorstep, Edwin Tunis, hardcover, 1st edition, Crowell, 1971, w/dust jacket........................**$30.00**

Christmas Bells Are Ringing, Sara & John E Brewton, red hardcover, 1st edition, Macmillan, 1951 ....**$20.00**

Clue of the Dead Duck, Scott Young, hardcover, Little Brown, 1962..**$10.00**

Coco the Gift Horse, Denise Hill, blue hardcover, 1st edition, Collins, London, 1966, w/dust jacket **$50.00**

Coming of Pout, Peter Blair, TS Hyman illustrations, hardcover, 1st edition, Little Brown, 1969, w/dust jacket **$20.00**

Cranberry Thanksgiving, Wende & Harry Devlin, pictorial hardcover, 1st edition, Parent's Magazine Press, 1971..**$20.00**

Crowd of Cows, John Graham, F Rojankovsky illustrations, hardcover, Harcourt Brace, 1968 ....**$15.00**

David & the Sea Gulls, Marion Downer, photo illustrations, hardcover, 1st edition, Lathrop, Lee, 1956 ....**$15.00**

Dog Days, Art Bernard, black & white illustrations, hardcover, 1st edition, Caldwell Caston, 1969, 204 pages........**$15.00**

Every One Has a Name, Richard Browner, Emma Landau illustrations, hardcover, 1st edition, Walck, 1961..**$10.00**

Explorer for an Aunt, Margaret Love, hardcover, Follet, 1967, w/dust jacket..**$15.00**

Faint George, Robert E Barry, oversize picture book, red, black & white illustrations, Houghton, 1957 ....**$25.00**

Fair Wind to Virginia, Cornelia Miegs, JC Wonstler illustrations, hardcover, 1st edition, Macmillan, 1955......**$10.00**

Farmer John Buys a Pig, John Cunliffe, Carol Barker illustrations, hardcover, 1st edition, London: Andrew Deutsch, 1964 ....**$20.00**

Forest House, Elizabeth Allen, Dutton, Paul Kennedy black & white illustrations, hardcover, Dutton, 1967 ....**$10.00**

Forty-Ninth Magician, Samuel Babbit, Natalie Babbit illustrations, hardcover, 1st edition, Pantheon Books, 1966...........**$20.00**

Frog Prince, Paul Galdone, pictorial hardcover, McGraw-Hill, 1975 ....**$10.00**

Good-Bye to Stony Crick, Kathryn Borland & Helen Speicher, Weekly Reader edition, hardcover, McGraw-Hill, 1975.**$10.00**

Grasshopper Year, Neola Tracy Lane, hardcover, 1st edition, Lippincott, 1960, w/dust jacket..............................**$20.00**

Green Isle, Katherine Burton, Frank Nicholas illustrations, hardcover, 1st edition, Hawthorn, 1963 ....**$10.00**

Hiding the Bell, Ruth Nulton Moore, AA Snyder illustrations, hardcover, 1st edition, Westminster Press, 1968...**$10.00**

Horse, Siegfried Stander, Victor Ambrus illustrations, gold hardcover, World Publishing, 1969 edition **$10.00**

Hosie's Alphabet, Hosea & Leonard Baskin, oversize hardcover picture book, Viking, 1972, w/dust jacket..**$35.00**

Hostage to Alexander, Mary Evans Andrews, 1st edition, hardcover, Longmans, 1961, w/dust jacket...........**$20.00**

Hour in the Morning, Gordon Cooper, Philip Gough illustrations, hardcover, Dutton, 1974 edition.................**$10.00**

I Met a Man, John Ciardi, Robert Osborn illustrations, hardcover, Houghton Mifflin, 1961, w/dust jacket.......**$40.00**

Iggie's House, Judy Blume, hardcover, 1st edition, Bradbury Press, 1970, w/dust jacket....................................**$20.00**

In Clean Hay, Eric Kelly, Maud & Miska Petersham color illustrations, hardcover, Macmillan, 1953 ....**$20.00**

Jamaica Boy, Bernard Wolf, photos by author, hardcover, 1st edition, Cowles, 1971 ....**$10.00**

Jennifer Prize, Eunice Young Smith, blue hardcover w/gilt letters, 1st edition, Bobbs-Merrill, 1951, w/dust jacket **$20.00**

Jimmy's Boa Ate the Wash, Trinks Hakes Noble, Steven Kellogg illustrations, Dial, Weekly Reader edition, 1960........**$15.00**

John Fisher's Magic Book, John Fisher, T dePaola illustrations, hardcover, 1st edition, Prentice-Hall, 1971 .**$10.00**

Joker & Jerry, Eleanor Helme & Paul Nance, Cecil Aldin black & white illustrations, Eyre & Spottiswood, 1955 edition..**$10.00**

Jolly Witch, Robert Burch, Leigh Grant illustrations, yellow hardcover, 1st edition, Dutton, 1975, 32 pages **$15.00**

Josef Chief of the Nez Perce, Dean Pollock, illustrated by author, hardcover, Binfords & Mort, 1950, 63 pages **$10.00**

Jumblies, Edward Lear, Edward Gorey illustrations, hardcover, 1st edition, Young Scott, 1968 .... **$25.00**

Kingdom of the Elephants, Alan Jenkins, hardcover, 1st edition, Follett, 1963 .... **$15.00**

Land of No Strangers, Gwen Marsh, Jean Garside illustrations, hardcover, 1st edition, Oxford University, 1951 ...... **$15.00**

Lesson for Janie, Dorothy Simpson, blue hardcover, illustrated endpapers, frontispiece, 1st edition, Lippincott, 1958.. **$15.00**

Little Tuck, Clara Baldwin, Paul Galdone illustrations, hardcover, 1st edition, Doubleday, 1959 .... **$15.00**

Magic Carpet, Eleanor Johnson, hardcover, Charles E Merrill, Treasure of Literature Readtext Series, 1954 .... **$30.00**

Magic Lasso, Hugh McClelland, hardcover, 1st edition, St Martin's Press, 1963 .... **$20.00**

Man Who Didn't Wash His Dishes, Phyllis Krasilovsky, Barbara Cooney illustrations, hardcover, Parents', 1950 .... **$15.00**

Merry-Go-Round Family, Mimi Bolton, hardcover, 1st edition, Coward McCann, 1954... **$10.00**

Mr Rogers' Song Book, Fred Rogers, Steven Kellogg illustrations, photo hardcover, oversize, Random House, 1970.. **$15.00**

Naughty Children, Christianna Brand, E Ardizzone illustrations, hardcover, 1st edition, Dutton, 1963 .... **$20.00**

No Room for a Dog, Marion Holland, Albert Orbaan illustrations, hardcover, Random House, 1959 .... **$15.00**

No Room for Nicky, Alicia Kaufmann, Vicki De Larrea illustrations, hardcover, Hawthorne, 1969 .... **$15.00**

Northern Exposure, Cyril Harris, L Vosburgh illustrations, hardcover, 1st edition, Norton, 1963, w/dust jacket **$15.00**

Path Above the Pines, Belle Dorman Rugh, hardcover, Houghton Mifflin, 1962, w/dust jacket.................. **$20.00**

Peter Bull, Helen Oechsli, Kelly Oechsli illustrations, oversize hardcover, 1st edition, Viking, 1971 .... **$15.00**

Pink Motel, Carol Ryrie Brink, S Greenwald illustrations, hardcover, 1st edition, Macmillan, 1959, w/dust jacket **$25.00**

Plaid Peacock, Sandy Alan, Pantheon, oblong picture book, Kelly Oechsli color illustrations, 1965.................. **$20.00**

Pookie at the Seaside, Ivy Wallace, pictorial hardcover, Collins, 1956... **$15.00**

Quiet Yelled Mrs Rabbit, Hilda Cole Espy, hardback, JB Lippincott, 1958.. **$10.00**

Representing Super Doll, Richard Peck, hardcover, 1st edition, Viking, 1974... **$10.00**

Riders at the Gate, Joseph Auslander, B Artzybasheff illustrations, hardcover, 1st edition, Macmillan, 1958...... **$20.00**

Runaway Summer of Davie Shaw, Mario Puzo, Stewart Sherwood illustrations, hardcover, 1st edition, Platt & Munk, 1966.. **$20.00**

Savage King of the Seven Seas, AF Scott, Jacques Le Scanff illustrations, hardcover, Geoffrey Chapman, 1968..**$20.00**

Seashells in Action, Audrey Newell, illustrated by author, hardcover, 1st edition, Walker, 1973, w/dust jacket........ **$20.00**

Secret Sea Richard Armstrong, hardcover, David McKay, 1966, w/dust jacket.................................... **$20.00**

Sign on Rosie's Door, Maurice Sendak, hardcover, early edition, Harper, 1960 .... **$20.00**

Sky Carnival, Willam F Hallstead, illustrated hardcover, David McKay, 1969, 149 pages.. **$10.00**

Summer's Coming In, Natalia Belting, Adrienne Adams illustrations, 1st edition, Holt, 1970, w/dust jacket **$25.00**

Thomas & the Red Headed Angel, Marion Garthwaite, L Bjorkiund illustrations, hardcover, Messner, 1959...**$20.00**

Up Periscope, Robb White, hardcover, 1st edition, Doubleday, 1956... **$15.00**

Warping of Al, Jessie Close, hardcover, 1st edition, Harper, 1950, w/dust jacket................................... **$15.00**

White Horse w/Wings, Anthea Davies, Brigitte Bryan illustrations, hardcover, 1st edition, Macmillan, 1968.....**$15.00**

Woggle of Witches, Adrienne Adams, Scribner, 1st edition, oversize hardcover, 1971, w/dust jacket **$20.00**

Yankee Doodle Painter, Anne Colver, Lee Ames illustrations, hardcover, 1st edition, Knopf, 1955, w/dust jacket..**$20.00**

Juvenile Series Books

Adventure Girls in the Air, Clair Bank, Burt, 1920, 2nd in series..**$7.00**

Adventures of Huckleberry Finn Mark Twain, Baldwin Hawes illustrations, World Publishing, 1940s **$10.00**

Ameliaranne Keeps Shop, Constance Heward, SB Pearce illustrations, 1928, 2nd in series....................**$30.00**

Augustus Goes South, Le Grand (Henderson), Bobbs-Merrill, illustrations by author, 1940s, oversize...............**$25.00**

Bobbsey Twins, Laura Lee Hope, Grosset & Dunlap, black & white illustrations, ca 1907, 1st edition, 1st in series..**$25.00**

Bomba the Jungle Boy, Roy Rockwood, Grosset, 1st edition, cloth covers, 1930s **$20.00**

Brother & Sister, Josephine Lawrence, Julia Greene illustrations, Cupples & Leon, ca 1920, sm.....................**$20.00**

Buster Brown Goes Swimming, RF Outcault, Cupples & Leon, illustrated paper-covered boards, ca 1905..**$75.00**

Curlytops at Cherry Farm, Howard R Garis, Cupples & Leon, 1920s, sm...**$30.00**

Doris Force at Cloudy Cove, Julia K Duncan, Goldsmith, Gooch cover illustration, ca 1930.........................**$10.00**

Father Takes Us to New York, Grace Humphrey, Penn, 1927..**$15.00**

Flyaways & Cinderella, Alice Dale Hardy, Grosset & Dunlap, 1907 ....**$20.00**

Girl Aviator on Golden Wings, Margaret Burnham, Donahue, 1920s **$15.00**

Girl Scouts in the Adirondacks, Lillian Elizabeth Roy, Grosset, 1915, 2nd in series................................**$15.00**

Grace Harlowe Overseas, Jessie Flower, Altemus, 1920s, 1st in series **$10.00**

Hardy Boys in Secret of the Old Mill, FW Dixon, Grosset & Dunlap, 1920s, 3rd in series.................................**$15.00**

Hunters of the Ozark (Deerfoot Series), Edward Ellis, Winston, 1890s **$15.00**

Jane Allen: Junior, Edith Bancroft, Cupples & Leon, 1920s, 4th in series..**$10.00**

Little House in the Big Woods, Laura Ingalls Wilder, Sewell illustrations, Harper Bros, color frontispiece **$65.00**

Mary Louise Stands the Test, Edith Van Dyne (Baum), Reilly, ca 1920..**$25.00**

Motor Boys Over the Rockies, Clarence Young, Cupples & Leon, 1920s..**$15.00**

Polly & Eleanor, Lillian Roy, Grosset, 1920s, 2nd in series..**$15.00**

Polly French Takes Charge, Francine Lewis, Young People Fiction, #1571:49, 1954, Whitman 282 pages, EX, $8.00. (Photo courtesy David and Virginia Brown)

Raggedy Ann Helps Grandpa Hoppergrass, Westfield Classic, McLoughlin, black & white & color illustrations ..**$40.00**

Rebecca of Sunnybrook Farm, Kate Douglas Wiggins, HM Gross illustrations, Riverside, 1931 ....**$20.00**

Royal Book of Oz, Ruth Plumly Thompson, John R Neill illustrations, Reilly & Lee, 1921, 1st edition..............**$125.00**

Ruth Fielding at the Red Mill, Alice B Emerson, Cupples & Leon, ca 1920s..**$15.00**

Snipp, Snapp, Snurr & the Magic Horse, Maj Lindman, Whitman, 1935, oversize **$45.00**

Spartan Twins, Lucie Fitch Perkins, Twins of the World series, Houghton, 1918....................................**$25.00**

Tom Slade Boy Scout, Percy Keese Fitzhugh, Grosset, ca 1910 ....**$15.00**

Triplets in Business, Bertha Moore, Eerdmans, 1940s....**$15.00**

Uncle Wiggily & the Cowbird, Mary Perks, Mary & Wallace Stover illustrations, 1943..**$30.00**

X Bar X Boys on the Ranch, Victor Appleton, Grosset, ca 1910 ....**$10.00**

Little Golden Books

Everyone has had a few of these books in their lifetime; some we've read to our own children so many times that we still know them word for word, and today they're appearing in antique malls and shops everywhere. The first were printed in 1942. These are recognizable by their blue paper spines (later ones had gold foil). Until the early 1970s, they were numbered consecutively; after that they were unnumbered.

First editions of the titles having a 25¢ or 29¢ cover price can be identified by either a notation on the first or second pages, or a letter on the bottom right corner of the last page

(A for 1, B for 2, etc.). If these are absent, you probably have a first edition.

Condition is extremely important. To qualify as mint, these books must look just as good as they looked the day they were purchased. Naturally, having been used by children, many show signs of wear. If your book is only lightly soiled, the cover has no tears or scrapes, the inside pages have only small creases or folded corners, and the spine is still strong, it will be worth about half as much as one in mint condition. A missing cover makes it worthless. Additional damage would of course lessen the value even more.

A series number containing an 'A' refers to an activity book, while a 'D' number identifies a Disney story.

For more information we recommend *Collecting Little Golden Books* by Steve Santi (who provided us with our narrative material).

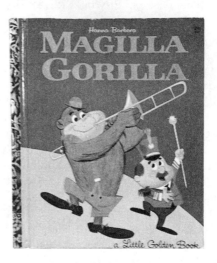

Magilla Gorilla, 1964, NM, $12.00. (Photo courtesy June Moon)

Activity book, 1955-63, hardcover, paper doll book w/paper dolls, EX **$35.00**

Activity book, 1955-63, hardcover, stamps, complete, EX..**$15.00**

Activity book, 1955-63, hardcover, wheel book w/wheel, EX **$10.00**

Band-Aid book, 1950-79, Helen Gaspard or Kathryn Jackson Malvern illustrations, w/out band-aid insert, EX ..**$10.00**

Eager Reader Series, 1974-75, boxed set of 8, EX.......**$35.00**

General titles, later editions w/nonfiction titles, EX, ea ..**$5.00**

General titles, later editions w/popular comic strip characters, EX, ea **$8.00**

General titles, 1950s 1st editions, antique gold foil spine w/leaves & flower pattern, hardcover, ea.............**$15.00**

General titles, 1960s, 1st editions, antique gold foil spine w/leaves & flower pattern, hardcover, ea.............**$12.00**

General titles, 1969-75, later printing, gold foil spine w/animal pattern, hardcover, ea **$4.00**

General titles, 1969-75, 1st edition, gold foil spine w/animal pattern, hardcover, ea..**$8.00**

Giant Little Golden Book, 1957-59, Disney titles, EX, ea ..**$20.00**

Giant Little Golden Book, 1957-59, individual titles, ea **$10.00**

Jig-Saw Puzzle Book, 1949-50, various authors & illustrations w/out puzzle, ea...**$10.00**

Jig-Saw Puzzle Book, 1949-50, various authors & illustrators, w/intact puzzle, EX...............$45.00

Popular illustrators Garth Williams & Eloise Wilkin, 1st editions, ea...............$20.00

Movie and TV Tie-Ins

Annie Oakley in Danger at Diablo, Whitman #1540:49, Doris Schroeder, illustrated, 282 pages...............$30.00

Bat Masterson, Wayne C Lee, Whitman #1550, 282 pages, EX/NM...............$20.00

The Beverly Hillbillies, A Saga of Wildcat Creek, **Doris Schroeder, #1572, 1963, Whitman, 212 pages, EX/NM, $15.00. (Photo courtesy David and Virginia Brown)**

Bewitched, The Opposite Uncle, William Johnston, Whitman #1572, 1970, 212 pages, EX/NM...............$35.00

Big Valley, Charles Hecklemann, Whitman #1569, 1966, 214 pages, EX/NM...............$25.00

Bonanza, Killer Lion, Steve Frazee, Whitman #1568, 1966, 212 pages, EX/NM...............$18.00

Circus Boy Under the Big Top, Dorothea J Snow, Whitman #1549, 1957, 282 pages, EX/NM...............$25.00

Combat, The Counterattack, FM Davis, Whitman #1520, 1964, 210 pages, EX/NM...............$20.00

Dr Kildare, The Magic Key, William Johnston, Whitman #1519, 1964, 210 pages, EX/NM...............$10.00

Dr Kildare Assigned to Trouble, RC Ackworth, Whitman #1547, 1963, 212 pages, EX/NM...............$12.00

Dragnet Case Stories, Richard Deming, Whitman #1527, 1957, 282 pages, EX/NM...............$25.00

Fury & the Mystery at Trapper's Hole, Troy Nesbit, Whitman #1557, 1959, 282 pages, EX/NM...............$18.00

Gene Autry & the Badmen of Broken Bow, Snowden Miller, Whitman #2355, 1951, 250 pages, EX/NM...............$15.00

Gene Autry & the Ghost Riders, Lewis B Patten, Whitman #1510:49, 1955, 282 pages, EX/NM...............$20.00

Gene Autry & the Thief River Outlaws, Bob Hamilton, Whitman #2303, 1944, 249 pages, EX/NM...............$14.00

Green Hornet, The Case of the Disappearing Doctor, Brandon Keith, Whitman #1570, 1966, 212 pages, EX/NM...............$35.00

Hawaii Five-0, Top Secret, Robert Sidney Bowen, Whitman #1511, 210 pages, EX/NM...............$15.00

Invaders Dam of Death, Jack Pearl, Whitman #1545, 1967, 212 pages, EX/NM...............$15.00

Janet Lennon, Adventure at Two Rivers, Barlow Meyers, Whitman #1536, 1961, 210 pages, EX/NM...............$12.00

John Payne & the Menace at Hawk's Nest, K Heisenfelt, Whitman #2385, 1943, 248 pages, w/dust jacket, EX/NM...............$22.00

Land of the Giants, Flight of Fear, Carl Henry Rathjen, Whitman #1516, 1969, 212 pages, EX/NM...............$30.00

Lassie, Forbidden Valley, Doris Schroeder, Whitman #1508, 1959, 282 pages, EX/NM...............$18.00

Lassie & the Mystery at Blackberry Bog, Dorothea J Snow, Whitman #1536, 1956, 282 pages, EX/NM...............$14.00

Lucy & the Madcap Mystery, Cole Fannin, Whitman #1505, 1963, 210 pages, EX/NM...............$35.00

Man From UNCLE, Affair of the Gunrunner's Gold, Kieth Brandon, Whitman #1543, 1967, 212 pages, EX/NM .$18.00

Mission Impossible, Priceless Particle, Talmage Powell, Whitman #1515, 1969, 212 pages, EX/NM...............$15.00

Monkees, Who's Got the Button?, William Johnston, Whitman #1539, 208 pages, EX/NM...............$25.00

Munsters & the Great Camera Caper, William Johnston, Whitman #1510, 1965, 212 pages, EX/NM...............$35.00

Patty Duke & Mystery Mansion, Doris Schroeder, Whitman #1514, 1964, 212 pages, EX/NM...............$20.00

Rat Patrol, The Iron Monster Raid, IG Edmonds, Whitman #1547, 1968, 210 pages, EX/NM...............$15.00

Rebel, HA De Rosso, Whitman #1548, 1961, 212 pages, EX/NM...............$20.00

Restless Gun, Barlow Meyers, Whitman #1559, 1959, 282 pages, EX/NM...............$25.00

Rifleman, Cole Fannin, Whitman #1569, 1959, 282 pages, EX/NM...............$20.00

Rin Tin Tin & the Call to Danger, Doris Schroeder, Whitman #1539, 1957, 282 pages, EX/NM...............$18.00

Ripcord, DS Halacy, Whitman #1522, 1962, 210 pages, EX/NM...............$25.00

Roy Rogers & the Brasada Bandits, Fannin Cole, Whitman #1500:49, 1955, 282 pages, EX/NM...............$25.00

Roy Rogers & the Gopher Creek Gunman, Don Middleton, Whitman #2309, 1945, 248 pages, w/dust jacket, EX/NM...............$30.00

Sea Hunt, Cole Fannin, Whitman #1541, 1960, 210 pages, EX/NM...............$25.00

Shirley Temple & the Spirit of Dragonwood, Kathryn Heisenfelt, Whitman #2311, 1945, 248 pages, w/dust jacket, EX/NM...............$25.00

Star Trek Mission to Horatius, Mack Reynolds, Whitman #1549, 1968, 210 pages, EX/NM...............$60.00

Tarzan & the Lost Safari, Edgar Rice Burroughs, Whitman #1522:49, 1957, 282 pages, EX/NM...............$12.00

Voyage to the Bottom of the Sea, Raymond F Jones, Whitman #1517, 1965, 212 pages, EX/NM...............$25.00

Walt Disney, Swiss Family Robinson, Steve Frazee, Whitman #1625, 1960, 210 pages, EX/NM...............$8.00

Walt Disney's Annette, Sierra Summer, Doris Schroeder, Whitman #1585, 1960, 282 pages, EX/NM............**$10.00**

Walt Disney's Bedknobs & Broomsticks, Walsh & DaGradi, Whitman #1570, 1971, 212 pages, EX/NM............**$12.00**

Bottle Openers

A figural bottle opener is one where the cap lifter is an actual feature of the subject being portrayed — for instance, the bill of a pelican or the mouth of a four-eyed man. Most are made of painted cast iron or aluminum; others were chrome or brass plated. Some of the major bottle-opener producers were Wilton, John Wright, L&L, and Gadzik. They have been reproduced, so beware of any examples with 'new' paint. Condition of the paint is an important consideration when it comes to evaluating a vintage opener.

For more information, read *Figural Bottle Openers, Identification Guide*, by the Figural Bottle Opener Collectors. Number codes in our descriptions correspond with their book.

Advisor: Charlie Reynolds (See Directory, Bottle Openers)

Club: Figural Bottle Opener Collectors
Linda Fitzsimmons
9697 Gwynn Park Dr., Ellicott City, MD 21043; 301-465-9296

Newsletter: *Just for Openers*
John Stanley
3712 Sunningdale Way, Durham, NC 27707-5684; 919-419-1546. Quarterly newsletter covers all types of bottle openers and corkscrews.

Alligator, F-136, cast iron, VG.......................................**$70.00**
Alligator, F-139, white metal..**$25.00**
Amish boy, F-31, painted cast iron, rare, 1953, 4x2" ..**$225.00**
Bear head, F-426, cast iron, 3¾" **$130.00**
Billy goat, F-74a, aluminum, 2¾x1⅞" **$15.00**
Bulldog head, F-425, cast iron, ca 1900, 4x3¾x1½", NM..**$75.00**
Cat, F-95, brass, 2¼x3"...**$40.00**
Cocker spaniel, F-80, brown & white, EX.................**$120.00**
Dachshund, F-83, brass...**$50.00**
Dolphin, F-152, chrome, Italy, 6½" **$110.00**
Donkey, F-60, cast iron, paint traces...........................**$20.00**
Donkey, F-61, cast iron...**$50.00**
Fish, F-46, abalone...**$35.00**
Flamingo, F-120, cast iron, hollow, Wilton Products, EX, from $100 to...**$135.00**
Foundryman, F-29, aluminum...**$16.50**
Jimmy Carter, 1975, M...**$55.00**
Lamppost Drunk, F-1, cast iron, 4⅛" **$15.00**
Lobster, F-167, cast iron, EX paint..............................**$32.00**
Lobster, F-168, cast iron, red & black paint................**$32.00**
Monkey, F-89b, aluminum, 2⅝" **$15.00**
Nude, F-177, brass...**$55.00**
Nude native girl kneeling, zinc, 1950s.........................**$35.00**
Palm tree, F-21, brass...**$25.00**

Parrot, F-108, cast iron...**$50.00**
Parrot, F-112, Wilton Products, sm, VG.....................**$65.00**
Pelican, F-129, cast iron, EX paint...............................**$75.00**

Rooster, F-97, multicolor paint on cast iron, 3¼", NM, $75.00.

Salted pretzel, F-230 ....**$50.00**
Sea gull, F-123, cast iron...**$60.00**
Setter, F-79, cast iron, EX multicolored paint.............**$80.00**
Shovel, F-221, brass...**$20.00**
Signpost Drunk, F-11, cast iron, VG paint..................**$18.00**
Squirrel, F-93, brass, 2⅝" **$15.00**
Trout, F-159, cast iron..**$120.00**

Boyd Crystal Art Glass

After the Degenhart glass studio closed (see the Degenhart section for information), it was bought out by the Boyd family, who added many of their own designs to the molds they acquired from the Degenharts and other defunct glasshouses. They are located in Cambridge, Ohio, and the glass they've been pressing in the more than 350 colors they've developed since they opened in 1978 is marked with their 'B in diamond' logo. All the work is done by hand, and each piece is made in a selected color in limited amounts — a production run lasts only about twelve weeks or less. Items in satin glass or an exceptional slag are especially collectible, so are those with hand-painted details, commanding as much as 30% more.

Note: An 'R' in the following lines indicates an item that has been retired.

Advisor: Joyce Pringle (See Directory, Boyd)

Airplane, Mirage...**$11.00**
Airplane, Nile Green...**$13.50**
Angel, Millennium Slag...**$17.00**
Angel, Vaseline Carnival...**$22.00**
Artie the Penguin, Classic Black....................................**$15.00**
Artie the Penguin, Vanilla Coral.....................................**$15.00**
Bow Slipper, Aqua Diamond **$8.75**

Bow Slipper, Harvest Gold......................................**$8.50**
Bunny on Nest, Sunkist Carnival..........................**$10.00**
Bunny Salt, Mountain Haze **$17.50**
Candy the small Carousel Horse, Chocolate Carnival...**$11.00**
Candy the small Carousel Horse, Maverick Blue.......**$12.00**
Candy the small Carousel Horse, Purple Frost.............**$8.00**
Cat Slipper, Ritz Blue..**$31.00**
Cat Slipper, Rosie Pink **$9.50**
Chick Salt, Caramel...**$15.00**
Chick Salt, Copper Glo...**$12.00**
Chick Salt, Mountain Haze.....................................**$12.00**
Chick Salt, Nutmeg Carnival....................................**$9.50**
Eli & Sarah, Chocolate...**$12.00**
Elizabeth, Alpine Blue (R)..**$8.50**
Fuzzy Bear, Capri Blue (R).......................................**$9.00**
JB Scotty, Confetti...**$280.00**
JB Scotty, Daffodil (R) **$35.00**
JB Scotty, Mountain Haze **$32.00**
JB Scotty, Mulberry...**$110.00**
JB Scotty, Spring Suprise (R)...................................**$85.00**
Jeremy the Frog, Green Bouquet **$15.00**
Jeremy the Frog, Pacifica (R) **$9.25**
Joey the Horse, Cashmire Pink...............................**$42.00**
Joey the Horse, Heatherbloom **$65.00**
Joey the Horse, Rubina **$70.00**
Lil Luck the Unicorn, Sunkist Carnival (R)................**$9.00**
Louise, Ice Green..**$80.00**
Melissa, Peacock Blue **$8.00**
Nancy Doll, Vaseline **$13.50**
Pooch the Dog, Oh Fudge......................................**$16.00**
Sammy the Squirrel, Cardinal Red..........................**$27.00**
Skippy Dog, Pippin Green **$8.00**
Taffy the large Carousel Horse, Capri Blue **$20.00**
Taffy the large Carousel Horse, Vaseline Carnival **$28.50**
Tucker Car, Peach..**$12.50**
Turkey Salt, Crystal Carnival **$10.00**
Willie the Mouse, Pale Orchid **$8.25**
Zack the Elephant, Bermuda Slag **$45.00**
Zack the Elephant, Ebony.......................................**$55.00**
Zack the Elephant, Sandpipper **$15.00**

Boyds Bears and Friends

The cold-cast sculptures designed by Gary M. Lowenthal such as we've listed here have become very dear to the heart of many collectors who enthusiastically pursue his Bearstones, Folkstones, and Dollstones lines, particularly first editions (1Es). Counterfeits do exist. Be sure to watch for the signature bear paw print on Bearstones, the star on Folkstones, and the shoe imprints on the Dollstones. To learn more about the entire line of Boyd's Collectibles, we recommend this Internet price guide: *Rosie's Secondary Market Price Guide to Boyds Bears & Friends*, www.RosieWells.com.

Bearstone, 1994, Arthur, #2003-03, 4th edition, MIB...**$35.00**

Bearstones, 1993, Bailey w/suitcase (rough texture), #2000, 1st edition, MIB..............................**$220.00**
Bearstones, 1993, Moriarty, #2005, 3rd edition, MIB ..**$60.00**
Bearstones, 1993-96, Bailey in the Orchard, #2006, 1st edition, M..**$60.00**
Bearstones, 1993-96, Neville, #2002, 2nd edition, MIB ..**$50.00**
Bearstones, 1993-97, Wilson With Love Sonnets, #2007, 58th edition, MIB...........................**$35.00**
Bearstones, 1994-96, Bessie, #2239, 1st edition, MIB .**$65.00**
Bearstones, 1994-96, Grenville the Santa Bear, #2030, 8th edition, MIB.......................**$55.00**
Bearstones, 1994-97, Ted & Teddy, Father & Son Read, ##2223, 41st edition, MIB......................**$25.00**
Bearstones, 1995-97, Otis, Tax Time, #2262, 4th edition, MIB **$35.00**

Cookie jar, Grenville, 10" x 9", $70.00.

Dollstones, issued August 1995, Megan w/Elliot & Annie...Christmas Carol, #3504, 1st edition, MIB..**$45.00**
Dollstones, issued August 1996, Jean w/Elliot & Debbie...The Baker, #3510, 1st edition, MIB.............................**$45.00**
Dollstones, issued January 1996, Sarah & Heather w/Elliot, Dolly & Amelia, Tea for Four, #3507, 1st edition, MIB..**$60.00**
Folkstone, issued January 1995, Jingle Moose, #2830, 5th edition, MIB............................**$70.00**
Folkstones, Ingrid & Olaf, 1E/691, candle holder, 4¼"..**$40.00**
Folkstones, issued Spring 1997, Constance & Felicity, #28205, 2nd edition, MIB.................................**$50.00**
Folkstones, issued 1998, Luminette, limited edition, MIB...**$45.00**
Folkstones, 1994-96, Angel of Freedom, #2820, 10th edition, MIB **$25.00**
Folkstones, 1995-97, Nicholas w/book list, #2802, 10th edition, ornament, MIB **$22.50**
Folkstones, 1996, Nanick & Segfried, #2807, Canadian, 7", MIB **$75.00**

Brastoff, Sascha

Who could have predicted when Sascha Brastoff joined the Army's Air Force in 1942 that he was to become a well-known artist! It was during his service with the Air Force that he became interested in costume and scenery design, performing, creating Christmas displays and murals, and drawing war bond posters.

After Sascha's stint in the Armed Forces, he decided to follow his dream of producing ceramics and in 1947 opened a small operation in West Los Angeles, California. Just six years later along with Nelson Rockefeller and several other businessmen with extensive knowledge of mass production techniques he built a pottery on Olympic Boulevard in Los Angeles.

Brastoff designed all the products while supervising approximately 150 people. His talents were so great they enabled him to move with ease from one decade to another and successfully change motifs, mediums, and designs as warranted. Unusual and varying materials were used over the years. He created a Western line that was popular in the 1940s and early 1950s. Just before the poodle craze hit the nation in the 1950s, he had the foresight, to introduce his poodle line. The same was true for smoking accessories, and he designed elegant, hand-painted dinnerware as well. He was not modest when it came to his creations. He knew he was talented and was willing to try any new endeavor which was usually a huge success.

Items with the Sascha Brastoff full signature are always popular, and generally they command the highest prices. He modeled obelisks; one with a lid and a full signature would be regarded as a highly desirable example of his work. Though values for his dinnerware are generally lower than for his other productions, it has its own following. The Merbaby design is always high on collectors' lists. An unusual piece was found last year — a figural horse salt shaker, solid white with assorted stars. More than likely it was made as part of a set, possibly the Star Steed pattern. It was marked 'Sascha' under the glaze between the front legs.

The 1940 Clay Club pieces were signed either with a full signature or 'Sascha.' In 1947 Sascha hired a large group of artists to hand decorate his designs, and 'Sascha B' became the standard mark. Following the opening of his studio in 1953, a chanticleer, the name Sascha Brastoff, the copyright symbol, and a hand-written style number (all in gold) were used on the bottom, with 'Sascha B.' on the front or topside of the item. (Be careful not to confuse this mark with a full signature, California, U.S.A.) Costume designs at 20th Century Fox (1946 – 47) were signed 'Sascha'; war bonds and posters also carried the signature 'Sascha' and 'Pvt.' or 'Sgt. Brastoff.'

After Brastoff left his company in 1962, the mark became a 'R' in a circle (registered trademark symbol) with a style number, all handwritten. The chanticleer may also accompany this mark. Brastoff died on February 4, 1993. For additional information consult *The Collector's Encyclopedia of Sascha Brastoff* by Steve Conti, A. DeWayne Bethany, and Bill Seay. Another source of information is *The Collector's Encyclopedia of California Pottery, Second Edition,* by Jack Chipman. Both are published by Collector Books.

Ashtray, peacock, gray, blue & green on white, 4x13"...**$40.00**

Ashtray, Rooftops, free-form, 15½" L.....................**$45.00**
Ashtray, Smoke-Tree, rust-orange, 9" sq.................**$55.00**
Bowl, bull moose in white, black & gray on yellow background, 3-footed, 3½x6" dia.........................**$40.00**
Bowl, leaf & fern, gold accents over black sponge background, marked F44, 13x12½x4¼".....................**$95.00**

Canister, Rooftops, C43, 13", $250.00. (Photo courtesy Steve Conti, A DeWayne Bethany, and Bill Seay)

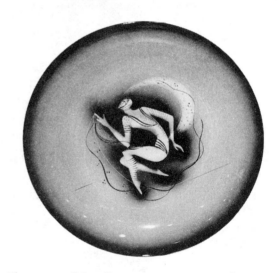

Charger, white figure on gray, 12", $200.00.

Cigarette box, black w/gold-shaded Oriental decor on lid, 4¾x7½x1¾"..**$40.00**
Creamer & sugar bowl, Surf Ballet, silver & blue marbling...**$50.00**
Dish, peacock, white w/black, gray, blues & greens, upturned edges, sq, 8x8"...................................**$60.00**
Dish, Surf Ballet, pink w/violet & gold, 2¼x6"..........**$45.00**
Figurine, Foresight bear, orange, resin, 9½"...............**$340.00**
Figurine, Hindsight bear, green, resin, 7"..................**$230.00**
Figurine, octopus, blue, resin, 10".........................**$260.00**
Figurine, rhino, blue, resin, 10x5".........................**$370.00**
Figurine, whale, orange, resin, 11".........................**$340.00**
Mug, Persian pattern, 5x3" dia................................**$40.00**
Nut dish, Star Steed, turquoise, C2 in gold on back, free-form, 2x7¼x5½"..**$80.00**
Plate, dove, charcoal on pink w/gold details, full signature, 10½" dia...**$85.00**

Punch set, Christmas tree design, 14½x7" bowl w/8 cups **$235.00**

Teapot, Surf Ballet, silver & blue marbling, 7½".........**$85.00**

Tile, city in clouds, blues, browns & greens, CP1, 21x16" **$300.00**

Tile, Temple Towers, CP3, 8x21" **$220.00**

Trinket box, Japanese pagodas in black & pink w/gold highlights, 8x5x2" **$55.00**

Vase, classic leaf motif on blue, #082, 8".....................**$65.00**

Vase, horse on 1 side, peacock on other, browns & grays on mottled gray background, gold trim, P1, 5x4x2"..**$45.00**

Vase, poodle on white, #066, 6x9" **$50.00**

Vase, Rooftops, teal, purple, rust, green & gold, cylindrical, #047, 8⅜x3⅝" dia **$65.00**

Vase, Star Steed, free-form, mk F21, 5¾x7"................**$50.00**

Vase, Star Steed, gold accents, sqd, 9⅜".....................**$95.00**

Vase, white w/maroon, light blue & gold bands, 2½x3" dia **$65.00**

Brayton Laguna

This company's products have proven to be highly collectible for those who appreciate their well-made, diversified items, some bordering on the whimsical. Durlin Brayton founded Brayton Laguna Pottery in 1927. The marriage between Durlin and Ellen (Webb) Webster Grieve a few years later created a partnership that brought together two talented people with vision and knowledge so broad that they were able to create many unique lines. At the height of Brayton's business success, the company employed over 125 workers and twenty designers.

Durlin's personally created items command a high price. Such items are hand turned, and those that were made from 1927 to 1930 are often incised 'Laguna Pottery' in Durlin's handwriting. These include cups, saucers, plates of assorted sizes, ashtrays, etc., glazed in eggplant, lettuce green, purple, and deep blue as well as other colors. Brayton Laguna's children's series (created by Lietta J. Dodd) has always been favored among collectors. However, many lines such as Calasia (artware), Blackamoors, sculpture, and the Hillbilly line are picking up large followings of their own. The sculptures, Indian, and Peruvian pieces including voodoo figures, matadors, and drummers, among others, were designed by Carol Safholm. Andy Anderson created the Hillbilly series, most notably the highly successful shotgun wedding group. He also created the calf, bull, and cow set which was done in several glazes. While the purple set has been the most popular, they are relatively common and often a hard-sell today. But when the three-piece set is found in an elusive glaze, it is even more valuable than the wedding group. Webton Ware is a good line for those who want inexpensive pottery and a Brayton Laguna mark. These pieces depict farmland and country-type themes such as farmers planting, women cooking, etc. Some items — wall pockets, for instance — may be found with only a flower motif;

wallhangings of women and men are popular, yet hard to find in this or any of Brayton's lines. Predominantly, the background of Webton Ware is white, and it's decorated with various pastel glazes including yellow, green, pink, and blue.

More than ten marks plus a paper label were used during Brayton's history. On items too small for a full mark, designers would simply incise their initials. Webb Brayton died in 1948, and Durlin died just three years later. Struggling with and finally succumbing to the effect of the influx of foreign pottery on the American market, Brayton Laguna finally closed in 1968.

For further study, read *The Collector's Encyclopedia of California Pottery Second Edition,* by Jack Chipman (Collector Books).

See also Cookie Jars.

Candle holder, Blackamoor seated on blue rug, 5"..**$100.00**

Figurine, baby sitting in diaper, lg cowlick in hair, big blue eyes, 4", EX...**$105.00**

Figurine, bull, head down, brown w/ivory horns, ca 1950s, USA N 551, 8x6½x14" **$30.00**

Figurine, cow, purple, 5½x9" **$200.00**

Figurine, donkey & cart, cart bottom & slats are wood, EX...**$130.00**

Figurine, Figaro (Pinocchio), pink w/black & white features & trim, 4½x3½"...**$125.00**

Figurine, Gay Nineties Bar, 3 men standing at bar, 8½x7½", from $100 to..**$125.00**

Figurine, lady w/2 Russian Wolfhounds, powder blue dress, yellow hair, white dogs, ca 1943, 11" **$135.00**

Figurine, Matilda, w/2 baskets, white shirt, yellow flowered vest, rose dress, ca 1930-37, 7⅝"........................**$110.00**

Figurine, panther, snarling, #23-26, black with jeweled collar, NM, $200.00. (Photo courtesy Lee Garmon)

Figurine, Pat (little girl) w/doll at back, 7", EX.........**$135.00**

Figurine, pouter pigeon, white & maroon, puffed chest & tail feathers spread, 5½", EX......................................**$50.00**

Figurine, Rosita, Spanish girl holding flower basket, 5½"...**$100.00**

Figurine, Sambo, Black boy in blue bibs, yellow hat, white shirt, 7¾" **$300.00**

Figurine, stylized bird, twisted neck & body, black w/gold trim, 9½x11", EX...**$165.00**

Figurine/planter, horse, light blue & lavender w/off-white mane, hooves & tail, planter in head, 5½x6½", EX.............**$25.00**

Flower holder, Sally, freckled face, 7", EX....................$45.00

Pitcher, orange-red w/green, early, 2⅝", EX..............$70.00

Planter, Blackamoor, kneeling, blue & yellow turban, pink shirt w/flowers, yellow pants, EX $130.00

Planter, lady in blue/green bloomer dress, seated on planter, 6¼x8½", EX..$50.00

Salt & pepper shakers, cat & dog, white w/blue & maroon crossing stripes, 4¼", 3½", pr $65.00

Salt & pepper shakers, Mammy & Chef, blue & white, 5", pr $200.00

Salt & pepper shakers, Provincial man & lady, brown, white & yellow, 5½", pr $100.00

Vase, sea horse, white ribbing w/turquoise trim, back pocket trimmed in rose, 8½" $225.00

Vase, white bonnet w/pink hand-painted roses & blue ribbon, 3x4", M..$35.00

Breweriana

Breweriana refers to items produced by breweries which are intended for immediate use and discard, such as beer cans and bottles, as well as countless items designed for long-term use while promoting a particular brand. Desirable collectibles include metal, cardboard, and neon signs; serving trays; glassware; tap handles; mirrors; coasters; and other paper goods.

Breweriana is generally divided into two broad categories: (pre- and postprohibition). Preprohibition breweries were numerous and distributed advertising trays, calendars, etched glassware and other items. Because American breweries were founded by European brewmasters, preprohibition advertising often depicted themes from that region. Brewery scenes, pretty women, and children were also common.

Competition was intense among the breweries that survived prohibition. The introduction of canned beer in 1935, the postwar technology boom, and the advent of television in the late 1940s produced countless new ways to advertise beer. Moving signs, can openers, enameled glasses, and neon are prolific examples of postprohibition breweriana.

A better understanding of the development of the product as well as advertising practices of companies helps in evaluating the variety of breweriana items that may be found. For example, 'chalks' are figural advertising pieces which were made for display in taverns or wherever beer was sold. Popular in the 1940s and 1950s, they were painted and glazed to resemble carnival prizes. Breweries realized in addition to food shopping, women generally assumed the role of cook — what better way to persuade women to buy a particular beer than a cookbook? Before the advent of the bottle cap in the early 1900s, beer bottles were sealed with a porcelain stopper or cork. Opening a corked bottle required a corkscrew which often had a brewery logo.

Prior to the advent of refrigeration, beer was often served at room temperature. A mug or glass was often half warm beer and half foam. A 1" by 8" flat piece of plastic was used to scrape foam from the glass. These foam scrapers came in various colors and bore the logo of the beer on tap.

Before prohibition, beer logos were applied to glassware by etching the glass with acid. These etched glasses often had ornate designs that included a replica of the actual brewery or a bust of the brewery's founder. After prohibition, enameling became popular and glasses were generally 'painted' with less ornate designs. Mugs featuring beer advertising date back to the 1800s in America; preprohibition versions were generally made of pottery or glass. Ceramic mugs became popular after prohibition and remain widely produced today.

Tap handles are a prominent way to advertise a particular brand wherever tap beer is sold. Unlike today's ornate handles, 'ball knobs' were prominent prior to the 1960s. They were about the size of a billiard ball with a flat face that featured a colorful beer logo.

The books we recommend for this area of collecting are *World of Beer Memorabilia* by Herb and Helen Haydock and *Vintage Bar Ware* by Stephen Visakay. (Both are published by Collector Books.)

See also Barware; Beer Cans.

Club: Beer Can Collectors of America
747 Merus Ct., Fenton, MO 63026
Annual dues: $27; although the club's roots are in beer can collecting, this organization offers a bimonthly breweriana magazine featuring many regional events and sponsors an annual convention; www.bcca.com

Ashtray, Adolph Coors Golden Brewery, ceramic dish w/raised center, 4 rests on rim, 1936 Colorado State Fair, EX+ $30.00

Ashtray, Hamm's, ceramic bear lying on back w/pendant around neck lettered Have a Hamm's, EX+ $65.00

Ashtray, Yuengling's, cast-iron arrowhead shape w/match holder, VG+...$60.00

Banner, Fox's DeLuxe Beer/The End of the Hunt, fox hunt & bottle graphics on cloth, ca 1940, 16x35", NM...$120.00

Bell/opener, Ring for Hopfheimer Beer on metal bell form w/opener as handle, 1930s, VG+ $45.00

Bingo card, Flock's Beer, cardboard w/blockout windows, 1930s, 8½x7½", VG+ $20.00

Booklet, A Trip Through the Adam Scheidt Brewery With a Camera, 16 pages w/black & white photos, 1930s, 8½x11", VG+ $45.00

Booklet, Debuque Brewing & Bottling Co, 42 pages w/scenes of brewery & color lithos of bottles, VG+ $180.00

Charger, Falstaff, tin w/tavern scene, 1970s, 24" dia, EX...$25.00

Display, Blatz barrel man playing banjo & lg bottle on stage w/It's Draft Brewed Blatz marquee, pot metal, light-up, EX..$85.00

Display, Blatz bottle man holding pennant & frothy mug, EX $45.00

Display, Busch Bavarian Beer can rotates on base, plastic w/paper label, EX...$30.00

Display, Falstaff, bottle, can & frothy stem glass encased in plastic bock of ice w/tongs, 1950s, 14x18", VG ...$35.00

Display, Falstaff, plaster figure holding Falstaff emblem & lg bottle on base reading America's Premium..., 16", VG+ **$200.00**

Display, Gibbons Beer, plaster relief sign w/hunting dog pointing, Is Good! lettered above, 11x20", EX ...**$200.00**

Display, Hamm's Beer, bear holding calendar sign on base lettered Big Bear Drinking Brotherhood, plastic, 16", EX+ **$85.00**

Display, Hamm's Beer, lighted barrel form w/flipping scenes featuring the Hamm's bear, EX+..........................**$135.00**

Display, Hamm's Beer Bear, promotional ceramic item made by the Red Wing Pottery Co., 1950s, 12", $475.00. (Photo courtesy June Moon)

Display, Pabst Blue Ribbon Beer, bar scene w/bartender behind bar, clock on wall & bottle, pot metal, EX................**$65.00**

Display, Schlitz, plastic & metal motion light w/revolving message in window on bottom part, 1960s, NM+........**$20.00**

Display, Utica Club Beer, plaster Utica waiter holding frothy glass on base lettered UC For Me, 9½", EX **$170.00**

Display, Valley Forge Beer, vacuum-formed 3-D figures of men boxing (1 white & 1 black), 1950s, 14", VG+, pr **$115.00**

Drinking glass, Anheuser-Busch, embossed pilsner, 6½", NM **$25.00**

Drinking glass, Puritan Beer, etched goblet, pre-prohibition, EX+ **$20.00**

Fan, Fort Pitt, cardboard, head images of couple toasting w/silhouette against moon in background, 1930s, 12", EX+ **$60.00**

Foam scraper, Chief Oskosh Beer, red on blue, 1940s, EX **$60.00**

Frisbee, Hudepohl Pure Grain Beer, plastic w/Happy Face in center, 1970s, 9¼" dia, EX......................................**$8.00**

Letter opener/ruler, Iroquois Beer & Ale, metal table knife shape w/ruler marks along edge, 1950s, EX+......**$12.00**

Match holder, Busch Beer/John Busch Brewing Co, celluloid, VG...**$100.00**

Mechanical pencil, Budweiser, name & logo, 1940s, EX+ **$18.00**

Model kit, Budweiser Clydesdale 8-Horse Hitch, AMT, 1970s, NMIB..**$25.00**

Model sprint car, Budweiser, diecast metal, 1980s, 1/24th scale, MIB **$35.00**

Mug, Coors 100th Anniversary, decal on white high gloss glaze, 1973, EX+ **$30.00**

Mug, Gluek Brewing Co, ceramic barrel form w/G-in-star logo embossed & outlined in blue on front, Red Wing, EX+ **$30.00**

Napkin, Camden Beer, paper, bottle graphics on white, 1950s, VG **$3.00**

Opener, Sprenger Brewing Co, cast-iron framed figure of a man holding up mug, wall-mount, EX **$260.00**

Patch, Alpen Brau Beer, cloth bottle-cap shape, white, gold & red, 1950s, 8" dia **$12.00**

Patch, Grossvater Beer/Old Cockney Ale, ribbon banner at top, white, yellow & blue on red, cloth, 1930s, 6x11", NM+ **$35.00**

Pin-back button, Play on the Budweiser 1941 3,000,000 Barrel team, white on red, 2½", EX **$40.00**

Pocket calendar, Daeufer's Peerless Beer, celluloid barrel shape w/graphics, 1934-35, NM **$70.00**

Pocketknife, Utica Club Beer, pearl-like handle, 1930s, G+ **$40.00**

Salt & pepper shakers, Utica Beer, Dooly & Shultz stein figures, ceramic, EX, pr...**$125.00**

Sign, Burgie!, diecut horse head in shadow-box frame marked Palomino at top, 1950s, 17½x14", EX......**$25.00**

Sign, Drewry's Beer, self-framed cardboard w/image of fisherman in boat reeling in fish, Reel Enjoyment!, 22x29", EX..**$85.00**

Sign, Falstaff Beer, Premium Quality... & shield logo on red plexiglass w/lighted footed base, for back bar use, EX **$115.00**

Sign, Hamm's Beer, faux stained glass w/name & image of bear on white, red & blue border, 1980s, 17½x16", NM+ **$65.00**

Sign, Hudepohl Beer, vacuum-formed baseball theme w/hitter swinging & catcher in position, Always A Hit!, 10x15", G+ **$115.00**

Sign, Lucky Lager, red letter L in script w/red & white neon tubing atop box lettered Lucky on Tap, 1960s, 18x16", NM **$40.00**

Sign, neon; Schlitz, white tubing, original transformerworks, 12" x 34", EX+, $150.00. (Photo courtesy Buffalo Bay Auction Co.)

Sign, Regal, cardboard shadow-box w/dog's head, lettered Beagle, Pointer, or Boxer on self-frame, 19x17", EX+, ea **$60.00**

Sign, Rolling Rock, neon lettering w/oblong neon tube frame, 1960s, NM...**$150.00**

Sign, Schmidt, lighted motion, The Brew That Grew With the Great Northwest, geese behind lg frothy glass, box frame, VG **$60.00**

Sign, Stegmaier Porter, diecut cardboard bottle shape w/wet-look, 16x4", EX **$10.00**

Sign, Stegmaier's Gold Medal Beer, cardboard hanger w/image of sign & butterfly on wood-look background, 17x12", VG+ **$45.00**

Sign, Sterling Super Bru, vertical pennant shape w/We Have... lettered above lg bottle, self-framed metal, 17½x9", EX **$150.00**

Stein, Anheuser-Busch/Budweiser, #CS-53, MIB **$65.00**

Stein, Anheuser-Busch/Ceramarte, A-&-Eagle logo, CSL2, w/lid, 1975, 9¾", EX..**$100.00**

Stein, Anheuser-Busch/Ceramarte, Bavarian house, ½-litre **$200.00**

Stein, Anheuser-Busch/Ceramarte, Busch, CS-44, 1980, EX **$100.00**

Stein, Anheuser-Busch/Ceramarte, Centennial Olympic Games, 1996, 5¾", EX..**$25.00**

Stein, Anheuser-Busch/Ceramarte, Clydesdale team in relief w/A-&-Eagle logo, pounded pewter lid, CSL29, 1976, EX **$100.00**

Stein, Anheuser-Busch/Ceramarte, Declaration of Independence, 1976, 7⅝", EX............................**$100.00**

Stein, Anheuser-Busch/Michelob, #CS-54, MIB **$40.00**

Stein, Anhueser-Busch, Budweiser Girl, Italy, 1973, 1-litre..**$200.00**

Stein, Anhueser-Busch, 10 Years Safe Service, 1978, 9".......**$100.00**

Stein, Anhueser-Busch, 30 Years Safe Service, 1994, 12½" ..**$100.00**

Stein, Anhueser-Busch/Albert Stahl, Budweiser Frog, figural, 9½", EX **$150.00**

Stein, Weber, ceramic w/white lettering & trim on deep blue high gloss glaze, 15", EX......................................**$120.00**

Tankard, Anheuser-Busch/Black & Tan, #CS-314, MIB..**$60.00**

Tankard, Anheuser-Busch/Budweiser, Joe E Louis, #CS-206, MIB **$35.00**

Tankard, Anheuser-Busch/Winchester, Calf Roping (#GM-19) or Bull Riding (#GM-22), MIB, ea....................**$35.00**

Tankard, Prima/Independent Brewing Assn, glass w/name & logo on porcelain & pewter lid, crown embossed on base, 6" **$55.00**

Tankard, Union/Shiller & Co, glass w/embossed pewter lid, 5¾", EX...**$160.00**

Tap knob, Acme the Favorite, chrome ball shape w/enameled metal insert, 1940s, NM+ **$100.00**

Tap knob, Bud King of Beers, baseball motif w/Phillies logo on Lucite, 1980s, EX+ **$10.00**

Tap knob, Koch's, wooden ball shape w/Koch's in red script lettering, 1950s, EX+ **$30.00**

Tap Knob, Michelob/Anheuser-Busch, red Bakelite w/gold & red enameled metal insert w/black lettering, 1940s, EX+ **$75.00**

Tap knob, Miller High Life, red Bakelite w/white-on-red painted metal insert, EX+ **$90.00**

Tap knob, Schlitz Malt Liquor, brown plastic bull's head w/advertising band around neck, 1960s, EX........**$10.00**

Thermometer, Old Reading Beer, dial gauge insert on round tin front w/decorative graphics, cardboard backing, 9", NM **$60.00**

Thermometer sign, Hamm's, reverse-painted glass w/image of bear leaning on thermometer, wood frame, 19x8", EX+ **$75.00**

Tip tray, Century Beer lettered on gold rim w/2 gents enjoying brew in center, round, EX **$100.00**

Tip tray, Miller High Life, rectangular w/slanted sides, 1950s, VG+...**$6.00**

Toy mascot figure, Hamm's Bear dressed as baseball player w/Hamm's 1 Bear on shirt, stuffed plush, 21", EX.**$60.00**

Tray, Golden Age Beer, round w/deep rim, shield logo on radiating stripes, Fernwood Brewing Co, VG+.....**$65.00**

Tray, Miller High Life, oval w/deep rim, girl seated on crescent moon against night sky, 15", EX **$40.00**

Tray, Ruppert Beer, round w/deep sides, cartoon image in center, 1950s, VG+...**$35.00**

Watch fob, Peru Beer Co, brass & enameled medallion, NM **$100.00**

Yardstick, Strohs Beer, painted wood trifold, red & yellow, 1960s, EX...**$15.00**

Breyer Horses

Breyer horses have been popular children's playthings since they were introduced in 1952, and you'll see several at any large flea market. Garage sales are good sources as well. The earlier horses had a glossy finish, but after 1968 a matt finish came into use. You'll find smaller domestic animals too. They are evaluated by condition, rarity, and desirability; some of the better examples may be worth a minimum of $150.00. Our values are for average condition; examples in mint condition are worth from 10% to 15% more.

For more information and listings, see *Schroeder's Collectible Toys, Antique to Modern*; and *Breyer Animal Collector's Guide* by Felicia Browell. (Both are published by Collector Books.)

Action Stock Horse Foal, bay pinto, 1984-86, Classic scale **$20.00**

Action Stock Horse Foal (Cricket), brown bay, Traditional scale, 1995-96..**$18.00**

Andalusian Foal (Proud Mare & Newborn Foal), apricot dun, Classic scale, 1993......................................**$10.00**

Appaloosa Performance Horse (JC Penney, Stallion), gray blanket, Traditional scale, ca 1984 ....**$55.00**

Arabian Mare, gray, Stablemate scale, 1996-97..............**$4.00**

Arabian Stallion (Desert Arabian Family), red bay w/black points, Classic scale, 1992-94 ....**$15.00**

Black Beauty (Dream Weaver), sorrel, limited edition, Traditional scale, 1991 ....**$35.00**

Black Beauty (King of the Wind Set), bay w/black points, Classic scale, 1990-93....................................**$15.00**

Bucking Bronco, matt gray, 1961-67 ....**$150.00**

Cantering Welsh Pony, chestnut, no ribbons, Traditional scale, 1979-81 ....**$50.00**

Draft Horse, dapple gray, Stablemate scale, 1989-94 .... **$9.00**

Family Arabian Mare, bay w/black points, Traditional scale, 1967-74 .... **$25.00**

Fighting Mestano, buckskin, Classic scale, 1994-97 .... **$20.00**

Fighting Stallion, bay, Traditional scale, 1961-87 .... **$30.00**

Fighting Stallion, glossy charcoal w/white mane, tail, stockings, Traditional scale, 1961-71 .... **$120.00**

Foundation Stallion, black, no markings, Traditional scale, 1977-87 .... **$25.00**

Galiceno, bay w/black points, Traditional scale, 1978-82 ... **$35.00**

Hobo (Hobo Gift Set), buckskin, Classic scale, 1975-81 .... **$60.00**

Jet Run (Trakehner Family), dark red w/chestnut star, Classic scale, 1992-94 .... **$15.00**

Jumping Horse (Sears), seal brown w/black points, Traditional scale, 1982-83 .... **$80.00**

Keen (Hanoverian Family), Classic scale, 1992-93 ...... **$15.00**

Kelso (Jeremy), brown, Classic scale, 1993-94 .... **$20.00**

Kelso (Sears, Draw Horses w/Sam Savitt), bay w/black points, Classic scale, full set, 1992 .... **$40.00**

Lipizzan Stallion (Toys R Us/Unicorn III), black w/gold accents, Classic scale, 1997 .... **$35.00**

Lying Down Unicorn (Toys R Us), glossy black or white, Traditional scale, 1997, ea **$25.00**

Man O' War, Traditional Scale, #47, 1969 – 95, $20.00. (Photo courtesy Carol Karbowiak Gilbert)

Mesteno, dark buckskin w/dark brown points, Classic scale, 1992-98 .... **$15.00**

Morgan, bay, bald face, Traditional scale, 1965-71 ..... **$55.00**

Mustang Foal (Trakehner Family), matt bay, 1992-94, Classic scale **$15.00**

Mustang Mare (Mustang Family), chestnut pinto, Classic scale, 1976-90 .... **$15.00**

Mustang Semi-Rearing (American Mustang), sorrel, Traditional scale, 1987-89 .... **$42.00**

Native Dancer, gray, Stablemate scale, 1976-94 .... **$7.00**

Nursing Foal, Sears, Pinto Mare & Suckling Foal Set, bay pinto, Traditional scale, foal only, 1982-83 .... **$28.00**

Pegasus (Lipizzan Stallion), alabaster (no trim color), Classic scale, 1984-87 .... **$50.00**

Proud Arabian Foal, rose-gray w/gray points, Traditional scale, 1989-90 .... **$25.00**

Quarter Horse Foal (Montgomery Ward, Appaloosa Family), black w/hind blanket, Classic scale, 1982 .... **$18.00**

Quarter Horse Yearling, liver chestnut, Traditional scale, 1970-80 .... **$35.00**

Rearing Stallion (Promises), dark bay pinto, Classic scale, 1994-95 .... **$15.00**

Ruffian, (Glory & Plank Jump Gift Set), dun w/black points, Classic scale, horse only, 1995-96 .... **$18.00**

Ruffian (Lula), bay w/black points, Classic scale, 1991-92 .... **$18.00**

Running Mare, woodgrain, Traditional scale, 1963-65 .. **$150.00**

Saddlebred, black, Stablemate scale, 1989-90 .... **$13.00**

Scamper (Barrel Racer), bay w/black points, Classic scale, 1998 .... **$20.00**

Seabiscuit, bay, Stablemate scale, 1976-90 .... **$9.00**

Seamps (Black Silks), black, 1997, Classic scale **$15.00**

Sham #410 (wheat-ear version), 1984 – 88, $40.00.
(Photo courtesy Carol Karbowiak Gilbert)

Sham (Arabian Stallion & Frisky Foal I), dappled bay w/black points, Traditional scale, 1994 .... **$35.00**

Shire (Riegseckers), palomino, Traditional scale, 1985 .**$125.00**

Stud Spider (Blanket Appaloosa), chestnut, Traditional scale, 1990-91 .... **$35.00**

Swamps (Black Silk), black, Classic scale, 1997 .... **$15.00**

Terrang, dark brown, Classic scale, 1975-90 .... **$20.00**

Western Prancing Horse, smoke, Traditional scale, 1961-76 .... **$30.00**

Other Animals

Bighorn Ram, matt tan, 1969-80 .... **$82.00**

Bison, matt brown w/dark head, 1994-96 .... **$22.00**

Boxer, tan/fawn, 1958-74 .... **$35.00**

Buffalo, brown, 1965-91 .... **$35.00**

Elephant, battleship gray, w/boy **$100.00**

Guernsey Cow, matt tan & white pinto, 1972-73 .... **$40.00**

Jasper the Market Hog, white & gray, 1974-2000 .... **$10.00**

Poodle, woodgrain, 1961-64 ....$300.00
St Bernard, 1972-80 ....$40.00

Brahma Bull, Traditional Scale, #70, glossy, 1958 – 93, from $40.00 to $50.00.

British Royal Commemoratives

While seasoned collectors may prefer the older pieces using circa 1840 (Queen Victoria's reign) as their starting point, even present-day souvenirs make a good inexpensive beginning collection. Ceramic items, glassware, metalware, and paper goods have been issued on the occasion of weddings, royal tours, birthdays, christenings, and many other celebrations. Food tins are fairly easy to find, and range in price from about $30.00 to around $75.00 for those made since the 1950s.

We've all seen that items related to Princess Diana have appreciated rapidly since her untimely and tragic demise, and in fact collections are being built exclusively from memorabilia marketed both before and after her death. For more information, we recommend *British Royal Commemoratives* by Audrey Zeder.

Advisor: Audrey Zeder (See Directory, British Royalty Commemoratives)

Beaker, Charles/Diana wedding, brown portrait w/decor, Doulton, 3½" $85.00
Bell, Charles/Diana wedding, crystal w/engraved decor, Prince of Wales feathers, 4" $45.00
Book, Charles/Diana in America by Levenson, hardback, 1985 ....$30.00
Booklet, Diana - Diary of a Princess, 1985, Austrian ..$30.00
Bookmark, Princess Diana memorial, blue woven silk w/gold decor...$20.00
Bookmark, Queen Mother 100 Birthday, white leather w/gold portrait & decoration $15.00
Bottle, Charles/Diana wedding, relief portrait w/decor, amber, Millville, 6x5" $40.00
Bottle, Prince William birth, multicolor cherubs, Wade ..$65.00
Bowl, Charles/Diana wedding, sepia portrait/multicolor, Price Kennsington, 4" $15.00

Cup & saucer, Prince William birth, black & white cherub decor, Worcester.....................................$85.00
Doll, Prince William, vinyl, blue & white romper suit, Nesbet, 18" $195.00
Egg cup, Charles/Diana divorce, sepia portrait w/decor, footed, Coronet.................................$55.00
Ephemera, Charles/Diana wedding, beer bottle labels, group of 7..$25.00
Ephemera, Charles/Diana wedding, paper coaster, Prince of Wales feathers decor.........................$5.00
Ephemera, Charles/Diana wedding, window sticker, black portrait, multicolor foil $10.00
Figure, Princess Diana, 1997 bobbing-head doll, limited edition of 500, 5¼" $100.00
Magazine, Hello, August 19, 1995, Diana cover, 10-page article $25.00
Magazine, Maclean's July 24, 2000, The Queen Mother at 100 ....$15.00
Magazine, Sunday Times 1977, The Queen & Her Ships .$20.00
Miniature, Charles/Diana wedding, loving cup, gold portrait w/decor, Wade, 2" $55.00
Miniature, Prince William first birthday, loving cup, multicolor portrait, 3x1¼" $55.00
Mug, Charles/Diana engagement, black & white individual portraits w/decor, cream, Stoneware.........$55.00
Mug, Charles/Diana wedding, purple, black & white portrait w/decor, stoneware $35.00
Mug, Prince Andrew 40th birthday, multicolor portrait w/decor, limited edition of 50, Chown.........$75.00
Mug, Prince Henry 2000, 16th birthday, multicolor portrait w/decor, limited edition of 50, Chown.........$75.00
Mug, Prince William first birthday, multicolor portrait w/decor, thumb-grip handle, Coronet........$45.00
Mug, Prince William 1982 birth, Bunnykins & birth decor, Doulton.......................................$65.00
Mug, Prince William 2000, 18th birthday, multicolor portrait w/decor, limited edition of 80, Chown.........$75.00
Mug, Princess Anne 1973 wedding, black w/gold portrait w/decor, Portmeirion...............................$60.00

Mug, Queen Elizabeth and Prince Philip 25th wedding anniversary, Wedgwood, 4", $165.00.

Novelty, Charles/Diana wedding, soap bar & plastic commemorative container, Morny $35.00

Novelty, Charles/Diana wedding tree ornament, multicolor portrait w/decor, round glass................................$20.00
Paperweight, Charles/Diana wedding relief portrait, amber glass, round, 3½"..$40.00
Paperweight, Princess Ann, 1977 cameo portrait on green, Baccarat $165.00
Pendant, Princess Diana, multicolor portrait, silver-tone bezel, 2"..$20.00
Pin-back button, Prince Charles, portrait on pale blue w/decor, 1953, 1"...$25.00
Plaque, Prince Henry 1984 christening, free-standing, Coronet, 4" $55.00

Plate, Prince Charles and Lady Diana, wedding commemorative, Coalport, $125.00.

Plate, Charles/Diana wedding, blue jasper, relief portrait w/decor, Wedgwood, 4".........................$55.00
Plate, Charles/Diana wedding, cobalt blue glass, gold portrait w/decor, 6x3 ....$25.00
Plate, Elizabeth II 1991 Washington visit, multicolor Queen/Bush portrait, 10" $195.00
Plate, Prince William 1982 birth, multicolor Charles/Diana portrait w/decor, Duchess, 8½" $35.00
Postcard, Prince William 18th birthday, blue w/portrait & multicolor 18s, Tanner....................$5.00
Postcard, Princess Diana memorial, opening of Peter Pan Gardens...$5.00
Pressed glass, Elizabeth II coronation plate, relief portrait, clear, 7" $35.00
Record, Elizabeth II 1977 jubilee, multicolor commerative cover, 2 records, 33⅓ rpm $35.00
Scrapbook, Elizabeth II 1959 Open Seaway, multicolor portrait cover, unused $35.00
Spoon, Prince Henry birth, enamel bowl w/portrait, silver plate $35.00
Stamps, Charles/Diana wedding, 1-stamp block, Seychelles, 4¾x4" $6.00
Stamps, Charles/Diana wedding, 4-stamp block, Korea, 7½ x 5½".....................................$25.00
Teapot, Charles/Diana wedding, flow-blue portrait w/decor, 4-cup, Staffordshire.......................$200.00
Textile, Elizabeth II jubilee scarf, multicolor portrait w/decor, 25x25" $35.00

Textile, Prince Charles 1969 investiture, child's apron, multicolor decor $75.00
Thimble, Prince William birth, gold w/multicolor decor, bone china, Spode.............................$35.00
Tile, Charles/Diana wedding, black & white portrait, pastel decor, round, 6" $35.00
Tin, Charles/Diana wedding, multicolor portrait in relief w/gold decor, 2x5" dia...................$45.00
Tin, Elizabeth II Jubilee, multicolor portrait in relief w/floral decor, 5½" dia.......................$35.00
Tin, Queen Mother 100th birthday, multicolor portrait w/decor on gold, 9x6.........................$40.00
Tray, Charles/Diana wedding, multicolor portrait, red, white & blue border, 7x6" $25.00

Brock of California

This was the trade name of the B.J. Brock Company, located in Lawndale, California. They operated from 1947 until 1980, and some of the dinnerware lines they produced have become desirable collectibles. One of the most common themes revolved around country living, farmhouses, barns, chickens, and cows. Patterns were Rooster, California Farmhouse, and California Rustic. Shapes echoed the same concept — there were skillets, milk cans, and flatirons fashioned into sugar bowls, creamers, and salt and pepper shakers. The company marketed a three-piece children's set as well. Also look for their '50s modern line called Manzanita, with pink and charcoal branches on platinum. With the interest in this style of dinnerware on the increase, this should be one to watch.

Carafe, farm scene, $35.00.

Bowl, candle holder; Rooster, on fence, 3-footed, 2¼x6½" dia, EX $45.00
Bowl, Forever Yours, 8¾" $24.00
Bowl, fruit/dessert; Forever Yours...........................$10.00
Bowl, girl milking cow, 9"...$22.00
Butter dish, farm scene, w/lid, ¼-lb $35.00

Coffeepot, Rooster, 8-cup, 10", from $50 to **$60.00**
Creamer, California Farmhouse...................................**$12.00**
Cup & saucer, California Farmhouse.........................**$18.00**
Cup & saucer, Forever Yours....................................**$12.00**
Dish, deviled egg; Rooster, holds 12 eggs, 13" dia **$30.00**
Lazy susan, farm scene, 5 sections w/center covered bowl, on wooden base, from $50 to **$60.00**
Plate, bread & butter; Forever Yours..........................**$5.00**
Plate, dinner; California Farmhouse **$20.00**
Plate, dinner; Forever Yours **$14.00**
Plate, dinner; Rooster **$18.00**
Skillet, Rooster **$28.00**
Sugar bowl, California Farmhouse, w/lid **$14.00**
Sugar bowl, Forever Yours, w/lid..............................**$28.00**
Tidbit tray, farm scene w/rooster on fence, trees & barn, 3-tiered, 6¾", 9" & 11" plates, 13½" H, from $55 to ..**$65.00**

Bubble Bath Containers

There's no hotter area of collecting today than items from the '50s through the '70s that are reminiscent of kids' early TV shows and hit movies, and bubble bath containers fill the bill. Most of these were made in the 1960s. The Colgate-Palmolive Company produced the majority of them — they're the ones marked 'Soaky' — and these seem to be the most collectible. Each character's name is right on the bottle. Other companies followed suit; Purex also made a line, so did Avon. Be sure to check for paint loss, and look carefully for cracks in the brittle plastic heads of the Soakies. Our values are for examples in excellent to near mint condition.

For more information, we recommend *Schroeder's Collectible Toys, Antique to Modern*, and *Collector's Guide to Bubble Bath Containers* by Greg Moore and Joe Pizzo. (Both are published by Collector Books.)

Advisors: Matt and Lisa Adams (See Directory, Bubble Bath Containers)

Brutus, Colgate-Palmolive, NM, $45.00; Popeye, Colgate-Palmolive, NM, $40.00.

Alvin (Chipmunks), Colgate-Palmolive, white sweater w/black A, cap head, NM **$30.00**
Anastasia, Kid Care, 1997, NM.................................**$8.00**
Augie Doggie, Purex, orange w/green shirt, original tag, EX..**$45.00**
Baloo Bear, Colgate-Palmolive, 1966, NM **$40.00**
Barney Rubble, Milvern (Purex), blue outfit w/yellow accents, NM..**$35.00**
Batman, Kid Care, blue & gray w/yellow belt, 1995, M ..**$10.00**
Bear, Tubby Time, cap head, EX................................**$35.00**
Beauty & the Beast, Cosrich, original tag, ea from $5 to **$8.00**
Bobo Bubbles, Lander, 1950s, NM **$30.00**
Bugs Bunny, Colgate-Palmolive, light blue & white, NM .**$25.00**
Cecil (Beany & Cecil), Purex, 1962, NM....................**$25.00**
Cement Truck, Colgate-Palmolive, blue & gray w/movable wheels, EX+..**$35.00**
Darth Vader, Omni, 1981, NM.................................**$20.00**
Dick Tracy, Colgate-Palmolive, 1965, NM..................**$50.00**
Dopey, Colgate-Palmolive, purple, yellow & red, 1960s, NM **$25.00**
El Cabong, Knickerbocker (Purex), black, yellow & white, rare, G+ **$50.00**
Ernie (Sesame Street), Minnetonka, holding rubber duckie, original tag, M **$8.00**

Felix the Cat, Colgate-Palmolive, 1960s, blue variation, $30.00. (Photo courtesy Greg Moore and Joe Pizzo)

Fozzie Bear, Muppet Treasure Island, Calgon, 1996, NM..**$10.00**
Frankenstein, Colgate-Palmolive, 1963, NM.................**$95.00**
Genie (Aladdin), Cosrich, M **$5.00**
GI Joe (Drill Instructor), DuCair Boescence, 1980s, NM ..**$15.00**
Gumby, M&L Creative Packaging, 1987, NM...............**$30.00**
Harriet Hippo, Merle Norman, in party hat, NM.........**$10.00**
Hunchback of Notre Dame, Kid Care, in robe w/sceptor, M **$5.00**
Incredible Hulk, Menjamin Ansehl, standing on rock, M..**$25.00**
Jiminy Cricket, Colgate-Palmolive, green, black & red or green, black & yellow, 1960s, EX+......................**$30.00**
Kermit the Frog, Calgon, Treasure Island outfit, w/tag, M...**$8.00**
King Louie (Jungle Book), Colgate-Palmolive, slip over, 1960s...**$15.00**

Lamb Chop (Shari Lewis), Kid Care, holding duck, w/tag, M $8.00

Lippy the Lion, Purex, purple vest, 1962, rare, EX $35.00

Mad Hatter, bronze w/pink hat & clock, Avon, 1970, EX ..$20.00

Magilla Gorilla, Purex, 1960s, NM $35.00

Marvin the Martian, Warner Bros, 1996, NM $15.00

Mr Do Bee, Manon Freres, 1960s, w/sticker, rare, NM ..$75.00

Mummy, Colgate-Palmolive, 1960s, NM.....................$100.00

Pebbles & Dino, Cosrich, Pebbles on Dino's back, M..$6.00

Pluto, Colgate-Palmolive, orange w/cap head, 1960s, NM..$25.00

Porky Pig, Colgate-Palmolive, red or blue tuxedo, 1960s, EX+ $25.00

Punkin' Puss, Purex, NM, $40.00.

Quick Draw McGraw, Purex, several variations, 1960s, NM, ea $30.00

Rainbow Brite, Hallmark, 1995, NM............................$10.00

Red Power Ranger, Centura (Canada), 1994................$20.00

Robocop, Cosway, 1990, NM..$15.00

Schroeder, Avon, 1970, MIB..$25.00

Simba, Kid Care, M..$6.00

Snoopy as Joe Cool, Minnetonka, 1996, NM $10.00

Snow White, Colgate-Palmolive, movable arms, 1960s, NM, $35.00.

Splash Down Space Capsule, Avon, 1970, MIB $20.00

Tasmanian Devil in Inner Tube, Kid Care, 1992, EX $8.00

Tennessee Tuxedo, Colgate-Palmolive, w/ice-cream cone, 1965, NM $30.00

Touche Turtle, Purex, standing, NM............................$40.00

Winkie Blink Clock, Avon, yellow w/blue hands & hat, 1975, MIB $15.00

Yoda (Star Wars), Omni, 1981, NM $20.00

Cake Toppers

In many ways, these diminutive couples reflect our culture — they actually capture miniature moments in time, and their style of dress reflects the many changes made in fashion down through the years. The earliest cake toppers (from before the turn of the twentieth century) were made of sugar and disintegrated rapidly. Next came bridal couples of carved wood, usually standing on plaster (gum paste) bases. When molded, this material could be made into lovely platforms and backdrops for the tiny figures. It was sometimes molded into columns with gazebo-style or lattice roofs under which the dainty couples stood hand in hand. Good Luck horseshoes representing all the best wishes for the bridal couple were popular as well.

By the 1920s and 1930s, plaster bases were still in use, but a flower bower replaced the columns and horseshoes. These bowers were constructed of wire and trimmed with cloth flowers, often lilies of the valley. The bridal figures of this period were usually porcelain or chalkware, and the brides' gowns became sleek and elegant, reflecting the Art Deco trend in fashion. Gone was the bustle and the prim pose. The groom looked equally elegant in black tie and tails. The pair now often took on a 'high society' air.

Then in the mid-1930s appeared the exact opposite — kewpies. These child-like figures with their wide-eyed, innocent faces were popular cake toppers well into the 1940s.

During WWII, military toppers became popular. It was now the groom who drew the most attention. He was dashing and patriotic in an Armed Forces uniform, and all branches of the military were represented. To complement the theme, a 48-star American flag or a red, white, and blue ribbon was often suspended from the center of the bower.

After the war, the bridal couple and the base they stood on were made of plastic — the latest rage. As for flowers and trim, there seemed no limit. Cabbage roses, strings of pearls, and huge gatherings of white netting added the final trim to oversized backdrops of hearts, cupids, birds, and bells. In the new millennium, fine china or delicate porcelain have become the materials of choice.

Cake toppers are fragile. Look them over carefully before purchasing. Expect to find them in all stages of completeness and condition. Chips, dents, broken parts, crumbling bases, or soiled clothing all seriously devalue a piece. Those in questionable or poor condition (unless extremely rare) are basically worthless. Prices suggested in the following listings apply to cake toppers that are compete with base, bower (or other finishing top), flowers, trim and lace, or clothing if applicable. A collectible topper should reflect minimal wear and obvious care.

Advisor: Jeannie Greenfield (See Directory, Cake Toppers)

Art-Deco era, chalkware w/shiny finish, gown & base are 1-pc, 6"...**$40.00**

Military couple arm-in-arm on plaster (gum paste) base, cloth bower of flowers & leaves on wire, 48-star flag in center...**$60.00**

1900s couple, carved wood figures on plaster stand...**$50.00**

1900s couple on plaster (gum paste) base, bower of cloth flowers w/painted plaster centers **$50.00**

1920s couple, single mold, poured lead.....................**$45.00**

1920s porcelain couple (3½") standing on cardboard 'steps' w/bow overhead, silver leaves & floral trim on bower **$45.00**

1930s couple on raised & sculpted base, cupola roof & columns w/lilies-of-the-valley trim, heavy, 10"...**$75.00**

1930s porcelain kewpies (crepe-paper attire) embrace under bower of cloth flowers, plaster embossed/sculpted base, 3"...**$50.00**

1940s couple, plaster/chalkware combination.............**$25.00**

1940s couple, all plastic, cloth flowers with green velvet and silver paper leaves in each of three large bells that serve as the backdrop, $40.00. (Photo courtesy Jeannie Greenfield)

1940s couple holding hands stands before table w/wedding ring, bower of cloth flowers & bell, plaster & chalkware **$50.00**

1950s (early) couple, chalkware.................................**$20.00**

1950s (early) couple, chalkware/plaster combination, flower bower w/pale peach-covered roses **$25.00**

1950s couple, heart-theme base, lg heart w/netting, flower center & upturned bell w/white glitter as backdrop, plastic **$20.00**

Calculators

It is difficult to picture the days when a basic four-function calculator cost hundreds of dollars, especially when today you get one free by simply filling out a credit application. Yet when they initially arrived on the market in 1971, the first of these electronic marvels cost from $300.00 to $400.00. All this for a calculator that could do no more than add, subtract, multiply, and divide.

Even at that price there was an uproar by consumers as calculating finally became convenient. No longer did you need to use a large mechanical monster adding machine or a slide rule with all of its complexity. You could even put away your pencil and paper for those tough numbers you couldn't 'do' in your head.

With prices initially so high and the profit potential so promising, several hundred companies jumped onto the calculator bandwagon. Some made their own; many purchased them from other (often overseas) manufacturers, just adding their own nameplate. Since the product was so new to the world, most of the calculators had some very different and interesting body styles.

Due to the competitive nature of all those new entries to the market, prices dropped quickly. A year and a half later, prices started to fall below $100.00 — a magic number that caused a boom in consumer demand. As even more calculators became available and electronics improved, prices continued to drop, eventually forcing many high-cost makers (who could not compete) out of business. By 1978 the number of major calculator companies could be counted on both hands. Fortunately calculators are still available at almost every garage sale or flea market for a mere pittance — usually 25¢ to $3.00.

For more information refer to *A Guide to HP Handheld Calculators and Computers* by Wlodek Mier-Jedrzejowicz, *Collector's Guide to Pocket Calculators* by Guy Ball and Bruce Flamm (both published by Wilson/Barnett), and *Personal Computers and Pocket Calculators* by Dr. Thomas Haddock.

Note: Due to limited line length, we have used these abbreviations: flr — fluorescent; fct — function.

Advisor: Guy D. Ball (See Directory, Calculators)

Club: International Association of Calculator Collectors 14561 Livingston St., Tustin, CA 92781-0345 Fax/phone: 714-730-6140; e-mail: mrcalc@usa.net Membership includes subscription to newsletter *The International Calculator Collector*

Related website: www.oldcalcs.com

Aristo M27, 4-fct, red LED, West Germany, c 1973, 2½x3½", from $85 to...**$95.00**

Bohn Omnitrex, 4-fct, %, green tube display, 5 AA batteries, 2-tone case, Taiwan, 1973, from $35 to................**$40.00**

Calfax 800-CD, 4-fct, red LED, 9V battery, Hong Kong, 3¼x5", from $65 to...**$75.00**

Canon LE-10, 4-fct, 10-digit red LED, scaled battery pack, battery power meter, boxy case, Japan, 1972, from $45 to...**$55.00**

Casio Mini (aka CM-602), 4-fct, 6-digit flr, 4 AA batteries, wrist strap, Japan, 1973, 6x3", from $35 to...........**$50.00**

Commodore US3, 4-fct, 8-digit tube display, 2 additional tubes indicate errors/low power, C-cell battery, 1972, from $55 to...**$95.00**

Daltone 80, 4-fct, %, red LED, 9V battery, sold as kit, 1975, 2½x4½", from $65 to...**$75.00**

Gillette PC-1, 4-fct, red LED, 9V battery, same style as Sinclair's Oxford series, 3x6¼", from $65 to.........**$75.00**

Interton PC-2010, 4-fct, 4 AA batteries, 3x5¼", from $35 to...**$45.00**

Kings Point FN-85 (aka financial computer), financial fct, flr, sealed battery, ca 1976, 3½x6½", from $55 to **$60.00**

Lloyd's 100, 4-fct, LCD, 4 C battery, flip-up display cover, very early LCD, 5½x9¼", from $60 to...................**$90.00**

Mancal 732, 4-fct, red LED, 4 AA batteries, unusual case, Japan, 2¾x5¼", from $50 to **$60.00**

Microlith 205 (Scientific), science fct, green flr, 9V battery, early F-function key example, Hong Kong, 1974, from $65 to **$75.00**

National Semiconductor 500, 4-fct, memory, green flr, paper printer, sealed battery, Japan, 3x5½", from $40 to.**$50.00**

Panasonic 830 (aka JE-830U), 4-fct, green flr, 2 D batteries, glossy white case, Japan, ca 1974, 5¾x6", from $60 to **$70.00**

Radofin #1525, 4-fct, %, gr flr, 2 AA batteries, Hong Kong, 2½x5¼", from $40 to..**$50.00**

Rockwell 22K, 4-fct, memory, %, sq root, blue flr, 3 AAA batteries, thin metal case, Japan, 1970s, 3x5½", $35 to **$45.00**

Sanyo CX-8001, 4-fct, constant, blue flr, 4 AA batteries, Japan c 1973, 3½x6", from $35 to....................................**$45.00**

Sharp EL-215S, 4-fct, memory, %, sq root, green flr, 2 AA batteries, Korea, 3¼x5¼", from $10 to......................**$20.00**

Sperry Remington Rand 661-D, 4-fct, 6-digit tube w/12 digit capability, 4 AA batteries, Japan, c 1972, from $35 to **$45.00**

Texas Instruments SR-16 II, science function, memory, red LED, sealed battery pack, ca 1975, 3x6", from $30 to **$40.00**

Texas Instruments TI-1400, 4-fct, %, red LED, 9V battery, c 1976-77, 2¾x5¾", from $25 to..............................**$30.00**

Toshiba BC-0808B, 4-fct, blue flr, 4 AA batteries, wrist strap, Japan, 3¾x5¾", from $40 to **$50.00**

Unisonic #1540L, 4-fct, memory, %, sq root, red LED, 2 AA batteries, Hong Kong, 3x6", from $20 to **$30.00**

Western Auto Citation, 4-fct, %, red LED, 9V battery, woodgrain colored face plate, USA, 2¾x5½", from $35 to **$45.00**

California Raisins

Since they starred in their first TV commercial in 1986, the California Raisins have attained stardom through movies, tapes, videos, and magazine ads. Today we see them every-where on the secondary market — PVC figures, radios, banks, posters — and they're very collectible. The PVC figures were introduced in 1987. Originally there were four, all issued for retail sales — a singer, two conga dancers, and a saxophone player. Before the year was out, Hardee's, the fast-food chain, came out with the same characters, though on a slightly smaller scale. A fifth character, Blue Surfboard (horizontal), was created, and three 5½" Bendees with flat pancake-style bodies appeared.

In 1988 the ranks had grown to twenty-one: Blue Surfboard (vertical), Red Guitar, Lady Dancer, Blue/Green Sunglasses, Guy Winking, Candy Cane, Santa Raisin, Bass Player, Drummer, Tambourine Lady (there were two styles), Lady Valentine, Boy Singer, Girl Singer, Hip Guitar Player, Sax Player with Beret, and four Graduates (styled like the original four, but on yellow pedestals and wearing graduation caps). And Hardee's issued an additional six: Blue Guitar, Trumpet Player, Roller Skater, Skateboard, Boom Box, and Yellow Surfboard.

Still eight more characters came out in 1989: Male in Beach Chair, Green Trunks with Surfboard, Hula Skirt, Girl Sitting on Sand, Piano Player, AC, Mom, and Michael Raisin. They made two movies and thereafter were joined by their fruit and vegetable friends, Rudy Bagaman, Lick Broccoli, Banana White, Leonard Limabean, and Cecil Thyme. Hardee's added four more characters in 1991: Anita Break, Alotta Style, Buster, and Benny.

All Raisins are dated with these exceptions: those issued in 1989 (only the Beach Scene characters are dated, and they're actually dated 1988) and those issued by Hardee's in 1991.

For more information we recommend *Schroeder's Collectible Toys, Antique to Modern* (Collector Books).

CALRAB-Applause, Bass Player, 1st commercial issue, 1988, M, $80.00.

Applause, Captain Toonz, w/blue boom box, yellow glasses & sneakers, Hardee's Second Promotion, 1988, sm, M **$3.00**

Applause, FF String, w/blue guitar & orange sneakers, Hardee's Second Promotion, 1988, sm, M **$3.00**

Applause, Michael Raisin (Jackson), w/silver microphone & studded belt, Special Edition, 1989, M.................**$20.00**

Applause, Rollin' Rollo, w/roller skates, yellow sneakers & hat marked H, Hardee's Second Promotion, 1988, sm, M...**$3.00**

Applause, SB Stuntz, w/yellow skateboard & blue sneakers, Hardee's Second Promotion, 1988, sm, M **$3.00**

Applause, Trumpy Trunote, w/trumpet & blue sneakers, Hardee's Second Promotion, 1988, sm, M **$3.00**

Applause, Waves Weaver I, w/yellow surfboard connected to foot, Hardee's Second Promotion, 1988, sm, M **$4.00**

Applause, Waves Weaver II, w/yellow surfboard not connected to foot, Hardee's Second Promotion, 1988, sm, M **$6.00**

Applause-Claymation, Banana White, yellow dress, Meet the Raisins First Edition, 1989, M **$20.00**

Applause-Claymation, Lick Broccoli, green & black w/red & orange guitar, Meet the Raisins First Edition, 1989, M **$20.00**

Applause-Claymation, Rudy Bagaman, w/cigar, purple shirt & flipflops, Meet the Raisins First Edition, 1989, M.....**$20.00**

CALRAB, Blue Surfboard, board connected to foot, Unknown Production, 1988, M...**$35.00**

CALRAB, Blue Surfboard, board in right hand, not connected to foot, Unknown Production, 1987, M...........**$50.00**

CALRAB, Guitar, red guitar, First Commercial Issue, 1988, M...**$8.00**

CALRAB, Hands, left hand points up, right hand points down, Post Raisin Bran Issue, 1987, M....................**$4.00**

CALRAB, Hands, pointing up w/thumbs on head, First Key Chains, 1987, M...**$5.00**

CALRAB, Hands, pointing up w/thumbs on head, Hardee's First Promotion, 1987, sm, M **$3.00**

CALRAB, Microphone, right hand in fist w/microphone in left, Post Raisin Brand Issue, 1987, M **$6.00**

CALRAB, Microphone, right hand points up w/microphone in left, Hardee's First Promotion, 1987, sm, M **$3.00**

CALRAB, Microphone, right hand points up w/microphone in left, First Key Chains, 1987, M.............................**$7.00**

CALRAB, Santa, red cap & green sneakers, Christmas Issue, 1988, M **$9.00**

CALRAB, Saxophone, gold sax, no hat, First Key Chains, 1987, M **$5.00**

CALRAB, Saxophone, gold sax, no hat, Hardee's First Promotion, 1987, sm, M **$3.00**

CALRAB, Saxophone, inside of sax painted red, Post Raisin Bran Issue, 1987, M **$4.00**

CALRAB, Singer, microphone in left hand not connected to face, First Commercial Issue, 1988, M **$6.00**

CALRAB, Sunglasses, holding candy cane, green glasses, red sneakers, Christmas Issue, 1988, M **$9.00**

CALRAB, Sunglasses, index finger touching face, First Key Chains, 1987, M...**$5.00**

CALRAB, Sunglasses, index finger touching face, orange glasses, Hardee's First Promotion, 1987, M.............**$3.00**

CALRAB, Sunglasses, right hand points up, left hand points down, orange glasses, Post Raisin Bran Issue, 1987, M **$4.00**

CALRAB, Sunglasses II, eyes not visible, aqua glasses & sneakers, First Commercial Issue, 1988, M **$6.00**

CALRAB, Sunglasses II, eyes visible, aqua glasses & sneakers, First Commercial Issue, 1988, M............................**$25.00**

CALRAB, Winky, in hitchhiking pose & winking, First Commercial Issue, 1988, M **$6.00**

CALRAB-Applause, AC, 'Gimme 5' pose, tall pompadour & red sneakers, Meet the Raisins Second Edition, 1989, M **$150.00**

CALRAB-Applause, Alotta Style, w/purple boom box, pink boots, Hardee's Fourth Promotion, 1991, sm, MIP..**$12.00**

CALRAB-Applause, Anita Break, shopping w/Hardee's bag, Hardee's Fourth Promotion, 1991, sm, M **$12.00**

CALRAB-Applause, Bass Player, w/gray slippers, Second Commercial Issue, 1988, M **$8.00**

CALRAB-Applause, Benny, w/bowling ball, orange sunglasses, Hardee's Fourth Promotion, 1991, sm, MIP **$20.00**

CALRAB-Applause, Boy in Beach Chair, orange glasses, brown base, Beach Theme Edition, 1988, M........**$15.00**

CALRAB-Applause, Boy w/Surfboard, purple board, brown base, Beach Theme Edition, 1988, M...................**$15.00**

CALRAB-Applause, Cecil Thyme (Carrot), Meet the Raisins Second Promotion, 1989, M................................**$175.00**

CALRAB-Applause, Drummer, black hat w/yellow feather, Second Commercial Issue, 1988, M **$8.00**

CALRAB-Applause, Girl w/Boom Box, purple glasses, green shoes, brown base, Beach Theme Edition, 1988, M **$15.00**

CALRAB-Applause, Girl w/Tambourine, green shoes & bracelet, Raisin Club Issue, 1988, M.....................**$12.00**

CALRAB-Applause, Girl w/Tambourine (Ms Delicious), yellow shoes, Second Commercial Issue, 1988, M....**$15.00**

CALRAB-Applause, Hands, Graduate w/both hands pointing up & thumbs on head, Graduate Key Chains, 1988, M **$85.00**

CALRAB-Applause, Hip Band Guitarist (Hendrix), w/headband & yellow guitar, Third Commercial Issue, 1988, M **$22.00**

CALRAB-Applause, Hip Band Guitarist (Hendrix), w/headband & yellow guitar, Second Key Chains, 1988, sm, M...**$65.00**

CALRAB-Applause, Hula Girl, yellow shoes & bracelet, green skirt, Beach Theme Edition, 1988, M **$15.00**

CALRAB-Applause, Lenny Limabean, purple suit, Meet the Raisins Second Promotion, 1989, M **$125.00**

CALRAB-Applause, Microphone (female), yellow shoes & bracelet, Third Commercial Edition, 1988, M..........**$9.00**

CALRAB-Applause, Microphone (female), yellow shoes & bracelet, Second Key Chains, 1988, sm, M...........**$45.00**

CALRAB-Applause, Microphone (male), left hand extended w/open palm, Third Commercial Issue, 1988, M ...**$9.00**

CALRAB-Applause, Microphone (male), left hand extended w/open palm, Second Key Chains, 1988, sm, M..**$45.00**

CALRAB-Applause, Mom, yellow hair, pink apron, Meet the Raisins Second Promotion, 1989, M **$125.00**

CALRAB-Applause, Piano, blue piano, red hair, green sneakers, Meet the Raisins First Edition, 1989, M..........**$35.00**

CALRAB-Applause, Saxophone, black beret, blue eyelids, Third Commercial Issue, 1988, M **$15.00**

CALRAB-Applause, Saxophone, Graduate w/gold sax, no hat, Graduate Key Chain, 1988, M **$85.00**

CALRAB-Applause, Singer, female, red-dish-purple shoes and bracelet, 1988, M, $12.00. (Photo courtesy Larry DeAngelo)

CALRAB-Applause, Sunglasses, Graduate w/index finger touching face, orange glasses, Graduate Key Chains, 1988, M...**$85.00**

CALRAB-Applause, Valentine, Be Mine, girl holding heart, Special Lover's Issue, 1988, M.................................**$8.00**

CALRAB-Applause, Valentine, I'm Yours, boy holding heart, Special Lover's Issue, 1988, M.................................**$8.00**

CALRAB-Claymation, Sunglasses/Singer/Hands/Saxophone or Graduate on yellow base, Post Raisin Bran, 1988, ea from $45 to...**$65.00**

Miscellaneous

Balloon, Congo line, 1987, M............................**$12.00**
Belt, lead singer w/mike on buckle, 1987, EX...........**$15.00**
Book, Birthday Boo Boo, 1988, EX......................**$10.00**
Bubble Bath, Rockin' Raisin, 24-oz, M..................**$4.00**
Cap, 1988, EX...**$5.00**
Coloring book, Sports Crazy, 1988, EX..................**$5.00**
Costume, Collegeville, 1988, MIB.......................**$10.00**
Game, California Raisin board game, MIB.................**$25.00**
Mugs, Christmas Issue, 1988, set of 4, MIB.............**$60.00**
Party invitations, M...................................**$15.00**
Pin-back button, California Raisins on Ice, 1988-89 Ice Capades, Applause.....................................**$8.00**
Postcard, Claymation/Will Vinton, 1988, M.............**$5.00**
Poster, California Raisin Band, 22x28", M..............**$8.00**
Sticker album, Diamond Publishing, 1988, M............**$15.00**
Sunshield, Congo Line, 1988, EX........................**$10.00**
Video, Hip To Be Fit, M................................**$18.00**
Wallet, yellow plastic, 1988, EX.......................**$20.00**
Wind-up toy, figure w/right hand up & orange glasses, 1987, MIB..**$8.00**
Wind-up toy, w/left hand up & right hand down, plastic, 1987, MIB...**$8.00**
Wristwatch, Official Fan Club, w/3 different bands, Nelsonic, 1987, MIB...**$50.00**

Winross truck, New America Highway Series, 1989, red Ford long-nose tandem axle with dual stacks, features Champion Raisins, M, from $225.00 to $300.00. (Photo courtesy Larry DeAngelo)

Camark Pottery

Camark Pottery was manufactured in CAMden, ARKansas, from 1927 to the early 1960s. The pottery was founded by Samuel J. 'Jack' Carnes, a native of east-central Ohio familiar with Ohio's fame for pottery production. Camark's first wares were made from Arkansas clays shipped by Carnes to John B. Lessell in Ohio in early to mid-1926. Lessell was one of the associates responsible for early art pottery making. These wares consisted of Lessell's lustre and iridescent finishes based on similar ideas he pioneered at Weller and other potteries. The variations made for Camark included versions of Weller's Marengo, LaSa, and Lamar. These 1926 pieces were signed only with the 'Lessell' signature. When Camark began operations in the spring of 1927, the company had many talented, experienced workers including Lessell's wife and step-daughter (Lessell himself died unexpectedly in December, 1926), the Sebaugh family, Frank Long, Alfred Tetzschner, and Boris Trifonoff. This group produced a wide range of art pottery finished in glazes of many types, including lustre and iridescent (signed LeCamark), Modernistic/Futuristic, crackles, and combination glaze effects such as drips. Art pottery manufacture continued until the early 1930s when emphasis changed to industrial castware (molded wares) with single-color, primarily matt glazes.

In the 1940s Camark introduced its Hand Painted line by Ernst Lechner. This line included the popular Iris, Rose, and Tulip patterns. Concurrent with the Hand Painted Series (which was made until the early 1950s), Camark continued mass production of industrial castware — simple, sometimes nondescript pottery and novelty items with primarily glossy pastel glazes — until the early 1960s.

Some of Camark's designs and glazes are easily confused with those of other companies. For instance, Lessell decorated and signed a line in his lustre and iridescent finishes using porcelain (not pottery) blanks purchased from the Fraunfelter China Company. Camark produced a variety of combination glazes including the popular drip glazes (green over pink and green over mustard/brown) closely resembling Muncie's — but Muncie's clay is generally white while Camark used a cream-colored clay for its drip-glaze pieces. Muncie's are marked with a letter/number combination, and the bottoms are usually smeared with the base color. Camark's bottoms have a more uniform color application.

For more information, we recommend the *Collector's Guide to Camark Pottery* by David Edwin Gifford, Arkansas pottery historian and author of *Collector's Encyclopedia of Niloak Pottery.* (Both books are published by Collector Books.)

Advisor: Tony Freyaldenhoven (See Directory, Camark)

Artware

Basket, Rose Green Overflow, unmarked, 6¾", from $100 to...**$120.00**

Humidor, Blue & White Stipple, cylindrical, Arkansas die stamp, from $140 to **$160.00**

Pitcher, Celestial Blue, multicolor parrot handle, gold Arkansas ink stamp, 6½", from $160 to..............**$180.00**

Pitcher, Green to Blue Combination Colors, early circular mold mark 414, 9", from $150 to **$200.00**

Pitcher, Royal Blue, 2nd Arkansas inventory sticker, 7", from $15 to...**$20.00**

Pitcher, waffle batter, Gray & Blue Mottle, parrot handle, early circular mold mark 200, 6¼", from $100 to **$120.00**

Stein, Autumn, Ruben's Trommers White Label, 1st block letter, 5½", from $30 to **$50.00**

Vase, Azurite Blue, shouldered, unmarked, 4¼", from $15 to **$25.00**

Vase, Barcelona or Spano, Yellow Bright, unmarked, 7¼", from $140 to...**$160.00**

Vase, Celestial Blue/Black Overflow, slightly shouldered, unmarked, incised X, 7", from $140 to **$160.00**

Vase, Frosted Green, 4-fold rim, Deco styling, 1st block letter, 8¼", from $50 to **$70.00**

Vase, Green White Overflow, Arkansas die stamp, 5¼", from $140 to...**$160.00**

Vase, Ivory, footed trumpet form, 1st block letter, 11¾", from $30 to...**$50.00**

Vase, Olive Green/Light Overflow, sm handles, 1st block letter, 6", from $140 to...**$160.00**

Vase, Orange Green Overflow, unmarked, 3", from $40 to...**$50.00**

Vase, Pastel Blue Green Overflow, handles, footed, 1st block letter mark, 9", from $120 to..........................**$140.00**

Vase, Purple Green Overflow, unmarked, 5¼", from $180 to...**$200.00**

Vase, Sea Green, rim-to-hip handles, unmarked, 4½", from $30 to...**$40.00**

Vase, Yellow Green Overflow, 1st block letter, fan form, 6", from $40 to...**$60.00**

Hand-Painted Ware

Basket, Bas Relief Morning Glory II, blue, unmarked, 9¾", from $100 to...**$120.00**

Bowl, Bas Relief Iris, blue, 5¼x14", from $80 to......**$120.00**

Creamer & sugar bowl, Festoon of Roses, gold trim, USA 830/830A, 2¼", 2", from $40 to **$60.00**

Pitcher & bowl, Festoon of Roses, rose pink, 2nd Arkansas inventory stickers, 9¾", 7¼", from $120 to **$140.00**

Vase, Festoon of Roses, ivory, low handles, gold trim, 573 USA, 9½", from $90 to **$110.00**

Vase, Festoon of Roses, rose pink, handles, unmarked, 7¾", from $80 to...**$100.00**

Wall pocket, Iris, 8½", from $300.00 to $400.00. (Photo courtesy David Gifford)

Industrial Castware

Figurine, lion, burgundy, Lions Club Camden Ark, unmarked, 3½x2¼", from $35 to..**$45.00**

Figurine, razorback hog, burgundy, mold mark 117, USA, 4¼", from $40 to...**$60.00**

Fishbowl, Tropical Fish, Mirror Black, unmarked, 8¼", from $150 to...**$200.00**

Fishbowl holder, Wistful Kitten, Mirror Black, unmarked, 9", from $60 to...**$80.00**

Flower frog, fish, early circular mold mark 413, 3½", from $40 to...**$60.00**

Shelf sitter, Humpty Dumpty, unmarked, 5½", from $140 to...**$160.00**

Vase, marked USA, Camark, N-112, 8½", from $30.00 to $40.00. (Photo courtesy David Gifford)

Vase, burgundy, low handles, mold mark 544 USA, 7½", from $25 to...**$35.00**

Vase, embossed flower w/integral leaf handles, burgundy, mold mark USA 571, 7½", from $35 to................**$45.00**

Wall hanger, climbing cat, emerald green, mold mark Camark, 16", from $60 to $80.00

Cambridge Glassware

If you're looking for a 'safe' place to put your investment dollars, Cambridge glass is one of your better options. But as with any commodity, in order to make a good investment, knowledge of the product and its market is required. There are two books we would recommend for your study, *Colors in Cambridge Glass,* put out by the National Cambridge Collectors Club, and *The Collector's Encyclopedia of Elegant Glass* by Gene Florence.

The Cambridge Glass Company (located in Cambridge, Ohio) made fine quality glassware from just after the turn of the century until 1958. They made thousands of different items in hundreds of various patterns and colors. Values hinge on rarity of shape and color. Of the various marks they used, the 'C in triangle' is the most common. In addition to their tableware, they also produced flower frogs representing ladies and children and models of animals and birds that are very valuable today. To learn more about them, you'll want to read *Animals and Figural Flower Frogs of the Depression Era* by Lee Garmon and Dick Spencer (Collector Books).

Advisor: Debbie Maggard (See Directory, Elegant Glassware)

Newsletter: *The Cambridge Crystal Ball*
National Cambridge Collectors, Inc.
P.O. Box 416, Cambridge, OH 43725-0416. Dues: $17 for individual member and $3 for associate member of same household

Apple Blossom, crystal, bowl, finger; w/plate, #3130.**$40.00**
Apple Blossom, crystal, bowl, flat, 12" **$55.00**
Apple Blossom, crystal, plate, sandwich; handles, 12½"..**$32.00**
Apple Blossom, crystal, tumbler, #3130, footed, 5-oz ...**$16.00**
Apple Blossom, pink or green, bowl, cereal; 6" **$55.00**
Apple Blossom, pink or green, plate, dinner; 9½" **$85.00**
Apple Blossom, pink or green, salt & pepper shakers, pr ..**$125.00**
Apple Blossom, pink or green, vase, 5" **$125.00**
Apple Blossom, yellow or amber, candlestick, keyhole, 1-light...**$35.00**
Apple Blossom, yellow or amber, comport, tall, 7" **$70.00**
Apple Blossom, yellow or amber, stem, cordial; #3130, 1-oz...**$110.00**
Apple Blossom, yellow or amber, stem, water; #3130, 8-oz...**$30.00**
Bookends, Scottie, crystal, hollow, pr......................**$175.00**
Candlelight, crystal, candlestick, #3900/67, 5" **$60.00**
Candlelight, crystal, comport, cheese; #3900/135, 5"...**$45.00**
Candlelight, crystal, bowl, #3900/28, footed, handles, 11½" **$85.00**
Candlelight, crystal, candlestick, #647, 2-light, 6"........**$75.00**
Candlelight, crystal, lamp, hurricane; #1617.............**$225.00**
Candlelight, crystal, plate, salad; #3900/22, 8" **$22.00**

Candlelight, crystal, stem, sherry; #7966, 2 oz.............**$85.00**
Candlelight, crystal, tumbler, juice; #3776, 5-oz **$30.00**
Candlelight, crystal, vase, bud; #274, 10".....................**$95.00**

Candlelight, crystal, water goblet, #3776, $45.00.

Caprice, blue or pink, bowl, salad; #57, 4 footed; 10".**$125.00**
Caprice, blue or pink, candlestick, keyhole; #647, 2-light, 5"...**$65.00**
Caprice, blue or pink, comport, #130, low foot, 6" **$50.00**
Caprice, blue or pink, tray, #42, oval, 9" **$50.00**
Caprice, blue or pink, vase, #245, 5½"......................**$165.00**
Caprice, crystal, blue or pink, tumbler, juice; #310, flat, 5-oz **$75.00**
Caprice, crystal, bonbon, #133, sq, footed, 6"............**$20.00**
Caprice, crystal, bowl, #49, 4-footed, 8" **$40.00**

Caprice, crystal, comport, 6" x 6", from $20.00 to $25.00.

Caprice, crystal, decanter, #187, w/stopper, 35-oz....**$195.00**
Caprice, crystal, ice bucket, #201 ....**$60.00**
Caprice, crystal, plate, #28, 4-footed, 14"...................**$35.00**
Caprice, crystal, plate, salad; #23, 7½" **$15.00**
Caprice, crystal, stem, cordial; #300, blown, 1-oz.......**$50.00**
Caprice, crystal, tumbler, #9, footed, 12-oz **$22.50**
Caprice, crystal, tumbler, water; #300, footed, 10-oz..**$20.00**
Caprice, crystal, vase, #337, crimped top, 4½"............**$55.00**

Chantilly, crystal, bowl, flared, 4-footed, 12".............$45.00

Chantilly, crystal, candlestick, keyhole; 2-light, 6" $40.00

Chantilly, crystal, creamer...$18.00

Chantilly, crystal, plate, salad; 8".................................$12.50

Chantilly, crystal, plate, torte; 14"...............................$45.00

Chantilly, crystal, salt & pepper shakers, handled, pr...$35.00

Chantilly, crystal, stem, claret; #3625, 4½-oz............$45.00

Chantilly, crystal, stem, cocktail; #3600, 2½-oz........$26.00

Chantilly, crystal, tumbler, juice; #3600, footed, 5-oz .$18.00

Chantilly, crystal, vase, globe, 5"..................................$55.00

Cleo, blue, bowl, cereal; 6"...$60.00

Cleo, blue, candy box, w/lid...$185.00

Cleo, blue, platter, 12"..$195.00

Cleo, blue, stem, wine; #3077, 3½-oz...........................$95.00

Cleo, blue, tumbler; #3022, footed, 12-oz.....................$95.00

Cleo, pink, green, yellow or amber, bowl, console; 12" $60.00

Cleo, pink, green, yellow or amber, pitcher, #38, 3½-pt..$225.00

Cleo, pink, green, yellow or amber, sugar cube tray........$185.00

Cleo, pink, green, yellow or amber, vase, 11" $195.00

Covered dish, turkey, blue, w/lid................................$550.00

Covered dish, turkey, pink, w/lid $400.00

Decagon, blue, bowl, bonbon; handles, 5½".............$22.00

Decagon, blue, bowl, soup plate; flat rim, 8½" $50.00

Decagon, blue, bowl, vegetable; round, 11" $48.00

Decagon, blue, plate, bread & butter; 6¼"................$10.00

Decagon, blue, tumbler, footed, 5-oz $20.00

Decagon, pastel colors, bowl, cream soup; w/liner ...$22.00

Decagon, pastel colors, ice bucket.............................$45.00

Decagon, pastel colors, plate, dinner; 9½"................$50.00

Decagon, pastel colors, saucer $3.00

Decagon, pastel colors, stem, water; 9-oz $20.00

Diane, crystal, basket, 2-handled, footed, 6" $30.00

Diane, crystal, bowl, baker; 10"..................................$60.00

Diane, crystal, candy box, w/lid, round $95.00

Diane, crystal, comport, 5½"..$35.00

Diane, crystal, pitcher, Doulton................................$335.00

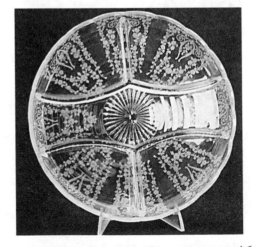

Diane, crystal, relish tray, five-part, 12", $65.00.

Diane, crystal, stem, cordial; #1066, 1-oz $65.00

Diane, crystal, stem, water; #1066, 11-oz...................$32.00

Diane, crystal, tumbler, sham bottom, 2½-oz.............$50.00

Diane, crystal, tumbler, tea; #1066, 12-oz $28.00

Diane, crystal, vase, globe; 5"......................................$55.00

Elaine, crystal, bowl, bonbon; footed, tab handled, 7"..$35.00

Elaine, crystal, bowl, finger; #3104, w/liner $40.00

Elaine, crystal, candlestick, 5".....................................$28.00

Elaine, crystal, lamp, hurricane; keyhole foot, w/prisms..$235.00

Elaine, crystal, plate, torte; 14"..................................$65.00

Elaine, crystal, salt & pepper shakers, handled, pr.....$45.00

Elaine, crystal, stem, cocktail; #3500, 3-oz................$30.00

Elaine, crystal, stem, hock; #3104, tall, 5-oz............$150.00

Elaine, crystal, stem, sherbet; #1402, tall $20.00

Elaine, crystal, vase, footed, 8"...................................$95.00

Figurine, swan, Apple Green, #1 style, 13½"...........$850.00

Figurine, swan, dark green, #3 style, 8½" $175.00

Flower frog, Bashful Charlotte, green, 11½" $375.00

Flower frog, Bashful Charlotte, Moonlight Blue Satin, 11½"..$800.00

Flower frog, Draped Lady, Dianthus, 8½"................$175.00

Flower frog, Draped Lady, light emerald, 8½"..........$225.00

Flower frog, Melon Boy, Dianthus...............................$425.00

Flower frog, Rose Lady, dark amber, tall base, 9¾" ..$275.00

Flower frog, turtle, ebony...$225.00

Gloria, crystal, bowl, bonbon; handles, 5½"...............$25.00

Gloria, crystal, stem, cocktail; #3035, 3-oz................$20.00

Gloria, crystal, stem, wine; #3130, 2½-oz..................$30.00

Gloria, crystal, tumbler, #3130, footed, 12-oz.............$25.00

Gloria, green, pink or yellow, butter dish, w/lid, w/handles..$350.00

Gloria, green, pink or yellow, pitcher, ball; 80-oz....$495.00

Gloria, green, pink or yellow, plate, dinner; sq........$110.00

Gloria, green, pink or yellow, sugar shaker, w/glass lid...$395.00

Imperial Hunt Scene, colors, creamer, flat...................$50.00

Imperial Hunt Scene, colors, ice tub............................$95.00

Imperial Hunt Scene, colors, stem, cocktail; #3085, 2½-oz $50.00

Imperial Hunt Scene, colors, tumbler, #3085, footed, 2½-oz $55.00

Imperial Hunt Scene, crystal, bowl, cereal; 6"............$20.00

Imperial Hunt Scene, crystal, stem, cocktail; #1402, 3-oz..$50.00

Imperial Hunt Scene, crystal, sugar bowl, footed $20.00

Mt Vernon, amber or crystal, bowl, #121, flared, 12½"..$35.00

Mt Vernon, amber or crystal, bowl, #43, deep, 10½" .$30.00

Mt Vernon, amber or crystal, bowl, finger; #23...........$10.00

Mt Vernon, amber or crystal, bowl, rose; #106, 6½"...$18.00

Mt Vernon, amber or crystal, coaster, #60, plain, 3" $5.00

Mt Vernon, amber or crystal, decanter, #52, w/stopper, 40-oz $85.00

Mt Vernon, amber or crystal, pitcher, ball; #95, 80-oz..$105.00

Mt Vernon, amber or crystal, relish, #200, 3-part, 11".$25.00

Mt Vernon, amber or crystal, sugar bowl, footed, #8 .$10.00

Mt Vernon, amber or crystal, vase, #42, 5"...............$15.00

Portia, crystal, basket, upturned sides, 2 handles $25.00

Portia, crystal, bowl, finger; #3124, w/liner................$45.00

Portia, crystal, cocktail icer, 2-pint..............................$75.00

Portia, crystal, pitcher, Doulton $355.00

Portia, crystal, salt & pepper shakers, flat, pr..............$30.00

Portia, crystal, stem, cordial; #3126, 1-oz....................$65.00

Portia, crystal, stem, goblet; #3130, 9-oz....................$28.00

Portia, crystal, tumbler, tea; #3130, 12-oz **$30.00**
Rosalie, amber, bowl, soup; 8½" **$35.00**
Rosalie, amber, bowl, 11½" **$55.00**
Rosalie, amber, ice bucket/pail.............................**$55.00**
Rosalie, amber, plate, 8⅜".................................**$10.00**
Rosalie, amber, platter, 15"................................**$100.00**
Rosalie, blue, pink or green, bowl, finger; w/liner.....**$70.00**
Rosalie, blue, pink or green, candlestick, keyhole; 5" ...**$40.00**
Rosalie, blue, pink or green, plate, cheese & cracker; 11"..**$75.00**
Rosalie, blue, pink or green, sugar bowl, footed........**$20.00**
Rosalie, blue, pink or green, vase, footed, 5½" **$75.00**
Rose Point, crystal, ashtray, #3500/130, oval, 4" **$90.00**
Rose Point, crystal, bowl, #3400/3, low foot, 11" **$175.00**
Rose Point, crystal, bowl, #3400/34, w/handles, 9½".**$85.00**
Rose Point, crystal, bowl, #3500/17, footed, 12".......**$130.00**
Rose Point, crystal, bowl, bonbon; #3400/204, cupped, deep, 3½"...**$85.00**
Rose Point, crystal, bowl, cream soup; #3400, w/liner ..**$175.00**
Rose Point, crystal, candlestick, #3900/74, 3-light, 6".**$65.00**
Rose Point, crystal, candy box, #3900/165, round....**$135.00**
Rose Point, crystal, cheese dish, #980, w/lid, 5".......**$595.00**
Rose Point, crystal, comport, #3400/74, 4-footed, 5"..**$75.00**
Rose Point, crystal, creamer, #944, flat.......................**$165.00**
Rose Point, crystal, decanter, #1320, footed, 14-oz...**$450.00**
Rose Point, crystal, marmalade, #157, w/lid, footed, 7-oz..**$210.00**
Rose Point, crystal, plate, canape; #693, 6⅛" **$195.00**
Rose Point, crystal, plate, dinner; #3400/64, 10½"....**$165.00**
Rose Point, crystal, relish, #3500/67, 6-pc, 12".........**$285.00**
Rose Point, crystal, relish, #3900/124, 2-part, 7" **$37.50**
Rose Point, crystal, stem, wine; #3500, 2½-oz **$65.00**
Rose Point, crystal, tumbler, #3400/115, 13-oz...........**$55.00**
Rose Point, crystal, tumbler, #498, straight sides, 8-oz..**$50.00**
Rose Point, crystal, vase, #1309, 5" **$120.00**
Rose Point, crystal, vase, #6004, footed, 12" **$110.00**
Rose Point, stem, claret; #3106, 4½-oz **$60.00**
Valencia, crystal, bowl, #1402/89, w/handles, 6" **$18.00**
Valencia, crystal, comport, #3500/37, 7" **$45.00**
Valencia, crystal, plate, salad; #3500/167, 7½" **$12.00**
Valencia, crystal, salt & pepper shakers, #3400/18, pr..**$65.00**
Valencia, crystal, stem, wine; #3500, 2½-oz **$40.00**
Valencia, crystal, tumbler, #3400/100, 13-oz...............**$25.00**
Wildflower, crystal, bowl, #3900/28, tab handles, footed, 11½"..**$47.50**
Wildflower, crystal, bowl, relish; 3-part, 6½"..............**$25.00**
Wildflower, crystal, cocktail shaker, #3400/175..........**$95.00**
Wildflower, crystal, plate, crescent salad **$175.00**
Wildflower, crystal, plate, salad; #3900/22, 8" **$17.50**
Wildflower, crystal, saucer, #3900/17 or #3400/54 ....**$3.50**
Wildflower, crystal, stem, water; #3121, 10-oz **$35.00**
Wildflower, crystal, vase, flower; #279, footed, 13" ..**$125.00**

Cameras

Camera collecting as an investment or hobby continues to grow in popularity, as evidenced by the interest shown in current publications and at numerous camera shows that emphasize both user and classic collectible types.

Buying at garage sales, flea markets, auctions, or estate sales are ways to add to collections, although it is rare to find an expensive classic camera offered through these outlets. However, buying at such sales to resell to dealers or collectors can be profitable if one is careful to buy quality items, not common cameras that sell for very little at best, especially when they show wear. A very old camera is not necessarily valuable, as value depends on availability and quality. Knowing how to check out a camera or to judge quality will pay off when building a collection or when buying for resale.

Some very general guidelines follow, but for the serious buyer who intends to concentrate on cameras, there are several reference books that can be obtained. Most are rather expensive, but some provide good descriptions and/or price guidelines.

There are many distinct types of cameras to consider: large format (such as Graflex and large view cameras), medium format, early folding and box styles, 35mm single-lens-reflex (SLR), 35mm range finders, twin-lens-reflex (TLR), miniature or subminiature, novelty, and other types — including the more recent 'point-and-shoot' styles, Polaroids, and movie cameras. Though there is a growing interest in certain types, we would caution you against buying common Polaroids and movie cameras for resale, as there is very little market for them at this time. Most pre-1900 cameras will be found in large-format view camera or studio camera types. From the 1920s to the 1930s, folding and box-type cameras were produced, which today make good collector items. Most have fairly low values because they were made in vast numbers. Many of the more expensive classics were manufactured in the 1930 – 1955 period and include primarily the Rangefinder type of camera and those with the first built-in meters. The most prized of these are of German or Japanese manufacture, valued because of their innovative designs and great optics. The key to collecting these types of cameras is to find a mint-condition item or one still in the original box. In camera collecting, quality is the most important aspect.

This updated listing includes only a few of the various categories and models of cameras from the many thousands available and gives current average retail prices for working models with average wear. Note that cameras in mint condition or like new with their original boxes may be valued much higher, while very worn examples with defects (scratches, dents, torn covers, poor optics, nonworking meters or range finders, torn bellows, corroded battery compartments, etc.) would be valued far less. A dealer, when buying for resale, will pay only a percentage of these values, as he must consider his expenses for refurbishing, cleaning, etc., as well as sales expenses. Again, remember that quality is the key to value, and prices on some cameras vary widely according to condition.

Typical collector favorites are old Alpa, Canon, Contax, Nikon, Leica, Rolleiflex, some Zeiss-Ikon models, Exakta, and certain Voigtlander models. For information about these makes as well as models by other manufacturers, please consult the advisor.

Advisor: C.E. Cataldo (See Directory, Cameras)

Agfa, Billy, early 1930s......................................**$15.00**
Agfa, Optima, 1960s, from $20 to......................**$50.00**
Agfaflex, various models, from $50 to..............**$100.00**
Ansco, Folding, Nr 1 to Nr 10, ea from $8 to **$30.00**
Ansco, Memar, 1956-59 ....**$25.00**
Ansco, Super Speedex, 3.5 lens, 1953-58 ....**$150.00**
Argus A, early model, 35mm Bakelite, 1936-41, from $20
   to..**$30.00**
Argus A2F, 1939-41, from $10 ....**$15.00**
Asahitflex I, 1st Japanese SLR.................................**$500.00**
Bell & Howell Foton, 1948................................**$1,200.00**
Braun Paxette I, 1952 ....**$30.00**
Canon A-1 ....**$165.00**
Canon IIB, 1949-53...**$250.00**
Canon III, 1952 ....**$275.00**
Canon L-1, 1956-57..**$400.00**
Canon S, 1938-46 (usually Nikkor Lenses), from $3,000
   to..**$4,500.00**
Canon S-11, 1947-49...**$375.00**
Canon T-50, from $50 to...............................**$75.00**
Canon 7, 1961-64..**$450.00**
Conley 4x5 Folding Plate, 1905 ....**$150.00**
Contax II or III, 1936-42, from $300 to......................**$450.00**
Detrola Model D, Detroit Corp, 1938-40....................**$20.00**
Eastman Baby Brownie Special, 1939-54 ....**$10.00**
Eastman Kodak Box Hawkeye No 2A, from $5 to........**$8.00**
Eastman Kodak No 2C Brownie Box, 1917-34, from $7
   to **$15.00**
Eastman Kodak No 3A Folding Pocket camera...........**$30.00**
Eastman Kodak Retina IIIc, from $125 to.....................**$180.00**
Eastman Kodak Signet 80....................................**$60.00**
Eastman Kodak-35, 1940-51 ....**$25.00**
Edinex, by Wirgin, from $20 to **$30.00**
Exakta, German made, various models, 1933-78, from $50
   to...**$800.00**
Exakta VX, 1951...**$80.00**
FED 1, USSR, prewar, from $80 to **$175.00**
Fujica AX-5 ....**$125.00**
Graflexs, Speed Graphics, various sizes, ea from $100 to..**$200.00**
Hasselglad 1000F, 1952-57, from $500 to..................**$700.00**

Kine Exakta, 1937 – 48, $190.00. (Photo courtesy C.E. Cataldo)

Kine Exakta 1, Ihagee, Dresden, 35mm Rangefinder, from
   $175 to...**$250.00**
Kodak Hawkeye, plastic......................................**$8.00**
Kodak Retina IIIC, from $350 to **$500.00**
Kodak Retina 1a, Typr (015), 1952, from $50 to........**$75.00**
Kodak 35, w/rangefinder, 1940-51 ....**$25.00**
Konica FS-1, from $50 to **$70.00**
Konica II, 35mm rangefinder, 1955 ....**$90.00**
Konica III, 1956-59 ....**$120.00**
Leica IID, 1932-38, from $250 to....................**$400.00**
Leica IIIc, from $200 to......................................**$300.00**
Leica IIIc, gray (ball-bearing model), 1942, from $2,500
   to..**$4,500.00**

Linex Stereo, Lionel Co., 1954, $100.00.
(Photo courtesy C.E. Cataldo)

Mamiyaflex 1, TLR, 1951, from $125 to **$200.00**
Minolta, folding cameras, 1934, from $150 to **$300.00**
Minolta SR-7 ....**$50.00**
Minolta XD-11, 1977..**$150.00**
Minolta XE-5...**$180.00**
Minolta-16, miniature, various models, from $15 to ...**$25.00**
Minox B, chrome, 1958-71.................................**$125.00**
Minox II, made in Wetzlar, Germany, from $250 to.**$400.00**
Nikon EM **$65.00**
Nikon F, various finders & meters, ea from $150 to.**$275.00**
Nikon FM, from $150 to.....................................**$195.00**
Nikon S2 Rangefinder, 1954-58, from $300 to...........**$500.00**
Olympus CM-2..**$150.00**
Olympus OM Series, many models, ea from $75 to.**$225.00**
Olympus Pen, half-frame, many models, ea from $50 to .**$225.00**
Olympus Pen EE, compact half-frame **$35.00**
Olympus 35IV, 1949-53 ....**$50.00**
Pentax ME..**$75.00**
Pentax Spotmatic, many models, ea from $50 to......**$125.00**
Plaubel-Makina II, 1933-39....................................**$200.00**
Polaroid 180, 185, 190, 195, ea from $100 to...........**$250.00**
Polaroid 195, w/Timonon f3.8 lens.........................**$200.00**
Praktica FX, 1952-57 ....**$40.00**
Regula, King, various models, fixed lens, ea..............**$25.00**
Regula, King, w/interchangeable lenses **$80.00**
Rolei 35, miniature, Germany, 1966-70...................**$275.00**

Rolleicord III, TLR, 1950 – 53, from $85.00 to $135.00. (Photo courtesy C.E. Cataldo)

Rolleicord/Rolleiflex, many models, ea from $75 to.**$800.00**
Rolleiflex Automat, 1937 ....**$125.00**
Rolleiflex 3.5F **$300.00**
Taron 35, 1955, from $15 to **$25.00**
Tessina, miniature, chrome, from $300 to **$500.00**
Topcon Uni, from $30 to..............................**$40.00**
Tower 45 (Sears), w/Nikkor Lens....................**$200.00**
Voigtlander Bessa, w/rangefinder, 1936............**$140.00**
Voigtlander Brilliant, TLR, metal body version, 1933..**$50.00**
Voigtlander Prominent 1, 35mm rangefinder, 1952-58, from
 $200 to..**$300.00**
Voigtlander Vitessa L, 1954 ....**$250.00**

Wirgin Edinex, 35mm, 1930 – 50, compact, $50.00. (Photo courtesy C.E. Cataldo)

Yashica A, TLR **$45.00**
Yashica Electro 35, 1966.............................**$25.00**
Zeiss Ikonta A, folder, 1933-40 ....**$80.00**
Zeiss-Ikon Box Tengor 43/2, 1934-38 ....**$40.00**
Zeiss-Ikon Juwell, 1927-39 ....**$500.00**
Zenit A, USSR...**$35.00**
Zorki 4, USSR..**$70.00**

Candlewick Glassware

This is a beautifully simple, very diverse line of glassware made by the Imperial Glass Company of Bellaire, Ohio,
from 1936 to 1982. (The factory closed in 1984.) From all explored written material found so far, it is known that Mr. Earl W. Newton brought back a piece of the French Cannonball pattern upon returning from a trip. The first Candlewick mold was derived using that piece of glass as a reference. As for the name Candlewick, it was introduced at a Wheeling, West Virginia, centennial celebration in August of 1936, appearing on a brochure showing the crafting of 'Candlewick Quilts' and promoting the new Candlewick line.

Imperial did cuttings on Candlewick; several major patterns are Floral, Valley Lily, Starlight, Princess, DuBarry, and Dots. Remember, these are *cuts* and should not be confused with etchings. (Cuts that were left unpolished were called Gray Cut — an example of this is the Dot cut.) The most popular Candlewick etching was Rose of Sharon (Wild Rose). All cutting was done on a wheel, while etching utilized etching paper and acid. Many collectors confuse these two processes. Imperial also used gold, silver, platinum, and hand painting to decorate Candlewick, and they made several items in colors.

With over 740 pieces in all, Imperial's Candlewick line was one of the leading tableware patterns in the country. Due to its popularity with collectors today, it is still number one and has the distinction of being the only single line of glassware ever to have had two books written about it, a national newsletter, and over fifteen collector clubs across the USA devoted to it exclusively.

There are reproductions on the market today — some are coming in from foreign countries. Look-alikes are often mistakenly labeled Candlewick, so if you're going to collect this pattern, you need to be well informed. Most collectors use the company mold numbers to help identify all the variations and sizes. The *Imperial Glass Encyclopedia, Vol. 1*, has a very good chapter on Candlewick. Also reference *Candlewick, The Jewel of Imperial*, by Mary Wetzel-Tomalka; and *Elegant Glassware of the Depression Era* by Gene Florence (Collector Books).

Advisor: Joan Cimini (See Directory, Imperial Glass)

Newsletter: *The Candlewick Collector* (Quarterly)
Virginia R. Scott, Editor
Subscriptions, $7.00 direct to
Connie Doll
17609 Falling Water Rd., Strongsville, OH 44136; 440-846-9610
e-mail: CWCollector@AOL.com

Ashtray, #400/64, individual............................**$8.00**
Ashtray, heart, #400/172, 4½" **$10.00**
Ashtray, sq, #400/651, 3¼".............................**$40.00**
Ashtrays, 4-pc bridge set, cigarette holder at side, #400/118 ....**$45.00**
Basket, beaded handle, #400/273, 5" **$255.00**
Bell, #400/108, 5"......................................**$75.00**
Bowl, deep, handles, #400/113A, 10" **$145.00**
Bowl, finger; #3800.....................................**$35.00**
Bowl, float; #400/92F, 12" **$40.00**

Bowl, handles, #400/52B, 6" $15.00
Bowl, handles, #400/72B, 8½" $22.00
Bowl, heart w/hand, #400/73H, 9" $175.00
Bowl, relish; #400/60, 7" $25.00
Bowl, round, #400/7F, 8" $37.50
Bowl, salad; #400/75B, 10" $40.00
Bowl, sq, #400/231, 5" $100.00
Cake stand, high foot, #400/103D, 11" $75.00
Candle holder, heart shape, #440/40HC, 5" $125.00
Candle holder, rolled edge, #400/79R, 3½" $14.00
Candy box, #400/259, shallow, 7" $135.00
Celery boat, oval, #400/46, 11" $65.00
Celery tray, handles, oval, #400/105, 13½" $40.00
Cigarette box, w/lid, #400/134 ....$40.00
Coaster, w/spoon rest, #400/226 ....$16.00
Compote, beaded stem, #400/48f, 8" $90.00
Creamer, beaded handle, 6-oz, #400/30 ....$8.00
Cup, coffee; #400/37...$7.50
Egg cup, beaded foot, lg bead foot, #400/19 .....$47.50
Hurricane lamp, handled, candle base, 2-pc, #400/76..$225.00
Jar tower, 3-section, #400/655 ....$550.00
Mayonnaise set, plate, divided bowl & 2 ladles, #400/84..$55.00
Mayonnaise set, scoop side bowl & spoon, #400/23..$40.00
Oil, beaded base, #400/164, 4-oz......................$55.00
Oil, etched Oil, w/stopper, #400/121 ....$65.00
Pitcher, no foot, beaded handle, #400/16, 16-oz $225.00
Pitcher, plain, #400/424, 64-oz.........................$50.00
Plate, handles, #400/42D, 5½" $11.00
Plate, handles, #400/72D, 10" $25.00
Plate, handles, crimped, #400/145C, 12" $45.00
Plate, luncheon; #400/7D, 9" $16.00
Plate, salad; #400/3D, 7"...................................$9.00
Plate, service; #400/92D, 14".............................$55.00
Plate, torte; handles, #400/113D, 14" $40.00
Plate, triangular, #400/266, 7½" $300.00
Plate, w/indent, #400/50, 8" $12.00
Platter, #400/131D, 16" $225.00
Salt & pepper shakers, beaded foot, straight sides, chrome
   tops, #400/247, pr...$20.00
Salt dip, #400/19, 2¼" $10.00
Salt spoon, w/ribbed bowl, #4000......................$11.00
Saucer, AD; #400/77AD $6.00
Stem, cocktail; #400/190, 4-oz $18.00
Stem, cordial; #3400, 1-oz $40.00
Stem, cordial; #3800, 1-oz $45.00
Stem, goblet; #4000, 11-oz $40.00
Stem, low sherbet; #3400, 5-oz $15.00
Sugar bowl, domed foot, #400/18 ....$105.00
Sugar bowl, plain foot, beaded handle, #400/31 ....$10.00
Tidbit server, 2-tier, cupped, #400/2701.............$95.00
Tray, #400/29, 6½" $15.00
Tray, condiment; #400/148, 5¼x9¼"...................$275.00
Tray, lemon; center handle, #400/221, 5½" $45.00
Tray, upturned handles, #400/42E, 5½" $20.00
Tumbler, #3800, 12-oz $33.00
Tumbler, cocktail; footed, #400/19, 3-oz............$18.00
Tumbler, iced tea; ftd, #3400, 12-oz $17.00

Tumbler, juice; #400/18, 5-oz $85.00
Tumbler, sherbet; #400/18, 6-oz $65.00
Tumbler, sherbet; low, #400/19, 5-oz..................$15.00
Tumbler, tea; #400/19, 14-oz $25.00
Tumbler, water; #400/18, 9-oz...........................$70.00
Vase, beaded foot, flared rim, #400/21, 8½" $225.00
Vase, beaded foot, straight side, $400/22, 10".........$195.00
Vase, bud; beaded foot (low), #400/107, 5¾" $65.00
Vase, bud; dome foot, #400/186, 7" $250.00
Vase, footed, beaded rim, #400/138B, 6" $145.00
Vase, rose bowl; footed, #400/132, 7½" $425.00

Candy Containers

Most of us can recall buying these glass toys as a child, since they were made well into the 1960s. We were fascinated by the variety of their shapes then, just as collectors are today. Looking back, it couldn't have been we were buying them for the candy, though perhaps as a child those tiny sugary balls flavored more with the coloring agent than anything else were enough to satisfy our sweet tooth.

Glass candy containers have been around since our country's centennial celebration in 1876 when the first two, the Liberty Bell and the Independence Hall, were introduced. Since then they have been made in hundreds of styles, and some of them have become very expensive. The leading manufacturers were in the east — Westmoreland, Victory Glass, J.H. Millstein, Crosetti, L.E. Smith, Jack Stough, T.H. Stough, and West Bros. made perhaps 90% of them — and collectors report finding many in the Pennsylvania area. Most are clear, but you'll find them in various other colors as well.

If you're going to deal in candy containers, you'll need a book that will show you all the variations available. A very comprehensive book, *Collector's Guide to Candy Containers* by Douglas M. Dezso, J. Leon Poirier, and Rose D. Poirier, was released early in 1998. D&P numbers in our listings refer to that book. Published by Collector Books, it is a must for beginners as well as seasoned collectors. Other references are *The Compleat American Glass Candy Containers Handbook* by Eilkelberner and Agadjaninian (revised by Adele Bowden); Jenny Long's *Album of Candy Containers, Vol. 1 and Vol. 2,* published in 1978 – 83, now out of print; and *Modern Candy Containers* by Jack Brush and William Miller (Collector Books).

Because of their popularity and considerable worth, many of the original containers have been reproduced. Beware of any questionable glassware that has a slick or oily touch. Among those that have been produced are Amber Pistol, Auto, Carpet Sweeper, Chicken on Nest, Display Case, Dog, Drum Mug, Fire Engine, Independence Hall, Jackie Coogan, Kewpie, Mail Box, Mantel Clock, Mule and Waterwagon, Peter Rabbit, Piano, Rabbit Pushing Wheelbarrow, Rocking Horse, Safe, Santa, Santa's Boot, Station Wagon, and Uncle Sam's Hat. Others are possible.

Our values are given for candy containers that are undamaged, in good original paint, and complete (with all original parts and closure). Repaired or repainted containers are worth much less.

See also Christmas; Easter; Halloween.

Advisor: Doug Dezso (See Directory, Candy Containers)

Club/Newsletter: *The Candy Gram*
Candy Container Collectors of America
Joyce L. Doyle
P.O. Box 426, North Reading, MA 01864-0426

Airplane, glass w/red plastic wings, cork closure at front, ca 1957, D&P #83, 4⅛" L, from $45 to **$60.00**

Army Bomber Airplane, JH Millstein Co/JNT PA Pat'd under tail, ca 1944, D&P #76, from $35 to **$50.00**

Bell, Stough's, Marked Liberty Bell, simulated crack, 2 on bottom, ca 1944, D&P #96, 2¼", from $35 to.......**$70.00**

Bulldog w/oblong base, push-in closure w/printing, TH Stough Co...Jeannette..., ca 1945, D&P #17, 3¾", from $40 to...**$50.00**

Candle holder, 12 vertical ribs, rope design at base, Banquet Mints, ca 1973, D&P #318, 4½x3", from $35 to....**$50.00**

Car, Boyd; 3 windows ea side, embossed spoked wheels, marked Boyd, ca 1993 to present, D&P #159, 3¼" L, from $20 to...**$30.00**

Chicken on nest, coarsely stippled chicken sitting on woven basket, unmarked, ca 1946, D&P #10, from $25 to........**$35.00**

Dog, Kiddies Breakfast Bell paper label, TH Stough Co Jeannette PA, ca 1955, D&P #29, 2¾", from $65 to **$75.00**

Gas Pump, red or yellow plastic w/glass bottle container inside, 1946-56, D&P #438, 6" **$100.00**

Gun, Beaded Border Grip; blown, stippled grip w/beaded border, Patented, ca 1949, D&P #390, 4⅛" L, from $18 to..**$25.00**

Gun, Stough's Whistling Jim - Straight Grip, black metal screw-cap closure, ca 1955, D&P #402, 3⅜" L, from $18 to..**$25.00**

Koala, stippled bear on smooth base, black plastic screw-on cap, marked San Diego Zoo, D&P #49, 6¾", from $15 to..**$20.00**

Lamp, white screw cap holds dark blue metal 2⅛" dia shade, TH Stough, 1970s, D&P #335, 3⅜", from $40 to ..**$60.00**

Lantern, Tiny Pear Shaped, #368, 2½", from $25.00 to $35.00. (Photo courtesy Doug Dezso, J. Leon Poirier, and Rose D. Poirier)

Lantern, Victory Glass Co, Candy Pellets... on bottom, ca 1943, D&P #374, from $15 to...............................**$20.00**

Locomotive, Stough's #8, blown, 2 raised rounded ribs around boiler, whistle cap, 1957, D&P #507, 3¼", from $25 to...**$35.00**

Musical Clarinet, came w/2 cello-wrapped peppermint sticks attached, Stough, ca 1948, D&P #450, 7½", from $25 to...**$35.00**

Nurser, Lynne Doll; cardboard push-in disc under nipple, vertical ribs, #5 on bottom, D&P #122E, from $25 to ..**$35.00**

Nurser, Waisted; white plain screw cap, ingredients listed on front, ca 1962, D&P #125B, 2¼", from $20 to **$30.00**

Rabbit Eating Carrot, coarsely lined fur, recessed ledge around base, ca 1946, D&P #55, 4½", from $60 to **$80.00**

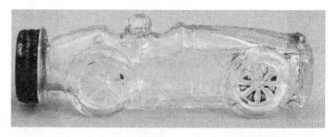

Racer With Number on Grill, 3⅝" long, from $95.00 to $145.00. (Photo courtesy Doug Dezso, J. Leon Poirier, and Rose D. Poirier)

Santa Claus, bottle type w/plastic head, JH Millstein..., ca 1947, D&P #282, 5", from $50 to.........................**$100.00**

Santa Claus, Sears, 5-point star embossed on bottom, styrofoam head, ca 1967, D&P #283, from $15 to **$20.00**

Santa w/skis, red & green plastic, E Rosen Co, Providence RI, ca 1945, D&P #287, 4½", from $15 to..................**$20.00**

Telephone; Lynne - Sunken Dial, squarish hollow candlestick, ca 1947, D&P #232, 4¾", from $50 to.........**$60.00**

Cape Cod by Avon

You can't walk through any flea market or mall now without seeing a good supply of this lovely ruby red glassware. It was made by Wheaton Glass Co. and sold by Avon from the 1970s until it was discontinued in 1997, after a gradual phasing-out process that lasted for approximately two years. The small cruet and tall candlesticks, for instance, were filled originally with one or the other of their fragrances, the wine and water goblets were filled with scented candle wax, and the dessert bowl with guest soap. Many 'campaigns' featured accessory tableware items such as plates, cake stands, and a water pitcher. Though still plentiful, dealers tell us that interest in this glassware is on the increase, and we expect values to climb as supplies diminish.

Advisor: Debbie Coe (See Directory, Cape Cod)

Bell, Hostess; marked Christmas 1979, 6½"...............**$22.50**
Bell, hostess; unmarked, 1979-80, 6½" **$17.50**

Bowl, dessert; 1978-90, 5" **$14.50**
Bowl, rimmed soup; 1991, 7½" **$24.50**
Bowl, vegetable; marked Centennial Edition 1886-1986, 8¾" **$45.00**
Bowl, vegetable; unmarked, 1986-90, 8¾" **$35.00**
Box, heart form, w/lid, 1989-90, 4" wide **$18.00**
Butter dish, w/lid, 1983-84, ¼-lb, 7" L **$24.00**
Cake knife, red plastic handle, wedge-shaped blade, Regent Sheffield, 1981-84, 8" **$18.00**
Candle holder, hurricane-type w/original clear chimney, 1985, 13" **$45.00**
Candlestick, 1975-80, 8¾", ea **$12.50**
Candlestick, 1983-84, 2½", ea **$9.75**
Candy dish, 1987-90, 3½x6" dia **$19.50**
Christmas ornament, 6-sided, marked Christmas 1990, 3¼" **$12.00**
Creamer, footed, 1981-84, 4" **$12.50**
Cruet, oil; w/stopper, 1975-80, 5-oz **$12.50**
Cup & saucer, 15th anniversary, marked 1975-1990 on cup, 7-oz **$24.50**
Cup & saucer, 1990-93, 7-oz **$19.50**
Decanter, w/stopper, 1977-80, 16-oz, 10½" **$20.00**
Goblet, champagne; 1991, 8-oz, 5¼" **$14.50**
Goblet, claret; 1992, 5-oz, 5¼" **$12.50**
Goblet, water; 1976-90, 9-oz **$12.50**
Goblet, wine; 1977-80, 3-oz, 4½" **$2.50**
Mug, pedestal foot, 1982-84, 6-oz, 5" **$12.50**
Napkin ring, 1989-90, 1¾" dia **$9.50**
Pie plate, server, 1992-93, 10¾" **$28.00**

Pitcher, water; footed, 1984 – 85, 60-ounce, $59.00.

Plate, bread & butter; 1992-93, 5½" **$9.50**
Plate, cake; pedestal foot, 1991, 3½x10¾" **$50.00**
Plate, dessert; 1980-90, 7½" **$9.50**
Plate, dinner; 1982-90, 11" **$35.00**
Platter, oval, 1986, 13" **$45.00**
Relish, rectangular, 2-part, 1985-86, 9½" **$19.50**
Salt & pepper shakers, marked May 1978, ea **$9.50**
Salt & pepper shakers, unmarked, 1978-80, ea **$6.00**
Sauce boat, footed, 1988, 8" L **$29.50**
Sugar bowl, footed, 1980-83, 3½" **$12.50**
Tidbit tray, 2-tiered (7" & 10" dia), 1987, 9¾" **$49.50**

Tumbler, straight-sided, footed, 1988, 8-oz, 3¾" **$9.50**
Tumbler, straight-sided, 1990, 12-oz, 5½" **$12.50**
Vase, footed, 1985, 8" **$24.00**

Cardinal China Company

This was the name of a distributing company who had their merchandise made to order and sold it through a chain of showrooms and outlet stores in several states from the late 1940s through the 1950s. (Although they made some of their own pottery early on, we have yet to find out just what they themselves produced.) They used their company name to mark cookie jars (some of which were made by the American Bisque Company), novelty wares, and kitchen items, many of which you'll see as you make your flea market rounds. *The Collector's Encyclopedia of Cookie Jars* by Joyce and Fred Roerig (Collector Books) shows a page of their jars, and more can be seen in *American Bisque* by Mary Jane Giacomini (Schiffer).

See also Cookie Jars.

Cake plate, roses on creamy white w/gold trim, I Knew You Were Coming So I Baked a Cake, pedestal foot ..**$35.00**
Cheese caddy, oaken bucket form, pink, yellow, green & black trim, 4x5½" **$15.00**
Cheese dish, w/mouse atop slab of cheese, 13x10" ...**$15.00**

Cheese plate, mouse atop wedge of cheese, gold trim, with knife, 9", $15.00.

Cheese tray, Deco-style cheese wedges, 5" L **$12.00**
Cookie server, 2-tier, pink flowers on white w/gold, I Knew You Were Coming So I Baked Some Cookies **$35.00**
Dresser dish, Doxie-dog **$18.00**
Egg dish, rooster in bright colors, green-painted scallops at rim, 2 sm & 1 lg well, 6" dia **$18.00**
Gravy boat, yellow, side handle, 2-spout **$12.00**
Measuring spoon holder, cottage w/peaked room, applied thermometer, NM **$50.00**
Measuring spoon holder, flowerpot shape w/basketweave base, w/spoons **$15.00**
Pie server, pink rose on white w/gold trim **$12.00**
Platter, Santa head, trimmed & Merry Christmas in 22k gold, 10x4" **$15.00**

Ring holder, elephant figural, shamrocks, flat back w/hole for hanging...**$15.00**
Scissors holder, nest w/chicken figural.....................**$25.00**
Spoon rest, double sunflower form, 6"......................**$14.00**
Spoon rest/tea bag holder, single 5-petal flower face .**$10.00**
Tray, ear-of-corn form, 11x4½" **$22.00**

Carnival Chalkware

From about 1910 until sometime in the 1950s, winners of carnival games everywhere in the United States were awarded chalkware figures of Kewpie dolls, the Lone Ranger, Hula girls, comic characters, etc. The assortment was vast and varied. The earliest were made of plaster with a pink cast. They ranged in size from about 5" up to 16".

They were easily chipped, so when it came time for the carnival to pick up and move on, they had to be carefully wrapped and packed away, a time consuming, tedious chore. When stuffed animals became available, concessionists found that they could simply throw them into a box without fear of damage, and so ended an era.

Today the most valuable of these statues are those modeled after Disney characters, movie stars, and comic book heroes.

Chalkware figures are featured in *The Carnival Chalk Prize, Vols I and II,* and *A Price Guide to Chalkware/Plaster Carnival Prizes* , all written by Thomas G. Morris. Along with photos, descriptions, and values, Mr. Morris has also included a fascinating history of carnival life in America.

Advisor: Tom Morris (See Directory, Carnival Chalkware)

Donkey, ca 1940 – 50, 12", $40.00. (Photo courtesy Tom Morris)

Bear, bank, standing, 1940-50, 11" **$45.00**
Betty Boop, Max Fleischer Studios, 1930-40, 14½"...**$320.00**
Bird w/nest, ca 1940-50, 9½".......................................**$40.00**
Bugs Bunny standing behind tree, 1940-50, 16" **$85.00**
Bulldog, sitting, chubby, ca 1935-45, 6¼" **$25.00**
Cat, sitting, tall & slim slinky look, 1945-50, 14½"......**$45.00**
Chicken, flat back, ca 1935-50, up to 4" **$9.00**
Clown, bank, sitting behind a drum, ca 1940-50, 12".**$65.00**
Clown, marked Happy, ca 1940-50, 7½" **$35.00**

Dog, sitting, flat back, 1935-50, up to 5" **$8.00**
Donald Duck, bank, head only, 1940-50, 10½" **$80.00**
Donald Duck, not copyrighted by Disney, ca 1934-50, 14"...**$90.00**
Donald Duck's nephew, wearing sailor cap, flat back, marked Junior, 1940-50, 6½".................................**$40.00**
Elephant, bank, sitting up, marked El Segundo Novelty Co, marked 1955, 12½"...**$50.00**
Elephant, standing, flat back, 1940-50, 10½"...............**$40.00**
Elephant (circus) sitting on drum, 1940-50, 12" **$60.00**
Ferdinand the Bull, sitting, ca 1940-50, 10½"..............**$75.00**
Horse, standing w/western saddle, ca 1940-50, 10½"...**$45.00**
Horse lamp, rearing, w/clock on base, original back glass, 1940-50, 13"...**$150.00**
Hula girl, 1 hand behind head w/lei & lg grass skirt, 1940-50, 16"...**$165.00**
Humpty Dumpty sitting on fence, lg smile, 1940-50, 11".**$45.00**
Indian chief on horseback, ca 1930-40, 11", from $50 to..**$65.00**
Lion, standing & growling, 1940-50, 9¼x12"...............**$45.00**
Majorette, marked El Segundo Novelty Co, 1949, 12"....**$65.00**
Mickey Mouse, standing w/hands in his pockets, 1940-50, 10"..**$75.00**
Owl on limb, bank, ca 1935-45, 10¼" **$55.00**
Pig, bank, marked Bank, sitting, several variations, 1940-50, 10¾"..**$55.00**

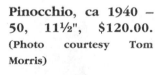

Pinocchio, ca 1940 – 50, 11½", $120.00. (Photo courtesy Tom Morris)

Pinocchio, no copyright marks found, 1 hand down, 1940-50, standing, 15"..**$185.00**
Popeye, boxing stance, 1940-50, 9¾" **$55.00**
Rabbit, sitting, flat back, ca 1945-50, 7½" **$20.00**
Scottie dog, sitting, ears pointed, ca 1935-45, 7"........**$20.00**
Ship lamp, light in base behind glass, unmarked, 1940-50, 16"...**$135.00**
Shirley Temple, full skirt, glows in the dark, 1935-50, 7" **$65.00**
Superman, wearing cape, S emblem on chest, 1940-50, 15"..**$295.00**
Wimpy standing w/hands behind his back, 1930-50, 13½" ...**$185.00**

Cash Family, Clinchfield Artware

Some smaller East Tennessee potteries are beginning to attract collector attention. Clinchfild Artware produced by the

Cash family of Erwin is one of them. The pottery was started in 1945 when the family first utilized a small building behind their home where they made three pottery pieces: a rolling-pin planter, a small elephant-shaped pitcher, and a buttermilk jug. Eventually they hired local artists to hand paint their wares. Cash products are sometimes confused with those made by the better-known Blue Ridge Pottery, due to the fact that many of the area's artisans worked first at one local company then another, and as a result, a style emerged that was typical of them all. Molds were passed around as local companies liquidated, adding to the confusion. But Cash's production was limited to specialty and souvenir pieces; the company never made any dinnerware.

For more information see *The Collector's Encyclopedia of Blue Ridge Dinnerware, Vol II,* by Bill and Betty Newbound (Collector Books).

Character jug, Pioneer Woman (head & shoulders), gingham print bonnet w/much cobalt **$225.00**
Jug, hillbilly w/jug, rifle, pipe & knife, brown on white, Tennessee across top, 6" **$25.00**
Jug, Over Handle shape, lavender irises, 5¾" **$48.00**
Mug, kitten in relief, blue on white, 4" **$35.00**
Pitcher, buttermilk; clovers, cobalt on white, 5" **$35.00**
Pitcher, buttermilk; floral, green on white, 7" **$32.50**
Pitcher, buttermilk; violets, lavender w/green leaves on white, 4" **$17.50**
Pitcher, buttermilk; violets, light blue on white, 5".....**$25.00**

Pitcher, chick with hand-painted flowers, from $35.00 to $45.00. (Photo courtesy Bill and Betty Newbound)

Pitcher, Jane, ivy, blue on white, 7¼"..........................**$35.00**
Pitcher, Karen, dogwood, pink on white, 5½"............**$32.50**
Pitcher, Spira, roses (open), red on white, 6½" **$60.00**
Planter, high-top shoe, flowers, red w/green leaves on white, 8¼x6¾x3¼" **$20.00**
Planter, kitten figural, sponge-like coloring, green eyes, 4½" **$45.00**
Planter, pipe shape w/pine cone decor on bowl, 8" L..**$25.00**

Planter, Scottie dog, white w/painted details, 7".........**$65.00**
Tumbler, duck w/bow around its neck, blue on white, 4" **$27.50**
Vase, Falling Leaves variation, bulbous (known as Flower Vase shape), 6"...**$25.00**
Vase, flowers (lg), white w/green leaves on white, slim, 9½" **$32.50**
Washbowl & pitcher, pink dogwood, 6½", 9½" dia ...**$55.00**

Cat Collectibles

Cat collectibles continue to grow in popularity as cats continue to dominate the world of household pets. Cat memorabilia can be found in almost all categories, and this allows for collections to grow rapidly! Most cat lovers/collectors are attracted to all items and to all breeds, though some do specialize. Popular categories include Siamese, black cats, Kitty Cucumber, Kliban, cookie jars, teapots, books, plates, postcards, and Louis Wain.

Because cats are found throughout the field of collectibles and antiques, there is some 'crossover' competition among collectors. For example: Chessie, the C&O Railroad cat, is collected by railroad and advertising buffs; Felix the Cat, board games, puppets, and Steiff cats are sought by toy collectors. A Weller cat complements a Weller pottery collection just as a Royal Doulton Flambe cat fits into a Flambe porcelain collection.

Since about 1970 the array and quality of cat items have made the hobby explode. And, looking back, the first half of the twentieth century offered a somewhat limited selection of cats — there were those from the later Victorian era, Louis Wain cats, Felix the Cat, the postcard rage, and the kitchen-item black cats of the 1950s. But prior to 1890, cat items were few and far between, so a true antique cat (100-years old or more) is scarce, much sought after, and when found in mint condition, pricey. Examples of such early items would be original fine art, porcelains, and bronzes.

There are several 'cat' books available on today's market; if you want to see great photos representing various aspects of 'cat' collecting, you'll enjoy *Cat Collectibles* by Pauline Flick, *Antique Cats for Collectors* by Katharine Morrison McClinton, *American Cat-alogue* by Bruce Johnson, *Collectible Cats, Book II* by Marbena "Jean" Fyke, and *The Cat Made Me Buy It* and *The Black Cat Made Me Buy It*, both by Muncaster and Yanow.

See also Black Cats; Character Collectibles; Cookie Jars; Holt Howard; Lefton.

Advisor: Karen Shanks (See Directory, Cat Collectibles)

Club: Cat Collectors

Newsletter: *Cat Talk*
Karen Shanks, President
PO Box 150784, Nashville, TN 37215
615-297-7403; www.catcollectors.com;
e-mail: musiccitykitty@yahoo.com
Subscription $20 per year US or $27 Canada

Bank, black w/white chest, musical, wind-up, Otagiri ..**$45.00**

Basket, wicker; cat woven in brown & tan, red button eyes, wooden ears, 7¼" **$22.50**

Bookends, antique white, compo, Universal Statuary Corp Original Sculpture B/W Marlotta **$50.00**

Bottle, perfume; blue w/embossed white kitten, metal, Made in China **$60.00**

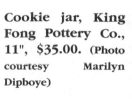

Cookie jar, King Fong Pottery Co., 11", $35.00. (Photo courtesy Marilyn Dipboye)

Creamer and sugar bowl, Japan, 4", from $20.00 to $25.00 for the set.

Doorstop, pink cat w/red hearts & blue bow, metal, American Folkart paper label, 10½" **$8.00**

Figurine, black cat on overstuffed white w/floral chair, ceramic, Katz & Co, England, 5¼x5½" **$25.00**

Figurine, brown cat w/pink ball, cold-cast porcelain, Made in Italy, 3" **$35.00**

Figurine, cat stalking, brass, 9½" **$44.00**

Figurine, cat w/mouse on tail, Lladro, 1984, 3" **$50.00**

Figurine, kitten in cream pitcher, licking 1 paw, pewter, marked 1983 Hudson Pewter USA, 1½" **$24.00**

Figurine, red tabby Persian, ceramic, Shafford, 1967, 10"...**$45.00**

Figurine, standing cat, white w/multicolored floral wreath around neck, marked Italy, 8½" **$65.00**

Figurine, white cat in front of old-time radio, on oval base, cold-cast porcelain, Border Fine Arts, 1987, 4¼" .**$65.00**

Matchbox holder, metal w/cat atop, detailed, 2½x1½x3"...**$50.00**

Pitcher, wine; elbow cut out for spout, tail is handle, marked WMF Germany, 8" **$30.00**

Plaque, black cats w/colorful row of houses, pink background, 11¾x5½" **$6.00**

Salt & pepper shakers, royal blue w/pink & green floral, applied pink flowers at neck, 2¼", pr **$10.50**

Teapot, light gray cat in Victorian dress w/yellow overskirt, carrying a fan-shaped purse & bouquet of flowers (spout) **$30.00**

Teapot, tail is handle, fish in paws is spout, soapstone, 5" **$50.00**

Toy, gray & white stuffed cat, meows & moves front paws, battery-operated **$24.00**

Tray, black w/long-haired white cat w/blue eyes, gold outlines, 12x18" **$45.00**

Tray, sleeping cat shaped, blue & cream, pottery, signed Sautler 76, 9½" **$22.00**

Character Cats

Aristocats, tumbler, made in France, $10.00. (Photo courtesy Marbena Fyke)

Cat in the Hat, bedspread, multicolored stripes w/cat in middle on white, twin size..**$35.00**

Cat in the Hat, bookends, cast iron, Midwest of Cannon Falls, MIB **$55.00**

Cat in the Hat, bookstand, red plastic, $15.00. (Photo courtesy Marilyn Dipboye)

Cat in the Hat, doll, plush, tag lettered Dr Seuss Enterprises, 30" **$25.00**

Cat in the Hat, jack-in-the-box, plays For He's a Jolly Good Fellow, Mattel, 1970, EX................................**$105.00**

Cat in the Hat, model kit, Revell #Z-2000, 1959, NM (VG box) **$285.00**

Cat in the Hat, ornament, hand-painted resin, 4½" **$18.00**

Cat in the Hat, tea set, porcelain, Perjinkities Division of Midwest, 5-pc..**$55.00**

Cat in the Hat, Thermos, Aladdin, 1970.....................**$35.00**

Cat in the Hat, trinket box, porcelain, 4"....................**$27.00**

Cat in the Hat, water globe, Whozit Friends Come To Visit, musical, 6½", MIB..**$50.00**

Chessie, candy jar, Sea Green Satin, embossed image, Fenton, limited edition, 8", EX.............................**$46.00**

Chessie, crib toy, figural, plush, musical, 1958, EXIB.**$95.00**

Chessie, cup & saucer, both white w/dark blue stripe, Chesapeake & Ohio Railway, Syracuse China....**$125.00**

Chessie, hanky, Chessie, Peake & kittens, scalloped border, Kimball, Switzerland, 12½x14" **$25.00**

Chessie, mirror, Peake, Chessie's Old Man, 2x3" **$12.00**

Chessie, plate, kitten on pillow, Golden Anniversary Issue, 5" dia **$50.00**

Chessie, playing card set, Chessie on 1 deck, Peak on other, NMIB..**$35.00**

Chessie, playing cards, B&O Chessie System Railroad, full deck, MIB (unopened) **$30.00**

Chessie, valentine card, kitten sleeping in heart, red w/printed paper lace background, 9¼x7¼" **$85.00**

Felix the Cat, ashtray, on pedestal, black metal, Felix the Cat Productions, 1990, 20", EX....................................**$60.00**

Felix the Cat, cigarette case & detachable lighter, enameled **$25.00**

Felix the Cat, clock, eyes & tail move back & forth, California Clock Co..**$60.00**

Felix the Cat, coin purse, black leather-like, Felix the Cat Productions, 1987...**$35.00**

Felix the Cat, color & wipe-off book, 1958, EX..........**$32.00**

Felix the Cat, cookie jar, black & white, Clay Art, 9½", M...**$32.00**

Felix the Cat, Felix (image of cat) Orange Dry bottle cap, cork inside, 1930s **$23.00**

Felix the Cat, hand towel & washcloth, Determined Products Inc, 1988...**$25.00**

Felix the Cat, Pep pin, shows Felix holding fish **$85.00**

Felix the Cat, pin-back button, Act Weird & Make Them Wonder, 1¼", M **$8.00**

Felix the Cat, postcard, Felix w/4 female cats on wall w/Oh! Felix - Last Night on the back porch, 1920s, unused............**$40.00**

Felix the Cat, salt & pepper shakers, 1 black, 1 white, 3¾", pr, MIB...**$22.50**

Felix the Cat, slide-tile puzzle, EX (G original card) ..**$30.00**

Felix the Cat, Soaky, red w/blue lettering on chest, Colgate, ca 1960s, 11", M on original stand **$70.00**

Felix the Cat, steering wheel spinner knob, Felix w/psychedelic colors in background **$15.00**

Figaro, book, figural, cloth, Dean's Rag Books, Great Britain, WDP, ca 1970s, 5½x7½", EX..............................**$35.00**

Figaro, figurine, marked Disney Japan, 2½".............**$38.00**

Figaro, pin, dancing, cloisonne...................................**$8.00**

Figaro, plush figurine, Disney Classics, ca 1980s, 5", MIB...**$15.50**

Figaro, snow globe, Pinocchio & Figaro look inside where Cleo is swimming, Enesco, MIB **$25.00**

Garfield, bank, sitting on green chair wearing Santa hat, Enesco, 1981, NM (VG box) **$45.00**

Garfield, bookends, Garfield on 1, Odie on the other, both sleeping, ceramic, Enesco, 1981, 4¼x4¼x5", pr ..**$45.00**

Garfield, bookends, pushing against wall, Enesco, pr from $150 to..**$175.00**

Garfield, Christmas ornament, Hallmark, 1992, 2½" ...**$10.00**

Garfield, doll, Souvenir of Colorado, 9½" **$25.00**

Garfield, figure, Garfield as Santa, vinyl, 6", EX.........**$25.00**

Garfield, figure, sitting, Dakin, w/tag, 1981, 9½x10½", EX .**$6.00**

Garfield, figurine, as Rodney Dangerfield, white base w/I Get No Respect in black letters, Enesco, 1981, 4½x3"..**$50.00**

Garfield, figurine, Let the Honeymoon Begin, Enesco, 1980, M (VG box) **$40.00**

Garfield, figurine, The Mad Telemarketer, I Quit on base, holds phone w/ripped cord, Enesco, 1978, 3x4".**$36.00**

Garfield, fishbowl (in belly), plastic, 18", M................**$45.00**

Garfield, music box, The Entertainer, plays piano w/Arlene on top, animated, Enesco, NM **$36.00**

Garfield, pin dish, Enesco, 4", $30.00.
(Photo courtesy Marbena Fyke)

Garfield, plate, Dreams Can Take You Anywhere, Danbury **$25.00**

Garfield, plate, One Dog Open Sleigh, Danbury Mint, w/styrofoam container, EX...**$50.00**

Garfield, plate, Winter Wonderland, Danbury Mint, w/styrofoam container, EX **$42.00**

Garfield, shoe lace holders **$5.00**

Garfield, trinket box, Be My Valentine, ceramic, Enesco ..**$30.00**

Garfield, yo-yo...**$10.00**

Kitty Cucumber, figurine, Priscilla feeding ducks, Schmid, MIB...**$32.00**

Kitty Cucumber, carousel, 4 figures ride on horses, plays Carousel Waltz, Schmid, 1989, 5½x8¼", NMIB **$70.00**

Kitty Cucumber, figurine, bride & groom, Schmid, 3x4", EX **$38.00**

Kitty Cucumber, figurine, Ginger in clown suit riding unicycle, EXIB (w/original pamphlet)...........................**$40.00**

Kitty Cucumber, figurine, Ginger, in pale blue bridesmaid dress w/bouquet of flowers & handkerchief, 1989, EX....**$18.50**

Kitty Cucumber, figurine, Kitty as witch w/broom, 1995, MIB **$45.00**

Kitty Cucumber, ornament, Kitty & snowman, #333-106, 3-D, 1987, 3¼", EX..**$90.00**

Kliban, apron, mice & cheese printed on white, EX ..**$20.00**

Kliban, bank, wearing red sneakers, 1979, 6½" **$85.00**

Kliban, bookends, cats in assorted positions among bookcases, Sigma, pr from $125 to............................**$150.00**

Kliban, box, cat & gramophone on lid, Sigma, from $375 to **$400.00**

Kliban, box, cat on back rests on lg red heart, Sigma, from $150 to...**$175.00**

Kliban, box, cat w/cowboy hat & kerchief sitting in white western hat, Sigma, from $150 to......................**$175.00**

Kliban, box, sitting in top hat, Sigma, from $75 to.....**$85.00**

Kliban, box, soaking in tub of blue water, Sigma, from $250 to..**$275.00**

Kliban, candy jar, sitting on stool playing guitar, Sigma, from $75 to..**$100.00**

Kliban, Christmas mug, cat in long hat handle, Sigma, from $35 to **$45.00**

Kliban, cookie jar, playing guitar, Sigma, from $165 to...**$180.00**

Kliban, creamer, figural, Sigma, from $55 to **$65.00**

Kliban, cup, graniteware w/cat on roller skates, red trim, signed B Kliban on bottom, 2¾", EX....................**$22.00**

Kliban, doll, Hula Fat Cat, in grass skirt & lei, plush, w/Kliban tag & Hawaii crazy shirt tag, 10", EX....................**$55.00**

Kliban, jigsaw puzzle, 100-pc, 7x7", MIB....................**$10.00**

Kliban, mug, cat's face, Sigma, from $15 to **$20.00**

Kliban, paperweight, Aloha Cat, steel **$8.00**

Kliban, picture frame, Love a Cat, cat at right, Sigma, from $100 to...**$125.00**

Kliban, pillow, pattern of tiny black cats on white on reverse side, 22" L, M **$22.00**

Kliban, pillow cases, wearing red sneakers, pr, EX **$30.00**

Kliban, plaque, from $70.00 to $90.00. (Photo courtesy Lee Garmon)

Kliban, rubber stamp, Butterfly Cats **$15.00**

Kliban, salt & pepper shakers, cat & phonograph, Sigma, pr, minimum value...**$300.00**

Kliban, salt & pepper shakers, cats hatching from eggs, Sigma, pr, minimum value **$350.00**

Kliban, sheets (1 fitted/1 flat), full size, 2-pc set, M ...**$45.00**

Kliban, soap dish, cat figural, soap rests on tummy, Sigma, from $140 to...**$160.00**

Kliban, sugar bowl, cat head w/red bow tie, w/lid, from Sigma, from $60 to **$75.00**

Kliban, T-shirt, Sashami, w/fish & chopsticks **$20.00**

Kliban, teapot, in tuxedo, from $175 to **$285.00**

Kliban, teapot, riding in airplane, tail handle, Sigma, from $375 to...**$450.00**

Kliban, wall plaque, waving portrait on white tray-like form, paper Japan label, Sigma, from $70 to..................**$90.00**

Cat-Tail Dinnerware

Cat-Tail was a dinnerware pattern popular during the late '20s until sometime in the '40s. So popular, in fact, that ovenware, glassware, tinware, even a kitchen table was made to coordinate with it. The dinnerware was made primarily by Universal Potteries of Cambridge, Ohio, though a catalog from Hall China circa 1927 shows a three-piece coffee service, and others may have produced it as well. It was sold for years by Sears Roebuck and Company, and some items bear a mark that includes their name.

The pattern is unmistakable: a cluster of red cattails (usually six, sometimes one or two) with black stems on creamy white. Shapes certainly vary; Universal used at least three of their standard mold designs, Camwood, Old Holland, Laurella, and possibly others. Some Cat-Tail pieces are marked Wheelock on the bottom. (Wheelock was a department store in Peoria, Illinois.)

If you're trying to decorate a '40s vintage kitchen, no other design could afford you more to work with. To see many of the pieces that are available and to learn more about the line, read *The Collector's Encyclopedia of American Dinnerware* by Jo Cunningham (Collector Books).

Advisors: Barbara and Ken Brooks (See Directory, Dinnerware)

Bowl, footed, 9½"...**$20.00**

Bowl, mixing; 8"..**$23.00**

Bowl, Old Holland shape, marked Wheelock, 6" **$7.00**

Bowl, soup; 8" **$15.00**

Bowl, straight sides, 6¼"..**$12.00**

Bowl, w/lid, from ice box set, 4" **$12.00**

Bowl, w/lid, from ice box set, 5" **$18.50**

Bowl, w/lid, from ice box set, 6" **$25.00**

Bowl, 6¼"...**$7.00**

Butter dish, 1-lb **$50.00**

Cake cover & tray, tinware **$35.00**

Cake plate, Mt Vernon..**$25.00**

Canister set, tin, 4-pc **$60.00**

Casserole, w/lid...**$30.00**

Coffeepot, electric..**$150.00**

Coffeepot, 3-pc **$70.00**
Cookie jar, from $100 to **$135.00**
Cracker jar, barrel shape, from $75 to...................... **$85.00**
Creamer **$20.00**
Cup & saucer, from $6 to... **$10.00**
Custard cup **$9.00**
Gravy boat, from $18 to... **$25.00**
Jug, ball; ceramic-topped cork stopper...................... **$37.50**
Jug, canteen.. **$38.00**
Jug, refrigerator; w/handle **$38.00**
Jug, side handle, cork stopper.................................. **$38.00**
Jug, 1-qt **$25.00**
Match holder, tinware... **$35.00**
Pickle dish/gravy boat liner **$20.00**
Pie plate... **$30.00**
Pie server, hole in handle for hanging, marked Universal
 Potteries **$25.00**
Pitcher, glass, w/ice lip, from $100 to...................... **$125.00**
Pitcher, milk/utility... **$22.00**
Pitcher, water **$40.00**

**Plate, chop; tab handles, 11", $30.00. (Photo
courtesy Barbara and Ken Brooks)**

Plate, dinner; Laurella shape, from $15 to................... **$20.00**
Plate, luncheon **$14.00**
Plate, salad or dessert; round.................................... **$6.50**
Plate, sq, 7¼" **$7.00**
Platter, oval, 11½", from $15 to **$20.00**
Platter, round, tab handles, 11"............................... **$30.00**
Platter, 13½" **$30.00**
Salad set (fork, spoon & bowl), from $50 to............... **$60.00**
Salt or pepper shaker, glass, made by Tipp, lg, ea from $25
 to **$35.00**
Saucer, from $3 to.. **$6.00**
Saucer, Old Holland shape, marked Wheelock............ **$6.00**
Scales, metal **$37.00**
Shaker set (salt, pepper, flour & sugar shakers), glass, on red
 metal tray, made by Tipp, from $60 to **$65.00**
Stack set, 3-pc w/lids, from $35 to............................ **$40.00**
Sugar bowl, open, from $8 to.................................... **$10.00**
Sugar bowl, w/lid, from $20 to **$25.00**
Tablecloth... **$90.00**

Teapot, 4-cup.. **$35.00**
Tray, for batter set **$75.00**
Tumbler, juice; glass.. **$30.00**
Tumbler, marked Universal Potteries, scarce, from $65 to ..**$70.00**
Tumbler, water; glass... **$35.00**

Waste can, tinware, from $35.00 to $40.00.
(Photo courtesy Barbara and Ken Brooks)

Ceramic Arts Studio

American-made figurines are very popular now, and these are certainly among the best. They have a distinctive look you'll soon learn to identify with confidence, even if you happen to pick up an unmarked piece. They were first designed in the 1940s and sold well until the company closed in 1955. (After that, the new owner took the molds to Japan and produced them over there for a short time.) The company's principal designer was Betty Harrington, who modeled the figures and knicknacks that so many have grown to love. In addition to the company's marks (there were at least seven, possibly more), many of the later pieces she designed carry their assigned names on the bottom as well.

The company also produced a line of metal items to accessorize the figurines. These were designed by Liberace's stepmother, Zona, who was also Betty's personal friend and art director of the figurine line.

Though prices continue to climb, once in a while one of many unmarked bargains can be found, but first you must familiarize yourself with your subject!

Advisors: BA Wellman (See Directory, Ceramic Arts Studio)

Ashtray, hippo, 5".. **$185.00**
Bank, Paisley Pig, 3 x 5½"....................................... **$150.00**
Bank, Skunky, 4", NM **$195.00**
Bell, Lillibelle, 6½".. **$95.00**
Bell, Winter Bell, 5¼".. **$90.00**
Bowl, Bonita, paisley shaped, 3¾" L **$65.00**
Candle holder, Bedtime Boy, 3¾" **$95.00**

Candle holder, Hear No Evil, angel on cloud, 5".......**$125.00**

Figurine, Al the hunter & Kirby the dog, 7¼", 2⅜", pr **$185.00**

Figurine, Alice in Wonderland, kneeling, 4½"..........**$200.00**

Figurine, angel, Blessing, arm up, 5¾".....................**$75.00**

Figurine, Aphrodite, 7¾"...**$225.00**

Figurine, Autumn Andy, 5" **$75.00**

Figurine, Bashful girl, 4½".......................................**$90.00**

Figurine, bass violin boy, 5" **$75.00**

Figurine, Beth, 5", from $55 to **$75.00**

Figurine, Billy, boxer (dog), sprawling, 2" L **$45.00**

Figurine, birch-wood canoe, 8" L............................**$125.00**

Figurine, black bear cub, 2¼"..................................**$65.00**

Figurine, Black boy & crocodile, 2½" H, 4⅝" L, pr..**$260.00**

Figurine, Burmese woman, 4½" **$125.00**

Figurine, chipmunk, 2"..**$45.00**

Figurine, Cinderella & Prince Charming, pr **$175.00**

Figurine, circus dog, 2½" **$50.00**

Figurine, collie pup, sleeping, 2¼" **$45.00**

Figurine, Comedy, 10"..**$85.00**

Figurine, cow & calf, snuggle, 5½", pr **$120.00**

Figurine, Daisy, 5½"...**$150.00**

Figurine, devil imp, sitting, rare, 3½".......................**$150.00**

Figurine, dog, Pomeranian, standing, 3" **$80.00**

Figurine, donkey, Dem, 4½".....................................**$85.00**

Figurine, Egyptian man & woman, rare, 9½", pr......**$650.00**

Figurine, Elsie, 5" **$95.00**

Figurine, Encore Man, 8½", from $100 to................**$135.00**

Figurine, ewe, 2" L...**$75.00**

Figurine, fox & goose, 3¼", pr **$195.00**

Figurine, Frisky the colt, 3¾"...................................**$125.00**

Figurine, Frisky the lamb, 3½", from $35 to................**$45.00**

Figurine, giraffe, small, $95.00.

Figurine, Grace & Greg, 9", pr..................................**$80.00**

Figurine, Guitar Man, on stool, scarce, 6½" **$250.00**

Figurine, Hansel & Gretel, 1-pc, 4½" **$65.00**

Figurine, harem girl, kneeling, 4¼"..........................**$80.00**

Figurine, horse, mother, 4¼" **$125.00**

Figurine, Inky & Dinky, skunks, 2¼", pr from $65 to....**$85.00**

Figurine, kangaroo mother, 4¾"...............................**$90.00**

Figurine, Katrina, chubby, 6¼".................................**$95.00**

Figurine, kitten w/ball, 2"...**$45.00**

Figurine, Lady Rowena on Charger, 8¼".....................**$225.00**

Figurine, leopards, fighting, 3½", 6¼" L, pr from $250 to **$285.00**

Figurine, lion & lioness, 5" L, 6½", pr......................**$450.00**

Figurine, Little Boy Blue, 4½"...................................**$35.00**

Figurine, Little Miss Muffet #2, 4¼"..........................**$80.00**

Figurines, Lover Boy and Willing, $135.00 for the pair.

Figurine, Lu-Tang (man), 6" **$45.00**

Figurine, Madonna, NM..**$185.00**

Figurine, Mr Monkey, scratching, 4"..........................**$95.00**

Figurine, Mrs Monkey, 3½".......................................**$95.00**

Figurine, Our Lady of Fatima, 9"...............................**$195.00**

Figurine, Palomino colt, 5¾"....................................**$150.00**

Figurine, Paul Bunyan, 4½"......................................**$75.00**

Figurine, Petrov & Petrushka, 5½", 5", pr.................**$100.00**

Figurine, Pioneer Sam & Pioneer Suzie, 5¼", 5", pr...**$95.00**

Figurine, pixie riding snail, 2¾" **$65.00**

Figurine, pixie sitting on bowl, 4½"..........................**$125.00**

Figurine, Polish boy & girl, 6¾", 6", pr.....................**$95.00**

Figurine, Poncho & Pepita, 4¼", 4½", pr **$100.00**

Figurine, Sambo, 3½"...**$325.00**

Figurine, Santa Claus, 2¼" **$125.00**

Figurine, Spaniel pup, sitting, 2" **$45.00**

Figurine, Sultan on pillow, 4¾"................................**$125.00**

Figurine, Wee Eskimo boy & girl, 3¼", pr.................**$35.00**

Figurine, zebra, 5" **$165.00**

Figurines, giraffe mother & baby, 6½", 5½", pr........**$185.00**

Head vase, Barbie, blond, 7½"..................................**$175.00**

Head vase, Becky, 5¼" **$165.00**

Head vase, Mei-ling, 5" **$150.00**

Head vase, Sven & Svea, 6¼", 5¾", M, pr from $300 to **$325.00**

Metal accessory, arched window w/cross, 14"...........**$80.00**

Miniature, pitcher, Diana the Huntress, bisque, 3½" ..**$45.00**

Plaque, cockatoo, 7½", from $50 to.........................**$85.00**

Plaque, Shadow Dancers A & B, 8", pr **$185.00**

115

Plaque, sprite, tail up, rare, 4½".....................$175.00
Plaque, Zor & Zorina, 9", pr...........................$95.00
Plaques, Dutch boy & girl, 9", pr.....................$125.00
Salt & pepper shakers, boy & chair, snuggle, pr........$75.00
Salt & pepper shakers, brown bear mother & cub, snuggle,
  pr...$90.00
Salt & pepper shakers, clown & dog in clown outfit, snuggle,
  pr..$195.00
Salt & pepper shakers, cow & calf, snuggle, 5¼", 2¼", pr ..$120.00
Salt & pepper shakers, deer mother & fawn, snuggle, 4¼", 2",
  pr..$125.00
Salt & pepper shakers, elf & mushroom, pr...............$65.00
Salt & pepper shakers, fish on tails, pr...............$125.00
Salt & pepper shakers, Gingham dog & Calico cat, 2¾", 2⅞",
  pr..$100.00
Salt & pepper shakers, monkey mother & baby, snuggle,
  pr..$110.00
Salt & pepper shakers, Oakie & Spring Leaf, snuggle, 4", 2½",
  pr...$85.00
Salt & pepper shakers, Paul Bunyan & tree, pr.........$200.00
Salt & pepper shakers, Sabu & elephant, snuggle, pr .$285.00

**Salt & pepper shakers, Sambo & Tiger, pr
from $495.00 to $525.00.**

Salt & pepper shakers, Thai & Thai-Thai, snuggle, 5" L,
  pr..$145.00
Salt & pepper shakers, Wee elephant boy & girl, 3¾", 3¼",
  pr...$85.00
Shelf sitter, banjo girl, 4", from $80 to.............$100.00
Shelf sitter, boy w/dog & girl w/cat, pr..............$130.00
Shelf sitter, Collie, mother, 5"......................$95.00
Shelf sitter, girl w/cat, 4¼".........................$75.00
Shelf sitter, Nip & Tuck, 4¼", 4", pr.................$60.00
Shelf sitter, Pete & Polly parrot, pr from $165 to....$185.00
Shelf sitter, Sun-Lin & Sun-Li, 5½", pr...............$75.00
Vase, Flying Ducks, round, 2".........................$45.00

Character and Promotional Drinking Glasses

In any household, especially those with children, I would venture to say, you should find a few of these glass-es. Put out by fast-food restaurant chains or by a company promoting a product, they have for years been commonplace. But now, instead of glass, the giveaways are nearly always plastic. If a glass is offered at all, you'll usually have to pay 99¢ for it.

Some are worth more than others. Among the common ones are Camp Snoopy, B.C. Ice Age, Garfield, McDonald's, Smurfs, and Coca-Cola. The better glasses are those with super heroes, characters from Star Trek and '30s movies such as *Wizard of Oz,* sports personalities, and cartoon characters by Walter Lantz and Walt Disney. Some of these carry a copyright date, and that's all it is. It's not the date of manufacture.

Many collectors are having a good time looking for these glasses. If you want to learn more about them, we recommend *Tomart's Price Guide to Character and Promotional Drinking Glasses* by Carol Markowski, and *Collectible Drinking Glasses, Identification and Values*, by our advisors Mark Chase and Michael Kelly (Collector Books).

There are some terms used in the descriptions that may be confusing. 'Brockway' style refers to a thick, heavy glass that tapers in from top to bottom. 'Federal' style, on the other hand, is thinner, and the top and bottom diameters are the same.

Advisors: Mark Chase and Michael Kelly (See Directory, Character and Promotional Drinking Glasses)

Newsletter: *Collector Glass News*
P.O. Box 308
Slippery Rock, PA 16057; 724-946-2838; fax: 724-946-9012 or e-mail: cgn@glassnews.com; www.glassnews.com

Al Capp, Dogpatch USA, ruby glass, oval portraits of Daisy
  or Li'l Abner, ea from $25 to......................$30.00
Al Capp, Shmoos, USF, 1949, Federal, 3 different sizes (3½",
  4¾", 5¼"), from $10 to.............................$20.00
Al Capp, 1975, footed, Daisy Mae, Li'l Abner, Mammy,
  Pappy, Sadie, ea from $40 to......................$80.00
Al Capp, 1975, footed, Joe Btsfplk, from $60 to.......$90.00
Animal Crackers, Chicago Tribune/NY News Syndicate, 1978,
  Eugene, Gnu, Lana, Dodo, ea from $7 to............$10.00
Animal Crackers, Chicago Tribune/NY News Syndicate, 1978,
  Louis, scarce, from $25 to........................$35.00
Apollo Series, Marathon Oil, Apollo 11, Apollo 12, Apollo 13,
  Apollo 14, ea from $2 to...........................$4.00
Apollo Series, Marathon Oil, carafe, from $6 to.......$10.00
Arby's, Bicentennial Cartoon Characters Series, 1976, 10 different, 6", ea from $20 to...........................$30.00
Arby's, Gary Patterson Thought Factory Collector Series,
  1982, 4 different cartoon sporting scenes, ea from $2
  to...$4.00
Arby's, Stained Glass Series, late 1970s, carafe, from $6
  to...$8.00
Arby's, Stained Glass Series, late 1970s, 5" or 6", ea from $2
  to...$4.00
Armour Peanut Butter, Transportation Series, 1950s, 8 different, ea from $3 to...............................$5.00
Beverly Hillbillies, CBS promotion, 1963, rare, NM ..$200.00

Bugs Bunny 50th Anniversary, from Ultramar (Canada), from $8.00 to $10.00 each. (Photo courtesy Collector Glass News)

Burger Chef, Burger Chef & Jeff, Now We're Glassified!, from $15 to **$25.00**

Burger Chef, Endangered Species Collector's Series, 1978, Bald Eagle, Orang-Utan, Panda, Tiger, ea from $5 to **$7.00**

Burger Chef, Presidents & Patriots, 1975, 6 different, ea from $7 to...**$10.00**

Burger King, Dallas Cowboys, Dr Pepper, 6 different, ea from $7 to...**$15.00**

Burger King, Mardi Gras, 1988, white glass mug w/red & yellow logo, from $8 to **$10.00**

Burger King, Mardis Gras, 1989, black glass mug w/white logo, from $8 to...**$10.00**

Burger King, Put a Smile in Your Tummy, features Burger King mascot, from $8 to...**$10.00**

Burger King, Where Kids Are King Series, pitcher, glass w/white label featuring Burger King & phrase, from $35 to **$40.00**

Burger King, Where Kids Are King Series, set of 4 glasses matching pitcher above, ea from $3 to **$5.00**

Children's Classics, Libbey Glass Co, Alice in Wonderland, Gulliver's Travels, Tom Sawyer, ea from $10 to ...**$15.00**

Children's Classics, Libbey Glass Co, Moby Dick, Robin Hood, Three Musketeers, Treasure Island, ea from $10 to **$15.00**

Children's Classics, Libbey Glass Co, The Wizard of Oz, from $25 to...**$30.00**

Dick Tracy, Domino's Pizza, M **$185.00**

Dick Tracy, 1940s, frosted, 8 different characters, 3" or 5", ea from $50 to...**$75.00**

Disney, 1980s, juice set, carafe (chiller) w/4 8-oz tumblers, complete w/box, from $15 to..............................**$20.00**

Disney All-Star Parade, 1939, 10 different, ea from $40 to...**$75.00**

Disney Characters, 1989, frosted juice, face images of Daisy, Donald, Goofy, Mickey, Minnie, Scrooge, ea from $5 to **$8.00**

Disney Characters, 1990, frosted tumbler, face images of Daisy, Donald, Goofy, Mickey, Minnie, Scrooge, ea from $5 to **$8.00**

Disney Film Classics, McDonald's/Coca-Cola/Canada, Cinderella, Fantasia, Peter Pan & Snow White & the Seven Dwarfs, ea **$15.00**

Domino's Pizza, Avoid the Noid, 1988, 4 different, ea .**$7.00**

Donald Duck, Donald Duck Cola, 1960s-70s, from $15 to **$20.00**

Elsie the Cow, Borden, Elsie & Family in 1976 Bicentennial Parade, red, white & blue graphics, from $5 to.....**$7.00**

Elsie the Cow, Borden, 1950s, white head image on waisted style, from $15 to...**$20.00**

Elsie the Cow, Borden,1960, yellow daisy image, from $10 to **$12.00**

ET, Pepsi/MCA Home Video, 1988, 6 different, ea from $15 to...**$25.00**

Flintstone Kids, Pizza Hut, 1986, 4 different, ea from $2 to **$4.00**

Flintstones, Welch's, 1962 (6 different), 1963 (2 different), 1964 (6 different), ea from $8 to.........................**$12.00**

Ghostbusters II, Sunoco/Canada, 1989, 6 different, ea from $5 to...**$8.00**

Goonies, Godfather's Pizza/Warner Bros, 1985, 4 different, from $4 to...**$8.00**

Great Muppet Caper, McDonald's, 1981, 4 different, 6", ea **$2.00**

Gulf Oil Co, Gulf Collector Series, 1980s, 6 different featuring early company history, ea from $3 to...............**$5.00**

Hanna-Barbera, Pepsi, 1977, Dynomutt, Flintstones, Josie & the Pussycats, Mumbly, Scooby, Yogi & Huck, ea from $20 to...**$35.00**

Happy Days, Dr Pepper, 1977, Fonzie, Joanie, Potsie, Ralph, Richie, ea from $8 to.......................................**$12.00**

Happy Days, Dr Pepper/Pizza Hut, 1977, Fonzie or Richie, ea from $10 to...**$15.00**

Happy Days, Dr Pepper/Pizza Hut, 1977, Joanie, Potsie, Ralph, ea from $8 to.......................................**$12.00**

Harvey Cartoon Characters, Pepsi, 1970s, action pose, baby Huey, Hot Stuff, Wendy, ea from $8 to **$15.00**

Harvey Cartoon Characters, Pepsi, 1970s, static pose, Baby Huey, Casper, Hot Stuff, Wendy, ea from $12 to.**$20.00**

Harvey Cartoon Characters, Pepsi, 1970s, static pose, Richie Rich, from $15 to...**$25.00**

Harvey Cartoon Characters, Pepsi, 1970s, static pose, Sad Sack, scarce, from $25 to **$35.00**

Hersey's Chocolate, A Kiss for You, from $3 to.........**$5.00**

Holly Hobbie, American Greetings/Coca-Cola, 1980 Christmas, 4 different: Christmas Is..., Wrap Each..., etc., ea $3 to...**$5.00**

Holly Hobbie, American Greetings/Coca-Cola, 1981 Christmas, 3 different: 'Tis the Season..., A Gift..., etc, ea $2 to...**$4.00**

Holly Hobbie, American Greetings/Coca-Cola, 1982 Christmas, 3 different: Wishing You..., Share in the Fun..., ea $2 to...**$4.00**

Hopalong Cassidy's Western Series, ea from $25 to ...**$30.00**

Indiana Jones & the Temple of Doom, 7-Up (w/4 different sponsors), 1984, set of 4 from $8 to **$15.00**

Indiana Jones: The Last Crusade, white plastic, 4 different, ea from $2 to...**$4.00**

James Bond 007, 1985, 4 different, ea from $10 to **$15.00**

Jungle Book, Disney/Canada, 1966, 6 different, numbered, 5", ea from $40 to...**$75.00**

Jungle Book, Disney/Canada, 1966, 6 different, numbered, 6½", ea from $30 to..**$60.00**

Jungle Book, Disney/Pepsi, 1970s, Bagheera or Shere Kahn, unmarked, ea from $60 to **$90.00**

Jungle Book, Disney/Pepsi, 1970s, Mowgli, unmarked, from $40 to...**$50.00**

Jungle Book, Disney/Pepsi, 1970s, Rama, unmarked, from $50 to...**$60.00**

King Kong, Coca-Cola/Dino De Laurentis Corp, 1976, from $5 to..**$8.00**

Leonardo TTV Collector Series, Go-Go Gopher, Pepsi, 6", from $15.00 to $25.00. (Photo courtesy June Moon)

Leonardo TTV Collector Series, Pepsi, Underdog, Simon Bar Sinister, Sweet Polly, 6", ea from $15 to..........................**$25.00**

Leonardo TTV Collector Series, Pepsi, Underdog, Simon Bar Sinister, Sweet Polly, 5", ea from $8 to **$15.00**

Masters of the Universe, Mattel, 1983, He-Man, Man-at-Arms, Skeletor, Teels, ea from $5 to **$10.00**

Masters of the Universe, Mattel, 1986, Battle Cat/He-Man, Man-at-Arms, Orko, Panthor/Skeletor, ea from $3 to **$5.00**

McDonald's, Classic '50s, 1993, fountain shape, 4 different, sm distribution, ea from $3 to **$5.00**

McDonald's, McDonaldland Collector Series, 1970s, 6 different, ea **$4.00**

McDonald's, mugs, smoked glass, embossed w/4 different McDonald's characters, ca 1977, ea from $8 to....**$10.00**

McDonald's, 1982 Knoxville World's Fair, Coca-Cola, flared tumbler, from $3 to...............................**$5.00**

Mickey Mouse, Mickey's Christmas Carol, Coca-Cola, 1982, 3 different, ea **$10.00**

Mickey Mouse, Through the Years, K-Mart, glass mugs w/4 different images (1928, 1937, 1940, 1955), ea from $3 to **$5.00**

Mickey Mouse, Through the Years, Sunoco/Canada, 1988, 6 different (1928, 1938, 1940, 1955, 1983, 1988), ea from $6 to **$10.00**

Mister Magoo, Polomar Jelly, many different variations & styles, ea from $25 to **$35.00**

Morris the Cat, 9-Lives, late 1970s, 2 different, mail-in premium, ea from $5 to..................................**$7.00**

NFL, Mobil Oil, low, footed, helmets on colored bands, Colts, Cowboys, Oilers, Steelers, ea from $2 to...............**$4.00**

NFL, Mobile Oil, low, flat, helmets on white bands, Bills, Buccaneers, Eagles, Red Skins, Steelers, ea from $3 to...**$5.00**

Norman Rockwell, Summer Series, Arby's, 1987, 4 different, tall, ea from $3 to **$5.00**

Norman Rockwell, Winter Series, Arby's, 1979, 4 different, short, ea from $3 to **$5.00**

Pac-Man, Bally Midway MFG/AAFES/Libbey, 1980, Shadow (Blinky), Bashful (Inky), Pokey (Clyde), Speedy (Pinky), ea $4 to...**$6.00**

Pac-Man, Bally Midway MFG/Libbey, 1982, 5⅜" flare top or mug, 6" flare top, ea from $2 to.............................**$4.00**

PAT Ward, Pepsi, late 1970s, action pose, Bullwinkle w/balloon, Dudley in canoe, Rocky in circus, 5", ea from $10 to...**$15.00**

PAT Ward, Pepsi, late 1970s, static pose, Boris, Mr Peabody, Natasha, 5", ea from $10 to...........................**$15.00**

PAT Ward, Pepsi, late 1970s, static pose, Boris & Natasha, 6", from $20 to...**$25.00**

PAT Ward, Pepsi, late 1970s, static pose, Bullwinkle, black or white lettering, 6", from $15 to.........................**$20.00**

PAT Ward, Pepsi, late 1970s, static pose, Bullwinkle, brown lettering, no Pepsi logo, 6", from $20 to..............**$25.00**

PAT Ward, Pepsi, late 1970s, static pose, Bullwinkle, 5", from $25 to...**$30.00**

PAT Ward, Pepsi, late 1970s, static pose, Dudley Do-Right, red lettering, no Pepsi logo, 6", from $15 to........**$20.00**

PAT Ward, Pepsi, late 1970s, static pose, Dudley Do-Right, black lettering, 6", from $15 to.........................**$20.00**

PAT Ward, Pepsi, late 1970s, static pose, Dudley Do-Right, 5", from $15 to...**$20.00**

PAT Ward, Pepsi, late 1970s, static pose, Rocky, black or white lettering, 6", from $15 to...........................**$20.00**

PAT Ward, Pepsi, late 1970s, static pose, Rocky, brown lettering, no Pepsi logo, 6", from $20 to...................**$25.00**

PAT Ward, Pepsi, late 1970s, static pose, Rocky, 5", from $20 to...**$25.00**

PAT Ward, Pepsi, late 1970s, static pose, Snidley Whiplash, black or white lettering, 6", from $15 to..............**$20.00**

PAT Ward, Pepsi, late 1970s, static pose, Snidley Whiplash, 5", from $10 to...**$15.00**

Peanuts Characters, Dolly Madison Bakeries, Snoopy for President, 4 different, ea from $4 to.......................**$6.00**

Peanuts Characters, Dolly Madison Bakeries, Snoopy Sport Series, 4 different, ea from $4 to **$6.00**

Peanuts Characters, milk glass mug, At Times Life Is Pure Joy (Snoopy & Woodstock dancing), from $3 to **$5.00**

Peanuts Characters, milk glass mug, Snoopy for President, 4 different, numbered & dated, ea from $5 to...........**$8.00**

Peanuts Characters, plastic, I Got It! I Got It!, I Have a Strange Tea, Let's Break for Lunch, ea from $5 to **$8.00**

Pepsi, Night Before Christmas, 1983-83, 4 different, ea from $4 to...**$6.00**

Popeye's Famous Fried Chicken/Pepsi, 1982, 10th Anniversary Series, 4 different, ea from $10 to **$15.00**

Rescuers, Pepsi, 1977, Brockway tumbler, Bernard, Bianca, Brutus & Nero, Evinrude, Orville, Penny, ea from $8 to...**$15.00**

Rescuers, Pepsi, 1977, Brockway tumbler, Madame Medusa or Rufus, ea from $25 to **$30.00**

Richie Rich, Harvey/Pepsi, 1973, from $8.00 to $10.00. (Photo courtesy **Collector Glass News**)

Smurf's, Hardee's, 1982 (8 different), 1983 (6 different), ea from $1 to...**$3.00**

Snow White & the Seven Dwarfs, Libbey, 1930s, verses on back, various colors, 8 different, ea from $15 to .**$25.00**

Star Trek, Dr Pepper, 1976, 4 different, ea from $20 to..**$25.00**

Star Wars, Burger King/Coca-Cola, 1977, 4 different, ea from $12 to...**$15.00**

Super Heroes, Marvel/7 Eleven, 1977, footed, Amazing Spider-Man, from $30 to..**$45.00**

Super Heroes, Marvel/7 Eleven, 1977, footed, Incredible Hulk, from $25 to **$35.00**

Super Heroes (Moon) Series, Pepsi/DC Comics, 1976, Superman, $15.00.

Super Heroes, Pepsi Super (Moon) Series/DC Comics, 1976, Green Lantern, Joker, Penguin, Riddler, ea from $35 to..........**$50.00**

Superman, NPP/M Polanar & Son, 1964, 6 different, various colors, 4¼" or 5¾", ea from $20 to......................**$35.00**

Universal Monsters, Universal Studio, 1980, footed, Creature, Dracula, Frankenstein, Mummy, Mutant, etc, ea from $100 to...**$160.00**

Walter Lantz, Pepsi, 1970s, Cuddles, from $60 to **$80.00**

Walter Lantz, Pepsi, 1970s, Woody Woodpecker, from $10 to...**$20.00**

Warner Bros, Marriot's Great America, 1975, 12-oz, 6 different (Bugs & related characters), ea from $25 to ..**$30.00**

Warner Bros, Pepsi, 1973, 16-oz, Bugs Bunny, white lettering, from $8 to..**$12.00**

Warner Bros, Pepsi, 1973, 16-oz, Henry Hawk, black lettering, from $25 to **$40.00**

Warner Bros, Pepsi, 1976, Interaction, Beaky Buzzard & Cool Cat w/kite or Taz & Porky w/fishing pole, ea from $8 to...**$10.00**

Warner Bros, Pepsi, 1976, Interaction, Foghorn Leghorn & Henry Hawk, from $10 to **$15.00**

Warner Bros, Pepsi, 1976, Interaction, others, ea from $5 to...**$10.00**

Western Heroes, Annie Oakley, Buffalo Bill, Wild Bill Hickok, Wyatt Earp, ea from $8 to.......................**$12.00**

Winnie the Pooh, Sears/WDP, 1970s, 4 different, ea from $15 to...**$25.00**

Wizard of Id, Arby's, 1983, 6 different, ea from $7 to ...**$10.00**

Wizard of Oz, Coca-Cola/Krystal, 1989, 50th Anniversary Series, 6 different, ea from $10 to **$15.00**

Wonderful World of Disney, Pepsi, 1980s, Alice, Bambi, Lady & the Tramp, Pinocchio, Snow White, 101 Dalmatians, ea **$25.00**

Ziggy, 7-Up Collector Series, 4 different, ea from $4 to ..**$7.00**

Character Banks

Since the invention of money there have been banks, and saving it has always been considered a virtue. What better way to entice children to save than to give them a bank styled after the likeness of one of their favorite characters! Always a popular collectible, mechanical and still banks have been made of nearly any conceivable material. Cast-iron and tin banks are often worth thousands of dollars. The ones listed here were made in the past fifty years or so, when ceramics and plastics were the materials of choice. Still, some of the higher-end examples can be quite pricey! (You can assume that all the banks we've listed here are ceramic, unless another type of material is mentioned in the description line.)

For more information see *Collector's Guide to Banks* by Jim and Beverly Mangus and *Collector's Guide to Glass Banks* by Charles V. Reynolds; several are shown in *The Collector's Encyclopedia of Cookie Jars* (there are three in the series) by Fred and Joyce Roerig. All of these books are published by Collector Books.

See also Advertising Character Collectibles; Cowboy Collectibles; Star Trek; Star Wars.

Advisor: Robin Stine (See Directory, Cleminson)

Alf, head figure, NMIP...**$25.00**

Andy Gump, litho tin, features Andy & Uncle Bim, 4", EX **$175.00**

Astro Boy, ceramic figure, 10", MIB............................$60.00
Baba Looey, plastic figure, 1960s, 9", EX....................$35.00
Bart Simpson, PVC figure sitting on stump, 6", M $16.00
Bart Simpson, PVC figure standing, Street Kids, 9", M .$6.00
Batman, ceramic figure, 1966, EX................................$40.00
Batman, plastic standing figure w/painted accents, Transogram, 1966, 19", EX....................................$125.00
Batman (Batman Returns), vinyl figure, 1991, 9", EX.$10.00
Beaky Buzzard, painted metal, Beaky standing beside barrel, 4", NM..$85.00
Benny the Ball (Topcats), ceramic figure, NM $65.00
Betty Boop, ceramic figure, Japan, 7", MIB................$45.00
Big Bird, plastic figure sitting on nest, 8", NM...........$15.00
Bionic Woman, plastic figure, Animals Plus Inc, 1976, 10", NM, from $30 to.......................................$40.00
Bugs Bunny, painted metal figure standing by barrel, 5½", NM $50.00
Bugs Bunny, plastic figure in bushel of carrots, 1972, 13", NM $25.00
Bugs Bunny, Uncle Bugs, vinyl figure, Great America, 1978, EX..$25.00

Bugs Bunny With Bag of Carrots, Warner Bros. Inc. 1981, 5½", from $50.00 to $55.00.
(Photo courtesy Jim and Beverly Mangus)

Bullwinkle, clock bank, Larami, 1969, MOC $50.00
Captain Marvel, metal dime register w/press-down trap, Fawcett, 2⅝" sq, VG...$100.00
Casper the Friendly Ghost, ceramic figure w/arms up, Japan, 6"..$45.00
Charlie McCarthy, composition & tin figure standing w/head tilted & hands in pockets, no monocle, 10", EX ..$250.00
Daffy Duck, painted metal figure leaning on tree trunk, 6", NM $135.00
Daffy Duck, painted metal figure standing by barrel, 4¼", NM $85.00
Do-Bee (Romper Room), plastic figure sitting on flowering meadow base, full color w/clear wings, 5", NM+..$60.00
Dukes of Hazzard, plastic General Lee car, AJ Renzi, 16", EX $15.00
Flintstones, Barney, hard plastic figure, Homecraft, 1973, 9", NM+ $30.00

Flintstones, Fred, hard plastic figure, Homecraft, 1973, 13", NM $30.00
Flintstones, Fred, vinyl figure holding bowling ball, 1977, 11", EX...$35.00
Flintstones, Pebbles, vinyl figure in chair, 1973, NM .$20.00
Flintstones, Pebbles, vinyl figure sleeping, EX+..........$25.00
Flintstones, Pebbles & Dino, blue vinyl, 13", EX+ $50.00
Heathcliff, plastic figure, EX+ $15.00
Humpty Dumpty, cast-metal figure, UK, 1970s, 4½", NM ..$30.00
Humpty Dumpty, litho tin figure, 5", EX $50.00
Incredible Hulk, vinyl head form, M............................$20.00
Li'l Abner, composition figure, Capp Enterprises, 1975, 7", M $100.00
Linus the Lion-Hearted, plastic figure, Transogram, 1965, 10", EX...$25.00
Little Lulu, plastic figure, Play Pal Plastics, 7½", NM ..$50.00
Mammy Yokum, composition figure, Al Capp, 1975, 7", M..$100.00

Miss Piggy, Sigma, 7¾", from $35.00 to $40.00. (Photo courtesy Jim and Beverly Mangus)

Pink Panther, ceramic figure, Japan, 8", M $45.00
Popeye, Daily Dime, metal register, KFS, 1956, 2⅝" sq, EX...$100.00
Porky Pig, Al Renzi, 1964, 15½", EX+ $50.00
Raggedy Ann, ceramic figure w/yarn hair sitting w/puppy, Pussy Willow Creations, 6", NMIB, from $25 to...$35.00
Raggedy Ann & Andy, papier-mache figures sitting arm-in-arm, 6", NM, from $20 to $25.00
Roadrunner, composition figure, VG+ $25.00
Robin (Batman), ceramic figure, Lego, 1966, NM $65.00
Scooby Doo, vinyl figure w/sheriff's badge, NM $25.00
Snoopy, ceramic figure as tennis player, Hat Series, 4", M .$30.00
Snoopy, ceramic figure on basketball, EX...................$20.00
Spider-Man, plastic bust figure, red, Renzi, 1979, 15", EX, from $15 to..$20.00
Top Cat, plastic figure standing in trash can, 1962, 10", NM.$45.00
Woodstock, ceramic figure, 6", M................................$15.00

Character Clocks and Watches

There is growing interest in the comic character clocks and watches produced from about 1930 into the 1950s and beyond. They're in rather short supply simply because they were made for children to wear (and play with). They were cheaply made with pin-lever movements, not worth an expensive repair job, and many were simply thrown away. The original packaging that today may be worth more than the watch itself was usually ripped apart by an excited child and promptly relegated to the wastebasket.

Condition is very important in assessing value. Unless a watch is in like-new condition, it is not mint. Rust, fading, scratching, or wear of any kind will sharply lessen its value, and the same is true of the box itself. Good, excellent, and mint watches can be evaluated on a scale of one to five, with excellent being a three, good a one, and mint a five. In other words, a watch worth $25.00 in good condition would be worth five times that amount if it were mint ($125.00). Beware of dealers who substitute a generic watch box for the original. Remember that these too were designed to appeal to children and (99% of the time) were printed with colorful graphics.

Some of these watches have been reproduced, so be on guard. For more information, we recommend *Comic Character Clocks and Watches* by Howard S. Brenner, and *Schroeder's Collectible Toys, Antique to Modern* (Collector Books).

See also Advertising and Promotional Wristwatches.

Clocks

Bart Simpson Alarm Clock, head image on face, yellow plastic case, Wesco/UK, MIB **$20.00**
Batman & Robin Talking Alarm Clock, 3-D figure of Batman running behind car at side of clock, Janex, 1974, EX......**$50.00**
Batman Alarm Clock, voice says 'Gothom City in trouble, Call for Batman,' Batlight shines on ceiling, 1993, NM ...**$40.00**

Bozo the Clown, alarm clock, Bozo's head moves, Larry Harmon/French, 1960s, EX, $150.00.

Dig 'Em Alarm Clock, 1979, NM..................................**$35.00**
Disneyland 35 Years of Magic Alarm Clock, features Sorcerer Mickey, dome shape, 1990, 4", MIB......................**$25.00**
Family Affair Alarm Clock, Buffy & Jody lettered on face, 1960s, M **$125.00**
Fred Flintstone Alarm Clock, image & Yabba Dabba Do on face, Fred's hands keep time, double bells, Germany, 1973, M..**$125.00**

Goofy Wall Clock, blue plastic w/full-color image of Goofy pointing time, Welby by Elgin, 1970s, 8" dia, NM...**$65.00**
Howdy Doody & Clarabelle Alarm Clock, Howdy & Clarabelle figures at right & bottom, Janex, 1974, EX................**$85.00**
Maggie Simpson Alarm Clock, MIB, from $100 to....**$125.00**
Mickey Mouse Wall Clock, green metal alarm clock shape w/Mickey's face, red hands, Hamilton, 1970s, 10" dia, EX...**$75.00**
Mickey's Clockshop, animated, musical, lights up, electric, Walt Disney, 1993, MIB..........................**$60.00**
Partridge Family Wall Clock, full-color photo image, Time Setters, 1972, 10" dia, NM, from $200 to............**$250.00**
Pinocchio Alarm Clock, various characters beside numbers surround Pinocchio, Bayard/France, 1967, EX...**$250.00**
Pluto Desk Clock, plastic figure w/bones as hands, tongue moves & eyes roll, rare, 9", NM **$200.00**

Raggedy Ann and Andy, talking alarm clock, NM, from $25.00 to $35.00.

Road Runner Travel Alarm Clock, Seth Thomas, 1970, 3" dia (when closed), MIB...**$185.00**
Simpsons Talking Radio Alarm Clock, Bart pouring beer in Homer's mouth, Wesco/UK, MIB.........................**$45.00**
Simpsons Wall Clock, Simpson family on black background w/white frame, JPI, 11x9", M.......................**$40.00**
Smokey the Bear Alarm Clock, white case w/blue double bells, Bradley, 1950s, 7", NMIB **$150.00**
Snoopy Alarm Clock, Snoopy & Woodstock dancing in front of rainbow, white metal case, 4x3", MIB, from $35 to **$45.00**
Snoopy Cuckoo Clock, plastic house w/2-D figures of Snoopy & Woodstock, Citizen, 1983, 16", M, from $175 to **$250.00**
Snoopy Pendulum Clock, Snoopy & Woodstock on face, plastic casing, Citizen, 1980s, 13", M, from $95 to......**$135.00**
Tweety Bird Talking Alarm Clock, battery-op, Janex, 1978, EX..**$75.00**

Pocket Watches

Bart Simpson, brushed steel sports diver style, made for Marks & Spencer (English store), 1997, MIP **$70.00**

Buck Rogers, colorful image of Buck & Wilma, embossed space monster on back, USA, 1935, 2" dia, EX..**$775.00**

Donald Duck, Donald w/hands on hips, chrome case w/Mickey Mouse embossed on back, Ingersoll, G.....................**$275.00**

GI Joe Combat Watch, w/compass & sighting lenses, Gilbert, EXIB...**$250.00**

Hopalong Cassidy, bust image of Hoppy on black background w/white numbers, chrome case, 1950s, 2" dia, EX **$150.00**

Mickey Mouse, gold-tone case w/train embossed on back, image w/moving arms, Bradley, 1970s, EX........**$125.00**

Mighty Mouse, flexing muscles, nickel-plated case, 1⅞" dia, EX+ **$100.00**

Popeye, Popeye surrounded by various characters between numbers, Ingersoll, 1935, 2" dia, EX.................**$850.00**

Popeye, silver-tone w/matching chain, w/hand-painted ceramic figure of Wimpy, Fossil, M (in litho tin can package) **$75.00**

Snoopy, gold-tone, w/hand-decorated red ceramic dog dish & original paperwork, limited edition of 500, Fossil, MIB..**$135.00**

Superman, 3-quarter figure, rectangular chrome case w/stopwatch feature, New Haven, EX **$600.00**

007 Spy Watch, w/secret lenses, Gilbert, EXIB **$300.00**

Wristwatches

Charlie's Angels Toy Fashion Watch, keeps time, GLJ Toys, 1977, MOC, from $35.00 to $45.00. (Photo courtesy Greg Davis and Bill Morgan)

Bart Simpson, Butterfinger candy bar premium, 1980s, M..**$20.00**

Boris & Natasha, black leather strap, in round black bomb-shaped case, Fossil, 1991, MIB.............................**$80.00**

Bugs Bunny & Gossamer, brown leather strap, Armitrom JPO #0476, NM **$60.00**

Captain Midnight, Ovaltine premium, 1988, M............**$40.00**

Casper the Friendly Ghost, Casper flies over mountains on blue dial, white vinyl strap, Bradley 1960s, NM...**$150.00**

Cat in the Hat & Dr Seuss, sold at the Universal Studios in Florida, M (red resin box w/Cat in the Hat top)..**$165.00**

Cinderella, Cinderella's arms keep time, complete w/3 interchangable bands, Bradley, EX (EX case), from $100 to **$150.00**

Cool Cat, full-figure image, Sheffield, 1960s, VG **$50.00**

Dennis the Menace, Dennis & Ruff on blue-trimmed face, 1960s, EX...**$75.00**

Dracula, Fossil, MIB **$265.00**

Elmer Fudd, Elmer in hunting outfit, white vinyl band, Sheffield, 1960s, NMIB **$150.00**

Evel Kneivel, Evel on motorcycle in stunt postion, white vinyl band, Bradley, 1976, EX **$150.00**

Farrah Fawcett, photo image, light blue strap, 1970s, NM, from $100 to...**$125.00**

Felix the Cat, w/polyresin Bag-O-Tricks bank, style #8, Fossil, MIB...**$75.00**

Flintstones, Fossil, 1993 M (lunch box case)..............**$45.00**

Flipper, glow-in-the-dark image of Flipper on face, ITF/MGM, M..**$125.00**

Fonz, photo image on face, vinyl band, Time Trends, 1976, MIB **$75.00**

Frankenstein, glow-in-the-dark, 1995, MOC...............**$25.00**

Gene Autry, bust image, original brown leather strap, Wilane, 1948, NM (EX box)..**$350.00**

Girl From UNCLE, black line drawing & numbers on pink face, 1960s, EX...**$65.00**

Goofy, runs backwards, Helbros, 1972, MIB **$1,400.00**

Hardy Boys, 1970s, NM, from $50 to **$75.00**

Howdy Doody, complete w/figure, Ideal Watch Co, MIB.**$650.00**

Johnny Quest, Fossil, M (original TV box).................**$45.00**

Josie & the Pussycats, complete w/3 bands, Bradley, 1971, MIB, from $300 to **$350.00**

Kaptain Kool & the Kongs, Kaptain Kool on face, 1977, from $75 to..**$100.00**

Lion King, Kodak premium, 1995, MIB **$5.00**

Man From UNCLE, line drawing of Napoleon talking on communicator, 1966, rare, EX.............................**$350.00**

Max Headroom, Coca-Cola, 1987, M..........................**$10.00**

Mayor Daley, hands keep time, striped band, WWC, 1971, VG **$50.00**

Mickey Mouse, Kelton, MIB....................................**$700.00**

Mickey Mouse, silver-tone case w/black leather strap, w/vintage wooden pull toy train, #LI-1452, Fossil, MIB..**$75.00**

Mickey Mouse, 50th Birthday, Registered Edition inscribed on back, red plastic strap, Bradley, 1977, MIP...**$125.00**

Mr Magoo, Nutrasweet, 1995, M...............................**$30.00**

Nightmare Before Christmas, features Lock, Shock & Barrel, Timex, MIB...**$175.00**

Partridge Family, family photo on face, 1970s, NM, from $150 to **$200.00**

Pepe Le Pew, plays I'm in the Mood for Love, black leather strap, Armitron, NM...**$35.00**

Porky Pig, image on rectangular face, red vinyl strap, 1940s-50s, EX..**$100.00**

Porky Pig, Porky tipping his hat, blue vinyl band, 1960s, NMIB..**$150.00**

Ren & Stimpy, Powdered Toast, Bigtime Enterprises, 1992, MIP **$40.00**

Robin Hood, Robin w/bow & arrow on face, original brown leather strap, Bradley, 1956, rare, NM....................**$75.00**

Rudolph the Red Nose Reindeer, red leather strap, Montgomery Ward, 1939, VG+ **$45.00**

Shaun Cassidy, cartoon image & Shaun Cassidy as Joe Hardy lettered on face, blue leather band, 1970s, NM....**$75.00**

Snoopy Hero-Time Watch, Snoopy on red dial with red band, MIB, with It's Hero Time patch, $100.00.

Superman, full-figure image on rectangular face, blue vinyl band w/red logo, 1940s-50s, VG..........................**$200.00**

Three Stooges, photo image, black band, Columbia Pictures, 1980, VG...**$125.00**

Welcome Back Kotter, flasher image of Barbarino on face, brown band, Pamco, 1976, MIP, from $75 to.....**$100.00**

Wonder Woman, image of Wonder Woman swinging on rope, hands keep time, blue band, Dabbs, 1977, EXIB..**$200.00**

Woody Woodpecker/Buzz Buzzard, Bradley, MIB ...**$110.00**

Yogi Bear, Swiss-made, Hanna-Barbera, late 1950s-early 1960s, NM..**$65.00**

Zorro, name in script on black face, original, black leather strap, US Time, 1955, EX...........................**$75.00**

Character Collectibles

Any popular personality, whether factual or fictional, has been promoted through the retail market to some degree. Depending on the extent of their fame, we may be deluged with this merchandise for weeks, months, even years. It's no wonder, then, that the secondary market abounds with these items or that there is such wide-spread collector demand for them today. There are rarities in any field, but for the beginning collector, many nice items are readily available at prices most can afford. Disney characters, Western heroes, TV and movie personalities, super heroes, comic book characters, and sports greats are the most sought after.

For more information, we recommend *Toys of the Sixties* and *Superhero Collectibles: A Pictorial Price Guide,* both by Bill Bruegman; *Collector's Guide to TV Toys and Memorabilia, 1960s and 1970s,* by Greg Davis and Bill Morgan; *Lone Ranger Collector's Reference and Value Guide* by Lee Felbinger; and *Roy Rogers and Dale Evans Toys and Memorabilia* by P. Allan Coyle. *Schroeder's Collectible Toys, Antique to Modern,* pub-

lished by Collector Books contains an extensive listing of character collectibles with current market values.

See also Advertising Characters; Beatles Collectibles; Bubble Bath Containers; California Raisins; Character and Promotional Drinking Glasses; Character Watches; Coloring Books; Cookie Jars; Cowboy Character Collectibles; Disney Collectibles; Dolls, Celebrity; Elvis Presley Memorabilia; Movie Stars Posters; Paper Dolls; Pez Candy Containers; Pin-Back Buttons; Puzzles; Rock 'n Roll Memorabilia; Shirley Temple; Star Trek; Star Wars; Toys; Vandor.

Note: Our listings are often organized by the leading character with which they're associated (for example, Pokey is in the listings that begin Gumby) or the title of the production in which they appear (Mr. T. is with A-Team listings).

Club: Barbara Eden's Official Fan Club
P.O. Box 556
Sherman Oaks, CA 91403; 818-761-0267

A-Team, Grenade Toss, Placo, 1983, MIB (sealed) **$75.00**
A-Team, party hats, set of 4 assorted, EX **$8.00**
Alf, finger puppet, plush, Coleco, 1987, M (EX box) .**$15.00**
Alf, sleeping bag, MIP **$15.00**
Alien, Glow Putty, 1979, MOC....................................**$20.00**
Alien, movie viewer, Kenner, 1979, EXIB **$45.00**
Annie, doll, w/party dress & shoes, Knickerbocker, 1982, MIB **$35.00**
Annie, napkins, Happy Birthday, 1980s, MIP **$6.00**
Archies, doll, Archie, stuffed cloth, 1960s, 18", MIP ...**$75.00**
Archies, Pick-Up Sticks, Ja-Ru, 1986, MOC.................**$10.00**
Archies, stencil set, 1983, MOC **$15.00**
Aristocats, Colorforms, 1960s, NMIB **$40.00**
Atom Ant, magic slate, Watkins-Strathmore, 1967, NM..**$40.00**
Baba Looey, doll, vinyl head w/stuffed body, Knickerbocker, 1959, 14", EX+...**$65.00**
Baby Huey, figure, inflatable vinyl w/bells inside, blue, white & yellow, Alvimar, 1960s, 9", EX **$25.00**
Banana Splits, Big Wind Music Set, Larami, 1970, MOC, from $30 to..**$40.00**
Banana Splits, figures, Drooper Sutton or Fleegle Sutton, 1973, MIP, ea...**$80.00**
Banana Splits, guitar, Snorky Elephant, plastic, 1960s, 10", VG+..**$25.00**
Banana Splits, Kut-Up Kit, Larami, 1973, MIP (sealed) .**$10.00**
Banana Splits, Paint-by-Number 'N Frame Set, Hasbro, 1969, MIB **$125.00**
Banana Splits, paper plate, 1969, 7", unused, EX **$20.00**
Banana Splits, pillow, Fleegle or Snork, Kellogg's 1960s, 10", EX, ea **$50.00**
Barney Google, figure, wearing sailor suit, Syroco, marked 1944 KFS, scarce, NM..**$100.00**
Batman, Batboat, inflatable vinyl, 1973, NM, from $35 to **$45.00**
Batman, bicycle ornament, plastic figure, Empire, 1966, 10", MOC...**$50.00**
Batman, Cartoon-a-Rama Animation Art Set, 1977, MIB (sealed) **$50.00**

Batman, figure, Robin, rubber w/elastic string, Fun Things/NPPI, 1966, 5", NM (EX card) **$65.00**

Batman, flashlight, blue plastic w/colorful decal, Nasta/NPPI, 1974, 3", EXIB **$75.00**

Batman, flicker ring, plastic, NM **$20.00**

Batman, flicker tile set (sold from vending machines), 6 different images of Batman characters, Vari-Vue, 1966, NM+ **$30.00**

Batman, Follow the Color Magic Rub-Off Set, Whitman, 1966, complete, NMIB **$125.00**

Batman, kite, inflatable vinyl, Sky, 1974, 45", MIP **$45.00**

Batman, magazine, Look, 1966, NM....................**$50.00**

Batman, magic slate, Golden, 1989, MIP (sealed).........**$5.00**

Batman, pinball game, Marx/NPPI, 1966, 21½x10", EX ..**$100.00**

Batman, poncho & mask, 1976, MIP.....................**$35.00**

Batman, poster, Batman & Robin swinging on rope in front of moon, glow-in-the-dark, Ciro Art Corp, 1966, 18x14", NM **$50.00**

Batman, slippers, blue simulated leather boot-type w/color image, 1966, M, from $100 to **$150.00**

Batman, wastebasket, metal w/images of logo & characters, Cheinco, 1966, 10x10", VG+ **$50.00**

Batman & Robin, mask, reversible images, General Electric TV, 1966, M **$20.00**

Batman & Wonder Woman, Etch-A-Sketch Action Pak, Ohio Art, 1981, MIP **$10.00**

Batman Returns, mask, Penguin, Latex, Morris, 1992, EX ..**$50.00**

Batman Returns, pencil topper, Penguin, MOC............**$6.00**

Battlestar Galactica, wallet, w/Cylon Raider, EX **$10.00**

Beany & Cecil, Colorforms Cartoon Kit, 1962, complete, EXIB, from $125 to...........................**$150.00**

Beany & Cecil, doll, Cecil, stuffed plush, Mattel, 1962, EX **$50.00**

Beany & Cecil, hand puppet, Beany, Zany Toys, 1952, VG (VG box) **$100.00**

Beany & Cecil, Skill Ball Game, Pressman, 1961, NMIB ..**$145.00**

Beetle Baily, doll, cloth w/vinyl head, Presents, w/original tags, M **$40.00**

Beetle Baily, Fold-A-Way Camp Swampy, MPC, 1964, MIB **$200.00**

Beetle Baily, puffy stickers, Ja-Ru, 1983, MIP (sealed)..**$20.00**

Ben Casey, charm bracelet, steel w/plastic pearls, Sears, 1962, NMOC...........................**$25.00**

Betty Boop, Colorforms Big Dress-Up Set, 1970s, complete, MIB **$45.00**

Betty Boop, figure, bendable, NJ Croce, 1988, 8", MOC..**$15.00**

Betty Boop, playing cards, Betty & Bimbo Art Deco graphics on blue, 1930s, complete, EX...........................**$115.00**

Beverly Hillbillies, charm bracelet, metal w/5 plastic photos, 1960s, NM, from $50 to...........................**$75.00**

Beverly Hillbillies, Clampett Family Songbook, includes 'Ballad of Jed Clampett,' Alfred Music Co, 1963, EX+ **$30.00**

Beverly Hillbillies, Magic Bubble Pipe, plastic corncob pipe, Kellogg's, 1960s, M, from $50 to **$75.00**

Bewitched, Magic Coffee Set, Amsco, 1965, complete, MIB, from $400 to...........................**$600.00**

Bionic Woman, paint-by-number set, Craftmaster, 1976, complete, MIB...........................**$30.00**

Bionic Woman, Play-Doh Action Playset, Kenner, 1977, NMIB...........................**$25.00**

Bonzo, postcard, Keep Your Eye on the Ball, image of Bonzo playing golf w/plastic bubble moving eyes, 1930s, NM...........................**$30.00**

Bozo the Clown, Circus Train or Circus Wagon, Multiple Toys, 1970, MIB, ea **$20.00**

Bozo the Clown, record player, Transogram, EX........**$65.00**

Bozo the Clown, sticker board, 1983, MIB.................**$15.00**

Bozo the Clown, Talking Telephone, 6 phrases, Hasbro, MIB **$50.00**

Brady Bunch, banjo, Larami, 1973, 14½", MIP, from $60 to **$70.00**

Brady Bunch, Brain Twisters, Larami, 1973, MOC **$25.00**

Brady Bunch, dominoes, Larami, 1973, MOC, from $40 to...........................**$50.00**

Brady Bunch, Fishing Fun Set, 1973, MOC **$40.00**

Brady Bunch, jump rope, Larami, 1973, MIP, from $50 to ..**$75.00**

Buck Rogers, Colorforms Adventure Set, 1979, MIB...**$30.00**

Bugs Bunny, camera, 1976, EXIB...........................**$140.00**

Bugs Bunny, candle holder, ceramic, NMIB...............**$25.00**

Bugs Bunny, Cartoon-O-Graph Sketch Board, 1950s, NMIB, $50.00.

Bugs Bunny, Cold Cups, 26 6-oz cups w/color graphics of Bugs, Daffy, Speedy, Sylvester, or Tweety, Fonda/WBP, 1959, EXIB...........................**$60.00**

Ben Casey's Doctor Bag, Transogram, with eight accessories, 1960s, EX, $38.00. (Photo courtesy June Moon)

Bugs Bunny, cup dispenser, 1989, MIP $10.00

Bugs Bunny, doll, dressed as baseball player, stuffed cloth, 1950s, rare, NM, from $300 to $400.00

Bugs Bunny, figure, bendable, 1988, 8", EX................$20.00

Bugs Bunny, napkins, birthday; Reed, 1980s, MIP........$6.00

Bugs Bunny, ring toss, Larami, 1981, MOC.................$15.00

Captain Action, flasher ring, several different, Vari-Vue, 1967, EX, ea $35.00

Captain America, bicycle license plate, pressed steel w/embossed image & name on green, Marx, 1967, 2x4", NM $40.00

Captain America, kite, plastic w/color image, Pressman, 1966, MIP...$65.00

Captain America, pendant, yellow vinyl w/paper insert showing Captain America, Dell Plastics, 1966, 7", EX (EX package) $65.00

Captain America, ring, from gumball machine, rubber, 1966, NM $50.00

Captain Kangaroo, Fun-Damental Activity Set, Lowe, 1977, M (NM sealed box) $20.00

Captain Kangaroo, table cover, images of the Captain, Mr Greenjeans & Dancing Bear, etc, Futura Designs, 1950s, NMIP $40.00

Captain Kangaroo, TV Eras-O-Board Set, Hasbro, 1956, complete, MIB $30.00

Captain Marvel, picture premium, color standing image w/facsimile inscription, Whiz Comics promo, 1940s, EX+.$100.00

Captain Planet, ring, Light & Sound, 1991, MOC........$25.00

Captain Planet, tin container, 1990, 6½" dia, EX.........$15.00

Care Bears, phonograph, 1983, MIB (sealed)............$125.00

Casper the Friendly Ghost, bat & ball set, inflatable vinyl, MOC...$15.00

Casper the Friendly Ghost, chalkboard, 12x18", MIP (sealed) $40.00

Casper the Friendly Ghost, figure, inflatable vinyl, 1981, 12", MIP $12.00

Casper the Friendly Ghost, Haunted Balloon House, Van Dam, 1960, MOC $30.00

Charlie Chan, card game, Whitman-McNaught Syndicate, 1939, complete, scarce, EX $85.00

Charlie Chaplin, musical statue, plays The Entertainer, Hamilton, 1992, MIB...$20.00

Charlie McCarthy, birthday card, talking; Birthday Greetings from Charlie McCarthy, CM Inc, 1939, 5½", EX ...$40.00

Charlie McCarthy, bubble gum wrapper, images of Charlie & Mortimer Snerd, 1940s, 3½x4", EX $30.00

Charlie McCarthy, matchbook, Tournament of Roses Parade, image of Edger Bergen & Charlie on cover, 1957, no matches, EX..$30.00

Charlie McCarthy, Mazuma play money, 1950s, MIP (unopened)...$55.00

Charlie's Angels, backpack, vinyl w/photo image, Travel Toys Inc, 1977, M, from $100 to.........................$150.00

Charlie's Angels, Cosmetic Beauty Kit, HG Toys, 1977, MIB, from $100 to...$125.00

Charlie's Angels, iron-on transfer, Cheryl Ladd, vinyl, 1977, 9x8", unused, M $10.00

Charlie's Angels, magic slate, Whitman, 1977, M, from $25 to...$30.00

Charlie's Angels, paint-by-number set, Hasbro, 1978, unused, NMIB, from $50 to...$75.00

Charlie's Angels, Poster Art Kit, HG Toys, 1977, complete, NMIB, from $50 to...$75.00

Charlie's Angels, target set, Placo Toys, 1977, MIB, from $60 to...$70.00

Chipmunks, figure, any character, PVC, NM, ea $5.00

Chipmunks, squeeze toy, Alvin, rubber, Holland, 1964, EX..$60.00

Chipmunks, walkie-talkie, Alvin, plastic, Helm Toys, 1985, NM, from $10 to..$15.00

CHiPs, bicycle siren, 1977, EX................................$25.00

CHiPs, binoculars, 1970s, MIB.................................$30.00

CHiPs, Book 'Em Set, Larami, 1983, MOC.................$30.00

CHiPs, Police Set, Buddy L, 1981, NRFB $100.00

Cosby Show, scrapbook, hardbound w/photo cover, 1986, 5x8", EX...$10.00

Creature From the Black Lagoon, figure, Remco, 4", NM ..$40.00

Curious George, magic slate, Fairchild, 1968, 9x12", M..$10.00

Dennis the Menace, doll, Stuff 'N Lace, Standard Toykraft, MIP...$40.00

Dennis the Menace, doll, vinyl w/cloth outfit, Dennis Play Products, 1957, 13", NMIB $165.00

Dennis the Menace, lamp, painted plaster 3-D image of Dennis w/drums & Ruff on round base, Hall, 1967, 17", EX $140.00

Deputy Dawg, Colorforms Cartoon Kit, 1962, complete, NMIB...$75.00

Deputy Dawg, pencil case, red cardboard w/decal, sectioned tray w/5 pencils & tools, Hasbro, 1961, 8x4", EX+ ..$25.00

Dick Tracy, canteen, Breathless Mahoney, MIB, from $20 to...$30.00

Dick Tracy, Crimestoppers Club Kit, complete w/many items, 1961, NM+ (w/brown box) $50.00

Dick Tracy, figure, Bonnie Braids, plastic, Charmore, 1951, 1¼", MOC..$50.00

Dick Tracy, finger puppet, marked Daily News Sync, 1961, EX $25.00

Dick Tracy, flashlight, blue w/red top, image of Dick Tracy on side, 1950s, EXIB..$50.00

Dick Tracy, hand puppet, Joe Jitsu, vinyl head w/cloth body, Ideal, 1961, 10", EX $30.00

Dick Tracy, Secret Service Phone Set, Quaker Oats premium, 1938, complete, M...$360.00

Dick Tracy, Special Agent Set, Larami, 1972, complete, NMIP $40.00

Dick Tracy, wallet, black vinyl w/Dick Tracy profile, 1973, NM $20.00

Dr Dolittle, bath toy, Fun Sponge, Amsco, NM..........$30.00

Dr Dolittle, Colorforms Cartoon Kit #456, NMIB $40.00

Dr Dolittle, hat, animal-skin print, Jacobson, NM $20.00

Dr Dolittle, party cups, w/animals & their names, Hallmark, (original wrappers) $20.00

Dr Dolittle, periscope, Bat-Zam #609, NMIP $30.00

Dr Dolittle, press-out book, Whitman, 1935, NM.......$25.00

Dr Kildare, nodder, painted composition, MGM Products, 1960s, 7", EX $65.00

Dr Kildare, telephone, plastic, Renzi, 1960s, NM $50.00

Dr Seuss, doll, Horton the Elephant or Thidwick the Big Hearted Moose, plush, Coleco, 1983, EX, ea from $50 to $75.00

Dr Seuss, doll, Yertle the Turtle, stuffed plush, Coleco, 1983, EX...$35.00

Dracula, doll, Hamilton Presents, 14", MIB $25.00

Dudley Do-Right, pen, yellow plastic w/silver figure on clip, 1970s, NM..$25.00

Dukes of Hazzard, ID Set, Grand Toy, MOC $10.00

Dukes of Hazzard, Speed Jumper Action Stunt Set, Knickerbocker, VG (VG box) $20.00

Dukes of Hazzard, tray, litho metal, 1981, 17x12", EX ..$20.00

Eight Is Enough, fan club kit, Fan Club Images, 1979, complete, NM (NM folder), from $40 to $50.00

Elmer Fudd, bud vase, ceramic, figural Elmer peering from behind tree stump, Shaw & Co, 1940s, 6½", EX...$100.00

Elmer Fudd, pull toy, paper litho on wood, Elmer in fire chief's car, EX...$300.00

Elvira, make-up kit, MOC, from $15 to....................$20.00

Emergency, fire helmet, plastic, Playco, 1975, EX⁺ $30.00

Emmett Kelly Circus, Colorforms, 1960, complete, NMIB..$40.00

ET, pillow, blue or purple, EX, ea................................$20.00

ET, sponge ball, 1982, M...$6.00

ET, tray, litho metal, 1982, 17x12", EX........................$15.00

ET, wind-up walker, LJN, 1982, 3", MOC.....................$20.00

Evel Knievel, bike flags, Schaper, 10x15", MIP $18.00

Family Affair, Buffy Make-Up & Hairstyling Set, Amsco, 1971, MIB, from $50 to......................................$70.00

Family Affair, Colorforms Cartoon Kit, 1970, complete, NMIB..$50.00

Family Affair, doll, Mrs Beasley, rag type in red or blue dress, Mattel, 1968, 10", EX, ea................................$15.00

Fantasy Island, iron-on transfers, several different, 1970s, M, ea $10.00

Fat Albert, figure, vinyl, 1973, 7", VG $10.00

Flash Gordon, beanie w/fins & goggles, 1950s, NM...$400.00

Flash Gordon, Colorforms, 1980, MIB $30.00

Flintstone Kids, figure, any character, Coleco, MOC, ea ..$15.00

Flintstones, ashtrays, ceramic, Fred & Wilma (brown & white) or Betty (black & white), Arrow, 1961, 5½x8", EX, pr $75.00

Flintstones, coin purse, Barney, 1975, NM $25.00

Flintstones, Crash Test Barney, 1993, MIB..................$15.00

Flintstones, Dyno Drilling Barney, 1993, MIB $15.00

Flintstones, figure, any character, bendable, Just Toys, MOC, ea $10.00

Flintstones, figure, any character, squeeze vinyl, Lanco, 1960s, NMIP, ea...$135.00

Flintstones, figure, Barney Rubble, plastic w/movable arms, 1980, 6", VG+...$15.00

Flintstones, figure, Dino, hard vinyl, orange, 1960s, 18", EX+ $22.00

Flintstones, figure, Fred & Barney, rubber, Knickerbocker, 11", EX, pr $30.00

Flintstones, finger puppet, Barney, Knickerbocker, 1972, MOC...$15.00

Flintstones, lamp, vinyl Fred figure, 11", NM $55.00

Flintstones, push-button puppet, Pebbles or Bamm-Bamm, Kohner, 1960s, EX, ea $25.00

Flintstones, push-button puppet, Wilma, Kohner, 1960s, NM..$35.00

Flintstones, Super Putty, 1980, MOC $15.00

Flintstones, telephone, green or red plastic w/cardboard dial, 6", EX..$125.00

Flipper, figure, stuffed plush w/sailor hat, Knickerbocker, 1976, 17", EX..$30.00

Flipper, jack-in-the-box, litho tin, Mattel, 1966, NM .$150.00

Flipper, magic slate, Whitman, 1967, NM $30.00

Flipper, Puncho Bag, inflatable vinyl, Coleco, 1966, MIP, from $50 to...$75.00

Flipper, stick-ons, plastic, 1965, MIP (sealed).............$50.00

Flying Nun, Oil Painting by Numbers, Hasbro, 1967, complete, NMIB, from $75 to $100.00

Flying Nun, Stitch-a-Story, Hasbro, 1967, complete, MIB..$85.00

Foghorn Leghorn, figure, ceramic, 1970s, NM $30.00

Foghorn Leghorn, figure, squeeze vinyl, NM.............$10.00

Foghorn Leghorn, flicker ring, EX..............................$40.00

Ghostbusters, yo-yo, sculpted plastic, Spectra Star, 1984, NM...$5.00

Gilligan's Island, figure, Gilligan, vinyl w/molded clothes, Turner, 9", M $20.00

Godzilla, toy figure, painted plastic, retractable tongue, wheeled feet & firing projectile in hand, Toho, 1977, 19", EX..$60.00

Goldilocks, Storykins, Hasbro, 1967, MIP, from $75 to..$100.00

Good Times, doll, JJ, cloth & vinyl, Shindana, 1975, 15", MIB..$50.00

Green Hornet, charm bracelet, w/5 charms, NMOC ..$100.00

Green Hornet, pennant, red felt w/image & lettering, Greenway Productions, 1966, 28", NM....................$75.00

Green Hornet, Print Putty, Colorforms, 1966, MOC....$75.00

Green Hornet, slide-tile puzzle, Roalex, scarce, NMOC..$285.00

Green Hornet, wallet, vinyl, Mattel, M.......................$100.00

Green Lantern, ring, glow-in-the-dark, DC Comics promotion, lg, unused, M...$15.00

Gremlins, Colorforms Deluxe Set, MIB......................$65.00

Gremlins, doll, Gizmo, plush, Quiron, 1984, rare, 14", MIB..$150.00

Gremlins, Rub 'N Play Transfers, Colorforms, MIP $10.00

Gremlins II, magic slate, Golden, 1990, M...................$8.00

Gumby & Pokey, Colorforms, 1988, MIB $10.00

Gumby & Pokey, figure, Pokey, bendable, Lakeside, 1965, MOC..$55.00

Gumby & Pokey, pencil top eraser, Pokey, 1967, 1", NM .$15.00

Happy Days, beanbag chair, red & white panels w/image of Fonzie holding thumbs up, 1970s, NM..............$125.00

Happy Days, guitar, Fonzie, 1976, MIB (sealed).........$75.00

Happy Days, paint-by-number set, Fonz, Craft Master, 1976, MIB..$25.00

Happy Days, Presto Magix, several different, APC, 1981, MIP, ea $10.00

Happy Days, puffy stickers, various, Imperial, 1981, MIP, ea $10.00

Happy Days, record player, Fonz, Vanity Fair, 1978, NM, from $50 to...$75.00

Hardy Boys, dolls, Kenner, 1978, 12", NRFB, ea.........$50.00

Hardy Boys, Poster Pen Set, Craft House, 1977, MIP .$45.00

Hardy Boys, Poster Put-Ons, 3 different styles, Bi-Rite, 1977, MIP, ea, from $10 to $15.00

Heckle & Jeckle, figure, hard rubber, 1958, 8", NM....$75.00

Hong Kong Phooey, candle, 1976, MIP.......................$25.00

Hong Kong Phooey, pillow doll, 1977, 18", EX..........$45.00

Howdy Doody, apple bag, Howdy Doody Washington State Apples, shows characters, 1950s-60s, holds 3 lbs, 17", unused, M...$8.00

Howdy Doody, doll, Princess Summerfall-Winterspring, squeeze vinyl, unused, NMIP $90.00

Howdy Doody, embroidery kit, Summerfall-Winterspring, Milton Bradley, 1950s, VG (VG box) $55.00

Howdy Doody, handkerchief, colorful image of Howdy spinning lasso, 1950s, 8x8", EX $25.00

Howdy Doody, marionette, Mr Bluster, Peter Puppet, 14", EX $265.00

Howdy Doody, night light, hard plastic cowboy figure on wood base, EX+.......................................$100.00

Howdy Doody, pen, posable plastic figure, Leadwords, 1988, 6", M..$5.00

Howdy Doody, pen, posable plastic w/pen in foot, NBC/KFS/Leadworks, 1988, 6"...............................$5.00

Howdy Doody, Phono Doodle phonograph, Shuratone, 1950s, EX, from $250 to $300.00

Howdy Doody, plate, ceramic, image of cowboy Howdy w/lasso, Smith-Taylor, 1950s, 8½" dia...................$55.00

Howdy Doody, sand forms, plastic facial molds of Howdy, Clarabell, Flub-a-Dub & Bluster, Ideal, 1950s, NM+, 4-pc set...$85.00

Howdy Doody, squeak toy, 13", $85.00. (Photo courtesy June Moon)

Howdy Doody, stationery, individual characters on ea sheet, w/envelopes, Graphic Products, 1971, MIB $25.00

Howdy Doody, swim ring, inflatable w/images of Howdy & friends, red & blue on yellow & red, 1950s, 21", NM $100.00

Howdy Doody, wall light, plastic relief image of Howdy on Santa's lap against fireplace, Royal Electric, 1950s, 14", VG+...$100.00

Huckleberry Hound, charm bracelet, gold-colored metal w/6 different characters, 1959, MOC............................$30.00

Huckleberry Hound, charm bracelet, w/6 charms, 1959, NM (EX illustrated card)..$35.00

Huckleberry Hound, Circus Playset, Cecil Coleman Ltd/Screen Gems, complete, EXIB $225.00

Huckleberry Hound, Colorforms Cartoon Kit, 1962, complete, NMIB..$65.00

Huckleberry Hound, figure, squeeze vinyl, Dell, 1962, 7", NMIP...$45.00

Huckleberry Hound, figure, squeeze vinyl w/top hat, umbrella & suitcase, Combex, 1960s, NM............$35.00

Huckleberry Hound, Flip Show, 1961, EXIB $40.00

Huckleberry Hound, Pinball Game, Lido, 1964, 7½", NMOC...$40.00

Huckleberry Hound, Pop-a-Part Target, Knickerbocker, 1959, VG+ (VG+ box) $60.00

Huckleberry Hound, speedboat, plastic, Regal Toy, 1960s, 17", NM...$200.00

Huckleberry Hound & Quick Draw McGraw, wall plaques, 1978, 12", EX, pr $50.00

I Dream of Jeannie, Knitting & Embroidery Kit, Harmony, 1975, MOC...$35.00

I Dream of Jeannie, magic slate, cartoon series, Rand McNally, 1975, NM...$45.00

In Living Color, doll, Homey the Clown, stuffed cloth, Acme, 1992, 24", MIB, from $25 to $35.00

Incredible Hulk, Colorforms Rub 'N Play, 1979, complete, MIB $30.00

Incredible Hulk, Crazy Foam, 1979, VG+ $25.00

Incredible Hulk, figure, rubber, 1979, 5", EX...............$8.00

Incredible Hulk, switchplate, glow-in-the-dark, 1976, MIP (sealed) $25.00

James Bond, beach towel, Sean Connery in red & black on white terrycloth, Glid Rose/Fon Products, 1965, 56x34", EX $100.00

James Bond, ID tags, 1984, M (on photo card) $35.00

James Bond, Thunderball Paint Set, British, 1965, EX $175.00

Josie & the Pussycats, chalkboard, 1970s, M, from $50 to $75.00

Josie & the Pussycats, Slick Ticker play watch, Larami, 1973, MOC, from $50 to...$75.00

Josie & the Pussycats, Vanity Set, Larami, 1973, MOC..$30.00

Katnip & Herman, kite, cardboard, Saalfield, 1960s, NMIP $25.00

King Leonardo, Paint-N-Press Art Set, True Talent, 1962, complete, EXIB $50.00

Knight Rider, sticker & album set, Gordy Ind, MOC $8.00

Land Before Time, doll, Little Foot, JC Penney Exclusive, stuffed cloth, EX..$35.00

Land of the Giants, flashlight/whistle, 1968, MOC......$60.00

Land of the Lost, Safari Shooter, Larami, 1975, MIP....$30.00

Lariat Sam, magic slate, Lowe, 1962, NM....................$30.00

Lassie, wallet, brown vinyl w/full-color image of Lassie, 1950s, EX...............$35.00

Laurel & Hardy, clothes hangers, diecut cardboard 2-sided images of duo w/plastic hooks, Henderson-Hoggard, 1967, EX, pr...............$85.00

Laurel & Hardy, magazine, 1000 New Jokes/Winter Edition, Babes in Toyland photo cover, 50 pages, Dell, 1935, G+ $40.00

Laurel & Hardy, magic slate, 1963, NM $35.00

Laverne & Shirley, iron-on transfers, several different, 1970s, MIP...............$15.00

Laverne & Shirley, pocketbook, Harmony, 1977, from $10.00 to $15.00. (Photo courtesy Greg Davis and Bill Morgan)

Leave It to Beaver, Eras-O-Picture Book, Hasbro, 1959, EX...............$85.00

Leave It to Beaver, figure, Beaver standing on lunch box base, 3½", M...............$35.00

Li'l Abner, tray, Dog Patch USA, 1968, EX...............$50.00

Little Audrey, figure, vinyl, 13", EX...............$50.00

Little Audrey, Shoulder Bag Leathercraft Kit, Jewel Leathergoods, 1961, complete, EXIB...............$75.00

Little Audrey, tote bag, vinyl w/Little Audrey & countries, 1960, 8x6x5", EX+...............$60.00

Little House on the Prairie, paint-by-number set, Craft House, 1979, MIB...............$40.00

Little Lulu, doll, stuffed cloth w/red dress & yarn hair, 1944, scarce, 15", EX...............$200.00

Little Lulu, jewelry box, Larami, 1973, MIP...............$15.00

Little Orphan Annie, mask, diecut paper litho, Ovaltine premium, 1933, 8½", EX...............$45.00

Lost in Space, writing tablet, June Lockhart cover, 1960s, 8x10", unused, NM+...............$30.00

Love Boat, doctor's set, Fleetwood, 1979, MOC...............$30.00

Magilla Gorilla, doll, bendable felt body w/vinyl head, complete w/felt accessories, Ideal, 1960s, 8", EX...............$85.00

Magilla Gorilla, pull toy, vinyl figure standing on plastic wagon, Ideal, 1964, EX...............$65.00

Man From Atlantis, Dip Dot Painting Kit, Kenner, 1977, NRFB...............$130.00

Masters of the Universe, He-Man Superblo, inflatable vinyl, Unique Art, 1984, expands to 7 feet, MIP...............$20.00

Masters of the Universe, Magetix Playset, American Publishing, 1985, MIP (sealed) $20.00

Mickey Mouse Club Show, Jimmy Dodd Magic Slate, 1954, NM, $36.00.

Mighty Mouse, figure, squeeze vinyl, Terrytoon, 1950s, 10", EX+...............$55.00

Mighty Mouse, How To Draw Cartoons Set, Gabriel, 1956, complete, EXIB...............$65.00

Mork & Mindy, Colorforms Magic Show, MIB...............$30.00

Mork & Mindy, Poster, Mork From Ork, 1970s, 36x24", EX...............$15.00

Mork & Mindy, sleeping bag, 1979, NM...............$20.00

Mr Magoo, magic slate, Rand McNally, 1975, EX+...............$20.00

Muppets, doll, Fozzie Bear, stuffed cloth, Fisher-Price, 1977-78, NM...............$10.00

Muppets, Dress-Up Doll, Great Gonzo, plush w/removable clothes, Fisher-Price, 1982-83, MIB...............$15.00

Muppets, oven mitt, Miss Piggy, 1981, NM...............$10.00

Muppets, push-button puppet, Kermit the Frog, Sony/Japan, 4", MOC...............$25.00

New Zoo Revue, figure, frog, vinyl, 1973, 3", EX...............$10.00

New Zoo Revue, figure, Henrietta Hippo, plush, 1977, 17", EX...............$60.00

New Zoo Revue, finger puppet, any character, vinyl, Rushton, 1970s, NM, ea...............$30.00

New Zoo Revue, pencil topper, any character, 1974, M, ea from $10 to...............$15.00

Nightmare on Elm Street, doll, Freddy Krueger, Matchbox, 16", NRFB...............$50.00

Nightmare on Elm Street, doll, Maxx Fx, Matchbox, 12", MIB...............$40.00

Nightmare on Elm Street, figure, Freddy Krueger, Bend & Twist vinyl, 10", MOC...............$25.00

Nightmare on Elm Street, figure, Stick-Up, 4", MOC...............$6.00

Partridge Family, bulletin board, red cork w/music staff logo in white, 1970s, 18x24", EX, from $75 to...............$100.00

Partridge Family, shopping bag, 1972, M...............$12.00

Peanuts, balance toy, Snoopy & the Balancing Woodstocks, Hasbro Preschool, 1982, MIB...............$15.00

Peanuts, beach bag, Beagle Beach, white w/zipper closure, Colgate premium, 9x8", M...............$20.00

Peanuts, doll, Charlie Brown, vinyl, 1950s, 9", VG...............$75.00

Peanuts, doll, Linus w/hand out, red shirt, MIP..........**$75.00**

Peanuts, doll, Lucy, rag-type w/red dress, Determined Toys, 1970s, 14", MIB.....................................**$20.00**

Peanuts, doll, Peppermint Patty, rag type, Determined Toys, 1970s, 14", MIB.................................**$20.00**

Peanuts, doll, Snoopy, inflatable, 1969, 18", EX..........**$10.00**

Peanuts, doll, Snoopy as Santa, plush, Applause, 1992, 15", MIP...**$35.00**

Peanuts, doll, Snoopy w/rattle, plush, 9", MIP..........**$10.00**

Peanuts, drum, tin & paper, shows Peanuts Marching Band & Good Grief Society w/Five & Frieda, Chein, 1963, VG+..**$45.00**

Peanuts, fishing pole, orange plastic featuring Snoopy, Zebco, VG...**$15.00**

Peanuts, hand puppet, Woodstock, velveteen w/yarn feathers, Determined, 1970s, 6", NM, from $15 to......**$20.00**

Peanuts, jack-in-the-box, Snoopy, NMIB...................**$75.00**

Peanuts, pull toy, Snoopy & Woodstock, plastic, Hasbro, EX...**$60.00**

Peanuts, See 'N Say, Snoopy Says, Mattel, 1968, MIB...**$75.00**

Peanuts, tea set, Snoopy, plastic, Berwick, 1979, 19 pcs, MIB...**$100.00**

Peanuts, windup figures, any character, M, ea from $5 to..**$10.00**

Pee Wee's Colorforms Play Set, Herman Toys Inc., 1987, 12x7, MIB, $25.00.

Phantom of the Opera, figure, hard plastic w/vinyl head, Hong Kong, 1950s, rare, 7", NM.........................**$150.00**

Phantom of the Opera, iron-on patch, classic pose w/logo below, 1965, 4x8", NM+.................................**$25.00**

Pink Panther, doll, plush, 6", M.................................**$10.00**

Pink Panther, slide-tile puzzle, Ja-Ru, 1981, MOC......**$15.00**

Pink Panther, washcloth, terry, Japan, unused, M......**$15.00**

Pixie & Dixie, hand puppets, Knickerbocker, 1962, unused, NMIB, ea...**$40.00**

Planet of the Apes, kite, Hi-Flier, MIP.......................**$75.00**

Planet of the Apes, Mix 'N Mold Set, Astronaut Virdon, Burke or Dr Zaius, rare, MIB, ea...................................**$100.00**

Planet of the Apes, squirt gun, Cornelius, plastic, AHI, 1970s, NM...**$75.00**

Popeye, Beach Boat, 1980, MOC..............................**$50.00**

Popeye, bowl, cereal; plastic, 1979, NM....................**$10.00**

Popeye, Colorforms Popeye the Weatherman, 1957, complete, EXIB..**$75.00**

Popeye, dexterity puzzle, Intelligence Test, fit 3 character heads in right indented areas, glass & tin frame, 5", NM...**$75.00**

Popeye, figure set, painted wood cut-out figures w/balloons, set of 4, EX..**$150.00**

Popeye, finger puppet set, Popeye, Olive Oyl, Sweet Pea, Whimpy & Brutus, 1960s, MOC.......................**$18.00**

Popeye, flashlight, pocket size, Larami, 1983, MOC...**$18.00**

Popeye, Flip Show, 1961, EXIB................................**$40.00**

Popeye, jack-in-the-box, Popeye in the Music Box, litho tin, Mattel, EX...**$150.00**

Popeye, knapsack, canvas, multicolor, w/tags, 1979, M..**$15.00**

Popeye, mask, Comic Club, diecut paper litho, Wrigley's Juicy Fruit premium, 1930s, 11x9", VG+...............**$65.00**

Popeye, roly poly, cloth w/vinyl head, Gund, M.....**$150.00**

Popeye, TV Stow-A-Way Slate, Lowe, 1957, 12x8", unused, NM...**$35.00**

Popeye & Wimpy, figures, matt green soft plastic, Marx, 1950s, 2½", NM+, pr.......................................**$40.00**

Porky Pig, figure, w/squeaker, Sun Rubber, NM.........**$50.00**

Porky Pig, ring, cloisonne, 1970s, M..........................**$12.00**

Power Rangers, yo-yo, litho tin, 1994, NM..................**$5.00**

Punky Bruster, plate, plastic, 1984, 9x10", EX...........**$20.00**

Quick Draw McGraw, bath soap, MIP.......................**$15.00**

Quick Draw McGraw, Lovable Smoking Traveler's Pet, plastic, M...**$20.00**

Quick Draw McGraw, Magic Rub-Off Pictures, Whitman, 1960, complete, EXIB.......................................**$65.00**

Quick Draw McGraw, Flintstones, and Huckleberry Hound wastebaskets, lithographed tin, EX, $60.00 each.
(Photo courtesy Mike's General Store)

Raggedy Ann, Busy Apron, Whitman, 1969, complete, MIP, from $30 to...**$35.00**

Raggedy Ann, Colorforms Easy Needlepoint, 1990, complete, MIB...**$15.00**

Raggedy Ann, Colorforms Sewing Cards, 1988, complete, MIB...**$15.00**

Raggedy Ann, planter, William Hirsch, 1940s, EX.......**$60.00**

Raggedy Ann, purse, plastic, Banner Bros, 1941, EX....**$100.00**

Raggedy Ann, sink, plastic, Hasbro/Romper Room, 1978, 20x14½", complete, NMIB, from $50 to...............**$65.00**

Raggedy Ann, stove, plastic, 1978, 7x15x20", VG.......**$30.00**

Raggedy Ann, talking telephone, plastic, battery-op, 1980, 9", M, from $40 to.....................................**$55.00**

Raggedy Ann, wall bag, vinyl w/4 pockets, Pussy Willow, 1981, MIP..**$25.00**

Raggedy Ann & Andy, Color Poster Pack, OSP Publishing, 1993, MIP..$15.00

Raggedy Ann & Andy, cork board, diecut figures, Manton Cork Corp, 23", NM, ea from $25 to $30.00

Raggedy Ann & Andy, crayon box, tin, Chein, 1974, VG+ $25.00

Raggedy Ann & Andy, Fun-Filled Playtime Box, Whitman, 1976, complete, NMIB $30.00

Raggedy Ann & Andy, highchair, doll; wood, Roth American Inc, NMIB, from $35 to $45.00

Raggedy Ann & Andy, tambourine, plastic, Kingsway, 1977, 6" dia, MIP, from $25 to $30.00

Raggedy Ann & Andy, watering can, tin litho, Chein, 1973, 9", NM..$45.00

Rat Fink, decal, black & white, 1990, 6", NM................$5.00

Rat Fink, ring, plastic w/detachable figure, Macman Ent, 1963, MIP..$30.00

Ricochet Rabbit, push puppet, Kohner, EX................$40.00

Rocky & Bullwinkle, doll, Rocky, stuffed cloth w/vinyl cap & goggles, 1991, EX.......................................$12.00

Rocky & Bullwinkle, figure set, Rocky, Natasha & Boris, bendable, 1991, MOC......................................$20.00

Rocky & Bullwinkle, sewing cards, Rocky & His Friends, Whitman, 1961, complete, NMIB.......................$100.00

Scooby Doo, stamper, Hanna-Barbera, 1983, MOC......$6.00

Scooby Soo, doll, stuffed cloth, paper label w/Scooby image, 1970, 11", EX...$25.00

Sesame Street, figure, Big Bird, squeeze vinyl, 3", EX..$5.00

Sesame Street, figure set, various characters, PVC, Applause, 1993, 8-pc, NM..$20.00

Sesame Street, Lacing Puppets, Cookie Monster & Bert or Oscar & Grover, Fisher-Price, 1984, MIP, ea..........$6.00

Shmoo, deodorizer figure, white ceramic, opening in back for wick, 1940s, 4½x6", NM...............................$100.00

Simpsons, activity album, w/slide-o-scope, Diamond, unused, NM...$15.00

Simpsons, doll, any character, rag-type, Dandee, 11", NM, ea..$18.00

Simpsons, doll, Bart, rag-type, Dandee, 17", NM........$25.00

Simpsons, doll, Bart, talker, stuffed cloth & vinyl, Dandee, 18", MIB...$75.00

Simpsons, doll, Homer, stuffed cloth w/vinyl head, Vivid Imaginations, 11", M....................................$35.00

Simpsons, figure, Lisa, Maggie or Marge, bendable, Jesco, 2", 3½" & 6", MOC, ea...................................$15.00

Simpsons, key chain, Bart, 3-D PVC figure on silver-tone ring, Street Kids, M.......................................$3.00

Simpsons, pajama bag, Bart, stuffed cloth figure holding toothbrush & pillow, Dandee, 24", M $40.00

Simpsons, pinball game, plastic, Jaru, MOC.................$5.00

Smurfs, Magic Talk Papa Smurf's Lab, Mattel Preschool, complete, MIB, from $40 to $50.00

Smurfs, Smurf Amaze-ing Action Maze, EX................$20.00

Sniffles, ceramic, cat figure sitting wearing sailor-type hat, Warner Bros, 1940s, 3½", VG+ $50.00

Space Jam, yo-yo, plastic w/Michael Jordan & Bugs Bunny Photo seal, Spectra Star, 1996, MIP....................$5.00

Space Kidettes, magic slate, Watkins-Strathmore, 1967, rare, NM..$40.00

Space Patrol, costume, coat, pants, cap & belt w/decoder buckle, Boys Wear by Billy the Kid, 1950s, VG.$135.00

Spider-Man, Color 'N Recolor Action Pictures, Avalon, 1977, unused, MIB...$50.00

Spider-Man, Colorforms Spider-Man & the Marvel Heroes Rub 'N Play Magic Transfer Set, 1978, MIB..........$50.00

Spider-Man, kazoo, Straco, MOC.............................$50.00

Spider-Man, postcards, set of 10 different, EX...........$10.00

Spider-Man, sunglasses, Nasta, 1986, MOC.................$10.00

Starsky & Hutch, Emergency Dashboard, Illco, 1977, MIB..$125.00

Starsky & Hutch, flashlight, Fleetwood, 1976, MOC...$65.00

Steve Canyon, scarf & goggles, silver plastic goggles & red scarf, EX+ (diecut card of Canyon) $65.00

Super Heroes (DC), calendar, 1976, Batman, Superman, Wonder Woman, etc, Neal Adams artwork, 12x11", M...$15.00

Super Heroes (DC), Super Shakers, Batman, Superman, Wonder Woman, Ideal, 1979, complete, unused, MIB.............$35.00

Super Heroes (Marvel), bumper sticker, Warning: I Brake for Marvel Super Heroes, Marvel Comics, 1978, 4x14", M..............$15.00

Super Heroes (Marvel), New Super Heroes Sparkle Paints, Kenner, 1967, unused, MIB................................$100.00

Supergirl, doll, Super Queen, vinyl w/cloth dress, red vinyl cape & boots, Ideal, 1967, 12", M, from $275 to .$325.00

Superman, Crazy Foam, American Aerosol, 1974, NM..$50.00

Superman, figure, vinyl, in flying pose, Transogram, 1940s, MOC (13x10") $200.00

Superman, iron-on transfer, red & black w/images of Superman in front of rocketship, 1950, 13x9", EX.$45.00

Superman, magic slate, Whitman, 1965, EX................$50.00

Superman, pencil, #2 lead, 1978, M.........................$20.00

Superman, planter, porcelain, 1976, sm, EX...............$15.00

Superman, push-button puppet, Kohner, 1966, 4", NM..$15.00

Superman, slide-tile puzzle, image of Superman flying over city, Toy Guidance, 1966, EX+.........................$40.00

Superman, valentine, Superman bust image on diecut heart w/2 kids on pop-out heart, 1940, 4½", NM.........$55.00

Superman, wallet, yellow vinyl w/coin holder & mini-magic slate w/pencil inside, 1966, M $30.00

Sylvester the Cat, figure, velour, 5", EX $10.00

Tarzan, Colorforms Cartoon Kit, 1966, complete, EXIB..$20.00

Three Stooges, puffy stickers, 1984, MIP (sealed).........$8.00

Tom & Jerry, figures, either character, bendable, MOC, ea...$10.00

Tom & Jerry, ring, Jerry, cloisonne, 1970s, M.............$12.00

Tom & Jerry, water pistols, Marx, 1960s, M................$65.00

Tom Corbett Space Cadet, Model-Craft Molding & Coloring Set #25, 1950s, VG (VG box)...........................$100.00

Tom Corbett Space Cadet, patch (from Tom Corbett Member Kit), blue, red & gold stitched fabric, Kellogg's, 1951, NM+..$60.00

Top Cat, doll, stuffed cloth body w/soft vinyl head w/tongue sticking out & in sitting position, Ideal 1960s, 6", MIB $150.00

Underdog, bop bag, inflatable vinyl, MIB $50.00
Underdog, pillow, inflatable vinyl, EX......................$15.00
Waldo, doll, vinyl, Mattel, 1991, 18", EX+...................$15.00
Weird-Ohs, magic slate, Davey the Way Out Cyclist, 1963, MIP (sealed) $30.00
Winky Dink, paint set, unused, MIB.........................$65.00
Winky Dink, Super Magic TV Kit, Winky Dink & You!, Standard Toycraft, 1968, unused, NMIB...............$125.00
Wizard of Oz, cup holder, plastic, 1989, 7", M...........$10.00
Wizard of Oz, magic kit, Armour Franks mail-in premium, Fun Inc, 1967, incomplete otherwise EX..............$45.00
Wizard of Oz, place mat, vinyl w/photo image, 1989, 12x16", EX...$15.00
Wolfman, doll, vinyl w/cloth clothes, Hamilton Presents, 1992, 14", EX...$30.00
Wolfman, figure, Playco Products, 1991, 10", MIB......$12.00
Wonder Woman, air freshener, 1975, MIP $40.00
Wonder Woman, cup & bowl, yellow & white Melmac type, EX $100.00
Wonder Woman, doll, inflatable vinyl, ca 1979, 24", MIP...$30.00
Wonder Woman, pencil, #2 lead, 1978, M $5.00
Wonder Woman, rub-on transfer, MIP.......................$30.00
Wonder Woman, scissors, child size, 1978, EX...........$10.00
Wonder Woman, sunglasses, 1976, MOC....................$15.00
Woody Woodpecker, cap, cloth baseball style featuring Woody's beak as hat bill, eyes & plastic crest feathers, 1950s, NM..$60.00
Woody Woodpecker, door knocker, Kellogg's premium, 1964, complete, MIB...............................$65.00
Woody Woodpecker, harmonica, plastic figure, early, 6", EX..$30.00
Woody Woodpecker, purse, vinyl w/image of Woody as Uncle Sam, 1970s, NM+..............................$20.00
Woody Woodpecker, ring, cloisonne, 1970s, M $12.00
X-Men, postcards, set of 10 different, EX $10.00

Yogi Bear, camera, 1960s, MIB, $65.00. (Photo courtesy June Moon)

Yogi Bear, decanter set, ceramic figural bottle w/cork neck & 4 cups hanging from back, Japan, 10", NM..........$60.00
Yogi Bear, figure, glazed china, Yogi standing on base lettered 'Don't Feed the Bears,' Ideas Inc, 1960s, 5½", EX+..$60.00
Yogi Bear, figure, sitting on log, vinyl, Dell, 1960, 6", EX..$30.00
Yogi Bear, pillow doll, w/bells inside, 1977, 15", EX .$20.00
Yogi Bear & Boo Boo, handkerchief, 1960s, 8" sq, EX..$10.00

Yogi Bear & Boo Boo, lamp, figural, NM...................$50.00
Ziggy, mirror, 1970s, MIP (sealed)............................$10.00

Cherished Teddies

First appearing on dealers' shelves in the spring of 1992, Cherished Teddies found instant collector appeal. They were designed by artist Priscilla Hillman and produced in the Orient for the Enesco company. Besides the figurines, the line includes waterballs, frames, plaques, and bells.

Abigail, in basket w/teddy bear, 1993, MIB $45.00
Abraham, Embrace the Earth, bear beside tree w/many animals around, MIB....................................$110.00
Alice, Cozy Warm Wishes Coming Your Way, 1993, MIB $110.00
Allison & Alexandria, both w/little teddy bears, #127981, 3", MIB $48.00
Bessie, dressed for Easter, #3H0/985, 1993, MIB $100.00
Beth, sits on reindeer rocking horse, #950807, 1992, MIB ..$50.00
Bucky & Brenda (w/papoose), Indian figures, 1993, 3", MIB $55.00
Charity, w/lamb, #3I0/477, MIB................................$80.00
Chelsea, holding a lamb, #E6/981, MIB.....................$135.00
Courtney, white floral dress & straw hat, #455/815, MIB..$80.00
Daisy, #E/706, Friendships Blossom With Love, MIB ..$375.00
Douglas, w/jack-in-the-box, #H2/136, 1992, MIB $50.00
Ernie, in Chicago Cubs uniform w/ball & bat, Limited Edition, MIB $195.00
Henrietta, wearing bonnet, holds basket, #3I2/537, MIB ..$70.00
Hilary Hugabear, holding pad of paper w/pencil in hand & 1 in her ear, #CT952, 1995, M..........................$60.00
Michelle & Michael, resting on pillow, #4H5/634, M..$45.00
Priscilla, There's No One Like Hue, #CRT-025, 1994, MIB...$160.00
Steven, hand in white jar w/red heart on front, #3E8/455, 1992, NRFB...$55.00
Sweetheart Ball, Jilly, Robin, Craig & Cheri, Darrel, Marian & Darla, complete set, 1995, M $70.00
Tammy, wearing poodle skirt, MIB...........................$60.00
Tasha, In Grandmother's Attic, #156353, MIB $75.00
Teddy & Roosevelt, big bear reading to sm bear, #3H1/614, MIB $90.00
Wedding Group, Bride, Groom, Groomsman, Bridesmaid, Flowergirl & Ring Bearer, M $70.00

Christmas Collectibles

Christmas is nearly everybody's favorite holiday, and it's a season when we all seem to want to get back to time-honored traditions. The stuffing and fruit cakes are made like Grandma always made them, we go caroling and sing the old songs that were written two hundred years ago, and the same Santa that brought gifts to the children in a time long forgotten still comes to our house and yours every Christmas Eve.

So for reasons of nostalgia, there are thousands of collectors interested in Christmas memorabilia. Some early Santa figures are rare and may be very expensive, especially when dressed in a color other than red. Blown glass ornaments and Christmas tree bulbs were made in shapes of fruits and vegetables, houses, Disney characters, animals, and birds. There are Dresden ornaments and candy containers from Germany, some of which were made prior to the 1870s, that have been lovingly preserved and handed down from generation to generation. They were made of cardboard that sparkled with gold and silver trim.

Artificial trees made of feathers were produced as early as 1850 and as late as 1950. Some were white, others blue, though most were green, and some had red berries or clips to hold candles. There were little bottle-brush trees, trees with cellophane needles, and trees from the '60s made of aluminum.

Collectible Christmas items are not necessarily old, expensive, or hard to find. Things produced in your lifetime have value as well. To learn more about this field, we recommend *Christmas Ornaments, Lights, and Decorations, Vols I, II, and III,* by George Johnson (Collector Books).

Candy container, Snowman, mica-covered cardboard, Made in Germany, 9", $47.00. (Photo courtesy George Johnson)

Artificial tree, crepe paper, ca 1940, from $30 to........**$40.00**
Artificial tree, green & white visca (like shredded rayon), ca 1950, 3½' to 5', from $30 to...................................**$45.00**
Artificial tree, green cellophane, ca 1935, from $20 to..**$35.00**
Candy container, cardboard w/scrap decoration, US, 1950s, 5½" wide, from $25 to **$35.00**
Candy container, cornucopia, printed cardboard, 3½", from $15 to...**$25.00**
Candy container, Santa, Bakelite head, molded glass body, 1940s, 6½", EX **$55.00**
Candy container, Santa, molded cardboard, potbelly, spring neck, West Germany, 9"..**$85.00**
Candy container, Santa, molded glass w/molded plastic head that screws off, 5¾", from $35 to **$45.00**
Candy container, Santa, papier-mache, red coat, blue pants, EX details, 4"..**$130.00**
Candy container, Santa, papier-mache, simple styling, USA, 7"...**$75.00**

Candy container, Santa in sleigh w/4 reindeer, red & white plastic, 15" L, Irwin Toys, 1950s, EX (EX window box) **$60.00**
Candy container, Santa w/sack on back, papier-mache, painted details, 8"...**$80.00**
Candy container, snowball, celluloid, 2"......................**$65.00**
Candy container, tambourine, printed paper, 3 sm brass bells, lid lifts, 2½"..**$125.00**
Decoration, reindeer, painted plaster w/lead antlers, Germany, from 2½" to 5", ea from $25 to...........**$60.00**
Display, Santa head, papier-mache w/paper eye inserts, relief image w/glitter on hat, 1940s, 17", EX+ **$110.00**
Display, Santa in sleigh w/whip & 2 reindeer (celluloid/glitter), 2 snowy trees (wire/wood), Japan, 1950s, 16", NM+..**$150.00**
Doll, Santa, plaster w/felt coat & hood, holds artificial tree, West Germany, 9", from $150 to **$175.00**
Lantern, Santa head, milk glass, double-faced, battery, Amico, Japan, 6", from $30 to..............................**$40.00**
Light bulb, Austrian man w/pipe, painted milk glass, screw-in base at top, Japan, ca 1925-50, 2¾", from $10 to ..**$15.00**
Light bulb, building on a rock, painted milk glass, Japan, ca 1950, 1½", from $50 to...**$60.00**
Light bulb, cross on a disk, milk glass, screw-in base at top, Japan, 1¾", from $25 to **$35.00**
Light bulb, dog in clown outfit, painted milk glass, screw-in base at top, Japan, ca 1950, 2¼", from $20 to **$50.00**
Light bulb, Donald Duck, Diamond Bright, Disney, Japan, head turned right, ca 1970, from $14 to **$18.00**
Light bulb, dressed duck, painted milk glass, screw-in base at top, Japan, 1920-55, 2¼", from $20 to **$25.00**
Light bulb, drummer marching, painted milk glass, screw-in base in top, Japan, ca 1950, 2½", from $35 to **$45.00**
Light bulb, flapper girl, painted milk glass, screw-in base at top, Japan, ca 1950, 2¾", from $55 to **$65.00**
Light bulb, generic bubble light, base in bottom has plastic cover, 4½" to 5½", ea from $2 to **$8.00**
Light bulb, Joey clown head, painted milk glass, Japan, screw-in base at top, Japan, ca 1935-50, 2", from $25 to **$35.00**
Light bulb, lion w/tennis racket, painted milk glass, screw-in base at top, Japan, ca 1955, 2¾", from $20 to **$30.00**
Light bulb, man in the moon on a star, painted milk glass, screw-in base at top, Japan, ca 1950, 2", from $15 to...**$25.00**
Light bulb, rabbit playing banjo, painted milk glass & frosted glass, screw-in base at top, Japan, 2¾", from $15 to **$25.00**
Light bulb, rooster in a tub, painted milk glass, screw-in base at top, Japan, 2¼", from $40 to **$50.00**
Light bulb, Santa head in chimney, painted milk glass, screw-in base at top, Japan, 2¼", from $15 to................**$20.00**
Light bulb, snowman w/stick, painted milk glass, screw-in base in top, Japan, ca 1930-55, 2" to 2½", from $6 to......**$12.00**
Light bulb, teddy bear sitting, painted milk glass, screws in at top, Japan, 2¾", from $25 to **$35.00**
Ornament, alligator, embossed legs, mold-blown, Inge Glass reissue, ca 1991, from $10 to **$12.00**

Ornament, alligator (standing), free-blown, 1950s, scarce, from $70 to..**$80.00**

Ornament, anchor, pressed cotton-covered cardboard, 3" to 6", from $20 to **$35.00**

Ornament, angel girl w/star, mold-blown, bumpy pattern on bottom, Inge Glass, 1950s, from $20 to **$30.00**

Ornament, angel head embossed on disk, mold-blown, 8-petal flower on back, 1950s, 2" dia, from $20 to.**$25.00**

Ornament, apple, spun cotton, Blumchen, 1990s, 3½", from $10 to..**$12.00**

Ornament, baby in buggy, mold-blown, 4-wheeled buggy w/folded hood, Inge Glass, 1980s, from $5 to.......**$8.00**

Ornament, basket, beaded glass, filled w/angel hair, 3-D, 2", from $8 to..**$12.00**

Ornament, basket, metal, 6 molded parts w/openwork, Made in West Germany, 1940s-50s, 2¼", from $15 to....**$25.00**

Ornament, bear dancing, mold-blown, reissued by Lauscha Glass, ca 1994, 3⅛", from $10 to..........................**$15.00**

Ornament, bear in bunting, mold-blown, reissued by Inge Glass, 1990s, 3¾", from $8 to **$12.00**

Ornament, bear in leather shorts & suspenders, mold-blown, 1980s, 3½", from $10 to **$12.00**

Ornament, bell, spun cotton covered w/crushed glass, 1¾", from $10 to..**$15.00**

Ornament, bell w/embossed church, mold-blown, embossed stars on sides & back, 2½", from $20 to...............**$30.00**

Ornament, berries on a leaf, small beads on stem w/attached fabric leaf, 3", from $2 to **$3.00**

Ornament, bird & pine tree, mold-blown, bumpy pattern, ca 1950, 2¾", from $10 to..**$12.00**

Ornament, bird on house, mold-blown (made of 2 pcs attached by sm spring), Germany, 1950s, 2¾", from $40 to..**$50.00**

Ornament, boy (chubby) riding sled, mold-blown, 1950s, 3¼", from $70 to..**$80.00**

Ornament, boy in flower basket, mold-blown, embossed daisies around waist, 1990s, 2½", from $8 to.......**$12.00**

Ornament, cat in a bag, mold-blown, reissued by Inge Glass, ca 1985-91, 3½", from $10 to.................................**$12.00**

Ornament, cherries, spun cotton, Blumchen & Co, 1990, 1¾", from $7 to...**$8.00**

Ornament, clown in a boot, mold-blown, conical hat, 1980s, 3", from $12 to...**$15.00**

Ornament, deer & pine trees embossed on disk, mold-blown, reissued by Lauscha Collection, 1970s, 2¼", from $8 to **$12.00**

Ornament, dog w/basket begging, mold-blown, ca 1970s, 5", from $20 to..**$25.00**

Ornament, duck (embossed) on disk, mold-blown, flower embossed on reverse, 1950s, 2½" dia, from $25 to **$35.00**

Ornament, dwarf face in pine cone, mold-blown, hands join under beard, 1980s, 3½", from $10 to...............**$15.00**

Ornament, dwarf w/pick, mold-blown, conical hat & flowing beard, pick in left hand, 1980s, 2½", from $8 to .**$10.00**

Ornament, elephant sitting on a ball, front legs raised, mold-blown, West Germany, 1970s, 4¼", from $8 to....**$12.00**

Ornament, fish, metal w/3 faceted jewels & embossed scales, William J Rigby of NY recast, 1980s-90s, 2¾", $8 to..**$10.00**

Ornament, frog playing bass violin, mold-blown, 1940s-50s, 4½", from $40 to..**$50.00**

Ornament, girl w/or w/out skis, spun cotton w/composition-plaster face, Japan, 4½", from $40 to...................**$45.00**

Ornament, Goldilocks, mold-blown, right hand at collar, 1970s, 3", from $15 to...**$18.00**

Ornament, grapefruit half, mold-blown, dimpled rind, Germany, 1990s, 3¼", from $12 to.......................**$15.00**

Ornament, grapes, mold-blown, egg-shaped bunch w/stylized leaves, Corning, 1½", from $1 to....................**$3.00**

Ornament, guardian angel w/2 children, mold-blown, 1970s, 3½", from $15 to...**$20.00**

Ornament, heart w/embossed church, comet & Merry Christmas, mold-blown, ca 1995, 2½", from $15 to.**$18.00**

Ornament, hummingbird, mold-blown w/spun glass wings, 1980s, from $10 to..**$12.00**

Ornament, lady bug beetle, mold-blown, 1970s, 2½", from $8 to..**$10.00**

Ornament, lemon, spun cotton, Blumchen, 1990s, 3½", from $8 to...**$9.00**

Ornament, lighthouse, mold-blown, 6-sided, 1950s-60s, 3", from $15 to..**$20.00**

Ornament, monkey w/fur ruffle, mold-blown, 1980s, from $10 to..**$15.00**

Ornament, owl on ball, mold-blown, Radco, 1995, 4", from $20 to..**$30.00**

Ornament, penguin, mold-blown, Japan, 1¾", from $15 to **$20.00**

Ornament, pickle, mold-blown, resembles Heinz Co trademark, 1985 reissue, 3½", from $10 to.............**$15.00**

Ornament, pig, mold-blown, basic oval shape w/little detail, Germany, 1980s, from $8 to **$10.00**

Ornament, pine cones (3) on branch, mold-blown, 2½", from $15 to..**$20.00**

Ornament, Punch clown, mold-blown, hunch back, waist-up version, 1970s, 3½", from $20 to.........................**$25.00**

Ornament, rooster, fabric, realistic paint, Russia, 1950s, 4", from $40 to..**$50.00**

Ornament, rooster on chicken coop, mold-blown, crude, Japan, 2¾", from $20 to **$30.00**

Ornament, sailor w/pilot's wheel, mold-blown, 1980s, 4", from $8 to..**$10.00**

Ornament, Santa, chenille w/paper face, Japan, 1950s, 5", from $5 to..**$10.00**

Ornament, Santa, composition face w/cloth or flannel clothes, Japan, ca 1925-50, 4", from $50 to **$70.00**

Ornament, Santa, mold-blown, heavy w/no delicate details, attributed to Corning Glass, ca 1939-40, 3", from $35 to..**$45.00**

Ornament, Santa head (double-faced), mold-blown, 1970s, 2¾", from $10 to...**$15.00**

Ornament, Santa on an icicle, mold- & free-blown, Radco, ca 1991, 9½", from $25 to....................................**$35.00**

Ornament, shell w/indented and ribbed front, mold-blown, 1950s-60s, 1¼", from $25 to..............................**$30.00**

Ornament, shell w/pearl, mold-blown, Italy, 1950s, from $75 to **$90.00**

Ornament, snowman clown, mold-blown, sm ruffle at neck, 3 buttons, 1950s, 4¼", from $15 to **$25.00**

Ornament, snowman w/walking stick, mold-blown, reissued by Inge Glass, 1991, 3", from $8 to.....................**$10.00**

Ornament, songbird, mold-blown w/spun glass wings, ca 1980s, 3½", from $10 to **$12.00**

Ornament, spider w/annealed legs, free-blown, clips on, 1950s, 2¾", from $35 to **$45.00**

Ornament, stork w/baby embossed onto egg shape, mold-blown, reissued by Inge Glass, ca 1993, from $8 to ..**$10.00**

Ornament, sun face & sun in the clouds (double-sided), mold-blown, Inge Glass, ca 1992, 2¼", from $10 to **$12.00**

Ornament, swan on pond embossed onto egg shape, 1980s reissue, 3", from $8 to **$12.00**

Ornament, watermelon slice, mold-blown, wedge shape, embossed seeds, Inge Glass, 1990, 4", from $8 to ..**$12.00**

Ornament, windmill w/embossed arms, mold-blown, 1950s, 2¼", from $15 to..**$20.00**

Ornament, woodpecker embossed on trunk, mold-blown, 1980s reissue, 4½", from $10 to...........................**$12.00**

Ornaments, fancy American shapes, mold made, ca 1935 – 40, from $2.00 to $5.00 each. (Photo courtesy George Johnson)

Sleigh, glitter-covered cardboard w/2 celluloid reindeer & celluloid Santa, Japan, 12", from $65 to **$75.00**

Squeak toy Santas, left: Rempel Mfg., 11½", from $5.00 to $10.00; right: Sanitoy, 8½", from $5.00 to $8.00. (Photo courtesy George Johnson)

Tree with bubble lights, ca 1950s, 20", from $100.00 to $125.00. (Photo courtesy George Johnson)

Trumpet, free-flown, foil noisemaker glued to end, 1950s-90s, 3½" to 5½", from $5 to................................**$10.00**

Village house, cardboard w/cellophane windows, Japan, lg, from $20 to..**$25.00**

Christmas Tree Pins

Once thought of as mere holiday novelties, Christms tree pins are now considered tiny prizes among costume jewelry and Christmas collectors. Hollycraft, Weiss, Lisner, and other famous costume jewelry designers created beautiful trees. Rhinestones, colored 'jewels', and lovely enameling make Christmas tree pins tiny works of art, and what used to be purchased for a few dollars now may command as much as one hundred, especially if signed. Pins are plentiful and prices vary. Buyers should be aware that many fakes and repros are out there. Many 'vintage looking' pins are actually brand new and retail for less than $10.00. Know your dealer, and if you are unsure, let it pass.

ART, traditional-style gold tree w/red, white & green stones, lg, from $65 to **$75.00**

Assesocraft, enameled partridge in pear tree design, 1970s, from $35 to..**$50.00**

Eisenburg, green & white stones w/red stones forming trunk, issued in 1950s, 1970s & 1980s, last issue price...**$47.50**

Hollycraft, lg multicolor rhinestones, ea set in a gold flower petal, from $125 to **$165.00**

Hollycraft, molded balls interspersed w/multicolor rhinestones, from $85 to..**$115.00**

Hollycraft, pastel rhinestones, various sizes & shapes, dated 1950, from $150 to................................**$200.00**

JJ (Jonette), multicolored stones in various gold or green enameled designs, 1950s-60s, ea from $35 to **$65.00**

Kenneth J Lane, hand-set rhinestones in pastels w/rows of clear rhinestones (his only design), 1960s, from $100 to..**$125.00**

Lisner, lg red, green & white stones, from $50 to.......**$65.00**

Trifari, unique jelly-like Swarovski crystals in blue & green, 1961, from $85 to **$110.00**

Unsigned, Austrian crystal sequins & colorful beads, med size, from $25 to $35.00

Unsigned, hand-set white rhinestones overall on triangular tree, 1950s, from $55 to...$75.00

Unsigned, Christmas tree set with rows of pavé rhinestones highlighted with colored stone 'ornaments,' ca 1950s – early 1960s, from $95.00 to $115.00. (Photo courtesy Jill Gallina)

Unsigned, white prong-set rhinestones w/dangling red beads, from $55 to...$75.00

Weiss, angular garland, aurora borealis stones (prong set), 1950s, from $85 to...$115.00

Weiss, geometric shape, multicolor rhinestones, 1950s, sm, from $45 to...$65.00

Cigarette Lighters

Collectors of tobacciana tell us that cigarette lighters are definitely hot! Look for novel designs (figurals, Deco styling, and so forth), unusual mechanisms (flint and fuel, flint and gas, battery, etc.), those made by companies now defunct, advertising lighters, and quality lighters made by Ronson, Dunhill, Evans, Colibri, Zippo, and Ronson. For more information we recommend *Collector's Guide to Cigarette Lighters, Vols. I* and *II,* by James Flanagan (Collector Books).

Newsletter: *On the Lighter Side*
Judith Sanders
Route 3, 136 Circle Dr.
Quitman, TX 75783; 903-763-2795; SASE for information

Advertising, Camel decals (front & back) on chromium, Japan, early 1960s, 2½x1½", from $20 to $30.00

Advertising, decals on front & back, chromium, Japan, late 1960s, 2¼x1½", from $5 to $10.00

Advertising, Frisco, chromium w/red & gold enamel, Vulcan, ca mid-1960s, 1¾x2", from $20 to........................$30.00

Advertising, General Electric, chromium, Zippo, ca 1963, 2¼x1¼", from $15 to..$25.00

Advertising, Hudson's Credit Jewelers, chromium & enamel tube style, Redlight, late 1940s, 3x⅜" dia, from $20 to $30.00

Advertising, Knott's Berry Farm, chromium & enamel, Japan, ca 1965, 1¾x2", from $10 to $20.00

Advertising, Playboy Bunny, black & white enameling on brass, Korea, mid-1960s, 2½x¾", from $10 to......$20.00

Art Deco, Spartan, chromium & enamel, Ronson, ca 1950, 2⅜x3", from $10 to..$20.00

Case/lighter combination, chromium, US Army Air Corp's emblem in blue w/gold trim, Evans, 1940s, 4¼x2½", from $75 to..$100.00

Case/lighter combination, chromium & enamel, lights cigarette as it slides from case, Magic Case, 1930s, 4¼", from $75 to..$100.00

Case/lighter combination, gold-plate w/embossed rays, Evans, 1930s, 4½x2½", from $80 to $100.00

Case/lighter combination, Pal, chromium & burgundy enamel, Ronson, ca 1941, 4⅛x2", from $50 to..............$80.00

Case/lighter combination, Sportcase, chromium & tortoise enamel w/gold fleur-de-lis, Ronson, ca 1936, 4⅛x2", from $50 to..$70.00

Case/lighter combination, Tuxedo, chromium & 2 shades of enamel, Ronson, 1930s, 4⅛x2⅝", from $75 to...$100.00

Decorative, chromium jockey figural, back of cap operates lighter, 1950s, 8½x2⅞" at base, from $150 to $200.00

Decorative, Decor, fabric under plastic cover can be changed to match decor, Ronson, ca 1954, 2¾x4¼" dia, from $30 to..$45.00

Decorative, Juno, silver plated, slim w/ornate decor, Ronson, ca 1952, 6¼x2" dia at base, from $30 to $50.00

Decorative, Minerva, floral on ivory porcelain, silver-plated top & base, Ronson, ca 1952, 3x2¾", from $30 to.........$50.00

Figural, camel (recumbent, w/howdah), metal, Japan, late 1940s, 2x3", from $25 to......................................$40.00

Figural, donkey w/lighter on back, brass, Japan, mid-1950s, 2x2½", from $15 to...$20.00

Figural, elephant, painted metal, Strikalite, late 1940s, 3x3½", from $25 to...$35.00

Figural, jockey, back of cap hinged to operate lighter, chromium, 8½", from $150.00 to $200.00. (Photo courtesy James Flanagan)

Figural, Scottie dog, painted metal, Strikalite, late 1930s, 2½x3", from $25 to......................................**$40.00**

Novelty, canteen, plastic, butane, cap removes to reveal lighter, Germany, late 1980s, 2¼x1⅜", from $15 to...............**$25.00**

Novelty, ceramic (pink) electric table type, MacDonald Specialties, late 1930s, 2½x3¼" dia, from $50 to .**$70.00**

Novelty, chromium & enamel table type, uses fluid & batteries, Silent Flame, 1940s, 3¾x2⅝" dia, from $25 to.........**$40.00**

Novelty, machine gun on tripod, chromium & metal, butane, mid-1980s, 5½x11⅞", from $50 to.........................**$70.00**

Novelty, mechanical pencil, gold-tone, lighter under cap, Albright in NY, mid-1950s, 5x½" dia, from $25 to ...**$40.00**

Novelty, rechargeable electric pocket type, Gulton, late 1950s, 2¾x1½", from $50 to **$75.00**

Occupied Japan, chromium & ceramic elephant, table type, ca 1948, 3½x4", from $75 to.............................**$100.00**

Occupied Japan, chromium & mother-of-pearl lift-arm pocket type, ca 1948, 1⅞x1⅝", from $100 to.............**$125.00**

Occupied Japan, chromium typewriter, lights by pressing space bar, ca 1948, 1¾x3½", from $150 to........**$175.00**

Occupied Japan, silver-plated cowboy, head is hinged, ca 1948, 4x1¾", from $90 to.....................................**$115.00**

Pocket, Banjo reproduction, gold plated, Ronson, 1960s, 2⅜x1⅞", from $60 to..**$80.00**

Pocket, brass w/leather cover, ladies', Germany, mid-1950s, 1⅜x1½", from $25 to...**$40.00**

Pocket, chromium, butane, Bentley, mid-1950s, 1½x2⅛", from $10 to...**$20.00**

Pocket, chromium, butane, Bentley in Austria, late 1950s, 2¼x1½", from $20 to...**$40.00**

Pocket, chromium, butane, Citation, late 1950s, 1¼x2¼", from $20 to...**$30.00**

Pocket, chromium, butane, Colibri in Ireland, early 1960s, 3x⅞", from $50 to...**$75.00**

Pocket, chromium, butane pipe lighter, Savinelli, mid-1970s, 2¾x1⅛", from $25 to...**$40.00**

Pocket, chromium, lift-arm type, Colibri, ca 1928, 2x1⅝", from $175 to..**$225.00**

Pocket, chromium w/black enamel silhouette of pinup girl, Zippo, ca 1994, 2¼x1½", from $10 to **$20.00**

Pocket, Comet, chromium & plastic, butane, Ronson, late 1950s, 2¼x1½", from $10 to **$15.00**

Pocket, Director, chromium, Berkley, late 1940s, 1¾x2⅛", from $25 to...**$40.00**

Pocket, gold plated, butane, lift arm, Dunhill in Switzerland, mid-1950s, 2½x⅞", from $250 to **$325.00**

Pocket, gold plated w/watch, Swiss made, 1960s, 2⅜x1⅛", from $70 to...**$90.00**

Pocket, Happy Days, brass finish, butane, lift arm, Yoshinaga Prince Co Ltd, ca 1988, 3¼x1", from $5 to...........**$10.00**

Pocket, Mini Cadet, chromium w/embossed leaves, Ronson in England, ca 1959, 1⅜x1¾", from $20 to **$40.00**

Pocket, painted chromium, Operation Desert Storm commemorative, Korea, early 1990s, 2¼x1½", from $10 to..**$15.00**

Pocket, platinum plate, Lektrolite, ca late 1930s, 1¾x1⅝", from $30 to..**$40.00**

Pocket, Princess, chromium w/leather band, Ronson, ca 1950s, 1⅞x1½", from $35 to **$50.00**

Pocket, Trickette, brass & rhinestones, Wisner, early 1950s, 1½x1¾", from $25 to..**$40.00**

Pocket, Win Sensor, chromium, butane, IC, late 1970s, 3¼x1", from $15 to..**$25.00**

Table, brass & blue & white ceramic, Penguin, ca late 1960s, 3¼x1⅞" dia, from $10 to **$20.00**

Table, brass & embossed leather, butane, Italy, mid-1970s, 4⅝x2½", from $20 to...**$30.00**

Table, brass w/leather band, Evans, late 1920s, 3¾x1⅞" dia, from $50 to..**$70.00**

Table, chromium, embossed tavern scene, lights by pushing button on top, Myflam, late 1940s, 2⅜x3", from $40 to...**$50.00**

Table, chromium, simple design, Evans, 1934, 2x1⅞", from $25 to...**$35.00**

Table, chromium & leather, DRP in Germany, late 1950s, 3¼x4", from $45 to...**$60.00**

Table, chromium w/leather cover, butane, Querria in France, late 1960s, 3¼x2⅛", from $40 to.........................**$50.00**

Table, Decor, made by Ronson, plastic cover may be removed to change fabric, ca 1954, 2¾" x 4¼", from $30.00 to $45.00.
(Photo courtesy James Flanagan)

Table, Mustang airplane, chromium, Negbaur in Germany, ca 1948, 3x6⅜x6¼" wingspan, from $75 to **$100.00**

Table, silver plate & glass, Hy Glo, late 1930s, 2½x2¼" dia, from $35 to...**$50.00**

Cleminson Pottery

One of the several small potteries that operated in California during the middle of the century, Cleminson was a family-operated enterprise that made kitchenware, decorative items, and novelties that are beginning to attract a considerable amount of interest. At the height of their productivity, they employed 150 workers, so as you make your rounds, you'll be very likely to see a piece or two offered for sale just about anywhere you go. Prices are not high; this may be a 'sleeper.'

They marked their ware fairly consistently with a circular ink stamp that contains the name 'Cleminson.' But even if you find an unmarked piece, with just a little experience you'll easily be able to recognize their very distinctive glaze colors. They're all strong, yet grayed-down, dusty tones. They made a line of bird-shaped tableware items that they marketed as 'Distlefink' and several plaques and wall pockets that are decorated with mottoes and Pennsylvania Dutch-type hearts and flowers.

In Jack Chipman's *The Collector's Encyclopedia of California Pottery, Second Edition,* you'll find a chapter devoted to Cleminson Pottery. Roerig's *The Collector's Encyclopedia of Cookie Jars* books have additional information. (All of these books are published by Collector Books.)

See also Clothes Sprinkler Bottles; Cookie Jars.

Advisor: Robin Stine (See Directory, California Pottery)

Bank, hope chest shape, Here's Hoping on white w/floral decoration, 3x4" **$25.00**
Bowl, Love Me on blue flowers & pink polka-dots, heart shape, 2¾" **$15.00**

Butter dish, lady lid, from $45.00 to $50.00.

Button holder, lady figural, 6¾" **$45.00**
Cigarette dispenser, wall hanging, 9x4" **$25.00**
Cleanser shaker, Cleanser Kate, 6½" **$40.00**
Creamer, rooster, 5½" **$35.00**
Cup, clown face w/hat lid, from $60 to......................**$80.00**
Cup & saucer, jumbo; Mom..**$16.00**
Darning egg, Darn It, girl form, original ribbon, 5"....**$60.00**
Dish, clown w/balloons holding hoop for poodle, 7¾" dia **$45.00**
Dish, red, 3-part, free-form, Galagray, 15x8"..............**$22.50**
Marmalade, flowerpot w/strawberry finial, 4", from $25 to..**$30.00**
Mug, Morning After, Never Again inside, 2¾"............**$15.00**
Napkin holder, pr of hands, white w/floral band at bottom, 2¼x5"..**$42.00**
Razor blade bank, man's face, 4" **$40.00**

Shakers, Deco lady, marked Cleminson Galagray Ware, 6½", pr..**$52.50**
Soap dish, girl in tub, scarce, 4x5", EX......................**$65.00**
String holder, heart shape, w/verse, 4½x5"................**$45.00**
Sugar shaker, represents girl, 3⅛x6" **$30.00**
Wall plaque, apple decoration, 8¼" dia....................**$22.00**
Wall plaque, God Bless Our Mobile Home, white w/blue mobile home, 6¾" **$32.00**
Wall plaque, mixed flowers, scalloped rim, 7" dia......**$12.50**
Wall pocket, coffee grinder, w/verse, 5½x7"..............**$30.00**
Wall pocket, coffeepot, Let's Have Another Cup of Coffee..**$35.00**
Wall pocket, Dumbo the Elephant, 5x3½x2½", EX **$45.00**
Wall pocket, kettle form, w/verse, 7¼"......................**$30.00**
Wall pocket, salt crock, 5¾x6½" **$65.00**
Wall pocket, Take Time for Tea, 7¾x6⅝" **$50.00**

Clothes Sprinkler Bottles

With the invention of the iron, clothes were sprinkled with water, rolled up to distribute the dampness, and pressed. This created steam when ironing, which helped to remove wrinkles. The earliest bottles were made of hand-blown clear glass. Ceramic figurals were introduced in the 1920s; these had a metal sprinkler cap with a rubber cork. Later versions had a true cork with an aluminum cap. More recent examples contain a plastic cap. A 'wetter-downer' bottle had no cap but contained a hole in the top to distribute water to larger items such as sheets and tablecloths. These were filled through a large opening in the bottom and plugged with a cork. Some 'wetter-downers' are mistaken for shakers and vice versa. In the end, with the invention of more sophisticated irons that produced their own steam (and later had their own sprayers), the sprinkler bottle was relegated to the attic or, worse yet, the trash can.

The variety of subjects depicted by figural sprinkler bottles runs from cute animals to laundry helpers and people who did the ironing. Because of their whimsical nature, their scarcity, and desirability as collectibles, we have seen a rapid rise in the cost of these bottles over the last couple of years.

See also Kitchen Prayer Ladies.

Advisor: Ellen Bercovici (See Directory, Clothes Sprinkler Bottles)

Cat, marble eyes, ceramic, American Bisque, from $300 to **$400.00**
Cat, variety of designs & colors, homemade ceramic, from $75 to..**$150.00**
Chinese man, Sprinkle Plenty, white, green & brown, holding iron, ceramic, from $95 to............................**$150.00**
Chinese man, Sprinkle Plenty, yellow & green, ceramic, Cardinal China Co, from $25 to............................**$50.00**
Chinese man, towel over arm, from $300 to............**$400.00**
Chinese man, variety of designs & color, handmade ceramic, from $50 to..**$150.00**

Chinese man, white & aqua, ceramic, Cleminson, from $40 to **$50.00**

Chinese man, white & aqua w/paper shirt tag, ceramic, Cleminson, from $75 to **$100.00**

Clothespin, face w/stenciled eyes & airbrushed cheeks, marked Cardinal.................................**$400.00**

Clothespin, face w/stenciled eyes & airbrushed cheeks & lips, from $200 to **$250.00**

Clothespin, hand decorated, ceramic, from $150 to **$200.00**

Clothespin, red, yellow & green plastic, from $20 to **$40.00**

Dearie Is Weary, ceramic, Enesco, from $350 to **$500.00**

Dutch boy, green & white ceramic, from $175 to **$250.00**

Dutch girl, white w/green & pink trim, wetter-downer, ceramic, from $175 to **$250.00**

Elephant, pink & gray, ceramic, from $60 to **$85.00**

Elephant, trunk forms handle, ceramic, American Bisque, from $400 to..**$600.00**

Elephant, white & pink w/shamrock on tummy, ceramic, from $100 to..**$150.00**

Emperor, variety of designs & colors, handmade ceramic, from $150 to...**$200.00**

Fireman, minimum value **$1,000.00**

Iron, blue flowers, ceramic, from $100 to **$150.00**

Iron, green ivy, ceramic, from $50 to **$75.00**

Iron, green plastic, from $35 to....................................**$55.00**

Iron, lady ironing, ceramic, from $45 to.....................**$75.00**

Iron, man & woman farmer, ceramic, from $200 to .**$275.00**

Iron, souvenir of Aquarena Springs, San Marcos TX, ceramic, from $200 to...**$300.00**

Iron, souvenir of Florida, pink flamingo, ceramic, from $250 to..**$325.00**

Iron, souvenir of Wonder Cave, ceramic, from $250 to ..**$300.00**

Mammy, ceramic, possibly Pfaltzgraff, from $250 to ..**$350.00**

Mary Maid, all colors, plastic, Reliance, from $15 to ..**$35.00**

Mary Poppins, Cleminson, from $250.00 to $350.00. (Photo courtesy Ellen Bercovici)

Myrtle, ceramic, Pfaltzgraff, from $250 to **$350.00**

Peasant woman, w/laundry poem on label, from $200 to **$300.00**

Poodle, gray and pink or white, ceramic, from $200.00 to $300.00.

Rooster, green, tan, and red detailing over white, ceramic, from $85.00 to $125.00.
(Photo courtesy Ellen Bercovici)

Clothing and Accessories

Watch a 'golden oldie' movie, and you can't help admiring the clothes — what style, what glamour, what fun! Due in part to the popularity of old movie classics and great new movies with retro themes, there's a growing fascination with the fabulous styes of the past — and there's no better way to step into the romance and glamour of those eras than with an exciting piece of vintage clothing!

'OOOhhh, it don't mean a thing, if it ain't got that S-W-I-N-G!' In 1935, Benny Goodman, 'King of Swing,' ushered in the swing era from Los Angeles' Polmar Ballroom. After playing two standard sets, he switched to swing, and the crowd went crazy! Swing's the 'in' thing in vintage clothing this year, and swing dance devotees are looking for the sassy styles of the late '30s through the mid-'40s to wear clubbing. Swing era gals' clothing featured short full or pleated skirts, wide padded shoulders, and natural waistlines. Guys, check out those wild, wide ties that were worn with 'gangster-look' zoot suits!

Clothes of the 1940s though the 1970s are not as delicate as their Victorian and Edwardian counterparts; they're easier to find and much more affordable! Remember, the more indicative of its period, the more desirable the item. Look for pieces with glitz and glamour — also young, trendy pieces that were expensive to begin with. Look for designer pieces and designer look-alikes. Although famous designer labels are hard to find, you may be lucky enough to run across one! American designers like Adrian, Claire McMardell, Charles James, Mainboucher, Hattie Carnegie, Norell, Pauline Trigere, and Mollie Parnis came to the fore during World War II. The '50s were the decade of Christian Dior; others included Balenciaga, Balmain, Chanel, Jacques Heim, Nona Ricci, Ann Fogarty, Oleg Cassini, and Adele Simpson. In the '60s and '70s, Mary Quant, Betsey Johnson, Givenchy, Yves St. Laurent, Oscar de la Renta, Galanos, Pierre Cardin, Rudi Gernreich, Paco Rabanne, Courreges, Arnold Scassi, Geoffrey Beene, Emilio Pucci, Zandra Rhodes, and Jessica McClintock (Gunne Sax) were some of the names that made fasion headlines.

Pucci, Lilli Ann of Calfornia, Eisenberg, and Adele Simpson designs contine to be especially sought after. Enid Colins imaginative bags are popular, but prices are lower than last year's. (See Purses.) Look for lingerie — '30s and '40s lace/hook corsets, and '50s pointy 'bullet' bras (like the ones in the old Maidenform Dream ads). For both men and women, look for '70s disco platform shoes (the wilder, the better), cowboy shirts and jackets, and fringed 'hippie' items. For men, look for bowling shirts, '50s 'Kramer' shirts, and '40s and '50s wild ties, especially those by Salvadore Dali.

Levi jeans and jackets made circa 1971 and before have a cult following, especially in Japan. Among the most sought-after denim Levi items are jeans with a capitol 'E' on a *red* tab or back pocket. The small 'e' jeans are also collectible; these were made during the late 1960s and until 1970 (with two rows of single stitching inside the back pocket). Worth watching for as well are the 'red line' styles of the '80s (these have double-stitched back pockets). Other characteristics to look for in vintage Levis are visible rivets inside the jeans and single pockets and silver-colored buttons on jackets with vertical pleats. From the same era, Lee, Wrangler, Bluebell, J.C. Penney, Oxhide, Big Yanks, James Dean, Doublewear, and Big Smith denims are collectible as well.

As with any collectible, condition is of the utmost importance. 'Deadstock' is a term that refers to a top-grade item that has never been worn or washed and still has its original tags. Number 1 grade must have no holes larger than a pinhole. A torn belt loop is permissible if no hole is created. There may be a few light stains and light fading. The crotch area must have no visible wear and the crotch seam must have no holes. And lastly, the item must not have been altered. Unless another condition is noted within the lines, values in the listing here are for items in number 1 grade. There are also other grades for items that have more defects.

While some collectors buy with the intent of preserving their clothing and simply enjoy having it, many buy it to wear. If you do wear it, be very careful how you clean it. Fabrics may become fragile with age.

For more information, refer to *Vintage Hats and Bonnets, 1770 – 1970, Identifications and Values,* by Sue Langley; *Antique and Vintage Clothing, 1850 – 1940* by Diane Snyder-Haug; *Collector's Guide to Vintage Fashions* (Collector Books) and *Vintage Fashions for Women, the 1950s & '60s,* by Kristina Harris (Shiffer); *Clothing and Accessories From the '40s, '50s, and '60s,* by Jan Lindenberger (Schiffer); *Vintage Denim* by David Little; *Shoes* by Linda O'Keefe; *Plastic Handbags* by Kate E. Dooner; *Fit To Be Tied, Vintage Ties of the '40s and Early '50s,* by Rod Dyer and Ron Spark; and *The Hawaiian Shirt* by H. Thomas Steele. For more information about denim clothing and vintage footwear see *How to Identify Vintage Apparel for Fun and Profit,* which is available from Flying Deuce Auction & Antiques (see Auction Houses).

Prices are a compilation of shows, shops, and Internet auctions. They are retail values and apply to items in excellent condition. Note: Extraordinary items bring extraordinary prices!

Advisors: Ken Weber, Clothing; Flying Deuce Auctions, Vintage Denim (See Directory, Clothing and Accessories)

Newsletter: *Costume Society of America*
55 Edgewater Dr., P.O. Box 73
Earleville, MD 21919
Phone: 410-275-1691 or Fax: 410-275-8936
www.costumesocietyamerica.com

Newsletter: *The Vintage Connection*
904 North 65 Street
Springfield, OR 97478-7021

Bomber jacket, leather, souvenir, reversible, 1940s-70s, men's...**$500.00**
Bowling shirt, 1950s, men's, (depends on embroidery) from $25 to..**$75.00**
Bra, peach rayon satin, marked Miss America on label, 1940s...**$6.00**
Circle skirt, flocked floral trim & sequins, 1950s.........**$45.00**
Collar, detachable, white cotton pique, 1950s..............**$6.00**
Cowboy shirt, cowboy on bucking bronco on back, 1950s.**$145.00**
Dress, black & white striped halter top w/black slightly full skirt, side zipper, 1950s...**$58.00**
Dress, black rose-print seersucker, V-neck, front zipper, Empire waistline, short sleeves, handmade, 1940s..............**$38.00**
Dress, black wool, very low neck w/4 sewn-in stripes, stand-up collar w/ties, ¾-sleeves, S Eisenberg, 1950s.**$155.00**
Dress, black/olive/gold herringbone striped knit, wide lapel w/notched collar, A-line skirt, Jeanne Durell, 2-pc, 1960s...**$28.00**
Dress, cocktail; black crepe w/gold sequins around V-neck, short sleeves, slightly full skirt, 1940s...................**$38.00**
Dress, cocktail; black crepe w/red velveteen yoke & gold soutache w/embroidery, red velveteen bolero, Paul Sachs, 1950s...**$210.00**

Dress, cocktail; black print, spaghetti straps, Princess style, w/bolero jacket, Helen of California, 1950s **$58.00**

Dress, cocktail; black rayon crepe w/chiffon bodice yoke, straight neck w/plunging back, back zipper, 1950s ..**$54.00**

Dress, cocktail; color-blocked crepe, V-neck, gathers along shoulders, short sleeves, unique orange belt, 1940s, EX...**$75.00**

Dress, cocktail; fuchsia floral jacquard, Princess style, dropped V-waistline w/gathers, Adele Simpson, 1950s **$85.00**

Dress, cocktail; green & black brocade, V-neck w/narrow skirt, ¾-sleeves, +coat w/shawl collar, Molly Modes NY, 1950s **$60.00**

Dress, cocktail; navy crepe w/chiffon drape, shawl collar, slim skirt w/inset pockets, Marcia Frocks NY, 1960s **$46.00**

Dress, cocktail; purple wool, scooped neck w/soutache trim & beadwork w/dangles, slim skirt, bolero jacket, 1960s **$65.00**

Dress, cocktail; screen-printed cotton, scoop neckline w/sequin pearls, short raglan sleeves, circle skirt, 1950s **$52.00**

Dress, cocktail; shiny floral print, spaghetti straps, reverse bolero jacket w/short sleeves, late 1950s...............**$76.00**

Dress, cocktail; silvery/aqua/black print, bustier style, spaghetti straps, sarong skirt, fully lined, 1950s ...**$58.00**

Dress, cocktail; washed silk, overlapped bodice, spread collar, elbow-length sleeves, Empire waist w/center panel, 1960s **$55.00**

Dress, cocktail; yellow & black crepe, keyhole-cut neck w/string tie, brass leaf studs, 3-pleat skirt, 1940s.**$85.00**

Dress, evening; black crepe w/rows of black fringe, short sleeves, full length (w/slight train), 1940s, EX ...**$185.00**

Dress, evening; pink crepe w/purple taffeta inset at chest, plunging V-neck w/sequins, short sleeves, slit skirt, 1940s..**$148.00**

Dress, evening; rayon chiffon bodice w/nude lining, long sleeves, bugle beads/sequins/rhinestones, satin skirt, 1960s...**$125.00**

Dress, formal; purple tulle, sequined top, strapless, pleated cummerbund, full skirt, Donald Original, 1960s ..**$35.00**

Dress, geometric cotton print, scooped neck, split cap sleeves, full panel skirt, black patent belt, 1950s.**$52.00**

Dress, gray iridescent, round neck w/collar, steel buttons, ¾-sleeves, pleated A-line skirt, 2-pc, P Stevens, 1960s.**$35.00**

Dress, jersey knit print, inset yoke, collar, short sleeves w/cuff, stitched-down pleats on skirt, belt missing, 1940s **$35.00**

Dress, linen blend, sq neck w/center notch, short sleeves w/bead fringe, wide belt, A-line skirt, 1960s............**$32.00**

Dress, navy rayon crepe, V-neck w/plaid detachable collar, ¾-sleeves, pleated drape at waist, 1940s..............**$38.00**

Dress, party; pink faille taffeta, sweetheart neck, gathered bodice, puff sleeves, tie belt, 1940s **$75.00**

Dress, pink rayon crepe, scoop neck w/applied hearts, ¾-sleeves, matching jacket w/cuffs, 1950s...............**$45.00**

Dress, printed chiffon, set-in sleeves w/shoulder pads, bias flounces drape skirt, mid-1940s, EX **$52.00**

Dress, printed cotton, round collar w/lace & rhinestone appliques, button front, pockets, short sleeves w/cuffs, 1940s..**$28.00**

Dress, rayon floral print, high draped neck w/pleats at shoulders, ¾-sleeves, sarong-style skirt, 1940s.............**$46.00**

Dress, white w/colorful dots, sweetheart neck, wide shoulder straps, pleated skirt, bolero jacket, Betty Barclay, 1950s..**$38.00**

Dress, wool, V-neck w/sm collar, cap sleeves, monkey fur trim on bodice & matching cape, 1950s **$65.00**

Dress, wool brocade on satin, straight neck w/scooped back, no sleeves, w/mandarin-style jacket, Jeanne Scott, 1960s .**$98.00**

Dress, 2-tone suede shirtwaist w/dropped waistline, short sleeves, Princess-line bodice, Marie Leavell, 1960s ..**$28.00**

Dressing gown, rayon taffeta w/flocked velvet birds, sweetheart neck w/sm collar, zipper front, puff sleeves, 1940s **$48.00**

Gloves, gauntlet style, brown cotton, 1940s...............**$15.00**

Gloves, white cotton, short, from $5 to.....................**$10.00**

Go-go boots, green vinyl, 1960s................................**$40.00**

Hat, black w/purple snood back, platter style, 1940s...**$45.00**

Hat, bubble toque, Jack McConnell, feathered, 1960s ..**$125.00**

Hat, red woven straw, black grosgrain ribbons and black net, 1940s, $48.00. (Photo courtesy Woodland Farms Antiques)

Hat, straw doll hat w/flowers & veil, 1940s, sm **$35.00**

Hat, straw trimmed w/cherries, 1950s, sm...................**$45.00**

Hat, topper, black straw w/lg red 'wing' & back-tied veil, 1940s..**$55.00**

Hat, toque, pink metallic brocade, 1960s **$12.00**

Hat, velvet turban w/knotted center front, Sears, 1940-41, from $35 to..**$55.00**

Hawaiian shirt, rayon or cotton print, men's, 1940s-50s, from $55 to..**$150.00**

Jacket, black wool, Princess style, sm stand-up collar, hooks & eyes closure, long sleeves w/cuffs, Lilli Ann, 1940s..**$125.00**

Lounging pajamas, Hawaiian print on rayon, wide legs, 1940s..**$95.00**

Mexican jacket, red felt w/cowboy scene & laced edge, 1950s......................**$58.00**

Nightgown, pink satin w/ivory lace, V-shaped yoke, cap sleeves, bias-cut long skirt, Weisman label, 1940s, EX......................**$58.00**

Panties, peach rayon, wide-leg step-ins, 1940s..........**$10.00**

Pants, blue garbardine w/western-style embroidery at pockets, ivory piping, zipper front, 1950s..................**$85.00**

Pantsuit, pink polyester, mandarin collar, tunic top w/zipper front, long sleeves, 2-pc, Saks Smartwear Minn, 1960s......................**$150.00**

Pop-it beads, plastic, 1950s......................**$5.00**

Scarf/kerchief, floral print on silk, 1950s......................**$15.00**

Shirt, wool gabardine, teal blue w/spread collar, men's, 1940s......................**$58.00**

Shoes, alligator pumps, plain, 1940s......................**$50.00**

Shoes, Disco-style platforms, brown leather-look vinyl, men's......................**$24.00**

Shoes, Disco-style platforms, gunmetal multicolor, 1970s......................**$65.00**

Shoes, evening, sq toes, silk w/gold & beaded lion head, 1960s-70s......................**$55.00**

Shoes, gold satin evening slippers, 1940s......................**$35.00**

Shoes, lace-up, brown leather w/round toes & basket-weave textures, men's, 1940s......................**$145.00**

Shoes, Lucite Cinderella heels, from $25 to......................**$55.00**

Shoes, purple satin with gold lamè leather platforms and piping, rhinestone buckles, 1940s, $185.00. (Photo courtesy Vintage Martini)

Shoes, saddle style, 1950s......................**$20.00**

Slip, net crinoline, 1950s......................**$15.00**

Slip, peach rayon satin, 1940s......................**$8.00**

Socks, argyle, brown & white, deadstock, men's, 1940s......................**$8.00**

Suit, beige linen blend w/triangular sailor collar, ¾-sleeves w/sm cuffs, 1940s, EX......................**$82.00**

Suit, black wool, shawl collar w/notched lapels, 4-button front, long sleeves w/rhinestone cuff studs, Leslie Fay, 1950s......................**$65.00**

Suit, blue wool, box-cut jacket w/notched lapels & 2 rhinestone buttons, A-line skirt, Milady NY, 1960s......................**$45.00**

Suit, brown w/red fleck & silver windowpane, men's, 1950s......................**$145.00**

Suit, brown wool, spread collar, piping details, Lilli Annette Diminuitive, set-in ¾-sleeves, 2-pc, 1940s, EX......................**$295.00**

Suit, double breasted, brown w/cream diagonal stripe, men's, 1940s......................**$225.00**

Suit, lavender/black tweed wool, long sleeves w/French cuffs, notched collar & lapel, Neiman Marcus, 2-pc, ca 1950, EX......................**$68.00**

Suit, navy faille, V-neck w/low collar, 3 covered buttons, Princess style, 7-gore skirt, 1940s......................**$52.00**

Suit, nubby wool crepe, single-button jacket, no collar, soutache trim, A-line skirt, Printzess...by Printz, 1940s......................**$95.00**

Suit, printed wool, sleeveless shell blouse w/scooped neck, A-line skirt, jacket w/rounded collar, C Dior NY, 1960s......................**$155.00**

Suit, purple grape wool, knife-pleated cape sleeves, mandarin collar, dropped waist w/knife-pleated skirt, 1960s, VG+......................**$58.00**

Suit, sharkskin, olive/blue, 3-button, narrow lapels, Rocraft, men's, 1960s......................**$210.00**

Suit, wool, burnt orange w/velvet braid trim, 3-pc, men's, 1970s......................**$95.00**

Sweater, beige cashmere w/fur collar, 1950s......................**$85.00**

Sweater, lamb's wool & cashmere shell w/floral seed pearl & sequin pattern, 1950s-60s......................**$45.00**

Sweater, wool shell w/aurora borealis sequins & seed pearls, fringed bottom, hand beaded in Hong Kong, 1960s......................**$78.00**

Sweater set (shell & cardigan), purple orlon, 1950s......................**$35.00**

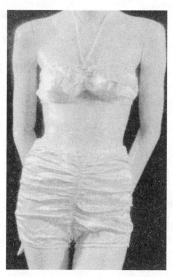

Swimsuit, pink lycra satin with gathered trunks, 1940s, $48.00. (Photo courtesy Vintage Martini)

Tie, Cornucopia Cascade, purple & red silk, Salvador Dali, men's, 1950s......................**$300.00**

Tie, narrow, black & silver diagonal stripes, men's, 1960s......................**$14.00**

Tie, red silk w/green Christmas wreath print, men's, 1940s...**$45.00**

Tuxedo, black wool, notched lapels, double-breasted style, men's, 1950s..................................**$95.00**

Tuxedo jacket, black, silver & blue brocade w/satin lapels, men's, 1960s..................................**$158.00**

Vintage Denim

Bib overalls, Levi Strauss 'Two Horse Brand,' 1920s, G-...**$500.00**

Bib overalls, Osh Kosh B'Gosh, vest back, Union Made, sanforized, black & gold tag, dark color, 32" waist...**$25.00**

Coat, chore; Lee 81-LJ, black lining, size med...........**$30.00**

Jacket, Headlight buckle-back 1st edition, med color, 1930-40s, size lg, G....................................**$250.00**

Jacket, Lee, pinstripe workwear, Union Made at top of label, 1950s, slight damage, size 42...............**$225.00**

Jacket, Lee 101-J, red label, 1950s...........................**$150.00**

Jacket, Lee 91-J, slanted e, 'union made' at top of label, long L, G-...**$110.00**

Jacket, Levi, big E, red cloth label, metal buttons, 1960s, EX, $125.00.
(Photo courtesy Manions Auctions)

Jacket, Levi, blanket-lined 1st edition, full leather (perfect) patch, dark color, 1930s, size 36.........**$700.00**

Jacket, Levi 506 XX, 1st edition, med color, size 38.**$250.00**

Jacket, Levi 506 XX, 1st edition, silver buckle, child's size...**$475.00**

Jacket, Levi 507 XX, 2nd edition, good color, some wear/damage, size sm.............................**$220.00**

Jacket, Levi 507XX, 2nd edition, size med.............**$500.00**

Jacket, Levi 559 XX, dark, size 38-40, NM...............**$50.00**

Jacket, Osh Kosh B'Gosh, indigo workwear, big button, corduroy collar, 1950s, size lg........................**$70.00**

Jeans, Levi big E, bell-bottoms w/paper flashers, beautiful Aztec design, 27" waist........................**$150.00**

Jeans, Levi big E, good grain, dark blue, 32" waist, EX..**$170.00**

Jeans, Levi XX, Conmar zipper, dark blue, 34" waist...**$200.00**

Jeans, Levi 501, double-stitched red lines, dark blue, 32" waist...**$95.00**

Jeans, Levi 501, leather patch, dark blue, 27" waist, EX...**$100.00**

Jeans, Levi 501, single-stitch red lines, dark blue, 36" waist...**$140.00**

Jeans, Levi 501 big E, #2 button, 36" waist............**$275.00**

Jeans, Levi 501 big E, #8 button, very dark, 30" waist..**$100.00**

Jeans, Levi 501 big E, red lines, dark blue, 32" waist...**$275.00**

Jeans, Levi 501 big E, S-patch, straight-stitched waistband, med color, 38" waist..........................**$275.00**

Jeans, Levi 501 sm e, red lines, #6 buttons, med blue, 33" waist, from $75 to...............................**$100.00**

Jeans, Levi 501 XX, leather patch, extremely dark, 37" waist...**$1,500.00**

Jeans, Levi 501 XX, leather patch, 1-sided red tag, professional repair, 32" waist.............................**$1,200.00**

Jeans, Levi 503 B XX, paper patch w/some damage, good color, 30" waist, VG..............................**$210.00**

Jeans, Levi 503 Z XX, leather patch, 1949, 26" waist..**$300.00**

Jeans, Levi 504 Z XX, 27" waist...............................**$325.00**

Jeans, Levi 505 big E, dark blue, 34" waist.............**$200.00**

Jeans, Levi 505 big E, med dark, 34" waist, professional repair...**$100.00**

Jeans, Levi 505 sm e, straight-stitched red lines, 34" waist, from $100 to..**$175.00**

Jeans, Levi 701 XX women's, w/original flashers, 24" waist...**$225.00**

Overalls, Hercules, indigo denim, w/flashers, 1940s, 34" waist...**$425.00**

Shirt, Levi, green, short horn tag, size lg.................**$40.00**

Shirt, Sears Roebuck, white painted snaps, 1950s, size med...**$60.00**

Coca-Cola Collectibles

Coca-Cola was introduced to the public in 1886. Immediately an advertising campaign began that over the years and continuing to the present day has literally saturated our lives with a never-ending variety of items. Some of the earlier calendars and trays have been known to bring prices well into the four figures. Because of these heady prices and the extremely widespread collector demand for good Coke items, reproductions are everywhere, so beware! Some of the items that have been reproduced are pocket mirrors (from 1905, 1906, 1908 – 11, 1916, and 1920), trays (from 1899, 1910, 1913 – 14, 1917, 1920, 1923, 1926, 1934, and 1937), tip trays (from 1907, 1909, 1910, 1913 – 14, 1917, and 1920), knives, cartons, bottles, clocks, and trade cards. In recent years, these items have been produced and marketed: an 8" brass 'button,' a 27" brass bottle-shaped thermometer, cast-iron toys and bottle-shaped door pulls, Yes Girl posters, a 12" 'button' sign (with one round hole), a rectangular paperweight, a 1949-style cooler radio, and there are others. Look for a date line.

In addition to reproductions, 'fantasy' items have also been made, the difference being that a 'fantasy' never existed as an original. Don't be deceived. Belt buckles are 'fantasies.' So are glass doorknobs with an etched trademark, bottle-shaped knives, pocketknives (supposedly from the 1933 World's Fair), a metal letter opener stamped 'Coca-Cola 5¢,' a cardboard sign with the 1911 lady with fur (9" x 11"), and celluloid vanity pieces (a mirror, brush, etc.).

When the company celebrated its 100th anniversary in 1986, many 'centennial' items were issued. They all carry the '100th Anniversary' logo. Many of them are collectible in their own right, and some are already expensive.

If you'd really like to study this subject, we recommend these books: *Goldstein's Coca-Cola Collectibles* by Sheldon Goldstein; *Collector's Guide to Coca-Cola Items, Vols I* and *II*, by Al Wilson; *Collectible Coca-Cola Toy Trucks* by Gael de Courtivron; *Petretti's Coca-Cola Collectibles Price Guide* by Allan Petretti; and *B.J. Summers' Guide to Coca-Cola* and *Pocket Guide to Coca-Cola*.

Advisor: Craig Stifter (See Directory, Soda Pop Collectibles)

Club: Coca-Cola Collectors Club
PMB 609, 4780 Ashform Dunwoody Rd, Suite A9166
Atlanta, GA 30338. Annual dues: $30.

Ashtray, ceramic, round white dish w/red disk logo on raised center, gold trim, Bill's Novelties, EX+................**$150.00**
Ashtray, metal, High in Energy Low in Calories, round w/red-on-white center, red rim w/4 rests, 1950s, EX **$30.00**
Ashtray, red Bakelite resembling deep-dish tray, raised center w/2 rests & logo, 1940s, NM+.........................**$75.00**
Bank, wooden early-style van w/stamped Drink Coca-Cola logo, w/driver & cases of bottles, Toystalgia Inc, 1980s, 7", M..**$30.00**
Banner, Be Really Refreshed, Coca-Cola Around the Clock!, image of clock at right of seafood barbecue & bottle, 1950s, M..**$50.00**

Bear, fur and plastic, electric action and sound, recent, 15", $35.00.

Belt, white vinyl w/repeated red & white contour logos, 1960, EX...**$20.00**
Bingo card, slide-tile type, Compliments Coca-Cola Bottling Co, 1940s, EX..**$25.00**
Blotter, How About a Coke, shows 3 ladies leaning forward w/bottles of Coke, Coca-Cola button at right, 1944, NM **$15.00**

Bottle carrier, aluminum, slanted top w/6 holes for bottles, Delicious & Refreshing logo on sides, 1950s, 5½x8", EX+..**$65.00**
Bottle holder, cardboard, Drive Refreshed/Handy Bottle Holder/Hang It in Your Car, red & white, 1950s, NM+...**$10.00**
Bottle topper, cardboard, Where Are the Five Missing Bottles of Coca-Cola?, man w/spy glass, 1950s, 7x3", NM.......**$20.00**
Calendar, 1966, Things Go Better With Coke, couple w/party tray above heads, complete, NM..........................**$75.00**
Calendar, 1972, lg yellow flower superimposed over rocks, complete, NM..**$30.00**
Calendar, 1976, Look Up America, NM+.....................**$75.00**
Calendar, 1979, Season Greetings/Santa 1978 December cover sheet, complete, M.......................................**$10.00**
Calendar, 1989, features Coca-Cola illustrators, NM+..**$10.00**
Calendar holder, diecut tin fishtail back panel w/replacement sheets, Coke Refreshes You Best!, 1960s, EX **$475.00**
Can, The Big Can for Lovers of Coke, 16-oz pull-tab, 1970s, NM **$10.00**
Cap, soda jerk; white cloth w/red trim & lettering, 1940s, NM+ **$75.00**
Cap, waitress; white crown topper trimmed in gold w/red Drink Coca-Cola lettering, elastic strap, 1950s, EX..**$50.00**
Carton display, diecut cardboard, For Picnic Fun on wooden sign next to picnic scene, 1952, 8x13", unused, NM..**$150.00**
Carton insert, cardboard, Party Time Is Refreshment Time!, party mask, horns & streamers shown, 1950s, 7x12", NM+ **$40.00**

Case, aluminum, 24-count, 'Drink Coca-Cola in Bottles' each side, 12½" x 17", EX, $75.00.

Christmas card, Merry Christmas From Our House to Yours, pictures Santa at open ice box, 1930s, EX............**$60.00**
Clock, Drink... fishtail logo on sq light-up, green face w/white 'sunburst' rays, numbers & dots, 15¼x15¼", EX **$275.00**
Clock, Things Go Better With Coke, button logo lower right, white w/green numbers, light-up, 16" sq, EX.........**$200.00**
Coaster, paper, Welcome Friend/Have a Coke, Sprite boy peering from behind Coke bottle, scalloped, 1950s, 3½" dia, NM **$15.00**
Cuff links, gold-tone fountain glass shape w/Enjoy Coca-Cola logo, 1970s, EX, pr **$55.00**
Decal, foil, Enjoy Coca-Cola, 1960s, 6x13", M............**$10.00**
Door sticker, Pull, diecut fishtail logo atop sign, 1964, 5x6", NM **$30.00**

Fan, paper w/wooden handle, resembling 1930s shield version w/Drink... & bottle in yellow spotlight, 1950s, EX..**$75.00**

Festoon, Know Your State Tree, 5 pcs, 1950s, 80", NM+ .**$425.00**

Game, ball & cup, wooden ball on tether attached to wooden handle w/cup on end, marked Coca-Cola Bottling Co, 1960s, EX..**$35.00**

Ice bucket, waxed cardboard, striped swag around top, red disk logos, EX+...**$50.00**

Ice pick/bottle opener, metal w/wooden handle, Compliments..., 1940s-50s, EX.............................**$40.00**

Key chain, metal bottle shape, 1950s, 2", NM.............**$5.00**

License plate attachment, Drink Coca-Cola in bottles on celluloid oval, metal frame, 6⅛x6½", VG..............**$275.00**

Lighter, clear plastic body showing fishtail logo w/metal flip top, 1960s, 2½x1¼", EX+.....................................**$30.00**

Lighter, metal slim type showing bottle & contour logo, 1970s, 2¾x¾", NM...**$25.00**

Matchbooks in vending machine box, machine pictured on 1 side w/DNS-80 on reverse of red covers, 12-pack, M (EX+ box)..**$225.00**

Menu board, tin chalkboard w/Drink... Be Refreshed diecut red oval logo above, Have a Coke below, 1950s, 26x18", NM..**$375.00**

Menu board, tin w/red embossed fishtail logo on white w/thin green stripes, arched top, green self-framed edge, NM..**$400.00**

Miniature bottle carton, cardboard carton & 6 glass bottles w/caps, 1940s, 2½x1½", NM...............................**$65.00**

Miniature bottle case, plastic w/24 plastic bottles, red on yellow, 1960s, 2½x3½", EX+..................................**$30.00**

Mug, ceramic, bell shaped w/handle, red lettering on white, 1970s, 5", NM...**$6.00**

Nail clipper, metal, w/applied bottle cap & chain, 1960s, 3x1", NM..**$15.00**

Note pad, the word Notes lettered in V-shape w/eagle emblem atop, 1943, 6x3½", NM............................**$15.00**

Pencil sharpener, metal can shape, contour logo, Germany, 1970s, 2½", EX...**$8.00**

Pin-back button, Member of Coca-Cola Bottle Club on white w/hand-held bottle, 1¼" dia, EX+..........................**$75.00**

Place mat, paper, Holiday Greetings, bough of holly w/lg red bow at right, bottle & button lower left, 1950s, 10x14", M..**$6.00**

Playing cards, double deck in cardboard '6-pack' holder w/contour logo, side of carton lettered A Gallon of Coke, EX..**$65.00**

Playing cards, Santa w/bottle of Coke & reading letter, 1979, complete, MIB...**$25.00**

Postcard, Go With a Winner, shows image of Cale Yarborugh & race car, Hardee's, 1985, unused, NM.................**$3.00**

Pretzel can, Diet Coke contour logo, 3½-gal, white w/red lid, 1993, NM...**$12.00**

Radio, plastic vending machine type w/Coke lettered sideways on front, 1982, 8½x4", NM+.........................**$70.00**

Sign, cardboard, diecut syrup bottle w/other side promoting Coke sales for good profits, 1950s, 12x6½", NM .**$50.00**

Sign, cardboard, Serve Yourself on white band above handheld paper cup on green w/button logo, 1949, 11x13", EX..**$185.00**

Sign, cardboard, Things Go Better With Coke, girl w/skates, 1964, 16x27", EX...**$100.00**

Sign, cardboard stringer, Enjoy Coke! Ice Cold Right Now!, bottle in snow bank, 1960s, 14x10", VG+..........**$100.00**

Sign, cardboard w/scrolled metal frame, Barbecue Sandwich, sandwich plate & Coke glass left of fishtail logo, 10x26", NM..**$60.00**

Sign, cardboard w/scrolled wire holder, shows BLT sandwich & glass of Coke, 1960s, 9x26", EX......................**$50.00**

Sign, celluloid, 1950s, 9", EX, $175.00.

Sign, flange, Have a Coca-Cola, yellow & white on red/yellow border, 1941, 18x18", EX+ **$385.00**

Sign, light-up, Drink Coca-Cola on disk w/metal wall bracket, 1950, NM..**$325.00**

Sign, light-up, lantern shape w/4 plastic panels showing logos, 1960s, NM...**$275.00**

Sign, neon (window), red Cocoa-Cola lettering w/white contour tubing framed w/white oblong tubing, 15x28x7", NM..**$240.00**

Sign, paper, Coca-Cola banner above lady w/food tray & bottles of Coke, Enjoy Food, green background, 1950s, 18x18", NM+...**$30.00**

Sign, paper, Your Choice of Sizes/Bring Home the Coke, girl pointing to regular & king-size bottles, 1960, 27", EX..**$25.00**

Sign, plastic w/metal hang rings, set of 4 w/race cars protruding from frames, Things Go Better..., 1960s, 16x13", VG-NM..**$575.00**

Sign, porcelain, Coca-Cola Sold Here Ice Cold, white & yellow on red, yellow border, 1940s, 12x29", EX...**$160.00**

Sign, tin, Deli, shows deli food & button logo on white, self-framed border, 1950, 16x50", NM.......................**$880.00**

Sign, tin, Enjoy... red dot logo/Things Go Better With Coke paper cup & Serve Yourself on snowflake ground, 22x25", NM..**$375.00**

Sign, tin, fishtail logo & bottle on white background w/thin green stripes, green self-framed rim, 12x32", NM.**$325.00**

Sign, tin button, Coco-Cola lettered over bottle on red, 1951, 24" dia, NM $400.00

Thermometer, celluloid stick-on type, Be Really Refreshed, geometric design w/fishtail logo, 6x2½", EX........$80.00

Thermometer, dial type, Drink Coca-Cola in Bottles, white on red, 1950s, 12" dia, NM $200.00

Thermometer, tin, Drink...in Bottles on red button top w/Quality Refreshment below, gray stripes on white, 1950, 9", EX.....................$325.00

Thermometer, tin bottle form, 29¼", NM.....................$70.00

Thermometer, tin cigar shape w/Drink...Sign of Good Taste/Refresh Yourself on red & white ground, 30x8", EX+ $525.00

Tie, cloth clip-on w/allover bottle-cap design, 1970s, 13x2½", NM+ $25.00

Toy car, Ford Taxi, red and white tin, friction, 'Refresh With Zest,' Taiyo/Dott, 1960s, 9", NMIB, $300.00.

Toy polar bear, w/Coke bottle, white plush, 1993, 7", MIB $15.00

Toy truck, Buddy L, metal, red & white w/Enjoy Coca-Cola contour logo, w/side-mount hand cart, 1970, MIB.$90.00

Toy truck, Marx, yellow plastic Ford style w/red Delicious & Refreshing logo on top center divider panel, 1950s, EX.....................$375.00

Tray, 1977, depicts various sporting events, from $40.00 to $50.00.

Tray, 1958, food cart, 10½x11¼", EX.....................$45.00

Tray, 1977, Romance or Wedding, 16x12½", NM, ea..$25.00

Tray, 1994, Santa w/elves in workshop, vertical, NM...$8.00

Writing tablet, Pause..., bottle on cover, 1950s, 10½x8", unused, NM+.....................$18.00

Coloring and Activity Books

Coloring and activity books representing familiar movie and TV stars of the 1950s and 1960s are fun to collect, though naturally unused examples are hard to find. Condition is very important, of course, so learn to judge their values accordingly. Unused books are worth as much as 50% to 75% more than one only partially colored. Several examples are shown in *Cartoon Toys & Collectibles, Identification and Value Guide,* by David Longest, and for those featuring the stars of TV shows, you'll enjoy *Collector's Guide to TV Memorabilia, 1960s & 1970s,* by Greg Davis and Bill Morgan. Both publications are available from Collector Books.

Adventures of Electro-Man Coloring Book, Lowe, 1967, unused, NM.....................$20.00

Alice in Wonderland Paint Book, Whitman, 1951, unused, EX.....................$50.00

Andy Panda Paint Book, Whitman, 1944, EX.............$40.00

Annette Coloring Book, WDP, 1964, unused, EX........$15.00

Baba Louie Coloring Book, Watkins-Strathmore, 1960, unused, EX.....................$15.00

Bambi Paint Book, Whitman/WDP, 1941-42, unused, EX.....................$55.00

Banana Splits Coloring Book, Whitman, 1969, unused, EX.....................$25.00

Beverly Hillbillies Coloring Book, Whitman, 1964, unused, EX.....................$30.00

Black Hole Coloring Book, Whitman, 1979, unused, EX.....................$12.00

Blue Fairy Story Paint Book, Whitman, 1939, unused, EX.....................$50.00

Bobbsey Twins Coloring Book, Whitman, 1954, unused, VG.....................$25.00

Brady Bunch Sticker Book, Whitman, 1973, unused, NM, from $50 to.....................$75.00

Bullwinkle Coloring Book, General Mills premium, 1963, unused, EX.....................$30.00

Captain America Coloring Book, Whitman, 1966, unused, EX.....................$50.00

Captain Kangaroo's Treasure House Punch-Out Book, Whitman, 1959, unpunched, NM.....................$65.00

Casper & Nightmare Coloring Book, Saalfield, 1964, unused, EX.....................$20.00

Charlie Chaplin Coloring Book, Saalfield, 1941, unused, M $50.00

Charlie McCarthy Paint Book, Whitman #690, 1938, EX..$45.00

Cinderella Paint Book, Whitman, 1950, unused, EX...$30.00

Dick Tracy Coloring Book, Saalfield, 1946, unused, EX.$45.00

Donald Duck Army Paint Book, Whitman, 1942, unused, EX..$45.00

Donna Reed Coloring Book, Saalfield, 1964, unused, NM...$30.00

Doris Day Coloring Book, Whitman, 1955, unused, EX ..$35.00

Dumbo the Elephant Coloring Book, 1972, unused, M...$25.00

Fat Albert & the Cosby Kids Coloring Book, Whitman, 1973, unused, EX..$8.00

Flash Gordon Paint Book, Whitman, 1936, unused, EX .$55.00

Flintstones Coloring Book, Charlton, 1971 unused, EX, from $10 to..$15.00

George of the Jungle Coloring Book, Whitman, 1968, unused, EX..$30.00

Geppetto Story Book, Whitman/WDP, 1939, unused, EX...$50.00

Gilligan's Island, Whitman #1135 1965, EX, $45.00.
(Photo courtesy Greg Davis and Bill Morgan)

Grizzly Adams Activity Book, Rand McNally, 1978, unused, NM..$20.00

Gunsmoke Coloring Book, Whitman, 1959, few pages colored, EX..$25.00

Hardy Boys Mystery Mazes, Tempo, 1977, unused, NM..$10.00

Hopalong Cassidy Coloring Book, Lowe, 1950, unused, NM...$75.00

How To Draw Super Heroes Sketchbook & Coloring Book, Golden, 1983, unused, EX $25.00

HR Pufnstuf Coloring Book, Whitman, 1970, unused, M..$35.00

J Worthington Foulfellow & Gideon Story Paint Book, Whitman, 1940, unused, NM.................$75.00

Jiminy Cricket Story Paint Book, Whitman, 1940, unused, NM...$75.00

Julia Coloring Book, Saalfield, 1969, unused, NM $25.00

Land of the Lost Coloring Book, Whitman, 1975, unused, NM...$25.00

Leave It to Beaver Coloring Book, Saalfield, 1958, unused, NM...$65.00

Little Lulu & Tubby Tom Paint Book, 1946, unused, VG...$40.00

Lone Ranger Coloring Book, Whitman, 1951, unused, EX...$65.00

Marvel Super Heroes Super Activity Book, Marvel, 1983, unused, EX $8.00

Mickey Rooney Paint Book, Merrill, 1940, unused, NM .$35.00

Mighty Mouse Sticker Book, Whitman, 1967, unused, NM...$50.00

Mrs Beasley Color and Read, Whitman, 1972, 16" x 7½", EX, from $15.00 to $20.00.

Mrs Beasley Coloring Book, Whitman, 1970, unused, NM...$25.00

My Favorite Martian Coloring Book, Whitman, unused, EX...$35.00

New Zoo Revue Coloring Book, Saalfield, 1974, unused, NM...$10.00

Old Yeller, Whitman, 1957, partially colored, NM+ $30.00

Oliver Sticker Book, 1968, unused, M $30.00

Parade of Comics Sticker Book, Saalfield, 1968, unused, NM...$50.00

Partridge Family Dot-to-Dot Book, World Distributors, 1972, unused, NM....................................$30.00

Peanuts Pictures To Color, Saalfield, 1960, unused, NM, from $25 to...$30.00

Peanuts Trace & Color, Saalfield, 1960s, set of 5, unused, MIB, from $25 to.............................$35.00

Pebbles & Bamm-Bamm Coloring Book, Whitman, 1964, unused, NM....................................$30.00

Pepper at School Sticker Book, Whitman, 1966, unused, EX..$20.00

Peppermint Patty Coloring Book, Artcraft, 1972, unused, NM..$12.00

Peter Pan Coloring Book, Whitman, 1952, unused, VG .$25.00

Pinocchio Story Paint Book, Whitman #1059, 1940, few pages colored, VG $45.00

Popeye Coloring Book, Samuel Lowe, 1961, unused, EX...$20.00

Popeye Paint Book, Whitman, 1937, oversized format, partially colored, VG+...............................$30.00

Popeye Paint Book, Whitman, 1937, oversized format, unused, EX $75.00

Quick Draw McGraw Coloring Book, Whitman, few pages colored, EX......$25.00

Raggedy Ann & Andy See-a-Word, Whitman, 1981, unused, NM, from $15 to......$20.00

Raggedy Ann Sticker Book, Whitman, 1962, unused, NM, from $25 to......$30.00

Rin Tin Tin Coloring Book, Whitman, 1955, unused, EX .$30.00

Rita Hayworth Dancing Star Coloring Book, Merrill, 1942, unused, EX $50.00

Roy Rogers & Dale Evans Ranch Tales Coloring Book, Whitman, 1953, several pages colored, EX..........$30.00

Shirley Temple Crosses the Country Coloring Book, Saalfield, 1939, unused, EX......$75.00

Six Million Dollar Man Coloring Book, Saalfield, 1976, unused, M......$15.00

Snow White & the Seven Dwarfs Paint Book, Whitman/WDE, 1938, unused, EX......$75.00

Space Angel Coloring Book, Saalfield, 1963, unused, EX......$35.00

Space Ghost Coloring Book, Whitman, 1965, unused, NM......$30.00

Steve Canyon Coloring Book, Saalfield, 1952, oversized, unused, NM......$50.00

Straight Arrow Color Book, Stephens, 1949, oversized, few pages colored, EX......$30.00

Superboy Coloring Book, Whitman, 1967, unused, NM ..$50.00

Superman Coloring Book, Whitman, 1965, unused, EX ..$30.00

Tammy's Vacation Coloring Book, Watkins-Strathmore, 1960s, unused, EX......$20.00

Tarzan Punch-Out Book, Whitman, 1967, unpunched, NM......$45.00

Tennessee Tuxedo Coloring Book, Whitman, 1975, unused, EX......$15.00

Terry & the Pirates Coloring Book, Saalfield, 1946, unused, NM, from $50 to......$75.00

That Girl Coloring Book, Artcraft, 1968, unused, NM.$25.00

Tweety Coloring Book, Whitman, Warner Brothers, from $25.00 to $45.00. (Photo courtesy David Longest)

Three Little Pigs Cut-Out Coloring Book, Pocket Books, 1953, unused, EX......$35.00

Thunderbirds Coloring Book, Whitman, 1968, unused, EX......$30.00

Tinker Toy Paint Book, Whitman, 1939, unused, NM ..$40.00

Uncle Martin the Martian Cut-Out Coloring Book, Golden Press, 1964, few pages colored, EX+ $35.00

Underdog Sticker Book, Whitman, 1973, unused, NM .$15.00

Universal City Studio Coloring Book, Saalfield, 1964, few pages colored, VG $30.00

Walt Disney Paint Book, Whitman, 1938, unused, EX..$100.00

Waltons Coloring Book, Whitman, 1975, unused, NM...$25.00

Winnie the Pooh & Friends Punch-Out Book, Golden, 1983, unpunched, NM......$15.00

Wizard of Oz Coloring Book, Whitman, 1962, unused, EX......$25.00

Yogi Bear & Great Green Giant Coloring Book, Modern Promotions, 1976, unused, EX......$20.00

101 Dalmatians Coloring Book, Whitman, 1960, unused, EX......$25.00

Comic Books

Though just about everyone can remember having stacks and stacks of comic books as a child, few of us ever saved them for more than a few months. At 10¢ a copy, new ones quickly replaced the old, well-read ones. We'd trade them with our friends, but very soon, out they went. If we didn't throw them away, Mother did. So even though they were printed in huge amounts, few survive, and today they're very desirable collectibles.

Factors that make a comic book valuable are condition (as with all paper collectibles, extremely important), content, and rarity, but not necessarily age. In fact, comics printed between 1950 and the late 1970s are most in demand by collectors who prefer those they had as children to the earlier comics. They look for issues where the hero is first introduced, and they insist on quality. Condition is first and foremost when it comes to assessing worth. Compared to a book in excellent condition, a mint issue might bring six to eight times more, while one in only good condition would be worth less than half the price. We've listed some of the more collectible (and expensive) comics, but many are worth very little. You'll really need to check your bookstore for a good reference book before you actively get involved in the comic book market.

Adventures in Paradise, Dell Four-Color #1301, 1962, EX......$18.00

Adventures of Cyclops & Phoenix, Marvel #1 ......$5.00

Adventures of Mighty Mouse, St John #2, 1952, EX ...$55.00

Al Capp's Wolf Gal, #2, 1952, VG+ $55.00

All-American Men of War, #5, VG $85.00

Alley Oop, #12, 1948, EX......$35.00

Andy Panda, Dell Four-Color #280, 1950, EX..........$25.00

Animal World, Dell Four-Color #713, VG+ $16.00

Annie Oakley, Dell #6, VG+ $30.00

Aquaman, Dell #1, 1962, EX......$175.00

Avengers, Marvel #1, 1963, EX $500.00
Bambi's Children, Dell Four-Color #30, VG $150.00
Bat Masterson, Dell Four-Color #1013, 1959, EX $35.00
Beany & Cecil, Dell #2, 1962, rare, EX $25.00
Ben Bowie & His Mountain Men, #11, EX $21.00
Ben Casey, Dell #1, 1962, photo cover, EX+ $18.00
Bewitched, Dell #2, 1965, NM, from $40 to $50.00
Bionic Woman, Charlton #1, 1977, NM $15.00
Bonanza, Gold Key #10, 1964, EX $15.00
Brave One, Dell Four-Color #773, VG $10.00
Buck Jones, Dell Four-Color #652, 1955, EX+ $20.00
Bugaloos, Charlton #1, 1972, NM, from $20 to $30.00
Bugs Bunny, #200, 1948, EX+ $50.00
Bullwinkle, Gold Key #1, 1962, EX $35.00
Bullwinkle & Rocky, Whitman #5, 1972, EX $10.00
Captain Marvel, Fawcett #132, 1951, VG $20.00
Captain Venture, Gold Key #1, 1968, EX $15.00
Casper the Friendly Ghost, #23, 1960, EX $10.00
Charlie Chan, Dell #1, 1965, EX+ $25.00
Cheyenne, Dell #16, 1960, EX+ $20.00
Christmas & Archie, Archie Comics #1, 1974, EX $10.00
Christmas in Disneyland, Dell #1, NM $95.00
Cindy, Marvel #38, 1950, EX $20.00
Circus Boy, Dell Four-Color #759, 1956, VG $20.00
Colt .45, Dell #5, 1960, EX $20.00
Conan the Barbarian, Marvel Treasury #4, 1975, oversized,
    NM $8.00
Courtship of Eddie's Father, #2, NM $20.00
Daisy Duck's Diary, #659, EX+ $15.00
Daredevil, Marvel Comics #1, 1964, G $150.00
Dark Shadows, Gold Key #5, 1970, NM $50.00
David & Goliath, Dell Four-Color #1205, 1961, VG $25.00
David Cassidy, Charlton #1, 1972, photo cover, NM $18.00
Dick Tracy, Dell #4, NM $100.00
Don Winslow, #61, 1948, EX $25.00
Donald Duck & Mickey Mouse in Disneyland, Dell Giant #1,
    EX $32.00
Dr Who & the Daleks, Dell #1, 1966, VG $15.00
Dudley Do-Right, #5, 1971, VG $15.00
Earthworm Jim, Marvel #1, 1995, NM $25.00
Fairy Tale Parade, Dell #3, 1943, VG+ $35.00
Fantastic Four, Marvel #48, 1966, VG $25.00
Fantastic Voyage, Gold Key #2, 1969, EX $10.00
Felix the Cat, Dell #6, 1964, EX $20.00

Flash, Why?, DC Comics, 1965, NM, from $30.00 to $40.00.

Flash Gordon, Dell #84, 1945, VG+ $140.00
Flintstones, Gold Key Giant #1, 1965, EX $50.00
Flipper, Gold Key #2, photo cover, EX $35.00
Fury, Dell Four-Color, #1296, 1962, EX $20.00
Gang Busters, DC Comics, #58, VG $15.00
Garrison's Gorillas, Dell #5, 1967, VG $20.00
Gidget, Dell #2, 1966, NM $30.00
Girl From UNCLE, Goldberg #1, 1978, G $15.00
Gomer Pyle, #3, 1967, EX $10.00
Great Grape Ape, #2, 1976, NM $5.00
Great Locomotive Chase, Dell Four-Color #712, Fess Parker
    photo cover, EX $20.00
Green Hornet, Dell #496, 1953, EX $35.00
Green Lantern, DC Comics #7, 1960, NM $200.00
Hand of Zorro, Dell Four-Color #574, 1954, EX $40.00
Hardy Boys, Gold Key #2, 1970, photo cover, NM $10.00
Harlem Globetrotters, #3, 1972, EX $5.00
Have Gun Will Travel, Dell Four-Color #983, 1959, G $8.00
Heckle & Jeckle, Dell #3, 1967, VG $8.00
Hennesey, Dell Four-Color #1200, 1961, VG+ $15.00
Henry, Dell #12, 1950, EX $10.00
High Chaparral, Gold Key #1, 1968, EX $10.00
Honey West, Gold Key #1, 1966, NM $75.00
Hopalong Cassidy, Fawcett #54, 1951, VG $10.00
House of Secrets, Dell #50, EX $40.00
Howdy Doody, Dell #15, 1952, EX $25.00
Huey, Dewy & Louie Back to School, Dell Giant #1,
    VG $15.00

Human Torch, Vol 1, #38, Chipiden Publishing, Aug., 1954, EX, $120.00.

I Love Lucy, Dell #29, 1960, VG+ $35.00
Incredible Hulk, Marvel #102, EX $75.00
Jerry Lewis, DC Comics #108, 1968, EX $8.00
Johnny Mac Brown, Dell Four-Color #645, EX $28.00
Josie & the Pussycats, Archie Comics #6, 1964, NM $20.00
Journey Into Mystery, Marvel #91, 1963, VG $25.00
Kidnapped, Dell Four-Color #1101, G+ $10.00
Krofft Supershow, Gold Key #1, 1976, NM $15.00
Lancer, Gold Key #1, 1968, EX+ $12.00
Lawman, Dell #8, 1961, VG+ $40.00
Little Audrey TV Funtime, Harvey Giant #1, 1962, VG ...$10.00

Lone Ranger, Dell #1, 1948, VG $100.00
Looney Tunes & Merry Melodies, Dell #34, 1944, EX ..$35.00
Lost World, Dell Four-Color #1145, G+ $25.00
Magilla Gorilla Vs Yogi Bear for President, Gold Key #3, 1964, EX $15.00
Marge's Little Lulu, Dell Four-Color #115, 1946, VG+ ..$150.00
Margie, Dell #2, 1962, VG $5.00
Maverick, Dell #980, EX $40.00
McHale's Navy, #3, VG+ $15.00
Mickey Mouse, Dell Four-Color #27, 1943, VG $165.00
Mickey Mouse & the Beanstalk, Dell Four-Color #157, 1947, EX $60.00
Mickey Mouse in Frontierland, Dell Giant #1, VG+ $35.00
Mod Squad, Dell #1, 1969, NM $40.00
Mr Ed, Gold Key #3, 1963, EX $25.00
Mutt & Jeff, DC Comics #39, 1948, EX $15.00
Nancy & Sluggo, Dell #145, EX+ $15.00
Nick Fury Agent of Shield, Marvel Comics, EX $15.00
No Time for Sergeants, Dell #2, 1965, EX $15.00
Our Gang, Dell #20, G $15.00
Peanuts, Gold Key #1, M $25.00
Peter Potamus, Gold Key #1, 1964, G $15.00

Phantom, Gold Key, 1964, EX, $25.00.

Picnic Party, Dell Giant #7, 1956, unused, EX $35.00
Playful Little Audrey, #1, EX+ $75.00
Pogo Possum, Dell #8, NM $75.00
Police Against Crime, Dell #3, 1954, VG $15.00
Popeye, Dell #48, 1959, EX $12.00
Raggedy Ann & Andy, Dell #452, 1952, NM, from $25 to $30.00
Range Rider, Dell #8, 1955, VG $15.00
Rawhide, Dell Four-Color #1097, 1960, photo cover, VG ..$25.00
Rawhide Kid, Dell #34, VG+ $15.00
Rex Allen, Dell #13, EX+ $30.00
Richie Rich, Dell #23, EX $20.00
Ricky Nelson, #998, 1959, VG+ $50.00
Road Runner, #25, EX $5.00
Rootie Kazootie, Dell #4, 1954, G $8.00
Roy Rogers, Dell #1239, 1950s, NM $35.00

Roy Rogers & Trigger, Dell #124, 1958, EX $35.00
Santa Claus Conquers the Martians, Dell #1, 1966, VG .$15.00
Santa Claus Funnies, Dell #205, 1948, EX $35.00
Scooby Doo, Marvel #1, 1977, M $25.00
Secret Agent, Gold Key #1, 1966, NM $100.00
Silly Symphonies, Dell #7, NM $75.00
Sir Walter Raleigh, Dell #644, 1955, G+ $10.00
Six-Gun Heroes, Fawcett #15, 1952, EX $35.00
Sleeping Beauty, #984, 1959, NM $90.00
Smilin' Jack, Dell #149, 1947, NM $75.00
Soldiers of Fortune, Dell #1, 1951, VG $35.00
Space Ghost, Gold Key #1, 1960s, VG $45.00
Spider-Man, Marvel #43, 1966, VG $35.00
Sports Thrills, Accepted #12, 1951, G $10.00
Star Wars, Marvel #1, 1977, M $45.00
Steve Canyon, Dell Four-Color #841, 1955, NM $35.00
Sugarfoot, #1098, G+ $20.00
Super Mouse, Dell #36, EX $12.00

Superman, DC Comics #1, 1939, NM, minimum value, $10,000.00. (Photo courtesy Bill Bruegman)

Superman's Pal Jimmy Olsen, Dell #23, VG $20.00
Tales of Suspense, Dell #10, VG+ $85.00
Tales of the Texas Rangers, #19, EX+ $25.00
Tales of Wells Fargo, Dell Four-Color #876, 1st issue, photo cover, EX $45.00
Tarzan, Dell Silver Age, #28, EX $40.00
Tarzan Saves the Proud Princess From Enemy Raiders, Dell, 1960, EX $25.00
Tarzan's Jungle Annual, Dell #2, 1953, EX $40.00
Terry & the Pirates, Dell #6, 1936, oversized, NM $150.00
Tessie the Typist, Marvel #21, 1949, VG $25.00
Tex Ritter Western, Fawcett/Charlton #33, EX $30.00
Texas Rangers in Action, #8, VG+ $15.00
Thief of Baghdad #1229, #1229, VG $30.00
Three Stooges, Dell #1170, 1961, VG $30.00
Tippy's Friends & Go-Go Animal, Tower #7, 1967, EX .$12.00
Tom & Jerry Summer Fun, Dell Giant #2, 1955, G $5.00
Tom Corbet Space Cadet, Dell #9, EX $50.00
Top Cat, Charlton #3, 1971, EX $15.00
Top Cat, Gold Key #5, 1963, NM $30.00

Turok, Dell #10, 1958, VG $45.00
Twilight Zone, #1, 1961, VG...$10.00
Two-Gun Kid, Marvel Comics, 1964, NM $20.00
Ultimate Spider-Man, Dynamic Forces, Marvel #1, NMIP..$75.00
Uncle Scrooge, Dell #386, 1952, VG $75.00
Underdog, #1, 1974, VG+ $20.00
Untouchables, Dell #207, 1962, EX $25.00
Vacation in Disneyland, Dell Giant #1, 1959, NM.....$150.00
Venus, #12, 1951, VG+ $40.00
Voyage to the Bottom of the Sea, Gold Key #6, 1966, EX...$15.00
Walt Disney's Old Yeller, Dell #869, 1957, EX............$25.00
Walt Disney's Picnic Party, Dell Giant #8, 1957, VG...$50.00
Walt Disney's Treasure Island, Dell #624, 1955, EX....$22.00
Walt Disney's Zorro, Dell #15, 1961, VG $45.00
War Comics, #48, 1957, VG..$10.00
Warlock, Marvel Premiere #1, 1972, NM....................$15.00
Western Roundup, Dell Giant #14, 1956, VG+ $15.00
Wings of Eagles, Dell #790, VG.....................................$30.00
Wonder Woman, Dell #34, G $30.00
Woody Woodpecker Back to School, Dell Giant #1, EX...$25.00
World of Wheels, #23, 1978, NM...................................$10.00
X-Men, Marvel #13, 1965, EX...$30.00
Yak Yak, Dell #1186, EX $30.00
Zane Grey's Stories of the West, #270, VG.................$15.00
77 Sunset Strip, Dell #1066, 1960, EX+ $30.00

Compacts and Purse Accessories

When 'liberated' women entered the work force after WWI, cosmetics, previously frowned upon, became more acceptable, and as a result the market was engulfed with compacts of all types and designs. Some went so far as to incorporate timepieces, cigarette compartments, coin holders, and money clips. All types of materials were used — mother-of-pearl, petit-point, cloisonne, celluloid, and leather among them. There were figural compacts, those with wonderful Art Deco designs, souvenir compacts, and some with advertising messages.

Carryalls were popular from the 1930s to the 1950s. They were made by compact manufacturers and were usually carried with evening wear. They contained compartments for powder, rouge, and lipstick; often held a comb and mirror; and some were designed with a space for cigarettes and a lighter. Other features might have included a timepiece, a tissue holder, a place for coins or stamps, and some even had music boxes. In addition to compacts and carryalls, solid perfumes and lipsticks are becoming popular collectibles as well.

For further study, we recommend *Vintage and Contemporary Purse Accessories* and *Vintage and Vogue Ladies' Compacts* by Roselyn Gerson; and *Collector's Encyclopedia of Compacts, Carryalls, and Face Powder Boxes, Volumes I* and *II,* by Laura Mueller.

Advisor: Roselyn Gerson (See Directory, Compacts)

Newsletter: The Compacts Collector Chronicle
Powder Puff
P.O. Box 40
Lynbrook, NY 11563. Subscription: $25 (4 issues, USA or Canada) per year

Carryalls

EAM, white metal w/gold-washed interior, chased floral borders, powder/rouge/lipstick/solid perfume/mirror, 4¼"..$250.00
Elgin American, Leaping Gazelles embossed on gold-tone, cut velvet carrier, hinged mirror, 4½x2½x1½", from $125 to $150.00

Evans, gold-tone with engine turning and rhinestone crown, 5½" x 3", from $130.00 to $160.00; Evans, gold-tone with multicolor stones on top, 5½" x 3", from $140.00 to $160.00. (Photo courtesy Roselyn Gerson/ Photographer Alvin Gerson)

Evans, Oversize, rose & gold-tone ribs on lid, graduated link chain, glued mirror, 6¾x3¼x1" $165.00
Evans, Petite, gold-tone basketweave, double access, music box charm bracelet on link chain, coin purse, ca 1955, 3¼"..$175.00
Evans, Petite, High Tide, gold-tone swirling waves, w/lighter, 3¼" sq, from $150 to...$175.00
Evans, Standard, cross-bar lid w/faux sapphires, 5 accessories, hinged mirror, 5½x3⅛x¾", from $100 to...............$125.00
Evans, Standard, gold-tone, Sunburst, broad mesh wrist strap, 6 accessories, 5½x3⅛x¾", from $75 to $100.00
Evans, Standard, mother-of-pearl w/gold-tone ribbed sides, snake wrist chain, glued mirror, 5½x3¼" $165.00
Evans, Standard, pearls, faux cabochon emeralds w/filigree, wrist chain, glued mirror, 5½x3¼" $275.00
Evans, Standard, silver-tone, double access, 6 accessories & glued mirror, 5½x3⅛x1", from $150 to...............$170.00
Unmarked, brushed silver-tone w/stenciled lady smoker, clip-on lipstick, wrist chain, double access, 3½".........$100.00
Unmarked, Standard, brushed gold-tone case w/rhinestone crown bijou, double access, 4 accessories, glued mirrors, 5¼"...$70.00

Volupte, black enamel w/attached rhinestone swag, hinged lid mirror, single access, 6x4x1", from $150 to...**$175.00**

Volupte, brushed silver-tone w/glossy gold-tone chevron & faux gemstone bijou clip, hinged mirror, 5x3x½", from $125 to..**$150.00**

Volupte, brushed silver-tone w/glossy gold-tone lid bars & rhinestones, twisted rope handle, hinged mirror, 5¼x3"..**$165.00**

Volupte, ribbed lid w/attached musical musical notes, snap closure, Swiss music box, hinged mirror, 5x3x½", from $125 to..**$150.00**

Wadsworth, Standard, green leather w/brushed gold-tone sides, ivory kid interior w/Ivorene framing, mirror, 6¼x3¼"..**$85.00**

Compacts

Adrienne, ivory enamel w/gold-tone box relief, framed mirror, 2¼" sq, from $35 to................................**$50.00**

Armand, lady's silhouette on white metal lid, framed mirror, 2¼" dia, from $45 to.................................**$60.00**

Coty, black 'cofferette' w/snap closure, lid crest, metallic mirror, 1⅞" sq, MIB, from $125 to..........................**$150.00**

Coty, blue & maroon enameled lid w/gold dots & center diamond motif, framed mirror, 2¾" dia, from $45 to..**$60.00**

Coty, glossy gold-tone w/aqua Bakelite shoulder & inset, incised logo, framed metallic mirror, 2¼x1½", from $45 to..**$60.00**

Coty, gold-tone ribs w/Coty crest, reverse gold foil label: French Flair, glued mirror, 2⅝" dia, from $15 to..**$25.00**

Coty, plastic classic logo lid inset, framed mirror, 2½" dia, from $25 to...**$30.00**

DeVilbiss, white enamel dogwood florets w/rhinestones on gold-tone, framed mirror, 2½x2¼", from $150 to .**$175.00**

Dorothy Gray, New Moon & Star on gold-tone, framed mirror, 3¼" dia, from $65 to......................................**$80.00**

Dorset Fifth Avenue, clear plastic dome over pink silk flowers on lavender velour on gold-tone, glued mirror, 3⅛" dia..**$40.00**

Dovell, blue enamel & gold-tone, center monogram cartouche, framed mirror, 2¼x1⅞x½", from $35 to....**$50.00**

Elgin American, green, rose & yellow gold-tone scrolls & flowers on brushed finish, 3¼x3", from $50 to....**$65.00**

Evans, black enameling w/attached fraternal crest, plated lid serves as mirror, 3" dia, from $45 to.....................**$60.00**

Fuller, engine-turned circles on gold-tone w/stylized monogram, Fuller Brush Co puff, glued mirror, 2¾" dia, $35 to...**$50.00**

Gallery Originals, brushed aluminum w/faux sapphires, paper instructions, glued metallic mirrors, 2¾" sq, from $35 to .**$50.00**

Girey, high-gloss gold-tone w/trough rim, attached rhinestone & crown bijou, framed mirror, 2¾x2¼x⅜", from $45 to **$60.00**

Jonteel, Bird of Paradise on white metal, octagonal, framed mirror, 1½" dia, w/finger ring chain, from $100 to........**$125.00**

Lucor, silver-tone on glossy gold-tone, center figure logo, glued mirror, 2¾" dia, from $25 to....................**$30.00**

Made in USA, petit-point pastoral scene on gold-tone, framed mirror, 3¼x2¼", from $75 to **$90.00**

Pompeian Co, brushed gold-tone w/Nouveau figure, incised tendrils, scrolled rim, framed mirror, 2½" dia, from $125 to..**$150.00**

Rex Fifth Avenue, cream enameling w/gold-tone monogram, framed mirror, oval, 2¾x2¼", from $45 to **$60.00**

Rhojan, gold-tone with Art Deco gazelle, puff with logo, glued mirror, 3½" square, from $125.00 to $150.00. (Photo courtesy Laura Mueller)

Richard Hudnut, engine-turned circles on gold-tone w/rhinestone-enhanced Du Barry crest, glued mirror, 2¾" dia **$45.00**

Richard Hudnut, multifloral lid on white metal, Art Moderne patterned puff, framed mirror, 2¼" dia, from $45 to.......**$60.00**

Schiaparelli, cerice enameling w/gold-tone lady silhouette, glued mirror, triangular, 2¼x1¾x⅜", from $225 to.............**$250.00**

Tre-Jur, Little One logo on white metal engine-turned banded lid, framed mirror, 2" dia, from $35 to.............**$50.00**

Unmarked, faux cloisonne case w/multicolored florals, framed mirror, 3⅛" dia, from $45 to **$60.00**

Unmarked, faux rosewood veneer enamel, indented dome w/in octagon shape, gold-tone interior, framed mirror, 2½"...**$75.00**

Unmarked, light blue enameling w/hand-painted florals on ivory Pearloid celluloid lid inset, framed mirror, 2¾" dia **$45.00**

Unmarked, ribbed circles on gold-tone w/monogram cartouch, glued mirror, 3¼" dia, from $35 to............**$50.00**

Unmarked, white porcelain dome lid w/transfer scene on gold-tone, glued mirror, 2½" dia, from $25 to **$40.00**

Volupte, lattice band relief on gold-tone, glued mirror, 2⅜" sq, from $25 to...**$40.00**

Woodworth, Art Nouveau w/silver-plated florals, Karess logo, framed mirror, 2", from $100 to **$125.00**

Woodworth, snowflake silver-plated lid, Viegay logo, framed mirror, 2", from $45 to..**$60.00**

Lipsticks

Barbara Gould, copper-tone w/Lucite base, 2¼", from $15 to **$25.00**

Boots, silver-tone w/simple engraved decor, 2⅛", from $15 to **$20.00**

Coty, gold-tone w/simple engraved decor, 1½", from $15 to **$20.00**

Evening in Paris, red, white & blue plastic, 2", from $25 to **$35.00**

Faoen, cobalt enamel, mini, 1⅜", from $5 to **$10.00**

Hampden, applied filigree set w/red, blue & green stones on gold-tone, 2", from $35 to **$50.00**

Hampden, purple translucent tube w/rhinestones at base, 2¼", from $30 to **$40.00**

Lucien Lelong, leopard-fur covered tube, 2¼", from $45 to **$60.00**

Mary Dunhill, aquamarine baked enamel w/personalized gold-tone initials, domed top, 2", from $25 to **$40.00**

Mary Dunhill, white enamel on silver-tone, red & clear rhinestones on domed lid, 2", from $25 to **$40.00**

Richard Hudnut, gold-tone w/engraved decor, 2⅝", from $55 to **$65.00**

Robert, gold-tone tube w/mobé pearl on top w/golden leaves & rhinestones, sticker, 2¾", from $40 to ...**$60.00**

Schildkraut, bezel-cut colored stones, sq sides, 2", from $45 to **$60.00**

Unmarked, black baked enamel tube w/glittery 'can-can' girls, 2¼", from $35 to **$50.00**

Unmarked, gold-tone filigree w/green stones, green cabochon stone at top, 2¼", from $45 to **$65.00**

Unmarked, gold-tone tube w/green & red crystal strawberry form at top of lid, 2⅞", from $50 to **$70.00**

Unmarked, gold-tone w/top decorated w/filigree, pearls & rhinestones, 2¼", from $45 to **$60.00**

Unmarked, silver, hand-engraved & decorated rope design, 2", from $45 to **$75.00**

Unmarked, sterling, faceted amethyst stone centered on lid, 2¼", from $100 to..**$125.00**

Unmarked, white enamel on gold-tone w/hand-painted roses, 2½", from $30 to **$45.00**

Weisner of Miami, aquamarine & clear crystals & rhinestones, top unscrews to reveal perfume bottle opening, 3", from $75 to..**$125.00**

Weisner of Miami, pearls & blue crystals, 2½", from $45 to **$65.00**

Wiesner of Miami, rhinestones allover, 2½", from $45 to **$65.00**

Mirrors

Accessocraft, gold-tone forward & backward tilting mirror & light combination, 2" dia, 5¼" L, from $15 to **$20.00**

Avon, clear plastic w/gold-tone stopper, perfume bottle combination, handle unscrews, 6½x3", from $15 to...**$25.00**

Carolee, polished gold-tone w/red & black enamel card symbols, 1995, 2¼" dia **$25.00**

Celluloid, lady figural, beveled mirror as part of skirt, 3½x2¼", from $50 to..**$75.00**

Faux tortoise plastic butterfly form, opens to reveal 2 oval & 1 rectangular mirror, 3x5¼", from $25 to.............**$35.00**

Florenza, blue stippled, 2" dia, 3⅞" L, from $20 to **$30.00**

Florenza, white & yellow gold-tone w/applied leaves, red & green stones, large faux pearl, 1½" dia, 4" L, from $35 to **$50.00**

Gold-tone, applied decoration extending to handle, 2½" dia, 4½" L, from $20 to..**$30.00**

Gold-tone, sliding fan shape w/Oriental scene, key chain combination, 2½x2", from $25 to **$40.00**

Gold-tone plastic w/Colonial transfer scene, 2½" dia, 4½" L, from $15 to **$20.00**

Gold-tone w/green enameling & red flowers, 2¼" dia, 5½" L, from $35 to **$50.00**

Gold-tone w/multicolor enameling, Toledo printed on center of lid, 1¾x4¾", from $25 to...............................**$35.00**

Gold-tone w/silver-tone in woven design, beveled, 2½" dia, from $20 to **$25.00**

Green marbleized enamel, beveled, Germany, 5¾x2¼", from $35 to **$45.00**

Ivorene plastic w/flapper girl gold profile & rhinestones, swings open, 3¾x2", from $30 to.........................**$50.00**

Petit-point on gold-tone, wire mirror retainer, mini, 3¼" including handle, from $20 to **$30.00**

Shirley Temple, 1990s, 3x2", from $5 to **$15.00**

Silver-tone, advertising, beveled, Standard Varnish Works, New York, Chicago, London, 2" dia, 3¾" L, from $35 to **$50.00**

Silver-tone, resembles bow, 3¼" dia, from $15 to......**$20.00**

Silver-tone w/engraved decoration, portrait under glass dome, beveled, Denmark, 2½" dia, 4½" L, from $25 to **$35.00**

Souvenir of Paris, black plastic, matchbook combination, 2¼" sq, from $5 to..**$10.00**

Sterling silver shield shape, engine turned, monogram on cartouch, beveled, 1¾x4", from $75 to................**$90.00**

Solid Perfumes

Carolee, antique gold-tone walnut-shaped pendant, 1¼x1½", from $40 to..**$50.00**

Corday, brushed gold-tone purse-shaped pendant, embossed foliage ea side, 1½x1⅞", from $35 to **$45.00**

Corday, gold-tone pendant w/ornate scroll design, unicorn on lid, 1½" dia, from $45 to **$55.00**

Corday, hammered gold-tone pendant framed w/free-swinging black plastic ring, 1¾x1¼", from $45 to **$50.00**

DuCair, blue ceramic pendant w/painted flowers, white silk neck cord, 1⅞x1¼", from $20 to..........................**$30.00**

Eli Metal Products, engraved gold-tone egg-shaped pendant, 1½x1", from $25 to **$30.00**

Estée Lauder, beige heart pendant w/gold cross-over stripes, black neck cord, contains Aliage, 1⅞", from $40 to .**$60.00**

Estée Lauder, brushed gold-tone purse-shape pendant w/scrolled flap, contains Youth Dew, 1½x1¼", from $50 to **$75.00**

Estée Lauder, gold-tone pendant w/blue marbleized cabochon stone in center of embossed rays, 2" dia, from $25 to **$40.00**

Estée Lauder, gold-tone pendant w/scroll design, 6 short chain suspensions, contains Azuree, 2x1", from $35 to..............$45.00

Estée Lauder, silver-tone engraved pendant w/ornate ball & tube chain, 1¼x1⅞", from $35 to.........$55.00

Gold-tone plastic fan form w/black cord, Celia Selivi engraved on inner lid, 2¼x1⅝", from $25 to.......$40.00

Goldette, pewter-colored pendant w/profile of man's face in relief, 1¾x1½", from $35 to.....................$45.00

Green enameled stylized bird form w/gold frame, pin w/swinging lid, 1½x1", from $30 to.....................$40.00

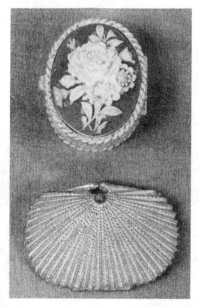

Light blue mottled metal oval, solid blue lid with white floral cameo, 1¾" x 1¼", from $15.00 to $25.00; Estée Lauder, gold-tone with ribbed rays centered with blue cabochon, 2" x 1½", from $20.00 to $30.00. (Photo courtesy Roselyn Gerson/Photographer Alvin Gerson)

Mary Chess, gold-tone pendant w/Wedgwood-style blue cameo, 1½x1¼", from $30 to....................$40.00

Matchabelli, antique gold-tone pendant w/strapwork-decorated lid, 1½" sq, from $30 to.....................$40.00

Max Factor, faux jade pendant w/gold-tone twisted & braided wire disk decoration, contains Khara, 2¼" dia, from $25 to .$40.00

Max Factor, gold-tone & porcelain Flower Song pendant, gold-tone bamboo frame, contains Hypnotique, 2x1½", from $35 to.............................$45.00

Max Factor, gold-tone fawn figural pendant, yellow-stone eyes, contains Hypnotique, 1¼x1¼", from $45 to .$55.00

Revlon, gold-tone conch shell pendant, 1¾x2¾", from $55 to....................................$65.00

Revlon, gold-tone owl-face pendant w/amethyst cabochon eyes, 1½" dia, from $55 to....................$65.00

Revlon, gold-tone pendant w/fish in relief, green-stone eyes, 1½" dia, from $45 to..........................$55.00

Rosenfeld by Florenza, gold-tone tiger's face w/black stripes & red eyes, 1½" dia, from $45 to $55.00

Silver (polished) doughnut-shape pendant, black silk neck cord, 1¾" dia, from $40 to...................$50.00

Silver-tone horseshoe shape w/engraved flowers & Oriental design, Singapore origin, 1½x1⅜", from $25 to...$35.00

Vanda, gold-tone cuckoo clock-shaped pendant w/rhinestones as numerals, 1¼x1¼", from $45 to...........$55.00

Viviane Woodward, Belle Fleur, gold-tone flower form, 1" dia, from $35 to $45.00

Condiment Sets

Whimsical styling makes these sets a lot of fun to collect. Any specie of animal or plant that ever existed and many that never did or ever will are represented, so an extensive collection is possible, and prices are still reasonable. These sets are usually comprised of a pair of salt and pepper shakers and a small mustard pot with spoon on a tray. Technically, the set must include a mustard pot to be considered a condiment set. Some never had a tray — but virtually all Japanese sets did. Others were figurals that were made in three parts. Though you'll find some with other backstamps, by and far the majority of these were made in Japan. (Ours are of generic Japanese origin unless a specific company is noted in our descriptions.) For more information, we recommend *Collector's Guide to Made in Japan Ceramics, Books I, II,* and *III,* by Carole Bess White; *Salt and Pepper Shakers, Vols I* through *IV,* by Helene Guarnaccia; and *Collector's Encyclopedia of Salt and Pepper Shakers, Figural and Novelty,* by Melva Davern. Note: without the matching ceramic spoon, prices on condiment sets should be 25% to 40% less than values listed here. See also Black Americana.

Advisor: Carole Bess White (See Directory, Japan Ceramics)

Carriage, raised slip decoration, from $80.00 to $100.00. (Photo courtesy Helene Guarnaccia)

Arabs (2) w/camel (mustard pot), ceramic, Japan, 1950s, from $80 to.................................$100.00

Black cats (3) w/ball of red yarn, ceramic, on braided rug tray, from $95 to.................................$110.00

Blue & orange lustre, ceramic, black Japan mark, 3 pcs on cloverleaf-shaped 3¾" tray, from $30 to.............$50.00

Blue lustre, ceramic, pepper shaker, built-in mustard pot & salt dip, red Japan mark, 4" L, from $30 to **$45.00**

Blue w/black & gold decor, green Japan mark, 3 pcs on slim 9" handled tray, from $45 to................**$65.00**

Boat, floral w/blue lustre, ceramic, pre-WWII, Japan mark, 3 pcs on boat tray, 6½" L, from $35 to...............**$55.00**

Bridal couple & preacher on tray, ceramic, Germany, 1920s, from $140 to.............................**$160.00**

Cats (3), orange lustre, ceramic, black tail of center cat is spoon, Japan, from $75 to **$90.00**

Cats & goldfish bowl, multicolor, ceramic, spoon handle is fish, 4 pcs on tray, from $95 to..................**$100.00**

Chef behind 2 pumpkins (1 is open salt), ceramic, Germany, 1920-30, from $95 to **$120.00**

Chickens (2) & chicken house (mustard) on grassy tray, ceramic, unmarked, from $35 to **$45.00**

Clowns (2 standing, 1 sitting), in red w/yellow pompon buttons & white ruffle, ceramic, Japan, 1930s, from $95 to.........................**$110.00**

Deco-style floral band on tan lustre, ceramic, Noritake mark, 3 pcs on 7½" tray w/cobalt handles, from $70 to.....**$100.00**

Desert scene, ceramic, shiny multicolor, red Japan mark, 5 pcs on 9¼" tray, from $65 to...............**$125.00**

Dog (nodder) pulling cart (mustard pot) w/2 barrels (shakers), ceramic, Germany, 1890s, from $140 to.....**$160.00**

Dogs (2) rowing boat, cat (mustard finial) sits between, ceramic, Germany, 1930s, from $125 to **$150.00**

Dogs w/radio headphones (3), ceramic, Germany, 1930s, from $100 to.....................**$120.00**

Donkey pulling cart w/3-pc top, ceramic, from $30 to ..**$40.00**

Dutch woman w/boy & girl on tray, ceramic, from $75 to.....................................**$95.00**

Dwarf w/2 toadstools on tray, ceramic, Crown Devon (English), 1950, from $90 to **$100.00**

Elephant tan lustre w/multicolor, ceramic, Japan mark, basket shakers at sides, lid on back for mustard, from $40 to.................................**$60.00**

Fish, silver lustre, ceramic, top of head & tip of tail are shakers, fin removes for mustard, Japan, from $100 to.........**$130.00**

Floral band on white w/tan lustre, ceramic, green Noritake mark, 3 pcs on 4¾" tray, from $50 to...................**$75.00**

Floral on tan to blue w/gold lustre, ceramic, black Japan mark, 5 pcs on 9¼" handled tray, from $65 to..**$125.00**

Flower basket, teal & multicolor lustre, black Japan mark, 3 pcs on 4" basket tray, from $40 to.......................**$60.00**

Flowers & mountains on blue w/multicolor lustre, ceramic, black Japan mark, 4 pcs on 5½" tray, from $65 to.......................**$105.00**

Frogs (2) & red flower (mustard) on green tray, Japan mark, 1950s, from $40 to.................................**$60.00**

Horses (2 shakers) pulling green carriage (mustard pot) on base, ceramic, Japan, 1950s, from $80 to **$100.00**

House, windmill & well on green tray, ceramic, Crown Devon #319, from $70 to **$90.00**

House (3-part), center section attached to white base, ceramic, Germany, ca 1920, from $120 to....................**$140.00**

Lobsters (3) on tray, ceramic, red & yellow, from $65 to..**$75.00**

Log cabin (attached to tray) amid 2 pine-tree shakers, ceramic, from $75 to.............................**$85.00**

Lotus blossoms, cream & tan lustre, ceramic, Goldcastle mark, 3 pcs on handled 5½" tray, from $30 to....**$50.00**

Man on tray stands amid 3 golf balls, ceramic, Crown Devon (English), 1930s, from $120 to............................**$160.00**

Man w/mug stands behind 3 barrels on tray, ceramic, post-WWII, Japan mark, 5¾" L, from $20 to **$35.00**

Monks (comic set of 3) on tray, ceramic, brown robes, Japan, 1960s, from $40 to **$60.00**

Natives & hut on tray, ceramic, Japan, 1950s, from $70 to...**$90.00**

Noah's ark, elephant & lion shakers, dove mustard finial, ceramic, Germany, 1930s, from $100 to **$140.00**

Owl on branch w/2 open dishes for salt & pepper, covered jar behind for mustard, ceramic, Germany, 1910-30, from $90 to.................................**$100.00**

Pigs (3) w/straw house, ceramic, Japan, 1950-60, from $120 to.................................**$160.00**

Rabbits (3), ceramic, black & white, Grafton (English), from $90 to.................................**$100.00**

Sailors (3) on tray, multicolor, ceramic, Japan, 1930s, from $95 to.................................**$120.00**

Swan in lake scenic w/blue & yellow lustre, ceramic, red Japan mark, 3 pcs on slim 9½" handled tray, from $45 to.................................**$65.00**

White opalescent w/orange lustre trim, ceramic, Noritake mark, 3 pcs on handled 4" tray, from $35 to **$65.00**

Winking chef w/spoon & 2 pots, ceramic, Goebel, M-31, from $120 to.................................**$160.00**

Wise monkeys (3), ceramic, tan & blue lustre, Japan mark, shakers & mustard jar on 5¾" L tray, from $60 to...........**$90.00**

Wise monkeys (3) on tray, ceramic, The Three Wise Monkeys on tray, Japan, 1950, from $80 to.......................**$120.00**

Woman & 2 children in boat, lustreware, ceramic, Japan, 1930s, from $60 to **$80.00**

Zeppelin w/scenic view on side, ceramic, Germany, 1920-30, from $80 to...............................**$100.00**

Cookbooks and Recipe Leaflets

Cookbook collecting is not new! Perhaps one of the finest books ever written on the subject goes back to just after the turn of the century when Elizabeth Robins Pennell published *My Cookery Books*, an edition limited to 330 copies; it had tipped-in photographs and was printed on luxurious, uncut paper. Mrs. Pennell, who spent much of her adult life travelling in Europe, wrote a weekly column on food and cooking for the *Pall Mall Gazette,* and as a result, reviewed many books on cookery. Her book was a compilation of titles from her extensive collection which was later donated to the Library of Congress. That this book was reprinted in 1983 is an indication that interest in cookbook collecting is strong and ongoing.

Books on food and beverages, if not bestsellers, are at the least generally popular. Cookbooks published by societies, lodges, churches, and similar organizations offer insight into regional food preferences and contain many recipes not found in other sources. Very early examples are unusually practical, often stressing religious observances and sometimes offering medical advise. Recipes were simple combinations of basic elements. Cookbooks and cooking guides of World Wars I and II stressed conservation of food. In sharp contrast are the more modern cookbooks often authored by doctors, dietitians, cooks, and domestic scientists, calling for more diversified materials and innovative combinations with exotic seasonings. Food manufacturers' cookbooks abound. By comparing early cookbooks to more recent publications, the fascinating evolution in cookery and food preparation is readily apparent.

Because this field is so large and varied, we recommend that you choose the field you find most interesting to you and specialize. Will you collect hardbound or softcover? Some collectors zero in on one particular food company's literature — for instance, Gold Medal Flour and Betty Crocker, the Pillsbury Flour Company's Pillsbury Bake-Offs, and Jell-O. Others look for more general publications on chocolate, spices and extracts, baking powers, or favored appliances. Fund-raising, regional, and political cookbooks are other types to consider.

Our advisor, Col. Bob Allen, has written *A Guide to Collecting Cookbooks* (Collector Books), a compilation of four large collections resulting in a much broader overview than is generally possible in a book of this type. It contains more than 300 color illustrations and in excess of 5,000 titles with current values. Also available is *Price Guide to Cookbooks and Recipe Leaflets* by Linda J. Dickinson.

Our suggested values are based on cookbooks in very good condition; remember to adjust prices up or down to evaluate examples in other conditions. For your convenience, our listings are grouped into categories representing various collecting areas.

Advisor: Bob Allen (See Directory, Cookbooks)

Club/Newsletter: *Cookbook Gossip*
Cookbook Collectors Club of America, Inc.
Bob and Jo Ellen Allen
P.O. Box 56
St. James, MO 65559-0056

Newsletter: *The Cookbook Collector's Exchange*
Sue Erwin
P.O. Box 32369
San Jose, CA 95152-2369

Pre-1900: Hardbound

American Cook Book, Mrs FL Gillette, 1887, w/notes about practical housekeeping, 3" thick..........................$125.00
American Heritage Cook Book, 1870..........................$125.00
American Practical Cookery Book, 1859....................$175.00
American Pure Food Cook Book, Sears & Roebuck & Co, 1899 ....$60.00

Boston School Kitchen Text Book, Mrs DA (Mary J) Lincoln, 1887, 237 pages $35.00
Clayton's Quaker Cook-Book, HJ Clayton, San Francisco, 1883, rare..$400.00
Cooking for Beginners, Marion Harland, 1884..........$120.00
Directions for Cooking, Eliza Leslie, 1841 ....$250.00
Family & Householders Guide, 1859, 238 pages $125.00
Family & Immigrants Complete Guide for Hand Book Hints, Recipes & Table Settings, J Marshall, 1849, 1856.$125.00
Family Nurse, Mrs Lydia Child, 1837..........................$325.00
French Dishes for American Tables, Pierre Caron/Mrs Frederic Sherman, New York, 1885, 1887, 231 pages...........$75.00
House Book or Manual of Domestic Economy, Miss Eliza Leslie, Philadelphia, 1840..............................$325.00
Kentucky Home Cook Book, Ladies of Maysville Kentucky, 1899, 387 pages $60.00
Motherly Talks w/Young Housekeepers, Mrs Harriet Beecher Stowe, 1873..$115.00
Mrs Hale's Receipts for the Million - Containing 545 Receipts, Mrs Sarah J Hale, 1851, 800 pages.....................$110.00
New Buckeye Cook Book, Home Publishing Co, 1888, 1,288 pages..$70.00
Peterson's New Cook Book, Hanna Mary Peterson, 1857..$175.00
Receipts, Louise D Speer, 2nd edition, 1898, 208 pages..$55.00
Temperance Cook Book, adapted from White House Cook Book, Saalfield, manilla cover, 1889.....................$75.00

Post-1900: Hardbound

America's Cook Book, Home Institute, New York Herald Tribune, 1938, 1941 ....$25.00
American Women's Cook Book, Ruth Berolzheimer, Consolidated Book Publishers, Chicago, 1938, 1939..$25.00
Amy Vanderbilt Success Casserole Cookery, Charlotte Adams, 1966 ....$15.00
Aromas & Flavors, Alice B Toklas, 1958, 1960...........$17.50
Art of Chinese Cooking, Mimie Ouei, 1960.................$15.00
Art of Good Cooking, Paula Peck, 1966, 368 pages...$12.50
Better Homes & Gardens Junior Cook Book, 1955, 78 pages..$20.00
Betty Furness Westinghouse Cook Book, Julia Kiene, 1st printing, 1954, 496 pages $25.00
Blender Cookbook, Seranne & Gaden, New York, 1961..$10.00
Brides Cook Book, Poppy Cannon, 1954, 1st edition, 400 pages..$17.50
Brunches & Coffee, Marion Courtney, 1969................$15.00
Cake - Art - Craft - Learn How To Decorate, Fred Abuer, Chicago, 1930..$30.00
Chafing-Dish Specialties, Nedda Cason Anders, 1954.$25.00
Complete American Cook Book, Stella Stanard, revised edition, 1957, 512 pages...$20.00
Complete Family Cook Book, Curtin Promotions Inc, NY, 3-ring binder, indexed, 1970, 416 pages.................$10.00
Congressional Club Cook Book, Foreword by Mrs Herbert Hoover, 1927, 1st edition $75.00
Cooking of India, Time-Life recipes, 1969.................$15.00

Cottage Kitchen, Marion Harland, 1907 ....$50.00

Delineator Cook Book, Mildred Maddocks Bently, Director Butterick Publishing, 1934, 1937.........................$30.00

Detroit News Menu Cook Book, Myrtle Calkins, 1933 .$35.00

Easter Idea Book, Charlotte Adams, Lenten dishes, etc, 1954.........................$20.00

Eating & Cooking Around the World - Fingers Before Forks, Erick Berry, Allena Champlin Best, 1963 ....$15.00

Everyday Foods, Harris & Lacy, Houghton Mifflin Co, 1930, 1932, 550 pages $30.00

Farm Journal's Complete Pie Cookbook, 1965, 308 pages..$10.00

Fireside Cook Book, James A Beard, 5th printing, 1949, 322 pages.........................$25.00

Food for Better Living, McDermott, Trilling & Nicholas, 1960.........................$15.00

Francis Parkinson Keyes Cook Book, 1955, 1st edition..$20.00

French Pastry Book, Crippen, 1932.........................$35.00

General Foods Cook Book, 1st edition, 1932, 370 pages...$35.00

Good Housekeeping Cook Book, Dorothy B Marsh, 1955 ....$20.00

Good Housekeeping's Book on Business of Housekeeping, Mildred M Bentley, 1926, 194 pages $35.00

Good Maine Food, Marjorie Mosser, 1939 ....$30.00

Good Neighbor Recipes, Erickson & Rock, 1952........$20.00

Heloise's Kitchen Hints, 3rd printing, 1963, 186 pages..$10.00

Highlander's Cookbook, recipes from Scotland, 1966 ...$10.00

Horizon Cook Book, American Heritage, Cooking From Biblical Times On, 2 volumes, 1968, 760 pages...$25.00

Hot Dog Cookbook, William Kaufman (autographed), 1966.........................$10.00

How America Eats, Clementine Paddleford, 1949, First Edition, 495 pages, $25.00. (Photo courtesy Col. Bob Allen)

How To Cook a Wolf, MFK Fisher, 1944, 261 pages ..$45.00

Ida Bailey Allen's Money-Saving Cook Book, 1st edition, 1940, 481 pages $35.00

Italian Desserts & Antipasto, Ala Mama Mia, Angela Catanzaro, 1958, 314 pages.........................$20.00

James Beard Menus for Entertainment, 1965.............$15.00

La Cucina - The Complete Italian Cook Book, Rose L Sorce, 1953 ....$25.00

Ladies' Home Journal Cook Book, Carol Traux, Doubleday & Co, NY, 1960 ....$20.00

Lily Wallace New American Cook Book, Lily Haxworth Wallace, 1941, 1942, 930 pages $25.00

Mama Mia Italian Cook Book, Angela Catanzaro, Liverright Publishing Corp, 1955, 286 pages $20.00

Margaret Mitchell's Cooking, Aluminum Cooking Utensil Company, 1932 ....$30.00

Marvel Cook Book, Georgette MacMillan, Street & Smith Corp, 1925 ....$35.00

Meals in Minutes, Better Homes & Gardens, 1963, 62 pages........................$12.50

Meta Given's Modern Encyclopedia of Cooking, 1st printing, 1947, 2 volumes, 1,724 pages $40.00

Molly Goldberg Cook Book, Molly Goldberg & Myra Waldo, 1955, 1959 ....$15.00

Mrs Mander's Cook Book, Olga Sarah Manders, 1968..$15.00

Mrs ST Rorer's Ice Creams, Water Ices & Frozen Puddings, 1913 ....$45.00

The New California Cook Book, Genevieve Callahan, 1946, 1955, $27.50. (Photo courtesy Col. Bob Allen)

New Pennsylvania Dutch Cook Book, 1958, 240 pages ..$20.00

Our Candy Recipes, Van Arsdale, 1932.........................$30.00

Outdoorsman's Cook Book, Arthur H Carhart, 1st printing, 1944 ....$25.00

Paula Peck's Art of Good Cooking, 1961....................$15.00

Potluck Party Recipes, Thora H Campbell, 1960.........$15.00

Prudence Penny's Cook Book, Home Economics editor of Los Angeles Examiner Newspaper, 1947, 2nd printing.........................$20.00

Quantity Cookery, Menu Planning & Cooking for Large Numbers, L Richards & N Treat, 1925, 200 pages.$400.00

Red & White International Cook Book, Red & White Corp Grocery Stores, 1930s.........................$35.00

Seven Hundred Sandwiches, Florence A Cowles, 1920, 1930.........................$30.00

Simple French Cookery, Edna Beilenson, Peter Pauper Press, 1958, 60 pages $20.00

Soup Book, Louis De Gouy, Chef of Waldorf-Astoria Hotel, NY, 1949 ....$25.00

Start to Finish, Ann Batchelder, 1954 ....$20.00

Stillmeadow Sampler, Gladys Tabor, 1959.................$25.00

Thousand Ways To Please a Husband w/Bettina's Best Recipes, Louise Bennett Weaver/Helen Cowles LeCron, 1917, 480 pages $74.00

West Coast Cook Book, Helen Evans Brown, 1952 reprint, 437 pages...$12.50

White House Cook Book, JH Ervin, Follet Publishing, 1st printing, Johnson family, 1964...............................$10.00

Woman's Exchange Recipes, Stella V Hough w/Kay Kopera, 1946 ....$25.00

365 Ways To Cook Hamburgers, Doyne Nickerson, Doubleday, 1958, 1960, 189 pages.......................$15.00

60 Minute Chef, Lillian Beuno McCue & Carol Traux, 1947...$17.50

Softcover, usually stapled

A&P News, Ann Page, published weekly, Great Atlantic & Pacific Tea Co, 1929 week of December 2, 4 pages..............$10.00

American Domestic Cook Book for 1867, Dr Herrick & Co, 32 pages...$35.00

Any Bride Can Cook, Maudie Owens, 1965, 1968, 81 pages...$5.00

Approved Recipes for Cooking w/Gas, AB Stoves Inc, Dorothy K Harris, 1936, 64 pages $14.00

Aubt Chick's Pies, Tarts, Ravioli, Cookies, Doughnuts, Nettie McBirney, The Chickadees, Tulsa Oklahoma, 1941, 39 pages...$10.00

Beech-Nut Book of Menus & Recipes, Ida Bailey Allen, 1923, 32 pages $20.00

Better Meals for Less, George E Cornforth, 1930, 128 pages...$14.00

Bond Bread - Name Your Favorite Recipe Book, 1935 ..$14.00

Bridal Shower Ideas, Roby Chatham, 1st edition, 1956 ..$10.00

Casseroles & Compliments w/Minute Rice, General Foods Corp, 1st printing, 1966 ....$8.00

Chef's Standby - Blue Ribbon Mayonnaise, John Behmann, Chicago, Richard-Hellman's, 1922, 14 pages $20.00

Clementine Paddleford's Cook Young Cookbook, food editor of This Week magazine, 1966, 124 pages.............$10.00

Cookies, Clara Gebhard & Mary Jane Albright, Wheat Flour Institute, Chicago, 1944, 16 pages $12.50

Cooking for Two - w/Menus & Recipes, Katherine Fisher, Director Good Housekeeping Institute, 1936, 12 pages $14.00

Cream Top Book of Tested Recipes, Cream Top Bottle Corp, 1935 ....$15.00

Culinary Arts Institute, 300 Ways To Serve Eggs #10, 1940, 1949, 1950, 1951, 1952, 48 pages $2.00

Del Monte Peaches — 11 Food Experts Tell Us How To Serve Them, CA Packing Corp, San Francisco, 1927, 16 pages...$20.00

Dr King's Guide to Health Cook Book, 1910.............$25.00

Dr Miles Cook Book, Cure All Co, 1910.....................$20.00

Duncan Hines Adventures in Good Cooking & the Art of Carving in the Home, 1960 ....$8.00

Edgewater Beach Hotel Salad Book, Mary Margaret McBride, 1959...$8.00

Enterprising Housekeeper, Helen Louise Johnson, Enterprise Mfg of PA, 1906, 90 pages+index.........................$20.00

Exciting World of Rice Dishes, General Foods Kitchen, General Foods Corp, 1959, 20 pages $10.00

Favorite Recipes in Country Kitchens, General Foods Corp, 1945 ....$12.50

Festive Manna, Mariam Field, Standard Brands Inc, 1966..$8.00

Fifty Two Sunday Dinners, Woman's World Magazine Co Inc, 1924 ....$20.00

Food & Fun, Here's a Book the Whole Family Will Enjoy, Arthur Godfrey, Star-Kist Tuna, 1953, 30 pages ...$15.00

Good Housekeeping Book of Cookies No 2, 1958, 68 pages..$8.00

Gorton's Sea Products, Gorton-Pew Fisheries Co, 1909..$25.00

Grandma's Old Fashioned Molasses, Duffy-Mott Company, 1946 ....$12.50

**Healthy Cookery, by Mary Dunbar,
Jewel Tea Co, 1926, $38.00.**

How To Get the Most Out of Your Mixmaster, Sunbeam Corp, 1936-37..$12.50

International Vegetarian Cookery, Sonya Richmond, 1965, 192 pages...$3.00

Little Book of Suggestions for the Careful Housekeeper, Woman's Club of Albany, New York, 1900s.........$20.00

Magnolias & Ambrosia - Creole Recipes, Dorothy V Doughty, 1967...$8.00

Margaret Mitchell's Meal Time Magic Desserts, Wear Ever Aluminum, 1951...$15.00

Money Saving Main Dishes, Human Nutrition Research Branch, Agricultural Research Service, 1955, 48 pages..$8.00

Oven Dinners - Menus & Recipes, Kroger, Jean Allen, 8 pages...$12.50

Peanut's Cook Book, Recipes by June Dutton, 1970, 64 pages $6.00

Sara & Aggies Household Handy Book, 1938, 31 pages ..$14.00

Sunset's Kitchen Cabinet Cook Book, 5th printing, 1938....$8.00

Today's Woman Book of Salads, Mrs Hyla Nelson O'Connor, 1953, 144 pages...$8.00

What's Cooking?, Mytinger & Casseberry Inc, 1st printing, 1952, 22 pages...$8.00

Charity, Fund-Raising, and Regional

Argo Presbyterian Cook Book, ladies' community project, Sullivan MO, spiral bound, 1959, 93 pages **$8.00**

Book Fare, by Book Fair, Greater St Louis Book Fair, book of recipes, 1967, softcover, 232 pages **$6.00**

Book Fare, Greater St Louis Book Fair, 1st edition, 1967, 232 pages..**$6.00**

Christian Home Cook Book, Church of God in Christ, Mennonite recipes, hardcover, 1966, 400 pages.....**$6.00**

Frost's Catskill Mountain Smoked Turkey, Kingston, NY, 1946, 24-page booklet **$8.00**

Helpful Hints, Jubilee Circle of First Methodist Church, 1931...**$12.00**

Household Guide w/Recipes, Arra Stutten Mixter, Hartford Gas Co, CT, 1935 ....**$12.00**

Radio

KTTR Presents My Favorite Recipes, Rolla MO, 1971, 132 pages..**$6.00**

KTTR Problems & Solutions Cook Book No 2, Rolla MO, 1970, 42 pages..**$6.00**

Your Neighbor Lady Book, WNAX 470 on Your Dial, Yankton-Sioux City, 1956, 72 pages **$10.00**

8 Years w/Your Neighbor Lady, Yankton-Sioux City, WNAX 570 on Your Dial, 1949, 72 pages **$12.50**

Food Company Advertising Recipe Books

Arm & Hammer Book of Valuable Recipes, 6th edition, 1915, 32 pages **$20.00**

Best Loved Foods of Christmas, Ann Pillsbury, 1958, 65 recipes, 65 pages **$10.00**

Betty Crocker's Dinner in a Dish Cookbook, 1965, 1st edition, 1st printing, hardcover spiral, 152 pages **$10.00**

Betty Crocker's Party Book, 1st edition, 1st printing, hardcover, spiral, 1960, 176 pages................................**$10.00**

Blue Bonnet Margarine Book of Creative Cooking, 1970, 30 pages..**$3.00**

Brer Rabbit Book of Molasses Magic, 1956, 24 pages ..**$10.00**

Calumet Book of Triumphs Form 516, 1934, 32 pages..**$12.00**

Carefree Cooking, Pet Milk Co, 1960, softcover, 16 pages **$6.00**

Ceresota Cook Book, Northwestern Consolidated Milling Company, Minneapolis MN, 1880s, 42 pages **$35.00**

Chiquita Banana's Cook Book, 1947, 24 pages...........**$12.50**

Clabber Girl Baking Book, 1937-38, 15 pages **$16.00**

Complete Jell-O Recipe Book, 1929, 48 pages...........**$15.00**

Corn Products Cook Book, Emma Church Hewitt, 1915, 40 pages..**$20.00**

Cream of Rice - World's Best Food, ca 1890, 27 pages ..**$30.00**

Crisco for Frying, For Shortening, for Cake Mixing, softcover, 1912, 32 pages **$20.00**

Delicious Nourishing Dishes for Breakfast, Luncheon & Dinner, Nabisco Shredded Wheat, Nabisco Co, 1950, softcover **$8.00**

Famous Recipes for Baker's Chocolate & Breakfast Cocoa, M Parloa, JM Hill, Fannie Farmer, AL Andrea, 1928, 64 pages..**$20.00**

Famous Recipes From New Orleans Collected for You by the Makers of Godchaux's Sugars - Look for the Blue Band, 1955 ....**$10.00**

Favorite Recipes From the KC Baking Powder Cook's Book, 1933..**$6.00**

Fleischmann's Recipes for Baking Raised Breads, 1917, 47 pages..**$20.00**

Golden Rule Cook Book, Mrs Ida Cogswell Baily Allen, 1918 ....**$25.00**

Hershey Recipe Book, Caroline B King, Hershey Chocolate Corp, 1930, 80 pages..**$16.00**

Horsford Almanac & Cook Book, 1883, 48 pages **$40.00**

Housewife's Year Book of Health & Homemaking, Kellogg Co, 1937, softcover, 36 pages **$12.00**

How To Can Finer Fruits & Save Sugar, Corn Products Refining Company, 1945, 32 pages **$10.00**

How To Make Your Cooking Different - Kitchen Bouquet, ca 1910, 6 pages **$20.00**

Jack & Mary's Jell-O Recipe Book, Jack Benny and Mary Livingston, 1937, first printing, 23 pages, $50.00. (Photo courtesy Col. Bob Allen)

Jell-O The Dainty Dessert, Nellie Duling Gans, 1908, 10 pages..**$75.00**

Kentucky Fried Chicken, late 1950s-early 1960s, 20 recipes, 24 pages, 5½x3½", NM **$25.00**

Knox Gelatine, Desserts, Salads, Candies & Frozen Dishes, 1941, softcover, 55 pages **$10.00**

Magic Eagle Brand Magic Discoveries for Quicker, Easier Cooking, softcover, 1935 ....**$12.00**

Mary Blake's Favorite Recipes, Carnation Co, 1954, softcover, 16 pages **$8.00**

New Cake Secrets, Francis Lee Barton, Swans Down, Igleheart Brothers Inc, 1931 ....**$15.00**

New Dr Price Cook Book for Use w/Dr Price's Baking Powder, 1921, softcover, 50 pages **$14.00**

New Fashioned Old Fashioned Recipes, Martha Lee Anderson, Arm & Hammer Baking Soda, 1952, softcover, 15 pages..**$6.00**

Old Favorite Honey Recipes, American Honey Institute, 1945, 52 pages **$12.50**

Pillsbury Cook Book, Mrs Nellie Duling Gans, 1911, 125 pages...**$25.00**

Pillsbury's Grand National Recipe & Baking Contest – 100 Prize-Winning Recipes, 1950, softcover, 96 pages, Bake-Off #1...**$75.00**

Rawleigh's Almanac Good Health Guide Cook Book, 1920...**$18.00**

Royal Baker & Pastry Cook, 1911, 46 pages **$20.00**

Rumford Complete Cook Book, Rumford Baking Powder, 1908, 1st edition, hardbound, 241 pages **$40.00**

Snowdrift Secrets, Sarah Tyson Rorer, 1913.................**$20.00**

Velvet Blend Cook Book - Milk Rich Carnation Recipes, Mary Blake, Home Service Dept, 1940s **$10.00**

Watkins' Almanac Home Doctor & Cook Book, 1907, 96 pages...**$25.00**

10 Cakes Husbands Like Best From Spry's Recipe Round-Up, Lever Bros, 1952, softcover **$5.00**

Recipe Leaflets

Dainty Dishes Made by Knox Gelatin, package inserts, cow's head, 1910, 2½x3¼", ea **$3.50**

Menus & Recipes, Kroger Food Foundation, 10-page fold-out, ca 1930...**$15.00**

Pastry Set, Recipes by Marjorie Noble Osborn, Author of Jolly Times Cook Book, Manufactured by Transogram Co, NY, 1948...**$3.00**

Protein Value of Plain Unflavored Gelatin, Knox package insert, 4-page folder, 1946.....................................**$3.50**

Red Magic Recipes, How To Cook With Heinz Ketchup, magazine recipe insert, ca 1960, 50¢. (Photo courtesy Col. Bob Allen)

Use Honey for Canning & Preserving, American Honey Institute, 8-page fold-out, 1945 ....**$2.00**

Cookie Cutters

In recent years, cookie cutters have come into their own as worthy kitchen collectibles. Prices on many have risen astronomically, but a practiced eye can still sort out a good bargain. Advertising cutters and product premiums, especially in plastic, can still be found without too much effort. Aluminum cutters with painted wood handles are usually worth several dollars each, if in good condition. Red and green are the usual handle colors, but other colors are more highly prized by many. Hallmark plastic cookie cutters, especially those with painted backs, are always worth considering, if in good condition.

Be wary of modern tin cutters being sold for antique. Many present-day tinsmiths chemically antique their cutters, especially if done in a primitive style. These are often sold by others as 'very old.' Look closely because most tinsmiths today sign and date these cutters.

Molds, instead of cutting the cookie out, impressed a design into the dough. To learn more about both types (and many other old kitchenware gadgets as well), we recommend *300 Years of Kitchen Collectibles* by Linda Campbell Franklin and *Kitchen Antiques, 1790 to 1940*, by Kathryn McNerney. Also read *The Cookie Shaper's Bible* by Phyllis Wetherill and our advisor, Rosemary Henry.

Advisor: Rosemary Henry (See Directory, Cookie Cutters)

Newsletter: *Cookies*
Rosemary Henry
9610 Greenview Ln.
Manassas, VA 20109-3320; Subscription: $12.00 per year for 6 issues

Newsletter: *Cookie Crumbs*
Cookie Cutter Collectors Club
Ruth Capper
1167 Teal Rd. SW
Dellroy, OH 44620; 216-735-2839 or 202-966-0869

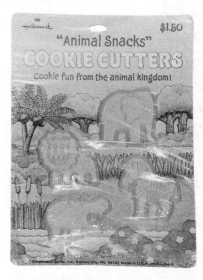

Animal Snacks Cookie Cutters, soft gold-colored plastic, Hallmark, 1978, mini, set of four, MIP, $15.00. (Photo courtesy Rosemary Henry)

Bugs Bunny, red plastic, 6½" **$10.00**

Camel, tin w/red-painted wood handle, ca 1940, 3½x3"..**$12.50**

Dekalb winged ear of corn, tin, w/recipe attached, 4¾" .**$10.00**
Elephant, tin w/green-painted wooden knob, 3x3½".**$22.50**
Flower, tin, marked Kreamer **$30.00**
Flower Garden set, 8 floral cutters, Aunt Chick, ea 2½" dia, MIB **$22.50**

Friar Tuck, orange plastic, Robin Hood Flour, 4", $6.50.

Happy Days, w/bunny, clown, jack-o'-lantern & snowman, red plastic, Aunt Chick's, set of 6, MIB w/instructions & recipes **$16.50**
Heart, tin, round metal handle, 6½" **$24.00**
Heart, tin w/green-painted wood handle, 3¼" **$12.50**
Kitten, tin, flat back, 4"..**$55.00**
Leaf, tin, handles, 4x2" **$45.00**
Looney Toons, Sylvester, Tweety, Elmer Fudd, Porky Pig & Yosemite Sam, red plastic, Wilton, 1978, set of 8, MIP **$14.00**
Mickey Mouse, tin, flat back, ca 1950s, 4½x2¾" **$35.00**
Minnie Mouse, tin, w/handle, 4x3" **$25.00**

Peanuts, Charlie Brown, Snoopy, Linus, and Lucy, colored plastic, Hallmark, 3½" to 4½", set of four, MIP, $50.00.

Pink Panther, pink plastic, Hallmark, 1970s **$14.50**
Prince Charming, red plastic, unmarked, ca 1961, 4¼" ..**$8.50**
Rabbit, tin, flat back, 2 finger holes, 6x6"....................**$40.00**
Rabbit, tin, marked Formay, 6⅛", from $30 to............**$40.00**
Raggedy Ann & Raggedy Andy, red & blue plastic, Hallmark, 1960s, MIP **$18.00**
Robin Hood, Robin Hood Flour, plastic, set of 5, NM..**$32.00**

Rocking horse, painted red, white & green, Hallmark, 1981, 4x3"..**$12.00**
Rooster, Brown Bag Art, brown clay, 1988, 6½x5".....**$20.00**
Rooster, tin, flat back, finger hole, 4x4"....................**$25.00**
Santa w/tree, tin, back stamped 3070 3/2, light rust, 10".**$25.00**
Scottie dog, tin w/green-painted wood handle, 2½x2¾" ..**$18.00**
Shamrock, tin, 5"..**$20.00**
Shaper, butterfly, hard plastic, Hallmark, 1986-87........**$6.50**
Shaper, Christmas tree, green, soft plastic, Hallmark, 1981 & 1984-85..**$3.00**
Shaper, dinosaur, yellow, Hallmark, 1987....................**$5.00**
Shaper, gingerbread boy, brown, Hallmark, 1992........**$4.50**
Shaper, graduation cap, Royal Blue, Hallmark, 1997..**$10.00**
Shaper, hippopotamus, lavender, Hallmark, 1988........**$5.00**
Shaper, Indian girl, gold tab, Hallmark, 1990-91..........**$5.00**
Shaper, pumpkin, orange, soft plastic, Hallmark, 1985-87 ..**$3.50**
Shaper, rocking horse, green, Hallmark, 1986-87........**$5.00**
Shaper, snowman, white, soft plastic, Hallmark, 1984-87, 4½"..**$3.50**
Shaper, tulip w/leaves, hard plastic, Hallmark, 1986-87 .**$6.50**
Snoopy, red plastic, round handle, Hallmark..............**$15.00**
Star, tin, 5 points, marked Kreamer, 3¼" **$17.50**
Tinkerbell, thin metal strip, no back, Disneyland, 8x3" .**$18.00**
Tom & Jerry set, w/Droopy, Tuffy, Barney Bear & Lucky Duck, red plastic, C 1956 Loew's Inc, NMIB........**$20.00**
Troll, tin, 3x2¼x1", M..**$17.50**
Zany Zoo set, plastic, 8 animals in clear plastic container w/yellow lid marked Cookies, Wilton **$12.50**

Cookie Jars

This is an area that for years saw an explosion of interest that resulted in some very high prices. Though the market has leveled off to a large extent, rare cookie jars sell for literally thousands of dollars. Even a common jar from a good manufacturer will fall into the $40.00 to $100.00 price range. At the top of the list are the Black-theme jars, then come the cartoon characters such as Popeye, Howdy Doody, or the Flintstones — in fact, any kind of a figural jar from an American pottery is collectible.

The American Bisque company was one of the largest producers of these jars from 1930 until the 1970s. Many of their jars have no marks at all; those that do are simply marked 'USA,' sometimes with a mold number. But their airbrushed colors are easy to spot, and collectors look for the molded-in wedge-shaped pads on their bases — these say 'American Bisque' to cookie jar buffs about as clearly as if they were marked.

The Brush Pottery (Ohio, 1946 – 71) made cookie jars that were decorated with the airbrush in many of the same colors used by American Bisque. These jars are strongly holding their values, and the rare ones continue to climb in price. McCoy was probably the leader in cookie-jar production. Even some of their very late jars bring high prices. Abingdon, Shawnee, and Red Wing all manufactured cookie jars, and there are a lot of wonderful jars by many other companies.

Joyce and Fred Roerig's books *The Collector's Encyclopedia of Cookie Jars, Vols. I, II,* and *III,* cover them all beautifully, and you won't want to miss Ermagene Westfall's *An Illustrated Value Guide to Cookie Jars Books I* and *II,* another wonderful reference. All are published by Collector Books.

Warning! The marketplace abounds with reproductions these days. Roger Jensen of Rockwood, Tennessee, is making a line of cookie jars as well as planters, salt and pepper shakers, and many other items which for years he marked McCoy. Because the 'real' McCoys never registered their trademark, he was able to receive federal approval to begin using this mark in 1992. Though he added '#93' to some of his pieces, the vast majority of his wares are undated. He used old molds, and novice collectors are being fooled into buying the new for 'old' prices. Here are some of his reproductions that you should be aware of: McCoy Mammy, Mammy With Cauliflower, Clown Bust, Dalmatians, Indian Head, Touring Car, and Rocking Horse; Hull Little Red Riding Hood; Pearl China Mammy; and the Mosaic Tile Mammy. Within the past couple of years, though, one of the last owners of the McCoy Pottery Company was able to make a successful appeal to end what they regarded as the fradulent use of their mark (it seems that they at last had it registered), so some of the later Jensen reproductions have been marked 'Brush-McCoy' (though this mark was never used on an authentic cookie jar) and 'B.J. Hull.' Besides these forgeries, several Brush jars have been reproduced as well (see Roerig's books for more information), and there are others. Some reproductions are being made in Taiwan and China, however there are also jars being reproduced here in the states.

Cookie jars from California are getting their fair share of attention right now, and then some! We've included several from companies such as Brayton Laguna, Treasure Craft, Vallona Starr, and Twin Winton. Westfield's and Roerig's books have information on all of these. Advisor Mike Ellis is the author of *Collector's Guide to Don Winton Designs* (Collector Books); and another of our advisors, Bernice Stamper, has written *Vallona Starr Ceramics,* which we're sure you will enjoy.

Advisors: April Tvorak, Enesco (see Directory, Figural Ceramics); Pat and Ann Duncan, Holt Howard (See Directory, Holt Howard); Rick Spencer, Shawnee (See Directory, Shawnee); Mike Ellis, Twin Winton (See Directory, Twin Winton); Bernice Stamper, Vallona Star (See Directory, Vallona Star); Lois Wildman, Vandor (See Directory, Vandor).

Newsletter: *Cookie Jarrin' With Joyce*
R.R. 2, Box 504
Walterboro, SC 29488

A Little Company, Diva, from $100 to $150.00
A Little Company, Earth Goddess $150.00
A Little Company, Edmund on Vacation (Black man), from $130 to...$150.00
A Little Company, Gospel Singer, from $135 to........$150.00

A Little Company, Pig, 1992, sm, med, or lg, ea, minimum value $110.00
A Little Company, Stella, from $165 to $180.00
Abingdon, Baby, Black, #561 ....$300.00
Abingdon, Choo Choo (Locomotive), #651 ....$150.00
Abingdon, Daisy Jar, marked Abingdon USA #677 .....$50.00
Abingdon, Fat Boy, marked Abingdon USA #495, 1941 .$250.00

Abingdon, Hippo, extensive decor, from $300.00 to $325.00. (Photo courtesy Fred and Joyce Roerig)

Abingdon, Hobby Horse, #602 ....$185.00
Abingdon, Humpty Dumpty, decorated, #663 ....$250.00
Abingdon, Jack-in-the Box, marked Abingdon USA #611, 1947 ....$275.00
Abingdon, Little Girl Cooky Jar, marked Abingdon USA #693, from $60 to...$75.00
Abingdon, Little Miss Muffet, marked Abingdon USA #622, 1949 ....$205.00
Abingdon, Little Old Lady, all white, marked Abingdon USA #471, from $175 to...$200.00
Abingdon, Little Old Lady, plaid apron, marked Abingdon USA #471, from $300 to $325.00
Abingdon, Money Bag, marked Abingdon USA #588, 1947..$75.00
Abingdon, Mother Goose, marked Abingdon USA #695 .....$295.00
Abingdon, Pineapple, marked Abingdon USA #664, 1949 ....$95.00
Abingdon, Wigwam, marked Abingdon USA #665, 1949 ..$250.00
Abingdon, Windmill, marked Abingdon USA #678, 1949, from $200 to...$225.00
Advertising, Aramis Bear, from $65 to $85.00
Advertising, Avon Bear, sponged or spattered pattern, from $50 to $65.00
Advertising, Barnum's Animal Crackers, Nabisco, carousel, from $30 to $60.00
Advertising, Betty Crocker, red spoon logo & stripes on white jar $90.00
Advertising, Blue Bonnet Sue, Benjamin & Medwin, 1989 Nabisco, from $60 to $80.00
Advertising, Chips Ahoy! Jar, blue lettering w/red trim on white, unmarked, from $45 to $55.00
Advertising, Eddie Bauer Bear, from $70 to $90.00
Advertising, Elsie the Cow, Pottery Guild, from $350 to ..$425.00

Advertising, Katy the Korn Top Pig, Bartlow Bros Inc Korn Top, Haeger USA.................................$110.00

Advertising, Keebler Sandies Jar, red & white graphics w/elf on white $80.00

Advertising, MooTown Snackers, no mark, from $175.00 to $200.00. (Photo courtesy Fred and Joyce Roerig)

Advertising, Oreo Cookie, Think Big, from $40 to $45.00

Advertising, Oreo Panda Bear, Nabisco, from $30 to .$60.00

Advertising, Pillsbury Doughboy Funfetti, Benjamin & Medwin, from $55 to.................................$65.00

Advertising, Proctor & Gamble USA World Soccer Ball, from $45 to...$55.00

Advertising, Quaker Oats, Regal, from $100 to........$125.00

Advertising, Snausages, talking dog, plastic, from $45 to...$65.00

Advertising, Sprout (Green Giant), 1990-1992.............$65.00

Advertising, Tony the Tiger, head figure, plastic, from $100 to..$125.00

American Bisque, Beehive, from $40 to $50.00

American Bisque, Boy Pig, airbrushed, unmarked $90.00

American Bisque, Carousel, from $100 to $125.00

American Bisque, Chef, standing, star on base, from $100 to..$135.00

American Bisque, Churn, #CJ-756 ....$25.00

American Bisque, Davy Crockett (against forest), marked USA...$750.00

American Bisque, Elephant, baby w/bib, from $150 to..$200.00

American Bisque, French Poodle, #CJ751, from $100 to..$125.00

American Bisque, Girl, w/blackboard, from $325 to ..$355.00

American Bisque, Jack-in-the Box, #CJ-753, from $125 to $135.00

American Bisque, Lamb, in overalls w/suspenders, from $60 to..$90.00

American Bisque, Magic Bunny, rabbit in hat, from $100 to $125.00

American Bisque, Owl, Collegiate, gold trim, from $125 to $135.00

American Bisque, Pennsylvania Dutch Girl or Boy, ea from $350 to...$385.00

American Bisque, Recipe Jar, #CJ-563.......................$110.00

American Bisque, Rooster, several variations, ea $60.00

American Bisque, Sadiron, from $100 to $125.00

American Bisque, Tortoise & Hare, w/flasher, from $525 to $625.00

American Bisque, Treasure Chest, #CJ-562............$200.00

American Bisque/Disney, Babes in Toyland, soldier standing guard at gate..$375.00

American Bisque/Hanna-Barbera, Yogi Bear............$475.00

Brayton Laguna, Grandma With Wedding Band, from $500.00 to $600.00.
(Photo courtesy Fred and Joyce Roerig)

Brayton Laguna, Mammy, yellow w/white apron, minimum value $900.00

Brayton Laguna, Matilda, from $435 to.....................$550.00

Brayton Laguna, Swedish Maiden, from $475 to......$535.00

Brush, Antique Touring Car.......................................$700.00

Brush, Boy w/Balloons $800.00

Brush, Cinderella Pumpkin, #W32, from $200 to......$275.00

Brush, Circus Horse, gr (+).......................................$950.00

Brush, Clown, yellow pants..$250.00

Brush, Cookie House, #W31......................................$125.00

Brush, Covered Wagon, dog finial, #W30, minimum value...$550.00

Brush, Cow w/Cat on Back, brown, #W10 (+)........$125.00

Brush, Davy Crockett, no gold, marked USA (+)......$300.00

Brush, Dog & Basket...$250.00

Brush, Donkey w/Cart, gray, ears down, #W33 ....$400.00

Brush, Elephant w/Ice Cream Cone (+) $500.00

Brush, Fish, #W52 (+) $500.00

Brush, Formal Pig, green hat & coat, no gold (+)....$300.00

Brush, Gas Lamp, #K1..$75.00

Brush, Granny, plain skirt, minimum value $400.00

Brush, Happy Bunny, white, #W25............................$225.00

Brush, Hen on Basket, unmarked..............................$125.00

Brush, Hillbilly Frog, minimum value (+) $4,500.00

Brush, Hillbilly Frog, reissue (may or may not be marked Reissue by JD)..$150.00

Brush, Hippo w/Monkey on Back, #W27, from $750 to...$850.00

Brush, Humpty Dumpty, w/beany & bow tie (+).....$275.00

Brush, Little Angel (+)...$800.00

Brush, Little Boy Blue, no gold, #K24 Brush USA, lg (+) **$800.00**

Brush, Little Girl, #017 (+) **$550.00**

Brush, Little Red Riding Hood, gold trim, marked, lg, minimum value (+) **$850.00**

Brush, Little Red Riding Hood, no gold, #K24 USA, sm ..**$550.00**

Brush, Nite Owl, 10½", from $100.00 to $125.00.
(Photo courtesy Fred and Joyce Roerig)

Brush, Old Clock, #W10 (+) **$165.00**

Brush, Old Shoe, #W23 ....**$125.00**

Brush, Peter, Peter Pumpkin Eater, #W24 (+) **$300.00**

Brush, Peter Pan, gold trim, lg **$800.00**

Brush, Peter Pan, no gold, sm **$550.00**

Brush, Puppy Police (+) **$585.00**

Brush, Sitting Pig, #W37 (+), from $400 to **$450.00**

Brush, Smiling Bear, #W46 (+) **$350.00**

Brush, Squirrel on Log, #W26 (+) **$100.00**

Brush, Squirrel w/Top Hat, green coat (+) **$250.00**

Brush, Stylized Owl **$350.00**

Brush, Stylized Siamese, #W41, from $400 to **$500.00**

Brush, Teddy Bear, feet together **$200.00**

Brush, Treasure Chest, #W28 ....**$150.00**

California Originals, Baseball Boy, marked 875 USA on lid & base, from $35 to **$45.00**

California Originals, Bear w/Beehive on Stump, from $35 to **$45.00**

California Originals, Bulldog on top of Cookie Safe, from $85 to **$100.00**

California Originals, Christmas Tree, from $450 to ...**$525.00**

California Originals, Clown on Elephant, #896 ....**$45.00**

California Originals, Elf Schoolhouse, from $60 to **$75.00**

California Originals, Frog w/Bow Tie, #2645 ....**$45.00**

California Originals, Frosty the Snowman, from $250 to..**$300.00**

California Originals, Hippo, from $25 to **$50.00**

California Originals, Keystone Cop (Bobbie), from $100 to **$125.00**

California Originals, Man in Barrel, from $135 to **$165.00**

California Originals, Mushrooms on Stump, from $15 to..**$25.00**

California Originals, Owl Sitting on Stump, from $50 to...**$60.00**

California Originals, Pelican, from $35 to **$65.00**

California Originals, Rabbit on Cookie Safe, from $65 to...**$85.00**

California Originals, Raggedy Ann or Raggedy Andy, ea from $100 to **$125.00**

California Originals, Rooster, from $35 to **$45.00**

California Originals, Sheriff on Cookie Safe, from $30 to **$50.00**

California Originals, Squirrel on Stump, from $50 to **$75.00**

California Originals, Train Engine, from $40 to **$60.00**

California Originals, Victrola, from $150 to **$250.00**

California Originals, Woody Woodpecker, antique finish, from $725 to **$865.00**

California Originals, Yellow Taxi **$175.00**

California Originals/DC Comics, Superman, brown, from $375 to **$425.00**

California Originals/DC Comics, Superman in Phone Booth, marked USA 846, 1978 ....**$600.00**

California Originals/DC Comics, Wonder Woman Cookie Bank, USA 847, 1878, 14" **$1,100.00**

California Originals/Disney, Donald Duck Leaning on Pumpkin, sepia wash on white, marked Walt Disney Productions 805 ....**$325.00**

California Originals/Disney, Ferdinand the Bull, from $100 to **$125.00**

California Originals/Disney, Tigger, #902 ....**$275.00**

California Originals/Disney, Winnie the Pooh, #900...**$200.00**

California Originals/Muppets Inc, Big Bird Chef, from $65 to **$85.00**

California Originals/Muppets Inc, Ernie & Bert Fine Cookies, #977, scarce **$425.00**

California Originals/Muppets Inc, Oscar the Grouch, #970 ....**$90.00**

Cardinal, Cookie Kate, #301 ....**$125.00**

Cardinal, Cookie Safe, from $50 to **$75.00**

Cardinal, French Chef Head, from $100 to **$125.00**

Cardinal, Little Girl, from $100 to **$125.00**

Cardinal, Pig Head, from $75 to **$100.00**

Cardinal, Sad Clown, from $100.00 to $125.00; Professor, from $100.00 to $125.00. (Photo courtesy Ermagene Westfield)

Cardinal, Smart Cookie Head, from $110 to **$135.00**

Certified International, Barney Rubble **$55.00**

Certified International, Buddy Bear, from $20 to **$25.00**

Certified International, Bugs Bunny Christmas, holding candy cane, from $85 to **$115.00**

Certified International, Chevy Corvette, from $50 to ..**$60.00**

Certified International, Dog on Jukebox, from $35 to ..**$40.00**

Certified International, Foghorn Leghorn, from $50 to..**$60.00**

Certified International, Fred Flintstone.........................**$55.00**

Certified International, Geranium, from $25 to **$35.00**

Certified International, Happy Hatters Funny Bunny, from $20 to **$25.00**

Certified International, Marvin the Martian, from $55 to..**$75.00**

Certified International, Raggedy Ann or Andy, ea from $50 to **$60.00**

Certified International, Tasmanian Devil w/NFL Team colors, from $35 to..**$50.00**

Certified International, Tweety Bird **$50.00**

Certified International, Yosemite Sam, from $35 to **$45.00**

Clay Art, Black Jazz Player, 1995...............................**$35.00**

Clay Art, Bloomin' Cat, from $50 to **$60.00**

Clay Art, Catfish, 8", 1989, from $35.00 to $45.00. (Photo courtesy Lee Garmon)

Clay Art, Cookie Patrol (policeman), from $30 to.......**$35.00**

Clay Art, Cow in the Corn, from $40 to......................**$50.00**

Clay Art, Dog Bone, 1991, from $35 to **$45.00**

Clay Art, Humpty Dumpty, 1991, from $100 to **$125.00**

Clay Art, James Dean, from $40 to.............................**$50.00**

Clay Art, Midnight Snack (fat couple hugging), from $50 to **$60.00**

Clay Art, Ragtime Piano Player (Black man) **$50.00**

Clay Art, Toaster, from $40 to....................................**$50.00**

Clay Art, Wizard of Oz, 1990, from $125 to **$150.00**

Cleminson, Cookstove...**$175.00**

Cleminson, Pig...**$275.00**

Cleminson, Potbellied Stove, 9".................................**$225.00**

Danawares/Disney, Donald Duck Jar, w/hat finial, multicolor on white **$125.00**

Danawares/Disney, Winnie the Pooh Treehouse........**$95.00**

DeForest of California, Birdhouse, snow-capped, from $100 to **$125.00**

DeForest of California, Chipmunk Holding Acorn, from $135 to..**$150.00**

DeForest of California, Clown, from $110 to **$145.00**

DeForest of California, Cocky (Dandee Rooster), from $350 to..**$400.00**

DeForest of California, Dachshund, from $135 to **$175.00**

DeForest of California, Elephant, from $45 to............**$55.00**

DeForest of California, Girl w/Ponytail, from $1,000 to ..**$1,100.00**

DeForest of California, Henny (Dandee Hen), from $200 to..**$225.00**

DeForest of California, Monkey w/Sailor Cap, from $150 to..**$165.00**

DeForest of California, Nun, from $285 to **$350.00**

DeForest of California, Owl, #5537.............................**$35.00**

DeForest of California, Pig Head, from $50 to...........**$55.00**

DeForest of California, Poodle, 1960 ....**$50.00**

DeForest of California, Puppy, #5515 ....**$55.00**

DeForest of California, Snappy Gingerbread Boy.....**$225.00**

Department 56, Beehive...**$35.00**

Department 56, Cantaloupe, from $65 to **$80.00**

Department 56, Fishing Creel Basket...........................**$65.00**

Department 56, McNutt's Chicken Coupe Car, from $125 to..**$150.00**

Department 56, Short Order Toaster **$60.00**

Department 56, Ugly Step Sisters, from $55 to...........**$85.00**

Department 56, Vegetable House, paper label, 1990, from $60.00 to $75.00. (Photo courtesy Fred and Joyce Roerig)

Department 56, Witch, from $150 to.........................**$200.00**

Disney China, Pocahontas & John Smith, PVC, from $10 to..**$12.00**

Doranne of California, Basket of Tomatoes, from $45 to..**$50.00**

Doranne of California, Butter Churn, from $35 to **$40.00**

Doranne of California, Catsup Bottle, #CJ-68 ....**$40.00**

Doranne of California, Cow on Moon, #J-2, from $375 to ..**$400.00**

Doranne of California, Deer, from $100 to................**$125.00**

Doranne of California, Doctor, #CJ-130, from $200 to..**$225.00**

Doranne of California, Dog w/Bow on head, from $60 to **$70.00**

Doranne of California, Dragon (Dinosaur or Puff the Magic Dragon), from $250 to......................................**$350.00**

Doranne of California, Elephant, #144, from $50.00 to $60.00. (Photo courtesy Fred and Joyce Roerig)

Doranne of California, Eggplant, from $60 to $70.00
Doranne of California, Fire Hydrant, from $25 to.......$50.00
Doranne of California, Garbage Can, from $20 to......$30.00
Doranne of California, Hen, #CJ 100 ....$45.00
Doranne of California, Ice Cream Cone, from $30 to.$40.00
Doranne of California, Ice Cream Soda, from $40 to .$45.00
Doranne of California, Jeep, from $125 to $150.00
Doranne of California, Lunch Box, from $50 to..........$60.00
Doranne of California, Mailbox, from $50 to $60.00
Doranne of California, Monkey in Barrel, from $100 to...$125.00
Doranne of California, Mother Goose, marked USA, from $150 to...$175.00
Doranne of California, Owl Winking, from $35 to $65.00
Doranne of California, Peanut, #CJ 18 ....$35.00
Doranne of California, Rabbit in Hat, from $65 to $85.00
Doranne of California, Rocking Horse, from $165 to ..$200.00
Doranne of California, School Bus, #CJ-120, from $125 to $150.00
Doranne of California, Turtle, from $35 to $45.00
Doranne of California, Walrus, from $60 to................$75.00
Enesco, Bear Pull Toy, 1996 ....$60.00
Enesco, Betsy Ross, from $200 to $235.00
Enesco, Clown Head, #E-5835, from $125 to............$150.00
Enesco, Mickey Mouse Cookie Time Clock, from $400 to..$450.00
Enesco, Old Woman in a Shoe, from $40 to $50.00
Enesco, Sweet Pickles Alligator, 1981, from $150 to...$175.00
Enesco, Three Little Pigs, from $40 to $50.00
Fitz & Floyd, Angel's Christmas $65.00
Fitz & Floyd, Bunny Hollow, from $75 to...............$100.00
Fitz & Floyd, Busy Bunnies Tree, from $150 to.......$175.00
Fitz & Floyd, Catarine the Great, from $165 to.........$200.00
Fitz & Floyd, Christmas Wreath Santa, from $150 to .$190.00
Fitz & Floyd, Clown, from $165 to...........................$175.00
Fitz & Floyd, Cookie Factory, c 1987, F&F Japan label, from $115 to...$125.00
Fitz & Floyd, Dinosaur Holding Sack of Cookies, from $75 to...$135.00
Fitz & Floyd, Elephant, from $45 to $55.00
Fitz & Floyd, Father Christmas Sleigh $200.00

Fitz & Floyd, Gooseberry Lane Truck, from $155 to ..$175.00
Fitz & Floyd, Hat Party Bear, from $125 to $145.00
Fitz & Floyd, Heidi Holstein $90.00
Fitz & Floyd, Herb Garden Rabbit............................$90.00
Fitz & Floyd, Holiday Cat...$130.00
Fitz & Floyd, Kangaroo, from $100 to $125.00
Fitz & Floyd, Kittens of Knightsbridge, from $75 to.$100.00
Fitz & Floyd, Kris Kringle Santa & Tree....................$240.00
Fitz & Floyd, Mayfair Bunny Rabbit, from $125 to ...$150.00
Fitz & Floyd, Mother Goose, from $150 to...............$200.00
Fitz & Floyd, Mr Snowman, from $75 to $100.00
Fitz & Floyd, Old World Santa, from $125 to...........$165.00
Fitz & Floyd, Peter the Great, from $65 to $85.00
Fitz & Floyd, Plaid Teddy Christmas Tree, from $125 to..$150.00
Fitz & Floyd, Prunella Pig, from $85 to $110.00
Fitz & Floyd, Queen of Hearts $125.00
Fitz & Floyd, Raccoon, from $75 to $100.00
Fitz & Floyd, Rose Terrace Rabbit.............................$90.00

Fitz & Floyd, Santa on Motorcycle, from $450.00 to $550.00. (Photo courtesy Fred and Joyce Roerig)

Fitz & Floyd, Santa's Magic Workshop, from $150 to ..$185.00
Fitz & Floyd, Scarecrow, from $85 to $125.00
Fitz & Floyd, Sheriff, from $295 to...........................$325.00
Fitz & Floyd, Strawberry Basket, from $60 to $75.00
Fitz & Floyd, Victorian House, from $165 to............$200.00
Flambro, Emmett Kelly Jr on Barrel, from $475 to ...$700.00
Fredericksburg Art Pottery, Cow on Moon, marked J 2 USA...$250.00
Fredericksburg Art Pottery, Dove, marked FAPCo USA..$30.00
Fredericksburg Art Pottery, Windmill, marked FAPCo ..$50.00
Goebel, Cat Head, from $100 to $125.00
Goebel, Owl, from $70 to...$80.00
Goebel, Parrot Head, wearing blue beany, from $70 to....$80.00
Hallmark, Christmas Bear, from $35 to $60.00
Hallmark, Santa, from $35 to $50.00
Happy Memories, Elvis Presley, from $400 to..........$500.00
Happy Memories, Hopalong Cassidy w/Topper, minimum value $550.00
Happy Memories, James Dean, from $350 to $400.00

Happy Memories, Scarlett O'Hara, in green drapery dress, 14¾", from $270 to **$300.00**

Harry James, Barney Rubble, from $175 to **$200.00**

Harry James, Top Cat, from $200 to **$250.00**

Harry James/Turner Entertainment, Tom & Jerry, 7" .**$200.00**

Hearth & Home (H&HD), Bridesmaid, from $50 to ...**$75.00**

Hearth & Home (H&HD), Carousel Horse **$55.00**

Hearth & Home (H&HD), Cheetah **$55.00**

Hearth & Home (H&HD), Hippo, from $40 to **$40.00**

Hearth & Home (H&HD), Sundance Kid, from $50 to ..**$100.00**

Hearth & Home (H&HD), Zebra, from $50 to **$60.00**

Hirsch, Basketball, from $100 to **$125.00**

Hirsch, Cookie Planet, from $90 to **$100.00**

Hirsch, Covered Wagon, from $65 to **$85.00**

Hirsch, Gingerbread House, from $35 to **$45.00**

Hirsch, Hen on Nest, from $60 to **$65.00**

Hirsch, Lot'sa Goodies! Chef, from $150 to **$175.00**

Hirsch, Monk, from $35 to **$65.00**

Hirsch, Peck O' Cookies Rooster, from $100 to **$125.00**

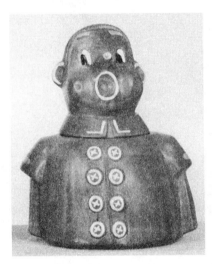

Hirsch, Pinocchio, #60, from $200.00 to $250.00.
(Photo courtesy Fred and Joyce Roerig)

Hirsch, Treasure Chest, all brown, marked WH '58, from $65 to **$75.00**

Hull, Barefoot Boy, blue pants & red hat.................**$425.00**

Hull, Daisy, from $35 to **$45.00**

Hull, Duck, from $40 to **$50.00**

Hull, Gingerbread Boy, brown, from $100 to **$135.00**

Lefton, Bossie, #6594, from $125 to **$150.00**

Japan, Alice's Adventures in Wonderland, house w/Alice's head coming out of roof & legs out front door, from $75 to **$95.00**

Japan, Cookie Time Clock w/Mouse Finial, blue w/multicolored trim...**$20.00**

Japan, Grandma, If All Else Fails Ask Grandma lettered on hat, orange **$20.00**

Japan, Hippo Fisherman **$35.00**

Japan, Horse Doctor..**$35.00**

Japan, Majorette Head, multicolored.........................**$25.00**

Japan, Pig Chef, white upper body w/multicolored accents, blue pants w/black belt **$30.00**

Japan, Professor Owl, w/scroll marked Cookies, brown ..**$20.00**

Japan, Tom & Jerry Cookies, brown jar w/cookies embossed allover, Tom finial & Jerry on side w/colorful lettering **$325.00**

Japan, Walt Disney Cookie Bus, minimum value, $500.00.

Lefton, Bluebird Love Nest, from $175 to.................**$200.00**

Lefton, Cat Head, from $95 to **$125.00**

Lefton, Egg w/Bunny, from $65 to............................**$85.00**

Lefton, Girl, #397, 8⅜", from $200 to......................**$225.00**

Lefton, Lamb Head, from $150 to **$160.00**

Maddux of California, Bear Shopper, from $150 to ..**$165.00**

Maddux of California, Beatrix Potter Rabbit.............**$100.00**

Maddux of California, Clown, very lg, from $325 to .**$395.00**

Maddux of California, Queen, #2104, from $125 to .**$140.00**

Maddux of California, Raggedy Ann, #2108, from $250 to..**$300.00**

Maddux of California, Strawberry...............................**$35.00**

Maddux of California, Walrus **$50.00**

McCoy, Animal Crackers Jar w/Clown Finial, marked USA, from $85 to..**$100.00**

McCoy, Apple, airbrushed blush, 1950-64 ....**$50.00**

McCoy, Apple, 1967..**$60.00**

McCoy, Asparagus Bunch, unmarked, 1977-79 ....**$50.00**

McCoy, Astronauts, from $750 to **$850.00**

McCoy, Bananas **$125.00**

McCoy, Barnum's Animals **$250.00**

McCoy, Basket of Potatoes...**$40.00**

McCoy, Bear, cookie in vest, no 'Cookies,' from $75 to ...**$85.00**

McCoy, Bear, cookie in vest, w/'Cookies'...................**$85.00**

McCoy, Bear & Beehive, marked #143 USA...............**$45.00**

McCoy, Bear Hugging Cookie Barrel, marked #142 USA, 1978, from $75 to...**$95.00**

McCoy, Betsy Baker, from $250 to **$300.00**

McCoy, Blue Willow Pitcher, #202 McCoy USA, 1973-75..**$75.00**

McCoy, Bobby Baker, #183, original..........................**$65.00**

McCoy, Boy on Baseball..**$250.00**

McCoy, Boy on Football, marked #222 McCoy USA, 1983 (+) **$275.00**

McCoy, Burlap Bag, red bird on lid............................**$50.00**

McCoy, Burlap Cookie Sack, marked #207 McCoy USA, 1985 ....**$40.00**

McCoy, Caboose $150.00
McCoy, Cat on Coal Scuttle $250.00

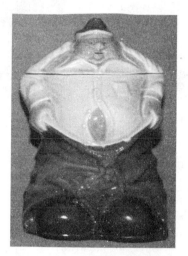

McCoy, Chairman of the Board, #162 USA, $550.00. (Photo courtesy Ermagene Westfall)

McCoy, Chilly Willy $50.00
McCoy, Chipmunk $125.00
McCoy, Christmas Tree, minimum value $800.00
McCoy, Churn, 2 bands $35.00
McCoy, Circus Horse, black $250.00
McCoy, Clown Bust (+) $75.00
McCoy, Clyde Dog $250.00
McCoy, Coalby Cat, from $325 to $375.00
McCoy, Coca-Cola Can $100.00
McCoy, Coffee Grinder $45.00
McCoy, Coffee Mug $45.00
McCoy, Colonial Fireplace $85.00
McCoy, Concave Jar w/Lilies, black gloss, marked USA, mid-1930s $40.00
McCoy, Cookie Bank, 1961 .... $165.00
McCoy, Cookie Barrel w/Sign, brown wood-grain, marked #146 McCoy USA, 1969-72, from $35 to $45.00
McCoy, Cookie Bell, unmarked, 1953-66 .... $50.00
McCoy, Cookie Boy $225.00
McCoy, Cookie Cabin $80.00
McCoy, Cookie Jug, single loop, 2-tone green rope ... $35.00
McCoy, Cookie Jug, w/cork stopper, brown & white ... $40.00
McCoy, Cookie Log, squirrel finial, from $35 to $45.00
McCoy, Cookie Safe $65.00
McCoy, Cookstove, black or white $35.00
McCoy, Corn, row of standing ears, yellow or white, 1977 .... $85.00
McCoy, Corn, single ear, yellow $175.00
McCoy, Cylinder, cobalt blue, marked USA #28 .... $40.00
McCoy, Cylinder, Flower Panels, modern motif, yellow, marked, #254 McCoy USA, 1970-71 .... $40.00
McCoy, Cylinder, mustard w/green drip glaze, marked USA #28 .... $45.00
McCoy, Cylinder, w/red flowers $45.00
McCoy, Cylinder w/Two Puppies, marked McCoy USA .. $200.00
McCoy, Dalmatians in Rocking Chair (+) $275.00

McCoy, Dog in Doghouse w/Bird on Top, unmarked, 1983 .... $250.00
McCoy, Dog on Basketweave, from $75 to $90.00
McCoy, Duck on Basketweave, from $75 to $90.00
McCoy, Duck w/Leaf in Bill, yellow w/red bill, 1964, from $65 to $85.00
McCoy, Dutch Treat Barn $50.00
McCoy, Eagle on Basket, from $35 to $50.00
McCoy, Early American Chest (Chiffoniere) $85.00
McCoy, Elephant w/Whole Trunk, unmarked, 1953 . $200.00
McCoy, Engine, black $175.00
McCoy, Forbidden Fruit, from $65 to $90.00
McCoy, Fortune Cookies, marked McCoy USA, 1965-68 . $65.00
McCoy, Freddie the Gleep, #189 (+), minimum value ... $500.00
McCoy, Frontier Family Jar (Cookies), unmarked, 1964-71 .... $55.00
McCoy, Fruit in Bushel Basket, from $65 to $80.00
McCoy, Garbage Can, marked #350 .... $35.00
McCoy, Gingerbread Boy on Ribbed Cylinder, marked USA, 1961 .... $75.00
McCoy, Grandfather Clock, black or brown $90.00
McCoy, Grandma w/Eyes Closed & Hands Folded, red & yellow w/white apron, marked, USA, 1972-73 .... $120.00
McCoy, Happy Face $80.00
McCoy, Hen on Basket, white $85.00
McCoy, Hen on Nest, marked USA, 1958-59, from $85 to .. $95.00
McCoy, Hobnail (Ball-Shaped), unmarked, 1940 ...... $100.00
McCoy, Hobnail (Heart-Shaped), unmarked, 1940, from $400 to $500.00
McCoy, Hot Air Balloon $40.00
McCoy, Hound Dog, head down, 1977 .... $35.00
McCoy, Ice Cream Cone $45.00
McCoy, Indian, brown (+) $350.00
McCoy, Jack-O'-Lantern $600.00
McCoy, Kangaroo, blue $300.00
McCoy, Kettle, bronze, 1961 .... $40.00
McCoy, Kissing Penguins, from $100 to $125.00
McCoy, Kitten on Basketweave, from $75 .... $90.00
McCoy, Kittens (2) on Low Basket, minimum value $600.00
McCoy, Kittens on Ball of Yarn $85.00
McCoy, Koala Bear $85.00
McCoy, Lamb on Basketweave $90.00
McCoy, Liberty Bell $75.00
McCoy, Little Clown $75.00
McCoy, Lunch Bucket, marked #377 USA $35.00
McCoy, Mac Dog $95.00
McCoy, Mammy, Cookies on base, white (+) $150.00
McCoy, Milk Can, Spirit of '76 .... $45.00
McCoy, Milk Can w/Gingham Flowers, marked #333 USA .. $40.00
McCoy, Milk Can w/Liberty Bell, marked USA #154, from $75 to $100.00
McCoy, Mouse Head, w/'Mickey Mouse' ears, yellow, 1978 .... $40.00
McCoy, Mouse on Clock $40.00
McCoy, Mr & Mrs Owl, from $75 to $90.00
McCoy, Nursery, decal of Humpty Dumpty, from $70 to .. $80.00
McCoy, Oaken Bucket, from $25 to $30.00

McCoy, Panda Bear w/Swirl Cookie, marked #141 USA, 1978...**$200.00**

McCoy, Pear, 1952 ....**$85.00**

McCoy, Pears on Basketweave **$70.00**

McCoy, Penguin w/Cookie Sign on Chest, white w/black & red trim or solid white, marked McCoy, 1940-43, from $175 to **$200.00**

McCoy, Picnic Basket, from $65 to **$75.00**

McCoy, Pig, winking **$300.00**

McCoy, Pineapple, marked McCoy USA, 1956-57 ....**$80.00**

McCoy, Pineapple, Modern, from $75 to....................**$90.00**

McCoy, Popeye, cylinder **$200.00**

McCoy, Potbelly Stove, black....................................**$30.00**

McCoy, Puppy, w/sign **$85.00**

McCoy, Raggedy Ann **$110.00**

McCoy, Red Barn, cow in door, rare, minimum value .**$350.00**

McCoy, Rooster, white, 1970-74.................................**$60.00**

McCoy, Sad Clown..**$85.00**

McCoy, Snoopy on Doghouse, marked United Features Syndicate (+), from $175 to **$200.00**

McCoy, Snow Bear, from $65 to.................................**$75.00**

McCoy, Strawberry, 1971-75.......................................**$65.00**

McCoy, Stump w/Frog, marked #216 McCoy USA, 1972 ...**$80.00**

McCoy, Stump w/Monkey, marked #253 McCoy USA (1970), from $50 to..**$60.00**

McCoy, Stump w/Rabbit, marked McCoy USA, 1971..**$50.00**

McCoy, Teapot (Cookies), metallic brown, marked McCoy USA, 1972 ....**$60.00**

McCoy, Tepee, slant top **$350.00**

McCoy, Timmy Tortoise **$45.00**

McCoy, Touring Car...**$100.00**

McCoy, Traffic Light...**$50.00**

McCoy, Tudor Cookie House **$125.00**

McCoy, Turkey, multicolored, marked McCoy USA, 1960 ....**$250.00**

McCoy, Uncle Sam's Hat, unmarked, 1973, from $650 to ..**$750.00**

McCoy, Upside Down Bear, panda **$50.00**

McCoy, WC Fields **$200.00**

McCoy, Windmill **$100.00**

McCoy, Wishing Well..**$40.00**

McCoy, Woodsy Owl, from $250 to **$300.00**

McCoy, Wren House, side lid **$175.00**

McCoy, Yosemite Sam...**$200.00**

McMe Productions, Cathy, 1994 ....**$160.00**

McMe Productions, Dale Evans, 1994 ....**$160.00**

McMe Productions, Roy Rogers Bust, 1994 ....**$160.00**

McMe Productions, Roy Rogers on Trigger, 1995 .....**$225.00**

Metlox, Apple, red w/brown & green stem **$65.00**

Metlox, Basset Hound, minimum value......................**$650.00**

Metlox, Beaver, Bucky **$175.00**

Metlox, Brownie Scout Head, 9⅛", minimum value.**$750.00**

Metlox, Calf's Head, Ferdinand, minimum value **$750.00**

Metlox, Clown, white w/black trim............................**$250.00**

Metlox, Cookie Girl, color glazed..............................**$80.00**

Metlox, Daisy Cookie Canister....................................**$45.00**

Metlox, Dinosaur (Dina), blue, 1987.........................**$175.00**

Metlox, Dinosaur (Mona), yellow, 1987....................**$175.00**

Metlox, Duck (Sir Francis Drake), white w/yellow bill & feet, green grass **$50.00**

Metlox, Flamingo, minimum value..............................**$500.00**

Metlox, Frog (Prince) w/Single Daisy, green w/white collar & yellow tie....................................**$250.00**

Metlox, Gingerbread, bisque, 3½-qt.............................**$125.00**

Metlox, Grapes, purple w/green leaf lid, from $200 to...**$250.00**

Metlox, Hippo (Bubbles) w/Water Lily on Back, yellow, minimum value **$350.00**

Metlox, Humpty Dumpty, seated w/feet **$275.00**

Metlox, Kangaroo w/Baby, minimum value..........**$1,000.00**

Metlox, Koala Bear **$125.00**

Metlox, Lamb w/Floral Collar **$300.00**

Metlox, Lion, yellow..**$175.00**

Metlox, Little Red Riding Hood, minimum value...**$1,250.00**

Metlox, Noah's Ark, bisque w/glazed accents, from $40 to **$50.00**

Metlox, Orange w/Blossom Finial **$65.00**

Metlox, Owl, brown **$45.00**

Metlox, Panda Bear, no lollipop..................................**$100.00**

Metlox, Parrot on Stump, green, minimum value **$350.00**

Metlox, Pineapple **$125.00**

Metlox, Pinocchio Head, 10¾" **$400.00**

Metlox, Pretzel Barrel **$125.00**

Metlox, Raccoon Cookie Bandit w/Apples................**$100.00**

Metlox, Rag Doll (Girl)..**$200.00**

Metlox, Scottie Dog, black..**$125.00**

Metlox, Spaceship w/Alien (Greetings Earth People), minimum value **$1,000.00**

Metlox, Strawberry, 9½"..**$70.00**

Metlox, Teddy Bear w/Cookie, light tan in blue sweater .**$45.00**

North American Ceramics, Andretti Race Car, from $315 to **$350.00**

North American Ceramics, Ford Victoria, from $200 to ..**$225.00**

North American Ceramics, Jingle Bear, from $150 to .**$175.00**

North American Ceramics, Moose, from $25 to **$35.00**

North American Ceramics, Porsche Convertible, from $125 to **$150.00**

North American Ceramics, Train Engine, from $75 to .**$110.00**

Omnibus, Alley Cat w/Bowling Ball **$40.00**

Omnibus, American Roadside Studebaker, from $45 to .**$65.00**

Omnibus, Around the World Santa, from $50 to.........**$65.00**

Omnibus, Cabbage Patch Rabbit (rabbit on cabbage), from $25 to **$35.00**

Omnibus, Chili Cow **$70.00**

Omnibus, Chunky the Snowman, from $35 to............**$50.00**

Omnibus, Clover Hill Dairy Cow **$120.00**

Omnibus, Cookie Mailbox, from $40 to **$45.00**

Omnibus, Daisy Cow, from $50 to..............................**$75.00**

Omnibus, Easter Cottage Sweet Shop, from $45 to **$50.00**

Omnibus, French Country Hen **$65.00**

Omnibus, German Santa **$75.00**

Omnibus, Gingerbread House, from $40 to **$45.00**

Omnibus, Halloween Pumpkin, from $45 to...............**$50.00**

Omnibus, Hometown Tea Shop, from $25 to **$30.00**

Omnibus, Humpty Dumpty, from $100 to.................**$125.00**

Omnibus, Keystone Cop, from $40 to **$50.00**

Omnibus, Miss Kitty, from $50 to **$65.00**

Omnibus, Noah's Ark Santa, from $45 to **$55.00**

Omnibus, Panda Bear, from $45 to **$50.00**

Omnibus, Rabbit on Cabbage **$60.00**

Omnibus, Safari Truck, from $45 to **$65.00**

Omnibus, Victorian Pig (pig couple), from $50 to **$65.00**

Omnibus, Vintage Santa (Santa in sleigh), from $55 to .. **$75.00**

Omnibus, Yule Tree, from $95 to **$115.00**

Red Wing, Bob White **$200.00**

Red Wing, Carousel, unmarked **$350.00**

Red Wing, Chef Pierre, blue, unmarked **$195.00**

Red Wing, Dutch Girl, yellow w/brown trim, marked . **$175.00**

Red Wing, Friar Tuck, green, marked **$175.00**

Red Wing, Happy the Children, verse on cylinder, from $100 to **$150.00**

Red Wing, King of Tarts, multicolor, marked (+) **$325.00**

Red Wing, Monk, beige, from $75 to **$100.00**

Red Wing, Monk, green, from $200 to **$275.00**

Red Wing, Pear, from $100 to **$125.00**

Red Wing, Peasant Design on Barrel Shape, brown w/painted-on colors **$120.00**

Regal, Cat, from $375 to **$425.00**

Regal, Churn Boy **$275.00**

Regal, Clown w/Cookie, green collar, marked, from $700 to **$750.00**

Regal, Dutch Girl, from $675 to **$725.00**

Regal, Fisherman/Whaler, unmarked, from $700 to . **$800.00**

Regal, Goldilocks, marked (+) **$375.00**

Regal, Kraft Marshmallow Bear, from $150 to **$215.00**

Regal, Little Miss Muffet, #705, from $350 to **$385.00**

Regal, Majorette, from $475 to **$675.00**

Regal, Oriental Lady with Baskets, from $700.00 to $750.00. (Photo courtesy Fred and Joyce Roerig)

Regal, Poodle (Fi Fi), marked, from $725 to **$725.00**

Regal, Toby Cookies, unmarked, from $750 to **$775.00**

Robinson-Ransbottom, Chef w/Bowl & Spoon, heavy gold trim, #411 .... **$225.00**

Robinson-Ransbottom, Hootie Owl, from $95 to **$115.00**

Robinson-Ransbottom, Jocko the Monkey **$375.00**

Robinson-Ransbottom, Ol' King Cole, multicolored w/black pipe & mug **$425.00**

Robinson-Ransbottom, Oscar the Doughboy, from $135 to **$165.00**

Robinson-Ransbottom, Pig Sheriff, heavy gold trim, #363 .... **$175.00**

Robinson-Ransbottom, Tiger Cubs, from $85 to **$100.00**

Robinson-Ransbottom, Whale w/Hat, marked **$525.00**

Shawnee, Cooky, white w/floral decals lg painted tulip & gold trim, marked USA **$300.00**

Shawnee, Cottage, marked USA #6 .... **$1,500.00**

Shawnee, Drum Major, gold trim, marked USA 10, minimum value **$575.00**

Shawnee, Dutch Boy (Jack), cold-painted, marked USA . **$100.00**

Shawnee, Dutch Boy (Jack), marked Great Northern USA #1025 .... **$325.00**

Shawnee, Dutch Girl (Jill), cold-painted, marked USA .. **$100.00**

Shawnee, Elephant (Jumbo), sitting upright, white w/yellow neck bow, marked USA #6 .... **$125.00**

Shawnee, Elephant (Lucky), sitting upright, decals & gold trim, marked USA **$825.00**

Shawnee, Fern Ware, yellow, marked USA **$85.00**

Shawnee, Fruit Basket, marked Shawnee 84 .... **$225.00**

Shawnee, Happy, white w/floral decals, blue & gold trim, marked USA **$300.00**

Shawnee, Jug, blue w/cold-painted flowers, marked USA **$105.00**

Shawnee, Little Chef, multicolor on cream, marked USA, $150.00.

Shawnee, Muggsy, decals & gold trim, marked Pat Muggsy USA **$1,000.00**

Shawnee, Muggsy, plain white w/blue trim, marked USA **$425.00**

Shawnee, Owl Winking, white w/trimmed face & neck, marked USA **$150.00**

Shawnee, Puss 'n Boots, decals & gold trim, marked Pat Puss 'n Boots USA, from $575 to **$625.00**

Shawnee, Sailor Boy, white w/cold-painted black trim, marked USA **$125.00**

Shawnee, Sailor Boy, yellow hair & gold neck tie, marked GOB & USA **$725.00**

Shawnee, Smiley the Pig, clover blossom, marked Pat Smiley USA..**$500.00**

Shawnee, Smiley the Pig, white w/blue neck scarf, black hooves & buttons, marked USA **$300.00**

Shawnee, Winnie the Pig, brown coat w/green collar, marked USA #61 ....**$425.00**

Shawnee, Winnie the Pig, clover blossom, marked Winnie USA **$475.00**

Shawnee (New), Billy in Dad's Sheriff Uniform........**$175.00**

Shawnee (New), Farmer Pig..**$175.00**

Shawnee (New), Sowly Pig...**$175.00**

Sierra Vista, Cottage, from $50 to **$65.00**

Sierra Vista, Dog on Drum, from $85 to.....................**$100.00**

Sierra Vista, Elephant, blue w/white, black & yellow plaid vest, from $125 to...**$150.00**

Sierra Vista, Grey Poodle, from $175.00 to $200.00. (Photo courtesy Ermagene Westfall)

Sierra Vista, Owl, from $75 to **$100.00**

Sierra Vista, Rooster, brown matt stain **$50.00**

Sierra Vista, Spaceship, matt brown, unmarked, from $375 to..**$425.00**

Sierra Vista, Squirrel, from $100 to.............................**$135.00**

Sierra Vista, Train, happy face on front **$95.00**

Sigma, Agatha, from $100 to..**$150.00**

Sigma, Beaver Fireman, from $125 to...........................**$150.00**

Sigma, Chef w/Dog, from $70 to....................................**$80.00**

Sigma, Circus Fat Lady **$200.00**

Sigma, Cubs Bear, from $125 to **$150.00**

Sigma, Duck w/Mixing Bowl, from $100 to **$125.00**

Sigma, Fat Cat, in pink dress w/red dots, from $225 to..**$275.00**

Sigma, Fat Cat, in tuxedo, from $225 to **$275.00**

Sigma, Kermit the Frog in TV, from $350 to **$400.00**

Sigma, Miss Piggy on Piano, from $235 to **$265.00**

Sigma, Panda Chef, from $65 to...................................**$75.00**

Sigma, Santa w/Bag of Goodies, from $65 to **$75.00**

Sigma, Snowman, from $100 to......................................**$125.00**

Sigma, Theodora Dog, from $125 to.............................**$150.00**

Sigma, Wind in the Willows, 1981, from $70 to..........**$90.00**

Star Jars, Bozo 50th Anniversary, 1995, from $225 to...**$275.00**

Star Jars, Cowardly Lion, 1994, from $250 to **$300.00**

Star Jars, Dorothy & Toto, 1994, from $325 to.........**$375.00**

Star Jars, Emerald City, 1996, 15½", from $500 to **$600.00**

Star Jars, Herman Munster, 1996, from $225 to.........**$275.00**

Star Jars, King Kong, 1996, from $250 to...................**$275.00**

Star Jars, Wicked Witch, 1994, from $325 to **$375.00**

Star Jars, Winged Monkey, 1994, from $325 to **$375.00**

Treasure Craft, Auntie 'Em, from $65 to **$75.00**

Treasure Craft, Bart Simpson, from $35 to.................**$50.00**

Treasure Craft, Baseball, from $35 to..........................**$40.00**

Treasure Craft, Bulldog Cafe, from $150 to **$175.00**

Treasure Craft, Cookie Balloon....................................**$40.00**

Treasure Craft, Cookie Chef, from $55 to **$75.00**

Treasure Craft, Droopy Dog (I'm So Happy) **$375.00**

Treasure Craft, Grandpa Munster **$275.00**

Treasure Craft, Herman Munster **$275.00**

Treasure Craft, Hobby Horse, plaid, from $40 to........**$50.00**

Treasure Craft, Meeko (Lion King), raccoon, from $45 to...**$55.00**

Treasure Craft, Pick-Up Truck, from $275.00 to $325.00. (Photo courtesy Fred and Joyce Roerig)

Treasure Craft, Policeman Bear **$40.00**

Treasure Craft, Santa w/Glass Bowl, from $175 to ...**$200.00**

Treasure Craft/Disney, Aladdin Genie Seated Holding Magic Lamp **$80.00**

Treasure Craft/Disney, Buzz Lightyear, from $185 to..**$240.00**

Treasure Craft/Disney, Donald Duck, seated w/arms folded, from $45 to...**$55.00**

Treasure Craft/Disney, Goofy, seated Indian style......**$60.00**

Treasure Craft/Disney, Simba (Lion King) **$95.00**

Treasure Craft/Henson, Fozzie Bear.........................**$50.00**

Treasure Craft/Henson, Miss Piggy, seated in glamorous pose **$50.00**

Treasure Craft/Henson, Miss Piggy on Column Jar.....**$75.00**

Twin Winton, Bear in Fire Truck, from $85 to.........**$110.00**

Twin Winton, Butler, from $300 to **$350.00**

Twin Winton, Church...**$500.00**

Twin Winton, Cinderella's Pumpkin Coach, from $165 to.**$200.00**

Twin Winton, Cookie Catcher, from $100 to.............**$125.00**

Twin Winton, Cowboy Rabbit, fully painted, from $125 to **$150.00**

Twin Winton, Dutch Girl, Collector Series, fully painted.**$200.00**

Twin Winton, Elf Bakery, elf finial, #50....................**$75.00**

Twin Winton, Grandma, #58 ....**$200.00**

Twin Winton, Hobby Horse, Collector Series, fully painted, from $175 to...**$190.00**

Twin Winton, Keystone Cop, from $85 to...............**$100.00**

Twin Winton, Lamb (For Good Little Lambs Only), Collector Series, fully painted, from $90 to **$100.00**

Twin Winton, Lion, from $65 to....................................**$85.00**

Twin Winton, Noah's Ark, from $100 to....................**$125.00**

Twin Winton, Pear w/Worm, wood stain w/painted detail, avocado green, pineapple yellow, orange or red, ea....**$300.00**

Twin Winton, Pirate Fox, wood stain **$75.00**

Twin Winton, Police Bear, Collector Series, fully painted, from $150 to...**$175.00**

Twin Winton, Ranger Bear, Collector Series, fully painted, from $90 to...**$110.00**

Twin Winton, Squirrel w/Cookie, from $40 to...........**$50.00**

USA Demand Marketing, Big Bird, Bert & Ernie, multicolored..**$45.00**

USA Pottery By JD, Nancy (seated) **$200.00**

Vandor, Baseball **$55.00**

Vandor, Beethoven Piano...**$65.00**

Vandor, Cowboy Mooranda, from $135 to **$185.00**

Vandor, Curious George on Rocketship......................**$60.00**

Vandor, Fred Flintstone, 1989, from $150 to **$175.00**

Vandor, Frog Head, from $200 to..............................**$275.00**

Vandor, Honeymooners Bus, from $120 to **$150.00**

Vandor, Howdy Doody, head figure, from $350 to ..**$400.00**

Vandor, I Love Lucy Characters in Car, minimum value ..**$150.00**

Vandor, Mona Lisa, 1992, from $50 to **$55.00**

Vandor, Popeye, from $420 to **$500.00**

Vandor, Radio, from $65 to **$100.00**

Vandor, Toaster **$125.00**

Viacom, Tommy Pickles (Rugrats), from $35 to..........**$45.00**

Wade, Brew Gaffer, 8⅜", from $75 to **$85.00**

Wade, Peasant Woman w/Tray of Cookies, 1991, 10½", from $90 to...**$110.00**

Warner Bros, Batman, from $100 to...........................**$150.00**

Warner Bros, Bugs Bunny in Rabbit Hole, 1996, from $40 to..**$45.00**

Warner Bros, Daffy Duck as Baseball Player, 1993, from $35 to..**$45.00**

Warner Bros, Foghorn Leghorn w/Dog & Henry Hawk, 1996, from $110 to..**$125.00**

Warner Bros, Marvin the Martian in Spaceship, 1993, from $100 to...**$125.00**

Warner Bros, Pepe LePew on Coffee Cup (Caffe Pepe), from $50 to...**$60.00**

Warner Bros, Pinky & the Brain, 1996, 12½", from $65 to **$75.00**

Warner Bros, Porky Pig in TV, 1995, 10½", from $50 to .**$60.00**

Warner Bros, Superman Bust, from $75 to...............**$100.00**

Warner Bros, Tasmanian Devil as Santa, 1995, from $65 to **$75.00**

Coors Rosebud Dinnerware

Golden, Colorado, was the site for both the Coors Brewing Company and the Coors Porcelain Company, each founded by the same man, Adolph Coors. The pottery's inception was in 1910, and in the early years they manufactured various ceramic products such as industrial needs, dinnerware, vases, and figurines; but their most famous line and the one we want to tell you about is 'Rosebud.'

The Rosebud 'Cook 'n Serve' line was introduced in 1934. It's very easy to spot, and after you've once seen a piece, you'll be able to recognize it instantly. It was made in solid colors — rose, blue, green, yellow, ivory, and orange. The rosebud and leaves are embossed and hand painted in contrasting colors. There are nearly fifty different pieces to collect, and bargains can still be found; but prices are accelerating, due to increased collector interest. For more information we recommend *Coors Rosebud Pottery* by Robert Schneider.

Note: Yellow and white tends to craze and stain. Our prices are for pieces with minimal crazing and no staining. To evaluate pieces in blue, add 10% to the prices below; add 15% for items in ivory.

Advisor: Rick Spencer (See Directory, Regal China)

Newsletter: *Coors Pottery Newsletter*
Robert Schneider
3808 Carr Pl. N
Seattle, WA 98103-8126

Apple baker, w/lid...**$55.00**

Baker, oval, deep, sm...**$25.00**

Baker, 9¼"...**$60.00**

Bean pot, lg...**$68.00**

Bean pot, sm...**$65.00**

Bowl, mixing; no rosebud, 6".......................................**$35.00**

Bowl, mixing; 8-pt..**$75.00**

Bowl, pudding; 2-pt..**$40.00**

Bowl, pudding; 7-pt..**$75.00**

Cake knife...**$85.00**

Casserole, Dutch; lg..**$95.00**

Casserole, Dutch; sm..**$72.00**

Casserole, straight sides, w/lid, 7"..............................**$55.00**

Casserole, straight side, w/lid , 8"...............................**$75.00**

Casserole, triple service; w/lid, 2-pt...........................**$64.00**

Casserole, w/lid, 9½"...**$100.00**

Creamer...**$30.00**

Cup & saucer **$45.00**

Dish, fruit/sauce...**$16.00**

Dish, oatmeal...**$25.00**

Dish, vegetable; deep...**$35.00**

Egg cup...**$50.00**

Honey pot, no spoon, w/lid, from $150 to...............**$180.00**

Jar, utility; w/lid **$85.00**

Loaf pan...**$50.00**

Muffin set, w/lid, rare..**$225.00**

Pie plate...**$35.00**

Pitcher, sm, w/lid...**$95.00**

Plate, dinner; 9¼"..**$20.00**

Plate, used under muffin cover, 6"...............................**$35.00**

Plate, 5"...**$9.00**

Plate, 7¼" $10.00
Platter, 9x12", from $42 to...........................$48.00
Ramekin, handled, 4¼" $40.00
Refrigerator set..$130.00
Salt & pepper shakers, individual, pr.............$85.00
Salt & pepper shakers, kitchen, pr.................$80.00
Salt & pepper shakers, tapered, range size, pr $85.00
Sugar bowl, w/lid $45.00
Sugar shaker...$80.00
Teapot, 2-cup...$200.00
Teapot, 6-cup, from $160 to $185.00
Tumbler, footed $125.00

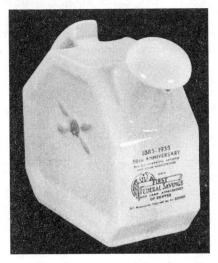

Water server, commemorative, $265.00.

Water server, w/stopper $120.00

Coppercraft Guild

During the 1960s and 1970s, the Coppercraft Guild Company of Taunton, Massachusetts, produced a variety of copper and copper-tone items which were sold through the home party plan. Though copper items such as picture frames, flowerpots, teapots, candle holders, trays, etc., were their mainstay, they also made molded wall decorations such as mirror-image pairs of birds on branches and large floral-relief plaques that they finished in metallic copper-tone paint. Some of their pictures were a combination of the copper-tone composition molds mounted on a sheet copper background. When uncompromised by chemical damage or abuse, the finish they used on their copper items has proven remarkably enduring, and many of these pieces still look new today. Collectors are beginning to take notice!

Bowl, footed, 4x7" dia, EX...........................$14.00
Bowl, leaf shape, brass loop handle, 2x4x5¼" $8.50
Box, money clip inside, Cache embossed on front, ⅝x3x4" $8.00
Bread tray, ornate etching in center, 12x6¾", EX $12.00
Candle bowl, 2x4½" dia, EX..........................$15.00

Glasses, clear glass w/copper bands at bottom, set of 4, 5½", EX..$13.50
Ice bucket, w/lid, 2 ring handles on sides, 5½x8", EX.$9.00
Mirror, eagle on top, scrollwork on sides, round mirror glass, 21x14½", 1959, EX................................$15.00
Napkin holder, praying hands embossed on sides, 1¼x4¼x7"..$7.00

Plaque, embossed copper with log cabin scene, 14", $14.00.

Plate, fireplace in center, acorns & leaves at border, 10½", EX $15.00
Serving dish, fluted, antique finish, 2¼x5¾" dia, EX..$15.00
Silent butler, spinning wheel embossed on top, 7½x5¼" (w/4½" wooden handle) $8.00
Tea set, demitasse; teapot, creamer & sugar bowl......$30.00
Tray, serving; ornate embossing in center, rope edge, 1½x14¾" dia, EX $12.50

Corkscrews

When the corkscrew was actually developed remains uncertain (the first patent was issued in 1795), but it most likely evolved from the worm on a ramrod or cleaning rod used to draw wadding from a gun barrel and found to be equally effective in the sometimes difficult task of removing corks from wine bottles. Inventors scurried to develop a better product, and as a result, thousands of variations have been made and marketed. This abundance and diversification invariably came to attract collectors, whose ranks are burgeoning. Many of today's collectors concentrate their attention on one particular type — those with advertising, a specific patent, or figural pullers, for instance.

Our advisor has written a very informative book, *Bull's Pocket Guide to Corkscrews* (Schiffer), with hundreds of full-color illustrations and current values.

Advisor: Donald A. Bull (See Directory, Corkscrews)

Cellerman's, full grip, button & fine wire worm, Universal, GF Hipkins, from $75 to $100.00

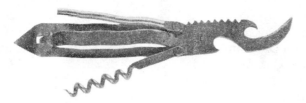

Combination tool, marked Depose France, from $40.00 to $50.00. (Photo courtesy Donald A. Bull)

Double lever, barmaid figural, aluminum, Italy, 1950s, from $50 to...**$90.00**

Double lever, duck head hand-painted resin handle, currently marketed, from $30 to................................**$40.00**

Figural handle, brass-plated bull's head, from $30 to.**$40.00**

Figural handle, golf ball w/frame, Made in England on ball, from $15 to..**$25.00**

Finger pull, 2-finger, marked Commercial, from $30 to..**$80.00**

Finger pull, 3-finger (eyebrow handle), unmarked, plain, from $5 to..**$25.00**

Flynut, handle w/threaded shank & worm, cast aluminum frame, from $50 to.....................................**$75.00**

Metal T handle, simple design, from $10 to................**$50.00**

Miniature, folding bow from ¾" to 1¾" (closed), plain, unmarked, from $20 to..**$40.00**

Nifty style, beer advertising, from $10 to....................**$50.00**

Picnic, worm w/short shaft, ring in top, unmarked brass hex head w/machined cap lifter, from $25 to............**$35.00**

Plastic, red 2-finger pull w/button, Hong Kong, from $2 to...**$3.00**

Pocket folder, So-Ezy Made in USA Pat Pend, from $40 to...**$50.00**

Prong puller, E-Z Cork Puller, toothed shaft w/folding cover, from $65 to...**$75.00**

Wood T-type, simple direct pull, from $10 to.............**$75.00**

Zig Zag, Lazy Tongs, many variations, from $30 to..**$100.00**

Cottage Ware

Made by several companies, cottage ware is a line of ceramic table and kitchen accessories, each piece styled as a cozy cottage with a thatched roof. At least four English potteries made the ware, and you'll find pieces marked 'Japan' as well as 'Occupied Japan.' You'll also find pieces styled as windmills and water wheels. The pieces preferred by collectors are marked 'Price Brothers' and 'Occupied Japan.' They're compatible in coloring as well as in styling, and values run about the same. Items marked simply 'Japan' are worth considerably less.

Bank, English, 5" L **$95.00**

Bowl, salad; English **$70.00**

Butter dish, English...**$65.00**

Butter pat, embossed cottage, rectangular, Occupied Japan..**$20.00**

Chocolate pot, English **$148.00**

Condiment set, 2 shakers & mustard on tray, Occupied Japan..**$50.00**

Condiment set, 2 shakers & mustard on 5" handled leaf tray **$80.00**

Condiment set, 3-part cottage on shaped tray w/applied bush, English, 4½" **$85.00**

Cookie jar, pink, brown & green, sq, Japan, 8½x5½"...........**$70.00**

Cookie jar, rectangular w/wicker handle, English or Occupied Japan...**$90.00**

Cookie jar, windmill, wicker handle, English (Price), rare, 5", minimum value **$165.00**

Cookie jar/canister, cylindrical, English, 8½x5".........**$140.00**

Cookie jar/canister, cylindrical, English, 8x3¾".........**$275.00**

Creamer, windmill, Occupied Japan, 2⅝" **$30.00**

Creamer & sugar bowl, English, 2½x4½" **$50.00**

Creamer & sugar bowl, w/lid, on tray, Occupied Japan..**$75.00**

Cup & saucer, English, 2½", 4½" **$50.00**

Demitasse pot, English **$100.00**

Dish w/cover, Occupied Japan, sm.............................**$40.00**

Egg cups, 4 on 6½" sq tray, English **$65.00**

Gravy boat & tray, English, rare, lg **$275.00**

Grease jar, Occupied Japan, from $25 to....................**$38.50**

Marmalade, English...**$45.00**

Mug, Price Bros, 3⅞"..**$55.00**

Pin tray, English, 4" dia **$22.00**

Pitcher, water; English, 8" **$165.00**

Salt & pepper shakers, windmill, Occupied Japan, pr..**$25.00**

Sugar bowl, windmill, w/lid, Occupied Japan, 3⅞"....**$30.00**

Sugar box, for cubes, English, 5¾" L.........................**$50.00**

Tea set, child's, Japan, serves 4 ....**$165.00**

Teapot, English, 4"..**$80.00**

Teapots, 6½", marked Price Bros. (English) and Occupied Japan, from $60.00 to $75.00.

Toast rack, 3-slot, English, 3½"...................................**$75.00**

Tumbler, Occupied Japan, 3½", 6 for **$65.00**

Cow Creamers

Cow creamers (and milk pitchers) have been around since before the nineteenth century, but, of course, those are rare. But by the early 1900s, they were becoming quite commonplace. In many of these older ones, the cow was standing on a platform (base) and very often had a lid. Not all cows on platforms are old, however, but it is a good indication of age. Examples from before WWII often were produced in England, Germany, and Japan.

Over the last fifty years there has been a slow revival of interest in these little cream dispensers, including the plastic Moo Cows, made by Whirley Industries, U.S.A, that were used in cafes during the '50s. With the current popularity of anything cow-shaped, manufacturers have expanded the concept, and some creamers now are made with matching sugar bowls. If you want to collect only vintage examples, nowadays you'll have to check closely to make sure they're not new.

Advisor: Shirley Green (See Directory, Cow Creamers)

Advertising, Dogpatch USA, white w/blue, Japan,
  3½x4" **$22.50**
Advertising, iridescent white, Worthing Parade, foreign,
  4½x6" **$28.00**
Advertising, Jell-O, multicolored, 5x6½" **$175.00**
Arms of University & City of Oxford shield on side, cream
  & orange lustre, marked Foreign, ca 1950, 6" L, from
  $35 to...**$40.00**
Arthur Wood, ironstone, w/sailboat on side, England,
  marked, 5½x7" **$85.00**
Borden Co, Elsie on side, mark on bottom, white w/gold
  trim, 5x7" **$55.00**
Burleigh, lazy cow, blue & white, on base, 5x6½".....**$60.00**
C Cooke, w/suckling calf on platform, w/lid, 5x6½" .**$225.00**
Calico, Burleigh, Staffordshire, England, ca 1975, 7" L, from
  $65 to...**$75.00**
China, Blue Onion design, blue & white, sitting cow,
  4x3½" **$20.00**
Czech, marigold iridescent, reclining cow on base,
  5½x7" **$55.00**
Delft, blue & white w/windmill Holland, 4x6½" **$22.00**
Delft style, blue w/sailing ship on left side, unmarked, ca
  1950, 6" **$45.00**
Goebel, full bee mark, brown & white, 4x6" **$35.00**
Guernsey printed on side, brass bell at neck, slash-
  type mouth, brown to white w/black hooves, from
  $20 to **$35.00**
Holstein, black & white, K403 on bottom, 4½x8" **$48.00**
Hummel, full bee mark, Germany, 1960s, 4x6", from $35
  to..**$45.00**
Jackfield-type, red clay, w/lid, 19th century, on platform,
  5½x7" **$175.00**
Japan, brown & white, sitting, 3¼", from $15 to **$25.00**
Japan, brown & white, tail handle, black mark, 5¼", from $22
  to..**$35.00**
Japan, brown to cream, shiny, 5¼" L, from $22 to.....**$35.00**
Japan, Dabs paper sticker, common mold, comes in various
  colors & designs, 1950s-60s, ea from $40 to **$50.00**
Japan, ironstone, black ring around eyes (known as Bull's Eye),
  crudely molded, reddish spots, green bell, 6" **$30.00**
Japan, lustre, creamer & sugar bowl, Texas longhorn, w/lid,
  5x6½" **$125.00**

Japan, yellow & white, 2½", from $15 to **$20.00**
Kenmar, pink w/bell, Japan, 5x6½" **$30.00**
Leersum castle image on side, brown & white, unmarked, ca
  1960, 6", from $32 to **$38.00**
Lefton, creamer & sugar bowl, tan w/white markings,
  4x5½" **$42.00**
McMaster, pottery, creamer & sugar bowl set, 4x6"....**$37.00**
Milton China Fine Bone China Staffordshire England, roses
  transfer on shiny white, 6½", from $25 to............**$30.00**
Occupied Japan, green & tan, lg body, 6x5" **$65.00**
Staffordshire, Chintz, multicolored, w/lid, on platform,
  5½x7" **$135.00**

Staffordshire Ware, Kent, Made in England, 1940s – 50s, 4¾x7" on platform with lid, scarce, from $100.00 to $150.00. (Photo courtesy Shirley Green)

Staucht Frae the Coo, white w/gold, Germany, 6x5½"..**$47.50**
TG Green, reclining, tan, England, 4x6" **$37.00**
Unmarked, brown glossy, stands w/tail curled, old,
  2¼x3" **$25.00**
Unmarked, purple & white w/yellow horns, 3-pc set,
  4x4½" **$17.50**
Unmarked, white glossy, recumbent w/legs tucked under,
  1920s, 6" **$50.00**
Unmarked, white porcelain, for child's tea set, 1½x2" ..**$15.00**

Unmarked, 1960s, 5½" x 8", from $55.00 to $65.00. (Photo courtesy Shirley Green)

Whirley, plastic, upright Moo Cow, 5x3" **$15.00**

Cowboy Character Collectibles

When we come across what is now termed cowboy character toys and memorabilia, it rekindles warm memories of childhood days for those of us who once 'rode the range' (often our backyards) with these gallant heroes. Today we can really appreciate them for the positive role models they were. They sat tall in the saddle; reminded us never to tell an un-truth; to respect 'women-folk' as well as our elders, animal life, our flag, our country, and our teachers; to eat all the cereal placed before us in order to build strong bodies; to worship God; and have (above all else) strong values that couldn't be compromised. They were Gene, Roy, and Tex, along with a couple of dozen other names, who rode beautiful steeds such as Champion, Trigger, and White Flash.

They rode into a final sunset on the silver screen only to return and ride into our homes via television in the 1950s. The next decade found us caught up in more western adventures such as Bonanza, Wagon Train, The Rifleman, and many others. These set the stage for a second wave of toys, games, and western outfits.

Annie Oakley was one of only a couple of cowgirls in the corral; Wild Bill Elliott used to drawl, 'I'm a peaceable man'; Ben Cartwright, Adam, Hoss, and Little Joe provided us with thrills and laughter. Some of the earliest collectibles are represented by Roy's and Gene's 1920s predecessors — Buck Jones, Hoot Gibson, Tom Mix, and Ken Maynard. There were so many others, all of whom were very real to us in the 1930s – '60s, just as their memories and values remain very real to us today.

Remember that few items of cowboy memorabilia have survived to the present in mint condition. When found, mint or near-mint items bring hefty prices, and they continue to escalate every year. Our values are for examples in good to very good condition.

For more information we recommend these books: *Roy Rogers, Singing Cowboy Stars, Silver Screen Cowboys, Hollywood Cowboy Heroes*, and *Western Comics: A Comprehensive Reference*, all by Robert W. Phillips. Other books include: *Collector's Guide to Hopalong Cassidy Memorabilia* by Joseph J. Caro, *Collector's Reference & Value Guide to The Lone Ranger* by Lee Felbinger, *W.F. Cody Buffalo Bill* by James W. Wojtowicz, and *Roy Rogers and Dale Evans Toys & Memorabilia* by P. Allan Coyle.

See also Toys, Guns; Toys, Rings.

Club/Newsletter: The Old Cowboy Picture Show
George F. Coan
PO Box 66
Camden, SC 29020; 803-432-9643

Club/Newsletter: Cowboy Collector
Joseph J. Caro, Publisher
P.O. Box 7486
Long Beach, CA 90807

Club/Newsletter: Hopalong Cassidy Fan Club International and *Hopalong Cassidy Newsletter*

Laura Bates, Editor
6310 Friendship Dr.
New Concord, OH 43762-9708; 614-826-4850

Newsletter: *Gene Autry Star Telegram*
Gene Autry Development Association
Chamber of Commerce
P.O. Box 158, Gene Autry, OK 73436

Newsletter: *The Lone Ranger Silver Bullet*
P.O. Box 553
Forks, WA 98331; 206-327-3726

Annie Oakley, bread label, black & white photo image on yellow background, Wonder Bread, EX...............**$35.00**
Annie Oakley, Castile Soap, Shooting Gallery, 2 rows of soap ducks, unused, NMIB...**$100.00**
Annie Oakley, outfit, red blouse & fringed skirt w/silkscreened image on pockets, Pla-Master, 1950, NMIB...**$200.00**
Bat Masterson, wallet, Croyder, 1950s, NMIB......**$75.00**
Dale Evans, fan, cardboard, 1950s, VG......................**$15.00**

Dale Evans, school bag, 1959 – 60, 9" x 14", EX, $150.00; M, $300.00. (Photo courtesy P. Allan Coyle)

Dale Evans, school bag, Queen of the West, Acme Brief Case Co, 1952 ....**$150.00**
Dale Evans, writing tablet, Dale w/Bullet on cover, Frontiers Inc, 1950s, 8x10", several sheets missing o/w EX..**$30.00**
Daniel Boone, Fess Parker Inflatable Indian Canoe, Multiple, 1965, NMIP..**$55.00**
Daniel Boone, Fess Parker Super Slate, Saalfield, 1964, 12x9", unused, EX+...**$45.00**
Daniel Boone, figure, plastic w/soft vinyl head & coonskin cap, American Tradition, 1964, 5", NM, from $75 to......**$100.00**
Daniel Boone, wallet, Fess Parker image, 1964, EX ...**$35.00**
Davy Crockett, Auto-Magic Picture Gun, complete w/film, Stephens, 1950s, EXIB...**$125.00**
Davy Crockett, bank, copper-tinted metal bust figure w/rifle, 5", NM (EX box) **$125.00**
Davy Crockett, bank, plaster figure, VG...................**$125.00**
Davy Crockett, Camera Ensemble, Herbert-George, complete, scarce, NM (EX box)...............................**$400.00**

Davy Crockett, doll, compo w/cloth clothes & coonskin hat, open/close eyes, 8", NMIB..................................**$175.00**

Davy Crockett, flashlight, litho tin w/red plastic top, 1950s, 3", EX..**$30.00**

Davy Crockett, Frontierland Pencil Case, brown vinyl holster form, no contents, 8", 1950s, VG+ **$65.00**

Davy Crockett, Guitare, EC France/WPD, 24", EX, $350.00.

Davy Crockett, napkins, Walt Disney's Official Davy Crockett Indian Fighter w/graphics, 30-ct, Beach Products, 1954, MIP **$55.00**

Davy Crockett, night light, head figure, 1950s, EX **$30.00**

Davy Crockett, ring, from gumball machine, 1960s, M..**$15.00**

Davy Crockett, slide-tile puzzle, black & white plastic w/image of Davy & friends, Roalex, 1950s, NMOC................**$50.00**

Davy Crockett, Thunderbird Moccasin Kit, Blaine, 1950s, complete, NM (EX box) **$175.00**

Davy Crockett, TV tray, litho tin w/image of Davy fighting Indian, WDP, 1955, 12x17", EX...........................**$100.00**

Davy Crockett, wallet, brown vinyl w/faux fur on Davy's hat, 1955, from $75 to **$100.00**

Davy Crockett, yo-yo, wood w/gold leaf stamp, tournament shape, Fli-Back, 1950s, NM **$90.00**

Gabby Hayes, Carry All Fishing Outfit, tubular canister w/graphic detail & carrying cord, no lid or contents otherwise EX..**$90.00**

Gabby Hayes, Sheriff Set, w/handcuffs & badge, John Henry, 1950, MOC, from $100 to.....................................**$125.00**

Gene Autry, Adventure Story Trail Map (Gene Autry & the Stagecoach Holdup), for Schafer's Bread labels 1-16, 1950, EX **$100.00**

Gene Autry, guitar, plastic, 31", EX............................**$150.00**

Gene Autry, stencil book, Stencil Art, 1950, unused, NM ..**$75.00**

Gunsmoke, ice cream box, All Star Ice Cream/Matt Dillon's Favorite/One Pint, head image in star frame, 1956, NM+ **$55.00**

Gunsmoke, promo card, L&M Presents Gunsmoke Saturday Nights, color photo of Arness w/cigarette, 1950s-60s, 7x6", NM+...**$40.00**

Hoot Gibson, program, Rodeo/Riverside Stadium, 1942, 2-color cover, w/biography page, 20 pages, 11x8½", EX+...**$30.00**

Hopalong Cassidy, belt, Switch-A-Buckle, NMOC **$225.00**

Hopalong Cassidy, bread wrapper, Hoppy's Favorite w/4 images, on foam-formed loaf, Barbara Ann Co, 1950s, 14x4", NM+..**$45.00**

Hopalong Cassidy, chaps, Hoppy image on black suede, 1950s, VG **$50.00**

Hopalong Cassidy, drum, 2 different images of Hoppy on drum tops, Rubbertone/Wm Boyd, 1950, 5" dia, EX **$225.00**

Hopalong Cassidy, Hold-Up Game, Enterprises of America, 1950, NMIB, $85.00.
(Photo courtesy Greg Davis and Bill Morgan)

Hopalong Cassidy, magazine, Song & Saddle/Barn Dance Hits & Western Pictures, photo w/Bill Boyd signature, 1947, VG..**$45.00**

Hopalong Cassidy, outfit, black pants w/red detail, black & white shirt w/red vinyl fringe, J Bard, 1950, EX ..**$200.00**

Hopalong Cassidy, Savings Club certificate & badge, bank promo, 8x10" certificate & 1⅜" dia tin badge, 1950, EX..**$65.00**

Hopalong Cassidy, stationery folio, w/writing paper & envelopes, Whitman, 1950, 10¾x8¼", VG+ **$60.00**

Hoplaong Cassidy, dominoes, Milton Bradley, 1950, complete, EXIB, from $75 to **$100.00**

Lone Ranger, Action Arcade, 1975, NMIB, from $100 to..**$125.00**

Lone Ranger, beanie, felt, white image & lettering on black w/red trim, 1940, NM, from $75 to **$100.00**

Lone Ranger, blotter, Bond Bread, 1940s, NM.............**$20.00**

Lone Ranger, coloring book, Merita Bread premium for Lone Ranger Health & Safety Club, TLR Inc, 1955, unused, EX **$55.00**

Lone Ranger, crayons, 1953, complete, NM (NM tin box), from $75 to...**$100.00**

Lone Ranger, doll, standing w/guns drawn & wearing chaps & mask, painted composition, Dollcraft/TLR, 10", NMIB **$800.00**

Lone Ranger First Aid Kit, American White Cross Labs Inc., EX, $65.00. (Photo courtesy David Longest)

Lone Ranger, harmonica, silver plated, 1947, NMIB, from $75 to...$125.00

Lone Ranger, magic slate, Whitman, 1978, EX, from $55 to $75.00

Lone Ranger, newspaper, Lone Ranger Roundup, Vol 1 #1, August 1939, Bond Bread Safety Club, 8 pages, rare, NM $100.00

Lone Ranger, pencil box, blue w/embossed gold image & lettering, 1940, NM $100.00

Lone Ranger, Punch-Out Set, 1947, complete, NMIB, from $175 to...$250.00

Maverick, TV Eras-O-Picture Book, Hasbro, 1959, MIB (sealed)..$100.00

Red Rider, Junior Braces, Slesinger, 1950, complete, rare, NM (EX box)..$225.00

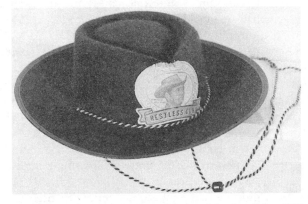

Restless Gun, cowboy hat, black felt, EX, $45.00. (Photo courtesy June Moon)

Rifleman, hat, felt, Tex-Felt Co, 1958, EX $70.00
Rin Tin Tin, display rack, ...Dog Supply Center, litho tin w/10 hooks for choker chains, Screen Gems, 1956, 8x4x21", VG..$135.00
Rin Tin Tin, Magic Picture Set, Transogram, 1956, complete, NMIB..$65.00
Rin Tin Tin & Rusty, belt buckle, EX...........................$65.00

Roy Rogers, Archery Set, Ben Pearson, 1950s, complete, scarce, EX (worn box) $275.00
Roy Rogers, bandanna, brown w/red & blue litho on tan, 1950s, EX..$55.00
Roy Rogers, bank, litho tin w/colorful image of Roy & Trigger, Ohio Art, 8", MIP $250.00
Roy Rogers, flashlight, red & white plastic, w/Trail Guide pamphlet, Bantam, 1974, 3", NM.........$165.00
Roy Rogers, harmonica, 1955, 4", NMOC $100.00
Roy Rogers, home movie, 8mm, Silver Fox Hunt, #505-C, Hollywood Film Entertainment, 1950s, complete, VG+ (w/box)..$55.00
Roy Rogers, Modeling Clay Set, Standard Toykraft, complete, NMIB.....................................$125.00

Roy Rogers, Official Riders Club membership kit, includes comic, membership card, and litho tin tab, 1950s, complete, M, $250.00; EX, $150.00. (Photo courtesy P. Allan Coyle)

Roy Rogers, phonograph, plastic & metal, RCA Victor, 1950s, rare, VG+.......................................$200.00
Roy Rogers, photograph, black & white, facsimile signed Many Happy Trails Roy Rogers, #RR-5X, 1940s, 8x10", EX $30.00
Roy Rogers, song folio, 2-color photo cover, 12 songs, 40 pages, Famous Music Corp, 1952, 12x9", M $45.00
Roy Rogers, tattoo transfers, Fawcett, EX (EX envelope)..$85.00
Roy Rogers, wood burning set, Burn-Rite, Rapaport Bros, complete, NM (EX box) $175.00
Roy Rogers & Dale Evans, Colorforms Dress-Up Kit, 1950s, complete, EXIB $150.00
Straight Arrow, powder horn, 1950s, rare, NM $100.00
Tom Mix, belt, white plastic w/red checkerboard & cowboy design, brass buckle w/secret compartment, 1930s, EX...$125.00
Tom Mix, postcard, dealer reminder to display 'Two for One' offer for telescope & birdcall, illustrated, NM+ $55.00
Tom Mix, spurs, glow-in-the-dark, MIB..................$150.00
Tonto, Castile Soap, figural, Kirk Guild, 1939, 4", EXIB...$55.00

Wild Bill Hickok, Bunkhouse Kit, Vorando Air Circulators, 1950s, NM (NM envelope) **$65.00**

Zorro, cape, Carnival Creations, NMOC.................**$65.00**

Zorro, Pencil Craft By Numbers, Hassenfeld Bros/WDP, complete, EXIB **$75.00**

Zorro, pinwheel, diecut plastic wheel w/graphics on wooden stick handle, WDP, 1950s, 18", EX+ **$85.00**

Zorro, Sun Pictures, complete, VG+ (VG+ opened package) **$55.00**

Zorro, wallet, brown or white vinyl w/Zorro & horse, EX, ea **$75.00**

Zorro, 3-D Cut-Outs, litho plastic, Aldon Industries, complete, NMIB, from $75 to **$100.00**

Cracker Jack Toys

In 1869 Frederick Rueckheim left Hamburg, Germany, bound for Chicago, where he planned to work on a farm for his uncle. But farm life did not appeal to Mr. Rueckheim, and after the Chicago fire, he moved there and helped clear the debris. With another man whose popcorn and confectionary business had been destroyed in the fire, Mr. Rueckheim started a business with one molasses kettle and one hand popper. The following year, Mr. Rueckheim bought out his original partner and sent for his brother, Louis. The two brothers formed Rueckheim & Bro. and quickly prospered as they continued expanding their confectionary line to include new products. It was not until 1896 that the first lot of Cracker Jack was produced — and then only as an adjunct to their growing line. Cracker Jack was sold in bulk form until 1899 when H.G. Eckstein, an old friend, invented the wax-sealed package, which allowed them to ship it further and thus sell it more easily. Demand for Cracker Jack soared, and it quickly became the main product of the factory. Today millions of boxes are produced — each with a prize in every box.

The idea of prizes came along during the time of bulk packaging; it was devised as a method to stimulate sales. Later, as the wax-sealed package was introduced, a prize was given (more or less) with each package. Next, the prize was added into the package, but still not every package received a prize. It was not until the 1920s that 'a prize in every package' became a reality. Initially, the prizes were put in with the confection, but the company feared this might pose a problem, should it inadvertently be mistaken for the popcorn. To avoid this, the prize was put in a separate compartment and, finally, into its own protective wrapper. Hundreds of prizes have been used over the years, and it is still true today that there is 'a prize in every package.' Prizes have ranged from the practical girl's bracelet and pencils to tricks, games, disguises, and stick-anywhere patches. To learn more about the subject, you'll want to read *Cracker Jack Toys, The Complete Unofficial Guide for Collectors*, and *Cracker Jack, The Unauthorized Guide to Advertising Collectibles*, both by our advisor, Larry White.

Advisor: Larry White (See Directory, Cracker Jack)

Airplane, litho tin, orange w/black & red circles........**$45.00**

Airplane card, paper, multicolored, marked CJR-2, miniature, 6 different, ea **$2.00**

Airplanes, WWII, paper kit, from $50 to **$100.00**

Alphabet charms, plastic, marked CJ Co, various colors, ea **$4.00**

Arrow-back pin/pocket clip, metal Liberty Bell shape, marked Liberty **$87.50**

Banjo, litho tin **$47.00**

Baseball bat **$65.00**

Bike sticker, paper w/bike wheel on cover, various colors, ID 1380, 10 different, ea **$5.00**

Book, Baby Bears, paper, Cracker Jack Box on back, 12 different, ea **$170.00**

Book, Children's Notes, paper....................................**$65.00**

Book, Six Little Kitty-Cats, EX, $115.00.
(Photo courtesy Mary and Larry White)

Booklet, Twig & Sprig, Cracker Jack box on back **$75.00**

Card games, all w/instructions, 1960s.........................**$10.00**

Charm, dirigible shape, metal w/celluloid insert **$95.00**

Circus animals, litho tin, 5 different, ea.....................**$135.00**

Clicker, Dutch Boy, tin litho **$45.00**

Clicker, Frog Chirper, black on green.........................**$30.00**

Clicker/screamer, metal **$40.00**

Compass **$125.00**

Cracker Jack Ball Player, others, 1914, set of 144, average price **$50.00**

Dexterity puzzle, Gee Cracker Jack Is Good............**$125.00**

Eyeglasses, paper & celluloid, marked Cracker Jack Wherever You Look...**$87.00**

Figure, baseball player, plastic, gray or blue, marked Cracker Jack Co, ea **$20.00**

Figure, boy, girl, soldier, Santa, etc, ceramic, marked Japan, ea **$18.00**

Figure, girl, earthenware **$40.00**

Figure, skunk, squirrel, fish, etc, plastic, 1950, EX, ea..**$10.00**

Finger Faces, clown, elephant, or jester, paper, ea.....**$36.00**

Game, Monkey Ring Toss, paper, red & green, 1940, EX..**$30.00**

Garage, litho tin..**$78.00**

Hand Kinema, elephant & crab, paper, marked Japan..**$40.00**

Horse & wagon, litho tin w/Cracker Jack & Angelus boxes, red, white & blue..**$65.00**

ID tag, plastic & paper, unassembled **$3.00**

Indian headdress, paper, marked Me for Cracker Jack..**$250.00**
Invisible magic picture, image of man fishing, What Will He Catch?...**$12.00**
Jewelry, plastic, wood or glass on string, from $5 to.**$10.00**
Jigsaw puzzle, various scenes, written in Japanese **$95.00**
Kaleidoscope cards, #46, set of 15, ea **$3.75**
Lapel pin, Cracker Jack Junior Detective, metal.........**$35.00**
Magic picture, image of man holding hoop, Who's Jumping Thru!..., plastic...**$1.00**
Martians, plastic, many different characters, 1960s, ea ..**$20.00**
Match shooter, gun, rifle, machine gun, etc, metal, marked Japan, ea...**$12.00**
Minute Movie, Cloudcrest Creations, paper, orange & black on white, 12 different, ea.......................................**$20.00**
Mirror, celluloid, glass & metal, round w/Cracker Jack box & logo, 4 different, ea **$125.00**
Nits, plastic, marked R&L Australia, set of 20, ea.........**$4.50**
Palm puzzle, fox, pirate, cow, etc, paper & celluloid, marked Cracker Jack Co, ea......................................**$80.00**
Palm puzzle, image of 2 carts, marked Germany **$45.00**
Paper doll, marked FW Rueckheim & Bro on back .**$127.00**
Pencil, wood, red lettering on white............................**$7.00**
Pencil stencils, B Series, 13, paper, multicolored, 20 different, ea **$10.00**
Picture panorama, circus, barnyard animals, etc, paper, EX, ea **$10.00**
Pinball games, 20 designs, Makatoy, Chicago, ea, from $8 to..**$12.00**
Pipe, dog's head, ceramic, red, pink & blue, Japan ...**$10.00**
Put-together prize, plastic, several different, unmarked, ea..**$10.00**
Puzzle, Last Round-Up, paper, red & green, 1940, EX .**$30.00**
Riddle book, paper, jester on front **$57.00**
Riddle card, paper, Cracker Jack on front, riddles on back **$20.00**
Ring, wheel, heart or other faux stone, pot metal, unmarked, ea **$12.00**
Rolling pin, wood, plain, doll size **$12.00**
Serving tray, metal w/Cracker Jack box **$130.00**
Shuffle game, paper, red, green & black....................**$26.00**
Slide card, Cracker Jack, fireman, pear, owl, etc, paper, ea...**$95.00**
Slide card, Cracker Jack Movies, paper, yellow front...**$120.00**
Song book, Uncle Sam...**$100.00**
Spinner game, Cracker Jack Golf **$90.00**
Spoon rider, astronaut, cowboy, monkey, etc, plastic, ea..**$7.50**
Squirt gun, early..**$90.00**
Stand-up, Herby..**$80.00**
State cards, state flag on 1 side, information on other .**$20.00**
Sticker, glow-in-the-dark, black & yellow, 1970, EX.....**$4.00**
Tattoos, #81, marked Cracker Jack — Borden, set of 14, ea **$2.50**
Tilt card, magician, elephant, pirate, etc, plastic & paper, 1950, ea...**$8.00**
Top, Always on Top, red, white & blue, w/Cracker Jack prize box...**$55.00**
Top, metal w/ABC design..**$30.00**

Train, Lone Eagle Flyer, litho tin, 4 different, ea.......**$120.00**
Trick mustache, paper, red or black, 1940, ea **$20.00**
Typewriter, litho tin..**$95.00**
Visor, marked Cracker Jack, paper, green **$125.00**
Wheel walker, elephant, police dog, pig, etc, unmarked, ea **$28.00**
Whistle, metal gun shape...**$20.00**
Whistle, Razz Zooka, paper, red & white **$37.50**
Zodiac coin, plastic, various colors, ea **$8.00**

Crackle Glass

At the height of productivity from the 1930s through the 1970s, nearly five hundred companies created crackle glass. As pieces stayed in production for several years, dating an item may be difficult. Some colors, such as ruby red, amberina, cobalt, and cranberry, were more expensive to produce. Smoke gray was made for a short time, and because quantities are scarce, prices tend to be higher than on some of the other colors, amethyst, green, and amber included. Crackle glass is still being produced today by the Blenko Glass Company, and it is being imported from Taiwan and China as well. For further information on other glass companies and values we recommend *Crackle Glass, Identification and Value Guide, Book I* and *Book II*, by Stan and Arlene Weitman (Collector Books).

Advisors: Stan and Arlene Weitman (See Directory, Crackle Glass)

Beaker, crystal w/applied olive-green leaves, Blenko, 1940s-50s, 9½", from $125 to **$150.00**
Bottle, perfume; blue w/crystal top, Bonita, 1931-53, 7", from $80 to...**$100.00**
Bottle, perfume; light blue w/matching flower stopper, unknown manufacturer, 4½", from $50 to...........**$75.00**
Candle holder, pale sea green, bottle shape, Blenko, 1960s, 5¼", from $55 to **$60.00**

Cruet, amberina, Rainbow, late 1940s – 60s, 7", from $45.00 to $75.00. (Photo courtesy Stan and Arlene Weitman)

Cruet, blue w/matching 3-ball stopper & pulled-back handle, Rainbow, late 1940s-60s, 6½", from $75 to...........**$85.00**

Cruet, sea green w/matching ball stopper, Pilgrim, 1949-69, 6", from $75 to...**$85.00**

Cruet, topaz w/matching drop-over handle & applied serpentine, unknown manufacturer, 5¼", from $35 to **$40.00**

Cup, amberina w/amber drop-over handle, Kanawha, 1957-87, 2¼", from $30 to..**$40.00**

Decanter, amberina, matching mushroom-shaped stopper, Rainbow, late 1940s-60s, 7¾", from $80 to **$105.00**

Decanter, charcoal w/blue tint, clear teardrop stopper, Blenko, 1960s, 11¾", from $100 to **$125.00**

Decanter, topaz w/matching ball stopper, Rainbow, late 1940s-60s, 8½", from $80 to................................**$100.00**

Goblet, olive green, unknown manufacturer, 5¾", from $50 to..**$75.00**

Jug, teal green w/matching drop-over handle, Pilgrim, 1949-69, miniature, 4", from $35 to.............................**$40.00**

Lamp, oil; amber, multicolor seaweed, unmarked Moser, late 1800s, 3¾x4"...**$375.00**

Pear, pale sea green w/dark green stem, Blenko, 1950s-60s, 5", from $60 to...**$100.00**

Pitcher, amberina, waisted, drop-over handle, Pilgrim, 1949-69, miniature, 3½", from $40 to......................**$45.00**

Pitcher, amberina w/amber pulled-back handle, Rainbow, late 1940s-60s, 5", from $55 to..............................**$60.00**

Pitcher, amethyst w/clear handle, waisted, Pilgrim, 1949-69, miniature, 3¼", from $50 to..................................**$55.00**

Pitcher, blue w/clear angular drop-over handle, crimped rim, Pilgrim, 1949-69, miniature, 3½", from $45 to......**$50.00**

Pitcher, blue w/clear drop-over handle, sq top, unknown maker, miniature, 4", from $45 to.........................**$50.00**

Pitcher, blue w/matching pulled-back handle, conical shape, Pilgrim, 1949-69, miniature, 4¼", from $35 to......**$40.00**

Pitcher, blue w/matching pulled-back handle, sq sides, Kanawha, 1957-87, 4", from $35 to **$40.00**

Pitcher, cranberry w/can neck, polished pontil, Moser, 5½"...**$575.00**

Pitcher, dark amber w/very dark drop-over handle, conical shape, Blenko, 1949-50, 17", from $125 to.........**$150.00**

Pitcher, emerald green w/clear drop-over handle, waisted, Pilgrim, 1949-69, 4", from $35 to..........................**$40.00**

Pitcher, emerald green w/matching drop-over handle, slim, mold blown, unknown manufacturer, 5¼", from $25 to...**$30.00**

Pitcher, green w/clear drop-over handle, trumpet neck, Pilgrim, 1949-69, miniature, 3½", from $35 to......**$40.00**

Pitcher, green w/matching pulled-back handle, Williamsburg Glass paper label, 1950-60, 4¾", from $55 to **$60.00**

Pitcher, hand-painted fish & seaweed on golden amber, applied handle, pinched sides, Moser, 5¾".......**$450.00**

Pitcher, lemon lime, clear pulled-back handle, flared cylinder w/narrow top, 1949-69, miniature, 4¼", $35 to ...**$40.00**

Pitcher, light amber w/clear pulled back handle, stick neck, unknown manufacturer, 5½", from $35 to............**$40.00**

Pitcher, light amber w/clear pulled-back handle, scalloped rim, unknown maker, miniature, 4½", from $35 to **$40.00**

Pitcher, olive green w/matching drop-over handle, bulbous w/wide mouth, Blenko, 1960s, 5¾", from $50 to ..**$55.00**

Pitcher, olive green w/matching pulled-back handle, Rainbow, 1940s-60s, 3¾", from $45 to.................**$50.00**

Pitcher, ruby w/amber drop-over handle, scalloped rim, unknown manufacturer, 4½", from $55 to............**$60.00**

Pitcher, ruby w/clear drop-over handle, teardrop shape w/sm opening at top, 1949-69, miniature, 3¾", from $40 to .**$45.00**

Pitcher, sea green w/matching drop-over handle, trumpet neck, Pilgrim, 1949-69, miniature, 3¾", from $35 to **$40.00**

Pitcher, tangerine w/clear drop-over handle, jug style, Pilgrim, 1949-69, 3¾", from $40 to........................**$45.00**

Pitcher, tangerine w/drop-over handle, pinched style, Rainbow, late 1940s-50s, 6", from $70 to.............**$75.00**

Pitcher, tangerine w/yellow pulled-back handle, flared cylinder, 1949-69, miniature, 4", from $40 to **$45.00**

Pitcher, wheat w/matching drop-over handle, bulbous w/sm neck, Blenko, 1960s, 9¾", from $75 to.............**$100.00**

Tray, cranberry, hand-painted egret in marsh scene, Moser, 1880s, 13½x7¼".......................................**$2,500.00**

Tumbler, crystal w/amber drop-over handle, unknown manufacturer, 5¼", from $35 to.................................**$50.00**

Tumbler, topaz, straight sides, unknown manufacturer, 6¾", from $35 to...**$50.00**

Vase, blue, Bischoff, 1940 – 63, 10½", from $100.00 to $125.00. (Photo courtesy Stan and Arlene Weitman)

Vase, blue w/applied decoration at base, 4-scallop top, Pilgrim, 1949-69, 3½", from $40 to.......................**$45.00**

Vase, blue w/applied serpentine to stick neck, Pilgrim, 1949-69, 6½", from $55 to..**$75.00**

Vase, golden amber, hand-painted seaweed scenes, unmarked Moser, miniature, 3¾" **$350.00**

Vase, olive green, double neck, Blenko, 1940s-50s, 4", from $50 to...**$75.00**

Vase, sea green, pinched, Blenko, late 1940s-50s, 3¾", from $55 to...**$75.00**

Vase, tangerine, footed, crimped rim, Blenko, 1950s, 8", from $120 to...**$145.00**

Vase, tangerine w/applied decor on stick neck, scalloped rim, Pilgrim, 1949-69, 4½", from $60 to................**$75.00**

Cuff Links

Cuff link collecting continues to be one of the fastest growing hobbies. Few collectibles are as affordable, available, and easy to store. Cuff links can often be found at garage sales, thrift shops, and flea markets for reasonable prices.

People collect cuff links for many reasons. Besides being a functional and interesting wearable, cuff links are educational. The design, shape, size, and materials used often relate to events, places, and products, and they typically reflect the period of their manufacture: examples are Art Deco, Victorian, Art Nouveau, Modern, etc. They offer the chance for the 'big find' which appeals to all collectors. Sometimes pairs purchased for small amounts turn out to be worth substantial sums.

Unless otherwise noted, the following listings apply to cuff links in excellent to mint condition.

Advisor: Gene Klompus (See Directory, Cuff Links)

Club: The National Cuff Link Society

Newsletter: *The Link*
Gene Klompus, President
P.O. Box 5700
Vernon Hills, IL 60010
Phone or Fax: 847-816-0035; Dues $30 per year; write for free booklet, *The Fun of Cuff Link Collecting.*'
e-mail: Genek@cufflink.com

Related Website: www.cufflink.com

Ace of spades, black & silver, rectangular, bold **$60.00**
Airplane, F14, 14k heavy gold, perfectly detailed replica, special **$275.00**
Baby shoes, gold color **$100.00**
Buddha, Mother of Pearl, on genuine onyx base, distinctive estate pr **$200.00**
Bugs Bunny, officially licensed...................................**$45.00**
Caduceus, +tie bar, classic medical symbol, sterling silver, w/gift box...**$95.00**
Camp David Presidential Retreat, official pr; federal eagle, same as given to dignitaries................................**$160.00**

Castle, ca 1960, from $35.00 to $50.00. (Photo courtesy Gene Klompus)

Chivas Regal, sterling silver, w/box bearing logo **$75.00**
Classic, double-sided, rich blue enamel over hallmarked sterling silver...**$130.00**
Dog (Bull Dog), figural, ivory, highly detailed, rare.**$200.00**

Elephant, double-sided, sterling silver, made in S Africa, ca 1940 ....**$125.00**
Estate prs, Nefertiti or Sphinx, 24k over sterling.......**$395.00**
FBI, official Federal Bureau of Investigation seal, rich colors...**$95.00**
Genuine Snapper, ca 1923, all different, 5 pr **$100.00**
Golfer, in swing pose, sterling silver golfer, black onyx background, round...**$80.00**
Greek Parthenon, double-sided, sterling silver, Greek key **$100.00**

Hand-in-circle peace sign, ca 1970, $45.00. (Photo courtesy Gene Klompus)

Horseheads, ivory, heavy dimensional detail, ca 1940 .**$250.00**
Inagural, Bush/Cheney 2001, 24k gold plate **$125.00**
Marilyn Monroe, first edition Playboy Magazine pose, oval...**$95.00**
Oil Derricks, sterling silver, detailed figural **$125.00**
Presidential, George Bush's famous sterling silver 'W 2000' **$195.00**
Salt & pepper shakers, classic design, high detail, sterling silver, distinctive **$85.00**
Star of David, sterling silver...**$85.00**
The Drunkard, original theatrical motif.......................**$85.00**
Wrap-arounds, silver or gold, 4 pr **$100.00**

Accessories

Stud set, mother-of-pearl & onyx, cuff links w/4 matching shirt studs **$95.00**
Stud set, Superman logo, cuff links w/4 studs, sterling silver, distictive...**$125.00**

Cup and Saucer Sets

Lovely cups and saucers are often available at garage sales and flea markets, and prices are generally quite reasonable. If limited space is a consideration, you might enjoy starting a collection, since they're easy to display en masse on a shelf or one at a time as a romantic accent on a coffee table. English manufacturers have produced endless bone china cups and saucers that are more decorative than functional and just as many that are part of their dinnerware lines. American manufacturers were just about as prolific as were the Japanese. Collecting examples from many companies and countries is a wonderful way to study the various ceramic manufacturers. Our advisors have written *Collectible Cups and Saucers, Identification and Values, Books I* and *II* (Collector Books), with hundreds of color photos organized by six collectible categories: early years (1700 – 1875), cabinet cups, nineteenth and twentieth century dinnerware, English tablewares, miniatures, and mustache cups and saucers.

Advisors: Jim and Susan Harran (See Directory, Cups and Saucers)

Coffee, Plain Blue Lace pattern, ribbed cup w/ring handle, Royal Copenhagen, 1922 to present, from $75 to..**$100.00**

Coffee, Rothchild Bird pattern, scalloped, Herend, 1950s to present, from $100 to **$125.00**

Demitasse, Colonial pattern, footed cup w/French Loop handle, Lenox, 1950s, from $40 to **$50.00**

Demitasse, dark blue leaf motif on ivory, scalloped, Noritake, current, from $20 to..**$30.00**

Demitasse, enameled floral design, footed cup w/24 ribs & sq handle, Lenox, 1950s, from $40 to **$50.00**

Demitasse, floral transfer, straight cup w/scalloped saucer, Rorstrand, 1950 to present, from $40 to **$50.00**

Demitasse, hand-painted gold floral, pedestal cup w/'broken' loop handle, Occupied Japan, 1945-52, from $35 to .**$45.00**

Demitasse, Husk pattern made for Williamsburg, Wedgwood, 1950s, from $25 to **$35.00**

Demitasse, Lavina, Royal Worcester, ca 1950s, from $30.00 to $40.00. (Photo courtesy Jim and Susan Harran)

Demitasse, Pansy, Dainty shape w/loop handle, Shelley, 1945-66, from $45 to..**$65.00**

Demitasse, Sleepy Hollow by Naomi Savage, can shape w/oval handle, cobalt saucer, Langenthal Porcelain, 1950s, from $40 to **$50.00**

Demitasse, strawberry-form cup on leaf saucer, Cemar California, ca 1946-57, from $40 to **$50.00**

Tea, autumn leaves on white w/gold, Tirschenreuth Bavaria, 1903-81, from $40 to...**$50.00**

Tea, bachelor buttons on white w/gold, footed & slightly waisted cup w/broken loop handle, Royal Vale, 1962+, from $30 to..**$40.00**

Tea, black w/pink inside cup, gilded branches & leaves, Leneige China, Burbank California, 1952, from $35 to..**$45.00**

Tea, bright floral on white w/gold, Duchess Bone China (AT Finney & Sons), 1947-60, from $30 to..................**$50.00**

Tea, Christmas candles & holly, footed cup w/angular loop handle, Tirschenreuth Bavaria, 1969 to present, from $60 to...**$75.00**

Tea, Chrysanthemum (Flower of the Month), puffed 8-flute design, Royal Albert, 1945+, from $30 to.............**$40.00**

Tea, Country Side chintz, Chester shape, Shelley, 1945-66, from $100 to..**$125.00**

Tea, dark red w/gold flowers, York shape, Aynsley, 1950s, from $30 to...**$40.00**

Tea, Dresden flowers on white, straight cup w/loop handle, low thumb rest, Carl Schumann, US Zone, 1945-49, from $40 to...**$50.00**

Tea, DuBarry chintz, Royal Flute shape w/'broken' loop handle, James Kent, 1934-80, from $85 to...............**$100.00**

Tea, floral on maroon, scalloped & footed cup w/coiled loop handle, Princess China/Occupied Japan, 1945-52, from $30 to...**$40.00**

Tea, floral transfer, waisted cup w/loop handle, Foley, 1930-35, from $30 to **$40.00**

Tea, gold leafy design on turquoise, corseted cup w/coiled loop handle, Synsley, 1950s, from $35 to............**$45.00**

Tea, leaf pattern on white w/gold trim, Rosenthal Studio Line, 1950s, from $50 to....................................**$60.00**

Tea, multicolor floral transfer, waisted & scalloped pedestal cup, Cauldon Potteries Ltd, 1950-62, from $30 to.**$40.00**

Tea, mums transfer, footed cup w/8 puffy flutes & 'broken' loop handle, crimped saucer, Paragon, 1957+, from $35 to...**$45.00**

Tea, pale peach w/pink & white floral transfer on inside of cup & on saucer, low Doris shape, Aynsley, 1950+, from $35 to..**$45.00**

Tea, peony & mixed floral transfer, footed & fluted cup, scalloped saucer, Aynsley, 1950s, from $40 to **$50.00**

Tea, San Souci pattern, molded cup w/unusual handle, Rosenthal, 1950s, w/dessert plate, from $75 to....**$90.00**

Tea, turquoise melon-shape cup w/gold floral decoration & 3 gold feet, Royal Sealy Japan, ca 1950+, from $35 to **$40.00**

Tea, yellow w/gold flowers on rim, York shape, Aynsley, 1950s, from $30 to **$40.00**

Tea, yellow w/violets on white inside cup, Adderleys Ltd, 1962, from $35 to...**$40.00**

Tea, Yule Tide, holly leaves & berries, footed & fluted cup, Queen Anne (Shore & Coggins), 1950+, from $30 to.............**$40.00**

Czechoslovakian Glass and Ceramics

Established as a country in 1918, Czechoslovakia is rich in the natural resources needed for production of glassware as well as pottery. Over the years it has produced vast amounts of both. Anywhere you go, from flea markets to fine antique shops, you'll find several examples of their lovely pressed and cut glass scent bottles, Deco vases, lamps, kitchenware, tableware, and figurines.

More than thirty-five marks have been recorded; some are ink stamped, some etched, and some molded in. Paper labels have also been used. *Czechoslovakian Glass and Collectibles* by Diane and Dale Barta and Helen M. Rose, and *Made in Czechoslovakia* by Ruth Forsythe are two books we highly recommend for further study.

Club: Czechoslovakian Collectors Guild International
P.O. Box 901395
Kansas City, MO 64190

Ceramics

Baby dish, 7" diameter from $40.00 to $45.00. (Photo courtesy Dale and Diane Barta and Helen M. Rose)

Box, dresser; lovers on lid, mirror inside, 3¼" dia **$65.00**
Box, duck figural, muted colors, 4¼", from $40 to **$45.00**
Candle holders, green mottled lustre, slim w/flared base, 6", pr from $40 to...**$45.00**
Covered sauce dish, lobster figural, 3½" **$35.00**
Creamer, duck figural, 3¾" **$60.00**
Creamer, figural cat handle, 4⅜" **$75.00**
Creamer, moose figural, 4⅞"..**$45.00**
Creamer, pearlescent lustreware w/green rim & handle, 3¾", from $20 to...**$25.00**
Creamer & sugar bowl, pink lustre, w/lid, 3¼", 4"....**$25.00**
Cup & saucer, rooster, from child's set **$25.00**
Figurine, cat, white w/pink details, 5", from $40 to ...**$45.00**
Figurine, Deco-style lady, white, 9¾" **$250.00**
Figurine, dog sitting, black & white, 4", from $30 to..**$35.00**
Flower holder, bird on stump, 5⅜"..............................**$40.00**
Match holder, hand-painted Oriental scene, green interior, scarce, 5", from $65 to......................................**$70.00**
Mug, tavern scene on white, Erphila, 4¼", from $30 to .**$35.00**
Mustard pot, pansies & black design on white, 3½" ..**$50.00**
Napkin ring, girl figural, 4" **$45.00**

Pitcher, batter; poppies & green leaves on white, w/lid, Erphila mark, from $50 to..................................**$55.00**
Pitcher, multicolor bubbles on blue & white, air brushed, Erphila mark, 7¼", from $65 to **$70.00**
Pitcher, toucan figural, cream, red & black, Erphila mark, 9", from $85 to..**$90.00**
Salt & pepper shakers, boy & girl figural, 3⅛", pr......**$45.00**
Teapot, girl finial, 8"..**$250.00**
Toby mug, Bumble figural, 5¼", from $50 to **$55.00**
Toothpick holder, rooster figural, cream & red, Erphila mark, 2", from $25 to..**$30.00**
Vase, Deco-style vining floral on black, white interior, 3" H...**$75.00**
Vase, green cactus, orange & pink flowers on white w/blue trim, orange handles, 7¾", from $40 to **$45.00**
Vase, Oriental scene, red & gold-flecked handles, marked Czecho-Slovakia & Chinese marking, 10½"......**$250.00**
Vase, painted bird & flowers, cylindrical, 4⅜" **$100.00**
Vase, yellow lustreware, handles, fluted black rim, 10"...**$50.00**
Wall pocket, bird among apples, 4¾"............................**$65.00**
Wall pocket, bird at wishing well, 6".............................**$60.00**
Wall pocket, bird on perch of birdhouse, 5½"............**$60.00**
Wall pocket, peacock on cobalt, 7¼" **$125.00**

Wall pocket, toucan, 7½", $60.00. (Photo courtesy Bill and Betty Newbound)

Wall pocket, woodpecker, 7¾" **$70.00**

Glassware

Candlestick, cameo, black vining decor on orange, 12½"...**$650.00**
Candlestick, mottled satin, cased in amber, 3⅛".........**$65.00**
Candlestick, pink transparent w/applied green decoration, 8"...**$65.00**
Candlestick, yellow to multicolor mottle at base, 4"...**$85.00**
Candy jar, green w/applied apricot pedestal base w/3 buttressed feet, w/lid, 6" **$275.00**
Candy jar, mottled colors, footed, w/lid, 5"..............**$150.00**
Perfume bottle, black opaque w/clear stopper, 5⅞"...**$250.00**
Perfume bottle, blue, shouldered, simple blue stopper, 5⅝"...**$185.00**

Perfume bottle, green pyramidal shape w/cuttings, spear-shaped stopper, 4⅝"...$145.00

Perfume bottle, boat with pink sail cut with various facets, paper label and signed, from $450.00 to $550.00. (Photo courtesy Monsen and Baer)

Perfume bottle, topaz, shouldered, frosted stopper, 6"..$200.00
Pitcher, blue transparent bubbly glass, 8⅝" $200.00
Pitcher, exotic bird painted on orange opaque w/black at rim, 11½"...$285.00
Puff box, cranberry opalescent hobnail, 3½" $175.00
Tumbler, enameled scene on crystal, 4¼" $50.00
Tumbler, green bubbly glass w/hand-painted hunt scene, 5¾"...$65.00
Tumbler, orange & green stacked segments, 4¾".......$50.00
Vase, blue & white varicolored, pink cased, embossed ribs, 6⅛"...$250.00
Vase, blue cased, pink ruffled top, 8½"....................$110.00
Vase, blue cased, pleated rim, crystal handles, 8¼" .$110.00
Vase, blue cased, rose ruffled top, 6" $100.00
Vase, blue opaque w/cobalt overlay, 7" $85.00
Vase, bud; multicolor mottle, 8¼" $75.00
Vase, bud; red cased, silver & black decor, 11¼".....$110.00
Vase, cane decoration, cased, 6" $200.00
Vase, cobalt w/silver birds on flowering branch, 13" $185.00
Vase, crystal w/red & black overlay, 8¼"..................$200.00
Vase, green cased in white w/black overlay, 8½" $125.00
Vase, green opaque w/3 cobalt angle handles, cobalt rim, 8¼"...$875.00
Vase, jack-in-the-pulpit; yellow opaque w/black trim at rim, 10½"...$65.00
Vase, milky white w/opalescent ball handles, 8⅝"...$275.00
Vase, mottled satin, cased in amber, 7⅜" $125.00
Vase, orange opaque w/black rim, footed trumpet form, 7¼"...$85.00
Vase, orange transparent w/yellow overlay, fan form, 8"..$200.00
Vase, painted desert scene, 8½" $815.00
Vase, red & white mottle w/applied black serpentine, black trim on ruffled rim, 8½" $160.00

Vase, red opaque w/applied black serpentine decoration, 6½"...$100.00
Vase, red opaque w/3 angled cobalt handles, cobalt rim, 5½" $575.00
Vase, stick form, mottled colors, 8½"..........................$65.00
Vase, varicolored ball form w/metal flower arranger top, 4¼" $100.00
Vase, varicolored w/green aventurine, black trim along rim, trumpet form, footed, 7" $150.00
Vase, white cased w/crystal handles, 7½" $65.00
Vase, white opaque w/red opaque overlay, 5½"........$95.00
Vase, white w/applied red serpentine decoration, fan form, 6¾"...$125.00
Vase, yellow, white & purple mottle, white cased, black trim, 8¼"...$200.00
Vase, yellow cased, red overlay at foot & lower body, 8" $125.00
Vase, yellow opaque w/black enamel decor, 8" $125.00
Vase, yellow opaque w/black trim at ruffled rim, slim flared cylinder, 8½" $75.00
Vase, yellow opaque w/Niagara Falls scene in black, 6¼"...$75.00
Wine, orange w/silver decor, clear stem, 3¾"............$40.00

Dakin

Dakin has been in the toy-making business since the 1950s and has made several lines of stuffed and vinyl dolls and animals. But the Dakins that collectors are most interested in today are the licensed characters and advertising figures made from 1968 through the 1970s. Originally there were seven Warner Brothers characters, each with a hard plastic body and a soft vinyl head, all under 10" tall. The line was very successful and eventually expanded to include more than fifty cartoon characters and several more that were advertising related. In addition to the figures, there are banks that were made in two sizes. Some Dakins are quite scarce and may sell for over $100.00 (a few even higher), though most will be in the $30.00 to $60.00 range. Dakin is now owned by Applause, Inc.

Condition is very important, and if you find one still in the original box, add about 50% to its value. Figures in the colorful 'Cartoon Theatre' boxes command higher prices than those that came in a clear plastic bag or package (MIP). More Dakins are listed in *Schroeder's Collectible Toys, Antique to Modern*, published by Collector Books.

Baby Puss, Hanna-Barbera, 1971, NM $100.00
Bambi, Disney, 1960s, MIP $35.00
Bamm-Bamm, Hanna-Barbera, 1970, w/club, EX $30.00
Barney Rubble, Hanna-Barbera, 1970, EX..................$40.00
Benji, 1978, cloth, EX $10.00
Bozo the Clown, Larry Harmon, 1974, EX..................$35.00
Bugs Bunny, Warner Bros, 1978, MIP (Fun Farm bag)..$20.00
Bullwinkle, Jay Ward, 1976, MIB (TV Cartoon Theater box) $60.00
Cool Cat, Warner Bros, 1970, w/beret, EX+ $30.00

Daffy Duck, Warner Bros, 1968, EX.................$30.00
Deputy Dawg, Terrytoons, 1977, EX.................$50.00
Dewey Duck, Disney, straight or bent legs, EX.........$30.00
Dino Dinosaur, Hanna-Barbera, 1970, EX $40.00
Donald Duck, Disney, 1960s, straight or bent legs, NMIP.$30.00
Dream Pets, Hawaiian Hound, cloth, w/surfboard & original tag, EX.................$15.00
Dream Pets, Kangaroo, cloth, w/camera, wearing beret, EX.................$10.00
Dudley Do-Right, Jay Ward, 1976, MIB (TV Cartoon Theater box) $75.00
Dumbo, Disney, 1960s, cloth collar, MIB $25.00
Elmer Fudd, Warner Bros, 1968, in tuxedo, EX $30.00

Foghorn Leghorn, 1970, 8½", EX, $75.00.

Fred Flintstone, Hanna-Barbera, 1970, EX..................$40.00
Goofy Gram, Dog, Congratulations Dumm-Dumm, EX..$25.00
Goofy Gram, Kangaroo, World's Greatest Mom, EX...$25.00
Goofy Gram, Pepe Le Peu, You're a Real Stinker, 1971, EX.................$40.00
Hokey Wolf, Hanna-Barbera, 1971, MIP..................$100.00
Huckleberry Hound, Hanna-Barbera, 1970, EX+ $60.00
Jack-in-the-Box, bank, 1971, EX.................$25.00
Lion in Cage, bank, 1971, EX $25.00
Mickey Mouse, Disney, cloth clothes, EX..................$20.00
Mighty Mouse, Terrytoons, 1978, marked Fun Farm, EX.$100.00
Minnie Mouse, Disney, 1960s, cloth clothes, EX.........$20.00
Monkey on a Barrel, bank, 1971, EX $25.00
Olive Oyle, King Features, 1976, MIB (TV Cartoon Theater box) $40.00
Opus, 1982, cloth, w/tag, EX.................$20.00
Pebbles Flintstone, Hanna-Barbera, 1970, EX..............$35.00
Pepe Le Peu, Warner Bros, 1971, EX $55.00
Pink Panther, Mirisch-Freleng, 1976, MIB (TV Cartoon Theater box).................$50.00
Popeye, King Features, 1974, cloth clothes, MIP $50.00
Porky Pig, Warner Bros, 1968, EX.................$30.00
Practical Pig, EX.................$45.00
Road Runner, Warner Bros, 1968, EX.................$30.00

Rocky Squirrel, Jay Ward, 1976, MIB (TV Cartoon Theater box) $60.00
Scooby Doo, Hanna-Barbera, 1980, EX $75.00
Scrappy Doo, Hanna-Barbera, 1982, EX $75.00
Seal on Box, bank, 1971, EX.................$25.00
Second Banana, Warner Bros, 1970, EX $35.00

Snagglepuss, 1971, 7½", EX, $100.00.

Speedy Gonzales, Warner Bros, M $35.00
Tweety Bird, Warner Bros, 1976, MIB (TV Cartoon Theater box) $40.00
Wile E Coyote, Warner Bros, 1968, MIB $30.00
Yosemite Sam, Warner Bros, 1976, MIP (Fun Farm bag)..$40.00

Advertising

Bay View Bank, 1976, EX+ $30.00
Bob's Big Boy, 1974, w/hamburger, EX+ $150.00
Buddie Bull, Buddig Meats, 1970s, cloth, EX $20.00
Cocker Spaniel, Crocker National Bank, 1979, cloth, 12", VG.................$20.00
Diaperene Baby, Sterling Drug Co, 1980, EX.............$40.00
Freddie Fast Gas Attendant, 1976, M $75.00
Glamour Kitty, 1977, complete w/crown, EX...........$200.00
Hobo Joe, bank, Hobo Joe's Restaurant, EX $60.00
Kernal Renk, American Seeds, 1970, rare, EX+.........$300.00
Li'l Miss Just Rite, 1965, EX+.................$60.00
Miss Liberty Bell, 1975, MIP.................$60.00
Quasar Robot, bank, 1975, NM $125.00
Sambo's Boy, 1974, vinyl, EX+ $80.00
Sambo's Tiger, 1974, vinyl, EX+ $125.00
Smokey Bear, 1976, M.................$25.00
St Bernard, Christian Bros Candy, 1982, cloth, VG.....$20.00
Woodsy Owl, 1974, MIP.................$60.00

Decanters

The first company to make figural ceramic decanters was the James Beam Distilling Company. Until mid-1992 they produced hundreds of varieties in their own US-based china factory. They first issued their bottles in the mid-'50s, and over the course of the next twenty-five years, more than twenty other companies followed their example. Among the more prominent of these were Brooks, Hoffman, Lionstone, McCormick, Old Commonwealth, Ski Country, and Wild Turkey. In 1975, Beam introduced the 'Wheel Series,' cars, trains, and fire engines with wheels that actually revolved. The popularity of this series resulted in a heightened interest in decanter collecting.

There are various sizes. The smallest (called miniatures) hold two ounces, and there are some that hold a gallon! A full decanter is worth no more than an empty one, and the absence of the tax stamp doesn't lower its value either. Just be sure that all the labels are intact and that there are no cracks or chips. You might want to empty your decanters as a safety precaution (many collectors do) rather than risk the possibility of the inner glaze breaking down and allowing the contents to leak into the porous ceramic body.

All of the decanters we've listed are fifths unless we've specified 'miniature' within the description.

See also Elvis Presley Collectibles.

Newsletter: *Beam Around the World*
International Association of Jim Beam Bottle and Specialties Clubs
Shirley Sumbles, Executive Administrator
2015 Burlington Ave., Kewanee, IL 61443; 309-853-3370

Newsletter: *The Ski Country Collector*
1224 Washington Ave., Golden, CO 80401

Anniversary, University of Toledo Centennial **$40.00**
Barton, Black & Gold Apothecary, 2½ Million Barrel Commemorative **$20.00**
Beam, Casino Series, Harold's Club Slot Machine, gray..**$10.00**
Beam, Casino Series, Harold's Club VIP, 1968 ....**$59.00**
Beam, Club Series, Hawaii Aloha w/Medallion...........**$15.00**
Beam, Club Series, Rocky Mountain Club **$10.00**
Beam, Convention Series, #10 Norfolk Waterman, pewter .**$29.00**
Beam, Convention Series, #11 Las Vegas Showgirl, brunette..**$45.00**
Beam, Convention Series, #16 Boston Minuteman, pewter **$55.00**
Beam, Convention Series, #2 Anaheim **$25.00**
Beam, Convention Series, #7 Louisville **$9.00**
Beam, Customer Series, Ponderosa Ranch...................**$13.00**
Beam, Customer Series, Travelodge Bear **$19.00**
Beam, Executive Series, 1968 Presidential **$14.00**
Beam, Executive Series, 1990 Nutcracker, Drummer Boy.**$29.00**
Beam, Foreign Series, Australia Koalas **$19.00**
Beam, Foreign Series, Fiji Islands **$9.00**
Beam, Fox Series, Green Coat **$29.00**
Beam, Fox Series, Uncle Sam Fox................................**$15.00**
Beam, Glass Series, Cleopatra, yellow **$12.00**
Beam, Organization Series, Ducks Unlimited #2, Wood Duck, 1975 ....**$46.00**
Beam, Organization Series, Kentucky Colonel **$10.00**

Beam, Organization Series, Pearl Harbor Survivors, 1976 ..**$11.00**
Beam, Organization Series, Shriner-Moila w/Camel....**$15.00**
Beam, Organization Series, Tall Cedars of Lebanon **$8.00**
Beam, People Series, Charlie McCarthy & Mortimer Snerd, pr **$85.00**
Beam, People Series, Martha Washington...................**$14.00**
Beam, Political Series, Donkey & Elephant on Drum, 1976, pr **$24.00**
Beam, Regal China Series, Antique Clock...................**$39.00**
Beam, Regal China Series, Coffee Mill **$20.00**
Beam, Regal China Series, London Bridge....................**$6.00**
Beam, Regal China Series, New York World's Fair **$15.00**
Beam, Sports Series, 1970 Preakness **$29.00**
Beam, Sports Series, 95th Kentucky Derby, red or pink, ea...**$18.00**
Beam, States Series, Arizona **$8.00**
Beam, States Series, Florida Shells, pr.......................**$14.00**
Beam, States Series, South Dakota, Mount Rushmore ..**$10.00**
Beam, Trophy Series, Bluejay **$10.00**
Beam, Trophy Series, Cats, Burmese or Siamese, ea ..**$18.00**
Beam, Trophy Series, Horse, Appaloosa, gray, 1962 .**$26.00**
Beam, Wheel Series, Casey Jones' Train, Caboose **$35.00**
Beam, Wheel Series, Casey Jones' Train, Locomotive & Tender..**$49.00**
Beam, Wheel Series, Casey Jones' Train, Tank Car.....**$35.00**
Beam, Wheel Series, Chevrolet Bel Air Convertible, turquoise..**$55.00**
Beam, Wheel Series, Firefighter, 1928 Fire Chief Car...**$119.00**
Beam, Wheel Series, Firefighter, 1930 Model A Fire Engine **$169.00**
Beam, Wheel Series, Mercedes, mocha....................**$52.00**
Beam, Wheel Series, Mercedes, red **$55.00**
Beam, Wheel Series, Police State Trooper, white........**$44.00**
Beam, Wheel Series, Police Tow Truck **$69.00**
Beam, Wheel Series, Thomas Flyer, ivory or blue, ea ...**$59.00**
Beam, Wheel Series, Train (General), Locomotive ...**$129.00**
Beam, Wheel Series, Train (General), Wood Tender.**$149.00**
Beam, Wheel Series, Train (Grant), Coal Tender **$69.00**
Beam, Wheel Series, Train (Grant), Locomotive **$85.00**
Beam, Wheel Series, Train (Turner), Locomotive **$119.00**
Beam, Wheel Series, Train (Turner), Wood Tender....**$75.00**
Beam, Wheel Series, 18-Wheeler Dump Truck **$45.00**
Beam, Wheel Series, 1903 Model A, black **$55.00**
Beam, Wheel Series, 1913 Model T, green **$55.00**
Beam, Wheel Series, 1956 Ford Thunderbird, gray or green, ea **$99.00**
Beam, Wheel Series, 1959 Ford Cadillac, pink...........**$59.00**
Beam, Wheel Series, 1963 Chevrolet Corvette, silver .**$85.00**
Beam, Wheel Series, 1963 Chevrolet Corvette, silver-blue, NY issue **$95.00**
Beam, Wheel Series, 1968 Chevrolet Corvette, blue...**$59.00**
Beam, Wheel Series, 1970 Dodge Challenger, Hot Rod, yellow **$49.00**
Beam, Wheel Series, 1978 Chevrolet Corvette, Florida exclusive, black **$129.00**
Beam, Wheel Series, 1978 Chevrolet Corvette, red, white or yellow, ea...**$85.00**

Beam, Wheel Series, 1985 San Francisco Cable Car ...**$59.00**
Collectors Art, Chevrolet Corvette Stingray, red, no label ..**$32.00**
Creative World, Romeo & Juliet, 1971, pr...................**$69.00**
Daniel Boone, Jug, Stoneware, 4/5 qt **$12.00**
Daviess County, American Legion, 1978, New Orleans..**$19.00**
Double Springs, Excalibur Phaeton.............................**$22.00**
Eagle Rare, Series I, #1..**$24.00**
Early Times, Bicentennial Series, USA.......................**$59.00**
Ezra Brooks, Dakota Cowgirl.....................................**$32.00**
Ezra Brooks, Foremost Astronaut **$19.00**
Ezra Brooks, Iowa Statehouse **$38.00**
Ezra Brooks, Lobster..**$22.00**
Ezra Brooks, Panda **$19.00**

Ezra Brooks, Quail, Heritage China, 1970, $12.00.

Ezra Brooks, Shrine Sphynx.......................................**$10.00**
Ezra Brooks, Wichita Centennial **$14.00**
Ezra Brooks, 1931 Duesenberg Phaeton, green **$28.00**
Famous First, Indy Racer #11, miniature.....................**$39.00**
Famous Grouse, very rare bisque finish.....................**$150.00**
Fraternal Order of Eagles, 1989, Las Vegas.................**$32.00**
Garnier, Partridge..**$15.00**
Garnier, Valley Quail, California **$19.00**
Grenadier, 18th Continental **$29.00**
Harvey's Bristol Cream, Coalport................................**$13.00**
Henry McKenna, 1-Quart Jug, stoneware **$16.00**
Hoffman, Goose w/Golden Egg Pitcher **$12.00**
Hoffman, World's Greatest Fan, Cincinnati Bengals....**$49.00**
Jack Daniels, Belle of Lincoln....................................**$29.00**
Jack Daniels, Crock, flat-sided, fifth **$20.00**
Jack Daniels, Flask, Fenton Glass..............................**$25.00**
Jack Daniels, Shot Glasses, Old #7, royal blue w/gold writing **$5.00**
Kessler, Football Player **$29.00**
Kontinental, Dock Worker..**$30.00**
Kontinental, Statue of Liberty **$25.00**
Lionstone, Firefighter #2, Carrying Child **$95.00**
Lionstone, Pheasant, 1977..**$45.00**
Lionstone Minis, Fireman #1 & #2, set.......................**$49.00**
Lionstone Minis, Tropical Birds, Macaw **$25.00**

Lord Calvert, #1 Canadian Goose...............................**$46.00**
Lord Calvert, #3 Canvasback......................................**$16.00**
Luxardo, Nubian, miniature **$8.00**
McCormick, Ciao Baby...**$26.00**
McCormick, Henry Ford, miniature..............................**$15.00**
McCormick, Packard Hood Ornament **$35.00**
McCormick, Patrick Henry **$19.00**
McCormick, Thomas Edison **$26.00**
Mike Wayne, John Wayne Statue, bronze, no label **$79.00**
Old Bardstown, Christmas Card **$14.00**
Old Bardstown, Tiger...**$29.00**
Old Commonwealth, Coal Miner Series, Standing w/Shovel #1 ....**$95.00**
Old Commonwealth, Firefighter Series, #2 Nozzleman.....**$69.00**
Old Commonwealth, Firefighter Series, #6 Breaking Through, Bookend **$69.00**
Old Commonwealth, Laredo Pass Boot **$15.00**
Old Commonwealth, Western Boot, miniature...........**$15.00**
Old Crow, Pawns, yellow or green, ea........................**$21.00**
Old Fitzgerald, South Carolina Tricentennial...............**$11.00**
Old Mr Boston, Amvets, 1975 National Convention **$9.00**
Old Mr Boston, West Virginia National Guard **$28.00**
Old Rip Van Winkle, Rip Van Winkle #2, Reclining....**$32.00**
Pacesetter, Green Machine, miniature.........................**$49.00**
Paramount, Ohio Governor James Rhodes...................**$25.00**
Philadelphia, Liberty Bell **$9.00**
PM Specialties, Firemark, made to hang on wall........**$65.00**
Raintree, Clown Set #2, set of 6 miniatures...............**$129.00**
Ski Country, Animals, Fox on Log..............................**$95.00**
Ski Country, Animals, Mountain Lion, miniature.........**$28.00**
Ski Country, Banded Waterfowl, Ducks Unlimited, Bufflehead, 1984, miniature **$29.00**
Ski Country, Banded Waterfowl, Ducks Unlimited, Mallard, 1980 ....**$75.00**
Ski Country, Birds, Black Swan **$45.00**
Ski Country, Birds, Cardinal, miniature.....................**$39.00**
Ski Country, Birds, Peacock......................................**$99.00**
Ski Country, Birds, Redwing Blackbird.......................**$45.00**
Ski Country, Birds, Whooping Crane, miniature **$39.00**
Ski Country, Christmas Series, Bob Cratchit **$54.00**
Ski Country, Christmas Series, Chickadees **$69.00**
Ski Country, Christmas Series, Scrooge, miniature.....**$24.00**
Ski Country, Circus Series, Horse, Palomino **$57.00**
Ski Country, Circus Series, PT Barnum, miniature......**$29.00**
Ski Country, Circus Series, Tiger on Ball **$44.00**
Ski Country, Customer Specialties, Ladies of Leadville, blue **$24.00**
Ski Country, Customer Specialties, Skier, Olympic **$29.00**
Ski Country, Customer Specialties, Voyage of Discovery, top of flagpole glued on, set of 3, miniature **$149.00**
Ski Country, Domestic Animals, Holstein Cow **$77.00**
Ski Country, Domestic Animals, Labrador w/Mallard .**$89.00**
Ski Country, Eagle Series, Birth of Freedom **$95.00**
Ski Country, Eagle Series, Hawk **$129.00**
Ski Country, Falcon Series, Peregrine, gallon size, 450 made **$295.00**
Ski Country, Fish Series, Rainbow Trout, miniature....**$35.00**

Ski Country, Game Birds Series, Pheasants in Corn, miniature..**$39.00**

Ski Country, Hawk Series, Osprey **$169.00**

Ski Country, Horned & Antlered Series, Bighorn Ram, 1973...**$45.00**

Ski Country, Indian Ceremonial Dancers Series, Buffalo, miniature..**$40.00**

Ski Country, Indian Ceremonial Dancers Series, Great Spirit **$99.00**

Ski Country, Indian Ceremonial Dancers Series, Talavai Kachina...**$55.00**

Ski Country, Owl Series, Baby Snow Owl, miniature.**$65.00**

Ski Country, Owl Series, Screech Owl Family...........**$109.00**

Ski Country, Waterfowl Series, Canada Goose, 1973, miniature...**$79.00**

Ski Country, Waterfowl Series, King Eider Duck.........**$55.00**

WC Fields, WC Fields Bust **$49.00**

Weller, Masterpiece...**$23.00**

Wild Turkey, Series I, #5...**$35.00**

Wild Turkey, Series I, #5-#8 Miniature Set **$149.00**

Wild Turkey, Series II, #1...**$25.00**

Wild Turkey, Series III, #12, Turkey & Skunks **$95.00**

Wild Turkey, Series III, #2, Turkey & Bobcat, miniature...**$45.00**

Wild Turkey, Series III, #5, Turkey & Raccoon...........**$95.00**

Wild Turkey, Series III, #9, Turkey & Bear Cubs........**$95.00**

DeForest of California

This family-run company (operated by Jack and Margaret DeForest and sons) was located in California; from the early 1950s until 1970 they produce the type of novelty ceramic kitchenware and giftware items that state has become known for. A favored theme was their onion-head jars, bowls, ashtray, etc., all designed with various comical expressions. Some of their cookie jars were finished in a brown wood-tone glaze and were very similar to many produced by Twin Winton. (See also Cookie Jars.)

Bank, Goody, pig figural, brown or pink, 1956, from $225 to...**$275.00**

Bean pot, pig figural, pink w/blue bow finial, Beans on lid, 1956, from $125 to..**$150.00**

Candy dish, pig figural, bow on lid, marked Candy on side, 1959, from $65 to...**$75.00**

Condiment, Cheezy or Big Cheese, cheese wedge shape w/smiling face, ea from $25 to.............................**$35.00**

Condiment, hamburger form w/smiling face, Relish on top of bun, 1956, from $25 to...**$30.00**

Condiment, Horse Radish on hat, smiling face, from $25 to...**$35.00**

Condiment, Onion, crying face, Derby hat lid, from $25 to...**$35.00**

Covered dish, peanut w/squirrel finial, from $15 to...**$20.00**

Creamer, pig figural, pink or brown, 1956, ea from $20 to..**$25.00**

Dip set, Peter Porker line, Dippy Pig, pig's head in center of tray, brown or pink, 1956, from $75 to **$95.00**

Hors d'oeurves, pig figural w/holes in back, from $25 to..**$30.00**

Lazy Susan, pig in center, brown or pink, 14" dia, from $175 to..**$200.00**

Pitcher, pig's head figural, brown or pink, 2-qt, from $65 to..**$75.00**

Plate, chop; Bar-B-Cutie, onion face, 15", from $65 to **$75.00**

Plate, dinner; Bar-B-Cutie, onion face, 11", from $35 to..**$45.00**

Platter, Hammy, 1956, from $60.00 to $70.00.
(Photo courtesy Fred and Joyce Roerig)

Range set, Perky (pig's face), drippings jar w/salt & pepper shakers, unmarked, 3-pc set, from $75 to **$95.00**

Relish dish, Hammy Jr, pig's face w/bow tie, pink or brown, 1957, 9x10", from $55 to **$65.00**

Rolling pin, Caution! Don't Dalley in This Galley, face on white, multicolor handles, from $55 to.................**$65.00**

Salt & pepper shakers, Bar-B-Cutie, onions, pr from $20 to..**$25.00**

Salt & pepper shakers, cheese wedges, unmarked, pr from $25 to..**$30.00**

Spooner rest, boy & girl faces form 2 rests, from $40 to..**$50.00**

Tea set, floral decor on shaded brown, stacking, 3-pc, from $40 to..**$50.00**

Tureen, Bar-B-Cutie, onion face, w/ladle, 8x12", from $175 to..**$195.00**

Degenhart

John and Elizabeth Degenhart owned and operated the Crystal Art Glass Factory in Cambridge, Ohio. From 1947 until John died in 1964, they produced some fine glassware. John was well known for his superior paperweights, but the glassware that collectors love today was made after '64, when Elizabeth restructured the company, creating many lovely moulds and scores of colors. She hired Zack Boyd, who had previously worked for Cambridge Glass, and between the two of them, they developed almost 150 unique and original color formulas.

Complying with provisions she had made before her death, close personal friends at Island Mould and Machine

Company in Wheeling, West Virginia, took Elizabeth's moulds and removed the familiar 'D in a heart' trademark from them. She had requested that ten of her moulds be donated to the Degenhart Museum, where they remain today. Zack Boyd eventually bought the Degenhart factory and acquired the remaining moulds. He has added his own logo to them and is continuing to press glass very similar to Mrs. Degenhart's.

For more information, we recommend *Degenhart Glass and Paperweights* by Gene Florence, published by the Degenhart Paperweight and Glass Museum, Inc., Cambridge, Ohio.

Club: Friends of Degenhart
Degenhart Paperweight and Glass Museum
P.O. Box 186, Cambridge, OH 43725; Individual membership: $5 per year; membership includes newsletter, *Heartbeat*, a quarterly publication and free admission to the museum

Baby Shoe (Hobo Boot) Toothpick Holder, Rose Marie..	$15.00
Basket Toothpick Holder, Amber	$12.00
Basket Toothpick Holder, Taffeta	$25.00
Beaded Oval Toothpick Holder, Aqua	$30.00
Bicentennial Bell, Crown Tuscan	$13.50
Bicentennial Bell, Lavender Blue	$12.00
Bicentennial Bell, Rose Marie Pink	$12.00
Bird Salt & Pepper, Crystal	$25.00
Bird Salt w/Cherry, Angel Blue	$15.00
Bird Salt w/Cherry, Baby Blue	$15.00
Bird Salt w/Cherry, Pearl Gray	$25.00
Bird Toothpick Holder, Canary	$15.00
Bird Toothpick Holder, Red	$45.00
Bow Slipper, Champagne	$15.00
Bow Slipper, Fawn	$15.00
Bow Slipper, Opal	$16.00
Bow Slipper, Wonder Blue	$25.00
Buzz Saw Wine, Amber	$15.00
Buzz Saw Wine, Pink	$25.00
Buzz Saw Wine, Red Carnival	$74.00
Chick Covered Dish, Light Powder Blue, 2"	$27.00
Child's Mug, Opal	$20.00
Colonial Drape Toothpick Holder, Vaseline	$20.00
Daisy & Button Hat, Frosty Jade	$15.00
Daisy & Button Salt, Custard, unmarked	$13.50
Daisy & Button Toothpick Holder, Bluebell	$25.00
Daisy & Button Toothpick Holder, Pink	$16.00
Daisy & Button Wine, Milk Blue	$40.00
Elephant Head Toothpick Holder, Amber	$20.00
Elephant Head Toothpick Holder, Amberina	$75.00
Forget-Me-Not Toothpick Holder, Bernard Boyd's Ebony	$25.00
Forget-Me-Not Toothpick Holder, Blue & White Slag	$30.00
Forget-Me-Not Toothpick Holder, Gray Slag	$20.00
Forget-Me-Not Toothpick Holder, Misty Green	$20.00
Forget-Me-Not Toothpick Holder, Twilight Blue	$20.00
Gypsy Pot Toothpick Holder, Bittersweet	$35.00
Hand, April Green	$12.00

Hand, Fog	$20.00

Hand, Tomato, 5", $25.00.

Heart & Lyre Cup Plate, Blue Green	$10.00
Heart & Lyre Cup Plate, Taffeta	$12.00
Heart Jewel Box, Ruby	$40.00
Heart Toothpick Holder, Chartreuse	$35.00
Heart Toothpick Holder, Ruby	$35.00
Hen Covered Dish, Amethyst, 5"	$50.00
Hen Covered Dish, Gold, 3"	$20.00
Hen Covered Dish, Opalescent, 3"	$25.00
High Boot, Crystal	$15.00
Kat Slipper (Puss & Boots), Ivory	$40.00
Kat Slipper (Puss & Boots), Rose Marie	$20.00
Lamb Covered Dish, Bernard Boyd's Ebony	$85.00
Lamb Covered Dish, Taffeta, 5"	$55.00
Mini Pitcher, w/o Sole, Mint Green	$25.00
Mini Slipper w/o Sole, Forest Green	$15.00
Mini Slipper w/Sole, Vaseline	$35.00
Owl, Chad's Blue	$50.00
Owl, Crystal Ice	$15.00
Owl, Custard #1	$50.00
Owl, Green Maverick	$75.00
Owl, Jim Dandy	$200.00
Owl, Maverick	$200.00
Owl, Mystery Surprise, from $100 to	$300.00
Owl, Spice Brown	$50.00
Owl, Sunset	$50.00
Pooch, April Day	$20.00
Pooch, Blue Jay	$20.00
Pooch, Bluebell	$15.00
Pooch, Daffodil Slag	$60.00
Pooch, Emerald Green	$20.00
Pooch, Henry's Blue	$25.00
Pooch, Milk White	$13.50
Pooch, Tomato Slag	$40.00
Portrait Plate, Red	$60.00
Priscilla, Bittersweet Slag	$200.00
Priscilla, Green Lavender Slag	$150.00
Priscilla, Jade	$150.00
Priscilla, Smoky Blue	$95.00
Robin Covered Dish, Dark Caramel, 5"	$100.00
Robin Covered Dish, Pigeon Blood, 5"	$90.00
Seal of Ohio Cup Plate, Pink	$12.00
Star & Dew Drop Salt, Crystal	$10.00
Star & Dew Drop Salt, Heatherbloom	$30.00

Stork & Peacock Child's Mug, Blue Green **$25.00**

Texas Boot, Cobalt, $20.00.

Texas Boot, Red **$25.00**
Texas Creamer & Sugar, Cobalt **$50.00**
Tomahawk (Hatchet), Bluebell **$25.00**
Turkey Covered Dish, Peach Blo, 5" **$50.00**
Wildflower Candle Holder, Amethyst **$25.00**
Wildflower Candle Holder, Milk Blue **$25.00**
Wildflower Candy Dish, Amber **$25.00**
Wildflower Candy Dish, Crown Tuscan, unmarked **$30.00**
Wildflower Candy Dish, Emerald Green **$25.00**
Wildflower Candy Dish, Twilight Blue **$25.00**

deLee Art Pottery

Jimmie Lee Adair Kohl founded her company in 1937, and it continued to operate until 1958. She was the inspiration, artist, and owner of the company for the 21 years it was in business. The name deLee means 'of or by Lee' and is taken from the French language. She trained as an artist at the San Diego Art Institute and UCLA where she also earned an art education degree. She taught art and ceramics at Belmont High School in Los Angeles while getting her ceramic business started. On September 9, 1999, at the age of 93, Jimmie Lee died after having lived a long and wonderfully creative life.

The deLee line included children, adults, animals, birds, and specialty items such as cookie jars, banks, wall pockets, and several licensed Walter Lantz characters. Skunks were a favorite subject, and more of her pieces were modeled as skunks than any other single animal. Her figurines are distinctive in their design, charm, and excellent hand painting; when carefully studied, they can be easily recognized. Jimmie Lee modeled almost all the pieces — more than 350 in all.

The beautiful deLee colors were mixed by her and remained essentially the same for 20 years. The same figurine may be found painted in different colors and patterns.

Figurines were sold wholesale only. Buyers could select from a catalog or visit the deLee booth in New York and Los Angeles Gift Marts. All figurines left the factory with name and logo stickers. The round Art Deco logo sticker is silver with the words 'deLee Art, California, Hand Decorated.' Many of the figures are incised 'deLee Art' on the bottom.

The factory was located in Los Angeles during its 21 years of production and in Cuernavaca, Mexico, for 4 years during WWII. Production continued until 1958, when Japanese copies of her figures caused sales to decline. For further study we recommend *deLee Art* by Joanne and Ralph Schaefer and John Humphries.

Advisors: Joanne and Ralph Schaefer (See Directory, deLee)

**Figurines, Hopalong and Cottontail, 5",
from $60.00 to $75.00 for the pair.**
(Photo courtesy Joanne and Ralph Schaefer and John Humphries)

Bank, Henny Penny, chicken w/bonnet, silver foil sticker, 6" **$25.00**
Bank, Money Bunny, w/purse in right hand, from $90 to .. **$125.00**
Candle holders, Twinkle & Star, angels designed to hold birthday candles, 4¾", pr **$65.00**
Cookie jar, Cookie, boy or girl chef, 12", from $250 to .. **$400.00**
Figurine, Annabelle, purple & blue flowers, blue bow on hat **$40.00**
Figurine, Babe, girl holding starfish, round sticker, rare, 4" **$85.00**
Figurine, Chesty, squirrel, 3½" **$25.00**
Figurine, Danny, original sticker, 8½" **$30.00**
Figurine, Dolores, incised mark, 8", from $75 to **$100.00**
Figurine, Hank, green pants, leans against vase, EX .. **$42.00**
Figurine, Horse Durves, horse, rare, 7" **$65.00**
Figurine, Joey, clown, 7½", from $110 to **$150.00**
Figurine, Kenny, brown jacket w/blue bow, holding puppy, from $40 to **$65.00**
Figurine, lamb, 3½" **$40.00**
Figurine, Maria, blue & pink flowers, blue bow, blond hair **$40.00**

Figurine, Miss Muffet, 5", from $90 to........................**$125.00**

Figurine, Nina, laced vest, brown hair, white scarf w/purple & blue flowers, double vases **$40.00**

Figurine, Panchita, blue trim w/blue & pink flowers on dress, brown hair, 12", from $35 to.........................**$50.00**

Figurine, Pat, girl holding skirt high, flower trim on white, 7" **$35.00**

Figurine, Pedro, bongo player, from $75.................**$125.00**

Figurine, poodle, outstretched limbs, 3½" H, from $135 to **$160.00**

Figurine, Siamese cat, 4" L..**$35.00**

Figurines, Grunt & Groan, pigs, floral decor, pr........**$50.00**

Figurines, Maui and Leilani, seated Hawaiian couple, ca 1950s, 9", minimum value, $350.00 for the pair. (Photo courtesy Jack Chipman)

Figurines, Siamese Dancers, male & female, 13", pr from $225 to..**$300.00**

Planter, angel w/hands folded, eyes downcast, 6½" ..**$35.00**

Planter, Daisy, pink skirt, aqua top, pink clay, 8", NM..**$30.00**

Planter, girl w/opening in apron, flower decor on white, 7" **$30.00**

Planter/vase, crescent shape w/scalloped edge, 3½x6"..**$32.50**

Vase, girl stands beside flower, sm flowers at her feet, rare, from $65 to...**$80.00**

Vase, girl w/2 baskets, long brown hair covered w/scarf, flower trim, 6½"..**$30.00**

Wall plaque, girl w/hands cupped under left knee, 7", from $75 to..**$100.00**

Wall pocket, bell w/cherries, black, red, & green, 5½" ..**$20.00**

Wall pocket, lady's head & shoulders, pendant necklace, light brown curls, rare, 5½", from $60.................**$80.00**

Wall pocket, skunk, silver label, 5x3½x2½".................**$35.00**

Depression Glass

Since the early '60s, this has been a very active area of collecting. Interest is still very strong, and although values have long been established, except for some of the rarer items, Depression glass is still relatively inexpensive. Some of the patterns and colors that were entirely avoided by the early wave of collectors are now becoming popular, and it's very easy to reassemble a nice table setting of one of these lines today.

Most of this glass was manufactured during the Depression years. It was inexpensive, mass-produced, and available in a wide assortment of colors. The same type of glassware was still being made to some extent during the '50s and '60s, and today the term 'Depression glass' has been expanded to include the later patterns as well.

Some things have been reproduced, and the slight variation in patterns and colors can be very difficult to detect. For instance, the Sharon butter dish has been reissued in original colors of pink and green (as well as others that were not original); and several pieces of Cherry Blossom, Madrid, Avocado, Mayfair, and Miss America have also been reproduced. Some pieces you'll see in 'antique' malls and flea markets today have been recently made in dark uncharacteristic 'carnival' colors, which, of course, are easy to spot.

For further study, Gene Florence has written several informative books on the subject, and we recommend them all: *The Pocket Guide to Depression Glass*, *The Collector's Encyclopedia of Depression Glass*, *Elegant Glassware of the Depression Era*, and *Very Rare Glassware of the Depression Years* (Collector Books).

See also Anchor Hocking and other specific companies.

Publication: *Depression Glass Daze*
Teri Steel, Editor/Publisher
Box 57, Otisville, MI 48463; 810-631-4593. The nation's marketplace for glass, china, and pottery

Adam, green, ashtray, 4½"..**$28.00**

Adam, green, butter dish, w/lid **$425.00**

Adam, green, coaster, 3¼"..**$20.00**

Adam, green, cup **$25.00**

Adam, green, plate, grill; 9"..**$23.00**

Adam, green, relish dish, divided, 8" **$25.00**

Adam, green, tumbler, iced tea; 5½"...........................**$65.00**

Adam, pink, bowl, cereal; 5¾" **$55.00**

Adam, pink, bowl, w/lid, 9" **$75.00**

Adam, pink, bowl, 9" **$45.00**

Adam, pink, candlesticks, 4", pr...................................**$95.00**

Adam, pink, plate, sherbet; 6" **$11.00**

Adam, pink, sherbet, 3"..**$33.00**

Adam, pink, sugar bowl...**$25.00**

American Pioneer, amber, cup......................................**$24.00**

American Pioneer, crystal or pink, bowl, handles, 5"..**$25.00**

American Pioneer, crystal or pink, candy jar w/lid, 1-lb..**$95.00**

American Pioneer, crystal or pink, lamp, tall, 8½" ...**$125.00**

American Pioneer, crystal or pink, pitcher, urn; w/cover, 7" **$195.00**

American Pioneer, crystal or pink, saucer....................**$4.00**

American Pioneer, green, candlesticks, 6½", pr........**$135.00**

American Pioneer, green, coaster, 3½" **$35.00**

American Pioneer, green, ice bucket, 6".....................**$75.00**

American Pioneer, green, mayonnaise, 4¼" **$90.00**

American Pioneer, green, vase, round, 9" **$250.00**
American Sweetheart, blue, saucer............................**$25.00**
American Sweetheart, cremax, bowl, cereal; 6" **$16.00**
American Sweetheart, monax, platter, oval, 13" **$80.00**
American Sweetheart, pink, bowl, vegetable; oval, 11" ..**$70.00**
American Sweetheart, red, plate, salad; 8" **$120.00**
American Sweetheart, smoke & other trims, bowl, soup; 9½" **$165.00**
Aunt Polly, blue, bowl, berry; 4¾" **$18.00**
Aunt Polly, blue, butter dish, w/lid............................**$250.00**
Aunt Polly, blue, sugar bowl **$35.00**
Aunt Polly, green or iridescent, bowl, w/handle, 5½" **$15.00**
Aunt Polly, green or iridescent, candy dish, w/handles ..**$75.00**
Aunt Polly, green or iridescent, plate, sherbet; 6".........**$6.00**
Aunt Polly, green or iridescent, vase, footed, 6½"......**$38.00**
Aurora, cobalt or pink, bowl, cereal; 5⅜" **$18.50**
Aurora, cobalt or pink, bowl, deep, 4½" **$65.00**
Aurora, cobalt or pink, plate, 6½" **$12.50**
Avocado, crystal, bowl, salad; 7½" **$12.00**
Avocado, crystal, tumbler..**$35.00**
Avocado, green, cup, footed, 2 styles **$38.00**
Avocado, pink, bowl, relish; footed, 6" **$30.00**
Avocado, pink, plate, luncheon; 8¼" **$17.00**
Beaded Block, crystal, pink, green or amber, bowl, round, 6¼" **$25.00**
Beaded Block, crystal, pink, green or amber, bowl, sq, 5½" **$35.00**
Beaded Block, crystal, pink, green or amber, candy dish, pear shaped..**$325.00**
Beaded Block, crystal, pink, green or amber, stemmed jelly, 4½" **$25.00**
Beaded Block, milk white, creamer **$45.00**
Block Optic, green, bowl, cereal; 5¼" **$12.00**
Block Optic, green, goblet, cocktail; 4" **$40.00**
Block Optic, green, ice bucket...................................**$45.00**
Block Optic, green, mug..**$40.00**
Block Optic, green, plate, dinner; 9" **$27.50**
Block Optic, green, tumbler, footed, 9-oz **$18.00**
Block Optic, green or pink, goblet, wine; 4½" **$40.00**
Block Optic, green or pink, sandwich server, center handle **$75.00**
Block Optic, pink, bowl, salad; 7¼" **$175.00**
Block Optic, yellow, candy jar, tall, w/lid, 2¼" **$75.00**
Block Optic, yellow, goblet, thin, 9-oz, 7¼" **$38.00**
Block Optic, yellow, plate, 12¾"................................**$30.00**
Bowknot, green, bowl, berry; 4½" **$25.00**
Bowknot, green, cup...**$12.00**
Bowknot, green, tumbler, 10-oz, 5" **$25.00**
Cameo, crystal, relish dish, footed, 3-part, 7½" **$175.00**
Cameo, green, bowl, soup; rimmed, 9" **$75.00**
Cameo, green, decanter, w/stopper, 10"...................**$195.00**
Cameo, green, goblet, wine; 4" **$80.00**
Cameo, green, jam jar, w/lid, 2" **$225.00**
Cameo, green, vase, 8"..**$55.00**
Cameo, pink, plate, luncheon; 8".............................**$35.00**
Cameo, yellow, bowl, vegetable; oval, 10" **$42.00**

Cherry Blossom, Delphite, pitcher, allover pattern, scalloped or round bottom, 36-oz, 6¾" **$80.00**
Cherry Blossom, Delphite, sherbet.............................**$16.00**
Cherry Blossom, green, butter dish, w/lid.................**$125.00**
Cherry Blossom, green, coaster **$12.00**
Cherry Blossom, green, plate, sherbet; 6"..................**$10.00**
Cherry Blossom, Jadite, plate, grill; 9" **$85.00**
Cherry Blossom, pink, bowl, flat soup; 7¾" **$100.00**
Cherry Blossom, pink, bowl, vegetable; oval, 9" **$52.00**
Cherry Blossom, pink, cake plate, 3 legs, 10¼"........**$35.00**
Cherry Blossom, pink, cup **$24.00**
Cherry Blossom, pink, plate, salad; 7" **$27.00**
Cherry Blossom, pink, saucer.....................................**$4.00**
Cherry Blossom, pink or green, platter, oval, 11" **$60.00**
Cherryberry, crystal or iridescent, bowl, berry; 4"........**$6.50**
Cherryberry, crystal or iridescent, butter dish, w/lid...**$150.00**
Cherryberry, crystal or iridescent, pickle dish, oval, 8¼" ..**$9.00**
Cherryberry, crystal or iridescent, plate, salad; 7½"......**$8.00**
Cherryberry, pink or green, comport, 5¾"..................**$28.00**
Cherryberry, pink or green, olive dish, handle, 5" **$22.00**
Chinex Classic, brownstone or plain ivory, bowl, vegetable; 7"...**$14.00**
Chinex Classic, brownstone or plain ivory, sherbert, low foot **$7.00**
Chinex Classic, castle decal, cup...............................**$15.00**
Chinex Classic, decal decorated, bowl, vegetable; 9"..**$25.00**
Chinex Classic, decal decorated, butter dish **$75.00**
Circle, green, bowl, 4½"...**$14.00**
Circle, green, goblet, wine; 4½" **$15.00**
Circle, green, sugar bowl **$7.00**
Circle, green, tumbler, flat, 15-oz **$25.00**
Circle, pink, creamer **$20.00**
Circle, pink, plate, luncheon; 8¼" **$10.00**
Cloverleaf, black, ashtray, match holder in center......**$65.00**
Cloverleaf, green, bowl, 8"...**$95.00**
Cloverleaf, green, cup **$9.00**
Cloverleaf, green, tumbler, flat, 9-oz, 4" **$65.00**
Cloverleaf, pink, green or yellow, bowl, dessert; 4"...**$40.00**
Cloverleaf, pink, plate, luncheon; 8"..........................**$11.00**
Cloverleaf, yellow, salt & pepper shakers, pr **$135.00**
Colonial, crystal, stem, claret; 4-oz, 5¼" **$20.00**
Colonial, green, cheese dish......................................**$250.00**
Colonial, green, spoon holder or celery, 5½" **$130.00**
Colonial, pink, bowl, low soup; 7" **$65.00**
Colonial, pink, platter, oval, 12" **$35.00**
Colonial, Royal Ruby, tumbler, water; 9-oz, 4" **$160.00**
Colonial Block, black, powder jar, w/lid....................**$22.50**
Colonial Block, crystal, bowl, 7"................................**$10.00**
Colonial Block, pink or green, butter tub **$45.00**
Colonial Fluted, green, bowl, lg berry; 7½" **$22.00**
Colonial Fluted, green, plate, luncheon; 8" **$8.00**
Colonial Fluted, green, sherbet................................**$7.00**
Columbia, crystal, bowl, cereal; 5" **$18.00**
Columbia, crystal, butter dish, w/lid **$20.00**
Columbia, crystal, plate, chop; 11" **$17.00**
Columbia, pink, plate, bread & butter; 6"..................**$15.00**
Coronation, pink, plate, sherbet; 6"............................**$3.00**

Coronation, pink, sherbet $10.00

Coronation, pink or Royal Ruby, bowl, berry; handled, 4¼" $7.00

Coronation, Royal Ruby, cup $6.50

Cremax, blue or decal decorated, bowl, soup; 7¾" ...$25.00

Cremax, blue or decal decorated, plate, sandwich; 11½"...$20.00

Cremax, cremax, cup, demitasse $11.00

Cremax, cremax, egg cup, 2¼" $12.00

Cube, green, butter dish, w/lid................................$65.00

Cube, pink, amber or white, sugar bowl, 2⅜" $3.00

Cube, pink, bowl, deep, 4½" $8.00

Cube, pink, candy jar, w/lid, 6½" $30.00

Cube, pink, coaster, 3¼" $10.00

Diamond Quilted, blue or black, candlesticks, 2 styles, pr $40.00

Diamond Quilted, blue or black, cup $17.50

Diamond Quilted, blue or black, vase, fan; dolphin handles..$75.00

Diamond Quilted, pink or green, bowl, cereal; 5".......$7.50

Diamond Quilted, pink or green, creamer $12.00

Diamond Quilted, pink or green, goblet, wine; 3 oz .$12.00

Diamond Quilted, pink or green, pitcher, 64-oz........$50.00

Diana, amber, candy jar, round, w/lid $40.00

Diana, crystal, creamer, oval......................................$9.00

Diana, crystal, salt & pepper shakers, pr.................$30.00

Diana, pink, ashtray, 3½" $3.50

Diana, pink, cup $20.00

Dogwood, green, tumbler, decorated, 10-oz, 4" $100.00

Dogwood, monax or cremax, bowl, berry; 8½" $40.00

Dogwood, pink, plate, salver; 12" $38.00

Dogwood, pink, platter, oval, 12" $750.00

Doric, Delphite, bowl, lg berry; 8¼".......................$150.00

Doric, Delphite, sherbet, footed $10.00

Doric, green, bowl, cream soup; 5" $450.00

Doric, green, creamer, 4" $14.00

Doric, green, tray, handled, 10".................................$30.00

Doric, pink, bowl, vegetable; oval, 9".......................$45.00

Doric, pink, plate, salad; 7" $20.00

Doric, pink, tumbler, footed, 10-oz, 4" $75.00

Doric & Pansy, green or teal, bowl, handled.............$45.00

Doric & Pansy, green or teal, cup..............................$16.00

Doric & Pansy, green or teal, salt & pepper shakers, pr..$425.00

Doric & Pansy, green or teal, tray, handled, 10".........$38.00

Doric & Pansy, pink or crystal, creamer....................$85.00

Doric & Pansy, pink or crystal, plate, dinner; 9" $15.00

English Hobnail, pink or green, ashtray, 3"..................$20.00

English Hobnail, pink or green, bowl, grapefruit; 6½"..$22.00

English Hobnail, pink or green, compote, round, footed, 5" $25.00

English Hobnail, pink or green, mayonnaise, 6".........$20.00

English Hobnail, pink or green, stem, wine; sq foot, 2-oz..$30.00

English Hobnail, pink or green, urn, w/lid, 15"........$395.00

English Hobnail, turquoise or ice blue, bonbon, handled, 6½"..$40.00

English Hobnail, turquoise or ice blue, bowl, rolled edge, 11"...$80.00

English Hobnail, turquoise or ice blue, cigarette box, w/lid, 4½x2½"..$55.00

English Hobnail, turquoise or ice blue, ice tub, 4".....$90.00

English Hobnail, turquoise or ice blue, tidbit, 2-tier...$85.00

Floral, green, sugar/candy bowl, w/lid.....................$20.00

Floral, green, vase, rose bowl, 3-legged...................$525.00

Floral, pink, butter dish, w/lid................................$105.00

Floral, pink, comport, 9"...$950.00

Floral, pink, salt & pepper shakers, flat, 6", pr..........$55.00

Floral & Diamond Band, green, tumbler, water; 4" $25.00

Floral & Diamond Band, iridescent, butter dish, w/lid.$275.00

Floral & Diamond Band, pink, bowl, nappy; handled, 5¾"..$15.00

Floral & Diamond Band, pink, sherbet........................$7.00

Florentine No 1, cobalt, bowl, berry; 5" $22.50

Florentine No 1, crystal or green, bowl, cereal; 6" $25.00

Florentine No 1, crystal or green, tumbler, ribbed, 9-oz, 4" $16.00

Florentine No 1, pink, creamer, ruffled $50.00

Florentine No 1, pink, plate, salad; 8½" $11.00

Florentine No 1, yellow, ashtray, 5½" $30.00

Florentine No 1, yellow, sugar bowl........................$12.00

Florentine No 2, cobalt, comport, ruffled, 3½" $65.00

Florentine No 2, cobalt, tumbler, water; 9-oz, 4" $70.00

Florentine No 2, crystal or green, butter dish, w/lid...$110.00

Florentine No 2, crystal or green, tumbler, footed, 5-oz, 4" $15.00

Florentine No 2, pink, bowl, berry; 4½".....................$17.00

Florentine No 2, pink, platter, oval, 11".....................$16.00

Florentine No 2, yellow, plate, dinner; 10"................$16.00

Flower Garden w/Butterflies, amber or crystal, plate, 2 styles, 8"...$15.00

Flower Garden w/Butterflies, amber or crystal, sandwich server, center handle $60.00

Flower Garden w/Butterflies, black, bowl, console; w/base, 8½"...$150.00

Flower Garden w/Butterflies, blue or canary yellow, candlesticks, 8", pr...$130.00

Flower Garden w/Butterflies, blue or canary yellow, plate, 10"...$48.00

Flower Garden w/Butterflies, pink, green or blue-green, plate, 7"..$21.00

Flower Garden w/Butterflies, pink, green or blue-green, sugar bowl..$75.00

Fortune, pink or crystal, bowl, dessert; 4½"..............$12.00

Fortune, pink or crystal, plate, luncheon; 8" $28.00

Fruits, green, bowl, berry; 8" $90.00

Fruits, green, cup..$8.00

Fruits, pink, tumbler, 1 fruit, 4" $18.00

Georgian, crystal, hot plate, center design, 5"...........$25.00

Georgian, green, bowl, cereal; 5¾".............................$25.00

Georgian, green, platter, closed-handled, 11½".........$68.00

Hex Optic, pink or green, bowl, ruffled berry; 4¼" ...$9.00

Hex Optic, pink or green, bucket reamer $65.00

Hex Optic, pink or green, ice bucket, metal handle ..$30.00

Hex Optic, pink or green, platter, round, 11"............$15.00

Hex Optic, pink or green, sugar shaker....................$235.00

Hobnail, crystal, decanter, w/stopper, 32-oz $32.00
Hobnail, crystal, tumbler, iced tea; 15-oz, 5¼"............$15.00
Hobnail, pink, cup...$6.00
Homespun, pink or crystal, bowl, cereal; closed handles, 5" $30.00
Homespun, pink or crystal, coaster/ashtray $6.50
Homespun, pink or crystal, plate, dinner; 9¼" $22.00
Homespun, pink or crystal, tumbler, iced tea; 12½-oz, 5 38" $35.00
Indiana Custard, French Ivory, bowl, cereal; 6½".......$30.00
Indiana Custard, French Ivory, creamer.....................$16.00
Indiana Custard, French Ivory, custard.....................$100.00
Indiana Custard, French Ivory, plate, dinner; 9¾" $32.00
Iris, crystal, bowl, salad; ruffled, 9½"........................$14.00
Iris, crystal, bowl, soup; 7½" $165.00
Iris, crystal, plate, luncheon; 8" $110.00
Iris, iridescent, fruit or nut set $150.00
Iris, iridescent, goblet, wine; 4" $28.00
Iris, iridescent, plate, sandwich; 11¾".......................$30.00
Iris, iridescent, sherbet, footed, 4"...........................$225.00
Iris, transparent green or pink, bowl, salad; ruffled, 9½"..$195.00
Iris, transparent green or pink, sugar bowl...............$150.00
Jubilee, pink, bowl, 3-footed, 13" $250.00
Jubilee, pink, sugar bowl $35.00
Jubilee, pink, vase, 12"...$350.00
Jubilee, yellow, bowl, fruit; handled, 9" $125.00
Jubilee, yellow, plate, sandwich; handled, 13½" $50.00
Laced Edge, opal, basket bowl..................................$225.00
Laced Edge, opal, bowl, 5"...$37.50
Laced Edge, opal, mayonnaise, 3-pc...........................$135.00
Laced Edge, opal, plate, dinner; 10" $85.00

Laced Edge, opalescent, tumbler, nine-ounce, $55.00. (Photo courtesy Gene Florence)

Lake Como, white, bowl, vegetable; 9¾" $50.00
Lake Como, white, cup, St Denis $30.00
Lake Como, white, sugar bowl, footed.......................$32.50
Laurel, jade green or decorated rims, bowl, berry; 4¾" $15.00
Laurel, jade green or decorated rims, plate, dinner; 9⅛" ..$25.00
Laurel, Poudre Blue, creamer, tall $40.00

Laurel, white opal or French Ivory, bowl, 11" $40.00
Laurel, white opal or French Ivory, salt & pepper shakers, pr $50.00
Lincoln Inn, cobalt or red, ashtray............................$17.50
Lincoln Inn, cobalt or red, finger bowl......................$20.00
Lincoln Inn, cobalt or red, plate, 12" $65.00
Lincoln Inn, pink, bowl, shallow................................$23.00
Lorain, crystal or green, bowl, vegetable; oval, 9¾"...$60.00
Lorain, crystal or green, relish, 4-part, 8"...................$25.00
Lorain, yellow, plate, luncheon; 8⅜" $28.00
Lorain, yellow, tumbler, footed, 9-oz, 4¾" $30.00
Madrid, amber, bowl, sauce; 5" $7.00

Madrid, amber, butter dish, $70.00.

Madrid, amber, gravy boat....................................$1,000.00
Madrid, blue, jam dish..$40.00
Madrid, blue, saucer $10.00
Madrid, green, hot dish coaster...............................$50.00
Madrid, green, plate, dinner; 10½".............................$55.00
Madrid, pink, bowl, low console; 11".........................$11.00
Madrid, pink, tumbler, 9-oz, 4¼"..............................$15.00
Manhattan, crystal, ashtray, sq, 4½" $18.00
Manhattan, crystal, bowl, salad; 9"............................$30.00
Manhattan, crystal, plate, sandwich; 14" $28.00
Manhattan, pink, comport, 5¾".................................$40.00
Manhattan, pink, relish tray, w/inserts, 14" $85.00
Mayfair (Federal), amber, bowl, cereal; 6"...................$18.00
Mayfair (Federal), amber, platter, oval, 12"..................$30.00
Mayfair (Federal), crystal, bowl, vegetable; oval, 10" .$18.00
Mayfair (Federal), crystal, cup $5.00
Mayfair (Federal), green, plate, dinner; 9½".................$15.00
Mayfair/Open Rose, blue, bowl, vegetable; 10" $80.00
Mayfair/Open Rose, blue, celery dish, 10" $75.00
Mayfair/Open Rose, blue, relish tray, 4-part, 8⅜".......$75.00
Mayfair/Open Rose, green, bowl, fruit; scalloped, deep, 12" $50.00
Mayfair/Open Rose, green, creamer, footed.............$225.00
Mayfair/Open Rose, green or yellow, plate, luncheon; 8½"...$85.00
Mayfair/Open Rose, green or yellow, sherbet, footed, 4¾"...$165.00
Mayfair/Open Rose, pink, bowl, vegetable; 7"............$30.00
Mayfair/Open Rose, pink, cake plate, footed, 10" $32.00
Mayfair/Open Rose, pink, plate, dinner; 9½"..............$60.00
Mayfair/Open Rose, pink, sherbet, footed, 3" $17.50

Mayfair/Open Rose, pink, tumbler, iced tea; 13½-oz, 5¼"..$65.00

Mayfair/Open Rose, yellow, celery dish, divided, 9"..$195.00

Miss America, crystal, coaster, 5¾"....................$16.00

Miss America, crystal, goblet, water; 10-oz, 5½"........$20.00

Miss America, green, bowl, cereal; 6¼"................$20.00

Miss America, green, tumbler, water; 10-oz, 4½".......$22.00

Miss America, pink, bowl, vegetable; oval, 10"..........$45.00

Miss America, pink, plate, dinner; 10¼".............$38.00

Miss America, Royal Ruby, creamer, footed.............$225.00

Miss America, Royal Ruby, sherbet........................$150.00

Moderntone, amethyst, plate, dinner; 8⅞"...............$13.00

Moderntone, amethyst, tumbler, 12-oz......................$90.00

Moderntone, cobalt, bowl, berry; 5".....................$28.00

Moderntone, cobalt, cup..$10.00

Moderntone, cobalt or amethyst, bowl, cereal; 6½"...$75.00

Moondrops, amber, tumbler, 9-oz, 4⅞"..................$15.00

Moondrops, amethyst, decanter, med, 8½"................$42.00

Moondrops, blue or red, ashtray.................................$30.00

Moondrops, blue or red, bowl, pickle; 7½"..............$35.00

Moondrops, blue or red, goblet, 5-oz, 4¾"...............$24.00

Moondrops, blue or red, gravy boat.....................$195.00

Moondrops, blue or red, mug, 12-oz, 5⅛"...............$40.00

Moondrops, crystal, plate, salad; 7⅛"....................$10.00

Moondrops, green, candy dish, ruffled, 8"................$20.00

Mt Pleasant, amethyst, black or cobalt, bowl, fruit; scalloped, 10"..$45.00

Mt Pleasant, amethyst, black or cobalt, plate, grill; 9"...$20.00

Mt Pleasant, amethyst, black or cobalt, sandwich server, center handle..$45.00

Mt Pleasant, pink or green, bonbon, rolled-up, handled, 7"..$16.00

Mt Pleasant, pink or green, sugar bowl......................$18.00

New Century, green or crystal, bowl, berry; 4½".......$30.00

New Century, green or crystal, bowl, casserole; w/lid, 9"..$95.00

New Century, green or crystal, plate, dinner; 10".......$18.00

New Century, green or crystal, salt & pepper shakers, pr.$40.00

New Century, green or crystal, tumbler, 10-oz, 5"......$22.00

New Century, pink, cobalt or amethyst, cup.............$20.00

New Century, pink, cobalt or amethyst, tumbler, 9-oz, 4¼"..$20.00

Newport, amethyst, salt & pepper shakers, pr...........$40.00

Newport, amethyst, sherbet....................................$15.00

Newport, cobalt, bowl, cereal; 5¼"........................$40.00

Newport, cobalt, cup..$14.00

Newport, cobalt or amethyst, plate, dinner; 8¾".......$30.00

No 610 Pyramid, crystal, bowl, master berry; 8½".....$30.00

No 610 Pyramid, green, ice tub...............................$115.00

No 610 Pyramid, pink, bowl, oval, 9½"...................$40.00

No 610 Pyramid, yellow, sugar bowl........................$40.00

No 612 Horseshoe, green, bowl, vegetable; oval, 10½".$30.00

No 612 Horseshoe, green, plate, sandwich; 11½"......$25.00

No 612 Horseshoe, green or yellow, bowl, salad; 7½"..$25.00

No 612 Horseshoe, green or yellow, plate, salad; 8⅜"..$12.00

No 612 Horseshoe, green or yellow, tumbler, footed, 9-oz..$32.00

No 612 Horseshoe, yellow, creamer, footed...............$20.00

No 612 Horseshoe, yellow, plate, grill; 10⅜"............$150.00

No 616 Vernon, crystal, plate, luncheon; 8"...............$12.00

No 616 Vernon, green or yellow, cup........................$18.00

No 616 Vernon, green or yellow, sugar bowl, footed ..$30.00

No 618 Pineapple & Floral, amber or red, bowl, salad; 7"...$10.00

No 618 Pineapple & Floral, amber or red, sugar bowl, diamond shape..$10.00

No 618 Pineapple & Floral, crystal, amber or red, plate, dinner; 9⅜"..$15.00

No 618 Pineapple & Floral, crystal, ashtray, 4½"........$17.50

No 618 Pineapple & Floral, crystal, vase, cone shape ..$60.00

Normandie, amber or pink, bowl, berry; 5"...............$10.00

Normandie, iridescent, sugar bowl............................$6.00

Normandie, pink, plate, dinner; 11"........................$125.00

Old Cafe, crystal, candy jar, w/Royal Ruby lid, 5½"...$25.00

Old Cafe, crystal, pink or Royal Ruby, cup...............$12.00

Old Cafe, crystal or pink, bowl, cereal; 5½".............$35.00

Old Cafe, crystal or pink, olive dish, oblong, 6"........$10.00

Old Cafe, Royal Ruby, tumbler, juice; 3".................$20.00

Old English, green or amber, tumbler, footed, 5½"...$40.00

Old English, pink, green or amber, bowl, flat, 4".......$22.00

Old English, pink, green or amber, candlesticks, 4", pr.$40.00

Old English, pink, green or amber, pitcher...............$75.00

Old English, pink, tumbler, 5½", $40.00; 4½", $28.00. (Photo courtesy Gene Florence)

Ovide, Art Deco, sherbet..$75.00

Ovide, black, candy dish, w/cover............................$45.00

Ovide, decor white, plate, luncheon; 8"...................$14.00

Ovide, green, fruit cocktail, footed...........................$4.00

Oyster & Pearl, crystal or pink, bowl, heart shape, handled, 5¼"..$15.00

Oyster & Pearl, Royal Ruby, plate, sandwich; 13½" ...$55.00

Oyster & Pearl, white or fired-on green or pink, candlesticks, 3½", pr..$30.00

Parrot, amber, bowl, lg berry; 8"............................$90.00

Parrot, amber, plate, grill; sq, 10½"........................$32.00

Parrot, amber, sugar bowl......................................$50.00

Parrot, green, bowl, berry; 5".................................$30.00

Parrot, green, plate, dinner; 9".............................**$58.00**
Parrot, green or amber, cup.................................**$42.00**
Patrician, amber, crystal, pink or green, tumbler, 5-oz, 4"..**$33.00**
Patrician, amber, crystal or green, plate, sherbet; 6"...**$10.00**
Patrician, amber, crystal or pink, jam dish.................**$30.00**
Patrician, amber or crystal, butter dish, w/lid.............**$95.00**

Patrician, amber, cracker jar, $90.00.

Patrician, amber or crystal, creamer, footed.............**$11.00**
Patrician, green, platter, oval, 11½"........................**$30.00**
Patrician, pink or green, plate, luncheon; 9".............**$16.00**
Patrick, pink, bowl, console; 11"............................**$165.00**
Patrick, pink, plate, salad; 7½"..............................**$25.00**
Patrick, yellow, cup...**$35.00**
Patrick, yellow, tray, handles, 11"..........................**$60.00**
Petalware, cremax, monax florette or decor, plate, dinner; 9".......................................**$16.00**
Petalware, cremax or monax, bowl, soup; 7".............**$65.00**
Petalware, crystal, bowl, lg berry; 9"......................**$8.50**
Petalware, pink, bowl, cereal; 5¾"..........................**$14.00**
Petalware, red trim floral, tumbler, 12-oz, 4⅝"..........**$37.50**
Primo, yellow or green, bowl, 4½"..........................**$25.00**
Primo, yellow or green, cake plate, 3-footed, 10"......**$45.00**
Primo, yellow or green, coaster/ashtray....................**$8.00**
Primo, yellow or green, plate, dinner; 10"................**$30.00**
Primo, yellow or green, tray, hostess; handles...........**$45.00**
Princess, green, butter dish, w/lid.........................**$100.00**
Princess, green, pink, topaz, or apricot, creamer, oval..**$20.00**
Princess, green, salt & pepper shakers, 4½", pr..........**$60.00**
Princess, green or pink, plate, salad; 8"..................**$18.00**
Princess, green or pink, platter, closed handles, 12"..**$30.00**
Princess, pink, bowl, berry; 4½"............................**$32.00**
Princess, pink, vase, 8".....................................**$65.00**
Princess, topaz or apricot, sugar bowl....................**$8.50**
Queen Mary, crystal, candy dish, #490, w/lid, 7¼"....**$22.00**
Queen Mary, crystal, relish tray, 4-part, 14"............**$12.00**
Queen Mary, pink, bowl, berry; flared, 5"...............**$12.00**
Queen Mary, pink, cup, lg...................................**$9.00**
Raindrops, green, bowl, cereal; 6".........................**$12.00**
Raindrops, green, plate, luncheon; 8".....................**$6.00**

Raindrops, green, tumbler, 10-oz, 5".......................**$9.00**
Ribbon, black, bowl, lg berry; flared, 8"..................**$40.00**
Ribbon, black, plate, luncheon; 8".........................**$14.00**
Ribbon, green, bowl, cereal; 5".............................**$45.00**
Ribbon, green, tumbler, 10-oz, 6"..........................**$35.00**
Ring, crystal, bowl, soup; 7"...............................**$10.00**
Ring, crystal, ice bucket....................................**$20.00**
Ring, crystal, salt & pepper shakers, 3", pr..............**$20.00**
Ring, green or w/decoration, butter/ice tub...............**$38.00**
Ring, green or w/decoration, plate, luncheon; 8".........**$5.00**
Ring, green or w/decoration, vase, 8".....................**$35.00**
Rock Crystal, blue, yellow or black, bowl, celery; oblong, 12"..**$45.00**
Rock Crystal, blue, yellow or black, cup, 7-oz...........**$27.50**
Rock Crystal, blue, yellow or black, lamp, electric...**$395.00**
Rock Crystal, blue, yellow or black, stem, cocktail; footed, 3½-oz...**$21.00**
Rock Crystal, crystal, bonbon, scalloped edge, 7½"...**$22.00**
Rock Crystal, crystal, bowl, salad; scalloped edge, 8"..**$27.50**
Rock Crystal, crystal, cake stand, footed, 2¾x11".......**$35.00**
Rock Crystal, crystal, candelabra, 3-light, pr...............**$65.00**
Rock Crystal, crystal, egg plate.............................**$35.00**
Rock Crystal, crystal, stem, 7-oz...........................**$16.00**
Rock Crystal, red, parfait, low footed, 3½-oz............**$85.00**
Rock Crystal, red, plate, bread & butter; scalloped edge, 6"...**$22.00**
Rock Crystal, red, saucer...................................**$22.00**
Rock Crystal, red, tumbler, old-fashioned; 5-oz.........**$60.00**
Rose Cameo, green, bowl, cereal; 5".......................**$22.00**
Rose Cameo, green, plate, salad; 7".......................**$15.00**
Rose Cameo, green, tumbler, footed, 2 styles, 5"........**$25.00**
Rosemary, amber, cup..**$7.50**
Rosemary, amber, sugar bowl, footed......................**$10.00**
Rosemary, green, bowl, berry; 5"...........................**$9.00**
Rosemary, green, plate, grill................................**$20.00**
Rosemary, pink, creamer, footed...........................**$25.00**
Roulette, crystal, plate, sandwich; 12"....................**$11.00**
Roulette, crystal, whiskey, 1½-oz, 2½"....................**$14.00**
Roulette, pink or green, bowl, fruit; 9"...................**$25.00**
Roulette, pink or green, sherbet............................**$6.00**
Round Robin, green, plate, sandwich; 12".................**$12.00**
Round Robin, green or iridescent, cup, footed............**$7.00**
Roxana, white, bowl, 4½x2⅜"..............................**$20.00**
Roxana, yellow, bowl, cereal; 6"...........................**$20.00**
Roxana, yellow, sherbet, footed............................**$12.00**
Royal Lace, amethyst, sherbet, in metal holder...........**$40.00**
Royal Lace, crystal, bowl, berry, 10".......................**$20.00**
Royal Lace, crystal, bowl, 3-legged, ruffled edge, 10"...**$55.00**
Royal Lace, crystal, cookie jar, w/lid......................**$35.00**
Royal Lace, crystal, pitcher, straight sides, 48-oz........**$40.00**
Royal Lace, green, candlesticks, straight edge, pr.......**$95.00**
Royal Lace, pink, bowl, vegetable; oval, 11"...............**$35.00**
Royal Lace, pink, platter, oval, 13".........................**$45.00**
Royal Lace, pink or green, tumbler, 12-oz, 5⅜"..........**$75.00**
S Pattern, crystal, pitcher (like Dogwood), 80-oz.......**$60.00**
S Pattern, crystal, sherbet, low footed....................**$4.50**

S Pattern, yellow, amber, or crystal w/trims, bowl, lg berry; 8½"..**$20.00**

S Pattern, yellow, amber, or crystal w/trims, plate, heavy cake; 13"...**$85.00**

Sandwich, amber or crystal, basket, 10" **$33.00**

Sandwich, amber or crystal, goblet, 9-oz..................**$13.00**

Sandwich, pink or green, candlesticks, 3½", pr..........**$45.00**

Sandwich, pink or green, mayonnaise, footed............**$35.00**

Sandwich, red, sugar bowl, lg **$45.00**

Sandwich, teal blue, bowl, hexagonal, 6"..................**$14.00**

Sharon, amber, bowl, cereal; 6".................................**$22.00**

Sharon, amber, jam dish, 7½".....................................**$40.00**

Sharon, green, candy jar, w/lid **$175.00**

Sharon, green, tumbler, thin, 9-oz, 4⅛".....................**$85.00**

Sharon, pink, butter dish, w/lid..................................**$60.00**

Sharon, pink, salt & pepper shakers, pr **$60.00**

Sharon, pink or green, bowl, vegetable; oval, 9½" **$35.00**

Ships, blue or white, cocktail mixer, w/stirrer **$30.00**

Ships, blue or white, ice bowl....................................**$40.00**

Ships, blue or white, plate, dinner; 9" **$40.00**

Ships, blue or white, tumbler, heavy bottom, 4-oz, 3¼"..**$27.50**

Ships, blue or white, tumbler, iced tea; 12-oz.............**$25.00**

Sierra, green, saucer **$9.00**

Sierra, green, sugar bowl **$28.00**

Sierra, pink, bowl, vegetable; oval, 9¼" **$75.00**

Sierra, pink, plate, dinner; 9" **$20.00**

Spiral, green, bowl, mixing; 7"...................................**$15.00**

Spiral, green, pitcher, bulbous, 54-oz, 7⅝"................**$40.00**

Spiral, green, preserve, w/lid.....................................**$35.00**

Spiral, green, sandwich server, center handle............**$25.00**

Starlight, crystal or white, bowl, cereal; closed handles, 5½"..**$7.00**

Starlight, crystal or white, bowl, 2¾x12" **$35.00**

Starlight, crystal or white, plate, bread & butter; 6"......**$3.00**

Starlight, pink, plate, sandwich; 13" **$18.00**

Strawberry, crystal or iridescent, bowl, deep berry; 7½" .**$20.00**

Strawberry, crystal or iridescent, plate, salad; 7½"......**$12.00**

Strawberry, pink or green, creamer, sm......................**$22.00**

Strawberry, pink or green, olive dish, handle, 5" **$20.00**

Sunburst, crystal, bowl, 10¾".....................................**$27.50**

Sunburst, crystal, cup **$10.00**

Sunburst, crystal, relish, 2-part...................................**$15.00**

Sunflower, green, ashtray, center design only, 5".......**$12.00**

Sunflower, pink, plate, dinner; 9"...............................**$22.00**

Swirl, Delphite, creamer, footed................................**$12.00**

Swirl, Delphite, tray, handles, 10½" **$27.50**

Swirl, pink, bowl, salad; 9"...**$26.00**

Swirl, pink, candy dish, open, 3 legs.........................**$15.00**

Swirl, pink, plate, salad; 8"...**$10.00**

Swirl, ultramarine, bowl, salad; rimmed, 9"...............**$32.00**

Swirl, ultramarine, coaster, 1x3¼"..............................**$16.00**

Swirl, ultramarine, tumbler, 9-oz, 4"..........................**$35.00**

Tea Room, green, salt & pepper shakers, pr...............**$75.00**

Tea Room, green, sundae, footed, ruffled top **$95.00**

Tea Room, green or pink, bowl, finger **$70.00**

Tea Room, green or pink, parfait...............................**$100.00**

Tea Room, pink, bowl, deep salad; 8¾".....................**$85.00**

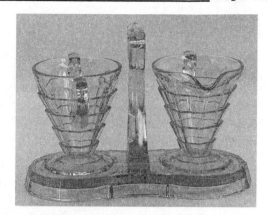

Tea Room, pink, creamer and sugar bowl on tray, $75.00.

Tea Room, pink, lamp, electric; 9"............................**$135.00**

Tea Room, pink, sugar bowl.......................................**$20.00**

Tea Room, pink, tumbler, footed, 11-oz **$45.00**

Thistle, green, plate, luncheon; 8"..............................**$24.00**

Thistle, green, saucer..**$12.00**

Thistle, pink, bowl, cereal; 5½"...................................**$33.00**

Thistle, pink, plate, grill; 10¼"....................................**$30.00**

Tulip, amethyst or blue, bowl, oval, oblong, 13¼" ..**$110.00**

Tulip, amethyst or blue, creamer **$24.00**

Tulip, crystal or green, cup...**$16.00**

Tulip, crystal or green, plate, 10"...............................**$34.00**

Twisted Optic, blue or canary yellow, bowl, 4¼x 11½" .**$55.00**

Twisted Optic, blue or canary yellow, bowl, 9" **$35.00**

Twisted Optic, blue or canary yellow, plate, salad; 7" .**$8.00**

Twisted Optic, blue or canary yellow, powder jar, w/lid...**$65.00**

Twisted Optic, pink, green or amber, basket, tall, 10"........**$60.00**

Twisted Optic, pink, green or amber, candlesticks, 8", pr..**$55.00**

Twisted Optic, pink, green or amber, mayonnaise.....**$30.00**

Twisted Optic, pink, green or amber, pitcher, 64-oz..**$45.00**

Twisted Optic, pink, green or amber, plate, sandwich; 10"..**$9.00**

Twisted Optic, pink, green or amber, vase, fan; handles, 8"..**$50.00**

Victory, black, amber, pink or green, bonbon, 7".......**$11.00**

Victory, black, amber, pink or green, cup..................**$12.00**

Victory, black, amber, pink or green, platter, 12" **$30.00**

Victory, black, bowl, rolled edge, 11".........................**$50.00**

Victory, blue, plate, bread & butter; 6".......................**$16.00**

Waterford, crystal, ashtray, 4".....................................**$7.50**

Waterford, crystal, bowl, cereal; 5½" **$19.00**

Waterford, crystal, coaster, 4".....................................**$4.00**

Waterford, crystal, relish tray, 5-part, 13¾"................**$18.00**

Waterford, pink, cake plate, handled, 10¼" **$20.00**

Waterford, pink, cup...**$15.00**

Waterford, pink, plate, salad; 7⅛"...............................**$15.00**

Windsor, crystal, bowl, pointed edge, 5" **$9.00**

Windsor, crystal, bowl, salad; 10½".............................**$15.00**

Windsor, crystal, sugar bowl, w/lid.............................**$12.00**

Windsor, green, tumbler, 12-oz, 5"..............................**$52.00**

Windsor, pink, tray, sq, handle, 4"..............................**$10.00**

Windsor, pink or green, bowl, boat shape, 7x11¾" ...**$40.00**

Disney

The largest and most popular area in character collectibles is without doubt Disneyana. There are clubs, newsletters, and special shows that are centered around this hobby. Every aspect of the retail market has been thoroughly saturated with Disney-related merchandise over the years, and today collectors are able to find many good examples at garage sales and flea markets.

Disney memorabilia from the late '20s and '30s was marked either 'Walt E. Disney' or 'Walt Disney Enterprises.' After about 1940 the name was changed to 'Walt Disney Productions.' This mark was in use until 1984 when the 'Walt Disney Company' mark was introduced, and this last mark has remained in use up to the present time. Some of the earlier items have become very expensive, though many are still within the reach of the average collector.

During the '30s, Mickey Mouse, Donald Duck, Snow White and the Seven Dwarfs, and the Three Little Pigs (along with all their friends and cohorts) dominated the Disney scene. The last of the '30s characters was Pinocchio, and some 'purists' prefer to stop their collections with him.

The '40s and '50s brought many new characters with them — Alice in Wonderland, Bambi, Dumbo, Lady and the Tramp, and Peter Pan were some of the major personalities featured in Disney's films of this era.

Even today, thanks to the re-releases of many of the old movies and the popularity of Disney's vacation 'kingdoms,' toy stores and department stores alike are full of quality items with the potential of soon becoming collectibles.

If you'd like to learn more about this fascinating field, we recommend *Stern's Guide to Disney Collectibles, First* and *Second Series*, by Michael Stern; *The Collector's Encyclopedia of Disneyana* by Michael Stern and David Longest; *Character Toys and Collectibles* and *Toys, Antique and Collectible*, both by David Longest; and *Schroeder's Collectible Toys, Antique to Modern*. All are published by Collector Books.

See also Character and Promotional Drinking Glasses; Character Banks; Character Watches; Cowboy Character Memorabilia; Dolls, Mattel; Enesco; Games; Hagen-Renaker; Pin-Back Buttons; Puzzles; Salt and Pepper Shakers; Toys; Valentines; Wade.

Note: in the following listings, many of the characters have been sorted by the name of the feature film in which they appeared.

Advisor: Judy Posner (See Directory, Character and Personality Collectibles)

Aladdin, bank, Abu, ceramic, monkey at pot of gold, from $25 to..**$35.00**
Aladdin, beanbag, Jasmine, 10", M.............................**$12.00**
Aladdin, figure set, 10 figures, Mattel, MIB **$12.00**
Alice in Wonderland, figure, Alice, porcelain, 1960, 5", EX **$25.00**
Alice in Wonderland, figure set, Alice, Cheshire Cat, Mad Hatter, March Hare, White Rabbit, ceramic, 1980s, to 6", MIB **$85.00**

Alice in Wonderland, stationery booklet w/envelopes, Whitman, 1951, complete, EX.............................**$60.00**
Alice in Wonderland, Stitch-A-Story, Hasbro, 1969, complete, NMIB..**$25.00**
Alice in Wonderland, tea set, Tea Time Dishes, Pasco, 1949, MIB **$40.00**
Bambi, figure, Bambi, celluloid, WD/Japan, 1940s, 2¼", EX+ **$25.00**
Bambi, figure, Flower the skunk, ceramic, American Pottery, 1940s, 4½", M..**$65.00**
Bambi, figure, Thumper & girlfriend, ceramic, American Pottery, 1940s, 4", pr **$85.00**
Bambi, planter, Bambi standing on green bowl base, ceramic, Leeds/WDP, 1940s-50s, 6½x9", NM+.................**$55.00**
Bambi, slippers, figural Bambi motif, Trimfoot/WDP, 1940s-50s, EX, pr...**$65.00**
Beauty & the Beast, doll, Beast, plush w/cloth clothes, Mattel, 1993, NMIB **$30.00**
Beauty & the Beast, tea set, Belle, china, 12-pc set, Schmid, MIB **$100.00**
Buzz Lightyear & Woody, salt & pepper shakers, ea on alphabet block, Treasure Craft, pr from $45 to **$65.00**
Chip 'N Dale, salt & pepper shakers, ceramic, Sango/Japan, M, pr **$35.00**
Cinderella, bank, litho tin book shape, 6", VG **$30.00**
Cinderella, figure, Cinderella & Prince dancing, bisque, Royal Orlean, 1981, 7", EX+...**$40.00**
Cinderella, figure, Mamma Mouse, ceramic, Evan K Shaw, 1950s, 3½" **$250.00**
Cinderella, pattern for apron, paper, JC Penney Co, 1950s, unused, VG+..**$15.00**
Cinderella, rubber stamp kit, 10 foam-backed stamps w/purple ink pad, EXIB...**$18.00**
Cinderella, wastebasket, metal, tells story w/graphics, 1950s, 19", EX **$50.00**
Daisy Duck, figure, Disneykin, 1st series, Marx, 1960s, NM..**$10.00**

Disney, top, Chein, 1973, various characters on blue and white striped top, tin, 6" dia, NM, $50.00. (Photo courtesy Linda Baker)

Disneyland, ashtray, ceramic, oblong w/horse & buggy scene, Disneyland lettered in gold, 1950s, 4¼x8¾", EX...**$45.00**

Disneyland, booklet, Sleeping Beauty Castle, w/lg centerfold from Sleeping Beauty movie, 1957, 11x8", EX **$30.00**

Disneyland, magazine (promotional), Vacationland Magazine, Winter 1958-59, EX **$65.00**

Disneyland, mirror, All Aboard The Disneyland Railroad..., wooden frame, 1977, 18x14", NM+ **$300.00**

Disneyland, musical map, 6-panel map w/5 uncut 78 rpm picture records promoting various park features, 15x43", NM **$85.00**

Disneyland, party decorations, 3 cardboard figures of Mickey, Pluto & Goofy, Dennison, 1950s-60s, NMIP (sealed) **$15.00**

Disneyland, place mat, die-cut paper w/perforated pop-up landmarks, 1950s-60s, 12x14", EX+ **$45.00**

Disneyland, pop gun, litho tin, WDP, 1950s, 6", VG ..**$40.00**

Disneyland, postcard fold-outs, Adventureland, Frontierland, Tomorrowland, ca 1963, unused, M, ea...............**$20.00**

Disneyland, salt & pepper shakers, coffeepot shape w/Main Street portraits & Sleeping Beauty Castle, porcelain, NM, pr...**$40.00**

Disneyland, shopping bag, white cartoon images of popular attractions on purple paper, store giveaway, 1950s-60s, VG+...**$30.00**

Donald Duck, bubble pipe, 1940s, MOC................**$65.00**

Donald Duck, figure, chalkware, 1940s, NM.............**$45.00**

Donald Duck, handkerchief, cotton, courting scene w/Daisy or beach scene w/Nephews, NM, ea **$45.00**

Dumbo, doll, Timothy the Mouse, plush, Character Novelty Co, 1940s, 8", VG+ **$100.00**

Dumbo, pin, silver-tone metal of circus ringmaster & Dumbo in full relief on double bars, WDP, 1940s, 2x2½", EX **$175.00**

Dumbo, push-button puppet, Toy Box, Japan, NM....**$20.00**

Dumbo, wall plaques, Dumbo & Timothy, die-cut cardboard, 14x9" & 8¼", 1951, NM, pr **$40.00**

Eeyore (Winnie the Pooh), sugar bowl, w/lid, marked Disney Made in China, from $40 to..................................**$50.00**

Fantasia, program, theatre souvenir booklet offered during 1st release, 32 pages, WDP, 1940, EX **$55.00**

Ferdinand the Bull, game, Put the Tail on Ferdinand..., Whitman, 1938, rare, VG (VG box).....................**$125.00**

Ferdinand the Bull, pin-back button, enameled in sq gold-tone filigree frame, flower in mouth, 1930s, 1¾", EX ...**$225.00**

Flip the Frog, planter, ceramic, raised image of Flip singing w/pig, bird, & cow, Japan, 1930s, 6", EX **$75.00**

Genie & Magic Lamp, salt & pepper shakers, blue Genie & gold lamp, Treasure Craft, pr from $28 to...........**$32.00**

Goofy, doll, Liberty Goofy, plush, Disney Stores, w/tag, 13", M...**$25.00**

Goofy, doll, Schuco, 1950s, 14", EX...................**$350.00**

Goofy, figure, Weebles, 1973, EX........................**$15.00**

Goofy, nodder, plastic, Marx, 1960s, 2¾", EX+..........**$45.00**

Goofy, yo-yo, plastic w/imprint seal, tournament shape, Festival, 1970s, MIP **$25.00**

Donald Duck, jack-in-the-box, Spear, composition figure with felt clothes, EX, $275.00. (Photo courtesy Michael Stern)

Donald Duck, projector, gray plastic, battery-operated, Stephens Products, 1950s, 8", VG........................**$50.00**

Donald Duck, Rolykin, 1960s, 1½", NM **$22.00**

Donald Duck, toy, Donald the Bubble Duck, bubble-blowing Donald as soda jerk, Morris Plastics, 1950s, NMIB .**$75.00**

Donald Duck, toy, Ice Cream truck, rubber, 1970s, 4½", VG+..**$10.00**

Ducktales, Colorforms, 1986, EXIB **$10.00**

Horace Horsecollar, wood figure, Fun-E-Flex, EX/NM, $2,500.00. (Photo courtesy David Longest and Michael Stern)

Hunchback of Notre Dame, figure set, PVC, Applause, 1996, 3", set of 6, M..**$20.00**

Jungle Book, figure, Disneykin, 2nd series, Bagheers, Shere Khan, Sonny (baby elephant), Marx, 1960s, ea....**$60.00**

Jungle Book, figure, Disneykin, 2nd series, Baloo, Marx, 1960s, NM..**$45.00**

Jungle Book, figure, Shere Khan lying down, ceramic, Enesco/WDP, 1967, 3x5½", EX **$50.00**

Lady & the Tramp, figure, Lady or Tramp, stuffed mohair w/plastic goggle eyes, Schuco, 1960s, 8", NM, ea **$250.00**

Lady & the Tramp, mug, ceramic w/decal, footed, from Tony's Town Square Restaurant, Florida, Buffalo China, 1970s, M......**$50.00**

Lady & the Tramp, plate, white china w/decal, Tony's Town Square Restaurant, Buffalo China, 1970s, 10", EX ..**$75.00**

Lady & the Tramp, platter, white china w/decal, from Tony's Town Square Restaurant, Buffalo China, 13½", EX......**$95.00**

Lady & the Tramp, wallet, red vinyl, WDP, 1950s, EX..**$40.00**

Laverne & Victor (Gargoyles), salt & pepper shakers, marked Disney Mexico, pr from $50 to......**$60.00**

Lion King, Colorforms, 1994, EXIB......**$8.00**

Lion King, Simba & Nala, salt & pepper shakers, lion cubs, pr from $25 to......**$35.00**

Lion King, Timon, spoon rest, meercat on leaf, from $10 to......**$12.00**

Little Mermaid, figure set, Ariel, Ursela, Flounder, Sebastian, ceramic, Disney/Japan, 1980s, up to 5½", MIB..**$100.00**

Little Mermaid, mobile (book store promotion), glossy cardboard, 5-pc, late 1980s, NM......**$50.00**

Little Mermaid, yo-yo, Ariel, plastic w/imprinted seal, Spectra Star, 1989, MIP......**$5.00**

Ludwig Von Drake, figure, squeeze vinyl, WDP, 1960s, NM......**$30.00**

Ludwig Von Drake, needlepoint kit, Hassenfeld, 1961, MIB......**$35.00**

Mary Poppins, cereal-box premium, figure pops out of chimney, blue plastic, 1964, 4x3" overall, MIP......**$45.00**

Mickey Mouse, bank, ceramic, Mickey waving, Japan, 1960s, 6", M......**$75.00**

Mickey Mouse, birthday card, Baby's First Birthday, Hall Bros, 1930s, 4½x4¼", VG......**$55.00**

Mickey Mouse, camera, features Mickey on train engine & Donald Duck's face, Helm Toy, 1960s, 5¾x5", EX .**$100.00**

Mickey Mouse, Christmas lights, Noma, 1930s, NMIB ...**$450.00**

Mickey Mouse, cookie box, Mickey Mouse Cookies, cardboard w/string handle, National Biscuit Co, 1937, 2x2x5", VG+......**$100.00**

Mickey Mouse, figural soap, WDE, 1930s, EX/NM, from $200.00 to $250.00. (Photo courtesy David Longest and Michael Stern)

Mickey Mouse, figure, bisque, Mickey as football player w/helmet in hand & foot on ball, 1960s, 6", EX ..**$65.00**

Mickey Mouse, figure, bisque, Mickey as tennis player, 1960s, 4", NM......**$40.00**

Mickey Mouse, fountain pen, head finial, band features Mickey running, engraved detail, Inkograph, 1935-38, 5", MIB......**$300.00**

Mickey Mouse, game, Pin the Tail on Mickey, red & black image of Mickey on oilcloth, Marks Bros, 1935, 22", VG+......**$100.00**

Mickey Mouse, Magic Movie Palette, store Christmas giveaway, WDE, 1930s, rare, 5½x8", VG+......**$125.00**

Mickey Mouse, menu, mask shape, Disneyland Hotel, 10¾x13¼", M......**$35.00**

Mickey Mouse, mirror, round w/Mickey's head on red, white & blue frame w/stars, Sentinel Creations, 1972, 16½", EX......**$125.00**

Mickey Mouse, pencil case, vinyl, w/Lunch Money pouch, face image of Mickey, 1950s, M......**$65.00**

Mickey Mouse, Rub 'N Play Magic Transfer Set, Colorforms, 1978, unused, MIB......**$30.00**

Mickey Mouse, salt & pepper shakers, Mickey in pants w/suspenders on round base w/name, ceramic, Brechner, 1961, NM, pr......**$200.00**

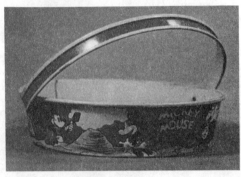

Mickey Mouse, sand sifter, Ohio Art, 1930s, EX, $225.00.
(Photo courtesy David Longest and Michael Stern)

Mickey Mouse, Sew-Ons, Lace & Dress Mickey & Minnie..., Colorforms, 1960s, MIB......**$40.00**

Mickey Mouse, store display, Drink Up w/Mickey's Fun Mugs, die-cut cardboard of Mickey's head, 1960s, 17x20", EX+......**$40.00**

Mickey Mouse, switch plate, My Room Is My Castle lettered on castle-shaped plate w/image of Mickey, plastic, 1960s, EX......**$25.00**

Mickey Mouse, tea set, porcelain, Mickey posing w/hands on hips in Bavarian costume, Germany, 1980s, 11-pc, MIB (sealed)......**$100.00**

Mickey Mouse & Donald Duck, blotter, cardboard litho w/military Mickey & Donald, Sunoco Oil, 1940s, 4x7", unused, NM+......**$30.00**

Mickey Mouse & Minnie, napkin holder, Mickey & the Beanstalk Tableware Collection, 1970s, 4½x5½", MIB......**$65.00**

Mickey Mouse Club, guitar, Mattel, 1955, 14" L, VG...**$75.00**

Mickey Mouse Club, harmonica, 1960s, NM......**$25.00**

Mickey Mouse Club, magic slate, features Jimmy Dodd, w/16-page activity/storybook, Strathmore, 1954, NM+......**$45.00**

Mickey Mouse Club, mask, Jimmy Dodd face, molded plastic, Ben Cooper, 1950s, EX......**$30.00**

Mickey Mouse Club, ring, adjustable metal, 1950s, EX..**$50.00**
Mickey Mouse Club, wallet, 1950s, NM **$30.00**
Minnie Mouse, bracelet, wood w/decaled image of Minnie, WDP, 1950s, NM **$25.00**
Minnie Mouse, figure, bisque, Minnie on roller skates w/hands touching toes, Giftware Ucago, 1960s, 4", EX...**$40.00**
Nightmare Before Christmas, banks, coin-snatch; 3 different, Japan, M, ea **$25.00**
Nightmare Before Christmas, figure set, Lock, Shock & Barrel, Hasbro, 1993, M (NM box) **$80.00**

Nightmare Before Christmas, figures, Lock, Shock, and Barrel, Hasbro, 1993, with three masks, MIB, $125.00. (Photo courtesy June Moon)

Nightmare Before Christmas, postcard book, M............**$6.00**
Percy & Meeko (Pocahontas), salt & pepper shakers, dog & raccoon, pr from $40 to **$50.00**
Peter Pan, bell, porcelain, Tinkerbell decal, gold trim, M ..**$50.00**
Peter Pan, Disneykid, Wendy, 1960s, 1", M................**$35.00**
Pinocchio, candy bar wrapper, features Jiminy Cricket, wax paper, Schutter Candy Co, 1940, 3⅛x8¼", VG.....**$85.00**

Pinocchio, doll, Ideal, jointed wood and composition, 1940s, 11", NM (NM rare box), $550.00. (Photo courtesy David Longest and Michael Stern)

Pinocchio, figure, Pinocchio, bisque, 1940s, 4", EX+..**$100.00**
Pinocchio, gum wrapper, Pinocchio Delicious Gum, shows Pinocchio w/bird's nest on end of long nose, Dietz Gum, 1940s, NM..**$100.00**
Pinocchio, hair clip, celluloid, featuring Pinocchio, WDP, 1940s, 2", NM **$30.00**

Pinocchio, pin, painted plastic Pinocchio figure, NEMO, 1940, 2", EX (EX card)...**$45.00**
Pinocchio, planter, book shape w/raised images of Pinocchio & Jiminy Cricket, ceramic, Dan Brechner Co, 1960s, 4", NM **$35.00**
Pinocchio, push-button puppet, Pinocchio, Toy Box, Japan, NM **$20.00**
Pinocchio, scrapbook, Pinocchio & Jiminy Cricket on wood-tone cover, Whitman, 1939, 10½x15½", EX.........**$45.00**

Pluto, doll, Schuco, 1950s, 13" long, EX, minimum value $350.00. (Photo courtesy Dunbar Gallery)

Pluto, figure, inflatable vinyl, 1960s, NM **$25.00**
Pluto, Rolykin, 1960s, 1½", NM **$22.00**
Rescuers Down Under, figure, Bernard or Bianca, bendable, Applause, 2", MIP, ea **$5.00**
Rescuers Down Under, figure, Bernard or Bianca, bendable, Justoys, 5", MIP, ca **$6.00**
Robin Hood, watering can, 1973, NMIB **$50.00**
Rocketeer, fan club membership card, M **$10.00**
Scrooge McDuck, bank, ceramic figure, EX **$25.00**
Sleeping Beauty, crib mobile, plastic, Kenner, 1958, EXIB **$85.00**
Sleeping Beauty, stamp book, Simon & Schuster, 1958, 32 pages, 8½x11", unused, NM+ **$30.00**
Snow White & the Seven Dwarfs, figure, Bashful, Evan K Shaw, 1950s, 2", M...**$125.00**

Snow White and the Seven Dwarfs, doll, Happy, Chad Valley, English, 12", EX, $300.00. (Photo courtesy David Longest and Michael Stern)

Snow White & the Seven Dwarfs, figure, Happy, Evan K Shaw, 1950s, 2", scarce, NM+ **$115.00**

Snow White & the Seven Dwarfs, figure, Snow White, Disneykin, Marx, 1950s, NMIB..............................$45.00

Snow White & the Seven Dwarfs, party invitation, features Happy, 1930s-40s, 3¾x7¼", NM+..........................$35.00

Snow White & the Seven Dwarfs, planter, Dopey figure next to pot, ceramic, Leeds, 1950s, 6", NM+.................$90.00

Snow White & the Seven Dwarfs, tea set, ceramic, Marx Toys/Japan/WDP, 1950s-60s, 16 pcs, EX............$250.00

Three Little Pigs, ashtray, lustreware, shows musical scene, M..$100.00

Three Little Pigs, plate, Big Bad Wolf, 1983 limited edition, Disney Collection/50th Anniversary series, 4½", EX................$32.00

Toy Story, bank, Alien figure, Sega, 11", M.................$30.00

Walt Disney, magazine, Walt Disney's, Vol III #3, April 1958, cover features Zorro on rearing horse, EX...........$25.00

Walt Disney World, bumper sticker, features Mickey & Minnie, 1970s, 2¾x15", NM+.................................$20.00

Who Framed Roger Rabbit, doll, Roger Rabbit, stuffed, 18", M...$55.00

Winnie the Pooh, ceiling fixture, painted glass, sq w/images of Pooh & friends, 1964, MIB.............................$100.00

Winnie the Pooh, figure, Eeyore, plush, Gund, 5", EX..$25.00

Winnie the Pooh, figure, Kanga w/Roo in pouch, plush, Gund, 1964, 7", EX+..$30.00

Winnie the Pooh, figure, Piglet, plush, Gund, 6", EX+..$30.00

Winnie the Pooh, figure, Pooh, plush, 6½", EX+........$30.00

Winnie the Pooh & Friends, mug tree, owl on top w/4 mugs w/characters on ea, from $50 to...........................$60.00

Winnie the Pooh & Friends, platter, embossed characters, marked Disney Made in China, from $40 to........$50.00

101 Dalmatians, poster, 1972, 41x27", NM...................$15.00

Dog Collectibles

Dog lovers appreciate the many items, old and new, that are modeled after or decorated with their favorite breeds. They pursue, some avidly, all with dedication, specific items for a particular accumulation or a range of objects, from matchbook covers to bronzes.

Perhaps the Scottish terrier is one of the most highly sought-out breeds of dogs among collectors; at any rate, Scottie devotees are more organized than most. Both the Aberdeen and West Highland terriers were used commercially; often the two are found together in things such as magnets, Black & White Scotch Whiskey advertisements, jewelry, and playing cards, for instance. They became a favorite of the advertising world in the 1930s and 1940s, partly as a result of the public popularity of President Roosevelt's dog, Fala. For information on Scottish terriers see *A Treasury of Scottie Dog Collectibles, Identification and Values, Vol. I – III,* by Candace Sten Davis and Patricia Baugh (Collector Books).

Poodles were the breed of the 1950s, and today items from those years are cherished collectibles. Trendsetter teeny-boppers wore poodle skirts, and the 5-&-10¢ stores were full of pink poodle figurines with 'coleslaw' fur. For a look back at these years, we recommend *Poodle Collectibles of the '50s and '60s* by Elaine Butler (L-W Books).

Many of the earlier collectibles are especially prized, making them expensive and difficult to find. Prices listed here may vary as they are dependent on supply and demand, location, and dealer assessment.

Advisor: Elaine Butler, Poodles (See Directory, Poodle Collectibles)

Club: Heart of America Scottish Terrier Club
Ms. Nancy McGray
507 Kurzweil
Raymore, MD 64083

Newsletter: *Canine Collectibles Quarterly*
Patty Shedlow, Editor
736 N Western Ave., Ste. 314
Lake Forest, IL 60045; Subscription: $28 per year

Border Collie, figurine, lying on floor in pile of clothes, Lowell Davis, Border Fine Art, Scotland, 1983, 4½".............$70.00

Bulldog, advertising pc, Hanley's Ale, flat open back, chalkware, 2½x9½x17"...$140.00

Bulldog, figurine, sitting, porcelain, w/Keramos stamp, 8"...$90.00

Bulldog, spittoon, brass w/relief bulldog on side, flared top, 10"...$60.00

Cocker Spaniel, book, Memories: Cocker Spaniel, John Galsworthy, illustrated by Maud Earl, published 1914 Scriber's, EX...$55.00

Cocker Spaniel, figurine, Lefton, #00412, 4½", from $20.00 to $25.00. (Photo courtesy Loretta DeLozier)

Cocker Spaniel, figurine, w/newspaper in mouth, Made in Japan, 4½x3½"...$25.00

Cocker Spaniel, plate, 2 puppies in apple crate, painted by Jim Lamb, 8½"...$110.00

Cocker Spaniel, TV lamp, 2 brown puppies, eyes light up, CLAES, 1950s, 11x5x8½".................................$65.00

Pekingese, book, Trouble; A Pet Dog, Louise Karr, published in New York, 1917, 59 pages, 5x7½", EX.........$160.00

Poodle, appliance cover, quilted, various shapes, sizes, designs, colors, ea from $8 to..............................$10.00

Poodle, apron, cotton, stamped for embroidery, from $4 to..............................$6.00

Poodle, apron, made from preprinted kit, from $4 to..............................$6.00

Poodle, ashtray, ceramic sitting dog at side, much extruded 'spinach,' unmarked, from $8 to..........................$12.00

Poodle, bank, ceramic w/cork stopper, rhinestone collar, Hand Painted...California by Pinto Products, from $20 to..............................$25.00

Poodle, bud vase, paper label: Josef Original, from $18 to..............................$22.00

Poodle, casserole, Chi Chi poodle pattern, marked Glidden 167, from $30 to..............................$40.00

Poodle, Christmas pot holder, embroidered poodle on terry cloth, from $4 to..............................$6.00

Poodle, clothes hamper, black vinyl w/printed scene, Lucite handle, no label, from $60 to..............................$75.00

Poodle, cocktail napkin, machine-embroidered poodle & edge, from $4 to..............................$7.00

Poodle, creamer & sugar bowl, ceramic, pink, yellow & blue on white, w/lid, Enesco, from $20 to..................$25.00

Poodle, decanter, ceramic, pink figural, head removes, Japan, from $15 to..............................$20.00

Poodle, decanter, figural, black on red clay, head removes, 6 cups attach to sides, Japan, from $15 to..............$20.00

Poodle, dish towel, printed linen, from $4 to..............$6.00

Poodle, dish towel, printed poodle on terry cloth, no label, from $4 to..............................$6.00

Poodle, figurine, ceramic, balancing parasol while riding unicycle (on base), from $20 to..............................$25.00

Poodle, figurine, ceramic, black dog on skis w/green cap, Japan, from $15 to..............................$20.00

Poodle, figurine, ceramic, holding paw up, much 'spinach,' paper label: Wales Made in Japan, from $8 to.....$12.00

Poodle, figurine, ceramic, stands w/basket in mouth, posed as Staffordshire dog, marked Italy, from $20 to...$25.00

Poodle, figurine, ceramic, upright mother w/2 puppies on chain leashes, unmarked, set from $10 to...........$15.00

Poodle, figurine, ceramic, w/angel wings, halo & violin, pink w/gold trim, from $20 to..............................$25.00

Poodle, figurine, ceramic, w/bridal headpiece & flowers, much extruded 'spinach' from $15 to...................$20.00

Poodle, figurine, ceramic, w/collar & beret, unmarked, from $12 to..............................$16.00

Poodle, figurine, ceramic, white w/white angora, illegible mark, from $12 to..............................$16.00

Poodle, greeting card, from $2 to..............................$6.00

Poodle, handkerchief, printed cotton, from $4 to.........$6.00

Poodle, kleenex holder, tin litho, Ransbury, from $18 to...$22.00

Poodle, lamp base, brown pottery, figural, Japan, from $20 to..............................$25.00

Poodle, laundry sprinkler, ceramic, gray, Japan, from $200 to..............................$300.00

Poodle, letter holder/stamp dispenser, ceramic & coiled wire, unmarked, from $18 to..............................$22.00

Poodle, lint brush, ceramic figural handle, Japan, from $15 to..............................$20.00

Poodle, lipstick holder, ceramic, 2 openings at back, Japan, from $6 to..............................$8.00

Poodle, magazine ad, Jantzen Sunclothes, family w/dog all in Jantzen plaid casual ware, ca 1950s, from $2 to....$8.00

Poodle, marionette puppet, Pelham, Made in England, FAO Schwarz, 1968, from $80 to..............................$100.00

Poodle, napkin ring, gold-tone metal w/rhinestone eyes, unmarked, from $8 to..............................$10.00

Poodle, pin, gold-tone metal, colored rhinestone eyes, from $8 to..............................$12.00

Poodle, pin, gold-tone metal w/openwork, marked Gerry, from $15 to..............................$20.00

Poodle, pin, red enameled metal, unmarked, from $4 to..............................$6.00

Poodle, pincushion, enameled nodder figure w/cushion on back, marked Florenza, from $30 to...................$35.00

Poodle, pitcher, ceramic, pink & blue dogs among flowers on white, Enesco, from $20 to..............................$25.00

Poodle, planter, ceramic, opening in back, Relpo 2030, from $15 to..............................$20.00

Poodle, planter, ceramic, pulling cart, much extruded 'spinach,' Napco, from $20 to..............................$25.00

Poodle, planter, ceramic, pulling cart, much extruded 'spinach,' rhinestones, marked 1G2253, from $20 to..............$25.00

Poodle, planter, ceramic, pulling cart, plaid & polka-dot decor, unmarked, from $10 to..............................$12.00

Poodle, plaque, ceramic, gold details, unmarked, 21x9", pr, from $100 to..............................$125.00

Poodle, postcard, from $1 to..............................$2.00

Poodle, powder box and perfume bottle, paper label marked Thames, sold through Sears ca 1950s, $15.00 to $20.00 each piece. (Photo courtesy Elaine Butler)

Poodle, purse, patent leather, poodle w/angel wings forms clasp, Korea, from $30 to..............................$35.00

Poodle, purse, straw, scene on side, Lucite handle, Princess Charming by Atlas Hollywood Fla, from $25 to...$30.00

Poodle, salt & pepper shakers, ceramic w/angora, Japan, pr, from $10 to..............................$12.00

Poodle, scarf, printed silk, no label, from $4 to...........$6.00

Poodle, skirt, Len Nay Originals, 1950s, from $60 to .**$75.00**
Poodle, squeeze toy, rubber, from $10 to **$15.00**
Poodle, stuffed toy, green beads, rabbit fur pompons, from $6 to...**$8.00**
Poodle, stuffed toy, Tammy Dream Pet, Dakin #1018, jointed legs, from $10 to **$15.00**
Poodle, stuffed toy, vinyl, Japan, from $4 to................**$6.00**
Poodle, tablecloth, printed poodles playing ball, no label, from $25 to..**$30.00**
Poodle, thermos bottle, Gi Gi & Beau in front of Eiffel Tower, Aladdin, from $30 to...**$35.00**
Poodle, tin container, Almond Kisses, Barton's Bonbonniere, tin litho, from $3 to **$6.00**
Poodle, trash can, dog w/umbrella tin light, Ransburg, from $20 to **$25.00**
Poodle, trash can, Dutch-cut poodle litho on tin, red interior, unmarked, from $20 to.......................................**$25.00**
Poodle, tray, tin litho, Melissa, sm, from $4 to.............**$6.00**
Poodle, tumbler, Fi Fi La Poodle on frosted glass, from $3 to **$6.00**
Poodle, tumblers, frosted glasses w/gold & black poodles w/rhinestone collars, 6 w/rack, from $50 to **$60.00**
Scottie, ashtray, metal, embossed dog in center, Japan, 1940s, 3x4", from $15 to **$25.00**
Scottie, bank, plastic, Reliable, ca 1950-60s, 7½", from $60 to **$80.00**
Scottie, bank, standing beside sphere, metal, 1950s, 4x3½x3½", from $80 to.....................................**$125.00**
Scottie, book, Argus & the Cat, Marjorie Flack, dog & cat cover, ca 1951, from $40 to **$60.00**
Scottie, book, Mac, Cecil Aldin, 1997 reprint, from $10 to **$20.00**
Scottie, bookends, flocked chalk, Made in Japan, ca 1950s, 5x4x5", pr from $15 to **$20.00**
Scottie, bookends, pot metal, head only, 1940s, 5x5x3", pr from $35 to...**$45.00**
Scottie, bootscraper, cast iron, ca 1970, 5x10", from $40 to **$60.00**
Scottie, bronze, playful pose, Austria, 2¼x1½x2¼", from $80 to..**$110.00**
Scottie, cake carrier, enameled scene on tin, 1950s, 10x11" dia, from $35 to **$55.00**
Scottie, Christmas ornament, pewter, Roosevelt-Vanderbilt Historical Association series, ca 1997 ....**$15.00**
Scottie, Christmas Stocking, red & black acrylic yarn, 1980s, from $15 to...**$30.00**
Scottie, clock, modeled after Scottie issued by Christofile Silversmiths of France, Times, 1997, 3x1¼x2½", from $50 to **$75.00**
Scottie, figurine, blue carnival glass, RM St Clair Elmwood Ind, ca 1978, 3x4x1½", from $150 to **$200.00**
Scottie, figurine, bronze, standing w/tail up, 1950s, 3½x4½x2", from $180 to...................................**$200.00**
Scottie, figurine, china, Made in USSR, 1980s, 1½x1½", from $20 to...**$25.00**
Scottie, figurine, composition, 1990s, 3½x6x7", from $10 to **$25.00**
Scottie, figurine, onyx, 2¼x4½", from $5 to...............**$10.00**
Scottie, figurine, pewter, 1950s, 1x2", from $10 to......**$20.00**
Scottie, handkerchief, printed cotton, 1940s, from $10 to ..**$20.00**
Scottie, ice cream mold, metal, 2-pc, 1950s, 6x8x2", from $125 to..**$150.00**
Scottie, letter holder/thermometer, wood, marked Souvenir of Monroe Mich, 1950s, 5x1¾x3¾", from $20 to .**$30.00**
Scottie, magazine ad, Carnation Milk, The Lucky Dog, baby spills milk, ca 1945, 13¾x10", from $7 to............**$10.00**

Scottie, mug, artist: Edwin Megargee, ca 1940s, from $20.00 to $40.00. (Photo courtesy Candace Sten Davis and Patricia Baugh)

Scottie, occasional card, 1920-50s, ea from $5 to........**$10.00**
Scottie, paperweight, brass, marked Made in England, ca 1940s, 3x¾x3", from $15 to **$18.00**
Scottie, party favor, plastic, 1950s, from $3 to............**$10.00**
Scottie, pencil box, cardboard & vinyl, ca 1940s, 2x11x4", from $20 to..**$25.00**
Scottie, picture record, Disney's Lady & the Tramp, 33⅓ rpm, from $30 to..**$60.00**
Scottie, planter, ceramic, painted roses & bow, Napco (Japan), ca 1940s, 3x7½", from $15 to **$20.00**
Scottie, planter, ceramic, standing beside mailbox, 1950s, 4x6x6", from $25 to **$35.00**
Scottie, planter, sitting beside basket, pastel pink & blue, Japan, 1940s, 3½x4½x2½", from $10 to **$12.00**
Scottie, print, Lady & the Tramp characters, premium w/video purchase, ca 1998, from $10 to **$20.00**
Scottie, salt & pepper shakers, ceramic, black & white, 1980s, 2½x3x1¼", pr from $20 to **$30.00**
Scottie, salt & pepper shakers, ceramic, red & black enameling, red lids, marked Richelain, 1940s, 3¼", pr from $10 to **$15.00**
Scottie, scarf, printed silk, 1950s, from $20 to............**$40.00**
Scottie, sign, Champion Spark Plugs, metal, Winter Ahead, dog in wintry scene, ca 1990s, M, from $15 to **$20.00**
Scottie, snow globe, Woof...Woof...Woof surrounding base, glass/composition, Made in China, 1990s, 2½", from $10 to **$20.00**
Scottie, steering wheel knob, Bakelite/reverse-painted glass/chrome, 1940s, from $80 to.......................**$120.00**
Scottie, stuffed toy, mohair, Schuco, 10x4x8", from $180 to **$225.00**

Scottie, stuffed toy, mohair, unmarked, 1950s, 9x4x7", from $25 to...$60.00

Scottie, stuffed toy, plush, Heritage Collection, Ganz, 1990s, 12x8x12", from $25 to $35.00

Scottie, sugar bowl, ceramic, black, Morton Potteries, 1940s, 3¼", from $15 to...$25.00

Scottie, swizzle stick, pewter figure on glass stick, 6", from $10 to...$15.00

Scottie, thimble, sterling silver, Tartan Terrier, 1990s, 1", from $25 to...$40.00

Scottie, towel, kitchen; printed linen, 1940s, from $5 to..$10.00

Scottie, trinket box, Scottie finial, plaid box, Limoges France, 1990s, 2x1½x2", from $90 to $120.00

Scottie, tumbler, dogs play above blue checkerboard, Hazel Atlas, 1930s, 4½", from $8 to..............................$18.00

Scottie, tumbler, green glass w/Scottic copper band, 1950s, 5¾", from $50 to...$80.00

Scottie, wood engraving, Highland Lass, Leo Meissner, ca 1953, from $150 to..$200.00

Sheltie, figurine, laying down, porcelain, unmarked, 2x4¼"..$35.00

Spaniel, figurine, marked Szeiler Made in England, 4¾x6¼"...$125.00

Welsh Corgi, figurine, looking down at mole emerging out of ground, cast bronze, Heredities, 1970s, 3⅛" $105.00

Dollhouse Furniture

Some of the mass-produced dollhouse furniture you're apt to see on the market today was made by Renwal and Acme during the 1940s and Ideal in the 1960s. All three of these companies used hard plastic for their furniture lines and imprinted most pieces with their names. Strombecker furniture was made of wood, and although it was not marked, it has a certain recognizable style to it. Remember that if you're lucky enough to find it complete in the original box, you'll want to preserve the carton as well.

Advisor: Judith Mosholder (See Directory Dollhouse Furniture)

Allied, bedroom set, ½" scale, MIB, $85.00. (Photo courtesy Marcie Tubbs)

Acme/Thomas, doll, Dutch boy or girl, flesh-colored, ea..$5.00

Acme/Thomas, rocking chair, green w/yellow, yellow w/green or yellow w/red, ea.............................$4.00

Acme/Thomas, seesaw, red or yellow horse heads, ea..$10.00

Acme/Thomas, stroller, white horse heads & blue w/white wheels...$18.00

Allied/Pyro, hutch, red or aqua, ea..............................$4.00

Allied/Pyro, lamp table, blue w/orange shade, unmarked..$18.00

Babyland Nursery, any pc, blue or pink, ea.................$5.00

Best, bunk bed or ladder, blue or pink, ea $5.00

Best, doll, baby; standing, hard plastic, 2".....................$4.00

Blue Box, chest, 4-drawer; light brown $4.00

Blue Box, table, dining; light brown.............................$5.00

Cheerio, chest of drawers, hard plastic, red $4.00

Cheerio, refrigerator, soft plastic, white, sm $2.00

Commonwealth, rake, yellow or red, ea.......................$4.00

Commonwealth, watering can, red or white, ea $6.00

Donna Lee, stove, white...$6.00

Donna Lee, table, kitchen; white..................................$6.00

Fisher-Price, bathroom set #253, M $6.00

Fisher-Price, dinette set #251, M...................................$4.00

Fisher-Price, fireplace, 1983 – 85, MOC, $3.00. (Photo courtesy Brad Cassity)

Fisher-Price, rocker #273, MOC $4.00

Ideal, cradle, blue or pink, ea $45.00

Ideal, hamper, blue..$6.00

Ideal, highboy, ivory w/blue $18.00

Ideal, lawn bench, blue or red, ea...............................$18.00

Ideal, lawn chair, white..$15.00

Ideal, potty chair, w/potty, blue..................................$15.00

Ideal, sink, bathroom; ivory w/black $8.00

Ideal, stove, ivory w/black...$15.00

Ideal, table, kitchen; ivory...$6.00

Ideal, table, kitchen; white..$20.00

Ideal Petite Princess, buffet, #4419-8, no accessories .$10.00

Ideal Petite Princess, buffet accessories, Royal #4419-8, ea...$4.00

Ideal Petite Princess, cabinet, Treasure Trove #4418-0 ..$10.00

Ideal Petite Princess, chest, Palace #4420-6, w/picture..$15.00

Ideal Petite Princess, range, #4507-0, no utensils........$50.00

Imagination, any pc, ea..$3.00

Irwin, dustpan, blue, bright yellow, green or orange, ea $4.00

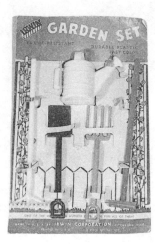

Irwin, garden set, MOC, $75.00.
(Photo courtesy Marcie Tubbs)

Irwin, plate or soup bowl, orange, ea $3.00
Irwin Interior Decorator, refrigerator, yellow.................$5.00
Irwin Interior Decorator, shower curtain, light green ...$4.00
Jaydon, buffet, reddish brown.......................................$4.00
Jaydon, chair, dining; reddish-brown swirl....................$2.00
Jaydon, sink, bathroom; ivory..$10.00
Marx, chair, barrel; hard plastic, red, ½".......................$3.00
Marx, chair, dining room; brown....................................$3.00
Marx, chest of drawers, hard plastic, blue or pink, ¾", ea...$5.00
Marx, doll, baby w/arms up; flesh-colored or pink, ea ..$4.00
Marx, doll, boy in diving position $4.00
Marx, doll, boy or girl sitting, ea $4.00
Marx Little Hostess, chaise, ivory w/bright pink.........$12.00
Marx Little Hostess, chest, block front, rust.................$12.00
Marx Little Hostess, fireplace, ivory $20.00
Marx Little Hostess, rocking chair, reddish brown......$12.00
Marx Little Hostess, table, lowboy; red.........................$12.00
Marx Little Hostess, tub & shower, no curtain $18.00
Marx Newlywed, bed, blue or deep pink, ea $15.00
Marx Newlywed, sofa, mustard or red, ea...................$15.00
Mattel Littles, armoire $8.00
Mattel Littles, dresser & lamp, in original box.............$12.00
Mattel Littles, sofa $8.00
MPC, any pc, ea..$3.00
Plasco, bed, brown headboard w/yellow spread..........$3.00
Plasco, bench, vanity; brown, dark brown, ivory or pink, ea $3.00
Plasco, nightstand, brown, marbleized med brown or tan, ea $3.00
Plasco, sink, bathroom; pink $4.00
Plasco, sofa, light blue w/brown base.........................$15.00
Plasco, stove, white w/blue base $5.00
Plasco, toilet, turquoise w/white $8.00
Reliable, fireplace, rust...$45.00
Reliable, table, dining; rust $25.00
Renwal, bathinette, blue w/decal $15.00

Renwal, chair, barrel; red w/brown base.....................$10.00
Renwal, clock, mantel; ivory or red, ea.......................$10.00
Renwal, desk, teacher's; brown $20.00
Renwal, doll, baby, plain $10.00
Renwal, doll, father; all tan, plastic rivets...................$25.00
Renwal, doll, mother, rose dress, metal rivets............$30.00

Renwal, living room set, MIB, from $100.00 to $125.00. (Photo courtesy Judith Mosholder)

Renwal, server, red, w/opening drawer......................$15.00
Renwal, table; brown or caramel, ea $8.00
Strombecker, chair, kitchen; red $6.00
Strombecker, lamp, floor; black base w/ivory shade..$15.00
Strombecker, sink; aqua or ivory, ea............................$8.00
Strombecker, table, trestle; red $8.00
Strombecker, toilet, ivory $10.00
Strombecker, urn, green or yellow, ea.........................$10.00
Superior, hutch, soft plastic, pink, sm...........................$1.00
Superior, lawn chair, soft plastic, yellow, sm $2.00
Superior, lawn chair/table, 2-seat; bright blue, bright yellow or pale green, no umbrella, ea $8.00
Superior, table, coffee; pale green or red, ea $8.00
Tomy Smaller Homes, bathroom scale.........................$15.00
Tomy Smaller Homes, range, counter-top; w/hood unit .$18.00
Tomy Smaller Homes, table, coffee..............................$10.00
Tootsietoy, cabinet, medicine; ivory.............................$25.00
Tootsietoy, chair, dining room; ivory $7.00
Tootsietoy, telephone, green $45.00
Tootsietoy, towel bar, ivory $20.00
Young Decorator, crib, blue..$45.00
Young Decorator, highchair, blue or pink, ea $45.00
Young Decorator, refrigerator, white............................$55.00
Young Decorator, stove, white $55.00

Dolls

Doll collecting is one of the most popular hobbies in the United States. Since many of the antique dolls are so expensive, modern dolls have come into their own and can be had at prices within the range of most budgets. Today's thrift-shop owners know the extent of 'doll mania,' though, so you'll seldom find a bargain there. But if you're willing to spend the time, garage sales can be a good source for your doll buying. Granted most will be in a 'well loved' condition, but as long as they're priced right, many can be re-dressed, rewigged, and cleaned up. Swap meets and flea markets may sometimes yield a good example or two, often at lower-than-book prices.

Modern dolls, those from 1935 to the present, are made of rubber, composition, magic skin, synthetic rubber, and many types of plastic. Most of these materials do not stand up well to age, so be objective when you buy, especially if you're buying with an eye to the future. Doll repair is an art best left to professionals, but if yours is only dirty, you can probably do it yourself. If you need to clean a composition doll, do it very carefully. Use only baby oil and follow up with a soft dry cloth to remove any residue. Most types of wigs can be shampooed with wig shampoo and lukewarm water. Be careful not to matt the hair as you shampoo, and follow up with hair conditioner or fabric softener. Comb gently and set while wet, using small soft rubber or metal curlers. Never use a curling iron or heated rollers.

In our listings, unless a condition is noted in the descriptions, values are for dolls in excellent condition.

For further study, we recommend these books: *Collector's Guide to Dolls of the 1960s and 1070s* by Cindy Sabulis; *Madame Alexander Dolls, 1965 – 1990,* by Pat Smith; *Doll Values, Antique to Modern, Third Edition,* and *Modern Collectible Dolls, Vols I, II, III,* and *IV,* by Patsy Moyer; *Black Dolls: 1820 – 1991* and *Black Dolls, Book II,* by Myla Perkins; *Chatty Cathy Dolls* by Kathy and Don Lewis; *Collector's Guide to Ideal Dolls* by Judith Izen; *Collector's Guide to Tammy* by Cindy Sabulis and Susan Weglewski; *Little Kiddles, An Identification Guide,* by Paris Langford (which includes other dolls as well); and *Collector's Encyclopedia of Vogue Dolls* by Judith Izen and Carol J. Stover. All these references are published by Collector Books.

See also Barbie and Friends; Shirley Temple; Toys (Action Figures and GI Joe); Trolls.

Magazine: *Doll Castle News*
37 Belvidere Ave., P.O. Box 247
Washington, NJ 07882
908-689-7042 or fax: 908-689-6320

Newsletter: Doll Collectors of America
30 Norwood Ave., Rockport, MA 01966-1730

Newsletter: *Doll Investment Newsletter*
P.O. Box 1982, Centerville, MA 02632

Newsletter: *Doll News*
United Federation of Doll Clubs
P.O. Box 14146, Parkville, MO 64152

Newsletter: *Modern Doll Club Journal*
Jeanne Niswonger
305 W Beacon Rd., Lakeland, FL 33803

Annalee

Barbara 'Annalee' Davis' was born in Concord, New Hampshire, on February, 11, 1915. She started dabbling at doll-making at an early age, often giving her creations to friends. She married Charles 'Chip' Thorndike in 1941 and moved to Meredith, New Hampshire, where they started a chicken farm and sold used auto parts. By the early 1950s, with the chicken farm failing, Annalee started crafting her dolls on the kitchen table to help make ends meet. She designed her dolls by looking into the mirror, drawing faces as she saw them, and making the clothes from scraps of material.

The dolls she developed are made of wool felt with 'hand-painted' features and flexible wire frameworks. The earlier dolls from the 1950s had a long white red-embroidered tag with no date. From 1959 to 1964, the tags stayed the same except there was a date in the upper right-hand corner. From 1965 to 1970, this same tag was folded in half and sewn into the seam of the doll. In 1970 a transition period began. The company changed its tag to a satiny white tag with a date preceded by a copyright symbol in the upper right-hand corner. In 1975 they made another change to a long white cotton strip with a copyright date. In 1982 the white tag was folded over, making it shorter. Many people mistake the copyright date as the date the doll was made — not so! It wasn't until 1986 that they finally began to date the tags with the year of manufacture, making it much easier for collectors to identify their dolls. Besides the red-lettered white Annalee tags, numerous others were used in the 1990s, but all reflect the year the doll was actually made.

For many years the company held a June auction on the premises; this practice has been discontinued. Annalee's signature can increase a doll's value by as much as $300.00, sometimes more, but at this time she is not signing *any* dolls. Only Chuck (her son) and Karen Thorndike are now signing them.

Remember, these dolls are made of wool felt. To protect them, store them with moth balls, and avoid exposing them to too much sunlight, since they will fade. Our advisor has been a collector for almost twenty years and a secondary market dealer since 1988. Most of these dolls have been in her collection at one time or another. She recommends 'If you like it, buy it, love it, treat it with care, and you'll have it to enjoy for many years to come.'

Our values are suggested for dolls in very good to excellent condition, not personally autographed by Annalee herself.

Advisor: Jane Holt (See Directory, Dolls)

Newsletter: *The Collector*
Annalee Doll Society
P.O. Box 1137, 50 Reservoir Rd., Meredith, NH 03253-1137
1-800-433-6557

Baby in pajamas, 1989, 18".............**$40.00**
Bunny, Sailor boy, 2000, 30"......................**$95.00**

Bunny artist, pink smock & blue beret, holds brush & palette, 1993, 7"............**$15.00**

Bunny w/carrot, 1985, 7"............**$25.00**

Caroller girl, 1974, 8"............**$50.00**

Christmas elf, green clothes, white pompon on hat, made many years to present, 10"............**$15.00**

Clown, Society Doll, deflated balloon, 1990, 8½", NM..**$40.00**

Colonial drummer boy, 1976, 18"............**$95.00**

Duck in raincoat, carrying umbrella, 1985, 5"............**$35.00**

Elf, pink, green or purple clothes, 1961, 26", ea **$250.00**

Equestriene mouse, 1982, 7", $100.00. (Photo courtesy Jane Holt)

Frog boy, purple & white checked rompers, 1980, 18"..**$75.00**

Frog bride and groom, 1980, 10", $300.00 for the pair. (Photo courtesy Jane Holt)

Indian maiden w/printed blanket, tan dress, 1991, 10"..**$50.00**

Leprechaun, dark green body, shamrock vest, 1977, 10"..**$55.00**

Leprechaun w/pot of gold, 1993, 5"............**$35.00**

Monk, black robe, 1963, 10"............**$150.00**

Mouse, biker boy, red & white striped shirt, streamline bicycle, 1978, 7"............**$30.00**

Mouse, housewife, holds mop, hair in rollers, 1983, 7"..**$35.00**

Mouse, Maid Marian, 1990, 7"............**$30.00**

Mouse, Pilgrim girl & boy, green plaid clothes, 1991, 12", pr............**$80.00**

Mouse, witch on broom (mobile), 1980, 7"............**$30.00**

Mouse, wizard, 1996, 3", M............**$25.00**

Mouse, woodchopper w/axe & logs, 1980, 7"............**$25.00**

Mrs Claus, sitting in rocker reading book, 1997, 18"..**$50.00**

Polar Bear, fishing, 1989, 7", in glass dome **$50.00**

Reindeer, 1977, red nose, 36"............**$100.00**

Santa Claus carrying book of Good Boys & Girls, 1970s-80s, 18"............**$65.00**

Santa in rocking chair soaking feet, 1991, 18"............**$55.00**

Skeleton Kid, 1996, 30"............**$125.00**

Snowy Owl, green ear muffs, 1990, 10"............**$35.00**

Thorny the Ghost, 1989, 18", M............**$125.00**

Unicorn, 1986, 10"............**$50.00**

Witch Kid, 1993, 30"............**$125.00**

Betsy McCall

The tiny 8" Betsy McCall doll was manufactured by the American Character Doll Company from 1957 through 1963. She was made from high-quality hard plastic with a bisque-like finish and hand-painted features. Betsy came in four hair colors — tosca, red, blond, and brunette. She had blue sleep eyes, molded lashes, a winsome smile, and a fully jointed body with bendable knees. On her back there is an identification circle which reads McCall Corp. The basic doll wore a sheer chemise, white taffeta panties, nylon socks, and Mary Jane-style shoes and could be purchased for $2.25.

There were two different materials used for tiny Betsy's hair. The first was a soft mohair sewn into fine mesh. Later the rubber skullcap was rooted with saran which was more suitable for washing and combing.

Betsy McCall had an extensive wardrobe with nearly one hundred outfits, each of which could be purchased separately. They were made from wonderful fabrics such as velvet, taffeta, felt, and even real mink. Each ensemble came with the appropriate footwear and was priced under $3.00. Since none of Betsy's clothing was tagged, it is often difficult to identify other than by its square snap closures (although these were used by other companies as well).

Betsy McCall is a highly collectible doll today but is still fairly easy to find at doll shows. The prices remain reasonable for this beautiful clotheshorse and her many accessories. For further information we recommend *Betsy McCall, A Collector's Guide*, by Marci Van Ausdall.

Advisor: Marci Van Ausdall (See Directory, Dolls)

Newsletter: *Betsy's Fan Club*
Marci Van Ausdall
P.O. Box 946, Quincy, CA 95971-0946; e-mail: dreams707@aol.com
Subscription $16.00 per year or send $4 for sample copy

Doll, American Character, original outfit, multi-jointed, 29", MIB............**$250.00**

Books and magazines featuring Betsy McCall, from $10.00 to $35.00. (Photo courtesy Marci Van Ausdall)

These are the dolls that bring back memories of childhood TV shows, popular songs, favorite movies, and familiar characters. Mego, Mattel, Remco, and Hasbro are among the largest manufacturers.

Condition is a very important worth-assessing factor, and if the doll is still in the original box, so much the better! Should the box be unopened (NRFB), the value is further enhanced. Using mint in box as a standard, deduct 30% to 35% for one that is mint (no box). Reduce the price for 'never removed from box' examples by about 40%. Values for dolls in only good or poorer condition drop at a rapid pace.

See also Elvis Presley Memorabilia.

Advisor: Henri Yunes (See Directory, Dolls)

Abbott & Costello (Who's on First), Ideal, 1984, gift set, 12", MIB **$100.00**

Doll, American Character, 8", EX, $200.00. In Town and Country outfit: $75.00. (Photo courtesy Marci Van Ausdall)

Angie Dickinson, Police Woman, Horsman, 1976, MIB, $60.00. (Photo courtesy June Moon)

Doll, American Character, Playtime outfit, 14", EX ...**$250.00**
Doll, Horsman, vinyl & rigid plastic body, sleep eyes, 1974, 12½", MIB...**$75.00**
Doll, Linda McCall (Betsy's cousin), 1959, 36", MIB.**$350.00**
Doll, original outfit w/pink tissue & booklet, 8", MIB, minimum value **$225.00**
Doll, starter kit #9300, blond hair w/side part, complete, EX (worn card), minimum value.............................**$275.00**
Doll, Uneeda, vinyl, rooted hair, 1964, 11½", MIB, minimum value **$95.00**
Doll, w/trunk & wardrobe, 14", M **$500.00**
Doll, wearing pink Prom Time formal, 8", EX **$150.00**
Outfit, April Showers, complete, EX **$45.00**
Outfit, Prom Time Formal, blue, EX **$50.00**
Outfit, Zoo Time, complete, VG...................................**$65.00**

Celebrity Dolls

Celebrity and character dolls have been widely collected for many years, but they've lately shown a significant increase in demand. Except for rarer examples, most of these dolls are still fairly easy to find at doll shows, toy auctions, and flea markets, and the majority are priced under $100.00.

Annisa Jones (Buffy, with Mrs. Beasley), Mattel, NMIB, $200.00. (Photo courtesy Henri Yunes)

Audrey Hepburn (Breakfast at Tiffany's), Mattel, 1998, black or pink outfit, 11½", MIB, ea **$85.00**
Charlie Chaplin, World Doll, 1989, 100th Anniversary, 11½", NRFB..**$55.00**
Cher, Mego, 1977, 2nd issue, Growing Hair, 12", NRFB (photo on box) **$80.00**

Cheryl Ladd (Kris), Mattel, 1978, 11½", NRFB............**$55.00**

Christy Brinkley, Real Models Collection, Matchbox, 1989, 11½", NRFB **$55.00**

Deidra Hall (Marlena), Mattel, 1999, 11½", NRFB.......**$85.00**

Desi Arnez (Ricky Ricardo), Hamilton Presents, 1991, 15½", MIB **$40.00**

Diana Ross, Mego, 1977, white & silver dress, 12", NRFB .**$125.00**

Dolly Parton, Eegee, 1987, 2nd edition, black jumpsuit or cowgirl outfit, 11½", NRFB, ea **$50.00**

Donny Osmond, Mattel, 1976, 11½", MIB **$60.00**

Drew Carey, Creation, 1998, 11½", NRFB...................**$30.00**

Elizabeth Taylor (The Bluebird), Horsman, 1976, w/3 outfits, 12", NRFB **$150.00**

Farrah Fawcett (Jill), Mego, 1976, 1st edition, white jumpsuit, 12", NRFB (photo on green box) **$60.00**

Jaclyn Smith (Kelly), Hasbro, 1977, jumpsuit & scarf, 8½", MOC..**$40.00**

Jaclyn Smith (Kelly), Mego, 1978, blue dress, rare, 12", NRFB **$125.00**

Jaleel White (Steve Urkel), Hasbro, 1991, cloth & vinyl, 17", MIB **$50.00**

Jimmy Osmond, Mattel, 1978, 9", MIB **$75.00**

John Stamos (Jesse), Tiger, 1993, 11½", MIB..............**$40.00**

John Wayne (Great Legends), Effanbee, 1982, Guardian of the West outfit, 18", MIB **$125.00**

Judy Garland (Great Legends/Wizard of Oz), Effanbee, 1984, w/Toto & basket, 14½", MIB **$100.00**

Kate Jackson (Sabrina), Mattel, 1978, red & white dress, 11½", NRFB **$60.00**

Kristy McNichol (Buddy), Mattel, 1978, w/extra outfit, 9", MIB **$40.00**

Madonna (Breathless Mahoney), Playmates, 1990, plastic, blue dress, 19", NRFB...**$60.00**

Marie Osmond, Mattel, 1976, 30", MIB **$115.00**

Marla Gibbs (Florence), 1978, 16", MIB....................**$100.00**

Mary Kate/Ashley Olsen (Michelle), cloth & vinyl, talker, 15", MIB **$40.00**

MC Hammer, Mattel, 1991, gold outfit w/boom box, 11½", MIB **$85.00**

Michael Jackson (King of Pop Singing Doll), Streetlife, 1995, rare, 11½", MIB..**$250.00**

Mr T, Galoob, 1983, 2nd edition, talker, vest & jeans, 12", MIB **$75.00**

Prince Charles, Goldberger, 1982, Palace Guard outfit, 12", rare, NRFB **$350.00**

Princess Diana, Danbury Mint, 1985, pink dress, 15", MIB **$110.00**

Sally Field (Flying Nun), Hasbro, 1967, 12", MIB **$200.00**

Sonny Bono, Mego, 1976, 12", NRFB (orange box) .**$150.00**

Soupy Sales, Sunshine Dolls, 1965, 6", NRFB............**$235.00**

Spice Girls (On Tour), Galoob, 1997, 2nd issue, 5 different, 11½", NRFB, ea **$65.00**

Susan Lucci (Erica Kane at Wedding), Mattel, 1999, 11½", NRFB **$85.00**

Sylvester Stallone (Rocky), Phoenix Toys, 1983, 8", MOC..**$45.00**

Vanilla Ice, THQ, 1991, issued in 3 different outfits, 12", NRFB, ea...**$50.00**

Vanna White, Totsy Toys, 1992, Mother's Day edition, w/baby, 11½", MIB...**$100.00**

Vanna White, Totsy Toys, 1992, special edition, silver, gold or platinum dress, MIB, ea **$125.00**

WC Fields, 1980, 16", M **$85.00**

Twiggy, Mattel, MIB, $300.00. (Photo courtesy Henri Yunes)

Vanna White in Wedding Dress, Totsy Toys, rare, MIB, $125.00. (Photo courtesy Henri Yunes)

Chatty Cathy and Other Mattel Talkers

One of the largest manufacturers of modern dolls is the Mattel company, the famous maker of the Barbie doll. But besides Barbie, there are many other types of Mattel's dolls that have their own devotees, and we've tried to list a sampling of several of their more collectible lines.

Next to Barbie, the all-time favorite doll was Mattel's Chatty Cathy. She was first made in the 1960s, in blond and brunette variations, and much of her success can be attributed to that fact that she could talk! By pulling the string on her back, she could respond with eleven different phrases. The line was expanded and soon included Chatty Baby, Tiny Chatty Baby and Tiny Chatty Brother (the twins), Charmin' Chatty, and finally Singing' Chatty. They all sold successfully for five years, and although Mattel reintroduced the line in 1969 (smaller and with a restyled face), it was not well received. For more information we recommend *Chatty Cathy*

Dolls, An Identification & Value Guide, by our advisors, Kathy and Don Lewis.

In 1960 Mattel introduced their first line of talking dolls. They decided to take the talking doll's success even further by introducing a new line — cartoon characters that the young TV viewers were already familiar with.

Below you will find a list of the more popular dolls and animals available. Most MIB (mint-in-box) toys found today are mute, but this should not detract from the listed price. If the doll still talks, you may consider adding a few more dollars to the price.

Advisors: Kathy and Don Lewis (See Directory, Dolls)

Baby Cheryl, 1965, 16", MIB.................................**$200.00**
Baby Colleen, Sears Exclusive, 1965, 15½", MIB......**$100.00**
Baby Drowsy, Black, 1968, 15", MIB.......................**$175.00**
Baby See 'N Say, 1964, MIB..................................**$150.00**
Baby Sing-A-Song, 1969, 16½", MIB.......................**$150.00**
Baby Small Talk, 1968, MIB...................................**$125.00**
Baby Whisper, 1968, 17½", MIB..............................**$200.00**
Bozo the Clown, stuffed cloth w/yarn hair, 1964, 18", MIB **$300.00**
Bugs Bunny, plush w/vinyl face, 1962, MIB.............**$300.00**
Captain Kangaroo, stuffed cloth w/felt hat, 1967, MIB **$150.00**
Casper the Friendly Ghost, stuffed terry cloth w/vinyl head, 1961, 15", NM.......................................**$125.00**
Charmin' Chatty, auburn or blond hair, blue eyes, 1 record, M **$250.00**
Chatty Baby, Black, M...**$650.00**
Chatty Baby, Black, w/pigtails, M.........................**$1,500.00**
Chatty Baby, early, brunette hair, brown eyes, M.....**$160.00**
Chatty Baby, open speaker, blond or brunette hair, blue eyes, M, ea...**$250.00**

Chatty Cathy, 1970, MIB, $85.00; loose, $55.00.
(Photo courtesy Kathy and Don Lewis/Mark Mazzetti)

Chatty Cathy, Black, page boy-style hair, 1962, M **$1,200.00**
Chatty Cathy, early, brunette hair, blue eyes, M **$85.00**

Chatty Cathy, later issue, open speaker, blond or brunette hair, blue eyes, M, ea...........................**$750.00**
Chatty Cathy, mid-year or transitional, brunette hair, brown or blue eyes, M, ea..............................**$650.00**
Chatty Cathy, patent pending, cloth over speaker or ring around speaker, blond hair, blue eyes, M, ea....**$750.00**
Chatty Cathy, reissue, blond hair, blue eyes, MIB **$80.00**

Chatty Cathy, vinyl, 1960 – 65, blond hair, two teeth, 20", $400.00. (Photo courtesy McMasters Doll Auctions)

Chatty Patty, 1980s, MIB **$50.00**
Cheerleader, 1970, several variations, MIB, ea...........**$75.00**
Dr Dolittle, 1969, 24", NMIB................................**$150.00**
Dr Dolittle's Pushmi-Pullyu, plush, 1968, NM...........**$125.00**
Gramma & Grampa, 1968, MIB..............................**$150.00**
Hi Dottie, Black, 1972, complete w/telephone, NM ...**$75.00**
King Kong, stuffed corduroy w/vinyl face, 1966, 12", NM **$150.00**
Linus the Lion-Hearted, plush w/vinyl face, 1965, NM..**$125.00**
Little Sister Look 'N Say, Sears Exclusive, 18", M........**$15.00**
Randi Reader, 1968, 19½", MIB..............................**$175.00**
Sally Ann Howes (Truly Scrumptious), pink dress, 1969, 11½", MIB...**$450.00**
Singing' Chatty, brunette hair, M **$275.00**
Sister Belle, 1961, MIB **$300.00**

Sister Belle, 1961, played with, non-talking, $25.00. (Photo courtesy Kathy and Don Lewis)

Teachy Talk, 1970, MIB	**$50.00**
Timey Tell, MIB	**$110.00**
Tiny Chatty Baby, brunette hair, brown eyes, M	**$300.00**

Dawn Dolls by Topper

Made by Deluxe Topper in the 1970s, this 6" fashion doll was part of a series sold as the Dawn Model Agency. They're becoming highly collectible, especially when mint in the box. They were issued already dressed in clothes of the highest style, or you could buy additional outfits, many complete with matching shoes and accessories.

Advisor: Dawn Diaz (See Directory, Dolls)

Case, Irwin Toy Ltd, Toronto, Canada (Topper), 1970, 8", $35.00.

Center: Dawn doll in original dress, loose, from $10.00 to $15.00; Wedding gowns modeled on each side, loose, from $10.00 to $15.00. (Photo courtesy Cindy Sabulis)

Dawn's Apartment, complete w/furniture	**$50.00**
Doll, Dancing Angie, NRFB	**$30.00**
Doll, Dancing Dale, NRFB	**$50.00**
Doll, Dancing Dawn, NRFB	**$30.00**
Doll, Dancing Gary, NRFB	**$40.00**
Doll, Dancing Glori, NRFB	**$30.00**
Doll, Dancing Jessica, NRFB	**$30.00**

Doll, Dancing Ron, NRFB	**$40.00**
Doll, Dancing Van, NRFB	**$50.00**
Doll, Dawn Majorette, NRFB	**$75.00**
Doll, Denise, NRFB	**$75.00**
Doll, Dinah, NRFB	**$75.00**
Doll, Gary, NRFB	**$30.00**
Doll, Jessica, NRFB	**$30.00**
Doll, Kip Majorette, NRFB	**$45.00**
Doll, Longlocks, NRFB	**$30.00**
Doll, Maureen, Dawn Model Agency, red & gold dress, NRFB	**$75.00**
Doll, Ron, NRFB	**$30.00**
Outfit, Bell Bottom Flounce, #0717, NRFB	**$25.00**

Holly Hobbie

In the late 1960s a young homemaker and mother, Holly Hobbie, approached the American Greeting Company with some charming country-styled drawings of children as proposed designs for greeting cards. Her concepts were well received by the company, and since that time thousands of Holly Holly items have been produced. Nearly all are marked HH, H. Hobbie, or Holly Hobbie.

Advisor: Donna Stultz (See Directory, Dolls)

Newsletter: *Holly Hobbie Collectors Gazette*
c/o Donna Stultz
1455 Otterdale Mill Rd.
Taneytown, MD 21787-3032; 410-775-2570
hhgazette@netscape.net
Subscription: $25 per year for 6 issues; includes free 50-word ad per issue, 'Free' sample issue available!

Doll, Baby Holly Hobbie, stuffed cloth with vinyl head and hands, original outfit, VG, $10.00 (MIB $25.00). (Photo courtesy Helen McCale)

Doll, Country Fun Holly Hobbie, 1989, 16", NRFB	**$20.00**
Doll, Grandma Holly, Knickerbocker, cloth, 14", MIB	**$20.00**
Doll, Grandma Holly, Knickerbocker, cloth, 24", MIB	**$25.00**
Doll, Holly Hobbie, Heather, Amy or Carrie, Knickerbocker, cloth, 6", MIB, ea	**$5.00**
Doll, Holly Hobbie, Heather, Amy or Carrie, Knickerbocker, cloth, 9", MIB, ea	**$10.00**

Doll, Holly Hobbie, Heather, Amy or Carrie, Knickerbocker, cloth, 16", MIB, ea **$20.00**
Doll, Holly Hobbie, Heather, Amy or Carrie, Knickerbocker, cloth, 27", MIB, ea **$25.00**
Doll, Holly Hobbie, Heather, Amy or Carrie, Knickerbocker, cloth, 33", MIB, ea **$35.00**
Doll, Holly Hobbie, 1988, scented, clear ornament around neck, 18", NRFB **$30.00**
Doll, Holly Hobbie, 25th Anniversary collector's edition, Meritus, 1994, 26", MIB **$25.00**
Doll, Holly Hobbie Bicentennial, Knickerbocker, cloth, 12", MIB **$25.00**
Doll, Holly Hobbie Day 'N Night, Knickerbocker, cloth, 14", MIB **$15.00**
Doll, Holly Hobbie Dream Along, Holly, Carrie or Amy, Knickerbocker, cloth, 9", MIB, ea **$10.00**
Doll, Holly Hobbie Dream Along, Holly, Carrie or Amy, Knickerbocker, cloth, 12", MIB, ea **$15.00**
Doll, Holly Hobbie Talker, cloth, 4 sayings, 16", MIB ..**$25.00**
Doll, Little Girl Holly, Knickerbocker, 1980, cloth, 15", MIB **$20.00**
Doll, Robby, Knickerbocker, cloth, 9", MIB................**$15.00**
Doll, Robby, Knickerbocker, cloth, 16", MIB..............**$20.00**
Dollhouse, M...**$200.00**
Sand pail, metal, Chein, 1976, 6", VG+ **$25.00**
Valentine Activity Book, 1978, 5x8", unused, EX........**$10.00**

Ideal Dolls

The Ideal Toy Company made many popular dolls such as Shirley Temple, Betsy Wetsy, Miss Revlon, Toni, and Patti Playpal. Ideal's doll production was so enormous that since 1907 over 700 different dolls have been 'brought to life,' made from materials such as composition, latex rubber, hard plastic, and vinyl.

Since Ideal dolls were mass produced, most are still accessible and affordable. Collectors often find these dolls at garage sales and flea markets. However, some Ideal dolls are highly desirable and command high prices — into the thousands of dollars. These sought-after dolls include the Samantha doll, variations of the Shirley Temple doll, certain dolls in the Patti Playpal family, and some Captain Action dolls.

The listing given here is only a sampling of Ideal dolls made from 1907 to 1989. This listing reports current, realistic selling prices at doll shows and through mail order. Please remember these values are for dolls in excellent condition with original clothing.

For more information please refer to *Collector's Guide to Ideal Dolls: Identification and Values, Second Edition,* by Judith Izen (Collector Books).

See also Advertising Characters; Shirley Temple; and Dolls subcategories: Betsy McCall, Celebrity Dolls, and Tammy.

Club: Ideal Collectors Club
Judith Izen
P.O. Box 623, Lexington, MA 02173

Subscription: $20 per year for 4 issues; includes free wanted/for sale ads in each issue

Baby Crissy, Black, 1973-76, pink dress, EX **$80.00**
Baby Crissy, 1973-76, pink dress, EX..........................**$65.00**
Baby Snoozie, 1965, re-dressed, EX, from $50 to.......**$75.00**
Belly Button Baby, 1970, push belly button & she moves, all original, EX, from $25 to...........................**$30.00**
Cinnamon, Curly Ribbons, 1974, EX **$45.00**
Cinnamon, Hairdoodler, 1973, EX................................**$40.00**
Crissy, Country Fashion, 1982-83, EX..........................**$20.00**
Crissy, Magic Hair, 1977, EX.......................................**$30.00**
Crissy, Magic Hair, 1977, NRFB **$100.00**
Crissy, Movin' Groovin', Black, 1977, EX **$100.00**
Crissy, Swirla Curla, Black, 1973, EX **$100.00**
Crissy, Twirly Beads, 1974, MIB **$65.00**
Dina, 1972-73, purple playsuit, EX.............................**$50.00**
Giggles, 1967, plastic & vinyl, 18", MIB, from $125 to .**$200.00**
Kissy, 1960s, 22", MIB, from $100 to **$125.00**

Mia (Velvet's Beautiful Friend), from the Crissy Grow Hair Family, 1971, MIB, $125.00. (Photo courtesy Cindy Sabulis)

Mia, 1971, turquoise romper, EX.................................**$50.00**
Patchwork Kids, 1976, several variations, 13", MIB, ea from $25 to...**$35.00**
Penny Playpal, 1959, re-dressed, 32", NM, from $300 to...**$350.00**
Rub-A-Dub Dolly, 1973, vinyl, nude, EX.....................**$20.00**
Tearie Dearie, 1964, all original, complete w/highchair, EX, from $35 to..**$45.00**
Toddler Thumbelina, 1960s, complete w/walker, NMIB, from $75 to..**$100.00**
Velvet, Beauty Braider, 1973, EX **$35.00**
Velvet, Look Around, 1972, EX....................................**$35.00**
Velvet, Swirly Daisies, 1974, MIB **$65.00**
Velvet, 1970, 1st issue, purple dress, EX.....................**$55.00**

Jem

The glamorous life of Jem mesmerized little girls who watched her Saturday morning cartoons, and she was a natural as a fashion doll. Hasbro saw the potential in 1985 when they introduced the Jem line of 12" dolls representing her, the rock stars from Jem's musical group, the Holograms, and other members of the cast, including the only boy, Rio, Jem's road manager and Jerrica's boyfriend. Each doll was poseable, jointed at the waist, head, and wrists, so that they could be positioned at will with their musical instruments and other accessory items. Their clothing, their makeup, and their hairdos were wonderfully exotic, and their faces were beautifully modeled. The Jem line was discontinued in 1987 after being on the market for only two years.

Accessory, Jem Speaker & Dressing Room, complete, NM **$100.00**
Doll, Aja, 1st issue, complete, M **$45.00**
Doll, Aja, 1st issue, nude, M **$15.00**
Doll, Glitter 'N Gold Rio, NRFB................................... **$35.00**
Doll, Glitter 'N Gold Rio, nude, M **$10.00**
Doll, Kimber, 1st issue, complete, M **$40.00**
Doll, Kimber, 1st issue, nude, M **$10.00**

Doll, Raya, complete, EX, $150.00; NRFB, $175.00.

Doll, Rock 'N Curl Jem, complete, M........................... **$20.00**
Doll, Rock 'N Curl Jem, nude **$7.00**
Doll, Roxy, complete, M **$50.00**
Doll, Roxy, NRFB... **$65.00**
Doll, Shana, 1st issue, NRFB... **$175.00**
Doll, Shana, 1st issue, nude, M **$35.00**
Doll, Stormer, 1st issue, NRFB...................................... **$65.00**
DOll, Stormer, 2nd issue, NRFB **$75.00**
Doll, Video, complete, 12½", MIB................................ **$40.00**
Outfit, Music Is Magic, complete, M............................ **$20.00**
Outfit, Share a Little Bit, complete, M......................... **$80.00**
Outfit, Share a Little Bit, NRFB.................................... **$125.00**
Outfit, Sophisticated Lady, complete, M **$20.00**
Outfit, You Can't Catch Me, complete, M.................... **$25.00**

Liddle Kiddles

These tiny little dolls ranging from ¾" to 4" tall were made by Mattel from 1966 until 1979. They all had poseable bodies and rooted hair that could be restyled, and they came with accessories of many types. Some represented storybook characters, some were flowers in perfume bottles, some were made to be worn as jewelry, and there were even spacemen 'Kiddles.'

Serious collectors prefer examples that are still in their original packaging and will often pay a minimum of 30% (to as much as 100%) over the price of a doll in excellent condition with all her original accessories. A doll whose accessories are missing is worth from 65% to 70% less. For more information, we recommend *Liddle Kiddles* by Paris Langford and *Schroeder's Collectible Toys, Antique to Modern* (both published by Collector Books).

Advisor: Dawn Diaz (See Directory, Dolls)

Club: Liddle Kiddle Klub
Laura Miller
3639 Fourth Ave., La Crescenta, CA 91214

Alice in Wonderliddle, complete, NM **$175.00**
Apple Blossom Kologne, #3707, MIP.......................... **$60.00**
Babe Biddle, #3505, complete, M................................ **$50.00**

Beach Buggy, #5003, 1967, NM, $50.00; Hot Dog Stand, #5002, 1967, M, $60.00. (Photo courtesy Tamela Storm and Debra Van Dyke)

Calamity Jiddle, #3506, complete w/high saddle horse, M..**$75.00**
Cinderiddle's Palace, #5068, plastic window version, M......**$50.00**
Dainty Deer, #3637, complete, M **$45.00**
Flower Pin Kiddle, #3471, MIP **$50.00**
Greta Grape, #3728, complete, M **$50.00**
Heart Charm Bracelet Kiddle, #3747, MIP **$50.00**
Heart Ring Kiddle, #3744, MIP **$50.00**
Henrietta Horseless Carriage, #3641, complete, M...... **$60.00**
Howard Biff Biddle, #3502, complete, M..................... **$75.00**
Kiddle & Kars Antique Fair Set, #3806, NRFB........... **$300.00**
Kiddles Sweet Shop, #3807, NRFB **$300.00**
Kleo Kola, #3729, complete, M.................................... **$50.00**
Lady Crimson, #A3840, NRFB...................................... **$100.00**
Laffy Lemon, #3742, MIP **$85.00**
Larky Locket, #3539, complete, EX **$25.00**
Liddle Biddle Peep, #3544, complete, M **$125.00**
Liddle Kiddles Kastle, 33522, M................................... **$55.00**
Liddle Kiddles Open House, #5167, MIB..................... **$40.00**
Liddle Kiddles Talking Townhouse, #5154, MIB......... **$50.00**
Limey Lou Spoonfulls, #2815, MIP **$25.00**

Lola Liddle, #3504, MIP, $50.00. (Photo courtesy Paris Langford)

Lolli-Mint, #3658, MIP	$60.00
Lottie Locket, #3679, complete, M	$35.00
Luscious Lime, #3733, glitter variation, complete, M	$75.00
Nappytime Baby, #3818, complete, M	$75.00
Olivia Orange Kola Kiddle, #3730, MIP	$80.00
Rah Rah Skediddle, #3788, complete, M	$135.00
Romeo & Juliet, #3782, MIP	$200.00
Shirley Strawberry, #3727, complete, M	$50.00
Sleeping Biddle, #3527, complete, M	$100.00
Snap-Happy Living Room, #5173, NMIP	$20.00
Snoopy Skediddler & His Sopwith Camel, M	$150.00
Teeter Time Baby, #3817, complete, M	$60.00
Tiny Tiger, #3636, MIP	$100.00
Vanilla Lilly, #2819, MIP	$25.00
Windy Fliddle, #3514, complete, M	$85.00

Littlechap Family

In 1964 Remco Industries created a family of four fashion dolls that represented an upper-middle class American family. The Littlechaps family consisted of the father, Dr. John Littlechap, his wife, Lisa, and their two children, teenage daughter Judy and pre-teen Libby. Interest in these dolls is on the rise as more and more collectors discover the exceptional quality of these fashion dolls and their clothing.

Advisor: Cindy Sabulis (See Directory, Dolls)

Bedroom or family room, EX, ea	$25.00
Carrying case, EX	$40.00
Doctor John's office, EX	$75.00
Doctor John's office, MIP	$325.00
Doll, Doctor John, MIB	$85.00
Doll, Judy, MIB	$75.00
Doll, Libby, MIB	$85.00
Doll, Lisa, MIB	$50.00
Outfit, Doctor John's, complete, EX, ea from $15 to	$30.00
Outfit, Doctor John's, NRFB, ea from $30 to	$70.00
Outfit, Judy, complete, EX, from $25 to	$40.00
Outfit, Judy's, NRFB, ea from $35 to	$75.00
Outfit, Libby's, complete, EX, ea from $20 to	$35.00
Outfit, Libby's, NRFB, ea from $35 to	$50.00
Outfit, Lisa's, complete, EX, ea from $20 to	$35.00
Outfit, Lisa's, NRFB, ea from $35 to	$75.00

Nancy Ann Storybook Dolls

This company was in business as early as as 1936, producing painted bisque dolls with mohair wigs and painted eyes. Later they made hard plastic 8" Muffie and Miss Nancy Ann Style Show dolls. Debby (11") and Lori Ann (7½") had vinyl heads and hard plastic bodies. In the 1950s and 1960s, they produced a 10½" Miss Nancy Ann and Little Miss Nancy Ann, both vinyl high-heeled fashion-type dolls. For information we recommend *Modern Collectible Dolls* by Patsy Moyer.

A Dillar a Dollar, painted bisque, brown mohair wig, all original, 1941-47, 5½", NM	$50.00
Annie at the Garden Gate, painted bisque, auburn mohair wig, original clothes, 1941-42, 5½", NM	$50.00

Commencement Series, hard plastic with black sleep eyes, Debut #75, 5", MIB, $100.00.

Debbie, hard plastic, in school dress, 10", MIB	$170.00
February, painted bisque, blond mohair wig, closed mouth, white dress, feather in hat, ca 1941-42, 6½", NM	$65.00
Goldilocks, painted bisque, blond mohair wig, all original, ca 1941-47, 5½"	$50.00
He Loves Me He Loves Me Not, painted bisque, blond mohair wig, original clothes, 1941-42, 5½", NM	$50.00
I'm Going a Milking, painted bisque, blond mohair wig, all original, 1941-42, 5½", NM	$50.00
Jennie Set the Table, painted bisque, closed mouth, auburn mohair wig, all original, 1941-42, 5½", NM	$50.00
Let Me Call You Sweetheart, hard plastic, auburn mohair wig, all original, 1947-49, 6½", NM	$50.00
Little Joan, painted bisque, auburn mohair wig, molded shoes, original clothes, 1941-42, 5½", NM	$50.00
Little Miss Nancy Ann, day dress, 8½", MIB	$50.00
Little Miss Pattycake, painted bisque, original dress, pink coat & bonnet, #234, 1938, 4½", NM	$300.00

Muffie, hard plastic, blue sleep eyes, auburn wig, straight-leg non-walker, all original, ca 1953, 8", NM............**$175.00**

Muffie, hard plastic, brown sleep eyes, blond wig, straight-leg non-walker, all original, ca 1953, 8", NM **$200.00**

Polly Put the Kettle On, painted bisque, brown mohair wig, closed mouth, all original, ca 1941-47, 5½", NM..**$35.00**

Stardust, hard plastic, auburn mohair wig, original lacy dress & hat, 1947-49, 6½", NM......................................**$50.00**

Style Show, hard plastic, non-walker, all original lacy outfit w/pink stole, #2404, 1960s, 18", NM...................**$600.00**

Summery Day, hard plastic, walker, sleep eyes, mohair wig, original clothes (replaced hat), 1950s, 18", NM..**$350.00**

Sunday's Child, painted bisque, reddish-blond mohair wig, all original, 1941-47, 5½", MIB **$75.00**

Thursday's Child, painted bisque, brown mohair wig, all original, 1941-47, 5½", MIB............................**$75.00**

Winter, painted bisque, brown mohair wig, original gold bracelet, ca 1941-42, 5½", MIB **$75.00**

Raggedy Ann and Andy

Raggedy Ann dolls have been made since the early part of the twentieth century, and over the years many companies have produced their own versions. They were created originally by Johnny Gruelle, and though these early dolls are practically nonexistent, they're easily identified by the mark, 'Patented Sept. 7, 1915.' P.F. Volland made them from 1920 to 1934; theirs were very similar in appearance to the originals. The Mollye Doll Outfitters were the first to print the now-familiar red heart on her chest, and they added a black outline around her nose. These dolls carry the handwritten inscription 'Raggedy Ann and Andy Doll/Manufactured by Mollye Doll Outfitters.' Georgene Averill made them from about 1938 to 1950, sewing their label into the seam of the dolls. Knickerbocker dolls (1963 to 1982) also carry a company label. The Applause Toy Company made these dolls for two years in the early 1980s, and they were finally taken over by Hasbro, the current producer, in 1983.

Unless noted otherwise, our values are for dolls in excellent/near-mint condition. If your doll has been played with but is still in good condition with a few minor flaws (as most are), you'll need deduct about 75% from these prices. Refer to *The World of Raggedy Ann Collectibles* by Kim Avery, and *Doll Values, Antique to Modern,* by Patsy Moyer (Collector Books).

Advisor: Kim Avery

Applause, Asleep/Awake Raggedy Ann & Andy, stuffed cloth, 12", ea from $25 to......................................**$30.00**

Applause, Raggedy Andy, Little Raggedys, Macmillan Inc, 12", from $25 to **$30.00**

Applause, Raggedy Andy, stuffed cloth, 1986, 25", from $45 to..**$50.00**

Applause, Raggedy Andy, stuffed cloth, 8", from $8 to..**$12.00**

Applause, Raggedy Ann & Andy (original versions), stuffed cloth, 20", ea from $45 to......................................**$55.00**

Applause, Sleepytime Raggedy Ann & Andy, stuffed cloth, 17", ea from $30 to...**$35.00**

Direct Connect International, Little Raggedy's Nighty Night Doll, stuffed cloth, 1991, 12", ea from $30 to.......**$35.00**

Georgene Novelties, Raggedy Ann, stuffed cloth, matching dress & feet, 1945-48, 22", from $225 to............**$250.00**

Georgene Novelties, Raggedy Ann, stuffed cloth, 50" (rare), from $575 to..**$650.00**

Georgene Novelties, Raggedy Ann & Andy, stuffed cloth, 1946-63, 15", ea from $80 to...............................**$95.00**

Georgene Novelties, Raggedy Ann & Andy, stuffed cloth, 1946-64, 19", ea from $95 to...............................**$125.00**

Georgene Novelties Co, Awake/Asleep Raggedy Andy, stuffed cloth, black-outlined nose, late 1930s-40, 13", from $300 to..**$325.00**

Georgene Novelties Co, Raggedy Andy, stuffed cloth, black-outlined nose, ca 1938-45, 19", from $325 to.....**$350.00**

Georgene Novelties Co, Raggedy Ann, stuffed cloth, 1946-63, 15", from $80 to...**$95.00**

Georgene Novelties Co, Raggedy Ann, stuffed cloth, 1946-63, 19", from $125 to...**$150.00**

Knickerbocker, Bedtime Raggedy Ann & Andy, stuffed cloth, iron-on eyes, Taiwan, 15", ea from $20 to............**$25.00**

Knickerbocker, Raggedy Andy, stuffed cloth, Malaysia, 15", from $25 to..**$30.00**

Knickerbocker, Raggedy Andy, stuffed cloth, original paper tag, Hong Kong, 40", from $155 to **$175.00**

Knickerbocker, Raggedy Andy, stuffed cloth, Taiwan, w/paper tag, 38½", MIB, from $165 to...............**$185.00**

Knickerbocker, Raggedy Andy, stuffed cloth, Taiwan, 19", MIB, from $85 to...**$95.00**

Knickerbocker, Raggedy Andy, stuffed cloth, unusual aqua outfit, Taiwan, 15", from $40 to.............................**$45.00**

Knickerbocker, Raggedy Ann, stuffed cloth, Hong Kong, 19", from $45 to..**$55.00**

Knickerbocker, Raggedy Ann, stuffed cloth, Hong Kong or Taiwan, 15", ea from $15 to..................................**$25.00**

Knickerbocker, Raggedy Ann, stuffed cloth, musical, Hong Kong, 15", from $35 to...**$40.00**

Knickerbocker, Raggedy Ann, stuffed cloth, Taiwan, 25", from $50 to..**$55.00**

Knickerbocker, Raggedy Ann, stuffed cloth, Taiwan, 31", from $80 to..**$95.00**

Knickerbocker, Raggedy Ann, stuffed cloth, Taiwan, 6", MIB, from $10 to..**$15.00**

Knickerbocker, Raggedy Ann & Andy, bean bag doll, Taiwan, 9", ea from $10 to..................................**$15.00**

Knickerbocker, Raggedy Ann & Andy, stuffed cloth, Hong Kong, 15", ea from $35 to................................**$45.00**

Knickerbocker, Raggedy Ann & Andy, stuffed cloth, Korea, 15", ea from $20 to..**$25.00**

Knickerbocker, Raggedy Ann & Andy, stuffed cloth marionettes, Taiwan, 12", MIB, ea from $65 to **$75.00**

Knickerbocker, Raggedy Ann & Andy Embraceables, stuffed cloth, #9216, 1973, 7", MIB, pr from $25 to.........**$30.00**

Knickerbocker, Raggedy Ann Teach & Dress, stuffed cloth, Hong Kong, late 1960s, 20", from $50 to.............**$55.00**

Playschool, Raggedy Ann, Black, stuffed cloth, 1994, 21", from $35 to...**$40.00**
Reliable Toy Co, Raggedy Ann & Andy, stuffed cloth, 19", ea from $175 to..**$195.00**

Strawberry Shortcake and Friends

Strawberry Shortcake came on the market with a bang around 1980. The line included everything to attract small girls — swimsuits, bed linens, blankets, anklets, underclothing, coats, shoes, sleeping bags, dolls and accessories, games, and many other delightful items. Strawberry Shortcake and her friends were short lived, lasting only until the mid-1980s.

Advisor: Geneva Addy (See Directory, Dolls)

Newsletter: *Berry-Bits*
Strawberry Shortcake Collector's Club
Peggy Jimenez
1409 72nd St., N Bergen, NJ 07047

Big Berry Trolley, 1982, EX..**$40.00**
Doll, Almond Tea, 6", MIB..**$25.00**
Doll, Angel Cake, 6", MIB...**$25.00**
Doll, Apple Dumpling, 6", MIB...................................**$25.00**
Doll, Apricot, 15", NM..**$35.00**
Doll, Baby Needs a Name, 15", NM............................**$35.00**
Doll, Berry Baby Orange Blossom, 6", MIB................**$35.00**
Doll, Butter Cookie, 6", MIB.......................................**$25.00**
Doll, Cafe Ole, 6", MIB..**$35.00**
Doll, Cherry Cuddler, 6", MIB....................................**$25.00**
Doll, Lime Chiffon, 6", MIB..**$25.00**
Doll, Mint Tulip, 6", MIB..**$25.00**

Doll, Raspberry Tart, #43120, MIB, $25.00.

Doll, Strawberry Shortcake, 12", NRFB **$45.00**
Doll, Strawberry Shortcake, 15", NM..........................**$35.00**
Dollhouse, M...**$150.00**
Dollhouse Furniture, attic, 6-pc, rare, M....................**$150.00**
Dollhouse Furniture, bathroom, 7-pc, rare, M.............**$90.00**

Dollhouse Furniture, bedroom, 7-pc, rare, M..............**$90.00**
Dollhouse Furniture, kitchen, 11-pc, rare, M **$100.00**
Dollhouse Furniture, living room, 6-pc, rare, M **$85.00**
Figure, Almond Tea w/Marza Panda, PVC, 1", MOC..**$15.00**
Figure, Lemon Chiffon w/balloons, PVC, 1", MOC.....**$15.00**
Figure, Merry Berry Worm, MIB **$35.00**
Figure, Mint Tulip w/March Mallard, PVC, MOC........**$15.00**
Figure, Purple Picman w/Berry Bird, poseable, MIB..**$35.00**
Figure, Raspberry Tart w/bowl of cherries, MOC........**$15.00**
Figure, Sour Grapes w/Dregs, Strawberryland Miniatures, MIP, from $15 to **$20.00**
Figurine, Cherry Cuddler w/Gooseberry, Strawberryland Miniatures, MIP, from $15 to..............................**$20.00**
Figurine, Lemon Mirange w/Frappo, PVC, 1", MOC...**$15.00**
Ice Skates, EX...**$35.00**
Motorized Bicycle, EX **$95.00**
Roller Skates, EX..**$35.00**
Sleeping Bag, EX **$25.00**
Storybook Play Case, M **$35.00**

Stroller, Coleco, 1981, large doll size, M, $85.00. (Photo courtesy June Moon)

Telephone, Strawberry Shortcake figure, battery-operated, EX...**$85.00**

Tammy and Friends

In 1962 the Ideal Novelty and Toy Company introduced their teenage Tammy doll. Slightly pudgy and not quite as sophisticated-looking as some of the teen fashion dolls on the market at the time, Tammy's innocent charm captivated consumers. Her extensive wardrobe and numerous accessories added to her popularity with children. Tammy had a car, a house, and her own catamaran. In addition, a large number of companies obtained licenses to issue products using the 'Tammy' name. Everything from paper dolls to nurses' kits were made with Tammy's image on them. Her success was not confined to the United States; she was also successful in Canada and several other European countries. See *Collector's Guide to Tammy, the Ideal Teen,* by Cindy

Sabulis and Susan Weglewski (published by Collector Books) for more information.

Advisor: Cindy Sabulis (See Directory, Dolls)

Accessory Pak, #9179-3, w/plate of crackers, juice, glasses, sandals & newspaper, NRFP **$20.00**
Accessory Pak, #9183-80, w/camera, luggage case & airline ticket, NRFP..**$15.00**
Accessory Pak, unknown #, w/frying pan, electric skillet & lids, NRFP, from $45 to................................**$50.00**

Car, MIB, $75.00. (Photo courtesy Cindy Sabulis)

Case, Dodi, green background, EX.............................**$30.00**
Case, Misty, Dutch door-type, black background, EX...**$30.00**
Case, Misty, pink & white background, EX................**$25.00**
Case, Misty & Tammy, hatbox style, EX....................**$30.00**
Case, Pepper, green or coral background, front snap closure, EX, ea.................................**$15.00**
Case, Pepper, hatbox style, turquoise background, EX ..**$40.00**
Case, Pepper, yellow or green background, EX, ea ...**$20.00**
Case, Pepper & Dodi, blue background, front opening, EX..**$30.00**
Case, Pepper & Patti, Montgomery Ward's Exclusive, red background, EX **$50.00**
Case, Tammy & Her Friends, pink or green background, EX, ea **$30.00**
Case, Tammy Beau & Arrow, hatbox style, blue or red, EX, ea **$40.00**
Case, Tammy Evening in Paris, blue, black, or red background, EX, ea **$20.00**
Case, Tammy Model Miss, double trunk, red or black, EX, ea **$25.00**
Case, Tammy Model Miss, hatbox style, blue or black, EX, ea **$30.00**
Case, Tammy Traveler, red or green background, EX, ea..**$45.00**
Doll, Bud, MIB, minimum value **$600.00**
Doll, Dodi, MIB **$75.00**
Doll, Glamour Misty the Miss Clairol Doll, MIB........**$150.00**
Doll, Grown Up Tammy, MIB **$85.00**
Doll, Grown Up Tammy (Black), MIB, minimum value ..**$300.00**
Doll, Misty, MIB..**$100.00**
Doll, Misty (Black), MIB, minimum value **$600.00**
Doll, Patti, MIB **$200.00**

Doll, Pepper, 'carrot'-colored hair, MIB **$75.00**
Doll, Pepper, MIB **$65.00**
Doll, Pepper (Canadian version), MIB.....................**$75.00**
Doll, Pepper (trimmer body & smaller face), MIB.....**$75.00**
Doll, Pos'n Dodi, M (decorated box).......................**$150.00**
Doll, Pos'n Dodi, M (plain box)...............................**$75.00**
Doll, Pos'n Misty & Her Telephone Booth, MIB.......**$125.00**
Doll, Pos'n Pepper, MIB...**$75.00**
Doll, Pos'n Pete, MIB...**$125.00**
Doll, Pos'n Tammy & Her Telephone Booth, MIB ...**$100.00**
Doll, Pos'n Ted, MIB..**$100.00**
Doll, Tammy, MIB...**$85.00**
Doll, Tammy's Dad, MIB...**$65.00**
Doll, Tammy's Mom, MIB...**$75.00**
Doll, Ted, MIB..**$50.00**
Outfit, Dad & Ted, sports car coat & cap, #9467-2, NRFP ..**$20.00**
Outfit, Pepper, After School, #9318-7, complete, M....**$25.00**
Outfit, Pepper, Miss Gadabout, #9331-0, MIP.............**$50.00**

Outfit, Snow Bunny, #9221, 1962, complete, NM, $50.00. (Photo courtesy Pat Smith)

Outfit, Tammy, Beach Party, #9056-3 or #9906-9, complete, M, ea...**$45.00**
Outfit, Tammy, Cutie Coed, #9132-2 or #9932-5, complete, M, ea..**$45.00**
Outfit, Tammy, Pizza Party, #9115-7 or #9924-2, complete, M, ea...**$30.00**
Outfit, Tammy's Mom, Evening in Paris, #9421-9, complete, M...**$35.00**
Pak clothing, #9224-7, w/pedal pushers, orange juice, newspaper & hanger, NRFP.................................**$25.00**
Pepper's Pony, MIB...**$200.00**
Tammy Bubble Bath Set, NRFB.................................**$75.00**
Tammy Hair Dryer, sq or round case, NM, ea............**$50.00**
Tammy's Car, MIB...**$75.00**
Tammy's Jukebox, M...**$50.00**

Tressy

Tressy was American Character's answer to Barbie. This 11½" fashion doll was made from 1963 to 1967. Tressy had a unique feature — her hair 'grew' by pushing a button on her stomach. She and her little sister, Cricket, had numerous fashions and accessories.

Advisor: Cindy Sabulis (See Directory, Dolls)

Apartment, M $150.00
Beauty Salon, M..$125.00
Case, Cricket, M $30.00
Case, Tressy, M $40.00

Doll, Cricket, blue or turquoise eyes, M, $25.00; Tressy, M, $35.00. (Photo courtesy Cindy Sabulis)

Doll, Pre-Teen Tressy, M..$60.00
Doll, Tressy in Miss America Character outfit, NM $65.00
Doll, Tressy w/Magic Make-up Face, M......................$25.00
Doll clothes pattern, M..$10.00
Gift Pack w/doll & clothing, NRFB, minimum value..$100.00
Hair Accessory Pak, NRFB, ea $20.00
Hair Dryer, M $40.00
Millinery, M $150.00
Outfits, MOC, ea $30.00

Uneeda Doll Co., Inc.

The Uneeda Doll Company was located in New York City and began making composition dolls about 1917. Later a transition was made to plastics and vinyl. Listings here are for dolls that are mint in their original boxes.

Baby Dollikins, vinyl head, hard plastic jointed body w/jointed elbows, wrists & knees, 1960s, 21".................$200.00
Baby Trix, hard plastic & vinyl, 1965, 19" $30.00
Baby Trix, vinyl head, hard plastic jointed body, drinks & wets, 1968, 12½"...$30.00
Bareskin Baby, hard plastic & vinyl, 1968, 12½" $20.00
Blabby, hard plastic & vinyl, 1962+, 14"......................$28.00
Coquette, Black, hard plastic & vinyl, 16" $36.00
Dollikin, hard plastic & vinyl, multi-jointed, 1960s, 20"...$125.00
Dollikin, multi-jointed, marked Uneeda/2S, 1957+, 19"..$175.00

Fairy Princess, hard plastic & vinyl, 1961, 32"..........$110.00
Freckles, ventriloquist doll, vinyl head, hands, rooted hair, cotton-stuffed cloth body, 1973, 30".....................$70.00
Freckles, vinyl head, rigid plastic body, #22 on head, 1960, 32" $100.00
Jennifer, hard plastic & vinyl, rooted hair w/side part, painted features, teen body, mod clothing, 1973, 18"..$25.00
Magic Meg, vinyl & plastic, rooted hair that grows, sleep eyes, 16" $25.00
Pir-thilla, vinyl, rooted hair, sleep eyes, blows up balloons, 1958, 12½"...$12.00
Pollyanna, vinyl & plastic, for Disney, 1960, 11" $35.00
Pollyanna, vinyl & plastic, for Disney, 1960, 17" $130.00
Pollyanna, vinyl & plastic, for Disney, 1960, 31" $150.00
Purty, vinyl & plastic, painted features, long rooted hair, 1973, 11"...$25.00
Rita Hayworth as Carmen, composition, red mohair wig, unmarked, cardboard tag, 1948, 14" $565.00
Serenade, vinyl & hard plastic w/rooted blond hair, blue sleep eyes, red & white dress, speaker in tummy, 1962, 21"..$55.00
Suzette, plastic & vinyl, 12"...$65.00
Tiny Teen, vinyl head, 6-pc hard plastic body, rooted hair, pierced ears, high-heels, 1957-59, 10½" $135.00

Toyland Fairy Princess, #27, 20", from $75.00 to $125.00. (Photo courtesy Cindy Sabulis)

Vogue Dolls, Inc.

Vogue Dolls Incorporated is one of America's most popular manufacturer of dolls. In the early 1920s through the mid-1940s, Vogue imported lovely dolls of bisque and composition, dressing them in the fashionable designs hand sewn by Vogue's founder, Jennie Graves. In the late '40s through the early '50s, they became famous for their wonderful hard plastic dolls, most notably the 8" Ginny doll. This adorable toddler doll skyrocketed into nationwide attention in the early '50s as lines of fans stretched around the block during store promotions, and Ginny dolls sold out regularly. A Far-Away-Lands Ginny was added in the late '50s, sold well through the '70s, and is still popular with collectors today. In fact, a modern-day version of Ginny is currently being sold by the Vogue Doll Company, Inc.

Many wonderful dolls followed through the years, including unique hard-plastic, vinyl, and soft-body dolls. These dolls include teenage dolls Jill, Jan, and Jeff; Ginnette the 8" baby doll; Miss Ginny; and the famous vinyl and soft-bodied dolls by noted artist and designer E. Wilkin. It is not uncommon for these highly collectible dolls to turn up at garage sales and flea markets.

Over the years, Vogue developed the well-deserved reputation as 'The Fashion Leaders in Doll Society' based on their fine quality sewing and on the wide variety of outfits designed for their dolls to wear. These outfits included frilly dress-up doll clothes as well as action-oriented sports outfits. The company was among the first in the doll industry to develop the concept of marketing and selling separate outfits for their dolls, many of which were 'matching' for their special doll lines. The very early Vogue outfits are most sought after, and later outfits are highly collectible as well. It is wise for collectors to become aware of Vogue's unique styles, designs, and construction methods in order to spot these authentic Vogue prizes on collecting outings.

Values here are only a general guide. For further information we recommend *Collector's Guide to Vogue Dolls* by Judith Izen and Carol J. Stover (Collector Books).

Baby Dear, vinyl head & limbs, cloth body, musical, 1960-64, 18", M **$275.00**
Baby Dear, vinyl head & limbs, cloth body, 1960-64, M..**$125.00**
Baby Dear, vinyl head & limbs, cloth body, 1960-64, 12", MIB **$250.00**
Baby Dear, vinyl head & limbs (later design), cloth body, crier, 1965, 12", M **$45.00**
Baby Dear-One, vinyl head & limbs, cloth body, open/closed mouth w/2 teeth, sleep eyes, 1962-63, 25", M ...**$250.00**
Betty Jane Make-Up, composition, sleep eyes, closed mouth, braids, original clothes, 14", 1940s, MIB, from $250 to **$345.00**
Brikette, soft & rigid vinyl, twist-&-turn swivel waist, swivel neck, flirty eyes, orange hair, 1959-60, 16", M ...**$175.00**
Crib Crowd baby, hard plastic, sleep eyes, caracul (lambskin) wig, 8", M, from $475 to over.............................**$500.00**
Cynthia, composition, jointed, open or closed mouth, sleep eyes, various wig & outfits, 1940s, 18", M, ea....**$450.00**
Ginnette, Cries Real Tears, vinyl, MIB **$125.00**
Ginnette, vinyl, jointed, open mouth, painted eyes, 8"..**$150.00**
Ginny, hard plastic, painted side-glancing arms, strung, mohair wig, 1948-50, 8", M, minimum value......**$300.00**
Ginny, hard plastic, sleep eyes, molded lashes, bent-knee walker, formal #1160, 1960, 8", M **$250.00**
Ginny, hard plastic, sleep eyes, molded lashes, bent-knee walker, Cook #1130 outfit, 1960, 8", M..............**$350.00**
Ginny, hard plastic, sleep eyes, molded lashes, straight-leg walker, Bon-Bons, 1955, 8", M, minimum value ..**$400.00**
Ginny, hard plastic, sleep eyes, molded lashes, straight-leg walker, Davy Crockett, 1955, 8", M....................**$500.00**
Ginny, hard plastic, sleep eyes, straight-leg walker, Candy Dandy, 1954, 8", M, from $300 to **$350.00**

Ginny, hard plastic, sleep eyes, straight-leg walker, My First Corsage, 1954, 8", MIB, from $350 to **$400.00**
Ginny, hard plastic, strung, sleep eyes, all original, 1950-53, 8", M, from $375 to...**$450.00**
Ginny, hard plastic, strung, sleep eyes, Bridal gown, 1953, 8", M, from $375 to **$400.00**
Ginny, hard plastic, strung, sleep eyes, Debutante outfit, 1952-53, 8", minimum value **$425.00**
Ginny, hard plastic, strung, sleep eyes, Poodlecut outfit, 1952, 8", M...**$600.00**
Ginny, hard plastic, strung, sleep eyes, school or play outfit, 1950-53, 8", M, ea...**$110.00**
Ginny, hard plastic (Dakin's mold), jointed, sleep eyes, molded lashes, First Ballet, recent, discontinued, 8", M...**$75.00**

Ginny, vinyl, Far-Away Lands Series (missing hat), 8", EX, from $20.00 to $25.00. (Photo courtesy Cindy Sabulis)

Ginny, vinyl, sleep eyes, bent arms, straight-leg non-walker, American Indian felt dress, 1968, 8", M, minimum value **$100.00**
Ginny, vinyl, sleep eyes, jointed arms, straight-leg non-walker, rooted hair, Far-Away Lands series, 1965-72, 8", M, ea **$80.00**
Ginny, vinyl & hard plastic, sleep eyes, bent-knee walker, rooted hair, all original, 1963-65, 8", M, minimum value **$150.00**
Jan, vinyl, sleep eyes, straight legs, 1969-60, MIB **$120.00**
Jan (Sweetheart), vinyl, sleep eyes, straight legs, 1964, MIB..**$150.00**
Jean from Young Folks series (Pantalette Doll), jointed composition, sleep eyes, mohair wig, 1947-48, 13", M, from $250 to...**$300.00**
Jeff, vinyl, blue sleep eyes, molded/painted black hair, 1958-60, 11", MIB...**$150.00**
Jill, hard plastic, sleep eyes, bent-knee walker, basic dress, 1957-58, 10½", M, from $125 to **$150.00**
Jill, hard plastic, sleep eyes, bent-knee walker, Could Have Danced All Night red dress #3130, 1960, 10½", MIB................**$300.00**

Jill, hard plastic, sleep eyes, bent-knee walker, long gown, 1959-60, 10½", MIB, minimum value **$200.00**

Jill, hard plastic, sleep eyes, bent-knee walker, ski clothes #3264, 1959, 10½", MIB.................................. **$275.00**

Jill (All New Jill), vinyl, sleep eyes, rooted hair, high-heeled feet, all original, 1962, 10½", M, from $150 to ... **$175.00**

Jill (Sweetheart), vinyl hair, sleep eyes, rooted hair, high-heeled feet, 1963, MIB, 10½", from $150 to **$175.00**

Jimmy, vinyl, jointed, open mouth, painted eyes, 1958, 8", M.. **$60.00**

Jimmy, vinyl, jointed, open mouth, painted mouth, clown clothes, 1958, 8", MIB, from $60 to **$150.00**

Li'l Loveable Imp, vinyl, sleep eyes, straight legs, rooted hair, 1964-65, 11", MIB.. **$175.00**

Lieutenant WAAC-ette or WAV-ette, composition, open or closed mouth, sleep eyes, 1943-44, 13", M, ea from $350 to **$400.00**

Littlest Angel, vinyl & hard plastic, sleep eyes, bent-knee walker, 1961-63, 10½", MIB **$100.00**

Love Me Linda, vinyl, painted eyes, 1965, 16", M, from $20 to **$45.00**

Mary Jane Make-Up, composition, closed mouth, sleep eyes, mohair wig, original clothes, 1940s, 13", MIB, from $250 to **$345.00**

Miss Ginny, vinyl, sleep eyes, straight legs, closed mouth, flat feet, 1965-71, 15", M, from $25 to **$55.00**

Patty, hard plastic, marked 14 on head, flocked organdy dress, 1949, 14", M, from $250 to **$300.00**

Skier from Sportswomen series, composition, unmarked, 1940s, 14", M **$400.00**

Sunshine Baby, composition, bent legs, molded hair, original gown & bonnet, late 1930s-mid 1940s, 8", M **$400.00**

Toddles Little Red Riding head, composition, mohair wig, all original, marked R&B faintly on back, 8", from $250 to **$300.00**

Too Dear, vinyl head & limbs, cloth body, closed mouth, sleep eyes, rooted hair, left arm bent, 1963-65, 17", M ... **$250.00**

Wash-A-Bye Baby, vinyl, painted eyes, 1975, M **$25.00**

Wee Imp, hard plastic, sleep eyes, bent-knee walker, freckles, orange wig, 1960, 8", M, from $300 to **$400.00**

Door Knockers

Though many of the door knockers you'll see on the market today are of the painted cast-iron variety (similar in design to doorstop figures), they're also found in brass and other metals. Most are modeled as people, animals, and birds; and baskets of flowers are common. All items listed are cast iron unless noted otherwise. Prices shown are suggested for examples without damage and in excellent original paint.

Advisor: Craig Dinner (See Directory, Door Knockers)

Bathing beauty w/finger at mouth, green 1920s swimsuit, unmarked 'Fish' pc, 5¼", beware of reproductions...**$795.00**

Birdhouse, cream w/red roof, green & cream trees, cream backplate, signed Hubley, #629, 3⅜ by 2⅜" **$425.00**

Buster Brown & Tige, cream shirt & pants, cream dog w/black spots, #200, 4⅜x2" **$635.00**

Butterfly, black, green, yellow & pink, under pink rose, cream & purple backplate, 3½x2½" **$225.00**

Butterfly on flowers, multicolor paint, 4x2½" **$635.00**

Cardinal on twigs, multicolor paint, rare, 5x3" **$285.00**

Castle, cream w/3 flags, blue sky, green trees, gold band, white oval backplate, 4x3" **$265.00**

Couple kissing among roses, brass, 5½" **$65.00**

Dog, brown, at entrance to cream doghouse, pink dish in front of dog, dark brown backplate, 4x3" **$865.00**

Dragon, tooled wrought iron, w/strike, 6½" **$115.00**

Flower basket, country style, unmarked, 3½x3" **$55.00**

Flower basket, yellow ribbon white basket, pink & blue flowers w/green leaves, yellow & white backplate, 4x2½" **$95.00**

Fox, brass, England **$45.00**

George Washington, multicolor paint, Waverly..., 4½x2¾" . **$85.00**

Highlander w/bagpipes, brass, marked Made in Great Britain, 6" **$85.00**

Ivy basket, light & dark green ivy in yellow basket, white backplate, 4½x2½" **$135.00**

Lady w/bonnet in profile, multicolor paint, Judd Co #619, 4x3" **$325.00**

Little girl knocking on door, blue dress, brown hat with black ribbon, holds black doll in left hand, rare, 3¾x2¾", $825.00. (Photo courtesy Craig Dinner)

Lion, bronze w/green patina, 6¼" **$105.00**

Mammy w/laundry basket over head, red & white dotted bandana, multicolored clothes, breasts form knocker, rare, 7¼" **$1,750.00**

Morning Glory, purple-blue single flower w/1 bud, green leaves as backplate, 3x3" **$310.00**

Parrot faces right, on brown branch, multicolored feathers, green leaves, cream & green backplate, 4¾x2¾" .. **$100.00**

Parrot on branch, multicolor paint, Hubley, 4¾x2¾" ... **$125.00**

Pear, original paint, flower backplate, 4¼x3" **$345.00**

Rooster, white variation, 4½x3" **$330.00**
Roses, pink & cream w/green leaves, brown stems, cream oval backplate, signed Hubley #626, 3x4" **$445.00**
Ship, gold waves & ship w/highlights, oval backplate w/blue waves, 4x2¾" **$225.00**
Sir Walter Scott bust, brass, England **$58.00**

Spider (orange, black, and yellow) on web (gray with black strings) with fly (yellow, black, and brown), 3½x1⅞", $865.00. (Photo courtesy Craig Dinner)

Victorian lady in profile (flesh tone), blond hair, yellow bonnet w/blue ribbon & red roses, cream backplate, #613, 4x3" **$425.00**
Woodpecker, red head w/black & white feathers, tree backplate, brown & green leaves w/pink flowers, 3¾x2½" **$125.00**
Zinnias, multicolor paint, marked Pat Pend LVL, rare, 3¾x2½" **$550.00**

Doorstops

There are three important factors to consider when buying doorstops — rarity, desirability, and condition. Desirability is often a more important issue than rarity, especially if the doorstop is well designed and detailed. Subject matter often overlaps into other areas, and if they appeal to collectors of Black Americana and advertising, for instance, this tends to drive prices upward. Most doorstops are made of painted cast iron, and value is directly related to the condition of the paint. If there is little paint left or if the figure has been repainted or is rusty, unless the price has been significantly reduced, pass it by.

Be aware that Hubley, one of the largest doorstop manufacturers, sold many of their molds to the John Wright Company who makes them today. Watch for seams that do not fit properly, grainy texture, and too-bright paint. Watch for reproductions!

The doorstops we've listed here are all of the painted cast-iron variety unless another type of material is mentioned in the description. Values are suggested for original examples in near-mint condition and paint and should be sharply reduced if heavy wear is apparent. Recent auctions report even higher prices realized for examples in pristine condition. For further information, we recommend *Doorstops, Identification and Values,* by Jeanne Bertoia.

Club: Doorstop Collectors of America
Jeanie Bertoia
1881 Spring Rd.
Vineland, NJ 08361; 856-692-1881; Membership $20.00 per year, includes 2 *Doorstoppers* newsletters and convention. Send 2-stamp SASE for sample.

Amish Man, hand in pocket, black wide-rim hat, full figure, solid, 8½x3¾", from $225 to **$275.00**
Aunt Jemima, white apron & red scarf, arms akimbo, wedge backed, 7½x3¾", from $250 to **$350.00**
Bellhop, blue uniform w/red trim, on base, #1244, 8⅞x4⅝", from $275 to **$350.00**
Boston Terrier, full figure, Hubley, National Foundry (& others), 10x10", from $75 to **$125.00**
Boston Terrier, profile, 9⅝x11¾", from $350 to **$450.00**
Buster Brown, dressed in sailor suit, 7¾x5¼", from $425 to **$475.00**
Camel, 2 humps, walking, full figure, 7x9", from $275 to **$350.00**
Cherubs, 2 w/grape cluster, 10x6⅜", from $375 to... **$450.00**
Chow Chow, standing w/head turned to right, full figure, 8½x9", from $300 to **$450.00**
Colonial Pilgrim, boy w/right hand out, 8¾x5⅜", from $350 to **$425.00**
Covered Wagon, 2 horses, Hubley, 3375, 5⅛x9½", from $150 to **$225.00**
Dachshund, seated, full figure, 8x12", from $400 to. **$550.00**
Deco Girl, holds skirt wide, cJo, #1251, 9x7½", from $350 to **$425.00**
Doll on Base, long pink tiered skirt on dress, matching bonnet, full figure, solid, 5½x4⅞", from $75 to **$125.00**
Donald Duck, holding stop sign, Walt Disney Productions 1971, 8⅜x5¼", from $250 to **$325.00**
Drum Major, full figure, solid, 13½x6½", from $350 to... **$425.00**
Dutch girl, w/yoke & 2 buckets, cJo, #1255, 7⅛x5¾", from $275 to **$350.00**
Elephant, trumpeting, Hubley, 8¼x12", from $100 to.. **$175.00**
Elk, head turned, rocky base, 11x10", from $175 to. **$250.00**
Fireplace, woman at spinning wheel at side, Eastern Specialty Co, 6¼x8", from $250 to **$325.00**
Fireside Cat, full figure, Hubley, Littco, others, 5⅝x10¾", from $175 to **$225.00**
Fisherman in Boat, standing in stern, 6¾x4", from $150 to **$225.00**
Flowered Doorway, floral arch surrounds door & bench, 7⅝x7½", from $325 to **$400.00**
Frog, full figure, 6x3½", from $75 to **$150.00**
Geisha, seated & playing instrument, full figure, Hubley, 7x6", from $200 to **$275.00**
Gnome, hands at waist, pointed hat, full figure, 10x4", from $250 to **$300.00**
Halloween Cat, arched back, AM Greenblat Studio #19 Copyright 1927, 9¼x6", from $300 to **$425.00**

Koala Bear on Log, #5 Taylor Cook, 1930, good original paint, 7", $470.00. (Photo courtesy Bertoia Auctions)

Lil Bo Peep, w/basket of flowers, 1 hand up to face, 6¾x5", from $225 to...$300.00

Little Dutch Woman, arms akimbo, white apron, blond hair, full figure, solid, 4x2⅝", from $100 to $125.00

Mary Quite Contrary, 15", EX, $1,000.00. (Photo courtesy Bertoia Auctions)

Messenger Boy, holding flowers, Hubley, #249 c FISH, 10x5⅜", from $500 to...$700.00

Monkey, thoughtful pose, full figure, 8½x4⅝", from $250 to...$325.00

Owl, on stump, 10x6", from $225 to.........................$300.00

Percheron, head straight ahead, full figure, Hubley, 9x7¾", from $175 to..$225.00

Pheasant, head turned, grassy base, #458, c Fred Everett, 8½x7½", from $350 to...$425.00

Pied Piper, sitting on toadstool playing horn, #120, 7¼x5", from $325 to..$350.00

Pirate w/Chest, sword in hand, 9¾x6", from $225 to..$300.00

Poinsettia, in white pot, cJo, #1232, 10x5", from $275 to...$350.00

Poppies, in footed vase, Hubley, #440, 10⅝x7⅞", from $125 to...$200.00

Poppies & Cornflowers, in striped vase, Hubley, #265, 7¼x6½", from $125 to...$175.00

Poppies & snapdragons, in basket, Hubley, #484, 7½x4¼", from $75 to...$150.00

Quail, 2 on grassy base, Hubley, #495, c Fred Everett, 7¼x6¼", from $350 to..$425.00

Rabbit by Fence, Albany Foundry, 6⅞x8⅛", from $435 to $450.00

Southern Belle, blue gown, holds hat & flowers, National Foundry, 11¼x6", from $150 to..........................$200.00

Spanish Girl, w/fan & mantilla, 9⅞x5½", from $325 to...$400.00

St Bernard, recumbent, full figure, Hubley, 3½x10½", from $375 to...$500.00

Sunbonnet Girl, facing left, 9x5½", from $400 to $450.00

Terrier, running, wedge, Spencer, Guilford Conn, 4x7", from $200 to...$250.00

Tiger Lilies, 3 lg flowers among green leaves, Hubley, #472, 10½x6", from $200 to..............................$275.00

Windmill, AA Richardson, 8x5⅝", from $150 to........$225.00

Woman holding hat (dangling near hem of skirt), rose in left hand, full figure, solid, 6⅜", from $150 to $200.00

Woman w/muff, head turned to right, full figure, solid, 9¼", from $225 to...$275.00

Zinnias, in handled urn, Hubley, #267, 7¼x7", from $125 to..$175.00

Duncan and Miller Glassware

Although the roots of the company can be traced back as far as 1865 when George Duncan went into business in Pittsburgh, Pennsylvania, the majority of the glassware that collectors are interested in was produced during the twentieth century. The firm became known as Duncan and Miller in 1900. They were bought out by the United States Glass Company who continued to produce many of the same designs through a separate operation which they called the Duncan and Miller Division.

In addition to crystal, they made some of their wares in a wide assortment of colors including ruby, milk glass, some opalescent glass, and a black opaque glass they called Ebony. Some of their pieces were decorated by cutting or etching. They also made a line of animals and bird figures. For information on these, see *Glass Animals of the Depression Era* by Lee Garmon and Dick Spencer (Collector Books).

Advisor: Roselle Schleifman (See Directory, Elegant Glass)

Canterbury, ashtray, crystal, 5" $12.00
Canterbury, basket, crystal, handled, oval, 10x4¼x7" ...$70.00
Canterbury, bowl, crystal, crimped, 7½x2¼"...............$15.00
Canterbury, bowl, crystal, crimped, 10½x5"...............$30.00
Canterbury, bowl, fruit; crystal, 5"...............................$8.00
Canterbury, bowl, rose; crystal, 5".............................$20.00
Canterbury, candlestick, crystal, 3-light, 6" $30.00
Canterbury, cigarette box, crystal, w/lid, 3½x4½" $18.00
Canterbury, cup, crystal..$10.00
Canterbury, plate, dinner; crystal, 11½"....................$27.50
Canterbury, plate, fruit; crystal, 1 handle, 6½" $6.00

Canterbury, stem, wine; crystal, #5115, 3½-oz, 6" **$27.50**
Canterbury, top hat, crystal, 3" **$18.00**
Canterbury, tumbler, juice; crystal, 5-oz, 4¼" **$7.50**
Canterbury, vase, cloverleaf; crystal, 4½" **$20.00**
Canterbury, vase, violet; crystal, crimped, 3" **$15.00**
Caribbean, bowl, finger; crystal, 4½" **$16.00**
Caribbean, bowl, salad; blue, 9" **$75.00**
Caribbean, candelabrum, crystal, 2-light, 4¾" **$40.00**
Caribbean, cup, punch; blue **$22.50**
Caribbean, pitcher, syrup; crystal, 9-oz, 4¼" **$65.00**
Caribbean, plate, crystal, 14" **$25.00**
Caribbean, plate, salad; blue, 7½" **$20.00**
Caribbean, salt dip, blue, 2½" **$25.00**
Caribbean, saucer, crystal **$4.00**
Caribbean, vase, blue, footed, 10" **$145.00**
Caribbean, vase, crystal, ruffled edge, footed, 5¾" **$22.00**
Figurine, Bird of Paradise, crystal......................**$700.00**
Figurine, donkey, crystal................................**$120.00**
Figurine, duck, ashtray, crystal, 4".....................**$20.00**
Figurine, duck, ashtray, red, 7".........................**$90.00**
Figurine, heron, crystal.................................**$150.00**
Figurine, swan, bowl, dark green, 10½" **$80.00**
Figurine, swan, crystal, solid, 5" **$35.00**
Figurine, swan, wheat cutting, 11" **$200.00**
Figurine, swordfish, crystal **$275.00**
Figurine, tropical fish, ashtray, pink, oval, 3½"........**$50.00**
First Love, ashtray, crystal, #30, 3½x2½" **$16.50**
First Love, bowl, crystal, #30, 11x1¾" **$55.00**
First Love, bowl, finger; crystal, #5111½, 4¼" **$35.00**
First Love, candle, crystal, #111, 1-light, 3"...........**$25.00**
First Love, candy dish, crystal, #115, w/5" lid, 6½" **$75.00**
First Love, cocktail shaker, crystal, #5200, 32-oz......**$175.00**
First Love, cup, crystal, #115...........................**$18.00**
First Love, mayonnaise, crystal, #115, 5½x2¾" **$35.00**
First Love, plate, crystal, #111, 7½" sq.................**$19.00**
First Love, plate, crystal, #115, 14" **$50.00**
First Love, salt & pepper shakers, crystal, #115, pr **$40.00**
First Love, sugar bowl, crystal, #111, 10-oz, 3" **$15.00**
First Love, urn, crystal, #525, 5" **$37.50**
First Love, vase, crystal, #505, footed, 10" **$115.00**
Sandwich, bowl, crystal, handled, 5½" **$15.00**
Sandwich, bowl, fruit; crystal, 3-part, 10" **$85.00**
Sandwich, bowl, salad; crystal, shallow, 12" **$40.00**
Sandwich, candy dish, crystal, 6" sq **$395.00**
Sandwich, creamer, crystal, footed, 7-oz, 4" **$9.00**
Sandwich, plate, hostess; crystal, 16" **$120.00**
Sandwich, plate, jelly; crystal, individual, 3" **$6.00**
Sandwich, saucer, crystal, w/ring, 6" **$4.00**
Sandwich, sugar bowl, crystal, 5-oz **$7.50**
Sandwich, vase, crystal, crimped, footed, 3" **$20.00**
Spiral Flutes, bowl, grapefruit; amber, green or pink, footed...**$20.00**
Spiral Flutes, bowl, lily pond; amber, green or pink, 10½"..**$40.00**
Spiral Flutes, bowl, mayonnaise; amber, green or pink, 4"..**$17.50**
Spiral Flutes, candlestick, amber, green or pink, 11½"....**$125.00**

Spiral Flutes, plate, torte; crystal, 13⅝".................**$27.50**
Spiral Flutes, stem, water; amber, green or pink, 7-oz, 6¼" **$17.50**
Spiral Flutes, vase, amber, green or pink, 6½"...........**$20.00**

Swan, blue opalescent, 9½", $200.00.

Tear Drop, bowl, crystal, 4 handles, 12" sq...............**$45.00**
Tear Drop, bowl, fruit nappy; crystal, 5" **$6.00**
Tear Drop, celery, crystal, handles, 11" **$15.00**
Tear Drop, creamer, crystal, 3-oz.........................**$5.00**
Tear Drop, olive dish, crystal, 2-part, 6" **$15.00**
Tear Drop, plate, torte; crystal, 14" **$35.00**
Tear Drop, relish tray, crystal, 3-part, 3-handled, 9" ...**$30.00**

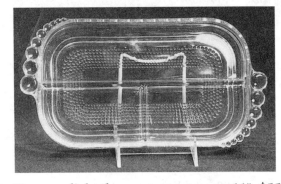
Tear Drop, relish, three-compartment, 11", $55.00.

Tear Drop, salt & pepper shakers, crystal, 5", pr........**$25.00**
Tear Drop, stem, crystal, 9-oz, 7".......................**$14.00**
Tear Drop, sweetmeat, crystal, center handle, 6½" **$35.00**
Tear Drop, tumbler, whiskey; crystal, footed, 2-oz, 2¼"..**$14.00**
Tear Drop, urn, crystal, w/lid, footed, 9" **$135.00**
Terrace, ashtray, crystal or amber, 4¾" sq...............**$22.00**
Terrace, bowl, crystal or amber, flared rim, 11x3¼"..**$32.50**
Terrace, cup, crystal or amber **$15.00**
Terrace, plate, amber or crystal, 7½" **$18.00**
Terrace, plate, cracker; cobalt or red, w/ring, handled, 11" **$110.00**
Terrace, relish tray, cobalt or red, 4-part, 9" **$100.00**
Terrace, stem, cocktail; crystal or amber, #5111½, 3½-oz, 4½" **$22.50**
Terrace, tumbler, cobalt or red **$40.00**

Easter Collectibles

The egg (a symbol of new life) and the bunny rabbit have long been part of Easter festivities; and since early in the twentieth century, Easter has been a full-blown commercial event. Postcards, candy containers, toys, and decorations have been made in infinite varieties. In the early 1900s many holiday items were made of papier-mache and composition and imported to this country from Germany. Rabbits were made of mohair, felt, and velveteen, often filled with straw, cotton, and cellulose.

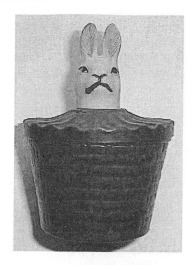

Candy container, celluloid, 3¾", NM, $100.00.

Candy container, chick (dressed), cardboard, spring neck, US Zone/W Germany **$65.00**
Candy container, egg form, molded cardboard, West Germany, 1940-60, 3-8", from $25 to **$40.00**
Candy container, rabbit (plain), cardboard, spring neck, W Germany/US Zone, 1940-50 ....**$75.00**
Candy container, rabbit begging, pulp, ca 1940-50, US ..**$55.00**
Candy container, rabbit sitting, pulp, no basket, USA, 1940-50 ....**$60.00**
Candy container, rabbit sitting w/basket on back, pulp, USA, 1940-50 ....**$95.00**
Egg, papier-mache, gold decor, 6" **$45.00**
Egg, papier-mache, w/brown composition dressed rabbit sitting inside on wooden bench, Germany, EX **$95.00**
Figure, bunny, bisque, Japan, 1940s, 3¾" **$45.00**
Figure, chick in suit, composition, Germany, 4½", EX.**$145.00**
Figure, rabbit, celluloid, translucent pink in green coat, holding orange carrot, 2".................................**$30.00**
Figure, rabbit, celluloid, white in black pants & shoes, red jacket, marked Peter Rabbit on shoe, 4", EX........**$85.00**
Figure, rabbit, cotton batten w/paper ears, Japan, 1930-50, 2-5", from $30 to **$45.00**
Figure, rabbit, cotton batten w/paper ears, Japan, 1930-50, 6" **$85.00**
Figure, rabbit in egg, compositon, multicolor paint, Germany, 5" **$95.00**
Figure, rabbit w/carrot, composition, brown & orange, Germany, 6" **$110.00**

Figurine, rabbit (dressed), celluloid, from 3-5", M **$65.00**
Nodder, duck, composition, yellow in orange dress & green bonnet, holding sm goose, 7"..............................**$85.00**
Nodder, duck, composition, yellow w/multicolor clothes, 7" **$135.00**
Toy, bunny pulling cart, lithographed tin, wind-up, Ohio Art **$75.00**

Egg Cups

Egg cups were once commonplace kitchen articles that were often put to daily use. These small egg holders were commonly made in a variety of shapes from ceramics, glass, metals, minerals, treen, and plastic. They were used as early as ancient Rome and were very common on Victorian tables. Many were styled like whimsical animals or made in other shapes that would specifically appeal to children. Some were commemorative or sold as souvenirs. Still others were part of extensive china or silver services.

Recent trends in US dietary patterns have caused egg cups to follow butter pats and salt dishes into relative obscurity. Yet today in other parts of the world, especially Europe, many people still eat soft-boiled eggs as part of their daily ritual, so the larger china companies in those locations continue to produce egg cups.

Though many are inexpensive, some are very pricey. Sought-after categories (or cross-collectibles) include Art Deco, Art pottery, Black memorabilia, chintz, golliwogs, majolica, personalities, pre-Victorian, railroad, and steamship. Single egg cups with pedestal bases are the most common, but shapes vary to include buckets, doubles, figurals, hoops, and sets of many types.

Pocillovists, as egg cup collectors are known, are increasing in numbers every day. For more extensive listings we recommend *Egg Cups: An Illustrated History and Price Guide,* by Brenda C. Blake (Antique Publications); and *Schroeder's Antiques Price Guide* (Collector Books).

Advisor: Brenda C. Blake (See Directory, Egg Cups)

Newsletter: *Egg Cup Collector's Corner*
Dr. Joan George, Editor
67 Stevens Ave., Old Bridge, NJ 08857; Subscription $20 per year for 4 issues; sample copies available at $5 each

Blue Onion, marked Vienna Woods Fine China, 4"....**$55.00**
Bunnies (2) support teal lustre cup on backs, Japan, 2½"..**$17.50**
Bunny girl beside flower cup, orange lustre & multicolor details, Japan, 3" **$17.50**
Buster Brown & Tige transfer, from breakfast set.....**$135.00**
Carnish Ware, double, TG Green, 4¼" **$80.00**
Chesterton, teal w/white trim, double, Harker, 1950s...**$10.00**
Chick, figural, milk glass, Westmoreland, #602 Line, 3¾"..**$40.00**
Chick emerging from egg figural, milk glass, unmarked, 3¼", from $8 to..**$10.00**
Clover w/vines, Belleek, 2½"...................................**$42.50**

Comical cat w/googly eyes holding cup between legs, marked Made in Japan, 3"......................................$50.00
Dog, figural, white w/brown paws, orange mouth, 1 brown ear, 1 orange, ceramic, Made in Japan, ca 1930, 2¾" $40.00
Doll Face, Morimura sticker, Nippon, 3½" $75.00

Double, chick on grassy mound, cups are eggshells, Portugal, $25.00.

Empress Dresden Flowers, flowers w/gold trim, Schumann, 4¾"..$70.00
Flow blue, Dainty, Maddocks.....................................$100.00
Golfing series, man hitting ball on 1 side, 2 men watching on other, Royal Doulton, D5497E, ca 1920, 2".........$440.00
Hallcraft, Fantasy pattern, Zeisel design $17.50
Harmony, Shelley, sm $42.00
Historic American Blue, double, Johnson Bros, 4" $40.00
Horse in desert scene, blue & green scene w/black rim & brown interior, Torquay, 2¼"...............................$55.00
Lady in apron figural, Cleminson, early.......................$35.00
Magnolia, cranberry-red floral on tan, double, Stangl, 1950s $13.00
Mickey Mouse figural, snouty nose, black & white, Japan, 1930s..$250.00
Motorcycle figural, yellow & black, ca 1940 ....$38.00
Old Cottage (chintz), double, Royal Winton.............$120.00
Prairie Mountain Wildflowers, china, Southern Pacific Railroad..$45.00
Raindrop, amber glass, double $38.00
Rosebud, Coors, 6-oz $25.00
Strawberry, double, Blue Ridge, 1950s $38.00
Swan w/cup on back, multicolor w/orange & white lustre, Japan, 2½" $16.00
Virginia Rose, Homer Laughlin, 4½" $75.00
Windmill scene w/gold trim, green Noritake mark, 3½" .$25.00

Egg Timers

Egg timers are comprised of a little glass tube (pinched in the center and filled with sand) attached to a figural base, usually between 3" and 5" in height. They're all the rage today among collectors. Most figural egg timers reached their heyday in the 1940s. However, Germany produced many beautiful and detailed timers much earlier. Japan followed suit by copying many German designs. Today, one may find timers from the United Kingdom as well as many foreign ports. The variety of subjects represented by these timers is endless. Included are scores of objects, animals, characters from fiction, and people in occupational or recreational activities. Timers have been made in many materials including bisque, china, ceramic, chalkware, cast iron, tin, brass, wood, and plastic.

Although they were originated to time a 3-minute egg, some were also used to limit the duration spent on telephone calls as a cost-saving measure. Frequently a timer is designed to look like a telephone, or a phone is depicted on it.

Since the glass tubes were made of thin, fine glass, they were easily broken. You may recognize a timer masquerading as a figurine by the empty hole that once held the tube. Do not pass up a good timer just because the glass is missing. These can be easily replaced by purchasing a cheap egg timer with a glass tube at your local grocery story.

Listings are for timers in excellent to mint condition with their glass tubes attached.

Advisor: Ellen Bercovici (See Directory, Egg Timers)

Bear, timer inserted to look like milk bottle, American Bisque...$95.00
Bear dressed as chef w/towel over arm, ceramic, Japan, 4"...$65.00
Bellhop, green, ceramic, Japan, 4½"............................$65.00
Bellhop on phone, ceramic, Japan, 3" $65.00
Black chef sitting w/right hand raised holding timer, ceramic, many sizes & shadings, German, from $95 to.....$120.00
Black chef standing w/lg fish, timer in fish's mouth, ceramic, Japan, 4¾"...$125.00
Black chef stanging w/frying pan, chalkware, Japan..$125.00
Bobby policeman, black outfit, German, from $95 to..$125.00
Bobby policeman, blue outfit, Japan, from $95 to ...$125.00
Boy skiing, ceramic, German, 3", from $65 to...........$85.00
Boy stands on head (plastic) which fills w/sand, ceramic, Cooley Lilly sticker, 3¾", from $50 to..................$65.00
Boy w/black cap stands & holds black bird, ceramic, unmarked, 3½", from $65 to...............................$85.00
Boy w/black cloak & cane, German, 3¾", from $65 to...$85.00
Boy w/red cap stands & holds different glass tubes in both hands, wooden, unmarked, 4½", from $35 to......$50.00
Bunny rabbit, floppy ears, timer in mouth, Japan, from $75 to...$95.00
Cat, timer sits in his back, wooden............................$45.00
Cat holding plate w/hole to hold timer which removes to change, ceramic, Japan, 3¾"...............................$50.00
Cat standing by base of grandfather clock, ceramic, German, 4¾"..$65.00
Cat w/ribbon at neck, ceramic, marked Germany......$85.00
Chef, combination music box, wooden, lg $175.00
Chef, winking, white clothes, timer in back, turn upside down to tip sand, ceramic, 4", from $50 to..........$65.00

Chef and lady baker, ceramic, incised crown mark, ca 1935 – 49, $100.00. (Photo courtesy J. Greenfield)

Chef in white on blue base holding spoon, ceramic, German, 4"..$60.00

Chef in yellow pants, white jacket, blue trim, holds platter of food, ceramic, Japan, 3½", from $50 to $75.00

Chef standing in blue w/white apron, towel over right arm, timer in jug under left, ceramic, Japan, 4½", from $50 to $65.00

Chicken, wings hold tube, ceramic, German, 2¾", from $50 to $65.00

Chicken on nest, green plastic, England, 2½"............$30.00

Clown on phone, standing, yellow suit, ceramic, Japan, 3¾", from $65 to..$85.00

Clown sitting w/legs to side, timer in right hand, ceramic, German, 3¼", from $85 to $95.00

Colonial lady w/bonnet, variety of dresses & colors, ceramic, German, 3¾" $65.00

Colonial man in knickers, ruffled shirt, waistcoat hides hat, ceramic, Japan, 4¾" $65.00

Dutch boy kneeling, ceramic, Japan, 2½", from $40 to..$50.00

Dutch boy standing, ceramic, German, 3½"................$65.00

Dutch girl on phone, standing, blue & white, ceramic, Japan, 3¾" $50.00

Dutch girl w/flowers, walking, chalkware, unmarked, 4½" $65.00

Fisherman, fish wrapped around neck, timer in fish's mouth, German...$95.00

Geisha, ceramic, German, 4½" $85.00

Goebel, double, chefs, man & woman, ceramic, German, 4" $100.00

Goebel, double, Mrs Pickwick, green, ceramic, German, 4" $150.00

Goebel, double, rabbits, various color combinations, ceramic, German, 4½"...$100.00

Goebel, double, roosters, various color combinations, ceramic, German, 4" $100.00

Goebel, lg owl w/holder on side $95.00

Goebel, little girl w/chick on tip of her shoe, from $95 to..$125.00

Goebel, single, chimney sweep, ceramic, German, 4¼"..$70.00

Goebel, single, Friar Tuck, ceramic, German, 4", from $45 to $75.00

Golliwog, bisque, English, 4½" $200.00

Kitchen maid w/measuring spoons, ceramic, DAVAR, from $100 to..$125.00

Kitten w/ball of yarn, chalkware.................................$50.00

Leprechaun, shamrock on base, brass, Ireland, 3¼" ..$40.00

Lighthouse, blue, cream & orange lustre, ceramic, German, 4½"..$85.00

Mammy, tin, lithographed picture of her cooking, pot holder hooks, unmarked, 7¾", from $150 to $195.00

Mexican boy playing guitar, ceramic, German, 3½"...$65.00

Mouse, brown 'Chef' on white apron Josef Original..........$50.00

Mouse, yellow & green, chalkware, Josef Originals, Japan, 1970s, 3¼" $35.00

Mrs Santa Claus, timer sits in bag next to her............$75.00

Newspaper boy, ceramic, Japan, 3¾" $85.00

Parlor maid w/cat, ceramic, Japan, 4" $65.00

Penguin, chalkware, England, 3¾"................................$50.00

Pixie, ceramic, Enesco, Japan, 5½".............................$40.00

Rabbit, holding carrot, timer in basket, Japan.............$65.00

Sailboat, lustreware, German...$95.00

Sailor, blue, ceramic, German, 4" $65.00

Sailor w/sailboat, ceramic, German, 4" $85.00

Santa Claus & present, ceramic, Sonsco/Japan, 5½"...$75.00

Scotsman w/bagpipes, plastic, England, 4½" $50.00

Sea gull, ceramic w/lustre finish, German...................$95.00

Sultan, Japan, 3½"...$75.00

Telephone, black glaze on clay, Japan, 2"...................$35.00

Telephone, candlestick type on base w/cup for timer, wooden, Cornwall Wood Prod, So Paris ME.................$25.00

Veggie man or woman, bisque, Japan, 4½", ea $95.00

Welsh woman, ceramic, German, 4½" $85.00

Windmill w/dog on base, Japan, 3¾"..........................$85.00

Elvis Presley Memorabilia

Since he burst upon the '50s scene wailing 'Heartbreak Hotel,' Elvis has been the undisputed 'king of rock 'n roll.' The fans that stood outside his dressing room for hours on end, screamed themselves hoarse as he sang, or simply danced until they dropped to his music are grown-up collectors today. Many of their children remember his comeback performances, and I'd venture to say that even their grandchildren know Elvis on a first-name basis.

There has never been a promotion in the realm of entertainment to equal the manufacture and sale of Elvis merchandise. By the latter part of 1956, there were already hundreds of items that appeared in every department store, drugstore, specialty shop, and music store in the country. There were bubble gum cards, pin-back buttons, handkerchiefs, dolls, guitars, billfolds, photograph albums, and scores of other items. You could even buy sideburns from a coin-operated machine. Look for the mark 'Elvis Presley Enterprises' (along with a 1956 or 1957 copyright date); you'll know you've found a gold mine. Items that carry the 'Boxcar' mark are from 1974 to 1977, when Elvis's legendary manager, Colonel Tom Parker, promoted another line of merchandise to augment their incomes during the declining years. Upon his death in 1977 and until 1981, the trademark became 'Boxcar Enterprises, Inc., Lic. by Factors ETC. Bear, DE.' The 'Elvis Presley Enterprises, Inc.' trademark reverted back to Graceland in 1982, which re-opened to the public in 1983.

Due to the very nature of his career, paper items are usually a large part of any 'Elvis' collection. He appeared on the cover of countless magazines. These along with ticket stubs, movie posters, lobby cards, and photographs of all types are sought after today, especially those from before the mid-'60s.

Though you sometime see Elvis 45s with $10.00 to $15.00 price tags, unless the record is in near mint to mint condition, this is just not realistic, since they sold in such volume. In fact, the picture sleeve itself (if it's in good condition) will be worth more than the record. The exceptions are, of course, the early Sun label records (he cut five in all) that collectors often pay in excess of $500.00 for. In fact, a near-mint copy of 'That's All Right' (his very first Sun recording) realized $2,800.00 at an auction held several years ago! And some of the colored vinyls, promotional records, and EPs and LPs with covers and jackets in excellent condition are certainly worth researching further. For instance, though his *Moody Blue* album with the blue vinyl record can often be had for under $25.00 (depending on condition), if you find one of the rare ones with the black record you can figure on about ten times that amount! For a thorough listing of his records as well as the sleeves, refer to *Official Price Guide to Elvis Presley Records and Memorabilia* by Jerry Osborne.

For more general information and an emphasis on the early items, refer to *Elvis Collectibles* and *Best of Elvis Collectibles* by Rosalind Cranor, P.O. Box 859, Blacksburg, VA 24063 ($19.95+$1.75 postage each volume). Also available: *Elvis Presley Memorabilia* by Sean O'Neal (Schiffer).

Note: The charm bracelet listed below from 1956 was reproduced in 1977, beware! Special thanks to Art and Judy Turner, Homestead Collectibles (see Directory, Decanters) for providing information on decanters. See also Magazines; Movie Posters; Pin-back Buttons; Records.

Advisor: Lee Garmon (See Directory, Advertising)

Balloon toy, California Toytime, image of Elvis as boxer (Kid Galahad) on balloon w/cardboard feet, 4", EX **$75.00**

Belt, white leather reproduction w/multicolor faux jewels, silver chains & buckles, EX..................................**$125.00**

Bracelet, charm; Loving You, on card w/pink print, from movie press book, Elvis Presley Enterprises, 1957, from $100 to..**$150.00**

Bracelet, charm; on card w/blue print, Canadian, Elvis Presley Enterprises, 1956.....................................**$125.00**

Bracelet, charm; on card w/deep pink print, Elvis Presley Enterprises, 1956..**$150.00**

Card set, Golden Boys, A&BC Gum, 1958, 36 cards ..**$80.00**

Cigarette lighter, Artist of the Century, color portrait, Zippo, 2000, 4 in series, ea from $25 to **$30.00**

Cigarette lighter, Zippo, 1980s, 6 in series, ea from $75 to..**$100.00**

Concert pin, laughing portrait, 3⅜"..............................**$12.00**

Decanter, McCormick, 1978, Elvis '77, plays Love Me Tender, 750 ml..**$125.00**

Decanter, McCormick, 1978, Elvis Bust, no music box, 750 ml..**$75.00**

Decanter, McCormick, 1979, Elvis '55, plays Loving You, 750 ml..**$125.00**

Decanter, McCormick, 1979, Elvis '77 Mini, plays Love Me Tender, 50 ml..**$55.00**

Decanter, McCormick, 1979, Elvis Gold, plays My Way, 750 ml..**$175.00**

Decanter, McCormick, 1980, Elvis '55 Mini, plays Loving You, 50 ml..**$65.00**

Decanter, McCormick, 1980, Elvis '68, plays Can't Help Falling in Love, 750 ml..**$125.00**

Decanter, McCormick, 1980, Elvis Silver, plays How Great Thou Art, 750 ml..**$175.00**

Decanter, McCormick, 1981, Aloha Elvis, plays Blue Hawaii, 750 ml..**$150.00**

Decanter, McCormick, 1981, Elvis '68 Mini, plays Can't Help Falling in Love, 50 ml..**$55.00**

Decanter, McCormick, 1981, Elvis Designer I White (Joy), plays Are You Lonesome Tonight, 750 ml..........**$150.00**

Decanter, McCormick, 1982, Aloha Elvis Mini, plays Blue Hawaii, 50 ml..**$175.00**

Decanter, McCormick, 1982, Elvis Designer II White (Love), plays It's Now or Never, 750 ml........................**$125.00**

Decanter, McCormick, 1982, Elvis Karate, plays Don't Be Cruel, 750 ml, $350.00. (Photo courtesy Lee Garmon)

Decanter, McCormick, 1983, Elvis Designer III White (Reverence), plays Crying n the Chapel, 750 ml..**$250.00**

Decanter, McCormick, 1983, Elvis Gold Mini, plays My Way, 50 ml..**$125.00**

Decanter, McCormick, 1983, Elvis Silver Mini, plays How Great Thou Art, 50 ml **$95.00**

Decanter, McCormick, 1983, Sgt Elvis, plays GI Blues, 750 ml..**$295.00**

Decanter, McCormick, 1984, Elvis & Rising Sun, Plays Green, Green Grass of Home, 750 ml....................**$495.00**

Decanter, McCormick, 1984, Elvis Designer I Gold, plays Are You Lonesome Tonight, 750 ml....................**$175.00**

Decanter, McCormick, 1984, Elvis Designer II Gold, plays It's Now or Never, 750 ml....................**$195.00**

Decanter, McCormick, 1984, Elvis Karate Mini, plays Don't Be Cruel, 50 ml....................**$125.00**

Decanter, McCormick, 1984, Elvis on Stage, plays Can't Help Falling in Love, 50 ml (decanter only)................**$195.00**

Decanter, McCormick, 1984, Elvis w/Stage, 50 ml (complete w/separate stage designed to hold decanter).....**$450.00**

Decanter, McCormick, 1984, Elvis 50th Anniversary, plays I Want You, I Need You, I Love You, 750 ml.......**$495.00**

Decanter, McCormick, 1984, Sgt Elvis Mini, plays GI Blues, 50 ml..**$95.00**

Decanter, McCormick, 1985, Elvis Designer I White Mini, plays Are You Lonesome Tonight, 50 ml............**$125.00**

Decanter, McCormick, 1985, Elvis Designer III Gold, plays Crying in the Chapel, 750 ml....................**$250.00**

Decanter, McCormick, 1985, Elvis Teddy Bear, plays Let Me Be Your Teddy Bear, 750 ml **$695.00**

Decanter, McCormick, 1986, Elvis & Gates of Graceland, plays Welcome to My World, 750 ml **$150.00**

Decanter, McCormick, 1986, Elvis & Rising Sun Mini, plays Green, Green Grass of Home, 50 ml **$250.00**

Decanter, McCormick, 1986, Elvis Designer I Gold Mini, plays Are You Lonesome Tonight, 50 ml............**$150.00**

Decanter, McCormick, 1986, Elvis Designer I Silver Mini, Plays Are You Lonesome Tonight, 50 ml............**$135.00**

Decanter, McCormick, 1986, Elvis Hound Dog, plays Hound Dog, 750 ml **$695.00**

Decanter, McCormick, 1986, Elvis Season's Greetings, plays White Christmas, 375 ml **$195.00**

Decanter, McCormick, 1986, Elvis Teddy Bear Mini, plays Let Me Be Your Teddy Bear, 50 ml **$295.00**

Decanter, McCormick, 1986, Elvis 50th Anniversary Mini, plays I Want You, I Need You, I Love You, 50 ml **$250.00**

Decanter, McCormick, 1987, Elvis Memories, cassette player base, lighted top, extremely rare, 750 ml, from $1,000 to..**$1,200.00**

Doll, Celebrity Collection, World Doll, 1984, 21", MIB **$110.00**

Doll, Comeback Special, Hasbro, 1993, NRFB **$45.00**

Doll, Hound Dog, Smile Toy Co, stuffed plush w/Elvis lettered on white neck ribbon, NM........................**$250.00**

Doll, in Army uniform, w/badges, dog tag & duffle bag, Mattel, 12", MIB..**$45.00**

Doll, in white jumpsuit, w/guitar, Eugene, 1984, 12", MIB **$52.00**

Doll, Teen Idol, Hasbro, 1993, NRFB..........................**$42.50**

Figurine, Aloha from Hawaii, lights up, w/guitar, MIB..**$40.00**

Figurine, in white w/guitar, hands raised, Royal Orleans, 10", MIB **$55.00**

Flasher ring, 1957, EX, minimum value....................**$100.00**

Guitar, Lapin, 1984, MOC (sealed) **$75.00**

Key chain, flasher, full figure on yellow background, 2½x2", EX..**$20.00**

Lamp, blue suede shoes, Elvis Presley Enterprises, 13x9¼x9¼", M **$45.00**

Menu, Sahara Tahoe Hotel, Elvis photo cover, 1974, 8½x11", M **$60.00**

Music box, Elvis stands on mirrored platform, plays Burning Love, Enesco, 1993, 7", MIB....................**$60.00**

Necklace, Love Me Tender, Elvis Presley Enterprises, 1956, from $175 to..**$225.00**

Overnight case, blue, Elvis Presley Enterprises, 1956, 6½x12x9", NM..**$650.00**

Overnight case, brown, Elvis Presley Enterprises, 1956, 6½x12x9", NM, from $750 to..............................**$850.00**

Paint-by-number set, Peerless Playthings, 1956, rare, complete, EX (EX box), minimum value................**$3,000.00**

Painting on velvet, singing closeup w/mike, 18¾x22¾" in carved wood frame..**$55.00**

Paperdoll book, Elvis, St Martin's Press, 1982, uncut, EX...**$30.00**

Pen, Tickle Me, feather type, EX................................**$35.00**

Pennant, Birthplace Tupelo..., Elvis Presley Enterprises, 1962, M **$30.00**

Pin-back button, full-color portrait on celluloid, Cioffi, Elvis Presley Enterprises, 1956, 3", EX....................**$55.00**

Pin-back button, Vari-Vue, flicker type, 1960s.............**$38.00**

Plate, Elvis at Gates of Graceland, Delphi, Bruce Emmett, 1988 limited edition..**$45.00**

Pocketknife, guitar form, portrait & 1935-1977, 6"......**$45.00**

Poster, Girl Happy, 1965, 41x27"...............................**$110.00**

Poster, Trouble w/Girls, 1-sheet, 1969, EX **$52.00**

Ring, brass w/full-color image under clear bubble, 1956, EX..**$200.00**

Scarf, concert giveaway, silky, M **$40.00**

Sideburn sticker from gumball machine, 1950s, EX....**$55.00**

Snow globe, blue suede shoes, porcelain musical base, Elvis Presley Enterprises, 5½", MIB............................**$30.00**

Songbook, #1, 15 songs, 15 pictures, 1956, 35-page, EX..**$52.50**

Tour photo, singing, down on 1 knee, full color, 8x10"..**$25.00**

Enesco

Enesco is a company that imports and distributes ceramic novelty items made in Japan. Some of their more popular lines are the Human Beans, Partners in Crime Christmas ornaments, Eggbert, Dutch Kids, and Mother in the Kitchen (also referred to as Kitchen Prayer Ladies, see also that category). Prices are climbing steadily. Several Enesco items are pictured in *The Collector's Encyclopedia of Cookie Jars, Volumes 1, 2,* and *3,* by Joyce and Fred Roerig (Collector Books).

Bank, Dear God Kids girl, 1982, from $40 to.............**$45.00**

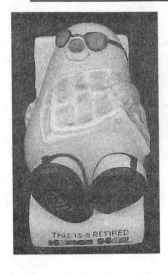

Bank, This is a Retired Human Bean, 1981, $30.00. (Photo courtesy Ron and Sherri Lewis)

Banks, Lucy & Me, Prayer Bears, 1987, 5x4", pr.......**$120.00**

Candy container, Dear God Kids, boy or girl, 1983, ea from $45 to..**$50.00**

Doll, Bong Bong, porcelain head & hands in clown clothes, 13, MIB **$80.00**

Figurine, Eggbert Stacking Doll, Policeman, egg-shaped, set of 4, M (EX box)...**$460.00**

Figurine, Having a Wash & Brush Up, girl in bubble-filled tub brushing her back, Memories of Yesterday Series, 1993, MIB **$45.00**

Figurine, I'll Always Treasure Your Friendship, Coral Kingdom, #910970, 1995, M.................................**$110.00**

Figurine, Kewpie w/pumpkin-shaped Halloween bag, #530662, 1993, 4¼", MIB...**$85.00**

Figurine, Mary Had a Little Lamb, 1995, 9", MIB **$80.00**

Figurine, Memories Are Best When Shared With You, Sisters & Best Friends Series, 1993, 4½x4½", MIB...........**$65.00**

Figurine, Mermaid, flowing hair & resting on shells & sea grass, 1990, 10x9½", NM **$175.00**

Figurine, Showering You With Hogs, parent pig w/baby pig in their raincoats, 3", MIB **$35.00**

Figurine set, To Hog & To Hold, Little Piggy Wedding set, 9 pcs, MIB **$145.00**

Figurine set, Willowbrook Victorian Summer House, 1994, MIB **$40.00**

Figurines, My Collection, shadow box w/2" figurines for ea month, 16" box, 1989, MIB **$40.00**

Jack-in-the-box, Pasha Cat, plays Memories from the musical Cats, 1987, 8¼", NM **$130.00**

Jack-in-the-box, Phantom of the Opera, plays, The Music of the Night, 1988, M (NM box)..............................**$185.00**

Jack-in-the-box, Rhett Butler, scenes of Rhett & Scarlett on laminated wood box, 1989, 6x8", M (EX box) **$75.00**

Jack-in-the-box, Snow White, NM (EX box)................**$55.00**

Mug, Barbie Nurse, 1994, MIB....................................**$30.00**

Music box, Country Cousins, The Carolers, plays We Wish You a Merry Christmas, 7x7½", NMIB...................**$85.00**

Music box, Eggbert, Lovebird, plays Love Me Tender, 1989, 6½", M (VG box) **$240.00**

Music box, Eiffel Tower, Small World of Music, mice explore the tower while 1 flies over in hot air balloon, 18", M.......**$75.00**

Music box, Knitting Pretty, plays Whistle While You Work, animated, MIB...**$85.00**

Music box, See the Flying Circus, Travels of Yesteryear, animated, plays Those Magnificent...Flying Machines, 1987, MIB **$70.00**

Music box, Take This Job & Shove It, mice on typewriter, plays Whistle While You Work, 1991, NMIB **$65.00**

Ornament, The Tin Man, 50th Anniversary of Wizard of Oz, MIB **$40.00**

Plate, Lucy & Me, 1982, 8½".....................................**$125.00**

Teapots, Mr & Mrs Humpty Dumpty, 1950s, 8" & 7", pr, M **$160.00**

Train set, Sugar Town Express, plays medley of 3 Christmas songs, battery-operated, 18 feet of track, 1995, MIB..**$40.00**

Eye Winker

Designed along the lines of an early pressed glass pattern by Dalzell, Gilmore, and Leighton, Eye Winker was one of several attractive glassware assortments featured in the catalogs of L. G. Wright during the '60s and '70s. The line was extensive and made in several colors: amber, blue, green, crystal, and red. It was probably pressed by Fostoria, Fenton, and Westmoreland, since we know these are the companies that made Moon and Star for Wright, who was not a glass manufacturer but simply a distributing company. Red and green are the most desirable colors and are priced higher than the others we mentioned. The values given here are for red and green, deduct about 20% for examples in clear, amber, or light blue.

Though prices may have softened slightly due to Internet influence, this line is still very collectible, and as the increased supply made available through online auctions gradually diminishes, we expect values to return to the level they were several months ago.

Advisor: Sophia Talbert (See Directory, Eye Winker)

Ashtray, allover pattern, 4½" dia, from $20 to **$25.00**

Bowl, 4 toes, 2½x5", from $22 to...............................**$28.00**

Butter dish, allover pattern, 4½" dia lid, 6" base, from $50 to **$65.00**

Candy dish, all over pattern, disk foot, w/lid, 5¼x5½" ..**$45.00**

Candy dish, oval, 4-toed, 5x3½"................................**$25.00**

Celery or relish, ruffled rim, oblong, 9½x5" **$40.00**

Compote, allover pattern except for plain flared rim, patterned lid, 10½x6"+finial **$70.00**

Compote, allover pattern except for plain flared rim & foot, patterned lid, 7x5", w/lid **$50.00**

Compote, allover pattern except for plain flared rim & foot, 7x7"..**$30.00**

Compote, jelly; patterned lid, plain foot & rim, 4¼x3½" ..**$40.00**

Compote, ruffled rim, plain foot, 4-sided, 7x6"...........**$40.00**

Compote, ruffled rim, 4-sided, 6x10", from $50 ....**$60.00**

Creamer & sugar bowl, allover pattern, disk foot, sm, 3¼" ...**$35.00**

Fairy lamp, allover pattern, disk foot, 2-pc, from $40 to...**$60.00**

Goblet, plain rim & foot, 6¼".......................................**$25.00**
Marmalade, w/lid, 5¼x4"...**$45.00**
Pitcher, ruffled rim, plain foot, 1-qt, from $70 to........**$75.00**
Pitcher, 28-oz, 7¾", minimum value **$50.00**
Salt & pepper shakers, 4", pr..**$30.00**
Salt cellar, allover pattern, ruffled rim, 1¾"................**$10.00**
Sherbet, plain rim & foot, 4½"..**$20.00**
Toothpick holder, allover pattern, ruffled rim, 2¼" **$15.00**
Tumbler, 8-oz, from $20 to **$28.00**
Vase, ruffled rim, 3-sided, 3-toed, 7¾"........................**$60.00**
Vase, 3-footed, scalloped, 6"..**$50.00**

Fast-Food Collectibles

Since the late 1970s, fast-food chains have been catering to their very young customers through their kiddie meals. The toys tucked in each box or bag have made a much longer-lasting impression on the kids than any meal could. Today it's not just the toys that are collectible, but also boxes, promotional signs used by the restaurant, the promotional items themselves (such as Christmas ornaments you can buy for 99¢, collector plates, glass tumblers, or stuffed animals), and the 'under 3' (safe for children under 3) toys their toddler customers are given on request.

There have been three kinds of promotions: 1) national — every restaurant in the country offering the same item, 2) regional, and 3) test market. A test market box might be worth $20.00, a regional box might be $10.00, and a national, $1.00. Supply dictates price.

To be most valuable, a toy must be in the original package, just as it was issued by the restaurant. Beware of dealers trying to 'repackage' toys in plain plastic bags. Most original bags were printed or contained an insert card. Vacuform containers were quickly discarded, dictating a premium price. Toys without the original packaging are worth only about one-half to two-thirds as much as those mint in package, which are the values we give in our listings.

Toys representing popular Disney characters draw cross-collectors, so do Star Trek, My Little Pony, and Barbie toys. It's not always the early items that are the most collectible, because some of them may have been issued in such vast amounts that there is an oversupply of them today. At the same time, a toy only a year or so old that might have been quickly withdrawn due to a problem with its design will already be one the collector will pay a good price to get.

Prices have dropped due to the influence of the Internet, and the values in our listings reflect the softer market. If you'd like to learn more about fast-food collectibles, we recommend *Tomart's Price Guide to Kid's Meal Collectibles* by Ken Clee; *The Illustrated Collector's Guide to McDonald's® Happy Meal® Boxes, Premiums and Promotions®*, *McDonald's® Happy Meal Toys in the USA*, *McDonald's® Happy Meal Toys Around the World*, and *Illustrated Collector's Guide to McDonald's® McCAPS*, all by Joyce and Terry Losonsky; *McDonald's® Collectibles* by Gary Henriques

and Audre Duval; and *Schroeder's Collectible Toys, Antique to Modern* (Collector Books).

See also California Raisins.

Note: Unless noted otherwise, values are given for MIP items (when applicable).

Club: McDonald's© Collector Club
1153 S Lee St., PMB 200
Des Plaines, IL 60016-6503
Membership: $15 per year for individual or out of state, $7 for juniors, or $20 per family or International members; includes annual dated lapel pin, quarterly newsletter, and annual members directory; send LSASE for club information, chapter list, and publication list; http://www.mcdclub.com

Newsletter: *Sunshine Express* **(monthly)**
and club's Sunshine Chapter
Bill and Pat Poe founders and current officers
220 Dominica Circle E.
Niceville, FL 32578-4085
850-897-4163; fax: 850-897-2606
e-mail: McPoes@aol.com
Club membership: as per above

Newsletter: *Collecting Tips*
Meredith Williams
Box 633, Joplin, MO 64802. Send SASE for information.

Arby's, Barbar's World Tour, pull-back racers, 1992, ea..**$3.00**
Arby's, Barbar's World Tour, squirters, 1992, ea...........**$2.00**
Arby's, Barbar's World Tour, stampers, 1991, ea...........**$3.00**
Arby's, Little Miss, 1981, ea..**$4.00**
Arby's, Looney Tunes Characters, 1987, oval base, ea .**$5.00**
Arby's, Looney Tunes Fun Fingers, 1989, ea.................**$5.00**
Arby's, Snow Domes, 1995, Yogi or Snagglepuss, ea ...**$5.00**
Arby's, Winter Wonderland Crazy Cruisers, 1995, ea **$4.00**
Burger King, Aladdin Hidden Treasures, 1994, ea........**$2.00**
Burger King, Beauty & the Beast, 1991, 4 different, ea ..**$4.00**
Burger King, Beetlejuice, 1990, 6 different, ea.............**$2.00**
Burger King, Captain Planet Flipover Star Cruiser, 1991, 4 different, ea...**$2.00**
Burger King, Crayola Christmas Bears, 1986, plush, 4 different colors, ea..**$5.00**

Burger King, Dino Crawlers, five in the series, 1994, $2.00 each.

Burger King, Glow-in-the-Dark Troll Patrol, 1993, 4 different, ea **$3.00**

Burger King, Go-Go Gadets, 1991, 4 different, ea **$3.00**

Burger King, Hunchback of Notre Dame, 1996, 8 different, ea **$4.00**

Burger King, It's Magic, 1992, 4 different, ea **$2.00**

Burger King, Kid Transporters, 1990, 6 different, ea.....**$2.00**

Burger King, Mini Sports Game, 1993, 4 different, ea ..**$3.00**

Burger King, Oliver & Co, 1996, 5 different, ea............**$3.00**

Burger King, Pranksters, 1994, 5 different, ea **$3.00**

Burger King, Silverhawks, 1987, pencil topper **$5.00**

Burger King, Super Powers, 1987, Aquaman tub toy ...**$6.00**

Burger King, Toy Story, 1995, Action Wing Buzz **$2.00**

Burger King, World Travel Adventure Kit, 1991, 4 different, ea **$2.00**

Dairy Queen, Alvin & the Chipmunks Music Makers, 1994, 4 different, ea **$3.00**

Dairy Queen, Dennis the Menace, 1994, 4 different, ea..**$2.00**

Dairy Queen, Rock-A-Doodle, 1991, 6 different, ea **$5.00**

Dairy Queen, Space Shuttle, 6 different, ea..................**$2.00**

Denny's, Dino-Makers, 5 different, ea.........................**$2.00**

Denny's, Flintstones Fun Squirters, 1991, 5 different, ea..**$2.00**

Denny's, Flintstones Vehicles, 1990, 3 different, ea **$2.00**

Denny's, Jetson's Go Back to School, 1992, 4 different, ea **$2.00**

Dominos Pizza, Donnie Domino, 1989, 4" **$3.00**

Dominos Pizza, Keep the Noid Out, 1987, 3 different, ea **$3.00**

Hardee's, Beach Bunnies, 1989, 4 different, ea............**$2.00**

Hardee's, Beakman's World, 1995, 4 different, ea.........**$2.00**

Hardee's, Dinobed Buddies, 1994, 4 different, ea.........**$2.00**

Hardee's, Fender-Bender 500 Racers, 1990, 5 different, ea...**$2.00**

Hardee's, Gremlin Adventures Read-Along Book & record, 1984, 5 different, ea.................................**$3.00**

Hardee's, Homeward Bound II, 1996, 5 different, ea ...**$2.00**

Hardee's, Kazoo Crew Sailors, 1991, 4 different, ea **$2.00**

Hardee's, Mouth Figurines, 1989, 4 different, ea...........**$2.00**

Hardee's, Pound Puppies, 1986, plush, 4 different, ea.**$2.00**

Hardee's, Smurf's Funmeal Pack, 1990, 6 different, ea.**$2.00**

Hardee's, Tattoads, 1995, 4 different, ea **$2.00**

Hardee's, Walt Disney Animated Film Classics, 1985, plush, 5 different, ea **$3.00**

Jack-in-the-Box, Bendable Buddies, 1975, 4 different, ea..**$5.00**

Jack-in-the-Box, Finger Puppets, 1994, 5 different, ea..**$5.00**

Jack-in-the-Box, Star Trek Next Generation, 1994, 6 different, ea...**$3.00**

Long John Silver's, Berenstain Bear Books, 1995, 4 different, ea **$2.00**

Long John Silver's, Free Willy II, 1995, 5 different, ea .**$2.00**

Long John Silver's, Map Activities, 1991, 3 different, ea ..**$2.00**

Long John Silver's, Sea Watchers, 1991, mini kaleidoscopes, 3 different, ea.................................**$2.00**

McDonald's, Amazing Wildlife, 1995, ea **$2.00**

McDonald's, Barbie/Hot Wheels, 1991, Hot Wheels, ea..**$2.00**

McDonald's, Barbie/Hot Wheels, 1998, Barbie, 4 different, ea **$2.00**

McDonald's, Barbie/Mini Streex, 1992, any including under age 3, ea **$2.00**

McDonald's, Batman, 1992, 6 different, ea **$2.00**

McDonald's, Berenstain Bears, 1987, any except under age 3, ea **$3.00**

McDonald's, Berenstain Bears, 1987, under age 3, Mama or Papa w/paper punch-outs, ea...........................**$5.00**

McDonald's, Crayola Stencils, 1987, any including under age 3, ea **$2.00**

McDonald's, Ducktails II, 1988, launch pad airport or Webby on tricycle, ea.................................**$4.00**

McDonald's, Flintstone Kids, 1988, under age 3, Dino.**$8.00**

McDonald's, Flintstone Kids, 1988, 4 different, ea........**$6.00**

McDonald's, Friendly Skies, 1994, United hanger w/Ronald plane **$3.00**

McDonald's, Ghostbusters, 1987, pencil case, Containment Chamber **$3.00**

McDonald's, Halloween McNuggets, 1993, any including under age 3, ea **$2.00**

McDonald's, Happy Pail, 1986, 5 different, ea **$3.00**

McDonald's, Hook, 1997, 4 different, ea......................**$2.00**

McDonald's, Jungle Book, 1989, 4 different, ea **$2.00**

McDonald's, Jungle Book, 1990, under age 3, Junior or Mowgli, ea **$6.00**

McDonald's, Little Mermaid, 1989, 4 different, ea.........**$2.00**

McDonald's, Littlest Pet Shop/Transformers, 1996, any including under age 3, ea.................................**$2.00**

McDonald's, Marvel Super Heroes, 1996, any including under age 3, ea **$3.00**

McDonald's, Mickey & Friends Adventure at Disney World (EPCOT Center), 1994, any, ea **$2.00**

McDonald's, Mickey's Birthdayland, 1988, any including under age 3, ea **$3.00**

McDonald's, Movables, 1988, any, ea **$5.00**

McDonald's, Muppet Babies, Gonzo, Fozzie, Miss Piggy, and Kermit, from $2.00 to $4.00 each. (Photo courtesy Gary Henriques and Audre Duvall)

McDonald's, Peanuts, 1990, any except under age 3, ea..**$2.00**

McDonald's, Peanuts, 1990, under age 3, Charlie Brown egg basket or Snoopy's potato sack, ea **$3.00**

McDonald's, Potato Heads, 1992, 8 different, ea...........**$3.00**

McDonald's, Rescuers Down Under, 1990, any including under age 3, ea **$2.00**

McDonald's, Runaway Robots, 1987, 6 different, ea.....**$2.00**

McDonald's, School Days, 1984, eraser, pencil or ruler, ea **$2.00**

McDonald's, Sea World of Texas, 1988, 4 different, ea **$8.00**

McDonald's, Space Jam, 1996, 8 different, ea...............**$2.00**

McDonald's, Space Rescue, 1995, any including under age 3, ea...**$2.00**

McDonald's, Stomper Mini 4x4, 1986, 15 different, M, ea .**$4.00**

McDonald's, Super Looney Tunes, 1991, any including under age 3, ea **$2.00**

McDonald's, Winter Worlds Ornaments, 1983, any, ea.**$3.00**

McDonald's, 101 Dalmatians Snow Dome Ornaments, 1996, 4 different, ea **$2.00**

McDonald's Star Trek, 1979, from $5 to.....................**$6.00**

Pizza Hut, Air Garfield kite or parachute, 1993, ca **$3.00**

Pizza Hut, Land Before Time hand puppets, 1988, any, ea ..**$2.00**

Pizza Hut, Pagemaster, 4 different, 1994, ea.................**$2.00**

Pizza Hut, Universal Monsters hologram cards, 1991, 3 different, ea...**$2.00**

Sonic, Brown Bag Bowlers, 1994, 4 different, ea..........**$3.00**

Sonic, Brown Bag Buddies, 1989 (4 different) or 1993 (3 different), ea **$3.00**

Sonic, Food Train, 1995, set of 7 cars w/engine.........**$14.00**

Sonic, Monster Peepers, 1994, 4 different, ea................**$2.00**

Sonic, Super Sonic Racers, 1995, 4 different, ea...........**$2.00**

Sonic, Wacky Sackers, 1994, set of 6 ....**$4.00**

Subway, Bobby's World, 1995, 4 different, ea...............**$2.00**

Subway, Cone Heads, 1993, 4 different, ea **$2.00**

Subway, Hackeysack Balls, 1991, 4 different, ea **$2.00**

Subway, Monkey Trouble, 1994, 5 different, ea............**$2.00**

Subway, Tale Tale, 1995, any including under age 3 ...**$2.00**

Taco Bell, Hugga Bunch, 1983, Fluffer, Gigglet or Tuggins, plush, ea **$3.00**

Taco Bell, Mask, 1995, It's Party Time switchplate or Milo w/mask, ea **$3.00**

Taco Bell, The Tick, 1996, Arthur w/wings or Sewer Urchin, ea..**$2.00**

Wendy's, Alf Tales, 1990, 6 different, ea **$2.00**

Wendy's, Cybercycles, 1994, 4 different, ea..................**$2.00**

Wendy's, Definitely Dinosaurs, 1988 (4 different) or 1989 (5 different), ea **$2.00**

Wendy's, Endangered Animal Games, 1993, any including under age 3, ea **$2.00**

Wendy's, Felix the Cat, 1990, plush figure....................**$2.00**

Wendy's, Furskins Bears, 1986, 4 different, plush, ea...**$3.00**

Wendy's, Gobots, 1986, Odd Ball/Monster **$3.00**

Wendy's, Potato Head II, 1988, 5 different, ea **$3.00**

White Castle, Camp White Castle, 1990, fork & spoon, ea **$2.00**

White Castle, Castleburger Friends, 1989, 6 different, ea..**$3.00**

White Castle, Glow-in-the-Dark Monsters, 1992, 3 different, ea...**$3.00**

White Castle, Holiday Huggables, 1990, 3 different, ea..**$3.00**

Fenton Glass

Located in Williamstown, West Virginia, the Fenton company is still producing glassware just as they have since the early part of the century. Nearly all fine department stores and gift shops carry an extensive line of their beautiful products, many of which rival examples of finest antique glassware. The fact that even some of their fairly recent glassware has collectible value attests to its fine quality.

Over the years they have made many lovely colors in scores of lines, several of which are very extensive. Paper labels were used exclusively until 1970. Since then some pieces have been made with a stamped-in logo.

Numbers in the descriptions correspond with catalog numbers used by the company. Collectors use them as a means of identification as to shape and size. If you'd like to learn more about the subject, we recommend *Fenton Glass, The Second Twenty-Five Years*, and *Fenton Glass, The Third Twenty-Five Years*, by William Heacock; *Fenton Glass, The 1980s*, by James Measell; and *Fenton Art Glass, 1907 to 1939*, and *Fenton Art Glass Patterns, 1939 to 1980*, both by Margaret and Kenn Whitmyer.

Advisor: Ferill J. Rice (See Directory, Fenton Glass)

Club: Fenton Art Glass Collectors of America, Inc.

Newsletter: Butterfly Net
P.O. Box 384
Williamstown, WV 26187; Full membership $20 per year; $5 for each associate membership; children under 12 free

Club: Pacific Northwest Fenton Association
P.O. Box 881
Tillamook, OR 97141, 503-842-4815; Subscription: $20 per year; includes quarterly informational newsletter

Baskets

Hobnail, blue opalescent, #3834, 4½", 1940s – 55, from $35.00 to $45.00.

Amethyst carnival, Spanish Lace, 8x8" **$48.00**

Bill Fenton's 50th Anniversary **$60.00**

Black, single-crimp, 2½" **$15.00**

Blue opalescent, Hobnail, #3830, 10" **$160.00**

Blue Ridge, #1923, 6" **$98.00**

Burmese, Hobnail, signed Bill Fenton, #GS007BR, 1996, 7" **$150.00**

Burmese satin, roses, #7437RB **$125.00**

Cranberry opalescent, Melon Heart Optic, #7122 ....**$75.00**
Crystal Velvet, grape, 3-toed, #8438 ....**$30.00**
Custard, log cabin, #7437CV **$50.00**
Emerald Crest on milk glass **$75.00**
French opalescent over blue, Coin Dot **$35.00**
Gold carnival w/hand-painted decoration, footed **$48.00**
Green w/white flowers, Christmas, Special Room **$45.00**
Lilac, Big Cookies **$325.00**
Lime sherbert, Hobnail, F2, 4½" **$128.00**
Butterfly and Berry, Heritage Green **$35.00**
Butterfly and Berry, Plum **$32.00**
Paneled, Velva Rose, 11" **$48.00**
Purple stretch, Levay, 3-toed **$55.00**
QVC, custard w/flowers, mini, 2½" **$55.00**
QVC 10th Anniversary, Burmese w/flowers, mini hat ..**$95.00**
Red carnival, Atlantis Fan, Singleton Bailey, limited edition,
    lg **$150.00**
Red carnival, NFGS, mini, 2½" **$60.00**
Salem Blue, Inverted Strawberry, sm, footed, #9537SR..**$38.00**
Topaz, Hobnail, F2, 4½" **$60.00**
Violets in Snow, crystal handle, #7436DV **$65.00**
Wisteria Threaded, Diamond Optic, 3-toed, #8425, 6½"..**$65.00**
75th Anniversary, pink stretch **$50.00**

Bells

Blue Rose/Blue Satin Medallion, #8267 ....**$45.00**
Daisy & Button, Lime Sherbet, #1966-LS, 1973-1980, from $20
    to **$25.00**
Daisy & Button, orange carnival, 1966-CO, 1971-74, from $30
    to **$35.00**
Desert Storm, hand-painted yellow ribbon, #7668YQ, 1,000
    made, 6"..**$40.00**
Hobnail, milk glass, #3667-MI, 1967-80s, from $20 to ..**$30.00**
Hobnail, ruby, #3667-RU, 1972-80s, from $20 to **$30.00**
Lily of the Valley, cameo opalescent, #8265-CO, 1979-80s,
    from $25 to...**$35.00**
Lily of the Valley, carnival, #8265-CN, 1979-80, from $30
    to **$35.00**
New Born on custard, #7564 ....**$30.00**
Patriot's, Bicentennial Patriot Red, #8467PR, 6½" **$35.00**
Spanish Lace, Violets in the Snow, #3567-DV, 1974-80s, from
    $50 to...**$60.00**
Studebaker, #7669-SU, limited edition of 5,000, 1986.**$85.00**

Carnival Glass

Note: Carnival glass items listed here were made after 1970.

Bell, Strawberry, amethyst..................................**$35.00**
Bowl, Butterfly & Berry, amethyst, #8428, heart shape, fantail
    interior, Special Room, 1990 ....**$75.00**
Bowl, Hearts & Flowers, amethyst, lg....................**$55.00**
Cheesie box, red, #9480, w/lid............................**$75.00**
Cuspidor, Water Lily & Cattails, red......................**$45.00**
Leaf plate, Rosalene...**$45.00**
Pagoda dish, amethyst, 2-pc **$45.00**

Pitcher, plum, #6869, 1997......................................**$95.00**
Vase, Atlantis, crystal iridized, limited edition..........**$150.00**

Crests

Apple Blossom, basket, #7436, handled, 6½", from $50 to.**$70.00**
Apple Blossom, cake plate **$125.00**
Apple Blossom, candle holder, #7271....................**$40.00**
Aqua, bowl, #203, 4½"......................................**$22.00**
Aqua, vase, tulip; triangular, #1924, 5" **$30.00**
Black, ashtray, #7377, from $35 to........................**$45.00**
Blue, bonbon, #7428, 8", from $45 to.....................**$55.00**
Emerald, bowl, dessert; #680 ....**$25.00**
Flame, tidbit, 2-tier, #7294, from $100 to..............**$125.00**
Gold, plate, #680, 6½"......................................**$10.00**
Peach, bowl, #7227, 7", from $45 to **$47.00**
Peach, vase, #6058, 6½"....................................**$45.00**
Peach, vase, #7495, 9", from $75 to **$85.00**
Peach, vase, double-crimp, #711, 6" **$40.00**
Plum, basket, hand-painted lilacs, inscribed Bill Fenton,
    #6730PJ, MIB w/certificate **$75.00**
Plum, basket, Spanish Lace, hand-painted lilacs on milk
    glass, #3538PJ, 1993, 8½"...............................**$55.00**
Plum, bell, Paisley, hand-painted lilacs on milk glass,
    #2746PJ, 1993, 7"..**$35.00**
Plum, jug, hand-painted lilacs on milk glass, #2765PJ, 1993,
    6½"..**$52.00**
Rose, vase, #4517, 11", from $200 to **$225.00**
Silver, bonbon, yellow roses, #7255YR, 5½" **$32.00**
Silver, cologne bottle, squat, #192.......................**$55.00**
Silver, mayonnaise set, #7203, 3 pcs **$40.00**
Silver, top hat, #7393, 1968, 8"..........................**$125.00**
Silver, vase, Spanish Lace, #3554SC, 4" **$22.50**
Silver Jamestown, vase, #7276, 12", from $125 to.....**$185.00**

Figurals and Novelties

Angel, Radiant; blue, #5542, 7½"..........................**$45.00**
Bear, green carnival, sitting, #5151.......................**$50.00**
Bear, Log Cabin on custard, sitting, #5151LC **$68.00**
Bear, Reclining; Raspberry Rosalene, #5233, Special Room,
    1989 ....**$30.00**
Bear, Reclining; red hearts, iced floral on white satin,
    #5139NIL...**$55.00**
Bear, Sitting; black opaque, #5151 ....**$56.00**
Bear, Sitting; Rosalene, #5151RE, Special Room, 1989
    Convention **$35.00**
Bird, Happiness; Iced Gold Butterfly & yellow floral on milk
    glass, #5197NIL..**$52.00**
Bird, Happiness; lavender satin, #5197 ....**$65.00**
Bird, Happiness; Log Cabin on custard, #5197 ....**$65.00**
Bird, Happiness; red carnival, #5917.....................**$52.00**
Bird, Short Tail; blue roses on blue satin, #5163 ....**$45.00**
Boot, Daisy & Button, amethyst carnival..................**$25.00**
Boy & Girl, Praying; white satin, #5100, pr................**$40.00**
Bridesmaid doll, hand-painted roses on Burmese,
    #5228BR..**$150.00**

Bridesmaid doll, white opalescent, Fenton Gift Ship, #5228 ....**$25.00**

Bunny, pink & lavender tulips on iridescent white, #5162TL, 1990 ....**$45.00**

Bunny, Violets in Snow, old, #5162DV......................**$60.00**

Butterfly on Branch, Favrene, #5171, 1991 Convention..**$48.00**

Butterfly on Branch, Heritage Green, #5171HG, 1984..**$20.00**

Butterfly on Branch, shiny Burmese, #5171BE, FAGCA 1992 Convention **$45.00**

Cat, Alley; Burmese satin, #C5177, QVC 1996.............**$90.00**

Cat, Happy; Burmese **$65.00**

Cat, Happy; Twilight Blue iridized, FAGCA................**$60.00**

Cat, Misty Blue satin iridized, #5165LR **$40.00**

Cat, pink floral on Pink Pearl, Cat Capers, #5169 09, 1991 ....**$45.00**

Cat, violet floral on White Satin, Seafoam Green Blush, #5165QVC...**$50.00**

Egg on pedestal, green roses on yellow satin, #5140GR, 1973 ....**$52.00**

Elephant, Kristen's Floral on white satin, #5158YB **$45.00**

Fawn, amethyst carnival, #5150CN...........................**$45.00**

Fawn, Iced Winter Rose, #5160TS, 1989 ....**$60.00**

Fish, paperweight, amethyst carnival, #5193...............**$50.00**

Fish, paperweight, blue carnival, #5193.....................**$35.00**

Fish, paperweight, Rosalene, #5193RE, 1991, 5", MIB w/certificate **$30.00**

Fox, red carnival, #5226RN, 1994, 5", from $40 to......**$45.00**

Frog, lavender & white petaled flowers on Roselene satin, #5166...**$60.00**

Kissing Kids, Rosalene, #5101RE, pr **$45.00**

Kitten, lavender floral on Jade Pearl, Cat Capers, #51918, 1993 ....**$45.00**

Mouse, Civil War; blue, #5148.................................**$59.00**

Mouse, iridized red/orange/yellow slag, #5148...........**$52.00**

Mouse, marigold, iridized by Crider, #5148 ....**$69.00**

Mouse, shiny blue Burmese, #5148UE.......................**$55.00**

Mouse, Spruce Green, 22k grape accents, #5148EM...**$45.00**

Owl, Celeste Blue carnival, blown.............................**$75.00**

September Morn nymph, Celeste Blue stretch, #2990KA, 1995, 4-pc **$95.00**

September Morn nymph, red, recent **$60.00**

Southern Girl, Rose Pearl, #5141, 1993, 8" **$75.00**

Squirrel, Meadow Beauty, French opalescent, #5215PD, 1998 ....**$45.00**

Sunfish, Rosalene, Special Glass, #5167RE, 1993 Convention, 2½" **$28.00**

Unicorn, autumn leaves on black, #5253AW, 1994 .....**$35.00**

Unicorn, carnival, #5253CN.....................................**$50.00**

Unicorn, Rusty Rose, #5253DK, 1993 ....**$25.00**

Unicorn, Twilight Blue, #5253TB, 1993 ....**$25.00**

Hobnail

Ashtray, French opalescent, med size **$38.00**

Ashtray, Springtime Green, ball form, #3648GT..........**$20.00**

Bowl, blue opalescent, pie-crimped, #3924, 9" **$55.00**

Bowl, cereal; milk glass, #3719MI **$40.00**

Bowl, cranberry opalescent, oval, #3927, 7"...............**$60.00**

Cake plate, blue opalescent, footed, 12" **$135.00**

Candle bowl, plum opalescent..................................**$75.00**

Candle holder, milk glass, w/finger hold, #3870........**$25.00**

Candle holders, teal opalescent, 6", pr **$69.00**

Candy dish, milk glass, w/lid, after 1967...................**$50.00**

Centerpiece, milk glass, tall, #3742, 3-pc, scarce **$115.00**

Champagne punch set, blue opalescent, #3611BO, 10-pc **$295.00**

Compote, Cameo opalescent, double-crimped, footed, 6" **$22.50**

Creamer & sugar bowl, cranberry opalescent, #389, 4"...**$250.00**

Creamer & sugar bowl, French opalescent, #3900, individual **$27.50**

Cruet, cranberry opalescent, #3863 ....**$90.00**

Epergne, milk glass, #3701MI, 4-pc, 10" **$75.00**

Ginger Jar, French opalescent, sm............................**$45.00**

Hand vase, milk glass, #3355MI, limited edition, 1992, 6" **$20.00**

Jug, milk glass, 70-oz, 9½".......................................**$75.00**

Mustard jar, French opalescent, #389, 3-pc.................**$35.00**

Pitcher, ice lip; #3665, $55.00; Cookie jar, $100.00. (Photo courtesy Gene Florence)

Pitcher, milk glass, rounded bottom, footed, before 1953 ....**$65.00**

Planter, crescent; milk glass, #3698, scarce, 10" **$30.00**

Punch cup, milk glass, #3847 ....**$20.00**

Relish, green opalescent, #3733GO...........................**$80.00**

Relish, milk glass, chrome handle, #3607MI..............**$24.00**

Relish, milk glass, divided, #3740, 12" **$25.00**

Relish, milk glass, 3-part, after 1967.........................**$45.00**

Rose bowl, blue opalescent, 4½" **$32.00**

Spoon holder, milk glass, #3612, rare **$79.00**

Syrup jug, lime green opal, 1950s, 5½" **$60.00**

Tankard, cranberry opalescent, #389 ....**$450.00**

Tumbler, milk glass, before 1953...............................**$10.00**

Vase, blue opalescent, scalloped, footed, 6"...............**$75.00**

Vase, cranberry opalescent, #3858, 8" **$145.00**

Vase, handkerchief; milk glass, #3750.......................**$22.00**

Vase, jack-in-pulpit; milk glass, #3356, limited edition,1992, 7½"..**$23.00**

Vase, milk glass, flat bottom, before 1953, 4".............**$40.00**

Vase, swung; blue opalescent, 18" $100.00

Lamps

Candle, Daisy on Cameo................................$90.00
Fairy, Black Crest, 1-pc $145.00
Fairy, hydrangeas on topaz opalescent, #2040, 7½".$145.00
Fairy, Log Cabin on custard, #7300CV $60.00
Fairy, Owl, blue satin, 2-pc................................$35.00
Fairy, Owl, Rosalene, #5108RE, 1976, 3½" $38.00
Fairy, Ruby, Gift Shop, #5405RU, 2-pc.....................$50.00
Fairy, Spiral Optic, Cameo opalescent, #7300, 2-pc....$68.00
Gone w/the Wind, Burmese, massive base, #9202, 36"..$950.00
Hurricane, Hobnail, peachblow, #3998.....................$110.00
Hurricane, Snow Crest on cranberry swirl, 2-pc $150.00

Spanish Lace with Silver Crest, Gone-With-the-Wind, #3509 SC, 1976 – 80s, $250.00. (Photo courtesy Margaret and Kenn Whitmyer)

Student, Burmese, artist signed, dated 1974, #7410, 21"...$525.00
Table, Butterfly & Flowering Branch, 1985 Connoisseur Collection, #7602EB, 22" $650.00

Miscellaneous

Box, hand-painted bunny, #4683B, 1991, 7" $40.00
Clock, opalescent w/hand-painted tulips, #8691TL.....$60.00
Compote, Jefferson, Bicentennial Patriot Red, #8476PR, limited edition $110.00
Compote, Provincial Bouquet on white satin, stemmed, #1628FS..$40.00
Ginger jar, blue roses on blue satin, #7288BL, 3-pc .$110.00
Ice bucket, Plymouth & Ming (double pattern), crystal, w/handle...$105.00
Jar, Macaroon (Big Cookies), amber, #1681 ....$195.00
Jug, rose overlay, melon shape, #192, 8".....................$65.00
Logo, chocolate glass, FAGCA 1982, oval, #9499CK ...$75.00
Perfume, blue overlay, long neck, 6"...........................$45.00
Perfume, copper rose on black glass, #7948KP $60.00
Perfume, Rose Trellis, heart stopper, #1710R5, MIB w/certificate..$95.00
Picture frame, peach rose on Cameo, #7596, 1985, 3¾x4¾" $40.00
Pitcher, Mary Gregory on cranberry, #3275DM, 6½" ..$125.00

Plate, Eagle, Bicentennial Patriot Red, #9418PR, 8¼" .$35.00
Plate, Garden of Eden, #9614NK, 8" $69.00
Rose bowl, Hanging Heart, turquoise, #8924.............$35.00
Tray, rabbit, pearlized Shell Pink, #4670, 1991, 6".....$14.00
Tumbler, roses on Burmese, 4" $50.00
Vase, bud; roses on Burmese satin, #7348................$75.00
Vase, Colonial, grapes on Stiegel Blue opalescent, 1991...$28.00
Vase, Hanging Heart, turquoise, #8954, 4".................$52.00
Vase, Peacock on Burmese, #8257, 1987 ....$100.00
Vase, Roses on Burmese satin, #7252 ....$125.00
Vase, Sophisticated Ladies, sand-carved black sphere, #7655SX, 10"...$225.00
Vase, Wisteria, Threaded Diamond Optic, 3-toed, #8455, 7"...$75.00

Wine bottle, New World, Cranberry opalescent, 1953, from $150.00 to $175.00. (Photo courtesy Margaret and Kenn Whitmyer)

Fiesta

You still can find Fiesta, but it's hard to get a bargain. Since it was discontinued in 1973, it has literally exploded onto the collectibles scene, and even at today's prices, new collectors continue to join the ranks of the veterans.

Fiesta is a line of solid-color dinnerware made by the Homer Laughlin China Company of Newell, West Virginia. It was introduced in 1936 and was immediately accepted by the American public. The line was varied. There were more than fifty items offered, and the color assortment included red (orange-red), cobalt, light green, and yellow. Within a short time, ivory and turquoise were added. (All these are referred to as 'original colors.')

As tastes changed during the production years, old colors were retired and new ones added. The colors collectors refer to as '50s colors are dark green, rose, chartreuse, and gray, and today these are very desirable. Medium green was introduced in 1959 at a time when some of the old standard shapes were being discontinued. Today, medium green pieces are the most expensive. Most pieces are marked.

Plates were ink stamped, and molded pieces usually had an indented mark.

In 1986 Homer Laughlin reintroduced Fiesta, but in colors different than the old line: white, black, cobalt, rose (bright pink), and apricot. Many of the pieces had been restyled, and the only problem collectors have had with the new colors is with the cobalt. But if you'll compare it with the old, you'll see that it is darker. Turquoise, periwinkle blue, yellow, and Seamist green were added next, and though the turquoise is close, it is a little greener than the original. Lilac and persimmon were later made for sale exclusively through Bloomingdale's department stores. Production was limited on lilac (not every item was made in it), and once it was discontinued, collectors were clamoring for it, often paying several times the original price. Sapphire blue, a color approximating the old cobalt, was introduced in 1996 — also a Bloomingdale's exclusive, and the selection was limited. Then came chartreuse (a little more vivid than the chartreuse of the '50s); gray was next, then Juniper (a rich teal); Cinnabar (maroon); Plum, and the last new color to be added, a strong yellow called Sunflower.

Items that have not been restyled are being made from the original molds. This means that you may find pieces with the old mark in the new colors (since the mark is an integral part of the mold). When an item has been restyled, new molds had to be created, and these will have the new mark. So will any piece marked with the ink stamp. The new ink mark is a script 'FIESTA' (all letters upper case), while the old is 'Fiesta.' Compare a few, the difference is obvious. Just don't be fooled into thinking you've found a rare cobalt juice pitcher or individual sugar and creamer set, they just weren't made in the old line. And if you find a piece with a letter H below the mark, you'll know that piece is new.

For further information, we recommend *The Collector's Encyclopedia of Fiesta, Ninth Edition,* by Sharon and Bob Huxford and *Post86 Fiesta* by Richard Racheter.

Newsletter: *Fiesta Collector's Quarterly*
China Specialties, Inc.
Box 471, Valley City, OH 44280. $12 (4 issues) per year

Club: Homer Laughlin Collectors Club (HLCC)
P.O. Box 16174
Loves Park, IL 61132-6174
Dues $20.00 per year, includes newsletter

Club: Homer Laughlin China Collector's Association (HLCCA)
P.O. Box 26021
Crystal City, VA 22215-6021
Dues $25.00 single, $40.00 couple; includes magazine

Ashtray, '50s colors...**$88.00**
Ashtray, red, cobalt or ivory.......................................**$60.00**
Ashtray, yellow, turquoise or light green.....................**$47.00**
Bowl, covered onion soup; cobalt or ivory...............**$725.00**
Bowl, covered onion soup; red...................................**$750.00**
Bowl, covered onion soup; turquoise, minimum value.**$7,500.00**

Bowl, covered onion soup; yellow or light green....**$650.00**
Bowl, cream soup; '50s colors.................................**$72.00**
Bowl, cream soup; med green, minimum value..**$4,2000.00**
Bowl, cream soup; red, cobalt or ivory.....................**$60.00**
Bowl, cream soup; yellow, turquoise or light green ..**$42.00**
Bowl, dessert; 6", '50s colors................................**$52.00**
Bowl, dessert; 6", med green................................**$500.00**
Bowl, dessert; 6", red, cobalt or ivory.....................**$52.00**
Bowl, dessert; 6", yellow, turquoise or light green.....**$38.00**
Bowl, footed salad; red, cobalt, ivory or turquoise..**$400.00**
Bowl, footed salad; yellow or light green...............**$340.00**
Bowl, fruit; 4¾", '50s colors..................................**$40.00**
Bowl, fruit; 4¾", med green.................................**$525.00**
Bowl, fruit; 4¾", red, cobalt or ivory......................**$35.00**
Bowl, fruit; 4¾", yellow, turquoise or light green......**$28.00**
Bowl, fruit; 5½", '50s colors..................................**$40.00**
Bowl, fruit; 5½", med green...................................**$75.00**
Bowl, fruit; 5½", red, cobalt or ivory......................**$35.00**
Bowl, fruit; 5½", yellow, turquoise or light green......**$28.00**
Bowl, fruit; 11¾", red, cobalt, ivory or turquoise.....**$340.00**
Bowl, fruit; 11¾", yellow or light green...................**$275.00**
Bowl, individual salad; med green, 7½"...................**$120.00**
Bowl, individual salad; red, turquoise or yellow, 7½"..**$85.00**
Bowl, nappy; 8½", '50s colors................................**$65.00**
Bowl, nappy; 8½", med green...............................**$140.00**
Bowl, nappy; 8½", red, cobalt, ivory or turquoise......**$55.00**
Bowl, nappy; 8½", yellow or light green...................**$40.00**
Bowl, nappy; 9½", red, cobalt, ivory or turquoise......**$65.00**
Bowl, nappy; 9½", yellow or light green...................**$52.00**
Bowl, Tom & Jerry; ivory w/gold letters..................**$260.00**
Bowl, unlisted salad; red, cobalt or ivory, minimum
 value..**$1,200.00**
Bowl, unlisted salad; yellow..................................**$105.00**
Candle holders, bulb; red, cobalt, ivory or turquoise, pr..**$130.00**
Candle holders, bulb; yellow or light green, pr..........**$95.00**
Candle holders, tripod; red, cobalt, ivory or turquoise,
 pr...**$650.00**
Candle holders, tripod; yellow or light green, pr.....**$485.00**
Carafe, red, cobalt, ivory, or turquoise...................**$340.00**
Carafe, yellow or light green.................................**$250.00**
Casserole, French; standard colors other than yellow, from
 $690 to...**$725.00**
Casserole, French; yellow....................................**$300.00**
Casserole, '50s colors...**$300.00**
Casserole, med green, minimum value...................**$900.00**
Casserole, red, cobalt, or ivory.............................**$225.00**
Casserole, yellow, turquoise, or light green.............**$165.00**
Coffeepot, demitasse; red, cobalt, ivory or turquoise..**$550.00**
Coffeepot, demitasse; yellow or light green.............**$425.00**
Coffeepot, '50s colors...**$350.00**
Coffeepot, red, cobalt or ivory..............................**$245.00**
Coffeepot, yellow, turquoise or light green.............**$195.00**
Compote, sweets; red, cobalt, ivory or turquoise.....**$100.00**
Compote, sweets; yellow or light green...................**$80.00**
Compote, 12", red, cobalt, ivory or turquoise..........**$200.00**
Compote, 12", yellow or light green.......................**$148.00**
Creamer, individual; red......................................**$365.00**

Creamer, individual; yellow $80.00
Creamer, regular; '50s colors $40.00
Creamer, regular; med green $90.00
Creamer, regular; red, cobalt or ivory $35.00
Creamer, regular; yellow, turquoise or light green $22.00
Creamer, stick-handled; red, cobalt, ivory or turquoise ..$70.00
Creamer, stick-handled; yellow or light green $45.00
Cup, demitasse; '50s colors $375.00
Cup, demitasse; red, cobalt or ivory $75.00
Cup, demitasse; yellow, turquoise or light green $65.00
Cup, see teacup
Egg cup, '50s colors $160.00
Egg cup, red, cobalt or ivory $70.00
Egg cup, yellow, turquoise or light green $58.00
Lid, for mixing bowl #1-#3, any color, minimum value ..$770.00
Lid, for mixing bowl #4, any color, minimum value .$1,000.00
Marmalade, red, cobalt, ivory or turquoise $325.00
Marmalade, yellow or light green $245.00
Mixing bowl #1, red, cobalt, ivory or turquoise $245.00
Mixing bowl #1, yellow or light green $180.00
Mixing bowl #2, red, cobalt, ivory, or turquoise $130.00
Mixing bowl #2, yellow or light green $115.00
Mixing bowl #3, red, cobalt, ivory, or turquoise $135.00
Mixing bowl #3, yellow or light green $125.00
Mixing bowl #4, red, cobalt, ivory or turquoise $160.00
Mixing bowl #4, yellow or light green $130.00
Mixing bowl #5, red, cobalt, ivory or turquoise $185.00
Mixing bowl #5, yellow or light green $155.00
Mixing bowl #6, red, cobalt, ivory or turquoise $265.00
Mixing bowl #6, yellow or light green $215.00
Mixing bowl #7, red, cobalt, ivory or turquoise $400.00
Mixing bowl #7, yellow or light green $350.00
Mug, Tom & Jerry; '50s colors $100.00
Mug, Tom & Jerry; ivory w/gold letters $65.00
Mug, Tom & Jerry; red, cobalt or ivory $80.00
Mug, Tom & Jerry; yellow, turquoise or light green ...$60.00
Mustard, red, cobalt, ivory, or turquoise $265.00
Mustard, yellow or light green $200.00
Pitcher, disk juice; gray, minimum value $3,000.00
Pitcher, disk juice; Harlequin yellow $60.00
Pitcher, disk juice; red $600.00
Pitcher, disk juice; yellow $45.00
Pitcher, disk water; '50s colors $275.00
Pitcher, disk water; med green, minimum value ...$1,200.00
Pitcher, disk water; red, cobalt or ivory $165.00
Pitcher, disk water; yellow, turquoise or light green ..$125.00
Pitcher, ice; red, cobalt, ivory or turquoise $160.00
Pitcher, ice; yellow or light green $140.00
Pitcher, jug, 2-pt; '50s colors $150.00
Pitcher, jug, 2-pt; red, cobalt or ivory $120.00
Pitcher, jug, 2-pt; yellow, turquoise or light green $85.00
Plate, cake; red, cobalt, ivory or turquoise, minimum value $1,000.00
Plate, cake; yellow or light green, minimum value ..$900.00
Plate, calendar; 1954 or 1955, 10" $45.00
Plate, calendar; 1955, 9" $50.00
Plate, chop; 13", '50s colors $100.00

Plate, chop; 13", med green $375.00
Plate, chop; 13", red, cobalt or ivory $55.00
Plate, chop; 13", yellow, turquoise or light green $40.00
Plate, chop; 15", '50s colors $145.00
Plate, chop; 15", red, cobalt or ivory $75.00
Plate, chop; 15", yellow, turquoise or light green $48.00
Plate, compartment; 10½", '50s colors $75.00
Plate, compartment; 10½", red, cobalt or ivory $45.00
Plate, compartment; 10½", yellow, turquoise or light green $40.00
Plate, compartment; 12", red, cobalt or ivory $60.00
Plate, compartment; 12", yellow or light green $50.00
Plate, deep; '50s colors $55.00
Plate, deep; med green $140.00
Plate, deep; red, cobalt or ivory $60.00
Plate, deep; yellow, turquoise or light green $35.00
Plate, 6", '50s colors $9.00
Plate, 6", med green $20.00
Plate, 6", red, cobalt, or ivory $7.00
Plate, 6", yellow, turquoise or light green $5.00
Plate, 7", '50s colors $13.00
Plate, 7", med green $32.00
Plate, 7", red, cobalt or ivory $10.00
Plate, 7", yellow, turquoise or light green $9.00
Plate, 9", '50s colors $22.00
Plate, 9", med green $45.00
Plate, 9", red, cobalt or ivory $18.00
Plate, 9", yellow, turquoise or light green $12.00
Plate, 10", '50s colors $52.00
Plate, 10", med green $135.00
Plate, 10", red, cobalt, or ivory $40.00
Plate, 10", yellow, turquoise or light green $32.00
Platter, '50s colors $58.00
Platter, med green $175.00
Platter, red, cobalt, or ivory $45.00
Platter, yellow, turquoise or light green $35.00
Relish tray, gold decor, complete, minimum value ...$250.00
Relish tray base, red, cobalt, ivory or turquoise $100.00
Relish tray base, yellow or light green $75.00
Relish tray center insert, red, cobalt, ivory or turquoise ..$60.00
Relish tray center insert, yellow or light green $50.00
Relish tray side insert, red, cobalt, ivory or turquoise ..$60.00
Relish tray side insert, yellow or light green $50.00
Salt & pepper shakers, '50s colors, pr $45.00
Salt & pepper shakers, med green, pr $185.00
Salt & pepper shakers, red, cobalt or ivory, pr $30.00
Salt & pepper shakers, yellow, turquoise or light green, pr $22.00
Sauce boat, '50s colors $78.00
Sauce boat, med green $180.00
Sauce boat, red, cobalt or ivory $85.00
Sauce boat, yellow, turquoise or light green $45.00
Saucer, demitasse; '50s colors $110.00
Saucer, demitasse; red, cobalt or ivory $22.00
Saucer, demitasse; yellow, turquoise or light green $18.00
Saucer, '50s colors $6.00
Saucer, med green $12.00

Saucer, original colors $4.00
Sugar bowl, individual; turquoise.........................$365.00
Sugar bowl, individual; yellow $120.00
Sugar bowl, w/lid, '50s colors, 3¼x3½" $72.00
Sugar bowl, w/lid, med green, 3¼x3½" $225.00
Sugar bowl, w/lid, red, cobalt or ivory, 3¼x3½".........$55.00
Sugar bowl, w/lid, yellow, turquoise or light green, 3¼x3½"...$45.00
Syrup, red, cobalt, ivory or turquoise $425.00

Syrup, yellow, turquoise, or light green, from $340.00 to $375.00.

Teacup, '50s colors $38.00
Teacup, med green...$58.00
Teacup, red, cobalt or ivory $35.00
Teacup, yellow, turquoise or light green.................$25.00
Teapot, lg; red, cobalt, ivory or turquoise...............$260.00
Teapot, lg; yellow or light green...........................$210.00
Teapot, med; '50s colors $325.00
Teapot, med; med green, minimum value $1,200.00
Teapot, med; red, cobalt or ivory $225.00
Teapot, med; yellow, turquoise or light green.........$160.00
Tray, figure-8; cobalt $100.00
Tray, figure-8; turquoise or yellow.......................$400.00
Tray, utility; red, cobalt, ivory or turquoise................$42.00
Tray, utility; yellow or light green..........................$38.00
Tumbler, juice; chartreuse or dark green $600.00
Tumbler, juice; red..$60.00
Tumbler, juice; rose $65.00
Tumbler, juice; yellow, turquoise or light green.........$40.00
Tumbler, water; red, cobalt, ivory or turquoise $85.00
Tumbler, water; yellow or light green $85.00
Vase, bud; red, cobalt, ivory or turquoise $125.00
Vase, bud; yellow or light green $80.00
Vase, 8", red, cobalt, turquoise or ivory, minimum value....$700.00
Vase, 8", yellow or light green, minimum value $600.00
Vase, 10", red, cobalt, ivory or turquoise.................$950.00
Vase, 10", yellow or light green............................$850.00
Vase, 12", red, cobalt, ivory or turquoise, minimum value..$1,300.00

Vase, 12", yellow or light green, mininum value...$1,100.00

Kitchen Kraft

Bowl, mixing; 6", light green or yellow.....................$72.00
Bowl, mixing; 6", red or cobalt $78.00
Bowl, mixing; 8", light green or yellow.....................$85.00
Bowl, mixing; 8", red or cobalt $95.00
Bowl, mixing; 10", light green or yellow.................$115.00
Bowl, mixing; 10", red or cobalt $125.00

Cake plate, Kitchen Kraft, light green or yellow, $55.00.

Cake plate, light green or yellow.............................$55.00
Cake plate, red or cobalt......................................$65.00
Cake server, light green or yellow $145.00
Cake server, red or cobalt...................................$155.00
Casserole, individual; light green or yellow $150.00
Casserole, individual; red or cobalt.......................$160.00
Casserole, 7½", light green or yellow $85.00
Casserole, 7½", red or cobalt...............................$90.00
Casserole, 8½", light green or yellow $105.00
Casserole, 8½", red or cobalt...............................$115.00
Covered jar, lg; light green or yellow $320.00
Covered jar, lg; red or cobalt...............................$325.00
Covered jar, med; light green or yellow $280.00
Covered jar, med; red or cobalt............................$295.00
Covered jar, sm; light green or yellow.....................$285.00
Covered jar, sm; red or cobalt $300.00
Covered jug, light green or yellow $280.00
Covered jug, red or cobalt..................................$290.00
Fork, light green or yellow $125.00
Fork, red or cobalt $135.00
Metal frame for platter..$26.00
Pie plate, Spruce green.......................................$305.00
Pie plate, 9", light green or yellow...........................$45.00
Pie plate, 9", red or cobalt...................................$48.00
Pie plate, 10", light green or yellow.........................$45.00
Pie plate, 10", red or cobalt.................................$48.00
Platter, light green or yellow $70.00
Platter, red or cobalt...$75.00

Platter, Spruce green	**$350.00**
Salt & pepper shakers, light green or yellow, pr	**$100.00**
Salt & pepper shakers, red or cobalt, pr	**$110.00**
Spoon, ivory, 12", minimum value	**$500.00**
Spoon, light green or yellow	**$135.00**
Spoon, red or cobalt	**$145.00**
Stacking refrigerator lid, ivory	**$225.00**
Stacking refrigerator lid, light green or yellow	**$75.00**
Stacking refrigerator lid, red or cobalt	**$85.00**
Stacking refrigerator unit, ivory	**$210.00**
Stacking refrigerator unit, light green or yellow	**$48.00**
Stacking refrigerator unit, red or cobalt	**$58.00**

Finch, Kay

Wonderful ceramic figurines signed by sculptor-artist-decorator Kay Finch are among the many that were produced in California during the middle of the last century. She modeled her line of animals and birds with much expression and favored soft color combinations often with vibrant pastel accents. Some of her models were quite large, but generally they range in size from 12" down to a tiny 2". She made several animal 'family groups' and some human subjects as well. After her death a few years ago, prices for her work began to climb.

She used a variety of marks and labels, and though most pieces are marked, some of the smaller animals are not; but you should be able to recognize her work with ease, once you've seen a few marked pieces.

For more information, we recommend *Kay Finch Ceramics, Her Enchanted World,* by Mike Nickel and Cindy Horvath (Schiffer); *Collectible Kay Finch* by Richard Martinez, Devin Frick, and Jean Frick; and *The Collector's Encyclopedia of California Pottery, Second Edition,* by Jack Chipman (both by Collector Books). Please note: Prices below are for items decorated in multiple colors, not solid glazes.

Advisors: Mike Nickel and Cindy Horvath (See Directory, Kay Finch)

Figurine, Dachshund puppy, #5320, 8", $750.00. (Photo courtesy Frances Finch Webb)

Ashtray, Bloodhound head, #4773, 6½x6½"	**$150.00**
Ashtray, swan, #4958, 4½"	**$70.00**
Bank, pig, Winkie, #185, 3¾x5"	**$150.00**
Candlesticks, turkey figural, #5794, 3¾", pr	**$225.00**
Cup, Missouri Mule, natural colors, 4¼"	**$125.00**
Figurine, Baby Ambrosia, cat, #5165, 5½"	**$200.00**
Figurine, bunny w/Jacket, #5005, 6"	**$175.00**
Figurine, Butch & Biddy, rooster & hen, #177 & #178, he: 8½", pr	**$150.00**
Figurine, camel, #464, 4½x5½"	**$450.00**
Figurine, choir boy, kneeling, #211, 5½"	**$60.00**
Figurine, dog, Dog Show Yorkshire, #4851, 2½x3"	**$500.00**
Figurine, elephant, Peanuts, #191, 8½"	**$350.00**
Figurine, Godey Man & Lady, #160, 7½", pr	**$125.00**
Figurine, guppy, fish, #173, 2½"	**$125.00**
Figurine, lamb, standing, #109, 5½"	**$95.00**
Figurine, long-eared donkey w/basket, #4769, 4"	**$125.00**

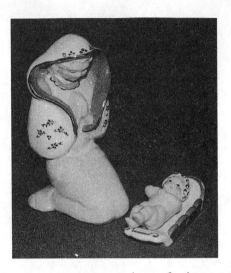

Figurine, Madonna, #4900, 6", $150.00; Infant in Cradle, #4990A, 4", $150.00.

Figurine, mama quail, #5984, 7"	**$425.00**
Figurine, parakeet on perch, #5164, 5¾"	**$225.00**
Figurine, rearing lamb, #109, 5½"	**$95.00**
Figurine, Scandie boy & girl, #126 & #127, 5¼", pr	**$150.00**
Figurine, Tootsie, owl, #189, 3¾"	**$35.00**
Figurine, Tubby, playful bear, #4847, 4¼"	**$225.00**
Shaker, kitchen; Puss, cat, #4616, 6"	**$400.00**
String holder, dog head, bow in hair, 4½x4"	**$400.00**
Toby jug, Santa Claus w/cap, scarce, #4950, 4"	**$150.00**
Wall plaque, sea horse, #5788, 16" L	**$225.00**

Fishbowl Ornaments

Prior to World War II, every dime store had its bowl of small goldfish. Nearby were stacks of goldfish bowls — small, medium, and large. Accompanying them were displays of ceramic ornaments for these bowls, many in the shape of Oriental pagodas or European-style castles. The fish died, the owners lost interest, and the glass containers along with their charming ornaments were either thrown out or relegated to the attic. In addition to pagodas and castles, other ornaments included bridges, lighthouses, colonnades, mermaids, and fish. Note that figurals such as mermaids are difficult to find.

Many fishbowl ornaments were produced in Japan between 1921 and 1941, and again after 1947. The older Japanese items often show clean, crisp mold designs with visible detail of the item's features. Others were made in Germany and some by potteries in the United States. Aquarium pieces made in America are not common. Those produced in recent years are usually of Chinese origin and are more crude, less colorful, and less detailed in appearance. In general, the more detail and more colorful, the older the piece. A few more examples are shown in *Collector's Guide to Made in Japan Ceramics* by Carole Bess White (Collector Books).

Advisor: Carole Bess White (See Directory, Japan Ceramics)

Bathing beauty in green suit on yellow lustre shell, red Japan mark, 2¼", from $50 to **$85.00**
Bathing beauty in shiny green suit on orange coral, black Japan mark, 4", from $35 to................................**$45.00**
Bathing beauty on shell, cinnamon & white lustre, red Japan mark, 3", from $40 to **$60.00**
Boy on dolphin, multicolored, black Japan mark, 3¾", from $25 to...**$40.00**
Castle, multicolored, black Japan mark, 2¼", from $18 to **$25.00**
Castle, multicolored (worn paint), black Japan mark, 3", from $3 to...**$5.00**
Castle, multicolored shiny, no mark, 4½", from $20 to .**$32.00**

Castle, tan and red with green and white rocks, red Japan mark, 5¼", from $20.00 to $32.00; Castle, multicolored, Japan mark, 3¾", from $22.00 to $30.00. (Photo courtesy Carole Bess White)

Castle, tan lustre w/green & white rocks, red Japan mark, 5¼", from $20 to..**$28.00**
Coral, shiny orange w/shadow of black sea diver, red Japan mark, 3½", from $18 to **$28.00**
Diver, orange, black mark, 3¼", from $15 to **$25.00**
Diver, white, black Japan mark, 4¾", from $15 to......**$25.00**
Fish, multicolored, black Japan mark, 2½", from $15 to..**$25.00**

Fish pair on waves, multicolored matt and shiny glazes, black Japan mark, 3¼", from $15.00 to $25.00. (Photo courtesy Carole Bess White)

Mermaid, painted bisque, black Japan mark, 4¾", from $45 to **$65.00**
Mermaid on conch shell, multicolored, black Japan mark, 3½", from $35 to...**$50.00**
Mermaid on snail, multicolored, red Japan mark, 4", from $45 to **$65.00**
Nude lady on starfish, painted bisque, black Japan mark, 4½", from $75 to...**$125.00**
Pagoda, multicolored, black Japan mark, 3½", from $18 to **$28.00**
Torii gate, multicolored, black Japan mark, 3¾", from $18 to **$30.00**

Fisher-Price

Probably no other toy manufacture is as well known among kids of today as Fisher-Price. Since the 1930s they've produced wonderful toys made of wood covered with vividly lithographed paper. Plastic parts weren't used until 1949, and this can sometimes help you date your finds. These toys were made for play, so very few older examples have survived in condition good enough to attract collectors. Watch for missing parts and avoid those that are dirty. Edge wear and some paint dulling is normal and to be expected. Our values are for toys with minimum signs of such wear. Mint condition examples will bring considerably higher prices, of course, and if the original box is present, add from 20% to 40% more.

For more information we recommend *Fisher-Price Toys*, by Brad Cassity; *Modern Toys, American Toys, 1930 – 1980*, by Linda Baker; *Fisher-Price, A Historical, Rarity Value Guide*, by John J. Murray and Bruce R. Fox (Books Americana); and *Schroeder's Collectible Toys, Antique to Modern*, published by Collector Books.

Advisor: Brad Cassity (See Directory, Toys)

Club: Fisher-Price Collector's Club
Jeanne Kennedy
1442 N Ogden, Mesa, AZ 85205; Monthly newsletter with information and ads; send SASE for more information

Museum: Toy Town Museum
636 Girard Ave., PO Box 238, East Aurora, NY 14052;
Monday through Saturday, 10 – 4.

Adventure People Alpha Probe, #325, 1980-84	**$25.00**
Adventure People Dune Buster, #322, 1979-82	**$15.00**
Adventure People White Water Kayak, 1977-80	**$15.00**
Basic Hardboard Puzzle, Weather, #563, 1975	**$10.00**
Bizzy Bunny Cart, #306, 1957-59	**$40.00**
Bouncing Buggy, #122, 1974-79, 6 wheels	**$5.00**
Bouncy Racer, #8, 1960-62	**$40.00**
Bucky Burro, #166, 1955-57	**$250.00**

Bulldozer, #311, 1976 – 77, 5½", EX+ $25.00; MIB, from $45.00 to $55.00. (Photo courtesy Brad Cassity)

Car & Camper, #686, 1968-70	**$65.00**
Chick Basket Cart, #304, 1960-64	**$40.00**
Chubby Cub, #164, 1969-72	**$20.00**
Cowboy Chime, #700, 1951-53	**$250.00**
Cry Baby Bear, #711, 1967-69	**$30.00**
Cuddly Cub, #719, 1971-77	**$5.00**
Ding-Dong Ducky, #724, 1949-50	**$225.00**
Dinky Engine, #642, 1959	**$60.00**
Dr Dolittle, #477, 1940-41	**$225.00**
Drummer Boy, #634, 1967-69	**$50.00**
Ferry Boat, #932, 1979-80	**$45.00**
Happy Hopper, #121, 1969-76	**$20.00**
Hot Dog Wagon, #445, 1940-41	**$250.00**
Husky Bulldozer, #311, 1978-79	**$20.00**
Husky Cement Mixer, #315, 1978-82	**$30.00**
Husky Farm Set, #331, 1981-83	**$25.00**
Jack-in-the-Box Puppet, #138, 1970-73	**$30.00**
Jiffy Dump Truck, #156, 1971-73	**$25.00**
Jumping Jack Scarecrow, #423, 1979	**$10.00**
Kiltie Dog, #450, 1936	**$400.00**
Lift & Load Railroad, #943, 1978-79	**$50.00**
Looky Chug-Chug, #189, 1958-60	**$85.00**
Magnetic Chug-Chug, #168, 1964-69	**$50.00**
Mini Snowmobile, #705, 1971-73	**$45.00**
Musical Elephant, #145, 1948-50	**$225.00**
Nifty Station Wagon, #234, 1960-62 & Easter 1963	**$250.00**

Oscar the Grouch, #177, 1877-84	**$20.00**
Play Family A-Frame, #990, 1974-76	**$60.00**
Play Family Animal Circus, #135, 1974-76	**$60.00**
Play Family Farm Barnyard, #117, 1972-74	**$25.00**
Play Family School, #923, 1971-78, 1st version	**$25.00**
Play Family Sesame Street Clubhouse, #937, 1977-79	**$70.00**
Pluto Pop-Up, #440, 1936	**$100.00**
Pop-Up-Pal Chime Phone, #150, 1968-78	**$40.00**
Prancy Pony, #617, 1965-70	**$30.00**
Puppy Playhouse, #110, 1978-80	**$10.00**
Push Bunny Cart, #401, 1942	**$225.00**
Push-Along Clown, #758, 1980-81	**$20.00**
Pushy Pig, #500, 1932-35	**$500.00**
Puzzle Puppy, #659, 1976-81	**$10.00**
Rabbit Cart, #52, 1950	**$75.00**
Roller Chime, #123, 1953-60 & Easter 1961	**$50.00**
Roly Raccoon, #172, 1980-82	**$10.00**
Rooster Cart, #469, 1938-40	**$400.00**
Running Bunny Cart, #495, 1941	**$225.00**
Scoop Loader, #300, 1975-77	**$25.00**
Space Blazer, #750, 1953-54	**$400.00**
Suzie Seal, #694, 1979-80	**$15.00**
Teddy Zilo, #741, 1967	**$45.00**
Tuggy Tooter, #139, 1967-73	**$40.00**
Uncle Timmy Turtle, #125, 1956-58, red shell	**$100.00**
Woodsey's Airport, #962, 1980-81	**$20.00**
Woodsey's Store, #961, 1980-81	**$35.00**

Fishing Lures

There have been literally thousands of lures made since the turn of the century. Some have bordered on the ridiculous, and some have turned out to be just as good as the manufacturers claimed. In lieu of buying outright from a dealer, try some of the older stores in your area — you just might turn up a good old lure. Go through any old tackle boxes that might be around, and when the water level is low, check out the river banks.

If you have to limit your collection, you might want to concentrate just on wooden lures, or you might decide to try to locate one of every lure made by a particular company. Whatever you decide, try to find examples with good original paint and hardware. Though many lures are still very reasonable, we have included some of the more expensive examples as well to give you an indication of the type you'll want to fully research if you think you've found a similar model. For such information, we recommend *Fishing Lure Collectibles, Second Edition,* by Dudley Murphy and Rick Edmisten; *The Fishing Lure Collector's Bible,* by R.L. Streater with Rick Edmisten and Dudley Murphy; *19th Century Fishing Lures* by Arlan Carter; *Collector's Guide to Creek Chub Lures & Collectibles* by Harold E Smith, M.D; and *Commercial Fish Decoys* by Frank R. Baron. All are published by Collector Books.

Advisor: Dave Hoover (See Directory, Fishing Lures)

Club: NFLCC Tackle Collectors
HC 3, Box 4012
Reeds Spring, MO 65737; Send SASE for more information about membership and their publications: *The National Fishing Lure Collector's Club Magazine* and *The NFLCC Gazette*

CA Clark Bait Co, Duckling #500, 2 trebles, ca 1946, 1⅞", from $40 to..**$60.00**

CA Clark Bait Co, Water Scout #300, no indentation (no-eye version), lg line tie, 2 trebles, ca 1930, 2¼", $75 to.....**$100.00**

Creek Chub, Baby Crawdad #402, albino coloring, 2 trebles, 2¼", from $20 to..**$30.00**

Creek Chub, Baby Jigger, 2 trebles, ca 1935, 3¼", from $100 to..**$150.00**

Creek Chub, Baby Pikie #30, orange w/black spots, 2 trebles, 1952-78, from $100 to **$150.00**

Creek Chub, Cray-Z-Fish #9924, yellow 'shrimp' color, from $15 to...**$20.00**

Creek Chub, Deluxe Wagtail Chub #806, painted to resemble goldfish, 2¾", from $125 to................**$150.00**

Creek Chub, Ding Bat #5100, 2 trebles, yellow w/red spots, ca 1937, 2", from $30 to..............................**$50.00**

Creek Chub, Dive Bomber, yellow w/3 red dots & red dash (Victory finish), 2 trebles, ca 1942, 2⅞", from $40 to.**$50.00**

Creek Chub, Fintail Shiner #2103, silver shiner paint on wood, metal tail, 4", from $300 to.......................**$400.00**

Creek Chub, Flat Injured Minnow #1505, red side chub paint on wood, 3¾", from $100 to **$150.00**

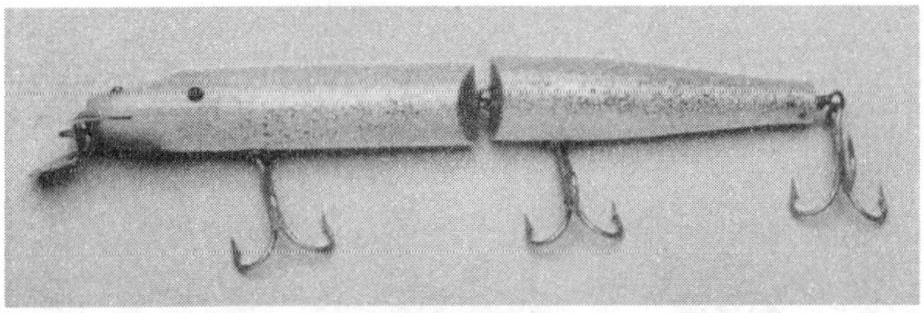

Creek Chub, Giant Jointed Pikie Minnow #800, 1957, glass eyes, 14" long, from $40.00 to $60.00. (Photo courtesy Dudley Murphy and Rick Edmisten)

Creek Chub, Husky Musky #630, orange spotted, 2 trebles, 5", from $200 to..**$250.00**

Creek Chub, Husky Pikie #3040 P, chrome, jointed body, 3 trebles, from $30 to **$50.00**

Creek Chub, Husky Plunker #5804, golden shiner paint on wood, 4¼", from $80 to......................................**$120.00**

Creek Chub, Injured Minnow #1524, Redwing Blackbird paint, propellers, 3 trebles, from $200 to **$300.00**

Creek Chub, Jointed Husky Pikie #3018, Silver Flash paint on wood, 6", from $30 to **$35.00**

Creek Chub, Jointed Piker #2603, New Silver Shiner paint, black back, from $25 to **$35.00**

Creek Chub, Mouse #6380, gray, 2 trebles, from $25 to..**$35.00**

Creek Chub, No-Eyed Wiggler #102, red & white painted wood, from $75 to...**$100.00**

Creek Chub, Skipper #4602, red head & white body, 2 trebles, 3", from $15 to...**$20.00**

Creek Chub, Snook Plunker #7134, blue flash paint on wood, 5", from $80 to...**$100.00**

Creek Chub, Snook Plunker #7135, painted as purple eel, from $150 to...**$200.00**

Creek Chub, Striper Strike #1916, Banana yellow, 2 trebles (1 hair covered), from $15 to.............................**$20.00**

Creek Chub, Wicked Wiggler #S1, feathered rear hook, 2 trebles, ca 1926, 2¾", from $50 to..............................**$65.00**

Creek Chub Darter #8038S, pearl paint, rear propeller, 2 trebles, ca 1955, from $35 to............................**$50.00**

Haas, Embossed Musky Liv-Minno, molded plastic & wood, thin plastic tail, 2 trebles, ca 1937, 6", from $150 to...**$200.00**

Haas, Single Hook Haas' Liv-Minno, tack & washer eyes, L-rig style line ties under chin, 1 treble, ca 1935, 4", from $150 to...**$200.00**

Heddon, DeLuxe Basser #8520, 2 heavy-duty trebles, clip hardware w/heavy-duty wire hanger, ca 1936, 4½", from $50 to..**$65.00**

Heddon, Great-Vamp #7540, pin near tail to hold hook mount in body, 3 trebles, ca 1937, 5", from $125 to **$150.00**

Heddon, King Zig-Wag #8350, 2 trebles, ca 1939, 5", from $50 to..**$75.00**

Heddon, Musky Surfusser #300, wire-through line tie & tail hanger, 6 trebles, ca 1939, 3¾", from $250 to..**$300.00**

Heddon, Punkinseed #740, line tie under chin (in mouth later), 2 trebles, ca 1940, 2½", from $50 to **$75.00**

Jamison, Musky Wig-Wag, red w/white body, 2 trebles, ca 1934, 6", from $100 to..**$125.00**

Jamison, Smacker, red head, white body, 1 dressed single hook, ca 1934, 6", from $10 to **$25.00**

Keeling, Moonlight Aristrocrat Torpedo, propellers, 3 trebles, ca 1930, 4", from $40 to..**$75.00**

Kellman, Flat Plug, yellow w/red dots, 1 treble & 1 single hook, ca 1930, 2⅜", from $50 to..........................**$75.00**

Kellman, Grasshopper, detailed carving (realistic), single hook, ca 1930, 1", from $125 to..........................**$150.00**

Paw Paw, Croaker Frog, real frogskin cover, 2 trebles, ca 1940, 3", from $50 to..**$60.00**

Paw Paw, Natural Hair Mouse, painted features, deer-hair body, 1 treble, ca 1930, 2½", from $75 to..........**$100.00**

Paw Paw, Pike Minnow, red w/white body, 3 trebles, ca 1935, 4½", from $15 to..**$30.00**

Paw Paw, River Chub, lg lip & body, River Runt type, 2 trebles, ca 1940, 2½", from $15 to............................**$30.00**

Pflueger, Baby Scoop #9300, glass eyes, 3-bladed propellers, 2 trebles, short wire leader, ca 1935, 3", from $40 to **$65.00**

Shakespeare, Jack Smith Lure, ball tail-hook hanger, belly fin, silver sparkle paint, 2 trebles, ca 1935, 3¾", from $50 to..**$75.00**

Shakespeare, Jim Dandy Floating Minnow, glass-eyed floater w/floppy propellers, 3 trebles, ca 1930, 3⅞", from $50 to **$75.00**

Shakespeare, Little Joe #6530, marked lip, glass eyes, scissors type tail-hook hanger, 1 treble, ca 1931, 2", from $45 to **$75.00**

Shakespeare, Slim Jim #43, typical scale finish, flat plate hook hardware, 3 trebles, ca 1930, 3¾", from $50 to ...**$75.00**

Shakespeare, Swimming Mouse Jr #6580, yellow & brown, 2 trebles, ca 1930, 2¾", from $30 to.........................**$45.00**

South Bend, Midg-Oreno #968, 2 belly mounted hooks, no tail hook, various types of eyes, ca 1933, 2¼", from $10 to..**$20.00**

South Bend, Plunk-Oreno #929, concave mouth, painted tack eyes, 1 single hook, ca 1939, 2", from $20 to **$40.00**

South Bend, Tarp-Oreno #979, painted tack eyes, 2 single hooks, ca 1938, 8", from $50 to............................**$75.00**

South Bend, Truck-Oreno #936, Whirl-Oreno & Surf-Oreno combination, 2 trebles, ca 1938, 9", from $300 to..**$400.00**

Strike Master, Night Hawk, spotted finish, lg plinking face, 2 trebles, ca 1928, 3¼", from $45 to.........................**$75.00**

Strike Master, Surface Teaser, thin front propeller, cup hook rigging, glass eyes, 2 trebles, ca 1928, 2⅞", from $45 to **$75.00**

Fitz & Floyd

If you've ever visited a Fitz & Floyd outlet store, you know why collectors find this company's products so exciting. Steven Speilberg has nothing on their designers when it comes to imagination. Much of their production is related to holidays, and they've especially outdone themselves with their Christmas lines. But there are wonderful themes taken from nature featuring foxes, deer, birds, or rabbits, and others that are outrageously and deliberately humorous. Not only is the concept outstanding, so is the quality.

See also Cookie Jars.

Bowl, serving; green w/multicolored parrot perched on side, oblong, 1986, 10x4"..**$110.00**

Candle holder, winged female creature, 1977, 10", $65.00. (Photo courtesy Lee Garmon)

Candle holders, witch standing in front of pumpkin, hole in pumpkin for candle, 1988, 6¼", pr....................**$105.00**

Candy jar, Hydrangea bear, multicolored, 1993, 8½"..**$155.00**

Candy jar, jack-o'-lantern w/ghost & black cat at sides, 1987, from $60 to..**$70.00**

Canister set, Woodland Spring, lg: 10" fox; med: 9½" rabbit; sm: 9" chipmunk, rubber-sealed lids...................**$120.00**

Clock, White Rabbit (Alice in Wonderland) stands among flowers holding lg pocketwatch, 1992...............**$175.00**

Covered jar, mother bunny pushing baby bunnies in cart, white w/pink highlights on ears, 1979, 4x7½x4".**$90.00**

Creamer & sugar bowl, bunnies, Cottontailors line, multicolored...**$105.00**

Figurine, cat, white w/tabby markings, 8"................**$110.00**

Figurine, owl on branch w/autumn leaves & acorns, 15" on 8x8" base..**$105.00**

Figurine, parrot, head down & wing up, multicolored, 1986, 12¼"...**$170.00**

Figurine, parrot, head up & wings down, multicolored, 1986, 10"..**$160.00**

Figurine, rooster standing among vegetables, multicolored, 16"...**$175.00**

Mirror, Alice in Wonderland, Storybook Collection, 1992...**$135.00**

Pitcher, black w/green leaves w/parrot on side, wings form handle, 8", MIB...**$110.00**

Pitcher, snowman figural, 1¾-qt, from $60 to............**$80.00**

Platter, serving; Hoedown Witch, multicolored, 1992, 12½x13½"..**$100.00**

Salad bowl, pumpkin shape, multicolored, w/lid, 8" H.**$130.00**

Salt & pepper shakers, Herschel Hippo, pr, from $20 to..**$25.00**

Salt & pepper shakers, parrots, multicolored, 1992, pr ..**$110.00**

Salt and pepper shakers, serving cats, from $22.00 to $25.00 for the pair.

Salt & pepper shakers, witch & cauldron, 1992, pr, from $20 to...**$25.00**

String holder, kangaroo, string in belly, baby kangaroo finial w/hole for string, 1978, 6" **$165.00**

Teapot, Abraham Lincoln, Figures From History Collection, gold eagle spout, 1995, 8¾" **$100.00**

Teapot, alligator w/fish in mouth, 1987, 32-oz, 9"....**$260.00**

Teapot, cauliflower shape, white & green, 1989, 4-oz, 7", NM..**$105.00**

Teapot, Cinderella & her coach, Storybook Collection, multicolored, 1995, 8x10", MIB...............................**$145.00**

Teapot, St Basil's Cathedral (Moscow), Famous Landmarks Around the World Collection, 1994, 11x9x5"......**$140.00**

Tureen, goose, Autumn Splendor Collection, 12x17", MIB .**$150.00**

Tureen, pheasant, multicolored, w/ladle (tail) & platter, 1990 ....**$165.00**

Tureen, pig shape, 15" L, w/13½x18" underplate & 10" ladle **$285.00**

Vase, white w/purple iris & green leaves in high relief, 14¼"..**$110.00**

Florence Ceramics

During the '40s, Florence Ward began modeling tiny ceramic children as a hobby at her home in Pasadena, California. She was so happy with the results that she expanded, hired decorators, and moved into a larger building where for two decades she produced the lovely line of figurines, wall plaques, busts, etc., that have become so popular today. The 'Florence Collection' featured authentically detailed models of such couples as Louis XV and Madame Pompadour, Pinkie and Blue Boy, and Rhett and Scarlett. Nearly all of the Florence figures have names which are written on their bases.

Many figures are decorated with 22k gold and lace. Real lace was cut to fit, dipped in a liquid material called slip, and fired. During the firing it burned away, leaving only hardened ceramic lace trim. The amount of lace work that was used is one of the factors that needs to be considered when evaluating a 'Florence.' Size is another. Though most of the figures you'll find today are singles, a few were made as groups, and once in awhile you'll find a lady seated on a divan. The more complex, the more expensive.

There are Florence figurines that are very rare and unusual, i.e., Mark Anthony, Cleopatra, Story Hour, Grandmother and I, Carmen, Dear Ruth, Spring and Fall Reverie, Clocks, and many others. These may be found with a high price; however, there are bargains still to be had.

Our wide range of values reflects the amounts of detailing and lace work present. If you'd like to learn more about the subject, we recommend *The Complete Book of Florence, A Labor of Love,* by Barbara and Jerry Kline, our advisors for this category, and Margaret Wehrspaun. (Ordering information many be found in the Directory.) Other references include *The Collector's Encyclopedia of California Pottery, Second Edition,* by Jack Chipman, and *The Florence Collectibles, An Era of Elegance,* by Doug Foland.

Advisors: Jerry and Barbara Kline (See Directory, Florence Ceramics)

Club: Florence Ceramics Collectors Club (FCCS)
Jerry Kline
PO Box 937
Kodak, TN 37764
865-933-9060 or fax: 865-933-4492

Adeline, fancy, 8¼" **$350.00**
Angel, 7¾"..**$140.00**
Ann, yellow, 6" **$150.00**

Barbara, child, 8½", from $200 to **$250.00**
Bea, 7¼" **$150.00**
Beth, 7½" **$125.00**
Blossom Girl, flower holder **$125.00**
Boy (bust), traditional, 12" **$200.00**
Charles, 8¾" **$325.00**
Charmaine, hands away, 8½" **$300.00**
Cindy, fancy, 8" **$325.00**
Claudia, 8¼" **$175.00**
Delia, hand showing, from $150 to........................**$200.00**
Denise, 10" **$500.00**
Diane, from $175 to **$200.00**

Dot and Bud, $700.00 each. (Photo courtesy Doug Foland)

Ellen, 7" **$125.00**
Ethel, plain, 7¼" **$125.00**
Gary, 8½" **$200.00**
Grace, plain, 7¾" **$150.00**
Halloween Child, 4" **$250.00**
Her Majesty, 7" **$200.00**
Jim, 6¾" **$80.00**
Josephine, 9" **$250.00**
Kay, flower holder, 7" **$60.00**
Lantern Boy, flower holder, 8¼" **$100.00**
Lillian, 7¼" **$150.00**

**Louis XV and Madame Pompadour, 12",
$800.00 for the pair.** (Photo courtesy Doug Foland)

Louis XVI, 10" $300.00
Madeline, from $200 to $300.00
Madonna, 10½" $150.00
Marsie, 8" $275.00
Matilda, 8½" $175.00
Mimi, flower holder, 6" $40.00

Musette, 8¾", $650.00.

Peg, flower holder, 7" $90.00
Rhett...$395.00
Sally, flower holder, 6¾" $40.00
Sarah, 7½" $130.00
Sue, 6" $75.00
Sue Ellen, 8¼" $175.00
Violet, wall pocket, w/gold, 7", from $200 to $250.00
Vivian, 10" $395.00
Winkin & Blinkin, ea 5½", pr $500.00

Flower Frogs

Flower frogs reached their peak of popularity in the United States in the 1920s and 1930s. During that time nearly every pottery and glass house in the Unted States produced some type of flower frog. At the same time numbers of ceramic flower frogs were being imported from Germany and Japan. Dining tables and sideboards were adorned with flowers sparingly placed around dancing ladies, birds, and aquatic animals in shallow bowls.

In the 1930s garden clubs began holding competitions in cut flower arranging. The pottery and glass flower frogs proved inadequate for the task and a new wave of metal flower frogs entered the market. Some were simple mesh, hairpin, and needle holders; but many were fanciful creations of loops, spirals, and crimped wires.

German and Japanese imports ceased during World War II, and only a very few American pottery and glass companies continued to produce flower frogs into the 1940s and 1950s. Metal flower frog production followed a similar decline; particularly after the water soluble florist foam,

Oasis, was invented in 1954. For further information we recommend *Flower Frogs for Collectors* (Schiffer) by our advisor, Bonnie Bull.

Advisor: Bonnie Bull (See Directory, Flower Frogs)

Ballerina, ceramic, pastels w/gold, 8 holes in base, US Zone Germany, 8½" $80.00
Bird on stump w/multiple openings, ceramic multicolored lustre, black Japan mark, 4½" or 5½", ea from $25 to...................................$45.00
Bird on white base, majolica-style, multicolor, ceramic, Japan mark, 6½", from $40 to $50.00
Birds (2) on base w/red berries, ceramic, multicolored lustre, black Japan mark, 5¾", from $30 to $45.00
Bleeding Heart pattern, pottery, Roseville, 1940s, 3½x5" ..$175.00
Crab, Muskota, Weller, pottery, naturalistic matt colors, 1920s, 2¼x5x4"..$265.00
Deer, white matt, pottery, Red Wing, 10½" $40.00
Dome shaped holder w/holes in dome & base, stamped sheet metal, green, G, 2"x4".................$23.00
Draped Lady, crystal frost, Cambridge Glass, 13¼" ..$175.00
Draped Lady, green frost, Cambridge Glass, 8½" $125.00
Duck, crystal, Heisey..$140.00
Ducks on base w/multiple openings, ceramic white w/orange lustre, black Japan mark, 5", from $25 to $40.00
Fish, pottery, marked Howard Pierce, 6"L................$155.00
Flower bud on blue lustre base w/multiple openings, ceramic, Japan mark, 2½", from $18 to $28.00
Frog, pottery, Royal Haeger, R-838, 4½" $55.00
Hairpin holder on round lead base, marked Blue Ribbon Flower Holder Co, Cuyahoga Falls, Ohio, green, VG, 2¼" $16.00
Interconnecting circles, 3, w/pins, metal, green, unused, marked Nagatani & Chicago, NM, 3½x3" $18.00
Lady in skimpy dress w/flowing skirt, glossy white ceramic, #8577, 6" $80.00
Lotus flower form, multicolor, ceramic, black Japan mark, 4½" dia, from $15 to.................................$20.00
Mermaid leaning beside water lily w/7 holes, ceramic lustreware, red Japan mark, 3¼" $120.00
Multi-loop holder, cast iron base w/holes & 8 sm feet, marked JPO, G, 4½" $29.00
Nude, draped Deco-style lady w/butterfly wings, white ceramic, 8 holes in base, unmarked, NM $150.00
Nude & flamingo, porcelain, Coronet, Registered Germany, 8¾"..$165.00
Nude on turtle, pastels, ceramic, Germany H-288, 7x4¾x5", NM $155.00
Nude posed before flower garland, ceramic, pastels, marked Germany, #10093 & #10098, ca 1930, 9¼" $125.00
Nude w/billowing drape, white ceramic, Deco style, holes in base, marked Registered Germany, 1930s, 11½"..$130.00
Nude w/drape flowing above head & over torso, white porcelain, Germany #4589, 8"...............................$90.00
Nude w/flower stands on base w/22 holes, porcelain, Germany, #8716, 7½x6" $150.00

Optic Swirl, amber glass bowl & frog w/clear 'vase' insert, Fostoria, 3x13½x11½", 3-pc set...........................**$110.00**

Pavlova, ceramic, Original Ivory, Cowan, #698, 6¼" **$150.00**

Pelican, majolica-style glaze, Japan mark, 6½", from $40.00 to $50.00; Bird, multicolored matt glazes, Japan mark, 6", from $25.00 to $35.00. (Photo courtesy Carole Bess White)

Pheasant, realistic paint (some wear), ceramic, Rosemeade, 4x5"...**$80.00**

Ruby glass, round, w/8 holes, Fenton, sm **$80.00**

Spring coils (7) on lead base, green, marked Spiro Flower & Candle Holder National Tinsel Mfg, VG, 3"..........**$30.00**

Swans encircle bowl, 2 swans on base form flower frog, ceramic multicolor lustre, black Japan mark, 5" frog, 7" dia bowl..**$75.00**

Turtle, amethyst glass, Fenton, 4" L............................**$85.00**

Two-tiered, metal, w/4 ball feet on bottom, stamped JB 247, Pat Applied For, F, 4x1¾" **$26.00**

Water lily pin holder, green metal, Beagle Mfg, marked Pat Pend, G, 1½"...**$26.00**

Fostoria

This was one of the major glassware producers of the twentieth century. They were located first in Fostoria, Ohio, but by the 1890s had moved to Moundsville, West Virginia. By the late '30s, they were recognized as the largest producers of handmade glass in the world. Their glassware is plentiful today and, considering its quality, not terribly expensive.

Though the company went out of business in the mid-'80s, the Lancaster Colony Company continues to use some of the old molds — herein is the problem. The ever-popular American and Coin Glass patterns are currently in production, and even experts have trouble distinguishing the old from the new. Before you invest in either line, talk to dealers. Ask them to show you some of their old pieces. Most will be happy to help out a novice collector. Read *Elegant Glassware of the Depression Era* by Gene Florence; *Fostoria Glassware, 1887 – 1982*, by Frances Bones; *Fostoria, An Identification and Value Guide, Volume II*, by Ann Kerr; and *Fostoria Stemware, The Crystal for America Series*, by Milbra Long and Emily Seate.

You'll be seeing a lot of inferior 'American' at flea markets and (sadly) antique malls. It's often priced as though it is American, but in fact it is not. It's been produced since the 1950s by Indiana Glass who calls it 'Whitehall.' Watch for pitchers with only two mold lines, they're everywhere. (Fostoria's had three.) Remember that Fostoria was hand-made, so their pieces were fire polished. This means that if the piece you're examining has sharp, noticeable mold lines, be leery. There are other differences to watch for as well. Fostoria's footed pieces were designed with a 'toe,' while Whitehall feet have a squared peg-like appearance. The rays are sharper and narrower on the genuine Fostoria pieces, and the glass itself has more sparkle and life. And if it weren't complicated enough, the Home Interior Company sells 'American'-like vases, covered bowls, and a footed candy dish that were produced in a foreign country, but at least they've marked theirs.

Coin Glass was originally produced in crystal, red, blue, emerald green, olive green, and amber. It's being reproduced today in crystal, green (darker than the original), blue (a lighter hue), and red. Though the green and blue are 'off' enough to be pretty obvious, the red is very close. Beware. Here are some (probably not all) of the items currently in production: bowl, 8" diameter; bowl, 9" oval; candlesticks, 4½"; candy jar with lid, 6¼"; creamer and sugar bowl; footed comport; wedding bowl, 8¼". Know your dealer!

Numbers included in our descriptions were company-assigned stock numbers that collectors use as a means to distinguish variations in stems and shapes.

Advisor: Debbie Maggard (See Directory, Elegant Glassware)

Newsletter/Club: *Facets of Fostoria*
Fostoria Glass Society of America
P.O. Box 826, Moundsville, WV 26041; Membership: $12.50 per year

American, crystal, bell..**$425.00**
American, crystal, bowl, boat; 12".............................**$17.50**
American, crystal, bowl, fruit; flared, 4¾" **$15.00**
American, crystal, bowl, jelly; 4¼x4¼"......................**$15.00**
American, crystal, bowl, nappy; 6"............................**$15.00**
American, crystal, bowl, nappy; 8".............................**$25.00**
American, crystal, butter dish, w/lid, ¼-lb **$25.00**
American, crystal, candlestick, round foot, 6¼"........**$195.00**
American, crystal, cup, punch; flared rim..................**$11.00**
American, crystal, goblet, #2056, low foot, 9-oz, 4⅜"...**$11.00**
American, crystal, hat, 3"...**$27.50**
American, crystal, mayonnaise, divided.......................**$17.50**
American, crystal, plate, bread & butter; 6".................**$12.00**
American, crystal, ring holder....................................**$200.00**
American, crystal, salt & pepper shakers, 3", pr **$20.00**
American, crystal, toothpick holder.............................**$25.00**
American, crystal, tray, 4-part, 10" sq........................**$85.00**

American, crystal, tumbler, juice; #2056, footed, 5-oz, 4¾" **$13.00**

American, crystal, tumbler, water; #2056, footed, 9-oz, 4⅞" **$15.00**

American, crystal, urn, pedestal foot, 6" sq **$30.00**

American, crystal, vase, flared, 8" **$80.00**

American, crystal, vase, flared, 10" **$90.00**

Baroque, blue, bowl, 2-part, 6½" **$35.00**

Baroque, blue, plate, 9½" **$65.00**

Baroque, blue, vase, 6½", $145.00; vase, 7", $165.00. (Photo courtesy Gene Florence)

Baroque, crystal, bowl, punch; footed.....................**$400.00**

Baroque, crystal, cup...**$10.00**

Baroque, crystal, tumbler, water; 9-oz, 4¼"................**$25.00**

Baroque, yellow, bowl, flared, 12"...............................**$32.50**

Baroque, yellow, tray, oval, 11" **$37.50**

Buttercup, crystal, bowl, salad; #2364, 10½" **$55.00**

Buttercup, crystal, candlestick, #2324, 4" **$17.50**

Buttercup, crystal, plate, #2337, 6" **$7.00**

Buttercup, crystal, plate, cracker; #2364, 11¼"..........**$30.00**

Buttercup, crystal, saucer, #2350...................................**$5.00**

Buttercup, crystal, vase, #4143, footed, 7½".............**$135.00**

Camellia, crystal, bowl, fruit; 5"..................................**$16.00**

Camellia, crystal, creamer, 4¼"....................................**$15.00**

Camellia, crystal, plate, dinner; 10¼" **$45.00**

Camellia, crystal, plate, salad; 7½" **$10.00**

Camellia, crystal, tray, muffin; handled, 9½" **$32.50**

Camellia, crystal, vase, oval, 8½" **$85.00**

Century, crystal, bowl, handled, 4½" **$12.00**

Century, crystal, bowl, lily pond; 9" **$30.00**

Century, crystal, ice bucket..**$65.00**

Century, crystal, plate, salad; 7½"..................................**$8.00**

Century, crystal, platter, 12" **$47.50**

Century, crystal, tray, muffin; handled, 9½" **$30.00**

Chintz, crystal, bowl, bonbon; #2496, 7⅝" **$32.50**

Chintz, crystal, plate, salad; #2496, 7½".....................**$15.00**

Chintz, crystal, platter, #2496, 12" **$100.00**

Chintz, crystal, vase, #4143, footed, 6" **$110.00**

Coin, amber, ashtray, #1372/124, 10" **$30.00**

Coin, amber, lamp, patio; oil, #1372/459, 16⅝" **$160.00**

Coin, blue, bowl, #1372/199, footed, 8½" **$90.00**

Coin, blue, lamp, coach; #1372/320, oil, 13½"..........**$225.00**

Coin, blue, pitcher, #1372/453, 32-oz, 6¼"................**$135.00**

Coin, blue, vase, bud; #1372/799, 8".............................**$40.00**

Coin, crystal, candle holder, #1372/326, 8", pr...........**$50.00**

Coin, crystal, nappy, #1372/495, 4½".............................**$22.00**

Coin, crystal, stem, wine; #1372/26, 5-oz, 4"..............**$35.00**

Coin, crystal, vase, #1372/818, footed, 10" **$45.00**

Coin, green, creamer, 1372/680.....................................**$30.00**

Coin, green, cruet, #1372/531, w/stopper, 7-oz........**$200.00**

Coin, green, sugar bowl, #1372/673, $65.00. (Photo courtesy Gene Florence)

Coin, olive, jelly, #1372/448..**$15.00**

Coin, ruby, ashtray, #1372/123, 5".............................**$22.50**

Coin, ruby, candle holder, #1372/326, 8", pr............**$125.00**

Coin, ruby, plate, #1372/550, 8"..................................**$40.00**

Coin, ruby, vase, bud; #1372/799, 8" **$45.00**

Corsage, crystal, bowl, #4119, footed, 4"....................**$22.00**

Corsage, crystal, candlestick, #2496, double...............**$45.00**

Corsage, crystal, ice bucket, #2496..............................**$75.00**

Corsage, crystal, plate, 8½"...**$12.50**

Corsage, crystal, saucer, #2440......................................**$5.00**

Corsage, crystal, sugar bowl, #2440.............................**$17.50**

Corsage, crystal, vase, bud; #5092, 8" **$60.00**

Corsage, plate, cracker; #2496, 11"...............................**$35.00**

Fairfax, amber, bowl, 3-footed, 6⅞"..............................**$15.00**

Fairfax, amber, plate, dinner; 10¼" **$20.00**

Fairfax, amber, stem, cocktail; 3-oz, 5¼" **$12.00**

Fairfax, green or topaz, candy dish, w/lid, flat, 3-part..**$55.00**

Fairfax, green or topaz, ice bucket **$40.00**

Fairfax, green or topaz, sauce boat liner.....................**$15.00**

Fairfax, green or topaz, tumbler, footed, 2½-oz **$18.00**

Fairfax, rose, blue, or orchid, baker, oval, 9" **$45.00**

Fairfax, rose, blue, or orchid, pitcher, #5000............**$300.00**

Fairfax, rose, blue, or topaz, cream soup, footed......**$23.00**

Heather, crystal, bowl, triangular, 3-footed, 7⅛" **$20.00**

Heather, crystal, oil, w/stopper, 5-oz **$50.00**

Heather, crystal, plate, dinner; lg center, 10½"...........**$45.00**

Heather, crystal, relish, 2-part, 7⅜" **$20.00**

Heather, crystal, sugar bowl, footed, 4" **$20.00**

Heather, crystal, vase, oval, 8½"...................................**$85.00**

Hermitage, amber, green or topaz, bowl, fruit; #2449½, 5" **$8.00**

Hermitage, azure, bowl, pedestal foot, deep, #2449, 8" .**$60.00**

Hermitage, crystal, bottle, oil; #2449, 3-oz $20.00
Hermitage, crystal, ice tub, #2449, 6" $17.50
Hermitage, wisteria, cup, #2449, footed $22.00
Jamestown, amber or brown, bowl, salad; #2719/211, 10"...$21.00
Jamestown, amber or brown, sauce dish, #2719/635, w/lid, 4½" $18.00
Jamestown, amber or brown, tumbler, iced tea; #2719/63, footed, 12-oz, 6" $10.00
Jamestown, amethyst, crystal or green, celery, #1719/360, 9¼" $32.50
Jamestown, amethyst, crystal or green, sauce dish, #2719/635, w/lid, 4½" $35.00
Jamestown, blue, pink or ruby, pickle, #2719/540, 8⅜"....$45.00
Jamestown, blue, pink or ruby, sugar bowl, #2719/679, footed, 3½" $25.00

Jenny Lind, milk glass, ca 1953 – 65, pitcher, #834, 8", $100.00; tumbler, #835, 4", $25.00. (Photo courtesy Lee Garmon)

June, crystal, decanter $425.00
June, crystal, sweetmeat $25.00
June, rose or blue, comport, #2400, 5" $75.00
June, rose or blue, sauce boat..............................$295.00
June, topaz, ashtray $40.00
June, topaz, plate, lemon $25.00
Kashmir, blue, cheese & cracker set $85.00
Kashmir, blue, stem, water; 9-oz $35.00
Kashmir, yellow or green, bowl, soup; 7" $35.00
Kashmir, yellow or green, plate, cake; 10" $35.00
Lido, crystal or azure, bowl, handles, 10½" $45.00
Lido, crystal or azure, cup, footed $15.00
Lido, crystal or azure, vase, 5" $75.00
Mayflower, crystal, bowl, finger; #869 ....$25.00
Mayflower, crystal, comport, 5½" $30.00
Mayflower, crystal, salt & pepper shakers, pr $65.00
Mayflower, crystal, vase, #2430, 8" $110.00
Meadow Rose, crystal or azure, bowl, handled, 4" sq..$11.00
Meadow Rose, crystal or azure, ice bucket, 4⅜" $100.00
Meadow Rose, crystal or azure, plate, dinner; 9½" $45.00
Navarre, blue or pink, stem, claret; #6106, 4½-oz, 6" $85.00
Navarre, blue or pink, tumbler, iced tea; #6106, footed, 13-oz, 5⅞" $60.00
Navarre, crystal, bowl, #2496, flared, 12"...............$62.50

Navarre, crystal, candlestick, #2496, 4" $25.00
Navarre, crystal, plate, salad; #2440, 7½" $15.00
New fgarland, amber or topaz, salt & pepper shakers, footed, pr $75.00
New Garland, amber or topaz, bowl, 12" $55.00
New Garland, amber or topaz, ice dish................$20.00
New Garland, rose, creamer, footed $17.50
New Garland, rose, plate, 9" $35.00
New Garland, rose, stem, wine; #6002 ....$25.00
Romance, crystal, bowl, salad; #2364, 9" $37.50
Romance, crystal, cup, #2350½, footed $20.00
Romance, crystal, plate, torte; #2364, 16" $95.00
Romance, crystal, vase, #4121, 5" $40.00
Royal, amber or green, bowl, #2267, footed, 7".........$35.00
Royal, amber or green, creamer, flat.....................$18.00
Royal, amber or green, pitcher, #1236 ....$395.00
Royal, amber or green, vase, #2292, flared $125.00
Seascape, opalescent, creamer, 3⅜" $25.00
Seascape, opalescent, sugar bowl, individual.............$25.00
Seville, amber, celery, #2350, 11" $15.00
Seville, amber, egg cup, #2350 ....$30.00
Seville, amber, plate, luncheon; #2350, 8½" $6.00
Seville, green, bowl, soup; #2350, 7¾" $27.50
Seville, green, tray, #2287, center handle, 11" $30.00
Sun Ray, crystal, bonbon, 3-toed............................$17.50
Sun Ray, crystal, onion soup; w/lid $40.00
Sun Ray, crystal, plate, 9½"...................................$28.00
Sun Ray, crystal, vase, 7".......................................$50.00
Trojan, rose, candlestick, #2375, flared, 3" $30.00
Trojan, rose, comport, #2400 or #5299, 6" $65.00
Trojan, rose, vase, #2417, 8" $175.00
Trojan, topaz, bonbon, #2375 ....$22.00
Trojan, topaz, pitcher, #5000...............................$335.00
Trojan, topaz, relish, #2375, 8½" $40.00
Versailles, blue, candlestick, #2394, 2" $40.00
Versailles, blue, pitcher, #5000............................$595.00
Versailles, pink or green, bowl, baker; #2375, 9"....$75.00
Versailles, pink or green, grapefruit, #5082½ $75.00
Versailles, yellow, comport, #5008, 3" $30.00
Versailles, yellow, sweetmeat, #2375.....................$35.00
Vesper, amber, bowl, soup; deep, 8¼" $45.00
Vesper, amber, stem, parfait; #5093......................$45.00
Vesper, blue, bowl, baker, #2350, oval, 10½" $135.00
Vesper, blue, ice bucket, #2378 ....$225.00
Vesper, blue, tumbler, #5100, footed, 12-oz $65.00
Vesper, green, bowl, fruit; #2350, 5½" $12.00
Vesper, green, plate, chop; 13¾"............................$40.00

Franciscan Dinnerware

Franciscan is a trade name of Gladding McBean, used on their dinnerware lines from the mid-'30s until it closed its Los Angeles-based plant in 1984. They were the first to market 'starter sets' (four-place settings), a practice that today is commonplace.

Two of their earliest lines were El Patio (simply styled, made in bright solid colors) and Coronado (with swirled borders and pastel glazes). In the late '30s, they made the first of many hand-painted dinnerware lines. Some of the best known are Apple, Desert Rose, and Ivy. From 1941 to 1977, 'Masterpiece' (true porcelain) china was produced in more than 170 patterns.

Many marks were used, most included the Franciscan name. An 'F' in a square with 'Made in U.S.A.' below it dates from 1938, and a double-line script 'F' was used in more recent years.

For further information, we recommend *The Collector's Encyclopedia of California Pottery, Second Edition,* by Jack Chipman.

Note: To evaluate maroon items in El Patio and Coronado, add 10% to 20% to suggested prices.

Advisors: Mick and Lorna Chase, Fiesta Plus (See Directory, Dinnerware)

Desert Rose, heart-shaped box, $165.00.
(Photo courtesy Mick and Lorna Chase)

Apple, ashtray, oval	**$137.50**
Apple, bowl, cereal; 6"	**$16.50**
Apple, bowl, mixing; sm	**$182.50**
Apple, bowl, vegetable; 8"	**$35.00**
Apple, candle holders, pr	**$160.00**
Apple, coffeepot	**$137.50**
Apple, compote, lg	**$82.50**
Apple, creamer, regular	**$24.00**
Apple, cup & saucer, demitasse	**$60.00**
Apple, cup & saucer, tea	**$16.50**
Apple, egg cup	**$38.50**
Apple, jam jar	**$137.50**
Apple, mug, cocoa; 10-oz	**$145.00**
Apple, pitcher, milk	**$82.50**
Apple, plate, coupe dessert	**$72.50**
Apple, plate, 8½"	**$14.00**
Apple, platter, 14"	**$72.00**
Apple, sherbet	**$27.50**
Apple, thimble	**$82.50**
Apple, tumbler, 10-oz	**$35.00**
Coronado, bowl, nut cup; from $16 to	**$18.00**

Coronado, bowl, salad; lg, from $35 to	**$50.00**
Coronado, bowl, sherbet/egg cup; from $15 to	**$18.00**
Coronado, pitcher, 1½-qt, from $35 to	**$60.00**
Coronado, plate, 9½", from $15 to	**$18.00**
Coronado, relish dish, oval, from $20 to	**$35.00**
Desert Rose, bowl, bouillon; w/lid	**$395.00**
Desert Rose, bowl, mixing; med	**$185.00**
Desert Rose, bowl, soup; footed	**$32.00**
Desert Rose, box, round	**$165.00**
Desert Rose, candle holders, pr	**$145.00**
Desert Rose, candy dish, oval	**$295.00**
Desert Rose, coffeepot	**$125.00**
Desert Rose, cookie jar	**$295.00**
Desert Rose, creamer, individual	**$40.00**
Desert Rose, cup & saucer, demitasse	**$55.00**
Desert Rose, ginger jar	**$225.00**
Desert Rose, mug, 7-oz	**$32.00**
Desert Rose, plate, chop; 12"	**$75.00**
Desert Rose, plate, 10½"	**$18.00**
Desert Rose, platter, 14"	**$65.00**
Desert Rose, shakers, tall, pr	**$75.00**
Desert Rose, teapot	**$125.00**
Desert Rose, tumbler, juice; 6-oz	**$55.00**
El Patio, bowl, cereal; from $15 to	**$20.00**
El Patio, bowl, onion soup; w/lid, from $45 to	**$60.00**
El Patio, bowl, serving; 8½" dia, from $18 to	**$20.00**
El Patio, creamer, from $12 to	**$15.00**
El Patio, fast-stand gravy, from $28 to	**$40.00**
El Patio, plate, 10½", from $20 to	**$25.00**
El Patio, plate, 9½", from $15 to	**$18.00**
El Patio, shakers, pr, from $20 to	**$35.00**
El Patio, teapot, from $65 to	**$95.00**
Forget-Me-Not, bowl, divided vegetable	**$45.00**
Forget-Me-Not, bowl, rimmed soup	**$28.00**
Forget-Me-Not, box, egg shape	**$195.00**
Forget-Me-Not, candy dish, oval	**$295.00**
Forget-Me-Not, cup & saucer, coffee	**$85.00**
Forget-Me-Not, egg cup	**$35.00**
Forget-Me-Not, jam jar	**$125.00**
Forget-Me-Not, napkin ring	**$65.00**
Forget-Me-Not, plate, coupe steak	**$195.00**
Forget-Me-Not, relish, 3-compartment	**$75.00**
Forget-Me-Not, vase, bud	**$75.00**
Ivy, cup & saucer, tall	**$55.00**
Ivy, gravy boat	**$38.00**
Ivy, mug, barrel form, 12-oz	**$60.00**
Ivy, plate, chop; 12"	**$90.00**
Ivy, plate, 6½"	**$7.50**
Ivy, plate, 10½"	**$22.00**
Ivy, sherbet	**$30.00**
Ivy, tile, sq	**$55.00**
Ivy, tumbler, 10-oz	**$38.00**
Meadow Rose, cup & saucer, tea	**$15.00**
Meadow Rose, gravy boat	**$32.00**
Meadow Rose, napkin ring	**$65.00**
Meadow Rose, pitcher, milk	**$75.00**
Meadow Rose, plate, side salad	**$40.00**

Meadow Rose, plate, 8½"	$12.00
Meadow Rose, relish, oval, 10"	$35.00
Meadow Rose, soup ladle	$95.00
Poppy, egg cup	$52.50
Poppy, mug, barrel form, 12-oz	$75.00
Poppy, plate, side salad	$60.00
Poppy, relish, oval, 10"	$52.50
Poppy, teapot	$195.00
Starburst, ashtray, individual	$20.00
Starburst, bonbon/jelly dish	$35.00
Starburst, bowl, divided, 8"	$25.00
Starburst, bowl, salad; ind	$25.00
Starburst, bowl, vegetable; 8½"	$45.00
Starburst, casserole, lg	$100.00
Starburst, cup & saucer	$25.00
Starburst, gravy ladle	$30.00
Starburst, mug, sm	$60.00
Starburst, oil cruet	$75.00
Starburst, pitcher, water; 10"	$85.00
Starburst, plate, 8"	$8.00

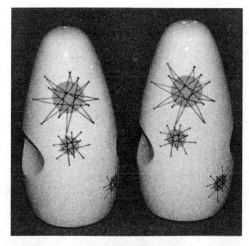

Starburst, shakers, bullet shape, large, $50.00 for the pair.

Starburst, vinegar cruet	$75.00

Frankoma

John Frank opened a studio pottery in Norman, Oklahoma, in 1933. The bowls, vases, coffee mugs, shakers, etc., he created bore the ink-stamped marks 'Frank Pottery' or 'Frank Potteries.' At this time, only a few hundred pieces were produced. Within a year, Mr. Frank had incorporated. Though not everything was marked, he continued to use these marks for two years. Items thus marked are not easy to find and command high prices. In 1935 the pot and leopard mark was introduced.

The Frank family moved to Sapulpa, Oklahoma, in 1938. In November of that year, a fire destroyed everything. The pot and leopard mark was never re-created, and today collectors avidly search for items with this mark. The rarest of all Frankoma marks is 'First Kiln Sapulpa 6-7-38,' which was applied to only about one hundred pieces fired on that date.

Grace Lee Frank worked beside her husband, creating many limited edition Madonna plates, Christmas cards, advertising items, birds, etc. She died in 1996.

Clay is important in determining when a piece was made. Ada clay, used until 1953, is creamy beige in color. In 1953 they changed over to a red brick shale from Sapulpa. Today most clay has a pinkish-red cast, though the pinkish cast is sometimes so muted that a novice might mistake it for Ada clay.

Rutile glazes were created early in the pottery's history; these give the ware a two-tone color treatment. However the US government closed the rutile mines in 1970, and Frank found it necessary to buy this material from Australia. The newer rutile produced different results, especially noticeable with their Woodland Moss glaze.

Upon John Frank's death in 1973, their daughter Joniece became president. Though the pottery burned again in 1983, the buildings were quickly rebuilt. Due to so many setbacks, however, the company found it necessary to file Chapter 11 in order to remain in control and stay in business. Mr. Richard Bernstein purchased Frankoma in 1991; it continues to operate.

Frank purchased Synar Ceramics of Muskogee, Oklahoma, in 1958; in late 1950, the name was changed to Gracetone Pottery in honor of Grace Lee Frank. Until supplies were exhausted, they continued to produce Synar's white clay line in glazes such as 'Alligator,' 'Woodpine,' 'White Satin,' 'Ebony,' 'Wintergreen' and a black and white straw combination. At the Frankoma pottery, an 'F' was added to the stock number on items made at both locations. New glazes were Aqua, Pink Champagne, and black, known as Gunmetal. Gracetone was sold in 1962 to Mr. Taylor, who had been a long-time family friend and manager of the pottery. Taylor continued operations until 1967. The only dinnerware pattern produced there was 'Orbit,' which is today hard to find. Other Gracetone pieces are becoming scarce as well.

If you'd like to learn more, we recommend *Frankoma Pottery, Value Guide and More,* by Susan Cox; and *Frankoma and Other Oklahoma Potteries* by Phyllis and Tom Bess.

Club/Newsletter: Frankoma Family Collectors Association
c/o Nancy Littrell
P.O. Box 32571, Oklahoma City, OK 73123-0771
Membership dues: $25; includes newsletter and annual convention

Ashtray, Aztec, Sapulpa clay, #471, 1962-65, 9"	$9.00
Ashtray, Elephant, Sorghum Brown, #459, 1951-52, 6½" dia	$75.00
Ashtray, Indian Bowl Maker seated at side, Sapulpa clay, #123, 1972-83	$42.00
Baker, Wagon Wheel, Red Bud, #94u, individual size	$6.00
Baker (baked beans), barrel form, Ada clay, w/lid, #97V, 2-qt	$40.00
Bank, Owl, Sapulpa clay, #384, 1980-82	$10.00

Bookend, Charger Horse, flat back, #111, 1972-75.....**$35.00**

Bowl, Crescent, Woodland Moss, #211, 1960-79, 12½"...**$18.00**

Bowl, free-form, Woodland Moss, #214, 1960-74, 12" ..**$13.00**

Bowl, serving; Sapulpa clay, round, 1980-91.................**$3.00**

Candle holder, Aladdin Lamp, Sapulpa clay, #309, 1968-70..**$21.00**

Candle holder, Wagon Wheel, does not have finger hold or cigarette rest, Sapulpa clay, #736, 1980-81.............**$7.50**

Candle holder, Wedding Ring, Ada clay, #300, 1949 ..**$15.00**

Christmas card, 1955, Leaf, 4".......................................**$65.00**

Christmas card, 1971, John & Grace Lee **$50.00**

Christmas card, 1987, Eagle w/Scroll **$50.00**

Cookie jar, no Trojan horse on lid, Ada clay, #99, mid-1940s...**$60.00**

Cornucopia, Woodland Moss, #56, 1960-75, 7" **$25.00**

Creamer, Cherokee Red, #92B, 1942............................**$20.00**

Creamer & sugar bowl, Lazybones, Peach Glow, w/lid, #4a/b...**$15.00**

Figurine, puma reclining, black, Ada Clay, $100.00.

Horseshoe, Turquoise, 1953..**$6.50**

Jardiniere, ringed, footed, Sapulpa clay, #70A, 1982 & later, 7"..**$34.00**

Mug, Donkey, Celery Green, 1981 ....**$25.00**

Mug, Elephant, Bush/Quayle, Peach, 1989..................**$15.00**

Mug, Elephant, Prairie Green, 1972...............................**$42.00**

Napkin ring, sq, Sapulpa clay, #262, 1982-88................**$3.00**

Pitcher, juice; Guernsey, Peach Glow, #93, w/lid, 1962-65, 25-oz, 7"..**$33.00**

Planter, Alamo, Sapulpa clay, #397, 1988-91, 6½" **$18.00**

Planter, hexagonal, Sapulpa clay, #37, 4" **$6.50**

Planter, log, Sorghum Brown, 1950-61, 11" **$17.00**

Planter, triangle, Woodland Moss, #239, 1969-70, 6"...**$10.00**

Plate, Chrismas 1986, For Thee I Play My Drum **$35.00**

Plate, Mayan Aztec, Woodland Moss, 7" **$5.50**

Plate, Teenagers of the Bible, Jonathan the Archer, 1975...**$30.00**

Plate, Wagon Wheel, Prairie Green or Desert Gold, 10", ea **$14.00**

Salt & pepper shakers, Ada clay, #44, 1936-38, sm, pr..**$12.00**

Salt & pepper shakers, puma, Sapulpa clay, #165H, 1953-57, pr...**$40.00**

Salt & pepper shakers, Red Bud, holes do not form S or P, #48H, pr...**$20.00**

Salt & pepper shakers, Sapulpa clay, #25H, 1966-74, pr.....**$16.00**

Salt & pepper shakers, Westwind, Mountain Haze, #6h, pr .**$6.00**

Sculpture, English Setter, Ada clay, 1942-49, 5¼x8" .**$100.00**

Sculpture, Indian Maiden, White Sand, #101, 12" **$35.00**

Sculpture, Phoebe, rubbed bisque, #130, 1972-75, 7".**$75.00**

Sculpture, planter, Swirl, #177, 1986+, 5½"...................**$5.50**

Sculpture, puma, reclining, flat back, #116, 9½".........**$35.00**

Sugar pack holder, Sapulpa clay, 1991...........................**$4.50**

Teacup, Plainsman, Desert Gold, #5cc, 5-oz **$5.00**

Teapot, Mayan Aztec, White Sand or Prairie Green, tall, straight, 6-cup...**$16.00**

Trivet, Cherokee Alphabet, Sapulpa clay, 6" dia **$10.00**

Trivet, Lazybones, Red Bud, 1957, 6" dia **$65.00**

Trivet, Rooster (Wagon Wheel dinnerware), Sapulpa clay, #94TR, 1965+...**$10.00**

Tureen, soup; w/warmer & lid, #246, 3-qt, 1980+......**$34.00**

Vase, boot w/star design, Ada clay, #507, 1942-1953 .**$10.00**

Vase, crocus bud; ivory, round, 1936-42, 8" **$20.00**

Vase, hexagon, Sapulpa clay, #65, 1966-78, 8"...........**$15.00**

Vase, pillow; Ada Clay, #60, 1942, 6½".......................**$30.00**

Vase, textured cylinder, Ada clay, 6" **$13.00**

Wall vase, Ram's Head, Ada Clay, #193, 1942.............**$75.00**

Freeman-McFarlin

This California-based company was the result of a union between Gerald McFarlin and Maynard Anthony Freeman, formed in the early 1950s and resulting in the production of a successful line of molded ceramic sculptures (predominately birds and animals, though human figures were also made) as well decorative items such as vases, flowerpots, bowls, etc. Anthony was the chief designer, and some of the items you find today bear his name. Glazes ranged from woodtones and solid colors to gold leaf, sometimes in combination. The most collectible of the Freeman-McFarlin figures were designed by Kay Finch, who sold some of her molds to the company in the early 1960s. The company produced these popular sculptures in their own glazes without Kay's trademark curlicues, making them easy for today's collectors to distinguish from her original work. This line was so successful that in the mid-'60s the company hired Kay herself, and until the late '70s, she designed numerous new and original animal models. Most were larger and more realistically detailed than the work she did in her own studio. She worked for the company until 1980. Her pieces are signed.

In addition to the signatures already mentioned, you may find pieces incised 'Jack White' or 'Hetrick,' both freelance designers affiliated with the company. Other marks include paper labels and an impressed mark 'F.McF, Calif USA,' often with a date.

Bowl, artichoke shape, white crackle, 12" dia **$45.00**

Bowl, marbleized blue & green w/green base & interior, #529, 3½x9½"...**$50.00**

Figurine, baby in diaper w/original pin, blue booties, w/gold bowling ball, 3"..**$25.00**

Figurine, comical cow, purple w/gold trim, 4x4" **$28.00**

Figurine, duck, brown tones, bill close to neck, 5x5" ..**$35.00**

Figurine, fawn on leaf, souvenir of Mt Rainier WA, ca 1940s, 1½x3" dia **$25.00**

Figurine, koala bear, gold, ca 1970s, 5x9" **$65.00**

Figurine, owl, red, 6"...$22.50
Figurine, roadrunner, ivory, marked Anthony (Anthony Freeman), 17½"..$40.00
Figurine, Siamese kitten sleeping, ca 1950, 3"..........$60.00
Figurine, turtle, gold-leaf finish, #162, 7½" L $35.00

Figurines, bird pair, gold leaf, #825/#826, signed Kay Finch, from $40.00 to $50.00 for the pair.
(Photo courtesy Devin Frick, Jean Frick, and Richard Martinez)

Figurines, snail family, papa, mamma & baby, dark & light brown striped, 8", 7" & 4", 3-pc set $170.00
Planter, Bassett hound, brown tones, 5½x7"..............$15.00
Planter, blue w/green drip, oblong, 10½" $25.00
Vase, bone white, 8-sided, fluted, 6".........................$30.00

Furniture

A piece of furniture can often be difficult to date, since many seventeenth- and eighteenth-century styles have been reproduced. Even a piece made early in the twentieth century now has enough age on it that it may be impossible for a novice to distinguish it from the antique. Sometimes cabinetmakers may have trouble identifying specific types of wood, since so much variation can occur within the same species; so although it is usually helpful to try to determine what kind of wood a piece has been made of, results are sometimes inconclusive. Construction methods are usually the best clues. Watch for evidence of twentieth-century tools — automatic routers, lathes, carvers, and spray guns.

For further information we recommend *Antique Oak Furniture* by Conover Hill; *Collector's Guide to Oak Furniture* by Jennifer George; *Heywood-Wakefield Modern Furniture* by Steven Rouland and Roger Rouland; *Collector's Encyclopedia of American Furniture, Vols I* and *II*, and *Furniture of the Depression Era*, all Robert and Harriett Swedberg; and *American Oak Furniture* by Katherine McNerney. All are published by Collector Books.

Armchair, Country ladderback, new paper rush seat, 3 arched slats, refinished, 58"...............................$120.00
Armchair, Deco style w/8-sided carved arms, original upholstery, Phoenix Chair Co, 34x24x22" $50.00
Armchair, Limbert #8073, 2 curved back slats, leather seats, Arts & Crafts, 35", VG..$200.00

Armchair, quarter-sawn oak w/barley twists & reeding, upholstered seat, 1920s, restored $250.00
Armchair rocker, oak w/banister back, original leather seat, factory made, generous proportions, 39"...........$130.00
Bed, brass w/stylized sunburst on headboard & footboard, ca 1930s, 42½x49" $500.00
Bed, bunk; maple, Conant-Ball, late 1940s, 81x42" ..$300.00
Bed, canopy; Sheraton, birch & pine w/tall posts, 20th century reproduction, single size $455.00
Bookcase, golden oak, 2 doors, brass fixtures, shelves adjust, gallery, apron, 58x36x12½"................................$800.00
Cabinet, china; solid oak, curved glass sides, sm crest, 1920s, 62x36x12" $795.00
Cabinet, in Wormley style, rattan door, adjustable shelves, 3 drawers, repainted, 1950s, 31x50x18" $240.00
Cabinet, sewing; mahogany w/banding design framing top, 1940s, 31x18x17"..$225.00
Cart, serving; Prober, bleached mahogany w/Pyrex top, Fifties Modern, 32x37".......................................$325.00
Cart/coffee table, black top & shelf, folds to form coffee table, 1980s, 37x24x28", VG..............................$110.00
Chair, club; brown upholstery, curved arms, Modernage, 29x35x35"..$850.00
Chair, desk; #39h, H-back, restored leather seats, Gustav Stickley, 33"..$500.00
Chair, desk; 3-slat back, recovered seat, brand, L & JG Stickley, 36", VG..$375.00
Chair, dining; solid oak, vase splat, leather seat, 1920s, 37" $90.00
Chair, dining; solid oak w/leather seat, 1920s, 40", 4 for...$415.00
Chair, Paulin/Hansen, Swan, original upholstery, Fifties Modern, 30", EX...$600.00
Chair, school; oak, 2-slat back, mass produced, 29"...$55.00
Chair, style of Miles van der Rohe, brown leather seat & back in tubular frame, 1960s, 32x18x26" $60.00
Chest of drawers, bleached mahogany, waterfall front, cedar lined, 1930s, 21x44x19"..................................$225.00

Chest of drawers, Dunbar, Berne, Indiana, light finish, five graduated drawers with recessed handles, ca 1950s, 31x28x18", $865.00.

Chest of drawers, oak, 4-drawer, bowed veneer fronts, brass pulls, modified cabriole feet, 40x30x19"............$365.00
Chest of drawers, oak w/thin pine on sides & bases of drawers (2 short over 3 long), wood knobs, curved apron, 50x30"..$300.00

Desk, lady's; golden oak, shaped drop-front, cut-out crest w/applied factory carvings, 52x26x16" **$450.00**

Desk, mahogany traditional style w/kneehole, 30x42x21".**$110.00**

Desk, oak, drop lid, wooden knobs, 1920s, 40x30x15" ..**$745.00**

Dresser, Princess type, quarter-sawn oak veneer top, plain sliced veneer sides, solid frame, mirror, 1920s, 74x40x21" **$495.00**

Footstool, French style w/cabriole legs, carved frame, upholstered top, 7x13x9" **$50.00**

Lamp, Bubble; Nelson/Miller, plastic/steel wire, Fifties Modern, 24" dia **$200.00**

Lounge chair, Charles Eames #670, manufactured by Herman Miller, tufted black leather in molded rosewood plywood shells, VG, $1,900.00.

Mirror, wall; domed plastic mirror in chrome frame, Ram label, 1970s, 18x36" **$150.00**

Rocker, concave crest rail, upholstered panel, Quaint metal tag, 42x27x29" **$175.00**

Shelf, oak w/worn black paint, shaped ends, 3 shelves, wall type, 33x29x7" **$165.00**

Shelves, pine w/old painted layers, 13x6½x6½" **$300.00**

Sofa, Chippendale-style camel-back w/EX upholstery, late 1900s, 82" **$470.00**

Sofa, Empire style, carved mahogany frame, old ivory brocade upholstery, 20th-century reproduction, stains, 78" **$175.00**

Sofa, mahogany Federal style w/carved feet, reeded cuffs, velvet upholstery, 32x74" **$440.00**

Stand, plant; Art Deco style, chrome-plated tubular frame w/4 glass shelves, 39x35x13" **$250.00**

Stand, plant; hardwood w/overall pressed florals, 28x21x18" **$125.00**

Table, breakfast extension; oak, 1930s, 30x43x30", +2 armless oak chairs **$295.00**

Table, coffee; blond veneer, open center, 1950s, 15x48" dia..**$700.00**

Table, coffee; brass w/original travertine top, 3-leg style, 1940s, 16x24" dia, EX **$325.00**

Table, library; oak, drawer opens from either side, Arts & Crafts, 30x42x27"..**$500.00**

Table, occasional; plain-cut walnut veneer top, selected hardwood base, 1940s, 27x18x15" **$215.00**

Table, occasional; white marble top on brass base, 1950s, 20x18" dia, VG...**$120.00**

Table, tea; mahogany Chippendale-style, tilt-top, tripod base w/ball & claw feet, recent manufacture, 29x31" ..**$500.00**

Table, trestle; walnut, thick boards w/cut-out ends, handmade, 46" **$220.00**

Umbrella stand, like #54, sq frame w/sq finials, copper liner, Gustav Stickley, 33" **$500.00**

Games

Games from the 1870s to the 1970s and beyond are fun to collect. Many of the earlier games are beautifully lithographed. Some of their boxes were designed by well-known artists and illustrators, and many times these old games are appreciated more for their artwork than for their entertainment value. Some represent a historical event or a specific era in the social development of our country. Characters from the early days of radio, television, and movies have been featured in hundreds of games designed for children and adults alike.

If you're going to collect games, be sure that they're reasonably clean, free of water damage, and complete. Most have playing instructions printed inside the lid or on a separate piece of paper that include an inventory list. Check the contents, and remember that the condition of the box is very important too.

If you'd like to learn more about games, we recommend *Toys, Antique and Collectible*, by David Longest; *Baby Boomer Games* by Rick Polizzi; *Schroeder's Collectible Toys, Antique to Modern* (all are published by Collector Books); and *Board Games of the '50s, '60s & '70s* by Stephanie Lane.

Club: American Game Collectors Association
49 Brooks Ave., Lewiston, ME 04240

Newsletter: *Game Times*
Joe Angiolillo
4628 Barlow Dr., Bartlesville, OK 74006

Adventures of Lassie, Whiting, 1955, EXIB.................**$50.00**

Alien, Kenner, 1979, EXIB...**$50.00**

Amazing Spider-Man, Milton Bradley, 1966, EXIB....**$250.00**

Astro Launch, Ohio Art, 1963, EXIB...........................**$75.00**

Baretta, Milton Bradley, 1976, EXIB...........................**$20.00**

Barnstormer, Marx, 1970, EXIB...................................**$35.00**

Batman & Robin Marble Maze, Hasbro, 1966, EXIB.**$100.00**

Battleboard, Ideal, 1972, NMIB....................................**$30.00**

Beany & Cecil Jumping Dishonest John, Mattel, 1962, NMIB **$35.00**

Black Hole Space Alert, Whitman, 1979, MIB **$35.00**

Blondie Hurry Scurry, Transogram, 1966, EXIB **$40.00**

Brady Bunch, Whitman, 1973, MIB..........................**$125.00**

Bugaloos, Milton Bradley, 1971, MIB, from $50 to **$60.00**

Camp Runamuck Card Game, Ideal, 1965, EXIB $25.00

Candyland, Milton Bradley, 1962, VG (VG box).........$50.00

Captain America, Milton Bradley, 1966, MIB............$100.00

Captain Kangaroo TV Lotto, Ideal, 1961, EXIB $25.00

Captain Kidd, Lowell, 1950s, EXIB.....................$50.00

Car 54 Where Are You?, Allison, 1963, EXIB $175.00

Championship Baseball, Lansing, 1966, EXIB $35.00

CHiPs, Ideal, 1981, MIB, from $25 to.......................$35.00

Chuck Conners Tin Can Alley Rifle Target, Ideal, 1976, EX+..$50.00

Cinderella, Parker Bros, 1964, EXIB $50.00

Cootie House, Schaper, 1966, EXIB $35.00

Dancing Princess, Hasbro, 1964, EXIB..................$35.00

Daniel Boone Card Game, Transogram, 1964, EXIB ..$30.00

Davy Crockett Radar Action, Ewing, 1955, EXIB $85.00

Deputy, Milton Bradley, 1960, EXIB $65.00

Deputy Dawg, Milton Bradley, 1960, EXIB $50.00

Dick Tracy Sunday Funnies, Ideal, 1972, EXIB $55.00

Dogfight, Milton Bradley, 1962, EXIB $40.00

Donald Duck Ring Toss, Transogram, 1961, EXIB.....$30.00

Donald Duck Wagon Train, 1977, NMIB $25.00

Dracula, Hasbro, 1963, EXIB...........................$150.00

Dukes of Hazzard, Ideal, 1981, EXIB....................$25.00

Emergency, Milton Bradley, 1973, EXIB $22.00

Family Ties, Applestreet, 1986, EXIB $30.00

Flash Gordon Target, 1952, EXIB $150.00

Flea Circus, Mattel, 1964, EXIB..........................$35.00

Flintstones, Milton Bradley, 1971, EXIB $25.00

Flintstones Stoneage, Transogram, 1961, EXIB............$40.00

Flipper Flips, Mattel, 1965, EXIB $55.00

Flying Nun, Milton Bradley, 1968, NMIB.................$50.00

Fugitive, Ideal, 1964, EXIB...............................$125.00

G-Men Clue Games, Whitman, EXIB.....................$85.00

Giant Cootie, Schaper, 1950s, EXIB......................$85.00

Gomer Pyle, Transogram, 1964, EXIB....................$50.00

Great Shakes Charlie Brown, Golden, 1988, MIB $12.00

Gunfight at the OK Corral, Ideal, 1973, EXIB $45.00

Gusher, Carrom, 1946, EXIB.............................$75.00

Have Gun Will Travel, Parker Bros, 1959, EXIB $75.00

Hawaiian Eye, Lowell, 1963, EXIB........................$85.00

Hearts Card Game, Whitman, 1951, NMIB $10.00

Hoopla, Ideal, 1966, EXIB................................$40.00

Hopalong Cassidy, Milton Bradley, 1950, EXIB $150.00

Howdy Doody's Own Game, Parker Bros, 1949, EXIB ..$100.00

Huckleberry Hound Juggle Roll, Transogram, 1960, EXIB..$60.00

Hunt for Red October, 1988, EXIB.......................$30.00

I Dream of Jeannie, Milton Bradley, 1965, NMIB........$70.00

Ipcress File, Milton Bradley, 1966, EXIB...................$25.00

Jack the Giant Killer, Lowell, 1950s, EXIB..................$40.00

Jeanne Dixon's Game of Destiny, 1969, MIB (sealed)..$20.00

Jetsons Fun Pad, Milton Bradley, 1963, EXIB............$75.00

Jingle Dingle's Weather, Lowell, 1954, EXIB.............$40.00

Journey to the Unknown, Remco, 1968, EXIB.........$100.00

King of the Cheese, Milton Bradley, 1959, EXIB.......$40.00

Kukla & Ollie, Parker Bros, 1962, EXIB....................$30.00

Land of the Lost, Milton Bradley, 1975, EXIB $25.00

Let's Face It, Hasbro, 1955, EXIB $30.00

Li'l Abner, Parker Bros, 1969, EXIB.............................$35.00

Lone Ranger & Tonto Spin To Win, Pressman, 1967, EXIB .$35.00

Looney Tunes, Milton Bradley, 1968, EXIB $50.00

Lost in Space 3-D Game, Remco, 1966, EXIB $225.00

M*A*S*H, Milton Bradley, 1981, MIB.....................$30.00

Magilla Gorilla, Ideal, 1964, NMIB.......................$100.00

Man From UNCLE Target Game, Marx, 1966, EXIB....$30.00

Marvel Super Heroes Card Game, Milton Bradley, 1978, MIB..$40.00

Mary Poppins, Milton Bradley, 1964, EXIB................$40.00

Mentor, Hasbro, 1961, EXIB.............................$40.00

Mickey Mouse Top Hat Target, Transogram, 1963, EXIB..$50.00

Mighty Comics Super Hero, Transogram, 1966, EXIB..$125.00

Mighty Mouse, Parker Bros, 1964, NMIB.................$65.00

Mighty Mouse Skill-Roll, Pressman, 1959, EXIB $65.00

Mission Impossible, Ideal, 1966, EXIB $75.00

Monster Old Maid, Milton Bradley, 1977, NMIB $30.00

Monstermania, Marx, 1977, MIB..........................$30.00

Moon Tag, Parker Bros, 1957, EXIB........................$85.00

Mr Ed, Parker Bros, 1960s, EXIB...........................$65.00

New Adventures of Pinocchio, Lowell, 1960, EXIB $50.00

Newlywed Game, Hasbro, 1969, NMIB $20.00

Outlaws, Transogram, 1961, EXIB........................$65.00

Pac-Man, Milton Bradley, 1982, NMIB $15.00

Partridge Family, 1971, VG (VG box).......................$35.00

Pathfinder, Milton Bradley, 1977, EXIB....................$20.00

Peter Gunn, Lowell, 1965, EXIB..........................$75.00

Peter Potamus, Ideal, 1964, EXIB.........................$185.00

Planet of the Apes, Milton Bradley, 1974, MIB $45.00

Pong, electronic video skill game, Sears, 1975, M (EX box), $65.00. (Photo courtesy June Moon)

Popeye & His Pals, Ideal, 1963, EXIB.....................$50.00

Prince Valiant, Transogram, 1955, EXIB....................$45.00

PT Boat 109, Ideal, 1963, VG (G box).......................$35.00

Rawhide, Lowell, 1960, EXIB..............................$85.00

Ride the Surf, 1963, EXIB................................$65.00

Rin-Tin-Tin, Transogram, EX (G box).......................$25.00

Seven Seas, Cadaco, 1960, EXIB...........................$35.00

Slap Tap, Ideal, 1967, EXIB $30.00

Snagglepuss, Transogram, 1961, EXIB $40.00

Space Pilot, Cadaco, 1951, EXIB...........................$75.00

Surfside 6, Lowell, 1962, EXIB.................................$65.00

Talking Football, Mattel, 1971, NMIB, $100.00. (Photo courtesy Martin and Carolyn Berens)

That Girl, Remco, 1969, EXIB....................................$70.00
Top Cat, Cadaco, 1961, NMIB....................................$45.00
Wagon Train, Milton Bradley, 1960, EXIB $50.00
Wanted Dead or Alive, Lowell, 1959, EXIB $75.00
West Point Story, Transogram, 1961, EXIB $50.00
Woody Owl's Give a Hoot, Whitman, 1976, NMIB.....$40.00
Yogi Bear Score-A-Matic Ball Toss, Transogram, 1960, EXIB $65.00
You Don't Say, Milton Bradley, 1963, EXIB................$20.00

Gas Station Collectibles

Items used and/or sold by gas stations are included in this very specialized area of advertising collectibles. Those with an interest in this field tend to specialize in memorabilia from a specific gas station like Texaco or Signal. This is a very regional market, with items from small companies that are no longer in business bringing the best prices. For instance, memorabilia decorated with Gulf's distinctive 'orange ball' logo may sell more readily in Pittsburgh than in Los Angeles. Gas station giveaways like plastic gas pump salt and pepper sets and license plate attachments are gaining in popularity with collectors. If you're interested in learning more about these types of collectibles, we recommend *Antique and Contemporary Advertising Memorabilia* by B.J. Summers and *Gas Station Memorabilia* by B.J. Summers and Wayne Priddy, both published by Collector Books.

See also Ashtrays; Automobilia.

Newsletter: *Petroleum Collectors Monthly*
Scott Benjamin and Wayne Henderson, Publishers
PO Box 556, LaGrange, OH 44050-0556; 440-355-6608.
Subscription: $29.95 per year in US, Canada: $38.50; International: $65.95 (samples: $5); website: www.pcmpublishing.com or www.oilcollectibles.com

Advisor: Scott Benjamin (See Directory Gas Station Collectibles)

Air pump, Eco Automatic Tireflater #97-9, metal w/plastic face, w/hose, 16", EX $450.00

Ashtrays, Texaco Service, metal, pinup girl images in centers on blue, 4¼" sq, set of 3 ....$180.00
Atlas/map book, Shell, snap-closure holder w/75 maps covering every state, Canada & Mexico, 1956, 18½x14", EX+ $30.00
Badge, Shell Approved Service, brass shell & scroll shape w/red & yellow enamel, 3½x3", EX.................$325.00
Belt Buckle, Mobil's red winged horse on white cloisonne inlayed on chrome emblem w/engraved initials, 1½x2", NM+ $100.00
Blotter, Gargoyle Lubricants, leather w/gilt lettering & stiched border, use w/rocking motion, EX.......................$60.00
Calendar, Esso, 1947, shows Father Time trying to take globe from Baby New Year, complete, framed, 16x10", EX (NOS) $30.00
Calendar, Richfield dealer, 1937, 12 illustrations w/January showing street cop & 2 kids on racer, 8x7", unused, EX $125.00
Calendar, Socony Gasoline/Motor Oils, 1929, Land — Water — Air, incomplete pad, 26½x13¼", EX+ $425.00
Cap, Mobiloil, red cloth w/lettering & winged horse emblem, NM+ $75.00
Cap, Phillips 66, tan cloth w/embroidered orange & black patch, black vinyl bill w/plastic mechanical pencil, EX $200.00
Clock, Mobil, tire frame w/glass front, Made in Germany, 4" dia, EX $200.00
Clock, Phillips 66 Tires/Batteries, round metal frame w/double bubble glass front, 15" dia, EX.......................$900.00
Compass, Union 76 Auto, w/suction cup mount, orange, blue & white, EX $15.00
Credit card, Union Oil 50th Anniversary, paper, complete w/tire & battery coupons, 1940, EX+ $50.00
Decal, Standard, diecut oval emblem w/torch, 32x40", unused, NM (NOS) $20.00
Display, Alemite Gas-co-lator, Filters Your Gas As You Drive, $5.25, plaster cast, 20x17x4", EX $425.00
Display rack, Mobil Radiator Flush, 2 cardboard signs flanked by 3-tiered wire stand, 40x25", VG $80.00
Doll, Buddy Lee in Phillips 66 uniform & cap, 13½", EX..$425.00
Globe, Derby, wide milk glass body w/2 lenses featuring white & blue Derby banner over white star on red, 13½", EX $200.00
Globe, Phillips 66, white plastic body w/2 lenses featuring the orange & black emblem on white, 13½", NM......$300.00
Globe, Sinclair Dino Gasoline, green plastic body w/red & green logo on 2 white lenses, 13½" dia, EX+ $190.00
Globe, Texaco, narrow milk glass body w/2 lenses featuring black name across top of red star logo, black rim, VG+ $475.00
Grease can, Indian Refining Co/Havoline Motor Grease, 1-lb, flat w/winged logo on screw lid $200.00
Mailbox, Santa Claus; green metal w/red, white & blue Standard logo, letters get the Santa Claus IN postmark, 17", EX+ $230.00
Manual, Standard Oil service station specifications w/working drawings, in binder, 9x11½", NM $160.00

Map holder, Phillips 66 emblem atop wooden 3-tiered rotating rack, w/assorted maps, 1950s, 22", EX.........**$650.00**

Map holder, Texaco Touring Service, green tin box w/red emblem, 9", EX+ **$100.00**

Measuring stick, Gargoyle Marine Oils, wooden fold-up type extends to 60", EX+ **$150.00**

Mechanical pen desk set, Standard, white porcelain base w/red, white & blue emblem, Service Station Cleanliness Award, EX **$135.00**

Oil bottle, Shell Lubricating Oil, 1½" sample size, 4-sided w/paper label, cork stopper, VIP Raceways giveaway, NM **$130.00**

Oil bottle rack, Mobiloil 'AF,' metal box w/4 wire legs & coiled handle holds 8 flat-sided bottles w/metal tops, VG+ **$1,100.00**

Oil bottle rack, Mobiloil porcelain shield on red can-type holder w/bent rod handle, holds 6 bottles w/thimble caps, VG+ **$325.00**

Oil can, Agalion Motor Oil, 1-gal, red w/lion head image, 11x8x3", VG **$350.00**

Oil Can, Keynoil Motor Oil, ½-gal, eagle logo, red & black on white label, 6½x8x3", VG............................**$475.00**

Oil can, Lion Head Motor Oil, 1-qt, Monarch of Oil above diagonal banner w/image lion's head, red & yellow, 5½", VG+...**$160.00**

Oil can, Marathon Handy Oiler, 4-oz, oval w/spout & cap, red & white w/runner mascot, NM **$35.00**

Oil can, Pep Boys Pure As Gold Motor Oil, 2-gal, yellow, 11½x8½x5¾", EX+ **$100.00**

Oil can, Tioplet Motor Oil, 1-qt, image of Indian chief pointing, red, white & blue, 5½", unopened, EX.......**$520.00**

Oil pour can, Penn-Rad 100% Pennsylvania Motor Oil engraved on tin tankard shape w/funnel spout, ½-gal, 11", EX+ **$20.00**

Paperweight, cast-iron St Louis Gas pump w/copper hose & nozzle, 7¾", repainted, EX.................................**$500.00**

Pocket mirror, Excelesior Motor Oils & Greases/Gasoline/Lubricating Oils/For All Purposes, patriotic design, 2" dia, EX...............................**$75.00**

Pocket watch, Shell Super X Motor Oil lettered on blue face w/white hands & numbers, chrome case, 1¾" dia, EX...**$185.00**

Poster, ...Step Ahead/Mighty Amoco, close-up image of marching drummer ready to beat drum, cardboard, 28x61", EX...**$100.00**

Poster, Golden Shell Motor Oil 25¢/Time To Change, shows baby's crying face & diaper on clothesline, 58x40", VG **$125.00**

Restroom key tags, Sunoco, Men's/Ladies' lettered on blue tabs above images of gas pumps, 7½x3½", NM ..**$110.00**

Sign, Beacon Flash Gasoline, 2-sided porcelain tombstone shape, orange & black on white, 28x22", VG **$600.00**

Sign, Gulf, sidewalk price rack w/3 pricing panels for Gulftane/Gulf No-nox/Good Gulf, 20¢ to 40¢ price range, 62", EX+ **$350.00**

Sign, Independent/No Smoking, oblong porcelain panel w/rounded corners, red & blue on white, 4x19", EX...............**$250.00**

Sign, Mobil, red diecut porcelain winged horse emblem w/white trim, 44" from hoof to wing, VG+.....**$1,100.00**

Sign, Mobiloil, porcelain lollipop w/winged horse on circle atop name panel, metal pole base, 64"x30½" dia, EX...**$700.00**

Sign, Purol Gasoline/The Pure Oil Co, porcelain pump, white on blue, oval, 15", VG.............................**$175.00**

Sign, Red Crown Gasoline, 2-sided porcelain circle w/name around crown logo, red & blue on white, 42", EX/VG+...**$650.00**

Sign, Service Entrance lettered in white, on blue diecut porcelain arrow w/white outline, 2-sided, 10x42", EX **$275.00**

Sign, Sky Chief Su-preme Gasoline/Super-Charged With Petrox, porcelain pump, red, green, white & black, 1959, 18", EX...**$100.00**

Sign, Socony-Vacuum Credit Cards Honored Here, 2-sided painted metal flange panel, blue on white, 14x23", VG **$50.00**

Sign, Sunoco Motor Oil/Mercury Made, porcelain w/rounded corners, yellow w/double pin-stripe border, early, 12x10", EX..**$350.00**

Sign, Super-Shell/Saves on Stop & Go Driving, paper, cartoon image of impatient motorist waiting on trolley, 33x53", VG+ **$900.00**

Snow globe, saleman's sample #KD 4, tanker & station in globe on base indicating place for dealer's name & message, VG **$200.00**

Soap dispenser, Phillips 66, stainless steel w/plastic window, push up to release soap, NM.............................**$160.00**

Soap dispenser, Shell, logo on cast-iron bowl that tips forward on base, 5", VG **$150.00**

Standee, Mobil, painted wood diecut image of station attendant holding pen & pad, 72", EX...................**$650.00**

Thermometer, Castrol, self-framed porcelain, Emaille Belg. T.P. Bruxeles, 1959, 30", EX, $175.00. (Photo courtesy Collectors Auction Service)

Thermometer, Mobil, dial w/glass front, Pam Clock Co, c 1957, 12" dia, EX **$400.00**

Thermometer, Trico Wiper Blades, dial-type wiper windshield shape, metal frame w/glass front, 9½x15", EX+ **$130.00**

Thermometer, Wakefield Castrol Motor Oil, self-framed porcelain, red & white on green, sq corners, ca 1959, 30", EX..$175.00

Thermometer/sign, Thermo Royal Anti-Freeze can graphic on red panel w/sm dial thermometer, 17½x11½", G..$250.00

Tie tack, Husky 10-year service award, gold-tone Husky dog standing on 2-star bar, ⅜x½", M.......................$275.00

Tire stand, Kenyon Tires, metal trapezoid shape w/winged tire logo, red & black, 8½x18½", VG+ $135.00

Winterfront, Jenney Gasoline/Best for Winter Driving, 2-sided cardboard designed to fit 1934 cars, blue, 14x21", NM $85.00

Winterfront, Mobilgas/For Friendly Service, 2-sided waxed cardboard w/winged horse emblem, red, white & blue, 12x20", EX $30.00

Gay Fad Glassware

What started out as a home-based 'one-woman' operation in the late 1930s within only a few years had grown into a substantial company requiring much larger facilities and a staff of decorators. The company, dubbed Gay Fad by her husband, was founded by Fran Taylor. Originally they decorated kitchenware items but later found instant success with the glassware they created, most of which utilized frosted backgrounds and multicolored designs such as tulips, state themes, Christmas motifs, etc. Some pieces were decorated with 22-karat gold and sterling silver. In addition to the frosted glass which collectors quickly learn to associate with this company, they also became famous for their 'bentware' — quirky cocktail glasses whose stems were actually bent.

Some of their more collectible lines are 'Beau Brummel' — martini glasses with straight or bent stems featuring a funny-faced drinker wearing a plaid bow tie; 'Gay Nineties' — various designs such as can-can girls and singing bartenders; '48 States' — maps with highlighted places of interest; 'Rich Man, Poor Man' (or Beggar Man, Thief, etc.); 'Bartender' (self-explanatory); 'Currier & Ives' — made to coordinate with the line by Royal China; 'Zombies' — extra tall and slim with various designs including roses, giraffes, and flamingos; and the sterling silver- and 22-karat gold-trimmed glassware.

Until you learn to spot it a mile away (which you soon will), look for an interlocking 'G' and 'F' or 'Gay Fad,' the latter mark indicating pieces from the late 1950s to the early 1960s. The glassware itself has the feel of satin and is of very good quality. It can be distinguished from other manufacturers' wares simply by checking the bottom — Gay Fad's are frosted; generally other manufacturers' are not. Hand-painted details are another good clue. (You may find similar glassware signed 'Briard'; this is not Gay Fad.) Listings below include Fire-King and Federal Glass pieces that were decorated by Gay Fad.

This Ohio-based company was sold in 1963 and closed altogether in 1965. Be careful of condition. If the frosting has darkened or the paint is worn or faded, it's best to wait for a better example.

Advisor: Donna S. McGrady (See the Directory, Gay Fad)

Ashtray, Trout Flies, clear..$6.00

Batter bowl, Fruits, milk white, signed w/F (Federal Glass), w/handle $70.00

Bent tray, Phoenix Bird, clear, signed Gay Fad, 13¾" dia..$17.00

Bent tray, Stylized Cats, clear, signed Gay Fad, 11½" dia...$18.00

Bent trays, classic design, paper label, 2 sq trays in metal frame..$22.00

Beverage set, Apple, frosted, 86-oz ball pitcher 6 13-oz round-bottom tumblers..................................$80.00

Beverage set, Colonial Homestead, frosted, 85-oz pitcher & 6 12-oz tumblers...$60.00

Beverage set, Magnolia, clear, 86-oz pitcher & 6 13-oz tumblers $75.00

Bowl, chili; Fruits, 2¼x5" $12.50

Bowl, mixing; Poinsettia, red w/green leaves on Fire-King Ivory Swirl, 8"...$45.00

Bowl, splash-proof; Fruits, Fire-King, 4¼x6½"...........$55.00

Bowls, nesting; Fruits, Fire-King, 6", 7½", 8¾", set of 3 .$45.00

Canister set, Red Rose, red lids, white interior, 3-pc ..$55.00

Casserole, Apple, open, oval, Fire-King Ivory, 1-qt....$45.00

Casserole, Apple, w/lid, Fire-King Ivory, 1-qt.............$65.00

Casserole, Fruits, divided, oval, Fire King, 11¾".........$40.00

Casserole, Fruits, w/lid, Fire-King, 1-qt........................$35.00

Casserole, Peach Blossom, w/au gratin lid, Fire-King, 2-qt..$35.00

Casserole, Rosemaling (tulips) on lid, clear, 2-qt, w/black wire rack...$30.00

Chip 'n Dip, Horace the Horse w/cart, knife tail, 3 bowls, double old-fashion glass as head, signed Gay Fad $60.00

Cocktail set, Poodle, metal frame 'body' w/martini mixer, double old-fashion glass as head & 4 5-oz glasses, signed Gay Fad $60.00

Cocktail shaker, Ballerina Shoes, red metal screw-top lid, frosted, 32-oz, 7".......................................$20.00

Cocktail shaker, full-figure ballerina, frosted, 28-oz, 9"..$35.00

Cruet set, Oil & Vinegar, Cherry, clear.......................$15.00

Decanter set, Gay '90s, Scotch, Rye, Gin & Bourbon, frosted or white inside $80.00

Goblet, Bow Pete, Hoffman Beer, 16-oz.....................$15.00

Ice tub, Gay '90s, frosted $16.00

Juice set, Tommy Tomato, frosted, 36-oz pitcher & 6 4-oz tumblers...$45.00

Loaf pan, Apple, Fire-King Ivory................................$35.00

Luncheon set, Fantasia Hawaiian Flower, 1 place setting (sq plate, cup & saucer) $15.00

Luncheon set, Ivy, sq plate, cup & saucer, tumbler, clear, 1 complete place setting, 4-pc $24.00

Martini mixer, 'A Jug of Wine...,' w/glass stirring rod, clear, signed Gay Fad, 10⅝" $16.00

Mix-A-Salad set, Ivy, 22-oz shaker w/plastic top, garlic press, measuring spoon, recipe book, MIB....................$70.00

Mug, Fruits, stackable, Fire-King, 3"...........................$12.00

Mug, Notre Dame, frosted, 16-oz $15.00

Mug set, Here's How in a different language on ea mug, frosted, 12-pc $72.00

Pilsner set, Gay '90s, portraits: Mama, Papa, Victoria, Rupert, Aunt Aggie, Uncle Bertie, Gramps & Horace, frosted, 8-pc **$90.00**

Pitcher, Currier & Ives, blue & white, frosted, 86-oz..**$60.00**

Pitcher, juice; Ada Orange, frosted, 36-oz **$22.00**

Pitcher, martini; cardinal & pine sprig, frosted, w/glass stirrer, 42-oz **$35.00**

Pitcher, Rosemaling (tulips), white inside, 32-oz **$28.00**

Pitcher, water; pears and cherries, frosted, $45.00. (Photo courtesy Donna McGrady)

Plate, Fruits, lace edge, Hazel Atlas, 8½"......................**$17.50**

Punch set, pink veiling, bowl & 8 cups in white metal frame..**$65.00**

Range set, Rooster, salt, pepper, sugar & flour shakers, frosted w/red metal lids, 8-oz, 4-pc **$40.00**

Refrigerator container, Distlefink on white, Fire-King, w/lid, 4x8"..**$50.00**

Salad set, Fruits, frosted, lg bowl, 2 cruets, salt & pepper shakers, 5-pc **$50.00**

Salad set, Outlined Fruits, lg bowl, 2 cruets, salt & pepper shakers, frosted, 5-pc.................................**$65.00**

Salt & pepper shakers, Morning Glory, frosted w/red plastic tops, pr **$16.00**

Stem, bent cocktail, Beau Brummel, clear, signed Gay Fad, 3½-oz...**$14.00**

Stem, bent cocktail, Souvenir of My Bender, frosted, 3-oz **$11.00**

Tea & toast, Magnolia, sq plate w/cup indent & cup, clear **$11.00**

Tom & Jerry set, Christmas bells, milk white, marked GF, bowl & 6 cups......................................**$70.00**

Tumbler, Christmas Greetings From Gay Fad, frosted, 4-oz..**$17.00**

Tumbler, Derby Winner Citation, frosted, 1948, 14-oz..**$50.00**

Tumbler, grouse, brown, aqua & gold on clear, signed Gay Fad, 10-oz...**$10.00**

Tumbler, Hors D'oeuvres, clear, 14-oz......................**$10.00**

Tumbler, Kentucky state map (1 of 48), pink, yellow or lime, frosted, marked GF, 10-oz **$6.00**

Tumbler, Oregon state map on pink picket fence, clear, marked GF...**$6.00**

Tumbler, Pegasus, gold & pink on black, 12-oz.........**$10.00**

Tumbler, Say When, frosted, 4-oz **$8.00**

Tumbler, Zombie, flamingo, frosted, marked GF, 14-oz.**$18.00**

Tumbler, Zombie, giraffe, frosted, marked GF, 14-oz.**$18.00**

Tumblers, angels preparing for Christmas, frosted, 12-oz, set of 8..**$72.00**

Tumblers, Dickens Christmas Carol characters, frosted, 12-oz, set of 8..**$50.00**

Tumblers, Famous Fighters (John L Sullivan & the others), frosted, 16-oz, 8 pc set..........................**$85.00**

Tumblers, French Poodle, clear, 17-oz, set of 8 in original box..**$96.00**

Tumblers, Game Birds & Animals, clear, 12-oz, 8-pc set, MIB **$75.00**

Tumblers, Ohio Presidents, frosted, 12-oz, set of 8....**$60.00**

Tumblers, Rich Man, Poor Man (nursery rhyme), frosted, marked GF, 16-oz, set of 8..................................**$95.00**

Tumblers, Sports Cars, white interior, 12-oz, 8 pc set...**$45.00**

Vanity set, butterflies in meadow, pink interior, 5-pc.**$60.00**

Vase, Red Poppy, clear, footed, 10" **$22.00**

Waffle set, Blue Willow, 48-oz waffle batter jug & 11½-oz syrup jug, frosted, pr.....................................**$95.00**

Waffle set, Little Black Sambo, frosted, 48-ounce batter jug, 11½" syrup jug, $275.00 for the pair. (Photo courtesy Donna McGrady)

Waffle set, Peach Blossoms, 48-oz waffle batter jug & 11½-oz syrup jug, frosted, pr..**$35.00**

Waffle set, Red Poppy, frosted, 48-oz waffle batter jug, 11½-oz syrup jug **$24.00**

Wine set, Grapes, decanter & 4 2½-oz stemmed wines, clear, 5-pc **$40.00**

Geisha Girl China

The late nineteenth century saw a rise in the popularity of Oriental wares in the US and Europe. Japan rose to meet the demands of this flourishing ceramics marketplace with a flurry of growth in potteries and decorating centers. These created items for export which would appeal to Western tastes and integrate into Western dining and decorating cultures, which were distinct from those of Japan. One example of the wares introduced into this marketplace was Geisha Girl porcelain.

Hundreds of different patterns and manufacturers' marks have been uncovered on Geisha Girl porcelain tea and dinnerware sets, dresser accessories, decorative items, etc., which were produced well into the twentieth century. They all share in common colorful decorations featuring kimono-clad ladies and children involved in everyday activities. These scenes are set against a backdrop of lush flora, distinctive Japanese architecture and majestic landscapes. Most Geisha Girl porcelain designs were laid on by means of a stencil, generally red or black. This appears as an outline on the ceramic body. Details are then completed by hand-painted washes in a myriad of colors. A minority of the wares were wholly hand painted.

Most Geisha Girl porcelain has a colorful border or edging with handles, finials, spouts, and feet similarly adorned. The most common border color is red which can range from orange to red-orange to a deep brick red. Among the earliest border colors were red, maroon, cobalt blue, light (apple) green, and Nile green. Pine green, blue-green, and turquoise made their appearance circa 1917, and a light cobalt or Delft blue appeared around 1920. Other colors (e.g. tan, yellow, brown, and gold) can also be found. Borders were often enhanced with gilded lace or floral decoration. The use of gold for this purpose diminished somewhat around 1910 to 1915 when some decorators used economic initiative (fewer firings required) to move the gold to just inside the border or replace the gold with white or yellow enamels. Wares with both border styles continued to be produced into the twentieth century. Exquisite examples with multicolored borders as well as ornate rims decorated with florals and geometrics can also be found.

Due to the number of different producers, the quality of Geisha ware ranges from crude to finely detailed. Geisha Girl porcelain was sold in sets and open stock in outlets ranging from the five-and-ten to fancy department stores. It was creatively used for store premiums, containers for store products, fair souvenirs, and resort memorabilia. The fineness of detailing, amount of gold highlights, border color, scarcity of form and, of course, condition all play a role in establishing the market value of a given item. Some patterns are scarcer than others, but most Geisha ware collectors seem not to focus on particular patterns.

The heyday of Geisha Girl porcelain was from 1910 through the 1930s. Production continued until the World War II era. During the 'Occupied' period, a small amount of wholly hand-painted examples were made, often with a black and gold border. The Oriental import stores and catalogs from the 1960s and 1970s featured some examples of Geisha Girl porcelain, many of which were produced in Hong Kong. These are recognized by the very white porcelain, sparse detail coloring, and lack of gold decoration. The 1990s has seen a resurgence of reproductions with a faux Nippon mark. These items are supposed to represent high quality Geisha ware, but in reality they are a blur of Geisha and Satsuma-style characteristics. They are too busy in design, too heavily enameled, and bear poor resemblance to items that rightfully carry Noritake's green M-in-Wreath Nippon mark. Once you've been introduced to a few of these reproductions, you'll be able to recognize them easily.

Note: Colors mentioned in the following listings refer to borders.

Advisor: Elyce Litts (See Directory, Geisha Girl China)

Ashtray, Temple A, Nippon mark, $25.00. (Photo courtesy Elyce Litts)

Berry set, Parasol C: Parasol, master w/5 individuals, red w/gold **$45.00**
Biscuit jar, Lady in Rickshaw, melon ribs, red-orange w/gold, footed..**$55.00**
Bonbon dish, Bamboo Trellis, red w/gold **$15.00**
Bowl, Dragon Boat, 6-lobed, blue w/gold, 7".............**$35.00**
Box, Mother & Daughter, covered, gold rim, 2x5x4" .**$32.00**
Celery dish, Foreign Garden, blue border....................**$45.00**
Cocoa pot, Battledore, ewer shape, yellow-green, 9".**$55.00**
Creamer, Boy w/Scythe, cobalt w/gold **$15.00**
Creamer, Long-Stemmed Peony, slender, fluted, blue w/gold **$12.00**
Cup & saucer, tea; Bamboo Trellis, dark green **$12.00**
Dresser box, Garden Bench B, cobalt w/gold, 6" dia **$38.00**
Egg cup, Cloud A, red..**$12.00**
Ewer, Garden Bench H, red w/gold lacing **$45.00**
Jug, Cherry Blossom, red-orange edge, 6½" **$35.00**
Lemonade set, Bellflower, brown w/trim, pitcher & 5 mugs..**$125.00**
Mug, lemonade; Geisha in Sampan B, cobalt w/gold ..**$12.00**
Napkin ring, Nippon mark, Temple A, oblong, scalloped edge, red **$35.00**
Nappy, Temple A, hand-fluted edge, single handle, sea-green border **$35.00**

Nut dish, Duck Watching A, red w/gold, footed, individual size **$8.00**

Plate, Bamboo Trellis, blue-green w/gold buds, simple decor, 6½" **$8.00**

Plate, Basket, swirl fluted, scalloped edge, dark apple green, 8½" **$30.00**

Plate, Bird Cage, red-orange w/gold, 6" **$10.00**

Puff box, Flower Gathering, ribbed, black stencil, red-orange edge, 3½" diameter..**$18.00**

Serving platter, Feather Fan, Nippon mark, handles, plus 6 matching cake plates **$75.00**

Shakers, Blind Man's Bluff, swirl-fluted body, light apple green, pr..**$22.00**

Sugar shaker, Parasol L, red-orange w/yellow lacing, handles, fluted body..**$28.00**

Tea set, River's Edge, green 3-banded border w/gold, pot, creamer, sugar bowl, 6 cups & saucers **$125.00**

Teapot, Kite A, brown w/gold......................................**$28.00**

Toothpick holder, Court Lady, blue w/gold, 5-sided, footed **$38.00**

Vase, Flower Gathering, 3 reserves on ornate ground, 3 footed, handles, 3" **$35.00**

GI Joe

The first GI Joe was introduced by Hasbro in 1964. He was 12" tall, and you could buy him with blond, auburn, black, or brown hair in four basic variations: Action Sailor, Action Marine, Action Soldier, and Action Pilot. There was also a Black doll as well as representatives of many other nations. By 1967 GI Joe could talk, all the better to converse with the female nurse who was first issued that year. The Adventure Team series (1970 – 1976) included Black Adventurer, Talking Astronaut, Sea Adventurer, Talking Team Commander, Land Adventurer, and several variations. At this point, their hands were made of rubber, making it easier for them to grasp the many guns, tools, and other accessories that Hasbro had devised. Playsets, vehicles, and clothing completed the package, and there were kid-size items designed specifically for the kids themselves. The 12" dolls were discontinued by 1976.

Brought out by popular demand, Hasbro's 3¾" GI Joes hit the market in 1982. Needless to say, they were very well accepted. In fact, these smaller GI Joes are thought to be the most successful line of action figures ever made. Loose figures (those removed from the original packaging) are very common, and even if you can locate the accessories that they came out with, most are worth only about $3.00 to $10.00. It's the mint-in-package items that most interest collectors, and they pay a huge premium for the package. There's an extensive line of accessories that goes with the smaller line as well. Many more are listed in *Schroeder's Collectible Toys, Antique to Modern.*

Note: A/M was used in the description lines as an abbreviation for Action Man.

12" Figures and Accessories

Accessory, Adventure Team Crocodile, EX, C6 ....**$15.00**
Accessory, Adventure Team Emergency Rescue, MIP.**$60.00**
Accessory, Adventure Team Jumpsuit, mesh, EX........**$12.00**
Accessory, Adventure Team Volcano Jumper, MIP **$50.00**
Accessory, Army Flag, EX **$45.00**
Accessory, Astronaut Helmet, w/microphone & visor, EX.**$30.00**
Accessory, Combat Construction, complete, EX........**$450.00**
Accessory, Communications Flag Set, #7704, complete, NM...**$125.00**
Accessory, Eight Ropes of Danger Underwater Diver Playset, MIB **$200.00**
Accessory, Grenade Launcher, A/M, EX **$15.00**
Accessory, Ice Pick, A/M, EX..**$5.00**
Accessory, Life Guards Shoulder Pouch, A/M, EX......**$45.00**
Accessory, Marine Dress Parade Set, #7710, MIP......**$175.00**
Accessory, Mine Detector & Harness, VG **$50.00**
Accessory, Royal Canadian Mounted Police, complete, EX...**$700.00**
Accessory, Russian Tunic, A/M, EX.............................**$35.00**
Accessory, Scuba Top, A/M, EX **$12.00**
Accessory, USAF Flag, EX **$45.00**
Adventure Team Headquarters, complete, EX (worn box) **$275.00**
Figure, Action Marine, complete, EX (G box)...........**$175.00**
Figure, Action Marine Medic Set, #7719, complete, NMIB...**$225.00**
Figure, Action Sailor, 30th Anniversary, 1994, NRFB ..**$140.00**

Figure, Action Sailor, MIB, $325.00. (Photo courtesy Cindy Sabulis)

Figure, Adventure Team Air Adventurer, complete, EX .**$150.00**
Figure, Adventure Team Land Adventurer, complete, EX (VG box) **$250.00**
Figure, Adventure Team Sea Adventurer, complete, EX (VG box) **$250.00**
Figure, Adventure Team Talking Astronaut, complete, VG (VG repro box).....................................**$300.00**
Figure, Annapolis Cadet, complete, NMIB................**$325.00**
Figure, Atomic Man, complete, NM **$100.00**
Figure, Black Action Soldier, Complete, M................**$900.00**
Figure, Combat Engineer, complete, M......................**$950.00**
Figure, Deep Sea Diver, complete, NM **$400.00**

Figure, German Tanker, A/M, complete $425.00

Figure, Hurrican Spotter, complete, NM $375.00

Figure, Landing Signal Officer, complete, M $475.00

Figure, Marine Medic, complete, NM...................$325.00

Figure, Navy Attack, rare version w/yellow life jacket, complete, NM..................$800.00

Figure, Royal Canadian Mounted Police, complctc, NM..$750.00

Figure, Scramble Pilot, complete, EX.....................$350.00

Figure, Secret Mission in Spy Island, mail-in, MIB......$40.00

Figure, State Trooper, complete, EX.....................$390.00

Figure, Tank Commander, complete, EX..................$525.00

Figure, Underwater Explorer, A/M, complete, NM ...$425.00

Figure, World War I Aviator Ace, mail-in, MIB...........$60.00

Vehicle, Action Pack Turbo Copter, MIB (sealed).......$50.00

Vehicle, Adventure Team Sea Sled, complete, EX.......$75.00

Vehicle, Blue Panther Navy Jet, complete, rare, M...$600.00

Vehicle, Five Star Jeep w/Trailer & Tripod, #7000, complete, NM..................$200.00

Vehicle, Team Vehicle, yellow ATV, VG.....................$55.00

3¾" Figures and Accessories

Accessory, AGP w/Super Trooper Figure, 1988, complete, MIB $30.00

Accessory, Battle Gear Accessory Pack #1, 1983, MIP ..$16.00

Accessory, Cobra Overlord's Dictator Vehicle, w/Overlord Figure, MIB..................$25.00

Accessory, Falcon Glider w/Grunt, complete, EX.....$100.00

Accessory, Heavy Artillery Laser w/Grand Slam, 1982, NRFB..$110.00

Accessory, Hovercraft, 1984 mail-in, MIP $40.00

Accessory, Missile Defense Unit, 1984, MIP $20.00

Accessory, Motorized Battle Wagon, 1991, MIP $35.00

Accessory, Phantom X-19 Stealth Fighter, 1988, MIB..$70.00

Accessory, SAS Parachutist Attack, Action Force, MIP ..$35.00

Accessory, Special Force Battle Gear, Action Force, MIP .$5.00

Accessory, Transportable Tactical Battle Platform, 1985, complete, NM..................$30.00

Figure, Dial-tone, MOC, $32.00.

Figure, Ace, 1983, MIP $25.00

Figure, Airtight, 1985, w/accessories, EX $12.00

Figure, Astro Viper, 1988, MIP..................$12.00

Figure, Baroness, 1984, w/accessories, EX $45.00

Figure, Big Boa, 1987, NMOC..................$35.00

Figure, Breaker, 1982, straight arm, VG (VG card) $85.00

Figure, Buzzer, 1985, MIP $35.00

Figure, Cobra, 1983, swivel-arm, NMOC $125.00

Figure, Cobra Officer, 1983, VG (VG card) $80.00

Figure, Colonel Courage, 1992, complete, M..................$5.00

Figure, Croc Master, 1987, EX (EX card)..................$30.00

Figure, Deep-Six, 1989, VG (VG card)..................$15.00

Figure, Drop-Zone, 1986, w/accessories, NM..............$10.00

Figure, Ferret, 1988, w/accessories, EX..................$8.00

Figure, Frag-Viper, 1988, NMOC..................$20.00

Figure, Gnawgahyde, 1989, NMOC..................$15.00

Figure, Heat-Viper, 1989, EX (EX card)..................$15.00

Figure, Lady Jaye, 1985, w/accessories, EX..................$20.00

Figure, Mainframe, 1986, EX (EX card)..................$20.00

Figure, Mega Marine Blast-Off, 1998, MOC..................$12.00

Figure, Mercer, 1987, w/accessories, NM..................$8.00

Figure, Night Force Outback, 1988, w/accessories, EX..$15.00

Figure, Outback, 1987, MOC..................$18.00

Figure, Quick Kick, 1985, MOC..................$35.00

Figure, Red Dog, 1987, w/accessories, NM..................$8.00

Figure, Roadblock, 1988, w/accessories, NM..............$10.00

Figure, Sci-Fi, 1986, w/accessories, EX..................$10.00

Figure, Slaughter's Renegades Mercer/Taurus/Red Dog, 1987, MOC..................$30.00

Figure, Snow Serpent, 1985, MOC..................$50.00

Figure, Star Brigade Carcass, w/accessories, EX..................$28.00

Figure, Storm Shadow, 1984, w/accessories, NM........$40.00

Figure, Sub-Zero, 1990, MOC..................$15.00

Figure, Thrasher, 1986, w/accessories, EX..................$6.00

Figure, Torpedo, 1983, MOC..................$60.00

Figure, Wet Suit, 1986, MOC..................$45.00

Figure, Zarana, 1986, w/earring, EX (EX card)..........$85.00

Gilner

Gilner was a California company that operated in Culver City from the mid-1930s until 1957. They produced florist ware, figurines, and other types of decorative pottery. Their pixie line is very popular with today's collectors.

Figurine, Black native boy dancing w/arms in air, w/original earrings..................$25.00

Figurine, female pixie in light green sitting w/legs stretched out in front, 3½x2¾"..................$30.00

Figurine, female pixie in red w/hands on flared skirt curtsying, 4"..................$35.00

Figurine, pixie in dark green in acrobatic position w/feet painted upwards, 3"..................$35.00

Figurine, pixie in red peeks from window of green tugboat window..................$60.00

Figurine, pixie lying on side w/head in hand, elbow on floor, green, 2½x5"..................$30.00

Figurine, Siamese woman on knees in costume, 11"..$20.00

Leaf dish, Black native w/metal hoop earrings in pale green dish, 4x8" $35.00

Planter, pixie couple in red sit & kiss beside pale green stump w/I Love U carved on it, 3x4" $60.00

Planter, pixie girl kneeling beside stump, solid green, 1951 ....$25.00

Planter, pixie playing piano, solid green, 4x4½" $28.00

Planter, pixie stands beside stump, solid red, 4x7" $45.00

Planter, pixies (2) in red sit on pale green log, 1940s, 5½x12½" $40.00

Planter, pixies (2) stand on ea side of 3 books, 1 reads Diary of a Pixie, other reads Pixie Pete & Pixie Tales, 7x5" $50.00

Planter, Polynesian boy resting on leaves beside hollow stump, 3¾x8½" $18.00

Salt & pepper shakers, pixie boy & girl sitting, 3", pr.$30.00

Wall pocket, pixie in red sitting on bunch of green grapes, 8x6½" $45.00

Wall pocket, pixie on teacup, maroon, white & yellow, rare, 4½x6½", from $95 to..............................$125.00

Wall pocket, pixie sitting on apple, 1950, hard to find, 6x6½", from $50 to..............................$75.00

Wall pocket, pixie sitting on rope handle of water bucket, dark green, 6x4½" $35.00

Glass Knives

Popular during the Depression years, glass knives were made in many of the same colors as the glass dinnerware of the era — pink, green, light blue, crystal, and more rarely, amber or white (originally called opal). Some were hand painted with flowers or fruit. The earliest boxes had poems printed on their tops explaining the knife's qualities in the pre-stainless steel days: 'No metal to tarnish when cutting your fruit, and so it is certain this glass knife will suit.' Eventually, a tissue flyer was packed with each knife, which elaborated even more on the knife's usefulness. 'It is keen as a razor, ideal for slicing tomatoes, oranges, lemons, grapefruit, and especially constructed for separating the meaty parts of grapefruit from its rind....' Boxes add interest by helping identify distributors as well as commercial names of the knives.

When originally sold, the blades were ground to a sharp cutting edge, but due to everyday usage, the blades eventually became nicked. Collectors will accept reground, resharpened blades as long as the original shape has been maintained.

Documented US glass companies that made glass knives are the Akro Agate Co., Cameron Glass Corp., Houze Glass Corp., Imperial Glass Corp., Jeannette Glass Co., and Westmoreland Glass Co.

Internet final-bid auction prices indicate what a person is willing to pay to add a new or different piece to a personal collection and may not necessarily reflect any price guide values.

Advisor: Michele A. Rosewitz (See Directory, Glass Knives)

Aer-Flo, crystal, 7½", from $30 to.....................$40.00

BK Co/ESP 12-14-20, crystal, hand-painted handle, 9".$35.00

BK Co/ESP 12-14-20, crystal, 9", from $15 to.............$18.00

BK Co/ESP 12-14-20, green, 9", from $40 to..............$60.00

Block, crystal, 8¼", from $12 to $25.00

Block, green, 8¼", from $37.50 to $55.00

Block, pink, 8¼", from $45 to $50.00

Cryst-o-lite (3 Flowers), crystal, 8½" $10.00

Dagger, crystal, 9", from $150 to......................$175.00

Dur-X, 3-leaf, blue, 8½" or 9"........................$50.00

Dur-X, 3-leaf, crystal, 8½" or 9".....................$20.00

Dur-X, 3-leaf, green, 8½" or 9".......................$50.00

Dur-X, 3-leaf, pink, 8½" or 9".......................$45.00

Dur-X, 5-leaf, blue, 9".................................$70.00

Dur-x, 5-leaf, crystal, 9".............................$40.00

Dur-X, 5-leaf, green, 9"...............................$60.00

Dur-X, 5-leaf, pink, 9"................................$60.00

Imperial Candlewick, crystal, 8½" $500.00

Plain handle, green, 8½" or 9", from $32 to.............$40.00

Steel-ite, crystal, 8½"................................$40.00

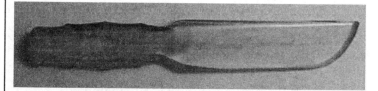

Steel-ite, green, 8½", $80.00. (Photo courtesy Michele A. Rosewitz)

Steel-ite, pink, 8½".....................................$80.00

Stonex, amber, 8½" $250.00

Stonex, crystal, 8½" $40.00

Stonex, green, 8½" $85.00

Stonex, opalescent, 8½" $350.00

Thumbguard, crystal, 9", from $25 to....................$40.00

Thumbguard, green, 9", from $350 to.....................$395.00

Vitex (Star & Diamond), blue, 8½" or 9"................$40.00

Vitex (Star & Diamond), crystal, 8½" or 9"..............$25.00

Vitex (Star & Diamond), pink, 8½" or 9"................$40.00

Golden Foliage

In 1935 Libbey Glass was purchased by Owens-Illinois but continued to operate under the Libbey Glass name. After World War II, the company turned to making tableware and still does today. Golden Foliage is just one of the many patterns made during the 1950s. It is a line of crystal glassware with a satin band that features a golden maple leaf as well as other varieties. The satin band is trimmed in gold, above and below. Since this gold seems to have easily worn off, be careful to find mint pieces for your collection. This pattern was made in silver as well.

Advisor: Debbie Coe (See Directory, Cape Cod)

Creamer & sugar bowl $15.00

Drink set, includes 6 jiggers & brass-finished caddy ..$49.00

Drink set, includes 8 tumblers (9-oz), ice tub & brass-finished caddy **$75.00**
Drink set, includes 8 tumblers (9-oz) & brass-finished caddy **$48.00**
Goblet, cocktail; 4-oz..**$6.00**
Goblet, cordial; 1-oz..**$9.50**
Goblet, pilsner; 11-oz..**$9.50**
Goblet, sherbet; 6½-oz..**$4.50**

Tumbler, water, ten-ounce, $7.50; goblet, water; nine-ounce, $6.50.

Ice tub, in metal 3-footed frame.................................**$22.50**
Pitcher, 5¼", w/metal frame **$16.50**
Salad dressing set, includes 3 bowls (4") & brass-finished caddy **$19.50**
Tumbler, beverage; 12½-oz.....................................**$9.50**
Tumbler, cooler; 14-oz...**$9.50**
Tumbler, jigger; 2-oz..**$7.00**
Tumbler, juice; 6-oz...**$5.00**
Tumbler, old fashioned; 9-oz.....................................**$6.00**

Graniteware

Though it really wasn't as durable as its name suggests, there's still a lot of granite ware around today, though much of it is now in collections. You may even be able to find a bargain. The popularity of the 'country' look in home decorating and the exposure it's had in some of the leading decorating magazines has caused granite ware prices, especially on rare items, to soar in recent years.

It's made from a variety of metals coated with enameling of various colors, some solid, others swirled. It's color, form, and, of course, condition that dictates value. (To evaluate items with wear and chipping, be sure to drastically reduce our values in proportion to the amount of damage.) Swirls of cobalt and white, purple and white, green and white, and brown and white are unusual, but even solid gray items such as a hanging salt box or a chamberstick can be expensive, because pieces like those are rare. Decorated examples are uncommon — so are children's

pieces and salesman's samples.

For further information, we recommend *The Collector's Encyclopedia of Granite Ware, Colors, Shapes, and Values,* by Helen Greguire (Collector Books).

Basin, blue & white med mottle inside & out, flared sides, 4⅜x12¾", EX.................................**$70.00**
Bowl, green & white lg mottle inside & out, black trim, pedestal foot, ca 1950, 3½x6⅝", EX.....................**$65.00**
Bowl, mixing; yellow & white lg swirl inside & out, black trim, ca 1950, 6x12¼", M.................**$50.00**
Bucket, green & white lg swirl, white interior, cobalt trim & ears, matching lid w/wire bail, 5¼x4½", M........**$650.00**
Butter melter, light blue & white lg mottle inside & out, ca 1980, 2⅝x2⅝", M **$25.00**
Coal hod, solid blue-gray inside & out, seamed, embossed GM, 15x10½" dia, EX.........................**$250.00**
Coffee boiler, bl-gray & white lg swirl, white interior, riveted handle & ears, seamed, Lava Ware, 10¼", EX....**$425.00**
Coffeepot, brilliant blue shading to lighter blue, white interior, black trim & handle, seamless, 9¼", EX.......**$325.00**
Coffeepot, green shading to ivory, white interior, black trim & handle, 9½x6", EX.............................**$225.00**
Coffeepot, light blue & white med swirl, white interior, black trim & handle, 6¾x4½", EX...............................**$160.00**
Coffeepot, reddish brown w/white specks (fine mottle), white interior, riveted spout & handle, seamless, 10¼", EX **$155.00**
Coffeepot, redipped dark blue w/white flecks over original dark green & white Chrysolite, seamless, 11", EX .**$165.00**
Colander, white, 2½x7½" (+handles), EX.................**$60.00**
Cream can, gray med mottle, matching lock cover, seamless, wire bail, 5¾x3¼", NM **$495.00**
Cup & saucer, gray & white med mottle, pearl Enameled Ware, 2¼x4½", 5¾", M....................**$125.00**
Cuspidor, gray lg mottle, riveted handle & seamed bottom, marked Agate Ware L&G Mfg Co, 5½x4¾", NM....**$425.00**
Double boiler, gray med mottle, seamless, wooden bail handles, marked L&G Mfg Co, 11¾x9¼" dia, EX **$115.00**
Double boiler, green veins of lg mottling w/white overall lumpy effect, green trim, Elite Austria, 8½x7", NM............**$265.00**
Foot tub, dark gray med mottle, seamed, oval, 8¾x18¾x12⅞", EX.................................**$195.00**
Foot tub, dark green & white lg mottle w/white interior, black handles & trim, seamless, 4½x18½x14¾", EX......**$495.00**
Fry pan, lavender-blue & white lg swirl, white interior, black trim & handle, 2x9⅞" dia, EX.............................**$325.00**
Kettle, gray lg mottle, seamless, matching lid, 6½x9" dia, EX......................................**$110.00**
Ladle, soup; green & white lg swirl, white interior, blue handle, 4½" dia, 13⅜" L, EX.............................**$250.00**
Measure, solid cobalt w/white interior, riveted lip & strap handle, seamed, 4¾x3½", EX.............................**$165.00**
Mold, melon; solid cobalt w/white interior, handled tin cover marked 10, 3¾x7¼x5½", M.................................**$115.00**
Mold, melon; solid med blue w/white interior, tin cover embossed No 50, 3⅝x7¾x5¾", NM....................**$155.00**

Mold, ribbed tube; cobalt w/white interior, 2⅞x8¼", EX...**$95.00**

Mold, ring; solid yellow w/white interior, 2¼x8⅛" dia, EX...**$65.00**

Mug, brown shading to light beige, western scenes, ca 1970, 3⅛x3½", M.............................**$45.00**

Mug, camp/mush; blue & white med mottle, white interior, black weld handle & trim, 5⅝x6⅞", EX **$165.00**

Mug, gray & white lg marbleized, white interior, seamless, 4⅛x4", EX...**$75.00**

Mug, red & white lg swirl, white interior, red trim, ca 1970, 3⅛x3½", M.............................**$30.00**

Mug, yellow & white checked pattern, white interior, black trim, ca 1980, 3x3⅜", NM.....................**$20.00**

Pan, egg; gray lg mottle, 5 eyes, riveted handle, 1¼x12" dia, NM...**$275.00**

Pan, egg; red inside & out, 7 eyes, 9⅞" dia, M **$110.00**

Pan, muffin; dark plum w/light gray & white lg mottling inside & out, 8-cup, 1⅝x14x7⅜", EX.................**$295.00**

Pan, pudding; red w/black trim, white interior, narrow rim, 2¾x9¾", NM...**$30.00**

Pan, pudding; white w/cobalt trim, Tru-Blue Quality Enamelware... label, 1½x7" dia, M.................**$35.00**

Pan, sauce; reddish orange w/white interior, black trim & handle, ca 1960, 2¾x6" dia, EX.................**$20.00**

Pan, tart; gray lg mottle, ⅞x6" dia, EX.................**$45.00**

Pie plate, dark brown & white med mottle inside & out w/black trim, 1x9½", EX **$15.00**

Pie plate, deep sea green shading to moss green, white interior, shallow, 9", M.................**$65.00**

Pitcher, blue & white fine mottle, white interior, light blue trim & handle, Elite Austria, 6½x5", EX.............**$325.00**

Pitcher, milk; gray lg mottle, squatty, seamless, weld handle, 6⅞x4½", NM...**$325.00**

Pitcher, water; green & white relish, white interior, cobalt trim, seamless, riveted handle, 7¾x5¾", EX......**$225.00**

Platter, cobalt & white lg mottle, white interior w/cobalt trim, 1¼x16¼x12¾", EX.................**$325.00**

Roaster, cream w/green trim, 4¼x8¾" (+handles), NM...**$145.00**

Skimmer, cobalt, white & green lg mottle front & back, black handle, 18" L, NM.................**$295.00**

Skimmer, dark gray, flat, perforated, Extra Agate Nickel-Steel Ware L&G Mfg Co mark, 3½" dia, 12" to top of handle, NM...**$70.00**

Soap dish, red w/embossed back, hangs, 5¾x3", EX.**$95.00**

Sugar bowl, blue & white lg mottle, white interior, cobalt trim, pedestal foot, marked Hong Kong, 1980, 2½x4¼", M...**$30.00**

Sugar bowl, blue & white lg mottle inside & out, black trim, 1898, 4½x4", M...**$55.00**

Tea steeper, brown & white med relish, white interior, cobalt trim & riveted handle, seamless, 4⅞x4", EX......**$195.00**

Tea strainer, gray med mottle, perforated bottom, ⅞x4" dia, NM...**$95.00**

Teakettle, blue & white lg swirl, white interior, black trim & ears, wooden bail, seamed, 7½x9", EX.............**$295.00**

Teakettle, white w/light blue chicken wire, white interior, seamed, 7½x8⅝", EX.................**$125.00**

Teapot, gray & light gray relish inside & out, squatty, Romania, ca 1989-91, 5x4⅝", M.................**$25.00**

Teapot, gray lg mottle, seamed body & spout, iron handle, 9¾x5¾", EX...**$325.00**

Teapot, green shading to white w/fruits & leaves, white interior, cobalt trim, seamed, ca 1970, 7¾", G+.........**$85.00**

Teapot, red & white lg swirl w/white interior, black trim, seamed, ca 1950, 7¾x4¾", NM **$195.00**

Wash basin, blue & white lg spatter, white interior, black trim, eyelet, 2⅝x10¼", EX.................**$145.00**

Wash basin, green & white lg mottle, white interior, black trim, eyelet, 3x11¾", EX.................**$155.00**

Wash basin, white w/gold bands, black trim, brass eyelet, Lisk Warrented No 2... label, 12" dia, EX+.............**$60.00**

Water pail, blue and white large mottle, white interior and black trim, bail handle, 11¼x8⅞", NM, $195.00. (Photo courtesy Helen Greguire)

Griswold Cast-Iron Cooking Ware

Late in the 1800s, the Griswold company introduced a line of cast-iron cooking ware that was eventually distributed on a large scale nationwide. Today's collectors appreciate the variety of skillets, cornstick pans, Dutch ovens, and griddles available to them, and many still enjoy using them to cook with.

Several marks have been used; most contain the Griswold name, though some were marked simply 'Erie.'

If you intend to use your cast iron, you can clean it safely by using any commercial oven cleaner. (Be sure to re-season it before you cook in it.) A badly pitted, rusty piece may leave you with no other recourse than to remove what rust you can with a wire brush, paint the surface black, and find an alternate use for it around the house. For instance, you might use a kettle to hold a large floor plant or some magazines. A small griddle or skillet would be attractive as part of a wall display in a country kitchen. It should be noted that prices are given for pieces in excellent condition. Items that are cracked, chipped, pitted, or warped are worth substantially less or nothing at all, depending on rarity.

Advisor: Grant Windsor (See Directory, Griswold)

Breadstick pan, #21, from $125 to **$175.00**
Cake mold, Santa...**$550.00**
Cornstick pan, #273..**$25.00**
Cornstick pan, #283, from $125 to **$175.00**
Dutch oven, #8, early tite-top, block trademarks, from $40
    to...**$60.00**
Dutch oven, #9, Erie trademark, round bottom **$60.00**
Gem pan, #11, French roll, wide band, 12 cups, from $30
    to...**$40.00**
Gem pan, #6, full writing...**$400.00**
Griddle, handled; #10, slant/EPU trademark **$65.00**
Griddle, handled; #8, Diamond trademark, from $75 to ..**$100.00**

Griddle, #8, marked Heat Slowly, $125.00.

Griddle, long; #8, block trademark.........................**$45.00**
Griddle, long; #11, slant/Erie trademark, from $100 to **$150.00**
Kettle, #8, Erie, regular (3-leg)..............................**$65.00**
Kettle, #9, Erie, flat bottom, #812..........................**$100.00**
Lemon squeezer, #1..**$180.00**
Rack, skillet display; all metal **$300.00**
Roaster, #3, oval, full writing cover w/trivet **$800.00**
Skillet, #2, block trademark, no heat ring, from $300
    to...**$400.00**
Skillet, #3, block trademark, no heat ring **$350.00**
Skillet, #3, sm trademark, grooved handle, from $5 to **$15.00**
Skillet, #4, block trademark, heat ring......................**$600.00**
Skillet, #5, Victor...**$475.00**
Skillet, #8, Erie trademark, outside heat ring, from $20
    to **$40.00**
Skillet, #8, sm trademark, grooved handle, from $10 to.....**$20.00**
Skillet, #10, block trademark, no heat ring.................**$50.00**
Skillet, #11, slant/EPU trademark **$350.00**
Skillet, #12, block trademark, from $75 to **$100.00**
Skillet, #15, oval..**$275.00**
Skillet, 5-in-1 breakfast, from $140 to **$160.00**
Skillet cover, #10, high smooth dome, block trademark, from
    $40 to...**$60.00**
Skillet cover, #11, low dome, top writing..................**$450.00**

Trivet, coffeepot; #1738, round, sm **$250.00**
Waffle iron, #2, sq, from $650 to.............................**$750.00**
Waffle iron, #8, Pat 1901...**$50.00**
Yankee bowl, #2, block trademark, smooth sides, from $75
    to...**$100.00**

Guardian Ware

The Guardian Service Company was in business from 1935 until 1955. They produced a very successful line of hammered aluminum that's just as popular today as it ever was. (Before 1935 Century Metalcraft made similar ware under the name SilverSeal, you'll occasionally see examples of it as well.) Guardian Service was sold though the home party plan, and special hostess gifts were offered as incentives. Until 1940 metal lids were used, but during the war when the government restricted the supply of available aluminum, glass lids were introduced. The cookware was very versatile, and one of their selling points was top-of-the-stove baking and roasting — 'no need to light the oven.' Many items had more than one use. For instance, their large turkey roaster came with racks and could be used for canning as well. The kettle oven used for stove-top baking also came with canning racks. Their Economy Trio set featured three triangular roasters that fit together on a round tray, making it possible to cook three foods at once on only one burner; for even further fuel economy, the casserole tureen could be stacked on top of that. Projections on the sides of the pans accommodated two styles of handles, a standard detachable utility handle as well as black 'mouse ear' handles for serving.

The company's logo is a knight with crossed weapons, and if you find a piece with a trademark that includes the words 'Patent Pending,' you'll know you have one of the earlier pieces.

In 1955 National Presto purchased the company and tried to convince housewives that the new stainless steel pans were superior to their tried-and-true Guardian aluminum, but the ladies would have none of it. In 1980 Tad and Suzie Kohara bought the rights to the Guardian Service name as well as the original molds. The new company is based in California, and is presently producing eight of the original pieces, canning racks, pressure cooker parts, serving handles, and replacement glass lids. Quoting their literature: 'Due to the age of the GS glass molds, we are unable to provide perfect glass covers. The covers may appear to have cracks or breaks on the surface. They are not breaks but mold marks and should be as durable as the originals.' They go on to say: 'These glass covers are not oven proof.' These mold marks may be a good way to distinguish the old glass lids from the new, and collectors tell us that the original lids have a green hue to the glass. The new company has also reproduced three cookbooks, one that shows the line with the original metal covers. If you want to obtain replacements, see the Directory for Guardian Service Cookware.

Be sure to judge condition when evaluating Guardian Service. Wear, baked-on grease, scratches, and obvious signs of use devaluate its worth. Our prices are for pieces ranging from average to exceptional condition. To be graded exceptional, the interior of the pan must have no pitting and the surface must be bright and clean. An item with a metal lid is worth approximately 25% more than the same piece with a glass lid. To most successfully clean your grungy garage-sale finds, put them in a self-cleaning oven, then wash them in soap and water. Never touch them with anything but a perfectly clean hotpad while they're hot, and make sure they're completely cooled before you put them in water. Abrasive cleansers only scratch the surface.

Advisor: Dennis S. McAdams (See the Directory, Guardian Service Cookware)

Ashtray, glass, w/knight & white stars logo, hostess gift, from $25 to..**$30.00**
Beverage urn, w/lid (no screen or dripper), common .**$20.00**
Beverage urn (coffeepot), glass lid, complete w/screen & dripper, 15"...**$50.00**
Can of cleaner, unopened..**$15.00**
Cookbook, Silver Seal, 1936, 48-pg, EX......................**$45.00**
Dome cooker, Tom Thumb, glass lid, w/handles, 3½x4⅞" dia, from $25 to..**$35.00**
Dome cooker, 1-qt, glass lid, w/handles, 6¾" dia, from $25 to...**$45.00**
Dome cooker, 2-qt, glass lid, w/handles, 4½x10½" dia, from $35 to...**$50.00**
Dome cooker, 4-qt, glass lid, w/handles, 6½x10½" dia, from $35 to...**$55.00**
Fryer, breakfast; glass lid, 10", from $45 to **$60.00**
Fryer, chicken; glass lid, 12", from $75 to **$100.00**

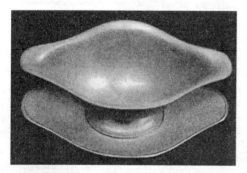

Gravy boat and undertray, from $30.00 to $50.00. (Photo courtesy Dennis McAdams)

Griddle broiler, octagonal, w/handles, polished center, 16½" dia, from $20 to **$40.00**
Handle, clamp-on style, from $10 to............................**$15.00**
Handles, slip-on style, Bakelite, pr, from $20 to.........**$35.00**
Ice bucket, glass lid, liner & tongs, 9", from $50 to ...**$90.00**
Kettle oven, glass lid, bail handle, w/rack, 8x12" dia, from $135 to...**$165.00**
Omelet pan, hinged in center, black handle on ea half, from $75 to...**$100.00**
Pot, triangular, w/glass lid, 7" to top of finial, 11" L, from $25 to..**$45.00**

Pressure cooker, minimum value **$125.00**
Roaster, glass lid, 4x15" L, from $85 to.....................**$100.00**
Roaster, turkey; glass lid, no rack, 16½" L, from $100 to..**$125.00**
Roaster, turkey; metal lid, w/rack, 16½" L, from $125 to..**$165.00**

Service kit, three cans of cleaner, brush, cookbook, clamp-on handle, slip-on handles, and steel wool, in original box, from $125.00 to $150.00. (Photo courtesy Dennis McAdams)

Tray, serving; hammered center, w/handles, 13" dia, from $20 to..**$30.00**
Tray/platter, w/handles, hammered surface, also used as roaster cover for stacking, 10x15" L, from $25 to...**$35.00**
Tumblers, glassware, stylized knight & shield in silver, & coasters w/embossed head of knight, 4 of each in metal rack **$80.00**
Tumblers & ashtray/coasters, glassware w/Guardian logo, white stars & gold trim, hostess gift, 6 of ea, from $275 to..**$325.00**
Tureen, bottom; glass lid, from $40 to.......................**$65.00**
Tureen, casserole; glass lid, from $65 to **$90.00**
Tureen, top; glass lid, from $30 to.............................**$45.00**

Gurley Candle Company

Gurley candles were cute little wax figures designed to celebrate holidays and special occasions. They are all marked Gurley on the bottom. They were made so well and had so much great detail that people decided to keep them year after year to decorate with instead of burning them. Woolworth's and other five-and-dime stores sold them from about 1940 until the 1970s. They're still plentiful today and inexpensive.

Tavern Novelty Candles were actually owned by Gurley. They were similar to the Gurley candles but not quite as detailed. All are marked Tavern on the bottom. Prices listed here are for unburned candles with no fading.

Advisor: Debbie Coe (See Directory, Cape Cod)

Christmas, angel, marked Gurley, 3" $3.50

Christmas, angel, marked Gurley, 5" $8.50

Christmas, baby angel on half moon, marked Gurley, 2½" $10.00

Christmas, Black caroler man w/red clothes, 3" $9.50

Christmas, blue grotto w/star, angel & baby, 4½" $10.00

Christmas, caroler man w/red clothes, 7" $8.50

Christmas, caroler set: lamppost, girl & boy carolers w/song books, cello player, in package $35.00

Christmas, choir boy or girl, 2¾", ea............................$6.00

Christmas, green candelabrum w/red candle, 5" $7.50

Christmas, grotto w/shepherd & sheep.......................$14.50

Christmas, lamppost, yellow cap & garland, 5½"..........$6.00

Christmas, reindeer, marked Tavern, 3½" $2.50

Christmas, Rudolph w/red nose, 3" $2.50

Christmas, Santa, 6¼" $12.00

Christmas, Santa sitting on present on sled, 3" $12.50

Christmas, snowman running w/red hat, 3" $8.50

Christmas, snowman w/red pipe & green hat, 5" $5.00

Christmas, white church w/choir boy inside, 6" $14.50

Christmas, 3" deer standing in front of candle, 5".........$6.50

Easter, chick, pink or yellow, 3" $5.00

Easter, pink birdhouse w/yellow bird, 3" $7.50

Easter, pink egg w/bunny inside, 3" $10.00

Easter, pink egg w/squirrel inside, 3" $12.00

Easter, pink winking rabbit w/carrot, 3¼" $4.50

Easter, rabbit, pink or yellow, 3" $5.00

Easter, white lily w/blue lip & green candle, 3"............$4.00

Halloween, black cat (4") w/orange candlestick beside it .$20.00

Halloween, black owl on orange stump, 3½" $9.00

Halloween, Frankenstein, later issue but harder to find, 6" $24.00

Halloween, ghost, white, 5" $20.00

Halloween, pumpkin w/black cat, 2½" $9.00

Halloween, pumpkin-face scarecrow, 5" $12.00

Halloween, skeleton, 8½" $35.00

Halloween, witch, black, 8" $20.00

Halloween, witch carrying jack-o'-lantern, 8½", $20.00.

Halloween, witch w/black cape, 3½" $9.00

Halloween, 4" cut-out orange owl w/7½" black candle behind it $24.00

Other Holidays, birthday boy, marked Tavern, 3" $6.00

Other Holidays, bride & groom, 4½", ea....................$14.50

Other Holidays, Eskimo & igloo, marked Tavern, 2-pc .$12.00

Other Holidays, Western girl or boy, 3", ea..................$9.50

Thanksgiving, acorns & leaves, 3½"..............................$6.50

Thanksgiving, gold sailing ship, 7½" $12.50

Thanksgiving, Indian boy & girl, brown & green clothes, 5", pr..$30.00

Thanksgiving, Pilgrim girl or boy, 2½", ea $4.50

Thanksgiving, turkey, 2½"...$3.00

Thanksgiving, turkey, 5¾" $15.00

Hadley, M. A.

Since 1940, the M.A. Hadley Pottery (Louisville, Tennessee) has been producing handmade dinnerware and decorative items painted freehand in a folky style with barnyard animals, baskets, whales, and sailing ships in a soft pastel palette of predominately blues and greens. Each piece is signed by hand with the first two initials and last name of artist-turned-potter Mary Alice Hadley, who has personally created each design. Some items may carry an amusing message in the bottom — for instance, 'Please Fill Me' in a canister or 'The End' in a coffee cup! Examples of this ware are beginning to turn up on the secondary market, and it's being snapped up not only by collectors who have to 'have it all' but by those who enjoy adding a decorative touch to a country-style room with only a few pieces of this unique pottery.

Horses and pigs seem to be popular subject matter; unusual pieces and the older, heavier examples command the higher prices.

Butter dish, dome lid with cow, 6¾" diameter, $50.00. (Photo courtesy Michael Sessman)

Ashtray set, 1 shaped as fisherman, 1 shaped as fish, pr...$20.00

Bank, penny; 'Penny Saved, Penny Earned' on side, 4½" .$25.00

Bank, pig, spotted $30.00

Bean pot, cow on 1 side, pig on other, w/lid, 7x11" dia..$70.00

Bell, clipper ship, metal clapper, 4x3" dia base **$38.00**
Bowl, cereal; heart, 6½" dia.....................................**$20.00**
Bowl, chicken, 3⅞x8¼" dia.....................................**$28.00**
Bowl, donkey, 7" dia..**$28.00**
Bowl, farmer & wife, 4½x11" dia.............................**$50.00**
Bowl, frog, 5" dia...**$28.00**
Bowl, horse, 3x7" dia..**$28.00**
Bowl, pasta; bird, 1¼x8" dia...................................**$30.00**
Bowl, w/boy & girl on lid, 6" dia.............................**$36.00**
Candle holder, triple; on pedestal, 5½x5½" **$35.00**

Canisters for 'Matches' and 'Salt,' wall mount, 5x5", from $45.00 to $50.00 each. (Photo courtesy Michael Sessman)

Casserole, pig & cow, w/lid, 4½x10½" dia **$45.00**
Clock, duck, from 9" plate **$45.00**
Coaster, frog, 4" dia **$22.50**
Creamer & sugar bowl, angel, 2¾" ea **$35.00**
Cup, frog **$28.00**
Cup, measuring; snowman, 3".................................**$20.00**
Cup, Santa's Milk Julep, 8-oz...................................**$36.00**
Cup & saucer, rooster on side, 'The End' inside cup .**$20.00**
Dog dish, 'My Dog' on outside, blue & pink bone on inside,
    2½x8" dia **$40.00**
Door plate, house shape, unglazed back, 4¼x6¾" **$30.00**
Egg cup, cow, 'The End' inside, 4¼x2¾" dia..............**$18.00**
Garlic jar, 'Garlic' on side w/holes, w/lid, 4" **$30.00**
Honey jar, 'Sweet to the Sweet' on front, beehive on back,
    w/lid, 4½"...**$28.00**
Hors d'oeuvre server, 15" dia platter w/bowl in center, house
    in center..**$95.00**
Letter holder, house shape, 5" **$36.00**
Mug, w/lamb & 'Lizzie' on sides, flared **$30.00**
Mustard jar, 'Mustard' on side, 4" **$20.00**
Napkin rings, house, barn, cow & pig, set of 4, NM..**$38.00**
Pie plate, rearing horse, 1½x9½" **$40.00**
Pitcher, cream; cow, 2¾" **$20.00**
Pitcher, roping cowboy, 5"...**$25.00**
Pitcher, syrup; maple tree w/spigot on 1 side, 'Syrup' on
    other, w/lid, 2-cup...**$40.00**
Pitcher, water; pig on side, 'The End' inside, 7½" **$50.00**
Plate, 'Reagan,' 9" **$25.00**
Plate, 'To My Teacher' w/stack of books & an apple, 3¾"
    dia **$20.00**

Plate, bread & butter; frog, 6"...................................**$20.00**
Plate, dessert; frog, 8"...**$25.00**
Plate, dinner; fisherman, 11"..................................**$28.00**
Salt & pepper shakers, chicken shape, 'S' & 'P' on back, 5½",
    pr...**$45.00**
Salt & pepper shakers, farmer on 1, wife on other, 4½",
    pr...**$25.00**
Spoon rest, fish shape, 7" L **$22.50**
Tea tile, donkey, 6x6"...**$25.00**
Toothbrush holder, cow, 5¼" **$28.00**
Toothbrush holder, horse, 5x6½" **$35.00**
Tray, serving; farming couple, 1¾" lip, 12" dia..........**$90.00**
Tumbler, donkey, 5" **$25.00**

Hagen-Renaker

This California-based company has been in business since 1946, first in Monrovia, later in San Dimas. They're most famous for their models of animals and birds, some of which were miniatures, and some that were made on a larger scale. Many bear paper labels (if they're large enough to accommodate them); others were attached to squares of heavy paper printed with the name of the company. They also used an incised 'HR' and a stamped 'Hagen-Renaker.' In addition to the animals, they made replicas of characters from several popular Disney films under license from the Disney Studio.

Advisor: Gayle Roller (See Directory, Hagen-Renaker)

Newsletter: The Hagen-Renaker Collector's Club Newsletter
c/o Jenny Palmer
3651 Polish Line Rd.
Cheboygan, MI 49721-9045

Console bowl, charcoal matt, brown edge, slim boat-like
    form, 16" L..**$45.00**
Figurine, Amir, Arabian stallion, San Dimas, B-707, 6¾",
    NM **$110.00**
Figurine, Arabian foal, standing w/tail up, white matt, A-298,
    2", from $30 to **$40.00**
Figurine, Boxer dog (female), crouched, Duchess, 3¼" tall, 6"
    L, from $55 to **$60.00**
Figurine, Brookside Steela, Hackney pony, San Marcos, matt
    finish, B-644, 5½", NM **$285.00**
Figurine, Brother Mouse, painted tail version, Monrovia sticker, mini **$20.00**
Figurine, Bruce, Boxer dog, recumbent, cropped ears, matt
    finish, 2¾x4"..**$45.00**
Figurine, Cat & Fiddle, from mouse band, #3062, 1992-93 ..**$25.00**
Figurine, Chihuahua puppy, begging, Pancho Villa, 1½".....**$25.00**
Figurine, Domino, Hereford bull, glossy, B-581, 5¼x8½" **$75.00**
Figurine, donkey foal, Harry, gray, San Marcos, 3¾" .**$40.00**
Figurine, draft horse w/harness, gray & white w/red details
    & silver accents, 1957, 2¾"....................................**$110.00**
Figurine, Geronimo, Brahma bull, B-579, 6x7¾" **$150.00**

Figurine, Hard Workin' Harry, Little Horrible, #389 .... **$50.00**
Figurine, Heather, Morgan mare, palomino, 1950s, 5", NM. **$235.00**
Figurine, Honora, American Saddlebred horse, Designers Workshop, Monrovia period, 8" **$215.00**
Figurine, horse, rearing, dun colored, A-2050, 1989-93, 3½" **$30.00**
Figurinc, Laddie, Collie puppy, scatcd, matt finish, Monrovia label **$45.00**
Figurine, Lady, dalmatian, sitting w/head up, 10½". **$335.00**
Figurine, Lippizan stallion, gray w/shading, San Marcos, 5¼x6" **$200.00**
Figurine, Man O' War, horse, San Dimas, B-742, 7" . **$150.00**

Figurine, Mischief, yearling with head down, B-680, 4", $300.00. (Photo courtesy Gayle Roller)

Figurine, Purple People Eater, Little Horrible, 1¼", rprs **$40.00**

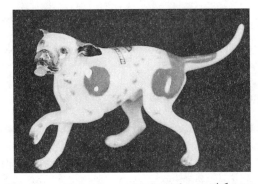

Figurine, Ranger, c 1953, 5" long, $65.00.

Figurine, Strictly From Hunger, Little Horrible, 1¾" **$65.00**
Figurine, Sun Cortez, mustang horse, San Marcos, 1980s, 6" **$165.00**
Wall decoration, Pompano, Suggestive Fossil, 7¼x12" . **$150.00**

Hall China Company

Hall China is still in production in East Liverpool, Ohio, where they have been located since around the turn of the century. They have produced literally hundreds of lines of kitchen and dinnerware items for both home and commercial use. Many of these have become very collectible.

They're especially famous for their teapots, some of which were shaped like automobiles, basketballs, doughnuts, etc. Each teapot was made in an assortment of colors, often trimmed in gold. Many were decaled to match their dinnerware lines. Some are quite rare, and collecting them all would be a real challenge.

During the 1950s, Eva Zeisel designed dinnerware shapes with a streamlined, ultra-modern look. Her lines, Classic and Century, were used with various decals as the basis for several of Hall's dinnerware patterns. She also designed kitchenware lines with the same modern styling. They were called Casual Living and Tri-Tone. All her designs are very popular with today's collectors, especially those with an interest in the movement referred to as '50s modern.'

Although some of the old kitchenware shapes and teapots are being produced today, you'll be able to tell them from the old pieces by the backstamp. To identify these new issues, Hall marks them with the shaped rectangular 'Hall' trademark they've used since the early 1970s.

For more information, we recommend *The Collector's Encyclopedia of Hall China*, Third Edition, by Margaret and Kenn Whitmyer (Collector Books).

Newsletter: *Hall China Collector's Club Newsletter*
P.O. Box 360488, Cleveland, OH 44136

Acacia, bowl, Thin Rim, 8½", from $25 to **$32.00**
Arizona, bowl, coupe soup; Tomorrow's Classic, 9", from $8.50 to **$10.00**
Arizona, butter dish, Tomorrow's Classic, from $145 to.. **$175.00**
Arizona, egg cup, Tomorrow's Classic, from $35 to ... **$47.00**
Arizona, ladle, Tomorrow's Classic, from $18 to **$22.00**
Arizona, plate, Tomorrow's Classic, 11", from $11 to . **$13.00**
Beauty, bowl, salad; 12", from $40 to **$50.00**
Beauty, casserole, round knob handle, from $40 to ... **$45.00**
Blue Blossom, bean pot, New England, #4, from $185 to. **$225.00**
Blue Blossom, canister, Radiance, from $350 to **$400.00**
Blue Blossom, creamer, morning set, from $45 to **$55.00**
Blue Blossom, jug, loop handle, from $175 to **$200.00**
Blue Bouquet, bowl, Radiance, 7½", from $20 to **$25.00**
Blue Bouquet, cake plate, from $40 to **$45.00**
Blue Bouquet, coffee dispenser, metal, from $40 to ... **$45.00**
Blue Bouquet, jug, Medallion, #3, from $32 to **$35.00**
Blue Bouquet, spoon, from $125 to **$135.00**
Blue Crocus, bowl, straight sides, 6", from $25 to **$28.00**
Blue Crocus, casserole, Thick Rim **$50.00**
Blue Floral, bowl, 9", from $26 to **$30.00**
Blue Floral, casserole, from $45 to **$50.00**
Blue Garden, batter jug, Sundial, from $265 to **$310.00**
Blue Garden, bean pot, New England, #4, from $175 to.. **$195.00**
Blue Garden, cookie jar, Sundial, from $325 to **$370.00**
Blue Garden, drip jar, Thick Rim, from $65 to **$75.00**
Blue Garden, water bottle, Zephyr, from $550 to **$575.00**
Blue Willow, bowl, plum pudding; 6", from $40 to ... **$50.00**
Bouquet, bowl, cereal; Tomorrow's Classic, 6", from $8.50 to **$10.00**
Bouquet, plate, Tomorrow's Classic, 8", from $8 to **$9.50**
Bouquet, vase, Tomorrow's Classic, from $80 to **$95.00**
Buckingham, bowl, celery; oval, Tomorrow's Classic, from $22 to **$24.00**

Buckingham, bowl, sq open vegetable; Tomorrow's Classic, 8¾", from $26 to...**$28.00**

Buckingham, candlestick, Tomorrow's Classic, 8", from $40 to...**$45.00**

Buckingham, plate, Tomorrow's Classic, 11", from $12 to..**$14.00**

Buckingham, vinegar bottle, Tomorrow's Classic, from $80 to...**$95.00**

Cactus, bowl, onion soup; individual, from $50 to.....**$60.00**

Cactus, bowl, Radiance, 9", from $32 to.................**$37.00**

Cameo Rose, bowl, cream soup; 5", from $85 to.......**$90.00**

Cameo Rose, bowl, vegetable; w/lid, from $50 to.....**$65.00**

Cameo Rose, cup, from $7.50 to.................**$8.50**

Cameo Rose, gravy boat w/underplate, from $27 to..**$32.00**

Cameo Rose, plate, 8", from $8 to.................**$9.50**

Cameo Rose, plate, 10", from $19 to.................**$25.00**

Cameo Rose, salt & pepper shakers, pr, from $40 to.**$45.00**

Caprice, bowl, salad; Tomorrow's Classic, 14½", from $32 to...**$37.00**

Caprice, egg cup, Tomorrow's Classic, from $45 to....**$47.00**

Caprice, sugar bowl, w/lid, Tomorrow's Classic, from $18 to...**$20.00**

Carrot/Golden Carrot, casserole, #70, 10" dia, from $60 to...**$70.00**

Carrot/Golden Carrot, stack set, Radiance, from $110 to...**$135.00**

Christmas Tree & Holly, bowl, plum pudding; 4½", from $25 to...**$30.00**

Christmas Tree & Holly, plate, 10", from $35 to........**$45.00**

Christmas Tree & Holly, sugar/coffee set, from $40 to......**$45.00**

Christmas Tree & Holly, tidbit tray, 2-tier, from $100 to..**$125.00**

Clover (Pink), baker, #503, 6" dia, from $18 to..........**$22.00**

Clover (Pink), jug, Medallion, from $50 to.................**$60.00**

Clover/Golden Clover, bowl, Thick Rim, 6", from $22 to ..**$26.00**

Clover/Golden Clover, cookie jar, Five Band, from $280 to...**$300.00**

Crocus, bread box, metal, from $110 to...................**$130.00**

Crocus, coffeepot, Meltdown, from $90 to.................**$110.00**

Crocus, gravy boat, from $32 to.................**$37.00**

Crocus, leftover, rectangular, from $65 to.................**$95.00**

Crocus, pie baker, from $85 to.................**$95.00**

Crocus, plate, 8¼", from $9 to.................**$12.00**

Crocus, plate, 10", from $90 to.................**$110.00**

Crocus, sugar bowl, w/lid, Art Deco, from $40 to.....**$45.00**

Crocus, tray, round, metal, from $50 to.................**$60.00**

Eggshell, bowl, custard; Dot, from $20 to.................**$22.00**

Eggshell, drip coffeepot, Dot, #691, from $225 to....**$270.00**

Eggshell, mustard jar, Plaid or Swag, from $90 to **$110.00**

Eggshell, shirred egg dish, Dot, from $27 to.............**$32.00**

Fantasy, baker, rectangular, from $150 to.................**$190.00**

Fantasy, bowl, cereal; Tomorrow's Classic, 6", from $8 to..**$10.00**

Fantasy, bowl, onion soup; w/lid, Tomorrow's Classic, from $35 to...**$37.00**

Fantasy, bowl, Thick Rim, 6", from $25 to.................**$30.00**

Fantasy, butter dish, Tomorrow's Classic, from $165 to..**$185.00**

Fantasy, casserole, Sundial, #1, from $55 to.............**$65.00**

Fantasy, casserole, Tomorrow's Classic, 2-qt, from $45 to **$55.00**

Fantasy, coffee server, Sundial, from $450 to...........**$550.00**

Fantasy, creamer, New York, from $40 to.................**$45.00**

Fantasy, creamer, Tomorrow's Classic, from $80 to..**$100.00**

Fantasy, drip jar, Thick Rim, from $80 to...................**$95.00**

Fantasy, jug, ball; #3, from $130 to.................**$160.00**

Fantasy, ladle, Tomorrow's Classic, from $18 to........**$22.00**

Fantasy, plate, Tomorrow's Classic, 11", from $11 to .**$13.00**

Fantasy, sugar bowl, w/lid, morning set, from $45 to..**$52.00**

Fantasy, syrup, Five Band, from $120 to.................**$150.00**

Fantasy, vase, Tomorrow's Classic, from $65 to.........**$75.00**

Fantasy batter bowl, Sundial, $350.00 to $450.00.

Five Band, batter bowl, red or cobalt, from $50 to....**$60.00**

Five Band, coffeepot, colors other than red or cobalt, ea from $45 to...**$55.00**

Five Band, cookie jar, red or cobalt, from $125 to...**$145.00**

Five Band, syrup, red or cobalt, from $65 to.............**$75.00**

Flamingo, casserole, Five Band, from $65 to.............**$75.00**

Flamingo, sugar bowl w/lid, Viking, from $40 to.......**$47.00**

Floral Lattice, canister, Radiance, from $250 to.......**$350.00**

French Flower, creamer, Bellevue, from $20 to.........**$25.00**

French Flower, sugar bowl, w/lid, Boston, from $32 to...**$37.00**

Frost Flowers, coffeepot, Tomorrow's Classic, 6-cup, from $90 to...**$110.00**

Frost Flowers, cup, Tomorrow's Classic, from $10 to.**$12.00**

Frost Flowers, plate, Tomorrow's Classic, 11", from $11 to...**$13.00**

Frost Flowers, saucer, Tomorrow's Classic, from $1 to.**$1.50**

Game Bird, bowl, Thick Rim, 6", from $25 to...........**$30.00**

Game Bird, mug, Irish coffee; from $60 to **$75.00**

Game Bird, plate, 10", from $60 to.................**$75.00**

Game Bird, sugar bowl, w/lid, New York, from $100 to.**$120.00**

Gold Label, bowl, salad; 9", from $15 to...................**$18.00**

Golden Glo, casserole, duck finial, from $40 to.........**$50.00**

Golden Glo, mug, #343, from $10 to.................**$12.00**

Harlequin, bowl, fruit; footed, Tomorrow's Classic, lg, from $40 to...**$45.00**

Harlequin, casserole, Tomorrow's Classic, 1¼-qt, from $35 to...**$40.00**

Harlequin, cookie jar, Tomorrow's Classic, from $250 to...**$300.00**

Harlequin, jug, ball; #3, Tomorrow's Classic, from $160 to **$190.00**

Heather Rose, bowl, cereal; 6¼", from $7.50 to **$10.00**

Heather Rose, cake plate, from $15 to......................**$18.00**

Heather Rose, coffeepot, Washington, 30-oz, from $45 to ..**$50.00**

Heather Rose, cookie jar, flared shape, from $75 to...**$85.00**

Heather Rose, jug, Rayed, from $20 to **$25.00**

Heather Rose, pickle dish, 9", from $9 to..................**$11.00**

Holiday, bowl, vegetable; sq, open, Tomorrow's Classic, 8¾", from $26 to..**$28.00**

Holiday, coffeepot, Tomorrow's Classic, 6-cup, from $100 to **$120.00**

Holiday, creamer, Tomorrow's Classic, from $12 to ...**$14.00**

Holiday, marmite & lid, Tomorrow's Classic, from $32 to...**$35.00**

Homewood, bowl, flat soup; 8½", from $12 to **$14.00**

Homewood, bowl, Radiance, 7½", from $18 to **$20.00**

Homewood, drip jar, Radiance **$25.00**

Homewood, salt & pepper shakers, handled, pr, from $40 to **$44.00**

Lyric, creamer, Tomorrow's Classic, from $11 to **$13.00**

Lyric, egg cup, Tomorrow's Classic, from $22 to **$25.00**

Lyric, salt & pepper shakers, Tomorrow's Classic, pr, from $28 to **$32.00**

Meadow Flower, bowl, custard; Thick Rim, from $28 to..**$32.00**

Meadow Flower, casserole, Radiance, from $60 to **$70.00**

Medallion, bowl, custard; Lettuce, from $16 to **$18.50**

Medallion, drip jar, Chinese Red, from $45 to............**$55.00**

Medallion, leftover, sq, Lettuce, from $55 to **$65.00**

Medallion, salt & pepper shakers, colors other than Lettuce, ivory, or Chinese Red, pr, from $40 to **$50.00**

Morning Glory, bowl, custard; straight sides, 3½", from $22 to..**$25.00**

Morning Glory, bowl, straight sides, 5", from $18 to..**$20.00**

Morning Glory, casserole, Thick Rim, from $37 to **$45.00**

Mums, bowl, cereal; 6", from $12 to **$14.00**

Mums, bowl, oval, 10¼", from $40 to.......................**$45.00**

Mums, bowl, Radiance, 7½", from $25 to...................**$27.00**

Mums, bowl, ruffled, tab handles, Medallion, 9½", from $75 to..**$90.00**

Mums, casserole, Radiance, from $45 to.....................**$50.00**

Mums, coffeepot, Terrace, from $100 to....................**$120.00**

Mums, creamer, Medallion, from $22 to **$25.00**

Mums, drip jar, Medallion, from $40 to **$45.00**

Mums, gravy boat, from $30 to **$35.00**

Mums, jug, Simplicity, from $200 to..........................**$225.00**

Mums, platter, oval, 11¼", from $30 to......................**$35.00**

Mums, sugar bowl, w/lid, New York, from $28 to **$35.00**

No 488, butter dish, Zephyr, 1-lb, from $500 to **$650.00**

No 488, casserole, Sundial, from $45 to **$55.00**

No 488, creamer, modern, from $20 to.......................**$25.00**

No 488, cup, from $18 to...**$20.00**

No 488, pretzel jar, from $250 to **$300.00**

No 488, saucer, from $1.50 to....................................**$2.50**

No 488, shirred egg dish, from $35 to **$40.00**

No 488, soup tureen, from $300 to **$350.00**

Orange Poppy, baker, French; fluted, from $20 to **$25.00**

Orange Poppy, bowl, salad; 9", from $18 to...............**$20.00**

Orange Poppy, bowl, vegetable; round, 9¼", from $45 to **$50.00**

Orange Poppy, canister set, round, 4-piece, metal, from $80 to **$100.00**

Orange Poppy, casserole, oval, 8", from $60 to..........**$65.00**

Orange Poppy, coffeepot, Great American, from $55 to ..**$65.00**

Orange Poppy, creamer, Great American, from $18 to.....**$20.00**

Orange Poppy, drip jar, Radiance, from $30 to **$35.00**

Orange Poppy, mustard jar, w/liner, from $45 to **$55.00**

Orange Poppy, salt & pepper shakers, handled, pr, from $40 to **$45.00**

Orange Poppy, soap dispenser, metal, from $145 to..**$185.00**

Orange Poppy, spoon, from $100 to **$120.00**

Orange Poppy, wastebasket, metal, from $85 to **$100.00**

Pastel Morning Glory, bean pot, New England, #4, from $185 to **$220.00**

Pastel Morning Glory, bowl, Radiance, 7½", from $25 to ..**$27.00**

Pastel Morning Glory, cake plate, from $40 to **$45.00**

Pastel Morning Glory, custard, Radiance, from $25 to..**$30.00**

Pastel Morning Glory, jug, w/lid, Radiance, #4, #5, or #6, ea from $160 to...**$190.00**

Pastel Morning Glory, pretzel jar, from $195 to........**$225.00**

Pastel Morning Glory, saucer, St Denis, from $6 to **$7.50**

Peach Blossom, ashtray, Tomorrow's Classic, from $7.50 to **$9.00**

Peach Blossom, egg cup, Tomorrow's Classic, from $42 to **$45.00**

Peach Blossom, plate, Tomorrow's Classic, 6", from $4.50 to **$5.50**

Peach Blossom, platter, Tomorrow's Classic, 17", from $32 to **$38.00**

Pinecone, bowl, celery; oval, Tomorrow's Classic, from $20 to **$24.00**

Pinecone, mug, Tomorrow's Classic, from $22 to.......**$27.00**

Pinecone, plate, E-Style, 9¼", from $8.50 to................**$9.50**

Pinecone, platter, Tomorrow's Classic, 12¼", from $22 to...**$28.00**

Pinecone, tidbit tray, E-Style, 3-tier, from $55 to.........**$65.00**

Primrose, ashtray, from $8 to.....................................**$10.00**

Primrose, bowl, flat soup; 8", from $10 to..................**$12.00**

Primrose, plate, 10", from $10 to...............................**$12.00**

Primrose, sugar bowl, w/lid, from $14 to...................**$16.00**

Red Poppy, bowl, Radiance, 6", from $18 to **$20.00**

Red Poppy, bowl, Radiance, 9", from $22 to **$27.00**

Red Poppy, clock, metal, teapot shape, from $125 to..**$175.00**

Red Poppy, creamer, modern, from $22 to **$25.00**

Red Poppy, cutting board, wood, from $40 to...........**$55.00**

Red Poppy, hot pad, metal, from $18 to **$22.00**

Red Poppy, jug, milk or syrup; Daniel, 4", from $42 to .**$47.00**

Red Poppy, plate, 6", from $4 to...............................**$5.00**

Red Poppy, plate, 10", from $65 to...........................**$85.00**

Red Poppy, salt & pepper shakers, Teardrop, pr, from $36 to **$44.00**

Red Poppy, sugar bowl, w/lid, modern, from $22 to.**$25.00**

Red Poppy, toaster cover, plastic, from $35 to...........**$45.00**

Red Poppy, tray, rectangular, metal, from $35 to **$50.00**

Red Poppy, tumbler, frosted, glass, 2 styles, ea from $22 to **$25.00**

Ribbed, bowl, salad; Chinese Red, 8¾", from $20 to .**$22.00**

Ribbed, casserole, Russet, 8", from $24 to...................**$28.00**

Ribbed, ramekin, Chinese Red, 6-oz, from $7.50 to......**$8.50**

Ribbed, salt & pepper shakers, handled, Russet, pr, from $14 to...**$17.00**

Rose Parade, bean pot, tab handles, from $115 to...**$135.00**

Rose Parade, bowl, straight sides, 9", from $35 to......**$40.00**

Rose Parade, casserole, tab handles, from $40 to.......**$45.00**

Rose Parade, salt & pepper shakers, Sani-Grid, pr, from $40 to...**$44.00**

Rose White, baker, French; fluted, from $35 to **$40.00**

Rose White, bowl, salad; 9", from $20 to **$25.00**

Rose White, bowl, straight sides, 7½", from $22 to....**$25.00**

Royal Rose, ball jug, #3, from $90.00 to $100.00. (Photo courtesy Margaret and Kenn Whitmyer)

Royal Rose, salt & pepper shakers, handled, pr, from $32 to **$36.00**

Rx, mug, Irish coffee; from $6 to **$8.00**

Sear's Arlington, bowl, oval, 9¼", from $18 to............**$20.00**

Sear's Arlington, cup, from $4 to **$5.00**

Sear's Arlington, gravy boat, w/underplate, from $22 to .**$25.00**

Sear's Arlington, plate, 10", from $6 to **$8.00**

Sear's Arlington, saucer, from $1 to...............................**$1.50**

Sear's Fairfax, bowl, fruit; 5¼", from $3.50 to **$4.50**

Sear's Fairfax, plate, 8", from $4.50 to...........................**$6.00**

Sear's Fairfax, sugar bowl, w/lid, from $14 to **$16.00**

Sear's Monticello, bowl, vegetable; w/lid, from $35 to..**$40.00**

Sear's Monticello, cup, from $5 to **$6.00**

Sear's Monticello, saucer, from $1 to.............................**$1.50**

Sear's Mount Vernon, bowl, cereal; 6¼", from $8 to ..**$10.00**

Sear's Mount Vernon, casserole, w/lid, from $37 to ...**$42.00**

Sear's Mount Vernon, plate, 10", from $11 to.............**$13.00**

Sear's Richmond/Brown-Eyed Susan, bowl, flat soup; 8", from $7 to...**$9.00**

Sear's Richmond/Brown-Eyed Susan, sugar bowl, w/lid, from $13 to...**$15.00**

Serenade, bowl, custard; Radiance, from $12 to.........**$14.00**

Serenade, bowl, oval, from $20 to **$25.00**

Serenade, cup, from $8 to..**$9.00**

Serenade, platter, 11¼", from $18 to............................**$20.00**

Serenade, salt & pepper shakers, handled, pr, from $32 to **$36.00**

Shaggy Tulip, coffeepot, Perk, from $65 to................**$75.00**

Shaggy Tulip, condiment jar, Radiance, from $300 to .**$350.00**

Silhouette, bowl, cereal; 6", from $14 to....................**$16.00**

Silhouette, bowl, Radiance, 9", from $20 to...............**$22.00**

Silhouette, bowl, salad; 9", from $16 to......................**$18.00**

Silhouette, cake safe, from $30 to...............................**$35.00**

Silhouette, canister, glass w/green decal, 1-gal, from $22 to...**$27.00**

Silhouette, casserole, Medallion, from $30 to.............**$40.00**

Silhouette, cup, from $12 to...**$14.00**

Silhouette, double boiler, enamel, from $45 to...........**$55.00**

Silhouette, jug, ball; #3, from $95 to..........................**$125.00**

Silhouette, jug, Medallion, #3, from $18 to.................**$22.00**

Silhouette, match safe, from $35 to..............................**$40.00**

Silhouette, mug, beverage; from $42 to.......................**$45.00**

Silhouette, plate, 6", from $5 to....................................**$6.50**

Silhouette, salt & pepper shakers, Medallion, pr, from $50 to...**$60.00**

Silhouette, saucer, St Denis, from $8 to **$10.00**

Silhouette, sifter, from $45 to.......................................**$55.00**

Silhouette, sugar bowl, w/lid, modern, from $22 to...**$25.00**

Silhouette, waffle iron, from $125 to **$150.00**

Silhouette, wax paper dispenser, from $45 to.............**$55.00**

Springtime, bowl, flat soup; 8½", from $11 to...........**$13.00**

Springtime, cake plate, from $14 to.............................**$16.50**

Springtime, casserole, Thick Rim, from $22 to...........**$27.00**

Springtime, cup, from $6 to...**$7.50**

Springtime, drip jar, Thick Rim, from $18 to...............**$22.00**

Springtime, pie baker, from $18 to...............................**$20.00**

Springtime, plate, 8¼", from $5 to **$6.00**

Springtime, saucer, from $1.50 to..................................**$2.50**

Stonewall, drip jar, open, #1188, from $40 to **$45.00**

Stonewall, leftover, rectangular, from $90 to.............**$110.00**

Stonewall, stack set, Radiance, from $115 to **$130.00**

Sundial, coffeepot, individual, red or cobalt, from $85 to..**$95.00**

Sundial, cookie jar, red or cobalt, from $200 to.......**$230.00**

Tulip, baker, French; fluted, from $20 to.....................**$22.00**

Tulip, bowl, fruit; 5½", from $6 to.................................**$8.00**

Tulip, bowl, Radiance, 6", from $14 to.......................**$16.00**

Tulip, bowl, Radiance, 9", from $25 to.......................**$30.00**

Tulip, casserole, Radiance, from $35 to.......................**$45.00**

Tulip, plate, 7", from $6 to..**$7.00**

Tulip, platter, oval, 13¼", from $30 to........................**$35.00**

Tulip, sugar bowl, w/lid, modern, from $22 to **$27.00**

Wild Poppy, baker, oval, from $95 to.......................**$125.00**

Wild Poppy, bowl, Radiance, 6", from $22 to............**$25.00**

Wild Poppy, coffeepot, Washington, 2-cup, from $170 to **$200.00**

Wild Poppy, cookie jar, Five Band, from $225 to.....**$265.00**

Wildfire, bowl, straight sides, 6", from $16 to............**$18.00**

Wildfire, casserole, tab handles, from $30 to **$35.00**

Wildfire, coffee dispenser, metal, from $25 to **$35.00**

Wildfire, coffeepot, S-lid, from $65 to.........................**$75.00**

Wildfire, gravy boat, from $22 to **$25.00**

Wildfire, jug, Sani-Grid, 5", from $55 to.....................**$65.00**

Wildfire, pie baker, from $45 to **$55.00**

Wildfire, plate, 10", from $50 to..................................**$65.00**

Wildfire, salt & pepper shakers, Teardrop, pr, from $36
to...**$44.00**
Yellow Rose, bowl, cereal; 6", from $9 to **$11.50**
Yellow Rose, creamer, Norse, from $18 to **$22.00**
Yellow Rose, cup, from $8 to **$10.00**
Yellow Rose, plate, 6", from $3.50 to..........................**$4.50**
Yellow Rose, saucer, from $1.50 to **$2.00**
Yellow Rose, sugar bowl, w/lid, Norse, from $27
to...**$32.00**

Teapots

Airflow, Chinese Red, 6-cup, from $125 to **$135.00**
Aladdin, cobalt, from $100 to **$125.00**

**Aladdin, Marine Blue with gold trim, from
$75.00 to $90.00.**

Albany, maroon w/gold label, 6-cup, from $95 to ...**$125.00**
Automobile, Delphinium, 6-cup, from $400 to **$450.00**
Bellevue, red, 2- or 4-cup, ea from $35 to **$45.00**
Boston, green w/early gold design, 4- to 8- cup, ea from $45
to...**$75.00**
Cleveland, Emerald, 6-cup, from $45 to **$55.00**
Donut, ivory w/standard decor, from $150 to..........**$175.00**
French, stock brown or stock green, 1- to 3-cup, ea from $20
to...**$25.00**
Globe, no drip, rose, 6-cup, from $45 to....................**$55.00**
Hollywood, maroon w/gold label, 6-cup, from $110
to...**$125.00**
Hook Cover, Cadet Blue, 6-cup, from $40 to **$45.00**
Illinois, maroon w/standard gold, 6-cup, from $190 to...**$220.00**
New York, Canary w/standard gold, 6- or 8-cup, ea from $35
to...**$45.00**
Newport, stock green, stock brown, or ivory, 5- or 7-cup, ea
from $30 to...**$35.00**
Ohio, black w/standard gold, from $200 to **$225.00**
Parade, ivory w/gold label, 6-cup, from $40 to **$45.00**
Philadelphia, Dresden w/standard gold, from $40
to...**$45.00**
Streamline, Chinese Red, 6-cup, from $115 to **$135.00**
Sundial, Canary, 6-cup, from $55 to............................**$65.00**
Windshield, ivory w/gold label & polka-dots, 6-cup, from
$50 to..**$60.00**

Hallmark

Since the early 1970s when Hallmark first introduced their glass ball and yarn doll ornaments, many lines and themes have been developed to the delight of collectors. Many early ornaments are now valued at several times their original price. This is especially true of the first one issued in a particular series. For instance, Betsy Clark's first edition issued in 1973 has a value today of $125.00 (MIB).

Our values are for ornaments that are mint and in their original boxes.

Advisor: The Baggage Car (See Directory, Hallmark)

Newsletter: The Baggage Car
3100 Justin Dr., Ste. B
Des Moines, IA 50322; 515-270-9080 or fax: 515-223-1398
Includes show and company information along with current listing

**Frosty Friends, second in series,
1981, MIB, from $150.00 to $175.00.**

Acorn Wreath, QXM5686, 1990, miniature, MIB **$12.00**
Across the Miles, QX304-4, 1992, MIB......................**$13.50**
All Pumped Up, handcrafted, QX5923, 1994, MIB......**$20.00**
Angel Melody, lighted acrylic, QLX7202, 1989, MIB...**$24.50**
Animal Home, handcrafted, QX149-6, 1978, MIB **$175.00**
Baby-Sitter, glass ball, QX264-2, 1985, MIB................**$12.50**
Baby's First Christmas, acrylic photo holder, QX516-2, 1980,
MIB **$30.00**
Betsy Clark, glass ball, 2nd edition, QX108-1, 1974, MIB...**$85.00**
Betsy Clark, satin ball, QX163-1, 1975, MIB...............**$42.50**
Bicentennial '76 Commemorative, satin ball, QX203-1, 1976,
MIB **$60.00**
Bobbin' Along, bear fishing atop mallard duck, QX5879,
1995, MIB **$40.00**
Chickadees, Birds of Winter, glass ball, QX204-1, MIB.......**$65.00**
Christmas Angel, acrylic w/holiday highlights, 1979, MIB..**$95.00**
Christmas Kitty, porcelain, 3rd edition, QX4377, 1991,
MIB...**$20.00**
Compact Skater, QX6766, 1998, MIB...........................**$21.00**
Country Wreath, straw & wood, QX470-9, 1987, MIB ..**$29.50**
Currier & Ives, glass ball, QX250-1, 1984, MIB..........**$22.50**

Currier & Ives, satin ball, QX164-1, 1975, MIB **$55.00**

Drummer Boy, yarn, QX123-1, 1975, MIB **$24.50**

Elves, glass ball, XHD103-5, 1973, MIB **$100.00**

Fills the Bill, pelican fishing, QX557-2, 1993, MIB...... **$17.50**

Friendship, glass ball, QX208-1, 1980, MIB **$20.00**

Grandmother, glass ball, QX205-7, 1983, MIB............ **$24.00**

Grandson, glass ball, QX2293, 1990, MIB................... **$27.50**

Jack & Jill, 3rd in Mother Goose series, handcrafted, QX5099, 1995, MIB **$30.00**

Jackpot Jingle, slot machine, QX5911, 1996, MIB....... **$24.00**

Jasmine & Aladdin, Disney, QXD4062, 1997, MIB..... **$30.00**

Last Minute Hug, QLX7181, 1988, MIB **$49.00**

Little Town of Bethlehem, QXN5864, 1992, miniature, MIB.. **$22.50**

Merry Koala, QX4155, 1986, MIB **$22.50**

Mother, porcelain & tin, QX5457, 1991, MIB.............. **$35.00**

Partridge, brass, QXM4525, 1989, MIB....................... **$12.00**

Puppy Love, Golden Retriever, brass, handcrafted, QX504-5, 1993, MIB **$30.00**

Santa's Workshop, handcrafted, QX450-3, 1982, MIB. **$85.00**

Squirrel, satin ball, QX138-2, 1977, MIB **$95.00**

Star of the Show, ballerina rabbit, QX6004, 1996, MIB.. **$20.00**

Sweetheart Surrey, QX447-9, 1987, MIB **$29.50**

Wooden Childhood, wooden airplane #5, QX4041, 1988, MIB **$22.50**

10 Years Together, bell, QX4013, 1986, MIB **$24.50**

25th Christmas Together, glass ball, QX211-6, 1982, MIB .. **$20.00**

1957 Corvette, Keepsake Ornament, 1991, MIB, from $75.00 to $90.00.

Halloween

Halloween is now the second biggest money-making holiday of the year, and more candy is sold at this time than for any other holiday. Folk artists are making new items to satisfy the demands of collectors and celebrators that can't get enough of the old items. Over one hundred years of celebrating this magical holiday has built a social history strata by strata, and wonderful and exciting finds can be made in all periods! From one dollar to thousands, there is something to excite collectors in every price range, with new collectibles being born every year. For further information we recommend *Collectible Halloween; More Halloween Collectibles; Halloween: Collectible Decorations & Games; Salem Witchcraft and Souvenirs; Postmarked Yesterday, Art of the Holiday Postcard;* and *Anthropomorphic Beings of Halloween* (all published by Schiffer); also see *Around Swanzey* and *The Armenians of Worcester* (Arcadia). The author of these books is Pamela E. Apkarian-Russell (Halloween Queen), a freelancer who also writes an ephemera column for *Unravel the Gavel, Barrs Postcard News, Antiques Journal, Postcard Collector, Antique Trader, Journal of Antiques and Collectibles, Joy of Halloween,* and others.

Advisor: Pamela E. Apkarian-Russell (See Directory, Halloween)

Publisher of Newsletter: *Trick or Treat Trader*
P.O. Box 499, Winchester, NH 03470; 603-239-8875
e-mail: halloweenqueen@cheshire.net
http://adam.cheshire.net/~halloweenqueen/home.html
Subscription: $15 per year in USA ($20 foreign) for 4 quarterly issues

Book, Best Witches, by Robert Heitmann, 1960, 30 pages, EX **$40.00**

Book, Witch Family, by Eleanor Estes, 1960, 186 pages, w/dust jacket, NM..**$30.00**

Book & record set, Georgie's Halloween, by Robert Bright, EX **$25.00**

Box, modern folk art, ghoul's face, painted paperboard w/wire bail handle, by Rich Connant **$40.00**

Candy box, cardboard w/image of owl on branch, EX...**$45.00**

Candy box, diecut witch w/owl & black cat on hat, EX.**$45.00**

Candy container, devil head w/veggie body, composition, 6", EX **$250.00**

Candy container, jack-o'-lantern, cardboard w/crepe-paper ruffle, Germany, 5½", EX...................................**$250.00**

Candy containers, cardboard, Western Germany, $75.00 each. (Photo courtesy Pamela Apkarian-Russell)

Candy holder, cat pulling pumpkin coach, cardboard, 2-sided, EX $45.00

Costume, Addams Family's Morticia, Ben Cooper, 1965, NM in EX box, $100.00.
(Photo courtesy American Pie Collectibles)

Costume, Bart Simpson, Ben Cooper (Canadian), MIB .**$12.00**
Costume, Batman, Ben Cooper, 1973, M (worn box).**$75.00**
Costume, Bionic Woman, Ben Cooper, 1975, MIB, from $30 to **$40.00**
Costume, Charlie Brown, Collegeville, 1980s, MIB **$15.00**
Costume, Cowardly Lion (Wizard of Oz), 1989, MIB .**$20.00**
Costume, Glow Worm, Ben Cooper, 1984, MIB **$20.00**
Costume, Jed Clampett, Ben Cooper, 1963, complete, NM (no box) **$50.00**
Costume, Jed Clampett, Ben Cooper, 1963, MIB, from $100 to **$125.00**
Costume, Maverick, 1959, EX (no box) **$50.00**
Costume, Space Ghost, Ben Cooper, 1965, complete, EX (EX box) **$75.00**
Costume, Wally Gator, 1960s, complete, EX (EX box)..**$50.00**
Cup, witch head in cone-shape hat, Malibu on hat & removable glasses...**$20.00**
Decoration, cat, Beistle, cardboard, thin jointed arms & legs, 27", VG **$50.00**
Decoration, Halloween a Go-Go Dancers, cardboard, 1960s, complete w/skeleton & girl, 14", MIB....................**$55.00**
Decoration, String 'em Outs, Dennison, pumpkins, VG...**$250.00**
Diecut, black cat on jack-o'-lantern, American, 1930s, 12", EX **$125.00**
Figure, ghost on jack-o'-lantern, Hallmark Merry Miniature, EX..**$15.00**
Figure, jack-o'-lantern man playing accordion, composition, EX..**$75.00**
Figure, owl, pulp, American, 1940s, 6½", NM..........**$150.00**
Figure, scarecrow, celluloid, EX.................................**$200.00**
Figure, witch, painted bisque, Japan, 1950s, 3", EX....**$40.00**
Figure, witch holding black cat, nodding head, hard plastic, 7", EX...**$150.00**
Figure, witch holding black cat, VC/USA, celluloid, 4½", VG **$250.00**
Figure, witch pulling cart w/ghost, celluloid, EX......**$250.00**

Finger puppet, Kooky Spookys, glow-in-the-dark, several variations, MIP, ea...**$10.00**
Game, Ring a Tail, Japan, 1930s, 3½" dia, scarce, EX (G box) **$195.00**
Game, Zingo Halloween Fortune & Stunt, 1930s, EX (EX box) **$45.00**
Hat, orange felt w/black cat & Jack-o'-lantern, EX **$20.00**
High Flyer Paddle Ball, China, MIP.............................**$5.00**
Horn, pipe shape w/jack-o'-lantern face, pressed cardboard w/wooden nose, Germany, EX **$145.00**
Jack-o'-lantern, paper on wire frame, folds up, EX **$25.00**
Jack-o'-lantern, pulp, smiling w/eyes crossed, pug nose, American, 1940s, 5", NM...................................**$150.00**
Jack-o'-lantern, soft plastic, battery-operated, Japan, 1950s, 4", MIB..**$65.00**
Lantern, black cat face on pedestal, pulp, American, 1940s, 5", EX...**$200.00**

Lantern, cardboard and tissue paper, four-panel, $125.00.
(Photo courtesy Pamela Apkarian-Russell)

Light bulb, milk glass sphere w/black skull & crossbones, Occupied Japan...**$45.00**
Make a Model Haunted House Kit, paper, England, unused, EX..**$15.00**
Mask, Batgirl, Ben Cooper, 1977, NM **$8.00**
Noisemaker, black cat, cardboard w/wooden handle, Germany, 1920s, 6", EX...............................**$75.00**
Noisemaker, frying pan shape w/black cat face, tin, sm, EX..**$50.00**
Noisemaker, jack-o'-lantern, litho tin w/plastic horn nose, EX..**$50.00**
Noisemaker/sparkler, jack-o'-lantern, tin, NMIB.........**$50.00**
Push-butter puppet, jack-o'-lantern man standing on pumpkin, plastic, EX **$35.00**
Rattle, plastic witch head atop wooden handle, 1950s, 8", EX..**$40.00**
Squeeze toy, Crying Pumpkin, Made in Boston USA, EX **$45.00**
Tambourine, children playing w/lg pumpkin, litho tin, Chein, 1930s, 7" dia, NM..**$100.00**
Tambourine, laughing devil's face, tin, EX...............**$110.00**
Yo-yo, jack-o'-lantern, tin, NM...................................**$10.00**
Yo-yo, skulls & crossbones, litho tin, 1960s, MIP **$10.00**

Harker Pottery

Harker was one of the oldest potteries in the country. Their history can be traced back to the 1840s. In the '30s, a new plant was built in Chester, West Virginia, and the company began manufacturing kitchen and dinnerware lines, eventually employing as many as three hundred workers.

Several of these lines are popular with collectors today. One of the most easily recognized is Cameoware. It is usually found in pink or blue decorated with white silhouettes of flowers, though other designs were made as well. Colonial Lady, Red Apple, Amy, Mallow, and Pansy are some of their better-known lines that are fairly easy to find and reassemble into sets.

If you'd like to learn more about Harker, we recommend *The Collector's Encyclopedia of American Dinnerware* by Jo Cunningham, published by Collector Books.

Amy, hi-rise jug, w/lid	**$75.00**
Amy, plate, dinner	**$10.00**
Amy, sugar bowl, open	**$10.00**
Basket of Flowers, bowl, vegetable	**$15.00**
Becky, bowl, utility	**$25.00**

Calico Tulip, condiment jars, $9.00 each; utility plate, $20.00.

Cameo Rose, platter	**$25.00**
Cameo Rose, shaker, pk	**$12.00**
Cherry, shakers, utility; pr	**$20.00**
Chesterton (Bermuda Blue), gravy boat	**$14.00**
Colonial Lady, casserole & spoon set	**$25.00**
Countryside, pepper shaker	**$20.00**
Countryside, scoop	**$40.00**
Dainty Flower, batter jug	**$28.00**
Dainty Flower, swirl cup	**$10.00**
Gladiola, bowl, mixing	**$40.00**
Ivy, pie baker	**$25.00**
Ivy, platter	**$25.00**
Mallow, plate, serving/utility; 12"	**$27.00**
Old Vintage, cup & saucer	**$12.00**

Pastel Tulip, cake plate, 11"	**$27.00**
Pastel Tulip, casserole, w/lid	**$36.00**
Petit Point, pitcher, disk; w/lid	**$80.00**
Petit Point Rose I or II, rolling pin	**$130.00**
Red Apple I, server, 12"	**$25.00**
Red Apple II, pitcher, 64-oz, 8"	**$75.00**
Republic, shaving mug, pastel roses	**$30.00**
Rose II, cake server	**$27.00**
Rose Spray, plate, breakfast; 9"	**$12.00**
Shellridge, sugar bowl, w/lid	**$12.00**
Spanish Gold, plate, luncheon	**$25.00**
White Rose, teapot	**$35.00**
Winter Asters, plate, dinner	**$15.00**

Hartland Plastics, Inc.

The Hartland company was located in Hartland, Wisconsin, where during the '50s and '60s they made several lines of plastic figures: Western and Historic Horsemen, Miniature Western Series, and the Hartland Sport Series of Famous Baseball Stars. Football and bowling figures and religious statues were made as well. The plastic, virgin acetate, was very durable and the figures were hand painted with careful attention to detail. They're often marked.

Though prices have come down from their high of a few years ago, rare figures and horses are still in high demand. Dealers using this guide should take these factors into consideration when pricing their items: values listed here are for the figure, horse (unless noted gunfighter), hat, guns, and all other accessories for that particular figure in near-mint condition with no rubs and all original parts. All parts were made exclusively for a special figure, so a hat is not just a hat — each one belongs to a specific figure! Many people do not realize this, and it is important for the collector to be knowledgeable. An excellent source of information is *Hartland Horses and Riders* by Gail Fitch.

In our listings for sports figures, mint to near-mint condition values are for figures that are white or near-white in color; excellent values are for those that are off-white or cream-colored. These values are representative of traditional retail prices asked by dealers; Internet values for Hartlands, as is so often the case nowadays, seem to be in a constant state of flux.

See also *Schroeder's Collectible Toys, Antique to Modern* (Collector Books).

Advisors: Judy and Kerry Irvin, Western Figures; James Watson, Sports Figures (See Directory, Hartland)

Bat Masterson, gunfighter, NMIB	**$500.00**
Bill Longley, NM	**$600.00**
Brave Eagle, NMIB	**$300.00**
Buffalo Bill, NM	**$300.00**
Champ Cowgirl, NM	**$150.00**
Chief Thunderbird, rare shield, NM	**$150.00**
Chris Colt, gunfighter, NM	**$150.00**

Clay Holister, gunfighter, NM, $225.00.

Dale Evans, purple, NM $250.00
Dan Troop, gunfighter, NM.......................................$500.00
Davy Crockett, NM $500.00
General Custer, NMIB..$250.00
General George Washington, NMIB $175.00
Gil Favor, prancing, NM..$650.00
Hoby Gillman, NM $250.00
Jim Bowie, w/tag, NM..$250.00
Johnny McKay, gunfighter, NM $800.00
Paladin, gunfighter, NM..$400.00
Rifleman, NMIB..$350.00
Ronald MacKenzie, NM...$1,200.00
Roy Rogers, semi-rearing, NMIB...............................$600.00
Seth Adams, NM $275.00
Sgt Preston, repro flag, NM.......................................$650.00
Tom Jeffords, NM $175.00
Tonto, NM $150.00
Warpaint Thunderbird, w/shield, NMIB....................$350.00
Wyatt Earp, w/tag, NMIB $250.00

Sports Figures

Babe Ruth, NM/M, from $175 to $200.00
Dick Groat, EX, from $800 to.................................$1,000.00
Dick Groat, w/bat, NM, minimum value $800.00
Don Drysdale, EX...$400.00
Duke Snider, EX, from $300 to..................................$325.00
Duke Snider, M, from $500 to $600.00
Eddie Mathews, NM/M, from $125 to $150.00
Ernie Banks, EX, from $245 to $265.00
Ernie Banks, 25th Anniversary, MIB..........................$40.00
Harmon Killebrew, NM/M, from $400 to...................$500.00
Henry Aaron, EX, from $175 to..................................$190.00
Henry Aaron, 25th Anniversary, MIB $50.00
Little Leaguer, 6", EX, from $100 to...........................$125.00
Little Leaguer, 6", NM/M, from $200 to.....................$250.00
Louie Aparacio, EX, from $200 to $225.00
Louie Aparacio, NM/M, from $250 to $350.00
Major Leaguer, 4", EX, from $50 to $75.00

Major Leaguer, 4", NM/M, from $100 to $125.00
Mickey Mantle, NM..$350.00
Nellie Fox, NM/M, from $200 to $250.00
Rocky Colavito, NM/M, from $600 to $700.00
Roger Maris, EX, from $300 to $350.00
Roger Maris, NM/M, from $350 to.............................$400.00
Stan Musial, EX, from $150 to $175.00
Stan Musial, NM/M, from $200 to..............................$250.00
Ted Williams, NM/M, from $225 to............................$300.00

Wally Joyner, 1988, MIP, $15.00.

Warren Spahn, NM/M, from $150 to $175.00
Willie Mays, EX, from $150 to $200.00
Willie Mays, NM/M, from $225 to $250.00
Yogi Berra, w/mask, EX, from $150 to $175.00
Yogi Berra, w/mask, NM, from $175 to $250.00
Yogi Berra, w/o mask, NM/M, from $150 to............$175.00

Head Vases

These are fun to collect, and prices are still reasonable. You've seen them at flea markets — heads of ladies, children, clowns, even some men and a religious figure now and then. A few look very much like famous people — there's a Jackie Onassis vase by Inarco that leaves no doubt as to who it's supposed to represent!

They were mainly imported from Japan, although a few were made by American companies and sold to florist shops to be filled with flower arrangements. So if there's an old flower shop in your neighborhood, you might start your search with their storerooms.

If you'd like to learn more about them, we recommend *Head Vases, Identification and Values*, by Kathleen Cole.

Newsletter: *Head Hunters Newsletter*
Maddy Gordon
P.O. Box 83H, Scarsdale, NY 10583, 914-472-0200
Subscription: $24 per year for 4 issues; also holds convention

Baby, Inarco (paper label) #E4392, brown-haired boy holding blue phone, Hello Gran'pa! on bib, 6" $45.00

Baby, Inarco #E3156, blond w/pink bow, painted eyes, ruffled collar, 5½"..**$45.00**

Baby, Relpo #459B, blond boy sucking finger, dark eyes, 5"...**$45.00**

Baby, unmarked, blond holding kitten, dressed in blue, 5½"..**$45.00**

Baby, unmarked, blond in pink ruffled bonnet w/pale blue bow, 5½"...**$45.00**

Baby, unmarked, pink bonnet w/3 applied flowers along rim, pink bodice, 6¼".......................................**$40.00**

Benjamin Franklin, unmarked, white hair, white shirt w/button, black collar, 6"....................................**$95.00**

Boy, unmarked, brown hair, knit cap & sweater, lg dark eyes, 5"...**$35.00**

Christmas girl, Napco #CX2348B, blond w/holly on brim of hat, red coat, holds present in red-gloved hands, 1956, 5½"...**$100.00**

Clown, Inarco #E-5071, tiny black hat, bald head, red nose & mouth, 4½"...**$40.00**

Clown, unmarked #9115, green hat w/red stripe, red ball nose, lg smile, ruffled collar, 6"..........................**$40.00**

Delsey (Tissue) Girl, Enesco (paper label), blond holding flowers, dark eyes, pastel flowers in hands, 5"....**$55.00**

Fireman (boy), Inarco (paper label), lg red hat w/#5, holding nozzle, black raincoat, 5"...........................**$75.00**

Girl, Inarco #E-1061, blond ponytail w/pink bow, hand to face, pink bodice w/white bow, 4½".................**$40.00**

Girl, Inarco #E-2767, blond w/lavender bow, white sweater & lavender jumper bodice, 5½".................**$45.00**

Girl, Inarco #2523, blond w/pigtails, green & white polka-dot scarf & bodice, 5½"................................**$50.00**

Girl, Reliable Glassware #K679C0, blond w/ponytails, green hat & bodice, hand up as if to wave, 1956, 6".....**$45.00**

Girl, unmarked, blond winking, flower hat, simple bow at neck of lavender collar, 5"............................**$55.00**

Girl, unmarked, holding parasol, flowers line top of opening, bow at neck, 4½"..................................**$75.00**

Girl w/parasol, Made in Japan, brown pigtails, flower applied to bodice, 5"...**$75.00**

Harlequin man, Japan, black mask, green ruffled collar, 5½"...**$85.00**

Lady, Glamour Girl, white w/gold-painted details, 6½"..**$20.00**

Lady, Inarco #E1755, Lady Aileen, blond lady w/emerald & gold tiara, 1964, 3½"..................................**$60.00**

Lady, Inarco #E190/L, blond curls, black hat w/bow, black bodice, pearl necklace & earrings, hand to face, 1961, 7"...**$125.00**

Lady, Inarco #E480, blond w/rose in hair, thick black lashes, pink bodice, hand to face, 1961, 3½"...................**$40.00**

Lady, Japan (paper label), black & gold hat & bodice, pearl necklace & earrings, hand to temple, 5½"............**$30.00**

Lady, Lefton, blond (no hat), pearl necklace & earrings, eyes looking to side, black-gloved hand to face, 6".....**$50.00**

Lady, Lefton (paper label) #2900, blond in flat-brimmed hat, strapless bodice, both hands to face, 6"............**$100.00**

Lady, Lefton #2251, blond w/long flip, white hat & bodice w/gold trim, white-gloved hand raised to face, 6"..**$95.00**

Lady, Mary Lou, black hat, yellow & white bodice w/black & gold trim, 5½"..**$250.00**

Lady, NAPCO #659/MA, lady in black, pierced rim to hat, hand to face, 1959, 5"...................................**$50.00**

Lady, Napcoware #C6431, blond w/long thick lashes, flowers on shoulder of black bodice, 6"..................**$50.00**

Lady, Napcoware #C7314, blond w/dark eyes, pearl necklace & earrings, black draped bodice, 9"..................**$100.00**

Lady, Parma #A219, blond w/flip on right, pearl earring in left ear, pearl necklace, green bodice, 8½".......**$300.00**

Lady, Relpo #A-1373S, pink pillbox hat covered in flowers, white-gloved hands to face, pink bodice, 4½".....**$45.00**

Lady, Rubens #495, blond in flat-brimmed hat, pearl necklace & earrings, white-gloved hands folded at chin, 5¾"...**$65.00**

Lady, Rubens #497M, blond w/flower in hair, thick black lashes, pearl necklace, leafy bodice, 6½".............**$60.00**

Lady, Rubens #499B, blond w/flower on hat, flowers along bodice, pearl earrings, 6".......................................**$75.00**

Lady, unmarked, blond hair, flat-rimmed hat, heavy lowered lashes, similar to Cleminson style, 6"..................**$35.00**

Lady, unmarked, blue wide-rimmed hat w/lg bow on right, gold eyelashes, blue & white bodice w/gold, 4".**$25.00**

Lady, unmarked, brunette w/head tilted, open painted eyes (heavy liner), green bodice, 7¼"..........................**$50.00**

Lady, unmarked, simple white & pink bonnet tied in bow at left side of chin, pearl earrings, green bodice, 5½"........**$60.00**

Mary Poppins, Enesco, 1950s, $450.00. (Photo courtesy Joel Cohen)

Mother & Child, Napcoware (paper label) #R-7076, pastel colors, 6½"..**$42.50**

Nun, Relpo (paper label), prayer pose w/hands folded, heavy black lashes, light blue & white attire, 6½"............**$35.00**

Oriental lady, Japan, wing-like protrusions at temples, gold trim, 5"..**$40.00**

Oriental lady, Lee Wards (paper label), geisha-like appearance, gold trim, 5"...**$40.00**

Teen girl, Ardco (paper label), #C3259, blond w/side-swept hair, pearl necklace & earrings, black & white bodice, 5½".**$55.00**

Teen girl, Enesco (paper label), blond frosted hair, heavy dark lashes, pearl necklace/earrings, scalloped bodice, 5½"...**$75.00**

Teen girl, Inarco #E3662, pale blond w/lg curls & green bow, green bodice, 2 dangling pearl earrings, 5½".......**$85.00**

Teen girl, Inarco #E4095, blond w/short bouffant hair, wide dark eyes, pearl earrings, white sweater & black jacket, 8"..**$200.00**

Teen girl, Lefton (paper label) #1343B, wide-brimmed white hat w/painted blue flowers, matching bodice w/collar, 6"..**$100.00**

Teen girl, Lefton #6638, waving light brown hair, wide dark eyes, pearl necklace & earrings, yellow bodice, 6½"...**$125.00**

Teen girl, Napco #C3205A, pale blond w/flowers lining opening, high-necked white bodice, pearl necklace, 1958, 6"..**$100.00**

Teen girl, Napco #C4072G, blond graduate in white w/gold trim, holds diploma in right hand, 1959, 6"........**$100.00**

Teen girl, Relpo #K1936, blond in hat w/turned brim, dark eyes, single pearl earring, black bodice, 7" **$350.00**

Teen girl, Relpo 32207, blond w/ponytails, pink hat & blue hair bow, pearl earrings, black bodice w/sm blue bow, 5½"...**$125.00**

Teen girl, Rubens #4121, blond w/braid across crown & pink bows, pink & white bodice, cold paint, pearl necklace, 6"..**$95.00**

Teen girl, unmarked, blond hair, dark eyes, single pearl earring, green bodice, 7"...................................**$450.00**

Teen girl, unmarked, blond w/heavy black lashes, pink scarf tied at neck, 5½"...**$150.00**

Teen girl, unmarked, long blond loose curls, lg flat pink bow in hair, pearl earring, white bodice, 7" **$350.00**

Teen girl, unmarked, streaky brown-blond hair w/sm red bow, pearl necklace, green bodice, hand w/ring to face, 7"..**$200.00**

Uncle Sam, unmarked, green, 6½"...............................**$30.00**

Heisey Glass

From just before the turn of the century until 1957, the Heisey Glass Company of Newark, Ohio, was one of the largest, most successful manufacturers of quality tableware in the world. Though the market is well established, many pieces are still reasonably priced; and if you're drawn to the lovely patterns and colors that Heisey made, you're investment should be sound.

After 1901 much of their glassware was marked with their familiar trademark, the 'Diamond H' (an H in a diamond) or a paper label. Blown pieces are often marked on the stem instead of the bowl or foot.

Numbers in the listings are catalog reference numbers assigned by the company to indicate variations in shape or stem style. Collectors use them, especially when they buy and sell by mail, for the same purpose. Many catalog pages (showing these numbers) are contained in *The Collector's*

Encyclopedia of Heisey Glass by Neila Bredehoft and *Heisey Glass, 1896 – 1957,* by Neila and Tom Bredehoft. These books and *Elegant Glassware of the Depression Era* by Gene Florence are excellent references for further study. If you're especially interested in the many varieties of glass animals Heisey produced, you'll want to get *Glass Animals and Flower Frogs of the Depression Era* by Lee Garmon and Dick Spencer. All are published by Collector Books.

Newsletter: *The Heisey News*
Heisey Collectors of America
169 W Church St., Newark, OH 43055; 612-345-2932

Charter Oak, crystal, comport, low foot, #3362, 6".....**$45.00**

Charter Oak, Flamingo, bowl, floral; #116 (oak leaf), 11"...**$45.00**

Charter Oak, Flamingo, plate, salad; #1246 (acorn & leaves), 6"...**$10.00**

Charter Oak, Flamingo, stem, saucer champagne; #3362, 6-oz..**$15.00**

Charter Oak, Hawthorne, plate, luncheon; #1246 (acorn & leaves), 8"...**$25.00**

Charter Oak, Moongleam, bowl, finger; #3362 ....**$20.00**

Charter Oak, Moongleam, stem, sherbet; #3362, low foot, 6-oz..**$22.00**

Chintz, crystal, comport, oval, 7"................................**$40.00**

Chintz, crystal, plate, luncheon; 8" sq........................**$10.00**

Chintz, crystal, salt & pepper shakers, pr...................**$40.00**

Chintz, crystal, tumbler, soda; #3389, 8-oz.................**$13.00**

Chintz, Sahara, bowl, finger; #4107............................**$20.00**

Chintz, Sahara, mayonnaise, dolphin foot, 5½"..........**$65.00**

Chintz, Sahara, stem, parfait; #3389, 5-oz...................**$35.00**

Chintz, Sahara, tray, celery; 10" **$30.00**

Crystolite, crystal, ashtray, 4½" sq.............................**$10.00**

Crystolite, crystal, creamer, regular............................**$30.00**

Crystolite, crystal, vase, short stem, 3" **$45.00**

Empress, Alexandrite, creamer, individual.................**$210.00**

Empress, Flamingo, bowl, mint; dolphin foot, 6" **$35.00**

Empress, Flamingo, bowl, pickle/olive; 2-part, 13".....**$35.00**

Empress, Flamingo, plate, 12"....................................**$45.00**

Empress, Moongleam, bonbon, 6"...............................**$30.00**

Empress, Moongleam, tray, relish; 3-part, 10" **$65.00**

Empress, Sahara, bowl, grapefruit; w/sq undertray **$30.00**

Greek Key, crystal, bowl, jelly; shallow, low foot, 4".**$40.00**

Greek Key, crystal, compote, w/lid, 5".....................**$130.00**

Greek Key, crystal, plate, 6" **$35.00**

Greek Key, crystal, sherbet, shallow, footed, 4½-oz ..**$30.00**

Greek Key, crystal, tumbler, flared rim, 7-oz..............**$60.00**

Ipswich, cobalt, bowl, floral, footed, 11"..................**$400.00**

Ipswich, pink, tumbler, soda; footed, 8-oz.................**$45.00**

Ipswich, Sahara, plate, 7" sq......................................**$50.00**

Lariat, crystal, ashtray, 4"..**$15.00**

Lariat, crystal, bowl, nut; individual, 4"....................**$32.00**

Lariat, crystal, candlestick, 3-light.............................**$45.00**

Lariat, crystal, tumbler, iced tea; footed, 12-oz..........**$28.00**

Lodestar, Dawn, candy jar, w/lid, 5"........................**$135.00**

Lodestar, Dawn, creamer...**$50.00**

Minuet, crystal, bowl, oval, #1514 ....$65.00
Minuet, crystal, plate, salad; 7" **$18.00**
Minuet, crystal, stem, cocktail; #5010, 3½-oz **$35.00**
Minuet, crystal, stem, sherbet; #5010, 6-oz **$25.00**
Minuet, crystal, vase, #5013, 5" **$50.00**
Minuet, crystal, vase, urn; #5012, 7½" **$90.00**
New Era, crystal, bowl, floral, 11" **$60.00**
New Era, crystal, pilsner, 8-oz **$25.00**
New Era, crystal, plate, bread & butter; 5½x4½" **$15.00**
New Era, crystal, plate, 9x7" **$25.00**
New Era, crystal, stem, champagne; 6-oz **$15.00**
Octagon, crystal, creamer, hotel **$10.00**
Octagon, Flamingo, plate, luncheon; 8" **$10.00**
Octagon, Hawthorne, saucer, #1231 ....**$12.00**
Octagon, Moongleam, bowl, vegetable; 9" **$30.00**
Octagon, Sahara, bowl, jelly; #1229, 5½" **$25.00**
Octagon, Sahara, tray, celery; 12" **$25.00**
Old Colony, Sahara, bowl, flared, footed, 13" **$40.00**
Old Colony, Sahara, bowl, nappy; 4½" **$14.00**
Old Colony, Sahara, plate, sq, 6" **$15.00**
Old Colony, Sahara, platter, oval, 14" **$45.00**
Old Colony, Sahara, stem, champagne; #3390, 6-oz...**$25.00**
Old Colony, Sahara, tumbler, soda; ft, #3380, 8-oz.....**$18.00**
Old Sandwich, cobalt, ashtray, individual.................**$45.00**
Old Sandwich, crystal, comport, 6" **$40.00**
Old Sandwich, crystal, creamer, 12-oz **$32.00**
Old Sandwich, crystal, tumbler, iced tea; 12-oz **$20.00**
Old Sandwich, Flamingo, pilsner, 10-oz **$32.00**
Old Sandwich, Flamingo, sundae, 6-oz **$30.00**
Old Sandwich, Moongleam, saucer............................**$15.00**
Old Sandwich, Sahara, plate, 8" sq **$27.00**
Orchid, crystal, bowl, floral; 11" **$70.00**
Orchid, crystal, bowl, salad; 7" **$60.00**

Orchid, crystal, butter dish, Waverly, $175.00.

Orchid, crystal, candlestick, Mercury, 1-light..............**$45.00**
Orchid, crystal, creamer, ft.......................................**$35.00**
Orchid, crystal, plate, torte; rolled edge, 14"..............**$65.00**
Orchid, crystal, plate, 6" **$13.00**
Orchid, crystal, stem, cocktail; #5025, 4-oz **$40.00**
Orchid, crystal, sugar bowl, individual **$35.00**
Orchid, crystal, tray, celery; 12" **$55.00**
Orchid, crystal, vase, fan; footed, 7" **$90.00**

Plantation, crystal, bowl, gardenia; 13" **$90.00**
Plantation, crystal, bowl, nappy; 5" **$30.00**
Plantation, crystal, candlestick, 3-light **$115.00**
Plantation, crystal, comport, 5" **$50.00**
Plantation, crystal, cup, punch **$35.00**
Plantation, crystal, plate, salad; 8" **$35.00**
Plantation, crystal, stem, pressed, 10-oz **$50.00**
Pleat & Panel, crystal, bowl, lemon; w/lid, 5".............**$20.00**
Pleat & Panel, crystal, pitcher, 3-pt **$45.00**
Pleat & Panel, crystal, vase, 8".................................**$30.00**
Pleat & Panel, Flamingo, bowl, nappy; 4½".................**$11.00**
Pleat & Panel, Flamingo, plate, sandwich; 14" **$32.50**
Pleat & Panel, Flamingo, platter, oval, 12".................**$42.50**
Pleat & Panel, Flamingo, stem, 8-oz **$35.00**
Pleat & Panel, Moongleam, plate, 6" **$8.00**
Pleat & Panel, Moongleam, saucer............................**$5.00**
Provincial, crystal, ashtray, sq, 3" **$12.50**
Provincial, crystal, bowl, floral **$40.00**
Provincial, crystal, coaster, 4" **$15.00**
Provincial, crystal, stem, wine; 3½-oz **$20.00**
Provincial, crystal, sugar bowl, footed **$25.00**
Provincial, crystal, tumbler, 8-oz...............................**$17.00**
Provincial, crystal, vase, pansy; 4"............................**$35.00**
Provincial, Limelight Green, bowl, nut/jelly; individual..**$40.00**
Queen Ann, crystal, bowl, floral; flared, 9" **$32.00**
Queen Ann, crystal, bowl, grapefruit; w/sq undertray .**$20.00**
Queen Ann, crystal, bowl, nut; dolphin foot, individual...**$20.00**
Queen Ann, crystal, comport, ft, 6"...........................**$25.00**
Queen Ann, crystal, mustard, w/lid **$60.00**
Queen Ann, crystal, plate, 8" sq **$10.00**
Queen Ann, crystal, stem, saucer champagne; 4-oz ...**$20.00**
Queen Ann, crystal, tumbler, tea; ground bottom, 12-oz...**$20.00**
Ridgeleigh, crystal, basket, bonbon; metal handle......**$25.00**
Ridgeleigh, crystal, bowl, nappy; bell or cupped, 4½" ...**$20.00**
Ridgeleigh, crystal, ice tub, handles.........................**$100.00**
Ridgeleigh, crystal, plate, sandwich; 13½".................**$45.00**
Ridgeleigh, crystal, salt & pepper shakers, pr **$45.00**
Ridgeleigh, crystal, stem, claret; pressed...................**$50.00**
Ridgeleigh, crystal, tumbler, juice; blown, 5-oz..........**$30.00**
Ridgeleigh, crystal, vase, 3½".................................**$25.00**
Rose, crystal, bowl, jelly; Queen Ann, handles, footed, 6"..**$55.00**
Rose, crystal, bowl, salad; Waverly, 7"......................**$60.00**
Rose, crystal, comport, Waverly, low foot, 6½"...........**$65.00**
Rose, crystal, plate, salad; Waverly, 7" **$20.00**
Rose, crystal, plate, torte; Waverly, 14" **$90.00**
Rose, crystal, stem, wine; #5072, 3-oz **$115.00**
Rose, crystal, tumbler, juice; #5072, footed, 5-oz **$55.00**
Saturn, crystal, bowl, finger **$15.00**
Saturn, crystal, bowl, fruit; flared rim, 12" **$35.00**
Saturn, crystal, marmalade, w/lid **$45.00**
Saturn, crystal, pitcher, juice **$40.00**
Saturn, crystal, stem, parfait; 5-oz............................**$10.00**
Saturn, Zircon Limelight, creamer **$180.00**
Saturn, Zircon Limelight, plate, luncheon; 8" **$55.00**
Saturn, Zircon Limelight, stem, 10-oz........................**$100.00**
Stanhope, crystal, cigarette box & lid, w/ or w/o round
    knob **$65.00**

Stanhope, crystal, plate, torte; handles, w/ or w/out T knobs..$35.00
Stanhope, crystal, stem, wine; #4083, 2½-oz...............$25.00
Stanhope, crystal, tumbler, soda; #4083, 12-oz............$25.00
Twist, crystal, bowl, French dressing..........................$80.00
Twist, crystal, pitcher, 3-pt.....................................$95.00
Twist, crystal, tumbler, iced tea; footed, 12-oz............$20.00
Twist, Flamingo, baker, oval, 9"...............................$35.00
Twist, Flamingo, tray, pickle; ground bottom, 7".........$35.00
Twist, Marigold, bonbon, handles, 6".........................$30.00
Twist, Moongleam, sugar bowl, ft..............................$37.50
Twist, Sahara, bowl, mint; handles, 6".......................$20.00
Victorian, crystal, bottle, French dressing...................$80.00
Victorian, crystal, butter dish, ¼-lb...........................$70.00
Victorian, crystal, cup, punch; 5-oz...........................$10.00
Victorian, crystal, salt & pepper shakers, pr................$65.00
Victorian, crystal, stem, sherbet; 5-oz........................$18.00
Victorian, crystal, vase, ft, 6".................................$100.00
Waverly, crystal, bowl, crimped edge, 10"...................$25.00
Waverly, crystal, bowl, floral; sea horse foot, 11".........$70.00
Waverly, crystal, butter dish, 6" sq...........................$65.00
Waverly, crystal, creamer, footed..............................$25.00
Waverly, crystal, honey dish, footed, 6½"....................$50.00
Waverly, crystal, stem, cocktail; #5019, 3½-oz............$15.00
Yeoman, crystal, parfait, 5-oz..................................$10.00
Yeoman, Flamingo, bowl, banana split; footed.............$23.00
Yeoman, Hawthorne, bowl, nappy; 4½"........................$15.00
Yeoman, Marigold, bowl, floral; low, 12"....................$55.00
Yeoman, Marigold, bowl, preserve; oval, 6".................$30.00
Yeoman, Moongleam, plate, 6"..................................$13.00
Yeoman, Sahara, creamer...$20.00

Figurals and Novelties

Rooster vase, 6½", $100.00.

Airedale, crystal..$650.00
Chick, crystal, head down or up, ea..........................$95.00
Colt, amber, kicking...$650.00
Colt, crystal, kicking..$200.00
Cygnet, baby swan, crystal, 2½"..............................$225.00
Doe head, bookend, crystal, 6¼", ea.........................$850.00

Dolphin, candlesticks, Moongleam, #110, pr.............$800.00
Duck, ashtray, crystal...$100.00
Elephant, amber, sm..$1,650.00
Filly, crystal, head forward.................................$1,000.00
Fish, bowl, crystal, 9½".......................................$450.00
Fish, match holder, crystal, 3x2¾"..........................$180.00
Giraffe, crystal, head to side.................................$275.00
Goose, crystal, wings half.....................................$100.00
Horse head, cigarette box, crystal, #1489, 4½x4".......$60.00
Irish setter, ashtray, crystal...................................$30.00
Kingfisher, flower block, Flamingo..........................$225.00
Mallard, crystal, wings half....................................$200.00
Piglet, crystal, sitting...$100.00
Rabbit, paperweight, crystal, 2¾x3¾".......................$225.00
Ringneck, pheasant, crystal, 11¾"...........................$175.00
Show horse, crystal...$1,250.00
Sparrow, crystal...$120.00
Tropical fish, crystal, 12"...................................$2,200.00
Wood duck, crystal, standing.................................$200.00

Hippie Collectibles

The 'Hippies' perpetuated the 'Beatnik' genre of rebellious, free-thinking, Bohemian nonconformity during the decade of the 1960s. Young people created a 'counterculture' with their own style of clothing, attitudes, music, politics, and behavior. They created new forms of art, theatre, and political activism. The center of this movement was the Haight-Ashbury district of San Francisco. The youth culture culminated there in 1967 in the 'Summer of Love.' Woodstock, in August 1969, attracted at least 400,000 people. Political activism against the Viet Nam War was intense and widespread. Posters, books, records, handbills, and other items from that era are highly collectible because of their uniqueness to this time period.

Advisor: Richard Synchef (See Directory, Beatnik and Hippie Collectibles)

Admission ticket, Woodstock Music & Art Fair, Globe Ticket Co, 1969, 1- or 3-day ticket................................$125.00
Book, Garage Sale, Ken Kesey, NY: Viking, 1973, contributors include Allen Ginsberg, Paul Krassner, Neal Cassidy, others..$225.00
Book, Journal of Psychedelic Drugs, Vol 2 #1, Marijuana, Dr Smith, San Francisco.....................................$45.00
Bumper sticker, Nixon's My Man, Nixon as hippie, 3-color, 12x3"...$50.00
Bumper sticker, Pat Paulsen for President, We Cannot Stand Pat, red, white & blue, 1968, 1x4"....................$80.00
Figurine, hippie man w/peace sign, 'High There,' American Greeting Corp, 1971, 6".................................$65.00
Figurine, hippie man w/sign: Fight Hate, Napcoware, 1970s, 6"...$75.00
Handbill, Straight Theatre, San Francisco, artist unknown, 1967, promoting venue in Haight Ashbury........$100.00

Magazine, Avant Garde, Ralph Ginsberg editon, NY, 1968-71, #1-12, ea from $40 to $200.00

Magazine, Psychedelic Review #6, 1965, important early scholarly writing about hallucinogens $160.00

Newspaper, Berkeley Barb, Vol 4 #2, January 13, 1967, The Human Be-In Issue..$80.00

Newspaper, Black Panther, 1967-74, per issue, from $40 to $250.00

Newspaper, SS New Left Notes, Vol 4 #24, July 8, 1969, Bring the War Home! issue $125.00

Paperback, Electric Tibet, N Hollywood: Dominion, 1969, study of San Francisco music scene.....................$50.00

Paperback, Hippies, The; by correspondents of Time, Joe Brown, NY: Time, 1967, surprisingly objective book..$60.00

Paperback, 1001 Ways To Beat the Draft, Tuli Kupferberg & Robert Bachlow, Grove Press, 1967, great period piece $70.00

Pin-back button, Free Spech, Free Speech Movement, in white on blue, Berkleley CA, 1964.......................$50.00

Poster, Can You Pass the Acid Test, Ken Kesey & The Merry Pranksters, Norman Hartweg artist, 1965, *the* '60s poster, $2,700.00. (Photo courtesy Richard Synchef)

Poster, Dick Gregory for President/Mark Lane for Vice, Peace & Freedom Party, 1968, 22x29" $400.00

Poster, Invocation for Maitreya, Lenore Kandel, poster by Michael Bowen, photos by Gene Anthony, blue & white on purple...$150.00

Poster, Kendrick & Assoc, Eller art, hippies face riot police, 1970, 22x29" $125.00

Poster, Would You Die To Save This Face?, stern-face photo of Lydon Johnson, International Poster Corp, 1968, 21x29" $60.00

Record, Can You Pass the Acid Test?, Ken Kesey & The Merry Pranksters, Sound City Productions, 1966, very rare..$550.00

Record, Leary, Timothy; LSD, NY/Pixie #1069, LP, 1966..$125.00

Record, Sound of Dissent, Mercury Records #61203, 1969, sounds of various speakers & antiwar demonstrations...........$75.00

Holt Howard

Now's the time to pick up the kitchenware (cruets, salt and peppers, condiments, etc.), novelty banks, ashtrays, and planters marked Holt Howard. They're not only marked but dated as well; you'll find production dates from the 1950s through the 1970s. (Beware of unmarked copy-cat lines!) There's a wide variety of items and decorative themes; those you're most likely to find will be from the rooster (done in golden brown, yellow, and orange), white cat (called Kozy Kitten), and Christmas lines. Not as easily found, the Pixies are by far the most collectible of all, and in general, Pixie prices continue to climb, particularly for the harder-to-find items.

Internet auctions have affected this market with the 'more supply, less demand' principal (more exposure, therefore in some cases lower prices), but all in all, the market has remained sound. Only the very common pieces have suffered.

Our values are for mint condition, factory-first examples. If any flaws are present, you must reduce the price accordingly.

Christmas

Ashtray, Santa in airplane marked North Pole Jet Stream, trays in wings, #6074, 6½x6¼" $110.00

Beverage set, smiling Santa face surrounded by white fur, top of ea pc is red w/white fur, 7" pitcher, +4 2½" shots...$75.00

Butter pats, holly leaves & berries, 2¾", set of 4........$32.00

Cake stand, musical: Jingle Bells, white w/3-D holly leaves & berries $85.00

Candelabrum, Santa trio, gift packages hold candles, 5x8"..$60.00

Candle holder, double; 3 choir boys hold lg song book $38.00

Candle holder, Santa in cowboy hat riding stagecoach pulled by 4 reindeer jumping over NOEL, 9" L $90.00

Candle holder, Santa in middle w/NOEL in gold, marked 1959 ....$40.00

Candle holder, 2 angel musicians on base w/cups at ea side, marked 1963, 4½x7½"...............................$40.00

Candle holder, 2 Santas stack on top ea other, marked #6007, 8¼"..$38.00

Candle holders, angels, white w/'spaghetti' trim on robes, cuffs & hoods, 1 w/bell, 1 w/package, 4", +snowflake hangers $70.00

Candle holders, camel figurals, 4", pr $50.00

Candle holders, children dressed as Wise Men, 3½", set of 3 ....$55.00

Candle holders, Santa in coach laden w/Christmas gifts, cowboy hat, 3x4", pr $42.00

Candle huggers, figural snowmen, Christmas tree hats, red scarfs, pr, from $30 to $35.00

Carousel, Santa holds metal spinner w/2 candles, spins from heat of flames..$50.00

Christmas tree, bottle-brush style w/fruit, foil ornaments & bird decorations, 15"....................................$40.00

Christmas tree, electric, 10" $70.00

Cookie jar, white w/red & green 'Cookie,' sm Santa w/sign reads 'Just Take 1,' 6x4" dia **$90.00**

Cookies/candy jar, roly-poly Santa figure, 3-pc, minimum value **$150.00**

Covered dish, green holly, with girl head finial, from $20.00 to $30.00.

Cups, Santa face w/snowflake eyes, stick handle is point of Santa's hat, set of 4 ....**$35.00**

Dish, Santa face, 7¼x5½" **$42.00**

Figurines, Santas shaped as letters: N, O, E, L, 3⅞", set of 4 ....**$65.00**

Head vase, girl w/drop earrings, holly head band, pearl necklace, 4" **$65.00**

Head vase, pitcher, smiling Santa, 7", w/3 matching 3" mugs **$50.00**

Match holder, Santa w/bongo drum, 4½"..............**$30.00**

Napkin holder, tree form, marked 1961, 5" **$40.00**

Place card holders/figurines, elves, 3", set of 4..........**$55.00**

Planter, angel standing before sq pot, 'spaghetti' trim on robe, cuffs & hood, 4¼x3¾x2¾" **$55.00**

Planter, angel w/hands in muff, silver trim in hair & on dress, dated 1958, 4" **$40.00**

Punch bowl, ladle & 8 cups, Santa face, dated 1962, 10-pc set...**$235.00**

Punch bowl, ladle & 8 cups, white w/holly sprig, paneled, 10-pc set **$65.00**

Salt & pepper shakers, angel figurals, 3½", pr............**$22.00**

Salt & pepper shakers, Christmas trees w/Santa's face on ea, 'S' & 'P,' 4½", pr **$25.00**

Salt & pepper shakers, Santa & his bag, Santa: 3", pr...**$35.00**

Salt & pepper shakers, Santa's head is salt, stacks on pepper body, from $30 to..**$40.00**

Salt & pepper shakers, standing Santas, 5½", pr.........**$18.00**

Salt & pepper shakers, stylized deer, 1 buck & 1 doe, pr..**$30.00**

Salt & pepper shakers, 2 stacked gift boxes, 'Merry Xmas' on top, pr...**$15.00**

Snack set, Santa waving on plate, red cup fits off-center well, 8½"...**$28.00**

Taper holder, elf in sleigh w/candy cane runners, 'spaghetti' trim at top of sleigh, 5" L **$28.00**

Tea set, pitcher/6 cups/cr+sug w/removable heads, winking Santa, 12-pc set.......................................**$115.00**

Tray, Santa, beard forms tray, 7¾", from $25 to **$30.00**

Votive candle holder, Santa, dated 1968, 3"..............**$20.00**

Wall pocket, Santa face, 'Greetings' across crown-like hat band, gold trim...**$175.00**

Kozy Kitten

Ashtray, cat on sq plaid base, 4 corner rests, from $60 to..**$75.00**

Bud vase, cat in plaid cap & neckerchief, from $75 to .**$100.00**

Butter dish, cats peeking out on side, ¼-lb, rare **$150.00**

Cookie jar, head form, from $40 to......................**$50.00**

Cottage cheese keeper, cat knob on lid **$75.00**

Creamer & sugar bowl, stackable, from $125 to.......**$150.00**

Letter holder, cat w/coiled wire back **$50.00**

Memo finder, full-bodied cat, legs cradle note pad, from $100 to **$125.00**

Powdered cleanser shaker, full-bodied lady cat wearing apron, w/broom, from $100 to......................**$125.00**

Salt & pepper shakers, cat's head, pr...........................**$30.00**

Salt & pepper shakers, head form, 1 in plaid cap, in wireware napkin holder frame...**$75.00**

Salt and pepper shakers, noisemakers in base, from $45.00 to $55.00. (Photo courtesy Marilyn Dipboye)

Salt & pepper shakers, 4 individual cat heads, stacked on upright dowel...**$175.00**

Sewing box, figural cat w/tape-measure tongue on lid ..**$100.00**

Spice set, stacking; from $150 to.............................**$175.00**

Spice set, 4 cat heads w/loop atop, hang on metal bar, ea 2½x3"...**$150.00**

String holder, head only, from $50 to **$60.00**

Sugar shaker, cat in apron carries sack w/word Pour, shaker holes in hat, side spout formed by sack, rare....**$125.00**

Tape measure, cat on cushion....................................**$85.00**

Wall pocket, cat's head, from $60 to...........................**$75.00**

Pixie Ware

Candlesticks, pr, from $45 to **$55.00**

Cherries jar, flat head finial on lid, w/cherry pick or spoon, from $150 to.......................................**$175.00**

Chili sauce, rare, minimum value................$400.00
Cocktail cherries, from $175 to....................$200.00
Cocktail olives, winking green head finial on lid, from $120
   to..$135.00
Cocktail onions, onion-head finial, from $160 to.....$175.00
Cruets, oil & vinegar, Sally & Sam, pr.................$275.00
Decanter, Devil Brew, striped base, rare, 10½", minimum
   value..$225.00
Decanter, Whiskey, w/winking head stopper, minimum
   value..$225.00
Decanter, 300 Proof, flat-head stopper w/red rose, minimum
   value..$225.00
Dish, flat-head handle w/crossed eyes & pickle nose, green
   stripes, minimum value...................................$100.00
French dressing bottle, minimum value, from $160 to.$180.00
Honey, very rare, from $400 to........................$500.00
Hors d'oeurve, head on body pierced for toothpicks, exag-
   gerated tall hairdo, saucer base, from $250 to...$300.00
Instant coffee jar, brown-skinned blond head finial, hard to
   find, from $250 to..$300.00
Italian dressing bottle, from $160 to.................$175.00
Jam & jelly jar, flat-head finial on lid, from $60 to.....$75.00
Ketchup jar, orange tomato-like head finial on lid, from $75
   to..$90.00
Mustard jar, yellow head finial on lid, from $75 to..$100.00

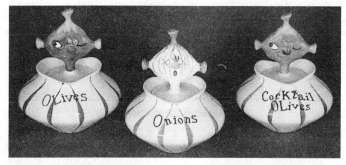

Olives, from $100.00 to $125.00; Onions, from $180.00 to $200.00; Cocktail Olives, from $120.00 to $135.00. (Photo courtesy Pat and Ann Duncan)

Onion jar, flat onion-head finial on lid, 1958, from $180 to...$200.00
Relish jar, green flat head on lid...............................$200.00
Russian dressing bottle, from $165 to.......................$175.00
Salt & pepper shakers, Salty & Peppy, attached flat head
   w/painted wood handle, pr, minimum value.....$200.00
Spice set, stacking; from $150 to..............................$175.00
Towel hook, flat head w/sm loop hanger, rare, minimum
   value..$200.00

Ponytail Princess

Candle holder, girl shares figure-8 platform w/flower-head
   candle cup, from $50 to....................................$60.00
Lipstick holder, from $50 to.......................................$65.00
Salt & pepper shakers, pr..$45.00
Tray, double; 2 joined flower cups, girl between, from $50
   to..$65.00

Rooster

Ashtray, figural rooster w/open-body rectangular receptacle,
   w/cigarette rest..$15.00
Bowl, cereal; 6"...$12.00
Bud vase, figural rooster, from $25 to.......................$30.00
Butter dish, embossed rooster, ¼-lb, from $50 to.......$65.00
Chocolate pot, tall & narrow w/flaring sides, embossed roost-
   er on front..$60.00
Cigarette holder, wooden w/painted-on rooster, wall mount,
   holds several packs..$150.00

Coffeepot, electric, from $60.00 to $85.00. (Photo courtesy Pat and Ann Duncan)

Coffeepot, embossed rooster, from $50 to..................$65.00
Cookie jar, embossed rooster...................................$150.00
Creamer & sugar bowl, embossed rooster, pr, from $35
   to..$50.00
Cup & saucer..$20.00
Dish, figural rooster w/open-body receptacle.............$15.00
Egg cup, double; figural rooster, from $18 to.............$25.00
Jam & jelly jar, embossed rooster.............................$60.00
Ketchup jar, embossed rooster.................................$35.00
Mug, embossed rooster (3 sizes), ea from $5 to........$10.00
Mustard jar, embossed rooster on front, w/lid............$35.00
Napkin holder...$40.00
Pincushion, 3¼x4"..$65.00
Pitcher, embossed rooster on front, cylindrical w/indents on
   side for gripping, no handle, tall......................$50.00
Pitcher, syrup; embossed rooster on front, tail
   handle...$30.00
Pitcher, water; flaring sides, tail handle, tall...............$50.00
Plate, embossed rooster, 8½", from $20 to.................$25.00
Platter, embossed rooster, oval, from $28 to..............$35.00
Recipe box, wood w/painted-on rooster, from $75
   to..$100.00
Salt & pepper shakers, figural rooster, tall, pr, from $30
   to..$40.00
Spoon rest, figural rooster, from $15 to....................$20.00
Tray, facing left, from $15 to...................................$20.00
Trivet, tile w/rooster in iron framework....................$40.00

Miscellaneous

Ashtray, golfer figural, 5½" $95.00

Ashtray, hunter w/gun to shoulder, smoke holes in ears & mouth, 5"..$35.00

Ashtray, little old lady w/bottle of booze, skirt forms tray, exposes her feet...$40.00

Ashtray, man figural w/open stomach receptacle & open mouth for exhaust, 5¼"...$35.00

Bank, Coin Kitty, bobbing head finial, from $100 to $135.00

Bank, Dandy-Lion, bobbing head, from $100 to $135.00

Bank, piggy, w/polka-dotted neck ribbon, 3x4".........$40.00

Bowl, fruit; watermelon shape, dated 1959, 2x6" dia, set of 4..$40.00

Candle holders, bride & groom, 4", pr $50.00

Candle holders, camel, sitting, w/red felt saddle & gold & silver trim, dated 1960, pr...$30.00

Cherry jar, Cherries If You Please lettered on sign held by butler, minimum value $250.00

Cocktail shaker, bartender theme, +4 tumblers...........$75.00

Coffee mug, Nixon's face on currency.........................$60.00

Desk accessories, Cock A Doddle Do (birds), sharpener, pencil holder, set..$60.00

Desk accessory, cat w/hole in head for pencils, wire back for papers, 6"..$40.00

Jam 'n Jelly jar, girl's head w/5-petal hat finial, from $60 to...$70.00

Ketchup jar, tomato-face finial w/leaf hair, 6"............$60.00

Martini shaker, butler (Jeeves), 9", from $175 to.......$200.00

Match holder, pink mouse w/cane, unmarked, 6"......$48.00

Mugs, Blue Willow, set of 4...$45.00

Napkin ring, sm white, yellow & green bird atop white ring, dated 1958, 1" dia..$110.00

Note pad holder, 3-D lady's hand $45.00

Olives jar, Olives If You Please lettered on sign held by butler (Jeeves), minimum value...............................$150.00

Paper clip, painted sq faces w/black back clip, rare, pr..$50.00

Pencil sharpener, whale figural, sharpener in mouth, 3¾" L...$55.00

Pitcher, blue forals on white, 1964-65, +4 mugs...........$75.00

Planter, bull, white w/ring in nose.............................$35.00

Planter, Granny holding 2 cards, planter boxes on ea side, 3¼x4½"..$30.00

Plate, Rake 'N Spade, MIB $20.00

Playing card holder, on base w/3-D bust of Granny holding playing cards, from $45 to $55.00

Salt & pepper shakers, chick figural w/yellow topknot, beak & feet, original tag marked Lil' Bo Peep, pr.........$50.00

Salt & pepper shakers, goose & golden egg, pr $40.00

Salt & pepper shakers, Moo Cow, working 'mooing' mechanism, 3¼", pr...$42.50

Salt & pepper shakers, New York Thruway souvenir, stylized girls w/wings marked Lil' Pepper & Lil' Salt, red & white, pr..$25.00

Salt & pepper shakers, poodle & cat, 4½", 4", pr.....$40.00

Salt & pepper shakers, Rock 'N Roll kids, heads on springs, pr $125.00

Salt & pepper shakers, tiger, big smile, 3½", pr..........$25.00

Snack set, tomato cup & lettuce leaf plate, 1962........$25.00

String holder, cat head, string comes out mouth, dated 1958 ....$40.00

Super scooper, Hot Stuff, red & white, w/lid, 6" $50.00

Tape dispenser, stylized poodle w/red neck band & pencil sharpener...$50.00

Tray, butler (Jeeves), 4¾" wide..................................$150.00

Utensil holder, chef in red & white, hands at front w/2 openings, 11½"..$30.00

Votive candle holder, pig, pastel, dated 1958, 5½".....$45.00

Wall pocket, pheasant w/scene, 6"..............................$38.00

Homer Laughlin China Co.

The first pottery made by The Laughlin Brothers of East Liverpool, Ohio, rolled off the production linein 1874. Mr. Homer Laughlin bought out his brother Shakespeare's interest in 1877, and the pottery became known as The Homer Laughlin China Company. Over the years, the company has been recognized as the largest producer of American dinnerware and has won numerous awards for quality and design. In keeping with the styles of the time, the early shapes were rather ornate, while the shapes from 1930 through 1970 were of a simpler design. Not only did the Homer Laughlin China Company apply a date to each piece of ware, but many times the name of the shape was also included n the backstamp.

For further information see *The Collector's Encyclopedia of Homer Laughlin Pottery* and *American Dinnerware, 1880s to 1920s*, both by Joanne Jasper (Collector Books). Also recommended is *Homer Laughlin China 1940's and 1950's*, *Homer Laughlin, A Giant Among Dishes*, both by Jo Cunningham (Schiffer), and *Homer Laughlin China Identification Guide to Shapes and Patterns* by Joe Cunningham and Darlene Nossaman (Schiffer). *The Collector's Encyclopedia of Fiesta, Ninth Edition,* by Sharon and Bob Huxford (Collector Books) has photographs and prices of several of the more collectible lines such as listed here.

See also Fiesta.

Advisor: Darlene Nossaman (See Directory, Dinnerware)

Club/Newsletter: Homer Laughlin China Collector's Association (HLCCA)
P.O. Box 26021
Crystal City, VA 22215-6021; Dues $25.00 single; $40.00 couple or family, includes *The Dish* magazine (a 16-page quarterly), free classifieds

Genessee: early 1900s (Pink Rose, Rose Spray, Gold Stamp and Band, Parisian Rose)

Bowl, fruit; 5" $5.00
Bowl, vegetable; oval, 9" $15.00
Casserole, w/lid, 9"...$45.00

Creamer $10.00
Cup & saucer, AD $16.00
Jug, 1½-pt $35.00
Pickle dish $22.00
Plate, 7" $7.50
Plate, 10" $10.00
Platter, 13" $18.00
Sauce boat $16.00
Saucer $3.00
Sugar bowl, w/lid $15.00
Teacup $6.00

Kraft Blue and Kraft Pink Shape, 1930s

Bowl, cereal; 6" $8.00
Bowl, cream soup; 5" $10.00
Bowl, fruit; 5½" $6.00
Bowl, vegetable; 8¾" dia $12.00
Creamer $8.00
Creamer, novelty $12.00
Egg cup, double $12.00
Plate, 6" $5.00
Plate, 9" $8.00
Plate, 10" $10.00
Platter, 10" $12.00
Saucer $3.00
Sugar bowl, w/lid $10.00
Teacup $7.00
Teapot $25.00

Newell: 1927 design (Yellow Glow, Puritan, Song of Spring, Southern Pride, Poppy)

Bowl, fruit; 5" $4.00
Bowl, vegetable; 9" $12.00
Casserole, w/lid $35.00
Creamer $10.00
Jug, 1½-pt $35.00
Plate, 7" $6.00
Plate, 10" $10.00
Platter, 12" $16.00
Sauce boat $15.00
Saucer $3.00
Sugar bowl, w/lid $15.00
Teacup $7.00

Virginia Rose

Bowl, fruit; 5" $5.00
Bowl, vegetable; 9" $18.00
Cake plate $25.00
Casserole, w/lid $45.00
Creamer $14.00
Plate, 7" $6.00
Plate, 10" $10.00
Platter, 13" $24.00
Rimmed soup $9.50

Sauce boat $18.00
Saucer $5.00
Sugar bowl, w/lid $16.00
Teacup $8.00
Tray, decal JJ59, rare, 8", from $28 to $35.00

Wells Art Glaze

Bowl, fruit; 5" $4.50
Bowl, vegetable; oval, 9" $18.00
Casserole, w/lid $48.00
Creamer $12.00
Muffin cover $45.00
Plate, 7" $6.00
Plate, 10" $10.50
Platter, 11" $18.00
Sauce boat $18.00
Saucer $18.00
Sugar bowl, w/lid $16.00
Teacup $7.00

Yellowstone 1927 (Moss Rose, Poppy Pastel, Golden Rose, Buttercup, Floral Spray)

Bowl, fruit; 5" $2.50
Bowl, vegetable; 9" $10.00
Butter dish $32.00
Casserole, w/lid $30.00
Creamer $6.00
Jug, 2½-pt $28.00
Plate, 6" $4.00
Plate, 10" $7.00
Platter, 13" $17.50
Sauce boat $10.00
Saucer $2.50
Sugar bowl, w/lid $10.00
Teacup $5.00

Horton Ceramics

Following the end of WWII, Mr. Horace Horton and his wife, Geri, returned to Mr. Horton's hometown, Eastland, Texas. With good clays nearby, Mr. Horton's keen business ability, and Mrs. Horton's skills in artistic design, they set about establishing a pottery in Eastland. Their wares were marketed mainly to floral shops, variety stores, and department stores. Mrs. Horton designed a logo of a rearing wild horse. Each piece has the mold number on the bottom as well as 'horton ceramics' in lower-case flowing script lettering. The pottery was sold in the early 1960s.

Advisor: Darlene Nossaman (See Directory, Horton Ceramics)

Jardinere, white, pink, black or green, #R12, 12x6", from $10 to $12.00

Jardinere, white, pink, black or green, Lone Cedar pot #308, 8x8", from $12 to **$14.00**

Mug, Sunshine Yellow or Forest Green, 6", from $5 to .**$7.00**

Novelty, powder horn, 2-tone brown w/real leather strap, 9", from $12 to..**$14.00**

Novelty, wind bell, yellow, brown or coral striped, 6x9", from $20 to...**$25.00**

Planter, bassinet, pink or blue, #B3, 4x6", from $10 to .**$12.00**

Planter, giraffe, yellow or brown, #G1, 9½", from $15 to...**$18.00**

Planter, #810, from $14.00 to $16.00. (Photo courtesy Darlene Nossaman)

Salt & pepper shakers, Sunshine Yellow or Forest Green, 4", pr, from $10 to **$12.00**

Vase, black, pink, coral, blue or green, #BV19, 9x1½", from $18 to..**$20.00**

Vase, white, pink, black or green, #E6, 6x6", from $10 to...**$14.00**

Hull

Hull has a look of its own. Many lines were made in soft, pastel matt glazes and modeled with flowers and ribbons, and as a result, they have a very feminine appeal.

The company operated in Crooksville (near Zanesville), Ohio, from just after the turn of the century until they closed in 1985. From the 1930s until the plant was destroyed by fire in 1950, they preferred the soft matt glazes so popular with today's collectors, though a few high gloss lines were made as well. When the plant was rebuilt, modern equipment was installed which they soon found did not lend itself to the duplication of the matt glazes, so they began to concentrate on the production of glossy wares, novelties, and figurines.

During the '40s and '50s, they produced a line of kitchenware items modeled after Little Red Riding Hood. Original pieces are expensive today and most are reproduced by persons other than Hull. (See also Little Red Riding Hood.)

Hull's Mirror Brown dinnerware line made from 1960 until they closed in 1985 was very successful for them and was made in large quantities. Its glossy brown glaze was enhanced with a band of ivory foam, and today's collectors are finding its rich colors and basic, strong shapes just as attractive now as they were back then. In addition to table service, there are novelty trays shaped like gingerbread men and fish, canisters and cookie jars, covered casseroles with ducks and hens as lids, vases, ashtrays, and mixing bowls. It's easy to find, and though you may have to pay 'near book'

prices at co-ops and antique malls, bargains are out there. It may be marked Hull, Crooksville, O; HPCo; or Crestone.

If you'd like to learn more about this subject, we recommend *The Collector's Encyclopedia of Hull Pottery* and *Ultimate Encyclopedia of Hull Pottery*, both by Brenda Roberts; and *Collector's Guide to Hull Pottery, The Dinnerware Lines*, by Barbara Loveless Gick-Burke.

Advisor: Brenda Roberts (See Directory, Hull)

Bank, Corky Pig, Mirror Brown, 5", from $50 to **$75.00**

Basket, Iris, flowers on pink to blue, #408, 7", from $285 to..**$365.00**

Basket, Magnolia, pink flowers on glossy pale pink, H-14, 10½", from $350 to.............................**$425.00**

Basket, Open Rose, pink & yellow roses on pale pink, simple handle, #140, 10½", $1,100 to....................**$1,300.00**

Basket, Orchid, flowers on pink to blue, #305, 7", from $750 to...**$850.00**

Basket, Serenade, 2 birds on floral branch on blue, #S4, 12x11½", from $400 to......................................**$500.00**

Basket, Wildflower, flowers on pink to blue, W-16, 10½", from $350 to...**$410.00**

Candle holder, Blossom Flite, floral on woven-look background, ring handle, #T-11, 3", from $45 to.........**$65.00**

Candle holder, Bow-Knot, blue to green, cornucopia form, B-17, 4", from $130 to **$165.00**

Candle holder, Calla Lily, flower on green to pink, 2¼", from $100 to..**$125.00**

Candle holder, Parchment & Pine, spiraling form, unmarked, 5" L, from $25 to.....................................**$35.00**

Candle holders, Magnolia, pink & yellow flowers on pale pink, #27, 4", pr, from $110 to **$150.00**

Casserole, Blossom, yellow flowers on ivory, open, #21, 7½", from $35 to...**$45.00**

Cornucopia, Dogwood, flowers on yellow to blue, #522, 3¾", from $95 to...**$125.00**

Cornucopia, Tokay, grapes on pink to green, #10, 11", from $55 to..**$80.00**

Cornucopia, Wildflower (# series), flowers on pink, #58, 6¼", from $165 to..**$215.00**

Cornucopia, Woodland, florals on pink, #W10, 11", from $175 to...**$210.00**

Creamer, Ebb Tide, green to ivory shell form, #E-15, 4", from $75 to...**$100.00**

Creamer, Open Rose, roses on pale pink, #115, 5", from $110 to...**$135.00**

Creamer, Water Lily, flower on Walnut to Apricot, #L-19, 5", from $65 to...**$95.00**

Ewer, Butterfly, butterfly & flowers in ivory w/gold handle, conical body, #B-15, 13½", from $165 to **$235.00**

Ewer, Mardi Gras/Granada, ivory to pink w/embossed flowers, #31, 10", from $145 to................................**$175.00**

Ewer, Orchid, flowers on pink to blue, slim, flared foot, #311, 13", from $675 to **$775.00**

Flowerpot, Sunglow, flowers on yellow, #97, 5½", from $30 to..**$40.00**

Jardiniere, Bow-Knot, flowers on blue to green, pink bow handles, B-19, 9⅜", from $950 to....................**$1,200.00**

Jardiniere, Iris, pink & yellow flowers on pink to blue, #413, 5½", from $165 to..**$195.00**

Jardiniere, Royal Imperial, speckled brown rim, pink speckled body w/embossed ribs, #75, 7", from $35 to.**$55.00**

Jardiniere, Water Lily, yellow flower on pink to ivory, sm handles, #L-23, 5½", from $110 to **$155.00**

Jardiniere, Water Lily, L-24, $340.00.

Lamp base, Rosella, ivory flowers w/green leaves on ivory, #L 3, ca 1946, 11", from $350 to..........................**$475.00**

Leaf dish, Rainbow, 12¼", from $30 to........................**$40.00**

Novelty, basket girl planter, glossy, #954, mid-1940s, 8", from $35 to...**$45.00**

Novelty, clown planter, #82, 6¼", from $45 to...........**$65.00**

Novelty, knight planter, #55, 8", from $80 to **$120.00**

Novelty, parrot planter, yellow, green & rose, #60, 6x9½", from $45 to...**$65.00**

Novelty, shrimp planter, yellow, #201, ca 1940, 5", from $30 to..**$40.00**

Pitcher, Bouquet, multicolor flowers on yellow to ivory, #22, 64-oz, from $175 to **$230.00**

Pitcher, Sunglow, flowers on bright yellow, ball shape, #55, 7½", from $145 to..**$185.00**

Planter, Poppy, multicolor flowers on blue to pink, sm handles, #602, 6½", from $145 to............................**$175.00**

Rose bowl, Iris, pink & blue flowers on ivory, sm integral handles, #412, 7", from $170 to..........................**$210.00**

Shakers, Floral, flower petals & brown centers form S&P, #44, 3½", pr, from $30 to **$40.00**

Sugar bowl, Magnolia, blue flowers on glossy pink, w/lid, H-22, 3¾", from $40 to...**$60.00**

Vase, Calla Lily, floral on green to pink, #540/33, 6", from $135 to..**$160.00**

Vase, Leaf, yellow to green, #100, 9", from $30 to **$40.00**

Vase, Magnolia, floral on pink to blue matt, 'tassels' hang from sm tab handles, #21, 12½", from $325 to ..**$425.00**

Vase, Magnolia, floral on yellow to pink matt, handles, #3, 8½", from $130 to..**$175.00**

Vase, Magnolia, flowers on glossy pale pink, swan handles, H-16, 12½", from $215 to......................................**$255.00**

Vase, Open Rose, swan form, pink & yellow roses on pale pink, #118, 6½", from $165 to **$195.00**

Vase, Sueno Tulip, yellow to blue, handles, #107-33, 8", from $155 to..**$200.00**

Vase, Water Lily, flower on yellow to pink, handles, #L-16, 12½", from $355 to..**$455.00**

Vase, Wildflower, flowers on pink to yellow, handles, W-4, 6½", from $65 to..**$85.00**

Vase, Woodland, floral on bright yellow to green, low handles, #W16, 8½", from $195 to **$275.00**

Wall pocket, Bow-Knot, cup & saucer form, flowers on cup, pink saucer, B-24, 6", from $265 to....................**$310.00**

Wall pocket, Rosella, ivory flowers on ivory, heart shape, R-10, 6½", from $150 to..**$180.00**

Window box, Woodland, flowers on pink, #W14, 10" L, from $160 to..**$210.00**

Dinnerware

Avocado, bowl, fruit; 5¼" **$5.00**

Avocado, coffee cup, 7-oz..**$6.00**

Avocado, gravy boat, w/tray...**$80.00**

Avocado, pepper shaker, w/cork, 3¾".............................**$6.00**

Avocado, pie plate, 9¼"..**$20.00**

Avocado, plate, salad; 6½" **$5.00**

Avocado, stein, 16-oz..**$8.00**

Centennial, casserole, 4½x11" **$110.00**

Centennial, creamer, unmarked, 4½"............................**$50.00**

Centennial, mug, unmarked, 4" **$50.00**

Centennial, pitcher, milk; unmarked, 7½" **$110.00**

Country Belle, bean pot, w/cover..................................**$35.00**

Country Belle, bowl, 8"..**$22.00**

Country Belle, condiment server, unlabeled................**$18.00**

Country Belle, cookie jar **$48.00**

Country Belle, plate, dinner...**$12.00**

Country Belle, souffle dish...**$29.00**

Country Squire, bowl, salad/spaghetti; 10¼"..............**$27.00**

Country Squire, pie plate **$22.00**

Country Squire, plate, dinner; 10¼" **$9.00**

Country Squire, shakers, cork bottoms, 3¾", pr **$16.00**

Country Squire, snack tray (from set) **$5.00**

Country Squire, steak plate, oval, 11¾x9" **$15.00**

Country Squire, water jug, 5-pt, 80-oz.........................**$32.00**

Crestone, bowl, 6", from $4 to...**$6.00**

Crestone, bowl, 9-oz, from $4 to.....................................**$6.00**

Crestone, carafe, 2-cup, 6½", from $45 to **$65.00**

Crestone, casserole, w/lid, 32-oz..................................**$25.00**

Crestone, coffee cup, 7-oz..**$6.00**

Crestone, coffee server, 8-cup, from $75 to **$125.00**

Crestone, creamer, 8-oz, from $20 to............................**$25.00**

Crestone, cup, 7-oz, from $4 to.......................................**$6.00**

Crestone, gravy boat, 10-oz **$20.00**

Crestone, gravy boat/syrup, 10-oz, from $30 to.........**$40.00**

Crestone, open baker, 32-oz, from $20 to **$25.00**

Crestone, pitcher, 38-oz...**$50.00**

Crestone, plate, bread & butter; 6½" **$5.00**

Crestone, plate, dessert; 7½"...**$7.00**

Crestone, plate, 10¼", from $10 to...............................**$12.00**

Crestone, steak plate, oval, 11¾x9" **$35.00**

Crestone, teapot, 5-cup, from $95 to **$145.00**	Mirror Brown, stein, 16-oz, from $8 to **$10.00**
Gingerbread Coal Car.. **$500.00**	Mirror Brown, sugar bowl, 12-oz, from $12 to **$15.00**
Gingerbread Man, child's bowl................................. **$80.00**	Mirror Brown, tray, 11x12", from $110 to................ **$155.00**
Gingerbread Man, child's cup.................................. **$80.00**	Provincial, creamer/jug, 8-oz..................................... **$16.00**
Gingerbread Man, coaster, 5x5"............................... **$30.00**	Provincial, ice jug, 2-qt... **$35.00**
Gingerbread Man, cookie jar, brown **$125.00**	Provincial, leaf serve-all, 12x7½".............................. **$45.00**
Gingerbread Man, server, brown, 10x10" **$30.00**	Provincial, mug/coffee cup, 9-oz............................... **$9.00**
Gingerbread Man, server, gray or sand, 10x10" **$50.00**	Provincial, plate, dinner; 10¼".................................. **$15.00**
Gingerbread Train Engine....................................... **$500.00**	Provincial, tidbit tray, 2-tier..................................... **$32.00**
Heartland, bowl, serving; oval................................. **$22.00**	Rainbow, bowl, 6", from $10 to.................................. **$15.00**
Heartland, coffee cup **$7.00**	Rainbow, bowl, 7", from $16 to.................................. **$22.00**
Heartland, custard.. **$8.00**	Rainbow, bowl, 8", from $20 to.................................. **$30.00**
Heartland, pitcher, 36-oz... **$40.00**	Rainbow, cup, 6-oz, from $4 to.................................. **$6.00**
Heartland, plate, dinner... **$12.00**	Rainbow, leaf, 7¼", from $12 to................................. **$16.00**
Heartland, platter, oval.. **$25.00**	Rainbow, leaf chip 'n dip, 12¼", from $30 to **$40.00**
Heartland, souffle dish **$29.00**	Rainbow, mug, 9-oz, from $4 to................................. **$6.00**
Mirror Almond, ashtray, 8", from $20 to **$25.00**	Rainbow, plate, salad.. **$5.00**
Mirror Almond, bowl, 10¼", from $25 to **$35.00**	Rainbow, plate, 8½", from $6 to................................. **$8.00**
Mirror Almond, bud vase, 9", from $16 to................ **$22.00**	Rainbow, plate, 10½", from $8 to............................... **$10.00**
Mirror Almond, Continental mug, 10-oz, from $12 to... **$16.00**	Rainbow, saucer, 5½", from $2 to............................... **$3.00**
Mirror Almond, cookie jar, 94-oz, from $30 to.......... **$45.00**	Rainbow, tidbit tray, 10", from $30 to........................ **$40.00**
Mirror Almond, corn dish, 9¼", from $30 to.............. **$40.00**	Ridge, creamer & sugar bowl, w/lid, 8-oz................. **$19.00**
Mirror Almond, covered bean pot, 12-oz, from $12 to..**$15.00**	Ridge, cup & saucer **$10.00**
Mirror Almond, creamer, 8-oz, from $12 to............... **$15.00**	Ridge, plate, dinner; 10¼".. **$8.00**
Mirror Almond, Dutch oven, 3-pt, from $30 to.......... **$40.00**	Ridge, plate, salad; 7¼"... **$5.00**
Mirror Almond, jug, 5-pt, from $40 to **$60.00**	Ridge, steak plate, 9½x12".. **$11.00**
Mirror Almond, mug, 9-oz, from $4 to **$6.00**	Ring, bowl, soup/salad; 12-oz.................................. **$9.00**
Mirror Almond, pie plate, 9¼", from $18 to............... **$24.00**	Ring, coffeepot... **$50.00**
Mirror Almond, plate, 8½", from $6 to....................... **$8.00**	Ring, creamer & sugar bowl **$24.00**
Mirror Almond, salt & pepper shakers, 3¾", pr, from $14 to **$18.00**	Ring, pitcher, 36-oz.. **$35.00**
Mirror Almond, sauce bowl, 5½", from $18 to........... **$26.00**	Ring, plate, dinner **$12.00**
Mirror Almond, server, 13⅜", from $75 to................ **$100.00**	Ring, platter, oval.. **$18.00**
Mirror Almond, snack set, from $20 to **$25.00**	Tangerine, bowl, divided vegetable, 10¾x7¼" **$22.00**
Mirror Almond, sugar bowl, 12-oz, from $12 to **$15.00**	Tangerine, bowl, fruit; 5¼".. **$5.00**
Mirror Almond, teapot, from $20 to **$30.00**	Tangerine, bowl, soup/salad; 6½"............................. **$7.00**
Mirror Brown, Bake & Serve, 6½", from $4 to............ **$5.00**	Tangerine, coffeepot, 8-cup...................................... **$45.00**
Mirror Brown, bowl, 6½", from $4 to **$5.00**	Tangerine, ice jug, 2-qt... **$28.00**
Mirror Brown, bowl, 10¼", from $20 to **$30.00**	Tangerine, plate, dinner; 10¼".................................. **$9.00**
Mirror Brown, bud vase, 9", from $16 to.................... **$22.00**	Tangerine, soup mug, 11-oz...................................... **$8.00**
Mirror Brown, butter dish, ¼-lb, from $20 to **$25.00**	Tangerine, steak plate, oval, 11¾x9".......................... **$15.00**
Mirror Brown, casserole w/duck lid, 2-pt, from $75 to ..**$100.00**	
Mirror Brown, cookie jar, 94-oz, from $30 to............. **$45.00**	
Mirror Brown, custard, from $4 to.............................. **$5.00**	
Mirror Brown, double server, 14½", from $140 to....**$165.00**	
Mirror Brown, French casserole, open, 3-pt, from $40 to..**$60.00**	
Mirror Brown, French casserole, w/lid, 5¼", from $14 to..**$18.00**	
Mirror Brown, gravy boat, 16-oz, from $35 to **$50.00**	
Mirror Brown, jug, 5-pt, from $40 to **$60.00**	
Mirror Brown, pie plate, 9¼", from $18 to................. **$24.00**	
Mirror Brown, plate, 6½", from $3 to.......................... **$4.00**	
Mirror Brown, plate, 10¼", from $8 to **$10.00**	
Mirror Brown, salad bowl, 6½", from $16 to **$25.00**	
Mirror Brown, server w/chicken cover, 13⅜", from $175 to **$225.00**	
Mirror Brown, shakers, pr, from $14 to **$18.00**	
Mirror Brown, steak plate, 14", from $20 to............... **$25.00**	

Imperial Glass

Organized in 1901 in Bellaire, Ohio, the Imperial Glass Company made carnival glass, stretch glass, a line called NuCut (made in imitation of cut glass), and a limited amount of art glass within the first decade of the century. In the mid-'30s, they designed one of their most famous patterns (and one of their most popular with today's collectors), Candlewick. Within a few years, milk glass had become their leading product.

During the '50s they reintroduced their NuCut line in crystal as well as colors, marketing it as 'Collector's Crystal.' In the late '50s they bought molds from both Heisey and Cambridge. Most of the glassware they reissued from these old molds was marked 'IG,' one letter superimposed over the other. When Imperial was bought by Lenox in 1973, an 'L' was added to the mark. The ALIG logo was added in 1981 when the company was purchased by Arthur Lorch. In 1982 the factory was sold to Robert Stahl of Minneapolis. Chapter 11 bankruptcy was filled in October that year. A plant resurgence continued production. Many Heisey by Imperial animals done in color were made at this time. A new mark, the NI for New Imperial, was used on a few items. In November of 1984 the plant closed forever and the assets were sold at liquidation. This was the end of the 'Big I.'

Numbers in the listings were assigned by the company and appeared on their catalog pages. They were used to indicate differences in shapes and stems, for instance. Collectors still use them.

For more information on Imperial we recommend *Imperial Glass* by Margaret and Douglas Archer; *Elegant Glassware of the Depression Era* by Gene Florence; *Imperial Carnival Glass* by Carl O. Burns; and *Imperial Glass Encyclopedia, Vol I, A to Cane, Vol II, Cane to M,* and *Volume III, M to Z,* edited by James Measell. To research Imperial's glass animals, refer to *Glass Animals of the Depression Years* by Lee Garmon and Dick Spencer.

See also Candlewick.

Note: To determine values for Cape Cod in colors, add 100% to prices suggested for crystal for Ritz Blue and Ruby; Amber, Antique Blue, Azalea, Evergreen, Verde, black, and milk glass are 50% higher than crystal.

Advisor: Joan Cimini (See Directory, Imperial)

Club: National Imperial Glass Collectors' Society, Inc. P.O. Box 534, Bellaire, OH 43906. Dues: $15 per year (+$3 for each additional member of household), quarterly newsletter: *Glasszette,* convention every June

Ashtray, #150, purple slag, 5" **$45.00**
Ashtray, Cape Cod, crystal, #160/150, double rest, 5½" .**$22.00**
Ashtray, heart shape, #294, ruby slag, 4½" **$25.00**
Basket, Cape Cod, crystal, footed, #160/40, 11" **$125.00**
Basket, Crocheted Crystal, 6" **$27.50**
Basket, Crocheted Crystal, 9" **$40.00**
Bottle, condiment; Cape Cod, crystal, #160/224, 6-oz .**$65.00**
Bottle, ketchup; Cape Cod, crystal, #160/237, 14-oz .**$210.00**
Bowl, Cape Cod, crystal, footed, #160/137B, 10"........**$75.00**
Bowl, Cape Cod, crystal, oval, #160/131B, 12" **$80.00**
Bowl, Cape Cod, crystal, oval, crimped, #160/131C, 12" ..**$90.00**
Bowl, Cape Cod, crystal, 2-handled, #160/145B, 9½"..**$37.50**
Bowl, console; Cape Cod, crystal, #160/75L, 13" **$42.50**
Bowl, cream soup; Diamond Quilted, pink or green, 4¾" **$10.00**
Bowl, dessert; Cape Cod, crystal, tab handled, #160/197, 4½" **$30.00**
Bowl, finger; Cape Cod, crystal, #1602, 4" **$12.00**
Bowl, fruit; Cape Cod, crystal, #160/3F, 6" **$12.00**
Bowl, fruit; Katy, blue opalescent, 4½" **$35.00**
Bowl, heart; Cape Cod, crystal, handled, #160/40H, 6"..**$25.00**
Bowl, Katy, green opalescent, #749B, 9" **$125.00**

Bowl, lily; Beaded Block, green, 4½" dia..................**$18.00**
Bowl, Narcissus; Crocheted Crystal, 7".....................**$40.00**
Bowl, salad; Cape Cod, crystal, #1608B, 11" **$40.00**
Bowl, soup; Cape Cod, crystal, tab handle, #160/198, 5½" **$18.00**
Bowl, vegetable; Cape Cod, crystal, oval, #160/221, 10"...**$80.00**
Butter dish, Cape Cod, crystal, handled, w/lid, #160/144, 5" **$45.00**
Cake stand, Cape Cod, crystal, #160/103D, 11" **$87.50**
Cake stand, Crocheted Crystal, footed, 12"................**$50.00**
Candle holder, Cape Cod, crystal, Aladdin style, #160/90, 5" **$85.00**
Candle holder, Cape Cod, crystal, saucer style, #160/175, 4½" **$30.00**
Candle holder, Crocheted Crystal, single, 6" W..........**$25.00**
Candle holder, Crocheted Crystal, 6" L **$25.00**
Candy jar, caramel slag, Louis XIV, 4-footed, #176, 6"..**$70.00**
Celery, Cape Cod, crystal, oval, #160/105, 8".............**$38.00**
Celery, Crocheted Crystal, oval, 10" **$28.00**
Cigarette holder, Cape Cod, crystal, footed, #1602 .....**$15.00**
Coaster, Cape Cod, crystal, w/spoon rest, #160/76.....**$10.00**
Comport, Cape Cod, crystal, #160/48B, 7"..................**$38.00**
Compote, #431C, ruby slag, crimped, footed, 6½" **$55.00**
Cordial, Decorated Western Apple, crystal, #176, 2-oz ..**$30.00**

Covered box, rooster, #158, green slag, $295.00. (Photo courtesy Sharon Thoerner)

Covered box, rooster, #158, jade slag.........................**$295.00**
Covered dish, duck on nest, #146, jade slag, 4½" **$65.00**
Creamer, Beaded Block, green **$25.00**
Creamer, Cape Cod, crystal, #160/30 ....**$10.00**
Creamer, caramel slag, flat, #666 ....**$30.00**
Creamer, Diamond Quilted, blue or black...................**$20.00**
Cup, coffee; Cape Cod, crystal, #160/37 ....**$8.00**
Cup, Katy, blue or green w/opalescent edge.............**$35.00**
Decanter, cask #1, Antique Blue **$55.00**
Egg cup, Cape Cod, crystal, #160/225 ....**$32.50**
Figurine, bull, amber, very rare...................................**$725.00**
Figurine, chick, milk glass, head down **$10.00**
Figurine, colt, caramel slag, balking...........................**$140.00**
Figurine, colt, Horizon Blue, kicking **$35.00**
Figurine, dog, Airedale, caramel slag.........................**$115.00**

Figurine, donkey, Meadow Green Carnival.................**$65.00**
Figurine, flying mare, amber, NI mark **$1,500.00**
Figurine, giraffe, amber, ALIG mark...........................**$375.00**
Figurine, mallard, light blue satin, wings down..........**$35.00**
Figurine, piglet, amber, standing **$40.00**
Figurine, ring-neck pheasant, amber, rare **$425.00**
Figurine, rooster, amber..**$390.00**
Figurine, Scottie, milk glass, 3½"...............................**$45.00**
Figurine, wood duck, caramel slag **$65.00**
Figurine, wood duckling, floating, Sunshine Yellow satin .**$20.00**
Figurine/paperweight, tiger, caramel slag.................**$150.00**
Figurine/paperweight, tiger, Jade, 8" L.......................**$95.00**
Goblet, Chroma, burgundy, #123 ....**$30.00**
Icer, Cape Cod, crystal, bowl, 2 inserts, #160/53/3, 3-pc ..**$50.00**
Jar, peanut; Cape Cod, crystal, handled, w/lid, #160/210, 12-oz **$65.00**
Jar, vanity; Reeded (Spun), pink, #701, 7⅝" **$40.00**
Ladle, mayonnaise; Crocheted Crystal...........................**$12.00**
Mayonnaise, Cape Cod, crystal, #160/52H, 3-pc set ...**$42.00**
Nappy, poppy; #478, jade slag, handled, 5½"...........**$55.00**
Pitcher, Cape Cod, crystal, #160/24, 2-qt **$85.00**
Pitcher, Dew Drop, opalescent, #624, 56-oz................**$80.00**
Plate, Beaded Block, opal, 8¾" **$30.00**
Plate, bread & butter; Cape Cod, crystal, #160/1D, 6½".**$10.00**
Plate, Cape Cod, crystal, cupped, #160/20V, 16".........**$60.00**
Plate, crescent salad; Cape Cod, crystal, #160/12, 8" ..**$50.00**
Plate, Crocheted Crystal, 14" **$30.00**
Plate, Crocheted Crystal, 17" **$45.00**
Plate, Katy, blue opalescent, 6" **$25.00**
Plate, mayonnaise; Crocheted Crystal, 7½"....................**$7.50**
Plate, salad; Crocheted Crystal, 8" **$9.00**
Plate, salad; Diamond Quilted, pink or green, 7" **$6.00**
Plate, windmill, caramel slag, #514, 10¾"....................**$60.00**
Puff box, Cape Cod, crystal, w/lid, #1601 ....**$45.00**
Relish, Crocheted Crystal, 3-pt, 11½" **$40.00**
Salt & pepper shakers, Cape Cod, crystal, #160/109, sq, pr..**$20.00**
Salt & pepper shakers, Cape Cod, crystal, footed, #160/116, pr..**$25.00**
Salt cellar, ruby slag, #61, 4-footed **$16.00**
Sherbet, Huckabee, pink, footed....................................**$30.00**
Stem, cocktail; Cape Cod, crystal, #1602, 3½-oz.........**$10.00**
Stem, luncheon; Cape Cod, crystal, #1602, 9-oz **$10.00**
Stem, sherbet; Crocheted Crystal, 6-oz.........................**$12.00**
Stem, water goblet; Crocheted Crystal, 9-oz, 7⅛" **$14.00**
Stem, wine; Crocheted Crystal, 4½-oz, 5½"..................**$17.50**
Sugar bowl, Cape Cod, crystal, footed, #160/31 ....**$12.00**
Toothpick holder, Azure Blue, #505, marked IG **$18.50**
Toothpick holder, ruby slag, #1, 1969-77.....................**$25.00**
Tumbler, #552, caramel slag, 11-oz **$80.00**
Tumbler, iced tea; Crocheted Crystal, footed, 12-oz ...**$18.00**
Tumbler, juice; Crocheted Crystal, footed, 6-oz, 6".....**$12.00**
Tumbler, tea; Cape Cod, crystal, footed, #160, 12-oz....**$19.00**
Tumbler, water; Cape Cod, crystal, #160, 10-oz..........**$15.00**
Vase, #965, caramel slag, footed, 9½".........................**$120.00**
Vase, Cape Cod, crystal, footed, #160/22, 7½" **$50.00**
Vase, caramel slag, footed, #529, 10" **$170.00**

Vase, fan; Diamond Quilted, dolphin handles, blue or black, ...**$75.00**
Vase, flip; Cape Cod, crystal, #1603, 11"....................**$165.00**
Vase, Katy, blue opalescent, #743B, 5¼" **$45.00**
Vase, Reeded (Spun), red, #701, 9" **$75.00**

Indiana Glass

In 1971 the Indiana Glass Co. introduce a line of new carnival glass, much of which was embossed with grape clusters and detailed leaves using their Harvest molds. It was first introduced in blue, and later gold and lime green were added. Prior to 1971 the Harvest molds had been used to produce a snowy white milk glass; blue and green satin or frosted glass; ruby red flashed glass; and plain glass in various shades of blue, amber, and green. Because this line was mass produced (machine-made) carnival, there are still large quantities available to collectors.

They also produced a line of handmade carnival called Heritage, which they made in amethyst and Sunset (amberina). Because it was handmade as opposed to being machine made, production was limited, and it is not as readily available to today's collectors as is the Harvest pattern carnival. There is a significant amount of interest in both lines today. Now that these lines are thirty years old, grandmother, mother, and aunt are leaving a piece or two to the next generation. The younger generation is off and running to complete Granny's collection via the Internet. This has caused a revival of interest in Indiana carnival glass as a collectible.

The company also produced a series of four Bicentennial commemorative plates made in blue and gold carnival: American Eagle, Independence Hall, Liberty Bell, and Spirit of '76. These are valued at $10.00 each unboxed, or $15.00 if in their original box. A large Liberty Bell cookie jar and a small Liberty Bell bank were also made in gold carnival; today the cookie jars are valued at $15.00 to $25.00 while the banks generally sell in the $5.00 to $10.00 range.

This glass is a little difficult to evaluate, since you see it in malls and flea markets with such a wide range of 'asking' prices. On one hand, you have sellers who themselves are not exactly sure what it is they have but since it's carnival assume it should be fairly pricey. On the other hand, you have those who just cleaned house and want to get rid of it. They may have bought it new themselves and know it's not very old and wasn't expensive to start with. (The Harvest Princess punch set sold for $5.98 in 1971.) So take heart, there are still bargains to be found, though they're becoming rarer with each passing year. The best buys on Indiana carnival glass are found at garage and estate sales.

In addition to the iridescent lines, Indiana Glass produced a line called Ruby Band Diamond Point, a clear, diamond-faceted pattern with a wide ruby-flashed rim band; some items from this line are listed below. Our values are for examples with the ruby flashing in excellent condition.

Over the last decade or so, the collectibles market has changed. Everyone seems to want to collect something, and the something they collect does not necessarily have to be old or scarce. Collecting has become a very pleasant pastime, and Indiana Glass seems to fit nicely into the new scheme of collecting. At any rate, this is one of the newer interests at the flea market/antique mall level, and if you can buy it right (and like its looks), now is the time!

See also King's Crown; Tiara.

Advisor: Donna Adler (See Directory, Indiana Glass)

Iridescent Amethyst Carnival Glass (Heritage)

This color is very difficult to find.

Basket, footed, 9x5x7".................................**$40.00**
Butter dish, 5x7½" dia, from $40 to.....................**$60.00**
Candle holders, 5½", pr, from $30 to....................**$40.00**
Center bowl, 4¾x8½", from $30 to.......................**$40.00**
Goblet, 8-oz, from $15 to...............................**$20.00**
Pitcher, 8¼", from $40 to...............................**$60.00**
Punch set, 10" bowl & pedestal, 8 cups, ladle, 11-pc, from $175 to.................................**$275.00**
Swung vase, slender & footed w/irregular rim, 11x3", from $30 to................................**$40.00**

Iridescent Blue Carnival Glass

Basket, Canterbury, 11" x 8" x 12", from $50.00 to $75.00.

Basket, Monticello, allover faceted embossed diamonds, 7x6" sq, from $25 to.................................**$35.00**
Butter dish, Harvest, embossed grapes, ¼-lb, 8" L, from $25 to..**$40.00**
Candle holders, Harvest, compote shape, 4", pr, from $25 to..**$35.00**
Candy box, Harvest, embossed grapes w/lace edge, w/lid, 6½", from $20 to................................**$35.00**
Candy box, Princess, diamond-point bands, pointed faceted finial, 6x6" dia, from $10 to......................**$15.00**
Canister/Candy jar, Harvest, embossed grapes, 7", from $15 to..**$35.00**
Canister/Cookie jar, Harvest, embossed grapes, 9", from $80 to..**$150.00**

Canister/Snack jar, Harvest, embossed grapes, 8", from $60 to..**$125.00**
Center bowl, Harvest, embossed grapes w/paneled sides, 4-footed, 4½x8½x12", common, from $15 to..........**$20.00**
Cooler (iced tea tumbler), Harvest, embossed grapes, 14-oz, set of 4, from $10 to.........................**$15.00**
Creamer & sugar bowl on tray, Harvest, embossed grapes, 3-pc, from $25 to...............................**$35.00**
Egg/Hors d'oeuvre tray, sectioned w/off-side holder for 8 eggs, 12¾" dia, from $40 to....................**$50.00**
Garland bowl (comport), paneled, 7½x8½" dia, from $15 to..**$20.00**
Goblet, Harvest, embossed grapes, 9-oz, from $10 to..**$12.00**
Hen on nest, from $15 to................................**$25.00**
Pitcher, Harvest, embossed grapes, 10½", common, from $25 to...**$40.00**
Plate, Bicentennial; American Eagle, from $10 to.......**$15.00**
Plate, hostess; Canterbury, allover diamond facets, flared crimped rim, 10", from $20 to..................**$25.00**
Punch set, Princess, complete w/ladle & hooks, 26-pc..**$125.00**
Punch set, Princess, incomplete, no ladle or hooks..**$60.00**
Tidbit, allover embossed diamond points, shallow w/flared sides, 6½".................................**$15.00**
Wedding bowl (sm compote), Thumbprint, footed, 5x5", from $10 to...**$15.00**

Iridescent Gold Carnival Glass

Basket, Canterbury, waffle pattern, flaring sides drawn in at handle terminals, 9½x11x8½", from $40 to..........**$65.00**
Basket, Monticello, lg faceted allover diamonds, sq, 7x6", from $30 to.....................................**$35.00**
Candy box, Harvest, embossed grapes, lace edge, footed, 6½x5¾", from $20 to.............................**$35.00**
Canister/Candy jar, Harvest, embossed grapes, 7", from $25 to..**$30.00**
Canister/Cookie jar, Harvest, embossed grapes, 9", from $50 to..**$75.00**
Canister/Snack jar, Harvest, embossed grapes, 8", from $40 to..**$60.00**
Center bowl, Harvest, oval w/embossed grapes & paneled sides, 4½x8½x12", from $15 to......................**$20.00**
Console set, Wild Rose, wide naturalistic petals form sides, 9" bowl w/pr 4½" bowl-type candle holders, 3-pc..**$30.00**
Cooler (iced tea tumbler), Harvest, 14-oz, from $8 to..**$12.00**
Egg plate, 11", from $15 to.............................**$35.00**
Goblet, Harvest, embossed grapes, 9-oz, from $8 to..**$12.00**
Hen on nest, 5½", from $10 to...........................**$20.00**
Pitcher, Harvest, embossed grapes, 10½", from $24 to..**$30.00**
Plate, hostess; diamond embossing, shallow w/crimped & flared sides, 10", from $12 to......................**$20.00**
Punch set, Princess, complete w/ladle & hooks, 26-pc..**$100.00**
Punch Set, Princess, incomplete, no ladle or hooks...**$50.00**
Relish tray, Vintage, 6 sections, 9x12¾", from $15 to.**$18.00**
Salad set, Vintage, embossed fruit, apple-shaped rim w/applied stem, 13", w/fork & spoon, 3-pc, from $15 to..................................**$20.00**

Tumbler, Harvest, 4", from $10 to $15.00
Wedding bowl, Harvest, embossed grapes, pedestal foot, 8½x8", from $22 to $28.00
Wedding bowl (sm compote), 5x5", from $9 to..........$12.00

Iridescent Lime Carnival Glass

Lime green examples are harder to find than either the gold or the blue.

Candy box, Harvest, 6½", from $20.00 to $40.00.

Canister/Candy jar, Harvest, embossed grapes, 7", from $20 to $30.00
Canister/Cookie jar, Harvest, embossed grapes, 9", from $50 to $80.00
Canister/Snack jar, Harvest, embossed grapes, 8", from $40 to $60.00
Center bowl, Harvest, embossed grapes, paneled sides, 4-footed, 4½x8½x12", from $15 to $20.00
Compote, Harvest, embossed grapes, 7x6", from $15 to $20.00
Console set, Harvest, embossed grapes, 10" bowl w/compote-shaped candle holders, 3-pc, from $50 to....$80.00
Cooler (iced tea tumbler), Harvest, embossed grapes, 14-oz, rare, from $12 to...$18.00
Creamer & sugar bowl on tray, Harvest, embossed grapes, 3-pc, from $25 to $35.00
Egg plate, 11", from $15 to $25.00
Goblet, Harvest, embossed grapes, 9-oz, from $10 to ..$15.00
Hen on nest, from $20 to..$25.00
Pitcher, Harvest, embossed grapes, 10½", from $30 to...$40.00
Plate, hostess; allover diamond points, flared crimped sides, 10", from $15 to $25.00
Punch set, Princess, complete w/ladle & hooks, 26-pc ..$125.00
Punch set, Princess, incomplete, no ladle or hooks ...$60.00
Salad set, Vintage, embossed fruit, apple-shaped rim w/applied stem, 13", w/fork & spoon, 3-pc, from $20 to $30.00
Snack set, Harvest, embossed grapes, 4 cups & 4 plates, 8-pc, from $50 to $75.00

Iridescent Sunset (Amberina) Carnival Glass (Heritage)

Basket, footed, 9x5x7", from $30 to $50.00
Basket, 9½x7½" sq, from $50 to $60.00
Bowl, crimped, 3¾x10", from $40 to $50.00
Butter dish, 5x7½" dia, from $35 to $40.00
Center bowl, 4¾x8½", from $40 to.............................$45.00
Creamer & sugar bowl $40.00
Dessert set, 8½" bowl, 12" plate, 2-pc, from $40 to ...$50.00
Goblet, 8-oz, from $12 to...$18.00
Pitcher, 7¼", from $40 to $55.00
Pitcher, 8¼", from $40 to $50.00
Plate, 14", from $30 to...$35.00
Punch set, 10" bowl, pedestal, 8 cups, & ladle, 11-pc, from $150 to...$225.00
Rose bowl, 6½x6½", from $25 to................................$35.00
Swung vase, slender, footed, w/irregular rim, 11x3" ..$65.00
Tumbler, 3½", from $10 to...$15.00

Patterns

Canterbury, basket, waffle pattern, Lime, Sunset or Horizon Blue, 5½x12", from $35 to $50.00
Monticello, basket, lg faceted diamonds overall, Lemon, Lime, Sunset or Horizon Blue, sq, 7x6", from $25 to........$40.00
Monticello, basket, lg faceted diamonds overall, Lemon, Lime, Sunset or Horizon Blue, 8¾x10½", from $35 to......$40.00
Monticello, candy box, lg faceted overall diamonds, w/lid, Lemon, Lime, Sunset or Horizon Blue, 5¼x6", from $15 to..$20.00
Ruby Band Diamond Point, bowl, salad; w/4 servers ..$45.00
Ruby Band Diamond Point, butter dish, from $20 to .$25.00
Ruby Band Diamond Point, chip 'n dip set, 13" dia, from $18 to..$25.00
Ruby Band Diamond Point, comport, 14½" dia, from $15 to..$25.00
Ruby Band Diamond Point, cooler (iced tea tumbler), 15-oz, from $8 to...$10.00
Ruby Band Diamond Point, creamer & sugar bowl, 4½", from $15 to...$20.00
Ruby Band Diamond Point, creamer & sugar bowl, 4¾", on 6x9" tray, from $15 to..$25.00
Ruby Band Diamond Point, decanter, 24-oz $30.00
Ruby Band Diamond Point, goblet, 12-oz, from $9 to ..$10.00
Ruby Band Diamond Point, On-the-Rocks, 9-oz, from $8 to..$10.00
Ruby Band Diamond Point, pitcher, 8", from $15 to ..$25.00
Ruby Band Diamond Point, plate, hostess; 12", from $12 to..$18.00

Indianapolis 500 Racing Collectibles

You don't have to be a Hoosier to know that unless the weather interfers, this famous 500-mile race is held in Indianapolis every Memorial day and has been since 1911. Collectors of Indy memorabilia have a plethora of race-related items to draw from and can zero in on one area or many, enabling them to build extensive and interesting collections. Some of the special areas of interest they pursue are autographs, photographs, or other memorabilia related to the drivers; pit badges; race programs and yearbooks; books and magazines; decanters and souvenir tumblers; model race cars; and tickets.

Advisor: Eric Jungnickel (See Directory, Indy 500 Memorabilia)

Pennant, 1960s, white lettering on red, 26" L, EX, $75.00.

Ashtray, pictures 1911 winning car & AJ Foyt's winning car, race scene, Hall of Fame, pottery, blue & white, 4x10", NM $12.00

Ashtray, white ceramic w/race cars, checkered flags & Indianapolis 500 banner inside, marked Taiwan, 5" dia $17.00

Book, Floyd Clymer's Indianapolis 500 Mile Race History, 1946, 11x8¼", EX+ $25.00

Book, Indy 500 Pace Cars, pictures & stories, 216 pages, 10x10", EX+ $15.00

Book, Racing Cars & Great Races, Frank Ross Jr, 191 pages, hardcover, black & white photos, 9½x6½", EX....$25.00

Decanter, Dan Gurney's #48 Olsonite Eagle, Beam, empty w/seal $30.00

Decanter, 1911 Marmon Wasp, yellow & black, Famous Firsts, Edition #1, 1968, hand-painted, Italy, 5x16½" L, NM $45.00

Diecast car, 1995 Corvette Pace Car, Officially Licensed Motor Speedway Product, Maistro, M (NM box)............$45.00

Diecast car, 1998 Corvette Convertible Pace Car, Officially Licensed Motor Speedway Product, Maisto, M (NM box)..$50.00

Jacket, 1982 Indy Camaro Limited Edition, blue w/silver pockets, Chevrolet on Stripe, made by Horizon, med, NM+ $105.00

License plate, Indianapolis 500 The 68th-May 27, 1984, in red & black on white background, M (still in plastic)..$55.00

License plate, issued to cars in parade, expiration date 5/31/93, EX...$80.00

Paperweight, clear Lucite w/gold race car w/Speedway terrace, ¾x2" dia, EX $20.00

Paperweight/accessory, Indianapolis Motor Speedway embossed on gold-painted plaster-cast racer w/driver, 1931, 8" L....................................$200.00

Photo, Preston Tucker on 1930s Harley-Davidson at 500, black & white on Kodak paper, 8x10", M $25.00

Pit badge, 1950, bronze, w/original backing card, VG+...$210.00

Pit badge, 1967, silver, w/original backing card, EX ..$60.00

Plate, coupe; race scene, gold trim, marked Jonroth, Designed & Import for CG Cramer, 7" dia, EX ..$150.00

Plate, vintage race cars & checkered flag border, Vernon Kilns, 10½" dia, EX....................................$85.00

Playing cards, 1981 Buick at 500, sold exclusively at Speedway, complete, M (VG+ box).....................$25.00

Postcard, Ralph DePalma w/mechanic in 1915 winning Mercedes car, Real Photo, unused, NM................$65.00

Poster, panoramic view of Indianapolis Motor Speedway, 13½x40", M (w/no folds) $30.00

Poster, 1990 Beretta Indy 500 Pace Car, original, 10½x15¼", NM $12.00

Press kit, 10 color slides w/black & white prints, dated 5/6/95, EX $65.00

Program, 1930, VG+ $135.00

Program, 1932, EX $150.00

Program, 1938, EX $90.00

Program, 1946, w/score sheet, EX................$75.00

Program, 20th Annual 500 Mile Sweepstakes, ads & stories, VG+..$150.00

Soda bottle, 7-Up, souvenir for 1978 500 Mile Race, winners & speeds from 1946-1977 on back, EX................$12.00

Stein, Budweiser, Special Events Series #9075, first in series, 1996, 5¾", NM+ $18.00

Ticket stub, 1940, press issue, EX $80.00

Tray, 1975 Indy 500/Falstaff, race scene & winners list, oval, 13x21", NM......................................$45.00

Tumbler, IMS logo, 1953 ....$25.00

Tumbler, IMS logo on front, winners listed on back, Tony Hulman facsimile signature, 1968....................$20.00

Tumbler, white & black silkscreen listing winners through 1967, gold trim, set of 6, MIB..........................$65.00

Yearbook, Floyd Clymer's 1950 Official Indianapolis 500 Mile; 112 pages, 11x8¼", VG+.......................$35.00

Yearbook, 1988, Hungness, EX+ $14.00

Italian Glass

Throughout the century, the island of Murano has been recognized a one of the major glassmaking centers of the world. Companies including Venini, Barovier, Aureliano Toso, Barvini, Vistosi, AVEM, Cenedese, Cappellin, Seguso, and Archimede Seguso have produced very fine art glass, examples of which today often bring several thousand dollars on the secondary market — superior examples much more. Such items are rarely seen at the garage sale and flea market level, but what you will be seeing are the more generic glass clowns, birds, ashtrays, and animals, generally referred to simply as Murano glass. Their values are determined by the techniques used in their making more than size alone. For instance, an item with gold inclusions, controlled bubbles, fused glass patches, or layers of colors is more desirable than one that has none of these elements, even though it may be larger. For more information concerning the specific companies mentioned above, see *Schroeder's Antiques Price Guide* (Collector Books).

Ashtray, green & amber, Murano, 3½x5½"................$75.00

Basket, Macchia Ambra Verde, Seguso paper label, 1952, 6x6½"..$500.00

Bottle, amber & green, unmarked Seguso, 15x3¾"..$200.00

Bottle, scent; clear cased w/red, green & blue sections, spherical, ball stopper, Seguso Murano, 4¾" $250.00

Bowl, Barovier E Toso, ribbed floriform, gold and opalescent with controlled bubbles, no mark, 3½" x 7½", $200.00.

Bowl, centerpiece; ruby red w/applied amber decoration at sides of bowl & along foot, Murano, 1940s-50s, 5x12" $95.00

Bowl, console; ruby, wide flat rim, shallow lobed bowl center, Made in Italy, 1¾x13¾"................$95.00

Bowl, Cordonato d'Oro, ribbed flower form, gold & opalescent, controlled bubbles, unmarked Barovier E Toso, 3½x7½" $200.00

Bowl, pink & white swirl w/silver inclusions, Venini, 1960s-70s, 2½x7½"...$65.00

Bowl, white & smoky topaz swirled glass canes, Venini, 4¼x9"...$150.00

Candlestick, flower form on coiled base, yellow & green w/gold & silver inclusions, ca 1940s.................$80.00

Decanter, clown figural, multicolor w/many applications, Murano, 15¼x5½"......................................$85.00

Decanter, crystal cylinder w/pink latticino stripes, hollow ball stopper, Murano, 1950s, 18½" $180.00

Decanter, deep amethyst crackle, hand blown, fluted neck, 13x5" $85.00

Decanter, gold leaf inclusions, crystal base, Murano, very heavy, 12x6"..$200.00

Ewer, multicolor stripes of white, pink, yellow, blue, green & gold, Venini, 12"......................................$150.00

Paperweight, purple & gold swirls, Venini/Murano, 6¼x3½" $125.00

Paperweight, red & yellow roses, Murano, 2¼x3¼"...$60.00

Sculpture, bluebirds on branch, applied leaves w/gold inclusions, Murano, 7x9½".................................$80.00

Sculpture, clown, yellow head, blue collar, red bow tie, striped body, black shoes, 12x7"......................$100.00

Sculpture, dove, pink w/red ribbon running through, ca 1950s, 5x11"..$70.00

Sculpture, duck, turquoise w/gold inclusions, 8", pr..$85.00

Sculpture, Eternity, clear, ruby & sapphire hues w/gold leaf accents, Murano, limited edition, 9½x17½"........$150.00

Sculpture, fish, blue body on clear base, 13"...........$85.00

Sculpture, pheasant, crystal w/blue sections, 15½"..$145.00

Sculpture, rooster, bright multicolors, AVEM, 8¼x9"...$250.00

Sculpture, rooster, multicolor streaks & spatters, red comb, 1950s, 9x5"...$60.00

Vase, blue w/pink interior w/in clear column, polished notches ea side, Murano, 8½x2" sq $75.00

Vase, blue-green & white latticinio, crimped body, Venini/Murano/Italia & paper label, 3½x4¼".....$150.00

Vase, bright green w/applied swirl, unmarked Cenedese, 13x4"..$700.00

Vase, clear w/internal vertical stripes & opaque gray band around body, Seguso, ca 1975, 13½"................$750.00

Vase, crystal cylinder w/vertical white filigree, pink & gold spirals, Murano, 1950s, 7¾".........................$300.00

Vase, handkerchief; crystal & white frosted, latticinio threads form ribbon-like panels, crimped shape, Venini, 7x9"...$400.00

Vase, handkerchief; light opaque blue & transparent blue, gold inclusions, Murano paper label, 4¾"..........$230.00

Vase, lattimo glass w/fine dusting of black gold, unmarked Murano, ca 1940, 7¼x7"................................$750.00

Vase, multicolor ribbons form body of vase, ruffled rim, 4x4"...$75.00

Vase, multilayered millefiori, striated multicolor handles, 3½"...$75.00

Vase, multilayered millifiori w/random silver & gold inclusions, Fratelli Toso, 6½".......................$265.00

Vase, pillow; black iridescent w/applied handles, in style of Martinuzzi, ca 1930, 6½x8".........................$600.00

Vase, Sommerso, organic shape w/clear, green & lattimo glass, AVEM, 1952, 13x6½".........................$750.00

Vase, tortoise shell pattern in yellow-amber & brown, bulbous, sm neck, flared rim, Made in Italy, 9x9½" .$75.00

Jade-ite Glassware

For the past few years, Jade-ite has been one of the fastest-moving types of collectible glassware on the market. It was produced by several companies from the 1940s through 1965. Many of Anchor Hocking's Fire-King lines were available in the soft opaque green Jade-ite, and Jeannette Glass as well as McKee produced their own versions.

It was always very inexpensive glass, and it was made in abundance. Dinnerware for the home as well as restaurants and a vast array of kitchenware items literally flooded the country for many years. Though a few rare pieces have become fairly expensive, most are still reasonably priced, and there are still bargains to be had.

For more information we recommend *Anchor Hocking's Fire-King & More, Kitchen Glassware of the Depression Years,* and *Collectible Glassware of the 40s, 50s, and 60s,* all by Gene Florence.

Ashtray, 6-sided, Jeannette, from $8 to......................$10.00

Baker, Ovenware, Fire-King, 1½x5", from $100 to...$125.00

Bowl, beater; w/beater, Jeannette, from $30 to **$35.00**

Bowl, candy/dessert; maple Leaf, Fire-King, from $25 to ..**$28.00**

Bowl, cereal; Shell, Fire-King, 6⅜".....................**$25.00**

Bowl, cereal; 1700 Line, Fire-King, 5⅞".......................**$35.00**

Bowl, Colonial Kitchen, Fire-King, 8¾", from $90 to..**$100.00**

Bowl, deep, #G305, Restaurant Ware, Fire-King, 10-oz.**$28.00**

Bowl, dessert; Jane Ray, Fire-King, 4⅞" **$12.00**

Bowl, mixing; Beaded Edge, Fire-King, 6", from $22.50
to...**$25.00**

Bowl, mixing; Ribbed, Fire-King, 4¾", from $90 to.....**$200.00**

Bowl, mixing; Splash Proof, Anchor Hocking, 2-qt, 7⅝", from
$60 to..**$65.00**

Bowl, mixing; Splash Proof, Anchor Hocking, 4-qt, 9½", from
$90 to...**$100.00**

Bowl, mixing; Swirl, Fire-King, 6", from $25 to **$28.00**

Bowl, mixing; Swirl, Fire-King, 8", from $25 to **$28.00**

Bowl, soup; Charm, Fire-King, 6"................................**$35.00**

Bowl, Tom & Jerry in black, McKee, 9", from $25 to.**$30.00**

Bowl, vegetable; Jane Ray, Fire-King, 8¼" **$25.00**

Bowl, vegetable; Shell, round, Fire-King, 8½"............**$28.00**

Bowl, vegetable; Three Bands, Fire-King, 8¼"............**$95.00**

Box, jewel; Fire-King, sq, from $75 to **$85.00**

Butter dish, crystal lid, Anchor Hocking, ¼-lb, from $110
to **$125.00**

Butter dish, ribbed base & ribbed crystal lid, Anchor
Hocking, ¼-lb, from $200 to **$250.00**

Candy dish, Fire-King, w/lid, 6¾", from $90 to **$95.00**

Canister, cereal, coffee, sugar, or tea, Jeannette, 48-oz, sq,
5½"..**$75.00**

Casserole, French; Ovenware, w/lid, 5"+handle, from $450
to **$500.00**

Crock, recessed knob handle, 40-oz, round, Jeannette, from
$55 to..**$60.00**

Cup, demitasse; Jane Ray, Fire-King **$40.00**

Cup, Ransom, 1700 Line, Fire-King, 9-oz....................**$22.00**

Cup, Sheaves of Wheat, Fire-King.................................**$60.00**

Cup, Swirl, Fire-King, 8-oz..**$40.00**

Cup, Three Bands, Fire-King, 8-oz..............................**$50.00**

Cup & saucer, Alice, Fire-King....................................**$10.00**

Cup & saucer, St Denis, Fire-King...............................**$20.00**

Custard cup, Ovenware, deep, ruffled top, Fire-King, from
$250 to..**$300.00**

Custard cup, Philbe, Fire-King, 6-oz, from $350 to...**$400.00**

Drippings bowl, black letters, w/lid, McKee, 4x5", from $85
to **$95.00**

Egg cup, single, from breakfast set, Fire-King, from $40
to **$45.00**

Grease jar, Fire-King, screw-on lid, from $75 to **$85.00**

Loaf pan, Ovenware, Fire-King, 5x9", from $45 to **$50.00**

Mug, Philbe, Fire-King, 8-oz, from $100 to **$125.00**

Mug, plain, Fire-King, 8-oz, from $20 to **$25.00**

Pitcher, ball jug, #G787, Restaurant Ware, Fire-King...**$600.00**

Pitcher, ball jug, Fire-King, 80-oz, from $500 to **$600.00**

Pitcher, milk; Beaded & Bar, Fire-King, 20-oz, from $200
to...**$250.00**

Pitcher, reamer; 2-cup, light colored, #3, from $30 to ..**$35.00**

Pitcher, Swirl, ball jug, Fire-King, 80-oz, from $1,250 to..**$1,500.00**

Plate, Alice, Fire-King, 9½" **$28.00**

Plate, dinner; Jane Ray, Fire-King, 9⅛".......................**$13.00**

Plate, dinner; Sheaves of Wheat, Fire-King, 9"...........**$85.00**

Plate, dinner; Swirl, Fire-King, 9⅛"............................**$80.00**

Plate, dinner; 1700 Line, Fire-King, 9⅛" **$25.00**

Plate, indent, #G310, Restaurant Ware, Fire-King, 8⅞" ..**$85.00**

Plate, pie/salad; #G297, Restaurant Ware, Fire-King, 6¾"...**$12.00**

Plate, Restaurant Ware, Fire-King, 10".......................**$150.00**

Plate, salad; Charm, Fire-King, 6⅝"............................**$40.00**

Plate, salad; Jane Ray, Fire-King, 7¾" **$12.00**

Plate, 3 compartments, child's, Fire-King, 7½", from $400
to...**$500.00**

Platter, Shell, oval, Fire-King, 9½x13" **$85.00**

Refrigerator container, Philbe, w/lid, Fire-King, 5⅛x9½",
from $65 to...**$75.00**

Saucer, demitasse; Restaurant Ware, Fire-King **$40.00**

Saucer, Sheaves of Wheat, Fire-King...........................**$20.00**

Saucer, Swirl, Fire-King, 5¾"......................................**$20.00**

Saucer, Three Bands, Fire-King, 5¾"...........................**$75.00**

Saucer, 1700 Line, Fire-King, 5¾"................................**$3.00**

Shaker, salt; emb letters, metal lid, McKee, from $50 to ...**$55.00**

Shakers, salt and pepper; horizontal rings, Fire King, range size, from $40.00 to $45.00 for the pair.

Shakers, toiletry; bi-carboniate soda, boric acid, epsom salts
or mouth wash, ea from $125 to........................**$135.00**

Skillet, Ovenware, Fire-King, 2-spout, 7", from $140 to ..**$165.00**

Skillet, Ovenware, 1-spout, Fire-King, 7", from $70 to .**$80.00**

Sugar bowl, Charm, Fire-King.....................................**$20.00**

Sugar bowl, Jane Ray, w/lid, Fire-King.......................**$32.50**

Sugar bowl, Shell, footed, Fire-King...........................**$25.00**

Tumbler, ringed bottom, 12-oz, Jeannette, from $22 to..**$25.00**

Japan Ceramics

This category is narrowed down to the inexpensive novelty items produced in Japan from 1921 to 1941 and again from 1947 until the present. Though Japanese ceramics marked Nippon, Noritake, and Occupied Japan have long been collected, some of the newest fun-type collectibles on today's market are the figural ashtrays, pincushions, wall pockets, toothbrush holders, etc., that are marked 'Made in Japan' or simply 'Japan.' In her books called *Collector's Guide to Made in Japan Ceramics* (there are three in series), Carole Bess White explains the pitfalls you will encounter when you try to determine production dates. Collectors refer to anything produced before WWII as 'old' and anything made after 1952 as 'new.' Backstamps are inconsistent as to wording and color, and styles are eclectic. Generally, items with applied devices are old, and they are heavier and thicker. Often they were more colorful than the newer items, since fewer colors mean less expense to the manufacturer. Lustre glazes are usually indicative of older pieces, especially the deep solid colors. When lustre was used after the war, it was often mottled with contrasting hues and was usually thinner.

Imaginative styling and strong colors are what give these Japanese ceramics their charm, and they also are factors to consider when you make your purchases. You'll find all you need to know to be a wise shopper in the books we've recommended.

See also Blue Willow; Cat Collectibles; Condiment Sets; Flower Frogs; Geisha Girl; Holt Howard; Kreiss; Lamps; Lefton; Napkin Dolls; Occupied Japan Collectibles; Powder Jars; Toothbrush Holders; Wall Pockets.

Advisor: Carole Bess White (See Directory, Japan Ceramics)

Newsletter *Made in Japan Info Letter*
Carole Bess White
P.O. Box 819
Portland, OR 97207; fax: 503-281-2817; Send SASE for information; no appraisals given; e-mail: CBESSW@aol.com

Ash receiver, pelican figural, lustreware, 2½", $22.50.

Ashtray, calico cat figure w/round dish on back showing mountain scene, multicolored, 2½", from $25 to .**$40.00**
Ashtray, calico elephant next to shamrock-shaped dish in tan lustre w/black rim, 2¼", from $18 to **$28.00**
Ashtray, frog sitting on bowl w/incurvate rim, 2 rests, multi-colored glossy & lustre, 2½", from $25 to **$35.00**
Ashtray, round dish w/2 rests, embossed strawberry decor on rim, blue & tan lustre, 4½", from $12 to **$20.00**

Ashtray, 3-sided horseshoe shape w/horse head on 1 side & card suits on other 2, tan lustre trim, 4", from $18 to **$32.00**
Bank, chiseled-look cat figure seated on hind legs, glossy, 4¼", from $20 to..**$35.00**
Basket, tulip shape w/floral decor on multicolor lustre, 6¼" W, from $50 to **$80.00**
Biscuit barrel, airbrushed blue & tan geometric designs on white, 6", from $50 to..**$80.00**
Bisquit barrel, octagonal w/wrapped handle, white w/painted cherry-branch decor, cherry finial, 6", from $50 to..**$70.00**
Bookends, Mexican man taking siesta on right-angled base, tan & orange w/light blue lustre, 4¼", pr from $28 to **$48.00**
Bookends, pelican on right-angled base, cream w/orange trim, 6", pr from $30 to **$55.00**
Bookends, sailboat on right-angled waves as base, multicolored, glossy, 4¾", pr, from $30 to........................**$50.00**
Bowl, octagonal w/reeded handle, geometric center w/lustre rim, 8" W, from $25 to...**$45.00**
Bowl, oval w/open handles, matt image of lady walking on path to house in distance, tan lustre rim, 8¼", from $35 to **$55.00**
Bowl, oval w/scalloped rim, cat handle, various lustre motifs, 7" W, ea from $30 to **$55.00**
Cache pot, frog hugging yellow blossom on base w/turtle, 4", from $30 to..**$45.00**
Cache pot, gentlemen trio in multicolored airbrushed glazes on base beside airbrushed ribbed pot, 4¾", from $20 to..**$30.00**
Cache pot, girl figure consoling dog w/toothache next to handled pot, multicolored, 5¾", from $25 to **$35.00**
Cache pot, Mexican figure sleeping beside horse w/head down, multicolored, 7" L, from $15 to..................**$25.00**
Cache pot, pixie figure nestled inside of log-shaped pot, glossy, 6" L, from $20 to **$35.00**
Candlestick, round flat cup on flared base, allover flowers & berries on blue, white trim, 7½", pr, from $135 to **$155.00**
Candy box, embossed profile bust of jester w/in floral wreath, floral band on side, lustre trim, 5½", from $35 to **$55.00**
Candy dish, crossed branch handles on bowl w/lg embossed flower & leaves, majolica style, 4½", from $35 to ..**$55.00**
Candy jar, cat figure pouncing, blue lustre body w/tan lustre base, rump is lid w/tail finial, 6¾", from $90 to ..**$150.00**
Chamberstick, blossom-form cup on 3-handled base w/embossed flowers, red, black, white & green, 2½", from $15 to..**$20.00**
Cigarette box, glossy marbled green & white w/black dog finial, 3", from $35 to...**$55.00**
Cigarette holder, round cup on pedestal base, multicolored flowers w/yellow lustre base, 3¼", from $40 to ..**$50.00**
Decanter set, figural bellhop holding 4 shot glasses in arms w/2 in pockets, multicolored, gold trim, 11", from $175 to **$250.00**

Figurine, boy in green top & brown pants w/begging dog on white base w/gold trim, 8¼", from $20 to **$30.00**

Figurine, coach w/2 horses, driver & passenger on oblong base, multicolored & white, 2½", from $8 to **$12.00**

Figurine, lady dancer holding multilayered ruffled skirt w/both hands, 6¾", from $45 to **$75.00**

Figurine, pheasant on oblong base, multicolored, glossy, majolica style, 6", from $35 to **$55.00**

Figurine, ram's head, cream matt, 7¼", from $30 to ... **$50.00**

Humidor, jar w/multicolored flowers on green crackle, concave sides, geometric design on lid, 6", from $45 to **$65.00**

Incense burner, man on elephant, multicolor lustre glazes, 6¼", from $45 to **$75.00**

Incense burner, porcelain Buddha figure w/tan lustre robe, black hair & scalloped band around base, 4¼", from $30 to **$40.00**

Incense burner, 2-pc pagoda, blue, tan & orange lustre w/gold finial, 6¼", from $25 to **$45.00**

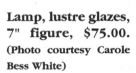

Lamp, lustre glazes, 7" figure, $75.00.
(Photo courtesy Carole Bess White)

Marmalade/jam pot, multicolored windmill scene w/yellow vertically ribbed base, wrapped handle, w/spoon, 4", from $25 to **$45.00**

Match holder, black cat figure rubbing against yellow pot, 2¼", from $28 to **$40.00**

Mayonnaise set, 4-footed bowl w/underplate & spoon, blue & tan lustre w/black trim, 5½", from $25 to **$40.00**

Pincushion, Dutch boy pushing wheelbarrow on grassy base, multicolored lustre, 3¼", from $18 to **$28.00**

Pincushion, Kewpie-style baby w/arm around green basket on gray rock, 4", from $30 to **$45.00**

Pitcher, basketweave donut shape w/multicolored embossed flowers on cream, from $30 to **$40.00**

Pitcher, black cat handle on green bulbous shape w/embossed hunt scene, 6¾", from $25 to **$40.00**

Pitcher, green & blue palm tree on orange w/tan lustre rim & handle, 8½", from $55 to **$115.00**

Plate, country scene w/swan on pond & house in distance, multicolored w/lustre trim, 8¼", from $20 to **$35.00**

Powder box, Colonial lady figural, bright blue dress, 7", from $30 to **$45.00**

Relish dish, divided heart shape, green crackle w/flower finial, 7½", from $18 to **$28.00**

Sandwich server, round w/open finial, multicolor flowers on striped border, lustre w/gold trim, 10", from $45 to .**$75.00**

Sauce boat & underplate, floral decor inside cup w/blue & tan lustre, 3", from $30 to **$60.00**

Soap dish/ring tray, early bathing beauty kneeling on shell-shaped dish, multicolored w/tan lustre, 3½", from $35 to **$55.00**

Sugar bowl & creamer, trumpeting elephant forms w/decorative back blankets, tan lustre, 4¼", from $50 to **$75.00**

Sugar bowl & creamer w/tray, sq w/diagonal spout, stylized flowers & crosshatching, dog finial, 3-pc set from $40 to **$55.00**

Sugar shaker, sq green basketweave w/multicolored embossed flowers, 5", from $15 to **$25.00**

Teapot, Satsuma style w/dragon spout & elephant finial, embossed elephant in gold on green, 5½", from $55 to **$100.00**

Teapot, sq w/wrapped handle, knob finial, triangles & stylized floral design on crackle glaze, 6¾", from $35 to **$65.00**

Teapot on tile, angled form w/3-color triangle motif on white, blue lustre trim, scalloped tile, 7¾", from $40 to **$65.00**

Teapot w/sugar bowl & creamer, angled forms w/black & white lustre triangle motif, 8", from $80 to **$130.00**

Teapot w/sugar bowl & creamer, granny figures in multicolored wash glazes, 8" pot, from $100 to **$125.00**

Toast rack, 5 bamboo-shaped dividers on base, blue & tan lustre, 5¼" L, from $40 to **$60.00**

Tray, oval w/open handles, multicolored lustre flowers on white w/orange rim, 10½", from $25 to **$35.00**

Vanity/ring box, round w/painted flower basket decor on dome lid, blue & tan lustre, 1¾", from $15 to **$20.00**

Vase, angled tulip shape w/handles, multicolored geometric motif trimmed in black, 6", from $30 to **$50.00**

Vase, bulbous urn w/rounded rim & base, stylized floral motif on pink crackle glaze, 7¼", from $35 to **$55.00**

Vase, bulbous w/long neck, bright multicolored stylized flowers painted over white crackle, 9¾", from $25 to **$45.00**

Vase, column shape w/embossed sailboats, glossy white on blue, 7¾", from $25 to **$45.00**

Vase, Satsuma-style urn w/6 tapering sides, rolled rim & base, geisha girl motif on crackle glaze, 5¾", from $20 to..**$40.00**

Vase, Satsuma-style urn w/sm loop handles & ruffled rim, bird motif, 6¼", from $20 to **$40.00**

Vase, sq w/wide flared rim, ribbed base, tropical island scene against yellow lustre sky, tan base, 7", from $50 to...**$85.00**

Vase, 3 cylinders w/embossed blossom & branch motif on round base, glossy white, 5½", from $10 to......... **$20.00**

Jewel Tea Company

At the turn of the century, there was stiff competition among door-to-door tea-and-coffee companies, and most of them tried to snag the customer by doling out coupons that could eventually be traded in for premiums. But the thing that set the Jewel Tea people apart from the others was that their premiums were awarded to the customer first, then 'earned' through the purchases that followed. This set the tone of their business dealings which obviously contributed to their success, and very soon in addition to the basic products they started out with, the company entered the food-manufacturing field. They eventually became one of the country's largest retailers. Today their products, containers, premiums, and advertising ephemera are all very collectible.

Advisors: Bill and Judy Vroman (See Directory, Jewel Tea)

Baking Powder, Jewel, cylindrical tin w/script logo & white lettering, 1950s-60s, 1-lb, from $20 to **$30.00**

Cake decorator set, late 1940s, from $50 to **$65.00**

Candy, Jewel Mints, round green tin, 1920s, 1-lb, from $30 to **$40.00**

Candy, Jewel Tea Spiced Jelly Drops, orange box w/orange & white lettering, from $20 to **$30.00**

Cereal, Jewel Quick Oats, cylindrical box w/white & orange lettering, from $40 to **$50.00**

Cocoa, Jewel or Jewel Tea, various boxes, ea from $25 to **$45.00**

Coffee, Jewel Blend, orange & gold w/white lettering & logo, paper label **$40.00**

Coffee, Jewel Private Blend, brown w/white lettering, 1-lb, from $15 to **$25.00**

Coffee, Jewel Special Blend, brown stripes on white, white & orange lettering on brown circle, 2-lb, from $15 to.. **$25.00**

Coffee, Royal Jewel, yellow w/brown & white, 1-lb, from $20 to **$35.00**

Coffee, West Coast, orange & brown w/white lettering, bell at top center, 1960s, 2-lb, from $25 to **$35.00**

Dishes, Melmac, 8 place settings, from $150 to **$170.00**

Extract, Jewel Imitation Vanilla, brown box w/orange & white lettering, 1960s, 4-oz, from $20 to **$30.00**

Extract, Jewel Lemon, orange, blue & white, 1916-19, from $40 to.. **$50.00**

Flour sifter, litho metal, EX **$485.00**

Garment bag, 1950s, MIP, from $25 to......................... **$30.00**

Laundry, Daintflakes, pink & blue box marked Soft Feathery Flakes of Pure Mild Soap, from $25 to **$30.00**

Laundry, Daybreak Laundry Set, from $15 to.............. **$20.00**

Laundry, Grano Granulated Soap, blue & white box marked Made For General Cleaning, 2-lb, from $25 to..... **$30.00**

Laundry, Pure Gloss Starch, teal & white box, from $25 to **$30.00**

Malted milk mixer, Jewel-T, from $40 to **$50.00**

Mix, Jewel Sunbrite Mix, Mason jar w/paper label & metal screw lid, 1960s, 26-oz, from $15 to **$25.00**

Mix, Jewel Tea Coconut Dessert, round tan tin w/brown & white logo & lettering, 1930s, 14-oz, from $30 to.. **$40.00**

Mix, Jewel Tea Devil's Food Cake Flour, 1920s, 10-oz, from $30 to.. **$40.00**

Mix, Jewel Tea Prepared Tapioca, tall sq orange & brown striped tin w/logo & brown lettering, 1930s, from $25 to **$35.00**

Mixer, Mary Dunbar, electric w/stand, bowl & original hang tag, white.. **$100.00**

Mixer, Mary Dunbar, hand-held style w/stand, 1940, from $40 to **$50.00**

Napkins, paper w/printed pattern, box of 200 .... **$25.00**

Nuts, Jewel Mixed Nuts, round brown-striped tin w/orange & brown lettering, 1960s, 1-lb, from $15 to **$20.00**

Peanut Butter, Jewel Tea, glass jar w/paper label & screw lid, 1930s, 1-lb, from $30 to **$40.00**

Pickle fork, Jewel-T, from $20 to **$25.00**

Razor blades, Jewel-T **$5.00**

Salesman's award, Ephraim Coffee cup w/saucer, 1939, 1-qt (given to top 400 salesmen), from $175 to........ **$350.00**

Scales, Jewel-T, from $45 to.. **$55.00**

Sweeper, Jewel, gold lettering on black, 1930s-40s, from $80 to **$100.00**

Sweeper, Jewel Little Bissell, from $40 to.................... **$50.00**

Sweeper, Jewel Suction Sweeper, early 1900s, lg **$150.00**

Sweeper, Jewel Suction Sweeper, tan lettering on dark tan, 1930s-40s, from $60 to **$100.00**

Tea bags, Jewel Tea, box w/dragon logo, gold & brown, 1948 .... **$65.00**

Jewelry

Today's costume jewelry collectors may range from nine to ninety and have tastes as varied as their ages, but one thing they all have in common is their love of these distinctive items of jewelry, some originally purchased at the corner five-&-dimes, others from department stores and boutiques.

Costume jewelry became popular, simply because it was easily affordable for all women. Today jewelry made before 1954 is considered to be 'antique,' while the term 'collectible' jewelry generally refers to those pieces made after that time. Costume jewelry was federally recognized as an American art form in 1954, and the copyright law was passed to protect the artists' designs. The copyright mark (c in a circle) found on the back of a piece identifies a post-1954 collectible.

Quality should always be the primary consideration when shopping for these treasures. Remember that pieces with colored rhinestones bring the higher prices. (Note: A rhinestone is a clear, foil-backed, leaded glass crystal — unless it is a colored rhinestone — while a stone is not foiled). A complete set (called a parure) increases in value by 20% over the total of its components. Check for a manufacturer's mark, since a signed piece is worth 20% more than one of comparable quality, but not signed. Some of the best designers are Miriam Haskell, Eisenberg, Trifari, Hollycraft, and Joseff.

Early plastic pieces (Lucite, Bakelite, and celluloid, for example) are very collectible. Some Lucite is used in combination with wood, and the figural designs are especially desirable.

There are several excellent reference books available if you'd like more information. Look for *Unsigned Beauties of Costume Jewelry* by our advisor Marcia Brown, who has also authored a new book entitled *Signed Beauties of Costume Jewelry*. Lillian Baker has written several including *50 Years of Collectible Fashion Jewelry* and *100 Years of Collectible Jewelry*. Books by other authors include *Collectible Costume Jewelry* and *Collectible Silver Jewelry* by Fred Rezazadeh; *Collectible Costume Jewelry* by Cherri Simonds; *Painted Porcelain Jewelry and Buttons* by Dorothy Kamm; *Vintage Jewelry for Investment and Casual Wear* by Karen L. Edeen; and video books *Hidden Treasures Series* by Christie Romero and Marcia Brown. All but the video are available through Collector Books.

See also Christmas Tree Pins

Advisor: Marcia Brown (See Directory, Jewelry)

Club/Newsletter: *Vintage Fashion and Costume Jewelry Newsletter Club*
P.O. Box 265, Glen Oaks, NY 11004

Bracelet, Cini, silver w/stylized floral links, from $100 to..**$150.00**

Bracelet, Coro, gold-plate and aurora borealis stones in Art Moderne styling, from $25.00 to $35.00. (Photo courtesy Lillian Baker)

Bracelet, Danecraft, silver flower form, from $40 to...**$70.00**
Bracelet, Danecraft, slim silver bangle w/embossed decor, from $30 to...**$40.00**
Bracelet, Emmons, antique gold-tone links w/purple & green unfaceted glass sq & rectangles, ¾" W, from $100 to...**$175.00**
Bracelet, JEB, silver & turquoise cuff type, from $350 to ..**$425.00**
Bracelet, Kerr, silver cuff w/stamped floral decor, from $45 to...**$65.00**
Bracelet, Miriam Haskell, 4 strands of light & bright aqua crystal beads, brass filigree clasp w/rhinestones, from $250 to...**$350.00**
Bracelet, unmarked, gold-plated, chunky style w/topaz emerald-cut & cabachon dangles spaced by pearl beads on chain...**$40.00**
Bracelet, unmarked, lime green cabochons form center row, smaller on outside rows....................**$48.00**
Bracelet, unmarked, pink plastic hinged cuff w/scattered clear rhinestones, wide.........................**$35.00**
Bracelet, unmarked, plastic flowers on chain **$12.00**
Bracelet, unmarked, red chaton rhinestones w/smaller rhinestones on 2 outer rows.....................**$30.00**
Bracelet, unmarked, single strand of hand-set clear rhinestones...**$18.00**

Bracelet, unmarked, 11 rows of gold rhinestones of various sizes, 2¼" W...................................**$110.00**
Bracelet, unmarked, 2 strands of faux graduated pearls w/rhinestone clasp.............................**$25.00**
Bracelet & earrings, Eisenberg, baguette Austrian crystal rhinestones, 1¾" W bracelet, knot earrings, 1950s, from $450 to...**$550.00**
Bracelet & earrings, Florenza, antique gold-tone w/triangular opal glass cabochons, faux pearls & colored rhinestones...**$200.00**
Bracelet & earrings, Schiaparelli, gold-plated scroll-leaf design, 1" W bracelet, 2½" earrings, from $250 to...........**$325.00**
Bracelet & earrings, unmarked, hinged cuff w/emerald-cut topaz rhinestones w/sm marquise & chatons.......**$90.00**
Brooch, Coro, enameled nosegay on gold-plate, glued-in rhinestones & faux pearls, 1930s, 3¾".............**$150.00**
Brooch, DeMario NY, gilt-brass flower cluster w/faux pearls & prong-set rhinestones, 1950s, 1½x2", from $150 to...**$175.00**
Brooch, Gerry's, base-metal begging poodle w/multicolor enameling, 1¾"...............................**$35.00**
Brooch, Gerry's, gold-tone turtle w/coral ceramic shell, green rhinestone eyes, 2½"...........................**$45.00**
Brooch, Hollycraft, base-metal monkey swinging from branch, multicolor enamel, 1950s, 2x2", from $40 to **$60.00**
Brooch, Jay Kel, sterling silver w/citrine-colored stones, from $40 to...**$50.00**
Brooch, Karu-Arke, antiqued-bronze leaf w/glued-in aquamarine, aurora borealis & sapphire rhinestones, from $100 to...**$135.00**
Brooch, Kramer, gold-tone metal leaf shape w/faux topaz marquise-cut cabochons (glued in), 1950s-early 1960s...**$80.00**
Brooch, Marcel Boucher, gold-plated ballerina w/etched tutu, 1¾", from $125 to.........................**$175.00**
Brooch, Mazer, silver flower form w/faux pearl & colored rhinestones...**$95.00**
Brooch, Reed Barton, African antelope, gold vermeil over sterling, Sterling hallmark, 2½", from $150 to **$200.00**
Brooch, Sarah Coventry, rhodium-plated abstract cushion w/clear chaton-cut rhinestones (glued in), from $55 to...**$75.00**
Brooch, Sorrento, silver lacy floral w/genuine jade stones...**$60.00**
Brooch, Trifari, gold-plated tiger w/black enamel stripes, 2¼" L, from $150 to.........................**$200.00**
Brooch, unmarked, aurora borealis, white marble beads & lavender navettes w/pearl center make a snowflake form...**$43.00**
Brooch, unmarked, baguette rhinestones in rows form Art Deco rectangle...**$48.00**
Brooch, unmarked, blue rhinestone butterfly w/gold-plated fringe...**$55.00**
Brooch, unmarked, blue rhinestone navettes & chatons form star, sm...**$35.00**
Brooch, unmarked, gold-plated elongated fish w/scattered rhinestones **$42.00**

Brooch, unmarked, gold-plated peacock w/hand-set rhinestones in tail display, enamel wings......................**$38.00**

Brooch, unmarked, pavé gold ribbon, 1930s..............**$95.00**

Brooch, unmarked, pink glass navette stones form overlapping leaves w/aurora borealis chaton trim...........**$35.00**

Brooch, unmarked, plastic parrot, multicolor w/rhinestone eye **$72.00**

Brooch, unmarked, pot-metal cat w/black enameling & clear rhinestones, 1940s.....................................**$68.00**

Brooch, unmarked, rhinestones swan, touches of black enamel on eyes, beak & feet.......................**$80.00**

Brooch, unmarked, sterling silver duck w/blue faceted glass body..**$65.00**

Brooch, Vendome, gold-tone diamond-shaped frame holds pink Austrian aurora borealis teardrop dangles, 1950s, 2½"...**$150.00**

Brooch, Viking, vermeil sterling stylized floral, from $50 to **$75.00**

Brooch, Weiss, multicolor rhinestones & Austrian crystals form flower, prong set, gold-plated, 1950s, 3½", from $100 to...**$145.00**

Brooch & earrings, Art, green tourmaline, blue aurora borealis & emerald green rhinestone, gun metal-plated, from $175 to..**$225.00**

Brooch & earrings, Danecraft, gold vermeil on siver w/cultured pearls, from $100 to **$150.00**

Brooch & earrings, ruby red & aurorea borealis rhinestones, prong set, rodium-plated, star brooch, from $130 to............**$175.00**

Brooch & earrings, Sarah Coventry, rhodium-plated hurricanes w/faux pearl centers, brooch: 2¾", from $85 to...**$110.00**

Brooch & earrings, unmarked, red, pink & aurora borealis Austrian crystals, navettes at end of silver-plated wires **$85.00**

Brooch & earrings, unmarked Austrian, gold & green rhinestone flowers on gold-plated stems **$145.00**

Brooches, Trifari, white enamel critters, values range from $68.00 to $80.00. (Photo courtesy Marcia Brown)

Clip, unmarked, blue rhinestone floral design............**$68.00**

Clip, unmarked, cat w/silver tail, blue glass stone body, pink rhinestone face...**$75.00**

Clip, unmarked, double-faceted rhinestones form teardrop...**$60.00**

Clip, unmarked, elongated red Bakelite spear shape surrounded by pavé diamente (rhinestones)...........**$125.00**

Clip, unmarked, lavender chatons w/pewter-metal finish..**$90.00**

Clip, unmarked, leaded glass multicolored stones......**$85.00**

Clip/brooch, Coro, rose & yellow gold-plate w/8 rectangular-cut faux topazes (all prong set, unfoiled), 4x2¾", from $150 to **$200.00**

Earrings, Eisenberg Original, rhinestones, sterling, clip-on, pr..**$60.00**

Earrings, unmarked, aurora borealis leaves, pr...........**$40.00**

Earrings, unmarked, aurora borealis rhinestone cluster, pr **$38.00**

Earrings, unmarked, button type rimmed w/clear rhinestones, pr from $12 to......................................**$18.00**

Earrings, unmarked, clear baguettes (3) w/6 sm chaton guards, pr...**$54.00**

Earrings, unmarked, faux pearl capped in peridot rhinestones ending in pearl drop, pr..........................**$36.00**

Earrings, unmarked, gold loops w/rhinestone in center, pr..**$18.00**

Earrings, unmarked, pearl rimmed w/clear rhinestones, pr..**$12.00**

Earrings, unmarked, pearl surrounded by 2 rows of pink rhinestones, pr **$28.00**

Earrings, unmarked, sapphire blue navettes form flower w/clear rhinestones, pr...**$45.00**

Earrings, unmarked, silver Art Novueau leaves ribbed w/rhinestones, pr...**$28.00**

Earrings, unmarked, strung pearls w/rhinestone rondels & balls, pr...**$50.00**

Earrings, unmarked, yellow plastic flower held by rhinestone in center, pr...**$14.00**

Earrings, unmarked, 4 blue cabochons rimmed by sm blue rhinestones, pr **$38.00**

Earrings, unsigned, chaton, pear & baguette rhinestones, prong-set, chromium-plate, 1950s, 3¼", from $115 to **$140.00**

Necklace, Celebrity Gems, antique gold-tone w/black plastic oval cabochon pendant (3¼") w/dangles, 1970s, from $50 to...**$80.00**

Necklace, Coro, gold-tone w/bright aqua rhinestones, 1940s, from $125 to..**$175.00**

Necklace, Eisenberg, rhinestones w/pear-cut Austrian crystal drop, rhodium-plate, from $700 to.....................**$800.00**

Necklace, Goldette, Bedouin-style faux perfume bottle pendant, pewter on silver-tone rope chain, 1960s, from $75 to...**$120.00**

Necklace, Japan, 3 strands of molded plastic & Venetian glass beads, silver-tone clasp & findings, 1950s, from $30 to...**$45.00**

Necklace, Pat Pending, gold-tone bolo-style rope chain w/prong-set citrine & topaz cabochons & rhinestones, 1960s-70s **$200.00**

Necklace, Trifari, Deco-style choker, clear rhinestones, rose gold-plate, front links ¾" W, from $110 to.........**$175.00**

Necklace, Trifari, snake chain with red glass flower petals, pavé leaves, $725.00. (Photo courtesy Marcia Brown)

Necklace, unmarked, celluloid snake studded w/rhinestones....................**$65.00**

Necklace, unmarked, flower garland of citrine & peridot blossoms **$85.00**

Necklace, unmarked, gold & brown cabachons feather out from iridescent chaton rhinestone, brown rhinestone chain **$30.00**

Necklace, unmarked, shaded green iridescent headlight rhinestones w/in loop of gold iridescent chatons..**$45.00**

Necklace, unmarked, simulated pearls w/brass filigree caps & rhinestone rondellas, 1-strand, from $75 to....**$115.00**

Necklace, unmarked, topaz & gold rhinestones w/acid-treated gray glass stones (giving dimpled effect), 1960s **$35.00**

Necklace, unmarked, 3 deep blue pear-shaped stones on simple rhinestone strand **$90.00**

Necklace, unmarked, 4 strands of simulated pearls w/rhinestone clasp, 12 strands dangle from clasp, choker style **$175.00**

Necklace & bracelet, Judy Lee, emerald-cut garnet rhinestones in antiqued brass, pendant necklace, 5-link bracelet......................**$150.00**

Necklace & bracelet, Renoir, copper links w/openwork, 1950s, ¾" W, from $110 to..................**$165.00**

Necklace & bracelet, unmarked, silver blue beads w/dangling blue chatons **$98.00**

Necklace & earrings, Sarah Coventry, smoked glass & clear rhinestones on rhodium-plate, 1960s, from $110 to **$145.00**

Necklace & earrings, unmarked, aqua, frosted prong-set rhinestones, gold-plate, 1950s, 1¼" dia earrings, from $200 to **$300.00**

Necklace & earrings, unmarked, black & clear rhinestones set in 4 rows, wheel spoke earrings **$75.00**

Necklace & earrings, unmarked, frosted green glass stones w/dark green rhinestones **$52.00**

Necklace & earrings, unmarked, pink sherbet cabochons (4 sizes) w/chains of pink chaton rhinestones **$75.00**

Necklace & earrings, unmarked, red & pink chatons w/graduated drops, center drop in earrings as well.......**$92.00**

Necklace & earrings, unmarked, simulated pearls & sapphire-blue rhinestones, glued in, rhodium-plated, 1950s, from $75 to **$100.00**

Necklace & earrings, unmarked, white glass cabochons intermingled w/clear chaton rhinestones **$40.00**

Ring, unmarked, black cabachon oval w/circle of rhinestones & black rhinestone trim....................**$32.00**

Ring, unmarked, frosted glass center w/aurora borealis chatons & leaves forming garland...............**$55.00**

Ring, unmarked, gold-plated, green chaton center, purple rhinestones, outer seed pearl row **$34.00**

Ring, unmarked, gold-plated navette diamond rhinestone w/diamond shape outline made by rows of green & clear rhinestones **$28.00**

Ring, unmarked, lg lavender center w/circle of clear rhinestones **$35.00**

Ring, unmarked, opaline clustres on gold-plate..........**$45.00**

Ring, unmarked, rhodium finish w/clear & emerald green rhinestone cluster................................**$18.00**

Ring, unmarked, tiger-eye cabochon, clear rhinestone circle..............................**$45.00**

Ring, unmarked, topaz chatons create chrysanthemum....**$55.00**

Johnson Bros.

There is a definite renewal of interest in dinnerware collecting right now, and just about any antique shop or mall you visit will offer a few nice examples of the wares made by this Staffordshire company. They've been in business since well before the turn of the century and have targeted the American market to such an extent that during the '60s and '70s, as much as 70% of their dinnerware was sold to distributors in this country. They made many scenic patterns, some of which may already be familiar to you. Among them are Friendly Village, Historic America, and Old Britain Castles. They produced lovely floral patterns as well, and with the interest today's collectors have been demonstrating in Chintz, dealers tell me that Johnson Brothers' Rose Chintz and Chintz (Victorian) sell very well for them, especially the latter. In addition to their polychrome designs, they made several patterns in both blue and pink transferware.

Though some of their lines, Friendly Village, for instance, are still being produced, most are no longer as extensive as they once were, so the secondary market is being tapped to replace broken items that are not available anywhere else. In addition to their company logo, much of their dinnerware is also stamped with the pattern name. Today they're a part of the Wedgwood group.

For more information on marks, patterns, and pricing, we recommend *Johnson Brothers Dinnerware Pattern Directory and Price Guide* by Mary J. Finegan.

Advisor: Mary J. Finegan (See Directory, Dinnerware)

Base Values (All patterns not listed in the following subheadings are priced in this section.)

Windsor Fruit, platter, 13", $45.00.

Bowl, rimmed soup	**$14.00**
Bowl, vegetable; round	**$25.00**
Bowl, vegetable; w/lid, minimum value	**$90.00**
Cup & saucer, jumbo	**$30.00**
Mug, coffee, minimum value	**$18.00**
Plate, bread & butter	**$6.00**
Plate, chop/cake	**$50.00**
Plate, dinner; minimum value	**$14.00**
Platter, lg, 14" or over, minimum value	**$60.00**
Saucer, tea	**$5.00**
Sugar bowl, w/out lid	**$30.00**

One Star Patterns

These patterns include Autumn's Delight, Coaching Scenes, Devonshire, Fish, Gamebirds, Garden Bouquet, Hearts and Flowers, Indies, Millstream, Olde English Countryside, Rose Bouquet, Sheraton, and Winchester.

Bowl, fruit/berry	**$9.00**
Bowl, soup; sq or round, 7"	**$13.00**
Butter dish, w/lid	**$55.00**
Coaster	**$9.00**
Creamer	**$32.00**
Egg cup	**$18.00**
Plate, buffet; 10½" to 11"	**$28.00**
Plate, luncheon	**$14.00**
Platter, sm, up to 12"	**$40.00**
Platter, turkey; 20½", minimum value	**$200.00**
Sauce/gravy boat	**$45.00**

Two Star Patterns

These patterns include Barnyard King, Century of Progress, Chintz-Victorian, Dorchester, English Chippendale, Harvest Fruit, His Majesty, Historic America, Merry Christmas, Old Britain Castles, Persian Tulip, Rose Chintz, Strawberry Fair, Tally Ho, Twelve Days of Christmas, and Wild Turkeys.

Bowl, soup/cereal; sq, round or lug handled	**$12.00**
Bowl, vegetable; oval	**$40.00**
Cup, tea	**$12.00**
Pitcher/jug, minimum value	**$55.00**
Plate, salad; sq or round	**$14.00**
Platter, med, 12" to 14"	**$55.00**
Salt & pepper shakers, pr	**$48.00**
Sugar bowl, w/lid	**$48.00**
Teapot or coffeepot, minimum value	**$100.00**
Tureen, minimum value	**$200.00**

Josef Originals

Figurines of lovely ladies, charming girls, and whimsical animals marked Josef Originals were designed by Muriel Joseph George of Arcadia, California, from 1945 to 1985. Until 1960 they were produced in California, but production costs were high, and copies of her work were being made in Japan. To remain competitive, she and her partner, George Good, found a company in Japan to build a factory and produce her designs to her satisfaction. Muriel retired in 1982; however, Mr. Good continued production of her work and made some design changes on some of the figurines. The company was sold in late 1985. The name is currently owned by Dakin/Applause, and a limited number of figurines with the Josef Originals name are being made. Those made during the ownership of Muriel are the most collectible. They can be recognized by these characteristics: the girls have a high-gloss finish, black eyes, and most are signed on the bottom. As of the 1970s a bisque finish was making its way into the line-up, and by 1980 glossy girls were fairly scarce in the product line. Brown-eyed figures date from 1982 through 1985; Applause uses a red-brown eye, although they are starting to release copies of early pieces that are signed Josef Originals by Applause or by Dakin. The animals were nearly always made with a matt finish and bore paper labels only. In the mid-1970s they introduced a line of animals with fuzzy flocked coats and glass eyes.

Our advisors, Jim and Kaye Whitaker, have three books which we recommend for further study: *Josef Originals, Charming Figurines (Revised Edition)*; *Josef Originals, A Second Look*; and *Josef Originals, Figurines of Muriel Joseph George*. These are all currently available, and each has no repeats of items shown in the other books.

Please note: All figurines have black eyes unless specified otherwise. As with so many collectibles, values have been impacted to a measurable extent since the advent of the Internet.

See also Birthday Angels.

Advisors: Jim and Kaye Whitaker (See Directory, Josef Originals; no appraisal requests please)

A Warm Hello, Thinking of You series, girl on phone, Japan, 5"	**$40.00**
Aquarius, from Zodiac Girls series, Japan, 4¾", from $30 to	**$40.00**
Birthstone Dolls, March Aquamarine & April Diamond, Japan, 3½", ea	**$20.00**

Buggy Bugs series, various poses, wire antenna, Japan, 3½" **$9.00**
Cat wall plaque, California, 4", from $35 to **$45.00**
Christmas, mice, Japan, 2¾", ea **$9.00**
Christmas, Pixie, Helper series, painting toy, Japan, 4¾".. **$25.00**
Christmas, Santa, w/kiss on forehead, Japan, 4¾" **$45.00**
Elephant, sitting, Japan, 3¾" **$20.00**

Flower Sprites, various poses, Japan, 3¾", $29.00 each. (Photo courtesy Jim and Kaye Whitaker)

Girl cutting cake, Japan, 6", from $40 to **$45.00**
It's a Wonderful World series, Japan, 3½", ea **$40.00**
Jeanne, from Colonial Days series, Japan, 9" **$110.00**
Lara's Theme music box, Japan, 6" **$55.00**
Lipstick, from First Time series, Japan, 4½", from $30 to.. **$35.00**
Little International, Puerto Rico, Japan, 4" **$35.00**
Love Letter, from Love Story - Romance series, Japan, 8" .**$110.00**
Mary Ann & Mama, California, 4", 7", pr **$115.00**
Ruby, from Little Jewels series, girl wearing crown w/set-in faux ruby, Japan, 3½" **$20.00**
Sports Angels series, angels playing various sports, Japan, 3½", ea **$24.00**
Three Coins in Fountain music box, girl by fountain, Japan, 6" **$65.00**
Tony, from First Love series, Japan, 5", from $35 to .. **$40.00**
Wee Three, cats in basket, California, 3" **$35.00**
Yorkshire, from Kennel Klub series, Japan, 3", from $12 to **$17.00**

Kanawha

The Kanawha Glass Company of Dunbar, West Virginia, produced a wide variety of fine glassware items from the 1930s until its closure in 1986. Known for fine crackle glass; red, pastel green, and blue slags; and lovely cased-glass pieces, this company's glassware is finding its way into the showcases of today's collectors. For more information we recommend *American Slag Glass* by Ruth Grizel (Collector Books).

See also Crackle Glass.

Basket, green slag, Hobnail, #296ed, ca 1971, 7" **$45.00**
Basket, milk glass, Hobnail, ruffled rim, 8x7x5" **$25.00**

Basket, milk glass w/orange overlay, ruffled rim, applied milk glass handle, 7½x6¾" **$27.50**
Basket, orange slag, threaded bottom, #331ed, ca 1971, 6½" **$45.00**
Cruet set, blue slag, Hobnail, #291ed, ca 1973, 6", pr....**$50.00**
Doll, orange satin slag, embossed dog beside her, original sticker, 8½" **$30.00**
Hat, blue, star panel, original sticker, 2½x3½" **$30.00**
Lady's shoe, dark to med blue, laces up front, bow tie, original sticker, 2¼x5½" **$30.00**
Pitcher, amberina, exaggerated straight-up style rim, amber handle, original sticker, 14½" **$27.50**
Pitcher, blue cased, bulbous body, clear blue handle, original sticker, 4" **$22.50**
Pitcher, green slag, #264ed, ca 1971, 4¼" **$25.00**
Salt & pepper shakers, blue slag, Hobnail, #290ed, ca 1973, 5", pr **$35.00**
Vase, amberina, pinched sides, ruffled flower-like top, 5¾x4¼" **$27.50**
Vase, blue cased, Diamond Quilt, wide scalloped & pleated rim, 5¼x6½" **$35.00**

Kaye of Hollywood

This was one of the smaller pottery studios that operated in California during the 1940s — interesting in that people tend to confuse the name with Kay Finch. Kay (Schueftan) worked for Hedi Schoop before striking out on her own; because her work was so similar to that of her former employer's, a successful lawsuit was brought against her, and it was at this point that the mark was changed from Kaye of Hollywood to Kim Ward.

Bust, lady w/blue & pink hat w/feathers, Kim Ward mark, 10½x7½", NM **$45.00**
Figurine/planter, Oriental lady holding 2 lg brown baskets, applied scarf, #3129, 1950s, 9½" **$32.00**
Planter, Asian boy w/2 lg pots, #3128, 9½" **$22.50**
Planter, Asian girl w/2 lg pots, $3129, 9½" **$22.50**
Planter, Cameo Waltz, girl w/opening in apron, Kim Ward Hollywood mark, 5" **$22.00**
Planter, girl in 2-tone green dress carrying open basket, 10" **$27.50**
Planter, girl w/2 open baskets, #34, Kim Ward mark, 9".. **$20.00**
Planter, Oriental girl kneels & holds basket, #382, 11x7"..**$32.50**
Planter, white-wigged gentleman in fine clothes stands beside lg pot, #105, early 1950s, 9½", NM **$37.50**
Planters, Dutch girl w/open baskets & boy w/lg openings in pockets, #A16 & #A17, Kim Ward Jr Hollywood mark, 5", pr **$47.50**

Keeler, Brad

California pottery is becoming quite popular among collectors, and Brad Keeler is one of the better known designers. After studying art for a time, he opened his own studio in 1939 where he created naturalistic studies of birds and animals. Sold through giftware stores, the figures were decorated by airbrushing with hand-painted details. Brad Keeler is remembered for his popular flamingo figures and his Chinese Modern Housewares. Keeler died of a heart attack in 1952, and the pottery closed soon thereafter. For more information, we recommend *The Collector's Encyclopedia of California Pottery, 2nd Edition,* by Jack Chipman.

Dish, green leaf shape w/red lobster, 2-section, #872, 12x7", from $40 to..**$50.00**
Dish, green leaves w/red tomato in center, 2-section, #887, 12x7⅛x3¾", from $45 to......................................**$55.00**
Dish, green w/red lobster on top, 3-section, #867, 11x9", from $45 to..**$55.00**
Figurine, black, gray & white cat w/blue eyes playing w/blue ball of string, 3"..**$30.00**

Figurine, blue jay, #735, 9¼", from $65.00 to $75.00.

Figurine, blue jay perched on stump, #18, 8¼", from $30 to **$60.00**
Figurine, duck, browns & greens, #50, 4¾" **$50.00**
Figurine, flamingo, head down, #31, 9½", from $85 to .**$100.00**
Figurine, rooster, multicolored, high fanned-out tail, #24, 8¼x10"...**$85.00**
Figurine, swan, #704, 16½"...**$125.00**
Figurine, Thumper, brown & white w/1 eye open, back paw scratching other eye, #981, 2½"...........................**$80.00**
Figurine, titmouse, yellow, on stump, #720F, 5½" **$40.00**
Figurines, doe (standing) & 2 spotted fawns (recumbent), 3-pc set **$55.00**
Figurines, pheasants, cock, #38A, 7x11½" L; hen, #38B, 6x7½" L, pr, from $125 to **$150.00**
Figurines, Siamese kittens, 1 standing on hind legs, 1 lying down, #657, 3", 2½", pr **$35.00**
Figurines, Siamese mother, #7988, 7", kitten, #939, 1⅞", pr .**$50.00**
Figurines, 2 kittens lying on their own green pillows, 1 on back, 1 sitting up licking paw, #941, 2½x3", pr...**$60.00**
Plate, red crab on green scalloped shape, 12½x11½" ..**$90.00**

Salt & pepper shakers, tomatoes, red, 1½", pr...........**$30.00**
Tray, 4 pale turquoise & brown leaf-shaped sections w/bird in center, #842, 10" dia...............................**$45.00**

Kentucky Derby Glasses

Since the the late 1930s, every running of the Kentucky Derby has been commemorated with a special glass tumbler. Each year at Churchill Downs on Derby day you can buy them filled with mint juleps. In the early days this was the only place where these glasses could be purchased. Many collections were started when folks carried the glasses home from the track and then continued to add one for each successive year as they attended the Derby.

The first glass appeared in 1938, but examples from then until 1945 are extremely scarce and are worth thousands — when they can be found. Because of this, many collectors begin with the 1945 glasses. There are three: the tall version, the short regular-size glass, and a jigger. Some years, for instance 1948, 1956, 1958, 1974, and 1986, have slightly different variations, so often there are more than one to collect. To date a glass, simply add one year to the last date on the winner's list found on the back.

Each year many companies put out commemorative Derby glasses. Collectors call them 'bar' glasses (as many bars sold their own versions filled with mint juleps). Because of this, collectors need to be educated as to what the official Kentucky Derby glass looks like.

These prices are for pristine, mint-condition glasses with no chips or flaws. All colors must be bright and show no signs of fading. Lettering must be perfect and intact, even the list of past winners on the back. If gold trim has been used, it must show no wear. If any of these problems exist, reduce our values by 50% to 75%, depending on the glass and the problem. Many more Kentucky Derby shot glasses, jiggers, cordials, and shooters in various colors and sizes were produced — too many to list here. But be aware that these may present themselves along the collecting trail.

Advisor: Betty L. Hornback (See Directory, Kentucky Derby and Horse Racing)

1940, aluminum **$800.00**
1940, French Lick, aluminum......................................**$800.00**
1941-1944, plastic Beetleware, ea from $2,500 to..**$4,000.00**
1945, jigger...**$1,000.00**
1945, regular **$1,600.00**
1945, tall **$450.00**
1946-47, clear frosted w/frosted bottom, L in circle, ea ..**$100.00**
1948, clear bottom...**$225.00**
1948, frosted bottom **$250.00**
1949, He Has Seen Them all, green on frosted **$225.00**
1950 ....**$450.00**
1951 ....**$650.00**
1952 ....**$225.00**
1953 ....**$175.00**

1954	$200.00
1955	$150.00
1956, 1 star, 2 tails	$275.00
1956, 1 star, 3 tails	$400.00
1956, 2 stars, 2 tails	$200.00
1956, 2 stars, 3 tails	$250.00
1957, gold & black on frost	$125.00
1958, Gold Bar	$175.00
1958, Iron Liege	$225.00
1959 60, ea	$100.00
1961	$110.00
1962, Churchill Downs, red, gold & black	$80.00
1963-64, ea	$55.00
1965	$75.00
1966-68, ea	$60.00
1969	$65.00
1970	$70.00
1971	$50.00
1972	$45.00

1973, $55.00. (Photo courtesy Betty Hornback/Photographer Dean Langdon)

1974, Federal, regular or mistake, ea	$200.00
1974, mistake (Canonero in 1971 listing on back), Libbey	$18.00
1974, regular (Canonero II in 1971 listing on back)	$16.00
1975-76, ea	$16.00
1976, plastic	$16.00
1977	$14.00
1978-79, ea	$16.00
1980	$22.00
1981-82, ea	$14.00
1983-85, ea	$12.00
1986	$14.00
1986 ('85 copy)	$20.00
1987-89, ea	$12.00
1990-92, ea	$10.00
1993-95, ea	$9.00
1996-97, ea	$8.00
1998-99, ea	$6.00

2000-2001, ea	$5.00
2002	$3.00

Bluegrass Stakes Glasses, Keeneland, Lexington, Kentucky

1996	$15.00
1997	$13.00
1998	$12.00
1999-2000, ea	$10.00
2001-2002	$8.00

Breeders Cup Glasses

1985, Aqueduct, not many produced	$300.00
1988, Churchill Downs	$40.00
1989, Gulfstream Park	$70.00
1990, Bellmont Park	$45.00
1991, Churchill Downs	$15.00
1991, Churchill Downs, mistake	$50.00
1992, Gulfstream Park	$30.00
1993, Santa Anita	$35.00
1993, Santa Anita, 10th Running, gold	$40.00
1994, Churchill Downs	$10.00
1995, Belmont Park	$20.00
1996, Woodbine, Canada	$30.00
1997, Hollywood Park	$20.00
1998, Churchill Downs	$10.00
1999, Gulfstream Park	$10.00
2000, Churchill Downs	$9.00
2001 Belmont Park, or 2002 Santa Anita	$7.00

Festival Glasses

1968	$95.00
1984	$20.00
1985-86, no glass made	$.09
1987-88, ea	$16.00
1989-90, ea	$14.00
1991-92, ea	$12.00
1993, very few produced	$75.00
1994-95, ea	$10.00
1996-98, ea	$8.00
1999-2000, ea	$7.00
2001-2002, ea	$6.00

Jim Beam Stakes Glasses

1980, 6"	$350.00
1981, 7"	$300.00
1982	$275.00
1983	$65.00
1984	$45.00
1985-86, ea	$25.00
1987-88, ea	$20.00
1988-90, ea	$16.00
1991-95, ea	$14.00

1996-98, ea $12.00
1999, sponsored by 'Gallery Furniture.com' $10.00
2000-2002, Spiral Stakes $8.00

Shot Glasses

1987, frosted red, 1½-ounce, $350.00. (Photo courtesy Betty Hornback/Photographer Dean Langdon)

1987, 1½-oz, black, ea $350.00
1987, 3-oz, black.......................................$700.00
1987, 3-oz, red......................................$1,500.00
1988, 1½-oz..$40.00
1988, 3-oz...$60.00
1989, 3-oz...$45.00
1989-91, 1½-oz, ea.....................................$35.00
1991, 3-oz...$40.00
1992, 1½-oz..$20.00
1992, 3-oz...$25.00
1993, 1½-oz or 3-oz, ea $15.00
1994, 1½-oz or 3-oz, ea $14.00
1995, 1½-oz or 3-oz, ea $14.00
1996, 1½-oz or 3-oz, ea $13.00
1997, 1½-oz or 3-oz, ea $12.00
1998, 1½-oz or 3-oz, ea $10.00
1999, fluted whiskey, 1½-oz............................$10.00
2000-2001, fluted whiskey, 1½-oz $8.00

WAMZ Radio Kentucky Derby Bar Glasses, Sponsored by Jim Beam

1991 ....$45.00
1992 ....$40.00
1993 ....$25.00
1994 ....$20.00
1995-96 ....$15.00
1997-99, ea $12.00
2000 ....$10.00

Kindell, Dorothy

Yet another California artist that worked during the prolific years of the '40s and '50s, Dorothy Kindell produced a variety of household items and giftware, but today she's best known for her sensual nudes. One of her most popular lines consisted of mugs, a pitcher, salt and pepper shakers, a wall pocket, bowls, a creamer and sugar set, and champagne glasses, featuring a lady in various stages of undress, modeled as handles or stems (on the champagnes). In the set of six mugs, she progresses from wearing her glamorous strapless evening gown to ultimately climbing nude, head-first into the last mug. These are relatively common but always marketable. Except for these and the salt and pepper shakers, the other items from the nude line are scarce and rather pricey.

Collectors also vie for her island girls, generally semi-nude and very sensuous.

Ashtray, 2 nudes under 7½" beachcomber's hat, common, from $50 to..$75.00
Champagne glass, black w/gold-colored nude, 6x4½" dia $275.00
Champagne glass, nude stem $150.00
Creamer & sugar bowl, nude handles, 2 on sugar bowl, 3½x3" dia $290.00
Ice bucket, nude on ea side, 5x11" dia $185.00
Mug, nude handles, 1 of the series of 6, common, 5¼"-6", ea from $35 to..$40.00
Mug, old cowboy w/white hair, beard & mustache, gray hat, 4½"...$135.00
Salt & pepper shakers, nude handles, 3x1¾", pr, from $50 to..$65.00
Shelf sitter, nude w/red cold-painted head band & towel at waist, 11"...$390.00

Turtle box, 12" wide, $165.00. (Photo courtesy Lewis and Merri Dey)

King's Crown, Thumbprint

Back in the late 1800s, this pattern was called Thumbprint. It was first made by the U.S. Glass Company and Tiffin, one of several companies who were a part of the US conglomerate, through the 1940s. U.S. Glass closed in the late 1950s, but Tiffin reopened in 1963 and reissued it. Indiana Glass bought the molds, made some minor changes, and during the 1970s, they made this line as well. Confusing, to say the least! Gene Florence's *Collectible Glassware of the 40s, 50s, and 60s* explains that originally the thumbprints were oval, but at some point Indiana changed theirs to circles. And Tiffin's tumblers were flared at the top, while Indiana's were straight. Our values are for the later issues of both companies, with the ruby flashing in excellent condition.

Bowl, finger; 4"	$17.50
Bowl, wedding/candy; footed, w/lid, 10½"	$165.00
Cake salver, footed, 12½"	$75.00
Cheese stand	$25.00
Lazy susan, w/ball-bearing spinner, 8½x24"	$295.00
Plate, bread & butter; 5"	$8.00
Plate, dinner; 10"	$40.00
Plate, party; 24"	$185.00
Plate, salad; 7⅜"	$12.00
Punch bowl, either style, ea	$450.00
Punch cup	$15.00
Relish, 5-part, 14"	$110.00
Stem, claret; 4-oz	$13.00
Stem, sundae/sherbet; 5½-oz	$10.00
Stem, wine; 2-oz	$7.50
Sugar bowl	$25.00
Tumbler, iced tea; footed, 12-oz	$20.00
Tumbler, juice; footed, 4-oz	$12.00
Tumbler, water; 8½-oz	$13.00
Vase, bud; 12¼"	$90.00

Kitchen Collectibles

If you've never paid much attention to old kitchen appliances, now is the time to do just that. Check in Grandma's basement — or your mother's kitchen cabinets, for that matter. As styles in home decorating changed, so did the styles of appliances. Some have wonderful Art Deco lines, while others border on the primitive. Most of those you'll find still work, and with a thorough cleaning you'll be able to restore them to their original 'like-new' appearance. Missing parts may be impossible to replace, but if it's just a cord that's gone, you can usually find what you need at any hardware store.

Even larger appliances are collectible and are often used to add the finishing touch to a period kitchen. Please note that prices listed here are for appliances that are free of rust, pitting, or dents and in excellent working condition.

During the nineteenth century, cast-iron apple peelers, cherry pitters, and food choppers were patented by the hundreds, and because they're practically indestructible, they're still around today. Unless parts are missing, they're still usable and most are very efficient at the task they were designed to perform.

A lot of good vintage kitchen glassware is still around and can generally be bought at reasonable prices. Pieces vary widely from custard cups and refrigerator dishes to canister sets and cookie jars. There are also several books available for further information and study. If this area of collecting interests you, you'll enjoy *300 Years of Kitchen Collectibles* by Linda Campbell, and *Kitchen Antiques, 1790 – 1940*, by Kathryn McNerney. Other books include: *Kitchen*

Glassware of the Depression Years and *Anchor Hocking's Fire-King & More* by Gene Florence; *Collector's Encyclopedia of Fry Glassware* by H.C. Fry Glass Society; *The '50s and '60s Kitchen, A Collector's Handbook and Price Guide*, by Jan Lindenberger; and *Fire-King Fever* and *Pyrex History and Price Guide*, both by April Tvorak.

See also Aluminum; Clothes Sprinkler Bottles; Fire-King; Glass Knives; Griswold; Kitchen Prayer Ladies; Porcelier; Reamers.

Advisor: Jim Barker, Appliances (See Directory, Appliances)

Appliances

Beater, Challenge, custard glass base, from $45 to	$55.00
Beater, Chicago Electric, Jade-ite bottom, from $85 to	$95.00
Beater, Kenmore, clear glass base w/handle, from $30 to	$35.00
Blender, Electra Mix, burgundy & white, Hollywood Liquefier Co, EX	$115.00
Blender, Knapp Monarch, red & white, 3 speeds, 1950s, 15½"	$25.00
Blender, Oster, clear glass canister w/chrome beehive base, screw-on white & turquoise icer attachment, MIB	$60.00
Blender, Osterizer Model 403, beehive-shaped base, 15¾", EX	$45.00
Blender, Sears, mustard yellow, 16 speeds, 1960s-early '70s, EX	$20.00
Blender, Vita Mix Mark 20, 2-speed, stainless steel, 1950s-60s, EX	$50.00
Blender, Waring-FC1-14, heavy metal base w/on-off switch (no other functions), EX+	$80.00
Bottle warmer, First Years Night & Day, MIB	$25.00
Bottle warmer, Safety 1st, Dusk to Dawn, w/night light, MIB	$30.00
Bottle/baby food warmer, Avent, heat control, aqua & white, MIB w/instructions	$38.00
Bottle/food warmer, Babytec Electronic, MIB	$20.00
Can opener, Sunbeam Model 64-S1, pink, 1950s, 9x5½x6½", EX	$25.00
Can opener/ice crusher, Oster, snowflake-pattern front, EX	$45.00
Can opener/knife sharpener, Hoover #8100, EX	$30.00
Coffee urn/percolator, Hamilton Beach, chrome, late 1950s-early '60s, MIB w/instructions	$75.00
Coffeepot, Sunbeam Coffee Master C30A, chrome w/black lid & handle, Deco styling, 12", EX	$20.00
Egg poacher, Wear Ever #18144, EX	$17.50
Juicer, Sunkist Juicit, milk glass top, bright chrome, 1950s, 9¾x5" dia, NM	$35.00
Mixer, Dormeyer Princess, chrome w/grill-like front, 1950s, 12x12" w/9" dia bowl, EX	$88.00
Mixer, Hamilton Beach Model G, 10-speed, juicer attachment, 1950s, EX	$30.00
Mixer, hand; Sunbeam Jr, chrome w/black handle, 2 beaters, MIB w/instruction booklet	$55.00
Mixer, hand; Sunbeam Mixmaster, pink, ca 1957, MIB	$65.00

Mixer, Kitchen Aid, Hobart Mfg, w/several attachments & 2 bowls, 1950s, 17x10x14" **$165.00**

Mixer, Manning-Bowman, Bakelite handle, heavy base w/rusty patina, 4-speed, working..........................**$50.00**

Mixer, Myers Bullet, chrome & green enamel, 2-speed motor, very heavy, EX..**$85.00**

Mixer, Sunbeam Mixmaster, white w/2 white bowls & juicer attachment, NM..**$40.00**

Mixer, Sunbeam Mixmaster Jr, copper, EX..................**$95.00**

Mixer, Sunbeam Stand Mixmaster #13C, 12-speed, copyright 1957, EX...**$35.00**

Mixer, Vidrio, cobalt glass base, from $125 to **$135.00**

Mixer, Vidrio, custard slag base, from $60 to.............**$70.00**

Percolator, chrome w/red Bakelite handle, engraved scrolling, complete w/creamer, sugar bowl & tray................**$45.00**

Percolator, Labelle, chrome ball shape w/flared foot, ca 1950s, EX..**$35.00**

Percolator, Mirro-Matic, black Bakelite top & handles, late 1950s, 8-cup, EX **$35.00**

Percolator, Sunbeam AP20, chrome w/black Bakelite handles, EX..**$30.00**

Popcorn popper, Dominion Electric Corp #1702, 400 watts, w/Fire-King sapphire lid (Philbe pattern), VG **$20.00**

Popcorn popper, Joe Namath, 4-qt, MIB **$24.00**

Popcorn Popper, Jolly Time, hand-rotating crank w/wooden knob, black-painted metal body w/wooden legs, 1940s-50s, EX...**$20.00**

Popcorn popper, Knapp Monarch Redi-Pop Automatic, aluminum, 6½", NM...**$22.00**

Popcorn popper, metal body w/Fire-King glass lid, black handle & feet, from $35 to...................................**$40.00**

Toaster, General Electric 139T82, chrome w/black Bakelite handles, 1940s-50s, EX **$40.00**

Toaster, Son Chief Speed-O-Matic, 2-slot, 4 plastic legs, white cord, EX..**$40.00**

Toaster, Sunbeam T-1-C, $75.00. (Photo courtesy Jim Barker)

Toaster, Sunbeam T-1-D, 2-slot, light & dark control, 2-prong plug, EX...**$55.00**

Toaster, Sunbeam T-20B, chrome, 2-slot, light & dark control, dated 1955 inside, EX..**$50.00**

Toaster, Toastmaster 1A5, bright chrome w/spear-like designs, dark brown plastic base, 7½x10¾x3½" .**$35.00**

Toaster, Westinghouse Turnover #231570, sides drop down, porcelain plug, Bakelite handles, 7x6x5"............**$42.50**

Toaster/oven, General Electric, chrome w/Bakelite knobs & handles, sliding tray in bottom, 9¼x12x8¾" **$45.00**

Miscellaneous Gadgets and Glassware

Apple parer/corer/slicer, White Mountain, green-painted cast iron w/red wood handle, NMIB......................**$15.00**

Apple peeler, Sinclair, cast iron, heart design on wheels, 10½x6¾" **$25.00**

Baker, sapphire blue ovenware, Anchor Hocking, round or sq, 1-pt, from $6 to...**$8.00**

Bean slicer, Alcoa, aluminum, spring loaded, 6".........**$12.50**

Beater, crank type w/green-painted wood handle, ultramarine bowl base, from $55 to **$60.00**

Beater, Ladd, green or pink glass base, complete, from $60 to..**$65.00**

Bowl, batter; green diamond-like shape in random pattern on milk glass, Federal, from $40 to.....................**$50.00**

Bowl, batter; yellow glass, stick handle, US Glass, from $35 to..**$40.00**

Bowl, mixing; Crisscross, Hazel-Atlas, 9⅝", from $25 to..**$28.00**

Bowl, mixing; Hex Optic, pink, Jeannette, flat rim, 9", from $25 to..**$30.00**

Bowl, mixing; milk glass, McKee, 9", from $25 to......**$28.00**

Bowl, mixing; Modern Tulip on milk glass, 1-qt, from $20 to..**$25.00**

Bowl, mixing; Ships, red on milk glass, 9", from $27.50 to..**$30.00**

Bowl, mixing; Swedish Modern, turquoise blue opaque glass, 3-qt, 8⅜", from $55 to **$60.00**

Bread box, Ampeco, painted tin w/Bread in blue on front, snap-on tin lid, 9½x13", VG **$25.00**

Bread box, Kromex, cutting board on door & removable shelf, 9½x11¼x16½"...**$50.00**

Bread box, Kromex, spun aluminum, 9½x17x11", EX..**$70.00**

Bread box, red & white painted metal, vertical (scarce), 1950s, 11x5" sq, EX **$55.00**

Bread box, roses & checkerboard pattern on tin, 10x17x10½", EX **$35.00**

Bread/cake box, Home Comfort, 13½x11x20", VG **$55.00**

Cake saver, Kromex w/black Bakelite on lid, glass underplate, in original box **$40.00**

Cake spatula/knife, all Bakelite, marbled yellow blade, brown 2-pc handle, EX **$30.00**

Can opener, Dazey Kwik-Kut Jr, single action, ca 1955, M in G- box **$12.00**

Can opener, Dazey Senior Model 60, chrome w/red handle, MIB **$22.50**

Can opener, red Bakelite, Best Co NYC USA, red handle & turner **$40.00**

Can opener, Rival Can-O-Matic Deluxe, chrome, w/removable cutter, MIB..**$15.00**

Can opener, Wear-ever, aluminum, hand-held pliers style, EX **$17.50**

Canister, caramel glass, 40-oz, from $75 to **$85.00**

Canister, Cereal in black letters on milk glass, McKee, sq, 48-oz, from $125 to **$135.00**

Canister, Delphite Blue, sq, 29-oz, 5", from $275 to.**$295.00**

Canister, Dutch decal on clear, sq, Hocking, from $20 to..**$22.50**

Canister, tea; fired-on green, metal lid, Hocking, from $25 to **$30.00**

Carving set, Community Silver, O monogram on handle, 16" knife, 12" fork, EX **$15.00**

Chopper, clear base, metal top, wood knob on handle w/up & down chopping action, from $18 to **$20.00**

Chopper, Handy Lightning Mincer Chicken & Noodler Cutter, 8", MIB **$30.00**

Chopper, nut; Hazel Atlas, glass w/tin top, red wooden knob on crank handle, 6¼" **$12.00**

Chopper/grinder, cast iron, hand-crank, top feed, 4 feet can be bolted down, unmarked, EX **$20.00**

Chopper/grinder, Rival Grind-O Mat #303, 1978, MIB w/instructions & recipe booklet **$15.00**

Chopper/grinder, Sunbeam, attachment for Mixmaster, ca 1950, NMIB..**$20.00**

Chopper/grinder, Universal #3, cast iron, clamps to table, 10½" **$25.00**

Cleaver/chopper, Foster Bros, 12" overall **$20.00**

Clock/timer, Intermatic A401, electric, 1950s, EX.......**$14.00**

Clock/timer, Telechron, electric, hangs on wall, 7" dia, EX **$25.00**

Cocktail shaker, Kromex w/clear set-off knobs, w/original label, 11x3½"..**$30.00**

Coffeepot, clear glass w/multicolor enameled rings, Glasbake, from $35 to **$40.00**

Cruet, amber glass, Farberware, from $25 to **$28.00**

Dripolator, clear glass w/blue bands, matching creamer & sugar bowl, from $45 to................................**$50.00**

Dripolator, Silex, clear glass w/embossed panels, from $50 to..**$60.00**

Egg beater, AJ Made in America, metal w/mixing bowl, 8½x5¼" dia **$25.00**

Egg beater, Best, all metal, EX................................**$15.00**

Egg beater, Big Bingo #71 Pat Apl'd For, ceramic base, EX **$12.00**

Egg beater, Edlund, tin, crank handle w/green wood knob, EX..**$18.00**

Egg beater, Genuine Dover The Other Stamping Co, red wooden handle, 11½", EX **$27.50**

Egg beater, Maynard Deluxe Master Mixer, red Bakelite handles, nylon blades, bearings & gears, 1955, MIB....**$40.00**

Egg beater, stainless steel blades, red Bakelite handles, 10" **$35.00**

Egg beater, tin w/yellow Bakelite handles, 12"..........**$20.00**

Egg beater, wire & tin, hand-crank, unmarked, 10½"...**$37.50**

Egg beater, Worlbeater, tin w/red Bakelite handle **$17.50**

Egg beater/mixer, glass bowl w/red metal lid & red wooden turning handle, 5" **$55.00**

Fork, meat; bone handle, 10½" **$15.00**

Funnel, pressed glass, lg mouth, 2¾x4¼" **$12.50**

Funnel, ribbed or plain green glass, 4½", from $35 to.**$40.00**

Ice pick, Broitzman's Milk & Cream embossed on metal side..**$15.00**

Ice pick, cast steel w/green wooden handle................**$6.50**

Ice pick, Standard Home Supply Star...Malt Extract, cast steel, 8½"..**$12.00**

Jar wrench, Gunnard, 8" **$10.00**

Lemon squeezer, hammered aluminum, 9"..................**$8.00**

Lemon squeezer, Vaughan Lemon & Lime, stainless steel, EX..**$6.50**

Measuring cup, crystal, Glasbake, 1-cup, from $20 to..**$25.00**

Measuring cup, fired-on green, 2-cup, from $25 to....**$30.00**

Measuring cup, Fluffo, Be Sure of Success..., clear glass, 1-cup, from $30 to **$35.00**

Measuring cup, Kellogg's, clear glass, rectangular, 1-cup, from $30 to **$38.00**

Measuring cup, McKee Glasbake Scientific, 1-cup, from $20 to..**$25.00**

Measuring pitcher, blue dots on milk glass, Hazel Atlas, 2-cup, from $40 to **$45.00**

Measuring pitcher, custard, McKee, 4-cup, from $50 to..**$55.00**

Measuring pitcher, green glass, Hocking, 2-cup, from $40 to..**$45.00**

Measuring pitcher, yellow opaque, McKee, 2-cup, from $130 to..**$140.00**

Pan, egg poacher; Mar-Crest, aluminum, 3 cups, black handle, 7½" dia **$10.00**

Pan, egg poacher; Mirro, aluminum, 4 cups, Bakelite handle, 8" dia, EX **$12.50**

Pea sheller, heavy cast aluminum w/rubber rollers, hand crank, 6x9¼", EX **$12.50**

Pea sheller, Lee's Green Pea Sheller, M in torn box w/instructions **$7.50**

Potato masher, Androck, red Bakelite handle **$10.00**

Potato masher, twisted wire & green wood handle, 16" (6" handle), NM **$20.00**

Potato masher/ricer, Foley Mfg, green wood handle, 6x6½" dia **$15.00**

Pretzel jar, pink, Hocking, from $125 to....................**$150.00**

Recipe box, Ransburg, Kitchen Bouquet, painted tin, EX.**$27.50**

Recipe box, Stylecraft, multicolor designs on bright red painted metal, 3½x3¼x5¼", EX................................**$20.00**

Refrigerator dish, Jennyware, ultramarine, round, 70-oz, from $75 to **$85.00**

Refrigerator dish, Tufglass, green, 5⅞" sq, from $25 to..**$27.50**

Rolling pin, clambroth, screw-on handles **$125.00**

Rolling pin, Krispy Krust, MIB....................................**$55.00**

Rolling pin, milk glass, wooden handles, 17½" **$50.00**

Rolling pin, wood w/green metal handles, 15½"..........**$17.50**

Rolling pin, wooden, red painted handles **$25.00**

Salad fork & spoon, clear pressed glass, 9¾", pr........**$14.00**

Salad fork & spoon, crystal w/blue handle, pr, from $70 to..**$75.00**

Salt & pepper shakers, dots on milk glass, metal lids, pr, from $35 to..**$40.00**

Salt & pepper shakers, Dutch skaters, red on milk glass, metal tops, Hazel Atlas, pr, from $30 to **$35.00**

Salt & pepper shakers, fired-on color, sq, Hocking, pr, from $30 to.....................**$35.00**

Salt & pepper shakers, forest green glass w/metal top, teardrop shape, sm, pr, from $20 to.....................**$30.00**

Salt & pepper shakers, lettering on black glass, 4½", pr, (deduct up to 50% for wear), from $55 to **$65.00**

Shaker, white, sq, McKee, 16-oz.....................**$45.00**

Sifter, Androck, 3-screen, painted tin (lady in kitchen), red handle, 5½", NM, from $40 to **$50.00**

Sifter, Androck Hand-i-Sift, painted tin (flowers), yellow handle, 5½x5", EX **$35.00**

Sifter, Bromwell's Measuring...Guaranteed, tin, 3-cup, M..**$25.00**

Sifter, Good Housekeeping, 2 green stripes on tin, EX.**$15.00**

Sifter, Nesco, aluminum, wood handle, handle connected to long tube that operates 3 arms that do sifting, NM.**$14.00**

Sifter, painted tin (blue & white flowers), crank handle w/blue wooden knob, 6¼x5" dia, NM **$35.00**

Spatula, Daisy, Schacht Rubber Mfg, green wooden handle, 9¾".....................**$10.00**

Spatula, S&H Green Stamps embossed on handle, all metal, 11", EX **$15.00**

Spatula, Swan's Down Cake Flour, 12¼", EX...............**$7.50**

Spoon, Rumford, used for mixing, beating & whipping, EX.....................**$8.00**

Sugar shaker, Kromex w/black cap marked Sugar, 5"..**$35.00**

Sugar shaker, red dots on custard, McKee, from $35 to..**$40.00**

Teakettle, white opaque glass w/metal whistle top, Glasbake, from $45 to.....................**$50.00**

Tidbit tray, Emerald-Glo, 2-tier, from $45 to **$50.00**

Timer, Hotpoint, aluminum w/black Bakelite setting lever, 4½x3¼".....................**$18.00**

Timer, Lux Maid of Honor, white w/blue numbers on metal, EX.....................**$18.00**

Timer, Mirro, aluminum, Robertshaw Controls Inc, EX, from $18 to.....................**$25.00**

Timer, Sessions, Fink Roselieve Co, metal, Deco styling, wall hanging, 4x4½", VG **$12.00**

Utensil, Formay Helper, metal, 10x3¼", EX.................**$12.50**

Utensil set, Lifetime Stainless Steel w/Bakelite handles, wooden holder, 13" knife, 11" fork, 12" skewer, NMIB **$15.00**

Warming dish, green transparent, with two inserts, $100.00. (Photo courtesy Gene Florence)

Wax paper holder, Kromex w/black Bakelite sides, 8½x14".....................**$45.00**

Whip, Artbeck, metal w/plastic push-down handle, M in original cardboard tube.....................**$10.00**

Whip, Fries, tin, 10½x8½".....................**$30.00**

Whisk, twisted wire, resembles snowshoe, EX **$3.50**

Whisk, wire, red wood handle, EX **$7.50**

Kitchen Prayer Ladies

The Enesco importing company of Elk Grove, Illinois, distributed a line of kitchen novelties during the 1960s that they originally called 'Mother in the Kitchen.' Today's collectors refer to them as 'Kitchen Prayer Ladies.' The line was fairly extensive — some pieces are common, others are very scarce. All are designed around the figure of 'Mother' who is wearing a long white apron inscribed with a prayer. She is more commonly found in a pink dress. Blue is harder to find and more valuable. Where we've given ranges, pink is represented by the lower end, blue by the higher. If you find her in a white dress with blue trim, add another 10% to 20%. For a complete listing and current values, you'll want to order *Prayer Lady Plus+* by April and Larry Tvorak. This line is pictured in *The Collector's Encyclopedia of Cookie Jars, Volumes 1* and *2*, by Joyce and Fred Roerig (Collector Books).

Advisor: April Tvorak (See Directory, Kitchen Prayer Ladies)

Air freshener **$150.00**

Bank, Mother's Pin Money, 5½", from $175 to **$250.00**

Bell, from $75 to.....................**$100.00**

Candle holders, pr.....................**$200.00**

Canister, pink, ea.....................**$300.00**

Canister set, pk, complete, from $1,200 to.............**$1,500.00**

Cookie jar, blue.....................**$495.00**

Cookie jar, pink.....................**$395.00**

Crumb tray or brush, from $125 to.....................**$200.00**

Egg timer, from $100 to **$135.00**

Instant coffee jar, spoon-holder loop on side **$150.00**

Mug.....................**$125.00**

Napkin holder, pink, from $25 to.....................**$30.00**

Picture frame, minimum value **$175.00**

Planter.....................**$75.00**

Plaque, full-figure **$100.00**

Ring holder.....................**$50.00**

Salt & pepper shakers, pr, from $15 to.....................**$22.00**

Soap dish, from $35 to.....................**$50.00**

Spoon holder, upright, from $65 to.....................**$75.00**

Sprinkler bottle, blue, minimum value **$600.00**

Sprinkler bottle, pink, minimum value **$500.00**

String holder, from $135 to.....................**$145.00**

String holder, wall mount, from $135 to.....................**$145.00**

Sugar bowl, w/spoon **$60.00**

Tea set, pot, sugar & creamer.....................**$300.00**

Toothpick holder, 4½", from $20 to.....................**$24.00**

Vase, bud; pink, from $100 to **$125.00**

Kreiss & Co.

Collectors are hot on the trail of figural ceramics, and one of the newest areas of interest are those figurines, napkin dolls, planters, mugs, etc., imported from Japan during the 1950s by the Kreiss company, located in California. Though much of their early production was run of the mill, in the late 1950s, the company introduced unique new lines — all bizarre, off the wall, politically incorrect, and very irreverent — and today it's these items that are attracting so much attention. There are several lines. One is a totally zany group of caricatures called Psycho-Ceramics. There's a Beatnick series, Nudies, and Elegant Heirs (all of which are strange little creatures), as well as some that are very well done and tasteful. Several will be inset with with colored 'jewels.' Many are marked either with an ink stamp or an in-mold trademark (some are dated), so you'll need to start turning likely-looking items over to check for the Kreiss name.

There's a very helpful book now on the market, called *Kreiss Novelty Ceramics*, written by and available from our advisors, Michele and Mike King.

See also Napkin Ladies.

Advisors: Michele and Mike King (See Directory, Kreiss; Psycho Ceramics)

Beatniks

Figure, man in blue, Work? Man I Deny Its Existence, 7" $75.00
Figure, short man in white coat w/blue stripes, sm blue hat, Like Man, Lend Me Your Ears, 5¼" $50.00
Figure, uppity man w/legs crossed, Dat Whatever It Is, I'm Against It, 4¾" (5½" on base)..............................$75.00
Figure, woman w/long stringy fibre hair, hands on hips, 6¾" $65.00

Christmas Psycho Ceramics

Ashtray, white w/Psycho Santa, Who Do I Look Like, Rin Tin Tin?, sq, 5½x5½"......................................$50.00
Figure, drunk man in black suit w/big red nose leaning against lamppost, Rudolph the Red Nose Reindeer, 5½"..$90.00
Figure, man dressed as Santa, It Was the Night Before Happyville, 6½" $75.00
Figure, man in party hat, kisses all over face, But Honey, It Was Just an Innocent Office Christmas Party, 5"..$75.00
Figure, pink creature w/Christmas tree on head, Somebody Stole the Tree, Dear, 6¼" $125.00
Figure, Psycho Santa leaning & waving, 5" $75.00
Figure, Psycho Santa stuck in chimney, 6¾"..............$75.00
Figure, screaming lady w/yellow hair, green dress, wearing party hat, Who Did the Mistletoe?, 5¼" $75.00
Figure, yellow cop w/red hat, green club, Okay, Which One of You Guys Parked Your Reindeer by the Red Curb?, 4½"..$100.00

Elegant Heirs

Figure, bum holding up drink, Man of Distinction, Hell, It's All I Could Afford, 7"..................................$60.00
Figure, bum w/cane & cigar, I May Look Busy, But I'm Only Confused, 7¼"..$75.00
Figure, convict w/ball & chain, On Vacation, 6¼"......$60.00
Figure, hairy woman in red dress & white apron, 5½".$50.00
Figure, man in yellow shirt & blue pants shaving his tongue, 6¼" $75.00
Figure, school boy wearing beanie, 6" $50.00

Moon Beings

Figure, brown long-necked creature, white hair, 4¾".$175.00
Figure, pink bird-like creature, 4¾"..........................$175.00
Figure, tan spotted bird-like creature, 4½"................$175.00

The Nudies

Figure, in plaid vest, cigar butt in mouth, 6½".........$100.00
Mug, black-haired creature w/hands at side, 4 ears, 4¼"..$100.00

Psycho Ceramics

Ashtray, blue distressed character holds pink ash bowl, 5", $100.00.
(Photo courtesy Michele and Mike King)

Ashtray, purple creature w/yellow hair, fingers in mouth, I Have a Nervous Cigarette Habit, 4¾" $110.00
Ashtray, yellow creature w/axe in head, Turn in Your Ulcer, Your Fired, 5"..$200.00
Ashtray, 1 maroon & 1 yellow figure holds ashtray, 2¾x6"..$125.00
Figure, angry creatures face-to-face, 1 blue & 1 yellow, 3"..$125.00
Figure, blue creature w/yellow hair & yellow ear plugs, My Mind's Made Up, Don't Confuse Me With Facts, 4¾"..........$225.00
Figure, blue wide-eyed creature, Looking for Someone With a Little Authority, I Have as Little as Anyone, 4¾".....$75.00
Figure, man in blue suit w/big teeth, Who Needs Experience, I'm a College Graduate, 4¾"..............................$75.00

Figure, pink, woebegone, I May Look Busy, But I'm Only Confused, 5"..$100.00

Figure, purple creature w/fingers in mouth, Whenever I Think, I Make Mistakes, 5"....................................$90.00

Figure, white Martian w/pink bull's-eye on belly, black ears & pink features, 3½x6"....................................$300.00

Figure, yellow w/big nose, I'm the Brains of This Outfit, 5"...$75.00

Figurine, yellow guy w/Devil biting his ear, I Can Resist Anything But Temptation, from $125 to...............$135.00

Pencil holder, yellow, woebegone, w/9 holes in head, Nobody Is Perfect, 4¾" $75.00

Miscellaneous

Crazy Creature, blue dragon-like creature w/yellow stripes..$175.00

Good Time Charlie, leaning against pink elephant w/sm pink elephant on hat, It Don't Pay if You Don't Play, 4½" $100.00

Good Time Charlie, riding pink elephant w/sm pink elephant in his back, A Little Fun Don't Hurt No One, 5¾" $100.00

Green-eyed monster, green dinosaur w/2 cave kids, cave kids 1½", dinosaur 6¾" $125.00

Green-eyed monsters, cave family, 2 adults, 4¾", 2 kids, 2½" $100.00

Space man and woman, red suits, clear plastic helmets, 6", $200.00 for the pair.

Lamps

Aladdin lamps have been made continually since 1908 by the Mantle Lamp Company of America, now Aladdin Mantle Lamp Company in Clarksville, Tennessee. Their famous kerosene lamps are highly collectible, and some are quite valuable. Many were relegated to the storage shelf or thrown away after electric lines came through the country. Today many people keep them on hand for emergency light.

Few know that Aladdin Industries, Inc. was one of the largest manufacturers of electric lamps from 1930 to 1956. They created new designs, colorful glass, and unique paper shades. These are not only collectible but are still used in many homes today. Many Aladdin lamps, kerosene as well as electric, can be found at garage sales, antique shops, and flea markets. You can learn more about them in the books *Aladdin Electric Lamps* and *Aladdin — The Magic Name in Lamps, Revised Edition,* written by J.W. Courter, who also periodically issues updated price guides for both kerosene and electric Aladdins.

Advisor: J.W. Courter (See Directory, Lamps)

Newsletter: *Mystic Lights of the Aladdin Knights*
J.W. Courter
3935 Kelley Rd., Kevil, KY 42053. Subscription: $25 (6 issues, postpaid 1st class) per year with current buy-sell-trade information. Send SASE for information about other publications.

Aladdin Electric Lamps

Bed lamp, #909 SS, Whip-o-lite fluted shade, EX, from $100 to...$125.00

Bed lamp, B-45, Whip-o-lite shade, EX, from $75 to .$100.00

Bedroom lamp, P-64, ceramic base, '50s Modern styling, 18", EX, from $25 to..$35.00

Bedroom lamp, P-70, metal & ceramic, EX, from $20 to......$30.00

Boudoir lamp, G-17, Opalique, Alacite, EX, from $100 to .$125.00

Figurine lamp, G-24, Cupid, short base, EX, from $200 to $250.00

Figurine lamp, M-123, lady, metal, EX, from $175 to ..$225.00

Magic Touch, MT-507, ceramic base, EX, from $300 to..$350.00

Pin-up lamp, M-350, cast white metal, plated, EX, from $50 to $70.00

Pin-up lamp, P-57, gun-'n-holster, ceramic, EX, from $125 to $150.00

Planter lamp, P-408, ceramic, EX, from $75 to $100.00

Table lamp, G-U, brass & marble, EX, from $75 to..$100.00

Table lamp, G-179, Opalique, EX, from $100 to.......$125.00

Table lamp, G-2, marble-like glass, EX, from $300 to ..$350.00

Table lamp, G-215, blue crystal bowl, EX, from $225 to ..$275.00

Table lamp, G-223, Alacite, EX, from $75 to.............$100.00

Table lamp, G-263A, Alacite, illuminated base, EX, from $50 to $60.00

Table lamp, G-345R, Alacite Pineapple, recipe lamp, EX, from $60 to..$70.00

Table lamp, M-367, iron base, spun glass shade, EX, from $20 to $30.00

Table lamp, M-49, brass metal, EX, from $25 to $35.00

Table lamp, M-93, w/Whip-o-lite shade, EX, from $175 to $225.00

Table lamp, MM-7, metal & moonstone, EX, from $200 to $250.00

Table lamp, P-470, ceramic, EX, from $30 to.............$50.00

TV lamp, TV-386, planter base, ceramic, EX, from $80 to $100.00

TV lamp, TV-426, metal w/foil shade, EX, from $20 to ..**$25.00**

Aladdin Kerosene Mantle Lamps

Caboose lamp, Model B-400, brass font, w/burner & good white shade, from $150 to **$200.00**

Floor lamp, Model #12, Verde Antique, #1253, EX, from $175 to..**$275.00**

Floor lamp, Model B, satin gold, B-298, EX, from $250 to **$325.00**

Hanging lamp, Model 23, brass w/glass shade, several types, EX, ea from $60 to **$100.00**

Shelf lamp, Model 23, Lincoln Drape, clear, w/burner, EX, from $90 to..**$100.00**

Table lamp, Model #12, Crystal Vase, variegated tan, 12", EX, from $200 to............................**$250.00**

Table lamp, Model A, Venetian, rose, EX, from $175 to ..**$275.00**

Table lamp, Model B, Corinthian, B-101, amber crystal, white metal connector, EX, from $100 to......................**$150.00**

Table lamp, Model B, Quilt, B-85, white moonstone, EX, from $300 to..**$350.00**

Table lamp, Model B, Simplicity, B-30, white, EX, from $125 to..**$175.00**

Table lamp, Short Lincoln Drape, B-60, Alacite, EX, from $500 to..**$600.00**

Wall bracket lamp, Model #6, complete w/font, correct burner, flame spreader & 2 part bracket, no shade, from $150 to..**$200.00**

Figural Lamps

Many of the figural lamps on the market today are from the '30s, '40s, and '50s. You'll often see them modeled as matching pairs, made primarily for use in the boudoir or the nursery. They were sometimes made of glass, but most were ceramic, so unless another material is mentioned in our descriptions, assume that all our figural lamps are ceramic. Several examples are shown in *Collector's Guide to Made in Japan Ceramics, Books I, II,* and *II,* by Carole Bess White (Collector Books).

See also Occupied Japan.

Advisor: Dee Boston (See Directory, Lamps)

Ballerina holding flower garland, marked Germany & Schneider #17282, 6½" **$135.00**

Birds on stump form base of lamp, blue & multicolor lustre, Japan mark, 5½", from $65 to **$95.00**

Chamberstick (candle light bulb), tan lustre w/multicolor florals, red Japan mark w/Nippon...Granted, 5½", from $25 to........**$40.00**

Clown (frowning child w/mandolin) stands on 8" base, marked Germany, 5½" **$135.00**

Colonial couple stand at base, multicolor details on white, black Japan mark, ca 1935, 7½", pr, from $55 to.**$85.00**

Colonial couple stand at base, white w/hand-painted details, flower decals, black Japan mark, 6¼", pr, from $50 to..**$75.00**

Colonial girl seated in white chair holds Pekingese puppy, marked Germany, 5½" **$145.00**

Dancing girl with tambourine to head, #2923II, 7", $175.00. (Photo courtesy Dee Boston)

Flapper in blue harem outfit w/yellow trim & black hair, unmarked, 6¾" **$125.00**

Girl holding skirt out, bright multicolor w/gold-trimmed base, marked Germany #89, 5½" **$145.00**

Girl w/book, boy w/mandolin (double figure), lustre finish, marked Schneider & Germany #16760, 7".........**$185.00**

Lady holding grape cluster & chalice, little detail, simple attire, marked Germany #6028, 6", pr................**$160.00**

Owl on base (2 pcs), blue & multicolor lustre, black Japan mark, 5½", from $60 to **$95.00**

Pierrot & lady in short dress stand at base, black Japan mark, 7", from $25 to **$45.00**

Scottie dog sits at base, shiny white w/glass eyes, black Japan mark, 6¾", from $50 to **$75.00**

Motion Lamps

Though some were made as early as 1920 and as late as the 1970s, motion lamps were most popular during the 1950s. Most are cylindrical with scenes such as waterfalls and forest fires and attain a sense of motion through the action of an inner cylinder that rotates with the heat of the bulb. Prices below are for lamps with original parts in good condition with no cracks, splits, dents, or holes. Any damage greatly decreases the value. As a rule of thumb, the oval lamps are worth a little more than their round counterparts. **Caution** — some lamps are being reproduced. Currently in production are Antique Autos, Trains, Old Mill, Ships in a Storm, Fish, and three psychedelic lamps. The color on the scenic lamps is much bluer, and they are in a plastic stand with a plastic top. There are quite a few small motion lamps in production that are not copies of the 1950s lamps. For further information we recommend *Collector's Guide to Motion Lamps* (Collector Books), which contains full-page color photographs and useful information.

Advisors: Jim and Kaye Whitaker (See Directory, Lamps)

Aquarium, Scene in Action #50, 1931, from $360 to...**$390.00**
Bicycles, Econolite, 1959, 11" **$125.00**
Birches, LA Goodman, 1956, from $200 to **$220.00**
Boy & Girl Scout, Rotovue Jr, 1950, 10" **$150.00**
Butterflies, Econolite, 1954, 11" **$85.00**
Church in snow scene, Econolite, 1957, 11" **$110.00**
Dance at Dawn, Rev-o-Lite #201, 1930s, from $160 to ..**$200.00**
Disneyland Express, Econolite, 1955, 11" **$175.00**
Elvgrin Pinup Girls **$350.00**
Forest Fire, LA Goodman, 1956, 11" **$65.00**
Fresh Water Fish, Econolite, 1950s, 11"....................**$95.00**
Hawaiian Scene, Econolite, 1959, 11" **$75.00**
Indian maiden, Gritt Inc, 1920s, 11".........................**$90.00**
Jets, Econolite #774, 1958 ....**$300.00**
Merry Go Round, Rotovue Jr, 1949, 10".....................**$95.00**
Michelob Advertising Lamp, Christmas design, 13".....**$95.00**
Mill Stream, Econolite, 1956, 11", from $65 to **$95.00**
Mountain Waterfall (Campers), LA Goodman, 1956, 11"..**$55.00**
Niagara Falls, LA Goodman, 1957, 11".......................**$35.00**
Op Art Lamp, black plastic, Visual Effects Inc, 1970s, 13"...**$25.00**
Oriental Fantasy, LA Goodman, 1957 ....**$150.00**
Planets, LA Goodman, 1957, from $200 to................**$240.00**
Sailboats, LA Goodman, 1954, 14" **$110.00**

Seattle World's Fair, Econolite, $175.00.

Spirit of '76, Creative Light Products, 1973, 11"...........**$45.00**
Steamboats, Econolite, 1957, 11" **$110.00**
Story Book (Hey Diddle Diddle), LA Goodman, 1956,
    11"...**$80.00**
The Bar Is Open, Visual Effects, Op Art, 1970s, 13"...**$35.00**
Trains Racing, LA Goodman, 1957, 11".......................**$85.00**
Venice Grand Canal, Econolite, 1963, 11" **$125.00**
White Christmas, flat front, Econolite, 11" **$125.00**

TV Lamps

By the 1950s, TV was commonplace in just about every home in the country but still fresh enough to have our undivided attention. Families gathered around the set and for the rest of the evening delighted in being entertained by Ed Sullivan or stumped by the $64,000 Question. Pottery producers catered to this scenario by producing TV lamps by the score, and with the popularity of anything from the '50s being what it is today, suddenly these lamps are making an appearance at flea markets and co-ops everywhere.

See also Maddux of California; Morton Potteries, Royal Haeger.

Ballerina & swan, Lane, 16", minimum value **$100.00**
Ballet dancer (male), painted plaster, signed American
    Statuary Co, Fiberglas shade, from $85 to **$95.00**
Bird, black & white, on brown log planter, 11x13" **$65.00**
Blue jay pr on stonework base w/green leaves, naturalistic
    colors, bisque...**$75.00**
Boy on dolphin, allover gold paint, signed Lane & Co, Van
    Nuys CA, from $95 to **$105.00**
Cockatoo w/brass base & planter, marked D21855M, from
    $75 to..**$90.00**
Cornucopia, woven, green gloss, bulb inside, from
    $45 to..**$55.00**
Crane, white w/gold spatter, on deep planter base,
    16"...**$80.00**
Deer & fawn heads before Fiberglas shade, from $75
    to **$95.00**
Deer leaping over scrolling foliage (planter), green or brown,
    from $60 to...**$70.00**
Dove pr, white w/gold spatter, Royal Fleet CA, 10x13½" ..**$60.00**
Duck, brown w/foamy gray wing tops, stylized, wood
    base...**$95.00**
Gazelle (leaping) w/planter, dark green, from $70 to ..**$90.00**
Horse & carriage, metal w/glass insert, from $85 to...**$100.00**
Horse beside stump, Deco style w/curly mane & tail, green,
    brown or chartreuse, ea from $85 to **$100.00**
Horse standing on rocky ledge, white, 12½x9½" **$60.00**
Horses (pr) facing/rearing, leafy molding between, tan ..**$80.00**
Lady & swan, terra cotta or turquoise high gloss, Lane, 16",
    minimum value **$100.00**
Musicians (black-painted pot metal) stand between frosted
    glass globe, from $120 to...................................**$135.00**
Owl, naturalistic, spread wings, Morton Pottery, marked
    Kron, lg, from $75 to...**$85.00**
Panther, black on green base, before red Fiberglas shade,
    from $65 to..**$75.00**
Sampan w/Oriental ea end, white/multicolor, reticulated
    windows, from $65 to **$75.00**
Siamese cats, 1 sitting/1 recumbent, plump, Kron, from $75
    to...**$90.00**
Siamese mother w/kitten, Kron, 1950s, 13¾x8".........**$77.50**
Tower of Pisa, soapstone, light inside, windows light up,
    from $135 to...**$145.00**
Yorkie dog, recumbent, plaster, Rock-O-Stone, from $75
    to...**$85.00**

L.E. Smith

Originating just after the turn of the century, the L.E. Smith company continues to operate in Mt. Pleasant, Pennsylvania, at the present time. In the 1920s they introduced a line of black glass that they are famous for today. Some pieces were decorated with silver overlay or enameling. Using their own original molds, they made a line of bird and animal figures in crystal as well as in colors. The company is currently producing these figures, many in two sizes. They were one of the main producers of the popular Moon and Star pattern which has been featured in their catalogs since the 1960s in a variety of shapes and colors.

If you'd like to learn more about their bird and animal figures, *Glass Animals of the Depression Era* by Lee Garmon and Dick Spencer has a chapter devoted to those made by L.E. Smith. See also *A Collector's Guide to Modern American Slag Glass* by Ruth Grizel.

See also Eye Winker; Moon and Star.

Basket, banana; Pineapple, pink, 7x5"........................**$18.00**
Basket, Bird of Paradise, ruby, upright feathers form deeply scalloped rim, center handle, ca 1980, 13½"........**$40.00**
Basket, bride's; Hobnail, yellow, 7"............................**$15.00**
Basket, Cane & Daisy, ruby, center handle, 1997, 13"..**$40.00**
Basket, Dominion, ruby, diamond-pattern base, flaring panels w/rounded tops, 1997, 7" W............................**$25.00**
Basket, Heritage, ruby, 7½x12½"................................**$50.00**
Basket, Pineapple, blue carnival, 14½" W..................**$35.00**
Basket, Pineapple, ruby, 14½" W................................**$40.00**
Basket, ruby, prs of narrow leaves, embossed/textured, 1997, 5¾" W...**$25.00**
Bookend, Goose Girl, ruby, 1979, 8"..........................**$45.00**
Bookend, horse, Almond Nouveau slag, rearing, 8", ea from $50 to..**$60.00**
Bookend, horse, crystal, rearing.................................**$35.00**
Bookend, rooster, ruby, 1960, 9"................................**$75.00**
Bookend, thrush, ruby carnival, 1980, 9"....................**$30.00**
Bookends, horse, amber, rearing, 8x5½", from $55 to .**$70.00**
Bookends, horse, green, rearing, 8x5½", pr.............**$125.00**
Bowl, berry; Robin Blue, footed, 4"............................**$16.00**
Bowl, console; black, #1022/4, 3-footed, ca 1930s, 6"..**$30.00**
Bowl, console; black, 3-footed, ca 1930s, 9"..............**$45.00**
Bowl, Dolly, ruby carnival..**$38.00**
Bowl, nappy, heart shape, Almond Nouveau slag, 6" ..**$25.00**
Bowl, turkey, dark blue, footed, oval, 7"....................**$65.00**
Bowl, Wigwam, flared...**$30.00**
Box, piano shape, black, 1992, 6½"............................**$45.00**
Butter dish, Almond Nouveau slag, 1980 ....**$45.00**
Candle holder, Almond Nouveau slag, #4041a, 7½", ea ..**$25.00**
Candle holder, angel, kneeling, slag, ea......................**$25.00**
Candle holders, angel, kneeling, green, pr.................**$26.00**
Candlestick, wigwam, black, ca 1935, 3¼"..................**$20.00**
Candy dish, ruby, cone shape, paneled w/embossed designs, 1990, 2½"..**$12.00**
Canoe, Daisy & Button, purple carnival.....................**$25.00**
Covered dish, duck, black, 1992, 7"............................**$45.00**
Covered dish, hen on nest, #820a, Almond Nouveau slag, 6"..**$50.00**
Covered dish, hen on nest, ruby, miniature, 1990, 3¼" L..**$15.00**
Covered dish, rooster, standing, Almond Nouveau slag, 9", from $75 to...**$85.00**
Covered dish, rooster, standing, white carnival..........**$75.00**
Cup & saucer, Do Si Do, black, ca 1930s....................**$12.00**
Cup & saucer, Mt Pleasant, black, ca 1930s **$12.00**
Dresser set, Colonial, cologne bottle & powder jar, purple...**$50.00**
Egg plate, ruby, 1990, 10¾"...**$60.00**
Figurine, bear, Almond Nouveau slag, #6654A, 4½"...**$45.00**
Figurine, bear, baby, head turned or straight, crystal, 3", ea...**$60.00**
Figurine, bear, papa, crystal, 4x6½"..........................**$250.00**
Figurine, bird, flying, Almond Nouveau slag, 9", from $45 to..**$50.00**
Figurine, bird, head up or down, Almond Nouveau slag, 5", pr..**$65.00**
Figurine, camel, recumbent, amber, 4½x6"................**$60.00**
Figurine, camel, recumbent, cobalt, 4½x6"................**$95.00**
Figurine, camel, recumbent, crystal, 4½x6"................**$50.00**
Figurine, cock, fighting, blue, 9"................................**$55.00**
Figurine, elephant, crystal, 1¾"..................................**$20.00**
Figurine, Goose Girl, amber, 5½"...............................**$35.00**
Figurine, Goose Girl, crystal, original, 6"...................**$25.00**
Figurine, Goose Girl, flame, 6"...................................**$40.00**
Figurine, Goose Girl, ice green carnival, 6"................**$60.00**

Figurine, Goose Girl, ruby, 1979, 6", $35.00.

Figurine, horse, recumbent, amberina, 9" L **$150.00**
Figurine, horse, recumbent, blue, 9" L......................**$115.00**
Figurine, horse, recumbent, green, 9" L....................**$100.00**
Figurine, lamb, black, marked C in circle, ca 1930s, 2¼" L **$18.00**
Figurine, Madonna praying, crystal............................**$35.00**
Figurine, rabbit, crystal, miniature.............................**$10.00**
Figurine, rooster, butterscotch slag, limited edition, #208...**$85.00**
Figurine, swan, Almond Nouveau slag, 5"..................**$55.00**
Figurine, swan, crystal lustre, limited edition, w/certificate, lg...**$55.00**
Figurine, swan, ice pink carnival, 2"...........................**$15.00**
Figurine, swan, milk glass w/decoration, 8½"............**$45.00**
Figurine, swan, open back, Almond Nouveau slag, #15a, 4½"..**$20.00**

Figurine, swan, open back, Almond Nouveau slag, #650, 9" **$45.00**

Figurine, thrush, blue frost.................................**$20.00**

Figurine, unicorn, pink, miniature.......................**$20.00**

Flowerpot, black, plain, ca 1930s, 3½" **$12.00**

Flowerpot & saucer, black, finely ribbed sides, ca 1930s, 5½"...**$35.00**

Lamp, candle; black base w/frosted ribbed shade, 1992, 7½"...**$35.00**

Lamp, fairy; turtle figural, green **$25.00**

Lamp, hurricane; black, low base w/clear chimey, 1992, 12"...**$35.00**

Lamp, hurricane; black, low base w/clear chimey, 9"..**$30.00**

Nappy, heart shape, #4630a, Almond Nouveau slag, 6"..**$25.00**

Novelty, boot on pedestal, green or amber, ea...........**$12.00**

Novelty, coal bucket, Almond Nouveau slag, #125a, 5".**$25.00**

Novelty, shoe skate, ice blue, limited edition, 4"........**$25.00**

Novelty, slipper, Daisy & Button, Almond Nouveau slag, 6" **$35.00**

Novelty, slipper, Daisy & Button, amber **$8.00**

Novelty, slipper, Daisy & Button, purple carnival.......**$25.00**

Nut dish, Mt Pleasant, black, #505, 8" dia **$25.00**

Paperweight, hexagon shape, black, 1992, 3" **$20.00**

Paperweight, oval, black, 1992, 5" **$20.00**

Paperweight, star shape, black, 1992, 5" **$23.00**

Pitcher, water; Heritage, ruby carnival......................**$40.00**

Pitcher, water; Hobstar, ice green, w/6 tumblers......**$125.00**

Pitcher, water; Tiara Eclipse, green **$70.00**

Plate, Abraham Lincoln, purple carnival, #706/1195, 9"...**$40.00**

Plate, George Washington Bicentennial, black, 1932, 8"..**$85.00**

Plate, Herald, Christmas 1972, purple carnival, lg **$40.00**

Plate, Jefferson Davis, 1972, purple carnival, lg..........**$40.00**

Plate, Mt Pleasant, black, ca 1930s, 8" **$12.00**

Plate, Robert E Lee, 1972, purple carnival, lg **$40.00**

Plate, Silver Dollar Eagle, 1972, purple carnival, lg....**$40.00**

Sandwich tray, black, shield-shape open center handle, ca 1930s, 10" dia **$40.00**

Soap dish, swan, clear, 8½" **$22.50**

Sugar bowl, Homestead, pink.......................................**$8.00**

Table set, Mt Pleasant, black, creamer & open sugar bowl, salt & pepper shakers & tray, ca 1930s, 5-pc.....**$170.00**

Toothpick holder, Daisy & Button, amberina..............**$12.50**

Tray, black, center open heart-shape handle, low gallery rim, ca 1930s, 6" dia **$15.00**

Tray, sandwich; Mt Pleasant, black, ca 1930s, 13½" dia.**$85.00**

Tumbler, Bull's Eye, ruby carnival..............................**$22.00**

Urn, black, 2 handles, footed, 8"..................................**$20.00**

Vase, bud; Almond Nouveau slag, #33a, 6½"..............**$35.00**

Vase, corn, crystal lustre, very lg................................**$37.00**

Votive, owl's head, Almond Nouveau slag, #668a, 2".**$25.00**

Lefton China

China, porcelain, and ceramic items with that now familiar mark, Lefton, have been around since the early 1940s and are highly sought after by collectors in the secondary market-

place today. The company was founded by Mr. George Zoltan Lefton, an immigrant from Hungary. In the 1930s he was a designer and manufacturer of sportswear, but eventually his hobby of collecting fine china and porcelain led him to initiate his own ceramic business. When the bombing of Pearl Harbor occurred on December 7, 1941, Mr. Lefton came to the aid of a Japanese-American friend and helped him protect his property from anti-Japanese groups. Later, Mr. Lefton was introduced to a Japanese factory owned by Kowa Koki KK. He contracted with them to produce ceramic items to his specifications, and until 1980 they made thousands of pieces that were marketed by the Lefton company, marked with the initials KW preceding the item number. Figurines and animals plus many of the whimsical pieces such as Bluebirds, Dainty Miss, Miss Priss, Cabbage Cutie, Elf Head, Mr. Toodles, and Dutch Girl are eagerly collected today. As with any antique or collectible, prices vary depending on location, condition, and availability. For the history of Lefton China, information about Lefton factories, marks, and other identification methods, we highly recommend the *Collector's Encyclopedia of Lefton China, Volumes I, II, III,* and *Lefton Price Guide* by our advisor Loretta DeLozier (Collector Books).

See also Birthday Angels; Cookie Jars.

Advisor: Loretta DeLozier (See Directory, Lefton)

Club: National Society of Lefton Collectors

Newsletter: *The Lefton Collector*
c/o Loretta DeLozier
PO Box 50201
Knoxville, TN 37950-0201; Dues: $25 per year (includes quarterly newsletter)

Ashtray, hand w/applied roses & sponged gold, #40452, from $55 to..**$65.00**

Ashtray, painted roses, 2 rests, gold trim, #132, 7", from $28 to...**$32.00**

Bank, Kewpie, thoughtful pose, #145, 6¾", from $65 to..**$75.00**

Bank, pink elephant sits w/trunk raised, blue stone eyes, #2429, 7", from $25 to...**$35.00**

Bonbon, violets on white, gold trim, #2334, from $30 to...**$35.00**

Box, candy; flowers & bow on egg shape, #4742, 4½", from $17 to..**$23.00**

Box, candy; Poinsettia, #4387, from $40 to **$45.00**

Box, powder; applied rhinestones & flowers, #90041, 4", from $45 to..**$55.00**

Box, powder; bone china, applied flowers on lid, heart shape, #550, 3¼", from $18 to.............................**$21.00**

Box, Spring Bouquet, hinged lid, #8134, 4", from $40 to..**$50.00**

Butter dish, Bossie the Cow, #6514, 7¾", from $22 to ..**$28.00**

Candle holder, boy dressed in Santa suit hugs fawn, #3051, 4", pr from $20 to **$25.00**

Candle holders, Forget-Me-Not, gold trim, #9827, 3", pr from $95 to...**$105.00**

Candle holders, lily form, white to green leaves at base, #2499, 3¾", pr from $25 to **$30.00**

Candle holders, pink applied roses on white w/sponge gold trim, #208, 4¾", pr from $45 to **$55.00**

Cigarette set, Lily of the Valley, box & 2 ashtrays, #242, from $55 to **$65.00**

Coffeepot, Floral Chintz, #8033, from $135 to **$155.00**

Compote, Fruits of Italy, #1205, 8⅝", from $8 to........**$12.00**

Compote, Rose Chintz, gold trim, #650, 7", from $38 to .**$42.00**

Compote, Violets on white w/sponged gold, #20406, 10½", from $70 to...**$80.00**

Cookie jar, Americana, roses on white, rose bud finial, #943, 7¼", from $125 to...**$145.00**

Creamer & sugar bowl, Cosmos, multicolor flowers on white w/gold, melon ribs, w/lid, #1078, from $55 to **$65.00**

Creamer & sugar bowl, Elegant Rose, w/lid, #2276, from $65 to...**$75.00**

Creamer & sugar bowl, Misty Rose, #5537, from $45 to..**$50.00**

Cup & saucer, AD; Elegant Rose, pink roses on pale pink, #634, from $32 to...**$36.00**

Cup & saucer, tea; violets, delicate legs on cup, #2996, from $35 to...**$40.00**

Decanter, Santa figural, #1383, 7¾", from $25 to.......**$35.00**

Egg cup, Golden Wheat, #20121, 3", from $15 to......**$20.00**

Egg cup, Lilac Chintz, #698, from $12 to....................**$18.00**

Figurine, Ballerina, #444, 5¾", set of 3, from $80 to ..**$95.00**

Figurine, Chickadee, #6609, 4½", from $20 to **$25.00**

Figurine, Christmas angel playing instrument, #1419, 3¼", from $15 to...**$20.00**

Figurine, fox & hare on base, #352, 9½", from $100 to ..**$125.00**

Figurine, Gay Nineties lady, pink w/gold sponge details, #1573, 7½", from $145 to...**$165.00**

Figurine, girl w/flowers & 2 pink poodles on chains, #692, 5¼", from $38 to...**$42.00**

Figurine, girl w/ponytail holds miniature identical doll, #8948, 4", from $48 to...**$52.00**

Figurine, Mildred (Colonial lady), bisque, #3046, 7", from $80 to...**$90.00**

Figurine, Persian cat, #1513, 3½", from $10 to...........**$15.00**

Figurine, Peter, Peter, Pumpkin Eater, #1247, 6¼", from $75 to...**$100.00**

Figurine, pixie on mushroom watching frog, #1191, 4", from $11 to...**$13.00**

Figurine, squirrel w/nut, bisque, #4749, 5", from $35 to...**$38.00**

Figurine, turkey, tail spread, #2255, 3", from $35 to...**$45.00**

Jam jar, Fruit Basket (Tutti Frutti), #1680, 4¾", from $32 to **$38.00**

Jam jar, pear w/leaf tray & spoon, #2844, from $32 to....**$38.00**

Lamp, kerosene; Green Holly, #4863, 5¾", from $45 to...**$55.00**

Mug, girl wearing Santa hat, #3545, 8", from $8 to.....**$12.00**

Mug, Rustic Daisy, flower on white basketweave, green handle, #4468, 3¾", from $8 to **$12.00**

Mug, Teddy Roosevelt figural, #2191, 4¼", from $45 to..**$50.00**

Mug, White Christmas, #1387, from $5 to....................**$10.00**

Music box, 2 children w/baby, plays Adeste Fideles, #267, 5¾", from $65 to...**$75.00**

Musical egg, applied Lily of the Valley, plays 'Hello Dolly,' #10456, $45.00. (Photo courtesy Loretta DeLozier)

Napkin holder, kitten figural, #1452, 5", from $15 to .**$20.00**

Perfume set, applied lilacs & stones, 2 bottles & powder jar, #233, from $160 to...**$180.00**

Picture frame, 2 cherubs at base, flowers & scrolling decor, oval, #7221, 7¼", from $65 to.....................................**$75.00**

Pitcher, Brown Heritage Floral, #1873, from $52 to....**$58.00**

Pitcher, Daisytime, daisies allover, plain white handle, #3406, 5¼", from $22 to...**$28.00**

Pitcher & bowl, Green Holly, #5174, 4", 5½" dia, from $15 to...**$20.00**

Planter, Angelfish (2) swimming on grassy base, #3174, 7½", from $38 to...**$42.00**

Planter, egg w/chick, #7880, 4½", from $10 to **$15.00**

Planter, hand holding open fan shape, roses & gold sponging, #282, from $95 to.......................................**$105.00**

Planter, horse & colt, brown w/black manes & tales, #2171, 6", from $25 to...**$30.00**

Planter, peacock, tail trailing, matt colors, #892, 6½", from $32 to...**$38.00**

Planter, ruffed grouse, matt finish, #580, 7", from $25 to..**$30.00**

Planter, Santa w/bag, #3656, 8", from $23 to **$27.00**

Plate, Brown Heritage Fruit, #562, 7¼", from $28 to..**$32.00**

Relish, White Holly, #6057, 12", from $25 to..............**$30.00**

Salt & pepper shakers, pink poodles, applied 'spinach,' #104, pr from $32 to...**$38.00**

Salt & pepper shakers, Rustic Daisy, white basketweave, green handles, #4124, 6¾", pr from $20 to **$25.00**

Shelf sitters, Colonial boy & girl, #1568, 5¼", pr from $30 to...**$40.00**

Snack set, Summertime, flowers on white, sm plate & cup, #261, from $28 to...**$32.00**

Switch plate, violets on white, #197, 5½x3½", from $15 to .**$20.00**

Teapot, Eastern Star insignia, #2725, from $60 to.......**$70.00**

Teapot, Elegant Rose, embossed swirl ribs, #2323, 5", from $110 to...**$135.00**

Teapot, Rose Chintz, #3185, miniature, from $50 to...**$60.00**

Teapot, Thumbelina, #1695, from $145 to.................**$195.00**

Teapot, violets on white, Dresden shape, #2439, from $215 to...**$265.00**

Tidbit tray, Festival, 2-tiered, #2624, from $65 to........**$85.00**

Vase, bud; Rose Chintz, #679, 6¼", from $25 to **$30.00**

Vase, cornucopia; applied lilacs & stones, #158, 5¾", from $60 to..**$65.00**

Vase, Flower Garland, applied floral branch on white bisque, slim ewer form, #2447, 7", from $28 to **$32.00**

Wall plaque, Colonial man & lady holding baskets of flowers, #1753, pr, from $130 to...............................**$160.00**

Wall plaque, Lord's Prayer, Elegant Rose, #6347, 8", from $24 to..**$34.00**

Wall pocket, Dainty Miss, #6767, 5", from $95 to **$125.00**

Letter Openers

If you're cramped for space but a true-blue collector at heart, here's a chance to get into a hobby where there's more than enough diversification to be both interesting and challenging, yet one that requires very little room for display. Whether you prefer the advertising letter openers or the more imaginative models with handles sculpted as a dimensional figure or incorporating a penknife or a cigarette lighter, for instance, you should be able to locate enough for a nice assortment. Materials are varied as well, ranging from silver plate to wood.

Advisor: Everett Grist (See Directory, Letter Openers)

Brass anchor, $18.00.

Advertising, Clarence A O'Brien, Registered Patent Attorney, brass...**$35.00**

Advertising, Kentucky Lithographing Co, Louisville KY, French ivory & steel **$14.00**

Advertising, Mobile Asphalt Co Inc, Whistler AL, white metal **$6.00**

Advertising, Yellow Pages, yellow plastic.....................**$3.00**

Agate & white metal **$8.00**

Arts & Crafts style, aluminum, cut-out dogwood on handle..**$15.00**

Bakelite, orange & yellow marbleized, Peekskill NY .**$25.00**

Bakelite handle, butterscotch w/hand-painted flowers, Ocean City MD **$25.00**

Brass, anchor handle, Souvenir of Nauvoo IL..............**$10.00**

Brass, chicken foot handle, feather shape blade **$15.00**

Brass, dagger w/enameled dragon, Taiwan.................**$12.00**

Brass, dragon figural handle...**$12.00**

Brass, engraved Oriental dragon, bottle-opener top...**$12.00**

Brass, lizard figural, tail is blade, marked China.........**$10.00**

Brass, nude 3-D woman handle, Great Smoky Mountains .**$18.00**

Brass, painted diamond shapes, marked KL1803 Israel ..**$8.00**

Brass, red-painted floral design, marked India..............**$6.00**

Brass, rose handle, embossed decor, marked India......**$8.00**

Brass, ruler handle (measures 3"), monogram.............**$8.00**

Brass, smiling Chinese elder figural **$15.00**

Brass, whale figural handle..**$12.00**

Brass & pewter, griffin-over-lion-head handle, engraved blade **$12.00**

Cloisonne enamel, brass & steel, pen-knife handle....**$20.00**

College, enamel & steel, Air Force Academy **$5.00**

College, leatherette & plastic, University of North Carolina, Chapel Hill..**$3.00**

Combination cigarette lighter w/fishing fly & ruler blade, plastic & steel, Mardi Gras '67, Japan **$40.00**

Combination magnifyer, red plastic w/brass shield, Annapolis, marked SP, made in USA.....................**$6.00**

Combination nail clipper & file, plastic & steel, fish handle, Missouri state shield w/mule **$10.00**

Combination paperweight, brass, represents sword & stone **$15.00**

Combination pen & ruler, plastic, Yorktown Hotel, Yorktown PA **$3.00**

Combination ruler, magnifier & tracing curve, plastic, Hong Kong **$3.00**

Copper, sword, Mitchell NC...**$5.00**

Enamel & brass, flower motif, red tassel **$30.00**

Gold-plated metal, gun figural, Alabama Polytechnic Institution...**$6.00**

Gold-plated w/rhinestone jewels in handle..................**$8.00**

Historical, aluminum, USS Alabama Battleship Memorial .**$8.00**

Historical, brass, WWII cartridge, Trench Art, South Pacific, ca 1942..**$25.00**

Historical, bronze, Paul Revere House, Boston MA......**$6.00**

Ivory, cvd dragon motif, double-sided........................**$55.00**

Leather handle, brown w/gold stamp, marked Italy.....**$6.00**

Lucite handle, encapsulated reverse-carved & filled rose, magnifier blade **$25.00**

Lucite handle, encapsulated reverse-carved & painted fish, Gulf Shores AL **$15.00**

Lucite handle w/3 encapsulated US pennies, paper label, Unique, Canada...**$15.00**

Mother-of-pearl, hand-painted orange & blossoms, Jacksonville FL **$15.00**

Onyx & gold-plate **$10.00**

Plastic, blue w/leather handle..**$3.00**

Plastic, owl, green...**$3.00**

Plastic, owl figural handle, Made in Italy, original........**$8.00**

Plastic & steel, religious motto, M-Cor, USA.................**$3.00**

Porcelain, hand-painted rose & leaves, signed R Riddle..**$45.00**

Pot metal, gold-colored lobster figural w/red enameling....**$8.00**

Resin, bust of Hawaiian greeter, foil sticker, Hawaiian Greeting, Poly-Art, LTD **$5.00**

Sheathed, brass opener w/American eagle, plastic sheath, made in India...**$12.00**

Sheathed, clear plastic w/magnifying blade, simple leather sheath...**$3.00**

Sheathed, exotic wood & stainless steel, Thrower 515 on sheeth, Japan...**$9.00**

Silver-plate & steel, floral decor, International Silver **$5.00**

Souvenir, Bakelite & steel, El Paso TX, Indian chief on leather sheath **$15.00**

Souvenir, brass & horn, Thailand **$12.00**

Souvenir, enamel on copper, Chile, marked Ind Chilena...**$12.00**

Souvenir, gold-plated & plastic, Great Smoky Mountains.....**$3.00**

Souvenir, painted pot metal, state of FL **$3.00**

Souvenir, plastic, Rainbow Falls, Watkins Glen NY, ruler blade **$4.00**

Souvenir, silver-plate, Boston, Midnight Ride of Paul Revere..**$10.00**

Souvenir, silver-plate, Nashville TN, Andrew Jackson ..**$8.00**

Souvenir, wooden dagger, Lincoln's Boyhood Home, KY.**$5.00**

Souvenir, wooden dagger, Lookout Mt TN....................**$5.00**

Stag handle, slim steel blade **$10.00**

Stainless steel, trowel form..**$8.00**

Steel, Norwegian dragon handle, TH Krystad, Norway ..**$15.00**

White metal, dagger form, London, Made in England..**$8.00**

White metal, golf clubs & bag form handle **$15.00**

White metal, letter holder in handle, Mailway **$6.00**

Wood, carved birds, scratch painted **$5.00**

Wood, carved rhino handle..**$5.00**

Wood, grapes carved in relief along handle................**$10.00**

Wood, hand-painted decor, simple to involved carving, ea from $10 to..**$35.00**

L.G. Wright

Until closing in mid-1990, the L.G. Wright Glass Company was located in New Martinsville, West Virginia. Mr. Wright started his business as a glass jobber and then began buying molds from defunct glass companies. He never made his own glass, instead many companies pressed his wares, among them Fenton, Imperial, Viking, and Westmoreland. Much of L.G. Wright's glass was reproductions of Colonial and Victorian glass and lamps. Many items were made from the original molds, but the designs of some were slightly changed. His company flourished in the 1960s and 1970s. For more information we recommend *The L.G. Wright Glass Company* by James Measell and W.C. 'Red' Roetteis (Glass Press).

Ashtray, Daisy & Button, ruby, 5½" **$12.00**

Basket, Daisy & Button, ruby, 7½"..............................**$22.00**

Basket, English Hobnail, black, made from Westmoreland mold, marked WG, 1990s, 9"..............................**$35.00**

Bell, Daisy & Button, ruby, 6½" **$35.00**

Bowl, Cherry, #7-16, slag glass, oval, 10", minimum value **$95.00**

Bowl, Cherry, #7-17, slag glass, oval, 5"......................**$45.00**

Bowl, Daisy & Button, amber, 5" **$15.00**

Bowl, sauce; Thistle, cobalt blue, 4½"......................**$12.50**

Bowl, sauce; Thistle, crystal, 4½"..............................**$12.00**

Bowl, Stork & Rushes, black carnival, beaded band, 1995, 8½"..**$45.00**

Butter dish, Cherry, #7-2, slag glass **$80.00**

Candy dish, Paneled Grape, amber, footed, w/lid, 6½x4" .**$35.00**

Canoe, Daisy & Button, ruby, 4¼"..............................**$20.00**

Compote, Palm Beach, apple green, ca 1930, 8½" **$95.00**

Compote, Wild Rose, green, 13"..............................**$25.00**

Covered dish, Atterbury duck, any color, unmarked, 11" ..**$70.00**

Covered dish, cat on nest, #80-2, cobalt blue slag, 5" ..**$75.00**

Covered dish, cow on nest, #80-3, cobalt blue slag, 5"..**$75.00**

Covered dish, cow on nest, #80-3, purple or caramel slag, 5"..**$50.00**

Covered dish, cow on nest, #80-3, ruby slag, 5".........**$65.00**

Covered dish, duck on flange base, amethyst w/white head **$65.00**

Covered dish, duck on flange base, milk glass or opaque blue w/milk glass head, ea..............................**$50.00**

Covered dish, flat-iron, amber, w/lid, 5x8½"..............**$50.00**

Covered dish, hen on nest, #70-8, amethyst w/white head or white w/amethyst head, 7½" **$65.00**

Covered dish, hen on nest, #70-8, blue slag, 8".........**$95.00**

Covered dish, hen on nest, #70-8, purple or caramel slag glass, 8" **$75.00**

Covered dish, hen on nest, #70-8, ruby slag, $295.00. (Photo courtesy Ruth Grizel)

Covered dish, hen on nest, #80-7, cobalt blue slag, 5".**$75.00**

Covered dish, hen on nest, #80-7, purple or caramel slag, 5"..**$50.00**

Covered dish, hen on nest, #80-7, ruby slag, 5" **$65.00**

Covered dish, hen on nest, amberina, red or vaseline, #70-8, 8", ea..**$75.00**

Covered dish, horse on nest, #80-8, cobalt blue slag, 5".**$75.00**

Covered dish, horse on nest, #80-8, purple or caramel slag, 5"..**$50.00**

Covered dish, lamb on nest, #80-9, cobalt blue slag, 5"..**$90.00**

Covered dish, lamb on nest, #80-9, purple or caramel slag, 5"..**$65.00**

Covered dish, lamb on nest, #80-9, ruby slag, 5" **$125.00**

Covered dish, owl's head, #80-10, ruby slag, 5" **$65.00**

Covered dish, owl's head on nest, #80-10, cobalt blue slag, 5"..**$75.00**

Covered dish, owl's head on nest, #80-10, custard, 5" .**$50.00**

Covered dish, owl's head on nest, #80-10, purple or caramel slag, 5"..**$50.00**

Covered dish, owl's head on ncst, #80-10, ruby slag, 5"...**$65.00**

Covered dish, owl's nead on nest, #80-10, amber, 5".**$45.00**

Covered dish, rooster on nest, #80-12, cobalt blue slag, 5"..**$75.00**

Covered dish, rooster on nest, #80-12, purple or caramel slag, 5" **$50.00**

Covered dish, rooster on nest, #80-12, ruby slag, 5" ..**$65.00**

Covered dish, swan on nest, #80-14, cobalt blue slag, 5" ..**$75.00**

Covered dish, swan on nest, #80-14, purple & caramel slag, 5" **$50.00**

Covered dish, swan on nest, #80-14, ruby slag, 5" **$90.00**

Covered dish, turkey on nest, #80-15, lilac mist, 5" ...**$55.00**

Covered dish, turkey on nest, #80-15, cobalt blue slag, 5" **$75.00**

Covered dish, turkey on nest, #80-15, purple or caramel slag, 5" **$50.00**

Covered dish, turkey on nest, #80-15, ruby slag, 5" ...**$65.00**

Covered dish, turtle, 'Knobby Back,' amber, lg..........**$95.00**

Covered dish, turtle, 'Knobby Back', dark green, lg.**$135.00**

Covered dish, turtle on nest, #80-16, amber, 5" **$20.00**

Covered dish, turtle on nest, #80-16, cobalt blue slag, 5" ..**$75.00**

Covered dish, turtle on nest, #80-16, purple or caramel slag, 5" **$50.00**

Covered dish, turtle on nest, #80-16, ruby slag, 5" **$65.00**

Creamer, Cherry #7-4, slag glass................................**$60.00**

Dish, Daisy & Button, ruby, oval, 4-footed, ca 1950s, 5" L ..**$12.00**

Goblet, Cherry, #7-12, slag glass **$30.00**

Goblet, Daisy & Button, ice blue, 5", set of 6.............**$75.00**

Goblet, Double Wedding Ring, ruby satin, 6¼" **$20.00**

Goblet, Paneled Grape, amber, 8-oz **$15.00**

Lamp, fairy; Diamond Point, 3-pc, 7"......................**$110.00**

Lamp, fairy; Thistle, crystal, 3-pc................................**$35.00**

Lamp, fairy; Wild Rose, green & crystal, ruffled base, 3-pc, 6" **$40.00**

Lamp, oil; Daisy & Button, ruby, 12" **$75.00**

Lamp base, Daisy & Fern, cranberry, bulbous inverted pear form, ornate metal base **$95.00**

Lamp shade, American Beauty, embossed roses, pink overlay, 1950s-60s, 6¾x10"..**$65.00**

Mustard jar, Ferdinand (bull's head), #77-46, purple slag..**$55.00**

Novelty, pump, #77-95, purple slag **$65.00**

Novelty, trough, #77-96, purple slag............................**$45.00**

Pitcher, Cherry, green, 5" **$32.00**

Pitcher, water; Cherry, #7-14, slag glass....................**$175.00**

Plate, Log Cabin, Crystal Mist, oval, limited edition, 1971, 9", from $40 to...**$50.00**

Plate, Paneled Grape, ruby, 7½", from $30 to............**$35.00**

Salt cellar, Cherry, crystal, master, 1¾x3¼" **$30.00**

Salt cellar, swan, crystal satin, 3¾" L...........................**$12.00**

Slipper, Daisy & Button, black, ca 1980s, 2¼x5¼" **$20.00**

Sugar bowl, Cherry, #7-5, slag glass, minimum value...**$50.00**

Sugar bowl, Paneled Grape, amber, sm......................**$15.00**

Sugar bowl, Thistle, cobalt blue, 4½" **$26.00**

Toothpick, Daisy & Button slipper, ruby, 1950 ....**$12.00**

Top hat, Daisy & Button, ruby, 2¼"..............................**$15.00**

Tray, Daisy & Button, light blue, 3-part, 7½x4½" **$25.00**

Tumbler, Cherry, #7-9, slag glass................................**$35.00**

Tumbler, iced tea; Cherry, #7-15, slag glass **$40.00**

Tumblers, Inverted Thumbprint, cranberry, ca 1970, set of 6, from $50 to...**$60.00**

Liberty Blue

'Take home a piece of American history!,' stated an ad from the 1970s for this dinnerware made in Staffordshire, England. Blue and white depictions of George Washington at Valley Forge, Paul Revere, Independence Hall — fourteen historic scenes in all — were offered on different place-setting pieces. The ad goes on to describe this 'unique...truly unusual...museum-quality...future family heirloom.'

For every five dollars spent on groceries you could purchase a basic piece (dinner plate, bread and butter plate, cup, saucer, or dessert dish) for fifty-nine cents on alternate weeks of the promotion. During the promotion, completer pieces could also be purchased. The soup tureen was the most expensive item, originally selling for $24.99. Nineteen completer pieces in all were offered along with a five-year open stock guarantee.

Beware of 18" and 20" platters. These are recent imports and not authentic Liberty Blue. For more information we recommend Jo Cunningham's book, *The Best of Collectible Dinnerware* (Schiffer).

Advisor: Gary Beegle (See Directory, Dinnerware)

Bowl, cereal; 6½", from $12 to....................................**$15.00**

Bowl, flat soup; 8¾", from $20 to.................................**$22.00**

Bowl, vegetable; oval, from $40 to **$45.00**

Bowl, vegetable; round, from $40 to **$45.00**

Butter dish, w/lid, ¼-lb...**$55.00**

Casserole, w/lid **$125.00**

Coaster..**$12.50**

Creamer, from $18 to..**$22.00**

Creamer & sugar bowl, w/lid, original box..................**$80.00**

Cup & saucer, from $7 to...**$9.00**

Gravy boat, from $32 to...**$38.00**

Gravy boat liner, from $22 to **$30.00**

Mug, from $10 to...**$12.00**

Pitcher, 7½"...**$125.00**

Plate, bread & butter; 6"..**$4.50**

Plate, luncheon; scarce, 8¾" **$24.00**

Plate, scarce, 7", from $9 to...**$12.00**

Plates, bread and butter, $4.50; dinner, from $6.00 to $8.00; fruit bowl, 5½", $6.50.

Platter, 12", from $35 to...$45.00
Platter, 14"..$95.00
Salt & pepper shakers, pr, from $38 to.............$42.00
Soup ladle, plain white, no decal, from $30 to..........$35.00
Soup tureen, w/lid..$425.00
Sugar bowl, no lid...$10.00
Sugar bowl, w/lid..$28.00
Teapot, w/lid, from $95 to..................................$145.00

License Plates

Some of the early porcelain license plates are valued at more than $500.00. First-year plates are especially desirable. Steel plates with the aluminum 'state seal' attached range in value from $150.00 (for those from 1915 to 1920) down to $20.00 (for those from the early 1940s to 1950). Even some modern plates are desirable to collectors who like those with special graphics and messages.

Our values are given for examples in good or better condition, unless noted otherwise. For further information see *License Plate Values* distributed by L-W Book Sales.

Advisor: Richard Diehl (See Directory, License Plates)

Newsletter: *Automobile License Plate Collectors*
Richard Dragon
P.O. Box 8400, Warwick, RI 02888-0400

Magazine: *License Plate Collectors Hobby Magazine*
Drew Steitz, Editor
P.O. Box 222
East Texas, PA 18046; phone or fax: 610-791-7979; e-mail: PL8Seditor@aol.com or RVGZ60A@prodigy.com; issued bimonthly; $18 per year (1st class, USA); send $2 for sample copy

1910, Massachusetts, porcelain $90.00
1912, Rhode Island, porcelain, touched up.............$70.00
1913, New Hampshire, procelain, triangular, Visitor...$100.00
1916, Wyoming, porcelain $250.00
1918, South Dakota, fair.......................................$18.50
1918, Massachusetts..$25.00
1925, Florida, repainted..$60.00
1926, Connecticut $14.50
1933, Nevada...$30.00
1933, New Jersey...$17.50
1934, Nebraska...$8.50
1935, Idaho...$20.00
1936, Texas, fair..$16.50
1938, Pennsylvania..$11.50
1940, Illinois...$9.50
1941, Rhode Island..$15.50
1942, Tennessee, state shape................................$60.00
1943, Kansas, tab..$8.50
1943, South Dakota, tab..$8.00
1946, Colorado, sample...$50.00
1948, Alaska...$200.00

1952, Illinois...$5.50
1954, Michigan..$12.50
1955, Wisconsin...$12.50
1958, Texas, pr...$18.00
1960, Louisiana..$45.00
1960, Utah...$12.50
1961, Kentucky..$10.50
1962, California, metal tab......................................$4.50
1962, New York, pr..$15.00
1962, Ohio...$6.50
1966, Alabama...$5.50
1966, Montana, tab $1.00
1966, New York, base undated................................$5.50
1966, Rhode Island..$8.50
1967, Missouri...$7.00
1968, Hawaii, base undated.....................................$8.50
1968, Iowa...$4.00
1968, South Carolina...$5.50
1969, Virginia, pr...$10.50
1970, Ohio...$3.50
1971, Nebraska..$4.00
1972, Indiana, fair...$1.00
1973, Rhode Island, scratched.................................$3.50
1973, Utah...$3.00
1973, Washington DC, inaugural............................$15.50
1974, Mississippi...$5.50
1976, Alaska, bear...$22.00
1976, Florida...$6.50
1976, Maryland, Bicentennial................................$50.00
1976, New Hampshire $5.50
1976, West Virginia, blue border map...................$12.50
1977, Oregon, Pacific Wonderland.........................$25.00
1978, Washington, base undated.............................$3.50
1978, Wyoming...$2.00
1979, North Carolina, First in Freedom................$10.50
1981, Washington DC, inaugural $10.50
1982, Kansas, wheat..$4.50
1985, Tennessee..$4.50
1986, North Dakota, Teddy.....................................$9.50
1988, Delaware..$5.50
1989, California, white...$2.50
1990, Georgia, peach...$3.50
1990, Minnesota, Celebrate $15.50
1991, Nebraska, windmill..$3.50
1992, Maine, lobster..$4.50
1992, New Mexico, cactus.......................................$3.50
1992, Texas, flag..$3.00
1993, Arkansas, Natural State.................................$4.50
1993, Texas, Lone Star...$3.50
1993, Wisconsin, farm scene...................................$2.50
1994, Michigan..$2.50
1996, Illinois..$2.50
1997, Hawaii, rainbow...$4.50
1997, Kentucky, horse...$4.50
1997, Nevada, Silver State.......................................$3.50
1997, Oklahoma, native...$7.50
1998, Indiana, amber waves....................................$6.00

1998, North Carolina, First in Flight $3.50
1999, Georgia, large peach...$4.50
1999, Michigan, bridge $8.50
2000, Arizona, scenic...$6.50
2000, Vermont $10.50

Little Red Riding Hood

This line of novelty cookie jars, canisters, mugs, teapots, and other kitchenware items was made by both Regal China and Hull. Today any piece is expensive. There are several variations of the cookie jars. The Regal jar with the open basket marked 'Little Red Riding Hood Pat. Design 135889' is worth about $350.00. The same with the closed basket goes for about $25.00 more. An unmarked Regal variation with a closed basket, full skirt, and no apron books at $600.00. The Hull jars are valued at about $350.00 unless they're heavily decorated with decals and gold trim, which can add as much as $250.00 to the basic value.

The complete line is covered in *The Collector's Encyclopedia of Cookie Jars* by Joyce and Fred Roerig (Collector Books), and again in *Little Red Riding Hood* by Mark E. Supnick.

Batter pitcher, $450.00. (Photo courtesy Pat Duncan)

Bank, standing, from $650 to $750.00
Bank, wall hanging $1,200.00
Butter dish, from $325 to..$350.00
Canister, cereal...$1,375.00
Canister, salt...$1,100.00
Canister, tea..$700.00
Canisters, coffee, sugar or flour, ea from $600 to.....$700.00
Cookie jar, closed basket, from $350 to $375.00
Cookie jar, open basket, from $300 to......................$350.00
Cracker jar, from $600 to $700.00
Creamer, top pour, no tab handle, from $400 to......$425.00
Creamer, top pour, tab handle, from $350 to............$375.00
Creamer & sugar bowl, open, 5", from $300 to........$350.00
Lamp, from $1,300 to...$1,500.00
Match holder, wall hanging, from $800 to................$850.00

Mustard jar, w/spoon, from $275 to..........................$350.00
Pitcher, milk; 8", from $325 to.................................$375.00
Pitcher, 7", from $325 to $350.00
Planter, hanging, from $375 to $450.00
Salt & pepper shakers, lg, 5", pr, from $165 to.........$200.00
Salt & pepper shakers, Pat Design 135889, med size, 4½", pr, from $800 to...$900.00
Salt & pepper shakers, 3¼", pr, from $60 to..............$90.00
Spice jar, sq base, ea from $650 to $750.00
Sugar bowl, w/lid, from $350 to $425.00
Sugar bowl lid only, minimum value.........................$175.00
Teapot, from $325 to..$375.00
Wolf jar, red base, from $925 to $975.00
Wolf jar, yellow base, from $750 to $800.00

Little Tikes

For more than twenty-five years, this company (a division of Rubbermaid) has produced an extensive line of toys and playtime equipment, all made of heavy-gauge plastic, sturdily built and able to stand up to the rowdiest children and the most inclement weather. As children usually outgrow these items well before they're worn out, you'll often see them at garage sales, priced at a fraction of their original cost. We've listed a few below, along with what we feel would be a high average for an example in excellent condition. Since there is no established secondary market pricing system, though, you can expect to see a wide range of asking prices.

Activity Garden, complete w/accessories, EX $100.00
Activity Gym Cube Slide, 32x32" assembled $55.00
Baby buggy/stroller, pink w/white wheels & handle, EX..$20.00
Beauty salon, w/swivel shair, hair dryer & other accessories, EX $115.00
Bowling set, 6 pins, ball & stand, EX $17.50
Canopy bed & night table, for Barbie, EX..................$70.00
Castle, slide, faux fireplace, EX $360.00
Community Playground, Toddle Tots, complete, NM.$25.00
Cozy Cottage Playhouse, microwave, oven, stove burner, clock decals, mail slot, sink, MIB......................$125.00
Cozy Cottage Toddler Bed, cottage-shaped headboard w/green shutters & blue roof, twin size, EX, from $175 to $200.00
Cozy Cruiser Trailer/Jogger, seats 2 children, can be pushed or towed behind a bicycle, EX..........................$110.00
Cube slide, lg size, 51x51x48", EX...........................$155.00
Doll house, Grand Mansion, w/furniture, people & accessories, EX...$190.00
Dump truck, Caterpillar, ride-on, rechargeable battery, EX..$105.00
Family Kitchen, complete w/accessories, EX $115.00
Hot Wheels Mountain, complete w/covered bridge, loop, crossover, EX..$70.00
Indy Race Car, battery-operated, high & low gear, forward & reverse, EX...$100.00
Log Cabin Playhouse, 57x48x59", EX.......................$100.00

Picnic table, yellow, teal & hot pink, EX.....................$35.00

Race Car Toddler Bed, race car shape, spoiler is bookshelf, hood raises for storage, twin size, EX.................$200.00

Rocket Airplane, ride-on pedal car, EX.......................$90.00

Stable, #5560, complete w/15-pc accessories, M (VG box) $80.00

Stencil set, 6 stencils w/carrying case, EX..................$15.00

Tractor & trailer, green pedal toy w/tilt-dump wagon, EX..$70.00

Up & Down Roller Coaster, coaster car w/10 feet of track & 2 hills, EX..$90.00

Waffle blocks, 6 red, 6 blue & 6 yellow blocks, 14x14x2", EX $180.00

Washer/dryer combination, comes w/iron & washer bin, 47x12¾x23" $75.00

Wave Climber, w/slide, EX...$90.00

Work Bench, Super Sized, complete w/accessories, 44x44x20", EX $100.00

Lladro Porcelains

Lovely studies of children and animals in subtle colors are characteristic of the Lladro porcelains produced in Labernes Blanques, Spain. Their retired and limited editions are popular with today's collectors.

Angel w/accordion, #1323, 1976-85 ....$400.00
Asian Love, #6156, 1994-98..$235.00
Baby's First Christmas, #5839, 1991-92.......................$60.00
Beagle puppy, #1072, 1969-90...................................$260.00
Call to Prayer, #5551, 1989-93 ....$340.00
Circus Magic, #5892, 1992-97.....................................$465.00
Clown w/saxophone, #5059, 1980-85 ....$675.00
Crane (nesting), #1599, 1989-97 ....$135.00
Doctor, #4602, 1971-1999..$230.00
Easter bunnies, #5902, 1992-96..................................$265.00
En Pointe (ballerina), #6371, 1997-2000....................$370.00
Forgotten, #1502, 1986-91 ....$230.00
Girl w/duck, #1052, 1969-98......................................$205.00
Girl w/watering can, #1339, 1977-78 ....$450.00
Graceful Dance (ballerina), #6205, 1995-98...............$340.00
Grand Parents Joy, 36553, 1998-2000.........................$670.00
Great Dane, #6558, 1998-2000 ....$670.00
Japanese girl decorating, #4840, 1973-97...................$525.00
Mallard duck, 35288, 1985-94 ....$570.00
Mayflower basket, 31629, 1989-91 ....$600.00
Motherhood, #4575, 1969-97......................................$300.00
Nippon lady, #5327, 1984-2000 ....$565.00
On the Beach, #1481, 1985-88...................................$440.00
Parisian Lady, #5321, 1985-95...................................$360.00
Phyllis (ballerina), #1356, 1978-93............................$235.00
Precious Love, #4856, 1974-85...................................$380.00
Seesaw, #1255, 1974-78...$670.00
Shepherdess w/dog, #1034, 1978-83 ....$225.00
Startled, #5614, 1989-91..$320.00
Stepping Out, #1537, 1988-2000 ....$320.00
Summer Angel, #6148, 1994-97 ....$260.00

Sunday Best, #5758, 1991-97 ....$785.00
Turtle Dove, #4450-M, matt, 1969-98 ....$265.00

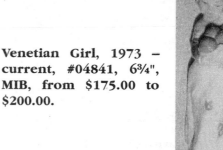

Venetian Girl, 1973 – current, #04841, 6¾", MIB, from $175.00 to $200.00.

Walk w/Father, #5751, 1991-94..................................$450.00

Longaberger Baskets

In the early 1900s in the small Ohio town of Dresden, John Wendell ('J.W.') Longaberger developed a love for hand-woven baskets. In 1973 J.W. and his fifth child, Dave, began to teach others how to weave baskets. J.W. passed away during that year, but the quality and attention to detail found in his baskets were kept alive by Dave through the Longaberger Company®.

Each basket is hand woven, using hardwood maple splints. Since 1978 each basket has been dated and signed by the weaver upon completion. In 1982 the practice of burning the Longaberger name and logo into the bottom of each basket began, guaranteeing its authenticity as a Longaberger Basket®.

New baskets can be obtained only through sales consulants, usually at a basket home party. Collector and speciality baskets are available only for a limited time throughout the year. For example, the 1992 Christmas Collection Basket was offered only from September through December 1992. After this, the basket was no longer available from Longaberger®. Once an item is discontinued or retired, it can only be obtained on the secondary market.

This information is from *The Ninth Edition Bentley Collection Guide*, published in June 2001. See the Directory for ordering information or call 1-800-837-4394.

Advisor: Jill S. Rindfuss (See Directory, Longaberger Baskets)

Baskets

Note: Values are for baskets only, unless accessories such as liners and protectors are mentioned in the description. Sizes may vary as much as one inch.

1979-93, Retired Mini Cradle™ (basket only), sm, rectangular, no color trim or weave, no handles, wood rockers, from $76 to **$115.00**

1983, Regular Line Darning™ (basket only), no color trim or weave, two leather ears, still in production but dark stain as shown is discontinued, 4" x 10", from $39.00 to $55.00. (From the collection of Nancy McDaniels)

1983, JW Medium Market™ (basket only), rectangular, blue weave & trim, 1 stationary handle, brass tag: Longaberger-JW Medium Market, from $1,421 to **$1,740.00**

1983-86, Retired Family Picnic™ (basket only), big, rectangular, no color trim or weave, 2 swinging handles, divided attached lid, from $330 to......................**$390.00**

1986, Incentive VIP™ (basket only), tall, rectangular, blue trim & accent weave, 2 swinging handles, brass tag, from $375 to...**$400.00**

1987, Easter Signature Single Pie™ (basket only), sq, red, blue & green weave, 1 stationary handle; all have Dave Longaberger's signature, from $182 to **$250.00**

1988, All-American Small Picnic™ (basket only), sq, red trim w/red & blue accent weave, 2 swinging handles, woven attached lid w/red & blue accent weave, from $201 to..................**$275.00**

1988, Holiday Hostess Large Market™ (basket only), rectangular, red & green weave w/red or green trim, 1 stationary handle, from $119 to..............................**$135.00**

1988-97, Heartland Medium Key™ (basket only), rectangular, Heartland Blue shoestring weave, 1 leather loop, metal bracket for hanging, burned-in Heartland logo on bottom, from $45 to..**$70.00**

1990-92, Hostess Collection Remembrance™ (basket only), rectangular, no color trim or weave, 2 swinging handles, woven attached lid, from $125 to **$175.00**

1991, JW Corn® (basket only), round, blue trim & accent weave, 2 leather handles, brass tag: Longaberger - JW Corn, from $334 to **$470.00**

1991, Mother's Day Medium Purse™ (basket only), rectangular, pink trim & accent weave, 1 swinging handle, from $95 to..**$115.00**

1992, Father's Day Paper™ (basket only), rectangular, higher in the back than in the front, Dresden blue & burgundy trim, no handles, from $70 to................................**$95.00**

1992-96, Hostess Collection Mail™ (basket only), tall, rectangular opening, no color weave, no handles, attached lid, metal hanger on back of basket for mounting, ⅜" weave, from $118 to...**$160.00**

1992-99, Booking/Promo Lavender™ (basket only), oval, no color trim or weave, 2 leather ears, ⅜" weave, from $32 to..**$53.00**

1993, All-Star Trio™ (w/liner & protector), rectangular, red & blue weave & trim, 2 leather ears, from $57 to ...**$95.00**

1993, Crisco Baking™ (basket only), oval, red & blue weave & trim, 2 leather ears, burned-in Crisco logo, from $105 to..**$120.00**

1993, Shades of Autumn Harvest™ (basket only), rectangular, green, rust & deep blue weave w/rust trim, swinging handle, from $75 to...**$100.00**

1994, Bee Basket™ (basket only), rectangular, rose pink & purple weave, 1 swinging handle, brass tag: Celebrate Your Success - 1994 - Bee Basket, from $167 to.......**$270.00**

1994, Boo™ (basket only), rectangular, orange & black weave & trim, 1 swinging handle, from $93 to..**$135.00**

1994, Holiday Hostess Sleigh Bell™ (basket only), round top, rectangular bottom, red or green trim w/red & green accent weave, 2 swinging handles, from $182 to.......**$250.00**

1995, Horizon of Hope™ (basket only), rectangular, no color weave or trim, 1 stationary handle, American Cancer Society logo on bottom, from $75 to **$95.00**

1995, Sweetheart Sentiments™ (basket only), sq, red trim & shoestring accent weave, 1 swinging handle, from $67 to..**$85.00**

1995, Traditions Family™ (basket only), oval, green trim & accent weave, 1 swinging handle, brass tag, w/box, from $173 to..**$240.00**

1995-96, Collectors Club Charter Membership™ (basket only), tall, rectangular opening, blue & green weave & trim, 2 swinging handles, commemorative brass tag, burned-in Collectors Club logo, from $105 to..**$178.00**

1995-97, Woven Traditions Spring® (basket only), sq, red, blue & green shoestring weave, 1 stationary handle, from $56 to..**$85.00**

1996, Employee Christmas Cracker™ (basket only), rectangular, red & green shoestring weave, no handles, from $65 to..**$95.00**

1997, Incentive $500 Million Celebration™ (basket only), rectangular, red & stained double trim, red accent weave, 2 swinging handles, brass tag, from $230 to........................**$275.00**

1997, 20th Century - First Edition™ (basket only), rectangular, natural w/flag design, 1 swinging handle, brass tag: 'First Edition,' from $62 to...**$105.00**

1998, Collector's Club Harbor™ (basket only), rectangular, blue & green double trim & accent weave, 2 swinging handles from $98 to...**$110.00**

1999, Lots of Luck™ (basket only), round, green chain link weave & trim, ⅜" weave, 1 stationary handle, no tag, from $90 to..**$130.00**

1999, May Series Daisy™ (basket only), round, blue weave & trim, 1 swinging handle, ⅜" weave, board bottom, from $67 to..**$85.00**

2000, Cheers™ (basket only), oval, stained, periwinkle & purple double trim, 1 stationary handle, board bottom w/burned-in logo, commemorative silver tag, from $61 to..**$71.00**

2000, Feature October Fields™ (basket only), tall, round, no color trim or weave, 1 swinging handle, from $70 to..$75.00

2001, Special Events Inaugural™ (basket only), rectangular, blue trim w/pewter star studs, red shoestring accent weave, 1 swinging handle, from $44 to................$45.00

Miscellaneous

1990, Father Christmas Cookie Mold™ - First Casting, brown pottery, inscription on back: Longaberger Pottery — First Casting - Christmas 1990, w/box, from $51 to..$60.00

1990-91, Roseville Grandma Bonnie's Apple Pie Plate,™ pottery, blue accents, embossing on bottom: Roseville, Ohio, w/box, from $43 to.......................$65.00

1999, Fruit Medley Pottery - Pitcher,™ Vitrified China, hand-painted fruit designs, logo on bottom, w/box, from $99 to..$195.00

Lu Ray Pastels

This was one of Taylor, Smith, and Taylor's most popular lines of dinnerware. It was made from the late 1930s until sometime in the early 1950s in five pastel colors: Windsor Blue, Persian Cream, Sharon Pink, Surf Green, and Chatham Gray.

If you'd like more information, we recommend *Collector's Guide to Lu Ray Pastels* by Kathy and Bill Meehan (Collector Books).

Juice tumblers, $50.00 each; Juice pitcher, $200.00.

Baker, vegetable; gray, oval, 9½" $30.00
Baker, vegetable; oval, 9½" $20.00
Bowl, coupe soup; flat..$15.00
Bowl, fruit; Chatham Gray, 5".....................................$16.00
Bowl, fruit; 5"...$5.00
Bowl, lug soup; tab handled $20.00
Bowl, mixing; 5½"..$125.00
Bowl, mixing; 10¼"...$150.00
Butter dish, gray, w/lid $90.00
Butter dish, w/lid..$50.00

Casserole, w/lid...$125.00
Chocolate cup, AD; straight sides..........................$80.00
Chocolate pot, AD; straight sides $200.00
Coaster/nut dish..$65.00
Creamer, from $8 to...$10.00
Cup/bowl, cream soup...$70.00
Egg cup, double; any color other than Chatham gray....$24.00
Egg cup, double; gray...$30.00
Epergne $110.00
Jug, water; footed..$125.00
Nappy, vegetable; round, 8½".................................$20.00
Pitcher, water; yellow, flat bottom $95.00
Plate, Chatham Gray, 9" $16.00
Plate, 6"...$3.00
Plate, 7"...$12.00
Plate, 8"...$20.00
Plate, 9"...$10.00
Platter, 11½"..$16.00
Platter, 13"...$19.00
Relish dish, 4-part..$95.00
Sauce/gravy boat, w/fixed stand, any color but yellow...$35.00
Sauce/gravy boat, w/fixed stand, yellow.................$22.50
Saucer, AD; gray...$10.00
Saucer, chocolate $30.00
Saucer, cream soup..$28.00
Sugar bowl, AD; individual, w/lid.............................$40.00
Sugar bowl, w/lid..$15.00
Teapot, curved spout...$125.00
Teapot, flat spout...$160.00
Tumbler, water..$80.00
Vase, bud...$400.00

Lunch Boxes

Character lunch boxes made of metal have been very collectible for several years, but now even those made of plastic and vinyl are coming into their own.

The first lunch box of this type ever produced featured Hopalong Cassidy. Made by the Aladdin company, it was constructed of steel and decorated with decals. But the first fully lithographed steel lunch box and matching thermos bottle was made a few years later (in 1953) by American Thermos. Roy Rogers was its featured character.

Since then hundreds have been made, and just as is true in other areas of character-related collectibles, the more desirable lunch boxes are those with easily recognizable, well-known subjects — western heroes; TV, Disney, and cartoon characters; and famous entertainers like the Bee Gees and the Beatles.

Values hinge on condition. Learn to grade your lunch boxes carefully. A grade of 'excellent' for metal boxes means that you will notice only very minor defects and less than normal wear. Plastic boxes may have a few scratches and some minor wear on the sides, but the graphics must be completely undamaged. Vinyls must retain their original shape; brass parts may be tarnished, and the hinge may show signs of beginning splits. If the box you're trying to evaluate is in any worse condition than we've described, to be realistic, you must cut these prices drastically. Values are given for boxes without matching thermoses, unless one is mentioned in the line. If you'd like to learn more, we recommend *Collector's Guide to Lunch Boxes* by Carole Bess White and L.M. White, and *Schroeder's Collectible Toys, Antique to Modern*, both published by Collector Books.

Note: Watch for reproductions marked 'China.'

Metal

A-Team, 1983, VG...**$20.00**
Action Jackson, 1973, w/thermos, NM......................**$175.00**
Animal Friends, 1975, EX.....................................**$30.00**
Atom Ant, 1966, G...**$40.00**
Battle of the Planets, 1979, EX **$40.00**
Betsy Clark, 1975, beige, w/thermos, EX...................**$25.00**
Black Hole, 1979, EX..**$50.00**
Bozo the Clown, 1963, dome top, w/thermos, NM..**$250.00**
Bullwinkle & Rocky, 1962, blue background, NM....**$700.00**
Campbell Kids, 1975, NM **$275.00**
Captain Astro, 1966, NM **$250.00**
Casey Jones, 1960, dome top, w/thermos, NM.........**$400.00**
Chavo, 1979, M..**$200.00**
Chitty-Chitty Bang-Bang, 1968, VG+ **$75.00**
Dick Tracy, 1967, w/thermos, NM...........................**$200.00**
Disney World, 1976, w/thermos, EX+ **$35.00**
Double Deckers, 1970, EX....................................**$60.00**
Dr Seuss, 1970, VG+..**$70.00**
Dragon's Lair, 1983, EX......................................**$25.00**
Dukes of Hazzard, 1980, EX..................................**$35.00**
Dynomutt, 1976, EX...**$50.00**
Fire House, 19759, w/thermos, NM **$425.00**
Flipper, 1967, EX **$100.00**

KISS, EX, $100.00. (Photo courtesy June Moon)

Gene Autry Melody Ranch, 1954, w/thermos, NM ...**$500.00**
Gentle Ben, 1968, EX **$95.00**
Get Smart, 1966, EX **$200.00**
Goober & the Ghost Chasers, 1974, VG+ **$50.00**
Goofy, 1984, EX+...**$30.00**
Great Wild West, 1959, EX...................................**$375.00**

Grizzly Adams, 1977, dome top, VG+.........................**$55.00**
Hansel & Gretel, 1982, EX...................................**$100.00**
Hee Haw, 1970, EX..**$70.00**
How the West Was Won, 1978, w/thermos, EX **$55.00**
Huckleberry Hound & Friends, 1961, VG....................**$75.00**
Incredible Hulk, 1978, EX...................................**$40.00**
James Bond 007, 1966, EX....................................**$250.00**
Jet Patrol, 1957, w/thermos, EX............................**$200.00**

Flipper, with thermos, EX, from $150.00 to $190.00.

Knight Rider, 1983, EX......................................**$35.00**
Korg, 1974, EX..**$35.00**
Krofft Supershow, 1976, VG **$50.00**
Land of the Giants, 1968, VG **$75.00**
Lassie, 1978, VG..**$35.00**
Laugh-In, 1968, w/thermos, EX..............................**$150.00**
Little Dutch Miss, 1959, VG.................................**$75.00**
Lost in Space, 1967, dome top, w/thermos, rare, NM ..**$600.00**
Marvel Super Heroes, 1976, EX..............................**$45.00**
Mickey Mouse Club, 1976, yellow, EX........................**$45.00**
Miss America, 1972, w/thermos, NM.........................**$150.00**
Monroes, 1967, EX...**$200.00**
Mork & Mindy, 1979, VG+.....................................**$30.00**
Munsters, 1965, w/thermos, M **$400.00**
Muppets, 1979, VG **$15.00**
Nancy Drew, 1977, w/thermos, NM, from $75 to.....**$100.00**
Pac Man, 1980, VG **$20.00**
Pathfinder, 1959, EX..**$400.00**
Pete's Dragon, 1978, EX.....................................**$45.00**
Pit Stop, 1968, EX+...**$175.00**
Planet of the Apes, 1974, VG................................**$60.00**
Polly Pal, 1974, w/thermos, EX **$35.00**
Popeye, 1964, EX+...**$100.00**
Rambo, 1985, M..**$35.00**
Return of the Jedi, 1983, VG................................**$30.00**
Robin Hood, 1956, w/thermos, EX **$150.00**
Secret Agent T, 1968, VG **$60.00**
Secret Nimh, 1982, w/thermos, M **$40.00**
Secret Wars, 1984, VG.......................................**$15.00**
Sesame Street, 1979, w/thermos, EX........................**$20.00**
Smokey Bear, 1975, NM **$350.00**
Snoopy, 1968, dome top, EX..................................**$65.00**
Star Trek, 1979, VG...**$45.00**

Steve Canyon, 1959, w/thermos, NM..........................$500.00
Superman, 1967, w/thermos, NM...............................$200.00
Three Little Pigs, 1982, EX.......................................$100.00
Track King, 1975, NM..$325.00
Voyage to the Bottom of the Sea, 1967, w/thermos, NM..$400.00
Wild Wild West, 1969, NM...$200.00
Yellow Submarine, 1968, w/thermos, NM $600.00
Zorro, 1958, VG..$90.00

Plastic

American Gladiators, 1992, red, EX.............................$9.00
Astrokids, 1988, w/thermos, EX.................................$8.00
Barney & Baby Bop, 1992, w/thermos, EX $8.00
Casper the Friendly Ghost, 1996, w/thermos, M.........$10.00
Chicklets Chewing Gum, 1987, w/thermos, M............$30.00
CHiPs, 1977, dome top, NM $30.00
Chuck E Cheese, 1996, w/thermos, NM $15.00
Dr Seuss, 1996, EX..$15.00
Ewoks, 1983, EX $15.00
Flintstones at the Zoo, 1989, w/thermos, EX $20.00
Garfield, 1980s, w/thermos, EX.................................$15.00
Ghostbusters, 1986, purple, EX $20.00
Hot Wheels, 1997, w/thermos, M..............................$20.00
Incredible Hulk, 1980, dome top, EX $40.00
Jabberjaw, 1977, NM...$30.00
Keebler Cookies, 1987, w/thermos, M $30.00
Little Orphan Annie, 1973, dome top, w/thermos, NM ..$40.00
Looney Tunes, 1977, EX...$10.00
Lucy Luncheonette, 1981, dome top, EX $15.00

Lunch With Kermit the Frog, 1988, dome-style box, EX, $20.00, matching plastic bottle, EX, $20.00. (Photo courtesy Carole Bess White and L.M. White)

Mickey Mouse & Donald Duck, 1984, w/thermos, EX ..$10.00
Mighty Mouse, 1979, EX+ $20.00
Nestle Quik, 1980, NM...$25.00
New Kids on the Block, 1990, w/thermos, EX.............$15.00
Popeye, 1979, dome top, EX $30.00
Rap It Up, 1992, EX...$15.00
Rocky Roughneck, 1977, EX......................................$20.00
Rover Dangerfield, 1990, w/thermos, EX....................$20.00

Six Million Dollar Man, 1974, M................................$35.00
Smurfette, 1984, pink, EX..$15.00
Star Trek Next Generation, 1989, w/thermos, M.........$20.00
Superman, 1980, EX+ $30.00
SWAT, 1975, dome top, w/thermos, EX.....................$40.00
Tom & Jerry, 1992, w/thermos, M.............................$20.00
Winnie the Pooh, 1990, w/thermos, M $25.00
101 Dalmatians, 1990, w/thermos, EX $10.00

Vinyl

Alvin & the Chipmunks, 1963, w/thermos, EX $150.00
Ballerina on Lily Pad, 1960s, EX...............................$100.00
Banana Splits, 1969, w/thermos, NM $450.00
Barbie, 1972, pink, EX...$35.00
Beany & Cecil, 1961, w/thermos, NM $200.00
Beauty & the Beast, softie, w/thermos, VG $8.00
Bobby Soxer, w/thermos, NM $150.00
Bullwinkle Lunch Kit, 1962, w/thermos, NM $285.00
Captain Kangaroo, 1964, w/thermos, EX...................$150.00
Casper the Friendly Ghost, 1966, w/thermos, NM....$375.00
Charlie's Angels, 1977, brunch bag, EX $125.00
Deputy Dawg, 1964, EX...$300.00
Dream Boat, NM...$125.00
Holly Hobbie, 1972, w/thermos, EX $40.00
Junior Nurse, 1963, w/thermos, EX...........................$120.00
Li'l Jodie, 1985, EX..$50.00
Linus the Lion-Hearted, 1965, w/thermos, NM $500.00
Lion in the Cart, 1985, EX..$40.00
Lion in the Van, 1978, NM $60.00
Mary Poppins, 1973, VG $50.00
Monkees, 1967, EX..$300.00
Pac Man, 1980, EX..$50.00
Peanuts, 1965, w/thermos, NM..................................$150.00
Peter Pan, w/thermos, NM...$20.00
Pink Panther, 1980, w/thermos, EX...........................$60.00
Ponytail Tid-Bit-Kit, 1959, w/thermos, NM...............$100.00
Princess, 1963, yellow, w/thermos, EX......................$50.00
Ringling Bros & Barnum & Bailey Circus, 1970, w/thermos, NM $200.00
Sabrina, 1972, NM..$200.00
Shari Lewis, 1963, w/thermos, EX.............................$125.00
Smokey Bear, w/thermos, NM...................................$250.00
Speedy Turtle, 1978, drawstring closure, M................$25.00
Tic Tac Toe, 1970s, EX..$50.00
Twiggy, 1967, w/thermos, EX $175.00
Underdog, 1972, w/thermos, NM...............................$425.00
Wizard in the Van, 1978, orange, VG+ $50.00
World of Barbie, 1971, pink, EX.................................$35.00
Yogi Bear, 1961, w/thermos, NM $200.00
Yosemite Sam, 1971, w/thermos, EX $150.00
Ziggy, 1979, EX...$85.00

Thermoses

Values are given for thermoses made of metal unless noted otherwise.

Banana Splits, 1970s, NM..**$185.00**
Bee Gees, 1978, plastic, M.......................................**$20.00**
Beverly Hillbillies, 1963, metal, EX **$50.00**
Campbell's Soup, 1968, EX **$60.00**
Casey Jones, 1960, EX..**$100.00**
Casper the Friendly Ghost, 1966, EX+ **$100.00**
Chitty-Chitty Bang-Bang, 1968, EX+ **$40.00**
Clash of the Titans, 1980, plastic, NM.....................**$10.00**
Evil Knievel, 1974, plastic, VG+.............................**$15.00**
Flying Nun, 1968, EX..**$60.00**
Fonz, 1976, M..**$50.00**
Green Hornet, 1967, EX **$90.00**
Hopalong Cassidy, 1950, EX....................................**$55.00**
Junior Miss, 1963, EX...**$75.00**
Kung Ku, 1974, plastic, EX **$15.00**
Little Dutch Miss, 1959, EX......................................**$45.00**
Mickey Mouse Club, 1976, plastic, EX **$7.00**
Partridge Family, 1973, plastic, M............................**$45.00**
Peanuts, 1966, EX...**$25.00**
Peter Pan, 1976, plastic, EX **$25.00**
Punky Brewster, 1984, plastic, NM...........................**$15.00**

Raggedy Ann and Andy, Aladdin, 1973, with thermos, EX, $80.00. (Photo courtesy Kim Avery)

Rifleman, 1960, EX **$125.00**
Roy Rogers, EX+...**$100.00**
Sabrina, 1972, plastic, EX...**$45.00**
Secret Agent, 1968, EX **$35.00**
Street Hawk, 1984, plastic, EX.................................**$35.00**
Superman, 1967, EX **$50.00**
Tim Horton Donuts, 1970s, plastic, EX......................**$35.00**
Waltons, 1973, plastic, EX **$22.00**
Yogi Bear, 1963, EX+...**$50.00**

Maddux of California

Founded in Los Angeles in 1938, Maddux not only produced ceramics but imported and distributed them as well. They supplied chain stores nationwide with well-designed figural planters, TV lamps, novelty and giftware items, and during the mid-1960s their merchandise was listed in every major stamp catalog. Because of an increasing amount of foreign imports and an economic slowdown in our own country, the company was forced to sell out in 1976. Under the new management, manufacturing was abandoned, and the company was converted solely to distribution. Collectors have only recently discovered this line, and prices right now are affordable though increasing.

Figurine, cockatoo on branch, 11", $45.00.

Figurine, flamingo, #0305, 9½" **$75.00**
Figurine, flamingo, wings up, 13¼" **$110.00**
Figurine, flamingo w/head down, 7" **$40.00**
Figurine, greyhound dog, #0927, 6x12" **$25.00**
Planter, flamingo, wings up, 11"................................**$110.00**
Planter, flamingo, wings up, 13".................................**$125.00**
Planter, flamingos (2) back-to-back form receptacle, 5x6½", from $60 to..**$70.00**
Planter, flamingos (7½", 11"), #1204, 13" overall **$125.00**
Planter, gazelle, #0542, 9¾" **$35.00**
TV lamp, basset hound, #0896, 12"...........................**$140.00**
TV lamp, couple dancing, #8008.................................**$82.50**
TV lamp, doe & fawn running, 11x10¼".....................**$65.00**
TV lamp, ducks, #0835, 8½x10" **$85.00**
TV lamp, gold-tone metal center w/black planter ea side, #0107W **$40.00**
TV lamp, horse, #0858, 13x11x6½" **$85.00**
TV lamp, orange w/red panel, #8019, 9x9½"..............**$40.00**
TV lamp, Prairie Schooner (covered wagon), #0844, 11"..**$35.00**
TV lamp, quail (3), #8016, 11½x9½" **$82.50**
TV lamp, swan planter, white porcelain, #0828, 12½"..**$50.00**
TV lamp, swans (2), #0825, 10x11½" **$50.00**
Vase, deer heads decor, pink, #0226.........................**$32.00**
Wall pocket, bird in metal holder (resembles cage), 7x7" cage...**$35.00**

Magazines

There are a lot of magazines around today, but unless they're in fine condition (clean, no missing or clipped pages, and very little other damage); have interesting features (cover illustrations, good advertising, or special-interest stories); or deal with sports greats, famous entertainers, or world-renowned personalities, they're worth very little. Issues printed prior to 1950 generally have value, and pre-1900 examples are now considered antique paper. Address labels on the fronts are acceptable, but if your magazine has one, follow these guidelines. Subtract 5% to 10% when the label is not intruding on the face of the cover. Deduct 20% if the label is on the face of an important cover and 30% to 40% if on the face of an important illustrator cover, thus ruining framing quality. If you find a magazine with no label, it will be worth about 25% more than one in about the same condition but having a label. For further information see *The Masters Price & Identification Guide to Old Magazines* (fifth edition now available); *Life Magazines, 1898 to 1994; Saturday Evening Post, 1899– 1965;* and several other up-to-the-minute guides covering specific magazine titles — all by our advisor Denis C. Jackson. See also TV Guides.

Advisors: Denis C. Jackson; Don Smith, Rare National Geographics (See Directory, Magazines)

Newsletter: *The Illustrator Collector's New*
(Sample issue: $3.50; Subscription $18.00 per year in U.S.)
Denis C. Jackson, Editor
P.O. Box 1958
Sequim, WA 98382; www.olypen.com/ticn
e-mail: ticn@olypen.com

American Cinematographer, 1979, January, NM..........**$30.00**
American Legion, 1923, March 23, Held cover, EX.....**$20.00**
American Needlewoman, 1926, May **$3.00**
Better Homes & Gardens, 1943, December, EX..........**$10.00**
Camera Craft, 1925, July, EX....................................**$15.00**
Car Collector, 1978, January, Vol 1 #1, EX...................**$7.00**
Child Life, 1954, December, Norman Rockwell, EX....**$20.00**
Collier's, 1950, April 8, Harry Truman, VG+.................**$10.00**
Collier's, 1955, November 11, Agatha Christie, EX......**$10.00**
Cosmopolitan, 1953, May, Marilyn Monroe/Oklahoma, EX..**$55.00**
Cosmopolitan, 1969, August, Elizabeth Taylor, VG+.....**$8.00**
Down Beat, 1941, January 15, Duke Ellington, NM+..**$24.00**
Esquire, 1943, May, Vargas illustrations, VG+..............**$30.00**
Esquire, 1951, September, Marilyn Monroe gatefold, VG+ **$150.00**
Esquire, 1973, March, Fat City Follies, EX+ **$8.00**
Family Circle, 1946, January 25, Bob Hope, M **$12.00**
Fortune, 1930s-40s, ea from $8 to **$75.00**
Fortune, 1932, August, Grant Wood illustration, EX ...**$20.00**
Fortune, 1940s, EX, ea from $8 to..............................**$10.00**
Garden & Home Builder, 1920s, VG, from $6 to **$8.00**
Good Housekeeping, 1935, May, Golden Anniversary issue, VG+..**$12.00**
Good Housekeeping, 1945, August, baby cover, EX+ ..**$8.00**
Good Housekeeping, 1967, May, Sonny & Cher, VG+ .**$8.00**
Gourmet, 1965, April, Lucius Beebe/Along the Boulevards, VG+ **$4.00**

Harper's Weekly, 1920, January, EX............................**$15.00**
Highway Traveler, 1940s-50s, VG, from $3 to **$5.00**
House Beautiful, 1923, October, EX............................**$30.00**
House Beautiful, 1959, October, Frank Lloyd Wright, EX...**$12.00**
Inside Sports, 1980, April, Nolan Ryan, EX **$25.00**
Inside Sports, 1993, March, swimsuit issue, EX............**$5.00**
Ladies' Home Journal, 1927, April, Rose O'Neill Kewpies, EX..**$25.00**
Ladies' Home Journal, 1947, May, Eleanor Roosevelt article, EX...**$4.00**
Ladies' Home Journal, 1960, December, Jacqueline Kennedy, VG+..**$5.00**
Ladies' Home Journal, 1960, January, Pat Boone, EX...**$5.00**
Life, 1937, October 6, Harpo Marx, EX......................**$30.00**
Life, 1939, December 11, Betty Grable, G **$8.00**
Life, 1942, Roy Rogers & Trigger, EX **$50.00**
Life, 1944, December 11, Judy Garland, EX **$35.00**
Life, 1945, May 21, Winston Churchill, G **$5.00**
Life, 1949, August 1, Joe DeMaggio, EX **$75.00**
Life, 1955, October 2, Rock Hudson, NM....................**$20.00**
Life, 1961, May 17, Alan B Shepard **$12.00**
Life, 1962, January 5, Lucille Ball, NM........................**$20.00**
Life, 1965, April 2, Gus Grissom & John Young, VG..**$16.00**
Life, 1965, July 30, Mickey Mantle, EX........................**$55.00**
Life, 1969, April 18, Mae West, VG..............................**$10.00**
Life, 1969, September 12, Coretta Scott King, VG.......**$14.00**
Life, 1971, July 23, Clint Eastwood, EX+.....................**$25.00**
Life, 1971, October 15, Opening of Disney World, EX..**$26.00**
Life, 1981, May, Reagan's attempted assassination, EX+ ...**$12.00**
Life, 1983, June, George Lucas & Star Wars, VG+.......**$15.00**
Literary Digest, 1918, April 27, NC Wyeth cover art, EX..**$20.00**
Look, 1937, December 21, Shirley Temple, VG **$20.00**
Look, 1937, May, Jean Harlow, Prohibition, EX..........**$15.00**
Look, 1938, June 7, Dionne Quints, EX.......................**$15.00**
Look, 1939, December 5, Hitler, VG+..........................**$10.00**
Look, 1939, February 28, Son of Frankenstein, EX.....**$10.00**
Look, 1940, February 27, Superman article, VG+........**$90.00**
Look, 1940, July, Linda Darnell, EX **$8.00**
Look, 1941, May 20, Gale Storm, EX.............................**$8.00**
Look, 1943, March 23, Lt Clark Gable, VG+ **$13.00**
Look, 1946, May 28, Nagasaki, EX...............................**$10.00**
Look, 1946, October 15, Ted Williams, EX...................**$85.00**
Look, 1956, November, James Dean, EX **$18.00**
Look, 1961, January 31, Clark Gable, EX.....................**$20.00**
Look, 1964, July 28, NY Nightlife, EX...........................**$8.00**
McCall's, 1931, July, 3 NC Wyeth illustrations, EX......**$22.00**
McCall's, 1940-49, EX, ea from $2 to...........................**$5.00**
McCall's, 1960, April, Marilyn Monroe, EX **$20.00**
McCall's, 1968, June, Jacqueline Kennedy, EX **$6.00**
McCall's, 1969, May, Fabulous Ford Women, VG+ **$5.00**
Modern Screen, 1939, Deanna Durbin, EX.................**$30.00**
Motion Picture, 1931, April, Marlene Dietrich, EX **$40.00**
Movie Life, 1968, October, Elvis, EX **$20.00**
Movie Mirror, 1935, December, Jeanette McDonald, EX..**$30.00**
Movie Mirror, 1940, February, Madeleine Carrol/Vivien Leigh article, VG+ **$35.00**
Movie Stars Parade, 1950, May, June Allyson, EX.......**$20.00**

Movieland, 1944, January, Ingrid Bergman, EX..........$25.00
National Geographic, 1915-16, ea $15.00
National Geographic, 1917-24, ea...............................$9.00
National Geographic, 1925-29, ea...............................$8.00
National Geographic, 1930-45, ea...............................$7.00
National Geographic, 1946-55, ea...............................$6.00
National Geographic, 1956-67, ea...............................$5.50
National Geographic, 1968-69, ea...............................$4.50
National Geographic, 1990-present, ea $2.00
Nevada, 1974, Summer, John Wayne, NM $10.00
Newsweek, 1940, February 26, war news, EX $6.00
Newsweek, 1975, June 16, Nolan Ryan, EX $20.00
Newsweek, 1987, August, Elvis Presley, EX+ $30.00
Newsweek, 1989, June 26, Batman, NM $8.00
On the QT, 1955, June, Vol 1 #1, EX $20.00
Parents, 1942, September, EX.......................................$5.00
Penthouse, 1976, July, Stephen King's 'The Ledge,' Gore
    Vidal, EX..$12.00
Penthouse, 1985, September, Madonna, EX $20.00
People, 1986, May 6, Bette Davis, EX+ $5.00
People Weekly, 1976, July 7, Paul McCartney, NM.......$8.00
Picture Play, 1936, July, Madge Evans, EX $25.00
Playboy, 1964, January, Marilyn Monroe nude photo, EX ..$35.00
Playboy, 1965, February, Beatles interview, EX $45.00
Playboy, 1981, September, Bo Derek, EX....................$12.00
Playboy, 1985, January, Goldie Hawn, EX+ $8.00
Playgirl, 1976, August, Robert Redford, EX+ $32.00
Popular Mechanics, 1942, Frozen Billions, VG+ $10.00
Redbook, 1934, November, Herbert Hoover, EX...........$8.00
Redbook, 1954, November, Grace Kelly, EX $15.00
Redbook, 1955, July, Marilyn Monroe.........................$55.00
Rolling Stone, 1975, November, 23, Pattie Hearst story,
    EX+..$20.00
Rolling Stone, 1985, May 9, Madonna, M, from $6 to...$8.00
Rolling Stone, 1986, #486, Billy Joel, EX......................$5.00
Rolling Stone, 1987, February 12, Pee Wee Herman, EX..$5.00
Saturday Evening Post, 1936, July 4, Captain America,
    NM $16.00
Saturday Evening Post, 1956, October 13, Eisenhower article,
    EX...$24.00
Saturday Evening Post, 1963, May 11, Leo Durocher,
    EX...$15.00
Saturday Evening Post, 1964, February 15, Sophia Loren,
    EX...$12.00
Saturday Evening Post, 1980, December, Muppets, EX...$5.00
Screen Guide, 1936, Ginger Rogers, EX......................$20.00
Screenland, 1934, February, Jean Harlow, EX.............$60.00
Screenland, 1939, October, Claudette Colbert, EX+ $25.00
Screenland, 1949, August, Maureen O'Hara, EX+ $18.00
Sporting News, 1947, December 3, Joe DiMaggio, EX .$38.00
Sporting News, 1974, August 17, Reggie Jackson, EX ..$8.00
Sports Illustrated, 1954, August 23, Yankee cards, EX ..$325.00
Sports Illustrated, 1958, May 12, Americas Cup, EX......$8.00
Sports Illustrated, 1969, October 20, World Series, M.$10.00
Sports Illustrated, 1972, March 13, Johnny Bench, EX..$10.00
Sports Illustrated, 1978, February 27, Leon Spinks, EX.$5.00
Sports Illustrated, 1990, August 6, Joe Montana, EX $6.00

Tattler, 1930s-40s, EX, ea from $4 to...........................$6.00
Time, 1937, December 27, Disney, EX $25.00
Time, 1944, July 17, Ernie Pyle, EX+...........................$8.00

Time, 1964, January 3, Martin Luther King, EX/VG, from $12.00 to $15.00.

Time, 1973, January 22, Marlon Brando, EX.................$5.00
Vogue, 1895, October 10, golf issue, EX.....................$70.00
Vogue, 1927, November 1, Bolin cover, EX.................$35.00
Woman's Day, 1940, September, Jimmy Stewart/J Edgar
    Hoover, VG...$6.00
Woman's Home Companion, 1904, February, features
    Edison's home, EX...$20.00

Pulp Magazines

As early as the turn of the century, pulp magazines were beginning to appear, but by the 1930s, their popularity had literally exploded. Called pulps because of the cheap wood-pulp paper they were printed on, crime and detective stories, westerns, adventure tales, and mysteries were the order of the day. Crime pulps sold for as little as 10¢; some of the westerns were 15¢. Plots were imaginative and spicy, if not downright risque. The top three publishers were Street and Smith, Popular, and the Thrilling Group. Some of the more familiar pulp-magazine authors were Agatha Christy, Clarence E. Mulford, Erle Stanley Gardner, Ellery Queen, Edgar Rice Burroughs, Louis L'Amour, and Max Brand. Until the 1950s when slick-paper magazines signed their death warrant, they were published by the thousands. Because of the poor quality of their paper, many have not survived. Those that have are seldom rated better than very good. A near-mint to mint example will bring a premium price, since it is almost impossible to locate one so well preserved. Except for a few very rare editions, many are in the average price range suggested below — some much lower.

Amazing Stories, 1931, August, G................................$15.00
Amazing Stories, 1932, October, VG $20.00
Amazing Stories, 1933, April, G+.................................$25.00
Amazing Stories, 1934, June, VG.................................$18.00
Amazing Stories, 1936, October, VG $20.00
Amazing Stories, 1945, September, VG $13.00
Amazing Stories, 1947, August, G+..............................$8.00

Amazing Stories, 1951, August, VG..................**$8.00**
Amazing Stories (Amazing Science Fiction), 1971, March, VG..................**$4.00**
American Boy, 1932, January, VG..................**$15.00**
Analog, 1964, November, VG..................**$6.00**
Analog Science Fiction, 1983, November, VG+.............**$3.00**
Argosy, 1932, November 5, VG..................**$25.00**
Argosy, 1942, March 7, EX..................**$15.00**
Argosy, 1962, August, VG..................**$12.00**
Asimov Science Fiction Magazine, 1986, May, EX........**$3.00**
Astounding, 1937, April, G+..................**$20.00**
Avon Fantasy Reader, 1947, February, VG..................**$15.00**
Avon Fantasy Reader, 1950, #12, G+..................**$10.00**
Bestseller Mystery, 1959, January, VG..................**$10.00**
Black Mask (Canadian), 1942, VG..................**$45.00**
Blue Book, 1935, Spetember, G..................**$8.00**
Charley Jones' Laugh Magazine, 1952, November, VG.**$8.00**
College Laughs, 1957, February, G+..................**$5.00**
Cosmic Frontiers, 1977, April, VG..................**$5.00**
Dark Fantasy, #20, VG..................**$8.00**
Dell Mystery Novels, 1955, January-March, #1, G+......**$8.00**
Detective Story Magazine, 1927, March 12, VG...........**$40.00**
Dime Mystery Magazine, 1949, October, NM.............**$13.00**
Doc Savage, 1938, September, VG..................**$65.00**
Ellery Queen, 1949, January, EX..................**$12.00**
Ellery Queen, 1956, July, VG..................**$18.00**
Ellery Queen, 1973, February, Vol 61 #2, VG.............**$3.00**
Ellery Queen, 1976, June, EX..................**$4.00**
Famous Fantastic Mysteries, 1939, December, Vol 1 #3, G+..................**$12.00**
Famous Fantastic Mysteries, 1940, March, Vol 1 #6, G.**$8.00**
Famous Fantastic Mysteries, 1941, October, Vol 3 #4, G..**$100.00**
Famous Fantastic Mysteries, 1948, April, Vol 9 #4, G...**$6.00**
Famous Fantastic Mysteries, 1950, February, Vol 11 #3, G+..................**$7.00**
Famous Fantastic Mysteries, 1952, December, Vol 14 #1, G+..................**$7.00**
Fantastic Adventures, 1939, September, Vol 1 #3, VG...**$20.00**
Fantastic Adventures, 1941, March, Vol 3 #2, G..........**$10.00**
Fantastic Adventures, 1947, March, Vol 9 #2, G............**$8.00**
Fantastic Adventures, 1948, December, Vol 10 #12.......**$7.00**
Fantastic Adventures, 1948, March, G..................**$5.00**
Fantastic Novels, 1948, March, Vol 1 #6, G+..................**$8.00**
Fantastic Novels, 1949, July, Vol 3 #2, G..................**$6.00**
Final Frontier, 1989, August, Vol 2 #4, EX..................**$5.00**
From Unknown Worlds, 1948, #1, G+..................**$15.00**
Galaxy, 1975, January, Vol 36 #1, VG+..................**$3.00**
Hitchcock Mystery Magazine, 1972, January, EX+......**$15.00**
Hitchcock Mystery Magazine, 1984, June, VG..............**$3.00**
Magazine of Fantasy & Science Fiction, 1971, June, Vol 40 #6, VG+..................**$5.00**
Magazine of Fantasy & Science Fiction, 1981, July, Vol 61 #1, VG+..................**$10.00**
Manhunt, 1953, February, Vol 1 #2, G+..................**$11.00**
Marvel, 1939, August, VG..................**$20.00**
Marvel, 1951, February, VG..................**$11.00**
Master Detective, 1942, January, EX..................**$8.00**

Mike Shane, 1972, November, Vol 31 #6, VG.............**$3.00**
Mystery Digest, 1957, May, Vol 1, #1, EX+..................**$6.00**
Other Worlds, 1949, November, Vol 1 #1, G+.............**$10.00**
Other Worlds, 1952, December, #24, VG..................**$5.00**
Planet Stories, 1939, Winter, Vol 1 #1, VG..................**$25.00**
Science Fiction Plus, 1953, March, Vol 1 #1, VG........**$10.00**
Space Journal, 1958, Spring, Vol 1 #2, VG+..................**$10.00**
Space Science Fiction, 1957, August, G..................**$9.00**
Super Science Stories, 1940, March, Vol 1 #1, G+.......**$15.00**
Super Science Stories, 1940, May, Vol 1, #1, G+.........**$15.00**
Suspense (American Release), 1951, Spring, Vol 1 #1, G+..**$6.00**
The Avenger, 1939, September, Vol 1 #1, Fair............**$10.00**
Twilight Zone, 1982, October, Vol 2, #7, EX..............**$10.00**
Twilight Zone, 1984, December, Vol 4 #5, EX............**$8.00**
Twilight Zone, 1986, February, Vol 5 #6, Stephen King, EX..................**$10.00**
Weird Stories, 1946, September, VG..................**$12.00**
Weird Tales, 1935, August, G..................**$20.00**
Weird Tales, 1948, March, Vol 40 #3, VG..................**$20.00**
Weird Tales, 1948, May, Vol 40 #4, VG+..................**$15.00**
Weird Tales, 1950, July, Vol 42, #5, G+..................**$15.00**
Weird Tales, 1951, Vol 43 #2, VG..................**$20.00**
Whisperer, 1940, October, Vol 1 #1, G..................**$10.00**
Wonder Stories, 1933, October, VG..................**$14.00**
Worlds Beyond, 1950, December, Vol 1 #1, G+..........**$13.00**

Marbles

There are three broad categories of collectible marbles, the antique variety, machine-made, and contemporary marbles. Under those broad divisions are many classifications. Everett Grist delves into all three categories in his books called *Big Book of Marbles, Antique and Collectible Marbles,* and *Machine Made and Contemporary Marbles* (Collector Books).

Sulfide marbles have figures (generally animals or birds) encased in the center. The glass is nearly always clear; a common example in excellent condition may run as low as $100.00, while those with an unusual subject or made of colored glass may go for more than $1,000.00. Many machine-made marbles are very reasonable, but if the colors are especially well placed and selected, good examples sell in excess of $50.00. Peltier comic character marbles often bring prices of $100.00 and up with Betty Boop, Moon Mulins, and Kayo being the rarest and most valuable. Watch for reproductions. New comic character marbles have the design printed on a large area of plain white glass with color swirled through the back and sides.

No matter where your interests lie, remember that condition is extremely important. From the nature of their use, mint-condition marbles are very rare and may be worth as much as three to five times more than one that is near-mint. Chipped and cracked marbles may be worth half or less, and some will be worthless. Polishing detracts considerably.

See also Akro Agate.

Advisor: Everett Grist (See Directory, Marbles)

Agate, contemporary, carnelian, 1¾" **$20.00**
Bennington, blue, ¾" **$1.00**
Bennington, fancy, ¾" **$2.00**
Christensen Agate, slag **$25.00**
Comic, Andy Gump **$80.00**
Goldstone, ¾" **$12.50**
Line Crockery, clay, 1¾" **$20.00**

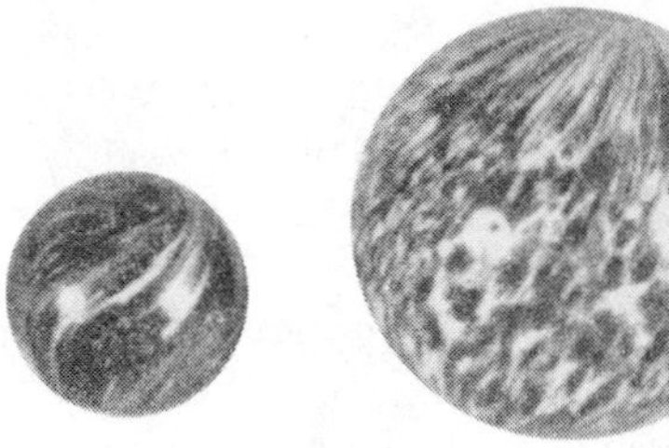

Lutz onionskin, green and white, 1¼", EX+, $350.00; onionskin, red, white, and blue, 2¼", EX, $250.00.

Marble King, bumblebee **$1.00**
Mica, blue, ¾" **$30.00**
Onionskin, ¾" **$80.00**
Opaque Swirl, green, ¾" **$40.00**
Peltier Glass, National line **$25.00**
Peltier Glass, slag **$15.00**
Pottery, 1¾" **$20.00**
Solid opaque, ¾" **$40.00**
Sulfide, bird, 2" **$100.00**
Sulfide, circus bear, 2" **$140.00**
Sulfide, fish, 1¾", M **$175.00**
Sulfide, lamb, 1¾" **$125.00**
Sulfide, parrot, 1½", EX **$100.00**
Sulfide, rooster, 1¾" **$150.00**

Match Safes

Match safes or vesta boxes, as they are known in England, evolved to keep matches dry and to protect against from unintentional ignition. These containers were produced in enormous quantities over a 75-year period from various materials including silver, brass, aluminum, and gold. Their shapes and designs were limitless and resulted in a wide variety of popular and whimsical styles. They have become very sought-after collectibles and can usually be recognized by a small, rough striking surface, usually on the bottom edge. Collectors should be cautious of numerous sterling reproductions currently on the market.

Advisor: George Sparacio (See Directory, Match Safes)

Alligator, figural, head forms lid, Souvenir St Augustine FL, brass, 2½x1½", EX **$400.00**
Alligator chasing Negro, Souvenir of FL, insert type, by August Goertz Co, plated brass, 2¾x1½", EX **$295.00**

Cat in the hat, original paint, 2½" x 1⅜", EX, $425.00. (Photo courtesy George Sparacio)

Cigar, bunch of 10, figural, nickel-plated brass, 2¾x1½", EX **$195.00**
Clown seated w/lg nose & single hair curl on head, figural, brass, 2½x1⅜", EX **$395.00**
Coffeepot, figural, brass, 1⅞x1¾", EX **$210.00**
Columbian World's Fair, Columbus & Jefferson, applied disk w/Chicago 1893, oval, nickel-plated brass, 2¾x1", EX **$125.00**
Cupid in garden, by Gorham Mfg Co, catalog #B1305, sterling, 2⅝x1¾", EX **$395.00**
Dragon motif, Japanese, brass, 2⅝x1½", EX **$140.00**
Erotica, couple copulating, automata type, nickel-plated, 2½x1½", EX **$3,200.00**
Fishing motif, fisherman catching trout, insert type, by August Goertz Co, 2¾x1½", EX **$75.00**
Frog, figural, Gorham Mfg Co, silver plate, 2x1½", EX ... **$395.00**
Gladstone, figural, flat back, plated brass, 1⅞x1½", EX .. **$175.00**
Gold Dust Twins, by Wm Schimoer Co, plated brass, 3x1⅝", EX **$275.00**
Golf motif, man hitting ball, sterling, 2½x1½", EX ... **$625.00**
Hidden photo, barrel shape, by Batin & Co, sterling, 2½x1⅝", EX **$275.00**
Hobo shoe, figural, advertising on sole, by Western Aluminum Co, aluminum, 3x1⅜", EX **$125.00**
Home Insurance/3-horse fire engine, by William Kerr, sterling, 2½x1⅜", EX **$625.00**
King George V & Queen Mary commemorative, book shaped, by Hamburg Rubber Co, vulcanite, 2x1½", EX **$85.00**
Knight in armor/castle motif, sterling, 2½x1⅜", EX . **$195.00**
Moreland Match enameled on sterling, 2¼x1⅝" **$375.00**
Morgan Tires, gutta percha, slip top lid, 2¾x1⅜", EX .. **$65.00**
Owl, figural, Japanese, brass, 2½x1½", EX **$425.00**
Owl on branch, figural, brass, 2¼x1¼", EX **$225.00**
Quincy Rock Mine/Copper Country Souvenir, copper, 2⅝x1½", EX **$165.00**
Rabbit & badger motif, Japanese, brass, 2½x1⅜", EX **$195.00**
Revolver, figural, plated brass w/vulcanite handles, 2⅜x3¾", EX **$365.00**
Risque motif on & inside lid, enamel on brass, French, 1⅞x1½", EX **$425.00**

Samurai warrior, stamped Kirin, Japanese, brass, 1⅞x1⅛", EX **$425.00**

Scalloped shell, figural, brass, 1⅞x2⅛", EX **$125.00**

Scarab, figural, plated brass, 2½x1⅛", EX **$350.00**

Schlitz Beer, double lid, stamp combo, by August Goertz Co, plated brass, 2¾x1½", EX **$95.00**

Shriners of North America motif, star set w/garnet, by Fairchild, sterling, 2⅜x1⅝", EX **$185.00**

Skunk w/sunken eyes, figural, brass, hinged jaw, 1¾x1½", EX **$135.00**

Smoking motif w/4 faces, by R Blackinton & Co, catalog #647, sterling, 2⅝x1¾", EX **$335.00**

Sorrento ware, inlaid decoration of lady, wood, 2¾x1½", EX **$90.00**

Suitcase, figural, nickel-plated brass, 1⅜x1⅞", EX **$215.00**

Swimmers in wave, by Kerr, catalog #941, sterling, 2¾x1⅞", EX **$395.00**

Max, Peter

Born in Germany in 1937, Peter Max came to the United States in 1953 where he later studied art in New York City. His work is colorful and his genre psychedelic. He is a prolific artist, best known for his designs from the '60s and '70s that typified the 'hippie' movement. In addition to his artwork, he has also designed housewares, clothing, toys, linens, etc. In the 1970s, commissioned by Iroquois China, he developed several lines of dinnerware in his own distinctive style. Today, many of those who were the youth of the hippie generation are active collectors of his work.

See also Hippie Collectibles.

Advisor: Richard Synchef (See Directory, Beatnik and Hippie Collectibles)

Cookie jar, Zero, 1989, by Sigma, from $175.00 to $200.00. (Photo courtesy June Moon)

Belt, red, white & blue w/stars & moons, Peter Max on metal buckle, EX **$135.00**

Book, Land of Blue, Franklin Watts Inc, 1970, EX **$60.00**

Book, Superposter Book, photo on front, 14 double-sided pages, Crown Publishing, 1971, 11x16", EX **$85.00**

Bowl, bull's-eye w/orange center w/radiating green, yellow & white, black border, EX **$40.00**

Clock, alarm; GE model #7270, face designed by Max, 5x3", EX **$110.00**

Clock, wall; 7-Up, psychedelic colors on flower-shape face, Everbrite Electric Signs, florescent lights inside, EX .**$105.00**

Cookbook, New Age Organic-Vegetarian; recipes by Peter Max & Ronwen Proust, 1971, EX **$70.00**

Cookbook, Teen Cuisine: A Beginner's Guide to French Cooking, Kirsch & Klein, Parents Magazine Press, 1969, EX **$60.00**

Greeting cards, yellow w/Love in red & picture of female face in profile, made by Regency, 25 cards & envelopes, EXIB **$90.00**

Model, Continental Boeing 777-200, Herpa Wings, MIB..**$85.00**

Pillow, Smiley face w/lots of teeth, vinyl, blow-up, 16x16", EX **$25.00**

Plate, butterfly design, by Iroquois China, 10", EX **$55.00**

Plate, gray w/design in center, porcelain, 1970s, 11½", EX..**$45.00**

Plate, multicolored flower, glass, 8½" **$65.00**

Poster, Cherry Creek Gallery, 1979, 28x22" **$65.00**

Poster, Grateful Dead, skull & lightning bolt design, Spring Tour 1988, 34x24" **$55.00**

Poster, Life Is Beautiful, Stay Alive, Don't Smoke Cigarettes, 1970s American Cancer Society, 16½x24¾", NM ..**$110.00**

Poster book, 24 posters, 1970, EX **$140.00**

Scarf, red lips in center w/geometric design, silk, 21x21" **$65.00**

Scarf, Saturn in center w/2 figures facing it, pink, purple, turquoise & white, 15x70", NM **$90.00**

Sign, 7-Up-The Uncola, metal, die-cut, 1970s, 23¾x12", EX **$85.00**

Tie, American flags w/black background, Neomax™, metal **$25.00**

Tray, butterfly design on yellow w/blue border, metal, round, EX **$65.00**

Tray, child w/Happy on hat, metal, round, NM **$65.00**

Tray, Love w/female head, red, green, pink & yellow, metal, 12⅞" dia **$50.00**

Watch, Save Our Ocean painting background, 1991, Japan, leather band, M **$45.00**

McCoy Pottery

This is probably the best-known of all American potteries, due to the wide variety of goods they produced from 1910 until the pottery finally closed only a few years ago.

They were located in Roseville, Ohio, the pottery center of the United States. They're most famous for their cookie jars, of which were made several hundred styles and variations. (For a listing of these, see the section entitled Cookie Jars.) McCoy is also well known for their figural planters, novelty kitchenware, and dinnerware.

They used a variety of marks over the years, but with little consistency, since it was a common practice to discontinue an item for awhile and then bring it out again decorated in a manner that would be in sync with current tastes. All of McCoy's marks were 'in the mold.' None were ink stamped, so very often the in-mold mark remained as it was when the mold was originally created. Most marks contain the McCoy name, though some of the early pieces were simply signed 'NM' for Nelson McCoy (Sanitary and Stoneware Company, the company's original title). Early stoneware pieces were sometimes impressed with a shield containing a number. If you have a piece with the Lancaster Colony Company mark (three curved lines — the left one beginning as a vertical and terminating as a horizontal, the other two formed as 'C's contained in the curve of the first), you'll know that your piece was made after the mid-'70s when McCoy was owned by that group. Today even these later pieces are becoming collectible.

If you'd like to learn more about this company, we recommend *The Collector's Encyclopedia of McCoy Pottery* and *The Collector's Encyclopedia of Brush-McCoy Pottery*, both by Sharon and Bob Huxford; and *McCoy Pottery, Collector's Reference & Value Guide, Vols 1, 2 & 3* by Bob and Margaret Hanson and Craig Nissen. All are published by Collector Books.

A note regarding cookie jars: beware of *new* cookie jars marked McCoy. It seems that the original McCoy pottery never registered their trademark, and for several years it was legally used by a small company in Rockwood, Tennessee. Not only did they use the original mark, but they reproduced some of the original jars as well. If you're not an experienced collector, you may have trouble distinguishing the new from the old. Some (but not all) are dated #93, the '#' one last attempt to fool the novice, but there are differences to watch for. The new ones are slightly smaller in size, and the finish is often flawed. He has also used the McCoy mark on jars never produced by the original company, such as Little Red Riding Hood and the Luzianne mammy. Only lately did it become known that the last owners of the McCoy pottery actually did register the trademark; so, having to drop McCoy, he has since worked his way through two other marks: Brush-McCoy and (currently) BJ Hull.

See Also Cookie Jars.

Advisor: Bob Hanson

Newsletter: *NM Xpress*
Carol Seman, Editor
8934 Brecksville Rd., #406, Brecksville, OH 44141

Ashtray, There's One in Every Bar, McCoy mark, from $35 to **$50.00**
Bank, Hung-Over Dog, leaning against barrel bank, 6x8", from $35 to...**$45.00**
Bank, Metz Beer, barrel form, unmarked, 8¼", from $50 to **$60.00**
Basket, yellow basketweave w/embossed flowers ea side of handle, Lancaster mark, 1967, 5x8", from $35 to.**$45.00**
Beverage server & stand, Esmond, from $40 to..........**$60.00**

Bookends, swallow, ivory w/hand decor, McCoy mark, 1956, 6x5½", pr from $200 to.......................................**$250.00**
Bowl, Pussy Cat Pussy Cat Where Have You Been?, white, 1940s, 6½", from $70 to.....................................**$100.00**
Bowl, serving; Islander Collection, white, 1979, from $20 to **$25.00**
Bowl, Triple Bulb, pink w/darker base spray, McCoy mark, 1950s, from $90 to..**$110.00**
Candle holder tray, green, 2 holders at opposite ends of 6-sided tray, NM mark, 1940s, 11½", from $125 to..**$150.00**
Candy dish, gondola form, gold trim, McCoy mark, 1955, from $60 to...**$75.00**
Coffeepot, Brown Antique Rose, 10-cup, ...**$45.00**
Console set, Starburst, centerpiece bowl & 2 candle holders, 1972, 3-pc set from $80 to...............................**$100.00**

Fish flower holders, 4¼", rose production glaze, from $80.00 to $200.00; rare coral glaze, from $250.00 to $300.00. (Photo courtesy Margaret and Bob Hanson and Craig Nissen)

Flower bowl, Sunburst Gold, 5½", from $30 to **$40.00**
Grease jar, cabbage figural, 1954, from $100 to........**$125.00**
Jar, porch; embossed foliage, green or white, NM mark, 1940s, 11x9½", from $150 to **$200.00**
Jardiniere, Butterfly, marked, 3½", from $25 to **$40.00**
Jardiniere, Swirl, orchid, McCoy mark, 1962, 7", from $20 to **$25.00**
Jardiniere & pedestal, Berries & Leaves (Stubby), unmarked, 1930s-40s, 7", 6½", from $200 to **$250.00**
Lamp, Mermaid, seated before shell, unmarked, 9¾x6", from $200 to..**$300.00**
Lamp, Wagon Wheel, unmarked, 1954, 8" w/original shade, from $75 to..**$100.00**
Lamp base, berries & leaves, matt brown & green w/tassels, 1930s, from $125 to...**$175.00**
Lamp base, berries & leaves, rose, 1930s, from $100 to...**$150.00**
Lamp base, Double Handle, brown onyx, 1930s, from $120 to...**$150.00**
Paperweight, baseball glove shape, 5", from $75 to.**$100.00**
Pitcher, ball jug, cobalt blue, made w/NM & McCoy USA marks, ea from $85 to **$125.00**
Pitcher, ball jug, Hobnail, yellow, unmarked, 1940s, 6", from $100 to..**$150.00**
Pitcher, pig figural, green, McCoy mark, 1940s, 5", from $500 to..**$600.00**
Pitcher, Strawberry Country, McCoy mark, 1970s, 32-oz, from $35 to...**$50.00**

Pitcher vase, Antique Rose, McCoy mark, 1959, 9", from $35 to...**$40.00**

Pitcher vase, parrot, green or brown spray, McCoy mark, 1952, 7", from $150 to....................................**$200.00**

Planter, baby carriage, What About Me?, gold trim, 1955, 7¾" x 6", from $100.00 to $120.00.
(Photo courtesy Margaret and Bob Hanson and Craig Nissen)

Planter, baby crib, pink or blue, unmarked, 1954, from $60 to...**$70.00**

Planter, bird (backwards), NM mark, from $50 to......**$60.00**

Planter, bird dog, speckled pointer on green & brown base, McCoy mark, 1959, 7¾", from $125 to..............**$175.00**

Planter, Cope monkey head, unmarked, 1940s, 5½", from $100 to...**$200.00**

Planter, dragonfly, pastel, 1940s, 3½", from $35 to.....**$45.00**

Planter, duck, white w/gold trim, McCoy mark, 1952, 5x8", from $50 to..**$65.00**

Planter, Dutch shoe, applied rose, McCoy mark, late 1940s, 7½", from $25 to...**$50.00**

Planter, goose pulling cart, variety of colors made, 1940s, 4¾x8", ea from $35 to..**$45.00**

Planter, Harmony, modernistic style w/linear decor, 1960, 12", from $25 to..**$35.00**

Planter, kitten w/ball of yarn, McCoy mark, #3026, 7x5½", from $80 to...**$100.00**

Planter, lamb, black, gray, or white, early 1940s, NM mark, 4½x6", from $50 to..**$60.00**

Planter, lion, pastel colors, NM mark, 1940s, 4x8¾", from $80 to...**$100.00**

Planter, pelican, floral decals & gold trim, NM mark, 1940s, 5¾x7¾", from $100 to.....................................**$150.00**

Planter, plow boy, brown blend, McCoy mark, 1955, 7x8", from $100 to...**$125.00**

Planter, shell, yellow or green, unmarked, 1955, 5x4", ea from $15 to..**$20.00**

Planter, swans (twin), yellow or white, McCoy mark, 1953, 8½", from $50 to..**$60.00**

Planter, turtle, green or chartreuse drip, McCoy mark, 1955, 12½x9", from $150 to.....................................**$200.00**

Planter, wheelbarrow & rooster, McCoy mark, 1955, from $100 to...**$125.00**

Plate, dinner; Canyon, brown matt, round, 1977, from $10 to...**$15.00**

Reamer, yellow or white, 1949, 8", from $60 to..........**$75.00**

Sand jar, embossed foliage, green or white, McCoy mark, 1955, 14x10", from $200 to.....................................**$250.00**

Stretch animal, dachshund, 1940s, from $175 to.......**$225.00**

Stretch animal, goat, 1940s, from $200 to..................**$250.00**

Vase, basket, green, McCoy mark, 1959, 8", from $40 to...**$50.00**

Vase, basketweave, 8", from $45 to............................**$60.00**

Vase, butterfly, handles, marked, 10", from $125 to.**$200.00**

Vase, Butterfly Castle Gate, pink, USA mark, 6x7", from $150 to...**$200.00**

Vase, cat figural, black, gray matt or white, 1960, 14", ea from $200 to..**$250.00**

Vase, cornucopia; yellow, McCoy mark, 1957, 7x6", from $30 to...**$40.00**

Vase, double tulip; white w/red tipping, McCoy mark, late 1940s, 8", from $85 to **$110.00**

Vase, Early American, blue dots in center of embossed diamonds on white, McCoy mark, 9x6", from $40 to..**$60.00**

Vase, Floraline, goblet form, green, marked, 6½", from $15 to...**$25.00**

Vase, Floraline, hourglass form, white, 7", from $20 to..**$25.00**

Vase, Floraline, twisted form w/sq top, marked, 9", from $25 to...**$30.00**

Vase, Floraline, white, round, marked, 4", from $15 to..**$20.00**

Vase, Hobnail V, NM mark, 9", from $125 to **$150.00**

Vase, Hyacinth, blue w/green leaves, McCoy mark, 1950, 8", from $100 to..**$125.00**

Vase, Ivy, hand-decorated, brown twig handles, McCoy mark, 1953, 9", from $100 to **$150.00**

Vase, Ivy, hand-decorated, much gold, McCoy mark, 1955, 9", from $200 to..**$300.00**

Vase, lizard handle, matt colors, unmarked, 9" or 10", ea from $300 to..**$400.00**

Vase, ribbed, cylindrical, McCoy mark, late 1940s, 10", from $50 to..**$60.00**

Vase, Sunflower, solid color, unmarked, mid-1950s, 9", from $40 to..**$60.00**

Vase, Vesta, blue, footed, 1962, 10", from $35 to.......**$45.00**

Wall pocket, butterfly, blue, NM mark, 7x6", from $250 to...**$350.00**

Wall pocket, clown, red cold paint, 1940s, 8", from $100 to...**$150.00**

Wall pocket, cuckoo clock, McCoy mark, 1950s, 8", from $125 to...**$150.00**

Wall pocket, lily, light pink, 6½", from $70 to.........**$100.00**

Wall pocket, pear, natural colors, 1950s, 7x6", from $65 to...**$80.00**

Wall pocket, urn, pink w/gold trim, McCoy mark, 1955, 4½x6½", from $50 to...**$75.00**

Wall pocket, violin, blue or brown, McCoy mark, mid-1950s, 10½", ea from $100 to...**$150.00**

Brown Drip Dinnerware

One of McCoy's dinnerware lines that was introduced in the 1960s is beginning to attract a following. It's a glossy brown stoneware-type pattern with frothy white decoration around the rims. Similar lines of brown stoneware were made by many other companies, Hull and Pfaltzgraff among them. McCoy simply called their line 'Brown Drip.'

Baker, oval, 10½"	**$10.00**
Baker, oval, 12½", from $18 to	**$22.00**
Bean pot, individual, 12-oz	**$4.00**
Bean pot, 1½-qt, from $15 to	**$20.00**
Bean pot, 3-qt, from $25 to	**$30.00**
Bowl, cereal; 6"	**$6.00**
Bowl, lug soup; 12-oz	**$8.00**
Bowl, lug soup; 18-oz	**$10.00**
Bowl, spaghetti or salad; 12½"	**$20.00**
Bowl, vegetable; divided	**$12.00**
Bowl, vegetable; 9"	**$12.00**
Butter dish, ¼-lb	**$15.00**
Candle holders, pr, from $18 to	**$22.00**
Canister, coffee	**$45.00**
Casserole, 2-qt	**$15.00**
Casserole, 3½-qt	**$20.00**
Casserole, 3-qt, w/hen-on-nest lid, from $45 to	**$50.00**
Corn tray, individual, from $15 to	**$20.00**
Creamer	**$5.00**
Cruet, oil & vinegar; ea from $12 to	**$15.00**
Cup, 8-oz	**$5.00**
Custard cup, 6-oz	**$4.00**
Gravy boat, from $12 to	**$15.00**
Mug, pedestal base, 12-oz	**$7.50**
Mug, 8-oz	**$5.00**
Mug, 12-oz, from $6 to	**$8.00**
Pie plate, 9", from $15 to	**$18.00**
Pitcher, jug style, 32-oz	**$20.00**
Plate, dinner; 10"	**$10.00**
Plate, salad; 7"	**$6.50**
Plate, soup & sandwich; w/lg cup ring	**$10.00**
Platter, fish form, 18"	**$32.00**
Platter, oval, 14", from $12 to	**$18.00**
Salt & pepper shakers, pr, from $6 to	**$9.00**
Saucer	**$5.00**
Souffle dish, 2-qt	**$9.50**
Teapot, 6-cup, from $18 to	**$22.00**
Trivet, concentric circles, round	**$12.00**

Melmac Dinnerware

The postwar era gave way to many new technologies in manufacturing. With the discovery that thermoplastics could be formed by the interaction of melamine and formaldehyde, Melmac was born. This colorful and decorative product found an eager market due to its style and affordability. Another attractive feature was its resistance to breakage. Who doesn't recall the sound it made as it bounced off the floor when you'd accidentally drop a piece.

Popularity began to wane: the dinnerware was found to fade with repeated washings, the edges could chip, and the surfaces could be scratched, stained, or burned. Melmac fell from favor in the late '60s and early '70s. At that time, it was restyled to imitate china that had become popular due to increased imports.

As always, demand and availability determine price. Our values are for items in mint condition only; pieces with scratches, chips, or stains have no value. Lines of similar value are grouped together. As there are many more manufacturers other than those listed, for a more thorough study of the subject we recommend *Melmac Dinnerware* by Gregory R. Zimmer and Alvin Daigle Jr.

See also Russel Wright.

Advisor: Gregory R. Zimmer (See Directory, Melmac)

Internet Information: Melmac Dinnerware Discussion List: www.egroups.com; search for MelmacDinnerware

Aztec, Debonaire, Flite-Lane, Mar-Crest, Restraware, Rivieraware, Stetson, Westinghouse

Bowl, cereal; from $2 to	**$3.00**
Bowl, fruit; from $1 to	**$2.00**
Butter dish, from $5 to	**$7.00**
Cup & saucer, from $2 to	**$3.00**
Gravy boat, from $5 to	**$6.00**
Plate, dinner; from $2 to	**$3.00**
Salt & pepper shakers, pr from $4 to	**$5.00**
Sugar bowl, w/lid, from $3 to	**$4.00**
Tumbler, 10-oz, from $7 to	**$8.00**

Boontoon, Branchell, Brookpark, Harmony House, Prolon, Watertown Lifetime Ware

Bowl, fruit; from $3 to	**$4.00**
Bowl, serving; from $8 to	**$10.00**
Butter dish, from $10 to	**$12.00**
Creamer, from $5 to	**$6.00**
Jug, w/lid, from $20 to	**$25.00**
Plate, bread; from $2 to	**$3.00**
Plate, compartment; from $10 to	**$12.00**
Plate, dinner; from $4 to	**$5.00**
Plate, salad; from $4 to	**$5.00**
Salt & pepper shakers, pr from $6 to	**$8.00**
Sugar bowl, from $6 to	**$8.00**
Tidbit tray, 2-tier, from $15 to	**$18.00**
Tray, bread; from $8 to	**$10.00**
Tumbler, 10-oz, from $12 to	**$15.00**

Fostoria, Lucent

Bowl, cereal; from $7 to	**$9.00**
Butter dish, from $15 to	**$18.00**
Creamer, from $8 to	**$10.00**
Cup & saucer, from $8 to	**$12.00**
Plate, bread; from $3 to	**$4.00**

Plate, dinner; from $6 to **$8.00**
Platter, from $12 to **$15.00**
Relish tray, from $15 to **$18.00**
Sugar bowl, w/lid, from $12 to **$15.00**

Bowl, divided serving; from $15.00 to $18.00.
(Photo courtesy Gregory R. Zimmer and Alvin Daigle Jr.)

Metlox Pottery

Founded in the late 1920s in Manhattan Beach, California, this company initially produced tile and commercial advertising signs. By the early '30s, their business in these areas had dwindled, and they began to concentrate their efforts on the manufacture of dinnerware, artware, and kitchenware. Carl Gibbs has authored *Collector's Encyclopedia of Metlox Potteries*, published by Collector Books, which we recommend for more information.

Carl Romanelli was the designer responsible for modeling many of the figural pieces they made during the late '30s and early '40s. These items are usually imprinted with his signature and are very collectible today. Coming on strong is their line of 'Poppets,' made from the mid-'60s through the mid-'70s. There were eighty-eight in all, whimsical, comical, sometimes grotesque. They represented characters ranging from the seven-piece Salvation Army Group to royalty, religious figures, policemen, and professionals. They came with a name tag, some had paper labels, others backstamps. If you question a piece whose label is missing, a good clue to look for is pierced facial features.

Poppytrail and Vernonware were the trade names for their dinnerware lines. Among their more popular patterns were California Ivy, California Provincial, Red Rooster, Homestead Provincial, and the later embossed patterns, Sculptured Grape, Sculptured Zinnia, and Sculptured Daisy.

Some of their lines can be confusing. There are two 'rooster' lines, Red Rooster (red, orange, and brown) and California Provincial (this one is in dark green and burgundy), and two 'homestead' lines, Colonial Homestead (red, orange, and brown like the Red Rooster line) and Homestead Provincial. Just remember the Provincial patterns are done in dark green and burgundy. See also Cookie Jars.

Advisor: Carl Gibbs, Jr. (See Directory, Metlox)

Antique Grape, creamer, 10-oz **$30.00**
Antique Grape, gravy, faststand, 1-pt **$45.00**
Antique Grape, pitcher, sm, 1½-pt **$55.00**
Antique Grape, sugar bowl, w/lid, 10-oz **$35.00**
Autumn Berry, butter dish, w/lid **$55.00**
Autumn Berry, mug, 8-oz **$22.00**
Autumn Berry, plate, dinner; 10¾" **$13.00**
California Aztec, plate, salad **$25.00**
California Confetti, bowl, vegetable; 9¼" **$50.00**
California Confetti, coaster **$25.00**
California Confetti, creamer **$32.00**
California Freeform, cup & saucer **$35.00**
California Freeform, flowerpot, 6" **$175.00**
California Freeform, pitcher, water **$300.00**
California Freeform, plate, dinner **$35.00**
California Ivy, bowl, salad; 11¼" **$90.00**
California Ivy, celery dish **$45.00**
California Ivy, egg cup **$38.00**
California Ivy, gravy boat, 12-oz **$38.00**
California Ivy, plate, dinner; 10¼" **$18.00**
California Peach Blossom, chop plate **$85.00**
California Peach Blossom, plate, dinner **$18.00**
California Provincial, candle holder **$60.00**
California Provincial, pepper mill **$60.00**
California Provincial, pipkin set **$450.00**
California Provincial, plate, dinner **$20.00**
California Provincial, platter, oval, 11" **$50.00**
California Provincial, teapot, w/lid, 42-oz (7-cup) **$145.00**
California Tempo, cup & saucer **$12.00**
Colonial Heritage, coffee carafe **$130.00**
Colonial Heritage, egg cup **$28.00**
Colonial Heritage, platter, oval, X-lg **$80.00**
Colorstax, baker, oval, 13" **$45.00**
Colorstax, bowl, cereal; 6½" **$18.00**
Colorstax, candlestick **$30.00**
Colorstax, pitcher, water; 2-qt **$75.00**
Homestead Provincial, bowl, salad; 11⅛" **$110.00**
Homestead Provincial, bowl, soup; 8" **$30.00**
Homestead Provincial, creamer, 6-oz **$32.00**
Homestead Provincial, plate, bread & butter; 6⅜" **$11.00**
Homestead Provincial, sprinkling can **$105.00**
Lotus, bowl, salad; 13½" **$95.00**
Lotus, chip 'n dip, shell **$55.00**
Lotus, gravy boat **$40.00**
Lotus, mug, 7-oz **$25.00**
Navajo, butter dish **$65.00**
Navajo, lug soup **$22.00**
Provincial Blue, ashtray, med, 6⅜" **$25.00**
Provincial Blue, cigarette box **$120.00**
Provincial Blue, cup & saucer, 6-oz **$20.00**
Provincial Blue, jam & mustard jars, ea **$75.00**
Provincial Blue, tumbler, 11-oz **$50.00**
Red Rooster, bowl, fruit; 6" **$14.00**
Red Rooster, buffet server, 12¼" **$70.00**
Red Rooster, plate, 10", from $13 to **$15.00**

Red Rooster, cookie jar, from $100.00 to $110.00. (Photo courtesy Joyce and Fred Roerig)

Red Rooster, sugar bowl, w/lid, 8-oz	$32.00
San Fernando, bowl, salad; 12½"	$70.00
Sculptured Daisy, cup & saucer	$14.00
Sculptured Daisy, platter, oval, 14¼"	$45.00
Sculptured Daisy, tumbler, 11-oz	$35.00
Sculptured Grape, bowl, soup; 8⅛"	$25.00
Sculptured Grape, pitcher, 2¼-qt	$80.00
Tickled Pink, chop plate, 13"	$45.00
Tickled Pink, plate, dinner; 10"	$13.00
Tickled Pink, salt & pepper shakers, pr	$30.00
True Blue, bowl, rim soup; 8⅛"	$20.00
True Blue, platter, oval, med, 12⅜"	$35.00
Vernon Antiqua, cup & saucer	$16.00
Vernon Antiqua, sugar bowl, w/lid, 10-oz	$32.00
Woodland Gold, coffeepot, w/lid, 8-cup	$100.00
Woodland Gold, mug, 8-oz	$25.00
Woodland Gold, salt & pepper shakers, pr	$26.00

Miscellaneous

Disney figurine, Alice in Wonderland	$400.00
Disney figurine, Baby Mouse (Cinderella)	$500.00
Disney figurine, Dumbo, mini, 1¾"	$200.00
Disney figurine, Faline	$165.00
Disney figurine, Sprite, Fantasia	$250.00
Miniature, alligator, 9"	$200.00
Miniature, canary on stump, 4⅝"	$125.00
Miniature, caterpillar	$140.00
Miniature, fawn, 5½"	$80.00
Miniature, penguin, 3"	$60.00
Miniature, terrier, very rare, 12½"	$500.00
Miniature, turtle, standing	$225.00
Nostalgia Line, American Royal Horse, colt, prone, 4¼x3"	$100.00
Nostalgia Line, Amish father, mother or child, ea	$70.00
Nostalgia Line, Chevrolet	$85.00
Nostalgia Line, locomotive	$65.00
Nostalgia Line, Santa	$90.00
Poppet, Angelina, angel, 7⅝"	$65.00
Poppet, Friar Tuck, 6½"	$55.00
Poppet, Grace, princess	$55.00

Poppet, Louisa, girl w/muff, 8½"	$55.00
Poppet, Penelope, nursemaid, 7¾"	$50.00
Poppet, Zelda, choral lady #2, 7⅝"	$85.00
Romanelli Artware, flower holder (Cornucopia Maid), 8¾"	$250.00
Romanelli Artware, vase, Sailfish, 9"	$160.00

Strawberry, fruit bowl, 10½" x 9½", from $50.00 to $55.00. (Photo courtesy Lee Garmon)

Milk Bottles

Between the turn of the century and the 1950s, milk was bought and sold in glass bottles. Until the '20s, the name and location of the dairy was embossed in the glass. After that it became commonplace to pyro-glaze (paint and fire) the lettering onto the surface. Farmers sometimes added a cow or some other graphic that represented the product or related to the name of the dairy.

Because so many of these glass bottles were destroyed when paper and plastic cartons became popular, they've become a scarce commodity, and today's collectors have begun to take notice of them. It's fun to see just how many you can find from your home state — or try getting one from every state in the union!

What makes for a good milk bottle? Collectors normally find the pyro-glaze decorations more desirable, since they're more visual. Bottles from dairies in their home state hold more interest for them, so naturally New Jersey bottles sell better there than they would in California, for instance. Green glass examples are unusual and often go for a premium; so do those with the embossed baby faces. (Watch for reproductions here!) Those with a 'Buy War Bonds' slogan or a patriot message are always popular, and cream-tops are good as well.

Some collectors enjoy adding 'go-alongs' to enhance their collections, so the paper pull tops, advertising items that feature dairy bottles, and those old cream-top spoons will also interest them. The spoons usually sell for about $6.00 to $10.00 each.

Advisor: John Shaw (See Directory, Milk Bottles)

Newsletter: *The Milk Route*
National Association of Milk Bottle Collectors, Inc.
Thomas Gallagher
4 Ox Bow Rd., Westport, CT 06880-2602; 203-454-1475

Newsletter: *Creamers*
Lloyd Bindscheattle
P.O. Box 11, Lake Villa, IL 60046-0011; Subscription: $5 for 4 issues

Alta Crest Farms, Spencer Mass, embossed lettering, 10 oz **$16.00**
Anderson Bros, Worcester, state not shown, blue pyro, round 10-oz **$11.00**
Araujo & Sons, Dighton Mass, maroon pyro, tall, round qt..**$30.00**
Baker & Son Dairy, Atlanta Mich, orange pyro, tall, round qt **$20.00**
Burroughs Brothers Walnut Grove Farm, Knightsen Calif, red pyro, round ½-pt **$11.00**
Candee's Dairy, Phoenix NY, SealRight waxed paper cone, unused, ½-pt **$10.00**
Cloverleaf Farms, Stockton Calif, red pyro, cream top, repro spoon, round qt.......................................**$25.00**
Cole Farm Dairy, Biddeford ME, black pyro, squat, sq ½-pt **$10.00**
Dumas Farm, Drink More Milk for Health, orange pyro, round ½-pt **$10.00**

Ethan Allen Creamery, Essex Junction, Vermont, orange pyro, tall square quart, $15.00. (Photo courtesy John Shaw)

Hunt's Dairy, Skowhegan ME, maroon pyro, sq qt **$14.00**
Hunt's Dairy, Skowhegan ME, red pyro, round ½-pt ...**$10.00**
Melrose Dairy, Ormond Fla, blue pyro, tall, round qt..**$20.00**
Model Dairy, Waukon Iowa, red pyro, tall, round qt .**$20.00**
Monson Milk Co, city & state not shown, orange & red pyro, tall, round qt **$25.00**
Natoma Farm, Hinsdale Ill, orange pyro, embossed, tall, round qt...**$28.00**
Natoma Farm, Hinsdale Ill, orange pyro, embossed on heel, tall, round qt **$81.00**
New Ulm Dairy, New Ulm Minnesota, red & blue pyro, Pearl Harbor 50th anniversary, sq qt **$18.00**

New Ulm Dairy, New Ulm Minnesota, 2-color, battle of Iwo Jima 50th anniversary, unused, sq qt **$11.00**
Orchard Grove Dairy, Eaton Rapids Mich, green pyro, tall, round qt..**$25.00**
Pine Grove Dairy, Skaneateales NY, green & orange pyro, little dull, tall, round qt **$23.00**
Plains Dairy, red & green pyro, Ayrshire cows on front, 1-pt...**$14.00**
Potomac Farms, state not shown, 5-color w/different color on ea side & shoulder, sq qt...............................**$16.00**
River Edge Dairy, Somerville NJ, red pyro, tall, round qt ..**$22.00**
St Mary's Dairy, George M Erich Prop, St Mary's PA, brown pyro, tall, round qt **$20.00**
Upland Farms, OL Parsons, Massachusetts Milk, orange pyro, tall, round qt **$21.00**
Zenda Farms, Clayton NY, orange pyro, STORE banner on sides & shoulder, round ¼-pt **$15.00**

Miller Studios

Imported chalkware items began appearing in local variety stores in the early '50s. Cheerfully painted hot pad holders, thermometers, wall plaques, and many other items offered a lot of decorator appeal. While not all examples will be marked Miller Studios, good indications of that manufacturer are the holes on the back where stapled-on cardboard packaging has been torn away — thus leaving small holes. There should also be a looped wire hanger on the back, although a missing hanger does not seem to affect price. Copyright dates are often found on the sides. Miller Studios, located in New Philadelphia, Pennsylvania, are the only existing American firm that makes hand-finished wall plaques yet today. Although they had over three hundred employees during the 1960s and 1970s, they presently have approximately seventy-five.

Advisors: Paul and Heather August (See Directory, Miller Studios)

Animals, poodle plaques, white w/black details & gold trim, 1978, 6", MIB, pr......................................**$25.00**
Bathometer, fish, aqua, green & salmon pink, dated 1977, 7½", from $20 to..**$25.00**
Bathometer, unicorn, ivory w/gold trim, 1983 ....**$13.00**
Bird, duckling, yellow w/black eyes & features, orange beak, 1963, 6" **$8.00**
Birds, bluebirds, blue w/orange belly, 1970, set of 3 ....**$15.00**
Birds, roosters, bright multicolors on black, pr, MIB..**$22.00**
Birds, swans, white w/blue tail feathers on black background, 1965, 3½x7", pr..**$10.00**
Figures, ballerinas, dancing in yellow dresses & shoes, gold trim, 1964, 13¾", 11", 8½", set of 3, EX...............**$10.00**
Figures, knights, gold w/white feather on helmet, 1965, pr **$25.00**
Fish, dated 1954, 5½x5½", 5½x6", pr, MIB **$25.00**
Fish, gaping mouths, w/bubbles, 4-pc set, 1970, 7" ...**$20.00**

Fish, mother & 3 babies, blues & greens w/red lips, 10x6½", 5x3" **$20.00**

Fish (2) fish, 1 starfish & 1 sea horse, 1967 ....**$15.00**

Fruit, peaches (3) & cherries (7) in cluster, #M51, M (VG box) **$12.00**

Hot pad holder, chicken, 1972, EX.................................**$9.00**

Memo pad, ear of corn, place for pencil holder, 1964 ..**$13.00**

Memo pad, owl w/pencil holder, original pad & pencil, 1970, 7x7", M..**$29.00**

Thermometer, well, 1970s, EX.....................................**$20.00**

Thermometer, bluebird and birdhouse, c 1984, $9.00.

Model Kits

By far the majority of model kits were vehicular, and though worth collecting, especially when you can find them still mint in the box, the really big news are the figure kits. Most were made by Aurora during the 1960s. Especially hot are the movie monsters, though TV and comic strip character kits are popular with collectors too. As a rule of thumb, assembled kits are valued at about half as much as conservatively priced mint-in-box kits. The condition of the box is just as important as the contents, and top collectors will usually pay an additional 15% (sometimes even more) for a box that retains the factory plastic wrap still intact. For more information, we recommend *Aurora History and Price Guide* by Bill Bruegman (Cap'n Penny Productions). *Schroeder's Toys, Antique to Modern,* contains prices and descriptions of hundreds of models by a variety of manufacturers. (The latter is published by Collector Books.)

Addar, Super Scenes, Jaws, 1975, NM (VG+ box).......**$30.00**

Addar, World Wildlife, Outlaw Mustang, 1975, MIB ...**$35.00**

AEF, Aliens, Ferro, 1980s, 1/35, MIB...........................**$26.00**

Airfix, Datsun 280-ZX Champion, 1980, M (EX+ sealed box)..**$35.00**

Airfix, Wildlife Series, Robins, 1979, MIB (sealed)......**$30.00**

AMT, '74 Corvette, MIB, from $40 to **$50.00**

AMT, Farrah's Foxy Vette, 1977, MIB..........................**$50.00**

AMT, Hang-Outs, Baseball, 1970s, MIB (sealed).........**$25.00**

AMT, The CAT, 1967, MIB..**$150.00**

AMT/Ertl, Dick Tracy Coupe, 1990, MIB (sealed).....**$20.00**

AMT/Ertl, Joker Goon Car, 1989, MIB (sealed)...........**$20.00**

AMT/Ertl, Star Wars, Han Solo, 1995, MIB (sealed) **$30.00**

Arii, Macross, Valkyrie VF-1J, MIB..............................**$15.00**

Aurora, American Buffalo, 1964, MIB (sealed).............**$100.00**

Aurora, Batboat, 1968, MIB, from $400 to..................**$500.00**

Aurora, Batman, 1966, MIB..**$285.00**

Aurora, Castle Creatures, Frog, 1966, MIB.................**$250.00**

Aurora, Comic Scenes, Batman, 1974, MIB **$85.00**

Aurora, Comic Scenes, Superman, 1974, MIB **$90.00**

Aurora, Forged Foil Cougar, 1969, MIB **$65.00**

Aurora, Frankenstein, 1961, MIB **$400.00**

Aurora, Green Beret, 1966, MIB (sealed) **$250.00**

Aurora, Land of the Giants, Spaceship, 1968, MIB ...**$325.00**

Aurora, Lunar Probe, 1960s, MIB **$175.00**

Aurora, Monster Scenes, Pain Parlor, 1971, MIB (sealed)..**$150.00**

Aurora, Mummy, 1963, MIB...**$250.00**

Aurora, Prehistoric Scenes, Jungle Swamp, 1971, MIB .**$100.00**

Aurora, Prince Valiant, 1959, MIB **$200.00**

Aurora, Spider-Man, 1974, MIB (sealed)....................**$160.00**

Aurora, Tarzan, 1967, MIB **$165.00**

Aurora, Tonto, 1967, MIB..**$200.00**

Aurora, Wacky Back-Wacker, 1965, MIB....................**$185.00**

Aurora, Whoozis, Kitty, 1968, MIB..............................**$65.00**

Aurora, Wolf Man, 1972, MIB.......................................**$120.00**

Aurora, Wolf Man's Wagon, 1964, MIB **$250.00**

Bachmann, Birds of the World, Barn Swallow, 1950s, MIB **$30.00**

Bandai, Galaman figure, NM (VG+ box) **$20.00**

Bandai, Kinggidran, 1990, MIB....................................**$40.00**

Billiken, Dracula, 1989, vinyl, MIB..............................**$275.00**

Billiken, Preditor, 1990, vinyl, MIB..............................**$110.00**

Dark Horse, Frankenstein, 1991, MIB **$130.00**

Dark Horse, King Kong, MIB...**$60.00**

Gerba, US Navy Vanguard Missile, 1950s, MIB.........**$200.00**

Hawk, Convair Mann Satellite, 1960, MIB **$100.00**

Hawk, Jupiter C/Explorer, 1966, MIB...........................**$50.00**

Hawk, Weird-Ohs, Daddy the Way Out Suburbanite, 1963, MIB **$100.00**

Hawk, Wild Woodie (Surfer Car), 1965, MIB **$30.00**

Horizon, Batman, 1989, MIB..**$80.00**

Horizon, Bride of Frankenstein, 1988, MIB **$75.00**

Horizon, Invisible Man, 1988, MIB...............................**$50.00**

Horizon, Marvel Universe, Dr Doom, 1991, MIB........**$40.00**

Horizon, Mole People, 1988, MIB **$50.00**

Horizon, Phantom of the Opera, 1988, MIB................**$50.00**

ITC, Scottish Terrier, 1960, MIB..................................**$30.00**

ITC, Stegosaurus Skeleton, 1950s, MIB.....................**$100.00**

Kaiyodo, Godzilla, 1991, soft vinyl, NM (VG+ box)...**$45.00**

Life-Like, Aerial Missiles on Helicopter, 1970s, MIB ...**$50.00**

Life-Like, Protoceratops, 1973, MIB.............................**$30.00**

Lindberg, Flying Saucer, 1952, MIB............................**$200.00**

Lindberg, Lighthouse, 1969, w/light, MIB **$30.00**

Lindberg, SST Continental, 1958, MIB........................**$175.00**

Lindberg, Wells Fargo Overland Stagecoach, 1960s, MIB...**$50.00**

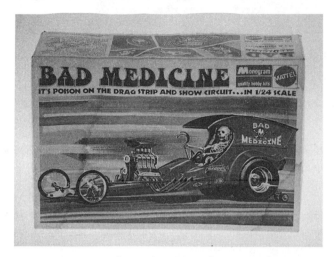

Monogram, Bad Medicine, #6055, 1970s, MIB, $60.00.

Monogram, Buck Rogers Marauder, 1979, MIB (sealed)....**$35.00**
Monogram, Dracula, 1991, MIB (sealed) **$30.00**
Monogram, Ghost of the Red Barn, 1969, MIB.........**$200.00**
Monogram, Green Hornet Dragster, 1960s, MIB **$55.00**
Monogram, Luminators, King Kong, MIB (sealed)......**$45.00**
Monogram, Luminators, Wolfman, MIB.......................**$20.00**
Monogram, Mummy, 1983, MIB (sealed)....................**$30.00**
Monogram, Snoopy on the Highwire, 1972, MIB **$30.00**
Monogram, Superman, 1974, MIB **$40.00**
Monogram, UFO, 1996, MIB (sealed)..........................**$35.00**
MPC, CB Freak, 1975, MIB.......................................**$50.00**
MPC, Glo Heads, Ape Man, 1975, MIB.....................**$60.00**
MPC, Ironside's Van, 1970, MIB...............................**$80.00**
MPC, Mummy Machine, 1970s, MIB (sealed) **$50.00**
MPC, Six Million Dollar Man, 1975, MIB **$50.00**
MPC, Star Wars, C-3PO, 1977, MIB (sealed) **$35.00**
MPC, Star Wars, X-Wing Fighter, 1978, MIB **$40.00**
MPC, TJ Hooker, Police Car, 1982, MIB......................**$30.00**
Pyro, Curler Super Surf Tricycle, 1970, MIB **$40.00**
Pyro, Der Baron & His Harley-Custom, 1970, MIB.....**$65.00**
Pyro, Ghost Ryder, 1970, MIB....................................**$50.00**
Pyro, Li'l Corporal, 1970, MIB....................................**$50.00**
Pyro, Rawhide, 1959, MIB.......................................**$250.00**
Pyro, Texas Cowboy, 1960s, MIB...............................**$60.00**
Pyro, Western Figures, Deputy Sheriff, 1961, MIB **$35.00**
Revell, Astronaut in Space, 1968, MIB **$100.00**
Revell, Beatles, Ringo Starr, 1964, MIB **$150.00**
Revell, Cat in the Hat, 1958, MIB.............................**$100.00**
Revell, Code Red, Emergency Van, 1981, MIB **$20.00**
Revell, Corporal Missile, 1958, MIB..........................**$100.00**
Revell, Eastern Airlines Golden Falcon, 1950s, MIB ...**$75.00**
Revell, Ed 'Big Daddy' Roth, Superfink, 1964, MIB ..**$300.00**
Revell, Flash Gordon & the Martian, 1965, MIB........**$225.00**
Revell, Flipper, 1965, MIB **$75.00**
Revell, Hardy Boys' Van, 1978, MIB............................**$35.00**
Revell, Historic PT-109, 1963, EXIB............................**$30.00**
Revell, John Travolta's Firebird Fever, 1979, MIB (sealed)...**$45.00**

Revell, McHale's Navy PT-73, 1965, MIB **$75.00**
Revell, Robotech, Nebo, 1984, MIB............................**$20.00**
Revell, Robotech, Vexar, 1982, MIB (sealed) **$30.00**
Revell, Space Pursuit, 1969, MIB.............................**$250.00**
Revell, X-17 Research Missile, 1957, MIB....................**$65.00**
Screamin', Bettie Page - Jungle Fever, 1994, MIB **$85.00**
Screamin', Star Wars, C-3PO, 1993, MIB **$45.00**
Testors, Davey the Cyclist, 1993, MIB (sealed) **$15.00**
Tomy, Lensmann, Grappler & Shuttle Truck, 1984, MIB .**$40.00**
Toy Biz, Thing, 1996, MIB (sealed)............................**$20.00**
Tsukuda, Mummy, MIB..**$75.00**
Tsukuda, Wolf Man, MIB...**$60.00**
Whiting, Space: 1999, Mammoth Model, 1976, MIB ...**$50.00**

Modern Mechanical Banks

The most popular (and expensive) type of bank with today's collectors are the mechanicals, so called because of the antics they perform when a coin is deposited. Over three hundred models were produced between the Civil War period and the first World War. On some, arms wave, legs kick, or mouths open to swallow up the coin — amusing nonsense intended by the inventor to encourage and reward thriftiness. Some of these original banks have been known to sell for as much as $20,000.00 — well out of the price range most of us can afford! So many opt for some of the modern mechanicals that are available on the collectibles market, including Book of Knowledge and James D. Capron, which are reproductions marked to indicate that they are indeed replicas. But beware — unmarked modern reproductions are common.

Reynolds Toys have been producing banks from their own original designs since 1971; some of Mr. Reynolds's banks are in the White House and the Smithsonian.

Advisor: Dan Iiannotti (See Directory, Banks)

Artillery Bank, Book of Knowledge, NM..................**$295.00**
Bad Accident, James Capron, M................................**$795.00**
Bush-Quayle, Reynolds #48S, 1989, edition of 100 ..**$260.00**
Butting Buffalo, Book of Knowledge, M **$350.00**
Cabin, Book of Knowledge, NM **$325.00**
Clinton, Reynolds #662, 1993, edition of 100...........**$310.00**
Cow (Kicking), Book of Knowledge, NM...................**$315.00**
Dentist Bank, Book of Knowledge, EX **$175.00**
Elephant, Jame Capron, M **$250.00**
Elephant, John Wright, NM **$175.00**
Humpty Dumpty, Reynolds #30m, 1975, edition of 20 ..**$1,250.00**
Jelly Bean King, Reynolds #04S, 1981, edition of 100 ..**$265.00**
Leap Frog, Book of Knowledge, NM **$335.00**
Lion & Monkeys, James Capron, M..........................**$875.00**
Magic Bank, James Capron, MIB...............................**$650.00**
Mary & Her Little Lamb, Reynolds #20M, edition of 20 ..**$850.00**
Milking Cow, Book of Knowledge, NM....................**$295.00**
Monkey, James Capron, MIB.....................................**$395.00**
Mule Entering Barn, James Capron, NM...................**$495.00**
Owl (Turns Head), Book of Knowledge, NM **$375.00**

Professor Pug Frog, James Capron, M $850.00
Race Course, James Capron, NM.............................$575.00
Santa Coming to a Child, Reynolds #28S, 1985, edition of
50 ....$165.00
St Nicholas, Reynolds #34M, 1975, edition of 50 ......$775.00
Super Bowl XXII Redskins, Reynolds #41S, 1988, edition of
50 ....$90.00
Tammany, Book of Knowledge, NMIB.....................$325.00
Teddy & the Bear, Book of Knowledge, NM $300.00
Tiniest Elephant, Reynolds #18S, 1984, edition of 50 ..$110.00

**Trick Dog, Capron, NM, $400.00; I Always Did
'Spise a Mule, Book of Knowledge, NM, $295.00.**

Uncle Louie, Reynolds #58M, 1977, edition of 50.....$350.00
Uncle Remus, Book of Knowledge, M......................$375.00
US & Spain, Book of Knowledge, NM......................$325.00

Mood Indigo by Inarco

This line of Japanese-made ceramics probably came out
in the 1960s, and enough of it was produced that a considerable amount has reached the secondary market. Because
of the interest today's collectors are exhibiting in items from
the '60s and '70s, it's beginning to show up in malls and co-
ops, and the displays are surprisingly attractive. The color of
the glaze is an electric blue, and each piece is modeled as
though it were built from stacks of various fruits. It was
imported by Inarco (Cleveland, Ohio) and often bears that
company's foil label.

Collectors are sticklers for condition (damaged items are
worth very little, even if they are rare) and prefer pieces with
a deep, rich blue color and dark numbers on the bottom that
are very legible. All pieces carry a number, and most collectors use these to keep track of their acquisitions. In addition
to the items described and evaluated below, here is a partial
listing of other known pieces (our research continues; watch
the next edition for more information):

E-2373 — Oblong Pitcher, 3" x 6" E-3095 — Fluted Vase, 7¾"
E-2374 — Covered Candy Dish, 9" E-3096 — Vase, 8"
E-2375 — Covered Dish, 6" E-3100 — Cigarette Lighter
E-2376 — Oval Dish, 8¼" E-3145 — Pitcher, 6"
E-2429 — Pitcher, 6" E-3267 — Oil Lamp
E-2431 — Coffee Cup, 4" E-3445 — Plate, 9½"

E-2432 — Hanging Plate, E-3462 — Pedestal
with fruit, 10" Cake Plate, 9½"
E-2719 — Relish Tray, 7½" E-3563 Candle Holder, 5"
E-2920 — Gravy Boat, with saucer, 8" E-4011 — Butter Dish,
with lid, 7½"

These pieces can be bought for as little as $5.00 to as
much as $30.00. Prices vary widely, and bargains can still be
had at many flea markets and garage sales.

Advisors: David and Debbie Crouse (See Directory, Mood
Indigo)

Bell, 5", from $5 to $15.00
Candle holder, goblet shape, 4½", pr $28.00
Centerpiece, stacked-up fruit on ribbed incurvate base,
12x6" $15.00
Cookie jar/canister, E-2374, 8" $18.00
Creamer & sugar bowl, w/lid, from $10 to $12.00
Cruet $17.50
Gravy boat, E-2373, 6½" $15.00
Jar, cylindrical, w/lid, 6½"..$15.00
Ladle, 9¾"...$25.00
Pitcher, E-2853, footed, 6"...$15.00
Salt & pepper shakers, E-2371, 3½", pr $12.00
Teapot, E-2430, 8"..$15.00
Trivet, 6" dia...$10.00

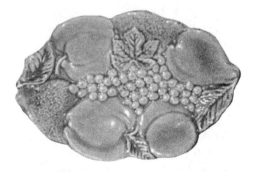

Tray, 8½" long, $28.00. (Photo courtesy David and Debbie Crouse)

Moon and Star

Moon and Star (originally called Palace) was first produced in the 1880s by John Adams & Company of
Pittsburgh. But because the glassware was so heavy to
transport, it was made for only a few years. In the 1960s,
Joseph Weishar of Wheeling, West Virginia, owner of Island
Mould & Machine Company, reproduced some of the original molds and incorporated the pattern into approximately
forty new and different items. Two of the largest distributors of this line were L.E. Smith of Mt. Pleasant,
Pennsylvania, who pressed their own glass, and L.G. Wright
of New Martinsville, West Virginia, who had theirs pressed
by Fostoria and Fenton. Both companies carried a large and

varied assortment of shapes and colors. Several other companies were involved in its manufacture as well, especially of the smaller items. All in all, there may be as many as one hundred different pieces, plenty to keep you involved and excited as you do your searching.

The glassware is already very collectible, even though it is still being made on a limited basis. Colors you'll see most often are amberina (yellow shading to orange red), green, amber, crystal, light blue, and ruby. Pieces in ruby and light blue are most collectible and harder to find than the other colors, which seem to be abundant. Purple, pink, cobalt, amethyst, tan slag, and light green and blue opalescent were made, too, but on a lesser scale.

Current L.E. Smith catalogs contain a dozen or so pieces that are still available in crystal, pink, cobalt (lighter than the old shade), and these colors with an iridized finish. A new color was introduced in 1992, teal green, and the water set in sapphire blue opalescent was pressed in 1993 by Weishar Enterprises. They are now producing limited editions in various colors and shapes, but they are marking their glassware 'Weishar,' to distinguish it from the old line. Cranberry Ice (light transparent pink) was introduced in 1994.

Unless another color is specified, our values are given for ruby and light blue. For amberina, green, and amber, deduct at least 30%. These colors are less in demand, and unless your prices are reasonable, you may find them harder to sell. Read *Mysteries of the Moon and Star* by George and Linda Breeze for more information.

Ashtray, allover pattern, moons form scallops along rim, 4 rests, 8" dia..**$25.00**
Ashtray, moons at rim, star in base, 6-sided, 5½".......**$18.00**
Ashtray, moons at rim, star in base, 6-sided, 8½".......**$25.00**
Banana boat, allover pattern, moons form scallops along rim, 9", from $28 to...**$32.00**
Banana boat, allover pattern, moons form scallops along rim, 12"..**$45.00**
Basket, allover pattern, moons form scallops along rim, footed, incurvate upright handles, 4", from $15 to.....**$22.00**
Basket, allover pattern, moons form scallops along rim, solid handle, 9", from $50 to...**$65.00**
Basket, allover pattern, moons form scallops along rim, solid handle, 6" **$40.00**
Bell, pattern along sides, plain rim & handle, from $35 to..**$45.00**
Bowl, allover pattern, footed, crimped rim, 7½", from $25 to..**$35.00**
Bowl, allover pattern, footed, scalloped rim, 12x5", from $35 to..**$45.00**
Butter dish, allover pattern, scalloped foot, patterned lid & finial, 6x5½" dia...**$45.00**
Butter dish, allover pattern, stars form scallops along rim of base, star finial, oval, ¼-lb, 8½"...........................**$50.00**
Butter/cheese dish, patterned lid, plain base, 7" dia, from $50 to..**$65.00**
Cake plate, allover pattern, low collared base, 13" dia, from $50 to..**$60.00**

Cake salver, allover pattern w/scalloped rim, raised foot w/scalloped edge, 5x12" dia, from $50 to............**$60.00**
Cake stand, allover pattern, plate removes from standard, 2-pc, 11" dia...**$75.00**
Candle bowl, allover pattern, footed, 8", from $25 to.......**$30.00**
Candle holder, allover pattern, bowl style w/ring handle, 2x5½", ea..**$18.00**
Candle holders, allover pattern, flared & scalloped foot, 6", pr from $40 to...**$50.00**
Candle holders, allover pattern, flared base, 4½", pr from $25 to..**$35.00**
Candle lamp, patterned shade, clear base, 2-pc, 7½", from $20 to..**$25.00**
Candy dish, allover pattern on base & lid, footed ball shape, 6"...**$25.00**
Canister, allover pattern, 1-lb or 2-lb, from $12 to......**$15.00**
Canister, allover pattern, 3½-lb or 5-lb, from $18 to..**$22.00**
Chandelier, dome shape, 14" dia, w/font, amber, from $250 to..**$300.00**
Chandelier, ruffled dome shape w/allover pattern, amber, 10"..**$75.00**
Cheese dish, patterned base, clear plain lid, 9½", from $65 to..**$70.00**
Compote, allover pattern, footed, flared crimped rim, 5", from $15 to...**$22.00**
Compote, allover pattern, raised foot, patterned lid & finial, 7½x6", from $30 to...**$40.00**
Compote, allover pattern, raised foot on stem, patterned lid & finial, 10x6", from $50 to.................................**$65.00**
Compote, allover pattern, raised foot on stem, patterned lid & finial, 12x8", from $60 to.................................**$75.00**
Compote, allover pattern, scalloped foot on stem, patterned lid & finial, 8x4", from $35 to..............................**$40.00**
Compote, allover pattern, scalloped rim, footed, 5½x8", from $28 to...**$35.00**
Compote, allover pattern, scalloped rim, footed, 5x6½", from $15 to...**$20.00**
Compote, allover pattern, scalloped rim, footed, 7x10", from $35 to...**$45.00**

Compote, rolled edge, 10" diameter, $45.00.

Console bowl, allover pattern, scalloped rim, flared foot w/flat edge, 8"..**$25.00**
Creamer, allover pattern, raised foot w/scalloped edge, 5¾x3"...**$35.00**

Creamer & sugar bowl (open), disk foot, sm, from $25 to **$35.00**

Cruet, vinegar; 6¾", from $65 to **$75.00**

Decanter, bulbous w/allover pattern, plain neck, foot ring, original patterned stopper, 32-oz, 12", from $75 to........**$90.00**

Epergne, allover pattern, 1-lily, flared bowl, scalloped foot, minimum value **$95.00**

Epergne, allover pattern, 2-pc, 9", minimum value **$65.00**

Goblet, water; plain rim & foot, 5¾", from $12 to **$15.00**

Goblet, wine; plain rim & foot, 4½", from $10 to.......**$14.00**

Jardiniere, allover pattern, patterned lid & finial, 9¾", minimum value...**$85.00**

Jardiniere/cracker jar, allover pattern, patterned lid & finial, 7¼", minimum value **$65.00**

Jardiniere/tobacco jar, allover pattern, patterned lid & finial, 6", minimum value...**$45.00**

Jelly dish, allover pattern, patterned lid & finial, stemmed foot, 10½", from $55 to **$65.00**

Jelly dish, patterned body w/plain flat rim & disk foot, patterned lid & finial, 6¾x3½".....................................**$35.00**

Lamp, fairy; cylindrical dome-top shade, 6", from $25 to .**$35.00**

Lamp, miniature; amber, from $115.00 to $125.00.

Lamp, miniature; blue, from $165 to..........................**$190.00**

Lamp, miniature; green **$135.00**

Lamp, miniature; milk glass, from $200 to **$225.00**

Lamp, miniature; red, from $175 to **$200.00**

Lamp, oil or electric; allover pattern, all original, amber, from $175 to..**$200.00**

Lamp, oil or electric; allover pattern, all original, red or light blue, 24", minimum value.................................**$325.00**

Lamp, oil; allover pattern, all original, common, 12", from $50 to **$75.00**

Lighter, allover patterned body, metal fittings, from $40 to **$50.00**

Nappy, allover pattern, crimped rim, 2¾x6", from $12 to **$18.00**

Pitcher, water; patterned body, ice lip, straight sides, plain disk foot, 1-qt, 7½", from $65 to **$75.00**

Plate, patterned body & center, smooth rim, 8".........**$35.00**

Relish bowl, 6 lg scallops form allover pattern, 1½x8"..**$35.00**

Relish dish, allover pattern, 1 plain handle, 2x8" dia, from $35 to..**$40.00**

Relish tray, patterned moons form scalloped rim, star in base, rectangular, 8"...**$35.00**

Salt & pepper shakers, allover pattern, metal tops, 4x2", pr from $25 to...**$35.00**

Salt cellar, allover pattern, scalloped rim, sm flat foot..**$8.00**

Sherbet, patterned body & foot w/plain rim & stem, 4¼x3¾", from $25 to...**$28.00**

Soap dish, allover pattern, oval, 2x6" **$12.00**

Spooner, allover pattern, straight sides, scalloped rim, raised foot, 5¼x4", from $45 to...**$50.00**

Sugar bowl, allover pattern, patterned lid & finial, sm flat foot, 5¼x4", from $35 to...**$40.00**

Sugar bowl, allover pattern, straight sides, patterned lid & finial, scalloped foot, 8x4½", from $35 to.............**$40.00**

Sugar shaker, allover pattern, metal top, 4½x3½" **$50.00**

Syrup pitcher, allover pattern, metal lid, 4½x3½", from $65 to...**$75.00**

Toothpick holder, allover pattern, scalloped rim, sm flat foot..**$10.00**

Tumbler, iced tea; no pattern at flat rim or on disk foot, 11-oz, 5", from $18 to...**$22.00**

Tumbler, juice; no pattern at rim, short pedestal foot, 4½", from $18 to...**$22.00**

Tumbler, juice; no pattern at rim or on disk foot, 5-oz, 3½", from $12 to...**$15.00**

Tumbler, no pattern at rim or on disk foot, 6½" **$30.00**

Tumbler, no pattern at rim or on disk foot, 7-oz, 4¼", from $12 to...**$15.00**

Mortens Studios

During the 1940s, a Swedish sculptor by the name of Oscar Mortens left his native country and moved to the United States, settling in Arizona. Along with his partner, Gunnar Thelin, they founded the Mortens Studios, a firm that specialized in the manufacture of animal figurines. Though he preferred dogs of all breeds, horses, cats, and wild animals were made, too, but on a much smaller scale.

The material he used was a plaster-like composition molded over a wire framework for support and reinforcement. Crazing is common, and our values reflect pieces with a moderate amount, but be sure to check for more serious damage before you buy. Most pieces are marked with either an ink stamp or a paper label.

Beagle, lying down, #554..**$55.00**

Bloodhound, #877 ....**$150.00**

Boston terrier, sitting, #793 ....**$70.00**

Chow pup, brown, #816, 3"...**$50.00**

Collie pup, #818, mini..**$55.00**

Colt, standing, #714 ....**$65.00**

Dachshund head plaque, lg, pr...................................**$475.00**

Doberman, #785 ....**$95.00**

Filly, chestnut brown, #716, 8½" $95.00
Fox terrier, black, #766..$95.00

German shepherd, sitting, 6½", from $75.00 to $100.00.

German shorthaired pointer, #849.............................$175.00
Greyhound, gray, #747, 6¾" $100.00
Irish setter, standing, #856, 5½x7¼" $95.00
Palomino, rearing, 9" $110.00
Pekingese, #553, mini...$65.00
Pointer, tail to leg, #851 ....$95.00
Pomeranian, #739 ....$95.00
Pug, #738, 4x5" $125.00
Stag, 7½x7" $150.00
Stallion, rearing, black, #662...$95.00

Morton Pottery

Six different potteries operated in Morton, Illinois, during a period of ninety-nine years. The first pottery, established by six Rapp brothers who had immigrated from Germany in the mid-1870s, was named Morton Pottery Works. It was in operation from 1877 to 1915 when it was reorganized and renamed Morton Earthenware Company. Its operation, 1915 – 1917, was curtailed by World War I. Cliftwood Art Potteries, Inc. was the second pottery to be established. It operated from 1920 until 1940 when it was sold and renamed Midwest Potteries, Inc. In March 1944 the pottery burned and was never rebuilt. Morton Pottery Company was the longest running of Morton's potteries. It was in operation from 1922 until 1976. The last pottery to open was the American Art Potteries. It was in production from 1947 until 1961.

All of Morton's potteries were spin-offs from the original Rapp brothers. Second, third, and fourth generation Rapps followed the tradition of their ancestors to produce a wide variety of pottery. Rockingham and yellow ware to Art Deco, giftwares, and novelties were produced by Morton's potteries.

To learn more about these companies, we recommend *Morton's Potteries: 99 Years, Vol. II*, by Doris and Burdell Hall.

Advisors: Doris and Burdell Hall (See Directory, Morton Pottery)

Morton Pottery Works — Morton Earthenware Company, 1877 – 1917

Baker, deep yellow ware, 8" dia $50.00
Chamber pot, yellow ware, w/lid, 10" dia.................$90.00
Milk boiler, brown Rockingham, 3½-pt $60.00
Milk jug, fancy applied handles, #36s, 1-pt................$50.00
Rice, nappy, fluted, yellow ware, 4½" $30.00
Stein, brown Rockingham, German motto top & bottom, 1-pt..$80.00

Cliftwood Art Potteries, Inc., 1920 – 1940

Candlesticks, black semi-lustre, 7", pr..........................$50.00
Clock, donut shape, Lux clock works, Herbage Green, 8½" $95.00
Figurine, bulldog, Nero, gray drip, 11" $95.00
Figurine, cat reclining, cobalt, 7x10¾".........................$55.00

Figurine, elephant, trumpeting, Old Rose, $50.00. (Photo courtesy Doris and Burdell Hall)

Figurine, lioness, chocolate drip, 7x12" $85.00
Figurine, tiger, dk tan w/hand-painted brown stripes, 5x16" $200.00
Lamp, donut shape w/clock insert, brown drip, 11" ..$150.00
Vase, bud; brown drip, 6" $35.00
Vase, heron figural, turquoise matt, 6".........................$20.00
Vase, tree trunk w/3 open limbs at top, Herbage Green, 9" $70.00
Wall pocket, green matt, teardrop shape, #216, 7½x5¾" ..$50.00

Midwest Potteries, Inc., 1940 – 1944

Cow creamer, brown drip w/yellow handle, 5" $24.00
Figurine, baseball player, batter, gray uniform, 7¼".$300.00
Figurine, crane, green/yellow spray, 11" $35.00
Figurine, duck w/2 ducklings behind, yellow & white, 3x6½x1¼"..$24.00
Miniature, goose, head bent, white & yellow w/gold, 1½"..$20.00

Miniature, rabbits kissing, white w/gold, 2½x3¼" **$30.00**
Miniature, squirrel, white & brown w/yellow acorn, 2¼" ..**$18.00**
Planter, fox, brown, 5¾x7" **$18.00**
Planter, lioness, yellow, 3¼x6½" **$14.00**

Planters: Calico Cat, blue and yellow spatter, $24.00; Gingham Dog, blue and yellow spatter, $24.00. (Photo courtesy Doris and Burdell Hall)

Wall mask, man's head caricature, Classical Greek style, white, 5x4½" **$35.00**
Wall mask, man's head caricature, 18th-C English mark, green, 5x6" **$40.00**

Morton Pottery Company, 1922 – 1976

Bank, bulldog, white **$25.00**
Bank, country schoolhouse, brown, 3x4x2½" **$30.00**
Bank, pig, black & white **$50.00**
Bank, pig, Skeedoodle, pink, #672, 5x6" **$50.00**
Bookends, books (2 open), pr **$14.00**
Bowl, mixing; Pilgrim Pottery line, blue, nested set of 6 ..**$150.00**
Christmas item, Santa cigarette box, hat is ashtray **$25.00**
Christmas item, Santa-face, plate, 12" **$50.00**
Christmas planter, Santa on chimney, red & white, #870..**$30.00**
Christmas planter, sleigh, white w/hand-painted holly & berries, #3015 ....**$24.00**
Easter planter, bunny w/carrot stands by basket, hand-painted decor, 5¾" **$20.00**
Easter planter, hen w/bonnet, yellow & blue, 4¾" **$16.00**
Figurine, buffalo, brown/black spray, 10x7" **$100.00**
Figurine, Pointer dog, brown spray, 6¾x4" **$24.00**
Miniature, elephant trumpeting, blue, 2½" **$10.00**
Pie bird, rooster, green, pink & white, 5¼" **$75.00**
Planter, dog figure on pr of rockers...........................**$18.00**
Political figurine, donkey, gray, marked Tawes, 2¼x2¼" ..**$25.00**
Political figurine, JFK Jr saluting father's casket, gray & lt tan, 7" **$50.00**
Stein, beer; leaf design, brown Rockingham, 5" **$18.00**

American Art Potteries, 1947 – 1961

Bowl, gray & yellow, butterfly, #135, 7x6½" **$18.00**
Doll parts: head, arms & legs, 3", set of 5 pcs...........**$60.00**

Figurine, frog, green & yellow, #400, 3x7" **$18.00**
Figurine, Hampshire hog, black w/white ribbon, green base, 5½x7½" **$40.00**
Figurine, rooster, gray & black spray, #305, 8" **$24.00**
Figuring, deer w/antlers, leaping, white w/gold, #502 ..**$40.00**
Planter, baby buggy, white, decor, 5½x7" **$20.00**
Planter, conch shell, orchid & light gray, #131, 7½x6" .**$24.00**
Planter, swan, pink & mauve w/gold, #391G.............**$27.00**
Planter, winged horse, pink, #49, 5x5" **$18.00**
Vase, cowboy boot, gray & pink, #312, 5½" **$15.00**
Vase/cornucopia, rose & gray, #204, 7½" **$18.00**

Moss Rose

Though a Moss Rose pattern has been produced by Staffordshire and American pottery companies alike since the mid-1800s, the ware we're dealing with here has a much different appearance. The pattern consists of a briar rose with dark green mossy leaves on stark white glaze. Very often it is trimmed in gold. In addition to dinnerware, many accessories and novelties were also made. Much of it was produced from the 1950s until the 1970s by Japanese manufacturers, but it was produced by many other firms as well.

Refer to *Schroeder's Antiques Price Guide* (Collector Books) for information on the early Moss Rose pattern.

Advisor: Geneva Addy (See Directory, Imperial Porcelain)

Gravy boat, Pompadour, attached tray, Rosenthal Germany, 9½", $85.00.

Bowl, Japan, 1950s, 4x7" **$20.00**
Bowl, oblong, unmarked, 2½x7½x10½" **$75.00**
Bowl, soup; Pompadour, Rosenthal, US Zone **$42.00**
Bowl, sterling base, unmarked, 4½x9½" **$195.00**
Bowl, sterling knob on lid, Rosenthal, 3¾x5⅛" dia ...**$40.00**
Bowl, vegetable; deep, Pompadour, Rosenthal, 2¾x7⅜x10⅞" **$65.00**
Bowl, vegetable; w/lid, Pomadour, Rosenthal **$150.00**
Cake plate, open handles, unmarked **$60.00**
Candle holders, Japan, 3", pr....................................**$15.00**
Coffeepot, Johann Haviland Bavaria Germany, 11¼".**$75.00**
Creamer & sugar bowl, Haviland & Co, 7" to finial....**$90.00**
Creamer & sugar bowl, Pompadour, Rosenthal **$70.00**

Cruets, oil & vinegar; Japan sticker, pr **$25.00**
Cup & saucer, demitasse; Japan................................**$8.00**
Cup & saucer, Royal Albert....................................**$22.50**
Egg boiler, electric, NM......................................**$55.00**
Egg coddler, Apco, Japan, paper labels, w/clamp & lid,
    3½"...**$32.00**
Mirror on stand, Japan **$15.00**
Plate, dinner; Johann Haviland Bavaria, 10", from $10 to.**$12.00**
Plate, dinner; Pompadour, Rosenthal, 10½" **$28.00**
Plate, dinner; Royal Albert, 11¼"...........................**$15.00**
Plate, unmarked, 7½" **$10.00**
Platter, Pompadour, Rosenthal, 13" dia **$70.00**
Relish, oval, Pompadour, Rosenthal, 6x9½" **$40.00**
Salt & pepper shakers, Johann Haviland Bavaria, 4¼", pr..**$30.00**
Salt & pepper shakers, Pompadour, Rosenthal, 5", pr ..**$60.00**
Salt & pepper shakers, Royal Albert, 3", pr **$30.00**
Tea set, Japan, 7½" teapot, creamer & sugar bowl, 4 plates &
    4 cups & saucers, 15-pc **$70.00**
Tea tile, Haviland, 6½" dia, from $125 to.................**$150.00**
Tidbit, 2-tier, Japan **$20.00**
Tray, Pompadour, Rosenthal, 13x10"........................**$65.00**
Tureen, soup; w/lid, Royal Albert............................**$140.00**
Wall pocket, violin shape, marked Japan, 9x4"..........**$58.00**

Motion Clocks (Electric)

Novelty clocks with some type of motion or animation were popular in spring-powered or wind-up form for hundreds of years. Today they bring thousands of dollars when sold. Electric-powered or motor-driven clocks first appeared in the late 1930s and were produced until quartz clocks became the standard, with the 1950s being the era during which they reached the height of their production.

Four companies led their field. They were Mastercrafters, United, Haddon, and Spartus in order of productivity. Mastercrafters was the earliest and longest-lived, making clocks from the late '40s until the late '80s. (They did, however, drop out of business several times during this long period.) United began making clocks in the early '50s and continued until the early '60s. Haddon followed in the same time frame, and Spartus was in production from the late '50s until the mid-'60s.

These clocks are well represented in the listings that follow; prices are for examples in excellent condition and working. With an average age of forty years, many now need repair. Dried-out grease and dirt easily cause movements and motions not to function. The other nemesis of many motion clocks is deterioration of the fiber gears. Originally intended to keep the clocks quiet, fiber gears have not held up like their metal counterparts. For fully restored clocks, add $50.00 to $75.00 to our values. (Full restoration includes complete cleaning of motor and movement, repair of same; cleaning and polishing face and bezel; cleaning and polishing case and repairing if necessary; and installing new line cord, plug, and light bulb if needed.) Brown is the most common case color for plastic clocks. Add 10% to 20% or more for cases in onyx

(mint green) or any light shade. If any parts noted below are missing, value can drop one-third to one-half. We must stress that 'as is' clocks will not bring these prices. Deteriorated, non-working clocks may be worth less that half of these values.

Note. When original names are not known, names have been assigned.

Advisors: Sam and Anna Samuelian (See Directory, Motion Clocks)

Haddon

Based in Chicago, Illinois, Haddon produced an attractive line of clocks. They used composition cases that were hand painted, and sturdy Hansen movements and motions. This is the only clock line for which new replacement motors are still available.

Granny rocking (Home Sweet Home) **$125.00**
Rocking Horse (Rancho), composition, from $150 to..**$200.00**
Teeter Totter, children on seesaw, from $125 to.......**$175.00**

Mastercrafters

Based in Chicago, Illinois, this company produced many of the most appealing and popular collectible motion clocks on today's market. Cases were made of plastic, with earlier examples being a sturdy urea plastic that imparted quality, depth, and shine to their finishes. Clock movements were relatively simple and often supplied by Sessions Clock Company, who also made many of their own clocks.

Airplane, Bakelite & Chrome, from $175 to **$225.00**
Blacksmith, plastic, from $75 to **$100.00**
Carousel, plastic, carousel front, from $175 to..........**$225.00**
Church, w/bell ringer, plastic **$100.00**

Fireplace, plastic, from $60.00 to $90.00.

Swinging Bird, plastic, w/cage front, from $125 to ..**$150.00**
Swinging Girl, plastic, from $100 to..........................**$125.00**
Swinging Playmates, plastic, w/fence, from $100 to.**$125.00**
Waterfall, plastic...**$100.00**

Spartus

This company made clocks well into the '80s, but most later clocks were not animated. Cases were usually plastic, and most clocks featured animals.

Cat, w/flirty eyes, plastic, from $25 to **$40.00**
Panda Bear, plastic, eyes move, from $25 to **$40.00**
Water Wheel (L style), plastic, from $20 to **$30.00**
Waterfall & Wheel, plastic, from $50 to........................**$75.00**

United

Based in Brooklyn, New York, United made mostly cast-metal cases finished in gold or bronze. Their movements were somewhat more complex than Mastercrafters'. Some of their clocks contained musical movements, which while pleasing can be annoying when continuously run.

Ballerina, woooden, from $75 to..............................**$125.00**
Bobbing Chicks, metal case, various colors, from $35 to...**$50.00**
Bobbing Chicks, wooden house, green & red, from $40
    to **$60.00**
Cowboy w/Rope, metal, wooden base, from $100 to ..**$150.00**
Dancers, metal w/sq glass dome, from $100 to........**$150.00**
Davy Crockett, metal, rare, 10"...................................**$650.00**
Fireplace, metal, gold, from $50 to **$75.00**
Fireplace, w/man & woman, spinning wheel & moving fire,
    from $125 to...**$150.00**
Fishing Boy, metal, fishing pole & fish move, from $125
    to **$150.00**
Huck Finn, fishing pole & fish move, from $150 to.**$175.00**
Hula Girl & Drummer, wooden, from $200 to..........**$250.00**
Majorette w/Rotating Baton, from $75 to **$125.00**
Owl, metal on wooden base, eyes move, from $75 to..**$100.00**
Windmill, pink plastic case, minor cracks in plastic, from $75
    to..**$125.00**

Miscellaneous

God Bless America, flag waves, from $75 to **$100.00**
Klocker Spaniel, from $50 to **$75.00**
Poodle, various colors, from $75 to **$100.00**

Motorcycle Collectibles

At some point in nearly everyone's life, they've experienced at least a brief love affair with a motorcycle. What could be more exhilarating than the open road — the wind in your hair, the sun on your back, and no thought for the cares of today or what tomorrow might bring. For some, the passion never diminished. For most of us, it's a fond memory. Regardless of which description best fits you personally, you will probably enjoy the old advertising and sales literature, books and magazines, posters, photographs, banners, etc., showing the old Harleys and Indians, and the club pins, deal-ership jewelry and clothing, and scores of other items of memorabilia such as collectors are now beginning to show considerable interest in. For more information and a lot of color photographs, we recommend *Motorcycle Collectibles With Values* by Leila Dunbar (Schiffer). See also License Plates.

Advisor: Bob 'Sprocket' Eckardt (See Directory, Motorcycles)

Badge, 1957 Gypsy Tour, enameled metal, 3⅛", EX ..**$55.00**
Banner, AMF/Harley-Davidson/The Great American
    Freedom Machines, 2 dirt bikers & #1 logo, paper,
    7x35", NM+ **$30.00**
Belt buckle, BMW logo above bike w/BMW below, solid
    brass, made by Baron #6223, 3x2", EX **$85.00**
Belt buckle, nickel w/satin face, Indian in red, raised cycle
    w/Old Indians Never Die on bottom, 3x2", M.....**$14.00**
Belt buckle, 1942 Gypsy Tour, gold-tone metal w/blue V in
    center (V for Victory 1942), 2x1¾", EX.................**$90.00**
Blotter, Firestone Gum-Dipped Motorcycle Tires, paper
    w/frontal view of cyclist, black & orange on white,
    EX+ **$100.00**
Brochure, Ace Four Cylinder Motorcycle, embossed cover, 14
    pages, 1924-26, 4x6", EX....................................**$165.00**

Brochure, Harley-Davidson, trifold featuring the 1936 #45 Twin, #75 Twin & #80 Twin, EX, $75.00.

Brochure, Indian, 1941...**$90.00**
Brochure, Triumph '68, The Ultimate in Motorcycling, dou-
    ble-sided, 8½x11" (folded), EX.............................**$40.00**
Catalog, accessory; 1958 Harley-Davidson, 30+ pages,
    8¼x10¾", EX..**$48.00**
License plate, 1949 Colorado, M (in torn original mailing
    envelope)..**$50.00**
Magazine, Harley-Davidson Enthusiast, May 1950, EX...**$15.00**
Pamphlet, 1958 Triumph Slick Shift Auto Clutch Operation, 2
    pages, EX..**$10.00**
Patch, Ducati on shield w/golden wings, 1960s, 12½x3½",
    EX...**$40.00**
Patch, red, white & blue flag-like #1 w/Honda in white on
    blue, 2¾x3", EX **$8.00**
Patch, Yamaha on shield on which eagle is perched, 1960s,
    8x9½", NM...**$45.00**
Pencil sharpener, die-cast, Puntgaaf, EX **$8.00**
Pennant, Harley-Davidson, golden yellow & red, 1950s, 5x3",
    EX+ **$130.00**
Pin-back button, Indian Motorcycles, Indian profile, white
    metal, 1930s, ¾x1¼", EX.....................................**$70.00**

Pin-back button, silver skull w/blue helmet, red eyes, Helmet Laws Suck on bottom, EX **$8.00**

Poster, Camel Pro Series Daytona 200 Motorcycle Classics, 1970s, rolled, 21x20", EX.................................**$60.00**

Poster, rider w/leather helmet, Thrills Spills above w/Races w/arrow, Goodyear Tires, 1940s-50s, 9x15", EX **$45.00**

Program, 1971 Loudon Motorcycle Races on 6/13/71, 40 pages, EX...**$12.00**

Sign, US Route 66, The Mother Road, black & white map background w/blue Indian Motorcycle, tin, 11x16". EX **$10.00**

Switch plate, red Indian Motorcycle w/Indian above in black, white background, M **$12.50**

Tin, Indian Motorcycle & Route 66, The Mother Road, EX **$14.00**

Watch fob, Indian Motorcycles, arrowhead shape w/Indian head, gold-colored metal, EX **$60.00**

Whistle, motorcycle cop; Commonwealth Plastics, 1950s, EX...**$45.00**

Movie Posters and Lobby Cards

Although many sizes of movie posters were made and all are collectible, the preferred size today is still the one-sheet, 27" wide and 41" long. Movie-memorabilia collecting is as diverse as films themselves. Popular areas include specific films such as *Gone With the Wind, Wizard of Oz*, and others; specific stars — from the greats to character actors; directors such as Hitchcock, Ford, Speilberg, and others; specific film types such as B-Westerns, all-Black casts, sports related, noir, '50s teen, '60s beach, musicals, crime, silent, radio characters, cartoons, and serials; specific characters such as Tarzan, Superman, Ellery Queen, Blondie, Ma and Pa Kettle, Whistler, and Nancy Drew; specific artists like Rockwell, Davis, Frazetta, Flagg, and others; specific art themes, for instance, policeman, firemen, horses, attorneys, doctors, or nurses (this list is endless). And some collectors just collect posters they like. In the past twenty years, movie memorabilia has steadily increased in value, and in the last few years the top price paid for a movie poster has reached $453,500.00. Movie memorabilia is a new field for collectors. In the past, only a few people knew where to find posters. Recently, auctions on the East and West coasts have created much publicity, attracting scores of new collectors. Many posters are still moderately priced, and the market is expanding, allowing even new collectors to see the value of their collections increase.

Advisors: Cleophas and Lou Ann Wooley, Movie Poster Service (See Directory, Movie Posters)

Ace Ventura Pet Detective, 1994, 1-sheet, 41x27", M..**$40.00**

Advise & Consent, Henry Fonda, 1962, Saul Bass artwork, ½-sheet, 28x22", NM.................................**$45.00**

Anastasia, 41" x 27", 1956, Bureau de Censure du Cinemas, Province de Quebec, VG, $50.00.

Aristocats, Disney, 1971, 1-sheet, 41x27", EX...........**$125.00**

Atomic Man, Gene Nelson, 1956, insert, 36x14", EX ..**$50.00**

Back From Eternity, Anita Ekberg, 1956, 1-sheet, 41x27", VG+...**$75.00**

Band of Angels, Clark Gable & Yvonne DeCarlo, 1957, insert, 36x14", EX **$50.00**

Beach Blanket Bingo, Frankie Avalon & Annette Funicello, 1965, 60x40", VG **$100.00**

Billy the Kid, Robert Taylor, 1955 reissue, insert, 36x14", VG **$35.00**

Bonnie Parker Story, Dorothy Provine, 1958, ½-sheet, 28x22", VG+ **$50.00**

Bride Goes Wild, June Allyson & Van Johnson, 1948, 1-sheet, 41x27", VG+ **$35.00**

Captain Lightfoot, Rock Hudson, 1955, insert, 36x14", EX **$50.00**

Cat on a Hot Tin Roof, Elizabeth Taylor, 1958, 1-sheet, 41x27", EX+...**$150.00**

Charade, Audrey Hepburn & Cary Grant, 1963, daybill, 30x13", NM...**$100.00**

Charlie Chan in Shanghai, 1935, Warner Oland & Keye Luke, lobby card, 14x11", EX.................................**$225.00**

Chinatown, Jack Nicholson, 1974, 1-sheet, 41x27", EX..**$150.00**

Countess From Hong Kong, Marlon Brando & Sophia Loren, 1967 , 1-sheet, 41x27", VG+.................................**$25.00**

Day the Earth Froze, 1963, insert, 36x14", VG+.........**$50.00**

Doc Savage, Ron Ely, 1975, 1-sheet, 41x27", EX........**$35.00**

Don't Knock the Rock, Bill Haley & the Comets, window card, 22x14", VG+...**$150.00**

Earth Vs the Flying Saucers, Hugh Marlow, 1956, 1-sheet, linen-backed, 41x27", EX **$75.00**

Escape From the Planet of the Apes, 1971, 76x43", EX..**$250.00**

Ferry Across the Mersey, Gerry & the Pacemakers, 1965, ½-sheet, 28x22", VG+ **$45.00**

Fight Never Ends, Joe Louis & the Mills Bros, 1947, 1-sheet, 41x27", restored on linen **$650.00**

Funny Girl, Barbara Streisand, 1972 reissue, 1-sheet, 41x27", EX+ **$35.00**

Gauntlet, Clint Eastwood, 1977, Frank Frazetta artwork, ½-sheet, 28x22", NM **$40.00**

Gigantis The Fire Monster (second Godzilla film), 1959, 1-sheet, 41x27", VG+ **$200.00**

Girl Hunters, Mickey Spillane, 1963, 1-sheet, 41x27", VG+ ..**$50.00**

Girls on the Beach, Beach Boys & the Crickets, 1965, 1-sheet, VG+ **$50.00**

Godzilla King of the Monsters, Raymond Burr, 1956, 1-sheet, linen-backed, 41x27", EX **$2,250.00**

Grease, John Travolta & Olivia Newton-John, 1978, 1-sheet, 41x27", VG+ **$85.00**

Gypsy, Natalie Wood, Karl Malden & Rosalind Russell, 1962, insert, 36x14", VG+ **$40.00**

Hard Day's Night, Beatles, lobby card, US version, 11x14", EX **$225.00**

Her Husband's Affairs, Lucille Ball & Franchot Tone, 1947, insert, 36x14", VG+ **$75.00**

High School Confidential, Jerry Lee Lewis, 1958, 1-sheet, 41x27", G+ **$65.00**

House of Seven Gables, Vincent Price & George Sanders, 1940, 1-sheet, 41x27", EX+ **$25.00**

How To Marry a Millionaire, Marilyn Monroe, Betty Grable & Lauren Bacall, 1953, daybill, 30x13", EX+...........**$200.00**

Hunchback of Notre Dame, 1996, 1-sheet, 41x27", M ..**$55.00**

I Married a Monster From Outer Space, Tom Tryon, 1958, ½-sheet, 28x22", VG+ **$135.00**

I Was a Teenage Werewolf, Michael Landon, 1957, 1-sheet, 41x27", restored on linen **$350.00**

If I Had My Way, Bing Crosby, 1940, 1-sheet, 41x27", VG+ **$100.00**

Invitation to the Dance, Gene Kelly, 1956, insert, 36x14", NM **$65.00**

Ivy, Joan Fontaine, 1947, 1-sheet, 41x27", VG+ **$125.00**

King Solomon's Mines, Deborah Kerr & Stewart Granger, 1962, 1-sheet, 41x27", EX **$50.00**

Kismet, Howard Keel & Ann Blyth, 1956, 1-sheet, 41x27", EX+ **$25.00**

Kissin' Cousins, Elvis Presley, 1964, 3-sheet, 41x81", EX **$85.00**

Land Unknown, 1957, 40x30", EX............................**$250.00**

Las Vegas Story, Jane Russell & Victor Mature, 1952, insert, 36x14", EX...**$150.00**

Little Mermaid, 1989, 1-sheet, 41x27", NM **$100.00**

Live & Let Die, Roger Moore as James Bond, 1973, 1-sheet, 41x27", VG+ **$85.00**

Mad Dogs & Englishmen, Joe Cocker film, 1971, 1-sheet, 41x27", VG+ **$40.00**

Madame, Sophia Loren, 1962, 1-sheet, 41x27", EX+ ...**$50.00**

Make Mine Mink, Terry Thomas, 1961, 1-sheet, 41x27", VG+ **$25.00**

Mame, Lucille Ball, 1974, 1-sheet, 41x27", NM...........**$35.00**

Man Called Adam, Sammy Davis Jr, 1966, 1-sheet, 41x27", VG+ **$50.00**

Man w/Nine Lives, Boris Karloff, 1940, 1-sheet, 41x27", restored on linen **$750.00**

Manchurian Candidate, Frank Sinatra & Laurence Harvey, 1962, 1-sheet, 41x27", EX **$65.00**

Moonraker, Roger Moore as James Bond, 1979, 1-sheet, 41x27", EX+ **$35.00**

Mr Magoo's Holiday Festival, 1970, 1-sheet, 41x27", VG ..**$25.00**

Munster Go Home, artwork of cast, 1966, 3-sheet, 41x81", VG+ **$150.00**

Muscle Beach Party, Frankie Avalon & Annette Funicello, 1964, 60x40", VG **$75.00**

Music Land, Disney, 1955, 1-sheet, 41x27", NM........**$250.00**

Naked & the Dead, Aldo Ray, Cliff Roberstson & Raymond Massey, 1958, lobby card set, 14x11" ea, VG **$35.00**

Night Without Sleep, Linda Darnell, 1952, 1-sheet, 41x27", EX+ **$40.00**

One Million Years BC, Raquel Welch, 1966, 60x40", VG+ ..**$10.00**

Pinocchio, 1962, 1-sheet, 41x27", EX **$40.00**

Planet of the Apes, Charlton Heston, 1968, window card, 22x14", M...**$100.00**

Please Not Now, Brigitte Bardot, 1963, ½-sheet, 28x22", VG+ ...**$45.00**

Prince Valiant, James Mason, Janet Leigh & Robert Wagner, 1954, window card, 44x14", VG+ **$65.00**

Road to Nashville, Johnny Cash & others, 1966, 1-sheet, 41x27", VG+ **$50.00**

Rodan, Japanese sci-fi, 1957, daybill, 30x13", NM **$100.00**

Rosemary's Baby, Mia Farrow, 1968, window card, 22x14", M..**$50.00**

Sands of Iwo Jima, John Wayne, 1950, title card, VG+..**$200.00**

Saturday Night Fever, John Travolta, 1977, 1-sheet, 41x27", VG+ **$65.00**

Shadow Returns, lobby card, 11x14", NM **$225.00**

Shock Corridor, Peter Breck (Big Valley fame), 1963, ½-sheet, 28x22", EX **$65.00**

Sleeping Beauty, 1970, 3-sheet, 41x81", M **$100.00**

Snow Queen (Hans Christian Andersen), George Dublin art, 1960, 1-sheet, 41x27", VG+ **$40.00**

South of Caliente, Roy Rogers, Dale Evans, and Trigger, 41" x 27", 1951, M, $500.00; EX, $300.00. (Photo courtesy P. Allan Coyle)

Speedway, Elvis Presley & Nancy Sinatra, 1968, 60x40", VG **$100.00**

St Louis Blues, Nat King Cole, 1958, ½-sheet, 28x22", EX ..**$30.00**

Such Good Friends, Otto Preminger film, 1-sheet, Saul Bass artwork, 41x27", EX+ **$25.00**

Tales From the Crypt, Cinerama, 1972, 41x27", NM ...**$50.00**

Tarzan the Fearless, 1933, linen-backed, 41x27", NM..**$800.00**

Ten Commandments, Charlton Heston, 1956, insert, 36x14", EX **$125.00**

That Tennessee Beat, Minnie Pearl, Statler Bros & Boots Randolph, 1966, 1-sheet, 41x27", EX.....................**$50.00**

Thunderball, Sean Connery, 1965, 1-sheet, 41x27", EX+..**$100.00**

Toy Story, 1995, 1-sheet, 41x27", NM+ **$40.00**

Two Lost Worlds, James Arness, 1950, insert, 36x14", VG+ **$100.00**

When Ladies Meet, Joan Crawford, Robert Taylor & Greer Garson, 1941, ½-sheet, 28x22", VG+..................**$150.00**

Where the Boys Are, Connie Francis, George Hamilton & Yvette Mimieux, 1961, 1-sheet, 41x27", VG+........**$45.00**

Wild Wild World of Jayne Mansfield, documentary, 1968, lobby card set, 14x11" ea, NM..................**$65.00**

Winnie the Pooh & Tigger Too, 1974, 1-sheet, 41x27", M..**$150.00**

Yellow Rolls Royce, Ingrid Bergman & Rex Harrison, 1965, 1-sheet, 41x27", EX **$35.00**

You're My Everything, Dan Dailey & Ann Baxter, 1949, 1-sheet, 41x27", EX **$50.00**

Ziegfield Girl, Tony Martin, 1941, lobby card, 14x11", EX .**$25.00**

Zulu, Michael Cane & Stanley Baker, 1963, 40x30", EX ...**$100.00**

Napkin Dolls

Cocktail, luncheon, or dinner..., paper, cotton, or damask..., solid, patterned, or plaid — regardless of size, color, or material, there's always been a place for napkins. In the late 1940s and early 1950s, buffet-style meals were gaining popularity. One accessory common to many of these buffets is now one of today's hot collectibles — the napkin doll. While most of the ceramic and wooden examples found today date from this period, many homemade napkin dolls were produced in ceramic classes of the 1960s and 1970s.

For information on napkin dolls as well as egg timers, string holders, children's whistle cups, baby feeder dishes, razor blade banks, pie birds, laundry sprinkler bottles, and other unique collectibles from the same era, we recommend *Collectibles for the Kitchen, Bath and Beyond*; for ordering information see our advisor's listing in the Directory.

Advisor: Bobbie Zucker Bryson (See Directory, Napkin Dolls)

Atlantic Mold, yellow & white lady, holding a lily, 11", from $65 to..**$75.00**

Betson's blue Colonial lady, bell clapper, marked Hand Painted, 9", from $75 to **$90.00**

California Originals, green & white, Spanish dancer, slits in rear only, foil label, 13", from $110 to...............**$125.00**

California Originals, toothpick holder basket over head, foil label, 13¾", from $65 to...........................**$85.00**

Enesco, Genie at Your Service, holding lantern, paper label, 8", from $100 to...................................**$135.00**

Goebel, native half doll on wire frame, marked Goebel, W Germany, ca 1957, 9½", from $135 to **$150.00**

Holland Mold, Daisy, No 514, 7¼", from $75 to.........**$95.00**

Holland Mold, Rebecca No H-265, 10½", from $150 to...**$195.00**

Holland Mold, Rosie, No H-827, 7½", from $65 to.....**$85.00**

Holt Howard, blue Sunbonnet Miss, marked Holt Howard 1958, 5", from $125 to **$150.00**

Japan, angel, blue, holding flowers, 5⅜", from $110 to..**$150.00**

Japan, lady in green w/pink umbrella, bell clapper, unmarked, 9", from $70 to **$85.00**

Japan, lady in pink dress w/blue shawl & yellow hat, 8½", from $65 to **$85.00**

Japan, Santa, marked Chess, 1957, 6¾", from $95 to...**$115.00**

Kreiss & Co, angel, candleholder in halo, 11", from $90 to **$110.00**

Kreiss & Co, pink doll w/poodle, jeweled eyes, necklace & ring, candle holder behind hat, marked, 10¾", from $100 to **$125.00**

Kreiss & Co, pink lady holding fan, candle holder behind fan, marked, 8¾", from $75 to............................**$95.00**

Kreiss & Co, yellow doll w/gold trim holding muff, jeweled eyes, candle holder in top of hat, marked, 10", from $95 to **$110.00**

Lady in blue or pink with candle holder behind hat, from $65.00 to $75.00. (Photo courtesy Bobbie Zucker Bryson)

Mallory Ceramics Studio, Christine, 9", from $135 to.**$150.00**

Man (bartender), holding tray w/candle holder, 8¾", from $85 to...**$100.00**

Marcia of California, woman w/molded apron & bowl on head, iridescent finish, 13", from $95 to **$150.00**

Marybelle, mold P71, Southern lady holding hat, 9¾", from $150 to...**$195.00**

Metal, silhouette of Deco woman, black & gold w/wire bottom, 8⅞", from $115 to **$135.00**

Miss Versatility Cocktail Girl, 13", from $75 to **$95.00**

Rooster, white w/red & black trim, slits in tail for napkins, w/egg salt & pepper shakers, from $35 to **$45.00**

Sevoy Etta, wood w/marble base, marked USD Patent No 159,005, 11½", from $35 to **$45.00**

Swedish doll, wooden, marked Patent No 113861, 12", from $25 to **$35.00**

Wooden Jamaican lady, movable arms, paper label: Ave 13 Nov 743, A Sinfonia, Tel 2350 Petropolis, 6", from $65 to.**$85.00**

Wooden pink & blue doll w/red strawberry toothpick holder on head, 8", from $60 to **$75.00**

Wooden, Japanese, from $30.00 to $40.00. (Photo courtesy Bobbie Zucker Bryson)

Wooden umbrella, marked Reg Prop No 382.649, Reproduction Prohibited, Industria Argentina, 8⅜", from $25 to **$45.00**

Yamihaya Bros, lady holding yoke w/bucket salt & pepper shakers, hat conceals candle holder, from $100 to **$135.00**

NASCAR Collectibles

Over the past decade, interest in NASCAR racing has increased to the point that the related collectibles industry has mushroomed into a multi-billion dollar business. Posters, magazines, soda pop bottles, model kits, and scores of other products are only a few examples of items produced with the sole intention of attracting racing fans. Also included as a part of this field of collecting are items such as race-worn apparel — even parts from the racing cars themselves — and these, though not devised as such, are the collectibles that command the highest prices! If you're a racing fan, you'll want to read *Racing Collectibles* by the editors of *Racing Collector's Price Guide* (Collector Books).

Antenna topper, Jeff Gordon's facsimile signature over #24 on 1 side, Hendrick's Motor Sports logo on other, M ..**$40.00**

Banner, Bud, Official Beer of NASCAR, A Raceday Favorite, shows track & stands, heavy vinyl, 48x72"...........**$35.00**

Book, NASCAR Transporters, by William Burt, inside look at the sophisticated transporters, 96 pages, softcover, 8x9", EX..**$25.00**

Book, Official NASCAR Annual, 1993, 300 pages, photos, info, schedules, EX **$20.00**

Car, inflatable; Dale Earnhardt Jr's #8, red w/black detail, EX...**$30.00**

Card set, Racer's Choice, Dale Earnhardt, 1996 Sun-drop, set of 3...**$20.00**

Card set, 1986 Sportstar Photographics, set of 13 .....**$700.00**

Clock, Dale Earnhardt, Sun-drop, 5,000 made, JEBCO......**$130.00**

Clock, Davey Allison, Mac Tools, 10,000 made, JEBCO.**$3,000.00**

Diecast, Coca-Cola Charlotte Motor Speedway Kenworth K100E semi, Racing Champions, 1992, NMIB......**$30.00**

Doll, Barbie, dressed like Kyle Petty, 50th Anniversary Edition, 1998, M (EX box)....................................**$20.00**

Knife, Case Trapper, blade etched/colored w/Dale Earnhardt signature, car & #3, gray pick bone handle, 3 blades, 4⅛"...**$90.00**

Knife, lock-back; 1998 Daytona Champion Earnhardt Commemorative, blue Frostwood handle, Frost Cutlery, w/sheath, MIB....................................**$45.00**

Lighter, Jeff Gordon #24 in red, 1995 Champion Winston Cup NASCAR in black w/red logo in center, Zippo, NM .**$30.00**

Magazine, Racing Pictorial, 1959, 1st issue...............**$150.00**

Magazine, Racing Pictorial, 1969-70 Annual **$30.00**

Magazine, Sports Illustrated, Dale Earnhardt, 2/26/01 ..**$20.00**

Mural, Earnhardt Jr/Budweiser, 2-part, 96x72" (together), M (in tube)...**$36.00**

Ornament, Dale Earnhardt kneeling on checkered floor, 3-D, Hallmark, MIB **$25.00**

Plate, Red Hot Ride, Dale Earndardt Jr, Hamilton Collection, 6½" dia **$40.00**

Postcard, #3 Dale Earnhardt, Goodwrench, GMAC, yellow Corvette **$40.00**

Poster, 1994 Chevrolet, Brickyard 400, 5 drivers, 36x24" ..**$30.00**

Poster, 1995 Busch Clash, 19 drivers, Daytona in background, 22x34" **$25.00**

Program, Atlanta, fall race, 1992, Richard Petty's last race and Jeff Gordon's first WC race, $45.00. (Photo courtesy Racing Collectibles)

Sign, Budweiser Official Beer 50th Anniversary, metal, 26x20" L, M..**$70.00**

Sign, Dale Earnhardt/Busch Beer, Dale standing in front of car w/crowd in background, metal, 35½x25½" ...**$50.00**

Sign, Sterling Martin's Coors Light car, metal, 36x16½"..**$48.00**

Sign, tin, hood-shaped, Rusty Wallace, Miller Lite, Harley-Davidson, 28x34" **$90.00**

Stand-up, Jeff Gordon, holding soda & a bag of Fritos, 30x72"...**$70.00**

Store display, Jim Beam, inflatable NASCAR-style car, 43x17x15" **$50.00**

Vehicle, Ernie Irvan, #36, 24k gold-plated Racing Champions, in leather case, 1998, MIB................................**$48.00**

Vehicle, radio controlled, Kenny Schrader's #36 M&M Racing Thunder, battery-operated, 5½x10½", MIB..........**$60.00**

Wall clock, Adam Petty Memorial, Adam standing in uniform, 8½" dia $30.00

Wall clock, 50th Anniversary, Dale Earnhardt, Snap On, made by Jebco, 11x23" $95.00

New Martinsville

Located in a West Virginia town by the same name, the New Martinsville Glass Company was founded in 1901 and until it was purchased by Viking in 1944 produced quality tableware in various patterns and colors that collectors admire today. They also made a line of glass animals which Viking continued to produce until they closed in 1986. In 1987 the factory was bought by Mr. Kenneth Dalzell who reopened the company under the title Dalzell-Viking. He used the old molds to reissue his own line of animals, which he marked 'Dalzell' with an acid stamp. These are usually priced in the $50.00 to $60.00 range. Examples marked 'V' were made by Viking for another company, Mirror Images. They're valued at $15.00 to $35.00, with colors sometimes higher.

Advisor: Roselle Schleifman (See Directory, Elegant Glass)

Batter set, cobalt, $300.00. (Photo courtesy Gene Florence)

Bonbon, Prelude, crystal, 3-footed, 6" $22.00
Bonbon, Radiance, ice blue or red, 6" $33.00
Bottle, oil; Prelude, crystal, 4-oz $45.00
Bowl, Meadow Wreath, crystal, flat, flared, 10" $35.00
Bowl, pickle; Radiance, ice blue or red, 7" $35.00
Bowl, Prelude, crystal, 3-footed, 15" $70.00
Bowl, relish; Meadow Wreath, crystal, 3-part, 8" $30.00
Candlestick, Meadow Wreath, crystal, 2-light, round footed $40.00
Candy box, Meadow Wreath, crystal, #42/26, 3-part, w/lid...$65.00
Candy dish, Moondrops, pink or green, w/lid............$55.00
Comport, Radiance, ice blue or red, 5" $30.00
Compote, Prelude, crystal, 6" $22.00
Cup, Moondrops, black...$35.00
Cup, punch; Radiance, amber......................................$7.00
Figurine, baby bear, crystal, head turned or straight, 3" ..$65.00
Figurine, chick, frosted, 1" $25.00
Figurine, elephant, bookend, crystal, 5½", ea.............$85.00
Figurine, horse, crystal, head up, 8"..........................$95.00
Figurine, pig, mama, crystal.......................................$325.00
Figurine, porpoise on wave, original.........................$750.00

Figurine, seal, baby, w/ball, crystal............................$60.00
Figurine, ships, bookends, crystal, ea $35.00
Figurine, swan, candle holders, ruby, pr $75.00
Figurine, woodsman, crystal, sq base, 7⅜" $135.00
Ladle, Radiance, amber, for punch bowl...................$110.00

Pitcher, Prelude, 78-ounce, $235.00.
(Photo courtesy Gene Florence)

Plate, bread & butter; Prelude, crystal, 6" $6.00
Plate, luncheon; Radiance, amber, 8" $10.00
Plate, Meadow Wreath, crystal, 11" $35.00
Plate, Moondrops, pink or green, 8" $20.00
Plate, Prelude, crystal, 16" $75.00
Stem, cordial; Prelude, crystal, ball stem, 1-oz...........$40.00
Sugar bowl, Moondrops, crystal, #37 ....$12.00
Tray, Prelude, crystal, for individual creamer & sugar bowl..$10.00
Vase, Meadow Wreath, crystal, #42/26, flared, 10"......$50.00

Nichols, Betty Lou

This California artist/potter is probably best known for her head vases, which display her talents and strict attention to detail to full advantage. Many of her ladies were dressed in stylish clothing and hats that were often decorated with applied lace, ruffles, and bows; the signature long eyelashes are apparent on nearly every model she made. Because these applications are delicate and susceptible to damage, mint-condition examples are rare and very valuable. Most of her head vases and figurines carry not only her name but the name of the subject as well.

Figurine, Anna, yellow polka-dot scarf, green top, hands on hips, 9", EX...$100.00
Figurine, Chris, yellow jacket, black hat & pants, 11¼", EX $80.00
Figurine, Dick, Christmas Angel, wide open bag, 6½", M $165.00
Figurine, Greta, blond girl holding open planter basket w/original plastic plants, 5½", M.......................$95.00

Figurine, Liz, lady w/basket that can be used as planter, cream dress w/green hand-painted decor, 10¼", M..........**$195.00**

Figurine, Melanie, carrying open hatbox, can be used as planter, 8½", M **$185.00**

Figurine, Virginia, frilly dress, may be used as planter, 10", M...**$1,125.00**

Figurine/flower holder, Margot, open baskets on ea side may be used as planter, 10½", NM.............................**$150.00**

Head vase, Becky, 5⅝", EX **$95.00**

Head vase, Demi-Dorable, 3½", M, from $100 to.....**$110.00**

Head vase, Ermintrude, wide-brimmed hat, 3 long curls, 8", EX **$200.00**

Head vase, Flora Belle, green, yellow & white plaid hat & dress w/ruffles, 11", EX.......................................**$260.00**

Head vase, Flora Belle, light brown, dark brown & white plaid dress & hat, ruffled collar, 11", M..............**$810.00**

Head vase, Jill, sm repair, 4", EX...................................**$95.00**

Head vase, Linda, blue w/white polka-dotted dress & hat, brown hair, 4½x5¾", M **$250.00**

Head vase, Mary Lou, repair to hat, 8", EX.............**$100.00**

Head vase, Mary Lou, ruffled collar, 5", NM **$195.00**

Head vase, Michelle, celery green dress, blond hair, 6x5", NM, from $225 to **$250.00**

Head vase, Nancy, ruffle at neck, 8", EX...................**$275.00**

Head vase, Nellie, blue w/white polka-dot dress w/cream ruffles, blue hat, 5", NM......................................**$180.00**

Head vase, praying nun, white habit, hands folded, M **$135.00**

Head vase, Sheila, green dress w/white w/black dotted ribbon at neck & matching hat, 7", EX **$200.00**

Head vase, Vicky, can be used as wall vase, 7", in rare mint condition, $650.00. (Photo courtesy Jack Chipman)

Head vase, Vicki, brunette dressed in ivory w/hand-painted roses, 8", EX+...**$375.00**

Nodding boy & girl, he: nods yes, 7½", she: nods no, 7", M, ea from $150 to **$175.00**

Planter, fence, yellow & brown, 3½x9½", M, from $100 to **$125.00**

Niloak Pottery

The Niloak Pottery company was the continuation of a quarter-century-old family business in Benton, Arkansas. Known as the Eagle Pottery in the early twentieth century, its owner was Charles Dean Hyten who continued in his father's footsteps making utilitarian wares for local and state markets. In 1909 Arthur Dovey, an experienced potter formerly from the Rookwood Pottery of Ohio and the Arkansas-Missouri based Ouachita Pottery companies, came to Benton and created America's most unusual art pottery. Introduced in 1910 as Niloak (kaolin spelled backwards), Dovey and Hyten produced art pottery pieces from swirling clays with a wide range of artificially created colors including red, blue, cream, brown, gray, and later, green. Connected to the Arts & Crafts Movement by 1913, the pottery was labeled as Missionware (probably due to its seeming simplicity in the making). Missionware (or swirl) production continued alongside utilitarian ware manufacturing until the 1930s when economic factors led to the making of another type of art pottery and later to (molded) industrial castware. In 1931 Niloak Pottery introduced Hywood Art Pottery (marked as such), consisting of regular glaze techniques including overspray, mottling, and drips of two colors on vases and bowls that were primarily hand thrown. It was short-lived and soon replaced with the Hywood by Niloak (or Hywood) line to increase marketing potential through the use of the well-recognized Niloak name. Experienced potters, designers, and ceramists were involved at Niloak; among them were Frank Long, Paul Cox, Stoin M. Stoin, Howard Lewis, and Rudy Ganz. Many local families had long ties to the pottery including the McNeills, Rowlands, and Alleys. Experiencing tremendous financial woes by the mid-1930s, Niloak came under new management which was led by Hardy L. Winburn of Little Rock. To maximize efficiency and stay competetive, they focused primarily on industrial castware such as vases, bowls, figurines, animals, and planters. Niloak survived into the late 1940s when it became known as the Winburn Tile Company of North Little Rock; it still exists today.

Virtually all of Niloak Missionware/swirl pottery is marked with die stamps. The exceptions are generally fan vases, wall pockets, lamp bases, and whiskey jugs. Be careful when you buy unmarked swirl pottery — it is usually Evans pottery (made in Missouri) which generally has either no interior glaze or is chocolate brown inside. Moreover, Evans made swirl wall pockets, lamp bases, and even hanging baskets that find their way on to today's market and are sold as Niloak. Niloak stickers are often placed on these unmarked Evans pieces — closely examine the condition of the sticker to determine if it is damaged or mutilated from the transfer process.

For more information, we recommend *The Collector's Encyclopedia of Niloak Pottery* (Collector Books) by our advisor David Edwin Gifford, a historian of Arkansas pottery.

Advisor: David Edwin Gifford (See Directory, Niloak)

Bowl, Mission, 8¾", from $275 to $325.00
Candlestick, Mission, flared foot, 7", from $125 to ...$175.00
Candlestick, Ozark Blue, hand thrown, Potteries sticker, 7",
    from $45 to...$65.00
Figurine, donkey on base, Peterson design, 2¾", from $75
    to...$125.00
Figurine, elephant, Ozark Blue, hollow, 2¼", from $50 to...$75.00
Figurine, Scottie dog, Mirror Black, Alley design, unmarked,
    3¾", from $50 to...$75.00
Figurine, swan, Ozark Blue, hollow, Potteries sticker, 2¾",
    from $50 to...$100.00
Figurine, Trojan horse, Ivory, larger second art mark, 8¾",
    from $125 to..$175.00
Flower frog, turtle, Canary Yellow, 1½x4¾", smallest Niloak
    block letters mark, from $50 to $100.00

**Ginger jar, Mission, 8½", $1,200.00;
vase, Mission, 10" x 5", $275.00.**

Planter, Burma camel, brown/tan, Niloak in low relief, 3¼",
    from $35 to..$45.00
Planter, clown & donkey, Star of the Big Top design, shiny
    w/colored details to clown's face, incised mark, 7", from
    $35 to..$45.00
Planter, clown drummer, medium blue, incised mark, 7½",
    from $25 to..$35.00
Planter, deer, Ozark Blue, free-standing, Niloak in low relief,
    10", from $100 to $200.00
Planter, elephant, opening in back, trunk raised, Ozark
    Dawn II, block letters mark, 4¼", from $45 to $65.00
Planter, poodle, Ozark Dawn II, Alley design, Niloak in low
    relief, 3½", from $100 to $150.00
Planter, rooster, dark green, Niloak in low relief, 8½", from
    $35 to..$45.00
Planter, squirrel, blue & tan matt, Niloak in low relief, 6",
    from $35 to..$45.00
Planter, wishing Well, Ozark Dawn II, Niloak in low relief,
    Alley design, 8", from $35 to $45.00
Shakers, geese, Ozark Dawn II, Alley design, Potteries stick-
    er, 2", pr, from $35 to..$45.00
Vase, Mission, cylindrical, 5½"......................................$90.00

Vase, Mission, waisted, 10", from $400 to.................$500.00
Vase, Mission, wide bands of color, 3x3½" $85.00
Vase, tulip form, Fox Red, Alley design, Niloak in low relief,
    7¼", from $15 to...$25.00

Novelty Radios

Novelty radios come in an unimaginable variety of shapes and sizes from advertising and product shapes to character forms, vehicles, and anything else the manufacturer might dream up. For information on these new, fun collectibles read *Collector's Guide to Novelty Radios* by Marty Bunis and Robert Breed, and *Schroeder's Collectible Toys, Antique to Modern* (Collector Books).

Alf, rectangular w/image on front, NM, from $50 to ..$60.00
Batman, 1973, bust figure, EX (EX box).....................$30.00

Batman, 1989 DC Comics, AM radio with belt clip and swing handle, 5½x3", from $75.00 to $100.00. (Photo courtesy Marty Bunis and Robert F. Breed)

Budweiser, can shape, complete w/battery that came in box,
    MIB $25.00
Bugs Bunny & Elmer Fudd, plastic, NM, from $50 to....$70.00
Cap'n Crunch Cereal box, Isis model 39, NM, from $35
    to..$50.00
Chicken & egg, clock/radio, AM/FM, quartz, Japanese clock
    movement, 6⅛x9", NM..$60.00
Del Monte Pineapple Chunks can, M $75.00
Dockers, FM only, made in Taiwan, 3¼x2¼", NM $30.00
Ford 250 camper, Philco-Ford Model P-23, NM, from $300
    to..$350.00
Heinz's Tomato Soup can, Hong Kong, NM, from $40 to .$60.00
Huffy Bikes, NM, from $35 to...$50.00
Incredible Hulk, Marvel Comics, 1978, 7", M $75.00
Kellogg's Special K, AM/FM, made in China, NM.......$50.00
Little Debbie Swiss Cake Rolls, Isis Model 103, NM, from $25
    to..$35.00
McDonald's, pop-can shape w/Speedee mascot, commemo-
    rating 30th anniversary, 1985, 5", NM $65.00
McIlhenny Tobasco Brand Pepper Sauce, AM/FM, made in
    China, 2¾x5", NM...$75.00

Mountain Dew Can, Hong Kong, NM, from $35 to....**$50.00**

Mug Root Beer, 1970s, can shape, MIB **$25.00**

Nixon, likeness of Nixon in victory sign pose, NM **$75.00**

Polaroid 600 Plus, film pack shape, 4x5", NM **$30.00**

Power Rangers, Micro Games of America, 1994, head figure, 5", NM, from $35 to.................................**$50.00**

Safety Kleen, parts-washing sink shape, PRI, NM.......**$50.00**

Sears Best Easy Living Paint can, Hong Kong, NM, from $35 to...**$50.00**

Snoopy doghouse, Determined, 1970s, plastic, 6x4", NMIB, from $50 to...**$60.00**

SOS Detergent box, 1989, NM, from $35 to **$50.00**

Teddy bear on mattress, Fun Designs, 1986, 8x8", NM, from $20 to...**$30.00**

Thunderbirds, ITC Entertainment Group Ltd, 1992, NM, from $75 to...**$100.00**

Wrangler, resembles leather w/stitching around edges, 3½x4¾", NM **$35.00**

Yogi Bear, Hanna Barbera/Markson, NM, from $100 to...**$125.00**

Novelty Telephones

Novelty telephones modeled after products or advertising items are popular with collectors — so are those that are character related. For further information we recommend *Schroeder's Collectible Toys, Antique to Modern* (Collector Books).

Snoopy and Woodstock, American Telephone Corporation, 1976, touchtone, EX, $100.00. (Photo courtesy June Moon)

Alvin (Alvin & the Chipmunks), 1984, MIB.................**$50.00**

Batmobile, Columbia, 1990, MIB, from $25 to **$35.00**

Batmobile (Batmobile Forever), MIB, from $35 to......**$50.00**

Beavis & Butthead, EX (EX box)..................................**$18.00**

Bugs Bunny, Warner Exclusive, MIB, from $60 to......**$70.00**

Charlie Tuna, 1987, MIB, from $50 to.........................**$65.00**

Garfield, recumbent, eyes closed until receiver is lifted, Tyco, EX...**$40.00**

Jeff Gordon, race car style, Columbia Tel-Com, MIB..**$25.00**

Keebler Elf, NM, from $60 to......................................**$70.00**

Mickey Mouse, Western Electric, 1976, EX.................**$175.00**

Opus the Penguin, receiver locks into back, Tyco, 1987, 14", EX..**$60.00**

Oscar Mayer Weiner, EX..**$65.00**

Roy Rogers, 1950s, plastic wall-type, 9x9", EX............**$50.00**

Snoopy & Woodstock, American Telecommunications Corp, Disney high/low volume switch underneath, 1976, EX...**$65.00**

Snoopy as Joe Cool, 1980s, MIB **$55.00**

Star Trek Enterprise, 1993, NM....................................**$25.00**

Strawberry Shortcake, M **$55.00**

Ziggy, 1989, MIB..**$75.00**

Occupied Japan Collectibles

Some items produced in Japan during the period from the end of WWII until the occupation ended in 1952 were marked Occupied Japan. No doubt much of the ware from this era was marked simply Japan, since obviously the 'Occupied' term caused considerable resentment among the Japanese people, and they were understandably reluctant to use the mark. So even though you may find identical items marked simply Japan or Made in Japan, only those with the more limited Occupied Japan mark are evaluated here.

Assume that the items described below are ceramic unless another material is mentioned. For more information, we recommend *Occupied Japan Collectibles* by Gene Florence (published by Collector Books).

Newsletter: *The Upside Down World of an O.J. Collector* The Occupied Japan Club c/o Florence Archambault 29 Freeborn St., Newport, RI 02840-1821. Published bimonthly; information requires SASE

Ashtray, metal, embossed knight w/shield, from $6 to...**$8.00**

Ashtray, metal, embossed map of Georgia, from $12.50 to...**$17.50**

Box, cigarette; pink roses on white, from $10 to........**$12.50**

Box, metal, embossed Pegasus, sm, from $10 to........**$12.00**

Cigarette lighter, champagne bucket, metal, from $15 to..**$17.50**

Cigarette lighter, gun form, metal w/pearl handles, from $17.50 to...**$20.00**

Creamer, windmill form, 2⅞", from $10 to..................**$12.00**

Crumb pan, metal, embossed scene, souvenir of New York, from $10 to...**$12.50**

Cup & saucer, demitasse; floral on pale yellow, can shape, from $6 to...**$8.00**

Cup & saucer, floral chintz, Merit, from $10 to...........**$12.50**

Cup & saucer, house scene w/lustre trim, from $10 to .**$12.00**

Cup & saucer, Livonia, magnolias on white, Mieto Norleans China, from $12.50 to...**$15.00**

Cup & saucer, Phoenix Bird, from $22.50 to...............**$25.00**

Cup & saucer, roses on white, from $10 to.................**$12.00**

Dinnerware set for 12, includes all service for 4 w/3 platters & serving bowls, from $400 to **$500.00**

Dinnerware set for 4 w/cups & saucers, 3 sizes of plates, cereal & soup bowls, creamer & sugar bowl w/lid, from $175 to...**$200.00**

Dinnerware set for 6, w/all items listed for service for 4 w/gravy boat & platter, from $225 to **$250.00**

Dinnerware set for 8, including all service for 6 & sm platter, from $275 to..**$350.00**

Doll, celluloid, pink baby, 5½", from $22.50 to..........**$25.00**

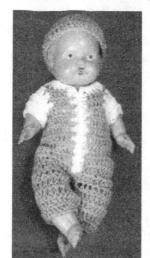

**Doll, celluloid, 7",
$45.00. (Photo courtesy Gene Florence)**

Doll, china, Black, 3¼", from $40 to.......................**$45.00**

Doll, china, 3¼", from $25 to **$30.00**

Doll, feather dancer, celluloid, 4¼", from $12.50 to...**$15.00**

Doll, football player, celluloid, 6", from $12 to..........**$15.00**

Doll, kewpie w/feathers, celluloid, from $22.50 to.....**$25.00**

Dresser set, floral decoration, two 4½" bottles and covered jar, $75.00 for the set. (Photo courtesy Florence Archambault)

Figurine, angel w/mandolin, 2⅝", from $4 to **$5.00**

Figurine, ballerina, 3⅝", from $17.50 to **$20.00**

Figurine, ballerina, 6⅛", from $35 to **$40.00**

Figurine, bird on tree branch, 3", from $12.50 to **$15.00**

Figurine, boy on fence w/basket, 4", from $6 to **$8.00**

Figurine, boy playing accordion, 2⅝", from $3 to **$4.00**

Figurine, boy w/begging dog, Hummel type, 5", from $35 to **$40.00**

Figurine, boy w/broken sprinkler, Hummel type, 4½", from $30 to...**$35.00**

Figurine, boy w/parrot, 5", from $12.50 to.................**$15.00**

Figurine, boy w/saxophone, 4⅝", from $8 to **$10.00**

Figurine, bride & groom, 4¼", from $20 to................**$25.00**

Figurine, cherub holding bowl, pastels, 5½", from $55 to **$65.00**

Figurine, cherub on base, pastel tones, 5¾", from $30 to **$35.00**

Figurine, cherub seated beside lg open flower, 4", from $30 to **$35.00**

Figurine, Colonial man & lady, fine hats, 12", pr, from $75 to **$90.00**

Figurine, Colonial man & lady, 4⅝", pr, from $30 to .**$35.00**

Figurine, cow w/horns, realistic, 2¾x4", from $8 to...**$10.00**

Figurine, Dutch girl, 3¼", from $5 to **$6.00**

Figurine, Dutch peasant couple, 8¼", pr, from $55 to..**$65.00**

Figurine, Eskimo boy & girl, 3", 2¾", pr, from $25 to**$30.00**

Figurine, flamingo, 7¼", from $25 to **$27.50**

Figurine, flower girl, 4⅝", from $15 to **$17.50**

Figurine, gentleman, fine detail, painted porcelain, 12", from $75 to **$100.00**

Figurine, girl in white dress (Florence copy), 7", from $20 to **$25.00**

Figurine, girl w/teddy bear, 5⅝", from $17.50 to........**$20.00**

Figurine, horse w/rider, 10¼", from $175 to.............**$200.00**

Figurine, horses (2) jumping fence, on base, 5", from $35 to **$45.00**

Figurine, Indian (American) w/baby, 5½", from $20 to **$25.00**

Figurine, Indian Chief, 5½", from $22.50 to **$25.00**

Figurine, lady bug w/bat, 2¼", from $6 to **$8.00**

Figurine, lady w/basket of flowers, painted bisque, 8", from $45 to **$50.00**

Figurine, lady w/mandolin, 4", from $6 to **$8.00**

Figurine, lamb or cow, celluloid, ea from $6 to...........**$8.00**

Figurine, man w/water sprinkler, painted bisque, 8", from $45 to **$50.00**

Figurine, newsboy, 5½", from $10 to..........................**$12.00**

Figurine, Oriental lady w/fan, 7½", from $12.50 to....**$15.00**

Figurine, Oriental man & woman, 6", pr, from $45 to..**$50.00**

Figurine, pastoral couple, 10½", pr, from $130 to **$140.00**

Figurine, pastoral couple by fence, 8⅛", pr, from $100 to **$125.00**

Figurine, peacock, tail down, 3⅛", from $6 to..............**$8.00**

Lamp, Colonial lady stands on base, 13", from $35 to .**$40.00**

Lighter, elephant figural, metal, from $15 to **$20.00**

Match holder, coal hod form, from $10 to **$12.50**

Mug, devil's head figural, from $35 to **$40.00**

Mug, Indian head, from $12.50 to................................**$15.00**

Mug, Santa figural, from $30 to **$35.00**

Pencil holder, Happy House, celluloid, from $20 to ..**$25.00**

Planter, donkey (blue stripes) w/2 baskets, from $6 to ...**$8.00**

Planter, donkey w/floral cart, from $9 to **$11.00**

Planter, girl w/mandolin, 3⅝", from $8 to...................**$10.00**

Planter, lady beside lg shell, 5½x6½", from $55 to **$65.00**

Planter, Oriental boy w/rickshaw, from $10 to **$12.00**

Plate, Cup of Gold, yellow flower on white, lattice rim, Rosetti, 8¼", from $22.50 to...................................**$25.00**

Salt & pepper shakers, cucumbers, pr from $30 to **$35.00**

Salt & pepper shakers, Dutch couple, pr from $12.50 to..**$15.00**

Salt & pepper shakers, squirrels, pr, from $12.50 to...**$15.00**

Salt & pepper shakers, strawberries on tray, 3-pc set, from $20 to.......**$25.00**

Salt & pepper shakes, Indians (shakers) in canoe, 3-pc set, from $22.50 to.......**$25.00**

Silent butler, copper, souvenir of Washington, DC, from $8 to.......**$10.00**

Sugar bowl, windmill form, w/lid, 3⅞", from $17.50 to.**$20.00**

Toby mug, MacArthur, from $65 to.......**$75.00**

Toby mug, parson, from $75 to.......**$100.00**

Tray, metal, United Nations souvenir, 4¾x2", from $8 to.......**$10.00**

Vase, lacquerware, leaf design, flared rim, 13", from $125 to.......**$150.00**

Wall plaque, cup & saucer, roses on white w/gold, 3¼", from $7.50 to.......**$9.00**

Wall plaque, man & lady seated in swings in relief, painted bisque, pr, from $50 to.......**$60.00**

Old MacDonald's Farm

This is a wonderful line of novelty kitchenware items fashioned as the family and the animals that live on Old MacDonald's Farm. It's been popular with collectors for quite some time, and prices are astronomical, though they seem to have stabilized, at least for now.

These things were made by the Regal China Company, who also made some of the Little Red Riding Hood items that are so collectible, as well as figural cookie jars, 'hugger' salt and pepper shakers, and decanters. The Roerigs devote a chapter to Regal in their book *The Collector's Encyclopedia of Cookie Jars* and, in fact, show the entire Old MacDonald's Farm line.

Advisor: Rick Spencer (See Directory, Regal China)

Teapot, duck's head, from $250.00 to $300.00.

Butter dish, cow's head.......**$220.00**

Canister, flour; cereal; or coffee; medium size, ea from $225 to.......**$250.00**

Canister, pretzels, peanuts, popcorn, chips or tidbits; lg, ea from $300 to.......**$350.00**

Canister, salt, sugar or tea; medium size, ea from $225 to.**$250.00**

Canister, soap or cookies; lg, ea from $350 to.......**$425.00**

Cookie jar, barn, from $295 to.......**$325.00**

Creamer, rooster, from $110 to.......**$125.00**

Grease jar, pig, from $200 to.......**$250.00**

Pitcher, milk; from $425 to.......**$450.00**

Salt & pepper shakers, boy & girl, pr.......**$80.00**

Salt & pepper shakers, churn, gold trim, pr.......**$95.00**

Salt & pepper shakers, feed sacks w/sheep, pr.......**$195.00**

Spice jar, assorted lids, sm, ea from $125 to.......**$150.00**

Sugar bowl, hen.......**$135.00**

Paper Dolls

One of the earliest producers of paper dolls was Raphael Tuck of England, who distributed many of their dolls in the United States in the late 1800s. Advertising companies used them to promote their products, and some were often included in the pages of leading ladies' magazines.

But over the years, the most common paper dolls have been those printed on the covers of a book containing their clothes on the inside pages. These were initiated during the 1920s and because they were inexpensive retained their popularity even during the Depression years. They peaked in the 1940s, but with the advent of television in the '50s, children began to loose interest. Be sure to check old boxes and trunks in your attic; you just may find some!

But what's really exciting right now are those from more recent years — celebrity dolls from television shows like 'The Brady Bunch' or 'The Waltons,' the skinny English model Twiggy, and movie stars like Rock Hudson and Debbie Reynolds. Our values are for paper dolls in mint, uncut, original condition. Just remember that cut sets (even if all original components are still there) are worth only about half as much. Damaged sets or those with missing pieces should be priced accordingly. Prices below are for uncut and original paper dolls in mint condition.

If you'd like to learn more about them, we recommend *Price Guide to Lowe & Whitman Paper Dolls* and *Price Guide to Saalfield and Merrill Paper Dolls* by Mary Young, and *Schroeder's Collectible Toys, Antique to Modern.*

Advisor: Mary Young (See Directory, Paper Dolls)

Newsletter: *Paper Dolls News*
Ema Terry
P.O. Box 807
Vivian, LA 71082; Subscription: $12 per year for 4 issues; want lists, sale items, and trades listed

Circus Paper Dolls, Saalfield #2610, 1952, from $35 to..**$50.00**

Darling Dolls w/Wavy Hair, Saalfield #6194, 1947, from $25 to.......**$40.00**

Debby Reynolds, Whitman #1178, 1953.......**$125.00**

Dolls of Other Lands, Whitman #2074, 1963, from $20 to.......**$45.00**

Dress Alike Dolls, Whitman #2058, 1951, from $60 to .**$100.00**
Elizabeth Taylor, Whitman #2057, 1957 ....**$150.00**
Elly May, Watkins-Strathmore #1819A, 1963 ....**$50.00**
Family of Dolls, Whitman #4574, 1960 ....**$40.00**
Fashion Reviews, Lowe #1246, 1949 ....**$45.00**
Flying Nun, Saalfield #1317, 1969......................**$75.00**
Gene Tierney, Whitman #992, 1947, from $125 to ...**$200.00**
Golden Girl, Merrill #1543, 1953, from $75 to **$100.00**
Goldilocks & the Three Bears, Saalfield #2245, 1939, from $100 to..**$200.00**
Grace Kelly, Whitman #2049, 1955 ....**$125.00**
Happiest Millionaire, Saalfield #4487, 1967, from $50 to...**$75.00**
Here Comes the Bride, Whitman #1189, 1952..............**$50.00**
High School Dolls, Merrill, #1551, 1948, from $75 to ..**$100.00**
I Love Lucy/Lucille Ball & Desi Arnez, Whitman #2101, 1953 ....**$100.00**

Jane Russell, Saalfield #4328, 1955, $95.00.
(Photo courtesy Mary Young)

Jill & Her Trunk Full of Clothes, Merrill #4828, 1943, from $35 to **$50.00**
Joanne Woodward, Saalfield #4436, 1958, from $75 to..**$125.00**
Judy Garland, Whitman #999, 1940...........................**$100.00**
Junior Miss Dolls, Platt & Munk, #229, 1942 ....**$45.00**
Let's Play w/the Baby, Merrill #1550, 1948, from $40 to..**$65.00**
Lindy-Lou 'n Cindy-Sue, Merrill #2564, 1954, from $65 to...**$90.00**
Little Friends From History, Rand McNally #186, 1936 .**$40.00**
Mary Hartline, Whitman #2104, 1952 ....**$75.00**
Mommy & Me, Whitman #977, 1954, from $30 to **$35.00**
Movie Starlets, Whitman #960, 1946...........................**$125.00**
Nurses, Whitman #1975, 1963.......................................**$40.00**
Partridge Family, Saalfield #5137, 1971 ....**$50.00**
Patty Duke, Whitman #4775, 1965, boxed...................**$50.00**
Penny's Party, Lowe #4207, 1952 ....**$25.00**
Pink Wedding, Merrill #1559, 1952, 8-page book, from $50 to...**$75.00**
Quiz Kids, Saalfield #2430, 1942, from $90 to **$175.00**
Raggedy Ann & Andy, Saalfield #2739, 1961, from $35 to..**$45.00**
Roy Rogers & Dale Evans, Whitman #1950, 1956, EX ...**$100.00**
Seven & Seventeen, Merrill #3441, 1945, from $100 to..**$140.00**
Shirley Temple Dolls & Dresses Her Movie Wardrobe, Saalfield #1773, 1938, from $200 to **$300.00**
Skediddle Kiddles, Whitman #4722, 1969, boxed **$35.00**

Slumber Party, Merrill #4854, 1943, from $65 to.........**$90.00**
Star Princess, Whitman #1839, 1979, from $10 to **$15.00**
Tammy & Her Family, Whitman #1997, 1964 ....**$60.00**
Tom the Aviator/Dick the Sailor/Harry the Soldier, Lowe #1074, 1941, ea from $50 to..................................**$75.00**
Tyrone Power & Linda Darnell, Merrill #3438, 1941, from $185 to..**$300.00**
Victory Paper Dolls, Saalfield #2445, 1943, from $85 to..**$125.00**
Waltons, Whitman #1995, 1974, from $50 to..............**$60.00**

Wishnik Cut-Outs, Whitman #1954, uncut, M, from $30.00 to $40.00.

Wonderful World of Brothers Grimm, Saalfield #1336, 1963, from $35 to..**$50.00**

Pencil Sharpeners

The whittling process of sharpening pencils with pocketknives was replaced by mechanical means in the 1880s. By the turn of the century, many ingenious desk-type sharpeners had been developed. Small pencil sharpeners designed for the purse or pocket were produced in the 1890s. The typical design consisted of a small steel tube containing a cutting blade which could be adjusted by screws. Mass-produced novelty pencil sharpeners became popular in the late 1920s. The most detailed figurals were made in Germany. These German sharpeners that originally sold for less than a dollar are now considered highly collectible!

Disney and other character pencil sharpeners have been produced in Catalin, plastic, ceramic, and rubber. Novelty battery-operated pencil sharpeners can also be found. For over fifty years pencil sharpeners have been used as advertising giveaways — from Baker's Chocolates and Coca-Cola's metal figurals to the plastic 'Marshmallow Man' distributed by McDonald's. As long as we have pencils, new pencil sharpeners will be produced, much to the delight of collectors.

Advisors: Phil Helley; Martha Hughes (See Directory, Pencil Sharpeners)

Bakelite, airplane, red, 2½" W, from $65 to **$75.00**
Bakelite, automobile shape, 2¼" L......................**$95.00**
Bakelite, Baby Hep, WDP, round.........................**$30.00**
Bakelite, Br'er Fox, round & fluted, 1⅜" **$50.00**
Bakelite, Cinderella, decal, round, EX **$85.00**
Bakelite, Cleo (fish) on yellow, WDP, 1¼x1¾", EX .**$110.00**
Bakelite, Donald Duck, decal, round, 1", EX **$55.00**
Bakelite, Goofy, round & fluted, 1½" **$55.00**
Bakelite, heart form, red, 1⅛x1⅛", EX+ **$70.00**
Bakelite, Huey, Dewey & Louie, decal on yellow, round, 1",
   EX **$90.00**
Bakelite, Joe Carioca, color decal, Plastic Novelties, 1940s, 1",
   EX+ **$55.00**
Bakelite, mantel clock, Germany, 2" **$65.00**
Bakelite, Pablo, round & fluted, 1" **$55.00**

**Bakelite, Panchito,
Disney, 1", $50.00.**

Bakelite, paneled cylinder, 2½" **$17.00**
Bakelite, Pete (dog from Little Rascals), octagonal, 1940s,
   1¼"...**$165.00**
Bakelite, pig, 1⅜" **$22.00**
Bakelite, Popeye, decal, round, EX..........................**$80.00**
Bakelite, shield w/flag, decal on butterscotch w/red swirls,
   round, 1"...**$85.00**
Bakelite, Snow White figural, WDE, 1¾"....................**$80.00**
Bakelite, Thumper, WDP, round, 1" **$55.00**
Bakelite, Walt Disney's train, figural, 1¾"................**$90.00**
Bakelite, 1" sharpener w/key chain w/Humble/Esso tag..**$30.00**
Bakelite, 1939 NY World's Fair **$80.00**
Bakelite, 3 Little Pigs, pig playing fiddle decal on green, WD,
   EX **$215.00**
Celluloid, Japan, pelican, 3"................................**$145.00**
Ceramic, Zorro figural, WDP, 6" **$75.00**
Metal, alarm clock, Japan......................................**$45.00**
Metal, banjo, w/glass back, Germany, 2¾" **$75.00**
Metal, British guard in guard house, Germany, 1½" ..**$80.00**
Metal, cash register, tin litho, Japan, EX+ **$90.00**
Metal, cat, Germany, 2x1¼", EX.............................**$130.00**
Metal, Charlie Chaplin, Germany, 2¼".....................**$150.00**
Metal, Felix the Cat, 1½" **$200.00**
Metal, Great Dane, Germany, 2"...............................**$90.00**
Metal, man, gold paint, Germany, 1950s, 1½" **$80.00**
Metal, piano player, Germany, 2"..............................**$90.00**
Metal, robot, jointed, crank on back works sharpener, Japan,
   6¼", EX **$48.00**
Metal, stop-&-go light, 2¼".....................................**$75.00**
Metal, zeppelin, gold paint, Germany, 3"................**$150.00**
Occupied Japan, Black Uncle Sam w/bow tie **$150.00**
Occupied Japan, bulldog head, 1½" **$95.00**

Occupied Japan, clown w/bow tie **$75.00**
Occupied Japan, Indian chief head...........................**$90.00**
Occupied Japan, smiling pig w/hat..........................**$80.00**
Plastic, Batman figure holding a red bat, 1973, 3", EX ..**$15.00**
Plastic, Bireley's soda bottle, 3".............................**$25.00**
Plastic, giraffe, press tail, head bobs, 4" **$18.00**
Plastic, Mummy (Universal Monsters), Universal Pictures,
   1960s, 3", EX **$40.00**
Plastic, Ronald McDonald, 2"..................................**$15.00**
Plastic, Snoopy Fire Truck, United Features, 1958......**$12.00**
Plastic, Sunbeam Bread, 1" **$15.00**

Pennsbury Pottery

From the 1950s throughout the 1960s, this pottery was sold in gift stores and souvenir shops along the Pennsylvania Turnpike. It was produced in Morrisville, Pennsylvania, by Henry and Lee Below. Much of the ware was hand painted in multicolor on caramel backgrounds, though some pieces were made in blue and white. Most of the time, themes centered around Amish people, barber shop singers, roosters, hex signs, and folksy mottos.

Much of the ware is marked, and if you're in the Pennsylvania/New Jersey area, you'll find a lot of it. It's fairly prevalent in the Midwest as well and can still sometimes be found at bargain prices.

Advisor: Shirley Graff (See Directory, Pennsbury)

Mug, Amish couple, 5", $30.00.

Ashtray, Amish, 5" dia **$25.00**
Ashtray, Pennsbury Inn, 8" **$45.00**
Bookends, Eagle, pr **$185.00**
Bottles, oil & vinegar; Black Rooster, pr...................**$150.00**
Bowl, Dutch Talk, 9" dia...**$90.00**
Bowl, pretzel; Amish, 12x8".....................................**$100.00**
Bowl, pretzel; Red Barn, 12x8" **$150.00**
Butter dish, Red Rooster, w/lid, 5x4" **$25.00**
Candle holders, Rooster, 4", pr.................................**$125.00**
Candy dish, Hex, heart shape, 6x6" **$50.00**
Coffee mug, Gay Ninety, 3¼".....................................**$35.00**
Compote, Red Rooster, footed, 5'............................**$40.00**

Cookie jar, Red Barn, w/lid $225.00
Egg cup, Red Rooster, 4"................................$20.00
Figurine, Blue Jay, #108, 10½" $650.00
Figurine, Cardinal, #120, 6½"................................$175.00
Figurine, Chickadee, #111, 3½"...............................$110.00
Figurine, Gold Finch, #102, pr...............................$150.00
Figurine, Magnolia Warbler, #112.............................$150.00
Figurine, Rooster & Hen, pr $450.00
Figurine, Scarlett Tanagers, #105, early model..........$160.00
Figurine, Wood Duck, #114, facing right, 10" $375.00
Figurine, Wren, #109, 3" $95.00
Mug, beer; Swallow the Insult, 5" $40.00
Mug, beverage; Folkart, 1-bird decor, 5".....................$35.00
Mug, coffee; Amish, 3¼" $30.00
Pitcher, Amish, 7¼" $100.00
Pitcher, Delft Toleware, 5" $55.00
Pitcher, Folkart, miniature, 2½" $30.00
Plaque, Eagle, #P214, 22".....................................$150.00
Plaque, Making Pie, 6" $60.00
Plaque, Washington Crossing the Delaware, 5" dia $25.00
Plate, Bible Reading, w/out primary colors, 9" dia.....$75.00
Plate, Black Rooster, 10"....................................$35.00
Plate, Blue Dowry, 10" $35.00
Plate, Christmas; Tree Tops, 1966...........................$45.00
Plate, Red Barn, 8"..$75.00
Plate, Red Rooster, 10" $35.00
Plate, warming; Picking Apples, electric, 6x6" $75.00
Relish tray, Red Rooster, 5 sections, 14½x11½"..........$85.00
Wall pocket, flower design w/red border, sq w/cut corners, 6½"...$75.00

Pepsi-Cola

People have been enjoying Pepsi-Cola since before the turn of the century. Various logos have been registered over the years; the familiar oval was first used in the early 1940s. At about the same time, the two 'dots' between the words Pepsi and Cola became one, though more recent items may carry the double-dot logo as well, especially when they're designed to be reminiscent of the old ones. The bottle cap logo came along in 1943 and with variations was used through the early 1960s.

Though there are expensive rarities, most items are still reasonable, since collectors are just now beginning to discover how fascinating this line of advertising memorabilia can be. There are three books in the series called *Pepsi-Cola Collectibles*, written by Bill Vehling and Michael Hunt, which we highly recommend. Another good reference is *Introduction to Pepsi Collecting* by Bob Stoddard. For more information we recommend *Antique and Collectible Advertising Memorabilia* by B.J. Summers (Collector Books).

Note: In the descriptions that follow, P-C was used as an abbreviation for Pepsi-Cola; the double-dot logo is represented by the equal sign.

Advisor: Craig Stifter (See Directory, Pepsi-Cola)

Newsletter: *Pepsi-Cola Collectors Club Express*
Bob Stoddard, Editor
P.O. Box 817
Claremont, CA 91711; Send SASE for information

Ashtray, glass, rectangular, bottle-cap logo in center w/Say Pepsi Please phrase, black border, 1960s, 4x4½", M, unused $75.00
Book cover, paper, Come Alive!, image of teen couple in gym, 1960s, 11x16", M..............................$5.00
Bookmark, cardboard feather shape w/bottle cap logo, red, white & blue, 1940s, 9x2", NM.........................$100.00
Bottle carrier, cardboard 6-pack, double-dot logo on white oval on blue & white striped ground, 1950s, EX+ $32.00
Bottle carrier, metal, holds 12 bottles, Pepsi-Cola Hits The Spot, 1950s, 5½x16" L, EX+ $300.00
Bottle carrier, plastic 6-pack, Pepsi-cap logo, 16-oz, 1960s-70s, EX+...$30.00
Bottle carrier, wooden 6-pack, A-frame type w/center divider, cut-out handle, stenciled logos, EX+ $140.00
Bottle display, cardboard card w/Pepsi=Cola Double Size 5¢ Ice Cold graphics, complete w/paper label bottle, NM $350.00
Change receiver, rubber, Say Pepsi Please in center w/geometric border, 1960s, 8x8", NM............................$25.00
Clock, Time for Pepsi=Cola in red w/lg block numbers in blue on white, shadow-box frame, electric, 14½x14½", VG+...$85.00
Coaster, stock paper, sq w/3-quarter bottle cap in center of daisy design, rounded corners, 1960s, 4x4", NM....$4.00
Doll, Santa, stuffed, 1970s, 33", NM $80.00
Door push bar, porcelain, yellow w/Have a Pepsi flanked w/modern Pepsi-Cola bottle-cap logos on white, 3x31½", EX+..$130.00

**Folding chair, 32",
EX, $150.00.** (Photo
courtesy Buffalo Bay)

Fountain pen, Bakelite case w/double-dot logo, red & blue on white, 1940s, NM...............................$80.00
Grocery cart bottle holder, metal, double-dot logo on panel attached to 2 spiraled wire holders, 1950s, 3x6", EX+.................$145.00
Headband, paper, 2 diecut feathers flank bottle-cap logo on blue & white striped background, 1950s, NM......$55.00

Paper cup, cone shape w/repeated bottle-cap design on white, 1950s, 10-oz, unused, M $22.00

Pin-back button, double-dot bottle-cap shape, 1940s, 1" dia, EX...$5.00

Pin-back button, Say Pepsi Please/Pepsi/bottle cap, 2½x2½", NM $25.00

Pocketknife, metal w/Pepsi=Cola 5¢ on white inlay, 1930s, 3", EX...$35.00

Santa, hollow papier-mache, 19", VG, $75.00.

Sign, cardboard, self-framed, plaid table w/bowls of soup, sandwiches & bottles, With Pepsi of Course!, 1950s, 21x19", NM...$230.00

Sign, cardboard slanted bottle cap w/Pepsi-Cola on white, 1950s, 13½", EX+ $60.00

Sign, cardboard stand-up, diecut dancing Santa in red long johns w/Pepsi bottle, Norman Rockwell art, 1950s, 20", EX+ $65.00

Sign, cardboard stand-up, diecut Santa holding up bottle & inset of bottle cap, 1956, 20", EX $60.00

Sign, celluloid oval, Refresh Without Filling, lady standing w/hands on hips & bottle cap, 1950s, 12x8", EX.$85.00

Sign, flicker disk, Take Home a Carton/Reach for a Pepsi w/3-quarter bottle cap, 10" dia, EX+..................$215.00

Sign, metal diecut bottle w/double-dot label, 1940s, 29x8", EX $550.00

Sign, paper, Pepsi=Cola/Bigger & Better at right of center 5¢ symbol w/paper-label bottle at left, 1930s, 6x20", NM $200.00

Sign, tin, Drink Pepsi=Cola/It Quenches Thirst in yellow & red on blue, yellow & blue contour background, 20x28", EX $150.00

Sign, tin bottle cap w/Pepsi-Cola in center, 19¼" dia, NM..$375.00

Sign, tin bottle shape w/Sparkling Pepsi=Cola 12 Fl Oz label, 44½x12¼", NM+ $1,350.00

Sign, tin disk w/cardboard backing & celluloid cover, bottle cap w/More Bounce to the Ounce tag, 1950s, 9" dia, EX $200.00

Sign, tin flange disk w/Buy Pepsi=Cola Here, red, white & blue, 16x17", NM $1,300.00

Sign, tin over cardboard w/celluloid, Pepsi=Cola 5¢ 12 Ounces/A Nickel Drink Worth a Dime, bottle in center, 12x5", NM+...$950.00

Sun visor, Say Pepsi Please phrase flanked by slanted bottle caps, 1950s, NM...$40.00

Thermometer, tin, Bigger/Better lettered above & below lg bottle at right of bulb on blue, 1930s, 15½", EX..$525.00

Thermometer, tin, The Light Refreshment, embossed bottle cap logo above, yellow, dated 1956, 27x7½", NM+......$185.00

Tray, Enjoy Pepsi=Cola/Hits the Spot, w/musical notes, 1940s, 10½x13¾", NM............................$100.00

Tray, modern Pepsi logo appearing to be submerged in ice, deep sides, rounded corners, 1970, 13¼" sq, EX+..$45.00

Tray, Pepsi-Cola lettering surrounding slanted bottle cap, deep sides, rounded corners, 1950s, 13½" sq, NM $100.00

Perfume Bottles

Here's an area of bottle collecting that has come into its own. Commercial bottles, as you can see from our listings, are very popular. Their values are based on several factors. For instance, when you assess a bottle, you'll need to note: is it sealed or full, does it have its original label, and is the original package or box present.

Figural bottles are interesting as well, especially the ceramic ones with tiny regal crowns as their stoppers.

Advisor: Monsen & Baer (See Directory, Perfume Bottles)

Club: International Perfume Bottle Association (IPBA)
Coleen Abbott, Membership Secretary
396 Croton Rd.
Wayne, PA 19087; Membership: $45 USA or $50 Canada

Bienaime, Caravane, clear w/faceted stopper & gold label, sealed, 4", in gold Oriental-decorated box $300.00

Bourjois, Evening in Paris, cobalt glass w/frosted stopper, silver label, empty, 4", MIB $225.00

Bourjois, Evening in Paris, cobalt glass w/silver label, 2", M in blue Bakelite clam-shell holder w/silver label $175.00

Bourjois, Kobako, clear w/molded foliage, metallic label, 3½", M in red & black inro box w/chrysanthemum decor...$355.00

Bourjois, On the Wind, orange cap, gold label, 1¾"..$145.00

Carbet, Gardenia, clear, rectangular, 5", MIB.............$65.00

Caron, Fleurs de Rocaille, clear urn shape, stopper w/bouquet under glass, empty, 3½", M in photo medallion box...$175.00

Caron, Le Baboc Blond, gold flower label, sealed, 3½", MIB $150.00

Caron, Royal Baine de Champagne, clear bottle w/gold foil cap & label, 6⅜", MIB.............................$75.00

Christian Dior, Diorissimo, gold metal encased flacon, 2¼", MIB $66.00

Christian Dior, Miss Dior, clear urn w/embossed rings, 4½", MIB $175.00

Ciro, Oh La La, clear waisted form w/black & red leather skirt, 2", MIB (box w/black garter & red bow)..$450.00

Corday, Toujours Moi, clear flattened round shape w/embossed decor, brown wash, gold label, empty, 3", MIB **$155.00**

Corday, Zigane, clear violin w/gold, 3", MIB **$220.00**

Coty, Elan, clear & frosted w/etched name, clear stopper, MIB **$175.00**

Coty, L'Aimant, amber glass w/gold label, originally designed by Lalique for Lilas Pourpre, MIB **$145.00**

Coty, L'Origan, cylindrical, on Lucite base w/silver guitar ..**$99.00**

Coty, Meteor, clear mini flask w/gold cap, black label, 1⅞", M in clear plastic case **$100.00**

Coty, Muse, clear shouldered form w/inner stopper & frosted glass overcap, gold label, 3¼", M in floral box....**$275.00**

Coty, Paris, flacon w/label on side, M in tasseled box **$35.00**

D'Orsay, Le Dandy, Intoxication & Voulez-Vouze, all clear w/gold caps, 2½", M, set of 3 in original white box **$25.00**

Devon Violets, black glass poodle on white plastic base, gold label on chest, 3", M in violet-decorated box.......**$110.00**

Dorothy Gray, Night Drums, clear tube w/rhinestone & metal cap, 2½", w/companion lipstick in satin pouch...**$50.00**

Dorothy Gray, Savoir Faire, black & gold masks on clear, 4" **$425.00**

DuBarry, Heart's Delight, clear w/white cap, empty, 2", M in white plastic case w/music along sides & glass Pierrot on top...**$300.00**

Elizabeth Arden, My Love, clear heart, brass cap, 2¾", MIB **$135.00**

Fragonard, Belle de Nuite, clear w/gold cap, M label, sealed, 2", MIB...**$150.00**

Grenoville, Oeillet Fanè, replica miniature with gold cap, flower bud stopper, 2", in its red and white box and outer box, $75.00.
(Photo courtesy Monsen and Baer Auctions)

Guerlain, Le Mouchoir de Monsieur, clear w/embossed swirls, label on bottom, empty, 4½" **$110.00**

Guerlain, Parure, clear w/green plastic lid, full, 1947, 1⅛" **$225.00**

Guerlain, Shalimar, marked Baccarat, sealed, in 7½x5" box, M **$330.00**

Helen of Troy, Pour la Brunette, black w/silver label, 3¼", M in half-box...**$225.00**

Helena Rubenstein, Apple Blossom Time Jeweled Perfumette, clear w/rhinestone-covered cap, 2¼", M in celluloid box **$55.00**

Hermes, Eau d'Hermes, clear w/sq sides, front labels, mushroom stopper, empty, 5½", M in leatherette box ..**$110.00**

Houbigant, Chantilly, gold metal ball shape, empty, 1¼", MIB **$55.00**

Isabey, Jasmin, clear flattened bulb w/pearly stopper, empty, 2⅜", in worn silk-lined box **$225.00**

Jean Desprez, Bal a Versailles, clear round flat shape, lyre stopper, 4¼", M in silk-lined box **$65.00**

Jean Patou, Caline, clear w/gold cap & gold enameling, 2¼", M in white box **$45.00**

Jergens, Ben-Hur, clear & frosted oval w/black & gold metallic label, 2½", M in stage-like presentation box.**$110.00**

Jergens, Jockey Club, frosted glass rectangle w/molded leaves, gold label, Ionic capital stopper, 4", M in holly box...**$125.00**

Lander, Jasmine, amber frosted lady in full gown, 4⅛" ..**$385.00**

Langlois, Narcisse, clear w/molded concentric rectangles, front label, cube stopper, empty, M in satin-lined box.....**$175.00**

Lanvin, Arpege, black glass ball w/raspberry gilt stopper, sealed, 2¼", M in original ecru & black box......**$200.00**

Lentheric, Tweed, gold metal compact for solid perfume, white cameo on green, 1¾", MIB.........................**$65.00**

Lilly Dache, Drifting, clear w/inner stopper, wood overcap, green labels, red velvet ribbon, sealed, 6½", M...**$50.00**

Lucien Lelong, Taglio, clear w/embossed medallion, empty, 1½", M in Lucite box..**$135.00**

Marcel, Rochas Femme, blue opaque w/long dauber, gold metal overcap, 2½", covered in black lace held by gold spring...**$125.00**

Mary Dunhill, Escape, clear cruet shape w/ball stopper, enameling & gold label, 4¼", MIB......................**$135.00**

Mary Dunhill, Flowers of Devonshire, clear w/8 ribs molded w/round balls, silver label, empty, 2½", M in silver box..**$150.00**

Matchabelli, Wind Song, gold/green enamel crown, 1½", MIB **$125.00**

Max Factor, Mystic, ca 1960s, 5½", $25.00.

Moiret, Pois de Senteur, eau de toilette clear bottle w/royal blue stopper, silver front label, empty, 5¾" **$100.00**

Molinard, Orval, clear round bottle w/scalloped edges & molded tiers, 2", M in box w/scenes of southern France **$75.00**

Molinard, Xmas Bells, black glass bell w/stopper, gold enameling, 2½", M.....................**$165.00**

Molinari, Coax Me, clear w/frosted stopper, front label, empty, ca 1940s, 2¾", M in drop-front box..........**$50.00**

Myrugia, Liria, clear cylinder w/gold front label, flattened stopper, 4⅜", M in tasseled box **$525.00**

Myrugia, Nueva Maja, clear w/rectangular panels & triangular facets, gold label, full, 3½", MIB w/senorita on front **$135.00**

Prince Alxis N Gagarin, blue glass w/gold enamel crown form w/coat-of-arms stopper, empty, 3¾".........**$150.00**

Prince George of Russia, Pierre Tappe, black wine-bottle form w/front label w/gold crown, black stopper, 3¼" **$100.00**

Raphael Paris, Replique, clear w/white label, stopper impressed w/letter R, sealed, 3⅜", M in white box w/red flower seal **$50.00**

Raphael Paris, Replique, original seal & label, 5x2½"...**$65.00**

Renaud, Orchidee, violet opaque w/black top, gold label, 2"....................**$245.00**

Renaud, Sweet Pea Ambre, gold opaque w/gold labels, empty, 4", MIB.....................**$320.00**

Revillon, Carnet de Bal, clear w/flat stopper, inverted brandy-snifter shape, empty, 2", M in green & white box..**$55.00**

Richard Hudnut, Le Debut Noir, black glass octagonal shape w/gilt stopper, empty, label missing, 2⅝" **$285.00**

Rieger, Crabapple, clear flask w/gold label, frosted stopper, empty, 3½", M in birds in crab apple tree decorated box.....................**$185.00**

Roger & Gallet, a L'Iris Blanc, clear decanter shape w/gold & blue label, sealed, 4", M in blue & gold box **$465.00**

Roger & Gallet, Night of Delight, clear flattened teardrop w/gold label, frosted stopper, empty, 3½", M in floral box.....................**$175.00**

Roger & Gallet, Violette de Parme, clear decanter shape w/pink label, empty, 2½", M in floral book-form box.....................**$75.00**

Rolex, Perpetually Yours, gold-metal pocketwatch form w/glass cover, 3", M in white satin-lined box **$600.00**

Schiaparelli, S, frosted & clear w/cursive S front, pink metallic ball cap, sealed, 3", M in pink & white box .**$150.00**

Schiaparelli, Shocking, clear dressmaker's dummy w/frosted stopper, measure label, glass flowers at neck, 3", MIB....**$385.00**

Schiaparelli, Zut, lady's torso in wave base, clear w/gold & green, 4¾".....................**$300.00**

Simonato, Incanto, enameled crown, gold label, 1950s, MIB **$230.00**

Solon Palmer, Brocade, clear triangular shape w/faceted spire stopper, front label, empty, 4", M in pink flocked box.....................**$55.00**

Solon Palmer, Glenecho, clear w/radiating circles & gold label, frosted flower stopper, 4¼" **$55.00**

Suzy, Scarlate de Suzy, clear w/red enameling, unopened, ⅛-oz, 2", M in round celluloid box **$55.00**

Vantine's, Sandalwood, clear w/frosted flower stopper, gold label, empty, 2", M in red lacquer box marked Made in Japan....................**$75.00**

Verlayne, Attente, clear fan shape w/Baccarat emblem, 3¼".....................**$90.00**

Weil, Cobra, clear ovoid w/flower-form stopper, blue velvet plinth, sealed, 4½", MIB....................**$135.00**

Yardley, frosted glass snowman w/brass hat-shaped cap & enameled details, 3½" **$275.00**

Pez Candy Dispensers

Though Pez candy has been around since the late 1920s, the dispensers that we all remember as children weren't introduced until the 1950s. Each had the head of a certain character — a Mexican, a doctor, Santa Claus, an animal, or perhaps a comic book hero. It's hard to determine the age of some of these, but if yours have tabs or 'feet' on the bottom so they can stand up, they were made in the last ten years. Though early on, collectors focused on this feature to evaluate their finds, now it's simply the character's head that's important to them. Some have variations in color and design, both of which can greatly affect value.

Condition is important; watch out for broken or missing parts. If a Pez is not in mint condition, most are worthless. Original packaging can add to the value, particularly if it is one that came out on a blister card. If the card has special graphics or information, this is especially true. Early figures were sometimes sold in boxes, but these are hard to find. Nowadays you'll see them offered 'mint in package,' sometimes at premium prices. But most intense Pez collectors say that those cellophane bags add very little if any to the value.

For more information, refer to *A Pictorial Guide to Plastic Candy Dispensers Featuring Pez* by David Welch; *Schroeder's Collectible Toys, Antique to Modern* (Collector Books); and *Collecting Toys #6* by Richard O'Brien.

Advisor: Richard Belyski (See Directory, Pez)

Newsletter: *Pez Collector's News*
Richard and Marianne Belyski, Editors
P.O. Box 124
Sea Cliff, NY 11579; 516-676-1183; www.peznews.com
Subscription: $19 for 6 issues

Angel, no feet **$60.00**
Baloo, w/feet **$20.00**
Barney Bear, no feet.................**$40.00**
Barney Bear, w/feet.................**$30.00**
Batman, no feet **$15.00**
Batman, no feet, w/cape.................**$100.00**
Batman, w/feet, blue or black, ea from $3 to **$5.00**
Captain America, no feet **$100.00**
Charlie Brown, w/feet, from $1 to **$3.00**

Charlie Brown, w/feet & tongue $20.00
Daffy Duck, no feet...$15.00
Dalmatian Pup, w/feet $50.00
Donald Duck, no feet..$15.00
Dumbo, w/feet, blue head...$25.00
Elephant, no feet, orange & blue, flat hat $90.00
Foghorn Leghorn, w/feet $95.00
Gorilla, no feet, black head $100.00
Gyro Gearloose, w/feet $6.00
Hulk, no feet, dark green..$60.00
Hulk, no feet, light green, remake $3.00
Indian Maiden, no feet..$175.00
Jiminy Cricket, no feet..$200.00
Knight, no feet..$300.00
Lamb, no feet $15.00
Lamb, w/feet, from $1 to $3.00
Lion w/Crown, no feet...$100.00
Mexican, no feet $250.00
Monkey Sailor, no feet, w/white cap $50.00
Mowgli, w/feet...$15.00
Nurse, no feet, brown hair $175.00
Octopus, no feet, black..$85.00
Papa Smurf, w/feet, red $6.00
Peter Pez (A), no feet..$65.00
Peter Pez (B), w/feet, from $1 to $3.00
Pink Panther, w/feet...$5.00
Policeman, no feet...$55.00
Pumpkin (A), no feet, from $10 to............................$15.00
Raven, no feet, yellow beak $60.00
Ringmaster, no feet..$300.00

Road Runner, no feet, $20.00;
Uncle Sam, no feet, $250.00.

Rudolph, no feet..$60.00
Scrooge McDuck (A), no feet $35.00
Scrooge McDuck (B), w/feet $6.00
Smurf, w/feet...$5.00
Smurfette, w/ft $5.00
Snow White, no feet...$175.00
Snowman (A), no feet...$10.00
Space Trooper Robot, no feet, full body $325.00
Sylvester (A), w/feet, cream or white whiskers, ea.......$5.00

Teenage Mutant Ninja Turtles, w/feet, 8 variations, ea from
 $1 to...$3.00
Tinkerbell, no feet...$275.00
Tyke, w/feet...$15.00
Uncle Sam, no feet..$250.00
Valentine Heart, from $1 to...$3.00
Winnie the Pooh, w/feet...$75.00
Witch, 3-pc, no feet..$10.00
Woodstock, w/feet, from $1 to $3.00
Woodstock, w/feet, painted feathers........................$15.00
Yappy Dog, no feet, orange or green, ea..................$65.00
Yosemite Sam, w/feet, from $1 to $3.00

Pfaltzgraff Pottery

Pfaltzgraff has operated in Pennsylvania since the early 1800s making redware at first, then stoneware crocks and jugs, yellow ware and spongeware in the 1920s, artware and kitchenware in the 1930s, and stoneware kitchen items through the hard years of the 1940s. In 1950 they developed their first line of dinnerware, called Gourmet Royale (known in later years as simply Gourmet). It was a high-gloss line of solid color accented at the rims with a band of frothy white, similar to lines made later by McCoy, Hull, Harker, and many other companies. Although it also came in pink, it was the dark brown that became so popular. Today these brown stoneware lines have captured the interest of young collectors as well as the more seasoned, and they all contain more than enough unusual items to make the hunt a bit of a challenge and loads of fun.

The success of Gourmet was just the inspiration that was needed to initiate the production of the many dinnerware lines that have become the backbone of the Pfaltzgraff company.

A giftware line called Muggsy was designed in the late 1940s. It consisted of items such as comic character mugs, ashtrays, bottle stoppers, children's dishes, a pretzel jar, a cookie jar, etc. All of the characters were given names. It was very successful and continued in production until 1960. The older versions have protruding features, while the later ones were simply painted on.

Village, an almond-glazed line with a folksy, brown stenciled tulip decoration, is now discontinued. It's a varied line with many wonderful, useful pieces, and besides the dinnerware itself, the company catalogs carried illustrations of matching glassware, metal items, copper accessories, and linens. Of course, all Pfaltzgraff is of the highest quality, and all these factors add up to a new area of collecting in the making. Several dinnerware lines are featured in our listings. To calculate the values of Yorktowne, Heritage, and Folk Art items not listed below, use Village prices.

For further information, we recommend *Pfaltzgraff, America's Potter,* by David A. Walsh and Polly Stetler, published in conjunction with the Historical Society of York County, York, Pennsylvania.

Christmas Heritage, bowl, soup/cereal; #009, 5½", from $2

to $3.50

Christmas Heritage, cheese tray, #533, 10½x7½", from $5 to $7.00

Christmas Heritage, pedestal mug, #290, 10-oz $4.50

Christmas Heritage, plate, dinner; #004, 10", from $4 to .$5.50

Gourmet Royale, ashtray, #AT32, skillet shape, 9", from $10 to $15.00

Gourmet Royale, ashtray, #321, 7¾", from $12 to $15.00

Gourmet Royale, au gratin, 11" long, $9.00.

Gourmet Royale, ashtray, 12", from $15 to $18.00

Gourmet Royale, baker, #321, oval, 7½", from $18 to ..$20.00

Gourmet Royale, baker, #323, 9½", from $20 to $24.00

Gourmet Royale, bean pot, #11-1, 1-qt, from $20 to ..$22.00

Gourmet Royale, bean pot, #11-2, 2-qt, from $28 to ..$30.00

Gourmet Royale, bean pot, #11-3, 3-qt $35.00

Gourmet Royale, bean pot, #11-4, 4-qt $45.00

Gourmet Royale, bean pot, #30, w/lip, lg, from $45 to ..$50.00

Gourmet Royale, bean pot warming stand $12.00

Gourmet Royale, bowl, #241, oval, 7x10", from $15 to ..$18.00

Gourmet Royale, bowl, cereal; #934SR, 5½" $6.00

Gourmet Royale, bowl, mixing; 6", from $8 to $14.00

Gourmet Royale, bowl, mixing; 8", from $12 to $14.00

Gourmet Royale, bowl, salad; tapered sides, 10", from $25 to $28.00

Gourmet Royale, bowl, soup; 2¼x7¼", from $6 to $8.00

Gourmet Royale, bowl, spaghetti; #219, shallow, 14", from $15 to $20.00

Gourmet Royale, bowl, vegetable; #341, divided, from $10 to $24.00

Gourmet Royale, butter dish, #394, ¼-lb stick type ...$12.00

Gourmet Royale, butter warmer, #301, stick handle, double spout, 9-oz, w/stand, from $18 to $22.00

Gourmet Royale, candle holders, tall, w/finger ring, 6", pr, from $25 to $35.00

Gourmet Royale, canister set, 4-pc, from $60 to $75.00

Gourmet Royale, casserole, hen on nest, 2-qt, from $75 to $95.00

Gourmet Royale, casserole, individual, #399, stick handle, 12-oz, from $10 to $12.00

Gourmet Royale, casserole, stick handle, 1-qt, from $15 to $18.00

Gourmet Royale, casserole, stick handle, 3-qt, from $25 to $30.00

Gourmet Royale, casserole, stick handle, 4-qt, from $32 to $40.00

Gourmet Royale, casserole-warming stand $10.00

Gourmet Royale, chafing dish, w/handles, lid & stand, 8x9", from $30 to $35.00

Gourmet Royale, cheese shaker, bulbous, 5¾", from $18 to $22.00

Gourmet Royale, chip 'n dip, #311, molded in 1 pc, 12", from $22 to $30.00

Gourmet Royale, chip 'n dip, 2-pc set, w/stand, #306, from $30 to $35.00

Gourmet Royale, coffee server, on metal & wood stand, 10¾", from $100 to $125.00

Gourmet Royale, creamer, #382, from $5 to $7.00

Gourmet Royale, cruet, coffeepot shape, fill through spout, 4", from $20 to $22.00

Gourmet Royale, cup, from $2 to $3.00

Gourmet Royale, cup & saucer, demitasse $18.00

Gourmet Royale, egg/relish tray, 15" L, from $22 to ..$28.00

Gourmet Royale, gravy boat, #426, 2-spout, lg, +underplate, from $14 to $16.00

Gourmet Royale, gravy boat, w/stick handle, 2-spout, from $15 to $20.00

Gourmet Royale, jug, #384, 32-oz, from $32 to $36.00

Gourmet Royale, jug, #386, ice lip, from $40 to $48.00

Gourmet Royale, ladle, sm, from $12 to $15.00

Gourmet Royale, ladle, 3½" dia bowl, w/11" handle, from $18 to $20.00

Gourmet Royale, lazy Susan, #220, 5-part, molded in 1 pc, 11", from $22 to $28.00

Gourmet Royale, lazy Susan, #308, 3 sections w/center bowl, 14", from $32 to $36.00

Gourmet Royale, mug, #391, 12-oz, from $6 to $8.00

Gourmet Royale, mug, #392, 16-oz, from $12 to $14.00

Gourmet Royale, pie plate, #7016, 9½", from $14 to .$18.00

Gourmet Royale, plate, dinner; #88R, from $3.50 to.....$4.50

Gourmet Royale, plate, egg; holds 12 halves, 7¾x12½", from $20 to $22.00

Gourmet Royale, plate, grill; #87, 3-section, 11", from $18 to $20.00

Gourmet Royale, plate, salad; 6¾", from $3 to $4.00

Gourmet Royale, plate, steak; 12", from $15 to $20.00

Gourmet Royale, platter, #320, 14", from $20 to $25.00

Gourmet Royale, platter, #337, 16", from $25 to $30.00

Gourmet Royale, rarebit, #330, w/lug handles, oval, 11", from $15 to $18.00

Gourmet Royale, relish dish, #265, 5x10", from $15 to ..$17.00

Gourmet Royale, roaster, #325, oval, 14", from $30 to ..$35.00

Gourmet Royale, roaster, #326, oval, 16", from $50 to ..$60.00

Gourmet Royale, salt & pepper shakers, #317/#318, 4½", pr, from $12 to $14.00

Gourmet Royale, salt & pepper shakers, bell shape, pr, from $25 to $35.00

Gourmet Royale, scoop, any size, from $15 to $18.00

Gourmet Royale, serving tray, round, 4-section, upright handle in center $22.00

Gourmet Royale, shirred egg dish, #360, 6", from $10 to ..$12.00

Gourmet Royale, souffle dish, #393, 5-qt, +underplate, from $65 to $70.00

Gourmet Royale, teapot, #381, 6-cup, from $18 to.....**$22.00**

Gourmet Royale, tray, tidbit; 2-tier, from $15 to **$18.00**

Gourmet Royale, tray, 3-part, 15½" L, minimum value..**$35.00**

Heritage, butter dish, #002-028, from $6 to **$8.00**

Heritage, cake/serving plate, #002-529, 11¼" dia, from $9 to **$12.00**

Heritage, cup & saucer, #002-002, 9-oz...........................**$3.00**

Heritage, soup tureen, #002-160, 3½-qt, from $25 to.**$35.00**

Muggsy, ashtray **$125.00**

Muggsy, bottle stopper, head, ball shape **$85.00**

Muggsy, canape holder, Carrie, lift-off head pierced for tooth-picks, from $125 to...**$150.00**

Muggsy, cigarette server..**$125.00**

Muggsy, clothes sprinkler bottle, Myrtle, Black, from $275 to..**$375.00**

Muggsy, clothes sprinkler bottle, Myrtle, white, from $250 to..**$350.00**

Muggsy, cookie jar, character face, minimum value.**$250.00**

Muggsy, mug, action figure (golfer, fisherman, etc), any from $65 to...**$85.00**

Muggsy, mug, Black action figure.............................**$125.00**

Muggsy, mug, character face, ea from $35 to **$38.00**

Muggsy, shot mug, character face, ea from $40 to.....**$50.00**

Muggsy, tumbler **$60.00**

Muggsy, utility jar, Handy Harry, hat w/short bill as flat lid, from $175 to...**$200.00**

Planter, donkey, brown drip, common, 10", from $15 to...**$20.00**

Planter, elephant, brown drip, scarce, from $90 to ..**$100.00**

Village, baker, #236, rectangular, tab handles, 2-qt, from $12 to...**$15.00**

Village, baker, #237, sq, tab handles, 9", from $10 to **$14.00**

Village, baker, #24, oval, 10¼", from $8 to **$10.00**

Village, baker, #240, oval, 7¾", from $6 to..................**$8.00**

Village, bean pot, 2½-qt...**$35.00**

Village, beverage server, #490, from $24 to.................**$28.00**

Village, bowl, butter; w/spout & handle, 8", from $35 to...**$42.00**

Village, bowl, fruit; #008, 5"...**$4.00**

Village, bowl, mixing; #453, 1-qt, 2-qt & 3-qt, 3-pc set, from $50 to...**$60.00**

Village, bowl, rim soup; #012, 8½" **$6.00**

Village, bowl, serving; #010, 7", from $8 to **$12.00**

Village, bowl, soup/cereal; #009, 6" **$4.50**

Village, bowl, vegetable; #011, 8¾", from $12 to **$15.00**

Village, bread tray, 12", from $15 to **$18.00**

Village, butter dish, #028..**$8.00**

Village, canisters, #520, 4-pc set, from $50 to **$60.00**

Village, casserole, w/lid, #315, 2-qt, from $18 to........**$25.00**

Village, coffee mug, #89F, 10-oz, from $6 to................**$8.00**

Village, coffeepot, lighthouse shape, 48-oz, from $30 to ..**$35.00**

Village, cookie jar, #540, 3-qt, from $18 to..................**$25.00**

Village, creamer & sugar bowl, #020, from $9 to **$12.00**

Village, cup & saucer, #001 & #002..............................**$3.50**

Village, flowerpot, 4½", from $15 to **$20.00**

Village, gravy boat, #443, w/saucer, 16-oz, from $12 to ..**$15.00**

Village, ice bucket, canister w/lid **$175.00**

Village, measuring cups, ceramic, 4 on hanging rack...**$45.00**

Village, measuring cups, copper, 4 on wooden rack w/pierced copper insert, EX...................................**$40.00**

Village, onion soup crock, #295, stick handle, sm, from $6 to...**$8.00**

Village, pedestal mug, #90F, 10-oz **$4.50**

Village, pitcher, #416, 2-qt, from $20 to......................**$25.00**

Village, plate, dinner; #004, 10¼", from $3 to..............**$4.50**

Village, platter, #016, 14", from $18 to **$22.00**

Village, quiche, 9"..**$20.00**

Village, soup tureen, #160, w/lid & ladle, 3½-qt, from $40 to...**$45.00**

Village, table light, #620, clear glass chimney on candle holder base, from $12 to **$14.00**

Pie Birds

Pie birds are hollow, china or ceramic kitchen utensils. They date to the 1800s in England, where they were known as pie vents or pie funnels. They are designed to support the upper crust and keep it flaky. They also serve as a steam vent to prevent spill over.

Most have arches on the base and they have one, and *only* one, vent hole on or near the top. There are many new pie birds on both the US and British markets. These are hand painted rather than airbrushed like the older ones.

The Pearl China Co. of East Liverpool, Ohio, first gave pie birds their 'wings.' Prior to the introduction in the late 1920s of an S-neck rooster shape, pie vents were non-figural. They resembled inverted funnels. Funnels which contain certain advertising are the most sought after.

The first bird-shaped pie vent produced in England was designed in 1933 by Clarice Cliff, a blackbird with an orange beak on a white base. The front of the base is imprinted with registry numbers. The bird later carried the name Newport Pottery; more recently it has been marked Midwinter Pottery.

Advisor: Linda Fields (See Directory, Pie Birds)

Newsletter: Pie Birds Unlimited
Patricia Donaldson, Editor
PO Box 192
Acworth, GA 30101-0192

Aluminum pie funnels, England, ea **$25.00**

Benny the baker, all white, Far East Imports, 4¾" ...**$150.00**

Bird, cobalt, stoneware, New Hampshire pottery, new, 4¼" **$20.00**

Black chef, yellow, red & white attire, brown spoon, Taiwan, 4½"...**$10.00**

Blackbird, thin neck, marked Scotland, from $60 to ..**$75.00**

Bluebird, black speckles, heavy pottery, US, 1950s....**$50.00**

Canary, yellow w/pink lips...**$40.00**

Chef, marked the Servex Chef, from $125 to...........**$140.00**

Cutie Pie, Josef Original (or A Lorrie Design), hen wearing bonnet, from $75 to..**$100.00**

Duck (or Swan) head, brown w/yellow beak, from $150 to $175.00

Dutch girl, multipurpose kitchen tool, from $150 to ..$195.00

Eagle, marked Sunglow, golden color, from $75 to....$85.00

Elephant, marked Nutbrown, white, tan or gray, respectively, from $75 to $175.00

Fred the Flour Grater, original has dots for eyes, from $65 to..$75.00

Funnel, marked, Gourmet Pie Cup, Reg No 369793...$75.00

Funnel, marked Grimwade Perfection $110.00

Funnel, pagoda, marked Nutbrown $95.00

Funnel, plain aluminum, from $10 to $15.00

Funnel, plain white w/rosebud on top, from $150 to .$175.00

Funnel, white, unmarked, England $15.00

Funnel, yellow ware, marked Mason Cash (paper label), new, from $15 to $18.00

Half Bird, black, w/scalloped or triangle bottom, from $75 to..$100.00

Long-neck Pie Duckling, American Pottery Co, blue, yellow or pink, 1940s, from $50 to $75.00

Pelican on stump, yellow bill & feet, England, from $50 to $70.00

Pie Boy, green sombreros on outfit, from $350 to ...$400.00

Royal Commemorative pie funnel, England $50.00

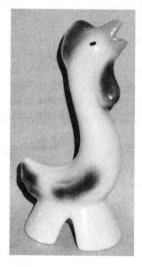

S-neck rooster, Pearl China Co., burgundy and blue on white, 1920 – 50, from $150.00 to $175.00. (Photo courtesy Linda Fields)

Welsh Lady, marked Cymru, from $95 to $125.00

Witch, holding pie, w/painted bird flying out, marked SB...$40.00

Pierce, Howard

Howard Pierce studied at the Chicago Art Institute, California's Pomona Colledge, and the University of Illinois. He married Ellen Van Voorhis of National City, California, who was also to become his business partner. Howard worked alongside William Manker for a short time, and today it is sometimes difficult tell one artist's work from the other's without first looking at the marks. This is especially true with some of their vases, nut cups, trays, and cups and saucers.

Howard was creative with his designs and selective with his materials. Since Howard worked at Douglas in Long Beach, California, during World War II, it is thought that pewter may have been one of the first mediums he worked with. The pewter lapel pins he created early on are considered very desirable by today's collectors and usually sell in the $200.00 to $300.00 range. He dabbled in polyurethane for only a short time as he found he was allergic to it. Today these polyurethane pieces — made nearly exclusively for his immediate family — are scarce and costly. They are extremly lightweight, usually figures of birds on bases. They were hand painted, and many of them have a powdery feel. Howard made a few pieces from aluminum and bronze. Bisque, cement, and porcelain (some with Mount St. Helen's ash) were also used for a limited number of items. (Be cautious not to confuse Howard's 'textured' items with the Mount St. Helen's ash pieces.) Howard's creativity extended itself to include paper as a workable medium as well, as he often made their own Christmas cards. His love for wildlife was constant throughout his career, and he found porcelain to be the best material to use for wildlife models.

Howard's earliest mark was probably 'Howard Pierce' in block letters. This was used on metalware (especially the lapel pins), but also can be found on a few very small ceramic animals. After the Pierces moved to Claremont, California, they used this mark: 'Claremont Calif. Howard Pierce,' usually with a stock number. A rubber stamp 'Howard Pierce Porcelains' was used later. Eventually 'Porcelains' was omitted. Not all pieces are marked, especially when part of a two- or three-piece set. As a rule, only the largest item of the set is marked.

In 1992 due to Howard's poor health, he and Ellen destroyed all the molds they had ever created. Later, with his health somewhat improved, he was able to work a few hours a week, creating miniatures of some of his original models and designing new ones as well. These miniatures are marked simply 'Pierce.' Howard Pierce passed away in February 1994.

Bowl, gondola shape, brown tones, black ink stamp, 5x9½", from $35 to...$50.00

Bowl, metallic blue w/black highlights, fluted, black ink stamp, 4½x7", from $100 to..............................$120.00

Creamer & sugar bowl, white gloss flowing over maroon, marked Howard Pierce Porcelain, #1XS, 2", from $85 to..$100.00

Figurine, bear cub, glossy brownish-green, ink stamp, 4¾x5¼", from $35 to...$50.00

Figurine, bird, gold overglaze w/occasional red showing through, unmarked, 5¾x4¾", from $35 to $50.00

Figurine, bison, white glossy, black ink stamp, 2½x3½", from $50 to..$75.00

Figurine, dachshund, brown, porcelain, black ink stamp, 3¼x10", from $85 to...$100.00

Figurine, dinosaur, brown ink stamp, black ink hand dated 1991, 5½x4½", from $80 to................................$100.00

Figurine, Ferdinand the Bull, brown & white, black ink stamp, 3¼x5½", from $75 to................................$85.00

Figurine, giraffe, black ink stamp, 10x4", from $75 to..**$85.00**

Figurine, girl & dog on base, high gloss, black ink stamp, 4½x3¼", from $65 to.................................**$70.00**

Figurine, horse, brown mottle, porcelain, black ink stamp, 8x10", from $250 to **$275.00**

Figurine, jackrabbit, brown & white, porcelain, impressed mark/#102P, 10½x4¾", from $75 to....................**$100.00**

Figurine, male ballet figure, black & white combination, black ink stamp, 7½", from $75 to.......................**$85.00**

Figurine, mountain sheep ram on rocky base, brown & white, black ink stamp, 7¼x3", from $80 to **$100.00**

Figurine, pelican, brown to white, black ink stamp, 7½x4½", from $75 to..**$85.00**

Figurine, pigeon, glossy white w/dark details, black ink stamp, 5¾x5¾", from $65 to...............................**$75.00**

Figurine, raccoon, brown tones, brown ink stamp, hand signed, dated 1991 in ink, 3¼x8½", from $75 to ..**$100.00**

Figurine, robin, orange breast, black ink stamp, 4½x3½", from $60 to...**$75.00**

Figurine, St Francis of Assisi, white matt, 5½", minimum value **$300.00**

Figurine, stylized cat w/slant eyes, black glossy, porcelain, ink stamp, 8x3", from $60 to **$75.00**

Figurine, toad, warty skin, brown tones, black ink stamp, hand signed in black ink, 3x3¾", from $50 to.....**$65.00**

**Figurine, unicorn, 5¾" x 5½",
signed, from $100.00 to $125.00.**
(Photo courtesy Darlene Hurst Dommel)

Figurines, covey of 3 quail, speckled brown, 2½", 4" & 6", set of 3 from $50 to..**$65.00**

Figurines, ducklings, brown w/speckles, unmarked, 2½x3", 2¾x3½", pr, from $25 to **$35.00**

Magnet, rabbit figural, unmarked, 3¼", from $50 to...**$75.00**

Planter, mint green matt w/leaf decor, impressed mark, 4¼x6½", from $50 to...**$75.00**

Planter, road runner on lg rock, black ink stamp, 7x13½", from $100 to..**$125.00**

Teapot, shepherd w/sheep in blue reserve on pale blue, flattened sides, impressed mark, 6", from $150 to ..**$200.00**

Vase, bisque fawn & tree in open center of chartreuse rectangle, impressed mark, 11½x6", from $85 to....**$100.00**

Vase, deer & tree beside vase, glossy white on black base, impressed mark, 7½x5", from $85 to.................**$100.00**

Vase, owls in relief, burnt sienna paint wash, impressed mark, 5½", from $50 to...**$75.00**

Vase, white fish scene in open center of green high-gloss body, impressed mark, 8x7", from $100 to **$125.00**

Pin-Back Buttons

Literally hundreds of thousands of pin-back buttons are available; pick a category and have fun! Most fall into one of three fields — advertising, political, and personality related, but within these three broad areas are many more specialized groups. Just make sure you buy only those that are undamaged, are still bright and unfaded, and have well-centered designs and properly aligned printing. The older buttons (those from before the 1920s) may be made of celluloid with the paper backing printed with the name of a company or a product.

See also Political.

Advisor: Michael McQuillen (See Directory, Pin-Back Buttons)

Alabama College pennant, American Tobacco Co, celluloid, 1¼" w/1¾" straight pin, NM **$22.00**

Bond Bread, For Stronger Bones..., First Flight Paris to New York, celluloid, #4 of set, Bastian Bros, NM.........**$38.00**

Chevrolet Watch the Leader, drum major on red, ¾", EX+ **$20.00**

Colt Frontier Six Shooter, sterling silver revolver form, marked Robbins Co Attleboro Mass, 1⅛" L..........**$75.00**

Corbin Brake, celluloid, Whitehead & Hoag paper label, sm stain, ⅞"...**$25.00**

Darth Vader, black & white portrait, Factors Etc Inc, 1977, 3", M **$10.00**

Disneyland, bust image of Winnie the Pooh w/bee on hand, 1960s, round, EX..**$15.00**

Disneyland, bicentennial w/America on Parade image of characters carrying the American flag, Disneyland on ribbon, EX...**$20.00**

Dizzy Dean Winners, embossed bronze-colored tin, ⅞", NM...**$75.00**

Du Pont Smokeless Powder, grouse scene, multicolored, ca 1910, 1¼", M..**$200.00**

Elsie the Borden Cow, Elsie portrait, red, white & black, tin litho, Borden Co, 1", VG...................................**$18.00**

Florida High School Music Festival, Tampa, April 27-28, 1951, celluloid, Russell Mfg Co, Wakefield Mass............**$18.00**

Ford logo in center, 1932 A Ford Year at top & bottom, V-8 & 4 overlapping, red, white & blue, ⅞", EX **$12.00**

Golden Guernsey Company, American Cattle Club, celluloid, paper insert, EX **$40.00**

Health for All, Santa pointing finger, National Tuberculosis Association, ⅞", M..**$25.00**

Hello Give Me Pearline, Pearline Soap premium, celluloid, Baltimore Badge & Novelty Co, paper insert, NM .**$22.00**

Howdy Doody Time, 1988, 2¼", from $5.00 to $7.00. (Photo courtesy Jack Koch)

I'm a Beech-nut, Wearer Qualified To Win, red & white tin litho, NM.................$15.00

I'm a Streak Freak, black & white on orange, 1973 SWIB Industries mark, 2¼", M.................$5.00

I'm Naughty But It's Nice, lady showing petticoats, High Admiral Cigarettes, celluloid, Whitehead & Hoag, EX.................$48.00

I'm The Guy That Done It All, Bud Fisher character, Tokio & Hassan Cigarettes, ¾", NM.................$25.00

I'm the Guy That Put the Bloom in Bloomers, Rube Goldberg character, Tokio & Hassan Cigarettes, ¾", NM.....$25.00

It's Spring, Go Get a Pontiac, birds on branch on white, ⅞", EX.................$20.00

John Lennon, In Memory of a Rock Superstar, Oct 9, 1940 - Dec 8, 1980, red, white & black, 3", NM.............$15.00

John Wayne Memorial, 3½".................$7.00

Join the American Party, Amoco, red, white & black, 1", VG.................$20.00

Just Kids Safety Club, Fatso portrait on white, Montreal Herald, 1930s, VG+.................$65.00

Just Kids Safety Club, Marjory, The Globe, 1930s, G..$30.00

Keystone Automobile Club, Keystone Safety, green & white, some crackling of ink, ⅞", VG.................$12.00

Let's Pull Together, push down on lever and Uncle Sam hangs Hitler, 1½", EX, $100.00.

Lindbergh portrait, Captain Charles 'Plucky' Lindbergh, New York 7:51 AM May 20th Paris 5:21 PM May 21st, 1¼", VG+.................$40.00

Little Miss Junket, lady in cooking attire, black & white, 1", NM.................$25.00

Lone Ranger, black & white portrait, tin litho, 1¾", NM.................$15.00

Marie Walcamp in the Red Ace, red, white & black, ⅞", EX.................$25.00

Member Magnolia 200 Club, tin litho, red, white & blue w/black, 1¾", NM.................$15.00

Merry Christmas - HUMMEL's, Santa portrait on white, 1¼" dia, w/ribbon & jingle bell, M.................$40.00

Mickey Mouse Club, Mickey's face on bull's-eye, 1950s, lg, MIP.................$75.00

Mobil Shield & Pegasus, Buant Birmingham, 1950s-early 1960s, 1¼", EX.................$10.00

Morticia (Addams Family), 1960s, 1", VG+.................$18.00

New Chevrolet Six, Queen of the Shows, lady's portrait, ⅞", EX.................$20.00

New Kids on the Block, group shot, tin litho, 1989, 6", NM.................$3.00

Nobody Loves a Fat Man, Rube Goldberg character, Tokio & Hassan Cigarettes, ¾", NM.................$25.00

Paramount Pictures, mountain scene, ¾", EX.................$15.00

Put-In-Bay, celluloid, Bastian Bros Co Rochester NY, 1½", EX.................$27.50

Radio Orphan Annie's Secret Society, embossed bronze-colored metal, 1", EX/NM.................$75.00

Renfrew of the Mounted, portrait reserve on red, 1¼", EX.................$25.00

Rock & Roll Hall of Fame Inductee Souvenir, 1986 (includes Chuck Berry, Elvis, Little Richard, others), 1¾x1⅞", M.................$10.00

Rod Cameron cowboy portrait on yellow, 1¼", EX....$15.00

Roy Rogers, portrait w/name below on white, tin litho, 1¾" dia, NM.................$15.00

Safety First/Stop/Drive Carefully, Spanky McFarland image encircled by lettering, Hal Roach Studios, 1930s, 1¼", EX..$65.00

Shirley Temple, The World's Darling Genuine Shirley Temple, An Ideal Doll, black & white, 1¼", NM.$45.00

Smile, I'm a Salesman of Florida Happiness, orange w/smiling face & hat, M.................$18.00

Spencer Shoe Baseball School, embossed bronze-colored tin, ¾", NM.................$50.00

Spend St Patrick's Day w/a Total Boar, The Original, Blue Boar Brand (beer), 2⅛", M.................$5.00

Sunset Carson, tin litho, 1¼", EX.................$20.00

Teddy Snow Crop Clean the Plate Club, polar bear head image in center, blue on white, 1950s, 3", NM....$30.00

Vote for Red Lion - The Motorists Choice, Gilmore Oil, tin litho, Vitachrome, Inc..., 1930s, VG.................$10.00

Watch Hudson which Means Essex Too, watchful eyes, red, white & black, 1⅜", VG.................$25.00

Welcome Home Our Heroes, WWII servicemen (3), red, white & blue, VG.................$15.00

Wilhelmina Queen of Holland, American Pepsin Gum, Whitehead & Hoag, ca 1901, NM.................$15.00

1933 Will Reward a Smile, smiling boy, red, white & black, Whitehead & Hoag, paper insert, NM.................$24.00

50 & candlestick phone, blue, white & black, celluloid, Whitehead & Hoag, NM.................$24.00

Kellogg's Pep Pins

Chances are if you're over fifty, you remember them — one in each box of PEP (Kellogg's wheat-flake cereal that was among the first to be vitamin fortified). There were eighty-six in all, each carrying the full-color image of a character from one of the popular cartoon strips of the day — Maggie and Jiggs, the Winkles, Dagwood and Blondie, Superman, Dick Tracy, and many others. Very few of these cartoons are still in print.

The pins were issued in five sets, the first in 1945, three in 1946, and the last in 1947. They were made in Connecticut by the Crown Bottle Cap Company, and they're marked PEP on the back. You could wear them on your cap, shirt, coat, or the official PEP pin beanie, an orange and white cloth cap made for just that purpose. The Superman pin — he was the only D.C. Comics Inc. character in the group — was included in each set.

Values are given for pins in near mint condition; prices should be sharply reduced when foxing or fading is present. Any unlisted pins are worth from $10.00 to $15.00.

Advisor: Doug Dezso (See Directory, Candy Containers)

Bo Plenty	$30.00
Corky, NM	$16.00
Dagwood, NM	$30.00
Dick Tracy, NM	$30.00
Early Bird, NM	$6.00
Fat Stuff, NM	$15.00
Felix the Cat, NM	$65.00
Flash Gordon, NM	$30.00
Flat Top, NM	$25.00
Goofy, NM	$10.00
Gravel Girtie, NM	$15.00
Harold Teen, NM	$15.00
Inspector, NM	$12.50
Jiggs, NM	$20.00
Judy, NM	$10.00
Kayo, NM	$20.00
Little King, NM	$15.00
Little Moose, NM	$15.00
Maggie, NM	$25.00
Mama De Stross, NM	$30.00
Mama Katzenjammer, NM	$25.00
Mamie, NM	$15.00
Moon Mullins, NM	$10.00
Navy Patrol, NM	$6.00
Olive Oyle, NM	$30.00
Orphan Annie, NM	$25.00
Pat Patton, NM	$10.00
Perry Winkle, NM	$15.00
Phantom, NM	$60.00
Pop Jenks, NM	$15.00
Popeye, NM	$30.00
Rip Winkle, NM	$20.00
Skeezix, NM	$15.00
Superman, NM	$35.00
Toots, NM	$15.00
Uncle Walt, NM	$15.00
Uncle Willie, NM	$12.50

Winkles Twins, NM	$90.00
Winnie Winkle, NM	$15.00

Pinup Art

Some of the more well-known artists in this field are Vargas, Petty, DeVorss, Elvgren, Moran, Ballantyne, Armstrong, and Phillips, and some enthusiasts pick a favorite and concentrate their collections on only his work. From the mid-thirties until well into the fifties, pinup art was extremely popular. As the adage goes, 'Sex sells.' And well it did. You'll find calendars, playing cards, magazines, advertising, and merchandise of all types that depict these unrealistically perfect ladies. Though not all items will be signed, most of these artists have a distinctive, easily identifiable style that you'll soon be able to recognize.

Unless noted otherwise, values listed below are for items in at least near-mint condition.

Advisor: Denis Jackson (See Directory, Pinup Art)

Newsletter: *The Illustrator Collector's News*
Denis Jackson, Editor
P.O. Box 1958
Sequim, WA 98382; 360-452-3810
ww.olypen.com/ticn
e-mail: ticn@olypen.com

Ad, diecut for auto lubricants, bikini-clad girl in sexy pose w/company mascot, signed Aslan, tin litho, 21x7", VG $110.00
Ad, diecut for Veedel, blond skater in white swimsuit w/red trim, tin litho, 14x5½", VG+ $325.00
Ad poster for motor oil, bikini-clad girl on water skis & girl in tight sweater & shorts on snow skis, 1950, 34x58", NM $125.00
Ad poster for Old Gold cigarettes, Armstrong, Suit Me to a Tee, 1930s, 11x10", EX, from $125 to $150.00
Ad sign for bath soap, nude girl peering from behind shower curtain holding bar of soap, tin over cardboard, 26x9", NM $100.00
Ad sign for motor oil, take-off of famous Marilyn Monroe pose standing over street air vent, tin, 19x7½", NM $175.00
Ashtray, glass w/painted image of Playmate holding key, 1960s, M $28.00
Ashtrays, metal, sq w/round center images of pinup girls, Texaco Service advertising on rims, set of 3, 4¼", EX $180.00
Blotter, Bolles, A Toasted Sandwitch (sic), 1930s, NM .. $25.00
Blotter, Elvgren, Booked for Tonight, 1951, NM $17.00
Blotter, Moran, Acute Shortage, 1941, EX+ $17.00
Blotter, Moran, Called in the Draft, 1944, EX+ $17.00
Book, Fun Hunting With MacPherson, 30 full-page pinups, 12x9", EX $150.00
Calendar, Elvgren, 1963, A Neat Package, 33x16", NM .. $90.00
Calendar, Elvgren, 1963, Out of This World, 33x16", NM ... $90.00

Calendar, Elvgren, 1978, stock car girl w/trophy, Napa Auto Parts, EX **$45.00**

Calendar, Moore/Esquire, 1950, spiral-bound, 12x8½", w/envelope, NM **$55.00**

Calendar, Moran, 1950, bathing beauty on diving board, auto supply advertising, 34x16", EX+ **$135.00**

Calendar, Mozert, 1968, Alluring, 33x16", NM **$65.00**

Calendar, Patton, 1932, Captivating, 11x5", EX............**$30.00**

Calendar, Playboy, 1962, Tina Louise, spiral-bound, 12½x8", EX+ **$60.00**

Calendar, Runci, 1957, Hats Off, 18x12", EX **$35.00**

Calendar, Sunblom, 1949, Sitting Pretty, 33x16", EX...**$65.00**

Calendar, Withers, 1943, Delightful Darlene, EX.........**$75.00**

Calendar, 1-month; Elvgren, 1971, February, Annette, 11x8", NM **$25.00**

Calendar, 1-month; Moran, Marilyn Monore in low-cut blouse & black skirt, EX **$50.00**

Calender, 1-month; Elvgren, 1964, April, Bird's Eye View, EX **$10.00**

Calendar, 1958, illustrated by Zoe Mozert, unused, $100.00. (Photo courtesy Buffalo Bay)

Cartoon, Petty, This Is His Secretary Speaking, Esquire September 1935, M **$18.00**

Date book, Bill Randall's...'57, 12 months w/cover page, ea month illustrated, spiral-bound, 16x9½", NM **$60.00**

Fan, Armstrong, brunette seated in red swimsuit, 1930s, 8x9½", EX...**$75.00**

Gatefold, Ludlow, Esquire's Fair Lady, Denise Darcel in low-cut gown & white gloves, 1955, 18x13", NM.......**$18.00**

Gatefold, Petty, So Take My Advise..., blond in navy chief's jacket, Esquire, EX+, from $75 to **$80.00**

Gatefold, Vargas, Torch Singer, blond in long black gown clapping hands, Esquire, February, 1945, EX.......**$40.00**

Gatefold, Vargas, V Mail for a Soldier, blond in blue & white ruffles, Esquire, 1943, NM **$45.00**

Greeting card, MacPherson, Nursery Rhymes for Grown-Ups, Shaw-Barton Publishing, 1950s, EX **$8.00**

Hot water bottle, painted plastic figure of Jayne Mansfield, Poynter Prod, 1957, 21", MIP..............................**$75.00**

Key chain telescope viewer, hold to light to view girl, extends to 1¼", EX+...**$15.00**

Label, Sweet Patootie, 1940s, 3x12", EX.......................**$3.00**

Letter opener, Elvgren, plastic nude in 8½" slotted folder w/painted dress, 'Designed by...,' 1950s, NM.......**$35.00**

Magazine, Escapade, October 1956, MacPherson article & pinups, EX..**$25.00**

Magazine cover, American, March 1936, Armstrong, brunette in veiled hat, EX...**$50.00**

Memo pad, Elvgren, Perfect Form, 1945-55, NM **$15.00**

Memo pad, Withers, I Like It This Way, 6x3", EX......**$12.00**

Mutoscope card, Armstrong, Heads Up, NM **$15.00**

Mutoscope card, Moran, On Top of the World, EX+ ..**$12.00**

Paper doll, Cherie, pull tab to remove clothes, 1940s, 3x5", NM..**$5.00**

Playing cards, Ballantine, double deck, Quick on the Draw (2 images), 1950s, MIB.......................................**$75.00**

Print, Armstrong, All My Love, 10½x8", EX...............**$25.00**

Print, Armstrong, Dreamy Eyes, 11½x10", NM...........**$40.00**

Print, D'Ancona, bare-shouldered brunette w/rose in hair & fan at her breast, 16x12", NM **$20.00**

Print, DeVorss, Hostess, 20x11, NM **$35.00**

Print, DeVorss, smiling brunette seated in blue gown w/sheer ruffled sleeves & legs exposed, 24x18", NM+ **$130.00**

Print, Fabian, Sheer Beauty, blond in pink on pink blanket, 1940s, 10x8", EX...**$20.00**

Print, Moran, Reflections, nude w/red hat on stool in front of mirror, 15x19", NM...**$95.00**

Punchboard, Elvgren, Fins 'n Deuces, 12x9½" w/5½x3½" label, EX **$28.00**

Punchboard, Sunshine Special, heavy cardboard, 1950s, 12" sq, EX **$30.00**

Puzzle, Elvgren, Help Wanted, Saalfield #1871, 1940s-50s, incomplete, EXIB **$50.00**

Sheet music, Armstrong, I Am Forever Thinking of You, M **$25.00**

Shot glass, Playboy Playmate w/key painted on glass, 1960s, 3", M **$45.00**

Stationery kit (for military serviceman), Thinking of You, folds out to reveal 23" pinup girl, Bell Engraving, 1940s, M **$35.00**

Steering knob, nude w/dog in her lap contained w/in clear plastic disk, 1950s, 1¾" dia, EX...........................**$25.00**

Trading cards, Elvgren, Brown & Bigelow, box of 90, 1993, 3½x2½", MIB **$20.00**

Playing Cards

Here is another collectible that is inexpensive, easy to display (especially single cards), and very diversified. Among the endless variations are backs that are printed with reproductions of famous paintings and pinup art, carry advertising of all types, and picture tourist attractions and world's fair scenes. Early decks are scarce, but those from the '40s on are usually more attractive anyway, so pick an area that interests you most and have fun! Though they're usually not dated, you may find some clues that will help you to determine an approximate date. Telephone numbers, zip codes, advertising slogans, and patriotic messages are always helpful.

See also Pinup Art.

Club/Newsletter: American Antique Deck Collectors; 52 Plus Joker Club
Clear the Decks, quarterly publication
Larry Herold, Auctioneer
300 E. 34th St., Apt. 6E
New York, NY 10016; e-mail: herojr@banet.net

ACE Transportation, transport modes shown on backs, Brown & Bigelow, ca 1950, bridge size, MIB (sealed) **$40.00**

Acme Fast Freight, Dependable Daily Service backs, double deck, MIB w/canasta rules booklet **$12.00**

Adventures of Sherlock Holmes, clues on cards, 52+2 Jokers+extra card, NMIB **$15.00**

Alaskan Totem Pole, Russell Artcraft, USPC, 1930s, MIB (sealed) **$20.00**

Alberly Coffee/Albers Super Markets, narrow, special aces, 1940s, 52+Joker+score card, G+ (G box) **$12.00**

Alka Seltzer, for 1980 Olympics, Sammy Davis & Speedy on red/blue backs, double deck, M (sealed in original package) **$100.00**

Amazing Spider Man, Marvel Comics Group, 1979, MIB (sealed) **$10.00**

American Indian Souvenir, Lazarus & Melzer, blanket back, photo on ea card, 52+Joker+title card, VGIB **$110.00**

American President Lines, eagle backs (1 blue/1 red), double deck, M in sealed wrapper **$20.00**

Baltimore & Ohio RR, 1953, 52 no joker, VG (no box) ..**$25.00**

Bar-Keeper's Friend, wide ad deck for cleanser, special aces, 52+special Joker, VG (no box) **$45.00**

Bicycle #808, club red backs, 1940, 52 no Joker, EX- (G box) **$22.00**

Bonanza TV show, original cast, 1970s, M (in sealed plastic box) **$15.00**

Canadian National Souvenir, narrow scenic, 1935, 52+Joker+score card, NMIB **$22.00**

Cir-Q-Lar Playing Cards, John Waddington, gold edge, 1930s, 52+Joker, EX+ (VG box) **$12.00**

Country Club of Ashland, lamppost backs (1 red/1 blue), double deck, MIB (sealed) **$10.00**

Cuba Souvenir, USPC, ca 1930, 52+Joker, EXIB **$50.00**

Delands Automatic (magic), SS Adams, 1940 stamp, 52+Joker, NMIB **$28.00**

Denver & Rio Grande, Main Line Through the Rockies, red backs, ca 1960, MIB (sealed) **$30.00**

Distant Early Warning, McLuhan, 1969, non-standard cartoon courts, MIB **$110.00**

Eagle Five Suit Bridge, 5th suit is eagle, USPC, 1938, 65+Joker+extra card, NMIB **$10.00**

East African, Fournier, Masai warrior painting on back, sepia photos on all cards, 1950s, 52+3 Jokers, NMIB **$28.00**

Edward K Cadogan Inc, NY, View of Boston Harbor backs, 1940s, 52+Joker+score card, VG (homemade box) ..**$10.00**

Elsie, Borden, courts, Aces & Jokers are comic cows, 1993, 52+2 Jokers, NMIB **$17.50**

Ford, Arrco, car or car facts on ea card, 1968, NMIB **$15.00**

Frisco Lines, double deck, 1958, ea 52+Joker, VGIB ..**$30.00**

Good Luck, nude color photo back, Hong Kong, 1940s, 52+2 Jokers, NMIB **$32.00**

Greyhound, Service to All 48 States, narrow, 1950s, MIB (sealed) **$35.00**

Humble Oil Co, Brown & Bigelow, 1960s, MIB (sealed)..**$10.00**

Illinois Central, Chicago skyline back w/white border, USPC, 1953, 52+2 Jokers, VGIB **$10.00**

Japan Airlines, kimono designs on backs, 1976, 52+JAL Jokers+score card, NMIB **$10.00**

Kansas City Southern, blue backs, 1953, MIB (sealed)..**$65.00**

Kem Streamline, torch backs (1 red/1 blue), double deck, 104+2 Jokers+2 cards relating to NY World's Fair, 1939, MIB **$40.00**

Kennedy Kards, Humor House, blue backs, 1953, M in sealed wrapper **$28.00**

KLM Royal Dutch Airlines, double deck, 1950s, ea 52+2 Jokers, NMIB **$40.00**

McConway & Torley Co, rail-coupler backs, Pittsburgh, 1910s, gold edge, 52+score card (no Joker), NMIB **$35.00**

Mexicana Airlines, Las Alas de Oro, 50th Anniversary, La Cubana, 1971, 52+2 Jokers, NMIB **$15.00**

Monticello Home of Thomas Jefferson, Atlantic Playing Cards, NY, double deck, 1935, NMIB **$10.00**

Moore-McCormack Lines, Arrco, cruise ships backs, yellow & blue borders, double deck, ea 52+2 Jokers, VG (worn box) **$10.00**

North Dakota land of Opportunity, narrow, double deck (2 different backs), ea 52+2 Jokers, ea VG+ (VG box), set **$10.00**

On the Spot, C. James Plumbing, Saturday Evening Post, double deck, EX, from $20.00 to $25.00.

Pan American World Airways, scenic photos from around the world on ea card, 1960s, 52+2 Jokers, EX (partial box) **$17.50**

Penang Souvenir, Malaysia's Pearl of Orient, Yong Guan Heng & Co, 1980s, 52+3 Jokers, EXIB **$12.00**

Premier Ranger Motor Oil, Brown & Bigelow for Premier Oil, motor oil can Joker, narrow, 1950s, 52+Joker+score card, EXIB **$28.00**

Quantas, Max Altitude, robot dog in spaceship on back, 1998, 52+2 Jokers, EXIB **$14.00**

Rookwood, Congress #606W, Indian head back framed in gold & gray, 52+Joker+extra card, EX- (G box)...**$35.00**

Samuel Hart & Co, Indian in headdress back, gold edge, 1930s, 52 no joker, VG+ (no box).........................**$10.00**

Scientific American, Rufus Porter Enterprises for US magazine, black & white scenes of Little Old NY, 1980s, MIB..**$22.00**

Standard TV, Hindustan Bombay, 1972, 52+2 Jokers+calendar card, EXIB **$17.50**

Tenth Olympiad, Wenger, film stars as courts, scenic aces, Olympic Games back, 52+Joe E Brown Joker, VG (VG box) **$95.00**

Texas Centennial, 6 flags as Aces & Joker, 1936, 52+Joker, EXIB...**$22.50**

TWA Collectors Series, Lockheed 749 - 1950 back, D&C TWA 125, 1970s, MIB (sealed) **$10.00**

Volvo Construction Equipment, picture of construction equipment on ea card, MIB (sealed).....................**$15.00**

W 5 (Double-U-Five) Scotch Whiskey, 52+nice advertising Joker, EXIB **$32.50**

Wayne Dog Food, white hunting dog back, Wayne dog food is ace high on Aces, 1960s-70s, 52+2 different Jokers, EXIB...**$10.00**

Welcome Aboard Air Force Two, double deck, 104 total, NMIB...**$55.00**

Western Stars, postcard size, Hollywood names on all cards, John Wayne is Joker, ca 1960, NM (no box)........**$40.00**

Yellowstone Park, for Haynes Inc by USPC, narrow, Old Faithful geyser backs, oval photo on ea card, 1930, 52+Joker, EXIB **$20.00**

Political Memorabilia

Political collecting is one of today's fastest-growing hobbies. Between campaign buttons, glassware, paper, and other items, collectors are scrambling to acquire these little pieces of history. Before the turn of the century and the advent of the modern political button, candidates produced ribbons, ferrotypes, stickpins, banners, and many household items to promote their cause. In 1896 the first celluloid (or cello) buttons were used. Cello refers to a process where a paper disc carrying a design is crimped under a piece of celluloid (now acetate) and fastened to a metal button back. In the 1920s the use of lithographed (or litho) buttons was introduced.

Campaigns of the 1930s through the 1990s have used both types of buttons. In today's media-hyped world, it is amazing that in addition to TV and radio commercials, candidates still use some of their funding to produce buttons. Bumper stickers, flyers, and novelty items also still abound. Reproductions are sometimes encountered by collectors. Practice and experience are the best tools in order to be aware.

One important factor to remember when pricing buttons is that condition is everything. Buttons with any cracks, stains, or other damage will only sell for a fraction of our suggested values. Listed below are some of the items one is likely to find when scrutinizing today's sales.

For more information about this hobby, we recommend you read Michael McQuillen's monthly column 'Political Parade' in *Antique Week* newspaper.

Advisor: Michael McQuillen (See Directory, Political)

Club: A.P.I.C. (American Political Items Collectors) of Indiana
Michael McQuillen
P.O. Box 50022
Indianapolis, IN 46250-0022
e-mail: mcquillen@politicalparade.com or website: www.politicalparade.com; National organization serving needs of political enthusiasts; send SASE for more information

Badge, Dwight D Eisenhower, Inauguration January 20, 1953, red, white & blue, w/ribbon & portrait medal below..........**$40.00**

Beer can, Gold Water, air-filled, steel, flat top, The Right Drink for the Conservative Taste, 12-oz size, M...**$15.00**

Book, Joint Appearances of Senator John F Kennedy & Vice President Richard M Nixon Presidential Campaign of 1960, NM **$25.00**

Book, The Emergence of John F Kennedy, Portrait, An Intimate Family Chronicle; Jacques Lowe, 224 pages, 1961, 8x11", EX **$20.00**

Bottle opener, Jimmy Carter's Happy Mouth, molded plastic vinyl head on wooden handle, Thomas Premiums, 1976, NMIB...**$22.00**

Bracelet, Eisenhower in gold-tone letters & elephant charm, 1950s, 7½", EX **$15.00**

Bumper sticker, Clinton - Gore, red, white & blue, M....**$2.00**

Bumper sticker, Jimmy Carter President, lettering at right angle, green & white, M..**$3.00**

Bumper sticker, President Nixon, red, white & blue, M ...**$4.00**

Bumper sticker, Release White House Watergate Witnesses, green & white, M **$4.00**

Bumper sticker, Take Your Country Back, Ross Perot '92, red, white & blue, M **$2.50**

Card game, Watergate Scandle, 1973, NMIB...............**$22.00**

Comb, Comb Nixon Out of Your Hair, white lettering on black plastic, ca 1969, 5x1", NM.........................**$15.00**

Cuff links, Presidental Seal w/Jimmy Carter's signature engraved on back, M **$135.00**

Inaugural ticket, Jimmy Carter, 1977, unused, M **$29.00**

License plate, Don't Blame Me I Voted (in black) Wallace (in red) on white, EX **$20.00**

License plate, Give Ike a Republican Congress, 1954, NM **$65.00**

License plate attachment, Roosevelt & Wallace, red, yellow & black, Donaldson Art Sign Co, ca 1941, VG.........**$80.00**

Lighter, Eisenhower Special, map w/Denver-to-Detroit campaign noted, June 15, 1952, Zippo, all original, EX............**$45.00**

Match cover, President Harry S Truman & Vice President Albert W Barkley Inaugural Dinner January 19, 1949, EX..**$15.00**

Paperback book, Do It!, Jerry Rubin, Simon & Schuster, 5th printing, ca 1970, EX **$14.00**

Pass, President's Platform, Eisenhower/Nixon, 1/20/53, 2½x4½", VG+ **$20.00**

Pennant, Chester A Arthur, green felt, slight discoloration, 7x3¼" **$15.00**

Photo, Nelson Rockefeller as Vice President, bold signature, 8x10", NM **$95.00**

Photo, Robert Kennedy, black & white glossy w/autopen signature, campaign literature on back, 8½x5½" **$8.50**

Pin-back button, Carter & Holtzman for America & New York Vote Democratic, green, white & black, 1¾", M **$6.50**

Pin-back button, Eisenhower - Nixon jugate portraits w/eagle over heads, celluloid, 2", EX **$40.00**

Pin-back button, John F Kennedy, The Man for the 60s, flasher, Vari-vue by Pictorial Productions, 2¾", VG.....**$20.00**

Pin-back button, Mamie Start Packing, The Kennedy's Are Coming, red, white & black tin litho, 4", M **$15.00**

Pin-back button, Re-Elect Reagan for President 1994, black & white portrait on red, white & blue, 1½", M..........**$5.00**

Pin-back button, Re-Elect Ron & George 1984 (Reagan & Bush), red, white & blue, 1¾", EX........................**$10.00**

Pin-back button, Richard M Nixon, I'm for Nixon, flasher, Vari-vue by Pictorial Productions Inc, 2¾", VG....**$15.00**

Pin-back button, Rockefeller for President, red, white & blue, 1⅛", M **$5.00**

Pin-back button, Ronald Reagan, Inauguration issue, 3½" **$6.00**

Pin-back button, Vote for Freeman - McCarthy, Vote DFL '58, flasher, Pictorial Productions, 2½", NM **$80.00**

Pin-back button, Walter F Mondale portrait, I Did It for Walter, flasher, Pictorial Productions Inc, 2½", M **$20.00**

Pin-back button, Women for Gore 2000, lady showing arm muscles, multicolor, 2¼", M **$3.00**

Poster, America Reagan Country, in cowboy hat, full color, matted & framed, 11x8½" **$30.00**

Poster, Carter - Mondale jugate, portraits on green & white, 17x11½", M..**$17.50**

Poster, George Wallace for President, comic portrait dressed in rebel uniform, Auto Initial Co, 24x18", NM......**$18.00**

Poster, Jimmy Carter for President, Vote Democratic, portrait on green & white, 17x11½", M............................**$17.50**

Poster, LBJ for the USA, portrait & US map, red, blue & black on white vinyl, 22x18", M **$10.00**

Poster, Lyndon Johnson US Senator, Roosevelt, Unity, Defense, cardboard, red, white & blue, 14x11", EX **$350.00**

Poster, Robert Kennedy portrait, Seek a Newer World, black & white, 25x19", M..**$25.00**

Poster, This Household Supports Clinton Gore 96, photograph of Clinton & Gore profiles, multicolor, 11¼x9¼", M..**$10.00**

Poster, This is a Hoover House, Service...Integrity, Women's Committee for Hoover, portrait center, EX **$70.00**

Puzzle, Forward America, FD Roosevelt, WWII era, 300+ pcs, EX in box **$55.00**

Puzzle, jigsaw; Nixon - Agnew, double-faced, Puzzle Factory, 1970, 500 pcs, 21¾x14¾", MIB (sealed)..............**$15.00**

Puzzle, political campaign buttons in 1¼" dia, Eaton Jigsaw, Treasure Collection, c 1980, 500+ pcs, MIB, sealed.**$17.50**

Textile, Alfred E Smith, portrait, ca 1928, 14x19" in antique gold 15½x10" frame, EX **$100.00**

Tie clasp, John F Kennedy, PT-109, boat shaped, marked Jolle, 1¾" **$35.00**

Porcelier China

The Porcelier Manufacturing Company was founded in East Liverpool, Ohio, in 1926. They moved to Greensburg, Pennsylvania, in 1930, where they continued to operate until closing in 1954. They're best known for their extensive line of vitrified china kitchenware, but it should also be noted that they made innumerable lighting fixtures.

The company used many different methods of marking their ware. Each mark included the name Porcelier, usually written in script. The mark can be an ink stamp in black, blue, brown, or green; engraved into the metal bottom plate (as on electrical pieces); on a paper label (as found on lighting fixtures); incised block letters; or raised block letters. With the exception of sugar bowls and creamers, most pieces are marked.

Our advisor for this category, Susan Grindberg, has written the *Collector's Guide to Porcelier China, Identification and Values* (Collector Books).

Advisor: Susan Grindberg (See Directory, Porcelier)

Bean pot, Basketweave Cameo, individual **$10.00**

Boiler, Beehive Floral Spray, 4-cup **$35.00**

Bowl, cereal; no decoration, commissioned for US Department of Defense **$6.00**

Bowl, spaghetti; floral decal **$85.00**

Canister, Barock-Colonial, ivory, red, or blue, ea **$40.00**

Canister, Country Life, ea **$35.00**

Casserole, no decoration, w/lid, 8½" dia....................**$30.00**

Ceiling fixture, triple; floral decal **$55.00**

Creamer, Reversed Field Flowers Hostess **$12.00**

Creamer, Scalloped Wild Flowers..............................**$15.00**

Creamer & sugar bowl, Rope Bow **$24.00**

Creamer & sugar bowl, Silhouette Hostess, w/lid.......**$24.00**

Decanter, Oriental Deco..**$60.00**

Egg cup, Hankscraft, platinum trim, from $8 to..........**$10.00**

Gravy boat, no decoration, commissioned for US Department of Defense **$25.00**

Jug, ball; Beehive Crisscross **$70.00**

Lamp, table; Antique Rose **$70.00**

Mug, Wildlife, gold trim **$35.00**

Percolator, Field Flowers, electric, #710......................**$75.00**

Percolator, Serv-All, platinum, electric, #3007 ....**$90.00**

Percolator, Tulips, electric, #10....................................**$85.00**

Pitcher, batter; Serv-All, gold or red & black, #3014...**$40.00**

Pitcher, disc; Flight..**$85.00**

Pitcher, disc; Hearth..**$70.00**

Pitcher, milk; no decoration; commissioned for US Department of Defense **$25.00**

Pitcher, Ribbed Band, 2-cup..$25.00
Pitcher, water; Field Flowers..............................$55.00

Pitcher, water; Flowerpot decal,
$55.00. (Photo courtesy Susan Grindberg)

Pot, Colonial, no decor, 6-cup.................................$35.00
Pot, Colonial, Silhouette, 6-cup $45.00
Pot, Dutch Boy & Girl, platinum or gold trim, 8-cup...$30.00
Pot, Geometric Wheat, 6-cup.................................$30.00
Pot, Oriental Deco, 4-cup $35.00
Pot, Paneled Rose, 8-cup $35.00
Pot, Rose & Wheat, 4-cup...$25.00
Salt & pepper shakers, hand-painted floral, sq, pr, from $20 to..$25.00
Sugar bowl, Black-Eyed Susan, w/lid, #710 ....$12.00
Teapot, Serv-All, gold or red & black, #3011 ....$35.00
Towel bar, various colors, pr, from $12 to $15.00
Urn, White Flower Platinum, electric..........................$95.00
Wall sconce, floral decal, 1-light................................$35.00

Powder Jars

Ceramic

With figural ceramics becoming increasingly popular, powder jars are desired collectibles. Found in various subjects and having great eye appeal, they make interesting collections. For more information we recommend *Collector's Guide to Made in Japan Ceramics* (there are three in series) by Carole Bess White (Collector Books).

Advisor: Carole Bess White (See Directory, Japan Ceramics)

Bamboo w/flower motif, black & white on orange, Japan, 3½" dia, from $15 to...$20.00
Colonial lady, blue hoop skirt, ¾-figure lid, Japan, 7", from $30 to...$40.00
Colonial lady w/rose in right hand, bouquet in other arm, Japan, 7", from $125 to $165.00

Dog pr, white w/black ears etc, atop basketweave lid (w/fruit decal) & bowl, Japan, 4", from $25 to...$45.00
Flapper, orange coat w/white trim, Japan, 4", from $70 to...$85.00
Flowers in relief (red, blue & green) over entire dome lid, yellow bowl, Japan, 3¾" dia.....................$20.00
Garden scene on white background w/blue border, solid blue jar w/gold trim, Noritake, 4¾" dia...............$65.00
Heart shape, Oriental lady w/fan in center of lid, Noritake, 3", from $300 to $400.00
Lady, hoop skirt as lid & bowl, gold & multicolored lustre, Goldcastle, 4", from $65 to $85.00
Lady, ½-figure in pink dress w/hands folded, floral decor on pink jar, Noritake, 5", from $295 to.....................$355.00
Landscape, fall scene in earth tones, green Noritake mark #27, 3½" dia $75.00
Oriental lady w/parasol in orange dress atop purple lustre scalloped lid & jar, Noritake, from $295 to $355.00
Pierrot, yellow costume w/multicolored trim, Goldcastle, 4¼", from $75 to...$100.00
Rabbit, ear cocked, on hexagonal lid & bowl, yellow w/multicolored trim, Japan, 5¼", from $45 to $65.00

Glass

Glassware items such as powder jars, trays, lamps, vanity sets, towel bars, and soap dishes were produced in large quantities during the Depression era by many glasshouses who were simply trying to stay afloat. They used many of the same colors as they had in the making of their colored Depression glass dinnerware that has been so popular with collectors for more than thirty years.

Some of their most imaginative work went into designing powder jars. Subjects ranging from birds and animals to Deco nudes and Cinderella's coach can be found today, and this diversity coupled with the fact that many were made in several colors provides collectors with more than enough variations to keep them interested and challenged.

Advisor: Sharon Thoerner, Glass Powder Jars (See Directory, Powder Jars)

Amethyst glass, very plain, New Martinsville, 4½" dia..$35.00
Annabella, pink transparent.....................................$175.00
Annette, pink frost...$200.00
Annette w/2 dogs, crystal $75.00
Ballerina, pink frost...$185.00
Bambi, marigold iridescent, Jeannette.........................$32.00
Blue carnival w/smocking design, Indiana Glass Co, 6½x6"...$25.00
Carrie, black, draped nude figural stem, painted flowers $195.00
Cleopatra II, crystal, shallow base, deep lid, 4¾".......$95.00
Colonial Lady, light blue opaque, Akro Agate..........$100.00

Crinoline Girl, crystal, off-the-shoulder gown, flowers in right hand, embossed bows on skirt...............**$40.00**

Crinoline Girl, green frost, off-the-shoulder gown, flowers in right hand, embossed bows on skirt.................**$165.00**

Curtsy, pink frost...**$140.00**

Dancing Girl, green frost, feminine features, rope trim at top of base........................**$120.00**

Dolly Sisters, green frost......................**$225.00**

Elephant (trunk down), green frost, lg.............**$85.00**

Elephant w/carousel base, pink frost............**$125.00**

Elephants Battling, pink frost.....................**$125.00**

Gretchen, green transparent, $195.00. (Photo courtesy Sharon Thoerner)

Horse & coach, pink frost, round.............**$350.00**

Jackie, green frost.....................................**$120.00**

Jackie, pink frost.......................................**$160.00**

Judy, green, New Martinsville....................**$75.00**

Lillian VII, pink frost, cone-shaped base.........**$195.00**

Martha Washington, crystal, Colonial lady between boy & girl......................**$100.00**

Minstrel, crystal..**$50.00**

Minstrel, pink frost....................................**$95.00**

Modernistic, pink satin, New Martinsville, original sticker label.......................**$115.00**

Obelisk, green frost, flat, no feet...............**$85.00**

Pagoda, blue frost w/Frances Mandel label.........**$40.00**

Parakeets, crystal frost............................**$155.00**

Poodle, iridescent, Jeannette....................**$50.00**

Roxana, green frost..................................**$135.00**

Royal Coach, pink frost w/white & gold overspray, black lid....................**$225.00**

Scottie, light blue opaque, Akro Agate.........**$150.00**

Scottie, pink transparent, Jeannette............**$70.00**

Southern Belle, green frost.......................**$195.00**

Sphinx, pink frost....................................**$110.00**

Terrier (sm, standing), pink frost..............**$125.00**

Three Birds, green or pink frost, ea...........**$125.00**

Twins, green frost....................................**$155.00**

Vamp, green frost, flapper's head forms finial.........**$155.00**

Vamp, pink frost, flapper's head forms finial...........**$120.00**

Wendy, fully painted................................**$145.00**

Precious Moments

Precious Moments is a line consisting of figurines, picture frames, dolls, plates, and other items, all with inspirational messages. They were created by Samuel J. Butcher and are produced by Enesco Inc. in the Orient. You'll find these in almost every gift store in the country, and some of the earlier, discontinued figurines are becoming very collectible. For more information, we recommend *Collector's Value Guide to Precious Moments by Enesco* (CheckerBee Publishing).

Our values are for examples in mint condition and retaining their original box.

Always in His Care, #225290, unmarked, 1990.........**$14.00**

Baby's First Christmas, #15911, Dove mark, 1985.......**$48.00**

Best Man (Bridal Party Series), #E2836, Cedar Tree mark, 1987..................**$35.00**

Bless-Um You, #527335, Butterfly mark, 1993, retired 1998.................**$44.00**

Blessed Are the Pure in Heart, #E3104, Hourglass mark, 1982, suspended 1991.................**$55.00**

Blessed Are the Pure in Heart, #E5392, Cross mark, 1984..**$40.00**

Blessings From My House to Yours, #E0503, Olive Branch mark, 1986, suspended 1986................**$80.00**

Bon Voyage, #522201, Bow & Arrow mark, 1989, suspended 1996.................**$150.00**

Bride, #E2846, Vessel mark, 1991................**$29.00**

Brotherly Love, #100544, Cedar Tree mark, 1987, suspended 1989.................**$98.00**

But Love Goes on Forever, #E3115, Fish mark, 1983.**$60.00**

Charity Begins in the Heart, #307009, Eyeglasses mark, 1998, retired 1998.................**$60.00**

Cheers to the Leader, #104035, Trumpet mark, 1994, retired 1997.................**$65.00**

Christmas Puppies Free, #528064, Ship mark, 1995, retired 1997.................**$26.00**

Cow With Bell, #E5638, Flame mark, 1990................**$37.00**

Dr Sam Sugar, #529850, Heart mark, 1996, retired 1997..**$24.00**

Dropping In for the Holidays, #531952, Heart mark, 1996, retired 1998.................**$49.00**

Especially for You, #E9282C, Cedar tree mark, 1987, suspended 1990.................**$35.00**

Friends Never Drift Apart, #522937, Butterfly mark, 1993..**$36.00**

Friends to the End, #104418, Vessel mark, 1991, suspended 1993.................**$36.00**

Friendship Hits the Spot, #306916, Star mark, 1999....**$32.00**

God Bless Our Family, #100501, Flower mark, 1988, retired 1999.................**$65.00**

God Sent His Love, #15881, Dove mark, 1985.........**$45.00**

Going Home, #52979, Ship mark, 1995.................**$65.00**

Grandfather, #529516, Butterfly mark, 1993, retired 1994...**$34.00**

Happy Birthday Dear Jesus, #524875, Vessel mark, 1991, suspended 1993.................**$33.00**

Have a Heavenly Christmas, #12416, Flower mark, 1988, suspended 1998.................................$24.00

Have I Got News for You, #105635, Vessel mark, 1991, suspended 1991.................................$50.00

He Careth for You, #E1377B, Cross mark, 1984, suspended 1984 ....$105.00

He Leadeth Me, #E1377A, no mark, before 1981, suspended 1984 ....$152.00

He Watches Over Us All, #E3105, Cross mark, 1984, suspended 1984.................................$68.00

Highway to Happiness, #649457, unmarked, 1999.....$20.00

I Belong to the Lord, #103632, Flower mark, 1988.....$42.00

I Haven't Seen Much of You Lately, #531057, Heart mark, 1996 ....$15.00

I Will Cherish the Old Rugged Cross, Vessel mark, 1991 ....$38.00

I'll Play My Drum for Him, #E2359, Hourglass mark, 1982 ....$96.00

Jesus Is the Light That Shines, #E0537, Fish mark, 1983 ....$75.00

Jesus Is the Only Way, #520756, 1989, retired in 1993, Bow and Arrow mark, MIB, $70.00.

Jesus Loves Me, #E7171, Cross mark, 1984, suspended 1985 ....$70.00

Jesus Loves Me, #E9278, Dove mark, 1985 ....$26.00

June (Calendar Girl Series), #110043, Butterfly mark, 1993.................................$56.00

Katie Lynne, #E0539, Cedar Tree mark, 1987, suspended 1988 ....$182.00

Let Heaven & Nature Sing, #E0532, Olive Branch mark, 1986, retired 1986 ....$40.00

Lord, Turn My Life Around, #520551, Flame mark, 1990, suspended 1996.................................$65.00

Love Is Patient, #E0535, Olive Branch mark, 1986, suspended 1986 ....$52.00

Love Is the Glue That Mends, #104027, Bow & Arrow mark, 1989, suspended 1990 ....$66.00

Love Rescued Me, #102385, Flower mark, 1988 ....$21.00

Loving You, #12017, Dove mark, 1985, suspended 1987..$60.00

Make a Joyful Noise, #522910, Flame mark, 1990, suspended 1996 ....$40.00

Many Moons in Same Canoe, Blessum You, #520772, Bow & Arrow mark, 1989, retired 1990.................................$332.00

May Your World Be Trimmed With Joy, #522082, G Clef mark, 1992, suspended 1996.................................$85.00

Mother Sew Dear, #E2850, Cross mark, 1984, retired 1984 ....$362.00

My Guardian Angel, #E7168, Cross mark, 1984, suspended 1984 ....$65.00

Oh Holy Night, #522848, Bow & Arrow mark, 1989 ..$36.00

Our First Christmas Together, #102350, Olive Branch mark, 1986 ....$36.00

Prayer Changed Things, #E5210, Cross mark, 1984, suspended 1984.................................$52.00

Precious Memories, #E2828, Cedar Tree mark, 1987, retired 199 ....$78.00

Pretty as a Princess, #526053, Heart mark, 1996.........$40.00

Puppies on Sled, #272892, Sword mark, 1997 ....$25.00

Reindeer, #102466, Olive Branch mark, 1986...........$192.00

Ring Those Christmas Bells, #525898, Ship mark, 1995, retired 1996 ....$142.00

Sammy, #528668, Ship mark, 1993, retired 1997.........$25.00

Say I Do, #261149, Eyeglasses mark, 1998 ....$60.00

Seek Ye the Lord, #E9261, Olive Branch mark, 1986, suspened 1986.................................$44.00

Serve With a Smile, #102431, Cedar Tree mark, 1987, suspended 1988.................................$30.00

Serving the Lord, #100161, Flower mark, 1988, suspended 1990 ....$68.00

Silent Night, #15814, Cedar Tree mark, 1987, suspended 1992.................................$98.00

Sure Would Love To Squeeze You, #456896, unmarked, 1998.................................$20.00

The Heavenly Light, #E5637, Flower mark, 1988........$37.00

The Lord Bless You & Keep You, #E7167, Fish mark, 1983, suspended 1985 ....$65.00

The Perfect Grandpa, #E7160, Fish mark, 1983, suspended 1986 ....$82.00

Timmy, #E5397, Flame mark, 1990, suspended 1991 .$156.00

To Thee With Love, #E0534, Fish mark, 1983, retired 1989 ....$60.00

Unicorn, #E2371, Flower mark, 1988, retired 1988.....$52.00

We Are God's Workmanship, #E9258, Fish mark, 1983..$45.00

Wishing You a Season Filled With Joy, #E2805, Cross mark, 1983, retired 1985 ....$90.00

You Are the Type I Love, #523542, Butterfly mark, 1993..$50.00

You Have Touched So Many Hearts, #112356, G Clef mark, 1992, retired 1997 ....$34.00

Purinton Pottery

The Purinton Pottery Company moved from Ohio to Shippenville, Pennsylvania, in 1941 and began producing several lines of dinnerware and kitchen items hand painted with fruits, ivy vines, and floral designs in bold brush strokes of color on a creamy white background. The company closed in 1959 due to economic reasons.

Purinton has a style that's popular today with collectors who like the country look. It isn't always marked, but you'll soon recognize its distinct appearance. Some of the rarer designs are Palm Tree, Peasant Garden, and Pennsylvania Dutch, and examples of these lines are considerably higher than the more common ones. You'll see more Apple and Fruit pieces than any, and in more diversified shapes.

For more information we recommend *Purinton Pottery, An Identification and Value Guide,* by Susan Morris.

Advisor: Susan Morris (See Directory, Purinton Pottery)

Apple, baker, 7" dia..$30.00
Apple, bowl, fruit; plain border, 12" $35.00
Apple, bowl, fruit; scalloped border, 12"...............$40.00
Apple, bowl, vegetable; open, 8½"........................$25.00
Apple, butter dish, 6½"...$65.00
Apple, coffeepot, 8-cup, 8" $90.00

Apple, grease jar, 5½", $85.00.
(Photo courtesy Susan Morris)

Apple, mug, juice; 6-oz, 2½" $15.00
Apple, pitcher, Rubel mold, 5" $75.00
Apple, plate, chop; plain border, 12".....................$35.00
Apple, platter, grill; indentations on surface, 12" $45.00
Apple, platter, meat; 12" $40.00
Apple, tray, roll; 11" $35.00
Chartreuse, bottles, oil & vinegar; tall, 1-pt, 9½", pr ..$75.00
Chartreuse, pitcher, beverage; 2-pt, 6¼".................$65.00
Chartreuse, tumbler, 12-oz, 5"..............................$20.00
Cresent Flower, teapot, 6-cup, 6" $85.00
Cresent Flower, vase, handled, 7½".....................$125.00
Daisy, grease jar, w/lid, 5½" $60.00
Daisy, jug, Rebecca; 7½"......................................$50.00
Fruit, bottle, vinegar; cobalt trim, 1-pt, 9½" $35.00
Fruit, cookie jar, red trim, oval, w/lid, 9" $60.00
Fruit, creamer, 3"...$15.00
Fruit, creamer & sugar bowl, miniature, 2" $30.00
Fruit, jug, Kent; 1-pt, 4½".....................................$30.00
Fruit, jug, oasis; 9½x9½" dia, minimum value.........$500.00
Fruit, plate, chop; 12"...$35.00

Fruit, plate, dinner; 9¾" $20.00
Fruit, shakers, range style, pr................................$40.00
Fruit, sugar bowl, w/lid, 4"...................................$25.00
Fruit, teapot, 4-cup, 5"...$55.00
Fruit, tumbler, 12-oz, 5"......................................$20.00
Heather Plaid, creamer, 3"...................................$20.00
Heather Plaid, mug, handled, 8-oz, 4" $25.00
Heather Plaid, plate, chop; 12"..............................$25.00
Heather Plaid, platter, meat; 12"...........................$30.00
Heather Plaid, shakers, pour 'n shake, 4¼", pr..........$60.00
Heather Plaid, teapot, 6-cup, 6"............................$65.00
Intaglio, bean pot, 3¼"...$50.00
Intaglio, butter dish, 6½".....................................$55.00
Intaglio, creamer, 3½"..$20.00
Intaglio, decanter, miniature, 5".............................$35.00
Intaglio, jug, 5-pt, 8"..$75.00
Intaglio, mug, juice; unusual grape design, 6-oz, 2½"..$20.00
Intaglio, plate, chop; 12".......................................$25.00
Intaglio, platter, meat; 12"....................................$30.00
Intaglio, tidbit tray, 2-tier, 10"..............................$55.00
Ivy-Blue & Red Blossoms, jardiniere (NAPCO mold), 5" ..$30.00
Ivy-Red Blossom, coffeepot, 8"..............................$65.00
Ivy-Red Blossom, teapot, 6-cup, 6" $55.00
Maywood, baker, 7"..$15.00
Maywood, plate, chop; 12"....................................$20.00
Maywood, platter, grill; 12"...................................$25.00
Maywood, teapot, 6-cup, 6½".................................$45.00
Ming Tree, canister, variation of original pattern, 7½".......$65.00
Ming Tree, plate, dinner; 9¾"................................$20.00
Mountain Rose, decanter, 5" $45.00
Mountain Rose, dish, w/lid, 9"...............................$75.00
Mountain Rose, jug, Dutch; 2-pt, 5¾".....................$85.00
Mountain Rose, marmalade jar, 4½"........................$65.00
Mountain Rose, planter, basket; 6¼".......................$50.00
Normandy Plaid, bowl, fruit; 12"............................$35.00
Normandy Plaid, bowl, spaghetti; 14½".....................$55.00
Normandy Plaid, cookie jar, oval, 9½" $60.00
Normandy Plaid, cruet, oil & vinegar; jug style, 5", pr ..$65.00
Normandy Plaid, grease jar, w/lid, 5½" $60.00
Normandy Plaid, jug, Kent; 1-pt, 4½".......................$30.00
Normandy Plaid, pitcher, beverage; 2-pt, 6¼".............$55.00
Normandy Plaid, teapot, 6-cup, 6" $65.00
Palm Tree, planter, basket; 6¼"............................$100.00
Palm Tree, plate, dinner; 9¼".............................$125.00
Peasant, plate, chop; hand signed by Dorothy Purinton, 12", minimum value................................$350.00
Peasant, vase, 6" $125.00
Peasant House, candy dish, NAPCO mold, 6"............$60.00
Pennsylvania Dutch, bowl, vegetable; divided, 10½"..$50.00
Pennsylvania Dutch, creamer, 3½"..........................$40.00
Pennsylvania Dutch, jug, honey; 6¼" $85.00
Pennsylvania Dutch, planter, basket; 6¼"...................$85.00
Pennsylvania Dutch, platter, meat; 12"......................$50.00
Pennsylvania Dutch, salt & pepper shakers, stacking; 2¼", pr..$50.00
Pennsylvania Dutch, saucer, 5½"............................$8.00
Petals, baker, 7"...$35.00

Petals, coffeepot, 8-cup, 8" $75.00
Petals, cookie jar, w/lid, 9" $85.00
Petals, cookie jar, 9" $85.00
Petals, dish, w/lid, 9" $65.00
Petals, pitcher, beverage; 2-pt, 6¼" $75.00
Pine Tree, jardiniere, 5" $40.00
Provincial Fruit, tumbler, 12-oz, 5" $20.00
Provincial Fruit, vase, 5" $30.00
Saraband, bowl, fruit; 12" $15.00
Saraband, bowl, range; w/lid, 5½" $20.00
Saraband, cookie jar, oval, 9½" $30.00
Saraband, plate, salad; 6¾" $4.00
Seaform, coffee server, 9" $125.00
Seaform, cup, 3¼" $20.00
Spatterware, mug, beer; 16-oz, 4¾" $25.00
Starflower, pitcher, 6" $65.00
Starflower, relish tray, 8" $45.00
Tea Rose, bowl, dessert; 4" $20.00
Tea Rose, planter, 5" $65.00
Tea Rose, plate, breakfast; 8½" $25.00
Turquoise, baker, 7" $30.00
Turquoise, plate, dinner; 9¾" $15.00

Purses

By definition a purse is a small bag or pouch for carrying money or personal articles, but collectors know that a lady's purse is so much more! Created in a myriad of wonderful materials reflecting different lifestyles and personalities, purses have become popular collectibles. Lucite examples and those decorated with rhinestones from the 1940s and 1950s are 'hot' items. So are the beautifully jeweled Enid Collins bags of the '50s and '60s. Tooled leather is a wonderful look as well as straw, silk, and suede. Look for fine craftsmanship and designer names. For further information, we recommend *Antique Purses* by Richard Holiner (Collector Books).

Enid Collins, In the Pink, from $200.00 to $250.00. (Photo courtesy Robert Lesley)

Enid Collins, bird in gold w/yellow stones in eyes & wings, rhinestones in stars, wooden box style, 6x11¼x4½" $165.00
Enid Collins, flowers in vase, jeweled, cloth, 8½x10x4", M $150.00
Enid Collins, Owl & Pussy Cat, jeweled, cloth, 8½x10½, NM $165.00
Enid Collins, trolley car, owl, money tree, sun & cat, jeweled, cloth, 10½", NM $175.00
Judith Leiber, beige snakeskin w/jewels, shoulder strap, dated 1984, M $155.00
Judith Leiber, black snakeskin, 2 compartments inside & 1 ea on front & back, 10½x10½"+strap $300.00
Judith Leiber, black suede clutch w/brass U-shaped handle embedded w/black rhinestones, 7½x8"+handle...$78.00
Judith Leiber, salmon snakeskin w/jeweled cabochon closure, 2 open pockets on outside, shoulder chain, 5½x9½" $175.00
Lamured Original, white plastic 'caviar' beads on brown fabric, Caviar Beadette Pat 9534, 6x6", M $40.00
Metal silver- & gold-tone basketweave w/hard plastic lid & handle, oval basket shape, EX................$35.00
Plastic, amber tortoise w/metal panels, hinged top w/snap closure, 4x6¼"+handle, EX $60.00
Plastic, black acrylic w/clear etched lid, resembles basket, swivel handles, NM $135.00
Plastic, black Lucite handle & frame, green material w/applied ribbon, rhinestones & seed pearls, Rialto, 14x12x3" $50.00
Plastic, clear & silver confetti body, clear handle, rhinestones & pearls along frame, snap closure, M $95.00
Plastic, clear carved Lucite lid, amber body, hinged handles, Gottlieb & Maresca, 1950s, 6x8½x4", EX...........$115.00
Plastic, clear carved Lucite top & ball feet, gray mottled body, long swivel handles, Deco styling, Rialto NY, 4x7" $175.00
Plastic, clear lid, white woven 'basket' body, brass latch, clear horseshoe handle, 4x8½x3½", EX+.....................$75.00
Plastic, clear lid w/colorful seashells, white marbleized body, gold-tone hinge, 3x8¼x4¾"+handle, EX...............$40.00
Plastic, clear Lucite w/deep spoon carving on top & handle, hinged in the back, 3½x8½x4½", EX...................$60.00
Plastic, clear Lucite w/gold glitter & rhinestones, oval basket shape, NM $70.00
Plastic, clear Lucite w/metal filigree sides & clasp, box type w/rhinestones on lid................................$80.00
Plastic, clear Lucite w/raised flowers & 10 lg rhinestones, silver trim on clasp, 4¼x7¼x1¾".............................$65.00
Plastic, creamy ivory laminate over round Lucite body w/deep carved floral pattern, 6x5"+horseshoe-shaped handle, EX..$80.00
Plastic, gray w/embedded gold threads, box style, Florida Handbags, EX...$80.00
Plastic, Lucite w/2 poodle dog appliques, lg dog has rhinestone collar & leash, 10x7x2"................................$95.00
Plastic, tortoise-shell Bakelite w/beaded center & beaded rose handle, metal clasps, 7x7" $185.00

Plastic, white lunch box shape w/swing handle, white clasp, mirror in lid, Wilardy, 9x7¼x5", EX....................**$110.00**

Plastic & straw w/poodle applique on side, 1950s, 9½x10x3½", EX....................**$80.00**

Rhinestone (prong-set) covered, hinged frame, Made in Czechoslovakia label inside, 4x4¾"....................**$55.00**

Rhinestone covered, hinged closure, 6x4½", NM **$135.00**

Rhinestone covered, hinged frame, 12 glass 'jewels' in clasp, chain handle, 6¼x6½"....................**$60.00**

Rhinestones & cut crystal, covered, hinged opening, chain strap, 5½x6", NM **$80.00**

Straw, silk & chenille flowers w/seashells, sequins & beads on front, straw button closure, Japan, 17x11½" +handles....................**$30.00**

Straw box type w/Lucite front side w/shell flowers under clear plastic, Adele Handbags Miami Florida, EX.**$40.00**

Tooled leather, 'turnloc' feature on the opening, Meeker Made, 6½x5", NM **$75.00**

Tooled leather, black w/intricate floral decor, silver buckle closure, strap handle, 7½x12"....................**$45.00**

Tooled leather, irises, 3-compartment, Cordova Shop Buffalo, ca 1930s, 6x7" **$95.00**

Tooled leather, white flowers & green leaves, front flap tucks into braided pc across front, ca 1960s, 6x8x4", EX.**$55.00**

Puzzles

The first children's puzzle was actually developed as a learning aid by an English map maker, trying to encourage the study of geography. Most nineteenth-century puzzles were made of wood, rather boring, and very expensive. But by the Victorian era, nursery rhymes and other light-hearted themes became popular. The industrial revolution and the inception of color lithography combined to produce a stunning variety of themes ranging from technical advancements, historical scenarios, and fairy tales. Power saws made production more cost effective, and wood was replaced with less expensive cardboard.

As early as the '20s and '30s, American manufacturers began to favor character-related puzzles, the market already influenced by radio and the movies. Some of these were advertising premiums. Die-cutters had replaced jigsaws, cardboard became thinner, and now everyone could afford puzzles. During the Depression they were a cheap form of entertainment, and no family get-together was complete without a puzzle spread out on the card table for all to enjoy.

Television and movies caused a lull in puzzle making during the '50s, but advancements in printing and improvements in quality brought them back strongly in the '60s. Unusual shapes, the use of fine art prints, and more challenging designs caused sales to increase.

If you're going to collect puzzles, you'll need to remember that unless all the pieces are there, they're not of much value, especially those from the twentieth century. The condition of the box is important as well. Right now there's a lot of interest in puzzles from the '50s through the '70s that feature popular TV shows and characters from that era. Remember, though a frame-tray puzzle still sealed in its original wrapping may be worth $10.00 or more, depending on the subject matter and its age, a well used example may well be worthless as a collectible.

To learn more about the subject, we recommend *Schroeder's Toys, Antique to Modern* (published by Collector Books). *Toys of the Sixties, A Pictorial Guide*, by Bill Bruegman (Cap'n Penny Productions) is another good source of information.

Newsletter: *Piece by Piece*
P.O. Box 12823
Kansas City, KS 66112-9998; Subscription: $8 per year

Alice in Wonderland, jigsaw, Jaymar, EXIB **$30.00**

Aquaman, jigsaw, Whitman, 100 pcs, MIB **$50.00**

Babes in Toyland, jigsaw, Whitman, 1961, 70 pcs, M (VG box) **$25.00**

Bart Simpson, jigsaw, Milton Bradley, 250 pcs, MIB (sealed) **$2.00**

Batman & Robin the Boy Wonder, jigsaw, APC, 1973, 81 pcs, EX (EX canister)....................**$15.00**

Beetle Baily, jigsaw, Jaymar, 1963, 60 pcs, NMIB **$25.00**

Ben Casey, jigsaw, Milton Bradley, 1962, 600 pcs, MIB (sealed) **$25.00**

Beverly Hillbillies, jigsaw, Jaymar, MIB, from $25 to..**$30.00**

Bionic Woman, jigsaw, Whitman, 1976, MIB, from $40 to....................**$50.00**

Blondie, frame-tray, Built-Rite, 1949, EX....................**$30.00**

Brady Bunch, frame-tray, Whitman #4558, EX............**$45.00**

Broken Arrow, frame-tray, Built-Rite, set of 4, MIB....**$65.00**

Captain America, frame-tray, 1966, EX....................**$25.00**

Captain America, jigsaw, Whitman, 1976, NMIB........**$30.00**

Charlie's Angels, jigsaw, HG Toys, 1976, 150 pcs, MIB, from $25 to....................**$30.00**

Chatty Baby, frame-tray, Whitman, 1960s, MIP..........**$30.00**

Chilly Willy, frame-tray, Walter Lantz, 1962-63, EX.....**$10.00**

Cinderella & the Prince at Midnight, jigsaw, Jaymar, 1950s, VG (G box) **$20.00**

Creatures of the Outer Limits, jigsaw, Milton Bradley, 1964, EXIB....................**$240.00**

Dark Shadows, jigsaw, Milton Bradley, 1969, NMIB...**$65.00**

Davy Crockett: Seige of the Fort, jigsaw, Jaymar, EXIB..**$35.00**

Dilly Dally the Human Bullet, frame-tray, Whitman, 1950s, EX....................**$40.00**

Donald Duck w/Daisy & Nephews in Haunted House, Golden/Western, 1983, 100 pcs, MIB (sealed)......**$20.00**

Donald Duck w/Uncle Scrooge & Nephews in Money Vault, jigsaw, Whitman/Western, MIB (sealed) **$23.00**

Donnie & Marie, jigsaw, Whitman, 1976, MIB **$35.00**

Dracula, jigsaw, 1974, EX (EX canister)....................**$20.00**

Eight Is Enough, jigsaw, APC, 1978, MIB **$25.00**

Fantastic Four, frame-tray, Whitman, 1968, scarce, NM ..**$50.00**

Fantastic Four, jigsaw, Third Eye, 1971, 500 pcs, MIB..**$100.00**

Farrah Fawcett, jigsaw, APC, 1977, 405 pcs, MIB, from $35 to....................**$40.00**

Fat Albert, jigsaw, Whitman, 1975, 100 pcs, EX (EX box)..**$20.00**
Flipper, jigsaw, Whitman, 1965, 100 pcs, MIB............**$25.00**
Fonz, jigsaw, HG Toys, 1976, EX (EX canister)..........**$25.00**
Frankenstein Jr, jigsaw, Whitman Big Little Book series, 1968,
    MIB...**$30.00**
Gabby Gator, frame-tray, Walter Lantz, 1962-63, EX...**$10.00**
Green Hornet, frame-tray, Whitman, 1966, set of 4, MIB, from
    $100 to..**$125.00**
Howdy Doody Goes West, frame-tray, Whitman, 1953,
    EX **$40.00**
HR Pufnstuf, frame-tray, Whitman, 1970, MIP............**$35.00**
Impossibles, frame-tray, Whitman, 1967, EX **$25.00**
Incredible Hulk, jigsaw, Third Eye, 1971, 500 pcs, MIB...**$100.00**
James Bond in Thunderball: Bond's Battle, jigsaw, Milton
    Bradley, 1965, EXIB...**$45.00**
Jonny Quest: Rescued, jigsaw, Milton Bradley, 1964,
    EXIB..**$90.00**

Lassie, jigsaw, Whitman, Big Little Book series, complete, 1960s, NMIB, $45.00. (Photo courtesy Larry Jacobs)

Lassie w/Forest Ranger, frame-tray, Wrather, 1966, EX **$15.00**
Lassie w/Puppies, frame-tray, Milton Bradley, 1959, EX..**$25.00**
Liddle Kiddles, frame-tray, Whitman, 1966, M **$55.00**
Love Boat, jigsaw, HG Toys, 1978, 150 pcs, MIB **$20.00**
Ludwig Von Drake, jigsaw, Whitman Jr, 1962, 70 pcs,
    EXIB **$60.00**
Marvel Super Heroes, jigsaw, Milton Bradley, 1966, 100 pcs,
    MIB **$125.00**
Mork & Mindy, jigsaw, Milton Bradley, 1978, 250 pcs,
    MIB **$15.00**
Mr Magoo, frame-tray, Whitman, 1965, NM...............**$20.00**
Munsters, jigsaw, Whitman, 1965, 100 pcs, EXIB........**$35.00**
Nancy & Sluggo, jigsaw, Whitman, 1973, NMIB **$15.00**
Nancy Drew, jigsaw, APC, 1970s, NM (NM canister)..**$30.00**
New Kids on the Block, jigsaw, Milton Bradley, 1990, 100
    pcs, MIB, from 10 to..**$15.00**
Patty Duke, jigsaw, Whitman Jr, 1963, 100 pcs, MIB, from $35
    to **$45.00**
Raggedy Ann, frame-tray, Milton Bradley, 1955, NM, from
    $25 to..**$35.00**
Raggedy Ann & Andy, frame-tray, Whitman, 1976, MIP..**$10.00**
Road Runner, frame-tray, 1966, NM **$20.00**

Road Runner, jigsaw, Whitman, 1980, EXIB **$20.00**
Silver Surfer, jigsaw, Third Eye, 1971, 500 pcs, MIB.**$100.00**
Simpsons, jigsaw, Milton Bradley, 100 pcs, MIB (sealed)...**$16.00**
Six Million Dollar Man, frame-tray, APC, 1976, MIP ..**$35.00**
Snoopy's House, jigsaw, Milton Bradley, 1989, 100 pcs,
    EXIB **$12.00**
Space Ghost, frame-tray, Whitman, 1967, NM............**$50.00**
Spider-Man, jigsaw, Whitman, 1982, 100 pcs, MIB
    (sealed)...**$8.00**
Star Wars Victory Celebration, jigsaw, Kenner, 1977, 500 pcs,
    M (sealed) box)..**$25.00**
Starsky & Hutch, jigsaw, HG Toys, 1976, MIB, from $25
    to **$30.00**
Steve Canyon in China, jigsaw, Jaymar, 1950s, EXIB..**$20.00**
Storybook Kiddies, frame-tray, Whitman, 1968, set of 4, MIB,
    from $50 to...**$65.00**
Street Hawk, jigsaw, Salters, 1984, 150 pcs, EXIB.......**$35.00**
Superboy, frame-tray, Whitman, 1968, NM.................**$50.00**
Superman, frame-tray, Whitman, 1965, EX.................**$20.00**
Superman, frame-tray, Whitman, 1966, NM................**$25.00**
Tammy & Pepper, jigsaw, Ideal, 100 pcs, VG (VG box).**$25.00**
Tiny Chatty Twins, frame-tray, Whitman, 1960s, MIP.**$30.00**
Tom & Jerry, frame-tray, 1965, NM **$20.00**
Top Cat, frame-tray, Whitman, 1961, NM **$20.00**
Underdog, frame-tray, Whitman #4522, 1965, M (sealed)..**$23.00**
Underdog, jigsaw, Whitman, 1975, 100 pcs, MIB **$25.00**
Village People, jigsaw, APC, 1978, MIB, from $65 to.**$85.00**
Wacky Races, frame-tray, Whitman, 1969, EX.............**$30.00**
Winnie the Pooh, frame-tray, Whitman, 1979, EX **$10.00**
Woodsy Owl, jigsaw, Whitman, 1976, 125 pcs, circular, 20"
    dia, EX (G+ box) **$25.00**
Wyatt Earp, jigsaw, Whitman, 1960s, NM (NM box)...**$25.00**

Pyrex

Though the history of this heat-proof glassware goes back to the early years of the twentieth century, the Pyrex that we tend to remember best is more than likely those mixing bowl sets, casseroles, pie plates, and baking dishes that were so popular in kitchens all across America from the late 1940s right on through the 1960s. Patterned Pyrex became commonplace by the late 1950s; if you were a new bride, you could be assured that your bridal shower would produce at least one of the 'Cinderella' bowl sets or an 'Oven, Refrigerator, Freezer' set in whatever pattern happened to be the most popular that year. Among the most recognizable patterns you'll see today are Gooseberry, Snowflake, Daisy, and Butterprint (roosters, the farmer and his wife, and wheat sheaves). There was also a line with various solid colors on the exteriors. You'll seldom if ever find a piece that doesn't carry the familiar logo somewhere. To learn more about Pyrex, we recommend *Kitchen Glassware of the Depression Years* by Gene Florence (Collector Books).

Bowl, blue, sq base, 12", from $35 to.........................**$38.00**
Bowl, cereal; blue, 5¾"..**$3.50**

Bowl, mixing; American Heritage, 6½", from $8 to....**$10.00**
Bowl, mixing; American Heritage, 8½", from $12.50 to..**$15.00**
Bowl, mixing; blue, 8½", from $10 to........................**$12.50**
Bowl, mixing; blue fired-on color, 6½", from $8 to....**$10.00**
Bowl, mixing; Butterprint Cinderella, 6¾", from $8 to ...**$10.00**
Bowl, mixing; Cinderella, 8¼", from $8 to **$10.00**
Bowl, mixing; Gooseberry, 8¼", from $8 to...............**$10.00**
Bowl, mixing; green fired-on color, 8½", from $10 to..**$12.50**
Bowl, mixing; mixed fired-on colors, set of 4, from $30
    to **$38.00**
Bowl, mixing; red fired-on color, 7½", from $10 to ...**$12.50**
Bowl, mixing; yellow fired-on color, 9½", from $12.50 to..**$15.00**
Bowl, vegetable; blue, 9" **$8.00**
Casserole, Cinderella, fired-on color, clear lid, from $15
    to **$20.00**
Creamer, blue **$4.50**
Cup & saucer, demitasse; blue **$20.00**
Divided dish, blue, from $30 to **$35.00**
Measuring cup, crystal, 1-cup, from $8 to **$10.00**
Measuring cup, crystal, 2-spout, from $22 to **$25.00**
Measuring cup, red, 16-oz, from $100 to.................**$125.00**
Pie plate, blue, 10", from $30 to............................**$35.00**
Plate, dinner; blue, 9¾" **$4.50**
Plate, sandwich; blue, 11½" **$5.50**
Refrigerator container, blue & white, 4¼x6¾", from $10
    to **$12.00**
Refrigerator container, red fired-on color, 3½x4¾", from $5
    to **$6.00**
Refrigerator dish, blue fired-on color, 4¼x6¾", from $8
    to **$10.00**
Refrigerator dish, Butterprint Cinderella, 6¼x6¾", from
    $12.50 to **$15.00**
Refrigerator dish, Gooseberry, 3½x4¾", from $6 to **$8.00**
Refrigerator dish, red, 4¼x6¾", from $135 to **$150.00**
Refrigerator dish, yellow fired-on color, 3½x4¾", from $7
    to **$8.00**
Refrigerator dish, yellow fired-on color, 7x9", from $12.50
    to **$15.00**

Railroadiana

It is estimated that almost two hundred different railway companies once operated in this country, so to try to collect just one item representative of each would be a challenge. Supply and demand is the rule governing all pricing, so naturally an item with a marking from a long-defunct, less prominent railroad generally carries the higher price tag.

Railroadiana is basically divided into two main categories, paper and hardware, with both having many subdivisions. Some collectors tend to specialize in only one area — locks, lanterns, ticket punches, dinnerware, or timetables, for example. Many times estate sales and garage sales are good sources for finding these items, since retired railroad employees often kept such memorabilia as keepsakes. Because many of these items are very

unique, you need to get to know as much as possible about railroad artifacts in order to be able to recognize and evaluate a good piece. For more information we recommend *Railroad Collectibles, Revised 4th Edition,* by Stanley L. Baker (Collector Books).

Advisors: Fred and Lila Shrader; John White, Grandpa's Depot (See Directory Railroadiana)

Dinnerware

Bowl, berry, D&RG, Blue Adam, no back stamp, 5½" ..**$18.00**
Bowl, salad; ATSF, Mimbreno, full back stamp, 3¼x7"..**$442.00**
Butter pat, CB&Q, Burlington Route, Violets & Daisies, bottom stamped, 3" **$72.00**
Butter pat, GN, Empire, no back stamp, 3" **$27.00**
Butter pat, SP&S, American pattern, no back stamp...**$27.00**
Chocolate pot, ATSF, California Poppy, no back stamp,
    6"..**$135.00**
Compote, N&W, Cavalier, pedestal foot, top mark,
    2½x7" **$865.00**
Creamer, Blue & Gold, no handle, no back stamp, 2¾" .**$54.00**
Creamer, D&RGW, Blue Adam, no handle, no back stamp,
    3"..**$29.00**
Creamer, PRR, Purple Laurel, no handle, bottom stamped ..**$75.00**
Cup & saucer, CNR, Queen Elizabeth, cup top logo ..**$47.00**
Cup & saucer, demitasse; C&O, Homestead, side logo .**$42.00**
Cup & saucer, demitasse; PRR, Broadway, both bottom
    stamped **$215.00**
Cup & saucer, GN, Spokane Rose, saucer bottom
    stamped **$78.00**
Egg cup, GTW, Blue & Gold, side logo, bottom stamped,
    2⅞"..**$270.00**
Gravy boat, B&O, Derby, no back stamp, 8" **$44.00**
Ice cream dish, B&O, Derby, tab handle, no back stamp,
    6"..**$38.00**
Plate, ACL, Palmetto, mitered corners, bottom stamped, top
    logo, 7" sq **$126.00**
Plate, CMStP&P, Traveler, full back stamp, 9½" **$195.00**
Plate, CP, Tremblant w/Railway, top logo, 9".............**$58.00**
Plate, ICRR, Coral, no back stamp, 9½"....................**$80.00**
Plate, NP, Monad, top logo, no back stamp, 5" **$51.00**
Plate, service, ICRR, inner courtyard scene, no back stamp,
    10½"..**$650.00**
Platter, CM&StP&P, top mark, no back stamp, 5x8½"..**$235.00**
Platter, UP, Portland Rose, full back stamp, 10x6½"..**$195.00**
Relish dish, SR, Peach Blossom, top logo, 12x6" **$220.00**
Sherbet, UP Winged Streamliner, pedestal foot, side logo,
    2½"..**$58.00**
Teapot, GM&O, side mark, 5¾" **$668.00**

Glassware

Ashtray, NYC, 20th Century Limited logo in center, 5½"
    dia **$50.00**
Ashtray, UP, red, white & blue enamel logo, 3½", from $6
    to **$12.00**

Bottle, milk; B&O Homestead Hotel, green enamel logo, 1-pt..$62.00

Bottle, milk; Missouri Pacific Lines, buzz saw logo, red pyro on clear, ½-pint, $25.00.

Bottle, milk; NYC, oval enamel logo, sq, ½-pt $12.00
Cruet & stopper, NP monad logo, 5¼".....................$385.00
Goblet, Amtrak Pioneer, train in oval, twisted stem, 7", from $35 to...$45.00
Roly-poly, PRR, detailed enamel picture of engine, 3" ..$11.00
Sherbet, CMStP&P, rectangular w/pedestal foot, white enamel logo, 2½x3½"..$81.00
Stem, cordial; ATSF, etched Sante Fe in cursive, 3¼".$48.00
Stem, wine; Amtrak Empire Builder, swirl stem, 4¼".$12.00
Stem, wine; CMStP&P rectangular white enamel logo, 4" ..$14.00
Swizzle stick, NYNH&H, New Haven Dining Car Service, cobalt, 4¾" $18.00
Tumbler, juice; GN, GN etched, 4" $137.00
Tumbler, water; B&O etched capitol dome logo, 5½"..$23.00
Tumbler, water; BAR blue enamel logo, 5" $26.00
Tumbler, whiskey; Maine Central, MCRR wheel-cut, 3" ..$89.00

Linens and Uniforms

Blanket, CN, cream w/blue stripes w/CN's maple leaf logo, wool, 44x64"..$49.00
Coat, waiter's; Pullman on inside label, white cotton.$22.00
Headrest seat cover, CRI&P, Route of the Rockets/Rock Island, 15x22"..$19.00
Headrest seat cover, NP, Monad YPL on lower edge .$16.00
Headrest seat cover, Southern Serves the South & logo, 5x19"..$10.00
Napkin, cocktail, NP, Monad YPL in color, 14" sq $21.00
Napkin, SP, City of San Francisco logo on cream, 20" sq $22.00
Napkin, UP, rust & cream w/UP on edges, 18" sq.$12.00
Pillowcase, C&O, stamped logo, 35x16".....................$11.00
Place mat, UP, Streamliner logo w/yellow border on white, 11x16" $17.00
Tablecloth, StL&SF, Frisco in script, white on white, 34" sq $32.00
Towel, hand; Property of the Pullman Company woven on blue center stripe $10.00
Towel, hand; Union Pacific woven on red center stripe .$4.00

Vest, conductor's, B&O, black wool, brass buttons, pre-1940..$95.00

Silverplate

Bouillon cup holder w/handles, Lehigh Valley, Reed & Barton, side logo, 4" interior dia $325.00
Butter pat, GN, International, top mark, 2¾" sq.......$680.00
Coffeepot, CMStP&P, International, logo finial, bottom stamped, 14-oz, 6"..$186.00
Coffeepot, NP, International, bottom stamped, 10-oz, 4½"..$36.00
Condiment holder w/hinged lid, Pullman, International, top mark, no glass insert, 3¼"..................................$135.00
Creamer, N&W, Reed & Barton, side logo in script, 3".$110.00
Crumber, NP, Dundee, Rogers, bottom stamped, 12".$360.00
Crumber tray, Reading, International, no handle, ornate, bottom stamped, 9x8"..$265.00
Fork, dinner; ATSF, Cromwell, International, bottom stamped $18.00
Fork, dinner; Pullman, Roosevelt, International, bottom stamped $24.00
Fork, seafood; B&O, Belmont, Reed & Barton, bottom stamped $35.00
Fork, seafood; PRR, Kings, Reed & Barton, top mark, Keystone logo, 6"..$46.00
Hot food cover w/finger hole, Pullman, International, bottom stamped, 6"..$87.00
Knife, dinner; ICRR, Dartmouth, International, top mark $15.00
Knife, dinner; SP, Modern (B), Reed & Barton, side mark ..$29.00
Nut pick, C&EI, Vendome, Reed & Barton, top mark .$185.00
Plate, ICRR, Reed & Barton, top mark & bottom stamped, Car 16, 5¾"..$295.00
Platter, NYNH&H, silhouette border, International, bottom stamped, 6x8½..$42.00
Spoon, demitasse; Fred Harvey, Churchill, Gorham, bottom stamped, 4¾" $26.00
Spoon, demitasse; PRR, Broadway, International, top mark, 4½"..$66.00
Spoon, ice tea; Southern RR, Century (B), bottom stamped, 7¾"..$19.00
Sugar tongs, CNR, Oval, Rogers, Canada, top logo, 4¼" ..$65.00
Sugar tongs, Louisville & Nashville, Cromwell, International, bottom stamped, 4¼" $72.00
Sugar tongs, MP, Empire (B), Rogers, bottom stamped, 4¼" $71.00
Syrup, NYC, hinged lid, attached underplate, bottom stamped, 6-oz, 4½"..$165.00
Tea strainer, UP, Meriden Brita, long handle, bottom stamped, 6¾"..$134.00
Teapot, CP, Elkington, side mark, 10-oz, 4½" $65.00
Teaspoon, Fred Harvey, Albany, International, bottom stamped, 5¾"..$15.00
Thermos, Pullman, Stanley Thermos, bottom stamped, 11", from $65 to..$100.00
Tray, bread; GN, International, top mark, 9½x6"........$86.00
Tray, UP, The Challenger, top mark, bottom stamped, 6" ..$75.00

Tureen, PRR, International & Reed & Barton, w/lid & under-plate, side logo, bottom stamped, 7½" $111.00

Miscellaneous

Ashtray, NYC, by Salem Pottery, NYC bird w/RR hat, 7½" sq $40.00

Ashtray, Pullman, metal w/1 rest, embossed: For Over 80 Years, 5½"..$28.00

Ashtray, SR, logo embossed center, brass, 5¼"..........$15.00

Ashtray, UP, Safety First, Bakelite, 3½" sq $12.00

Badge, breast; Panama Canal Railroad Co, celluloid w/picture, 2½" dia...$82.00

Badge, cap & breast; B&O Police, silver-tone..........$435.00

Badge, cap; El Paso Union Passenger Depot, contour ..$190.00

Badge, cap; Louisville & Nashville, flagman, contour ...$102.00

Badge, cap; SP, SPCo, fireman, 3¾x1" $194.00

Badge, lapel; CMStP&P, waiter, enamel on silver-tone, 1½x1⅝"..$26.00

Badge, wallet; CP, Department Investigation Constable..$78.00

Bell, trolley; original pull string & brackets, 12" dia, 20" bracket to bracket..$41.00

Berth key, Pullman, brass $38.00

Blotter, AC&Y, 1950s, 4x8" $8.00

Blotter, CB&O, Oct/Nov/Dec 1936 calendar, 3½x8½"..$8.00

Blotter, DSS&A, map of routes, 9x4" $16.00

Book, CNR, Uniform Code of Operation Rules, revised 1962, 128 pages..$9.00

Book, Meet the Maine Central, 1981, 64 pages, 8½x11"..$10.00

Book, PRR, List of Reportable Locations, 1964, 125 pages, 7x9"..$15.00

Book, PRR, Veteran Employees, 1850 to 1880, gold embossed hardcover, 130+ pages........................$90.00

Booklet, ATSF, Big Trees & Yosemite, 1924, 16 pages, 8x9"..$66.00

Booklet, D&RG, Anderson, 1936, 172 pages, 7x9" $13.00

Booklet, NP, King of the Land of Fortune: Apples, 16 pages, 5¼x8½"......................................$32.00

Booklet, NP, Ranch Vacations, 1948, 15 pages, 8½x11"..$15.00

Bookmark, CMStP&P, gold embossed train on leather, 4½x1¼"..$28.00

Box, cigar; UP Herald on cover & inside, brass hinges..$25.00

Box, railway fuses, Equitable Powder Manufacturing Company, wood, 12x12x15" $15.00

Button, CP, dome w/beaver, brass, ⅞".............................$6.00

Button, MP, buzz-saw logo on gold-tone metal, ⅞" $6.00

Button, NY, Susquehanna & Western, silver-tone metal, ⅞"..$2.00

Button, Parker Railway News Company, gold-tone metal, American Railway Supply Company, ⅞"..............$16.00

Button, Pennsylvania, P superimposed over L, old brass, ⅞"..$3.00

Button, Pullman, gold-tone metal, ⅞" $2.00

Button, UP Overland Route, gold-tone, St Louis Button Company, ⅞"..$12.00

Calendar, ATSF, 1953, pocket-size $5.00

Calendar, C&O, Chessie, spiral-bound booklet, 1961, complete $10.00

Calendar, CB&Q, Burlington Route, 1956, pocket-size ..$16.00

Calendar, CB&Q, Burlington Route, 1962, pocket-size .$4.00

Calendar, ICRR, 1957, 13-month pad, 18x27" $78.00

Calendar, Missouri Pacific Lines, $85.00. (Photo courtesy B.J. Summers)

Calendar, PRR, various Pennsylvania scenes, 1945 to 1972, plastic, pocket-size, from $4 to............................$18.00

Calendar, UP, 1932, pocket-size $54.00

Calendar, UP, 1952, pocket-size $6.00

Coaster, paper, C&O Chessie, various locations, ea from $3 to $5.00

Coasters, paper, various railroads, ea from 50¢ to........$4.00

Cuspidor, N&W embossed, black cement, 11" $38.00

Hard hat, RI, complete w/inner head band................$19.00

Jug, StL&SF, stoneware, 2-gal....................................$300.00

Knife, office; B&O, brass handle, 4" plus 1" spade shape blade $37.00

Ledger, FDDM&S, receipts for deliveries, 1957 ....$21.00

Letter opener, SP&S, full-color logo, metal 5½" $38.00

Lighter, Erie logo one side, streamliner other side, Zippo, 1950s $88.00

Lighter, GN, logo w/Rocky, original box....................$46.00

Lighter, PRR, Keystone logo plus original box, Zippo, 1940s to 1950s $96.00

Lighter, PRR, red enamel Keystone logo, brushed chrome, Zippo snap top, 1980s....................................$21.00

Lighter, StL&SF, logo one side, map other, Vulcan, 1960s to 1970s $22.00

Lighter, WP, Feather River logo, black & red enamel on brown chrome, Zippo snap top, 1980s.................$18.00

Magazine, CMStP&P, Milwaukee Road, October 1969 ..$11.50

Magazine, N&W, April, 1962 ....$4.00

Map, Market Street Railway, San Francisco, California, 1942, 16x16", folds to 4x8"..$26.00

Map, PRR, 1942, full color, folds to pocket size, 22x17"..$8.00

Map, UP map of United States, 1947, 18x24", folds to 9x4"..$10.00

Match holder to fit matchbook, KCS, hammered aluminum...$48.00

Matchbook, Fred Harvey w/picture of Los Angeles Union Station, unused...**$8.00**

Matchbook, ICRR logo, unused **$1.00**

Menu, C&NW, 1960, 7½x10".............................**$21.00**

Menu, CP, breakfast, 1955, 8x5"..............................**$5.00**

Menu, Elk's Club excursion, Santa Fe/Fred Harvey, 1954..**$35.00**

Menu, ICRR, City of Miami, 1967, 6x9" **$11.00**

Menu, PRR, It Pays To Dine Early or Late, 1939, 3½x5" ...**$9.00**

Menu, PRR, WWII era, early 1940s, wartime restrictions, 11x7" **$33.00**

Menu, SCL, detailed coastal map on cover, 1940s, 9½x6"..**$64.00**

Menu, UP, City of San Francisco, luncheon, 1950, 7x9½" **$5.00**

Menu card, ATSF, 1969, 6½x3½" **$4.00**

Menu card, CRI&P, breakfast, 1975, 6½x10" **$5.00**

Note pad, UP, 50 sheets, 5x7" **$5.00**

Paperweight, PRR embossed cast iron, silver, pancake-style w/knob, 5"...**$37.00**

Pass, Texas Electric Railway, 1944 to 1945 ....**$15.00**

Pen, ATSF, Santa Fe logo, Practice Safety, Sheaffer.......**$6.00**

Pencil, mechanical; StL&SF, Frisco Line, black & red pearlized **$30.00**

Pencil clip, various railroads w/name &/or logo, 1990s, from $1 to..**$6.00**

Photograph, locomotive, various railroads, 8½x11", from $4 to **$12.00**

Placemat, paper, CMStP&P, Milwaukee Road, 10x14" ...**$5.00**

Playing cards, SP, scenics/Coast Daylight, case, 2¼" ..**$36.00**

Pocketknife, StL&SF, Case XX, 4-blade, w/original sheath & box, 5" **$90.00**

Postcard, ATSF, colorful map of area served, unmailed..**$5.00**

Postcard, C&A depot, Mexico, Missouri, real photograph **$26.00**

Postcard, Wabash depot, Kirksville, Missouri, 1910, real photograph **$21.00**

Ruler, CP, wood w/metal strip, 18".............................**$22.00**

Sack, paper, Fred Harvey, linens only, 18x26" **$4.00**

Swizzle stick, C&NW logo, red & black plastic...........**$12.00**

Swizzle stick, GN, white & red plastic w/Rocky...........**$5.00**

Swizzle stick, plastic, plain w/railroad name on shank, ea up to **$2.00**

Tag, baggage, MKT diecut logo string tag...................**$14.00**

Tag, baggage, Vermont Railroad, manufactured by Robbins, Boston, brass, 1¾" **$52.00**

Tape measure, UP, metal case, 6" metal tape, 1¾" dia.**$8.00**

Ticket punch, Pullman, General Railway Equipment Company, side logo..**$42.00**

Timetable, employee; Bessemer & Lake Erie, 1955, 55 pages..**$38.00**

Timetable, employee; Detroit, Toledo & Ironton, 1982 ..**$13.00**

Timetable, employee; MKT system, 1982.....................**$5.00**

Timetable, employee; Toledo terminal, 1971 ....**$17.00**

Timetable, public; Maine Central, 1958.......................**$7.00**

Timetable, public; SP&S, 1957, 12 pages **$14.00**

Timetable, public; WP, 1951 through 1955, 8 pages, ea ..**$4.00**

Timetable card, CM, 1915 ....**$36.00**

Token, baggage; Kentucky & Indiana Railway, brass, octagonal, ⅝" **$23.00**

Token holder, Philadelphia Rapid Transit issue, tokens slide out, chrome, 2¼x¾ **$20.00**

Water can, NKPRR, galvanized, lift-off lid, 12" **$16.00**

Wax sealer, UP, Nebraska, brass head, turned wood handle **$188.00**

Razor Blade Banks

Razor blade banks are receptacles designed to safely store used razor blades. While the double-edged disposable razor blades date back to as early as 1904, ceramic and figural razor blade safes most likely were not produced until the early 1940s. The development of the electric razor and the later disposable razors did away with the need for these items, and their production ended in the 1960s.

Shapes include barber chairs, barbers, animals, and barber poles, which were very popular. Listerine produced a white donkey and elephant in 1936 with political overtones. They also made a white ceramic frog. These were used as promotional items for shaving cream. Suggested values are based on availability and apply to items in near-mint to excellent condition. Note that regional pricing could vary.

Advisor: Debbie Gillham (See Directory, Razor Blade Banks)

Barbershop quartet, four singing barber heads, from $95.00 to $125.00. (Photo courtesy Debbie Gillham)

Barber, wood w/Gay Blade bottom, unscrews, Woodcraft, 1950, 6", from $65 to **$75.00**

Barber, wood w/key & metal holders for razor & brush, 9", from $60 to...**$80.00**

Barber bust w/handlebar mustache, coat & tie, from $50 to **$70.00**

Barber chair, sm, from $100 to **$125.00**

Barber head, different colors on collar, Cleminson, from $25 to **$35.00**

Barber holding pole, Occupied Japan, marked Blades on back, 4", from 65 to..**$75.00**

Barber holding pole, Occupied Japan, 4", from $50 to .**$60.00**

Barber pole, red & white, w/ or w/o attachments & various titles, from $20 to...**$25.00**

Barber pole w/barber head & derby hat, white, from $40 to...**$60.00**

Barber pole w/face, red & white, from $30 to............**$40.00**

Barber standing in blue coat & stroking chin, from $65 to...**$85.00**

Barber w/buggy eyes, pudgy full body, Gleason look-alike, from $65 to...**$75.00**

Box w/policeman holding up hand, metal, marked Used Blades, from $75 to..**$100.00**

Dandy Dans, plastic w/brush holders, from $25 to....**$35.00**

Friar Tuck, Razor Blade Holder (on back), Goebel..**$300.00**

Frog, green, marked For Used Blades, from $60 to....**$70.00**

Grinding stone, For Dull Ones, from $80 to.............**$100.00**

Half barber pole, hangs on wall, may be personalized w/name, from $40 to...**$60.00**

Half shaving cup, hangs on wall, marked Gay Blades w/floral design, from $75 to..**$100.00**

Indian head, porcelain, marked Japan, 4" **$25.00**

Listerine donkey, from $20 to.....................................**$30.00**

Listerine elephant, from $25 to...................................**$35.00**

Listerine frog, from $15 to...**$25.00**

Looie, right- or left-hand version, from $85 to..........**$110.00**

Man shaving, mushroom shape, Cleminson, from $25 to...**$35.00**

Man shaving, mushroom shape, Cleminson, personalized, from $45 to...**$55.00**

Razor Bum, from $85 to..**$100.00**

Safe, green, marked Blade Safe on front, from $40 to..**$60.00**

Shaving brush, ceramic, wide style w/decal, from $45 to...**$65.00**

Souvenir, wood-burned outhouse, For Gay Old Blades, by Crosby, found w/names of several states, from $35 to...**$45.00**

Tony the Barber, Ceramic Arts Studio, from $85 to....**$95.00**

White ceramic outhouse, Specialist in Used Blades on bottom, from $75 to...**$90.00**

Reamers

Reamers were a European invention of the late 1700s, devised as a tool for extracting liquid from citrus fruits, which was often used as a medicinal remedy. Eventually the concept of freshly squeezed juice worked its way across the oceans. Many early U.S. patents (mostly for wood reamers) were filed in the mid-1880s, and thanks to the 1916 Sunkist 'Drink An Orange' advertising campaign, the reamer soon became a permanent fixture in the well-equipped American kitchen. Most of the major U.S. glass companies and pottery manufacturers included juicers as part of their kitchenware lines. However, some of the most beautiful and unique reamers are ceramic figures and hand-painted, elegant china and porcelain examples. The invention of frozen and bottled citrus juice relegated many a reamer to the kitchen shelf.

However, the current trend for a healthier diet has garnered renewed interest for the manual juice squeezer.

Most of the German and English reamers listed here can be attributed to the 1920s and 1930s. Most of the Japanese imports are from the 1940s.

Advisor: Bobbie Zucker Bryson (See Directory, Reamers)

Newsletter: *National Reamer Collectors Association*
Debbie Gillham
301-977-5727 e-mail: reamers@erols.com or
http://www.reamers.org

Ceramic

Baby's, 2-pc, pink w/white kitten in blue pajamas, pink, blue, green & white top, Japan, 4", from $75 to..**$85.00**

Baby's Orange, 2-pc, red & white, Japan, 4½" **$55.00**

Black face & hands, red coat & blue pants, 4¾", from $500 to...**$600.00**

Bucket, 2-pc, blue & white, pagoda image, rattan handle, from $75 to...**$100.00**

Camel, kneeling, luster w/light green top, 4¼", from $225 to...**$275.00**

Chick, 2-pc, yellow w/orange bill & green handle, Germany, Goebel, 3½", from $135 to **$150.00**

Child's, 2-pc, orange lustre w/red, blue & yellow flowers, 2", from $100 to...**$125.00**

Clown, brown body & hat, blue button & collar, 6", from $95 to...**$125.00**

Clown, head in saucer, maroon & white, 4" dia, from $175 to...**$225.00**

Clown, lime green & white, 4¾", from $95 to.........**$125.00**

Clown, Sourpuss, w/saucer, 4¾", from $115 to **$135.00**

Clown, 2-pc, green & yellow w/pig head, 5", from $200 to...**$275.00**

Clown, 2-pc, sitting cross-legged, green w/white ruffled coat & hat, German, 5", from $275 to........................**$350.00**

Clown, 2-pc, wearing tuxedo, 5½", from $125 to.....**$150.00**

Clown head, 2-pc, white body w/orange stripes & black polka-dots, 4¾", from $75 to...............................**$100.00**

Cottage, Carlton Ware (England), yellow w/orange & green trim, 4", from $95 to...**$125.00**

Cup, 2-pc, yellow & white spatter pattern, Stangl, 6¼", from $50 to...**$75.00**

Elephant, white, 1-pc, w/multicolored blanket, marked Newbach, 5¾", from $115 to **$150.00**

Fish, 2-pc, orange & white, marked Jaeft, 3¾", from $185 to...**$225.00**

Floral w/gold, Nippon, 2-pc **$195.00**

Floral w/gold, Royal Rudolstadt, 2-pc, from $150 to ..**$200.00**

Germany, Goebel, Winnie-the-Pooh, orange w/white top, 4½"...**$300.00**

Grapefruit, 2-pc, top has green clown reamer head, bottom is grapefruit half, ca 1940s, Japan, 4", from $85 to...**$115.00**

House, 2-pc, beige w/green trees & tan branches, blue door & windmill, Japan, 4½", from $150 to **$185.00**

Lady's head w/black hair in green lustre ruffled saucer, 3¾", from $275 to.................................**$350.00**

Lemon, 2-pc, yellow w/green leaves, gold trim, Japan, 4", from $65 to.................................**$85.00**

Lime, 2-pc, Orange for Baby, green w/pebble finish, 4⅜", from $75 to.................................**$100.00**

Mexican, sitting, holding green cactus, w/orange coat, black pants & yellow hat, 5½", from $225 to.............**$300.00**

Orange, orange with white lettering and cone, green leaves and brown handle marked 'Kiddies Orange Juice,' Goebel Germany, two-piece, 4", from $85.00 to $110.00. (Photo courtesy Bobbie Zucker Bryson)

Orange, 2-pc, Orange for Baby, yellow w/blue flowers, Goebel, 3½".................................**$135.00**

Pear, 3-pc, white w/black, outlined, leaves on top, marked Japan, from $55 to.................................**$75.00**

Pitcher, lemon slice, yellow w/green handle, 6¾", from $40 to.................................**$50.00**

Pitcher, 2-pc, beige w/multicolor flowers & black trim, Japan, 8¾".................................**$50.00**

Pitcher, 2-pc, beige w/red & yellow flowers, black trim, Japan, 8½", w/6 cups, from $50 to.................**$65.00**

Pitcher, 2-pc, black w/gold wheat, 8".................................**$45.00**

Pitcher, 2-pc, cream w/red & black cattails, Universal Cambridge, 9", from $165 to.................**$185.00**

Pitcher, 2-pc, rose w/yellow & lavender flowers, green leaves, Japan, 7", +6 cups, from $60 to.............**$75.00**

Red Wing USA, yellow, 6¾".................................**$125.00**

Rose, yellow w/green leaves, Germany, 1¾", from $200 to.................................**$225.00**

Saucer, cream, tan & maroon w/blue trim, England, 3¼" dia, from $90 to.................................**$100.00**

Saucer, white w/pink flowers & green leaves, Germany, 4½" dia, from $85 to.................................**$100.00**

Saucer, 2-pc, France, Ivoire Corbelle, Henriot Quimper #1166, 4¼", from $350 to.................**$400.00**

Sleeping Mexican, 2-pc, green shirt, red pants, gold top, Japan, 4¾", from $175 to.................**$200.00**

Teapot, 2-pc, blue, green & white, England/Shelley, 3½", from $95 to.................................**$125.00**

Teapot, 2-pc, white w/red flowers & trim, Prussia/Germany/Royal Rudolstadt, 3¼".................**$150.00**

Teapot, 2-pc, white w/yellow & maroon flowers, Nippon, 3¼".................................**$90.00**

USA, Ade-O-Matic Genuine Coorsite Porcelain, green, 9".................................**$150.00**

USA, Jiffy Juicer, US Pat 2,130,755, Sept 2, 1928, yellow, 5¼".................................**$85.00**

Glass

Crystal, Crisscross, Hazel-Atlas, from $20 to.............**$25.00**

Crystal, embossed Tcheco-Scovaquie on handle, from $30 to.................................**$35.00**

Crystal, Glasbake, McKee on handle, from $65 to......**$75.00**

Crystal, RADNT, from $135 to.................................**$150.00**

Crystal, sm tab, Cambridge, from $18 to.................**$20.00**

Crystal, 2-pc, referred to by collectors as 'Buttons & Bows,' unknown maker, from $55 to.................**$60.00**

Crystal, 2-pc, Westmoreland, from $65 to.................**$70.00**

Crystal w/elephant decor on base, 2-pc, Fenton, from $110 to.................................**$125.00**

Frosted crystal, 2-pc, Jenkins, from $50 to.............**$55.00**

Green, Circle pitcher w/reamer top, Hocking, from $45 to.................................**$50.00**

Green, Crisscross, tab handle, Hazel-Atlas, from $40 to.................................**$45.00**

Green, Hex Optic, bucket reamer, from $40 to.........**$45.00**

Green, marked Argentina, from $125 to.................**$150.00**

Green, Orange Juice Extractor, from $55 to.............**$65.00**

Green, pointed cone, Federal, from $25 to.............**$28.00**

Green, tab handle, Federal, from $25 to.................**$28.00**

Green, 2-cup pitcher set w/sunflower in bottom, from $130 to.................................**$150.00**

Green, 2-pc w/embossed oranges or lemons, Westmoreland, ea from $175 to.................................**$195.00**

Green, 4-cup pitcher set, marked A&J, Hazel-Atlas, from $45 to.................................**$50.00**

Green, 4-cup pitcher set, US Glass, from $140 to.....**$150.00**

Green, 6-sided cone, vertical handle, Indiana Glass, from $85 to.................................**$95.00**

Green (light), straight sides, Fry, from $35 to.............**$38.00**

Jadite (dark), embossed Sunkist, from $45 to.............**$55.00**

Milk glass, embossed Fleur-de-Lis, from $75 to.........**$85.00**

Milk glass, embossed Valencia, from $120 to...........**$150.00**

Milk glass, 4-cup stippled pitcher set, Hazel-Atlas, from $35 to.................................**$40.00**

Pearl (white opalescent), straight sides, Fry, from $35 to......**$40.00**

Pink, flattened loop handle, Westmoreland, from $110 to...**$125.00**

Pink, handled w/spout opposite, Indiana Glass, from $85 to.................................**$95.00**

Pink, Jennyware, from $125 to.................................**$135.00**

Pink, ribbed, looped handle, Federal, from $40 to.....**$45.00**

Pink, tab handle, lg, 5⅞", from $40 to.................**$50.00**

Pink, 2-cup pitcher set, Hazel-Atlas, from $150 to....**$160.00**

Pink (light), 2-cup pitcher set, US Glass, from $55 to...**$60.00**

Pink w/decor, 2-pc, Westmoreland, from $200 to....**$225.00**

Seville Yellow, embossed Sunkist, from $50 to...........**$55.00**

Skokie Green, pointed cone, 5¼", from $65 to.........**$75.00**

Records

Records are still plentiful at flea markets and some antique malls, but albums (rock, jazz, and country) from the '50s and '60s are harder to find in collectible condition (very good or better). Garage sales are sometimes a great place to buy old records, since most of what you'll find there have been stored more carefully by their original owners.

There are two schools of thought concerning what is a collectible record. While some collectors prefer the rarities — those made in limited quantities by an unknown who later became famous, or those aimed at a specific segment of music lovers — others like the vintage Top-10 recordings. Now that they're so often being replaced with CDs, we realize that even though we take them for granted, the possibility of their becoming a thing of the past may be reality tomorrow.

Whatever the slant your collection takes, learn to visually inspect records before you buy them. Condition is one of the most important factors to consider when assessing value. To be judged as mint, a record may have been played but must have no visual or audible deterioration — no loss of gloss to the finish, no stickers or writing on the label, no holes, no skips when it is played. If any of these are apparent, at best it is considered to be excellent, and its value is up to 90% lower than a mint example. Many of the records you'll find that seem to you to be in wonderful shape would be judged only very good, excellent at the most, by a knowledgeable dealer. Sleeves with no tape, stickers, tears, or obvious damage at best would be excellent; mint condition sleeves are impossible to find unless you've found old store stock.

LPs must be in their jackets, which must be in at least excellent condition. Be on the lookout for colored vinyl or picture discs, as some of these command higher prices; in fact, older Vogue picture disks commonly sell in the $25.00 to $75.00 range, some even higher. It's not too uncommon to find old radio station discards. These records will say either 'Not for Sale' or 'Audition Copy' and may be worth more than their commercial counterparts. Our values are based on original issue — remember to cut these prices drastically when condition is less than described.

If you'd like more information, we recommend *American Premium Record Guide* by L.R. Docks.

Advisor: L.R. Docks (See Directory, Records)

45 rpm

Two conditions are noted in our description lines. The first is the condition of the record itself; the second is the condition of the jacket, without which many 45s are of no value.

Alpert, Herb & Tijuana Brass; My Favorite Things/The Christmas Song, A&M 1001, EX/NM........................**$2.00**

America, I Need You/Riverside, WB 7580, NM/VG **$2.50**

Anka, Paul; Dance on Little Girl, ABC-P 10220, EX/EX..**$10.00**

Anka, Paul; I Miss You So/Late Last Night, ABC-P 10011, M/EX...**$10.00**

Armstrong, Louis & Orchestra; The Night Before Christmas/When the Saints Go Marching In, Continental 1001, EX/EX...**$2.50**

Avalon, Frankie; Just Ask Your Heart/Two Fools, Chancellor 1040, EX/EX..**$10.00**

Avalon, Frankie; Why/Swinging on a Rainbow, Chancellor 1045, M/EX...**$10.00**

Bare, Bobby; To Whom It May Concern/I Don't Believe I'll Fall in Love Today, RCA 8083, NM/EX **$5.00**

Beach Boys, Getcha Back/Male Ego, CBS 493, M/M....**$2.50**

Beatles, Got To Get You Into My Life/Helter Skelter (reissue), Capitol 4274, EX/EX **$3.00**

Beatles, Let It Be/You Know My Name, Apple 2764, EX/EX...**$15.00**

Beatles, Love Me Do/PS I Love You (yellow label), Tollie 9008, EX/EX...**$25.00**

Belafonte, Harry; Danny Boy/Take My Mother Home, RCA 6790, EX/EX..**$4.00**

Benatar, Pat; Hit Me w/Your Best Shot/Prisoner of Love, Chrysalis 2464, NM/EX..**$2.00**

Blondie, Atomic/Die Young Stay Pretty, Chrysalis 2410, M/EX..**$2.00**

Blue Oyster Cult, Shooting Shark/Dragon Lady, Columbia 4298, M/M..**$2.00**

Blues Brothers, Gimme Some Lovin'/She Caught the Katy, Atlantic 3666, M/EX **$2.50**

Bolton, Michael; Sittin' on the Dock of the Bay/Call My Name, Columbia 7680, M/EX.................................**$2.50**

Bon Jovi, Bad Medicine/99 in the Shade, Mercury 870657, M/EX..**$2.00**

Boone, Pat; Bernardine/Love Letters in the Sand, Dot 15570, NM/EX..**$8.00**

Bread, It Don't Matter to Me, Elektra 45701, NM/EX **$3.00**

Browne, Jackson; Stay/Rosie, Asylum 45485, M/M.......**$3.00**

Bryant, Anita; Hey Good Lookin'/Bonaparte's Retreat, Columbia 42847, M/EX..**$5.00**

Cannon, Freddy; Way Down Yonder in New Orleans, Swan 4043, NM/EX...**$6.00**

Carpenters, Please Mr Postman/This Masquarade, A&M 1646, NM/EX...**$4.00**

Darin, Bobby; You Must Have Been a Beautiful Baby/Sorrow Tomorrow, Atco 6206, EX/EX.................................**$7.50**

Davis, Sammy Jr; Rhythm of Life, Decca 734605, NM/EX..**$4.00**

Eddy, Duane; Bonnie Come Back/Lost Island, Jamie 1144, EX/EX...**$4.00**

Fabian, Hound Dog Man/This Friendly World, Chancellor 1044, M/EX...**$12.50**

Garland, Judy; Life Is Just a Bowl of Cherries/April Showers/Come Rain or Come Shine, Capitol T734, EX/EX...**$5.00**

Harrell, Doug; Hospitality Blues/Exsanguination Blues, Colonial 501, EX/EX...**$10.00**

James, Sonny; Only Love Can Break a Heart, Capitol 13232, M/EX..**$4.00**

Lauren, Rod; If I Had a Girl/No Wonder, RCA 7645, NM/NM...**$10.00**

Lawrence, Steve; Girls Girls Girls/Little Boy Blue, UA 233, EX/EX..**$4.00**

Madonna, Crazy for You, Geffen 29051, M/M..............**$2.50**

Mathis, Johnny; The Twelfth of Never/Chances Are, Columbia 40993, EX/EX......................................**$4.00**

Nelson, Rick; Fools Rush In/Down Home, Decca 31533, M/EX..**$12.50**

Nelson, Rick; Stood Up/Waitin' in School, Imperial 5483, NM/EX..**$12.50**

O'Brian, Hugh; TV's Wyatt Earp Sings: One Silver Dollar/Same to You/Pale Horse/On Boot Hill, ABC-P 203 EP, NM/EX..**$10.00**

Oliver, Jean & The Arrangement; Crellie 334, NM/EX..**$4.00**

Page, Patti; Fibbin'/You Will Find Your Love (in Paris), Mercury 71355, EX/EX......................................**$5.00**

Paul & Paula, Ba-Hey-Be/Young Lovers, Philips 40096, NM/EX..**$6.00**

Peter & Gordon, I Don't Want To See You Again/I Would Buy You Presents, Capitol 5272, NM/EX **$5.00**

Presley, Elvis; Are You Lonesome Tonight/I Gotta Know, RCA 1781, EX/EX......................................**$8.00**

Presley, Elvis; Crying in the Chapel/I Believe in the Man in the Sky, RCA 447-0643, EX/EX......................**$8.00**

Presley, Elvis; Stuck on You/Fame & Fortune, RCA 47-7740, M/NM..**$18.00**

Sadler, Sgt Barry; Ballad of the Green Berets/Letter From Vietnam, RCA 8739, M/EX......................................**$4.00**

Starr, Ringo; It's All Down to Goodnight Vienna, Apple #1882, NM/VG, $5.00.

Tillotson, Johnny; Earth Angel/Pledging My Love, Cadence 1377, EX/EX..**$8.00**

Wallace, Jerry; Mission Bell Blues/Little Coco Palm, Challenge 59060, NM/EX......................................**$8.00**

78 rpm

Aladdins, Cry Cry Baby, Aladdin 3275, EX..................**$30.00**

Autry, Gene; In the Shadow of the Pine, Champion 16050, EX..**$50.00**

Beard, Dean; Rakin' & Scrapin', Atlantic 1137, EX......**$20.00**

Bowen, Jimmy; I'm Sticking w/You, Roulette 4010, EX...**$15.00**

Carter Family, Keep on the Sunny Side, Bluebird 5006, EX **$12.00**

Charles, Ray; What'd I Say, Atlantic 2006, EX **$30.00**

Cochran, Eddie; Sittin' in the Balcony, Liberty 55056, EX..**$30.00**

Crescendos, Oh Julie, Nasco 6005, EX..................**$20.00**

Crosby, Bing; Shine, Brunswick 6485, EX **$12.00**

Domino, Fats; Don't You Know I Love You, Imperial 5492, EX..**$12.00**

Five Satins, To the Aisle, Ember 1019, EX..................**$15.00**

Gracie, Charlie; Butterfly, Cameo 105, EX..................**$15.00**

Hawkins, Dale; Susie-Q, Checker 863, EX..................**$20.00**

Helms, Bobby; My Special Angel, Decca 30423, EX...**$20.00**

James, Sonny; First Date, First Kiss, First Love, Capitol 3674, EX..**$10.00**

King, BB; Got the Blues, Bullet 315, EX..................**$12.00**

Luke, Robin; Susie Darlin', Dot 15781, EX **$20.00**

Lymon, Frankie (& The Teenagers); I'm Not a Juvenile Delinquent, Gee 1026, EX......................................**$12.00**

Mathis, Johnny; Tell Me Why, Talent 738, EX..........**$15.00**

Mills Brothers, Smoke Rings, Brunswick 6225, EX......**$10.00**

Nelson, Rick; Be Bop Baby, Imperial 5463, EX **$20.00**

Nelson, Rick; Teenager's Romance, Verve 10047, EX.**$20.00**

Rays, Silhouettes, Cameo 117, EX **$20.00**

Reynolds, Jody; Endless Sleep, Demon 1507, EX **$15.00**

Robbins, Marty; Story of My Life, Columbia 41013, EX.**$15.00**

Silhouettes, Headin' for the Poorhouse, Ember 1032, EX ..**$10.00**

Six Teens, A Casual Look, Flip 315, EX......................**$15.00**

Smith, Bessie; After You've Come, Columbia 14197-D, EX **$50.00**

Smith, Kate; When the Moon Comes Over the Mountain, Columbia 2516D, EX **$10.00**

Storm, Warren; Mama Mama Mama, Nasco 6015, EX.**$15.00**

Tucker, Sophie; Some of These Days, Columbia 826-D, EX..**$10.00**

Turbans, When You Dance, Herald 458, EX..............**$15.00**

LP Albums

Atkins, Chet; Galloping Guitar, RCA Victor 3079, 10", EX..**$50.00**

Berry, Chuck; Chuck Berry Is on Top, Chess 1435, EX......**$50.00**

Cadets, Rockin' 'n Rollin', Crown 5015, EX **$50.00**

Cleftones, Heart & Soul, Gee 705, EX......................**$100.00**

Darin, Bobby (& the Jaybirds); This Is Bobby Darin, Atco 115, EX **$20.00**

Dells, Oh What a Night, Vee Jays 1010, black label, EX...**$25.00**

Fabian, Hold That Tiger, Chancellor 5003, EX **$40.00**

Flamingos, Flamingos, End 205, EX **$75.00**

Foley, Red; Souvenir Album, Decca 8294, EX............**$20.00**

Gilley, Mickey; Lonely Wine, Astro 101, EX..............**$175.00**

Haley, Bill; Rockin' the Joint, Decca 8775, EX............**$40.00**

Hamblen, Stuart; It Is No Secret, RCA Victor 1253, EX...**$16.00**

Holly, Buddy; That'll Be the Day, Decca 8707, multicolored label, EX..**$40.00**

Husky, Ferlin; Sittin' on a Rainbow, Capitol 976, EX..**$20.00**

Jones, George; Salutes Hank Williams, Mercury 20596, EX **$30.00**

King, BB; My Kind of Blues, Crown 5188, EX $20.00
Little Richard, Fabulous Little Richard, RCA 2114, EX..$30.00
Miracles, Hi We're the Miracles, Tamla 220, EX $75.00

**Nelson, Rick; Album Seven by Rick,
Imperial IR, Stereo 12082, VG, $5.00.**

Orbison, Roy; Crying, Monument 4007, EX $30.00
Platters, Remember When, Mercury 20410, EX $15.00
Presley, Elvis; Elvis, RCA Victor 1382, EX $40.00
Reeves, Jim; Girls I Have Known, RCA Victor 1685, EX..$15.00
Rivieras, Campus Party, Riviera 701, EX $60.00
Ronettes, Presenting the Fabulous Ronettes, Phillies 4006,
    EX..$80.00
Smith, Carl; Let's Live a Little, Columbia 1172, EX......$15.00
Snow, Hank; Country Classics, RCA Victor 1233.........$20.00
Tokens, The Lion Sleeps Tonight, RCA Victor 2514, EX..$30.00
Valens, Richie; His Greatest Hits, Del-Fi 1225, EX $25.00
Waters, Muddy; The Best of Muddy Waters, Chess 1427, black
    label, EX $75.00
Whitman, Slim; Country Favorites, Imperial 9064, EX ..$25.00
Young, Faron; This Is Faron Young, Capitol 1096, EX .$20.00

Red Wing

For almost a century, Red Wing, Minnesota, was the center of a great pottery industry. In the early 1900s several local companies merged to form the Red Wing Stoneware Company. Until they introduced their dinnerware lines in 1935, most of their production centered around stoneware jugs, crocks, flowerpots, and other utilitarian items. To reflect the changes made in 1935, the name was changed to Red Wing Potteries Inc. In addition to scores of lovely dinnerware lines, they also made vases, planters, flowerpots, etc., some with exceptional shapes and decoration.

Some of their more recognizable lines of dinnerware and those you'll most often find are Bob White (decorated in blue and brown brush strokes with quail), Tampico (featuring a collage of fruit including watermelon), Random Harvest (simple pink and brown leaves and flowers), and Village Green (or Brown, solid-color pieces introduced in the '50s). Often

you'll find complete or nearly complete sets, and when you do, the lot price is usually a real bargain.

If you'd like to learn more about the subject, we recommend *Red Wing Stoneware, An Identification and Value Guide,* and *Red Wing Collectibles,* both by Dan and Gail DePasquale and Larry Peterson. B.L. and R.L. Dollen have written *Red Wing Art Pottery, Books I* and *II.* All are published by Collector Books.

Advisors: Wendy and Leo Frese, Artware (See Directory, Red Wing); and B.L. and R.L. Dollen, Dinnerware (See Directory, Red Wing)

Club/Newsletter: *Red Wing Collectors Newsletter*
Red Wing Collectors Society, Inc.
Doug Podpeskar, membership information
624 Jones St., Eveleth, MN 55734-1631; 218-744-4854. Please include SASE when requesting information.

Artware

Ashtray, bronze-green gloss, leaf form, #746, 9", from $22
    to..**$30.00**
Ashtray, silver-green gloss, rectangular, #3002, 12", from $24
    to..**$32.00**
Bowl, burnt-orange gloss w/lime-green interior, cloverleaf
    shape, #1412, 8", from $32 to **$40.00**
Bowl, centerpiece; unmarked bird figurine in center, blue
    glossy lustre & coral, #1037, 8", from $75 to........**$90.00**
Bowl, console; ivory semi-matt, scalloped edge, silver wing
    label, #1620, 10", from $40 to **$50.00**
Bowl, dark green gloss w/yellow interior, leaf shape, #1429,
    10", from $32 to **$40.00**
Bowl, florals embossed on semi-matt ivory w/brown wash,
    6-sided, #1322, 5½", from $38 to **$54.00**
Bowl, Garden Club style, ivory semi-matt w/green interior,
    #1092, 10½", from $32 to **$40.00**
Bowl, Monarch Gothic, green semi-matt w/brown trim, #937,
    10", from $40 to **$52.00**
Bowl, pink semi-matt, sq, #1037, 7½", from $30 to....**$38.00**
Bowl, white matt, low, concave, #835, 8", from $35
    to..**$46.00**
Candle holders, ivory semi-matt, scalloped edge, #1619, 4½",
    pr, from $30 to **$40.00**
Candle holders, Textura, gray gloss w/pink interior, #B2111,
    5x5" sq, pr, from $28 to **$34.00**
Candle holders, turquoise, leaf motif, #1286, pr, from $60
    to..**$76.00**
Compote, black semi-matt, #M5008, 6", from $42 to..**$54.00**
Compote, flecked Nile Blue w/Colonial Buff interior, gold
    wing label, modern style, #5022, 7", from $48 to ..**$60.00**
Compote, ivory semi-matt, medium pedestal, #M1597, 7",
    from $30 to..**$36.00**
Compote, Prismatique, Mandarin Orange semi-matt w/Celadon
    interior, footed, low, #788, 5½", from $56 to...........**$68.00**
Compote, Stereoline, burnt-orange gloss, wide boat style,
    #665, 11", from $32 to **$40.00**

Figurine, Oriental lady, yellow gloss, #1308, 10", from $100 to...**$130.00**

Figurine, swans, flecked pastel green gloss, #B2506, 9", from $135 to...**$165.00**

Planter, basketweave on yellow gloss w/brown semi-matt interior, rectangular, #432, 13", from $26 to **$34.00**

Planter, Birch Bark, ivory semi-matt w/brown wash, cinnamon interior, log form, #730, 11", from $85 to ..**$110.00**

Planter, cart form, Celadon Yellow semi-matt, #M1531, 9x7", from $45 to...**$70.00**

Planter, deer figure, turquoise gloss, #1338, 5½", from $85 to...**$100.00**

Planter, gray gloss w/coral interior, sq, #1378, 5½", from $32 to...**$45.00**

Planter, leaves embossed on gray gloss, coral interior, #677, 8½", from $28 to...**$36.00**

Planter, loops embossed on flecked Zephyr Pink gloss, round, #643, 4", from $34 to.....................................**$40.00**

Planter, violet; black semi-matt, #B1403, 5", from $42 to...**$54.00**

Planter, violin form, flecked Zephyr Pink gloss, #M1484, 13", from $45 to...**$55.00**

Vase, Belle, Snow White textured matt w/orange interior, footed, #842, 8", from $36 to **$45.00**

Vase, blue glossy, swirled, #952, 6", from $48 to.......**$60.00**

Vase, blue semi-matt w/white interior, fan form, #892, 7½", from $36 to...**$48.00**

Vase, Chromoline, blue gloss & yellow combination, hand-painted rings, footed, #637, 8", from $72 to.........**$90.00**

Vase, Cinnamon semi-matt w/light green interior, gladiolus style, #416, 12", from $62 to **$75.00**

Vase, Cypress Green semi-matt, compote shape, #1120, 9", from $38 to...**$52.00**

Vase, Decorator Glazed, blue gloss w/gunmetal interior, crackle surface, #1301, 5", from $48 to.................**$60.00**

Vase, flecked Nile Blue gloss, hanging type, silver wing label, #1467, 10½", from $38 to **$46.00**

Vase, flecked Nile Blue gloss w/Colonial Buff interior, fish-handled pitcher form, #220, 10", from $98 to **$130.00**

Vase, flecked yellow gloss, snifter type, #M1442, 8½", from $46 to...**$58.00**

Vase, flecked yellow gloss, spike trimmed, #M1457, 7½", from $42 to...**$56.00**

Vase, flecked Zephyr Pink gloss, pitcher from, #1559, 9½", from $38 to...**$48.00**

Vase, flowers embossed on semi-matt ivory, green interior, low handles, #1360, 7½", from $36 to **$48.00**

Vase, glossy tan w/brown leaf trim, green interior, #1103, 8½", from $48 to...**$64.00**

Vase, ivory semi-matt w/green interior, flat handles, #1168, 7", from $42 to...**$56.00**

Vase, leaves embossed on green, ivory interior, handles, #1115, 7¼", from $52 to...**$68.00**

Vase, pink semi-matt, ivory interior, double handles, #1111, 7½", from $48 to...**$62.00**

Vase, pink semi-matt, ivory interior, footed, #1237, 8", from $48 to...**$56.00**

Vase, Prismatique, Celadon gloss w/Mandarin Orange interior, #798, 8", from $60 to **$74.00**

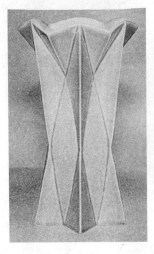

Vase, Prismatique, Persian Blue, white interior, straight angle style, #797, 11", from $68.00 to $82.00. (From the collection of Bev and Duane Brown/Photo courtesy B.L. and R.L. Dollen)

Vase, Stereoline, Bronze Green semi-matt w/Pea Green interior, tulip form, #1440, 6", from $26 to **$34.00**

Vase, Textura, flecked tan gloss w/dark green interior, footed, #B2105, 10", from $38 to **$46.00**

Vase, Tropicana, dark green gloss w/yellow interior, desert flower reserve, #B2004, 10", from $38 to.............**$46.00**

Vase, white semi-matt, fan shaped, handles, #946, from $28 to...**$36.00**

Vase, yellow gloss w/gray interior, fish handle, #220, 10", from $90 to...**$120.00**

Wall pocket, pink semi-matt/ivory, sconce type, #1254, 7", from $72 to...**$95.00**

Dinnerware

Blossom Time, cup & saucer, from $12 to **$16.00**

Blossom Time, plate, dinner; 10½", from $20 to **$26.00**

Bob White, casserole, w/lid & stand, 2-qt, from $60 to..**$75.00**

Bob White, cookie jar, from $125 to.....................**$175.00**

Bob White, cup & saucer, from $14 to **$22.00**

Bob White, hors d'oeuvre holder, from $50 to **$60.00**

Bob White, plate, dinner; 11", from $22 to **$32.00**

Bob White, salt & pepper shakers, bird form, pr, from $42 to...**$40.00**

Bob White, salt & pepper shakers, tall, pr, from $40 to....**$45.00**

Bob White, water cooler, 2-gal, w/stand, from $625 to ..**$775.00**

Brittany, plate, dinner; 10", from $18 to **$22.00**

Ebb Tide, cup & saucer, from $10 to **$15.00**

Ebb Tide, plate, dinner; 10", from $18 to **$14.00**

Harvest, plate, dinner; 10½", from $85 to **$125.00**

Iris, cup & saucer, from $25 to **$30.00**

Iris, plate, dinner; 10½", from $30 to **$35.00**

Iris, spoon rest, from $40 to **$50.00**

Iris, sugar bowl, w/lid, from $25 to **$30.00**

Lotus, cup & saucer, from $13 to **$21.00**

Lotus, plate, dinner; 10½", from $20 to **$24.00**

Lotus, plate, salad; 7", from $8 to.....................**$12.00**

Magnolia, bowl, salad; from $10 to **$15.00**

Morning Glory, plate, dinner; 10½", from $22 to........**$28.00**

Nassau, plate, dinner; 10¼", from $80 to $100.00
Orleans, plate, dinner; 10", from $18 to $22.00
Pepe, bean pot, w/lid, from $32 to............................$40.00

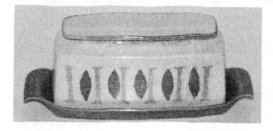

Pepe, butter dish, from $40.00 to $45.00. (Photo courtesy Ted Haun)

Pepe, tray, bread; from $30 to.....................................$38.00
Plum Blossom, bowl, sauce; from $7 to $10.00
Plum Blossom, cup & saucer, from $12 to $18.00
Plum Blossom; plate, dinner; 10½", from $18 to $24.00
Provincial Oomph, bowls, mixing; 6", 8", & 10", complete set from $65 to...$80.00
Provincial Oomph, pitcher, 60-oz, from $35 to..........$45.00
Provincial Oomph, plate, dinner; 10", from $15 to.....$20.00
Random Harvest, casserole, w/lid, from $36 to $40.00
Random Harvest, creamer, from $22 to $26.00
Random Harvest, cup & saucer, from $15 to $18.00
Random Harvest, gravy boat, from $25 to...................$30.00
Random Harvest, pitcher, water; 2-qt, from $40 to.....$48.00
Random Harvest, plate, dinner; 10½", from $22 to....$28.00
Random Harvest, relish tray, from $26 to $34.00
Random Harvest, sugar bowl, w/lid, from $25 to......$30.00
Round-Up, saucer, from $25 to....................................$30.00
Round-Up, sugar bowl, w/lid, from $52 to $65.00
Swirl, pitcher, royal blue gloss w/white interior, 64-oz, from $75 to...$100.00
Tampico, cup & saucer, from $30 to............................$38.00
Tampico, plate, dinner; 10½", from $28 to..................$35.00
Tampico, water cooler, 2-gal, from $525 to..............$700.00
Two Step, plate, dinner; 10½", from $22 to $28.00
Two Step, salt shakers, pr, from $18 to $25.00
Village Green, beverage server, w/lid, 8-cup, from $30 to..$40.00
Village Green, mug, beverage; from $18 to................$25.00
Village Green, pitcher, 10-cup, from $32 to $46.00
Village Green, syrup jug, from $12 to.........................$18.00
Village Green, teapot, 6-cup, from $30 to $40.00
Willow Wind, plate, dinner; 10½", from $26 to $30.00

Regal China

Perhaps best known for their Beam whiskey decanters, the Regal China company (of Antioch, Illinois) also produced some exceptionally well-modeled ceramic novelties, among them their 'hugger' salt and pepper shakers, designed by artist Ruth Van Tellingen Bendel. (Of all pieces about 15% are Bendel and 85% are Van Tellingen.) Facing pairs made to 'lock' together arm-in-arm, some huggies are signed Bendel while others bear the Van Tellingen mark. Another popular design is her Peek-a-Boo Bunny line, depicting the coy little bunny in the red and white 'jammies' who's just about to pop his buttons. (The cookie jar has been reproduced.)

See also Cookie Jars; Old MacDonald's Farm.

Van Tellingen Shakers

Bears, brown, pr, from $25 to $28.00
Boy & dog, white, pr $68.00
Bunnies, solid colors, pr, from $28 to.......................$32.00
Ducks, pr..$38.00
Dutch boy & girl, pr, from $45 to $50.00
Mary & lamb, pr...$60.00
Peek-a-Boo, red dots, lg (has been reproduced), pr, from $450 to..$500.00
Peek-a-Boo, red dots, sm, pr, from $250 to $275.00
Peek-a-Boo, white solid, sm, pr..............................$200.00
Sailor & mermaid, pr, from $225 to $260.00

Miscellaneous

Monkey bank, c C Miller, from $110 to....................$120.00
Salt & pepper shakers, A Nod to Abe, 6th S & P Convention 1991 Chicago Illinois, 3-pc set, from $225 to $250.00
Salt & pepper shakers, cat, sitting w/eyes closed, white w/hat & gold bow, pr..$225.00
Salt & pepper shakers, clown, pr.............................$450.00
Salt & pepper shakers, Dutch Girl, pr $275.00
Salt & pepper shakers, FiFi, pr.................................$450.00
Salt & pepper shakers, fish, mk C Miller, 1-pc...........$55.00
Salt & pepper shakers, French Chef, white w/gold trim, pr, from $250 to..$350.00
Salt & pepper shakers, Humpty Dumpty, unmarked, pr, from $150 to..$175.00
Salt & pepper shakers, Snuggle-Hug Bears, Copr 1958 R Bendel, pr, from $125 to..................................$150.00
Salt & pepper shakers, Snuggle-Hug Bunnies, Copr 1958 R Bendel, pr, from $125..$150.00
Salt & pepper shakers, tulip, pr.................................$50.00
San Joaquin Snack Jar, James B Beam Distilling Co Genuine Regal China 1977, 12", from $100 to.................$125.00

Restaurant China

Restaurant china, also commonly called cafe ware, diner china, institutional china, hotelware, or commercial china, is specifically designed for use in commercial food service. In addition to restaurants, it is used on board airplanes, ships, and trains, as well as in the dining areas of hotels, railroad stations, airports, government offices, military facilities, corporations, schools, hospitals, department and drug stores, amusement and sports parks, churches, clubs, and the like. Though most hotelware produced in America before 1900 has a heavy gauge nonvitrified body, vitrified commercial china made post-1910 includes some of the finest quality ware ever produced, far surpassing that of nonvitrified household products. A break- and chip-resistant rolled or welted edge is characteristic of American ware produced from the 1920s through the 1970s and is still frequently used, though no longer a concern on the very durable high alumina content bodies introduced in the 1960s. In addition, commercial tableware is also made of porcelain, glass-ceramic, glass laminate, glass, melamine, pewter-like metal, and silverplate. Airlines use fine gauge china in first class, due to space and weight factors. And beginning in the late 1970s, fine gauge porcelain and bone china became a popular choice of upscale restaurants, hotels, and country clubs. To reduce loss from wear, most decoration is applied to bisque, then glazed and glaze fired (i.e. underglaze) or to glaze-fired ware, then fired into the glaze (i.e. in-glaze). Until the 1970s many restaurants regularly ordered custom-decorated white, deep tan, blue, or pink-bodied patterns. However, it is estimated that more than 90% of today's commercial ware is plain or embossed white.

For decades collectors have searched for railroad and ship china. Interest in airline china is on the rise. Attractive standard (stock) patterns are now also sought by many. Western motifs and stencil airbrushed designs are especially treasured. The popularity of high quality American-made Oriental designs has increased. Most prefer traditional medium-heavy gauge American vitrified china, though fine china collectors no doubt favor the commercial china products of Pickard or Royal Doulton. While some find it difficult to pass up any dining concern or transportation system top-marked piece, others seek ware that is decorated with a military logo or department store, casino, or amusement park name. Some collect only creamers, others butters or teapots. Some look for ware made by a particular manufacturer (e.g. Tepco), others specific patterns such as Willow or Indian Tree, or pink, blue, or tan body colors. It is currently considered fashionable to serve home-cooked meals on mismatched top-marked hotelware. Reminiscent of days gone by, pre-1960s restaurant or railroad china brings to mind pre-freeway cross-country vacations by car or rail when dining out was an event, unlike the quick stops at today's fast-food and family-style restaurants. For a more through study of the subject, we recommend *Restaurant China, Identification & Value Guide for Restaurant, Airline, Ship & Railroad Dinnerware, Volume 1* and *Volume 2,* by Barbara Conroy (Collector Books); her website with a list of contents and details of her books along with many pages of additional restaurant china information is listed in the Directory.

In the lines below, TM indicates top-marked or side-marked. Please note: Commercial food service china is neither advertising nor souvenir china, since it is not meant to be removed from the restaurant premises.

Advisor: Barbara Conroy (See Directory, Dinnerware)

Restaurant China Online Club: Restaurant Ware Collectors Network; www.restaurantwarecollectors.com/main.htm

Yahoo Clubs: RWCN Restaurant Ware Collectors
http://clubs.yahoo.com/clubs/rwcnrestaurantwarecollectors

Restaurant, Hotel, Department and Drug Store, Casino, and Company Cafeteria China

Arthurdale Inn TM 5½" plate, tan body, Carr 1950s, from $11 to..**$14.00**

Barclay Hotel 10¼" service plate, Syracuse, ca 1970s, from $28 to...**$35.00**

Biltmore Hotel TM 6¾" sq salad, Lune Lamelle, Buffalo, 1930s, from $40 to **$50.00**

Bonanza Hotel & Casino TM 10½" plate, Syracuse, from $30 to..**$40.00**

Bonanza restaurant chain TM 9½" plate, Wallace Desert Ware, late 1950s, from $40 to **$50.00**

Branding Iron-Border pattern sugar bowl w/lid, Tepco, from $38 to...**$45.00**

Canadian Pacific Empress Hotel TM cream pitcher, Steelite backstamp, mid-1970s, from $15 to.....................**$20.00**

Clinton Hotel TM 9" plate, Grindley Hotel Ware, 1930s, from $12 to...**$15.00**

Coronado Beach Hotel 10¾" service plate, Iroquois, 1950s, from $30 to...**$40.00**

Crocker Bank TM 9" plate, Sterling Medallion, 1977, from $15 to..**$20.00**

Dog House TM 6½" plate, Laughlin, 1964, from $30 to.....**$40.00**

Early California-Brown pattern mug, Tepco, from $40 to ..**$50.00**

Emerson Hotel TM match stand, Hutschenreuther Black Knight backstamp, 1920s, from $24 to.................**$30.00**

Far East Cafe TM, 7" plate, Tepco, 1950s-60s, from $15 to **$20.00**

General Motors TM 9¼" plate, Sterling, 1968, from $50 to **$60.00**

Gold Rush Gear pattern cream pitcher, Russel Wright design, 1958 date code, from $40 to **$50.00**

Golfcrest Country Club TM 10½" service plate, Shenango, 1981, from $18 to...**$24.00**

Hacienda Hotel & Casino TM cream pitcher, McNicol, late 1950s, from $60 to **$80.00**

Hotel Dennis 9¾" service plate, Lamberton backstamp, 1920s, from $50 to...**$65.00**

Hotel Kimball 10" service plate, Lamberton backstamp, 1911-23, from $70 to **$90.00**

Jackie Jenson's Bow & Bell TM 5½" plate, Laughlin, 1965, from $40 to...**$50.00**

Kings Arms TM soup, Dunn Bennett Vitreous Ironstone backstamp, 1950s-60s, from $10 to **$12.50**

Kings Castle Hotel & Casino TM 11" service plate, pewter-like, Wilton, from $24 to **$30.00**

Liggett's Drug Store TM 7" plate, Warwick, 1945, from $30 to..**$40.00**

Marineland of the Pacific TM 6¼" plate, Syracuse, 1962, from $50 to...**$60.00**

Mark Hopkins Motel TM Irish coffee mug, Hall, 1950-60s, 10-oz, from $12 to **$15.00**

Maxim's TM 12" plate, Rego, 1980s, from $15 to........**$20.00**

Metropolitan Life Insurance Co TM cup & saucer, Syracuse, 1964, from $30 to...**$40.00**

Miramar Hotel TM 7¼" plate, Mayer, 1940s, from $14 to...**$18.00**

Neptune's Palace TM 6½" plate, Jackson, 1980, from $12 to...**$15.00**

Ox Head-Brown pattern cup & saucer, Homer Laughlin, 1969 date code, from $35 to...**$45.00**

Palace Hotel TM cup & saucer, Palace Hotel backstamp, Shenango, ca 1940s-50s, from $20 to...................**$25.00**

Palace Hotel TM 11½" lg platter, Buffalo, dated 1917, from $30 to...**$40.00**

Red Willow pattern fruit, McCobb shape, 1975, from $12 to...**$15.00**

Rusty Pelican TM mug, Chefware backstamp, 1970s, from $12 to...**$15.00**

Sam's Hof Brau TM mug, Tepco, 1950s-60s, from $40 to ..**$50.00**

San Francisco Giants (stadium restaurant) TM 7¼" plate, Syracuse, 1961, from $75 to.................................**$100.00**

San Francisco Press Club TM 9½" plate, Shenango, 1963, from $18 to...**$24.00**

Schuler's Family Restaurants TM 5½" plate, tan body, Iroquois, from $11 to...**$14.00**

Sears Restaurants TM mug, Syracuse, 1973, from $18 to ..**$24.00**

Southwest Desert pattern cup, Wallace, 1940s, from $20 to...**$25.00**

Tien Hu Crimson pattern 9½" platter, Buffalo, early 1980s, from $8 to...**$10.00**

Transportation and Military China

Air New Zealand Tasman Empire pattern 5¾" plate, Noritake backstamp, 1980s, from $10 to.................................**$15.00**

Alaska Airlines Gold Coast pattern cup, Racket backstamp, 1980s, from $18 to...**$22.00**

Alcoa Steamship Co Alcoa Cavalier pattern fruit, Syracuse backstamp, 1960s, from $30 to.................................**$40.00**

American Airlines American Eagle II pattern cup, Syracuse Airlite backstamp, 1946, from $35 to **$50.00**

American President Lines President Wilson pattern butter pat, Shenango backstamp, late 1930s-early 1940s, from $35 to...**$45.00**

Amtrak National pattern cream pitcher, Hall backstamp, 1970s-ca 1980s, from $10 to.................................**$15.00**

Avianca Columbia Cali pattern cup & saucer, Noritake backstamp, 1960s-70s, from $50 to **$60.00**

Baltimore & Ohio Centenary pattern 6¾" plate, railroad & Shenango backstamps, ca 1949-68, 6¾", from $90 to **$115.00**

Baltimore Mail Line City of Baltimore pattern 7¼" plate, Scammell Trenton backstamp, 1930s, from $50 to..**$60.00**

British Airways Concorde 7" casserole, Royal Doulton backstamp, 1976-ca 1985, from $18 to.........................**$22.00**

Canadian Pacific Foliage pattern crescent salad, Ridgways backstamp, post-1955, from $40 to **$50.00**

Chesapeake Steamship Co Chesapeake Steamship pattern cake cover, no backstamp, 1930s, from $95 to ..**$110.00**

Chicago, Indianapolis & Louisville Monon pattern 7¼" platter, Shenango backstamp, 1951-ca 1967, 7¼", from $100 to...**$125.00**

Delaware & Hudson Canterbury pattern fruit, ca 1926-46, from $75 to...**$100.00**

Delta Airlines Widget pattern footed cup, Mayer, 1970s-80s, from $5 to...**$7.00**

Delta Queen Steamboat Co Mississippi Queen pattern 10¾" service plate, Syracuse backstamp, ca 1987, from $40 to...**$50.00**

Department of Navy TM cup & saucer, Jackson backstamp, ca 1982, from $18 to...**$24.00**

Eastern Air Lines Eastern Platinum Line pattern cup & saucer, Rego backstamp, 1980s-91, from $15 to **$18.00**

Eastern Steamship Lines Eastern Green pattern double egg cup, Buffalo (unmarked), 1920s, from $75 to **$100.00**

Erie Susquehanna pattern 10" celery, Buffalo backstamp, 1920s, from $100 to...**$125.00**

Hawaiian Airlines Honolulu pattern 5" plate, Abco backstamp, 1980s-90s, from $10 to.............................**$12.00**

Holland America Line 'Rotterdam' pattern, 8" pickle, NASM script initials, 1970, from $25.00 to $30.00. (Photo courtesy Barbara Conroy)

Home Lines Oceanic pattern 9½" plate, Richard Ginori backstamp, 1980s, from $18 to.................................**$22.00**

Japan Airlines Initials pattern 9" plate, Noritake backstamp, 1960s, from $30 to...**$40.00**

KLM Royal Class pattern napkin holder, Hutschenreuther backstamp, late 1980s-95, from $8 to...................**$10.00**

Knutsen OAS Knutsen pattern butter pat, Fuji Trading Co backstamp, from $24 to...**$30.00**

Malaysian Airline System Golden Club pattern salt & pepper shakers, Noritake backstamp, 1980s, pr, from $28 to.**$35.00**

Moore-McCormack Lines Rio pattern celery, 1950s, from $45 to...**$60.00**

National Airlines Sun King pattern 7" casserole, Sterling China backstamp, 1970s, from $24 to **$30.00**

New York Central Dewitt Clinton pattern cup, railroad backstamp, ca 1925-51, from $35 to **$40.00**

Northwest Airlines Regal Imperial pattern 6¾" plate, Royal Doulton backstamp, 1983-ca 1987, from $20 to...**$25.00**

NYK Line Kamakaura Maru pattern cup & saucer, AD; Sango backstamp, from $45 to...**$60.00**

Pan American World Airways TM 6½" ashtray, Noritake backstamp, 1970s, from $40 to.................................**$50.00**

Prudential Lines Santa Magdalena pattern 8" plate, Jackson backstamp, ca 1978, 8", from $22 to **$28.00**

Qantas Airways Alice Springs pattern butter, Royal Grafton backstamp, ca 1970s-85, from $18 to **$22.00**

Royal Caribbean Cruise Line Nordic Prince pattern ashtray, Schmidt Porcelana backstamp, 1970s, from $12 to .**$15.00**

Seaboard Air Line Railway Miami pattern 11" celery, OPCO backstamp, 1920s, from $150 to **$175.00**

States Line California pattern 6¼" plate, Jackson backstamp, ca 1976, from $18 to **$24.00**

Union Pacific Challenger pattern 6½" plate, Syracuse Econo-Rim backstamp, ca 1937-54, from $55 to **$65.00**

United Air Lines United Blue TM 6" L casserole, Hall backstamp, 1946-54, from $28 to **$35.00**

United Airlines Connoisseur pattern 5½" plate, Noritake backstamp, 1992-96, from $7 to **$9.00**

United States Army Medical Department TM cream pitcher, Shanango backstamp, 1930s, from $18 to **$24.00**

United States Lines Leviathan pattern cream pitcher, Jackson backstamp, dated 1926, from $125 to **$160.00**

United States Senate TM cup & saucer, Scammell's Trenton backstamp, ca 1920s, from $100 to **$140.00**

US Navy Captain's mess flag TM 6½" plate, Buffalo backstamp, early 1960s, from $15 to **$20.00**

Rock 'n Roll Memorabilia

Ticket stubs and souvenirs issued at rock concerts, posters of artists that have reached celebrity status, and merchandise such as dolls, games, clothing, etc., that was sold through retail stores during the heights of their careers are just the things that interest collectors of rock 'n roll memorabilia. Some original, one-of-a-kind examples — for instance, their instruments, concert costumes, and personal items — often sell at the large auction galleries in the East where they've realized very high-dollar prices. For more information, Greg Moore has written *A Price Guide to Rock and Roll Collectibles* which is distributed by L-W Book Sales. *Collector's Guide to TV Toys & Memorabilia* by Greg Davis and Bill Morgan contains additional information and photos (it is published by Collector Books).

Note: Most posters sell in the range of $5.00 to $10.00; those listed below are the higher-end examples in excellent or better condition.

See also Beatles Collectibles; Elvis Presley Memorabilia; Magazines; Movie Posters; Pin-Back Buttons; Records.

Advisor: Bojo/Bob Gottuso (See Directory, Character and Personality Collectibles)

ABBA, annual, 1978, EX................................**$25.00**

ABBA, press kit, includes 8x10" photos+6 bio sheets, etc, 1997, VG+...**$16.00**

AC/DC, back patch, Angus stabbed w/guitar, If You Want Blood, 1991, 11½x14" tapering to 9½" at bottom, M.............**$22.00**

AC/DC, bandana, The Razors Edge, Brockum, 1990, 21x21", M...**$15.00**

AC/DC, pin-back button, Angus devil character & logo enameling on silver-tone, 1996, 1½"............................**$12.00**

AC/DC, tour book, Blow Up Your Video, England, 1988, oversize, 18 pages, VG+......................................**$25.00**

Adam Ant, concert ticket, Riverside CA, Mar 31, 1983, for special guest, unused **$12.00**

Adam Ant, pin-back button, chest-up photo portrait, 1½", M...**$2.00**

Aerosmith, concert ticket, Springfield MA, Nov 3, 1974, general admission, unused..................................**$49.00**

Aerosmith, pass, Get a Grip '93-'95, nail-in-nose image, VIP, cloth, EX..**$18.00**

Aerosmith, tour book, Get a Grip, 1993-94, full size, 22 pages, EX..**$26.00**

Air Supply, pin-back button, Air Supply logo, red & white on blue, 1¾" dia, EX......................................**$3.00**

Alice Cooper, concert ticket, Keil Auditorium, St Louis MO, January 16, 1988, unused..............................**$18.00**

Allman Bros, tour book, Richard Betts American Music Show, 1974, 18 pages, EX **$65.00**

Anthrax, necklace, silver-tone Anthrax logo on link chain, all metal, Brockum, M...................................**$15.00**

Anthrax, patch, iron-on diecut of Anthrax logo, 10".....**$8.00**

Anthrax, pin-back button, goofy face on silver-tone metal, Brockum, 1990, 1¼", M.....................................**$8.00**

B-52s, book, The B-52s, Della Martini, Wise Publications, 1990, M w/poster.......................................**$15.00**

Backstreet Boys, pin-back button, group photo, 1997, 2"+, M...**$3.00**

Barry Manilow, sweatshirt, Manilow checkered logo, collared, zipper front, Jerzees, 1997......................**$45.00**

Bay City Rollers, annual, 1977, EX............................**$25.00**

Beach Boys, pass, logo & surfer, cloth, mid-1980s.....**$10.00**

Beach Boys, shorts, embroidered Beach Boys, Sunkist logo & 25th Anniversary Tour, poly/cotton, promotional, M..**$30.00**

Billy Joel, patch, Storm Front flag, flag shape, 3x3½", M...**$8.00**

Bon Jovi, book, Bon Jovi Live!, full-color pull-out poster, Omnibus, 1996.......................................**$10.00**

Bon Jovi, patch, Cross Road, cross logo, silkscreened, made in England, 11x14".......................................**$15.00**

Bruce Springsteen, book, Down Thunder Road, Marc Eliot w/Mike Appel, softcover, 350+ pages, EX............**$10.00**

Bruce Springsteen, tour book, Born in the USA World Tour 1984-85, 34 pages, M....................................**$45.00**

Bruce Springsteen, tour book, World Tour 1993, 30 pages, NM...**$25.00**

Bryan Adams, book, Inside Story, Hugh Gregory, United Kingdom import, 1992, M....................................**$12.00**

Cheap Trick, T-shirt, Woke Up w/a Monster, repeating logos on back on black, 1994, M..............................**$36.00**

Cheap Trick, tour book, Cheap Trick in Concert, 1979, 26 pages...**$35.00**

Cher, mug, Heart of Stone, heart & sword logo, 1990..**$35.00**

Cher, tour book, Heart of Stone Tour, 1989, 20+ pages, EX **$45.00**

David Bowie, tour book, Glass Spider Tour, 1987, 24 pages, VG **$20.00**

David Cassidy, annuals, 1974 & 1975, EX, ea **$30.00**

David Cassidy, concert poster, Curtis Hixon Hall, Tampa FL, Sept 26, lg image of David, early 1970s, 22x15", VG+ **$40.00**

Def Leppard, patch, Hysteria triangle silkscreened on black, sew on, 1987, 3¼x4" **$8.00**

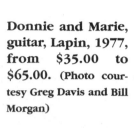

Donnie and Marie, guitar, Lapin, 1977, from $35.00 to $65.00. (Photo courtesy Greg Davis and Bill Morgan)

Doors, poster, shirtless Jim Morrison, oblong, black & white w/red border, 1994, 36x12", NM...............................**$8.00**

Duran Duran, book, Duran Duran in Their Own Words, Omnibus Press, 1983, softcover, 32 pages, VG+ w/G- poster..**$15.00**

Duran Duran, pin-back button, Duran Duran & group image on white, 1983, 1¼", VG **$2.00**

Eagles, pin-back button, Don Henley & star logo on blue, concert issue..**$3.00**

Eagles, tour book, 1976, 26 pages, EX......................**$25.00**

Elton John, poster, Breaking Hearts Tour, medium stock paper, 1986, 14x17", EX **$25.00**

Elton John, tour book, Breaking Hearts, gold cover, 26 pages, EX..**$10.00**

Fleetwood Mac, magazine, BAM, group on cover w/multi-page article, October 23, 1987, VG **$35.00**

Fleetwood Mac, pass, After Show Guest, The Other Side of the Mirror Tour, octagonal cloth, 1989....................**$8.00**

Fleetwood Mac, postcard, The Wave, band shown waving, 1990, M **$6.00**

Iron Maiden, bandana, Evil That Men Do, face & bars on black, 22" sq..**$12.00**

Iron Maiden, wallet, Angel & Gambler artwork on black nylon, tri-fold **$18.00**

James Taylor, shirt, James Taylor Ball of Sound embroidered on dark green, short sleeve, cotton, EX................**$28.00**

Janet Jackson, book, Out of the Madness, unauthorized biography, Bart Andrews, paperback, 1994, 300+ pages, M **$15.00**

Jimmi Hendrix, clothes hanger, cardboard, Saunders, 1960s, unpunched, EX+..**$125.00**

Jimmy Buffett, T-shirt, parrot holding a Corona & J Buffett, crew across back, c 1986, M **$45.00**

Joe Cocker, T-shirt, Night Calls World Tour 1992 on black, M **$15.00**

KISS, belt buckle, black w/silver letters & border, 1977, M **$30.00**

KISS, book, The Dynasty Tour, M **$70.00**

KISS, chair, inflatable, M **$80.00**

KISS, Colorforms Adventure Set, MIB.......................**$120.00**

KISS, concert ticket, Psycho Circus, Omaha Civic Arena, December 16, 1988, unused **$15.00**

KISS, costume, Gene Simmons, 1978, sm, EXIB.......**$160.00**

KISS, jigsaw puzzle, Casse-Tete, 1977, NMIB.............**$50.00**

KISS, key chain, 4 different, Aucoin, 1977, NM, ea **$50.00**

KISS, necklace, MIB (w/photo card)..........................**$35.00**

KISS, pin-back button, group image & KISS logo, KISS Co, 1984, 1¼", M..**$5.00**

KISS, sleeping bag, Aucion Management, 1978, NM ..**$500.00**

KISS, T-shirt, KISS Revenge World Tour 1992, group image, M..**$22.00**

KISS, window shade, KISS Dynasty, Por View Screen Co, 35x64", MIP **$30.00**

Led Zeppelin, necklace, diecut crucifix w/black enamel & Led Zeppelin on link silver-tone chain, Winterland, 1990..**$12.00**

Led Zeppelin, poster, 4 individual color photos on black w/4 logos at bottom, 1991, 24x36", EX......................**$16.00**

Led Zeppelin, sticker, stage photo & Zoso logo, refractive plastic, 1995, 5" sq **$6.00**

Led Zeppelin, T-shirt, Page Plant Official Concert Tour, double-sided printing, 1995, lg, unused, M................**$10.00**

Lynyrd Skynyrd, baseball cap, Lynyrd Skynyrd & LS wing logo embroidered on black, M **$15.00**

Lynyrd Skynyrd, concert ticket, Lynyrd Skynyrd Tribute Tour, May 19, 1988, unused..**$10.00**

Lynyrd Skynyrd, pin-back button, Second Helping, face images, 1983, 1¼", VG **$8.00**

Madonna, calendar, 12 color images, Winterland, 1997, 12x12", M, sealed..**$12.00**

Madonna, pin-back button, Girlie Show logo & XXX, 1½", M **$3.00**

Madonna, poster, Blond Ambition World Tour 1990, bareback Madonna, 24x36", M..**$15.00**

Meat Loaf, T-shirt, Bat Out of Hell on front, Everything Louder Than Everything Else World Tour 93, 94, 96, M **$17.00**

Meat Loaf, tour book, Bat Out of Hell II Back Into Hell, 1993, 24 pages, EX **$18.00**

Metallica, book, Metallica Live!, Mark Putterford, Omnibus Press, 1994, M w/poster..**$10.00**

Metallica, patch, diecut embroidered logo, white on black, iron-on, 10"..**$7.00**

Michael Jackson, pass, History World Tour, Michael image & Before Show on cloth..**$12.00**

Michael Jackson, pin-back button, Dangerous, 1½", M.**$3.00**

Michael Jackson, T-shirt, lion face, Michael Jackson Dangerous King of Pop, M $20.00

Monkees, annual, 1967, EX+..........................$50.00

Monkees, book, Who's Got the Button, Whitman, 1968, hardcover, EX $20.00

Monkees, concert ticket, 20th Anniversary Tour, Mississippi, 1986 ....$15.00

Monkees, fan club kit, folder w/lg assortment of material, incomplete, 1967, 11½x8¾", EX+..................$85.00

Monkees, finger puppets, vinyl w/cloth clothes, Remco, 1970, EX, ea $35.00

Monkees, flip book, black & white photo images that appear in motion when flipped quickly, 1967, EX..........$12.00

Monkees, pass, Justus 1997 World Tour, guitar logo on cloth $10.00

Monkees, pin-back button set, 4-pc w/head images of ea member, 1966, MIB..................$40.00

Motley Crue, postcard, repeating Motley Crue & star logos, 1994, unused $5.00

Motley Crue, sticker, skull & handcuffs, 1983, 4½" dia...$5.00

New Kids on the Block, T-shirt, cartoon images, New Kids logos on black, M $15.00

New Kids on the Block, T-shirt, Jonathan photo & New Kids logo, M $16.00

New Kids on the Block, tapestry, 5 head-to-foot images w/logos, door size, 1989, M..................$15.00

New Kids on the Block, video, Hangin' Tough, 30 minutes, 1989, M, sealed $18.00

Osmonds, annual, 1976, EX..................$25.00

Ozzy Osbourne, patch, Ozzy logo iron-on transfer, 3½". $3.00

Ozzy Osbourne, tapestry, Ozzy Osbourne & bat logos on black satin, 1986, 20x20", M..................$15.00

Partridge Family, book, Partridge Family Album, Joey Green w/forward by Shirley Jones, softcover, 1994, 330 pages, EX..................$12.00

Pat Benatar, sticker, Pat w/open mouth & Benatar logo, 1984, 4½"..................$6.00

Paula Abdul, tour book, Under My Spell, M $12.00

Pink Floyd, T-shirt, screaming face & Pink Floyd (both sides) on black, M..................$15.00

Queen, book, New Visual Documentary, Ken Dean, Omnibus Press, 1991, M..................$15.00

REM, coaster, REM New Adventures in Hi-Fi & landscape, cardboard, 3½x3½" sq, M..................$12.00

Richard Marx, tour book, Repeat Offender World Tour, 1989, 26 pages, EX $30.00

Rod Stewart, concert pin, Rod Stewart World Tour 1978-79, gold-tone w/red enamel, 1" rectangle, NM..................$8.00

Rod Stewart, scarf, Rod in red leather, European Tour 1983, EX..................$45.00

Rolling Stones, book, It's Only Rock 'n Roll...My On the Road Adventures, Chet Flippo, St Martin's Press, 1985, EX..................$20.00

Rolling Stones, pin-back button, diecast devil's head, all metal, 1994, 2"..................$18.00

Rolling Stones, poster, David Byrd (nude) artwork, full color, 1969, 14x21", M..................$18.00

Rolling Stones, program, Steel Wheels North American Tour 1989, 22 pages, VG..................$18.00

Rolling Stones, shorts, Rolling Stones Steel Wheels on white cotton..................$13.00

Rolling Stones, tour book, American Tour '81, EX......$15.00

Rolling Stones, tour book, European Tour '82, VG.....$20.00

Scorpions, tour book, Crazy World tour 1990-91, 22 pages, M..................$15.00

Steve Miller, T-shirt, Steve Miller Band Live in the USA repeating logo, Spring Tour 1996, M..................$15.00

Sting, sweat shirt, Sting & Soul Cages embroidered on black, zipper front, NM..................$30.00

Sting, tour book, Soul Cages, 1991, 31 pages, NM $15.00

Ted Nugent, sticker, shirtless Ted w/mouth open & arm raised, 1982, 4½" dia $3.00

Three Dog Night, concert poster, An Evening With..., Curtis-Hixon Hall, Tampa FL, August 13, 1970s, 22x14", NM.............$30.00

U2, patch, Rattle & Hum w/guitar player image, woven, felt back, 3x4"..................$8.00

U2, scarf, U2 Zooropa 93 logo, yellow silkscreen on blue, knit fabric, 7x46"..................$25.00

U2, T-shirt, Zooropa logo & US stars logo, 1993 on black, M..................$15.00

Van Halen, tour book, Texas World Music Festival, 1978, oversize, 18 pages, NM $65.00

Various artists, Color & Re-Color book, over 400 full-figure rock star combinations possible, Magic Wand, 1967, 14", EX+ $50.00

Who, promo button, Who Are You, MCA Cords, 1978, 2¼", VG+..................$12.00

Rookwood

Although this company was established in 1879, it continued to produce commercial artware until it closed in 1967. Located in Cincinnati, Ohio, Rookwood is recognized today as the largest producer of high-quality art pottery ever to operate in the United States.

Most of the pieces listed here are from the later years of production, but we've included some early pieces as well. With few exceptions, all early Ohio art pottery companies produced an artist-decorated brown-glaze line — Rookwood's was called Standard. Among their other early lines were Sea Green, Iris, Jewel Porcelain, Wax Matt, and Vellum.

Virtually all of Rookwood's pieces are marked. The most familiar mark is the 'reverse R'-P monogram. It was first used in 1886, and until 1900 a flame point was added above it to represent each passing year. After the turn of the century, a Roman numeral below the monogram was used to indicate the current year. In addition to the dating mark, a die-stamped number was used to identify the shape.

The Cincinnati Art Galleries routinely hold large and important cataloged auctions. The full-color catalogs sometime contain company history and listings of artists and designers with their monograms (as well as company codes and trademarks). Collectors now regard them as an excellent source for information and study.

Ashtray, #1084, 1947, owl beside tray, white matt, 4¼" H...**$200.00**

Ashtray, #2602, 1934, frog beside tray, light green gloss, 3x6½"...**$550.00**

Ashtray, #6097, 1950, frog figural, green matt w/crystalline effect, 2⅞"...**$375.00**

Bowl, console; #6826, 1950, celadon green gloss, 4x12½"...**$60.00**

Box, 1955, Oriental decor, turquoise gloss, 3¼" H.........**$160.00**

Box, #2839, 1945, green gloss, 4¾" sq, NM.............**$150.00**

Candle holders, #2836, 1930, lotus form, green over pink, 3½", pr..**$250.00**

Creamer & sugar bowl, #547, 1946, green matt, NM..**$50.00**

Figurine, #6661, 1945, kitten, white matt, 1½x3½"...**$900.00**

Paperweight, #1855, 1934, geese (2) figural, ivory matt, 4¼"..**$200.00**

Paperweight, #6156, 1932, gazelle figural, white matt, 5⅜"...**$400.00**

Paperweight, #6160, 1946, rabbit figural, ivory matt, 3"..**$300.00**

Paperweight, #6383, 1946, canary figural, ivory matt, 3⅝", NM **$130.00**

Pencil holder/ashtray, ca 1950, pink gloss w/black wooden ball in center, 3½"..**$30.00**

Tile, #2043, 1930, molded cockatoo, 5½"..................**$200.00**

Tile, #3077, 1930, molded parrot, pastels, 5¾" sq **$180.00**

Tray, #1139, 1950, molded rook, mottled tan gloss, X, 5½" **$150.00**

Tray, #7149, 1949, mottled gray gloss, 7½" dia..........**$90.00**

Tray, #7216, 1964, mottled purple gloss, 7½" dia **$300.00**

Tray, #7232, 1944, orange gloss, 7" dia......................**$50.00**

Tray, pin; #1084, 1939, owl figure, 4½".....................**$250.00**

Trivet, #2351, 1943, molded sea gull, multicolor, 5⅞" dia ..**$325.00**

Trivet, 33077, 1940, molded parrot, multicolor **$325.00**

Vase, #2330, 1934, green matt, 3 angular handles, 4⅞" ..**$200.00**

Vase, #2428, 1940, green matt, 3 handles, 5½".........**$200.00**

Vase, #2587E, 1948, Candy Apple Red gloss, 5" **$130.00**

Vase, #5292DD, 1954, celadon green gloss, X, 7".......**$70.00**

Vase, #6029, 1930, green matt, 6¼" **$200.00**

Vase, #6098, 1948, burgundy gloss, 5" **$130.00**

Vase, #6204C, 1951, turquoise glossy drip over gray mottled gloss, 7" **$180.00**

Vase, #6303, 1932, goldstone w/copper dust crystalline, 4½" **$500.00**

Vase, #6311, 1938, Coromandel Red gloss, 7½".......**$400.00**

Vase, #6317F, 1933, Coromandel w/red, orange & gray tones, 4" **$350.00**

Vase, #6337, 1944, tan gloss, 6½"..............................**$100.00**

Vase, #6350, 1937, molded cardinal & butterflies, blue matt, 4½" **$170.00**

Vase, #6432, obscured date, molded flowers on green gloss, 3½" **$60.00**

Vase, #6434, 1954, floral, light blue gloss, 5½" **$110.00**

Vase, #6434, 1954, floral, yellow gloss, 5½" **$110.00**

Vase, #6474, 1958, molded flowers on tan gloss, flattened form, 4"..**$60.00**

Vase, #6503, 1936, brown drip w/blue highlights over ribbed body, 4¼"..**$160.00**

Vase, #6632, 1945, molded flowers on ivory matt, 5"..**$120.00**

Vase, #6632, 1946, molded flowers on peach matt, 5½"..**$150.00**

Vase, #6660F, 1950, thick Bengal Brown, 3¼" **$140.00**

Vase, #7081, 1951, celadon green gloss, 3" **$150.00**

Vase, #7086, 1951, banded form, yellow & gray gloss, 7"...**$700.00**

Vase, #7137, 1959, red gloss, 9".................................**$140.00**

Vase, #7137, 1959, yellow gloss, 7¾".........................**$80.00**

Vase, #778, 1946, cream gloss, 10"............................**$150.00**

Vase, #778, 1951, peach gloss, 9½"............................**$220.00**

Vase, bud; #6591, 1959, calla lily form, Violet Gray, 4¾"..**$150.00**

Rooster and Roses

Back in the 1940s, newlyweds might conceivably have received some of this imported Japanese-made kitchenware as a housewarming gift. They'd no doubt be stunned to see the prices it's now bringing! Rooster and Roses (Ucagco called it Early Provincial) is one of those lines of novelty ceramics from the '40s and '50s that are among today's hottest collectibles. Ucagco was only one of several importers whose label you'll find on this pattern; among other are Py, ACSON, Norcrest, and Lefton. The design is easy to spot — there's the rooster, yellow breast with black crosshatching, brown head and, of course, the red crest and waddle, large full-blown roses with green leaves and vines, and a trimming of yellow borders punctuated by groups of brown lines. (You'll find another line having blue flowers among the roses, and one with a rooster with a green head and a green border. These are not considered Rooster and Roses by purist collectors, though there is a market for them as well.) The line is fun to collect, since shapes are so diversified. Even though there has been relatively little communication among collectors, more than eighty items have been reported and no doubt more will surface.

Advisor: Jacki Elliott (See Directory, Rooster and Roses)

Ashtray, rectangular, part of set, 3x2"............................**$9.50**

Ashtray, round or sq, sm, from $15 to.........................**$25.00**

Ashtray, sq, lg, from $35 to...**$40.00**

Basket, flared sides, 6", from $45 to **$65.00**

Bell, from $55 to...**$95.00**

Bell, rooster & chicken on opposing sides, rare, from $95 to...**$125.00**

Biscuit jar, w/wicker handle, from $65 to...................**$95.00**

Bonbon dish, pedestal base, minimum value **$55.00**

Bowl, cereal; from $14 to..**$25.00**

Bowl, rice; on saucer, from $25 to **$35.00**

Bowl, 8", from $45 to..**$55.00**

Box, trinket; w/lid, round, from $25 to **$35.00**

Box, 4½x3½", from $25 to...**$35.00**

Bread plate, from $15 to...**$25.00**

Butter dish, ¼-lb, from $20 to **$25.00**

Candle warmer (for tea & coffeepots), from $25 to...**$45.00**

Candy dish, flat chicken-shaped tray w/3-dimensional chicken head, made in 3 sizes, from $75 to **$100.00**

Candy dish, w/3-dimensional leaf handle, from $25 to ..**$45.00**

Canister set, round, 4-pc, from $150 to **$175.00**

Canister set, sq, 4-pc, from $100 to **$150.00**

Canister set, stacking, rare, minimum value.............**$150.00**

Carafe, no handle, w/stopper lid, 8", from $65 to **$85.00**

Carafe, w/handle & stopper lid, 8"...........................**$85.00**

Casserole dish, w/lid, from $65 to **$85.00**

Castor set in revolving wire rack, 2 cruets, mustard jar & salt & pepper shakers, rare, from $125 to................**$150.00**

Chamberstick, saucer base, ring handle, from $25 to.**$35.00**

Cheese dish, slant lid, from $40 to...........................**$55.00**

Cigarette box w/2 trays, hard to find, from $65 to.....**$75.00**

Coaster, ceramic disk embedded in round wood tray, rare, minimum value..**$45.00**

Coffee grinder, rare, minimum value **$150.00**

Coffeepot, 'Coffee' in neck band, w/creamer & sugar bowl, both w/appropriately lettered neck bands, 3 pcs, from $75 to...**$85.00**

Condiment set, 2 cruets, salt & pepper shakers w/mustard jar on tray, miniature, from $50 to...........................**$75.00**

Condiment set, 2 cruets, salt & pepper shakers w/mustard jar atop wire & wood holder, 4 spice canisters below, minimum value **$125.00**

Cookie jar, ceramic handles, from $85 to **$100.00**

Creamer & sugar bowl, w/lid, lg...............................**$25.00**

Creamer & sugar bowl on rectangular tray, from $65 to ..**$75.00**

Cruets, cojoined w/twisted necks, sm.......................**$45.00**

Cruets, oil & vinegar, flared bases, pr......................**$45.00**

Cruets, oil & vinegar, sq, lg, pr from $30 to...............**$35.00**

Cup and saucer, $25.00; dinner plate, from $25.00 to $35.00; side salad, crescent shape, hard to find, from $50.00 to $60.00. (Photo courtesy Jacki Elliott)

Cruets, oil & vinegar, w/salt & pepper shakers in shadow box, from $55 to **$75.00**

Demitasse pot, w/6 cups & saucers, minimum value.**$175.00**

Egg cup, from $20 to..**$25.00**

Egg cup on tray, from $35 to **$45.00**

Egg plate, from $55 to..**$65.00**

Flowerpot, buttress handles, 5", from $35 to..............**$45.00**

Hamburger press, wood w/embedded ceramic tray, round, minimum value...**$24.00**

Instant coffee jar, no attached spoon holder on side, minimum value..**$35.00**

Instant coffee jar, spoon-holder tube on side, rare.....**$45.00**

Jam & jelly containers, cojoined, w/lids & spoons, from $35 to **$45.00**

Jam & jelly containers, cojoined, w/lids & spoons, w/loop handles & lids, very rare **$85.00**

Jam jar, attached underplate, from $35 to..................**$45.00**

Ketchup or mustard jar, flared cylinder w/lettered label, ea from $25 to...**$30.00**

Lamp, pinup, made from either a match holder or a salt box, ea from $75 to **$100.00**

Lazy Susan on wood pedestal, round covered box at center, 4 sections around outside (2 w/lids), from $150 to..**$250.00**

Marmalade, round base w/tab handles, w/lid & spoon, minimum value, from $35 to.................................**$55.00**

Match holder, wall mount, from $65 to **$85.00**

Measuring cup set, 4-pc w/matching ceramic rack, from $45 to **$65.00**

Measuring spoons on 8" ceramic spoon-shaped rack, from $40 to **$55.00**

Mug, rounded bottom, medium, from $20 to.............**$25.00**

Mug, straight upright bar handle, lg, from $20 to.......**$35.00**

Napkin holder, from $30 to **$40.00**

Pipe holder/ashtray, from $30 to **$50.00**

Pitcher, bulbous, 5", from $25 to **$30.00**

Pitcher, lettered Milk on neck band, from $22.50 to ..**$35.00**

Pitcher, 3½", from $15 to **$20.00**

Planter, rolling pin shape, rare, minimum value.........**$50.00**

Plate, luncheon; from $15 to **$25.00**

Platter, 12", from $35 to..**$55.00**

Recipe box, part of shadow box set, from $25 to **$35.00**

Relish tray, 2 round wells w/center handle, 12", from $35 to..**$40.00**

Relish tray, 3 wells w/center handle, from $55 to **$65.00**

Rolling pin, minimum value **$50.00**

Salad fork, spoon & salt & pepper shakers w/wooden handles, on ceramic wall rack, minimum value........**$55.00**

Salad fork & spoon w/wooden handles on ceramic wall-mount rack, from $45 to **$65.00**

Salt & pepper shakers, drum shape w/long horizontal ceramic handle, lg, pr, from $30 to................................**$40.00**

Salt & pepper shakers, w/applied rose, sq, pr...........**$23.00**

Salt & pepper shakers, w/handle, pr, from $15 to......**$20.00**

Salt & pepper shakers, w/lettered neck band, pr.......**$25.00**

Salt & pepper shakers, 4", pr, from $15 to **$20.00**

Salt box, wooden lid...**$60.00**

Salt box, wooden lid, from $45 to **$55.00**

Shaker, cheese or sugar, 7", from $20 to **$30.00**

Skillet, 4"..**$18.00**

Slipper, 3-dimensional rose on toe, rare, from $85 to **$125.00**

Snack tray w/cup, oval, 2-pc, minimum value............**$45.00**

Snack tray w/cup, rectangular, 2-pc, from $50 to.......**$60.00**

Spice rack, 3 rows of 2 curved-front containers, together forming half-cylinder shape w/flat back **$85.00**

Spice set, 9 sq containers in wood frame w/pull-out ceramic tray in base, from $75 to......................................**$95.00**

Spoon holder, w/lg salt shaker in well on side extension, from $20 to..**$25.00**

Stacking tea set, teapot, creamer & sugar bowl, from $70 to **$90.00**

Syrup pitcher, w/2 sm graduated pitchers on tray, minimum value **$60.00**

Tazza (footed tray), 3x6" dia.......................................**$45.00**

Teapot, from $55 to..**$65.00**

Toast holder, minimum value **$75.00**

Tray, closed tab handles ea end, 11", from $25 to **$30.00**

Tray, round w/chamberstick-type handle on 1 side, 5½", from $15 to **$20.00**

Tumbler, from $15 to...**$20.00**

Vase, round w/flat sides, 6", from $20 to **$30.00**

Wall hanger, teapot shape, pr.....................................**$90.00**

Wall pocket, lavabo, 2-pc, mounted on board, from $85 to **$125.00**

Wall pocket, scalloped top, bulbous bottom, from $55 to **$65.00**

Wall pocket, teapots, facing ea other, pr, minimum value ..**$90.00**

Watering can, from $25 to...**$30.00**

Roselane Sparklers

Beginning as a husband and wife operation in the late 1930s, the Roselane Pottery Company of Pasadena, California, expanded their inventory from the figurines they originally sold to local florists to include a complete line of decorative items that eventually were shipped to Alaska, South America, and all parts of the United States.

One of their lines was the Roselane Sparklers. Popular in the '50s, these small animal and bird figures were airbrush decorated and had rhinestone eyes. They're fun to look for, and though prices are rising steadily, they're still not terribly expensive.

If you'd like to learn more, there's a chapter on Roselane in *The Collector's Encyclopedia of California Pottery, Second Edition,* by Jack Chipman.

Advisor: Lee Garmon (See Directory, Advertising, Reddy Kilowatt)

Angelfish, 4½", from $20 to **$25.00**

Basset hound, sitting, 4", from $15 to **$18.00**

Basset hound pup, 2", from $12 to **$15.00**

Bulldog, fierce expression, looking right, 2", from $12 to..**$15.00**

Bulldog, fierce expression, looking up & right, jeweled collar, lg, from $22 to **$25.00**

Bulldog, sitting, slender body, looking right, 6"..........**$25.00**

Cat, mama holding babies, 5", from $40 to **$45.00**

Cat, recumbent, head turned right, tail & paws tucked under body, from $20 to..**$25.00**

Cat, Siamese, looking straight ahead, no collar, 5" **$45.00**

Cat, Siamese, sitting, looking straight ahead, jeweled collar, 7", from $40 to **$50.00**

Cat, sitting, head turned right, tail out behind, from $25 to **$28.00**

Cat, standing, head turned right, tail arched over back, jeweled collar, 5½", from $25 to **$30.00**

Chihuahua, sitting, left paw raised, looking straight ahead, 7"...**$28.00**

Cocker spaniel, 4½", from $15 to..............................**$20.00**

Deer, standing, head turned right, looking downward, 5½"...**$25.00**

Deer w/antlers, standing, jeweled collar, 4½", from $22 to **$28.00**

Elephant, sitting on hind quarters, 6"........................**$28.00**

Elephant, trunk raised, striding, jeweled headpiece, 6" ..**$28.00**

Fawn, legs folded under body, 4x3½"........................**$25.00**

Fawn, upturned head, 4x3½" **$20.00**

Fawn, 4½x1½"...**$20.00**

Kangaroo, mama holding babies, 4½", from $40 to ...**$45.00**

Kitten, sitting, 1¾" **$12.00**

Owl, very stylized, lg round eyes, teardrop-shaped body, lg **$25.00**

Owl, 3½" **$15.00**

Owl, 5¼" **$25.00**

Owl, 7"...**$30.00**

Owl baby, 2¼", from $12 to **$15.00**

Pheasants (1 pink, 3¾", 1 blue, 5"), looking back, pr, from $30 to **$35.00**

Pig, lg..**$25.00**

Pouter pigeon, 3½"...**$20.00**

Racoon, standing, 4½", from $20 to **$25.00**

Whippet, sitting, 7½", from $25 to **$28.00**

Rosemeade

The Wahpeton Pottery Company of Wahpeton, North Dakota, chose the trade name Rosemeade for a line of bird and animal figurines, novelty salt and pepper shakers, bells, and many other items which were sold from the 1940s to the 1960s through gift stores and souvenir shops in that part of the country. They were marked with either a paper label or an ink stamp; the name Prairie Rose was also used. See *Collector's Encyclopedia of Rosemeade Pottery* by Darlene Hurst Dommel (Collector Books) for more information.

Advisor: Bryce Farnsworth (See Directory, Rosemeade)

Club: North Dakota Pottery Collectors' Society
Sandy Short
Box 14, Beach, ND 58621; 701-872-3236. Annual dues: $15; sponsors annual convention and includes 4 newsletters

Ashtray, Breckenridge Minnesota Centennial, 1857 (train) 1957 at top, 5", from $175 to...........................**$200.00**

Ashtray, Fargo Structural Products Inc, green, triangular, 6¼", from $100 to...**$125.00**

Ashtray, gopher at side, Gopher State Minnesota, 5", from $150 to...**$200.00**

Ashtray, Mallard hen, 3½x6½", from $325 to............**$350.00**

Bank, bear, aqua, 3¾x6", minimum value.................**$400.00**

Bank, hippopotamus, 2¾x5¾", minimum value.......**$500.00**

Bell, peacock, 5½", from $200 to.............................**$300.00**

Bowl, incurvate rim, Rosemeade NO DAK mark, 1½x4¼", from $75 to...**$100.00**

Covered dish, hen on basket, white on black base, 5½x5½", from $350 to...**$400.00**

Creamer & sugar bowl, blue, mini, 2x3", 2x1¾", from $75 to...**$100.00**

Creamer & sugar bowl, Prairie Rose, 2¾", 2", from $75 to **$100.00**

Cup, hand thrown, twisted handle, 2¼", from $75 to.**$100.00**

Figurine, bison, black gloss, 2½x3½", from $100 to.**$150.00**

Figurine, coyote howling, 4½x3⅞", from $250 to.....**$300.00**

Figurine, pheasant hen, 4x11½", from $350 to.........**$400.00**

Figurines, ducks, yellow, mini, 1¾x1½", pr, from $200 to.**$250.00**

Flower holder, frog, blue, 2¾x3¼", from $30 to........**$50.00**

Paperweight, teddy bear, Teddy Roosevelt Memorial Park, 3½", from $300 to..**$350.00**

Pitcher, bulbous, flared rim, red gloss, 2⅝", from $35 to..**$50.00**

Planter, circus horse, various colors, 5x6½", ea from $75 to **$100.00**

Planter, deer, yellow shaded to green matt, 3¾x5¼", from $50 to...**$75.00**

Planter, kangaroo, 4¾x6", from $100 to **$125.00**

Planter, lamb, 6x6½", from $150 to...........................**$200.00**

Planter, mermaid, 4¾x3¼", from $200 to.................**$250.00**

Planter, pheasant cock, 3¾x9¼", minimum value **$500.00**

Planter, swan, made in many colors, 4¾x5", ea from $35 to...**$65.00**

Planter, wooden shoe w/floral design, 2¾x5¼", from $85 to **$100.00**

Plaque, northern pike in relief, 3½x6", from $225 to ..**$275.00**

Plate, Dakota Centennial, w/decal, 7¼", from $50 to.**$75.00**

Posy ring, heart shape, 7", from $125 to **$150.00**

Relish dish, 2-compartment, 5½x9", from $50 to........**$75.00**

Salt & pepper shakers, Black Angus bull, 1¾", pr, from $300 to...**$350.00**

Salt & pepper shakers, Boston terrier, 2½", pr, from $250 to **$300.00**

Salt and pepper shakers: flamingos on stumps, pr, from $85 to...**$100.00**

Salt & pepper shakers, pelicans, pink, 3¼", pr, from $85 to **$100.00**

Salt & pepper shakers, Prairie Rose, 2½", pr, from $35 to .**$50.00**

Salt & pepper shakers, rooster & hen, 3½", 2¼", pr, from $50 to...**$85.00**

Salt & pepper shakers, skunks, 2¾", pr, from $40 to .**$60.00**

Salt & pepper shakers, turkey gobbler & hen, 1½x1¾", 1x2", pr,. from $175 to...**$225.00**

Salt & pepper shakers, wheat shock, 3¾", pr, from $125 to **$150.00**

Salt & pepper shakers, wire-haired fox terrier, tan ears, 2", pr, from $40 to...**$50.00**

Spoon rest, pansy, 4", from $75 to.........................**$100.00**

Spoon rest, spoon form, Fort Lincoln State Park souvenir, 8¾", from $100 to..**$125.00**

Spoon rest, water lily on leaf, 4¾", from $75 to......**$100.00**

Toothpick holder, pheasant, 4x5", from $75 to........**$100.00**

Tray, Indiana state map, 5¼", from $100 to.............**$125.00**

Vases, 5½", $45.00; 7½", $50.00; bowl, 4" x 8", $55.00.

Vase, black/blue crackle, trumpet neck, 5", from $75 to..**$100.00**

Vase, 3-color swirl, flared rim, 4⅛", minimum value ..**$200.00**

Roseville Pottery

This company took its name from the city in Ohio where they operated for a few years before moving to Zanesville in the late 1890s. They're recognized as one of the giants in the industry, having produced many lines of the finest in art pottery from the beginning to the end of their operations. Even when machinery took over many of the procedures once carefully done by hand, the pottery they produced continued to reflect the artistic merit and high standards of quality the company had always insisted upon.

Several marks were used over the years as well as some paper labels. The very early art lines often carried an applied ceramic seal with the name of the line (Royal, Egypt, Mongol, Mara, or Woodland) under a circle containing the words Rozane Ware. From 1910 until 1928 an Rv mark was used, the 'v' being contained in the upper loop of the 'R.' Paper labels were common from 1914 until 1937. From 1932 until they closed in 1952, the mark was Roseville in script, or R USA. Pieces marked RRP Co Roseville, Ohio, were not made by the Roseville Pottery but by Robinson Ransbottom of Roseville, Ohio. Don't be confused. There are many jardinieres and pedestals in a brown and green blended glaze that are being sold at flea markets and antique malls as Roseville that were actually made by Robinson Ransbottom as late as the 1970s and 1980s. That isn't to say they don't have some worth of their own, but don't buy them for old Roseville.

Most of the listings here are for items produced from the 1930s on — things you'll be more likely to encounter today. If you'd like to learn more about the subject, we recommend *The Collector's Encyclopedia of Roseville Pottery, Vols 1* and *2* (revised editions, 2001 pricing by Mike Nickel) by Sharon and Bob Huxford (Collector Books); *A Price Guide to Roseville Pottery by the Numbers* by John Humphries (L&W Book Sales); *Roseville in All Its Splendor* by Jack and Nancy Bomm (L&W Book Sales); and *Collector's Compendium of Roseville Pottery, Vols 1* and *2*, by R.B. Monsen (Monsen & Baer).

Advisor: Mike Nickel (See the Directory, Roseville)

Newsletter: *Rosevilles of the Past*
Nancy Bomm, Editor
P.O. Box 656
Clarcona, FL 32710-0656; Subscription: $19.95 per year for 6 to 12 newsletters

Apple Blossom, vase, #390-12, blue, 12½", from $450 to ..**$500.00**
Apple Blossom, vase, #390-12, green or pink, 12½", ea from $400 to..**$450.00**
Apple Blossom, window box, #368-8, blue, 2½x10½", from $200 to..**$225.00**
Artwood, planter, #1056-10, 6½x10½", from $85 to ...**$95.00**
Artwood, vase, #1057-8, 8", from $85 to......................**$95.00**
Baneda, candle holder, #1087, pink, 5½", pr, from $600 to..**$675.00**
Baneda, vase, #610, green, from $725 to **$800.00**
Bittersweet, cornucopia, #857-4, 4½", from $100 to.**$125.00**
Bittersweet, vase, #881-6, 6", from $100 to **$125.00**
Blackberry, hanging basket, 4½x6½", from $1,000 to.**$1,200.00**
Blackberry, jardiniere, 7", from $750 to **$850.00**
Bleeding Heart, candlesticks, #1139, blue, 5", pr, from $275 to..**$325.00**
Bleeding Heart, plate, #382-10, pink or green, 10½", from $150 to..**$175.00**
Bushberry, hanging basket, blue, 7", from $450 to ..**$500.00**
Bushberry, mug, #1-3½", orange, from $150 to........**$175.00**
Bushberry, vase, #34-8, blue, 8", from $250 to **$275.00**
Cameo II, flowerpot, 5½", from $350 to....................**$450.00**
Cameo II, wall pocket, 9½", from $500 to **$600.00**
Capri, planter, #C-110-10, 5x10½", from $45 to **$55.00**
Capri, vase, #582-9, from $50 to..................................**$60.00**
Carnelian I, bowl, w/handles, 3x9", from $80 to........**$90.00**
Carnelian I, vase, fan shape w/scallops, w/handles, 8", from $100 to..**$125.00**
Carnelian II, planter, w/handles, 3x8", from $100 to.**$125.00**
Carnelian II, planter, 3x8", from $100 to **$125.00**
Carnelian II, vase, pot w/handles, 5", from $200 to.**$250.00**
Clemana, bowl, #281, tan, 4½x6½", from $200 to....**$225.00**
Clemana, vase, #756, blue, 9½", from $550 to..........**$600.00**
Clematis, flower arranger, #192-5, blue, 5½", from $100 to..**$125.00**
Clematis, flowerpot w/saucer, #668-5, green or brown, 5½", from $150 to..**$175.00**

Columbine, cornucopia, #149-6, blue or tan, 5½", from $150 to..**$175.00**
Columbine, hanging basket, pink, 8½", from $375 to ..**$425.00**
Corinthian, hanging basket, 8", from $200 to............**$250.00**
Corinthian, vase, 8½", from $150 to............................**$175.00**
Cosmos, center bowl, #374-14, green, 15½", from $300 to..**$350.00**
Cosmos, vase, #134-4, blue, 4", from $175 to **$200.00**
Cremona, fan vase, 5", from $125 to..........................**$150.00**
Cremona, urn, 4", from $150 to..................................**$175.00**
Dahlrose, hanging basket, #343, 7½", from $250 to.**$300.00**
Dahlrose, pillow vase, #419, 5x7", from $200 to.......**$250.00**
Dawn, bowl, #318-14, pink or yellow, 16", from $275 to .**$325.00**
Dawn, vase, #833-12, pink or yellow, 12", from $600 to...**$700.00**
Dogwood I, double bud vase, 8", from $150 to **$175.00**
Dogwood I, tub, 4x7", from $125 to..........................**$150.00**
Dogwood II, hanging basket, 7", from $250 to........**$300.00**
Dogwood II, jardiniere, 8", from $250 to **$300.00**
Donatello, ashtray, 3", from $175 to **$225.00**
Donatello, plate, 8", from $450 to.............................**$500.00**
Earlam, bowl, #218, 3x11½", from $400 to................**$450.00**
Earlam, vase, #522, 9", from $800 to.........................**$900.00**
Falline, center bowl, #244, blue, 11", from $500 to ..**$600.00**
Falline, vase, #647, blue, 7½", from $1,300 to.......**$1,500.00**
Ferella, bowl w/frog, #211, red, 5", from $1,100 to.**$1,200.00**
Florane (late line), bud vase, 7", from $30 to **$35.00**
Florane (late line), sand jar, 12", from $100 to.........**$135.00**
Florentine, ashtray, 5", from $150 to.........................**$175.00**
Florentine, jardiniere, 5", from $150 to **$175.00**
Floxglove, flower frog, #46, blue, 4", from $125 to..**$150.00**
Foxglove, tray, #424, green/pink, 15", from $350 to...**$400.00**
Freesia, flowerpot w/saucer, #670-5, green, 5½", from $225 to..**$250.00**
Freesia, jardiniere, #669-4, blue, 4", from $125 to **$150.00**
Freesia, window box, #1392-8, tangerine, 10½", from $150 to..**$175.00**
Fuchsia, candlesticks, #1132, green, 2", pr, from $150 to.**$175.00**
Fuchsia, vase, #893-6, blue, 6", from $250 to...........**$300.00**
Futura, center bowl, #196, 3½", from $700 to...........**$800.00**
Futura, vase, #384, 8", from $600 to **$700.00**
Futura, vase, #400, 7½", from $1,000 to.................**$1,100.00**
Imperial I, compote, 6½", from $175 to **$225.00**
Imperial I, planter, 14x16", from $350 to..................**$400.00**
Imperial II, bowl w/frog, flared rim, 5x12½", from $500 to..**$550.00**
Imperial II, vase, lg ribbing, tapered, incurvate rim, 5", from $350 to..**$400.00**
Iris, pillow vase, #922-8, blue, 8½", from $325 to **$375.00**
Iris, pillow vase, #922-8, pink or tan, 8½", from $275 to..**$300.00**
Ivory II, cornucopia, #2, 5½x12", from $75 to...........**$95.00**
Ivory II, jardiniere, #574-4, 4", from $40 to **$50.00**
Ixia, hanging basket, 7", from $250 to......................**$300.00**
Ixia, vase, #856-8, 8½", from $200 to.......................**$250.00**
Jonquil, center bowl, #219, 3½x9", from $325 to **$375.00**
Jonquil, jardiniere, #621, 4", from $250 to...............**$275.00**
La Rose, bowl, 3", from $125 to **$150.00**

La Rose, wall pocket, 9", from $300 to......................**$350.00**
Laurel, bowl, #252, gold, 3½", from $350 to............**$400.00**
Laurel, vase, #676, gold, 10", from $550 to..............**$650.00**
Lotus, pillow vase, #L4-10, 10½", from $275 to.......**$325.00**
Lotus, planter, #L9-4, 3½x4", from $100 to...............**$125.00**
Luffa, candlesticks, #1097, 5", pr, from $500 to........**$600.00**
Luffa, vase, #683, 6", from $350 to............................**$600.00**
Magnolia, ashtray, #28, 7", from $100 to..................**$125.00**

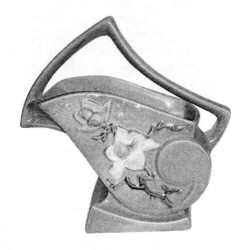

Magnolia, basket, #386-12, from $275.00 to $325.00.

Magnolia, conch shell, #453-6, 6½", from $95 to......**$110.00**
Magnolia, vase, #91-8, 8", from $125 to.....................**$150.00**
Mayfair, cornucopia, #1013-6, 3x6½", from $60 to......**$75.00**
Mayfair, planter, #113-8, 3½x8½", from $70 to...........**$85.00**
Ming Tree, bookends, #559, 5½", pr, from $95 to....**$110.00**
Ming Tree, bowl, #526-9, 4x11½", from $95 to.........**$110.00**
Mock Orange, planter, #931-8, 3½x9", from $125 to..**$150.00**
Mock Orange, vase, #973-8, 8½", from $150 to.......**$175.00**
Moderne, compote, #297-6, 6", from $250 to............**$275.00**
Moderne, vase, #789-6, 6", from $225 to...................**$250.00**
Montacello, basket, tan, 6½", from $900 to............**$1,000.00**
Montacello, vase, blue, 8½", from $650 to...............**$750.00**
Morning Glory, center bowl, #270, ivory, 4½x11½", from $350 to..**$375.00**
Morning Glory, pillow vase, #120, green, 7", from $550 to..**$600.00**
Moss, bowl, pillow vase, #781, pink/green or orange/green, ea from $200 to **$225.00**
Moss, candlesticks, #1109, blue, 2", pr, from $150 to.**$175.00**
Mostique, hanging basket, 7", from $400 to..............**$500.00**
Mostique, jardiniere, 8", from $250 to.......................**$300.00**
Normandy, hanging basket, 7" **$300.00**
Orian, candle holders, #1108, turquoise, 4½", pr, from 275 to...**$325.00**
Orian, compote, #272, yellow, 4½x10½", from $225 to..**$250.00**
Peony, bookends, #11, 5½", pr, from $200 to...........**$250.00**
Peony, mug, #2-3½", 3½", from $100 to...................**$125.00**
Peony, planter, #387-8, 10", from $85 to....................**$95.00**
Pine Cone, ashtray, #499, blue, from $200 to **$225.00**
Pine Cone, bowl, #320-5, 4½", green, from $175 to.**$225.00**

Pine Cone, candlestick, #1099-4½", blue, 5", ea from $275 to..**$350.00**
Pine Cone, vase, #121-7, brown, 7", from $275 to ...**$325.00**
Poppy, basket, #348-12, gray/green, 12½", from $500 to..**$550.00**
Poppy, bowl, #336-10, pink, 12", from $275 to **$300.00**
Primrose, vase, #760-6, tan, 7", from $150 to...........**$175.00**
Raymor, casserole, #199, 7½", from $40 to.................**$50.00**
Raymor, condiment tray, 8½", from $40 to..................**$50.00**
Raymor, corn server, #162, 12½", from $45 to **$50.00**
Raymor, ramekin, #156, w/lid, 6½", from $35 to........**$40.00**
Raymor, salad bowl, #161, 11½", from $35 to............**$40.00**
Rosecraft Blended, jardiniere, 4", from $90 to..........**$110.00**
Rosecraft Blended, vase, #35, 10", from $125 to.......**$150.00**
Rosecraft Hexagon, bowl, green, handled, 7½", from $250 to..**$275.00**
Rosecraft Hexagon, candlestick, brown, 8", ea from $350 to..**$400.00**
Rosecraft Panel, vase, green, 6", from $200 to..........**$250.00**
Rosecraft Panel, window box, brown, 6x12", from $400 to..**$450.00**
Rosecraft Vintage, vase, handled, 4", from $175 to ..**$200.00**
Rosecraft Vintage, window box, 6x11½", from $550 to ..**$650.00**
Royal Capri, leaf dish, #533-10, 2x10½", from $200 to....**$225.00**
Royal Capri, vase, #583-9, 9", from $250 to...............**$275.00**
Rozane 1917, bowl, incurvate rim, 3½", from $100 to..**$125.00**
Rozane 1917, compote, 6½", from $150 to **$175.00**
Russco, double bud vase, 8½", from $100 to...........**$125.00**
Russco, triple cornucopia, heavy crystals, 8x12½", from $300 to..**$350.00**
Savona, candlesticks, handled, 3½", pr, from $125 to .**$150.00**
Savona, window box, 2½x9", from $75 to **$100.00**
Silhouette, vase, #784-8, from $100 to **$125.00**
Silhouette, vase, #789-14, 14", from $350 to............**$400.00**
Snowberry, ewer, #1TK-15, blue or pink, 16", from $600 to..**$700.00**
Snowberry, vase, #1RB-6, blue or pink, 6", from $200 to .**$225.00**
Snowberry, vase, #1V-6, green, 6", from $70 to..........**$85.00**
Sunflower, bowl, #208, 4", from $650 to **$750.00**
Sunflower, vase, #486, 5", from $800 to **$900.00**
Teasel, vase, #888-12, dark blue or rust, 12", from $500 to..**$600.00**
Teasel, vase, #888-12, light blue or tan, 12", from $450 to..**$550.00**
Thornapple, hanging basket, 7", from $250 to..........**$300.00**
Thornapple, triple bud vase, #1120, 6", from $200 to .**$250.00**
Topeo, center bowl, red, 3x11½", from $100 to **$125.00**
Topeo, double candlesticks, blue, 5", pr, from $550 to...**$600.00**
Tourmaline, candlesticks, flared base, 5", pr, from $175 to .**$200.00**
Tourmaline, cornucopia, 7", from $75 to...................**$100.00**
Tuscany, flower arranger, handles droop to flared base, pink, 5½", from $100 to...**$125.00**
Tuscany, vase, flat sided w/flaring rim, drooping handles, pink, 6", from $125 to **$150.00**
Velmoss, bowl, #266, green, 3x11", from $175 to.....**$225.00**
Velmoss, vase, #719, red, 9½", from $400 to............**$450.00**
Velmoss Scroll, bowl, 3", from $125 to **$150.00**
Velmoss Scroll, vase, 10", from $275 to **$325.00**

Volpato, candlesticks, 9½", pr, from $250 to............**$300.00**
Volpato, covered urn, 8", from $300 to **$350.00**
Water Lily, candlesticks, #1155, rose w/green, 5", 4½", pr,
from $225 to...**$250.00**
Water Lily, flower frog, #48, brown w/green, 4½", from $140
to..**$165.00**
White Rose, basket, #362-8, 7½", from $200 to **$250.00**
White Rose, vase, #987-9, 9", from $150 to...............**$200.00**
Wincraft, basket, #210-12, 12", from $500 to............**$600.00**
Wincraft, vase, #288-15, 16", from $375 to **$425.00**
Windsor, basket, #330, rust, 4½", from $900 to **$1,000.00**
Windsor, lamp base, #551, 7", rust, from $1,000 to .**$1,250.00**
Zephyr Lily, bud vase, #201-7, 7½", from $175 to....**$200.00**
Zephyr Lily, cornucopia, #204-8, brown, 8½", from $150
to **$175.00**
Zephyr Lily, tray, green, 14½", from $200 to **$225.00**

Royal China

The dinnerware and kitchenware lines made by Royal China of Sebring, Ohio (1934 – 1986), have become very collectible, those cataloged here in particular. The most sought after today have as their origins supermarket and gas station promotions; some were given away, and others distributed by stamp companies. They were also retailed through major outlet stores such as Sears Roebuck and W.T. Grant.

The Royal China Company is credited with revolutionizing the dinnerware industry through the introduction of Kenneth Doyle's stamping maching in 1948. Prior to this innovative technique, decals were laboriously applied by hand.

Veteran collectors find that the number of patterns produced by Royal seems almost endless, and many can turn up in unexpected colors. For example, Currier & Ives is not restricted to blue but can be found in pink, yellow, green, black, and even multiple colorations. To simplify pattern identification, focus on the pattern's border which will be consistent (most of the time). Memory Lane features a border of oak leaves and acorns. Bucks County, an exclusive of W.T. Grant, sports a Pennsylvania Dutch tulip-motif garland. Fair Oaks has magnolia blossoms surrounded by periwinkle edging. The Willows (Blue Willow, Pink Willow, Yellow, etc.) speak for themselves. Colonial Homestead and Old Curiosity Shop are typically found in green and are often mistaken one for the other. Here's how to tell the difference: Old Curiosity Shop's border depicts metal hinges and pulls, while Colonial Homestead's features wooden boards with pegged joints. Most Currier & Ives dinnerware pieces regardless of color will have the famous scroll border designed by art director Gordon Parker.

Be on the lookout for matching accessories by a variety of manufacturers. These were done in all sorts of media including paper, plastic, glass, and metal. A wide variety of coordinating items may be found including clocks, lamps, placemats, and bakeware that match a number of Royal patterns. These items are disappearing fast but none quicker than the matching glassware, most notably Gay Fad. From

three-ounce juice tumblers to 14-ounce Zombic glasses, these items were produced in several treatments and styles in clear, frosted, and milk glass.

Our advisor is happy to answer any questions on American clay products from figurines to dinnerware via e-mail. For further reading on this subject with an emphasis on Currier & Ives, we highly recommend *A Collector's Guide for Currier & Ives Dinnerware by the Royal China Company* by Elden R. Aupperle (with 2001 Price Guide, 112 pages, soft cover) as well as the newsletter and clubs listed below.

Note: Our Currier and Ives prices are for items in the blue pattern. This line was made on a very limited basis in pink as well. To evaluate that color, you'll have to double our values.

Advisor: BA Wellman (See Directory, Dinnerware)

Newsletter: *Currier and Ives China by Royal*
c/o Jack and Treva Hamlin
145 Township Rd. 1088, Proctorville, OH 45669; 740-886-7644

Club: C&I Dinnerware Collectors
E.R. Aupperle, Treasurer
29470 Saxon Road
Toulon, IL 61483; 309-896-3331, fax: 309-856-6005

Blue Heaven, bowl, fruit nappy; 5½"..............................**$3.00**
Blue Heaven, bowl, vegetable; 10" **$20.00**
Blue Heaven, creamer **$5.00**
Blue Heaven, cup & saucer **$5.00**
Blue Heaven, gravy boat..**$15.00**
Blue Heaven, plate, dinner; 10"......................................**$6.00**
Blue Heaven, platter, tab handles, 10½"......................**$20.00**
Blue Heaven, sugar bowl..**$8.00**
Blue Willow, ashtray, 5½"..**$12.00**
Blue Willow, bowl, cereal; 6¼"......................................**$15.00**
Blue Willow, bowl, fruit nappy; 5½" **$6.50**
Blue Willow, bowl, soup; 8¼"..**$12.00**
Blue Willow, bowl, vegetable; 10" **$22.00**
Blue Willow, butter dish, ¼-lb **$35.00**
Blue Willow, casserole, w/lid **$95.00**
Blue Willow, creamer..**$6.00**
Blue Willow, cup & saucer **$6.00**
Blue Willow, gravy boat, double spout **$18.00**
Blue Willow, pie plate, 10"..**$30.00**
Blue Willow, plate, bread & butter; 6¼".........................**$3.00**
Blue Willow, plate, dinner; 10".......................................**$6.00**
Blue Willow, plate, salad; rare, 7¼" **$7.00**
Blue Willow, platter, oval, 13" **$32.00**
Blue Willow, platter, serving; tab hdls, 11"..................**$20.00**
Blue Willow, salt & pepper shakers, pr.........................**$25.00**
Blue Willow, sugar bowl, w/lid......................................**$15.00**
Blue Willow, teapot..**$125.00**
Blue Willow, tray, tidbit; 2-tier.....................................**$65.00**
Buck's County, ashtray, 5½" **$15.00**
Buck's County, bowl, soup; 8½" **$18.00**
Buck's County, bowl, vegetable; 10"............................**$28.00**

Buck's County, casserole, w/lid $125.00
Buck's County, creamer.................................$8.00
Buck's County, cup & saucer.........................$8.00
Buck's County, gravy boat, double spout...................$28.00
Buck's County, plate, bread & butter; 6¼" $4.00
Buck's County, plate, dinner; 10" $12.00
Buck's County, platter, oval $35.00
Buck's County, platter, serving; tab hdls, 11" $20.00
Buck's County, salt & pepper shakers, pr $25.00
Buck's County, sugar bowl, w/lid........................$18.00
Buck's County, teapot $145.00
Colonial Homestead, bowl, cereal; 6¼" $15.00
Colonial Homestead, bowl, fruit nappy; 5½" $4.00
Colonial Homestead, bowl, soup; 8¼" $9.00
Colonial Homestead, bowl, vegetable; 10" $20.00
Colonial Homestead, casserole, angle handles, w/lid..$75.00
Colonial Homestead, chop plate, 12"...................$18.00
Colonial Homestead, creamer.........................$5.00
Colonial Homestead, cup & saucer $5.00
Colonial Homestead, gravy boat, double spout.........$15.00
Colonial Homestead, pie plate $25.00
Colonial Homestead, plate, bread & butter; 6".............$2.00
Colonial Homestead, plate, dinner; 10"...................$4.00
Colonial Homestead, plate, salad; rare, 7¼" $7.00
Colonial Homestead, platter, oval, 13" $24.00
Colonial Homestead, platter, serving; tab handles, 10½"....$15.00
Colonial Homestead, salt & pepper shakers, pr.........$18.00
Colonial Homestead, sugar bowl, w/lid.....................$15.00
Colonial Homestead, teapot..............................$95.00
Currier & Ives, ashtray, 5½", from $15 to $18.00
Currier & Ives, bowl, cereal; round (various sizes made) ..$15.00
Currier & Ives, bowl, fruit nappy; 5½"........................$5.00
Currier & Ives, bowl, salad/cereal; tab handles, 6¼"..$35.00
Currier & Ives, bowl, soup; 8½".........................$14.00
Currier & Ives, bowl, vegetable; deep, 10", from $30 to..$35.00
Currier & Ives, bowl, vegetable; 9" $25.00
Currier & Ives, butter dish, Fashionable, ¼-lb, from $40 to...$35.00

Currier & Ives, casserole, angle handles, $115.00.

Currier & Ives, casserole, tab handles, w/lid.............$250.00
Currier & Ives, clock plate, blue numbers, 2 decals, from
  $150 to...$200.00
Currier & Ives, clock plate, non-factory.....................$50.00
Currier & Ives, creamer, angle handle...........................$8.00
Currier & Ives, creamer, round handle, tall, rare $48.00

Currier & Ives, cup & saucer $6.00
Currier & Ives, gravy boat, double spout, from $20
  to...$25.00
Currier & Ives, gravy boat, tab handles, w/liner (like 7"
  plate), from $100 to...................................$135.00
Currier & Ives, gravy ladle, 3 styles, ea from $35 to ..$50.00
Currier & Ives, lamp, candle; w/globe, from $250 to ..$300.00
Currier & Ives, pie baker, 10", (depending on picture) from
  $30 to..$90.00
Currier & Ives, plate, bread & butter; 6⅜", from $3 to.$5.00
Currier & Ives, plate, calendar; ca 1969-86, ea from $25
  to...$75.00
Currier & Ives, plate, chop; Getting Ice, 11½", from $35
  to $45.00
Currier & Ives, plate, chop; Getting Ice, 12¼" $38.00
Currier & Ives, plate, chop; Rocky Mountains, 11½"..$65.00
Currier & Ives, plate, dinner; 10"........................$7.00
Currier & Ives, plate, luncheon; very rare, 9".............$25.00
Currier & Ives, plate, salad; rare, 7" $15.00
Currier & Ives, platter, oval, 13" $35.00
Currier & Ives, platter, tab handles, 10½" dia, from $20
  to...$30.00
Currier & Ives, salt & pepper shakers, pr, from $30 to..$35.00
Currier & Ives, sugar bowl, angle handles $18.00
Currier & Ives, sugar bowl, no handles, flared top $48.00
Currier & Ives, sugar bowl, no handles, w/lid...........$35.00
Currier & Ives, teapot, many different styles & stampings,
  from $110 to...$150.00
Currier & Ives, tidbit tray, 2- or 3-tier, abundant, from $50
  to...$125.00
Currier & Ives, tumbler, iced tea; glass, 12-oz, 5½"....$18.00
Currier & Ives, tumbler, juice; glass, 5-oz, 3½", from $8
  to...$12.00
Currier & Ives, tumbler, old-fashioned; glass, 3¼", from $8
  to...$15.00
Currier & Ives, tumbler, water; glass, 4¾" $15.00
Fair Oaks, bowl, divided vegetable.......................$45.00
Fair Oaks, bowl, soup...................................$15.00
Fair Oaks, bowl, vegetable; 9"..........................$30.00
Fair Oaks, butter dish...................................$45.00
Fair Oaks, casserole, w/lid...............................$135.00
Fair Oaks, creamer.......................................$12.00
Fair Oaks, cup & saucer..................................$8.00
Fair Oaks, plate, bread & butter...........................$3.00
Fair Oaks, plate, dinner; 10" $12.00
Fair Oaks, platter, tab handles, 10½" $22.00
Fair Oaks, salt & pepper shakers, pr $22.00
Fair Oaks, sugar bowl, w/lid $18.00
Fair Oaks, teapot $125.00
Memory Lane, bowl, cereal; 6¼"..........................$15.00
Memory Lane, bowl, fruit nappy; 5½" $3.00
Memory Lane, bowl, soup; 8½".............................$9.00
Memory Lane, bowl, vegetable; 10"........................$25.00
Memory Lane, butter dish, ¼-lb...........................$30.00
Memory Lane, creamer....................................$6.00
Memory Lane, gravy boat $18.00
Memory Lane, gravy boat liner, from $12 to $15.00

Memory Lane, gravy ladle, plain, white, for all sets, from $35
to...**$50.00**
Memory Lane, plate, bread & butter; 6⅜".....................**$2.00**
Memory Lane, plate, chop; 12"....................................**$25.00**
Memory Lane, plate, chop; 13"....................................**$35.00**
Memory Lane, plate, dinner...**$8.00**
Memory Lane, plate, luncheon; rare, 9¼".....................**$15.00**
Memory Lane, plate, salad; rare, 7"..............................**$10.00**
Memory Lane, platter, oval, 13"...................................**$30.00**
Memory Lane, platter, tab handles, 10½"......................**$15.00**
Memory Lane, salt & pepper shakers, pr......................**$25.00**
Memory Lane, sugar bowl, w/lid..................................**$15.00**
Memory Lane, tumbler, iced tea; glass.........................**$15.00**
Memory Lane, tumbler, juice; glass.............................**$8.00**
Old Curiosity Shop, bowl, fruit nappy; 5½"..................**$4.00**
Old Curiosity Shop, bowl, soup/cereal; 6½"..................**$15.00**
Old Curiosity Shop, bowl, vegetable; 9".......................**$22.00**
Old Curiosity Shop, bowl, vegetable; 10".....................**$25.00**
Old Curiosity Shop, casserole, w/lid............................**$90.00**
Old Curiosity Shop, creamer..**$6.00**
Old Curiosity Shop, cup & saucer................................**$5.00**
Old Curiosity Shop, plate, bread & butter; 6⅜".............**$3.00**
Old Curiosity Shop, plate, dinner; 10"..........................**$5.00**
Old Curiosity Shop, platter, tab handles, 10½".............**$15.00**
Old Curiosity Shop, salt & pepper shakers, pr..............**$20.00**
Old Curiosity Shop, sugar bowl, w/lid.........................**$12.00**
Old Curiosity Shop, teapot..**$115.00**

Royal Copley

This is a line of planters, wall pockets, vases, and other novelty items, most of which are modeled as appealing animals, birds, or human figures. They were made by the Spaulding China Company of Sebring, Ohio, from 1942 until 1957. The decoration is underglazed and airbrushed, and some pieces are trimmed in gold (which can add 25% to 50% to their values). Not every piece is marked, but they all have a style that is distinctive. Some items are ink stamped; others have (or have had) labels.

Royal Copley is really not hard to find, and unmarked items may sometimes be had at bargain prices. The more common pieces seem to have stabilized, but the rare and hard-to-find examples are showing a steady increase. Your collection can go in several directions; for instance, some people choose a particular animal to collect. If you're a cat lover, they were made in an extensive assortment of styles and sizes. Teddy bears are also popular; you'll find them licking a lollipop, playing a mandolin, or modeled as a bank, and they come in various colors as well. Wildlife lovers can collect deer, pheasants, fish, and gazelles, and there's also a wide array of songbirds.

If you'd like more information, we recommend *Collector's Guide to Royal Copley Plus Royal Windsor & Spaulding, Books I* and *II,* by Joe Devine.

Advisor: Joe Devine (See Directory, Royal Copley)

Ashtray, butterfly shape, paper label only, USA on bottom, 5x9", from $20 to...**$25.00**
Bank, pig w/bow tie, eyes open or closed, paper label only, 6¼", from $60 to...**$75.00**
Bank, teddy bear, paper label only, rare, 7½", from $125 to...**$150.00**
Candy/tidbit, triangular w/brass center handle, 7⅛", from $25 to...**$30.00**
Coaster, antique automobile, unmarked, from $35 to...**$40.00**
Coaster, Dutch painting, unmarked, from $35 to........**$40.00**
Creamer, leaves form body, made in several colors, 3", ea from $20 to...**$24.00**
Figurine, Airedale dog, paper label only, 6½", from $25 to...**$30.00**
Figurine, dog w/ears slightly raised, seated, paper label, 8½", from $35 to...**$40.00**
Figurine, dove, paper label only, 5", from $12 to........**$15.00**
Figurine, gull, wing molded to base, paper label only, 8", from $60 to...**$70.00**
Figurine, hen #1, multicolor, paper label only, 5½", from $30 to...**$35.00**
Figurine, hen #2, multicolor, paper label only, 6", from $35 to...**$40.00**
Figurine, kingfisher, wide variations in color, 5", ea from $45 to...**$50.00**
Figurine, kinglet, paper label, sm, 3½", from $26 to..**$28.00**
Figurine, lark on fancy stump, paper label only, 5", from $12 to...**$16.00**
Figurine, parrot on stump, predominantly blue, paper label, 8", from $40 to...**$45.00**
Figurine, rooster, multicolor, 8", from $40 to..............**$45.00**
Figurine, spaniel dog, paper label only, 6¼", from $30 to..**$35.00**
Figurine, swallow, many variations in color, paper label, 8", ea from $25 to...**$30.00**
Figurine, wren, wide variations made in color, paper label, 6¼", ea from $20 to...**$24.00**
Lamp, 2 birds in bower, paper label only, 8", from $50 to...**$60.00**
Pitcher, floral decal on ivory, gold stamp, 6", from $12 to...**$16.00**
Pitcher, Pome Fruit, apples in relief on blue, green stamp, 8", from $65 to...**$75.00**
Planter, bamboo, 3 runners, paper label only, 5¾", from $12 to...**$15.00**
Planter, barefoot boy, paper label only, 7½", from $35 to...**$40.00**
Planter, Blackamoor, made to hang or rest on table, raised letters, 8", from $40 to...**$45.00**
Planter, boat shape, turquoise w/brown specks, marked USA, 4¾x12½", from $14 to...**$16.00**
Planter, coach, beige, teal or deep rose to plum, green stamp, 3¼x6", ea from $18 to...**$20.00**
Planter, Cocker Spaniel w/basket, paper label only, 5½", from $35 to...**$40.00**
Planter, deer on sled (Little Huck), Spaulding label, 6", from $60 to...**$65.00**

Planter, dog (brown and white) and mailbox, 8", $35.00.

Planter, dog w/right foot raised, paper label only, scarce, 7½", from $65 to $75.00

Planter, duck & mail box, US Mail on mail box, paper label only, 6¾", from $75 to $85.00

Planter, Dutch boy w/bucket, paper label only, 6", from $25 to $30.00

Planter, elephant w/ball, paper label only, 7½", from $25 to $30.00

Planter, finch perched at side of lg apple, paper label only, 6½", from $30 to..$35.00

Planter, hat, made to hang or rest on table, raised mark, 5½", from $40 to..$45.00

Planter, Indian boy & drum, paper label only, 6½", from $20 to $25.00

Planter, kitten (playful) & boot, paper label only, 7½", from $50 to..$55.00

Planter, kitten w/ball of yarn, yellow yarn, gold trim, 8¼", from $60 to..$70.00

Planter, Linley decal, floral on white, gold stamp, 4", from $12 to..$15.00

Planter, mallard sitting, paper label only, 5", from $30 to...$35.00

Planter, Oriental girl w/basket on ground, aka 'pregnant lady,' raised mark, 7¾", from $15 to $20.00

Planter, pirate's head, made to hang or rest on table, raised mark, 8", from $45 to $50.00

Planter, poodle, white, prancing beside pink planter, 6", from $70 to..$75.00

Planter, pup w/suitcase, name tag reads Skip, paper label only, 7", from $45 to..$50.00

Planter, ram's head, paper label only, 6½", from $25 to..$30.00

Planter, rooster, head down, tail up, raised mark, 7¾", from $30 to $35.00

Planter, rooster & wheelbarrow, handles resting on bench, 8", from $135 to..$150.00

Planter, tanager beside stump, green stamp or raised letters, 6¼", from $20 to..$25.00

Planter, wood duck (mature), paper label only, 7¼", from $35 to..$40.00

Planter/vase, mallard beside stump, paper label only, 8", from $40 to..$45.00

Planter/wall pocket, girl w/wide-brimmed hat, hangs or rests on table, raised mark, 7½", from $40 to $45.00

Plaque/planter, fruit plate, will hang or rest on table, 6¾", from $30 to..$35.00

Vase, Congratulations w/baby decal on pink or blue cylinder, 8", from $60 to $65.00

Vase, Dogwood, realistic floral, 8¼", from $20 to......$24.00

Vase, Harmony, tricolor leaves, 7½", from $50 to......$55.00

Vase, Homma, white stem & leaves on black, 8½", from $16 to...$18.00

Vase, Oriental dragon in relief, footed, paper label only, 5½", from $12 to..$15.00

Vase, rooster, 2 runners, flowing tail, multicolor, 7⅛", from $40 to..$45.00

Vase, Trailing Leaf & Vine, paper label only, 8½", from $25 to..$30.00

Vase/planter, horse's head, paper label only, 6¼", from $20 to..$25.00

Vase/planter, Oriental floral decor on white, footed, sq sides, paper label only, 5½", from $12 to $15.00

Royal Haeger

Many generations of the Haeger family have been associated with the ceramic industry. Starting out as a brickyard in 1871, the Haeger Company (Dundee, Illinois) progressed to include artware in their production as early as 1914. That was only the beginning. In the '30s they began to make a line of commercial artware so successful that as a result a plant was built in Macomb, Illinois, devoted exclusively to its production.

Royal Haeger was their premium line. Its chief designer in the 1940s was Royal Arden Hickman, a talented artist and sculptor who also worked in mediums other than pottery. For Haeger he designed a line of wonderfully stylized animals and birds, high-style vases, and human figures and masks with extremely fine details.

Paper labels were used extensively before the mid-'30s. Royal Haeger ware has an in-mold script mark, and their Flower Ware line (1954 – 1963) is marked 'RG' (Royal Garden).

Collectors need to be aware that certain glazes can bring two to three times more than others. For those wanting to learn more about this pottery, we recommend *Haeger Potteries Through the Years* by David D. Dilley (L-W Book Sales).

Advisor: David D. Dilley (See Directory, Royal Haeger)

Club: Haeger Pottery Collectors of America
Lanette Clarke
5021 Toyon Way
Antioch, CA 94509, 925-776-7784; Monthly newsletter available

Ashtray, free-form, Green Agate, Royal Haeger R-873 USA...$15.00

Ashtray, free-form heart shape, Mandarin Orange, Royal Haeger 135 c USA, 1⅜x11½"................................$10.00

Ashtray, Gold Tweed, #127, Royal Haeger USA, Haeger Gold Tweed 22k Gold, 2x10¼x9½" **$20.00**

Bank, dog, 1 ear raised, winking, white transparent, Haeger 8034 c, 8½x7½" **$85.00**

Basket, Rose of Sharon, Chartreuse w/red flowers on side, Royal Haeger R-575 USA, 8x7" **$75.00**

Bookends, calla lily bookends, Amber, Royal Haeger R-475 USA, 6⅛x4½x4½", pr **$60.00**

Bookends, ram figural, Ming Green-Blue w/brown & blue spots, R-132 (unmarked), 8x8½x4", pr **$150.00**

Bowl, applied flowers, Cloudy Blue & White, R-373 (unmarked), 1950s, 6½x19x6" **$75.00**

Bowl, boat shape, Mandarin Orange, #373-H, marked Royal Haeger, 4x15x7" **$30.00**

Bowl, shell form, Chartreuse & Silver Spray, Royal Haeger R-297 USA, 2¾x14x7½" **$30.00**

Bowl, starfish, Pearl Grey Drip, Royal Haeger R-967 USA & crown foil label, 2⅜x14½x14¼" **$45.00**

Bowl, 3-footed, dark & light blue, #25, Haeger in diamond shape, 3¼x6" **$60.00**

Bowl, 4-scallop rim, Lilac, Royal Haeger R-333 c USA, foil label: Handcrafted Haeger, 4½x16¼x7" **$35.00**

Candle holder, double fish, Mauve Agate, R-203 (unmarked), 5" **$35.00**

Candle holders, flower & leaf, light blue w/green accents, R-185, foil label: Royal-Haeger By Royal Hickman, 2½", pr **$65.00**

Candle holders, leaf form, Ebony, R-437 (unmarked), 2¾x4¾", pr **$15.00**

Candy bowl, lily on lid, Mallow & Aqua, Royal Haeger R-431 USA, 6x7½" dia **$65.00**

Cigarette lighter, Mandarin Orange, Japan, Royal Haeger 813-H USA, 10¾"x4⅛" dia base **$25.00**

Figurine, leopard, snarling, Chartreuse, R-1131 (unmarked), 7¾x7½x3½" **$75.00**

Figurine, mare & foal on base, Amber, Royal Haeger R-451 USA, 11x13x4" **$150.00**

Figurine, panther on base, black on speckled base, marked Haeger Designs of Dundee, 9¾x18¾x5⅛" **$75.00**

Figurine, rabbit, blue, #3248 (unmarked), 1940s, 5x4x4" minimum value **$15.00**

Figurine, wren house, Mauve Agate, Royal Haeger R-287 USA, 9¼x7¼x4¼" **$75.00**

Flower frog, swan, green white & beige, #57 (unmarked), 4x3x3¼" **$25.00**

Goblet, gold, #3928, marked Haeger USA c, 1962-69, 9⅜", minimum value **$15.00**

Lamp, Fawn, Ebony, #5195, marked w/foil label: Royal-Haeger, Dundee Illinois, replaced shade, 24½" .**$150.00**

Lamp, Tree of Life, Green Agate w/Chartreuse, #5401, foil label: Royal Haeger Dundee Ill, 7½" (21½" to finial top) **$45.00**

Lamp base, Bow, Mauve Agate, R-455 (unmarked), 13½x5" **$100.00**

Lavabo, pink, R-1506/R-1507, 2-pc set **$75.00**

Pitcher, rooster handle, Persian Blue, Royal Haeger USA H-608, 9x6¾x4" **$40.00**

Planter, Brown Earth Graphic Wrap, #4185X, 5½x8" dia, minimum value...**$60.00**

Planter, bullfighter, Haeger Red, #502-H, marked Royal Haeger, 13x5½" **$125.00**

Planter, Colonial flower girl, chartreuse, #3318 (unmarked), 9x6½x4¾" **$35.00**

Planter, cornucopia, white, #3061, Haeger - USA, 5½x12x4" **$50.00**

Planter, duck, Jade Crackle, Royal Haeger R-1844 USA, 6½x8x7" **$30.00**

Planter, giraffe, Ebony Cascade, Royal Haeger USA, 15¾x11x6" **$175.00**

Planter, hippos (2), Bennington Brown Foam, #5070, 5x10½" **$45.00**

Planter, horse, white, #3314 (unmarked), 6x7½x3" **$45.00**

Planter, Madonna, white, #990, Haeger - USA, 13¼x10¼x10¼" **$55.00**

Planter, pilgrim's hat, light brown, Haeger - USA c - #394, 4⅝x7¾x7½" **$25.00**

Planter, pouter pigeon, Mauve Agate, R-108, Royal Haeger by Royal Hickman USA, 8½x11⅞x4½" **$75.00**

Planter, Southern belle, topless, pink, #3054, Haeger USA, designed by Royal Hickman, 8x4⅞" **$75.00**

Planter, triple ball, Oxblood, foil label: Genuine Haeger, R-852, 3⅝x11¼x4¾" **$40.00**

Planter, trout, pearl carnival w/gold fins, Royal Haeger R-284 USA, 9¼x8x4", minimum value **$100.00**

Toe Tapper, w/violin, #8296, brown textured, 9¼x3¾", minimum value...**$35.00**

Vase, Brown Earth Graphic Wrap, #4233-X, marked c Royal Haeger USA, 11x5" dia base **$60.00**

Vase, dark rose, angle handles, #39 (unmarked), 6⅞x8½"..**$50.00**

Vase, deer (2, abstract style), white, #3108 (unmarked), ca 1942, 7½x5x2" **$25.00**

Vase, double lily, green, #186 (unmarked), ca 1936, 6x4½x3¾" **$25.00**

Vase, feather plume form, white, Royal Haeger R-248 USA, 10x6x3⅜" **$25.00**

Vase, floral in relief, green, #463 (unmarked), ca 1930, 6½x5⅞x4" **$30.00**

Vase, Morning Glory (3 trumpets), Mauve Agate, Royal Haeger R-452 USA, 16½" **$90.00**

Vase, pitcher, form, speckled black, marked Haeger USA, 10⅛x2⅝" **$10.00**

Vase, rooster figural, white, #3220 (unmarked), 14x7x4" ..**$75.00**

Vase, Textured, Sunset Yellow, S-400, foil label: Studio Haeger, 10¼" **$100.00**

Vase, white w/blue bow at base of trumpet neck, Royal Haeger USA R-455, ca 1936, 14x5" **$75.00**

Rozart

George and Rose Rydings (Kansas City, Missouri) were aspiring potters, who in 1969 set about to produce a line of fine underglaze art pottery. They inherited some vintage American-made artware which they very much admired and set about trying to unravel the enigma of ceramic chemistry used by the old masters. Early in the 1970s, Fred Radford, grandson of Albert Radford, a well-known, remarkably talented artist who had made his presence felt in the Ohio pottery circles (ca 1890s – 1904), offered them ideas about glazing techniques, chemistry, etc., and allowed them to experiment with his grandfather's formula for Jasperware (which he had produced in his own pottery). It was then that the Ryding's pottery acquired a different look — one very reminiscent of the wares made by the turn-of-the century American art pottery masters.

Rozart (as they named their pottery) has created may lines since its beginning: Twainware, Sylvan, Cameoware, Rozart Royal, Rusticware, Deko, Krakatoa, and Sateen to mention a few. All of their pottery is marked in some fashion. Though some items have been found with paper labels, they did not come from the Rydings. You will almost always find the initials of the artist responsible for the decorating and a date code, created in one of two ways: two digits, for example '88' denoting 1988, or a month (represented by a number) separated by a slash followed by the two-digit year. The earliest mark known is 'Rozart' at the top of a circle, 'Handmade' in the center, and 'K.C.M.O.' (Kansas City, Missouri) at the bottom. In the early years, a stylized paint brush was sometimes added to the mark as well. Other marks followed over the years, including a seal which was used extensively.

The Rydings venture quickly involved several family members, some of which developed their own lines, themes, and designs. George signs his pieces in one of three ways: 'GMR,' 'GR,' or 'RG' (with a backwards R). In the early years George worked on Twainware, Jasperware, and Cameoware. He has many wheel-thrown pieces to his credit.

Rose, who is very knowledgable about Native Americans, does scenics and portraits, using painstaking care to authenticate the exact history of a particular tribe and their culture. Her mark is either 'RR' or 'RRydings,' both written on an angle.

Four of the seven Rydings children have worked in the pottery as well, becoming decorators in their own right. Anne Rydings White designed and executed many original pieces in addition to her work on the original Twainware line, which she signed 'AR.' (Before her marriage, she used this mark or simply 'Anne.') She is still actively involved; her later creations are signed 'ARW. Susan Rydings Ubert has specialized in design pieces (mostly Sylvan) and is an accomplished sculptor and mold maker. She signs her pieces with an 'S' over the letter R. Susan's daughter, Maureen, does female figures in the Art Deco style. Rebecca 'Becky' Ridings White, now a commercial artist, early on designed such lines as Fleamarket (depicting typical flea market scenes and merchandise), Nature's Jewels, and Animal, which she marked with the name of the line as well as her initials (B over the letter R). (When collecting Rozart, use caution if you want a particular artist's work; with two Rydings children married to two unrelated White families, it would be easy to confuse the artists and their place in history.)

Of all the children, Cynthia Rydings Cushing has always been the most prolific. Her Kittypots line depicts animated cats and kittens involved in a variety of activities on vases, jars, etc., utilizing their Rusticware glazes and shapes (usually 3" to 4"

high). Her earlier work is signed with a 'C' over the 'R'; today she uses the initials 'CRC.'

The Rozart Pottery is still active today, and while prices for the older pieces have been climbing steadily for several years, they are still affordable.

Figurine, poodle, reclining, Kraktoa line, 1970, 6" L....**$125.00**
Ginger jar, flower motif, w/lid, ca 1975, 3¾"..............**$75.00**
Jardiniere, Cameoware, 3 sculptured frogs, mid-1980s, 11"..**$95.00**
Jardiniere, Western theme, Cindy Cushing, w/base, 1981, 16"..**$150.00**
Jug, Rusticware, Cleopatra, mid-1980s, 22"...............**$350.00**
Sign, Rozart Pottery in script, base across front, 1998, 5½"..**$20.00**
Sign, Rozart Pottery in script, sm vertical base, 1989, 5½"..**$35.00**
Tankard, part of the Twainware series, very scarce w/lid, Anne Rydings, 1974, 9½"..............................**$325.00**
Tile, Danielle nude, Deko line, Ubert, 1998, 10" **$68.00**
Tile, Two Moons Chief Joseph, Rose Rydings, 1974, 6" sq...**$55.00**
Vase, Animal by Becky Rydings, 2 handles, 1988, 9¾"...**$95.00**
Vase, Deko line w/dancing nude, narrow base, mid-1980s, 12"..**$210.00**
Vase, Kittypots, three cat groupings in continuous sequence on sides, signed CR, 12"..........................**$300.00**
Vase, Nature's Jewels by Becky Rydings, butterfly motif, 4"..**$24.00**
Vase, Rusticware, Indian Chief, Anne Rydings, 8" **$175.00**
Vase, stonewall w/flowers, wheel-thrown, GR, 7½"...**$95.00**
Vase, Twainware, Tom the Retired Painter, limited edition of 2,500, 6"...**$155.00**
Vase, winter scene, Dove Gray glaze, GR, 1999, 9"..**$100.00**
Water set, pitcher & 4 mugs, horse motif, marked CRC..**$235.00**

RumRill

RumRill-marked pottery was actually made by other companies who simply provided the merchandise that George Rumrill marketed from 1933 until his death in 1942. Rumrill designed his own lines, and the potteries who filled the orders were the Red Wing Stoneware Company, Red Wing Potteries, Shawnee (but they were involved for only a few months), Florence, and Gonder. Many of the designs were produced by more than one company. Examples may be marked RumRill or with the name of the specific pottery.

For more information we recommend *Red Wing Art Pottery, Books I* and *II* by B.L. and R.L. Dollen (Collector Books).

Advisors: Wendy and Leo Frese, Three Rivers Collectibles (See Directory, Rum Rill)

Basket, Vingage Group #615, 12½".........................**$120.00**
Basket, Vintage Group #619, double handles...........**$110.00**

Bowl, #509, Seafoam, 5".................................$25.00
Bowl, console; Athena #571, deep blue..................$825.00
Bowl, Grecian Group #302, Dutch Blue, double handles, 6"...**$55.00**

Covered bowl, ivory with brown wash, by Red Wing, $70.00.

Vase, bud; #290, Dutch Blue, 9½".............................$75.00
Vase, bud; Novelty Group #510, Scarlet & Bay, 8".....**$70.00**
Vase, Double Nude #568, Seashell, 11"....................$685.00
Vase, Fluted Group #267, Lilac, 9"........................**$125.00**
Vase, Indian Group #291, Scarlet & Bay, 5½".............$40.00
Vase, Ivy Ball #601-6, Suntan w/green interior..........$75.00
Vase, Manhattan Group #543, Dutch Blue, triple floral...$250.00
Vase, Miscellaneous Group #686, Riviera, 11"............**$70.00**
Vase, Neoclassic #668, fan form, Suntan w/green interior, 10", NM **$100.00**

Russel Wright Designs

One of the country's foremost industrial designers, Russel Wright, was also responsible for several lines of dinnerware, glassware, and spun aluminum that have become very collectible. American Modern, produced by the Steubenville Pottery Company (1939 – 1959) is his best known dinnerware and the most popular today. It had simple, sweeping lines that appealed to tastes of that period, and it was made in a variety of solid colors. Iroquois China made his Casual line, and because it was so serviceable, it's relatively easy to find today. It will be marked with both Wright's signature and 'China by Iroquois.' His spun aluminum is highly valued as well, even though it wasn't so eagerly accepted in its day, due to the fact that it was so easily damaged.

If you'd like to learn more about the subject, we recommend *The Collector's Encyclopedia of Russel Wright, Second Edition,* by Ann Kerr (Collector Books).

Note: Values are given for solid color dinnerware unless a pattern is specifically mentioned.

American Modern

The most desirable colors are Canteloupe, Glacier Blue, Bean Brown, and White; add 50% to our values for these colors. Chartreuse is represented by the low end of our range; Cedar, Black Chutney, and Seafoam by the high end; and Coral and Gray near the middle. To evaluate patterned items, deduct 25%.

Bowl, divided vegetable, from $85 to.....................**$120.00**
Bowl, salad; from $75 to...................................**$100.00**
Coffeepot, AD; from $100 to **$150.00**
Cup, from $8 to **$10.00**
Pitcher, water; from $100 to **$135.00**
Plate, salad; 8", from $12 to...............................**$15.00**
Salt & pepper shakers, pr, from $12 to...................**$16.00**

Highlight

Bowl, salad/vegetable; round, from $65 to **$75.00**
Bowl, vegetable; oval, from $65 to **$75.00**
Creamer, from $35 to..**$40.00**
Cup, from $25 to...**$30.00**
Plate, dinner; from $25 to..................................**$30.00**
Platter, round, sm, from $55 to............................**$60.00**

Iroquois Casual

To price Brick Red, Aqua, and Cantaloupe Casual, double our values; for Avocado, use the low end of the range. Oyster, White, and Charcoal are at the high end.

Bowl, fruit; redesigned, 5¾", from $12 to **$14.00**
Carafe, wine/coffee; from $100 to.........................**$200.00**
Cover for 4-qt casserole, from $20 to **$25.00**
Creamer, stacking, from $15 to.............................**$18.00**
Cup & saucer, redesigned, from $18 to **$22.00**
Pitcher, w/lid, 1½-qt, from $120 to.......................**$150.00**
Plate, luncheon; 9½", from $8 to..........................**$10.00**
Sugar bowl, stacking, from $15 to.........................**$18.00**

Knowles

The high end of the range should be used to evaluate solid-color examples.

Bowl, fruit; 5½", from $8 to...............................**$10.00**
Bowl, serving; round or oval, ea from $30 to............**$35.00**
Centerpiece server, from $75 to **$150.00**
Plate, salad; 8½", from $8 to..............................**$10.00**
Sugar bowl, w/lid, from $25 to **$30.00**

Plastic

These values apply to Home Decorator, Residential, and Flair (which is at the high end of the range). Copper Penny and Black Velvet items command 50% more. Meladur items are all hard to find in good condition, and values can be basically computed using the following guidelines (except for the fruit bowl, which in Meladur is valued at $7.00 to $8.00).

Bowl, divided vegetable; #714, from $20 to...............**$25.00**

Bowl, fruit; #707, from $13 to.....................................$15.00
Plate, bread & butter; #705, from $3 to $6.00
Plate, dinner; #703, from $8 to $10.00
Platter, #710, from $20 to...$25.00
Sugar bowl, w/lid, #712, from $12 to $15.00
Tumbler, #715, from $15 to...$18.00

Spun Aluminum

Cheeseboard, from $75 to...$100.00
Cooking items, ea from $150 to $200.00
Hot relish server w/ceramic inserts, from $200 to....$225.00
Muddler, from $75 to..$100.00
Serving accessory, lg, from $175 to.........................$225.00
Serving accessory, sm, from $100 to........................$125.00
Vase, 12", from $150 to $175.00
Waste basket, from $125 to..$150.00

Sterling

Values are given for undecorated examples.

Bowl, onion soup; 10-oz, from $20 to........................$25.00
Bowl, salad; 7½", from $14 to $18.00

Bowl, soup/cereal; from $12.00 to $14.00. (Photo courtesy Ann Kerr)

Cream pitcher, 9-oz, from $14 to...............................$16.00
Creamer, individual, 1-oz, from $10 to $12.00
Cup, 7-oz, from $10 to $15.00
Plate, dinner; 10¼", from $10 to $15.00
Plate, service; from $16 to...$20.00

White Clover (for Harker)

Bowl, fruit; clover decor, from $10 to........................$12.00
Bowl, vegetable; 8¼", from $27 to.............................$30.00
Casserole, clover decor, w/lid, 1-qt, from $45 to........$55.00
Pitcher, clover decor, w/lid, 2-qt, from $75 to $100.00
Plate, chop; clover decor, 11", from $25 to $28.00
Plate, dinner; clover decor, 9¼", from $14 to..............$16.00
Saucer, clover only, from $3 to...................................$4.00

Salt Shakers

Probably the most common type of souvenir shop merchandise from the '20 through the '60s, salt and pepper shakers can be spotted at any antique mall or flea market today by the dozens. Most were made in Japan and imported by various companies, though American manufacturers made their fair share as well. When even new shakers retail for $10.00 and up, don't be surprised to see dealers tagging the better vintage varieties with some hefty prices.

'Miniature shakers' are hard to find, and their prices have risen faster than any others'. They were all made by Arcadia Ceramics (probably an American company). They're under 1½" tall, some so small they had no space to accommodate a cork. Instead they came with instructions to 'use Scotch tape to cover the hole.'

Advertising sets and premiums are always good, since they appeal to a cross section of collectors. If you have a chance to buy them on the primary market, do so. Many of these are listed in the Advertising Character Collectibles section of this guide.

Recent sales have shown a rise in price for some low-line shakers that are being purchased not by salt shaker collectors but people with a connection to the theme or topic they represent. (Doctors will buy doctor-related shakers, etc.) Fishing shakers are on the rise especially breed fish. High-end shakers are getting soft. Many of the vintage rare sets are being reproduced and redesigned so collectors can own a set at a more reasonable cost.

There are several good books which we highly recommend to help you stay informed: *Salt and Pepper Shakers, Identification and Values, Vols I, II, III,* and *IV,* by Helene Guarnaccia; and *The Collector's Encyclopedia of Salt and Pepper Shakers, Figural and Novelty, First* and *Second Series,* by Melva Davern. All are published by Collector Books.

See also Advertising Character Collectibles; Breweriana; Condiment Sets; Holt Howard; Occupied Japan; Regal China; Rosemeade; Shawnee; Vandor; and other specific companies.

Advisor: Judy Posner (See Directory, Salt and Pepper Shakers)

Club: Novelty Salt and Pepper Club
c/o Irene Thornburg, Membership Coordinator
581 Joy Rd.
Battle Creek, MI 49017; Publishes quarterly newsletter and annual roster. Annual dues: $20 in USA, Canada, and Mexico; $25 for all other countries

Advertising

Anheuser-Busch Bud Man, ceramic, Ceramarte Brazil, 1991, 3½", pr, MIB **$28.00**
Camel Cigarettes Max & Ray camels, hard plastic, dated 1993, 4¼", pr..**$49.00**
Canada Dry Soda bottles, glass w/metal tops, applied decals, embossed Muth & Son Buffalo NY mark, 4", pr ..**$49.00**

Dooley & Shultz Utica Beer steins, ceramic, unmarked, taller: 4½", pr...**$125.00**

Esslingers Beer bottles, foil labels, metal tops, 4", pr..**$29.00**

Esso gas pump, plastic, red & white or blue & white, pr, from $18 to...**$30.00**

Fingerhut truck & trailer, plastic, white w/blue & black, 1¾x3¾", 2-pc set..**$29.00**

Firestone Tires, ceramic, from $40.00 to $50.00 for the pair. (Photo courtesy Helene Guarnaccia)

Fox Head 400 Beer bottles, glass w/metal tops, 4", pr..**$39.00**

Homepride Flour Fred, hard plastic, black & white, 3½", pr...**$55.00**

Jones Dairy milk bottle, glass w/decal labels, metal tops, Muth of Buffalo, 3½", pr..............................**$75.00**

Kentucky Fried Chicken Colonel Sanders, hard plastic, black base for pepper, white for salt, 4¼", pr................**$75.00**

Kentucky Fried Chicken Colonel Sanders, white plastic, c 1965, pr, from $45 to...........................**$60.00**

Magic Chef, chef figure in black & white, ceramic, pr, from $65 to...**$70.00**

Nugget Casino's Nugget Sam, ceramic, multicolor, Japan, 1950s, 4", pr **$75.00**

Old Life Soda bottles, glass w/decal labels, metal tops, 4½", pr...**$75.00**

Peerless Beer men, hard plastic gnome-type characters, 1950s, 5", pr **$95.00**

Poppin' & Poppie Fresh, white plastic w/blue details, pr, from $20 to...**$25.00**

Pure Oil Company gas pumps, plastic, 2¾", pr........**$195.00**

Quaker State Motor Oil cans, heavy cardboard, 1940s-50s, 1½", pr..**$40.00**

Schlitz Beer bottles, metal caps, pr, from $16 to........**$20.00**

Smokey the Bear, ceramic, w/shovel or bucket, yellow hats, pr, from $45 to....................................**$50.00**

St Lawrence Dairy cream-top bottles, glass w/metal tops, 3¼", pr...**$50.00**

Tappan Chefs, ceramic, dressed in white, detailed faces, red shoes, pr, from $25 to............................**$30.00**

Vess Soda bottles, glass w/applied decals, plastic screw tops, pr...**$45.00**

White Satin gin bottles, green glass w/metal tops & paper labels, 4¾", pr...................................**$24.00**

Animals, Birds, and Fish

Angelfish, bone china, realistic, pr, from $10 to **$18.00**

Angelfish, ceramic, realistic, Japan, pr, from $10 to....**$20.00**

Bird & nest on stump, ceramic, EX details, Japan, 3-pc set, from $15 to..**$18.00**

Bird mother perched beside nest containing 2 babies (shakers), ceramic, Japan, 3-pc set, from $10 to..........**$12.00**

Birds (shakers) on branch, silver-plated metal, 3-pc set, from $20 to...**$25.00**

Cardinals on leafy branch, ceramic, hand-painted, Japan, 3-pc set, from $18 to **$20.00**

Cat & mouse, ceramic, realistic appearance, unglazed bottoms, unmarked, cat: 1¾x3¼", pr **$28.00**

Chickens, ceramic, black & red paint, cojoined 1-pc set, from $10 to...**$12.00**

Chipmunks dressed as fireman & doctor, ceramic, sm, pr from $8 to...**$18.00**

Cow w/milk can (shaker) ea side, ceramic, 3-pc set from $8 to...**$20.00**

Dachshunds, ceramic, realistic appearance, pr, from $12 to..**$25.00**

Deer, ceramic, 1 recumbent/1 standing, cartoon-like appearance, Japan, pr, from $10 to **$12.00**

Dinosaurs, pottery, realistic appearance, green Japan ink mark, 1950s, 2½x3", pr..............................**$59.00**

Elephant w/basket (shaker) ea side, ceramic, pink & yellow dominating colors, 3-pc set, from $55 to.............**$45.00**

Hippos, pottery, white w/painted details, red Japan mark, 1½x3½", pr..**$29.00**

Horse holds round bale of hay, ceramic, hugger type, pr, from $7 to...**$15.00**

Horses rearing, ceramic, brown tones, realistic appearance, pr, from $15 to..**$18.00**

Kangaroo mama w/baby in pouch, ceramic, multicolor, Made in Japan, ¾", pr...**$28.00**

Large-mouth bass, ceramic, realistic, Japan, pr, from $6 to **$20.00**

Lobsters, ceramic, realistic appearance, Japan, 1950s, pr, from $8 to...**$10.00**

Mice, ceramic, comic appearance, Japan, pr, from $5 to...**$7.00**

Monkey (1 shaker) hangs from palm tree (2nd), ceramic, Made in Japan, pr, from $15 to **$18.00**

Monkey driving car, ceramic, multicolor, dressed, steering w/feet, Japan mark, 1950s, pr..............................**$49.00**

Moose heads, ceramic, realistic appearance, Victoria Ceramics Japan, 1950s, 3", pr..............................**$28.00**

Mouse holds 2 slices of cheese (shakers), ceramic, 3-pc set, from $7 to...**$10.00**

Pelicans, ceramic, realistic appearance, Japan, 1950s, 3", pr **$26.00**

Pheasants, ceramic, 1 w/tail up, 2nd w/tail down, Japan, pr, from $7 to...**$9.00**

Pig couple dressed in pink, posed as if to dance, ceramic, Japan, pr, from $12 to **$15.00**

Pigs, bone china, pink w/painted details, mini, pr, from $8 to...**$15.00**

Pigs, ceramic, black & white Hampshire hogs, realistic appearance, pr, from $18 to................................**$20.00**

Pigs, pottery, sitting & leaning, pastels, Japan mark, 2½", pr................................**$22.00**

Pigs w/snub noses, pottery, pink w/black details, Japan paper label, 1930s, 3", pr **$35.00**

Purple cows, bisque, original paint, Victoria Ceramics Japan, 1950s, 2½', pr...............................**$25.00**

Raccoons, ceramic, realistic appearance, Japan, pr, from $10 to.......................**$15.00**

Rooster & chicken, clear glass w/pottery heads, Made in Czechoslovakia, 3", pr **$29.00**

Rooster & hen, ceramic, red, white & black, realistic apperance, rooster w/head up, hen pecking, pr, from $10 to **$12.00**

Roosters, pink bisque, multicolor w/gold, Japan paper label, 1950s, 3½", pr **$25.00**

Scotty dog, porcelain, multicolor paint, Germany, 1930s-40s, 2½", pr...............................**$28.00**

Sea gulls, pottery, multicolor, flat unglazed bottoms, 1950s, 2¾", pr **$22.00**

Seals, ceramic, applied whiskers, realistic appearance, Japan, ca 1950, pr, from $8 to.......................**$10.00**

Siamese cats, ceramic, blue rhinestone eyes, Victoria Ceramics Made in Japan, taller: 3⅞", pr.............**$21.00**

Siamese kittens, ceramic, tan to near-black, realistic appearance, pr, from $6 to.......................**$8.00**

Skunk (Disney Flower look-alike), ceramic, Japan, pr, from $30 to...............................**$35.00**

Skunks, bisque, pastel pink, Bradley Exclusives foil label, 2½", pr...............................**$28.00**

Swans, ceramic, shaker holes in chests, pr, from $7 to...............................**$10.00**

Teddy bears, ceramic, piggy-back type, dressed up, crudely made & painted, red Japan mark, 4¼", pr **$20.00**

Tigers, ceramic, 1 recumbent, 1 pacing, Made in Japan, pr, from $18 to...............................**$20.00**

Trout, ceramic, realistic paint, Japan, pr, from $15 to **$20.00**

Turkey tom & hen, ceramic, EX details, Japan, pr, from $10 to...............................**$12.00**

Turtles, ceramic, comic appearance, 1 standing on back legs, Japan, 1950s, pr, from $12 to................**$15.00**

Turtles, ceramic, realistic appearance, Japan, 1950s, pr, from $5 to...............................**$7.00**

Zebras, ceramic, realistic appearance, Japan, pr, from $8 to **$10.00**

Black Americana

Boy & girl (heads only), red clay, black glaze, she w/red bow, he w/blue chef's cap, sm, pr, from $35 to..**$40.00**

Boy & girl dressed as Mammy & Chef, ceramic, light brown skin, Japan, 1950s, pr, from $60 to.......................**$70.00**

Boy & girl sitting in basket, ceramic, multicolor, Japan, 3-pc set, from $90 to.......................**$100.00**

Boy riding alligator, ceramic, multicolor, Japan, pr, from $85 to...............................**$90.00**

Boy sitting & eating watermelon slice (2nd shaker), ceramic, multicolor, Japan, pr, from $125 to **$125.00**

Boy sitting on cotton bale, ceramic, multicolor, Japan, 4", pr, from $125 to...............................**$150.00**

Boy sitting on toilet, ceramic, multicolor, Japan, pr, from $55 to...............................**$65.00**

Boys atop ears of corn, ceramic, multicolor, Japan, pr...**$65.00**

Cotton pickers (man & lady), pottery, stamped New Orleans, early, pr, from $50 to...............................**$60.00**

Mammy & Butler, ceramic, painted details, Japan, pr, from $90 to...............................**$100.00**

Mammy & Chef, ceramic, black glaze w/red, white & gold details, 5", pr, from $40 to...............................**$45.00**

Mammy & Chef, ceramic, dressed in red w/yellow & black trim, Pearl China, 7½", pr, from $125 to............**$135.00**

Mammy & Chef, ceramic, dressed in yellow, Pearl China Co, pr, from $100 to...............................**$125.00**

Mammy & Chef, ceramic, dressed in yellow w/red & black trim, 7", pr, from $75 to...............................**$85.00**

Mammy & Chef, ceramic, he holds spoon lettered Pepper, she has plate lettered Salt, 6", pr, from $150 to .**$175.00**

Mammy & Chef, ceramic, red, white & blue, Japan, 8", pr, from $125 to...............................**$135.00**

Mammy & Chef, ceramic, red, white & blue, 6½", pr, from $65 to...............................**$75.00**

Mammy & Chef, ceramic, unmarked, from 4" to 5", pr, from $30 to...............................**$35.00**

Mammy & Chef, ceramic, white skin but Black features, Japan, 4", pr, from $35 to...............................**$45.00**

Matador & bull, ceramic, multicolor, nice detail, Japan, pr, from $55 to...............................**$45.00**

Minstrel singer head & white gloves, ceramic, Japan, pr, from $125 to...............................**$150.00**

Native boy & palm tree, ceramic, exaggerated features, pr, from $40 to...............................**$50.00**

Native man & lady w/baskets on heads, ceramic, black skin, Japan, pr, from $55 to **$65.00**

Native mother w/baby on back, ceramic, nesting type, exaggerated features, Japan, pr, from $75 to **$85.00**

Character

Aladdin & lamp, ceramic, multicolor w/bright gold trim, Vallona Star, 4⅞", pr...............................**$69.00**

Babar & girlfriend (elephants), ceramic, dressed-up couple, unmarked, 3½", pr...............................**$55.00**

Bimbo (Betty Boop's dog), ceramic, cold-painted features, unmarked, 1930s, 2½", pr...............................**$125.00**

Cow & the Moon, ceramic, multicolor, Japan, pr, from $20 to.**$25.00**

Doc & Sleepy (of Snow White's 7 Dwarfs), ceramic, multicolor, black Foreign mark, 1930s, 2¾", pr..........**$125.00**

Ferdinand the Bull, ceramic, multicolor, Disney, Japan, late 1930s, 2¾", pr **$90.00**

Goose & golden egg, ceramic, gold & white, unmarked, 1950s, 3" goose, pr...............................**$30.00**

Goose & golden egg, ceramic, gold & white, Vallona Star, 1950s, goose: 5¾", pr...............................**$39.00**

Heckle & Jeckle magpies, ceramic, H719 on bottoms, Japan paper labels, light paint wear, 3½", pr....................$85.00

Humpty Dumpty, ceramic, head (1 shaker) sits atop body (2nd), Japan, pr, from $95 to..........................$100.00

Jerry Colonna pushing luggage cart (suitcase shakers), ceramic, Made in Japan foil label, 5", 3-pc set.....$55.00

Jonah & whale, ceramic, figure stands in opening at side of whale, Japan, pr, from $40 to...........................$50.00

Kewpie babies, porcelain, crying, pastels, marked M756, Made in Japan label, 3¼", pr.................................$38.00

Mary Had a Little Lamb, ceramic, blond girl stands w/lamb at her feet, Relco (Japan), 1950s-60s, 4", pr.............$35.00

Mickey & Minnie, ceramic, seated on bench, Disney, ca 1960, complete set from $125 to.................................$125.00

Miss Muffet & spider, ceramic, multicolor, Poinsettia Studio paper label, Miss Muffet: 2½", pr.........................$85.00

Moon Mullins, glass w/hard plastic hat tops, cold-painted features, Made in Japan label, 1930s, 3", pr.........$95.00

Mouse & cheese (from Farmer in the Dell), ceramic, Japan, pr, from $10 to...................................$12.00

Mouse & clock (Hickory Dickory Dock), ceramic, mouse fits atop clock, Japan, pr, from $15 to.......................$18.00

Old King Cole in chair, ceramic, stacking type, Hand Painted Royal Japan label, 1940s-50s, 4¼", pr..................$45.00

Old Mother Hubbard & dog, ceramic, gold trim, Poinsettia Studio label, 3½", pr...$95.00

Oswold & Homer, ceramic, multicolor, Napco Japan #1C3635, c 1958 Walter Lantz Productions, 4", NM, pr...$150.00

Paul Bunyan & Babe, ceramic, unmarked Japan, 1950s, 5½", 3½", pr...$32.00

Pebbles & Bamm-Bamm, ceramic, multicolor, Harry James, 4", pr..$49.00

Pinocchio, glazed porcelain bisque, multicolor, Disney, Made in Japan, 5", pr......................................$150.00

Pinocchio, heavy porcelain, hand-painted, Japanese copy, pr, from $125 to....................................$135.00

Pluto, ceramic, cold paint, c Walt Disney Productions, 1940s, 3¼", pr...$49.00

Pluto w/bone & Pluto w/cup & saucer, ceramic, multicolor, Disney, Japan, 3½", pr.................................$125.00

Preacher Crow & Dandy (crows from Dumbo), ceramic, Disney, Japan foil labels, 1940s-50s, 4", pr...........$89.00

Raggedy Ann, ceramic, unmarked vintage import, 4", pr..$39.00

Shmoos, ceramic, boy in graduate hat & tassel, girl in bonnet & neck scarf, figures on green grass, UFS, 1940s, 4", pr...$95.00

Silly Symphony Pig, ceramic, Japan, 1930s, 4", pr......$69.00

Tom Sawyer & fence, ceramic, multicolor, Parkcraft, 3"..$45.00

Tortoise & Hare, ceramic, multicolor, Vallona Star, tortoise: 3", hare: 3½" L, pr..$55.00

Woody & Winnie Woodpecker, Walter Lantz 1990, sold at Universal in Florida only, pr.................................$49.00

Yosemite Sam, ceramic, multicolor, Lego paper label, 1960s, pr...$125.00

Fruit, Vegetables, and Other Food

Apples, porcelain, hand-painted, Japan, pr, from $5 to..$7.00

Cabbage, ceramic, realistic appearance, sm, pr, from $5 to .$7.00

Ears of corn, ceramic, hand-painted, standing up, Japan, pr, from $4 to...$6.00

Ham & egg, ceramic, egg in shell, ham unsliced, realistic appearance, Japan, pr, from $18 to......................$20.00

Hamburger & hot dog in buns, ceramic, realistic appearance, Japan, pr, from $8 to...$10.00

Loaf of bread & stick of butter, ceramic, realistic appearance, Japan, pr, from $3 to...$5.00

Oranges on tray, ceramic, EX details, 3-pc set, from $8 to .$10.00

Peas in pod, ceramic, green paint, 1-pc w/holes at ea end, from $12 to...$15.00

Pie wedge & whipped cream, ceramic, realistic appearance, Japan, pr, from $10 to...$12.00

Potatoes, ceramic, realistic appearance, Japan, pr, from $4 to..$6.00

Tomatoes, ceramic, red and green, marked Japan, 3½", $12.00 for the pair.

Tomatoes, porcelain, realistic appearance, Japan, 2", pr, from $4 to...$6.00

Holidays and Special Occasions

Christmas, candles w/holly & berries, ceramic, white w/green, red & gold, Japan, pr, from $7 to.........$10.00

Christmas, Santa & Mrs Claus, ceramic, she w/muff, he waving, Japan, pr, from $12 to..................................$15.00

Christmas, Santa & Mrs Claus in rockers, ceramic, red & white w/gold trim, Japan, pr, from $15 to...........$25.00

Christmas, Santa & tree, ceramic, red, white & green, Japan, pr, from $8 to...$10.00

Christmas, Santa faces, gold hats, Japan, sm, pr, from $10 to ..$20.00

Christmas, Santa faces (1 winking), ceramic, red hat, Japan, pr, from $12 to...$15.00

Christmas, Santa's boots, ceramic, red & white w/gold trim, Japan, pr, from $7 to...$10.00

Christmas, snowman & snowlady, ceramic, black, white & yellow, Japan, pr, from $8 to..............................$18.00

Gift packages, ceramic, fancy bows, unmarked, 1950s, pr....$18.00

Household Items

Alarm clocks, ceramic, hand-painted, comic faces, lightweight, Japan, pr, from $8 to...........................$10.00

Blenders, plastic, clear & silver-tone w/black tops, pr, from $18 to...**$20.00**

Boots & saddle, ceramic, unglazed bottoms, unmarked, 1950s, 3½", pr **$18.00**

Cash register, plastic, push key & drawer comes out revealing shakers, from $35 to **$40.00**

Chefs, wooden, bobbing heads, painted details, pr, from $4 to **$6.00**

Cigar resting in ashtray, ceramic, brown, white & yellow, unglazed bottom, unmarked, 1½x2¼", pr **$30.00**

Clocks, wooden, cross-cut from branch leaving bark around edge, Time for Salt/Time for Pepper, pr, from $3 to .**$5.00**

Coffeepots, plastic, silver-tone & black, pr, from $10 to.**$12.00**

Fireplace & chair, ceramic, hand-painted, lightweight, Japan, pr, from $6 to **$8.00**

Mixer, plastic, bowl is for sugar, beaters are shakers, from $12 to...**$15.00**

Piano, plastic, when keys are pushed shakers pop out of top, from $12 to **$15.00**

Pipe on pipe holder, ceramic, multicolor, Trevewood, 2x3¾", pr...**$22.00**

Pressing iron, plastic, silver-tone & black, pr, from $6 to.**$8.00**

Seltzer bottles, pottery, hand decorated, gold tops, Elbee Art Cleveland Ohio Hand Decorated, 1950s, pr.........**$22.00**

Teakettles, ceramic, hand-painted, lightweight, Japan, pr, from $8 to...**$10.00**

Telephone, plastic, old-fashioned wall type, turn crank & shakers come out front, from $10 to....................**$12.00**

Television, plastic, when knob is turned shakers come out of top, from $12 to **$15.00**

Typewriter and inkwell, ceramic, shiny black, unmarked, $24.00. (Photo courtesy Helene Guarnaccia)

Washing machine, plastic, sugar bowl tub & wringers are shakers, 3-pc set, from $12 to...............................**$15.00**

Watering cans, ceramic, chickens painted on side, unscrew sprinkler to fill, lightweight, Japan, pr, from $10 to.**$15.00**

Wheelbarrows, ceramic, hand-painted, lightweight, Japan, pr, from $8 to...**$10.00**

Wood plane & square rule, ceramic, unmarked American, 1¾x3", pr...**$22.00**

Miniatures

Ace of Hearts & Deuce of Clubs, ceramic, Arcadia Ceramics, pr..**$30.00**

Ace of Hearts & stack of gold coins, ceramic, Arcadia Ceramics, pr **$55.00**

Baby shoes, ceramic, bronze colored, unmarked, 1x2", pr..**$28.00**

Barn & hay wagon, ceramic, multicolor, Arcadia Ceramics, barn: 1⅜", pr..**$60.00**

Baseball glove w/ball & hat w/bat, ceramic, Arcadia Ceramics, pr **$95.00**

Bowling pin & ball, ceramic, Arcadia Ceramics, pr, from $30 to..**$35.00**

Candlesticks, ceramic, gold & white, Arcadia Ceramics, 1½", pr..**$30.00**

Coffeepot & grinder, ceramic, Arcadia, pr, from $25 to.**$30.00**

Cup of coffee & piece of pie, ceramic, Arcadia Ceramics, from $25 to..**$30.00**

Lighthouse & sailboat, ceramic, Arcadia Ceramics, pr, from $35 to..**$40.00**

Pipe & slippers, ceramic, multicolor, unmarked, 2⅜", 2¼", pr..**$22.00**

Rainbow & pot of gold, ceramic, Arcadia Ceramics, pr, from $35 to..**$55.00**

Snake charmer & basket, ceramic, Arcadia Ceramics, pr, from $75 to..**$85.00**

Strawberries, ceramic, realistic appearance, Arcadia Ceramics, 1¼", pr..**$22.00**

Telescope & planet, ceramic, multicolor w/gold, Arcadia Ceramics, telescope: 2⅛", pr.................................**$95.00**

People

Baseball batter & catcher, pottery, holes in eyes, multicolor, flat unglazed bottoms, 1950s, pr..........................**$85.00**

Baseball batter & umpire, ceramic, multicolor, original corks, Japan paper label, 5", pr **$75.00**

Boy & girl, ceramic, Hummel-like appearance, EX hand-painting, Japan, pr, from $15 to............................**$20.00**

Boy & girl, ceramic, sitting & reading on original wooden bench, EX details, pr, from $15 to........................**$18.00**

Boy boxers, ceramic, multicolor, fierce expressions, Japan, pr, from $25 to..**$30.00**

Boys in space suits, ceramic, power packs on backs, Japan, 1950s, 3¾", pr **$49.00**

Bride & groom, ceramic, gold trim, Japan, 4¼", pr **$28.00**

Bride & groom, ceramic, multicolor, sitting on wooden bench, Japan, 3½", complete set **$28.00**

Canadian Mounted Police, pot metal, original hand-painting, light wear on silver bases, 3⅞", pr........................**$39.00**

Chefs, ceramic, full-bodied figural w/Salt or Pepper on tummies, Japan, pr, from $6 to **$8.00**

Chefs, ceramic, head & shoulders figurals w/white hats, turned-up mustaches & bow ties, Japan, pr, from $8 to........**$10.00**

Child in top hat (2nd shaker), ceramic, stacking, red Japan mark, 5", pr **$45.00**

Clown boy & girl w/pointed hats, ceramic, multicolor, Japan lg, pr, from $12 to..**$15.00**

Clown musicians, pottery, hand-painted, Japan stamp, 1930s, 3½", pr..**$29.00**

Clown on drum (2nd shaker), ceramic, multicolor, Japan, pr, from $22 to..**$28.00**

Clown's playing leapfrog, ceramic, multicolor, Japan, pr, from $20 to..**$25.00**

Confucious figures, ceramic, Be Swift To Hear But Slow To Speak & One Laugh Is Worth a Hundred Sighs, Japan, 1950s, pr..**$45.00**

Cowboy & cow girl, ceramic, Kewpie-like faces, Japan, pr, from $8 to..**$18.00**

Devil heads, chalkware, original paint, 1940s, 2⅞", pr..**$24.00**

Dutch boy & girl, ceramic, multicolor paint, Japan, pr, from $8 to..**$10.00**

Dutch boy & girl, ceramic, sitting on original wooden bench, sm, from $8 to..**$10.00**

Dutch boy & girl kissing, ceramic, red, white, blue & yellow, Japan, pr, from $12 to..**$15.00**

Dutch bride & groom, ceramic, blue & white w/blond hair, Japan, pr, from $8 to..**$10.00**

Dutch couple, ceramic, hugging, 1-pc set w/openings in sides, from $15 to..**$18.00**

Dutch girl w/yoke across shoulders supports 2 buckets (shakers), ceramic, 3-pc set, from $15 to................**$18.00**

Eisenhower, General; ceramic, stacking set forms bust, flat unglazed bottoms, unmarked, 1950s, 3½", 2-pc..**$79.00**

Eisenhower busts, ceramic, Ike on backs, flat unglazed bottoms, 1950s, 3½", pr..**$69.00**

George & Martha Washington decals on sq shakers, ceramic, pr, from $10 to..**$12.00**

Indian boy & girl, ceramic, he w/headdress & she w/feather in hair, multicolor, pr, from $15 to..**$18.00**

Indian brave w/drum & chief w/headdress, ceramic, detailed hand-painting, pr, from $18 to..**$20.00**

Indian chief & lady, ceramic, bust-type figures, bright multicolor paint, rugged features, pr, from $12 to..**$15.00**

Indian chief & teepee, ceramic, multicolor, pr, from $15 to..**$18.00**

Indian chief busts, pot metal, bronze paint, pr, from $8 to..**$10.00**

Indian chief in canoe, ceramic, multicolor, pr, from $18 to..**$20.00**

Indian man & lady, ceramic, comic appearance, unmarked, pr, from $15 to..**$20.00**

Indian man & lady, chalkware, multicolor paint, early, pr, from $18 to..**$20.00**

John F Kennedy in rocking chair, ceramic, painted details, pr, from $55 to..**$60.00**

Kewpies, ceramic, delicate tinted bisque-like finish, Japan, pr, from $45 to..**$50.00**

Man & woman, ceramic, frowning/smiling turnabouts, gold trim, Japan, 5", pr..**$25.00**

Man in doghouse & lady w/rolling pin, ceramic, Vallona Star, lady: 3½", pr..**$125.00**

Martian men, ceramic, I Just Arrived From Mars/Hi Ho I'm a Li Li Lo on reverse, red Japan sticker, 1950s, 3½", pr..**$39.00**

Mexican man asleep, ceramic, head & arms (1 shaker) atop seated body, pr, from $15 to..**$18.00**

Nude man singing in bathtub, ceramic, painted details, white tub, unmarked, 1950s, 2½x3¼", pr..**$69.00**

Pixie baseball batter & catcher, dressed in red, red Japan mark, 3½", pr..**$75.00**

Pixie chefs, ceramic, multicolor, Ucago Ceramics Japan foil labels, 4½", pr..**$39.00**

Pixies riding rocket ships, ceramic, unmarked Japan, 1950s, 2¾x3½", pr..**$59.00**

Porter, wooden, $45.00. (Photo courtesy Helen Guarnaccia)

Praying boy & girl, ceramic, white w/gold trim, Japan, pr, from $10 to..**$12.00**

Richard & Pat Nixon, ceramic, decal on bell-like shape, pr, from $8 to..**$15.00**

Southern belles, ceramic, multicolor, shiny, green PY Japan mark, 2¾", pr..**$38.00**

Teepees, ceramic, white w/painted details, pr, from $5 to..**$7.00**

Totem poles, ceramic, multicolor, pr, from $10 to......**$12.00**

Zodiac girls, ceramic, multicolor, red Japan mark, 4½", pr..**$55.00**

Souvenir

Alamo building replica, pot metal, bronze paint, Japan, 1¾x2½", pr..**$49.00**

Alcatraz Prison inmate, ceramic, multicolor, Exclusive BP Japan label, 4½", pr..**$34.00**

Bahama policemen, ceramic, brown skin tones, black & white uniforms, 1950s, 4¼", pr..**$32.00**

Connecticut state map & Yale graduation map, ceramic, Parkcraft, pr..**$49.00**

Dice & Cards, ceramic, black & white, souvenir of Reno Nevada, Exclusive BP Japan label, 3½", pr.........**$26.00**

Havana Cuba book & cigar, ceramic, Parkcraft, 3¼x2" book, 4¾" cigar, pr......................................**$49.00**
Hemisfair '68 Tower Building, ceramic, 5½", pr **$45.00**

Kennedy Space Center, space vehicles, ceramic, from $20.00 to $25.00. (Photo courtesy Helene Guarnaccia)

Missouri state map & mug, ceramic, Parkcraft stamp, 2½", pr **$49.00**
Nevada, potty & window, ceramic, 1950s, window: 2¾", pr **$24.00**
Ohio state map & tire, ceramic, Parkcraft, pr..............**$49.00**
Singing Towers, Lake Wales Fla, silver-tone metal, 3½", pr **$55.00**
St Lawrence Seaway ship, ceramic, smokestacks are shakers, 1950s, 2x6½", 3-pc set....................**$50.00**
Washington Monuments, Bakelite, 4¼", pr..................**$65.00**

Miscellaneous

Anthropomorphic corn people, ceramic, no lace trim, Japan, pr, from $15 to **$18.00**
Anthropomorphic pear people, ceramic, red & green, simple design, Japan, pr, from $8 to **$10.00**
Anthropomorphic train engines w/cartoon faces, ceramic, unmarked Japan, 2x3¼", pr **$29.00**
Anthropomorphic vegetable couple, porcelain, lace trim, Japan, pr, from $20 to **$25.00**
Anthropomorphic vegetable ladies, ceramic, 1 w/basket, 2nd w/broom, EX details, Japan, pr, from $40 to........**$45.00**
Anthropomorphic vegetable people tennis players, ceramic, hand-painted, Japan, pr, from $65 to **$75.00**
Car & camper, ceramic, glossy paint, ca 1940s, pr, from $25 to **$30.00**
Cowboy boots, painted pot metal, pr, from $10 to **$12.00**
Golf bag & ball, ceramic, flat unglazed bottoms, probably American (unmarked), bag: 3¼", pr..................**$22.00**
Green thumb & trowel, ceramic, hand w/green thumb interlocks around handle of trowel, 1950s, 1½x5¼", pr .**$28.00**
Humpty Dumpty-type egg heads, ceramic, Gayet California Pottery, 1⅞", pr......................................**$19.00**
Lawnmower, plastic, wheels & handle move realistically, shakers move up & down like pistons, red & white, from $22 to..**$25.00**
Locomotives, ceramic, realistic, lightweight, pr, from $8 to **$10.00**
Logging truck tractor & trailer, pottery, multicolor, green Japan mark, 2x4¾", pr......................................**$26.00**

Pixie heads, ceramic, multicolor, marked 6981 Japan, 3¼", pr..**$32.00**
Race cars, ceramic, 22k gold paint, ca 1940s, pr, from $25 to **$28.00**
Seashells, ceramic, realistic appearance, Japan, pr, from $4 to **$6.00**
Shotgun shells, Bakelite, realistic metal base, pr, from $12 to **$15.00**

Schoop, Hedi

One of the most successful California ceramic studios was founded in Hollywood by Hedi Schoop, who had been educated in the arts in Berlin and Germany. She had studied not only painting but sculpture, architecture, and fashion design as well. Fleeing Nazi Germany with her husband, the famous composer Frederick Holander, Hedi settled in California in 1933 and only a few years later became involved in producing novelty giftware items so popular that they were soon widely copied by other California companies. She designed many animated human figures, some in matched pairs, some that doubled as flower containers. All were hand painted and many were decorated with applied ribbons, sgraffito work, and gold trim. To a lesser extent, she modeled animal figures as well. Until fire leveled the plant in 1958, the business was very productive. Nearly everything she made was marked.

If you'd like to learn more about her work, we recommend *The Collector's Encyclopedia of California Pottery, Second Edition,* by Jack Chipman (Collector Books).

Bowl, shell form, ivory w/gold, black interior, 1950s, 12" L..**$42.50**
Candle holder, double, spiral-twist base & branches..**$45.00**
Dresser box, Deco lady, base is half of her long full skirt, hands together under her chin, 7"........**$85.00**
Figurine, girl w/flowing skirt holds billowing apron w/1 hand, 7½" **$70.00**
Figurine, girl w/jump rope, tooled gray hair, grey eyes, pink pinafore w/silver flakes, on gray pedestal, 9", NM .**$110.00**
Figurine, Hula dancer, long grass skirt, fingertips together at waist, 11" **$300.00**
Figurine/flower holder, Marguerita, basket on her head, pinks, cream & green, 12", NM **$110.00**
Figurine/planter, Balinese dancer w/fan (planter), gold trim, 12" **$95.00**
Figurine/planter, dancing girls w/swirling skirts, green shades w/gold trim, 10½", facing pr, EX............**$120.00**
Figurine/planter, girl holding open book stands before lg open book (planter), blue, mauve & green 8½"..**$70.00**
Figurine/planter, girl in Tyrolean-style hat holds skirt wide, 11", from $85 to......................................**$100.00**
Figurine/planter, girl w/lg funnel-shaped basket on her right, flowers in her left hand, 9" **$60.00**
Figurine/planter, lady dancing in gown w/long sleeves & plunging neckline, fan held above her face, open basket, 13" **$95.00**

Figurine/planter, lady in off-shoulder gown w/umbrella in left hand (planter), picture hat, 13".....................**$145.00**

Figurine/planter, lady in pink dress w/pleated skirt holds flowers & lg vase, 9¼x6⅞", NM.........................**$110.00**

Figurine/planter, lady w/basket (planter) & poodle, long black dress, pink shoes.....................................**$215.00**

Figurine/planter, lady w/parasol, Phantasy line, green dress, gold trim, 11"...**$90.00**

Figurine/planter, lady w/striped skirt holds basket & chicken, boy w/striped hat holds striped baskets, pr.......**$140.00**

Figurine/planter, Repose, lady seated w/long black hair, gold trim, 12"..**$165.00**

Figurines, Chinese musicians (boy & girl), yellow & green, ca 1946, 11", pr, NM..**$175.00**

Figurines, dancing couple (portraying Comedy & Tragedy), pink, gold & black, 12¾", 12¼", pr **$300.00**

Figurines, dancing girls, ea carrying ceramic basket suspended on cord in 1 hand, 2nd outstretched, 13", 12", facing pr...**$300.00**

Figurines, Dutch boy & girl, pastel pinks & blues, 11½", 11", pr **$175.00**

Figurines, Oriental lady w/fan (flower holder) & man w/hand outstretched, 11¼", 12", pr, EX...............**$45.00**

Figurines/planters, Dutch boy & girl, she holds pot low, he has 1 on his back, pink & blue, 9", 10½", pr.......**$90.00**

Figurines/planters, French peasants, ea w/basket, she wearing lg hat, both w/hand extended, 13", 12½", pr.......**$175.00**

Figurines/planters, rooster, tan w/yellow, white & black, 8½", facing pr **$125.00**

Planter, horse w/saddle, 7" **$60.00**

Plate, poodle, black & gray on white, 7½" sq **$85.00**

Plate, sailboats at dock, mountains in background, shades of blue/teal, signed, sq **$100.00**

Vase, Art Deco-style fish on pink sculpted shape w/round opening in center...**$75.00**

Scouting Collectibles

Collecting scouting memorabilia has long been a popular pastime for many. Through the years, millions of boys and girls have been a part of this worthy organization founded in England in 1907 by retired Major-General Lord Robert Baden-Powell. Scouting has served to establish goals in young people and help them to develop leadership skills, physical strength, and mental alertness. Through scouting, they learn basic fundamentals of survival. The scouting movement came to the United States in 1910, and the first World Scout Jamboree was held in 1911 in England. If you would like to learn more, we recommend *A Guide to Scouting Collectibles With Values* by R.J. Sayers (ordering information is given in the Directory).

Advisor: R.J. Sayers (See Directory, Scouting Collectibles)

Boy Scouts

Armband, 1957 National Jamboree, white felt w/red lettering, for Staff **$25.00**

Armband, 1973 National Jamboree, Service Corps......**$20.00**

Ashtray, 1973 National Jamboree, w/logo.....................**$3.00**

Bank, Scout w/staff, gray-painted iron **$45.00**

Banner, 1971 World Jamboree, fringed **$5.00**

Baseball hat, 1967 World Jamboree, w/diamond patch..**$5.00**

Belt buckle, 1959 World Jamboree Special Issue, w/logo..**$45.00**

Belt buckle, 1960 National Jamboree, full first class.....**$3.00**

Binoculars, Offical Boy Scouts, plastic in vinyl case, 1950s **$20.00**

Book, National Jamboree Insignia Checklist, Ellis, 1988..**$8.00**

Book, Souvenir; 1977 National Jamboree **$4.00**

Book, The Patch Collector's Handbook, Bearce-Myers, 1990...**$7.00**

Book, 1963 Official World Jamboree, Golden Leaves of Marathon...**$10.00**

Bookends, 1960 National Jamboree, Official...............**$15.00**

Box, gadget; 1957 National Jamboree, pressed wood w/figures along side..**$10.00**

Bust, Baden-Powell, silver-tone metal, 6"..................**$100.00**

Canteen, plastic w/plastic screw top, 1970..................**$4.00**

Cigarette lighter, 1964 National Jamboree, staff pc, w/logo...**$10.00**

Compass, Sylva Pathfinder, plastic, sq, 1950..................**$6.00**

Decal, A Boy Scout Lives Here, scout w/staff, English, 1940s...**$4.00**

Figure, Scout hiking w/canteen, painted iron **$12.00**

Figure, Scout making fire, painted iron **$15.00**

First-Aid Kit, Bauer & Black, in khaki case, rectangular ..**$15.00**

Flag, Local Cub Pack, blue wool, pack numbers sewn on, 1940 ....**$25.00**

Flashlight, green plastic w/full emblems, L-shape **$10.00**

Handkerchief, khaki w/red logo, 1970 ....**$2.00**

Hatchet, Tru-Temper, oak handle, 1950s.....................**$12.50**

Medal, Eagle, Robins type 3, sterling with flat back (no BSA), 2nd class bar with hanging knot, $75.00.

Money clip, 1969 National Jamboree, gold-tone w/logo .**$3.00**

Neckerchief, Official 1951 World Jamboree, cotton **$50.00**

Pamphlet, District Operation, BSA series, 1957.............**$2.00**

Pamphlet, Scoutmasters First 6 Weeks, BSA issue.........**$4.00**

Pamphlet, Universal Indian Sign Language, BSA issue.**$9.00**

Paperweight, 1967 World Jamboree, clear plastic w/logo in center **$8.00**

Patch, jacket; 1955 Official World Jamboree, woven material, 6"..**$35.00**

Pedometer, Official BSA issue, belt-loop holder, 1950s-70s...**$10.00**

Pen, ink; Parker Bros, w/1940s emblem.....................**$7.50**

Pin-back, Baden-Powell in center, crossed flags.........**$40.00**

Plate, Our Heritage, Rockwell-Gorham, ceramic.........**$50.00**

Record, Morse Code Made Easy, 78 rpm....................**$15.00**

Record, 1950 Scout Marches, Official Boy Scout issue, 45 rpm..**$8.00**

Ring, full first class, sterling **$10.00**

Smoking pipe, Baden-Powell on side of stem, 4½" .**$100.00**

Smoking pipe, Meershaum, carved face of Baden-Powell in ivory, rare...**$100.00**

Souvenir book, 1957 World Jamboree, issued at Jamboree..**$15.00**

Statue, Baden-Powell in uniform, bronze, w/sword in scabbard, 9¾"...**$150.00**

Tea tin, shows Major Baden-Powell on top, 4x4x6½" ..**$45.00**

Window sticker, Get Out & Vote **$5.00**

Girl Scouts

Armband, Farm Aid **$15.00**

Badge, Wing Scouting, cloth.....................................**$20.00**

Brownie wings, 1931..**$10.00**

Camera, Falcon, 1940 ....**$30.00**

Certificate, Brownie Law; embossed, 1920 ....**$15.00**

Cookie cutter set, green handle.................................**$20.00**

Cup, collapsible; aluminum, 1950 ....**$5.00**

Doll in uniform, Flexy-Wood, jointed w/painted features, 1928-30 ....**$40.00**

Doll in uniform, Terri Lee, hard plastic, 1949-53, 16"..**$20.00**

Emblem, Girl Scout Hospital Aide.............................**$20.00**

Flag, Official Brownies, smaller type, 1930s.................**$25.00**

Handbook, Official Leaders; tan cover, 1920..............**$30.00**

Medal, Life Saving, bronze, Maltese cross, 1916 ....**$200.00**

Memory book & calendar, 1934 ....**$10.00**

Paper dolls, boxed w/all figures, 1958 ....**$20.00**

Patch, Treasurers, green twill, 1937...........................**$10.00**

Pin, 1923-34 GSA Tenderfoot....................................**$4.00**

Pin, 1939 World's Fair Service **$200.00**

Postcard, Brownie, child by lake, 1930s.....................**$10.00**

Program, 1940 Mariners, sm anchor guard pin **$15.00**

Whistle, Official, cylinder type, 1920s.........................**$20.00**

Sebastians

These tiny figures were first made in 1938 by Preston W. Baston and sold through gift stores, primarily in the New England area. When he retired in 1976, the Lance Corporation chose one hundred designs which they continued to produce under Baston's supervision. Since then, the discontinued figures have become very collectible.

Baston died in 1984, but his son, P.W. Baston, Jr., continues the tradition.

The figures are marked with an imprinted signature and a paper label. Early labels (before 1977) were green and silver foil shaped like an artist's palette; these are referred to as 'Marblehead' labels (Marblehead, Massachusetts, being the location of the factory) and figures that carry one of these are becoming hard to find and are highly valued by collectors.

Adams Academy, w/steeple......................................**$100.00**

Andrew Jackson..**$35.00**

Becky Thatcher...**$23.00**

Betsy Ross..**$23.00**

Calvary...**$500.00**

Candy Store..**$80.00**

Christmas Morning..**$30.00**

Clown..**$50.00**

Darned Well He Can..**$275.00**

Doctor...**$75.00**

Elizabeth Monroe..**$65.00**

Farmer...**$35.00**

Gathering Tulips..**$100.00**

George Washington w/cannon **$35.00**

Grocery Store, Marblehead era...................................**$65.00**

Hanna Dustin, pen stand..**$300.00**

Jack & Jill, blue label...**$40.00**

JF Kennedy...**$60.00**

Little Sister, blue label..**$40.00**

Mrs Obocell..**$400.00**

Old North Church, autographed Woody Baston, blue...**$45.00**

Paul Revere **$45.00**

Pilgrims, 1947, $125.00; Colonial Watchman, $90.00.

Prince Philip...**$200.00**

Ronald Reagan, Young Republican **$85.00**

Sam Weller...**$60.00**

Shoemaker, green label...**$70.00**

Skipping Rope...**$35.00**

Son of the Desert..**$225.00**

Swanboat, Masons...**$200.00**

Weaver & Loom, Marblehead era................................**$65.00**

White House, gold...**$100.00**

Shawnee Pottery

In 1937 a company was formed in Zanesville, Ohio, on the suspected site of a Shawnee Indian village. They took the tribe's name to represent their company, recognizing the Indians to be the first to use the rich clay from the banks of the Muskingum River to make pottery there. Their venture was very successful, and until they closed in 1961, they produced many lines of kitchenware, planters, vases, lamps, and cookie jars that are very collectible today.

They specialized in figural items. There were 'Winnie' and 'Smiley' pig cookie jars and salt and pepper shakers; 'Bo Peep,' 'Puss 'n Boots,' 'Boy Blue,' and 'Charlie Chicken' pitchers; Dutch children; lobsters; and two lines of dinnerware modeled as ears of corn.

Values sometimes hinge on the extent of an item's decoration. Most items will increase by 100% to 200% when heavily decorated with decals and gold trimmed.

Not all of their ware was marked Shawnee; many pieces were simply marked U.S.A. (If periods are not present, it is not Shawnee) with a three- or four-digit mold number. If you'd like to learn more about this subject, we recommend *Shawnee Pottery, The Full Encyclopedia,* by Pam Curran; *The Collector's Guide to Shawnee Pottery* by Duane and Janice Vanderbilt; and *Shawnee Pottery, Identification & Value Guide,* by Jim and Bev Mangus.

See Also Cookie Jars.

Advisor: Rick Spencer (See Directory, Shawnee)

Club: Shawnee Pottery Collectors' Club
P.O. Box 713
New Smyrna Beach, FL 32170-0713; Monthly nationwide newsletter. SASE (c/o Pamela Curran) required when requesting information. Optional: $3 for sample of current newsletter

Ashtray, panther paw, black & white, marked USA ...**$27.00**
Creamer, Pennsylvania Dutch, decorated w/heart & flowers, marked USA 12 ....**$60.00**
Creamer, Puss 'n Boots, w/gold, marked Shawnee USA 85 ....**$140.00**
Creamer, Smiley the Pig, embossed cloverleaf w/gold, marked Patented Smiley USA **$185.00**
Figurine, donkey, no mark, 6½"......................................**$12.00**
Figurine, gazelle, w/gold, marked USA 614, 5".........**$85.00**
Grease jar, cottage, marked USA 8......................**$375.00**
Pitcher, Bo Peep, marked USA Pat Bo Peep, 40-oz....**$90.00**
Pitcher, Space Saver, embossed flower, marked USA 40, 20-oz **$26.00**
Planter, Bicycle Built for Two, marked Shawnee USA 735 ....**$75.00**
Planter, bull, w/gold, marked 668..............................**$25.00**
Planter, circus horse, marked USA **$20.00**
Planter, clown w/pot, marked USA 619......................**$15.00**
Planter, Colonial Lady, marked USA 616 ....**$35.00**
Planter, cub bear & wagon, w/gold, marked USA 731..**$50.00**
Planter, dog & jug, marked USA 610 ....**$10.00**
Planter, dolphin, marked USA **$12.00**
Planter, dove w/planting dish, w/gold, marked Shawnee 2025 ....**$45.00**

Planter, duckling, marked Shawnee USA 720.............**$26.00**
Planter, elephant, marked USA....................................**$20.00**
Planter, hobby horse, marked Shawnee 600 ....**$20.00**
Planter, Irish setter, marked USA **$10.00**
Planter, kitten, marked, USA 723................................**$35.00**
Planter, lovebirds, marked USA **$12.00**
Planter, lying deer, marked USA **$25.00**
Planter, Madonna, marked USA **$30.00**
Planter, pig & basket, marked USA **$10.00**
Planter, pixie, marked USA 536 ....**$10.00**
Planter, rabbit, marked USA..**$16.00**
Planter, rabbit & cabbage, marked USA......................**$10.00**
Planter, terrier & doghouse, marked USA...................**$25.00**
Planter, three pigs, marked USA **$16.00**
Salt & pepper shakers, Chanticleers, gold & decorated, pr...**$190.00**
Salt & pepper shakers, Chanticleers, sm, pr...............**$35.00**
Salt & pepper shakers, ducks, sm, pr **$35.00**
Salt & pepper shakers, Dutch Kids, blue & gold, lg, pr, from $85 to...**$95.00**
Salt & pepper shakers, elephants, white, turquoise & flax blue, sm, pr..**$25.00**
Salt & pepper shakers, flower clusters, sm, pr...........**$25.00**
Salt & pepper shakers, flowerpots, gold pot & flower, sm, pr, from $55 to...**$65.00**

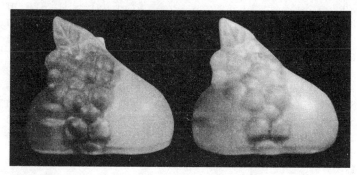

Salt and pepper shakers, Fruit, small, from $25.00 to $35.00 for the pair. (Photo courtesy Duane Vanderbilt)

Salt & pepper shakers, Jack & Jill, gold & decals, lg, pr, from $200 to...**$225.00**
Salt & pepper shakers, Jumbo, sm, pr.....................**$100.00**
Salt & pepper shakers, milk cans, w/gold, sm, pr, from $75 to **$85.00**
Salt & pepper shakers, Muggsy, gold & decals, pr, minimum value **$400.00**
Salt & pepper shakers, Puss 'n Boots, sm, pr, from $35 to..**$45.00**
Salt & pepper shakers, Smiley & Winnie, heart set, sm, pr **$60.00**
Salt & pepper shakers, Smiley the Pig, blue neckerchief w/gold & decals, lg, pr **$295.00**
Salt & pepper shakers, Smiley the Pig, green neckerchief, lg, pr **$135.00**
Salt & pepper shakers, Smiley the Pig, peach neckerchief, sm, pr..**$50.00**
Salt & pepper shakers, sunflower, sm, pr...................**$35.00**
Salt & pepper shakers, Swiss Kids, lg, pr **$45.00**
Salt & pepper shakers, watering cans, sm, pr............**$26.00**

Teapot, cottage, marked USA 7, 5-cup, rare, minimum value **$650.00**
Teapot, fern embossed, peach, yellow, blue, or green, marked USA, 8-cup..**$60.00**
Teapot, horseshoe design, yellow, flax blue, or turquoise, marked USA, 8-cup....................**$45.00**
Teapot, Pennsylvania Dutch, marked USA 14, 14-oz..**$70.00**
Teapot, swirl, blue, green, or yellow, marked USA....**$35.00**
Teapot, Wave pattern, blue, yellow, or green, marked USA, 5-cup...**$50.00**
Vase, cornucopia, marked Shawnee USA 865, 5"........**$16.00**
Vase, cornucopia girl or boy, marked USA 1275 or USA 1265, 5", ea....................................**$14.00**
Wall pocket, clock, w/gold, marked USA 530.............**$45.00**
Wall pocket, red feather, no mark...............................**$45.00**

Corn Ware

Bowl, fruit; King or Queen, marked 92 ....**$48.00**
Butter dish, Queen, w/lid, marked Shawnee 72 ....**$55.00**
Casserole, Queen, marked Shawnee 74, lg, from $50 to ..**$55.00**
Creamer, King, w/gold, marked 70, from $95 to **$110.00**
Dish, vegetable; King, marked Shawnee 95, 9"...........**$55.00**
Mug, King or Queen, marked Shawnee 69, 8-oz........**$50.00**
Pitcher, King or Queen, marked 71, from $60 to........**$70.00**
Plate, Queen, marked Shawnee 68, 10".......................**$40.00**
Platter, King or Queen, marked 96, 12" **$55.00**
Relish tray, King, marked Shawnee 79, from $40 to...**$45.00**
Salt shakers, King or Queen, lg, pr............................**$40.00**
Salt shakers, King or Queen, sm, pr **$28.00**
Saucer, Queen, marked 91...**$18.00**
Sugar shaker, White Corn, marked USA, from $60 to...**$70.00**
Teapot, King, marked Shawnee 65, 10-oz **$175.00**

Lobster Ware

Bowl, batter; handled, marked 928 ....**$55.00**
Creamer & sugar bowl, w/lid, marked 910 ....**$90.00**
Hors d'oeuvre holder, marked USA, 7¼"....................**$280.00**
Salad set, marked 924, 9-pc **$135.00**
Salt & pepper shakers, claw shape, marked USA, pr .**$40.00**
Salt & pepper shakers, full body, marked USA, pr...**$225.00**
Spoon holder, double; marked USA 935, 8½".............**$250.00**

Valencia

Ashtray...**$24.00**
Bowl, fruit; no mark, 5" **$17.00**
Bowls, nesting; 8 sizes, ea **$22.00**
Casserole, 7½"...**$50.00**
Coaster...**$15.00**
Cup & saucer, AD; no mark.......................................**$22.00**
Cup & saucer, tea; no mark **$18.00**
Egg cup **$18.00**
Fork, 9½"...**$35.00**
Marmite, 4½"...**$24.00**
Nappy, 9½" **$20.00**

Plate, chop; no mark, 13"..**$25.00**
Plate, compartment...**$24.00**
Plate, no mark, 6½"...**$12.00**
Sugar bowl, w/lid **$25.00**
Teapot, regular, no mark, 8-cup **$65.00**
Tray, utility **$18.00**
Waffle set, 5 pcs..**$100.00**

Sheet Music

Flea markets are a good source for buying old sheet music, and prices are usually very reasonable. Most examples can be bought for less than $5.00. More often than not, it is collected for reasons other than content. Some of the cover art was done by well-known illustrators like Rockwell, Christy, Barbelle, and Starmer, and some collectors like to zero in on their particular favorite, often framing some of the more attractive examples. Black Americana collectors can find many good examples with Black entertainers featured on the covers and the music reflecting an ethnic theme.

You may want to concentrate on music by a particularly renowned composer, for instance George M. Cohan or Irving Berlin. Or you may find you enjoy covers featuring famous entertainers and movie stars from the '40s through the '60s, for instance. At any rate, be critical of condition when you buy or sell sheet music. As is true with any item of paper, tears, dog ears, or soil will greatly reduce its value.

If you'd like a more thorough listing of sheet music and prices, we recommend *The Sheet Music Reference and Price Guide* by Anna Marie Guiheen and Marie-Reine A. Pafik (Collector Books), and *The Collector's Guide to Sheet Music* by Debbie Dillon.

Aladdin's Genie Dances, Kenneth Kimes, 1951.............**$5.00**
All American Girl, Al Lewis, Photo cover: Ted Fiorito, 1932 ....**$10.00**
Alouette, New Musical Version, Rudy Vallee, 1945 ....**$8.00**
Am I That Easy To Forget?, Carl Belew & WS Stevenson, 1958...**$5.00**
And Russia Is Her Name, EY Harburg & Jerome Kern, 1943 ....**$10.00**
And Then I Remember, Janis Moss Rosenburg, 1956 ...**$5.00**
Are These Really Mine?, Sunny Skylar, David Saxon & Robert Cook, 1945...........................**$3.00**
Are You Livin' Old Man?, Redd Evans, Irene Higginbotham & Abner Silver, 1945 ....**$5.00**
Backward, Turn Backward; Dave Coleman, 1954.........**$5.00**
Baia, Ary Barroso & Ray Gilbert, Movie: The Three Caballeros (Disney), 1945 ....**$15.00**
Barking Dog, Al Stillman, Photo cover: Crew Cuts, 1954.**$5.00**
Beau James, Baker, Movie: Beau James, Photo cover: Bob Hope & Vera Miles, 1957.........................**$5.00**
Beauty Must Be Loved, Sammy Fain & Irving Kahal, 1934..**$5.00**
Bernardine, Johnny Mercer, Movie: Bernardine, Photo cover: Pat Boone & Terry Moore, 1957 ....**$5.00**

Beyond the Reef, Jack Pitman, photo cover: Bing Crosby, 1949...$3.00

Blue Harlem, Edward Kennedy & Duke Ellington, 1935 ....$10.00

Blue Mirage, Sam Coslow & Lotar Olias, 1954.............$5.00

Boy Named Sue, Shel Silverstein, Photo cover: Johnny Cash, 1969..$5.00

Brazil, Bob Russell, Movie: Saludos Amigos (Disney), 1939...$15.00

Bumming Around, Pete Graves, 1953 ....$3.00

Bus Stop Song, Darby, Movie: Bus Stop, Photo cover: Marilyn Monroe & Don Murray, 1956..................$10.00

Bye & Bye, Lorenz Hart & Richard Rogers, Musical: Dearest Enemy, 1925..$5.00

Can't Help Falling in Love, Peretti, Creatore & Weiss, Movie: Blue Hawaii, Photo cover: Elvis Presley, 1961 ....$5.00

Carlotta, Cole Porter, Movie: Can Can, 1943.................$5.00

Chicka Boom, Bob Merrill, 1953...................................$5.00

Cling a Little Closer, Mitchell Parish & Erwin Kent, 1947 .$5.00

Cold, Cold Heart; Hank Williams, Photo cover: Tony Bennett...$3.00

Comme Ci, Comme Ca; Joan Whitney & Alex Kramer, Photo cover: Frank Sinatra, 1947 ....$5.00

Coney Island Baby, Peter Alonzo, 1962........................$5.00

Cornbelt Symphony, Nev Simons, 1948........................$5.00

Curiosity, Joan Whitney, Alex Kramer & Sam Ward, 1947 ..$5.00

Cutest Little Red-Headed Doll, Jack Wolf & Carl Sigman, 1947...$5.00

Darling Lili, Mercer & Mancini, Movie: Darling Lili, Photo cover: Julie Andrews, 1970................................$5.00

Daughter of Jole Blon, Bart Dawson, 1948 ....$5.00

Dinner for One Please, James, Michael Carr, Photo cover: Jackie Heller, Cover artist: B Harris, 1935...............$5.00

Don't Forget To Say 'No' Baby, Hoagy Carmichael & Johnny Mercer, 1942..$5.00

Donna Maria, Claude Debussy & Allie Wrubel, 1941 ...$5.00

Down in the Depths, Cole Porter, Movie: Red, Hot & Blue, 1936...$5.00

Eleventh Hour, King Palmer & Carl Sigman, Photo cover: Al Hibbler, 1956..$3.00

Enchanted Sea, Frank Metis & Randy Starr, 1959..........$5.00

Eyes of Blue, Stone & Young, Movie: Shane, Photo cover: Alan Ladd, Jean Arthur & Van Heflin, 1953 ....$5.00

Faith Can Move Mountains, Ben Raleigh & Guy Woods, Photo cover: Johnnie Ray, 1952..............................$5.00

Fire & Rain, James Taylor, Photo cover: James Taylor, 1969..$5.00

Five Minutes With Mr Thornhill, Claude Thornhill, 1942..$5.00

Flea in Her Ear, Cahn & Kaper, Movie: A Flea in Her Ear, Photo cover: Rex Harrison, 1968 ....$5.00

For Once in My Life, Ronald Miller & Orlando Murden, Photo cover: Tony Bennett, 1967 ....$5.00

For the Good Times, Kris Kristofferson, 1968 ....$5.00

Forever & Ever, Malia Roasa & Franz Winkler, Photo cover: Perry Como, 1947 ....$5.00

Furlough Waltz, Claude Marquis, Photo cover: Guy Lombardo, 1945...$5.00

Giant, Webster & Tiomkin, Movie: Giant, Photo cover: James Dean, Liz Taylor & Rock Hudson, 1956...............$10.00

Gideon Bible, Steve Allen, Photo cover: Steve Allen, 1954..$5.00

Girl That I Marry, Irving Berlin, Movie: Annie Get Your Gun, 1947 ....$10.00

Go Away Little Girl, Carole King, Photo cover: Donny Osmond, 1962...$5.00

Goin' Out of My Head, Teddy Randozzo & Bobby Weinstein, 1964..$5.00

Going Down, William J Harry & William L Baker, Photo cover: Robert Baker, 1947 ....$5.00

Goodbye Sue, Rule, Ricca & Loman, Photo cover: Robert Downey, 1943 ....$3.00

Goodnight, Sleep Tight; Sylvia Fine, Movie: The Five Pennies, Photo cover: Danny Kaye & Louis Armstrong, 1959..$5.00

Goodnight Irene, Huddie Ledbetter & John Lomax, Photo cover: The Weavers & Gordon Jenkins, 1950.........$3.00

Great Divide, Gimbel & Schifrin, Movie: Bullet, Photo cover: Steve McQueen & Jacqueline Bisset, 1969..............$5.00

Green Beret, PG Fairbanks & CWD Ken Whitcomb, 1964..$5.00

Guitar Boogie, Arthur Smith, Photo cover: Arthur Smith, 1946..$5.00

Guy Is a Guy, Oscar Brand, Photo cover: Doris Day, 1952..$5.00

Have I Told You Lately That I Love You, Scott Wiseman, Photo cover: Bing Crosby & Andrew Sisters, 1946 ....$10.00

Have Mercy, Buck Ram & Chick Webb, 1939 ....$5.00

He's a Right Guy, Cole Porter, Movie: Something for the Boys, 1942 ....$5.00

He's One-A in the Army, Redd Evans, WWII, 1941....$10.00

Heart, Richard Alder & Jerry Ross, Musical: Damn Yankees, 1955..$5.00

Heartbroken, Springer & Ebb, Photo cover: Judy Garland, 1953...$10.00

Hearts of Stone, Jackson, 1954 ....$5.00

Here, There & Everywhere; John Lennon & Paul McCartney, Photo cover: Beatles, 1966...............................$25.00

Here You Are, Leo Robin & Ralph Rainger, 1943 ....$5.00

Ho Ho Song, Red Buttons & Joe Darion, Photo cover: Red Buttons, 1953...$5.00

Holy Grail, Albert Stillman & Georg Fredrick Handel, 1945..$5.00

Honorable Profession of the Forth Estate, Irving Berlin, Musical: Miss Liberty, 1949....................................$10.00

Hot Toddy, Hendler & Flanagan, 1953 ....$5.00

How Cute Can You Be?, Bill Carey & Carl Fischer, 1946..$5.00

I Beg of You, Elvis Presley, 1957 ....$20.00

I Don't Care If the Sun Don't Shine, Mack Davis, Photo cover: Tony Martin, 1949...$5.00

I Don't Want To Be Hurt Anymore, McCarthy, Photo cover: Nat King Cole, 1962...$3.00

I Hate You Darling, Cole Porter, Movie: Let's Face It, 1943..$5.00

I Hear a Dream, Leo Robin & Ralph Rainger, Movie: Gulliver's Travels, 1939..$5.00

425

I Love You, Cole Porter, Movie: Mexican Hayride, 1943 .**$5.00**

I Paid My Income Tax Today, Irving Berlin, 1942 ....**$5.00**

I Surrender Dear, Gordon Clifford & Harry Harris, Photo cover: Bing Crosby, 1931 ....**$5.00**

I Want To Hold Your Hand, Beatles, 1978 ....**$25.00**

I Went to the Wedding, Jessie Mae Robinson, Photo cover: Patti Page, 1952 ....**$5.00**

I Wuv a Wabbit, Milton Berle, Ervin Drake & Paul Martell, Cover Artist: Barbelle, 1945....................................**$8.00**

I'll Have a Vanilla, Redmond Farrar & Arthur Terker, Photo cover: Eddie Cantor, 1934 ....**$10.00**

I'll Know, Jo Swerling, Abe Burrow & Frank Loesser, Musical: Guys & Dolls, 1950...................................**$5.00**

I'll Sing You a Thousand Love Songs, Warren and Dubin, 1936, $15.00. (Photo courtesy Guiheen & Pafik)

I'm an Indian Too, Irving Berlin, Movie: Annie Get Your Gun, 1946..**$5.00**

I'm At the Mercy of Love, Benny Davis & J Fred Coots, Musical: Cotton Club Parade, 1936..........................**$8.00**

I'm Hans Christian Andersen, Frank Loesser, Movie: Hans Christian Andersen, Photo cover: Danny Kaye, 1951..**$5.00**

I'm Not Your Steppin' Stone, Monkees, 1966 ....**$5.00**

I'm Popeye the Sailor Man, Sammy Lerner, Movie: Popeye the Sailor, Photo cover: Popeye, Olive, Wimpy & Bluto, 1934 ....**$25.00**

I've Got the Sun in the Morning, Irving Berlin, Movie: Annie Get Your Gun, 1946...**$10.00**

If I Give My Heart to You, Jimmie Crane, Al Jacobs & Jimmy Brewster, Photo cover: Doris Day, 1953 ....**$5.00**

If I Had My Life To Live Over, Henry Tobias, Moe Jaffe & Larry Vincent, Photo cover: Buddy Clark, 1948 ...**$10.00**

If I Ruled the World, Leslie Bricusse & Cyril Ornadel, Photo cover: Tony Bennett, 1963 ....**$5.00**

Ike, Mr President, Photo cover: White House, 1953...**$25.00**

In a World of My Own, Bob Hilliard & Sammy Fain, Movie: Alice in Wonderland (Disney), 1951......................**$10.00**

In the Mission of Augustine, Jack Chiarelli, 1953..........**$3.00**

Is He the Only Man in the World?, Irving Berlin, 1962...**$5.00**

It Might Have Been, Cole Porter, Movie: Something To Shout About, 1943 ....**$5.00**

It's Impossible, A Manzanero & Sid Wayne, Photo cover: Perry Como, 1968 ....**$5.00**

Jesse James, Jerry Livingston, Photo cover: Eileen Barton, 1954..**$5.00**

Just an Old Love of Mine, Peggy Lee & Dave Barbour, Photo cover: Peggy Lee & Dave Barbour, 1947 ....**$5.00**

Katrina, Don Raye & Gene DePaul, Movie: Adventures of Ichabod Crane & Mr Toad (Disney), 1949...........**$10.00**

Lady Bird Cha, Cha, Cha; Cover Artist: Norman Rockwell, 1968 ....**$25.00**

Lavender Blue, Larry Morey & Eliot Daniel, Movie: So Dear to My Heart (Disney), 1948................................**$10.00**

Let's Go to Church, Steve Allen, Photo cover: Jimmy Wakely & Margaret Whiting, 1950..**$5.00**

Little Boy's Christmas, Claire, Elliot & Hettel, 1959.......**$3.00**

Little White Cloud That Cried, Johnnie Ray, Photo cover: Johnnie Ray, 1951 ....**$5.00**

Lookin' Out My Back Door, John Fogerty, Photo cover: Creedence Clearwater Revival, 1970.......................**$3.00**

Magic Mountain, Allen & George, Movie: The Magic Mountain, 1964..**$3.00**

March of the Cards, Bob Hilliard & Sammy Fain, Movie: Alice in Wonderland (Disney), 1951 ....**$10.00**

Mexico, Charles Wolcott & Ray Gilbert, Movie: The Three Caballeros (Disney), 1945 ....**$10.00**

Mister Tap Toe, Terry Gilkyson, Richard Dehr & Frank Miller, Photo cover: Doris Day, 1952 ....**$5.00**

More, Norman Newell, R Ortolani & N Oliviero, Movie: Mondo Cane, 1963 ....**$3.00**

My Buddy's Girl, Herb Newman & Murry Schwimmer, 1956...**$3.00**

My Heart Cries for You, Carl Sigman & Percy Faith, Photo cover: Guy Mitchell, 1950.......................................**$5.00**

My Mother Would Love You, Cole Porter, Movie: Panama Hattie, 1942...**$5.00**

My One & Only Love, Robert Mellin & Guy Wood, 1953 ....**$3.00**

Nice To Be Around, Williams & Williams, Movie: Cinderella, Photo cover: James Caan & Marsha Mason, 1973 ..**$3.00**

Noah Found Grace in the Eyes of the Lord, Robert Schmertz, 1951..**$5.00**

Oh Gee! Oh My!; PG Wodehouse & George & Ira Gershwin, 1949..**$5.00**

Old Chaperone, Ramey Idriss & George Tibbles, 1947 ..**$5.00**

Oop Shoop, Shirley Gunter & The Queens, Photo cover: The Crew Cuts, 1954 ....**$3.00**

Otty the Otter, Shaindling & Pattarini, Movie: The Great Adventure, 1955 ....**$3.00**

Pearly Shells, Webley Edward & Leon Pober, Photo cover: Billy Vaughn, 1964 ....**$5.00**

Play Me a Hurtin' Tune, Sylvia Dee & Sid Lippman, Photo cover: Andrews Sisters & Guy Lombardo, 1952 .....**$4.00**

Power of Love, Colla, Hayes & Lewis, Movie: Back to the Future, Photo cover: Huey Lewis & the News, 1985 .**$3.00**

Rainbow, Russ Hamilton, 1957 ....**$5.00**

Riding on a Rainbow, Berkeley Graham & Carley Mills, 1951...**$3.00**

Rose in Her Hair, Harry Warren & Al Dubin, Movie: Broadway Gondolier, Photo cover: Dick Powell, 1935..............**$8.00**

Ruby Tuesday, Mick Jagger & Keith Richards, Photo cover: Rolling Stones, 1967...**$5.00**

Second Hand Rose, Grant Clarke & James F Hanley, Photo cover: Barbara Streisand, 1965.................................**$3.00**

Sew the Buttons On, John Jennings, Musical: Riverwind, 1963...**$3.00**

Silver in the Moon, HA Pooley, 1945..........................**$3.00**

Sixteen Reasons, Bill & Doree Post, Photo cover: Connie Stevens, 1959...**$3.00**

So Near & Yet So Far, Cole Porter, Movie: You'll Never Get Rich, 1941 ....**$5.00**

Someone Who Cares, Harvey, Movie: Fools, Photo cover: Jason Robards & Katharine Ross, 1971.....................**$3.00**

Song of the Dreamer, Eddie 'Tex' Curtiss, Photo cover: Johnnie Ray, 1955 ....**$5.00**

Spellbound Concerto, Miklos Rozsa, 1946.....................**$5.00**

Sue Me, Jo Swerling, Abe Burrows & Frank Loesser, Musical: Guys & Dolls, 1950...................................**$5.00**

Sweet Eloise, Mack David & Russ Morgan, Photo cover: Buddy Franklin, Cover artist: Sig-Ch, 1942 ....**$3.00**

Syncopated Clock, Leroy Anderson, 1946......................**$5.00**

Teenager's Mother, Curtis R Lewis & JL McFarland, Photo cover: Bill Haley, 1958 ....**$5.00**

That Old Dream Peddler, Al Stewart & Pepe Delgado, 1947 ..**$5.00**

Theme From the Monkees, Tommy Boyce & Bobby Hart, Photo cover: Monkees, 1966.......................**$5.00**

There's a Rising Moon, Paul Francis Webster & Sammy Fain, Movie: Young at Heart, 1954.................**$5.00**

They Say It's Wonderful, Irving Berlin, Movie: Annie Get Your Gun, 1946.......................................**$10.00**

Thumper Song, Bliss, Sour & Manners, Movie: Bambi, 1942...**$10.00**

To the Door of the Sun, Norman Newell, Mario Panzeri, Lorenzo Pilat & Carrado Conti, Photo cover: Al Martino, 1974 ......**$3.00**

Travelin' Man, Jerry Fuller, 1961 ....**$5.00**

Very Good Advice, Bob Hilliard & Sammy Fain, Movie: Alice in Wonderland (Disney), 1951 ....**$10.00**

Welcome Song, Kermit Goell & Fred Spielman, 1945...**$5.00**

What Is a Wife?, Gene Pillar & Ruth Roberts, Photo cover: Steve Allen & Gary Moore, 1955 ....**$5.00**

When I Marry Mr Snow, Richard Rodgers & Oscar Hammerstein II, Movie: Carousel, Cover artist: BJH, 1945...**$5.00**

When the Sun Comes Out, Ted Koeler & Harold Arlen, 1941...**$3.00**

Where in the World?, Buddy Kaye & Carl Lampl, Photo cover: Mindy Carson, 1950 ....**$5.00**

Shell Pink Glassware

This beautiful soft pink, opaque glassware was made for only a short time in the late 1950s by the Jeannette Glass Company. Though a few pieces are commanding prices of more than $200.00 (the Anniversary cake plate, the cigarette box with the butterfly finial, and the lazy Susan tray), most pieces carry modest price tags, and the ware though not as easy to find as it was a few years ago is still available for the collector who is willing to do some searching. Refer to *Collectible Glassware from the 40s, 50s, and 60s,* by Gene Florence (Collector Books) for photos and more information.

Ashtray, butterfly shape...................................**$28.00**

Base, for lazy Susan, w/ball bearings **$160.00**

Bowl, Florentine, footed, 10" **$30.00**

Bowl, Gondola, 17½" **$40.00**

Bowl, Holiday, footed, 10½" **$45.00**

Bowl, Lombardi, design in center, 4-footed, 11".......**$42.00**

Bowl, Napco #2250, w/berry design, footed.............**$15.00**

Bowl, Pheasant, footed, 8".................................**$37.50**

Bowl, Wedding, w/lid, 6½"................................**$22.50**

Cake plate, Anniversary **$225.00**

Cake stand, Harp, 10"......................................**$45.00**

Candle holders, Eagle, 3-footed, pr....................**$85.00**

Candle holders, 2-light, pr **$45.00**

Candy dish, Floragold, 4-footed, 5¼"...................**$20.00**

Candy dish, sq, w/lid, 6½"................................**$30.00**

Candy jar, Grapes, 4-footed, w/lid, 5½" **$20.00**

Candy jar bottom, National **$10.00**

Celery/relish, 3-part, 12½" **$45.00**

Cigarette box, butterfly finial **$235.00**

Compote, Napco #2256, sq...............................**$12.50**

Compote, Windsor, 5½" x 6", $20.00.

Cookie jar, w/lid, 6½" **$100.00**

Creamer, Baltimore Pear....................................**$15.00**

Cup, punch; 5-oz **$6.00**

Honey jar, beehive shape, notched lid **$40.00**

Pitcher, Thumbprint, footed, 24-oz......................**$27.50**

Pot, Napco #2249, crosshatch design...................**$15.00**

Powder jar, w/lid, 4¾"......................................**$45.00**

Punch base, 3½" **$35.00**

Punch bowl, 7½-qt...**$125.00**

Punch ladle, pink plastic...**$20.00**
Relish, Vineyard, octagonal, 4-part, 12" **$42.00**
Stem, sherbet; Thumbprint, 5-oz **$12.50**
Stem, water goblet; Thumbprint, 8-oz............................**$12.50**
Sugar bowl, Baltimore Pear, footed, w/lid..................**$11.00**
Tray, Harp, 2-handled, 12½x9¾"...................................**$60.00**
Tray, lazy Susan, 5-part, 13½" **$55.00**
Tray, snack; w/cup indent, 7¾x10"...............................**$9.00**
Tray, Venetian, 6-part, 16½"..**$40.00**
Tray, 5-part, 2 handles, 15¾" **$85.00**
Tumbler, juice; Thumbprint, footed, 5-oz **$8.00**
Vase, cornucopia, 5" **$15.00**
Vase, heavy bottom, 9"...**$150.00**
Vase, 7" **$30.00**

Shirley Temple

Born April 23, 1928, Shirley Jane Temple danced and smiled her way into the hearts of America in the movie *Stand Up and Cheer*. Many successful roles followed and by the time Shirley was eight years old, she was #1 at box offices around the country. Her picture appeared in publications almost daily, and any news about her was news indeed. Mothers dressed their little daughters in clothing copied after hers and coiffed them with Shirley hairdos.

The extent of her success was mirrored in the unbelievable assortment of merchandise that saturated the retail market. Dolls, coloring books, children's clothing and jewelry, fountain pens, paper dolls, stationery, and playing cards are just a few examples of the hundreds of items that were available. Shirley's face was a common sight on the covers of magazines as well as in the advertisements they contained, and she was the focus of scores of magazine articles.

Though she had been retired from the movies for nearly a decade, she had two successful TV series in the late '50s, *The Shirley Temple Story-Book* and *The Shirley Temple Show*. Her reappearance caused new interest in some of the items that had been so popular during her childhood, and many were reissued.

Always interested in charity and community service, Shirley became actively involved in a political career in the late '60s, serving at both the state and national levels.

If you're interested in learning more about her, we recommend *Shirley Temple Dolls and Collectibles* by Patricia R. Smith; *Toys, Antique and Collectible,* by David Longest; and *Shirley in the Magazines* by Gen Jones.

Note: The pin-back button we describe has been reproduced, so has the cobalt glassware with Shirley's likeness. Beware!

Advisor: Gen Jones (See Directory, Character and Personality Collectibles)

Newsletter: *Lollipop News*
P.O. Box 6203
Oxnard, CA 93031; Dues: $14 per year

Newsletter: *The Shirley Temple Collectors News*
8811 Colonial Rd.
Brooklyn, NY 11209; Dues: $20 per year; checks payable to Rita Dubas

Shirley Temple, autograph as adult, common, $10.00. (Photo courtesy Pat Smith)

Birthday card puzzle, Hallmark, 1986, M......................**$12.50**
Book, Captain January/The Little Colonel, 1940s, EX+, w/dust jacket...**$45.00**
Book, Little Playmates, 16 pages of pictures, EX........**$45.00**
Book, Littlest Rebel, 1939, EX, w/dust jacket..............**$35.00**
Book, Shirley Temple Treasury, Four Books in One, hardbound 205 pages, 1959, w/dust jacket, EX...........**$25.00**
Book, Story of Shirley Temple, Little Big Book, 1935, VG+ **$65.00**
Bowl, cereal; white portrait on cobalt glass, 1930s, original only **$60.00**
Bracelet, w/3 charms, 1936, NM..................................**$45.00**
Clothes hanger, blue cardboard, 1934, M **$65.00**
Doll, bisque, unlicensed Japanese, all original, 6", M..**$250.00**
Doll, celluloid, all original, Japan, 5", NM.................**$185.00**
Doll, celluloid, all original, Japan, 8", NM.................**$245.00**
Doll, composition, Ideal, 11", NM **$975.00**
Doll, composition, Ideal, 13", NM **$750.00**
Doll, composition, Ideal, 16", NM **$800.00**
Doll, composition, Ideal, 18", NM **$975.00**
Doll, composition, Ideal, 20", NM............................**$1,100.00**
Doll, composition, Ideal, 22", NM............................**$1,200.00**
Doll, composition, Ideal, 27", NM............................**$1,750.00**
Doll, Danbury Mint, as Little Colonel, Rebecca of Sunnybrook Farm or Heidi, 1996, 16", MIB.........**$25.00**
Doll, vinyl, sleep eyes, open/closed mouth, rooted hair, blue nylon dress, purse/pin, Ideal, 1959-63, 15", MIB.**$495.00**
Doll, vinyl, sleep eyes, open/closed mouth w/teeth, synthetic wig, yellow dress, white purse, Ideal, 1957, 12", NM **$250.00**
Doll clothes, dress w/attached slip, blue w/lace trim, ca 1957, w/tag, for 12" doll, EX **$110.00**
Doll clothes, dress w/attached slip, blue w/white lace & appliqued flowers, tagged, 1957, fits 15" doll, EX .**$125.00**

Doll clothes, raincoat & hat set, fits 12" doll, ca 1957 58, M (EX box) $75.00

Doll clothes, Rebecca of Sunnybrook Farm outfit, w/tag, complete, fits 12" doll $125.00

Figurine, porcelain, Nostalgia, 1982, M......................$75.00

Handkerchief, Littlest Rebel, 1936, M........................$38.00

Magazine, Hit Parade, 1946, VG..................................$15.00

Magazine ad, black & white close-up photo, from 1934, 5x3½" $6.00

Magazine ad, for movie I'll Be Seeing You, w/Ginger Rogers & Joseph Cotten, full page, 10⅜x14" $18.00

Movie film, Pie Covered Wagon, Ken Films #222, 8mm, EX in box w/photo lid..$25.00

Paper dolls, Shirley Temple Dolls & Dresses, 1934 authorized edition, uncut, EX+..$125.00

Phone card, photo, #25 in series of 48, 2¼x1¼" $35.00

Photograph, black & white glossy, early, 8x10" w/6 smaller shots along side $15.00

Plate, Baby Take a Bow..$65.00

Poster, Shirley in tattered dress, 14x11", M..................$20.00

School tablet, 1935, M..$40.00

Scrapbook, spiral-bound, Saalfield, 1936, EX..............$50.00

Sheet music, Animal Crackers in My Soup, from Curly Top, Shirley as Heidi on cover, EX................................$20.00

Spoon, silver plate w/photo on handle $14.00

Valentine, I've Gone Overboard, 1930s, NM $4.00

Shot Glasses

Shot glasses are small articles of glass that generally hold an ounce or two of liquid; they measure about 3" height or less in height. They've been around since the 1830s have been made in nearly every conceivable type of glass.

Shot glass collectors are usually quantity collectors often boasting of hundreds or even a thousand glasses! The most desirable to collectors are whiskey sample or advertising glasses from the pre-Prohibition era. Most carry etched white lettering that comprises messages relating to a distiller, company, proprietor, or other alcohol-related advertising. Shot glasses like these sell for around $50.00 to $75.00, but recently many rare examples have been auctioned off at prices in excess of $100.00.

These values are only estimates and should be used as a general guide. The club welcomes your suggestions and comments. For more information, we recommend *Shot Glasses: An American Tradition*, and *The Shot Glass Encyclopedia*, both by Mark Pickvet.

Note: Values for shot glasses in good condition are represented by the low end of our ranges, while the high end reflects estimated values for examples in mint condition.

Advisor: Mark Pickvet (See Directory, Shot Glasses)

Black porcelain replica, from $3 to $4.00

Carnival colors, plain or fluted, from $65 to $85.00

Carnival colors, w/patterns, from $150 to $200.00

Culver 22kt gold, from $6 to..$8.00

Depression, colors, from $8 to $12.00

Depression, colors w/patterns or etching, from $15 to .$25.00

Depression, tall, general designs, from $12 to $15.00

Depression, tall, tourist, from $5 to $7.50

Frosted w/gold designs, from $6 to $8.00

General, advertising, from $4 to $5.00

General, etched designs, from $5 to $7.50

General, porcelain, from $4 to......................................$6.00

General, w/enameled design, from $3 to $4.00

General, w/frosted designs, from $3 to $4.00

General, w/gold designs, from $6 to $8.00

General tourist, from $3 to..$5.00

Inside eyes, from $5 to..$7.50

Iridized silver, from $5 to..$7.50

Mary Gregory or Anchor Hocking Ships, from $135 to ..$180.00

Nudes, from $25 to..$35.00

Plain, w/or w/out flutes, from 75¢ to $1.00

Pop or soda advertising, from $12.50 to....................$15.00

Porcelain tourist, from $3.50 to....................................$5.50

Rounded European designs w/gold rims, from $4 to...$5.00

Ruby flashed, from $35 to..$45.00

Southern Airways, 20th year (1949 – 69), $22.00 at auction. (Photo courtesy Shot Glass Exchange)

Square, general, from $5 to..$7.50

Square, w/etching, from $7.50 to $10.00

Square, w/pewter, from $12.50 to $15.00

Square, w/2-tone bronze & pewter, from $15 to $17.50

Standard glass w/pewter, from $8 to $12.00

Taiwan tourist, from $2 to..$3.00

Tiffany, Galle, or fancy art, from $500 to $750.00

Turquoise & gold tourist, from $6 to............................$8.00

Whiskey or beer advertising, modern, from $5 to $7.00

Whiskey sample glasses, from $45 to $85.00

19th-century cut patterns, from $75 to......................$125.00

Silhouette Pictures

These novelty pictures are familiar to everyone. Even today a good number of them are still around, and you'll often see them at flea markets and co-ops. They were very popular in their day and never expensive, and because they were made for so many years (the '20s through the '50s), many variations are available. Though the glass in some is flat, in others it is curved. Backgrounds may be foil, a scenic print, hand tinted, or plain. Sometimes dried flowers were added as accents. But the characteristic common to them all is that the subject matter is reverse painted on the glass. People (even complicated groups), scenes, ships, and animals were popular themes. Though quite often the silhouette was done in solid black to create a look similar to the nineteenth-century cut silhouettes, colors were sometimes used as well.

In the '20s, making tinsel art pictures became a popular pastime. Ladies would paint the outline of their subjects on the back of the glass and use crumpled tinfoil as a background. Sometimes they would tint certain areas of the glass, making the foil appear to be colored. This type is popular with with collectors of folk art.

If you'd like to learn more about this subject, we recommend *The Encyclopedia of Silhouette Collectibles on Glass; 1996 – 97 Price Guide for Encyclopedia of Silhouette Collectibles on Glass;* and *Vintage Silhouettes on Glass and Reverse Paintings* (copyright 2000, all new items pictured) by Shirley Mace. These books show examples of Benton Glass pictures with frames made of metal, wood, plaster, and plastic. The metal frames with the stripes are most favored by collectors as long as they are in good condition. Wood frames were actually considered deluxe when silhouettes were originally sold. Recently some convex glass silhouettes from Canada have been found, nearly identical to the ones made by Benton Glass except for their brown tape frames. Backgrounds seem to be slightly different as well. Among the flat glass silhouettes, the ones signed by Diefenbach are the most expensive. The wildflower pictures, especially ones with fine lines and good detail, are becoming popular with collectors.

Advisor: Shirley Mace (See Directory, Silhouette Pictures)

Convex Glass

Boy (w/dog) shows mother fish he caught, BG 45-109, Benton Glass **$35.00**
Boy on rocking horse followed by girl carrying flag, BG 68-103, Benton Glass **$45.00**
Child plays w/cat while mother watches, BG 68-7B, Benton Glass **$60.00**
Child watches birds in tree from window's ledge, ER 7D-7, CE Erickson Co, advertising **$28.00**
Couple sit while having drinks, BG 68-29, Benton Glass...**$40.00**
Horse & rider jumping fence, PW 5d-4, multicolor, round, Peter Watson's Studio **$25.00**
Indian chief stands w/horse overlooking wagon train in valley, BG 45-203, Benton Glass **$35.00**
Lady looks upon well on hill, BG 45-182, Benton Glass ..**$30.00**
Man & boy overlook the sea, BG 45-122, Benton Glass...**$35.00**
Man looking into mirror as tailor checks fit, BG 3½ 4½-28, Benton Glass **$30.00**
Man sits blowing bubbles from long pipe as boy watches, BG 45-118, Benton Glass **$35.00**

Mother & Son w/Dearest Mother poem in upper corner, BG 68-129, Benton Glass..**$35.00**
Scottie dog chases butterfly, BG 45-186, Benton Glass .**$30.00**
Snowland Splendor, deer watches man w/team of sled dogs, BA 45-2, advertising, Baco Glass Plaque, 1950 ....**$32.00**
Woman shoots bow & arrow while man looks on, BG-45-77, Benton Glass..**$30.00**

Flat Glass

Beau Brummel, man in tails w/top hat & cane, RE 57-125, clear cellophane behind glass, Reliance Products **$18.00**
Boy & his dog fishing, FI 44-2, dried wildflowers, marked Fisher **$30.00**
Boy fishing while flock of geese fly overhead, NE 5½ 7½-1, Newton Manufacturing **$30.00**
Courtship, RE 44-83, Reliance Products **$22.00**
Double Dutch, Dutch boy & girl hold hands, RE 711-33, Reliance Products..**$33.00**
Elfin Music, RI- 57-760, C&A Richards **$140.00**
Girl w/flowers, FL 3½ 3½-3, wildflowers, hand-painted, Flowercraft..**$32.00**
Girl w/3 ducks under tree on a windy day, DE 921-11, Deltex Products..**$30.00**
Hidden Pool, plaster, 2 nude ladies take a swim, BB 68-10, Buckbee-Brehm **$20.00**
John Alden, man in long coat sits in chair smoking pipe, RI 44-592, signed Virginia Dowd, C&A Richards, Boston, Mass **$22.00**
Kittens (2) watch butterfly, BH 48-1, Blaine Hudson .**$10.00**

Lady admiring young boy's catch, Benton Glass #45-109, $45.00. (Photo courtesy Shirley and Ray Mace)

Lady standing on stool lighting candles on fireplace mantel, AP 810-20, Art Publishing **$25.00**
Lady walking Scottie has her hat blown off in the wind, DE 810-15, foil background, Deltex Products............**$35.00**
Little Red Riding Hood (w/wolf), RE 810-15, black w/silver foil background, Reliance Products......................**$35.00**
May I See You Home?, man about to kiss lady's hand, BB 46-1, Buckbee-Brehm **$28.00**

Out Where the West Begins, 2 cowboys w/coffee at campfire, horses beyond, NE 810-4, Newton Manufacturing **$35.00**
Swan Pond, RE 711-2, Reliance Products **$30.00**
The Answer, lady taking mail from box, BB 46-4, painted on glass, Buckbee-Brehm, 1930 ....**$25.00**

Silverplated and Sterling Flatware

The secondary market is being tapped more and more as the only source for those replacement pieces needed to augment family heirloom sets, and there are many collectors who admire the vintage flatware simply because they appreciate its beauty, quality, and affordability. Several factors influence pricing. For instance, a popular pattern though plentiful may be more expensive than a scarce one that might be passed over because it very likely would be difficult to collect. When you buy silverplate, condition is very important, since replating can be expensive.

Pieces with no monograms are preferred. To evaluate monogrammed items, deduct 20% from fancy or rare examples; 30% from common, plain items; and 50% to 70% if they are worn.

Interest in silverplated flatware from the 1950s and 1960s is on the increase as the older patterns are becoming harder to find in excellent condition. As a result, prices are climbing.

Dinner knives range in size from 9⅜" to 10"; dinner forks from 7⅜" to 7¾". Luncheon knives are approximately 8½" to 8¾", while luncheon forks are about 6¾" to 7". Place knives measure 8⅞" to 9¼", and place forks 7⅛" to 7¼".

Our values are given for flatware in excellent condition. Matching services often advertise in various trade papers and can be very helpful in locating the items you're looking for.

If you'd like to learn more about the subject, we recommend *The Standard Encyclopedia of American Silverplate* by Frances M. Bones and Lee Roy Fisher, and *Silverplated Flatware* by Tere Hagan (Collector Books).

Advisor: Rick Spencer (See Directory, Regal)

Silverplate

Adam, iced beverage spoon, Community **$9.00**
Adam, jelly slice, Community **$12.00**
Adam, salad fork, Community **$7.00**
Adonis, 1933, grapefruit spoon, Heirloom.....................**$5.00**
Adonis, 1933, seafood fork, Heirloom...........................**$5.00**
Adoration, 1930, dinner knife, hollow handle, 1847 Rogers...**$7.00**
Adoration, 1930, iced beverage spoon, 1847 Rogers **$9.00**
Adoration, 1930, infant spoon, 1847 Rogers..................**$8.00**
Adoration, 1930, salad fork, 1847 Rogers......................**$7.00**
Affection, 1961, cold meat fork, Community...............**$15.00**
Affection, 1961, pickle fork, solid handle, Community.**$8.00**
Alamo, 1913, bread knife, serrated blade, R Wallace..**$24.00**
Ambassador, cocktail fork, 1847 Rogers........................**$9.00**
Ambassador, oval soup spoon, 1847 Rogers **$8.00**
Ambassador, pie server, 1847 Rogers..........................**$24.00**
Anjou, chocolate spoon, 1899 Wallace.........................**$12.00**

Anjou, round soup spoon, 1899 Wallace.....................**$8.00**
Anniversary, 1923, gravy ladle, 1847 Rogers **$16.00**
Anniversary, 1923, original wooden box, 1847 Rogers..**$20.00**
Anniversary, 1923, pie server, 1847 Rogers **$20.00**
Anniversary, 1923, service for 8, 40 pcs, 1847 Rogers..**$135.00**
Argosy, 1926, ice cream fork, 1847 Rogers.................**$16.00**
Athena, 1916, ice cream fork **$14.00**
Banbury, 1950, individual butter spreader, Rogers **$5.00**
Beloved, 1960, pierced pie server, Meridian Silver **$16.00**
Berlin, 1899, fruit knife, hollow handle, American Silver..**$15.00**
Berlin, 1899, strawberry fork, American Silver **$15.00**
Bordeaux, 1945, jelly slice, Nobility **$8.00**
Bridal Wreath, 1915, butter pick, Oneida.....................**$9.00**
Bridal Wreath, 1915, teaspoon, Oneida........................**$4.00**
Bright Future, 1954, berry spoon, Holmes & Edwards ..**$20.00**
Caprice, 1939, gravy ladle, Nobility Plate **$16.00**
Caprice, 1939, iced beverage spoon, Nobility Plate......**$9.00**
Caprice, 1939, seafood fork, Nobility Plate...................**$7.00**
Caprice, 1939, tomato server, Nobility Plate................**$20.00**
Charter Oak, 1906, coffee spoon, 1847 Rogers...........**$10.00**
Charter Oak, 1906, cold meat fork, 1847 Rogers **$35.00**
Charter Oak, 1906, dinner knife, hollow handle, 1847 Rogers..**$30.00**
Charter Oak, 1906, lunch fork, 1847 Rogers...............**$15.00**
Charter Oak, 1906, salad fork, 1847 Rogers **$48.00**
Charter Oak, 1906, tablespoon, 1847 Rogers..............**$16.00**
Chevalier, 1895, oyster ladle, Rogers & Bros..............**$39.00**
Coronation, 1936, master butter knife, Oneida **$7.00**
Coronation, 1936, original 2-drawer box, Oneida.......**$35.00**
Coronation, 1936, oval soup spoon, Oneida **$7.00**
Coronation, 1936, service for 8, 48 pcs, Oneida.......**$175.00**
Coronation, 1936, sugar shell spoon, Oneida...............**$7.00**
Daffodil, 1950, berry spoon, 1847 Rogers...................**$25.00**
Daffodil, 1950, child's fork, 1847 Rogers **$14.00**
Daffodil, 1950, child's spoon, 1847 Rogers.................**$14.00**
Daffodil, 1950, pickle fork, solid handle, 1847 Rogers.**$12.00**
Daffodil, 1950, pierced relish spoon, 1847 Rogers......**$15.00**
Daffodil, 1950, 4-pc dinner setting, 1947 Rogers **$18.00**
Daisy II, 1910, berry spoon, Wm Roger & Sons **$22.00**
Dawn, 1949, cold meat fork, Rogers & Bros..............**$12.00**
Dawn, 1949, gravy ladle, Rogers & Bros **$15.00**
Dawn, 1949, luncheon knife, hollow handle, Rogers & Bros...**$9.00**
Dawn, 1949, luncheon knife, hollow handle, Rogers & Bros...**$6.00**
Dawn, 1949, pierced pie server, solid handle, Rogers & Bros...**$18.00**
Dawn, 1949, sugar shell spoon, Rogers & Bros **$6.00**
Dundee, master spoon, solid handle, 1847 Rogers.....**$20.00**
El California, 1961, 2-pc salad-serving set, Wm Rogers..**$24.00**
Emerson/Waldorf, 1915, lettuce fork, Rockford...........**$25.00**
Enchantment, 1957, cold meat fork, Oneida **$15.00**
Fairmount, 1911, sugar tongs, Carrolton **$15.00**
Fantasy, 1941, cream ladle, Tudor Plate **$10.00**
Fantasy, 1941, individual butter knife, Tudor Plate.......**$5.00**
Fantasy, 1941, round soup spoon, Tudor Plate............**$6.00**
Fantasy, 1941, tablespoon, Tudor Plate.........................**$7.00**

First Colony, 1975, sugar shell spoon, 1881 Rogers......**$7.00**
First Love, 1937, beef fork, 1847 Rogers...................**$18.00**
First Love, 1937, curved baby spoon, 1847 Rogers.....**$24.00**
First Love, 1937, gravy ladle, 1847 Rogers..................**$20.00**
First Love, 1937, pierced pie server, 1847 Rogers.......**$25.00**
First Love, 1937, service for 12, 72 pcs, 1847 Rogers...**$275.00**
Flower, 1906, dinner knife, solid handle, Rogers.........**$7.00**
Geneva, 1881, ice tongs, Rogers..................................**$42.00**
Geneva, 1881, oyster ladle, Rogers **$50.00**
Grand Elegance, 1959, berry spoon, Rogers................**$15.00**
Grand Elegance, 1959, cold meat fork, Rogers **$12.00**
Grosvenor, 1921, beef fork, Community.....................**$18.00**
Grosvenor, 1921, lg cake server, Community.............**$30.00**
Grosvenor, 1921, sugar tongs, Community..................**$24.00**
Harmony, 1938, baby fork, Rogers.............................**$10.00**
Harmony, 1938, baby spoon, Rogers **$10.00**
Honor, 1937, master butter knife, Wm Rogers **$5.00**
Imperial, 1904, berry spoon, gold-washed bowl, Holmes &
    Edwards **$24.00**
Imperial, 1904, bouillon spoon, Holmes & Edwards ..**$12.00**
Interlude, 1971, berry spoon, International **$18.00**
Interlude, 1971, mayonnaise ladle, International **$16.00**
Interlude, 1971, pickle fork, solid handle, International ..**$10.00**
June, 1932, master butter knife, Tudor Plate **$5.00**
June, 1932, oval soup spoon, Tudor Plate....................**$6.00**
June, 1932, sugar shell spoon, Tudor Plate **$5.00**
King Cedric, 1933, jelly slice, Community **$6.00**
King Cedric, 1933, pie server, hollow handle, Community.**$16.00**
King Cedric, 1933, salad fork, Community **$6.00**
King Edward, 1951, bonbon spoon, National...............**$8.00**
King Edward, 1951, child's fork, National.....................**$8.00**
Kremlin, 1883, dessert fork **$12.00**
La France, 1920, master butter knife **$6.00**
Laurel/Helene, tomato server, Rogers **$16.00**
Malibu, 1956, salad fork, Wm Rogers.........................**$6.00**
Marquise, 1900, 3-tined pie fork, Rogers/Hamilton **$10.00**
May Queen, 1951, berry spoon, Holmes & Edwards..**$20.00**
May Queen, 1951, cold meat fork, Holmes & Edwards..**$14.00**
May Queen, 1951, pierced serving spoon, Holmes &
    Edwards **$9.00**
May Queen, 1951, teaspoon, Holmes & Edwards.........**$3.00**
Nine Flowers, 1933, sugar shell spoon, Wallace **$6.00**
Olive, 19th Century, egg spoon, various manufacturers ..**$16.00**
Olive, 19th Century, nut pick, various manufacturers ..**$8.00**
Olive, 19th Century, sm pie fork, various manufacturers..**$10.00**
Olive, 19th Century, 2-prong butter pick, various manufac-
    turers **$12.00**
Oregon, 1900, mustard ladle, long handle, Royal Plate..**$24.00**
Orleans, 1964, dinner fork, Oneida.............................**$9.00**
Orleans, 1964, master butter knife, Oneida **$7.00**
Orleans, 1964, sugar shell spoon, Oneida **$7.00**
Parisian, 1887, demitasse spoon, Reed & Barton **$15.00**
Pearl, 1900, baby food pusher, Williams.....................**$15.00**
Pearl, 1900, jelly trowel, Williams.............................**$20.00**
Queen Bess, round soup spoon.................................**$5.00**
Queen Bess, 5-pc dinner setting **$15.00**
Reflection, 1959, fruit spoon, 1847 Rogers...................**$9.00**

Reflection, 1959, pierced relish spoon, 1947 Rogers...**$12.00**
Reflection, 1959, 2-pc baby set, 1847 Rogers **$20.00**
Reflection, 1959, 3-pc youth set, 1847 Rogers............**$30.00**
Rhythmic, 1957, dessert place spoon, Holmes & Edwards.**$7.00**
Rhythmic, 1957, dinner knife, hollow handle, Holmes &
    Edwards **$5.00**
Rhythmic, 1957, salad fork, Holmes & Edwards **$5.00**
Rhythmic, 1957, sugar shell spoon...........................**$7.00**
Rhythmic, 1957, teaspoon, Holmes & Edwards..........**$4.00**
Sierra, 1914, cocktail fork..**$10.00**
Sierra, 1914, corn scrapper.......................................**$16.00**
Silver Tulip, 1956, pierced pie server, International......**$8.00**
Southern Splendor, 1962, dinner knife, hollow handle,
    Rogers & Bros **$6.00**
Southern Splendor, 1962, salad fork, Rogers & Bros ..**$6.00**
Southern Splendor, 1962, teaspoon, Rogers & Bros......**$4.00**
Sweet Briar, 1948, oval soup spoon, Tudor Plate **$5.00**
Union Pacific Railroad, early 1900s, bouillon spoon ..**$18.00**
United Airlines, 1950s, sm lunch fork **$15.00**
United Airlines, 1950s, sm lunch knife, solid handle..**$15.00**
United Airlines, 1950s, sm teaspoon **$10.00**
Victorian Classic, 1973, pierced relish spoon, 1881
    Rogers **$9.00**
Victorian Classic, 1973, sugar shell spoon, 1881 Rogers..**$6.00**
Vintage, 1904, pickle fork, long handle, 1847 Rogers...**$45.00**
Vintage, 1904, 3-pc roast carving set, 1847 Rogers...**$225.00**
Wentworth, 1938, iced beverage spoon, Holmes & Tuttle..**$6.00**
Western Airlines, 1940s, coffee spoon.......................**$12.00**
Windsor, twisted butter knife, 1847 Rogers................**$18.00**

Sterling

America, bonbon spoon, Concord Silver....................**$22.00**
America, cold meat fork, Concord Silver....................**$39.00**
America, gravy ladle, Concord Silver **$40.00**
American Classic, cocktail fork, Easterling..................**$19.00**
American Classic, pierced tablespoon, Easterling **$50.00**
American Classic, place knife, Easterling....................**$30.00**
American Classic, salad fork, Easterling.....................**$28.00**
American Victorian, butter spreader, flat handle, Lunt..**$16.00**
American Victorian, lemon fork, Lunt........................**$25.00**
Apollo, ice cream spoon, Alvin Silver........................**$29.00**
Aspen, salad fork, Gorham **$25.00**
Aspen, teaspoon, Gorham...**$17.00**
Blithe Spirit, sugar server, Gorham............................**$24.00**
Blithe Spirit, 4-pc place setting, Gorham **$95.00**
Blossom Time, 2-pc roast carving set, International ...**$90.00**
Blossum Time, 4-pc place setting, International **$78.00**
Brocade, cream soup spoon, International...................**$22.00**
Brocade, serving spoon, International **$42.00**
Camellia, cocktail fork, Gorham **$20.00**
Camellia, service for 12, 77-pc set, w/servers, Gorham..**$1,500.00**
Damask Rose, carving set, roast, 2-pc, Oneida.........**$130.00**
Damask Rose, iced beverage spoon, Oneida.............**$28.00**
Damask Rose, jelly server, Oneida **$32.00**
Damask Rose, lemon fork, Oneida **$30.00**
Damask Rose, teaspoon, Oneida................................**$9.00**

Diadem, master butter knife, hollow handle, Reed & Barton $30.00
Diadem, 4-pc dinner size setting, Reed & Barton.....$150.00
Diamond Star, place spoon, Steiff.............................$30.00
Discovery, cocktail fork, Wallace..............................$22.00
Discovery, pierced tablespoon, Wallace $55.00
Drury Lane, place fork, Towle...................................$30.00
Drury Lane, teaspoon, Towle $19.00
El Grandee, fish knife, hollow handle, Towle............$32.00
El Grandee, 4-pc dinner setting, Towle.....................$130.00
Everlasting Orchid, cream soup spoon, Westmoreland.$26.00
Everlasting Orchid, 4-pc place setting, Westmoreland..$72.00
Fontana, bonbon spoon, Towle $38.00
Fontana, pickle fork, Towle $32.00
Formality, cocktail fork, State House $20.00
Formality, grill knife, State House $18.00
Formality, iced beverage spoon, State House $20.00

Francis I, twelve each: luncheon knives and forks, salad and seafood forks, teaspoons, soup and bouillon spoons, and butter knives; six each: fish knives and forks; and twenty-three other various serving pieces, Reed and Barton, 167 troy ounces, $3,850.00.

French Renaissance, sugar spoon, Reed & Barton......$30.00
French Renaissance, 4-pc lunch setting, Reed & Barton..$110.00
Gadroonette, casserole spoon, Manchester $58.00
Gadroonette, ice cream fork, Manchester....................$26.00
Gadroonette, 4-pc place setting, Manchester..............$64.00
Grandeur, demitasse spoon, Oneida $16.00
Grandeur, lemon fork, Oneida $22.00
Hunt Club, demitasse spoon, Gorham.......................$16.00
Hunt Club, sugar tongs, Gorham...............................$38.00
Joan of Arc, pie server, hollow handle, International.$25.00
Joan of Arc, salad serving fork, International.............$85.00
Joan of Arc, wedding cake knife, International $45.00
Joan of Arc, 4-pc place setting, International.............$95.00
King Richard, citrus spoon, Towle $32.00
King Richard, 4-pc place setting, Towle....................$125.00
Kirk, baby spoon, Cynthia $20.00
Kirk, cream soup spoon, Cynthia...............................$29.00
Kirk, demitasse spoon, Betsy Patterson $19.00

Lace Point, gravy ladle, Lunt....................................$55.00
Lace Point, pickle fork, Lunt.....................................$22.00
Lace Point, teaspoon, Lunt.......................................$18.00
Lunt, dinner fork, Chateau.......................................$32.00
Lunt, flat individual butter knife, Chateau.................$20.00
Lunt, tablespoon, Chateau..$38.00
Margaret Rose, cream soup spoon, National..............$19.00
Margaret Rose, sauce ladle, National........................$39.00
Margaret Rose, 4-pc grill setting, National $45.00
Marquise, lunch fork, Tiffany....................................$52.00
Marquise, pie fork, Tiffany..$59.00
Martha Washington, chocolate spoon, Frank Smith....$24.00
Martha Washington, fruit spoon, Frank Smith $20.00
Minuet, berry spoon, International............................$58.00
Minuet, sugar sifter, International.............................$75.00
Minuet, youth fork, International...............................$26.00
Minuet, 5 o'clock spoon, International $18.00
Mount Vernon, salt spoon, Lunt $25.00
Nocturne, salad fork, Gorham..................................$25.00
Nocturne, steak carving set, Gorham........................$55.00
Old Lace, cold meat fork, Towle................................$55.00
Old Lace, place knife, Towle......................................$30.00
Old Master, cream soup spoon, Towle $30.00
Old Master, dinner knife, hollow handle, Towle $34.00
Old Master, strawberry fork, Towle............................$30.00
Repousse, lettuce fork, Kirk......................................$130.00
Repousse, medium berry spoon, Kirk........................$200.00
Repousse, 4-pc place setting, Kirk $125.00
Richelieu, dinner fork, Tiffany..................................$92.00
Richelieu, fruit spoon, Tiffany $80.00
Richelieu, salad fork, Tiffany.....................................$95.00
Richelieu, tablespoon, Tiffany...................................$135.00
Rose, bacon fork, Steiff...$72.00
Rose, ice cream slice, Steiff.......................................$52.00
Rose, salad serving spoon, Steiff...............................$94.00
Rose, steak knife, Steiff...$35.00
Silver Rose, cold meat fork, Oneida...........................$42.00
Silver Rose, 4-pc place setting, Oneida.......................$70.00
Silver Wheat, cheese server, hollow handle, Reed & Barton.$28.00
Silver Wheat, cream soup spoon, Reed & Barton.......$26.00
Tranquility, baby fork, Fine Arts................................$22.00
Tranquility, salad fork, Fine Arts $24.00
Tranquility, tablespoon, Fine Arts..............................$42.00
Trianon, pierced sugar tongs, Dominick & Haff $90.00
Willow, dessert spoon, Gorham.................................$28.00
Willow, olive fork, Gorham $24.00
Willow, place knife, modern, Gorham........................$26.00
Wodefield, berry spoon, Kirk....................................$85.00
Wodefield, fish serving fork, Kirk..............................$110.00
Wodefield, fruit spoon, Kirk.....................................$29.00
Wodefield, ice cream spoon, Kirk $30.00

Simmons, Robert

Simmons was one of many talented California artisans who during the middle of the twentieth century produced a wide variety of ceramic novelty and decorative items which today's collectors appreciate for their excellent form and beauty. Especially popular are his animal figurines (of which his dogs are a favorite), representing both domestic and exotic species.

Bank, chicken, 1950s, 5x4" **$30.00**
Figurine, bull terrier, original Butch silver sticker **$42.00**
Figurine, chow chow, original Nimpo #168 silver sticker, 5½" **$45.00**
Figurine, cocker Spaniel, original Ruggles silver sticker, 3" **$40.00**
Figurine, collie dog, original Queenie #147 sticker, 10½" L, from $60 to **$65.00**
Figurine, collie dog, original sticker, 12" **$75.00**
Figurine, English setter, original Ace #486 sticker, 7x9¼" ..**$110.00**
Figurine, foal, gray, 1950s, 4½" **$29.00**
Figurine, French bulldog, original Jigs #2064 silver sticker, 4" **$40.00**
Figurine, German shepherd, green over brown, 1950s, 6¾" **$22.50**
Figurine, giraffe, original Snip #20174 sticker, 6½x4½" ..**$50.00**
Figurine, great dane, original Champ #113 silver sticker, 5½" **$45.00**
Figurine, Hereford bull, 5½x9" **$35.00**
Figurine, kitten, gray, 3⅜" **$20.00**
Figurine, kitten, Trixie, 2¾" **$22.00**
Figurine, poodle, black, 5" **$65.00**
Figurine, Scottish terrier, original Chauncy #114 sticker, 5½" **$35.00**
Figurine, squirrel, original Nippy #2037 sticker, 7½" ..**$20.00**
Figurine, St Bernard puppy, original Bernie #149 silver sticker, 5" **$35.00**
Figurine, Twinkle, calf, 1950s, 3⅜" **$25.00**
Figurines, squirrels, 1 sitting (2¾"), 2nd w/tail up (slightly taller), pr **$25.00**
Salt & pepper shakers, puppies (playful), brown & white, 3½", pr **$12.50**

Skookum Indian Dolls

The Skookums Apple Packers Association of Wenatchee, Washington, had a doll made from their trademark. Skookum figures were designed and registered by a Montana woman, Mary McAboy, in 1917. Although she always made note of the Skookum's name, she also used the 'Bully Good' trademark along with other information to inform the buyer that 'Bully Good' translated is 'Skookums.' McAboy had an article published in the March 1920 issue of *Playthings* magazine explaining the history of Skookum dolls. Anyone interested can obtain this information on microfilm from any large library.

In 1920 the Arrow Novelty Company held the contract to make the dolls, but by 1929 the H.H. Tammen Company had taken over their production. Skookums were designed with life-like facial characteristics. The dried apple heads of the earliest dolls did not last, and they were soon replaced with

heads made of a composition material. Wool blankets formed the bodies that were then stuffed with dried twigs, leaves, and grass. The remainder of the body was cloth and felt.

Skookum dolls with wooden legs and felt-covered wooden feet were made between 1917 and 1949. After 1949 the legs and feet were made of plastic. The newest dolls have plastic heads. A 'Skookums Bully Good Indians' paper label was placed on one foot of each early doll. Exact dating of a Skookum is very difficult. McAboy designed many different tribes of dolls simply by using different blanket styles, beading, and backboards (for carrying the papoose). The store display dolls, 36" and larger, are the most valuable of the Skookums. Prices range from $2,000.00 to $2,500.00 per doll or $4,500.00 to $5,000.00 for the pair.

Advisor: Jo Ann Palmieri (See Directory Skookum Dolls)

Child, plastic legs, marked Skookum Bully Good, 6", from $35.00 to $50.00.

Child, plastic legs, 8" to 10", from $50 to **$75.00**
Female w/papoose, wooden legs, 8" to 10", from $75 to ...**$150.00**
Female w/papoose, wooden legs, 10" to 12", from $150 to.**$250.00**
Female w/papoose, wooden legs, 14" to 16", from $250 to.**$300.00**
Male, wooden legs, 8" to 10", from $125 to **$175.00**
Male, wooden legs, 10 to 12", from $175 to **$250.00**
Male, wooden legs, 14" to 16", from $300 to **$400.00**

Smiley Face

The Smiley Face was designed in 1963 by Harvey Ball, a commercial artist that had been commissioned by an insurance company to design a 'happy' logo to use on office supplies and pin-back buttons — seems spirits were low due to unpopular company policies, and the office manager was looking for something that would cheer up her employees. 'Operation Smile' was a huge success. Who would have thought that such a simple concept — tiny eyes with a curving line to represent a big smile in black on a bright yellow background — would have become the enduring icon that it did. Mr. Young was paid a mere $45.00 for his efforts, and no one even bothered to obtain a trademark for Smiley! Over the year, many companies have designed scores of products featuring the happy face. The McCoy Pottery Comany was one of them; they made a line of cookie jars, mugs, banks, and planters. No matter if you collect Smiley or McCoy, you'll want to watch for those!

The Smiley face is enjoying renewed popularity today — you'll find many 'new' examples in those specialty catalogs we all get so many of. But if you buy the vintage Smileys, expect to pay several times their original retail price. Right now, these are hot!

Antenna ball, graduate, tasseled mortarboard attached to Smiley ball, made for car antenna, M **$4.00**
Bank, 1971 Play Pal, lg, EX...**$30.00**
Carpet sweeper, Sweep-A-Smile, Wagner, 1960s, NM..**$115.00**
Clock, Lux Time Division, Lebanon Tennessee, wall type, 7" dia, EX **$15.00**
Cocktail set, shaker & 4 tumblers, printed faces on clear glass, metal lid, Hazelware, 6-pc set, MIB............**$85.00**
Cookie Jar, McCoy, 11x7"..**$80.00**
Disco ball nightlight, plugs into outlet, switch on cord, 6½", M...**$17.50**
Mug, Smiley clown face, McCoy, 4", from $15 to.......**$20.00**
Napkin holder & salt & pepper shakers, ceramic, Made in China, 3-pc set **$55.00**
Necktie, Make the Children Smile/Save the Children on back, EX..**$17.50**
Pez dispenser, different colors, ea w/Smiley face top, complete set of 6, all M in packages **$20.00**
Playing cards, yellow face on box, cards have blue faces, 1960s, mini deck, cards: 2¼x1¾", MIB, from $3 to .**$5.00**
Salt & pepper shakers, yellow plastic, MIB.................**$10.00**
Sugar dispenser, hard plastic, clear w/white top, Shirley Inc Warren PA Patent Pending, 1960s, EX...................**$15.00**
Suncatcher, yellow glass, finished in brass, M..............**$6.00**
Tumblers, faces on clear glass, 1970s, 4¼", 6 for **$15.00**

Snow Domes

Snow dome collectors buy them all, old and new. The older ones (from the thirties and forties) are made in two pieces, the round glass globe that sits on a separate base. They were made here as well as in Italy, and today this type is being imported from Austria and the Orient.

During the fifties, plastic snow domes made in West Germany were popular as souvenirs and Christmas toys. Some were half-domes with blue backs; others were made in bottle shapes or simple geometric forms.

There were two styles produced in the seventies. Both were made of plastic. The first were designed as large domes with a plastic figure of an animal, a mermaid, or some other character draped over the top. In the other style, the snow dome itself was made in an unusual shape.

Snow domes have become popular fun-type collectibles, and there are two good references we recommend for further reading: *Snow Domes* by Nancy McMichael and *The Collector's Guide to Snow Domes* by Helene Guarnaccia.

Advisor: Nancy McMichael (See Directory, Snow Domes)

Newsletter: Snow Biz
P.O. Box 53262
Washington DC 20009

Character, Tinker Bell, Made in England, 4", EX.........**$40.00**
Christmas, Santa's Workshop North Pole NY, plastic dome on footed base, 3", VG **$25.00**
Figural, Sea Captain, ship in plastic belly, 5¾", EX **$50.00**
Musical, Chicago landmarks, plays My Kind of Town ..**$35.00**
Musical, Garfield as Santa w/Odie pulling sleigh over houses, plays Here Comes Santa Claus, Enesco, 1980s, 5", EX...**$45.00**
Musical, kittens, glass globe on polyresin hand-painted base, plays Memory, 5½", MIB.......................................**$32.00**
Musical, Little Mermaid, plays Under the Sea, 7", EX.**$55.00**
Musical, Snow White, plays So This Is Love, Disney, lg, EX...**$70.00**
Souvenir, Hearst Castle San Simeon California, plastic dome on solid base, 2", EX...**$25.00**
Souvenir, Old Yellowstone National Park, brown bear, black glass base, 1930s-40s, 3¾", EX..............................**$35.00**
Souvenir, Paris buildings against blue sky, plastic dome on blue plastic footed base, marked Made in France, 2x3", EX...**$25.00**

Souvenir, Royal Canadian Mounted Police, Canadian flag and mountains in background, $18.00. (Photo courtesy Helene Guarnaccia)

Souvenir, Royal Canadian Mounted Police, figure on horseback, plastic dome on footed base, EX **$18.00**
Souvenir, Trafalgar Square & Nelson's Column, blue background, Made in Hong Kong, 1960s, 3¾", EX **$30.00**
Souvenir, Wildwood by the Sea, sailing ships in plastic dome w/footed base, 2½x3", EX....................................**$22.00**
Souvenir, Yosemite National Park, girl on sled, black plastic base, ca 1950, EX...**$45.00**
Souvenir, Zoological Park North Carolina, elephant figure atop plastic dome w/2 elephants inside, solid base, 5", EX..**$35.00**
Souvenir, 1982 World's Fair, tall plastic dome on solid base, 3½", EX...**$28.00**

Souvenir of Paris, Eiffel tower & buildings, plastic, marked made in France, 2¼x3"...**$25.00**

Wedding, Bride & Groom, plastic, Pez, 4½", MIB **$30.00**

Soda-Pop Memorabilia

A specialty area of the advertising field, soft-drink memorabilia is a favorite of many collectors. Now that vintage Coca-Cola items have become rather expensive, interest is expanding to include some of the less widely collected sodas — Grapette, Hires Root Beer, and Dr. Pepper, for instance.

See also Coca-Cola; Pepsi-Cola.

Advisor: Craig Stifter (See Directory, Soda-Pop Memorabilia)

Newsletter: National Pop Can Collectors
5417 Midvale Dr. #4
Rockford, IL 61108-2325; Send for free information

Barq's, door sticker, In in lg letters on red band above Drink...It's Good & lg bottle, Case of Emergency..., NM+ **$15.00**

Barq's, sign, embossed tin, Drink...It's Good on blue w/tilted bottle over orange dot at right, 12x30", EX+......**$250.00**

Big Ben's, sign, cardboard, Refresh!/Take a Break/Try...Big Ben's Lemon Bubbles, NM.............................**$15.00**

Bireley's, sign, cardboard, girl flirting w/boy in pool, I Go Overboard for You & Bire-ley's, 1945, 20x34", NM .**$230.00**

Bireley's, sign, metal bottle cap shape w/view of dot logo in interior of cap, 1960s, 29" dia, NM......................**$175.00**

Bireley's, thermometer, tin, Not a Bubble in a Bottle!/Non-Carbonated, w/bottle graphic, 16x5", EX+..........**$200.00**

Canada Dry, bottle topper, diecut cardboard image of boy & girl heads sipping from lg glass, 1950s, NM+.......**$70.00**

Canada Dry, door push, tin, name above tilted bottle w/A Beverage...Mixer...Chaser at bottom on white, 9x3", NM+ **$100.00**

Canada Dry, sign, porcelain kick-plate type, Canada Dry Beverages w/crown & shield logo on white, 10x30", EX+ **$50.00**

Cherry Smash, bottle topper, diecut cardboard image of Colonial boy w/glass, 11½x7", EX **$30.00**

Cliqout Club Ginger Ale, calendar, 1942, complete, EX..**$100.00**

Dad's Root Beer, clock, glass & metal light up w/bottle cap logo, Drink...Tastes Like Root Beer Should, 16" sq, NM...**$225.00**

Dad's Root Beer, sign, diecut cardboard bottle w/advertising tab at bottle neck, ½ Gal Papa Size 18¢, 28x9", VG+ **$125.00**

Dad's Root Beer, thermometer, tin, orange w/Just Right...For Dad's the Old Fashioned Root Beer & bottle graphic, 26", EX **$325.00**

Diet-Rite Cola, lighter, aluminum w/flip top, Sugar-Free in script above product name in lower-case lettering, VG **$15.00**

Double Cola, sign, cardboard, girls having a party by fireplace, oval logo upper right, 1950s, 24x18", EX+............**$200.00**

Double Cola, sign, cardboard stand-up, serviceman holding up bottle while talking on phone, 1940s, 14x11", EX+..**$60.00**

Double Cola, sign, diecut cardboard hanger, Get a Lift on balloon w/boy & girl in oval logo gondola, 1950s, 9", NM...**$18.00**

Dr Pepper, badge, metal w/cloisonne grid logo above celluloid window for name, 'at 10-2 & 4 o'clock' at bottom, NM+..**$300.00**

Dr Pepper, bottle/can opener, metal, pointed end for opening cans, The Friendly Pepper Upper, 1960s, 3½", EX+ **$15.00**

Dr Pepper, clock, round w/glass front & wide white case, grid logo, electric, Telechron, 15" dia...............**$200.00**

Dr Pepper, clock, white tin bottle cap w/red 10-2-4 & white Dr Pepper on red center band, 18½" dia, NM.....**$480.00**

Dr Pepper, key holder, rubber, gold on black, oblong w/diagonal corners, 1½x2", 1940s-50s, NM+........**$15.00**

Dr Pepper, menu board, oval logo w/V-shaped emblem on panel above chalkboard, Dr Pepper... lower left, 1960s, 20", NM+...**$275.00**

Dr Pepper, miniature bottle, embossed clear glass, 1940s, 3½", EX...**$80.00**

Dr Pepper, mirror, image of boy & girl kissing, 1970, 19x13", NM...**$20.00**

Dr Pepper, seed (flower) packet, paper, Free With Carton of Dr Pepper, 1950s, 4½x3½", EX+ **$25.00**

Dr Pepper, sign, cardboard, Certainly!, lady at football game being offered a Dr Pepper, self-framed, 20x32", NM **$325.00**

Dr Pepper, sign, cardboard, Try Frosty Pepper..., shows glass, bottle & float nestled in snow, 1960s, 15x25", NM+ **$50.00**

Dr Pepper, sign, paper, Have a Picnic at the New York World's Fair on Us!, logo/graphics/auto ad, dated 1964, 25x15", M...**$100.00**

Dr Pepper, thermometer, dial, Hot or Cold & oval logo on 2-tone divided background, 18", EX+ **$125.00**

Dr Pepper, thermometer, tin, Hot or Cold & oval logo on red, stepped sides, curved ends, 27x8", EX **$150.00**

Dr Pepper, tray, Drink a Bite To Eat, girl holding 2 bottles, 1939, EX **$325.00**

Dr Pepper, watch, metal case w/leather strap, Fossil, 1980s, MIB **$80.00**

Frostie Root Beer, mugs, clear glass w/red & yellow mascot logo, set of 4, 1950s-60s, 5", EX+ **$30.00**

Frostie Root Beer, sign, tin bottle cap w/Drink... & image of Frostie w/bottle, 12½" dia, EX+.........................**$275.00**

Frostie Root Beer, thermometer, tin, mascot & bottle cap above w/6-pack below on white, 36x8", EX......**$150.00**

Frostie Root Beer, thermometer, tin, white w/You'll Love It! above bottle w/bulb, 11½x3", NM **$130.00**

Grapette, mechanical pen, plastic, 1950s, 5", EX **$28.00**

Grapette, sign, cardboard, shopper singing 'Helps Your Day Along...Like a Song,' w/oval logo, 1950s, 9x22", NM...**$180.00**

Grapette, sign, cardboard, Thirsty or Not! in upper left corner, girl w/bottle & flowers in lower left, 28x24", NM+ **$185.00**

Grapette, syrup bottle, clear glass elephant shape w/screw cap, 1950s, 20-oz, NM $30.00

Grapette, thermometer, bottle cap dial type, Thirsty or Not w/oval logo on white, 11" dia, EX $100.00

Green River, bottle display, First for Thirst/5¢, cardboard stand-up holding original bottle, EX $75.00

Hires, door push bar, porcelain, A Refreshing Welcome 'Hires to You!,' red & blue on aqua, 3x31", VG+ $160.00

Hires, door push/pull handle, tin, vertical, blue & white stripes Drink Hires & tilted bottle, 13x3", NM....$150.00

Hires, menu board, cardboard, R-J logo above row of menu slots, 1950s, 24x20", EX+ $150.00

Hires, sign, celluloid, Drink Hires Root Beer, 1950s, 9", EX $100.00

Hires, sign, embossed tin, Hires R-J Root Beer logo flanked by In Bottles & Ice Cold on blue background, 10x28", NM $50.00

Hires, thermometer, tin, blue & white vertical stripes, Drink Hires above w/tilted bottle below, 27x8", EX $180.00

Kist Beverages, calendar, 1951, image of Lou Gehrig in sky behind boy on pitcher's mound, 33x16", complete, EX $230.00

Kist Beverages, clock, Enjoy...logo in red, white & black on white w/black numbers, wood shadow-box frame, 16x16", NM+ $200.00

Kist Beverages, menu board, self-framed tin, Enjoy...For Good Food Here, red, white & yellow, 20x9", EX+ $65.00

Kreemo Root Beer, bottle carrier, 6-pack, red tin w/red & white label, handled, EX+ $30.00

Mission Orange, door push plate, tin, Drink & bottle cap above bottle, Naturally Good! below, orange & blue, 1950s, NM+ $175.00

Mission Orange, fan, cardboard w/wooden handle, Keep Cool With..., 1930s, 11½x8", VG+ $10.00

Moxie, ashtray, aluminum w/embossed logos on flat rim between 3 rests, 1960s, 5½" dia, EX+ $20.00

Moxie, sign, cardboard stand-up, Drink...It's Always a Pleasure To Serve You on disk atop striped base, 1950s, 7", NM $120.00

Moxie, sign, cardboard stand-up, diecut bust image of pointing Moxie man w/disk logo, 1950s, 8x11", NM+ $145.00

Moxie, sign, cardboard stand-up, diecut image of hand-held bottle, 1950s, 21x9", NM (NOS) $100.00

Nehi, bottle carrier, cardboard, 6-pack, 1940s, EX $15.00

Nehi, bottle topper, cardboard, Taste the Reason Millions Drink Nehi, 4 head images drinking from straws, 1934, EX $65.00

Nehi, sign, metal, Curb Service/Nehi/Sold Here Ice Cold, blue on yellow, 1940s, 28x20", EX $65.00

Nesbitt's, picnic cooler, 1950s, EX $65.00

NuGrape, belt, vinyl, NuGrape in white repeated on burgundy, 1960s, NM $8.00

NuGrape, porcelain ovoid shape w/You Need a NuGrape Soda in blue on yellow, Imitation Grape Flavor below, 6x11½", NM+ $225.00

NuGrape, sign, tin, A Flavor You Can't Forget/NuGrape Soda on yellow rectangles over red w/hand-held bottle, 14x32", EX $160.00

NuGrape, thermometer, dial w/glass front, Have Fun With ...Delicious Anytime! & tilted bottle on white, 12" dia, NM $100.00

NuGrape, thermometer, tin bottle shape w/illustrated look, 17x5", NM $200.00

NuGrape, thermometer, tin bottle shape w/realistic look, 16½x4¼", EX $130.00

NuGrape, thermometer, tin panel w/Have....Fun With NuGrape & tilted bottle on white, 13½x5¾", NM $245.00

Orange-Crush, clock, There's Only One...Carbonated Beverage on orange diamond logo, wooden frame, 15½x15½", NM $250.00

Orange-Crush, menu board, tin over cardboard w/menu slots flanking bottle cap, Today's Specials above, 23x35", VG+ $185.00

Orange-Crush, opener, metal wall-mount w/embossed product name, 1950, 3x3", NM $30.00

Orange-Crush, scoreboard, baseball; self-framed tin, blackboard area on orange w/advertising, Scioto Sign Co, 18x54", EX $675.00

Orange-Crush, sign, celluloid button hanger, Enjoy...Naturally It Tastes Better on orange ground, 9", NM+ $150.00

Orange-Crush, sign, embossed plastic, cartoon image of couple sharing a bottle at fountain table, 12x11", NM+ $190.00

Orange-Crush, sign, 2-sided tin disk, orange w/Ask for Orange-Crush Carbonated Beverage, 23½" dia, EX............$185.00

Orange-Crush, thermometer, dial, white upper part w/Drink Orange-Crush on lower orange part w/scalloped top, 12" dia, EX $350.00

Orange-Crush, tray, 6 bottles viewed like spokes of a wheel, deep sides, 1940s, 10" dia, NM $160.00

Royal Crown Cola, bottle display, cardboard & foil, button sign atop pleated fan shape next to bottle, 1930s, 14x8", NOS $135.00

Royal Crown Cola, box of straws, RC Makes You Feel Like New, 1940s, EX $225.00

Royal Crown Cola, calendar, 1953, features Arlene Dahl, complete, NM $225.00

Royal Crown Cola, carton display, cardboard diecut image of boy saying 'Look! What You Get for a Quarter...,' 1940, NM $95.00

Royal Crown Cola, clock, glass front w/metal frame, 1950s, 16x16" $100.00

Royal Crown Cola, sign, cardboard, RC Does Taste Best! Says Gene Tierney, her image & logo, 1940s, 11x28", NM $300.00

Royal Crown Cola, sign, embossed tin, Drink.../Take Home a Carton, 25¢ 6-pack on white dot at right, 22x58" (framed), EX $375.00

Royal Crown Cola, sign, tin bottle shape, 1950s, 11½x3", NM+ $350.00

Royal Crown Cola, thermometer, embossed tin, red diamond logo above bulb next to bottle graphic on white, 14x6", NM $185.00

Royal Crown Cola, trolley sign, cardboard, Lucille Ball says 'RC Tastes Best!,' 1940s, 11x28", EX+ $200.00

Seven-Up, ashtray, round glass dish w/bubble logo in center, 1950s-60s, 4½" dia, EX+ **$40.00**

Seven-Up, ashtray, round glass dish w/4 protruding rests, Fresh Up With logo in center, 1950s, 3¼" dia, NM+ **$15.00**

Seven-Up, calendar, 1954, bust image of woman & bubble logo above full pad, 20½x9¾", VG+ **$120.00**

Seven-Up, clock, round w/glass front, lg logo in center w/lg black numbers 1-12, Pam, 15" dia, NM+ **$300.00**

Seven-Up, cooler, metal lunch box type w/swing handles, 7-Up the Uncola on sides, red, white & green, 1970s, 8x14", EX+ **$15.00**

Seven-Up, display bottle, plastic, 1960s, 28", EX **$85.00**

Seven-Up, menu board, hand-held bottle & bubble logo on panel above chalkboard, rounded corners, 27½x19½", EX **$200.00**

Seven-Up, sign, cardboard, Time Out — Fresh Up With (7-Up bubble logo), 2 hockey boys, ornate self-frame, 15x22", VG..**$35.00**

Seven-Up, sign, cardboard hanger, bubble logo above For Thirst/For Taste/For Lift diecut panels, 1960s, 10x5", NM+ **$50.00**

Seven-Up, sign, cardboard stand-up, diecut image of grocer w/case, Here's Your Family Fresh Up, 1948, 12x10", NM **$50.00**

Seven-Up, sign, cardboard w/2-pc wire frame, lg tilted bottle & golfer, Blast Thirst w/the Quick Quencher!, 21x34", EX **$175.00**

Seven-Up, sign, cardboard 2-sided diecut hanger, 'Tis the Uncola Season, image of Santa in holly wreath, 10" dia, EX...**$35.00**

Seven-Up, sign, light-up, Fresh Up With...in a Cup! tilted paper cup in center, You Like It... at bottom, 13x21x4", EX+ **$475.00**

Seven-Up, sign, tin, Fresh Up With above tilted bottle on white raised field w/green flat rim, 47x17½", EX..........**$400.00**

Seven-Up, thermometer, dial w/glass front, The Quality Drink, 10" dia, EX...**$225.00**

Seven-Up, thermometer, porcelain, 15", NM, $75.00. (Photo courtesy Dunbar Gallery)

Squirt, change mat, plastic, Try the Fresh Approach for a Change!, bottle/grapefruit next to hologram logo, 9x12", EX+ **$75.00**

Squirt, decal, Squirt boy holding bottle, 1940s, unused, NM **$5.00**

Squirt, menu board, tin, Squirt boy, lg bottle & advertising on panel above chalkboard, 1954, 27x19", EX+ **$225.00**

Squirt, Party Fun Book, w/games, puzzles, etc, 1953, VG..**$22.00**

Squirt, sign, cardboard hanger, Squirt boy w/lg bottle seated on picture frame, 2-sided, 1940s, 6½x5", EX+......**$65.00**

Squirt, sign, cardboard stand-up, Call for Squirt & Gin, shows Snowball the snowman on phone & lg bottle, 1956, 14", NM **$60.00**

Squirt, sign, paper, offer for 18" mascot doll & soft drink coupon for $2.95, doll & 6-pack pictured, 1962, 10x21", M **$50.00**

Squirt, sign, paper, 5¢ Sale/One Party Size 5¢ With Purchase of One Carton at Regular Price, w/Squirt boy, 11x34", NM+ **$160.00**

Squirt, sign, tin, Switch to Squirt/Never an After-Taste, boy pushing lg bottle, yellow & red, dated 1958, 10x28", EX..**$135.00**

Squirt, thermometer, metal, Drink Squirt on diagonal banner above bottle & grapefruit w/bulb at side, 1971, 13½", NM **$90.00**

Sun Crest, clock, light-up, round w/image of bottle surrounded by numbers, NM...............................**$350.00**

Top Notch Beverages, sign, cardboard hanger, name & graphics above list of flavors, 14x7", EX+ **$45.00**

Vernors, bank, metal can shape, Original Vernors, Its Different Flavor Aged in Oak Bucket, 1960s, M ..**$15.00**

Vernors, clock, Drink...Deliciously Different in green on yellow dot, bearded leprechaun head at 6 o'clock, 20" dia, NM+ **$900.00**

Whistle, bag rack, tin advertising panel on wire holder, orange & blue on white, 17x37", VG+...............**$625.00**

Whistle, decal, bottle cap image on yellow, Refreshing Fruit Flavor below, VG+...................................**$5.00**

Whistle, menu board, Thirsty? Just Whistle above board w/elves in ea corner, embossed, 27x20", NM **$285.00**

Whistle, sign, cardboard, elf at top lowering Whistle letters vertically w/rope, elf on bottle below, 23x2¾", EX..**$170.00**

Whistle, sign, cardboard diecut stand-up, Thirsty?...above boy in knickers running w/bottle, 1939, 27x13", EX+ **$475.00**

Soda Bottles With Painted Labels

The earliest type of soda bottles were made by soda producers and sold in the immediate vicinity of the bottling company. Many had pontil scars, left by a rod that was used to manipulate the bottle as it was blown. They had a flat bottom rather than a 'kick-up,' so for transport, they were laid on their side and arranged in layers. This served to keep the cork moist, which kept it expanded, tight, and in place. Upright the cork would dry out, shrink, and expel itself with a 'pop,' hence the name 'soda pop.'

Until the '30s, the name of the product or the bottler was embossed in the glass or printed on a paper label (sometimes pasted over reused returnable bottles). Though a few paper labels were used as late as the '60s, nearly all bottles produced from the mid-'30s on had painted-on (pyro-glazed) lettering, and logos and pictures were often added. Imaginations ran rampant. Bottlers waged a fierce competition to make their soda logos eye catching and sales inspiring. Anything went! Girls, airplanes, patriotic designs, slogans proclaiming amazing health benefits, even cowboys and Indians became popular advertising ploys. This is the type you'll encounter most often today, and collector interest is on the increase. Look for interesting, multicolored labels, rare examples from small-town bottlers, and those made from glass in colors other than clear or green.

A Good Beverage, clear glass, 8-oz $100.00
All American, clear glass, 8-oz.................................$10.00
Big Ten, clear glass, 10-oz $10.00

Bobby Sox, seven-ounce, EX, $25.00.

Booth's, clear glass, 12-oz...$10.00
Brown Cow, clear glass, Dyersburg TN, 8-oz $15.00
Cohasset, clear glass, 7-oz..$10.00
Cott Nectar Beverages, clear glass, 12-oz $15.00
Don's, clear glass, 7-oz...$15.00
Five Points, green glass, 1-qt.....................................$15.00
Fleck's, clear glass, 7-oz $10.00
Frost King, clear glass, 7-oz $45.00
Gill's, clear glass, 10-oz..$20.00
Hernon Bros, clear glass, 1-qt $15.00
Hollywood, clear glass, 12-oz.....................................$15.00
Indian Mound Spring, green glass, 7-oz $15.00
Keck's, clear glass, 6½-oz $15.00
Kenton's, clear glass w/white painted label, 8-oz.........$7.50
Life, clear glass, man & woman pictured, 12-oz $7.50
LLL Triple, green glass, 7-oz $15.00
Mac Fuddy, clear glass, 10-oz.....................................$35.00
Made Rite, clear glass, 10-oz......................................$10.00
Mini Pop, clear glass, 4-oz...$10.00
Mrs Lombardi's, clear glass, 12-oz..............................$75.00
New Yorker, clear glass, 1-qt $25.00
Nugget, clear glass, 12-oz..$15.00
Orange Ball, clear glass, 12-oz $15.00

Pep-Up, clear glass, 7-oz..$15.00
Pioneer, clear glass, 7-oz...$8.00
Quench, green glass, 8-oz...$15.00
Rech's, clear glass, 12-oz..$10.00
Sahara Dry, green glass, 7-oz $20.00
Scot, green glass, 1-qt..$20.00
Tab, clear glass, 10-oz..$10.00
Tea-Cola, clear glass, 6½-oz..$15.00
Virginia Bell, clear glass, 10-oz...................................$20.00
Waukesha, clear glass, 7-oz...$10.00
Wise-Up, green glass, 7-oz..$15.00

Sporting Goods

Catalogs and various ephemera distributed by sporting good manufacturers, ammunition boxes, and just about any other item used for hunting and fishing purposes are collectible. In fact, there are auctions devoted entirely to collectors with these interests.

One of the most best-known companies specializing in merchandise of this kind was the gun manufacturer, Winchester Repeating Arms Company. After 1931, their mark was changed from Winchester Trademark USA to Winchester-Western. Remington, Ithaca, Peters, and Dupont are other manufacturers whose goods are especially sought after.

Advisor: Kevin R. Bowman (See Directory, Sports Collectibles)

Ax, camp; Marbles #9, strong logo, 16" original handle, EX+, w/original marked sheath $155.00
Bag, game/blind; Ducks Unlimited, heavy canvas w/leather re-enforcement, 3-compartment, Federal, 1987, 13x12x5", EX $30.00
Book, Complete Book of the Wild Turkey, Roger Latham, c 1956, 1st edition, hardcover, 265 pages, EX w/dust jacket $120.00
Bow, Bear Archery Kodiak Magnum, 1966, 52", NM..$175.00
Bow, Mach 5X, 29-31" draw, 70-80 lbs, 60% letoff, PSE overdraw/TM hunter, wood grip, RS hunting sight, NM..$225.00
Box, ammunition; Federal Cartridge Mohawk Skeet Shells, 1-pc cardboard, VG $30.00
Box, ammunition; Federal Hi Power Shot Shells, wooden, 9½x9¾", EX...$25.00
Box, ammunition; Peters Victor Rustless 20 Gauge Shells, holds 7 shots $40.00
Box, ammunition; Remington Arms Co, wooden, 14x9x9", EX $35.00
Box, ammunition; Remington 12-gauge 3" shells, wooden, holds 500, EX $55.00
Box, ammunition; Sharps Carbin .52 Cal, wooden, dovetailed, sq nails, EX $35.00
Box, ammunition; Western World Champion, wooden, 15x9x9", EX..$20.00
Box, ammunition; Wetherby .300 Magnums, tiger & bullet on front, EX $20.00

Box, ammunition; Winchester Repeater Speed Loads 12 Gauge Shotshells, G **$50.00**

Brochure, Winchester, Skeet Parade, schedule of events, 5½x7½" (folded), EX..............................**$40.00**

Call, crow, Hoosier, cedar barrel form, scratches/dings, 4½", G **$70.00**

Call, deer; Herter's, MIB w/instruction papers **$25.00**

Call, duck; Boyd Martin Duck, turned walnut barrel & stopper, metal reed, MIB w/instructions..................**$110.00**

Call, duck; Chick Major-Don Cahill Dixie Mallard, MIB .**$85.00**

Call, duck; Earl Dennison, laminated wood (cherry, walnut, maple), dated 1982, 6¼", EX **$45.00**

Call, duck; Pappy's Duck Calls of Jonesboro IL, w/label, 6", VG..............................**$40.00**

Call, goose; Ken Marin signature on maple, ca 1987, M .**$80.00**

Call, turkey; ML Lynch Fool Proof Model 101, box call, dated 1965, NMIB..............................**$70.00**

Can, Dupont Blasting Caps 100 No 5, tin, 2⅛x2½x1⅜", EX **$45.00**

Can, Hercules Bullseye Pistol Powder, 3⅝" sq, VG **$17.50**

Catalog, Bear Archery Equipment, 1958, EX **$65.00**

Catalog, Healthways Swim & Water Sports Accessories, black & white, 1950s, 32 pages, EX **$45.00**

Catalog, Heddon Fishing Tackle, color, 1936, 36 pages, EX..............................**$185.00**

Catalog, New Webley Air Pistol, 1930s, 8 pages, 5x7½", EX..............................**$20.00**

Catalog, Pfleuger Full Line Tackle, many illustrations, 1934, EX **$150.00**

Catalog, Winchester, color cover, 1934, 152 pages, VG+ ..**$65.00**

Envelope, Remington, VG, $40.00.
(Photo courtesy Kevin Bowman)

Fish grabber, Marble Arms, steel, mechanically sound, ca 1920s, G..............................**$80.00**

Jacket, shooting; tan w/leather shoulders, elbows & forearms, Imperial, w/club patches, 1940s, EX...........**$45.00**

Knife, fish; Russell Green River, wood checkered handle, saw top edge, 5", G, w/original sheath **$25.00**

Knife, hunting; Stuart Cohen, staghorn handle, 6" blade, 11½" overall, w/tooled leather sheath **$185.00**

Knife, Marbles Ideal, ½-guard, leather handle, aluminum pommel, strong logo, 6", VG, w/original unmarked sheath **$110.00**

Poster, Remington Shur Shot, man shooting targets, diecut, 20½x13", EX..............................**$375.00**

Reel, fly; Winchester Trademark Made in USA #1136, plastic crank handle, 2½" dia, EX **$110.00**

Reel, Meek Bluegrass, BF Meed & Sons #33, Carter's Pat, July 5, 04, Nov 28, 05, EX **$180.00**

Reel, Newel P454-F, 5-to-1 gear ratio, 540-yard capacity of 40# mono line, EX..............................**$225.00**

Reel, Penn International 965 Baitcaster, 1-pc aluminum frame, stainless steel spindle, 4.75-to-1 ratio, Made in USA, EX..............................**$155.00**

Reel, Shimano TLD 30, 2-speed, 1-pc frame, MIB **$250.00**

Tin, Powder Mills Dead Shot Powder, red-painted tin w/stenciled front, original cap, 6x4" oval, VG................**$75.00**

Vise, fly-tying; Thompson Model A, MIB w/papers & accessories..............................**$35.00**

Watch fob, metal, Savage Rifles/Savage Arms Co, embossed Indian head w/enameled head band, early, 1⅝" dia, NM **$325.00**

Sports Collectibles

When the baseball card craze began sweeping the country well over a decade ago, memorabilia relating to many types of sports began to interest sports fans. Today ticket stubs, autographed baseballs, sports magazines, and game-used bats and uniforms are prized by baseball fans, and some items, depending on their age or the notoriety of the player or team they represent, may be very valuable. Baseball and golf seem to be the two sports most collectors prefer, but hockey and auto racing are gaining ground. Game-used equipment is sought out by collectors, and where once they preferred only items used by professionals, now the sports market has expanded, and collectors have taken great interest in the youth equipment endorsed by many star players now enshrined in their respective Hall of Fame. Some youth equipment was given away as advertising premiums and bear that company's name or logo. Such items are now very desirable.

See also Autographs; Indianapolis 500 Memorabilia; Magazines; Motorcycle Memorabilia; Pin-Back Buttons; Puzzles.

Advisors: Don and Anne Kier (See Directory, Sports Collectibles)

Badge, Masters, 1978, green & white, EX....................**$40.00**

Bag, Detroit Tigers logo on nylon, game giveaway, 26x18", M **$16.50**

Baseball, Cleveland Indian 1970s team signatures (24 total), Frank Robinson signature in sweet spot, NM.....**$160.00**

Baseball, D&M, Model #DB30, Special League on sweet spot, red stitching, VG (VG box)..............................**$120.00**

Baseball, Detroit Tigers 1950 team signatures (27 total), NM **$210.00**

Baseball, Joe DiMaggio #5 in blue ballpoint on ink, w/Certificate of Authenticity, M..........................**$165.00**

Baseball, Rawlings XPG12, Tony Kubek facsimile signature, EX **$125.00**

Baseball, Wilson Custom Fit A2074 CF2, MLB Trapeze Style, M **$145.00**

Baseball bat, Easton Connexion, 2⅝" extended barrel, scandium alloy, 34", 31-oz, M, unused......................**$145.00**

Baseball bat, Easton Redline C-Core, Total Peen finish, Maxlite design, leather grip, alloy shell, 33", 28-oz, NM...................**$170.00**

Baseball bat, Louisville Slugger, Ted williams decal, EX ..**$130.00**

Baseball bat, Louisville Slugger TPS Autumn Gold, 2⅝" barrel, 33", 30-oz, EX................................**$100.00**

Baseball bat, McLaughlin-Millard Inc Northern Adirondack White Ash Dolgeville New York No 262 Gehrig Model, VG, 33"......................**$165.00**

Baseball bat, Spaulding Mickey Mantel Model 1843, 1960s, 33", EX+......................**$125.00**

Baseball bat, Steve Carlton Game Model #P89, 34½", M ..**$220.00**

Baseball glove, Mickey Mantle authentic signature, EX.....**$245.00**

Baseball glove, Rawlings XFCB17, Brooks Robinson facsimile signature, NM..................**$75.00**

Baseball glove, Spaulding #42-135, Roger Maris facsimile signature, full size, NM **$200.00**

Baseball glove, Wilson Conform infielder's, brown, 11½", EX......................**$65.00**

Baseball glove, Wilson Famous Player, Louis Aparicio, 1960s, MIB **$200.00**

Basketball, Buffalo Braves, American Motors promotion, ca 1970s, M......................**$120.00**

Basketball, Spaulding, Larry Bird signature in silver, w/certificate of authenticity, M......................**$90.00**

Basketball, Wilson Evolution, Michael Jordan signature (authentic), M......................**$200.00**

Basketball, Wilson Official B1550, ca 1950s, EX.......**$180.00**

Basketball, Wilt Chamberlain signature, w/photo taken at autographing session, 1998, M **$200.00**

Basketball shoes, Air Jordan XIII, white leather w/red suede, M......................**$95.00**

Basketball shoes, Allen Iverson Answer IV, MIB **$85.00**

Basketball shoes, Nike Air Jordan VII edition, 1993, rare, M......................**$200.00**

Book, Babe Ruth's Own Book of Baseball, A Burt, 1928, VG w/dust jacket......................**$130.00**

Book cover, Yankees team photo w/Mickey Mantle sitting in center, 1968, NM......................**$25.00**

Book, How To Play the Infield & How To Play the Outfield, Spaulding's, 1922, VG+......................**$55.00**

Boxing gloves, Rocky Marciano, Benlee, 1950s, NM (VG box) **$330.00**

Calendar, Jackie Robinson image, 1952, 10x17", VG+ ..**$70.00**

Calendar, Joe DiMaggio teaching boy to bat, Mayo, 1957, 33x16", VG+......................**$150.00**

Calendar, Mickey Cochrane Showing Them How, Vincent Civiletti, 1961, 33x16", EX......................**$95.00**

Catcher's mask, goggle-eyed, Model 305, Draper-Maynard Co, all original, EX......................**$395.00**

Figure, Muhammad Ali, pewter, Sports Illustrated, MIB .**$20.00**

Football, Wilson's The Duke, 1960s, MIB..................**$165.00**

Game, All Star Baseball Game, Cadaco, 1968, NM **$70.00**

Game, Electronic Basketball, Mattel, 1978, MIB.........**$55.00**

Game, Jackie Robinson's Batter Up Baseball, 1951, EX .**$260.00**

Game, Muhammad Ali's Boxing Ring, Mego, c 1976, M (VG box) **$100.00**

Game, Talking Baseball, Mattel, 1971, EXIB **$120.00**

Golf ball, Winchester (Spaulding #1), EX...................**$75.00**

Golf club, Jock Hutchison, Winchester, wood shaft, putter, EX **$100.00**

Golf club, Winchester Ranger, wood shaft, midiron, leather wrapped handle, 40"......................**$110.00**

Helmet, football; Medalist Gladiator Hydra-Flo, 1970s style cage, EX......................**$80.00**

Jacket, Dodgers (Brooklyn), lined, Timberline Co of Milwaukee, 1950s, NM......................**$130.00**

Jacket, Giants, chain w/baseball on zipper, Richline Co, 1950s, child's size, NM+......................**$85.00**

Knife, Babe Ruth, baseball shape, kids' souvenirs at Yankee Stadium, 3" L, EX+......................**$110.00**

Light, neon, Coors Light & basketball, 28x20", M.....**$150.00**

Magazine, Dell Sports Basketball, Oscar Robertson cover, 1959, EX......................**$45.00**

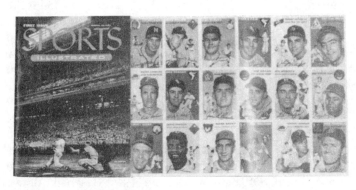

Magazine, *Sports Illustrated*, first issue, August 16, 1954, complete with color 'Trading Card Collectors' fold-out, EX, $185.00.

Paperweight, catcher's mitt shape, St Louis Cardinals souvenir, leather w/Cardinals' mascot in palm, 4", EX............**$40.00**

Pencil, mechanical; Joe DiMaggio stamp on barrel, all wood, EX......................**$35.00**

Pennant, Brooklyn Dodgers, 1940s, VG+ **$110.00**

Pennant, Chicago Cubs, felt, 1950s, 30", EX.............**$115.00**

Pennant, Chicago Cubs, felt, 1960, full size, EX..........**$85.00**

Pennant, Cincinnati Royals, great logo on felt, 1960s, 30", EX+......................**$300.00**

Pennant, Cleveland Indians, picture on front, names of players on back, slight fading, 1961, EX...................**$110.00**

Pennant, Detroit Lions, red felt, 1960s, 29", EX..........**$80.00**

Pennant, Detroit Tigers, white on green felt, full size, 1950s, EX **$120.00**

Pennant, Hank Aaron Home Run King, 30" L, M........**$25.00**

Pennant, New York Yankees 1936 American League Championship, 24" L, EX **$270.00**

Pennant, Princeton Football, tiger (mascot) jumping through the letter P, 1920s, 33" L, EX......................**$95.00**

Pennant, San Francisco Giants, black felt, 1950s-60s, 30", NM ...**$75.00**

Pillowcase, LA Dodgers, logo, standard size, 20x26", MIB (sealed) **$10.00**

Pin-back button, Hank Aaron portrait, 1950s, EX.......**$90.00**
Pin-back button, Mark McGuire, 3".............................**$12.00**
Pin-back button, Mickey Mantle portrait, retirement issue, 4", EX..**$20.00**
Program, basketball; NCAA Western Finals, 1950, EX .**$100.00**
Program, basketball; Rochester Royals, 1946-47, EX...**$165.00**
Program, football; AFL Championship, San Diego Chargers vs Buffalo Bills, December 1961, EX **$150.00**
Program, football; Super Bowl X Game Day, Dallas Cowboys & Pittsburgh Steelers, January 18, 1976, 120 pages, EX...**$100.00**
Program, football; 49ers & Lions, 1957, EX...............**$115.00**
Program, Indianapolis Clowns, history & photos, 1960s, EX...**$35.00**
Program, Kentucky Derby, Churchill Downs, May 1st 1948, VG...**$160.00**
Program, night baseball; Ted Williams' hands photo cover, no score card, 1960, NM **$90.00**
Program, Roller Derby, Riverside Stadium, Washington DC, EX .**$75.00**
Program, 1st Annual Pro Bowl, 1951, NM.................**$450.00**
Program, 1912 Toledo Baseball, Toledo vs Indianapolis, VG+ **$35.00**
Program, 1938 Sugar Bowl, Louisiana State vs University of Santa Clara, mc, EX+ **$180.00**
Scorecard, Augusta National (Masters), Fred Couples signed autograph, EX **$35.00**
Scorecard, New York Yankees & St Louis Browns at Yankee Stadium, 1948, EX...**$45.00**
Scorecard, Washington Capitols & Chicago Stags, 1946, EX..**$85.00**
Stamp Album, Official Sportsstamp 1949 Baseball Album, National League Edition, EX **$195.00**
Ticket, Indianapolis 500, 1936, EX **$70.00**
Ticket, Kentucky Derby Admission, 1951, EX............**$45.00**
Ticket, St Louis Cardinals, Old Sportsman's Park, September 1930, EX...**$35.00**
Ticket, World Series Game #7, Tigers & Cardinals, 1968, EX..**$75.00**
Ticket stub, World Series Game #7, Dodgers, 1956, EX..**$285.00**
Ticket stub, 1951 World Series, 6th game, Joe Dimaggio's last game & Mickey Mantle's 1st World Series, EX ...**$110.00**
Watch fob, Champions lettered on baseball shape, inlaid enameling w/Sporting Goods store advertising on back, 1½", NM **$100.00**
Yearbook, Converse Basketball Year Book, 1936-37, EX....**$185.00**
Yearbook, New York Yankees, 1962, EX..................**$110.00**
Yearbook, St Louis Browns, 1952, EX.......................**$130.00**

St. Clair Glass

Since 1941, the St. Clair family has operated a small glasshouse in Elwood, Indiana. They're most famous for their lamps, though they've also produced many styles of toothpick holders, paperweights, and various miniatures as well. Though the paperweights are usually stamped and dated, smaller items may not be marked at all. In addition to vari-

ous colors of iridescent glass, they've also made many articles in slag glass (both caramel and pink) and custard.

Right now, interest is high on Betsy Ross sulfides (they range from $350.00 to $375.00), the black Scottie dog ($500.00), signed lamps, and all items made by St. Clair brothers Ed and Paul, both of whom produced only a limited amount of glassware. For more information, we recommend *St. Clair Glass Collector's Book, Vol II,* by our advisor, Ted Pruitt.

Advisor: Ted Pruitt (See Directory, St. Clair)

Animal dish, dolphin, blue, Joe St Clair.....................**$175.00**
Animal dish, reclining colt, cobalt custard, from $135 to...**$160.00**
Bell, Christmas, from $100 to **$125.00**
Bell, fruit pattern, blue carnival, from $90 to............**$100.00**
Bird, blue & clear, lg, from $75 to **$95.00**
Candle holder, sulfide, multicolor floral, from $75 to.**$85.00**
Compote, ruffled rim, low ped base, pink slag, from $150 to..**$175.00**
Creamer, Holly Band, aqua opal **$85.00**
Doorstop, mallard..**$625.00**
Figurine, owl on round base, various colors, ea from $100 to..**$125.00**
Paperweight, apple form w/stem & leaf, blue carnival, blown...**$100.00**
Paperweight, flowers, sm, from $40 to **$50.00**
Paperweight, Kewpie, windowed, from $200 to.......**$225.00**
Paperweight, lily, Ed St Clair, from $400 to..............**$425.00**
Paperweight, rose, feathered or windowed, from $800 to **$1,200.00**
Paperweight, speckled, from $90 to..........................**$100.00**
Paperweight, sulfide, cameo, windowed/etched, from $300 to..**$325.00**
Paperweight, sulfide, James Madison on cobalt blue, 1971 ....**$150.00**
Paperweight, sulfide, kitten, from $150 to................**$175.00**
Plate, Lyndon B Johnson, from $20 to.......................**$25.00**
Ring holder, clear w/yellow flower, from $60 to **$90.00**
Ring holder, teapot form w/spout, from $75 to **$85.00**

Ring holder, teapot shape, 4½", from $75.00 to $85.00.

Salt cellar, wheelbarrow form, various colors, ea from $25 to **$30.00**

Toothpick holder, Argonaut Shell, various colors, ea from $25 to..**$30.00**

Toothpick holder, Cactus, carnival, from $25 to..........**$30.00**

Toothpick holder, Indian, blue opaque, from $25 to..**$30.00**

Toothpick holder, sheaf of wheat, various colors, ea from $45 to..**$50.00**

Toothpick holder, sulfide, flower, from $65 to............**$75.00**

Tumbler, Grape & Cable, red......................................**$30.00**

TV Lamp, unsigned, from $975 to.........................**$1,000.00**

Vase, paperweight base, clear trumpet neck, from $75 to..**$85.00**

Wine, Hobstar, crystal carnival, from $35 to................**$45.00**

Wine glass, Paneled Grape, cobalt, from $35 to.........**$45.00**

Stanford Corn

Teapots, cookie jars, salt and pepper shakers, and other kitchen and dinnerware items modeled as ears of yellow corn with green shucks were made by the Stanford company, who marked most of their ware. The Shawnee company made two very similar corn lines; just check the marks to verify the manufacturer.

Butter dish..**$60.00**

Casserole, 8½" L..**$50.00**

Cookie jar...**$100.00**

Creamer & sugar bowl..**$60.00**

Cup..**$20.00**

Pitcher, 7½"..**$65.00**

Plate, 9" L..**$35.00**

Relish tray..**$45.00**

Salt & pepper shakers, sm, pr....................................**$30.00**

Salt & pepper shakers, 4", pr.....................................**$35.00**

Spoon rest..**$30.00**

Teapot..**$75.00**

Tumbler..**$35.00**

Stangl Birds

The Stangl Pottery Company of Flemington and Trenton, New Jersey, made a line of ceramic birds which they introduced in 1940 to fulfill the needs of a market no longer able to access foreign imports due to the onset of WWII. These bird figures immediately attracted a great deal of attention. At the height of their productivity, sixty decorators were employed to hand paint the birds at the plant, and the overflow was contracted out and decorated in private homes. After WWII, inexpensive imported figurines once again saturated the market, and for the most part, Stangl curtailed their own production, though the birds were made on a very limited basis until as late as 1978.

Nearly all the birds were marked. A four-digit number was used to identify the species, and most pieces were signed by the decorator. An 'F' indicates a bird that was decorated at the Flemington plant.

For more information see *Collector's Encyclopedia of Stangl Artware, Lamps, and Birds* by Robert L. Runge, Jr. (Collector Books).

Advisors: Popkorn Antiques (See Directory, Stangl)

Club: Stangl/Fulper Collectors Club
P.O. Box 538
Flemington, NJ 08822; Yearly membership: $25 (includes quarterly newsletter)

Audubon Warbler, #3755, 4¼"......................................**$500.00**

Black-Throated Green Warbler, #3814, 3"..................**$165.00**

Bobolink, #3595, 4¾"..**$160.00**

Broadbill Hummingbird, #3629, 4½"............................**$150.00**

Canary (right), #3746, rose flower, 6¼"......................**$250.00**

Cliff Swallow, #3852, 3½"..**$170.00**

Cock Pheasant, #3492...**$200.00**

Cockatoo, #3405, 6"..**$50.00**

Duck, Gazing; #3250D, 3¾"..**$130.00**

Duck, Flying; #3443, gray, 9"......................................**$265.00**

Duck, Standing; #3250A, 3¼"......................................**$115.00**

Evening Grosbeak, #3813, 5"......................................**$150.00**

Goldfinch, #3849..**$140.00**

Goldfinches (group), #3635...**$215.00**

Gray Cardinal, #3596, 5"...**$70.00**

Hen Pheasant, #3491, 6¼x11"....................................**$185.00**

Hummingbird pr, #3599D..**$325.00**

Indigo Bunting, #3589, 3½"...**$85.00**

Lovebird, #3401, revised, 3½"......................................**$65.00**

Oriole, #3402, beak down, 3½"....................................**$100.00**

Painted Bunting, #3452, 5"..**$100.00**

Parakeet pr, #3582D, blue, 7"......................................**$215.00**

Parrot, #3449, 5½"..**$160.00**

Parula Warbler, #3583, 4¼"...**$75.00**

Penguin, #3274, 6"...**$475.00**

Red-Breasted Nuthatch, #3851, 3¾"............................**$70.00**

Rooster, #3285, early, 4½"..**$140.00**

Wren, #3401, dark brown, revised, 3½".......................**$55.00**

Wrens, #3401D, revised version, 6", $135.00 (early version, 6½", $500.00).

443

Stangl Dinnerware

The Stangl Company of Trenton, New Jersey, grew out of the Fulper company that had been established in Flemington early in the 1800s. Martin Stangl, president of the company, introduced a line of dinnerware in the 1920s. By 1954, 90% of their production centered around their dinnerware lines. Until 1942 the clay they used was white. Although most of the dinnerware production was solid-color glazes until WWII, they also did many hand-painted, but not carved patterns in the 1930s and early 1940s. In 1942, however, the first of the red-clay lines that have become synonymous with the Stangl name was created. Designs were hand carved into the greenware then hand painted. More than one hundred different patterns have been cataloged. From 1974 until 1978, a few lines previously discontinued on the red clay were reintroduced with a white clay body. Soon after 1978, the factory closed.

If you'd like more information on the subject, read *The Collector's Encyclopedia of Stangl Dinnerware* by Robert C. Runge, Jr. (Collector Books) and *Stangl Pottery* by Harvey Duke.

Advisors: Popkorn Antiques (See Directory, Stangl)

Amber-Glo, bowl, salad; 1954-60, 12", from $50 to **$55.00**
Amber-Glo, butter dish...**$35.00**
Amber-Glo, gravy boat..**$10.00**
Amber-Glo, plate, 12½"..**$30.00**
Amber-Glo, salt & pepper shakers, 1954-60, pr, from $12 to..**$16.00**
Amber-Glo, sugar bowl, open **$22.00**
Antique Gold, plate, chop; scrolled pattern, 14½"......**$60.00**
Antique Gold, teapot, treasured **$125.00**
Bittersweet, gravy boat...**$15.00**
Bittersweet, mug, tapered **$35.00**
Blueberry, butter dish...**$65.00**
Blueberry, creamer **$25.00**
Blueberry, platter, kidney shape..................................**$90.00**
Blueberry, platter, oval, 11½" **$115.00**
Cosmos, cup, AD **$18.00**
Cosmos, teapot **$150.00**
Country Garden, bowl, cereal.......................................**$22.00**
Country Garden, bread tray **$50.00**
Country Garden, cake stand **$30.00**
Country Garden, pitcher, 1-qt **$60.00**
Country Garden, plate, 11" **$45.00**
Festival, candy dish, 1-handle......................................**$45.00**
Festival, casserole, w/serving lid, 8"............................**$75.00**
Festival, sherbet **$35.00**
Fruit, bowl, open vegetable; 2-part, oval.....................**$45.00**
Fruit, coffeepot, 1942+, 8-cup, from $90 to..............**$120.00**
Fruit, cruet, w/stopper...**$50.00**
Fruit, relish dish, 1942+, from $35 to **$45.00**
Fruit & Flowers, bowl, divided vegetable; oval **$50.00**
Fruit & Flowers, cruet w/stopper, 1958-70s, from $35 to..**$45.00**
Fruit & Flowers, cup & saucer.....................................**$18.00**

Fruit & Flowers, egg cup **$25.00**
Fruit & Flowers, platter, oval, 1958-70s, 11½", from $95 to..**$110.00**
Fruit & Flowers, warmer, 1958-70s, from $30 to.........**$40.00**
Harvest, bowl, oval, 9", from $45 to **$55.00**
Harvest, plate, 1940-45, 10", from $35 to....................**$45.00**
Harvest, salt & pepper shakers, pr...............................**$20.00**
Harvest, sugar bowl, w/lid, 1940-45, from $25 to.......**$30.00**
Kiddieware, bowl, cereal; Flying Saucer, 1960, from $300 to..**$400.00**
Kiddieware, bowl, cereal; Little Bo Peep, 1953, from $90 to **$110.00**
Kiddieware, bowl, cereal; Woman-in-the-Shoe, 1968, from $125 to..**$150.00**
Kiddieware, cup, Ginger Boy, 1957, from $110 to ...**$135.00**
Kiddieware, dish, ABCs, divided, whiteware..............**$80.00**
Kiddieware, divided dish, ABC, 1956, from $80 to.....**$95.00**
Kiddieware, divided dish, Cookie Twins, 1957, from $200 to..**$250.00**
Kiddieware, plate, Goldilocks, 1946, 9", from $200 to..**$250.00**
Kiddieware, plate, Peter Rabbit, Terra Rose **$195.00**
Magnolia, bowl, coupe soup **$30.00**
Magnolia, mug, coffee, 2-cup **$45.00**
Mountain Laurel, casserole; w/lid, 1944, 8", from $75 to..**$100.00**
Mountain Laurel, plate, chop; 1944, 12½", from $80 to **$90.00**
Mountain Laurel, teapot, 1944, from $110 to **$135.00**
Sculptured Fruit, cup & saucer, 1966-70s, from $13 to ..**$16.00**
Sculptured Fruit, plate, 1966-70s, 10", from $12 to **$15.00**
Star Flower, bowl, lug soup; 1952, from $10 to.........**$15.00**
Star Flower, bowl, salad; 10", from $40 to.................**$50.00**
Star Flower, cup & saucer, from $13 to **$16.00**
Star Flower, gravy boat & undertray **$30.00**
Star Flower, plate, 8", from $10 to..............................**$15.00**
Star Flower, tidbit, 1952, 10", from $8 to **$10.00**
Thistle, bowl, divided vegetable; oval **$45.00**
Thistle, butter dish, from $50 to **$60.00**
Thistle, plate, 11", from $30 to to...............................**$35.00**
Town & Country, bowl, porridge; straight sides, blue, 1974-78, 7½", from $35 to...**$50.00**
Town & Country, bowl, soup/cereal; black or crimson, from $20 to **$30.00**
Town & Country, butter dish, brown, green, honey, or yellow, ea from $20 to **$35.00**
Town & Country, candlestick, blue, chamberstick shape, 1974-78, #5299, 7½", from $45 to.........................**$55.00**
Town & Country, deviled egg plate, paneled, brown, green, honey or yellow, 1974-78, 11½", from $50 to......**$80.00**
Town & Country, flowerpot, blue, 5", from $35 to.....**$45.00**
Town & Country, mug, stacking; blue, 1974-78, from $50 to **$60.00**
Town & Country, platter, oval, blue, 1974-78, 11½", from $60 to **$70.00**
Town & Country, sugar bowl, black or crimson, from $25 to **$30.00**
Town & Country, wall pocket, blue, 1974-1978, from $75 to **$100.00**
Wild Rose, bowl, lug soup...**$15.00**

Wild Rose, bowl, oval divided vegetable; 1955-early 1960s, 8", from $30 to **$45.00**

Wild Rose, cake stand, from $20 to **$25.00**

Wild Rose, egg cup, 1955-early 1960s, from $15 to....**$20.00**

Wild Rose, mug, 2-cup, from $40 to **$45.00**

Wild Rose, pitcher, 1955-early 1960s, 2-qt, from $75 to...**$85.00**

Wild Rose, plate, 1955-early 1960s, 10", from $20 to..**$25.00**

Wild Rose, plate, 1955-early 1960s, 8"to **$15.00**

Star Wars

In the late '70s, the movie 'Star Wars' became a box office hit, most notably for its fantastic special effects and its ever-popular theme of space adventure. Two more movies followed, 'The Empire Strikes Back' in 1980 and 'Return of the Jedi' in 1983. After the first movie, an enormous amount of related merchandise was released. A large percentage of these items was action figures, made by the Kenner company who used the logo of the 20th Century Fox studios (under whom they were licensed) on everything they made until 1980. Just before the second movie, Star Wars creator, George Lucas, regained control of the merchandising rights, and items inspired by the last two films can be identified by his own Lucasfilm logo. Since 1987, Lucasfilm Ltd. has operated shops in conjunction with the Star Tours at Disneyland theme parks.

What to collect? First and foremost, buy what you yourself enjoy. But remember that condition is all-important. Look for items still mint in the box. Using that as a basis, if the box is missing, deduct at least half from its mint-in-box value. If a major accessory or part is gone, the item is basically worthless. Learn to recognize the most desirable, most valuable items. There are a lot of Star Wars bargains yet to be had!

Original packaging helps date a toy, since the package or card design was updated as each new movie was released. Naturally, items representing the older movies are more valuable than later issues. For more coverage of this subject, refer to *Schroeder's Collectible Toys, Antique to Modern* (Collector Books).

Note: Though the market was inundated with scores of collectors' items promoting *Episode 1,* the latest movie in the series, very few have attracted enough interest to cause significant trading on the secondary level.

Bank, C3-PO, Roman Ceramics, M **$75.00**

Bank, Jabba the Hut figural, ceramic, Sigma, from $75 to **$85.00**

Book, Return of the Jedi, Ballantine, 1983, 1st edition, softcover, EX **$10.00**

Bookends, Darth Vader & Chewbacca, ceramic, Sigma, pr, minimum value **$275.00**

Candle holder, Yoda beside tree trunk, ceramic, Sigma, minimum value **$200.00**

Case, Darth Vader, EX **$15.00**

Doll, Chewbacca, Kenner, 1978-79, synthetic fur w/plastic eyes & nose, 20", EX **$25.00**

Figure, Admiral Ackbar, Return of the Jedi, M (VG card)..**$35.00**

Figure, AT-AT Commander, Return of the Jedi, M (VG+ card)..**$40.00**

Figure, AT-ST Driver, Power of the Force, 1995-present, MOC (green w/slide)..**$60.00**

Figure, Ben Obi-Wan Kenobi, Empire Strikes Back, M (NM card)..**$120.00**

Figure, Ben Obi-Wan Kenobi, Star Wars, M (NM unpunched card) (12-back)..**$800.00**

Figure, Ben Obi-Wan Kenobi, Tri-logo, M (NM card)..**$125.00**

Figure, Bib Fortuna, Return of the Jedi, M (NM card), from $50 to **$75.00**

Figure, Boba Fett, Power of the Force, 1995-present, MOC (green) **$15.00**

Figure, Boba Fett, Star Wars, complete, EX, from $15 to..**$20.00**

Figure, Boss Nass, Episode I/Wave 3, MOC................**$12.00**

Figure, C-3PO, Power of the Force, removable limbs, M (NM card)..**$120.00**

Figure, C-3PO, Star Wars, 12", MIB (sealed)..............**$600.00**

Figure, Chewbacca, Power of the Force, 1995-present, MOC (green) **$12.00**

Figure, Chewbacca, Star Wars, 12", M (VG box).......**$250.00**

Figure, Clone Emperor, Power of the Force, 1995-present, MOC **$30.00**

Figure, Darth Vader, Power of the Force, M (EX card)..**$125.00**

Figure, Darth Vader, Star Wars, complete, NM, from $12 to **$15.00**

Figure, Death Squad Commander, Star Wars, M (EX+ card) (12-back) **$275.00**

Figure, Death Star Droid, Empire Strikes Back, M (NM unpunched card) (45-back) **$150.00**

Figure, Death Star Gunner, Power of the Force, 1995-present, MOC (red) **$15.00**

Figure, Dengar, Tri-logo, M (EX+ card) **$60.00**

Figure, Emperor's Royal Guard, Return of the Jedi, M (NM card)..**$75.00**

Figure, FX-7, Empire Strikes Back, complete, NM **$8.00**

Figure, General Madine, Return of the Jedi, M (EX card)..**$35.00**

Figure, Greedo, Return of the Jedi, M (NM card) **$75.00**

Figure, Han Solo, Empire Strikes Back, Hoth gear, M (NM card)..**$130.00**

Figure, Han Solo, Star Wars, lg head, complete, NM..**$20.00**

Figure, IG-88, Tri-logo, M (EX card) **$240.00**

Figure, Imperial Dignitary, Power of the Force, complete, NM **$55.00**

Figure, Imperial Gunner, Power of the Force, M (VG+ card)..**$80.00**

Figure, Jawa, Empire Strikes Back, M (VG+ card) **$60.00**

Figure, Jawa, Star Wars, 12", M (EX box) **$250.00**

Figure, Lando Calrissian, Empire Strikes Back, M (NM card) **$100.00**

Figure, Lobot, Empire Strikes Back, M (EX card)........**$60.00**

Figure, Logray, Return of the Jedi, complete, NM **$10.00**

Figure, Luke Skywalker, Power of the Force, battle poncho, NM **$70.00**

Figure, Luke Skywalker, Power of the Force, 1995-present, Jedi Knight outfit, MOC (green) **$15.00**

Figure, Luke Skywalker, Return of the Jedi, Jedi Knight outfit, blue saber, NM **$50.00**

Figure, Luke Skywalker, Return of the Jedi, X-Wing pilot outfit, M (EX+ card) **$60.00**

Figure, Luke Skywalker, Tri-logo, Jedi Knight outfit, M (NM card)...**$125.00**

Figure, Nien Numb, Return of the Jedi, NM (NM card) ..**$50.00**

Figure, Pit Droid, Episode I/Wave 9, 2-pack, MOC **$15.00**

Figure, Princess Leia Organa, Empire Strikes Back, Bespin outfit, M (VG card) **$95.00**

Figure, Princess Leia Organa, Empire Strikes Back, turtleneck, complete, NM...**$35.00**

Figure, Princess Leia Organa, Power of the Force, 1995-present, 12', MIB **$25.00**

Figure, Princess Leia Organa, Return of the Jedi, turtleneck, M (NM card)..**$100.00**

Figure, Prune Face, Return of the Jedi, NM (NM card)........**$40.00**

Figure, Rancor Keeper, Return of the Jedi, complete, NM ..**$12.00**

Figure, Rebel Commando, Return of the Jedi, M (NM card)..**$30.00**

Figure, R2-D2, Episode I/Wave 5, MOC......................**$20.00**

Figure, R2-D2, Star Wars, complete, EX....................**$12.00**

Figure, R5-D4, Power of the Force, 1995-present, MOC (red) **$15.00**

Figure, Sand People, Star Wars, M (NM card) (12-back)..**$350.00**

Figure, Sandtrooper, Power of the Force, 1995-present, MOC (red) **$20.00**

Figure, Squid Head, Return of the Jedi, M (EX card) .**$35.00**

Figure, Stormtrooper, Return of the Jedi, M (NM+ card)..**$100.00**

Figure, Taun Taun, Empire Strikes Back, M (EX box) ..**$50.00**

Figure, TIE Fighter Pilot, Power of the Force, 1995-present, 12", MIB...**$35.00**

Figure, Tusken Raider, Tri-logo, M (NM card) **$125.00**

Figure, Ugnaught, Tri-logo, M (NM card) **$125.00**

Figure, Walrus Man, Empire Strikes Back, M (EX card) ..**$100.00**

Figure, Wicket W Warrick, Return of the Jedi, complete, NM **$20.00**

Figure, Yoda, Empire Strikes Back, brown or orange snake, complete, NM, ea from $30 to **$35.00**

Figure, Yoda, Power of the Force, 1995-present, w/hologram, MOC (red) **$40.00**

Figure, Zuckuss, Return of the Jedi, M (EX+ card) **$75.00**

Figure, 8D8, Return of the Jedi, M (NM card).............**$40.00**

Game, Destroy Death Star, VG **$20.00**

Lazer Rifle, Empire Strikes Back, Kenner, 1980, plastic, battery-operated, 18½", EX **$75.00**

Mug, Biker Scout, Sigma, ceramic, MIB.....................**$30.00**

Mug, Imperial Biker Scout's face, ceramic, Sigma, from $60 to...**$75.00**

Mug, Wicket W Warrick's face, ceramic, Sigma, from $25 to...**$35.00**

Music box, C-3PO, ceramic, Sigma, minimum value ..**$200.00**

Pencil tray, C-3PO, ceramic, Sigma, from $30 to **$40.00**

Playset, Bespin Freeze Chamber, Micro Collection, MIB .**$90.00**

Playset, Cantina Adventure Set, Sears, MIB...............**$225.00**

Playset, Cloud City, Empire Strikes Back, M (EX box)...**$275.00**

Playset, Death Star Escape, Micro Collection, M (EX box) **$50.00**

Playset, Ewock Fire Cart, M (NM box)........................**$40.00**

Playset, Ewock Village, Return of the Jedi, M (NM box) ..**$75.00**

Playset, Hoth Ice Planet, M (VG box)........................**$100.00**

Playset, Imperial Attack Base, M (decals applied), EX+ Canadian box)..**$85.00**

Playset, Rebel Command Center, Empire Strikes Back, M (EX box) **$250.00**

Poster set, Craftmaster, 1979, w/2 posters, MIB (sealed) .**$30.00**

Record, Ewoks Join the Fight, 45 rpm, w/booklet, M (sealed) **$10.00**

Sculpture, Hans Solo, clay, Star Jars Inc, from $250 to ..**$275.00**

Sculpture, Obi-Wan (Ben) Kenobi, clay, Star Jars Inc, from $250 to **$275.00**

Soap dish, Landspeeder shape, ceramic, Sigma, from $40 to **$60.00**

Teapot, Taun Taun figural, ceramic, Sigma, minimum value **$200.00**

Trading cards, Topps, first series, 1977, MIP, $49.00.

Vase, Yoda beside tree, ceramic, Sigma #501, from $70 to **$80.00**

Vehicle, A-Wing Fighter, Power of the Force, 1995-present, MIB **$25.00**

Vehicle, B-Wing Fighter, Return of the Jedi, NM (NM box) **$225.00**

Vehicle, Darth Vader's TIE Fighter, Power of the Force, 1995-present, MIB...**$20.00**

Vehicle, Endor Forest Ranger, Tri-logo, MIB (sealed) .**$65.00**

Vehicle, Ewock Combat Glider, Return of the Jedi, MIB..**$40.00**

Vehicle, Landspeeder, Star Wars, MIB.......................**$145.00**

Vehicle, Millennium Falcon, Empire Strikes Back, diecast, MIB **$175.00**

Vehicle, Scout Walker, Empire Strikes Back, MIB **$85.00**

Vehicle, Snowspeeder, Empire Strikes Back, EX (worn box)...**$45.00**

Vehicle, Star Destroyer, Power of the Force, 1995-present, electronic, MIB..**$25.00**

Vehicle, TIE Fighter, Star Wars, diecast, MOC **$150.00**

Vehicle, X-Wing Fighter (Battle Damaged), Empire Strikes Back, M (EX box)...**$125.00**

Yo-Yo, Darth Vader, Dairy Queen promo, Humphrey, 1970s, rare, NM...**$25.00**

Stauffer, Erich

From a distance, these child-like figures closely resemble Hummel figurines. They're marked 'Designed by Erich Stauffer' in blue script, often with a pair of crossed arrows or a crown. They always carry a number, sometimes with the letter S or U before it. As an added bonus, you may find a paper label bearing the title of the featured subject. Arnart Imports Inc. imported Erich Stauffer figurines from Japan from the late 1950s through the 1980s. Some of these pieces may be found with original Arnart blue and gold stickers.

Figurines range in size from 4½" up to 12½" tall. The most common is the single figure, but some may have two or three children on a single base. The most interesting are those that include accessories or animals to complete their theme. Note that Arnart Imports also made a similar line, but those pieces are smaller and not of the same quality. As a rule, figures marked Erich Stauffer and/or Arnart Imports would be valued at $4.00 to $5.00 per inch in height, sometimes a bit more if the accessories are unique and if stickers and tags are present.

Note: The majority of the listings that follow were gleaned from Internet auction sales. They indicate not only the winning bid but also include postage, insurance, and occasionally handling charges as well, since those costs must be added to the winning bid to arrive at an accurate reflection of the final costs.

Advisor: Joan Oates (See Directory, Erich Stauffer Figurines)

#S8536, girl sewing to repair shoe, 8"..........................**$35.00**
#S8542, nurse, girl on bench in nurse's outfit, duck at feet, 5"..**$55.00**
#U5843, Music Time, girl w/accordion, 6½".............**$16.00**
#U8561, boy w/hammer in 1 hand, bandaged thumb on other, 7½"..**$20.00**
#3248, Sandy Shoes, boy dumping sand from shoe, 6½"..**$20.00**
#44/115, Nurse, white gown, 5½"..............................**$55.00**
#55/1537, Little Bohemian, girl version, 5"................**$15.00**
#55/1537, Little Bohemian, male version, 5"..............**$15.00**
#55/1547, Little Sport, 5½"..**$15.00**
#55/2029, Dancing Time, 3 children dance in circle w/hands clasped...**$32.50**
#55/511, boy sits beside water bucket, 5"..................**$10.00**
#8028, Spring Time, boy sits on fence w/musical horn, duck at feet w/bird on fence, 3½x5½"........................**$25.00**
#8212, boy stands in front of fence............................**$15.00**
#8213, boy artist sits on fence w/painting items, duck at feet...**$30.00**
#8248, boy playing horn, goose at feet, 6½".............**$38.00**
#8268, girl picking corn, 5¼"....................................**$14.00**
#8268, girl pouring tea/coffee into cup, 5¼"............**$12.50**
#8326, Collie, sitting, 1960s, 4¾x7"..........................**$35.00**

#8343, boy & dog under umbrella.............................**$18.00**

#8394, Life on the Farm, boy with two ducks, 5", $22.00. (Photo courtesy Joan and Ken Oates)

#8395, girl sits on fence w/music book, duck at feet, 5"..**$22.00**
#8396, boy by fence w/umbrella, 5"...........................**$12.50**

Steiff Animals

These stuffed animals originated in Germany around the turn of the century. They were created by Margaret Steiff, whose company continues to operate to the present day. They are identified by the button inside the ear and the identification tag (which often carries the name of the animal) on their chest. Over the years, variations in tags and buttons help collectors determine approximate dates of manufacture.

Teddy bear collectors regard Steiff bears as some of the most valuable on the market. When assessing the worth of a bear, they use some general guidelines as a starting basis, though other features can come into play as well. For instance, bears made prior to 1912 that have long gold mohair fur start at a minimum of $75.00 per inch. If the bear has dark brown or curly white mohair fur instead, that figure may go as high as $135.00. From the 1920 to 1930 era, the rule of thumb would be about $50.00 minimum per inch. A bear (or any other animal) on cast-iron or wooden wheels starts at $75.00 per inch; but if the tires are hard rubber, the value is much lower, more like $27.00 per inch.

It's a fascinating study which is well covered in *Teddy Bears and Steiff Animals, First, Second,* and *Third Series,* by Margaret Fox Mandel. Also see Cynthia Powell's *Collector's Guide to Miniature Teddy Bears.*

Newsletter/Club: *Collector's Life*
The World's Foremost Publication for Steiff Enthusiasts
Beth Savino
P.O. Box 798
Holland, OH 43528; 1-800-862-TOYS; fax: 419-473-3947

Baby Chick, spotted Dralon w/felt comb, plastic feet & beak, all ID, 1971, 4", NM..**$85.00**

Baby Duck, yellow mohair w/brown airbrushed markings, orange felt beak & feet, all ID, 1959-61, 5½", EX..**$200.00**

Bear, gold mohair, glass eyes, original blue ribbon, raised script button, 1950s, 13", NM..............**$500.00**

Bear, gold mohair w/felt pads, glass eyes, all ID, 1950, 6", EX **$225.00**

Bear, Margaret Strong, cream, original button & tag, 1984-86, 9", NM..............**$125.00**

Bear, white mohair, glass eyes, original blue ribbon, raised script button, 1950s, 6", EX..............**$500.00**

Bendy Panda, mohair, all ID, 1960s, 3", NM **$325.00**

Biggie Beagle, mohair, plastic eyes, original red collar, all ID, 1960s, 7½", M..............**$185.00**

Bison, mohair w/felt horns, all ID, 1950, 8", M **$225.00**

Camel, mohair & felt, all ID, 1950, 5¾", NM............**$135.00**

Clownie Clown, original outfit, chest tag, 16", EX, from $200 to..............**$400.00**

Clownie Clown, original outfit, chest tag, 5", M **$100.00**

Cockie Dog, seated, black & white, original collar, no ID, 4½", EX..............**$85.00**

Coco Monkey, gray mohair w/white fringe around face & ears, glass eyes, original red leather collar, all ID, 5½", NM **$150.00**

Cosy Koala, all ID, 1970, 5", M..............**$65.00**

Crabby Lobster, felt w/vivid airbrushing, glass eyes, all ID, 4½", M **$350.00**

Donkey, velvet w/rope tail & leather harness, raised script button & stock tag, 1959-67, 4½", M..............**$165.00**

Dormili Rabbit, tan & white, all ID, 1986-88, 7", M **$65.00**

Elephant, w/anniversary blanket, all ID, 1959-67, 2½", M .**$150.00**

Floppy Beagle, sleeping, mohair, original ribbon, chest tag, 8", NM..............**$125.00**

Floppy Hens, mohair & felt, all ID, 1958, rare, 7" & 8", pr **$300.00**

Froggy Frog, seated, velvet, glass eyes, all ID, 1968, 3", NM..............**$135.00**

Giraffe, velvet, all ID, 1959-67, 6", M..............**$150.00**

Halloween Cat, black velvet & mohair, glass eyes, chest tag, raised script button & remnant stock tag, 1950s, 4", EX..............**$165.00**

Hedgehog, incised button & stock tag, 1966-67, 2¼", NM..............**$35.00**

Hide-A-Gift Rabbit, all ID, 1950, 5½", M, from $175 to...**$185.00**

Hoppy Rabbit, mohair, glass eyes, original ribbon & bell, all ID, 1968, 9", NM **$200.00**

Hoppy Rabbit, mohair, plastic eyes, original ribbon & bell, all ID, 1968, 7½", NM..............**$165.00**

Jackie Bear, raised script button & remnant stock tag, 1950s, rare, 9½", EX..............**$900.00**

Jumbo Elephant, mohair w/red felt bib, all ID, 1968, 9", M **$385.00**

Koala Bear, jointed head, all ID, 1959-61, 4½", M....**$425.00**

Lamb (from Mary Had a Little Lamb), all ID, 1986, 5", M..............**$75.00**

Leo Lion, seated, incised button, 1960, 5", NM..........**$85.00**

Lioness, mohair, glass eyes, fully jointed, raised script button & stock tag, 1951-57, rare, 6", M **$250.00**

Lora Parrot, mohair & felt, incised button & stock tag, 1968, 9", EX..............**$150.00**

Manni Rabbit, mohair, glass eyes, w/squeaker, original ribbon & bell, no ID, 1950s, 16", NM..............**$950.00**

Max & Moritz, all ID, 1950s, rare, 3½", MIP.............**$385.00**

Maxi Mole, mohair, all ID, 1965, 4", M..............**$135.00**

Molly Dog, white mohair w/red-brown tipping, glass eyes, swivel head, all ID, 1958, rare, 10", EX **$450.00**

Moosy Moose, all ID, 1963-64, rare, 4½", M.............**$425.00**

Nelly Snail, velveteen & vinyl, all ID, 1962, 6", EX ..**$200.00**

Niki Rabbit, mohair, glass eyes, fully jointed, original ribbon, raised script button & stock tag, 7", M..............**$400.00**

Nosy Rhinoceros, gray mohair with felt horn and ears, chest tag, raised script button and stock tag, 1954, 5", M, $110.00.

Original Teddy, gold mohair, black bead eyes, fully jointed, chest tag, 1950s, 3½", EX..............**$265.00**

Orsi Bear, caramel mohair, amber glass eyes, raised script button & chest tag, 1956, 8½", NM..............**$850.00**

Peggy Penguin, chest tag, 1959, 5", NM **$100.00**

Peky Dog, plush & felt, chest tag, 1950, 3", EX..........**$75.00**

Pieps Mouse, white mohair, all ID, M..............**$100.00**

Pony, mohair, glass eyes, original red leather saddle & plastic reins, chest tag, 1950s, 5", NM **$125.00**

Raccy Raccoon, mohair, glass eyes, stock tag, 6", EX **$100.00**

Renny Reindeer, chest tag, 1950s, 4½", M..............**$185.00**

Skunk, mohair & velvet, glass eyes, chest tag, 1962-63, 4¼", M..............**$250.00**

Snunki Ram, tan mohair w/black face & feet, original chest tag, 1950s, 6", NM..............**$125.00**

Squirrel, puppet, mohair w/felt hands & feet, glass eyes, 8½", NM..............**$75.00**

Teddy Baby, tan, all ID, 1985-86, 15", M..............**$250.00**

Tessie Schnauzer, gray mohair, glass eyes, original red collar, chest tag, 4½", NM..............**$150.00**

Tysus Dinosaur, all ID, 1980s, 7½", MIB..............**$125.00**

Woolie Bird, raised script button & stock tag, 1949, 2", NM..............**$50.00**

Woolie Frog, incised button & stock tag, 1960s, 2½", NM..............**$35.00**

Woolie Mouse, white, no ID, 1960, 1½", M.................$35.00
Woolie Skunk, raised script button, 1950s, 1½", NM ..$150.00

String Holders

Today we admire string holders for their decorative nature. They are much sought after by collectors. However, in the 1800s, they were strictly utilitarian, serving as dispensers of string used to wrap food and packages. The earliest were made of cast iron. Later, advertising string holders appeared in general stores. They were made of tin or cast iron and were provided by companies pedaling such products as shoes, laundry supplies, and food. These advertising string holders command the highest prices.

These days we take cellophane tape for granted. Before it was invented, string was used to tie up packages. String holders became a staple item in the home kitchen. To add a whimsical touch, in the late 1920s and 1930s, many string holders were presented as human shapes, faces, animals, and fruits. Most of these novelty string holders were made of chalkware (plaster of Paris), ceramics, or wood fiber. If you were lucky, you might have won a plaster of Paris 'Super Hero' or comic character string holder at your local carnival. These prizes were known as 'carnival chalkware.' The Indian string holder was a popular giveaway, so was Betty Boop and Superman.

Our values reflect string holders in excellent condition.

Advisor: Ellen Bercovici (See Directory, String Holders)

Apple & berries, chalkware, from $35 to.....................$50.00
Apple w/face, ceramic, PY, from $100 to..................$150.00
Baby face, chalkware, from $175 to $250.00
Balloon, ceramic, from $35 to $65.00
Bananas, chalkware, newer vintage, from $35 to $50.00
Beehive, cast iron, original tan paint, lg.....................$95.00
Bird on branch, scissors in head, ceramic, from $85 to..$100.00
Birdcage, red & white w/green leaves & yellow bird, chalkware, from $100 to..$150.00
Black child w/pink bandana, ceramic $195.00
Boy, top hat & pipe, eyes to side, chalkware, from $50 to $60.00
Bride & bridesmaids, ceramic, from $75 to...............$125.00
Butler, Black man w/white lips & eyebrows, ceramic, minimum value $300.00
Cabbage, ceramic, Japan...$100.00
Cat's head, ceramic, black & green eyes, from $65 to $85.00
Chef, chalkware, from $50 to $75.00
Cherry cluster, chalkware, from $125 to.....................$150.00
Clown w/string around tooth, chalkware, from $200 to..$300.00
Dog, Scottie, ceramic, from $125 to...........................$200.00
Dutch girl's head, chalkware, from $50 to $75.00
Elephant, yellow, England, ceramic, from $60 to $75.00
Gourd, chalkware, from $125 to $150.00
Granny in rocking chair, ceramic, PY, from $100 to.$150.00
Groom & bridesmaids, ceramic, from $75 to $125.00

House, Cleminson, ceramic, from $125 to.................$175.00
I Hate Housework, composition, from $35 to............$50.00
Indian head w/headdress, from $250 to....................$350.00
Iron w/flowers, ceramic, from $200 to $300.00
Jester, chalkware, from $125 to $175.00
Kitten w/ball of yarn, ceramic, homemade $65.00
Lady's head, Art Deco, ceramic, from $125 to $150.00
Little Red Riding Hood, chalkware, minimum value .$250.00
Maid, Sarsaparilla, ceramic, 1984, from $95 to..........$125.00
Mammy, plaid apron, polka-dot shirt, ceramic, Japan, from $95 to...$185.00
Mexican head w/sombrero, composition, from $50 to..$75.00
Mouse, composition, Josef Originals, from $50 to $60.00
Oriental man w/coolie hat, ceramic, marked Abingdon, from $350 to...$500.00
Parrot, chalkware, brightly colored, from $125 to $150.00

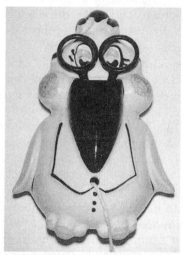

Penguin, ceramic, from $85.00 to $100.00. (Photo courtesy Ellen Bercovici)

Pig w/flowers, ceramic, from $100 to........................$125.00
Pirate & gypsy, wood fiber, pr, from $100 to............$125.00
Prayer Lady, by Enesco, ceramic...............................$200.00
Prince Pineapple, chalkware, from $225 to...............$275.00
Rooster & flowers on heart shape, ceramic, String Along..., 7x6"..$48.00
Rose, chalkware, from $125 to $150.00
Rosie the Riveter, chalkware, from $125 to...............$200.00
Teapot, wooden, red paint, decal of Black man, 6x4½", from $95 to...$125.00
Witch in pumpkin, winking, ceramic, from $125 to .$175.00

Swanky Swigs

These glasses, ranging in size from 3⅛" to 5⅝", were originally distributed by the Kraft company who filled them with their cheese spread. They were introduced in the 1930s and can still be found in the supermarket today in a clear small glass with indented designs of different patterns. There are approximately 223 different variations of colors and patterns ranging from sailboats, bands, animals, dots, stars, checkers, etc.

In 1999 a few Kraft Australian Swanky Swigs started turning up. We now have American, Canadian, and the Australian Kraft Swanky Swigs. They have been verified as Kraft Australian swigs because of the Kraft ads in magazines.

Here is a listing of some of the harder-to-find examples: In the small (Canadian) size (about 3¹⁄₁₆" to 3¼") look for Band No. 5 (two red and two black bands); Galleon (2 ships on each example, made in five colors — black, blue, green, red, and yellow); Checkers (made in four color combinations — black and red, black and yellow, black and orange, and black and white, all having a top row of black checks); and Fleur-De-Lis (black fleur-de-lis with a bright red filigree motif).

In the regular size (about 3⅜" to 3⅞") look for Dots Forming Diamonds (diamonds made up of small red dots); Lattice and Vine (white lattice with flowers in these combinations — white and blue, white and green, and white and red); Texas Centennial (a cowboy and horse in these colors — black, blue, green, and red); three special issues with dates of 1936, 1938, and 1942; and Tulip No. 2 (available in black, blue, green, and red).

In the large (Canadian) size (about 4³⁄₁₆" to 5⅝" you'll find Circles and Dot (circles with a small dot in the middle, in black, blue, green, and red); Star No. 1 (small scattered stars, made in black, blue, green, and red); Cornflower No. 2 (in dark blue, light blue, red, and yellow); Provincial Cress (made only in red/burgundy with maple leaves); and blue.

Even the lids are collectible and are valued at a minimum of $3.00, depending on condition and the advertising message they convey.

For more information we recommend *Swanky Swigs* by Ian Warner; *Collectible Glassware of the 40s, 50s, and 60s* and *The Collector's Encyclopedia of Depression Glass*, both by Gene Florence; and *Collectible Drinking Glasses* by Mark Chase and Michael Kelly.

Note: All are American issue unless noted Canadian.

Advisor: Joyce Jackson (See Directory, Swanky Swigs)

Antique #1, black, blue, brown, green, orange or red, Canadian, 3¼", ea **$8.00**
Antique #1, black, blue, brown, green, orange or red, Canadian, 1954, 4¾", ea **$20.00**
Antique #1, black, blue, brown, green, orange or red, 1954, 3¾", ea **$4.00**
Antique #2, lime green, deep red, orange, blue or black, Canadian, 1974, 4⅝", ea **$20.00**
Bachelor Button, red, green & white, 1955, 3¾" **$3.00**
Bachelor Button, red, white & green, Canadian, 1955, 3¼" **$6.00**
Bachelor Button, red, white & green, Canadian, 1955, 4¾" **$15.00**
Band #1, red & black, 1933, 3⅜" **$3.00**
Band #2, black & red, Canadian, 1933, 4¾" **$20.00**
Band #2, black & red, 1933, 3⅜" **$3.00**
Band #3, white & blue, 1933, 3⅜" **$3.00**
Band #4, blue, 1933, 3⅜" **$3.00**
Bicentennial Tulip, green, red or yellow, 1975, 3¾", ea ... **$15.00**
Blue Tulips, 1937, 4¼" **$20.00**
Bustlin' Betty, blue, brown, green, orange, red or yellow, 1953, 3¾", ea **$4.00**
Bustlin' Betty, blue, brown, green, orange, red or yellow, Canadian, 1953, 3¼", ea **$8.00**
Bustlin' Betty, blue, brown, green, orange, red or yellow, Canadian, 1953, 4¾", ea **$20.00**
Carnival, blue, green, red or yellow, 1939, 3½", ea **$6.00**
Checkerboard, white w/blue, green or red, Canadian, 1936, 4¾", ea **$20.00**
Checkerboard, white w/blue, green or red, 1936, 3½", ea **$20.00**
Circles & Dot, any color, 1934, 3½", ea **$7.00**
Circles & Dot, black, blue, green or red, Canadian, 1934, 4¾", ea **$20.00**
Coin, clear & plain w/indented coin decor around base, Canadian, 1968, 3⅛" or 3¼", ea **$2.00**
Coin, clear & plain w/indented coin decor around base, 1968, 3¾" **$1.00**
Colonial, clear w/indented waffle design around middle & base, 1976, 3¾", ea .... **$.50**
Colonial, clear w/indented waffle design around middle & base, 1976, 4⅜", ea **$1.00**
Cornflower #1, light blue & green, Canadian, 1941, 4⅝", ea **$20.00**
Cornflower #1, light blue & green, Canadian, 3¼", ea . **$8.00**
Cornflower #1, light blue & green, 1941, 3½", ea **$4.00**
Cornflower #2, dark blue, light blue, red or yellow, Canadian, 1947, 3¼", ea **$8.00**
Cornflower #2, dark blue, light blue, red or yellow, Canadian, 1947, 4¼", ea **$40.00**
Cornflower #2, dark blue, light blue, red or yellow, 1947, 3½", ea **$4.00**
Crystal Petal, clear & plain w/fluted base, 1951, 3½", ea . **$2.00**
Dots Forming Diamonds, any color, 1935, 3½", ea **$50.00**

Ethnic Series, 1974, Canadian, 4⅝": Poppy Red India, Lime Green Calypso, Royal Blue Spanish, Yellow Scottish, $20.00 each. **(Photo courtesy Joyce Jackson)**

Forget-Me-Not, dark blue, light blue, red or yellow, Canadian, 3¼", ea **$8.00**
Forget-Me-Not, dark blue, light blue, red or yellow, 1948, 3½", ea **$4.00**
Galleon, black, blue, green, red or yellow, Canadian, 1936, 3⅛", ea **$30.00**
Hostess, clear & plain w/indented groove base, Canadian, 1960, 3⅛" or 3¼", ea **$2.00**

Hostess, clear & plain w/indented groove base, Canadian, 1960, 5⅝", ea **$5.00**

Hostess, clear & plain w/indented groove base, 1960, 3¾", ea **$1.00**

Jonquil (Posy Pattern), yellow & green, Canadian, 1941, 3¼" **$8.00**

Jonquil (Posy Pattern), yellow & green, Canadian, 1941, 4⅝", ea **$20.00**

Jonquil (Posy Pattern), yellow & green, 1941, 3½", ea.**$4.00**

Kiddie Kup, black, blue, brown, green, orange or red, Canadian, 1956, 3¼", ea **$6.00**

Kiddie Kup, black, blue, brown, green, orange or red, Canadian, 1956, 4¾", ea **$20.00**

Kiddie Kup, black, blue, brown, green, orange or red, 1956, 3¾", ea **$3.00**

Lattice & Vine, white w/blue, green or red, 1936, 3½", ea **$50.00**

Petal Star, clear, 50th Anniversary of Kraft Cheese Spreads, 1933-1983, ca 1983, 3¾", ea **$2.00**

Petal Star, clear w/indented star base, Canadian, 1978, 3¼", ea...**$2.00**

Petal Star, clear w/indented star base, 1978, 3¾", ea......**$.50**

Plain, clear, like Tulip #1 w/out design, 1940, 3½", ea...**$4.00**

Plain, clear, like Tulip #3 w/out design, 1951, 3⅞", ea...**$5.00**

Provincial Crest, red & burgundy, Canadian, 1974, 4⅝", ea...**$25.00**

Sailboat #1, blue, 1936, 3½", ea **$12.00**

Sailboat #2, blue, green, light green or red, 1936, 3½", ea...**$12.00**

Special Issue, Cornflower #1, light blue flowers/green leaves, Greetings From Kraft, etc, 1941, 3½" **$410.00**

Special Issue, Lewis-Pacific Dairyman's Assoc, Kraft Foods, Sept 13, 1947, Chehalis WA, 3½".......................**$100.00**

Special Issue, Posy Pattern Tulip, red tulip w/green leaves, Greetings From Kraft, CA Retail Assoc, etc, 1940, 3½" **$350.00**

Special Issue, Posy Pattern Violet, Greetings From Kraft, CA Retail Assoc, Grocers Merchants, Del Monte, 1942, 3½" **$350.00**

Special Issue, Sailboat #1, blue, Greetings From Kraft, CA Retail Assoc, Grocers Merchants, Del Monte, 1936, 3½" **$350.00**

Special Issue, Tulip #1, red, Greetings From Kraft, CA Retail Assoc, Grocers Merchants, Del Monte, 1938, 3½" **$350.00**

Sportsmen Series, red hockey, blue skiing, red football, red baseball or green soccer, Canadian, 1976, 4⅝", ea ..**$20.00**

Stars #1, black, blue, green or red, 1935, 3½", ea **$7.00**

Stars #1, black, blue, green, red or yellow, Canadian, 1934, 4¾", ea..**$20.00**

Stars #1, yellow, 1935, 3½", ea..................................**$25.00**

Stars #2, clear w/orange stars, Canadian, 1971, 4⅝", ea **$5.00**

Texas Centennial, black, blue, green or red, 1936, 3½", ea...**$30.00**

Tulip (Posy Pattern), red & green, Canadian, 1941, 3¼", ea..**$8.00**

Tulip (Posy Pattern), red & green, Canadian, 1941, 4⅝", ea...**$20.00**

Tulip (Posy Pattern), red & green, 1941, 3½", ea **$4.00**

Tulip #1, black, blue, green or red, Canadian, 1937, 4⅝", ea...**$20.00**

Tulip #1, black, blue, green, red or yellow, Canadian, 3¼", ea..**$8.00**

Tulip #1, black, blue, green, red or yellow, 1937, 3½", ea...**$4.00**

Tulip #2, black, blue, green or red, 1938, 3½", ea **$25.00**

Tulip #3, dark blue, light blue, red or yellow, Canadian, 1950, 4¾", ea..**$20.00**

Tulip #3, dark blue, light blue, red or yellow, Canadian, 3¼", ea..**$8.00**

Tulip #3, dark blue, light blue, red or yellow, 1950, 3⅞", ea...**$4.00**

Violet (Posy Pattern), blue & green, Canadian, 1941, 3¼", ea..**$8.00**

Violet (Posy Pattern), blue & green, Canadian, 1941, 4⅝", ea...**$20.00**

Violet (Posy Pattern), blue & green, 1941, 3½", ea.......**$4.00**

Wildlife Series, black bear, Canadian goose, moose or red fox, Canadian, 1975, 4⅝", ea **$20.00**

Syroco

Syroco Inc. originated in New York in 1890 when a group of European wood carvers banded together to produce original hand carvings for fashionable homes of the area. Their products were also used in public buildings throughout upstate New York, including the state capitol. Demand for those products led to the development of the original Syroco reproduction process that allowed them to copy original carvings with no loss of detail. They later developed exclusive hand-applied color finishes to further enhance the product, which they continued to improve and refine over ninety years.

Syroco's master carvers use tools and skills handed down from father to son through many generations. Woods used, depending on the effect called for, include Swiss pear wood, oak, mahogany, and wormy chestnut. When a design is completed, it is transformed into a metal cast through their molding and tooling process. A compression mold system using wood fiber was employed from the early 1940s to the 1960s. Since 1962 a process has been in use in which pellets of resin are injected into a press, heated to the melting point, and then injected into the mold. Because the resin is liquid, it fills every crevice, thus producing an exact copy of the carver's art. It is then cooled, cleaned, and finished.

Other companies have produced similar items, among them are Multi Products, now of Erie, Pennsylvania. It was incorporated in Chicago in 1941 but in 1976 was purchased by John Hronas. Multi Products hired a staff of artists, made some wood originals, and developed a tooling process for forms. They used a styrene-based material, heavily loaded with talc or calcium carbonate. A hydraulic press was used to remove excess material from the forms. Shapes were dried in kilns for seventy-two hours, then finished and, if the design required it, trimmed in gold. Their products included bears, memo pads, thermometers, brush holders, trays, plaques, nut bowls, napkin holders, etc., which were sold mainly as souvenirs. The large clocks and mirrors were made before the 1940s and may sell for as much as $100.00 and more, depending on condition. Syroco used gold trim, but any other painted decoration you might encounter was very likely done by an outside firm. Some collectors prefer the painted examples and tend to pay a little more to get them. You may also find similar products stamped 'Ornawood,' 'Decor-A-Wood,' and 'Swank'; these are collectible as well.

See also Motion Clocks.

Ashtray, double, glass bowls, cigarette compartment in center, from $10 to **$20.00**

Ashtray, floral at sides, rectangular receptacle, from 2 to 4 rests, Syroco, 4x6", from $6 to................................**$10.00**

Ashtray, florals at sq sides, round receptacle, from 2 to 4 rests, Syroco, 5½x5½", from $7 to........................**$10.00**

Ashtray, steer & building on sides, marked Alamo TX, from $3 to...**$10.00**

Barometer, ship's captain at wheel, round mechanism at wheel's center, from $10 to.................................**$15.00**

Bookends, Diana the Huntress w/hound, pr, from $10 to..**$15.00**

Bookends, End of the Trail, pr, from $10 to **$15.00**

Bookends, lg wild rose, pr, from $10 to.....................**$15.00**

Bookends, Mount Rushmore, pr, from $10 to.............**$15.00**

Bookends, Scottie dog w/front legs on bench, 6½x4½", pr...**$50.00**

Bookends, Scottie dogs with glass eyes, OrnaWood, 7½", $75.00. (Photo courtesy Candace Sten Davis and Patricia J. Baugh)

Box, bear, waterfall & trees on lid, marked Yellowstone Nat Park, 3½x4½", from $5 to **$7.00**

Box, cowboy boots & saddle on lid, w/paper label...**$12.50**

Box, deer & trees, 4½x6", from $4 to **$6.00**

Box, floral design at sides & on lid, Syroco, 5½x5½", from $5 to...**$10.00**

Box, rope design on lid, velvet lining, Syroco, 6x6", from $10 to...**$15.00**

Box, standing dog on lid, 4x6", from $5 to **$10.00**

Box, swirl design, 5½x7", from $8 to........................**$10.00**

Brush holder, ship w/white triple mainsails, 4½", from $7 to...**$12.00**

Brush holder, 2 drunks w/keg, 5", from $5 to **$10.00**

Brush holder, 4 puppies in basket, from $8 to **$10.00**

Clock, cuckoo; blue bird cuckoo, key wound, 4½x4"..**$55.00**

Clock, white & gold scroll design, 8-day wind-up, 26" ..**$40.00**

Coat racks, Raggedy Ann & Andy, Andy (#7510) sits on fence, Ann (#7509) leans on fence, 9x12", pr **$20.00**

Figure, musician, painted, from $10 to **$15.00**

Figure, seated Indian, from $6 to **$10.00**

Figurine, buffalo, red nostrils & black eyes, 3¼x2¼x1½" ..**$35.00**

Figurine, bullfighter, 1968, 20x34½" **$30.00**

Figurine, Cape Cod fisherman & woman, painted, pr, from $6 to...**$15.00**

Figurine, Pinocchio, fingers crossed behind back, name on base, marked Walt Disney Prod Multi Products Chicago, 5" **$48.00**

Figurines, peacocks on dogwood branch, gold, 8¼", 12½", pr **$20.00**

Mirror, oval w/gold scrollwork border, #2369, made by Dart Industries for Syroco, 24½x16½" **$28.00**

Picture frame, 3x2½" **$6.00**

Picture frame, 8x5½", from $6 to **$12.00**

Pin holder, baby shoe shape, green velvet for pins, 3x2½" **$15.00**

Pipe holder, 2 horses at gate, 3 rests, from $12 to **$15.00**

Plaque, cat on hind legs playing violin like a cello, 5½x3½"...**$70.00**

Plaque, Washington DC, brown, 9⅛x6½"....................**$12.50**

Plaque, 10-point buck embossed on shield, 3-D effect, 10½" **$15.00**

Plate, barn & silo pastorial scene at center, fruits & vegetables at rim, 8", from $2 to **$5.00**

Plate, pine cones & leaves, 4", from $2 to.................**$5.00**

Thermometer, Black figure, marked Multi Prod 1949, 5½" **$50.00**

Thermometer, captain at ship's wheel, painted, marked Copyright Thad Co, 4"...**$15.00**

Thermometer, figural, man w/umbrella stands beside thermometer, 6" **$20.00**

Thermometer, Scottie dogs at sides, magnet at bottom, 4", from $5 to...**$10.00**

Tie rack, bartender behind bar w/bottles, painted, 6x9½", from $10 to...**$20.00**

Tie rack, Boy Scout insignia in center w/tents on sides, 10¼" L **$35.00**

Tie rack, pointer dog at top, metal hangers, 7x12", from $10 to...**$20.00**

Tray, flowers, marked Multi Products, 11" L, from $8 to.**$14.00**

Wall hanging, Aquarius sign (Zodiac), #7042, 1½" **$10.00**

Wall plaque, crucifix, white, 8", from $5 to................**$10.00**

Wall plaque, Our Mother of Perpetual Help, 4x5", from $5 to...**$10.00**

Wall plaque, Scottie dog, repainted, 6", from $2 to **$8.00**
Wall shelf, floral w/acanthus leaf, bead trim at top edge, Multi Products, 9x7", pr, from $7 to **$12.00**

Taylor, Smith, and Taylor

Though this company is most famous for their pastel dinnerware line, Lu Ray, they made many other patterns, and some of them are very collectible in their own right. They were located in the East Liverpool area of West Virginia, the 'dinnerware capitol' of the world. Their answer to HLC's very successful Fiesta line was Vistosa. It was made in four primary colors, and though quite attractive, the line was never developed to include any more than twenty items. Other lines/shapes that collectors especially look for are Taverne (also called Silhouette — similar to a line made by Hall), Conversation (a shape designed by Walter Dorwin Teague, 1950 to 1954), and Pebbleford (a textured, pastel line on the Versatile shape, made from 1952 to 1960).

For more information we recommend *Collector's Guide to Lu-Ray Pastels* by Bill and Kathy Meehan (Collector Books), which covers several dinnerware lines in addition to LuRay.

Note: To evaluate King O'Dell, add 15% to the values we list for Conversation. For Boutonniere, add 15% to our Ever Yours values; and for Dwarf Pine, add the same amount to the values suggested for Versatile.

See also LuRay Pastels.

Brown-Eyed Susan, bowl, soup.....................................**$6.50**
Brown-Eyed Susan, plate, bread & butter.....................**$4.50**
Brown-Eyed Susan, plate, dinner **$7.00**
Brown-Eyed Susan, saucer...**$2.50**
Buttercup, bowl, rimmed soup....................................**$5.00**
Buttercup, plate, dinner..**$5.00**
Buttercup, plate, salad..**$4.00**
Buttercup, saucer **$1.50**
Cathay, bowl, fruit/dessert **$1.50**
Cathay, bowl, rimmed soup.......................................**$2.00**
Cathay, bowl, vegetable; round..................................**$7.50**
Cathay, cup, short mug shape **$1.50**
Cathay, plate, bread & butter......................................**$1.50**
Cathay, plate, dinner; from $3 to................................**$5.00**
Cathay, saucer...**$2.50**
Conversation, bowl, cereal...**$7.00**
Conversation, bowl, fruit/dessert................................**$5.50**
Conversation, bowl, vegetable; oval, lg **$12.50**
Conversation, plate, bread & butter **$5.00**
Country Store, plate, bread & butter **$5.00**
Country Store, plate, dinner.......................................**$7.00**
Country Store, saucer..**$3.00**
Daisy Wreath, cup & saucer.......................................**$5.00**
Daisy Wreath, plate, dinner..**$6.50**
Dutch Onion, creamer (open).....................................**$4.00**
Dutch Onion, cup & saucer...**$3.50**
Echo Dell, bowl, cereal..**$7.50**

Echo Dell, bowl, vegetable; round..............................**$7.00**
Echo Dell, creamer, open...**$7.50**
Echo Dell, cup & saucer **$7.00**
Echo Dell, plate, bread & butter..................................**$5.00**
Echo Dell, plate, chop..**$12.50**
Echo Dell, plate, dinner **$7.50**
Echo Dell, sugar bowl, w/lid.......................................**$10.00**
Etruscan, cup & saucer..**$5.00**
Etruscan, plate, bread & butter...................................**$3.00**
Etruscan, plate, dinner...**$5.00**
Ever Yours, bowl, fruit/dessert **$6.00**
Ever Yours, gravy boat (no underplate)......................**$9.00**
Ever Yours, plate, bread & butter................................**$4.50**
Ever Yours, saucer **$4.00**
Ever Yours, sugar bowl, w/lid **$7.50**
Flor del Sol, plate, salad...**$3.00**
Florabunda, bowl, coupe soup....................................**$5.00**
Florabunda, bowl, vegetable; round **$10.00**
Florabunda, creamer (open) **$5.00**
Florabunda, plate, bread & butter................................**$3.00**
Florabunda, plate, dinner..**$5.00**
Florabunda, platter, round **$10.00**
Florabunda, sugar bowl, w/lid.....................................**$7.50**
Golden Jubilee, bowl, cereal.......................................**$8.00**
Golden Jubilee, bowl, fruit/dessert..............................**$6.50**
Golden Jubilee, bowl, vegetable; oval **$17.50**
Golden Jubilee, coffeepot...**$30.00**
Golden Jubilee, creamer (open)...................................**$15.00**
Golden Jubilee, plate, bread & butter..........................**$6.50**
Golden Jubilee, plate, dinner.......................................**$12.00**
Golden Jubilee, plate, salad..**$7.50**
Golden Jubilee, platter, medium..................................**$20.00**
Golden Jubilee, sugar bowl, w/lid................................**$17.50**
Holiday Wreath, cup & saucer.....................................**$4.50**
Holiday Wreath, plate, chop..**$10.00**
Holiday Wreath, saucer **$2.50**
Indian Summer, bowl, soup...**$5.00**
Indian Summer, bowl, vegetable; round......................**$15.00**
Indian Summer, bowl, vegetable; sm **$10.00**
Indian Summer, creamer...**$7.00**
Indian Summer, cup & saucer.....................................**$7.00**
Indian Summer, gravy boat w/underplate & ladle......**$22.50**
Indian Summer, plate, dinner......................................**$7.00**
Indian Summer, plate, luncheon..................................**$5.00**
Indian Summer, platter, lg...**$17.50**
Lazy Daisy, bowl, fruit/dessert....................................**$5.00**
Lazy Daisy, bowl, soup...**$7.50**
Lazy Daisy, bowl, vegetable; round, lg........................**$15.00**
Lazy Daisy, bowl, vegetable; round, sm **$10.00**
Lazy Daisy, cup & saucer...**$7.50**
Lazy Daisy, plate, bread & butter................................**$5.00**
Lazy Daisy, plate, dinner...**$6.50**
Lazy Daisy, plate, luncheon..**$5.00**
Lazy Daisy, platter, 13½"...**$18.00**
Lazy Daisy, salt & pepper shakers, pr **$10.00**
Lazy Daisy, sugar bowl, w/lid **$12.50**
Pastoral, bowl, fruit/dessert...**$6.00**

Pastoral, plate, bread & butter $6.00
Pastoral, saucer $5.00
Pebbleford, bowl, salad..$4.00
Pebbleford, cup & saucer..$4.00
Pebbleford, plate, bread & butter..............................$3.50
Pebbleford, plate, dinner...$9.00
Pebbleford, plate, salad...$5.00
Pebbleford, platter, 13" L..$8.00
Reveille, creamer (open) $7.50
Reveille, plate, bread & butter $3.00
Reveille, plate, dinner...$6.50
Reveille, saucer $2.50
Sierra, bowl, soup/cereal...$7.50
Sierra, plate, dinner...$9.00
Sierra, plate, salad...$7.00
Taverne (Silhouette), bowl, cereal; Laurel shape $20.00
Taverne (Silhouette), bowl, vegetable; w/lid..............$50.00

Taverne (Silhouette), butter dish, Laurel shape, $150.00. (Photo courtesy Bill and Kathy Meehan)

Taverne (Silhouette), creamer, Laurel shape...............$15.00
Taverne (Silhouette), creamer, w/lid, Laurel shape $20.00
Taverne (Silhouette), cup & saucer, St Denis, Laurel
    shape...$42.00
Taverne (Silhouette), Laurel shape, 10" $25.00
Versatile, bowl, vegetable; 8½x6¾"...........................$12.50
Versatile, cup & saucer $7.50
Versatile, gravy boat (no underplate)..........................$17.50
Versatile, plate, dinner $7.50
Vistosa, egg cup, footed, from $25 to.........................$35.00
Vistosa, plate, bread & butter; from $10 to $15.00
Vistosa, plate, chop; 15", from $40 to $50.00
Vistosa, plate, dinner; 9", from $15 to........................$20.00
Vistosa, salt & pepper shakers, pr...............................$32.00
Wood Rose, cup & saucer...$6.00
Wood Rose, plate, dinner...$7.50
Wood Rose, saucer..$2.50

Tiara Exclusives

Collectors are just beginning to take notice of the glassware sold through Tiara in-home parties, their Sandwich line in particular. A branch of the Lancaster Colony Corp., the Tiara Division closed in 1998. Several companies were involved in producing the lovely colored glassware they marketed over the years, among them Indiana Glass, Fenton, Dalzell Viking, and L.E. Smith.

In 1990 and 2000, Home Interiors offered a small selection of Tiara Sandwich Glass dinnerware in an attractive transparent purple color called Plum. They have also marketed Tiara's square honey box and children's dish set. Some of this glassware may be currently available through Home Interiors.

Advisor: Mandi Birkinbine (See Directory, Tiara)

Crown Dinnerware

In the mid-1980s Tiara made Crown Dinnerware in Imperial Blue. This is the pattern most collectors know as King's Crown Thumbprint. The color is a rich medium blue and brighter than cobalt.

Cup $3.00
Goblet, stemmed, 8-oz, from $3 to $5.00
Plate, bread; 8"..$5.00
Plate, dinner; 10"..$7.00
Saucer $2.00

Honey Boxes

One of Tiara's more popular items was the honey box or honey dish. It is square with tiny tab feet and an embossed allover pattern of bees and hives. The dish measures 6" tall with the lid and was made in many different colors, ranging in value from $15.00 up to $60.00, depending on the color.

Amber, from $15 to $25.00
Black, from $25 to $35.00
Chantilly (pale) Green, from $45 to............................$60.00
Clear, from $35 to $45.00
Light blue, from $25 to..$50.00
Spruce (teal) Green, from $20 to.................................$35.00

Sandwich Pattern

In the late 1960s, Tiara contracted with Indiana to produce their famous line of Sandwich dinnerware (a staple at Indiana Glass since the late 1920s). Over the years, it has been offered in many colors: ruby, Spruce (teal), crystal, amber, green, pink (officially named Peach), blue, and others in limited amounts. The dark, midnight blue color was named Bicentennial Blue. In 1976, Tiara Exclusives presented the Sandwich Glass Bicentennial Collector's Series in observance of America's Bicentennial. According to the Tiara brochure, this Colonial Blue Sandwich glass (sometimes also called Anniversary or Midnight Blue by collectors) was approved for a production of 15,000 sets. We've listed a few pieces of Tiara's Sandwich, and though the market is unstable and tends to vary from region to region, our estimates will serve to offer an indication of current asking prices. Because this glass is not rare and is relatively new, collectors tend to purchase only items in perfect condition. Chips or scratches will decrease value significantly.

With most items, the quickest way to tell Anchor Hocking's Sandwich from Tiara and Indiana Sandwich is by looking at the flower in the pattern. The Tiara/Indiana flower is outlined with a single line and has convex petals. Anchor Hocking's flower is made with double lines, so has a more complex appearance, and the convex area in each petal is tiny. Tiara's Chantilly Green Sandwich is a pale green color that resembles the light green glass made by Indiana Glass during the Depression era. Use of a black light can help determine the age of pale green Sandwich glass. The green Sandwich made by Indiana Glass during the Depression will fluoresce yellow-green under a black light. Tiara's Chantilly Green reflects the purple color of the black light bulb, but does not fluoresce yellow-green. To learn more about the two lines, we recommend *Collectible Glassware from the 40s, 50s, and 60s*, by Gene Florence (Collector Books). Also available are *Collecting Tiara Amber Sandwich Glass*, *Collecting Tiara Bicentennial Blue Sandwich Glass*, and *Collecting Tiara Chantilly Green Sandwich Glass*, all by our advisor, Mandi Birkinbine (see the Directory for ordering information).

Ashtray, amber, 1¼x7½" **$15.00**
Basket, amber, tall & slender, 10¾x4¾" **$50.00**
Bowl, amber, slant slides, 1¾x4¾" **$5.50**
Bowl, amber, 6-sided, 1¼x6¼" **$12.00**
Bowl, console; amber, footed, flared rim, 3⅞x11"...**$40.00**
Bowl, salad; amber, crimped, 4¾x10", from $15 to....**$18.00**
Bowl, salad; amber, slant-sided, 3x8⅜".......................**$20.00**
Bowl, salad; Chantilly Green, slant-sided, 3x8⅜", from $15 to **$25.00**
Butter dish, amber, domed lid, 6" H, from $20 to **$25.00**
Butter dish, Bicentennial Blue, from $25 to **$35.00**
Butter dish, Chantilly Green, domed lid, 6" H **$35.00**
Cake plate, Chantilly Green, footed, 4x10", from $55 to..**$70.00**
Candle holders, amber, flared foot, 3¾", pr **$18.00**
Candle holders, amber, scalloped rim, footed, 3¼x5½", pr **$25.00**
Candle holders, Chantilly Green, 8½", pr **$45.00**
Candy box, amber, w/lid, 7½", from $65 to.................**$80.00**
Canister, amber, 26-oz, 5⅝", from $12 to....................**$20.00**
Canister, amber, 38-oz, 7½", from $12 to....................**$20.00**
Canister, amber, 52-oz, 8⅞", from $18 to....................**$26.00**
Celery tray/oblong relish, Bicentennial Blue, 10⅜x4⅜"..**$18.50**
Clock, amber, wall hanging, 12" dia, from $20 to.......**$25.00**
Clock, amber, wall hanging, 16" dia, from $45 to.......**$55.00**
Compote, amber, 8" **$25.00**
Creamer & sugar bowl, Bicentennial Blue, round, flat, pr, from $20 to...**$25.00**
Cup, coffee; amber, 9-oz...**$4.00**
Cup, punch; & saucer, crystal, 2⅝x3⅜" **$6.00**
Cup, snack; amber **$4.00**
Dish, club, heart, diamond or spade shape, amber, 4", ea from $3 to...**$5.00**

Dish, club, heart, diamond or spade shape, clear, 4", ea...**$3.00**
Egg tray, amber, 12", from $12 to...............................**$18.00**
Egg tray, Chantilly Green, from $15 to **$22.00**
Egg tray, Spruce Green, 12" **$15.00**
Fairy lamp, amber, egg shape, pedestal foot, 2-pc, 5¾", from $14 to...**$18.00**
Fairy lamp, Chantilly Green, from $18 to **$26.00**
Fairy lamp, Regal Blue, 2-pc, 5¾" **$25.00**
Goblet, table wine; amber, 8½-oz, 5½" **$7.50**
Goblet, water; amber, 8-oz, 5¼", from $6 to.................**$8.00**
Goblet, water; Bicentennial Blue, 8-oz, 5¼", from $8 to .**$12.00**
Goblet, water; clear, 5¼", from $5 to............................**$8.00**
Goblet, water; Spruce Green, 8-oz, 5¼", from $4 to **$5.50**
Gravy boat, amber, 3⅛x7⅜", from $45 to **$60.00**
Mug, amber, footed, 5½"...**$8.00**

Napkin holder, amber, footed fan shape, 4" x 7½", from $22.00 to $28.00. (Photo courtesy Mandi Birkinbine)

Pitcher, amber, 8¼", from $45 to................................**$65.00**
Plate, dinner; amber, 10", from $9.50 to **$12.50**
Plate, dinner; Chantilly Green, from $8 to..................**$12.00**
Plate, salad; amber, 8" **$7.00**
Plate, salad; Chantilly Green, 8¼", from $4 to **$8.00**
Platter, amber, sawtooth rim, 12", from $8.50 to........**$12.00**
Puff box, Horizon Blue, 2x3¾" dia **$22.00**
Salt & pepper shakers, amber, 4¾", pr, from $18 to ..**$25.00**
Sherbet, amber, 3x3⅝"...**$5.00**
Tray, amber, footed, 1¾x12¾"......................................**$35.00**
Tray, Chantilly Green, 3-part, 12" **$19.00**
Tray, divided relish, amber, 4-compartment, 10", from $25 to..**$30.00**
Tray, tidbit; Horizon Blue, center silver-colored metal handle, 8¼" dia **$17.50**
Tumbler, juice; amber, 8-oz, 4", from $12 to..............**$14.00**
Tumbler, water; amber, 10-oz, 6½" **$8.00**
Vase, amber, ruffled, footed, 3¼x6½" **$16.00**
Vase, bud; amber, 3⅝", from $15 to.............................**$25.00**
Wine set, amber, decanter, tray & 8 goblets...............**$55.00**

Tire Ashtrays

Manufacturers of tires issued miniature versions containing ashtray inserts that they usually embossed with advertising messages. Others were used as souvenirs from World's Fairs. The earlier styles were made of glass or glass and metal, but by the early 1920s, they were replaced by the more familiar rubber-tired variety. The inserts were often made of clear glass, but colors were also used, and once in awhile you'll find a tin one. The tires themselves were usually black; other colors are rarely found. Hundreds have been produced over the years; in fact, the larger tire companies still issue them occasionally, but you no longer see the details or colors that are evident in the pre-WWII ashtrays. Although the common ones bring modest prices, rare examples sometimes sell for up to several hundred dollars. For ladies or non-smokers, some miniature tires were called pin trays.

For more information we recommend *Tire Ashtray Collector's Guide* by Jeff McVey.

Advisor: Jeff McVey (See Directory, Tire Ashtrays)

Armstrong Rhino-Flex, Miracle SD, name on tire in gold, glass insert w/picture of rhino & name, 6" dia **$35.00**

Bridgestone, D-Lug, Tubeless, clear glass insert w/logo name in center, 3x8¾" dia..**$30.00**

Firestone, Champion, Safety-Lock Cord, gum dipped, clear glass insert w/embossed F & pledge, 6" dia.........**$45.00**

Firestone, HD, High Speed, amber glass insert, embossed Century of Progress 1934, 2 extended rests, 5⅜" dia **$90.00**

Firestone, red & black plastic insert w/3 extended rests, 6" dia **$10.00**

General, Heavy Duty Cushion, 40-12, green glass insert w/match holder, 2 snuffs, 1 rest, name in bottom, 4⅝" dia....**$125.00**

General, Steelex Radial, glass insert, black letters 'goes a long way to make friends,' 6½" dia..............................**$20.00**

Goodrich Silvertown, Golden Ply 600-16 4-ply, clear glass insert, 6⅛" dia..**$45.00**

Goodrich Silvertown, Lifesaver Radial HR 70-15, clear glass insert, 6" dia **$25.00**

Goodyear, American Eagle Radial, Flexten, clear insert, white decal w/name & eagle, 5¾" dia **$20.00**

Goodyear, Balloon All Weather 6.00-21, green glass insert w/6-nut disc wheel, 5½" dia..................................**$80.00**

Goodyear, Hi-Miler Cross Rib, nylon, clear glass insert w/logo name in blue letters, 6¼" dia **$25.00**

Hood Arrow, Heavy Duty 6 Ply, 600-20, 6⅜" dia.......**$65.00**

Kelly Springfield, Commercial Heavy Tread, 10.0x20, clear glass insert, 6" dia...**$35.00**

Kelly Springfield, Voyager, Aramid Belted Radial, clear insert w/green decal, 6" dia **$20.00**

Miller, Miller Deluxe, Long Safe Mileage, Geared to the Road, clear insert w/name on bottom, 7" dia **$80.00**

Mohawk, Akron O, glass insert w/yellow bottom & local ad from Urbana IL, 1930s, 5⅜" dia.............................**$45.00**

Pennsylvania, Jeannette PA, Low Pressure, glass insert w/pressed pattern bottom, old, 5½" dia **$50.00**

Pennsylvania Tires, pink glass insert, 5¼" dia **$50.00**

Seiberling, All-Tread, solid, clear glass insert, 6⅝" dia ...**$25.00**

Seiberling, Patrician De Luxe 4-ply, green glass insert w/cream decal on bottom w/local ad, 3½" dia....**$45.00**

Seiberling, Sealed-Aire, 760-15, clear glass insert, 5⅞" dia ..**$30.00**

Vogue Tyre, Custom Built, Steel Radial, black plastic insert w/logo of lions in center, 6" dia............................**$35.00**

Tobacco Collectibles

Until lately, the tobacco industry spent staggering sums advertising their products, and scores of retail companies turned out many types of smoking accessories such as pipes, humidors, lighters, and ashtrays. Even though the smoking habit isn't particularly popular nowadays, collecting tobacco-related memorabilia is!

See also Advertising Character Collectibles, Joe Camel; Cigarette Lighters.

Club/Newsletter: *Tobacco Jar*
Society of Tobacco Jar Collectors
Charlotte Tarses, Treasurer
3011 Falstaff Road #307
Baltimore, MD 21209; Dues: $30 per year ($35 outside of U.S.)

Cigar box, Royal Princess Hand Made 5¢, wood, complete w/inner label, ca 1930, EX....................................**$90.00**

Cigar cutter, El Tino/The 5¢ Cigar, reverse-painted glass key-wind cutter, 8¼x6¾x5", VG+..............................**$360.00**

Cigar cutter, Griswold Manufacturing Co of Erie PA, #2492 & lg S, Red J, 18¾x7½", EX......................................**$85.00**

Cigar cutter, Griswold Mfg #2494S, Piper-Heidsieck, 19x4½x8", EX..**$85.00**

Cigar cutter, Star, cast iron, 9-lb, 19x7", EX **$75.00**

Cigar display, brass-colored pot-metal teepee flanked by 2 Indians seated on base holding cigars, 13x9", VG+...**$110.00**

Cigarette pack, Clown Balanced Blend Cigarettes, yellow, VG+...**$25.00**

Cigarette vendor, Auto Smoker, Lighted & Fresh Old Gold on front plate, 11", EX..**$850.00**

Decal, Philip Morris & Co Ltd, cigarette pack, for use on inside of glass, 3¼x2½"..**$45.00**

Door push, Duke's Mixture/The 'Roll' of Fame, image of hand pouring from pouch into other hand on blue ground, 6x9", EX..**$425.00**

Fan pull, Bagley's Clam Bake Fine Cut Chewing, diecut cardboard image of Old Salt w/tobacco packet, 8", EX **$170.00**

Humidor, drunk man w/cigarette laying on wine barrel, hand-carved wood, Anri, Made in Italy, 1920s, 6½"........**$55.00**

Humidor, Dunhill, chrome, removable aluminum liner, monogram, dated 1938, 6x5½", EX......................**$55.00**

Humidor, Green River Tobacco, glass, original paper label, 7x6¼"..**$185.00**

Humidor, Green River Tobacco, stoneware, brown & white w/paper label, resembles whiskey jug **$150.00**

Lunch pail, King Koal Tobacco, 5x8x4", EX.............**$365.00**

Lunch pail, Mayo's Cut Plug, 3-tiered, collapsible, w/different logo on ea layer, gold on blue, 5x8", VG+..........**$35.00**

Lunch pail, North Pole Smoking Tobacco, tall box, bail handle, graphics on blue, 6x4x6", VG+ $350.00

Lunch pail, Red Crest Cut Plug, cardboard w/leather handle & clasp, silhouette image of rooster & lettering, 8" L, VG+...$85.00

Lunch pail, US Marine Smoke or Chew, light blue, EX+ .$525.00

Lunch pail, Winner Cut Plug Smoke & Chew, racing scene, EX $575.00

Pipe, Barbi, squat Danish bulldog shape, straight grain, 6-sided shank w/dark wood insert, AA grade, EX............$325.00

Pipe, Barbi, tight straight grain, red w/black stem, BB grade, EX $250.00

Pipe, Dunhill Bruyere 5102, full bent, bird's-eye grain, 6⅛"...$130.00

Pipe, Dunhill Shell Briar, billiard shape, Made in England, refurbished bit, NM......................................$180.00

Pipe, Dunhill-London A, Made in England, 13 Patent #1343253/20 T 35, EX $145.00

Pipe, GBD Unique, Made in London England, 1½" polished briar stem, oversize, 7¼" L, EX $245.00

Pipe, JD Cooke, straight bulldog shape, magnum size, 7½", EX $225.00

Pipe, Joura, straight-grain Danish brandy style, A grade, 2" bowl, 5½" L, EX...$400.00

Pipe, Larsen (Teddy), straight-grain, squat Dublin w/pointed bottom, vulcanite fishtail stem, unused, M.........$185.00

Pipe, Mark Tinsky, straight grain (light stain, sandblasted), 1986, M..$145.00

Pipe, meerschaum, fox head, white stem, old repair .$535.00

Pipe, meerschaum, risque lady, amber stem, VG $525.00

Pipe display rack, Smoke WDC Pipes lettered on round back resembling target w/easel stand, clip holders, 20", EX..$30.00

Pocket mirror, Cycle Cigarettes, 2⅛" dia, VG $35.00

Pocket mirror, Lucky Strike Cigarettes, shaped like cigarette pack, dated 1938, 3x2", NM+................................$190.00

Pocket tin, Big Ben Pipe & Cigarette Smoking Tobacco, vertical, clock image, red, black & yellow, VG+....$215.00

Pocket tin, Black & White Roll Cut, vertical, diagonal 2-color, 4½", EX...$375.00

Pocket tin, Central Union New Cut Smoking, vertical, lady in crescent moon, gold on red, 4½", EX+...............$325.00

Pocket tin, Central Union Tobacco, vertical, 4½", EX..$260.00

Pocket tin, Century/P Lorillard & Co, flat, black on red w/rounded corners, miniature, 1¼x2⅛x⅜", EX+ $170.00

Pocket tin, Globe, flat, black on red, 2⅜x3¾x⅝", EX+ $200.00

Pocket tin, Hi Plane, vertical, hinged lid, single prop, EX...$60.00

Pocket tin, Lord Kenyon Blend Super Mild, vertical, blue & white, 3", EX $375.00

Pocket tin, Lucky Strike, vertical, white (rare), 4½", EX+ ..$375.00

Pocket tin, Pat Hand Cube Cut Granules, vertical, oval, red, 2¾", EX+ $275.00

Pocket tin, Regal Cube Cut, vertical, fold-over flip top, white, 4", EX+..$375.00

Pocket tin, Three Feathers Choice Granulated Plug Cut, vertical, 4¼", EX+ $325.00

Pocket tin, Times Square Smoking Mixture, vertical, cityscape on blue, 4½", EX+ $300.00

Pocket tin, Yankee Doodle Flake Cut, 2-oz, 3¼x2¼", EX..$65.00

Pocket tin, 15¢ Tiger Bright Sweet Chewing Tobacco, vertical, black on cream, 3", EX.............................$275.00

Sign, Chesterfield, paperboard, Betty Grable on poster hanging on wooden wall w/soldier's hat & brush on shelf, 22", EX..$25.00

Sign, Chesterfield, tin flange, Buy...Here, oval above diecut image of Regular & King Size packs, 16½x12", VG.............$100.00

Sign, Gail & Ax Navy Tobacco, paper, Now in the New Pocket Pouches/Foil Lined/10¢, image of sailor, wood frame, 42", VG+...$500.00

Sign, Heart of Havana Harvester Cigar 5¢, tin, heart-shaped image of woman on yellow self-framed oval, 13", EX $165.00

Sign, Mayo's Plug, tin, Tags Good to July 1911, 9½x13½", VG...$170.00

Sign, Model, tin, litho image of Model man as store Indian, Compare Model's Smoking Qualities/Did You Say 10¢?, 15", VG $65.00

Sign, Model Smoking Tobacco, cardboard stand-up, diecut Indian figure holding pocket tin, 22", EX............$35.00

Sign, Philip Morris, heavy paper, Now!.../King Size or Regular above Johnny displaying 2 packs, 23½x18", EX $35.00

Sign, Philip Morris, paper, Safety First/Call for..., image of Johnny calling at left, 23x41", EX+ $65.00

Sign, Sun-Ray Cigar, paper, Pleasing to All/Mild & Fragrant, lettering over sunburst-type rays, white on blue, 9x15", NM $40.00

Sign, The Old Reliable/Peg Top, cardboard, name lettered on image of cigar, yellow background, 14x48", NM+ ..$130.00

Sign, two-sided flange, Camel/Prince Albert, tin litho, 17½" x 10½", VG, $400.00. (Photo courtesy Buffalo Bay)

Sign, We Sell Cigarettes, Smoke Kool w/Snow-Fresh Filter, tin, 12x30", EX..$55.00

Store bin, Game Fine Cut, rectangular w/slip lid, game bird graphics, 7x12x8", EX+.......................................$800.00

Store bin, Sweet Cuba Fine Cut 5¢, slant top w/hinged lid, yellow, 8x9½", VG+ **$200.00**

Store canister, Sterling Fine Cut 5¢ Wax Bags, round w/slip lid, red & green plaid background, 7", EX **$65.00**

Thermometer, Mail Pouch Tobacco, tin, Treat Yourself to the Best/Chew..., yellow & white on blue, white border, 39", EX+ **$300.00**

Thermometer, Snow Bird Cigars 10¢, wooden feather shape, Allen & Dunning Co, EX+....................................**$250.00**

Thermometer/sign, Winston Cigarettes, tin litho, round, EX **$40.00**

Tin, Kennebec Cigars, simulated wood-grain resembling cigar box, hinged lid, interior lithoed label, 4½x8½", VG **$35.00**

Tin, Lucky Strike Cigarettes, red, white, green & black, 3½x2¾" dia, VG+ **$40.00**

Tin, Seal of North Carolina Plug Cut, round w/smaller slip lid, 6", VG+ **$285.00**

Tin, Stag Tobacco for Pipe & Cigarettes, sq w/round lid, graphics on red, 5x6", EX+ **$575.00**

Tin, Surburg's High Grade, oblong w/dome top, blue & blue-green w/silver, 7", VG+ **$180.00**

Tin, Sure Shot Chewing Tobacco, Indian w/drawn bow, hinged lid, 6½x15x10", EX..................**$365.00**

Tin, War Eagle Cigars, 2 for 5¢, red, white & yellow, 5¼x5", EX..**$55.00**

Tip tray, El Verso Havana Cigars, litho image of man in chair by lamp table, dark blue, 6½x4½", EX.................**$90.00**

Tobacco silk, Lehigh University, Richmond Straight Cut Cigarettes Factory 25, 2nd Dist Va, 3⅞x5¼", EX..**$65.00**

Tobacco tag, Gray Horse Tobacco, ⅝x⅞", EX............**$80.00**

Tobacco tag, Schoolfield & Watson, overview of railroad tracks, wide gauge, EX...**$65.00**

Tobacco tag, Twin City, Winston Salem, detailed drawings of towns, EX **$145.00**

Toothbrush Holders

Novelty toothbrush holders have been modeled as animals of all types, in human forms, and in the likenesses of many storybook personalities. Today all are very collectible, especially those representing popular Disney characters. Most of these are made of bisque and are decorated over the glaze. Condition of the paint is an important consideration when trying to arrive at an evaluation.

For more information, refer to *Pictorial Guide to Toothbrush Holders* by Marilyn Cooper.

Advisor: Marilyn Cooper (See Directory, Toothbrush Holders)

Bear w/pants & jacket holds tray w/1 hole, wall hanging, Gayton, 6½", from $70 to....................................**$80.00**

Bow w/top hat, 2 holes, wall hanging, Japan, 5½", from $70 to **$85.00**

Cat standing on front paws, 1 hole, wall hanging, Japan, 5⅜", from $90 to..**$100.00**

Children in auto, 2 holes, wall hanging, Japan, 5", from $70 to..**$80.00**

Clown w/bug on nose, holds tray w/3 holes, wall hanging, Japan, 5⅛", from $125 to...................................**$150.00**

Cowboy next to cactus, 3 holes, wall hanging, Japan, 5½", from $85 to...**$95.00**

Dog, begging, 1 hole, wall hanging, Japan, 3⅞", from $85 to..**$95.00**

Dog begging, lustreware, 2 holes, wall hanging, 3¾", from $100 to..**$125.00**

Donkey w/mane, 2 holes, mane holds 1 brush, wall hanging, Japan, 5¾", from $100 to **$125.00**

Dutch boy & girl sitting on mantel, 3 holes, stands, Japan (Goldcastle), 4¼", from $110 to **$125.00**

Elephant w/trunk in air, 3 holes, wall hanging, Japan, 5½", from $85 to...**$100.00**

Frog w/mandolin, 1 hole, stands, Japan (Goldcastle), 6", from $95 to..**$110.00**

Girl w/basket standing before fence, 2 holes, wall hanging, Japan, 5¼", from $75 to **$85.00**

Little Red Riding Hood, shaker top, Germany, 4¼", from $350 to..**$425.00**

Little Red Riding Hood, 2 holes, wall hanging, Japan, 5½", from $95 to..**$110.00**

Old Woman in Shoe, 3 holes, wall hanging, Japan, 4½", from $80 to...**$95.00**

Pinocchio & Figaro, 1 hole, stands, Shafford, 5¼", from $450 to..**$475.00**

Sailors on anchor, 2 holes, wall hanging, Japan, 5½", from $60 to...**$70.00**

Schnauzer dog, sitting, 2 holes, Germany, 3⅛", from $90 to..**$110.00**

Skeezix, metal, 2 holes, wall hanging, K USA, 6", from $150 to..**$175.00**

Swami, sitting, 1-hole, Japan, 4", from $90 to **$100.00**

Three Bears, 2 holes, wall hanging, Japan, 5", from $75 to..**$85.00**

Three Bears w/bowls, 3 holes, stands, KIM ISUI, 4", from $85 to..**$95.00**

Uncle Willie, 2 holes, wall hanging, FAS-Japan, 5⅛", from $95 to..**$105.00**

Toys

Toy collecting has long been an area of very strong activity, but over the past decade it has literally exploded. Many of the larger auction galleries have cataloged toy auctions, and it isn't uncommon for scarce nineteenth-century toys in good condition go for $5,000.00 to $10,000.00 and up. Toy shows are popular, and there are clubs, newsletters, and magazines that cater only to the needs and wants of toy collectors. Though once buyers ignored toys less than thirty years old, in more recent years, even some toys from the '80s are sought after.

Condition has more bearing on the value of a toy than any other factor. A used toy in good condition with no major flaws will still be worth only about half (in some cases much less) as much as one in mint (like new) condition. Those mint and in their original boxes will be worth considerably more than the same toy without its box.

There are many good toy guides on the market today including: *Modern Toys, American Toys, 1930 to 1980,* by Linda Baker; *Collecting Toys* and *Collecting Toy Trains* by Richard O'Brien; *Schroeder's Collectible Toys, Antique to Modern; Elmer's Price Guide to Toys* by Elmer Duellman; *Toys of the Sixties, A Pictorial Guide,* by Bill Bruegman; *Occupied Japan Toys With Prices* by David C. Gould and Donna Crevar-Donaldson; and *Cartoon Toys and Collectibles* by David Longest. More books are listed in the subcategory narratives that follow. With the exception of O'Brien's (Books Americana), Bruegman's (Cap't Penny Productions), and Gould's and Crevar-Donaldson's all the books we've referred to are published by Collector Books.

See also Advertising Character Collectibles; Breyer Horses; Bubble Bath Containers; Character Collectibles; Disney Collectibles; Dolls; Fast-Food Collectibles; Fisher-Price; Halloween; Hartland Plastics Inc.; Model Kits; Paper Dolls; Games; Puzzles; Star Trek; Star Wars; Steiff Animals; Trolls.

Action Figures and Accessories

Back in 1964, Barbie dolls were taking the feminine side of the toy market by storm. Hasbro took a risky step in an attempt to capture the interest of the male segment of the population. Their answer to the Barbie doll craze was GI Joe. Since no self-respecting boy would admit to playing with dolls, Hasbro called their boy dolls 'action figures,' and to the surprise of many, they were phenomenally successful. Today action figures generate just as much enthusiasm among toy collectors as they ever did among little boys.

Action figures are simply dolls with poseable bodies. Some, the original GI Joes, for instance, were 12" tall, while others were 6" to 9" in height. In recent years, the 3¾" figure has been favored. GI Joe was introduced in the 3¾" size in the '80s and proved to be unprecedented in action figure sales. (See also GI Joe.)

In addition to the figures themselves, each company added a full line of accessories such as clothing, vehicles, play sets, weapons, etc. — all are avidly collected. Be aware of condition! Original packaging is extremely important. In fact, when it comes to the recent issues, loose, played-with examples are seldom worth more than a few dollars.

For more information, refer to *Collectible Action Figures* by Paris and Susan Manos (published by Collector Books).

Club: The Mego Adventurers Club
Old Forest Press, Inc.
PMB 195, 223 Wall St.
Huntington, NY 11743; Membership: $18.95 per year ($30 foreign); Includes 6 issues of *Mego Head,* the official club newsletter

Advanced Dungeons & Dragons, figure, Strongheart or War Duke, 3¾", MOC, ea $20.00

Adventures of Indiana Jones, accessory, Desert Convoy Truck, Kenner, MIB $70.00
Adventures of Indiana Jones, accessory, Mola Ram, Kenner, MOC $70.00
Adventures of Indiana Jones, figure, Indiana Jones, Kenner, 3¾", MOC $200.00
Adventures of Indiana Jones, figure, Toht, Kenner, 3¾", MOC $30.00
Battlestar Galactica, accessory, Cylon Raider, Mattel, M (NM Canadian box), ea...$60.00
Battlestar Galactica, figure, Imperious Leader or Ovion, Mattel, 3¾", MOC, ea from $10 to........................$15.00
Best of the West, accessory, Circle X Ranch, Marx, MIB, from $135 to $160.00
Best of the West, figure, Captain Maddox, Marx, complete, NM (EX Fort Apache Fighters box).....................$115.00
Best of the West, figure, Johnny West, Marx, complete, EX...$45.00
Best of the West, figure, Sam Cobra, Marx, complete, M..$60.00
Best of the West, figure, Sam Cobra, Marx, later version w/quick-draw grip, MIB...$40.00
Best of the West, figure, Sheriff Garrett, Marx, complete, NM (VG box) $175.00
Best of the West, figure, Zeb Zachary, Marx, complete, EXIB..$135.00
Best of the West, horse, Pancho, sorrel w/black tack, Marx, complete, NM..$45.00
Big Jim, accessory, Jungle Truck, Mattel, M $45.00
Big Jim, accessory, Sea Rescue, Mattel, complete, NM..$15.00
Big Jim, figure, any character, Mattel, complete, EX, ea from $20 to..$25.00
Big Jim, figure, Big Jeff, #7316, NRFB.........................$50.00
Black Hole, figure, Maximillian, Mego, MOC..............$35.00
Black Hole, figure, Vincent, Mego, MOC....................$50.00
Blackstar, figure, Vizir, MOC.......................................$25.00
Blackstar, figure, White Knight, MOC $30.00
Buck Rogers, figure, any character, Mego, 12", MIB, ea.....$65.00
Buck Rogers, figure, any character, Mego, 3¾", MOC, ea..$20.00
Captain Action, accessory, Action Cave, Ideal, M.....$100.00
Captain Action, accessory, Buck Rogers outfit, complete, Ideal, M..$95.00
Captain Action, accessory, Lone Ranger outfit, complete, Ideal, NM..$200.00
Captain Action, figure, Action Boy, Ideal, 12", complete, EX $360.00
Captain Action, figure, Captain America, complete, Ideal, 12", M..$200.00
Captain Action, figure, Phantom, Ideal, 12", MIB $175.00
Captain Action, figure, Steve Canyon, Ideal, 12", MIB..$215.00
Captain Planet & the Planeteers, figure, Commander Clash, Tiger/Kenner, MOC...$12.00
CHiPs, accessory, motorcycle, Mego, MIB...................$50.00
CHiPs, figure set, Jon, Ponch & Sarge, Mego, 8", MOC..$45.00
Dragon Heart, figure, Draco, Medusa or Razorthorn, MOC, ea $12.00
Dragon Heart, figure set, Draco w/Bowen or Evil Griffen Dragon w/King, MIB (sealed), ea........................$15.00

Dukes of Hazzard, figure, any character, Mego, 8", MOC, ea from $30 to..$35.00

Justice League of America, accessory, Aquaman playset, Multiple/Canada, 1967, complete, NM (NM box), from $275 to..$350.00

Justice League of America, accessory, Batman playset, Multiple/Canada, 1967, MIB, from $500 to.........$600.00

Lone Ranger Rides Again, accessory, Prairie Wagon, Gabriel, MIB $40.00

Lone Ranger Rides Again, accessory, Tribal Teepee, Gabriel, MIB $35.00

Lone Ranger Rides Again, figure, any character, Gabriel, 9", MIB, ea $50.00

Lost in Space, figure, Don West or Will Robinson, Trendmasters, 8", MIB, ea $40.00

Lost in Space, figure, Judy Robinson, Trendmasters, 8", MIB..$35.00

Lost in Space, figure, Tybo the Carrot Man, Trendmasters, 8", MIB $45.00

M*A*S*H, accessory, Military Base, complete, Tri-Star, NMIB..$40.00

M*A*S*H, figure, any character, Tri-Star, 3¾", MOC, ea .$20.00

Major Matt Mason, accessory, Rocket Launch Pack, Mattel, complete, EX..$20.00

Major Matt Mason, figure, Doug Davis, w/helmet, Mattel, EX..$60.00

Major Matt Mason, figure, Jeff Long, w/helmet, Mattel, VG $75.00

Marvel Super Heroes, accessory, Batcave, Mego, MIB ..$200.00

Marvel Super Heroes, figure, Aquaman, Mego, complete, 8", M..$125.00

Marvel Super Heroes, figure, Captain America, Mego, complete, 8", M..$60.00

Marvel Super Heroes, figure, Falcon, Mego, 8", MIB (sealed) $190.00

Marvel Super Heroes, figure, Human Torch, Mego, 8", EX $40.00

Marvel Super Heroes, figure, Penguin, Mego, 8", MIB .$90.00

Marvel Super Heroes, figure, Riddler, Mego, 8", MIB ..$200.00

Marvel Super Heroes, figure, Superman, Mego, 8", MOC..$145.00

Marvel Super Heroes, figure, Wonder Woman, complete, Mego, 8", M..$100.00

Masters of the Universe, figure, any character except Flying Fists He-Man or Hurricane Hordack, MOC, ea from $15 to..$20.00

Masters of the Universe, figure, Flying Fists He-Man or Hurricane Hordack, MOC, ea $40.00

Micronauts, accessory, Hydrocopter, MIB (sealed) $80.00

Micronauts, figure, Andromeda, Mego, MIB................$50.00

Micronauts, figure, Betatron, Mego, MIB $25.00

Official World's Greatest Super Heroes, accessory, Batcopter, Mego, NMIB..$175.00

Official World's Greatest Super Heroes, figure, Aquaman or Tarzan, 8", M, ea $45.00

Official World's Greatest Super Heroes, figure, Human Torch or Shazam, Mego, 8", MOC, ea..$50.00

Official World's Greatest Super Heroes, figure, Penguin, Mego, 8", MOC (sealed) $125.00

Planet of the Apes, figure, Astronaut, Mego, 8", M.....$65.00

Planet of the Apes, figure, Peter Burke, Mego, 8", MOC ..$110.00

Planet of the Apes, figure, Soldier Ape, complete, Mego, 8", M..$55.00

Power Lords, figure, any character, MOC, ea from $20 to ..$30.00

Princess of Power, accessory, Crystal Castle, complete, Mattel, MIB..$100.00

Princess of Power, any character, Mattel, MOC, ea.....$20.00

Rambo, accessory, Weapons Pak, Coleco, 1985, MOC ..$10.00

Rambo, figure, any character except Rambo, Coleco, 6", MOC, ea..$15.00

Rambo, figure, Rambo, Coleco, 6", MOC....................$20.00

Rapid Development Force, figure, any character, Time Products, 1992, 12", MIB, ea..$12.00

Robotech, accessory, Bioroid Hovercraft, Matchbox, MOC..$15.00

Robotech, figure, Corg, Matchbox, MOC....................$12.50

Robotech, figure, Dana Sterling, Lisa Hayes, Max Sterling or Miriya (purple or red version), Matchbox, MOC, ea..$15.00

Robotech, figure, Rick Hunter or Rook Bartley, Matchbox, MOC..$17.50

Six Million Dollar Man, figure, Oscar Goldman, Kenner, 12", MIB, $100.00. (Photo courtesy Cindy Sabulis)

Skeleton Warriors, figure, any character, MOC, ea from $8 to..$10.00

Spawn, figure, any character from 1st or 2nd series, Todd Toys, MOC, ea..$25.00

Spawn, figure, any character from 3rd or 4th series, Todd Toys, MOC, ea..$12.00

Stargate, accessory, Winged Glider, MIB (sealed).......$25.00

Stargate, figure, any character, MOC, ea from $6 to ...$10.00

Super Powers, accessory, Batmobile, Kenner, 1985, MIB.$100.00

Super Powers, figure, Aquaman, complete, Kenner, NM $15.00

Super Powers, figure, Cyclotron, complete, Kenner, M ..$25.00

Super Powers, figure, Golden Pharaoh, Kenner, MOC ...$30.00

Super Powers, figure, Superman, Kenner, MOC (unpunched) **$40.00**

Super Powers, figure, Ted Tornado, Kenner, MOC.....**$45.00**

Superman: Man of Steel, accessory, Superboy VTOL Cycle, Kenner, 1995, MOC.................................**$12.00**

Superman: Man of Steel, figure, Powerflight Superman, Laser Superman, Superboy or Conduit, Kenner, 1995, MOC, ea..**$8.00**

SWAT, accessory, Van, LJN, MIB **$75.00**

SWAT, figure, any character, MIP, ea **$30.00**

Tales of the Cryptkeeper, figure, any character except Talking Cryptkeeper, Ace Novelty, MOC, ea......**$100.00**

Tales of the Cryptkeeper, figure, Talking Cryptkeeper, Ace Novelty, MIB **$20.00**

Tarzan, figure set, Tarzan & Giant Ape or Tarzan & Jungle Cat, Mattel, MIB, ea **$200.00**

Team America, figure, any character, Ideal, 1982, MOC, ea from $8 to..**$12.00**

Terminator 2, any character except John Conner, Kenner, MOC, ea..**$20.00**

Terminator 2, figure, John Conner, MOC...................**$25.00**

Tigersharks, accessory, Sharkhammer vehicle, LJN, MIB ..**$50.00**

Tigersharks, figure, any character, LJN, MOC, ea from $15 to...**$20.00**

Toxic Crusaders, figure, any character, Playmates, MOC, ea **$10.00**

Venom, figure, any character from 1st or 2nd series, Toy Biz, MOC, ea...**$15.00**

Waltons, accessory, Country Store, Mego, MIB **$85.00**

Waltons, accessory, Farmhouse, Mego, MIB.............**$125.00**

Waltons, figure sets, Grandma & Grandpa, Johnboy & Mary Ellen or Mom & Pop, Mego, 8", MIB, ea **$35.00**

Willow, figure, Kael w/Horse or Shosha w/Horse, Tonka, MIP, ea **$10.00**

Willow, figure, Ufgood w/Baby, Tonka, rare, MIP **$15.00**

Wizard of Oz, figure, any character except Scarecrow or Wicked Witch, Mego, 8", MOC, ea.......................**$35.00**

Wizard of Oz, figure, Scarecrow or Wicked Witch, Mego, 8", MOC, ea..**$45.00**

World Wrestling Federation, figure, Bam Bam Bigalow, LJN, MOC, from $35 to................................**$50.00**

World Wrestling Federation, figure, Honky Tonk Man, Hasbro, MOC..**$10.00**

World Wrestling Federation, figure, Nasty Boys, Hasbro, MOC, from $25 to................................**$35.00**

World Wrestling Federation, figure, Typhoon, Hasbro, MOC..**$15.00**

Battery Operated

It is estimated that approximately 95% of the battery-operated toys that were so popular from the '40s through the '60s came from Japan. The remaining 5% were made in the United States by other companies. To market these toys in America, many distributorships were organized. Some of the largest were Cragstan, Linemar, and Rosko. But even American toy makers such as Marx, Ideal, Hubley, and Daisy sold them under their own names, so the trademarks you'll find on Japanese battery-operated toys are not necessarily that of the manufacturer, and it's sometimes just about impossible to determine the specific company that actually did make them. After peaking in the '60s, the Japanese toy industry began a decline, bowing out to competition from the cheaper diecast and plastic toy makers.

Remember that it is rare to find one of these complex toys that has survived in good, collectible condition. Batteries caused corrosion, lubricants dried out, cycles were interrupted and mechanisms ruined, rubber hoses and bellows aged and cracked, so the mortality rate was extremely high. A toy rated good, that is showing signs of wear but well taken care of, is generally worth about half as much as the same toy in mint (like new) condition. Besides condition, battery-operated toys are rated on scarcity, desirability, and the number of 'actions' they perform. A 'major' toy is one that has three or more actions, while one that has only one or two is considered 'minor.' The latter, of course, are worth much less.

In addition to the books we referenced in the beginning narrative to the toy category, you'll find more information in *Collecting Battery Toys* by Don Hultzman (Books Americana) and *Collector's Guide to Battery Toys* by Don Hultzman (Collector Books).

Alps, Bubble Blowing Monkey, w/bubble solution, NMIB ..**$175.00**

Alps, Chippy the Chipmunk, 1950s, MIB.................**$225.00**

Alps, Cragstan Crap Shooting Monkey, MIB, from $150.00 to $175.00.

Alps, Cyclist Clown, 1950s, 9", EX **$300.00**

Alps, Drumming Bunny, 1960s, MIB........................**$125.00**

Alps, Frankie the Roller Skating Monkey, 1950s, 12", EXIB **$115.00**

Alps, Hooty the Happy Owl, 1960s, 9", MIB.............**$185.00**

Alps, Princess the Begging Poodle, 1950s, 8", EX......**$65.00**

Alps, Shaggy the Friendly Pup, 1960s, 8", EX **$65.00**

Aoshin, Monkee Mobile, 1967, 12", NMIB.................**$525.00**

Asahitoy, Musical Car, 1950s, 9", EX **$225.00**

Bandai, Air Control Tower, litho tin, 1960s, 11, EX ..**$400.00**

Bandai, Flipper the Spouting Dolphin, MIB.............**$125.00**

Bandai, Pete the Policeman, M.................................$125.00
Bandai, Swimming Duck, 1950s, 8", EX $140.00
CK, Clucking Clara, MIB, from $175 to $225.00
Cragstan, Dilly Dalmatian, 1950s, 9½", EX $100.00
Cragstan, Oldtimer Train Set, 1950s, MIB $225.00
Cragstan, Yo-Yo Clown, 1960s, 9", NM $250.00
Daiya, Josie the Walking Cow, 1950s, NM $150.00
Ideal, Clancy the Great, 1960s, MIB.......................$285.00
Illco, Mickey Mouse Loop-the-Loop, MIB................$175.00
K, Highway Skill Driving, litho tin w/plastic cars, 1960s,
    NMIB...$150.00
K, Merry Rabbit, 1950s, 11", NM $200.00
KO, Musical Dancing Sweethearts, 1950s, 10", rare, NM..$300.00
Linemar, Bubbling Pup, 1950s, 7½", EX $150.00
Linemar, Busy Secretary, 1950s, 7½", MIB...............$300.00
Linemar, Butterfly w/Flapping Wings, 1950s, 10" W, EX..$100.00
Linemar, Doxie the Dog, 1950s, 9", EX....................$50.00
Linemar, Feeding Bird Watcher, 1950s, 9", EX..........$250.00
Linemar, Jocko the Drinking Monkey, 1950s, 11", VG..$75.00
Linemar, Musical Hall, 1950s, EX.............................$200.00
Linemar, Walking Cat, 1950s, 6", EX........................$65.00
Marusan, Magic Clown Man, litho tin w/cloth clothes, 1950s,
    11", NM...$450.00
Marx, Aircraft Carrier, 20", EXIB.............................$450.00
Marx, Barking Spaniel Dog, 1950s, 7", EX................$100.00
Marx, Colonel Hap Hazzard, 1968, 11", EX..............$700.00
Marx, Mickey Mouse Krazy Car, 7", EXIB.................$125.00
Marx, Race-A-Kart, 1960s, 10½", EX........................$150.00
Mego, Chee Chee Chihuahua, 1960s, 8", EX.............$50.00
Mego, Dashee the Derby Hat Dachshund, remote, 1971, 8",
    EX..$85.00
Mego, Roll-Over Rover, 1970s, 9", EX......................$65.00
Mikuni, Rooster, 7", EXIB.......................................$60.00
MT, ABC Fairy Train, litho tin, 14", EX (EX box)......$175.00
MT, Bunny the Cashier, litho tin, 1950s, 7½", EX.....$300.00
MT, Mickey Mouse Trolley, 1960s, EX......................$225.00
MT, Tom & Jerry Highway Patrol, 1960s, 8", VG......$100.00
Remco, Bulldog Tank, 1960s, 22", EXIB....................$150.00
Remco, Firebird 99 Dashmobile, 1960s, 13", EX.......$225.00
Remco, Johnny Speedmobile, mostly plastic, 1960s, rare, 15",
    EX..$285.00
Remco, Tumbling Monkey, EX.................................$125.00
Rosko, Chap the Obedient Dog, 1960s, MIB.............$125.00
Rosko, Dennis the Menace Zylophone Player, 9", MIB...$375.00
S&E, Popcorn Vendor (bear), 1960s, 7", EX.............$300.00
S&E, Snappy Alligator, EXIB...................................$100.00
SAN, Pistol Pete, 11", NMIB....................................$360.00
SAN, Smoking Pop Locomotive, 1950, 10½", EX......$110.00
TN, Brave Eagle, 1950s, 11", EX...............................$140.00
TN, Handy Hank Mystery Tractor, 1950s, EX............$200.00
TN, Loop-the-Loop Monkey, 1960s, 10", EX..............$75.00
TN, Magic Action Bulldozer, 1950s, 9½", EX............$200.00
TN, Merry-Go-Round Truck, 1950s, rare, 11", NM....$375.00
TN, Slurpy Pup, 1960s, 6½", MIB.............................$125.00
TN, Worried Mother Duck & Baby, 1950s, 11", MIB...$200.00
Tomiyama, Donny the Smiling Dog, 1961, 8½", MIB..$175.00
TPS, Happy Plane, 1960s, 9" L, EX...........................$115.00

TPS, Stunt Plane, 1960s, 10½" W, MIB.....................$250.00
Y, Cragstan Crapshooter, 1950s, 9", MIB..................$175.00
Y, Grand-Pa Car, 1950s, 9", EX.................................$75.00
Y, Hasty Chimp, 1960s, 9", MIB...............................$125.00
Y, Waddles Family Car, 1960s, MIB..........................$150.00
YM, Yo-Yo Monkey, 1960s, 12", EX..........................$150.00

Guns

Some of the bestselling kinds of toys ever made, toy guns were first patented in the late 1850s. Until WWII most were made of cast iron, though other materials were used on a lesser scale. After the war, cast iron became cost prohibitive, and steel and diecast zinc were used. By 1950 most were made of either diecast material or plastic. Hundreds of names can be found embossed on these little guns, a custom which continues to the present time. Because of their tremendous popularity and durability, today's collectors can find a diversity of models and styles, and prices are still fairly affordable.

See also Cowboy Character Collectibles.

Newsletter: *Toy Gun Collectors of America*
Jim Buskirk, Editor and Publisher
3009 Oleander Ave., San Marcos, CA 92069; 760-559-1054.
Published quarterly, covers both toy and BB guns. Dues: $17 per year

Actoy Wyatt Earp Frontier Marshall Cap Guns & Holster,
    complete w/2 9" cap guns & embossed leather holster,
    NMIB...$450.00
Daisy Marshal of the West Gun Set, complete w/2 8" cap pis-
    tols, double-barrel shot gun, holster & ammunition,
    NMIB...$125.00
Esquire Lone Ranger Pony Boy Gun & Holster Set, 2 guns
    & double leather holster w/jewels & medallions, 1947,
    MIB $300.00
Fleetwood Starsky & Hutch Repeater Cap Gun, 1976, MIP,
    from $40 to..$50.00
George Schmidt Hopalong Cassidy Pistol, cameo grips, 9",
    EX $250.00

Hamilton Secret Agent Hideaway Pistol, 5½", VGIB, $75.00.

Hubley, Flintlock Jr Cap Pistol, diecast w/nickel-plated finish & brown swirl plastic grips, 1955, 7½", NMIB **$50.00**

Hubley Davy Crockett Flintlock Buffalo Rifle, 25", EX **$150.00**

Hubley Scout Rifle, lever action, diecast w/nickel-plated finish, 1960, EX **$125.00**

Hubley Texan Cap Pistol, dicast w/nickel-plated finish & star logo, white plastic steer grips, 1950s, 9", VG **$150.00**

Hubley Zorro Coyote Holster Set, diecast w/black & gold leather holster, NM (EX box) **$175.00**

Ideal Man From UNCLE Cap Pistol, black plastic w/silver detail, diecast works, stickers on sides, VG **$65.00**

John Henry Dick Tracy Shoulder Holster Set, complete, 1950, MIP **$85.00**

Kilgore Big Horn Six-Shooter Cap Pistol, diecast w/nickel-plated finish, heavy scroll work, 7", NMIB **$75.00**

Kilgore Buc-a-roo Single Shot Cap Pistol, diecast w/brown plastic grips, 1950s, NMIB **$125.00**

Kilgore Fast-Draw Single Holster Set, plastic w/studded & jeweled faux leather holster, 1950s, NMIB **$125.00**

Kilgore Roy Rogers Cap Pistol, diecast w/nickel-plated finish, white plastic horse-head grips, revolving cylinder, M **$300.00**

Knickerbocker Dragnet Detective Special Repeating Revolver, black-painted diecast w/Badge 714 inlaid on grips, 6", NMIB......................................**$75.00**

Leslie-Henry Gunsmoke Cap Pistol, diecast w/nickel-plated finish, brown plastic horse-head grips, 9", NM ..**$150.00**

Leslie-Henry Smoky Joe Cap Pistol, diecast w/nickel-plated finish, translucent amber grips, 1950s, 9", VG....**$100.00**

Leslie-Henry Texas Ranger Gun & Holster Set, diecast w/white grips, brown leather holster w/studs & jewels, 1950s, NMIB **$150.00**

Leslie-Henry Wagon Train Cap Pistol, diecast w/chrome finish, black textured stag grips, 1950s, 9", VG **$125.00**

Leslie-Henry Wild Bill Hickok Cap Pistol, diecast w/gold finish, white plastic horse-head grips, 1950s, 9½", EX......**$175.00**

Lone Star Batman Ray Gun, blue plastic w/black detail, 1970, rare, 7½", EX......................................**$250.00**

Lone Star Starsky & Hutch Shoulder Holster Set, 1976, MOC..**$125.00**

Maco USA Machine Gun, plastic w/yellow cardboard barrel, complete w/plastic tripod & bullets, 1950s, 12", MIB.......**$175.00**

Marx Bullet Shooting Snub Nose Cap Pistol, diecast w/black-painted finish, brown plastic grips, 1960, NM......**$75.00**

Marx Dick Tracy Siren Pistol, red finish, VG **$75.00**

Marx Flash Gordon Click Ray Pistol, litho tin, 10", NM (NM box) **$250.00**

Marx Tom Corbett Space Cadet Atomic Rifle, MIB ...**$350.00**

Mattel Agent Zero-M Radio Rifle, black plastic diecast works, 1964, 22½", EX **$165.00**

Mattel Fanner 45 Shootin' Shell, 11¼", EX **$250.00**

Mattel Fanner 50 Cap Pistol No 543, diecast w/chrome finish, plastic stag grips, 1957, NM (NM box)................**$275.00**

Mattel Shootin' Shell Remington Derringer No 622, 1959, MIB **$100.00**

Mattel Shootin' Shell Winchester Carbine, 26", M **$165.00**

Nichols Stallion .38 Cap Pistol, diecast w/nickel plated finish, white plastic grips, 9½", NM..............................**$125.00**

Ohio Art Astro Ray Signal Dart Gun, red plastic w/white trim, 1960s, 10", EX (EX box) **$250.00**

Remco Captain Buck Flash Buzz Ray Gun, plastic, battery-operated, 1965, 9", EX....................................**$100.00**

Schmidt Buck 'N Bronc Deputy Cap Pistol, diecast w/nickel-plated finish, metal grips w/copper finish, 1950, 8½", VG...**$125.00**

Stevens Pawnee Bill Cap Gun, cast iron, 1940, 7½", VG ..**$125.00**

Stevens Peacemaker Repeating Cap Pistol, diecast w/nickel-plated finish, black plastic horse head grips, 9", EX (VG box) **$150.00**

Tigrett Hopalong Cassidy Zoomerang Gun, red plastic, shoots coil of paper w/spring action, 1950, 9", NMIB..**$175.00**

TN Quick-Draw Rifle, litho tin, friction, 1960, 12½", EX..**$85.00**

Topper Sixfinger Spy Gun, plastic, 1965, 3½", NMOC..**$85.00**

Wesco Lugar Automatic, hard plastic, complete w/10 pellets, 1950s, 7", NMIB **$100.00**

Wyandotte Red Ranger Jr Cap Pistol, diecast w/silver finish, white plastic horse-head grips, 1957, 8", EX **$100.00**

Wyandotte Water Pistol, red-painted pressed steel, 1940s, 7", EX (G box)...**$50.00**

Ramp Walkers

Though ramp-walking figures were made as early as the 1870s, ours date from about 1935 on. They were made in Czechoslovakia from the '20s through the '40s and in this country during the '50s and '60s by Marx, who made theirs of plastic. John Wilson of Watsontown, Pennsylvania, sold his worldwide. They were known as 'Wilson Walkies' and stood about 4½" high. But the majority has been imported from Hong Kong.

Advisor: Randy Welch (See Directory, Toys)

Astro, Hanna-Barbera/Marx **$150.00**

Astro & Rosey, Hanna-Barbera/Marx **$75.00**

Big Bad Wolf & Mason Pig, Disney/Marx...................**$50.00**

Boy & Girl Dancing, plastic **$45.00**

Brontosaurus w/Monkey, Marx **$40.00**

Bull, plastic..**$20.00**

Bunny Pushing Cart, plastic....................................**$60.00**

Chipmunks Carrying Acorns, plastic **$35.00**

Cow, plastic, w/metal legs, sm **$20.00**

Dairy Cow, plastic **$20.00**

Dog, Czechoslovakian **$35.00**

Donald Duck Pulling Nephews in Wagon, Disney **$35.00**

Duck, plastic **$20.00**

Farmer Pushing Wheelbarrow, plastic.......................**$30.00**

Fiddler & Fifer Pigs, Disney/Marx **$50.00**

Figaro the Cat w/Ball, Disney/Marx..........................**$30.00**

Fred & Wilma on Dino, Hanna-Barbera/Marx.............**$60.00**

Goat, plastic **$20.00**

Goofy Grape, Funny Face Drink Mix, w/plastic coin weight **$60.00**

Hap and Hop Soldiers, $25.00. (Photo courtesy Randy and Adriene Welch)

Horse w/English Rider, plastic, lg $50.00
Indian Chief, plastic.....................$70.00
Jiminy Cricket w/Cello, Disney/Marx...................$30.00
Kangaroo w/Baby Pouch, plastic $30.00
Lion w/Clown, Marx........................$40.00
Mad Hatter w/March Hare, Disney/Marx..................$50.00
Mammy, Wilson $40.00
Mickey Mouse & Pluto Hunting, Disney/Marx...........$40.00
Mickey Mouse Pushing Lawn Roller, Disney/Marx ..$35.00
Monkeys Carrying Bananas, plastic...............$60.00
Nursemaid Pushing Baby Stroller $20.00
Olive Oyl, Wilson.........................$175.00
Pig, plastic $20.00
Pinocchio, Wilson.........................$200.00
Policeman, Czechoslovakian.......................$60.00
Popeye Pushing Spinach Can Wheelbarrow, King Features/Marx.........................$30.00
Reindeer, plastic.........................$45.00
Sailors SS Shoreleave, plastic.....................$25.00
Santa w/Gold Sack, Marx.......................$45.00
Soldier, Wilson $30.00
Sydney Dinosaur, Long John Silver's, 1989, yellow & purple or lavender & pink, w/plastic coin weight, ea $15.00
Tin Man Robot Pushing Cart, plastic..................$150.00
Top Cat & Benny, Marx $65.00
Yogi Bear & Huckleberry Hound, Hanna-Barbera/Marx...$50.00
Zebra w/Native, Marx.......................$40.00

Rings

Toy rings are a fairly new interest in the collecting world. Earlier radio and TV mail-order premiums have been popular for some time but have increased in value considerably over the past few years. Now there is a growing interest in other types of rings as well — those from gumball machines, World's Fairs souvenirs, movie and TV show promotions, and any depicting celebrities. They may be metal or plastic; most

have adjustable shanks. New rings are already being sought out as future collectibles.

Note: All rings listed here are considered to be in fine to very fine condition. Wear, damage, and missing parts will devaluate them considerably.

Advisors: Bruce and Jan Thalberg (See Directory, Toys)

Billy West Club, cowboy on horse, silver- & gold-tone on brass versions, 1940s, from $65 to $125.00
Gene Autry Flag, gold-plated on plastic base, Dell Comics made gold & silver versions, 1950s, from $75 to ..$150.00
Howdy Doody, glow photo (under dome), gold-plated on brass base, 1950s, from $100 to $150.00
Lone Ranger, National Defenders, eagle on top, mirror inside, gold-plated on brass, adjustable, 1940s, from $100 to.........................$200.00
Lucky Skull, gold-plated on brass, high-relief Skull, ribs on sides, detailed, 1950s, from $65 to $85.00
Mickey Mouse Club, gold-plated on white cast metal, enameled Mickey in circle, red, white & black, 1980s, from $85 to.........................$100.00
Shmoo Lucky Ring, gold-plated on brass, high relief Shmoo on top & sides, 1950s, from $75 to.........$100.00
Sky King Teleblinker, sm telescope & built-in clicker for signaling, metal, lg, 1950s, from $100 to.........$200.00

Robots and Space Toys

Japanese toy manufacturers introduced their robots and space toys as early as 1948. Some of the best examples were made in the '50s, during the 'golden age' of battery-operated toys. They became more and more complex, and today some of these in excellent condition may bring well over $1,000.00. By the '60s, more and more plastic was used in their production, and the toys became inferior.

Answer Game Machine Robot, Japan, lithographed tin, battery-op, 15", EX (EX box), minimum value $550.00
Billy Blastoff Space Scout, Eldon, 1968, battery-op, 4½", EX.........................$200.00
Captain Lazer, litho tin, battery-op, M.........$150.00
Columbia Space Shuttle, litho tin, battery-op, MIB...$375.00
Cragstan Flying Saucer, litho tin, battery-op, MIB.....$475.00
Jupiter Rocket Launching Pad, TN, 1960s, several actions, litho tin, battery-op, 7", NM $375.00
Lunar Hovercraft, TPS, battery-op, MIB.........$325.00
Moon Crawler X-12, battery-op, M.........$100.00
Moon Explorer, Japan, advances w/engine sound & spinning antenna, tin, crank action, 7½", EX..........$300.00
Radicon Robot, MT, 1950s, several actions, litho tin, battery-op, extremely rare, 15", EX, minimum value ..$4,000.00
Rocket Racer #3, Japan, 1950s, advances w/sound, litho tin w/celluloid driver, friction, 6½", EX..........$100.00
Solar X Space Rocket, TN, 1960s, advances w/several actions, litho tin, battery-op, 15½", NM $300.00
Sonicon Racer, MT, 1960s, litho tin, battery-op, 13", EX ..$200.00

Space Jeep, Daiya, 1950s, litho tin, friction, 7", NM .**$485.00**

Space Pioneer Vehicle, MT, 1960s, 3 actions, litho tin, battery-op, 12", EX **$300.00**

Space Rocket Patrol Ship, Courtland, 1950s, litho tin w/red plastic dome, friction, 7", NM **$150.00**

Space Satellite, W Germany, 1950s, spaceship & Sputnik rotate around globe, litho tin, lever action, NMIB............**$225.00**

Sparky Robot, wind-up, litho tin, sparking action, KO/Japan, 1950, 8", NMIB, $585.00. (Photo courtesy Phil Helley)

Zoomer the Robot, TN, advances w/lighted eyes, battery-op, 8", NM............**$725.00**

Slot Car Racers

Slot cars first became popular in the early 1960s. Electric raceways set up in storefront windows were commonplace. Huge commercial tracks with eight and ten lanes were located in hobby stores and raceways throughout the United States. Large corporations such as Aurora, Revell, Monogram, and Cox, many of which were already manufacturing toys and hobby items, jumped on the bandwagon to produce slot cars and race sets. By the end of the early 1970s, people were losing interest in slot racing, and its popularity diminished. Today the same baby boomers that raced slot cars in earlier days are revitalizing the sport. Vintage slot cars have made a comeback as one of the hottest automobile collectibles of the 1990s. Want ads for slot cars frequently appear in newspapers and publications geared toward the collector. As you would expect, slot cars were generally well used, so finding vintage cars and race sets in like-new or mint condition is difficult. Slot cars replicating the 'muscle' cars from the '60s and '70s are extremely sought after, and clubs and organizations devoted to these collectibles are becoming more and more commonplace. Large toy companies such as Tomy and Tyco still produce some slots today, but not in the quality, quantity, or variety of years past.

Advisor: Gary Pollastro (See Directory, Toys)

Accessory, Aurora Model Motoring 4-Way Stop Track, 9", EX............**$15.00**

Accessory, Aurora Speedline Finish Set, 1968, MOC ..**$25.00**

Accessory, Eldon Power Track, MOC............**$10.00**

Accessory, Monogram Lane Change Track, MIB........**$20.00**

Accessory, Strombecker Grandstand, #9399, EX **$25.00**

Accessory, Tyco Stick Shift 4-Speed Controller, EX **$10.00**

Car, Aurora, Ford Baja Bronco, #1909, red, EX..........**$15.00**

Car, Aurora AFX, Blazer, #1917, black, blue & white, VG....**$12.00**

Car, Aurora AFX, Dodge Fever Dragster, white & yellow, EX............**$15.00**

Car, Aurora AFX, Ford Thunderbird Stock Car, NMIB ..**$25.00**

Car, Aurora AFX, Matador Taxi, white, EX **$20.00**

Car, Aurora AFX, Pontiac Firebird, black & gold, EX .**$25.00**

Car, Aurora AFX, Porsche 917, white & blue, MIB **$40.00**

Car, Aurora AFX, Volkswagen Bug, lime w/blue tanks, EX.**$30.00**

Car, Aurora G-Plus, Capri, white w/green & blue stripe, EX............**$15.00**

Car, Aurora G-Plus, Indy Valvoline, black, VG............**$12.00**

Car, Aurora G-Plus, Lotus F1, #1783, black & gold, EX..**$20.00**

Car, Aurora Thunderjet, Alfa Romeo Type 33, #1409, yellow, EX............**$25.00**

Car, Aurora Thunderjet, Cheetah, #1403, green, EX ...**$35.00**

Car, Aurora Thunderjet, Ferrari 250, red & white, EX...**$50.00**

Car, Aurora Thunderjet, Hot Rod Coupe, red, VG......**$25.00**

Car, Aurora Vibrator, Van Body Trailer, #1586, gray, G .**$20.00**

Car, TCR, Jam Car, yellow & black, EX........................**$15.00**

Car, TCR, Mack Truck, EX........................**$15.00**

Car, TCR, Mercury Stock Car, purple & chrome, VG..**$15.00**

Car, Tyco, '97 Corvette, yellow, EX........................**$15.00**

Car, Tyco, A-Team Van, black & red, EX....................**$20.00**

Car, Tyco, Caterpillar #96, black & yellow, EX **$20.00**

Car, Tyco, Firebird, #6914, cream & red, VG **$12.00**

Car, Tyco, Highway Patrol, #56, black & white, w/sound, EX........................**$16.00**

Car, Tyco, Mustang, #1, orange w/yellow flames, EX...**$20.00**

Car, Tyco, Porsche Carrera, #8527, yellow & black, EX..**$25.00**

Car, Tyco, Thunderbird, #15, red & yellow, VG **$10.00**

Set, AMT, Cobra Racing Set, NMIB............**$185.00**

Set, Atlas, Racing Set #1000, HO scale, G (G box)...**$100.00**

Set, Aurora, Jackie Stewart Oval 8, VG (VG box).......**$85.00**

Set, Aurora AFX, Revamatic Slot Car Set, EX (EX box)...**$75.00**

Set, Cox, Baja Bug Raceway, Super Scale, NMIB......**$150.00**

Set, Eldon, Raceway 24, 1/24 scale, VG (VG box)...**$195.00**

Set, Ideal, Alcan Highway Torture Track, 1968, complete, MIB **$50.00**

Set, Tyco, International Pro Racing Set, #930086, EX ...**$125.00**

Vehicles

These are the types of toys that are intensely dear to the heart of many a collector. Having a beautiful car is part of the American dream, and over the past eighty years, just about as many models, makes, and variations have been made as toys for children as the real vehicles for adults. Novices and advanced collectors alike are easily able to find something to suit their tastes as well as their budgets.

One area that is especially volatile includes those '50s and '60s tin scale-model autos by foreign manufacturers —

Japan, U.S. Zone Germany, and England. Since these are relatively modern, you'll still be able to find some at yard sales and flea markets at reasonable prices.

There are several good references for these toys: *Collecting Toy Cars and Trucks* by Richard O'Brien; *Hot Wheels, A Collector's Guide,* by Bob Parker; *Collector's Guide to Tootsietoys* by David Richter; *Collector's Guide to Tonka Trucks, 1947 – 1963,* by Don and Barb deSalle; and *Matchbox Toys, 1948 to 1993, Collector's Guide to Diecast Toys and Scale Models,* and *Toy Car Collector's Guide* by Dana Johnson.

Newsletter: *The Replica*
Bridget Shine, Editor
Highways 136 and 20, Dyersville, IA 52040; 319-875-2000

Newsletter: *Matchbox USA*
Charles Mack
62 Saw Mill Rd., Durham, CT 06422; 203-349-1655

Chein, Racer #52, tin w/wooden wheels, EX............**$200.00**
Corgi, #154, Ferrari Formula I....................................**$50.00**
Corgi, #163, Santa Pod Dragster................................**$50.00**
Corgi, #210 Citroen DS19...**$90.00**
Corgi, #217, Fiat 1800...**$80.00**
Corgi, #229, Chevrolet Corvair, MIB.........................**$70.00**
Corgi, #237, Oldsmobile Sheriff's Car, MIB..............**$100.00**
Corgi, #253, Mercedes Benz 220SE...........................**$90.00**
Corgi, #262, Lincoln Continental Limo, gold............**$100.00**
Corgi, #264, Oldsmobile Toronado............................**$85.00**
Corgi, #307, Renault..**$20.00**
Corgi, #329, Opel Senator, silver, MIB **$50.00**
Corgi, #353, Road Scanner.......................................**$60.00**
Corgi, #371, Porsche Carrera....................................**$40.00**
Corgi, #386, Bertone Runabout................................**$50.00**
Corgi, #401, VW 1200...**$60.00**
Corgi, #425, London Taxi...**$25.00**
Corgi, #437, Cadillac Ambulance.............................**$100.00**
Corgi, #445, Plymouth Sports Suburban.....................**$90.00**
Corgi, #464, Commer Pickup Truck **$65.00**
Corgi, #479, Mobile Camera Van..............................**$150.00**
Corgi, #506, Sunbeam Imp Police.............................**$125.00**
Corgi, #801, Ford Thunderbird **$25.00**
Cragstan, Beach Jeep, litho tin, friction, 7", NMIB **$95.00**
Cragstan, Ford Fairlane 500 Skyliner, red w/white top that slides into trunk, chrome detail, friction, 11", NMIB..........**$400.00**
Cragstan, Radar Jeep, battery-operated, w/searchlight & 2 figures, tin, 11", NMIB **$100.00**
Daiya, New Car w/Boat Trailer, painted tin, friction, NMIB **$300.00**
Dinky, #102, MG Midget, MIB..................................**$210.00**
Dinky, #130, Ford Consul Cortina **$95.00**
Dinky, #169, Fire Corsair **$100.00**
Dinky, #179, Studebaker President, MIB **$170.00**
Dinky, #204, Ferrari, MIB...**$65.00**
Dinky, #243, Volvo Police Racer, MIB.......................**$65.00**
Dinky, #282, Austin 1800 Taxi..................................**$80.00**

Dinky, #405, Universal Jeep, MIB.............................**$60.00**
Dinky, #440, Mobilgas Tanker, MIB..........................**$150.00**
Dinky, #505, Maserati 2000, MIB.............................**$135.00**
Dinky, #506, Aston Martin, MIB...............................**$140.00**
Dinky, #520, Chrysler New Yorker, MIB....................**$225.00**
Dinky, #532, Lincoln Premiere, MIB **$210.00**
Dinky, #555, Ford Thunderbird, MIB.........................**$200.00**
Dinky, #584, Covered Truck, MIB.............................**$155.00**
Dinky, #622, 10-Ton Army Truck..............................**$145.00**
Dinky, #667, Armored Patrol Car, MIB **$60.00**
Dinky, Corvette Stingray, MIB **$80.00**
Hot Wheels, AW Shoot, red line tires, olive, 1976, NM+...**$40.00**
Hot Wheels, Beatnik Bandit, red line tires, ice blue w/white interior, 1968, NM **$40.00**
Hot Wheels, Camaro Z-28, black walls, metal-flake red, 1984, MIP...**$12.50**
Hot Wheels, Classic Nomad, red line tires, blue, 1970, M ..**$85.00**
Hot Wheels, Custom, T-Bird, red line tires, purple w/white interior, 1968, NM+...**$200.00**
Hot Wheels, Demon, red line tires, blue, 1970, NM+.**$34.00**
Hot Wheels, Emergency Squad, red line tires, red, 1976, M...**$35.00**
Hot Wheels, Fire Eater, red line tires, red, 1977, M....**$25.00**
Hot Wheels, Gulch Stepper, black walls, red, 1987, MIP..**$7.00**
Hot Wheels, Hot Heap, red line tires, magenta w/white interior, 1968, M...**$150.00**
Hot Wheels, Ice T, red line tires, light yellow, 1971, M..**$75.00**
Hot Wheels, Jeep Scrambler, black walls, metal-flake red, 1988, MIP..**$16.00**
Hot Wheels, Light My Firebird, red line tires, red w/white interior, 1970, NM+ **$60.00**
Hot Wheels, Mirada Stocker, black walls, yellow, 1982, MIP...**$15.00**
Hot Wheels, Nitty Gritty Kitty, red line tires, metallic brown, 1970, NM **$100.00**
Hot Wheels, Open Fire, red line tires, magenta, 1972, NM+...**$175.00**
Hot Wheels, Paramedic, black wall tires, yellow, 1977, NM+ **$20.00**
Hot Wheels, Road Torch, black walls, red, 1987, MIP..**$20.00**
Hot Wheels, Sand Crab, red line tires, yellow, 1970, NM+ ..**$30.00**
Hot Wheels, Thunderbird Stocker, black walls, white, 1984, MIP...**$35.00**
Hot Wheels, Upfront 924, black walls, yellow w/red, orange & black tampo, 1979, NM+ **$5.00**
Hot Wheels, VW Bug, black walls, turquoise w/pink, light green & blue tampo, 1991, NM **$10.00**
Hot Wheels, Wind Splitter, black walls, metallic blue, 1984, MIP...**$9.00**
Huki, Volkswagen, yellow tin w/plastic seats, friction, 6", NMOC **$75.00**
Ichiko, Renault Floride, red w/black top, chrome detail, friction, 8", EXIB **$150.00**
Ichiko, Toyota 2000 GT, red w/chrome detail, friction, 1960s, 16", VG **$300.00**
Marusan, Greyhound Lines Red Ribbon Bus, litho tin, friction, 12½", M..**$750.00**

Marusan, Jet Racer, litho tin, friction, 8½", NM (EX box)...**$500.00**

Marx, Lumar Wrecker Service Truck, pressed steel, 16", EX...**$200.00**

Marx, Motor Market Grocery Truck, pressed steel, red w/blue stake bed, 14", NM (G box)..................................**$300.00**

Matchbox, K-06-D, Motorcycle Transporter, 1975, MIP..**$15.00**

Matchbox, Y-04-A, Sentinel Wagon, 1956, unpainted metal wheels, MIP..**$55.00**

Matchbox, 06 F, Ford Pickup, Super Fast, red w/white top, green base, silver grille, 1970, M...........................**$20.00**

Matchbox, 11-E, Scaffolding Truck, Super Fast, silver, 1970, complete, M..**$24.00**

Matchbox, 13-G, Snorkel Fire Engine, w/closed cab, regular wheels, 1977, MIP, from $5 to **$10.00**

Matchbox, 15-F, Fork Lift Truck, Super Fast, red w/black steering wheels, yellow hoist, gray fork, Lansing labels, NM+ **$10.00**

Matchbox, 17-C, Hoveringham Tipper, regular wheels, red cab w/orange tipper, 1963, MIP **$20.00**

Matchbox, 17-H, AMX Pro Stocker, maroon w/Dr Pepper tampo, MIP...**$6.00**

Matchbox, 19-F, Road Dragster, regular wheels, red, MIP, from $10 to...**$15.00**

Matchbox, 20-E, Range Rover Ambulance, regular wheels, olive cab, 1975, MIP **$50.00**

Matchbox, 23-F, Mustang GT350, regular wheels, 1979, MIP **$12.00**

Matchbox, 30-E, Beach Buggy, Super Fast, lavender, 1970, EX+ **$11.00**

Matchbox, 36-C, Opel Diplomat, Super Fast, 1970, MIP..**$20.00**

Matchbox, 36-E, Hot Rod Draguar, regular wheels, 1970, MIP **$20.00**

Matchbox, 43-E, Dragon Wheels, Super Fast, green base, dash-dot wheels, 1972, EX+ **$10.00**

Matchbox, 55-D, Mercury Parkline Police Car, regular wheels, blue dome light, 1968, M **$10.00**

Matchbox, 66-C, Greyhound Bus, regular wheels, clear windows, 1967, MIP **$70.00**

Matchbox, 66-C Greyhound Bus, regular wheels, amber windows, 1967, MIP **$10.00**

Matchbox, 74-C, Daimler Bus, Super Fast, Esso Extra Petrol, red w/red & pink base, thin wheels, 1970, M......**$20.00**

Matchbox, 75-D, Alfa Carabo, 1971, M **$10.00**

NGS, Chevrolet Corvair Sedan, red w/chrome detail, friction, 8", NMIB...**$200.00**

Smith-Miller, Chevrolet Materials Truck, pressed steel w/wooden flat bed, green, 14", VG **$350.00**

Smith-Miller, Ford Materials Truck, pressed steel, yellow, 14", VG..**$375.00**

Smith-Miller, PIE Tractor-Trailer, pressed steel cab w/aluminim trailer, rear doors open, red, 24", VG.................**$500.00**

Structo, Road Grader, pressed steel, red w/black tires, 1940s, 18", MIB..**$200.00**

Structo, US Mail Truck, #928, pressed steel, 17", NM .**$300.00**

Taiyo, Chevy Corvette, red w/chrome detail, battery-operated, 1968, 10", EX **$125.00**

TN, Cadillac, gray w/chrome detail, friction, 1950s, 8½", EX...**$150.00**

TN, Mercedes Benz Sports Car, red w/chrome detail, friction, EXIB...**$125.00**

TN, Searchlight Jeep, battery-operated, 1950s, 8", EX..**$140.00**

Tonka, Army Jeep, marked GR 2-2431, 11", EX........**$150.00**

Tonka, Cement Truck, #620, 1963, M **$200.00**

Tonka, Gambles Semi, 1956, EX................................**$325.00**

Tonka, Nationwide Moving Van, #39, 1958, EX........**$275.00**

Tonka, Standard Oil Tanker Semi, 1961, G **$350.00**

Tonka, Troop Carrier, #380, 1964, 14", NM **$200.00**

Tootsietoy, Auburn Roadster, #1016, light green, 6", EX..**$50.00**

Tootsietoy, Lincoln Capri, 2-door, red & white, 6", NM...**$40.00**

Tootsietoy, Mack US Mail Service Truck, #4645, red & tan, 3", EX..**$50.00**

Tootsietoy Truck, Ford Touring Car, #4570, green w/gold metal wheels, 3", EX...**$35.00**

Wyandotte, Ambulance, pressed steel, white w/red decal, wooden wheels, opening rear door, 1940s, 11", VG.........**$200.00**

Wyandotte, Cord Auto and House Trailer, blue, replaced wooden trailer wheels, 24", VG, $350.00.

Wyandotte, Woody Roadster Convertible, pressed steel, retractable top/opening trunk, red & yellow trim, 1940s, 13", VG **$250.00**

Y, North American Van Lines Truck, litho tin, friction, 13", NM (EX box) **$150.00**

Wind-Ups

Windup toys, especially comic character or personality related, are greatly in demand by collectors today. Though most were made through the years of the '30s through the '50s, they carry their own weight against much earlier toys and are considered very worthwhile investments. Mechanisms vary; some are key wound while others depended on lever action to tighten the mainspring and release the action of the toy. Tin and celluloid were used in their manufacture, and although it is sometimes possible to repair a tin windup, experts advise against putting your money into a celluloid toy whose mechanism is not working, since the material may be too fragile to tolerate the repair.

Alps, Bunny Cycle, tin & celluloid, 6", EXIB............**$275.00**

Alps, Happy Life, girl on bench w/umbrella, tin & celluloid, 9½", NMIB..**$475.00**

Alps, Mr Butts the Cigarette Boy, litho tin w/cloth clothes, 9", NMIB..**$300.00**

Alps, Peacock, litho tin, 6", EX................................**$150.00**

Alps, Roaring Lion, plush over tin, 7", MIB..............**$100.00**

Alps, Traveling Boy, litho tin & celluloid, 4½", NMIB .**$175.00**

ASC, Batmobile, litho tin, friction, rare, 11", NM (EX box) **$1,200.00**

Baldwin, Little red Hen, litho tin, 5", NM (EX box)..**$200.00**

Bandai, Monkey Cycle, litho tin, 5", NMIB..............**$350.00**

Borgfeldt, Mickey & Minnie Acrobats, tin w/celluloid figures, 13", VG **$400.00**

Chein, Barnacle Bill, litho tin, 6", EX **$300.00**

Chein, Fancy Groceries Truck, litho tin, 6", EX **$350.00**

Chein, Pelican, litho tin, 5", NM **$150.00**

CK, Deep Sea Diver, celluloid, prewar, 4½", MIB **$200.00**

CK, King Merry (2 parrots in cage), celluloid, 12", EXIB .**$200.00**

Irwin, Crawling Baby, composition w/cloth clothes, 6", EXIB...**$100.00**

K, Cycling Quacky, litho tin, 6", EXIB **$175.00**

K, Western Ranger, litho tin, 5", NM (EX box)..........**$170.00**

KO, Ali & His Flying Carpet, litho tin, 1950s, NM, from $165 to..**$190.00**

KO, Merry Ball Blower Circus Car, EX (EX box), $125.00.
(Photo courtesy June Moon)

Kohler, Duck, litho tin, 1950s, NM..............................**$75.00**

Lindstrom, Dancing Dutch Boy, litho tin, EXIB **$275.00**

Lindstrom, Johnny Clown, litho tin, 8", VG...............**$275.00**

Linemar, Banjo Player, litho tin, 5", NM....................**$200.00**

Linemar, Barney on Dino, litho tin & celluloid, 8½", NMIB **$675.00**

Linemar, Casper the Ghost, litho tin, 5", EX..............**$265.00**

Linemar, Disney Airplane, litho tin, friction, rare, 6" W, EX (VG box) **$950.00**

Linemar, Donald Duck Drummer, litho tin, VG **$400.00**

Linemar, Fishing Boy, litho tin, 6", NM (EX box) **$240.00**

Linemar, Flintstone Turnover Tank, litho tin, 1961, 4", MIB..**$925.00**

Linemar, Jiminy Cricket, litho tin, 1960s, EX **$400.00**

Linemar, Ludwig Von Drake (swinging arms), litho tin, NM...**$350.00**

Linemar, Ludwig Von Drake on Go Cart, litho tin, 1960s, NM **$450.00**

Linemar, Old Jalopy, litho tin, 5", VG **$100.00**

Linemar, Pluto on Motorcycle, litho tin, friction, 1960s, 3", NM **$350.00**

Linemar, Prehistoric Animal (Dinosaur), litho tin, 8", NM (EX box) **$275.00**

Marx, Auto Mac the Automatic Wonder Truck Driver, plastic, 11½", VG **$150.00**

Marx, Ballet Dancer, litho tin, 6", VG (VG box) **$225.00**

Marx, Dum Dum & Touche Turtle, plastic, friction, 1963, rare, 4", MIB **$200.00**

Marx, Funny Tiger, litho tin, 1960s, 6½", NMIB........**$200.00**

Marx, Goofy the Walking Gardener, litho tin, 9x8", EX ..**$350.00**

Marx, Hopping Billy the Bird, litho tin, 1960s, NMIB..**$100.00**

Marx, Mary Poppins, plastic, 1964, 8", NMIB **$175.00**

Marx, Milton Berle Car, litho tin, 5½", VG+ **$250.00**

Marx, Mystic Motorcycle, litho tin, 4½", VG.........**$175.00**

Marx, Pluto the Drum Major, litho tin w/rubber tail & ears, 1940s, NMIB..**$500.00**

Marx, Sparkling Hot Rod Racer, plastic, friction, 1950s, 8", EXIB...**$150.00**

Marx, Super Heroes Express Train, litho tin, 1967, 12", NMIB...**$650.00**

Marx, Walking Owl, plush over tin, 8", EX (VG box)..**$150.00**

MT, Monkey & Bee, celluloid, 4", NM (EX box).......**$250.00**

MT, Santa Claus, celluloid, 4", NM (EX box).............**$200.00**

Nylint, Howdy Doody Cart, litho tin, 9", NM............**$425.00**

Occupied Japan, Bellhop, celluloid, 4", VG **$125.00**

Occupied Japan, Easter on Parade, tin & celluloid, 8", NMIB...**$200.00**

Occupied Japan, Lion Teaser, celluloid, 6", NMIB **$350.00**

Ohio Art, Giant Ride Ferris Wheel, litho tin w/plastic seats, 17", NMIB **$400.00**

Schuco, Acrobat Bear, mohair w/glass eyes, 1950s, 5", EX (VG box) **$500.00**

Schuco, Donald Duck, litho tin w/felt jacket, 6", VG ..**$375.00**

TN, Blacksmith Teddy, plush & litho tin, 6", EXIB...**$200.00**

TN, Circus Clown, litho tin & celluloid, 5", NM (EX box)..**$200.00**

TN, Kennel Frolics (dog chases rabbit), litho tin w/celluloid figures, 3", NM (EX box) **$300.00**

TPS, Happy Hippo, litho tin, 6", NM (NM box)........**$500.00**

TPS, Pango-Pango African Dancer, litho tin, NM (NM box) **$300.00**

TPS, Waiter, litho tin w/rayon trousers & apron, 6½", EX **$235.00**

TT, Ski Boy, litho tin w/celluloid head, friction, 4", NM **$150.00**

Unique Art, Bombo the Monkey, litho tin, EX (VG box)...**$200.00**

Unique Art, Finnegan Porter, litho tin, 14", NMIB **$350.00**

Unique Art, Gurdy the Goose, litho tin, 9", G **$75.00**

Unique Art, Hee-Haw (donkey cart), litho tin, 10½", G..**$200.00**

Unique Art, Kiddy Cyclist, litho tin, 9", EX...............**$375.00**

Unique Art, Lincoln Tunnel, litho tin, 24", G **$250.00**

Unique Art, Police Motorcycle, litho tin, 8½", G **$325.00**

Wolverine, Drum Major, litho tin, 13½", EX **$275.00**

Wolverine, Jet Roller Coaster, litho tin, 21", G **$225.00**

Wolverine, Mystery Car, silver-painted tin, 13", EXIB...**$375.00**

Wolverine, Over & Under (race car on track), litho tin, 2½" car, EXIB...**$300.00**

Wolverine, Sulky Racer, plastic, 9", EXIB..................**$150.00**

Wyandotte, Carousel w/Swans & Airplanes, litho tin, musical, 4½" dia, VG...$275.00

Wyandotte, Easter Bunny Motorcycle (w/sidecar), litho tin, 9½", G $200.00

Wyandotte, Man on the Flying Trapeze, litho tin, 9", NM (EX box) $250.00

Transistor Radios

Introduced during the Christmas shopping season of 1954, transistor radios were at the cutting edge of futuristic design and miniaturization. Among the most desirable is the 1954 four-transistor Regency TR-1 which is valued at a minimum of $750.00 in jade green. Black may go for as much as $300.00, other colors from $350.00 to $400.00. The TR-1 'Mike Todd' version in the 'Around the World in Eighty Days' leather book-look presentation case goes for $4,000.00 and up! Some of the early Toshiba models sell for $250.00 to $350.00, some of the Sonys even higher — their TR-33 books at a minimum of $1,000.00, their TR-55 at $1,500.00 and up! Certain pre-1960 models by Hoffman and Admiral represented the earliest practical use of solar technology and are also highly valued. Early collectible transistor radios all have civil defense triangle markings at 640 and 1240 on the frequency dial and nine or fewer transistors. Very few desirable sets were made after 1963.

Values in our listings are for radios in at least very good condition — not necessarily working, but complete and requiring very little effort to restore them to working order. Cases may show minor wear. All radios are battery-operated unless noted otherwise. For more information we recommend *Collector's Guide to Transistor Radios* (there are two editions), by Marty and Sue Bunis (Collector Books).

Advisors: Marty and Sue Bunis (See Directory, Radios)

Admiral, #Y2091, Imperial 8, horizontal, AM, battery, 1961...$25.00

Admiral, #Y2603, Super 7, vertical, 7 transistors, AM, battery, 1960 ....$20.00

Admiral, #4P22, horizontal, 4 transistors, AM, battery, 1957 ....$40.00

Airline, #GEN-1259A, vertical, 10 transistors, AM/FM, battery, 1964 ....$15.00

Airline, #GTM-1233A, horizontal, 9 transistors, AM, 2 shortwaves, battery, 1963 ....$20.00

Aiwa, #AR-670, vertical, 6 transistors, AM, battery, 1964..$15.00

Alaron, #DC3280, Deluxe Eight, horizontal, 9 transistors, AM, shortwave, battery, 1964..$25.00

Alpha, #Q62, vertical, 6 transistors, AM, battery, 1962...$40.00

Ambassador, #A-884, horizontal, 8 transistors, AM, battery, 1965 ....$25.00

Aristo Tone, #MT-601, 6 transistors, AM, battery.........$15.00

Arvin, #60R19, horizontal, 4 transistors, AM, battery, 1959 ....$25.00

Arvin, #61R16, vertical, 6 transistors, AM, battery, 1961..$35.00

Arvin, #65R79, horizontal, 9 transistors, AM/FM, battery, 1965...$10.00

Automatic, #PTR-15B, horizontal, AM, battery, 1958 ..$30.00

Blaupunkt, #22503, Lido, horizontal, 9 transistors, AM/FM, shortwave, battery, 1963.......................................$25.00

Bulova, #278, horizontal, 4 transistors, AM, battery, 1958..$60.00

Bulova, #870, vertical, 6 transistors, AM, battery, 1963..$30.00

Channel Master, #6550, Swing-Along, portable radio/phonograph, AM, battery, 1962......................................$50.00

Channel Master, VHF Monitor, horizontal, 9 transistors, AM, battery, 1965...$20.00

Columbia, #600BX, vertical, 6 transistors, AM, battery, 1960 ....$30.00

Commodore, #610A, HiFi, vertical, 6 transistors, AM, battery...$25.00

Coronado, #43-9900, vertical, 6 transistors, AM, battery, 1960 ....$30.00

Crosley, #JM-8BK, Enchantment, book shape, 3 subminiature tubes & 2 transistors, AM, battery, 1956 ....$150.00

Crown, #TR-555, vertical, 5 transistors, AM, battery, 1960 ....$40.00

Delmonico, #7YR707, sq, 7 tranistors, AM, battery, 1965 .$55.00

Dewald, #K-701A, horizontal, 6 tranistors, AM, battery, 1956 ....$150.00

Emmerson, #855, horizontal, 6 transistors, AM, battery, 1957...$40.00

Emmerson, #888, Transmitter, horizontal/clock, 8 transisters, AM, battery, 1958.......................................$125.00

Essex, #TR-6K, vertical, 6 transistors, AM, battery.......$15.00

Excel, #6T-2, Aristocrat, horizontal, AM, battery, 1959...$35.00

Falcon, #6THK, vertical, 6 transistors, AM, battery, 1964 ..$20.00

Futura, #250, radio/phonograph, 6 transistors, AM, battery, 1962 ....$35.00

General Electric, #P-850D, vertical, AM, battery, 1964..$30.00

General Electric, #P711A, horizontal, 4 transistors, AM, battery, 1957...$40.00

General Electric, #P750A, horizontal, 6 transistors, AM, battery, 1958...$25.00

Global, #GFM-931, horizontal, 10 transistors, AM/FM, battery...$40.00

Global Imperial, #HT-8054, vertical, 8 transistors, AM, battery...$25.00

Hi-Delity, horizontal, 8 transistors, AM, shortwave, battery, 1964 ....$45.00

Hilton, #TR108, vertical, 10 transistors, AM, battery ...$25.00

Hitachi, #TH-759, horizontal, 7 transistors, AM, battery, 1962...$40.00

Hoffman, #OP708, horizontal, 8 transistors, AM, battery, 1962 ....$30.00

Holiday, #HS921, Super DX, vertical, 9 transistors, AM, battery...$20.00

ITT, #615, vertical, 6 transistors, AM, battery, 1963.....$20.00

Jaguar, #6T-250, vertical, 6 transistors, AM, battery, 1960..$40.00

Jefferson-Travis, #JT-D210, vertical, 4 transistors, AM, battery, 1961 ....$30.00

Jefferson-Travis, #JT-H204, Deluxe 8, vertical, 8 transistors, AM, battery, 1961 ....$40.00

Juliette, #AT-65, vertical, 6 transistors, AM, battery, 1965 ....**$15.00**

Kensington, #HT-1268, vertical, 10 transistors, AM, battery **$20.00**

Kowa, #KT-62A, horizontal, 6 transistors, AM, battery, 1961 ....**$30.00**

Lafayette, #FS-93, horizontal, 9 transistors, AM, weather/marine, battery, 1962 ....**$35.00**

Lefco, #6YR-15A, vertical, 6 transistors, AM, battery...**$30.00**

Lloyd's, #TF-912, horizontal, 9 transistors, AM/FM, battery, 1965 ....**$15.00**

Lloyd's, #6K87B, sq, 6 transistors, AM, battery............**$40.00**

Magnavox, #AM-23, vertical, 6 transistors, AM, battery, 1960..**$35.00**

Majestic, #6G780, vertical, 6 transistors, AM, battery ..**$40.00**

Matsushia, #T-50, horizontal, 6 transistors, AM, battery, 1962 ....**$30.00**

Motorola, #X14E, vertical, 6 transistors, AM, battery, 1960 ....**$50.00**

Motorola, 7X23E Power 10, 1959, horizontal, navy blue, seven-transistor, 'jet plane' design, AM, battery, 4" x 6½" x 2", $110.00. (Photo courtesy Marty and Sue Bunis)

Motorola, #7X24S, horizontal, 7 transistors, AM, battery, 1959 ....**$110.00**

Nobility, #832N, vertical, 8 transistors, AM, battery **$10.00**

Norelco, #L3X09T/54, horizontal, 7 transistors, AM, 2 shortwaves, battery, 1962 ....**$25.00**

North American, #NT-602, horizontal, 6 transistors, AM, battery, 1964 ....**$20.00**

Olson, #RA-315, vertical, 4 transistors, AM, battery, 1960 ....**$40.00**

Olympic, #447, horizontal, 4 transistors, AM, battery, 1957 ....**$135.00**

OMGS, #TRN-8023, Suburbia, horizontal, 12 transistors, AM, battery **$35.00**

Panasonic, #RF-820, horizontal, 9 transistors, AM/FM, battery, 1964 ....**$20.00**

Penncrest, #1130, horizontal, 6 transistors, AM, battery..**$25.00**

Philco, #NT-815BK, horizontal, AM, 2 shortwaves, battery, 1965 ....**$20.00**

Raytheon, #T-100-3, horizontal, AM, battery, 1956 ...**$200.00**

RCA, #1-BT-58, Globe Trotter, horizontal, 7 transistors, AM, battery, 1959......................................**$25.00**

RCA, #1-T-4H, vertical, 8 transistors, AM, battery, 1960 .**$35.00**

Realtone, #TR-1820, vertical, 8 transistors, AM, battery, 1962..**$25.00**

Ross, #RE777, Jubilee, vertical, 7 transistors, AM, battery, 1964 ....**$15.00**

Sanyo, #AFT-9S, Transworld, horizontal, 9 transistors, AM/FM, shortwave, battery **$25.00**

Seminole, #801, horizontal, 8 transistors, AM, battery, 1963 ....**$40.00**

Sentinel, #1E500, horizontal, AM, battery **$150.00**

Sharp, #FW-503, horizontal, 12 transistors, AM/FM, marine, battery, 1964 ....**$25.00**

Silvertone, #1203, vertical, 6 transistors, AM, battery, 1961 ..**$25.00**

Sony, #TR-620, vertical, 6 transistors, AM, battery, 1961 ..**$70.00**

Sony, #TR-84, Super Sensitivity, horizontal, 8 transistors, AM, battery, 1961 ....**$35.00**

Summit, #S109, vertical, 10 transistors, AM, battery **$30.00**

Supreme, #TR0861, vertical, 6 transistors, AM, battery, 1962..**$45.00**

Sylvania, #3305TA, horizontal, 6 transistors, 'T6' logo, AM, battery, 1958..**$35.00**

Symphonic, #SF-400, horizontal, 9 transistors, AM/FM, shortwave, battery, 1963......................................**$20.00**

Toshiba, #3TP-315Y, vertical, 3 transistors, AM, battery, 1959..**$75.00**

Toshiba, #8TM-294B, horizontal, 8 transistors, AM, battery **$50.00**

Trutone, #DC3704, Jr, vertical, 6 transistors, AM, battery **$15.00**

United Royal, #802, horizontal, 8 transistors, AM, shortwave, battery **$20.00**

Universal, #RE-64, Deluxe, vertical, 6 transistors, AM, battery **$10.00**

Viscount, #602, VIP, vertical, 6 transistors, AM, battery, 1962..**$40.00**

Vorando, #V-700, vertical, 8 transistors, AM, battery, 1965 ....**$40.00**

Watterson, #601, horizontal/table, 6 transistors, AM, battery, 1958 ....**$20.00**

Westinghouse, #H611P5, horizontal, 5 transistors, AM, battery, 1957 ....**$75.00**

Yashica, #YT-300, horizontal, 9 transistors, AM, shortwave, battery, 1961 ....**$25.00**

York, #TR-121, horizontal, 12 transistors, AM/FM, battery, 1965 ....**$20.00**

Zennith, Royal 200, vertical, 7 transistors, AM, battery, 1959 ....**$45.00**

Zephyr, #ZR-620, vertical, 6 transistors, AM, battery, 1962 ....**$40.00**

Trolls

The legend of the troll originated in Scandinavia. Nordic mythology described them as short, intelligent, essentially unpleasant, supernatural creatures who were doomed to forever live underground. During the '70s, a TV cartoon special and movie based on J.R.R. Tolkien's books, *The Hobbit* and *The Lord of the Rings*, caused an increase in trolls' popularity. As a result, books, puzzles, posters, and dolls of all types were available on the retail market. In the early '80s, Broom Hilda and Irwin Troll were featured in a series of books as well as Saturday morning cartoons. Today trolls are enjoying a strong comeback.

Troll dolls of the '60s are primarily credited to Thomas Dam of Denmark. Many, using Dam molds, were produced in America by Royalty Des. of Florida and Wishnik. In Norway A/S Nyform created a different version. Some were also made in Hong Kong, Japan, and Korea, but those were of inferior plastic and design.

The larger trolls (approximately 12") are rare and very desirable to collectors. Troll animals by Dam, such as the giraffe, horse, cow, donkey, and lion, are bringing premium prices.

For more information, refer to *Collector's Guide to Trolls* by Pat Peterson.

Advisor: Pat Peterson (See Directory, Trolls)

Astronaut, Dam, 1964, 11", EX $125.00
Ballerina, bright red hair, green eyes, Dam, MIP $55.00
Bride-Nik, Uneeda Wishnik, 1980s, reissue, original gown & veil, red hair, amber eyes, 6", NM $20.00
Cook-Nik, Uneeda Wishnik, bendable, original outfit, blue hair, brown eyes, 5", EX.................................$20.00
Eskimo, red & white painted-on clothes, brown hair & eyes, Dam, 1965, 5½", EX...................................$75.00
Fire Chief, Treasure Trolls, blue hair & eyes, 4", M....$12.00
Girl w/accordion, Norwegian, Nyform, printed-on clothes, brown hair, amber eyes, 6", NM $50.00
Hula-Nik, Uneeda Wishnik, purple rooted skirt, orange hair (faded), yellow eyes, 5", EX................................$30.00
Indian, felt outfit w/yellow feather in black hair, green eyes, Dam, 7", NM...$50.00
Koko Monkey, Norfin's Ark/Dam, 2½" $4.00
Nursnik, Uneeda Wishnik, 1970s, 6", MOC $50.00
Robin Hood, red hair, brown eyes, complete w/bow & arrow, Russ Storybook series, 4½", NM................$15.00
Sock-It-To-Me, Uneeda Wishnik, original outfit, white hair, amber eyes, 6", NM $50.00
Tartan Girl, original outfit w/matching ribbons in black hair, amber eyes, Dam, 1964, 12", M, from $145 to...$165.00
Uglie Elephant, Made in Japan, blue painted body, black rabbit-fur hair, amber eyes, 3½", NM $25.00
Wizard, Treasure Trolls, lt purple hair, blue eyes, 4", M ...$15.00

TV Guides

This publication goes back to the early 1950s, and granted, those early issues are very rare. But what an interesting, very visual way to chronicle the history of TV programming!

Values in our listings are for examples in fine to mint condition; be sure to reduce them significantly when damage of any type is present. For insight into *TV Guide* collecting, we recommend *The TV Guide Catalog* by Jeff Kadet, the *TV Guide* Specialist.

Advisor: Jeff Kadet (See Directory, *TV Guides*)

1953, April 24, Ralph Edwards.....................................$51.00
1953, May 15, David & Ricky Nelson $117.00
1953, October 2, Red Skelton.....................................$88.00
1954, January 1, Bing Crosby.......................................$64.00
1954, June 25, Howdy Doody & Buffalo Bob..........$450.00
1954, March 26, Jackie Gleason...................................$89.00
1954, Oct 23, Walt Disney & Friends $150.00
1955, April 16, Garry Moore $35.00
1955, February 5, Edward R Murrow.........................$31.00
1955, March 19, Art Carney as Ed Norton $90.00
1956, February 18, Jimmy Durante............................$34.00
1956, June 9, Patti Page...$14.00
1956, September 8, Elvis Presley...............................$375.00
1957, April 27, Groucho Marx $32.00
1957, February 2, Jane Wyman...................................$23.00
1957, September 28, Burns & Allen $68.00
1958, April 26, Guy Williams as Zorro....................$205.00
1958, August 16, cast of Wagon Train........................$68.00
1958, November 1, Jack Paar......................................$25.00
1959, May 9, Edd Byrnes of 77 Sunset Strip...............$45.00
1959, November 7, Jack Benny...................................$71.00
1960, April 30, June Lockart & Lassie $66.00
1960, July 16, Lucille Ball...$87.00
1961, January 28, Ronnie Howard & Andy Griffith ..$175.00
1961, March 25, Alfred Hitchcock $45.00
1961, March 25, Donna Reed......................................$31.00
1962, August 25, Lawrence Welk................................$15.00
1962, January 13, cast of Hazel $34.00
1962, May 12, Don Knotts...$66.00
1963, January 26, Martin Milner & George Maharis of Route 66 ....$150.00
1963, July 6, Martin Milner & Glenn Corbett of Route 66 ..$115.00
1963, November 16, cast of Mr Novak.......................$33.00
1964, June 13, Fred Flintstone $150.00
1964, March 7, Richard Chamberlain..........................$17.00
1964, September 26, Dan Blocker of Bonanza............$82.00
1965, April 24, Andy Griffith.....................................$82.00
1965, August 21, Fess Parker as Daniel Boone $36.00
1965, January 2, cast of The Munsters $234.00
1966, June 18, cast of Bewitched $48.00
1966, March 26, Adam West as Batman....................$150.00
1966, March 5, Barbara Feldon by Andy Warhol $36.00
1967, February 11, cast of Mission Impossible............$48.00
1967, July 29, The Rat Patrol $45.00
1967, November 18, William Shatner & Leonard Nimoy of Star Trek $95.00
1968, July 20, cast of The Big Valley..........................$66.00
1968, March 16, Sally Fields as The Flying Nun..........$26.00
1968, November 9, Get Smart Wedding......................$26.00
1969, December 6, Doris Day......................................$48.00
1969, February 22, cast of Lancer...............................$40.00

1969, October 4, Bill Cosby $20.00
1970, December 12, Ed Sullivan & the Muppets $22.00
1970, February 28, cast of Mod Squad $22.00
1970, June 27, Liza Minelli $16.00
1971, December 11, James Garner $13.00
1971, May 29, cast of All in the Family $37.00
1971, October 2, Jimmy Stewart $9.00
1972, January 29, David Janssen $40.00
1972, March 4, Johnny Carson $18.00
1972, October 28, Charlie Brown Special $24.00
1973, December 15, Katharine Hepburn $10.00
1973, June 23, David Carradine of Kung Fu $16.00
1973, March 31, Lucille Ball & Desi Arnaz $42.00
1974, August 3, cast of Emergency $95.00
1974, January 19, Bob Hope $10.00
1974, March 2, Jimmy Stewart of Hawkins $14.00
1975, April 12, Cher $24.00
1975, July 5, Tony Orlando & Dawn $17.00
1975, May 10, Muhammad Ali $10.00
1976, August 12, cast of The Waltons $17.00
1976, December 11, Valerie Harper of Rhoda $19.00
1976, May 22, cast of Laverne & Shirley $19.00
1977, December 31, cast of Kojak $24.00
1977, January 29, Wonder Woman $55.00
1977, June 4, Alan Alda of M.A.S.H. $14.00
1978, February, Charlie's Angels $27.00
1978, November 25, Suzanne Summers $19.00
1978, September 16, cast of Battlestar Galactica $20.00
1979, February 3, cast of CHiPs $20.00
1979, June 30, cast of Dukes of Hazzard $28.00
1979, November 10, The Bee Gees $19.00
1980, May 31, cast of Vegas $17.00
1980, November 22, Pam Dawber of Mork & Mindy .$13.00
1980, September 20, Priscilla Presley $17.00
1981, January 17, Ronald Reagan $19.00
1981, May 9, Larry Hagman & Patrick Duffy of Dallas ..$20.00
1981, November 21, John Lennon $13.00
1982, February 27, cast of Dynasty $13.00
1982, July 10, cast of Facts of Life $21.00
1982, September 18, Victoria Principal....................$22.00
1983, December 10, Tom Selleck $15.00
1983, January 8, John Madden $10.00
1983, June 25, David Hasselhoff & KITT of Knight Rider ..$24.00
1984, December 22, cast of Webster $10.00
1984, January 21, TV Game Show Hosts $17.00
1984, June 23, Connie Sellecca $13.00
1985, March 2, Michael Landon $22.00
1985, May 18, Christopher Columbus $7.00
1985, November 9, Charles & Diana $19.00
1986, April 5, cast of Family Ties $13.00
1986, December 20, cast of Our House $11.00
1986, January 18, cast of Night Court $13.00
1987, December 26, cast of A Year in the Life $22.00
1987, February 28, Valerie Bertinelli.....................$15.00
1987, July 4, Barbara Walters $8.00
1988, July 16, 6 Most Beautiful Women $15.00
1988, March 5, Oprah Winfrey $6.00

1988, September 24, cast of The Cosby Show............$9.00
1989, January 14, cast of Moonlighting $22.00
1989, October 7, Delta Burke & Gerald McRaney $15.00
1989, September 22, Rosanne Barr & Bill Cosby $15.00
1990, June 9, Bart Simpson & The Ninja Turtles........$16.00
1990, March 17, The Simpsons $20.00
1991, April 13, Burt Reynolds & Marilu Henner...........$8.00
1991, April 6, Baseball TV Preview $11.00
1991, May 11, cast of LA Law $11.00
1994, December 17, Kathie Lee Gifford....................$9.00
1994, February 26, Whitney Houston......................$13.00
1994, Juy 2, Reba McIntire $28.00
1995, April 8, Jennie Garth $10.00
1995, August 5, Tom Selleck $7.00
1995, January 28, Super Bowl.............................$9.00
1996, April 6, Gillian Anderson & David Duchovny of X-Files $15.00
1996, February 24, Tori Spelling.........................$5.00
1996, June 22, NASCAR'S Jeff Gordon $24.00
1997, April 26, Tom Hanks $8.00
1997, April 5, Rosie O'Donnell $15.00
1997, June 7, LeAnn Rimes $15.00
1998, February 28, cast of Ally McBeal $8.00
1998, January 24, Sonny Bono............................$22.00
1998, March 28, cast of Law & Order $7.00
1999, July 17, Dennis Frans of NYPD Blue $10.00
1999, May 1, Kentucky Derby Special $25.00
1999, November 20, Tribute to Walter Payton............$23.00

Twin Winton

The genius behind the designs at Twin Winton was sculptor Don Winton. He and his twin, Ross, started the company while still in high school in the mid-1930s. In 1952 older brother Bruce Winton bought the company from his two younger brothers and directed its development nationwide. They produced animal figures, cookie jars, and matching kitchenware and household items during this time. It is important to note that Bruce was an extremely shrewd business man, and if an order came in for a nonstandard color, he would generally accommodate the buyer — for an additional charge, of course. As a result, you may find a Mopsy (Raggedy Ann) cookie jar, for instance, in a wood stain finish or some other unusual color, even though Mopsy was only offered in the Collector Series in the catalogs. This California company was active until it sold in 1976 to Roger Bowermeister, who continued to use the Twin Winton name. He experimented with different finishes. One of the most common is a light tan with a high gloss glaze. He owned the company only one year until it went bankrupt and was sold at auction. Al Levin of Treasure Craft bought the molds and used some of them in his line. Eventually, the molds were destroyed.

One of Twin Winton's most successful concepts was their Hillbilly line — mugs, pitchers, bowls, lamps, ashtrays, decanters, and novelty items molded after the mountain boys in Paul Webb's cartoon series. Don Winton was the company's only designer, though he free-lanced as well. He designed for Disney, Brush-McCoy, Revell Toys, The Grammy Awards, American Country Music Awards, Ronald Reagan Foundation, and numerous other companies and foundations.

Twin Winton has been revived by Don and Norma Winton (the original Don Winton and his wife). They are currently selling new designs as well as some of his original artwork through the Twin Winton Collector Club on the Internet at twinwinton.com. Some of Don's more prominent pieces of art are currently registered with the Smithsonian in Washington, D.C.

If you would like more information, read *A Collector's Guide to Don Winton Designs* by Michael L. Ellis and *The Collector's Encyclopedia of Cookie Jars* (three in the series) by Joyce and Fred Roerig. All are published by Collector Books.

Note: Color codes in the listings below are as follows: A — avocado green; CS — Collectors Series, fully painted; G — gray; I — ivory; O — orange; P — pineapple yellow; R — red; and W — wood stain with hand-painted detail. Values are based on actual sales as well as dealers' asking prices.

See also Cookie Jars.

Advisor: Mike Ellis (See Directory, Twin Winton)

Club: Twin Winton Collector Club
Also Don Winton Designs (other than Twin Winton)
266 Rose Lane
Costa Mesa, CA 92627; 714-646-7112 or fax: 7414-645-4919; website: twinwinton.com; e-mail: ellis5@pacbell.net

Ashtray, Bambi, W, 6x8" **$100.00**
Ashtray, kitten, W, 6x8" **$100.00**
Bank, bull, W, I, G, A, P, O, R, 8" **$65.00**
Bank, cop, W, I, G, A, P, O, R, 8" **$65.00**
Bank, Dobbin, W, I, G, A, P, O, R, 8" **$40.00**
Bank, Dutch girl, W, I, G, A, P, O, R, 8" **$50.00**
Bank, elf, W, I, G, A, P, O, R, 8" **$50.00**
Bank, friar (aka monk, Friar Tuck), W, I, G, A, P, O, R, 8"..**$40.00**
Bank, poodle, W, I, G, A, P, O, R, 8" **$65.00**
Bank, squirrel on nut, W, I, G, A, P, O, R, 8"............**$50.00**
Bank, wooly mammoth, made for Ford dealership, 5"..**$75.00**
Candle holder, Aladdin lamp form, W, I, G, A, P, O, R, 6½x9½" **$45.00**
Candle holder, Strauss, W, I, G, A, P, O, R, 10x5" **$15.00**
Candle holder, Strauss, W, I, G, A, P, O, R, 6x4½" **$12.00**
Candle holder, Verdi, W, I, G, A, P, O, R, 9½x4" **$15.00**
Candy jar, elephant, W, I, G, A, P, O, R, 9x6" **$45.00**
Candy jar, nut w/squirrel finial, W, I, G, A, P, O, R, 9x8"...**$75.00**
Candy jar, Old Woman in Shoe, child on roof, W, I, G, A, P, O, R, 10x10" **$75.00**
Canister, Bucket, Coffee, W, I, G, A, P, O, R, 5x6" **$30.00**
Canister, Farm, Flour, W, I, G, A, P, O, R, 10x6"..........**$65.00**
Canister, Farm, Tea, W, I, G, A, P, O, R, 5x3" **$30.00**
Canister, Pot O' Sugar, W, I, G, A, P, O, R, 7x6" **$30.00**
Canister, Pot O' Tea, W, I, G, A, P, O, R, 5x4" **$20.00**

Creamer, Artist Palette Line, 4" dia **$40.00**
Creamer & sugar bowl, hen & rooster, W, G, I, TW-221, 5x6", pr..**$20.00**
Expanimal, chipmunk, 4 pcs that can be used as bookends, servers or planters, W, 7½" H.............**$125.00**
Expanimal, poodle, 4 pcs that can be used as bookends, servers or planters, W, 7½" H.............**$125.00**
Figurine, Boo Boo bear, made for Idea Inc, 4"..........**$75.00**
Figurine, boy shot putting w/Stanford logo on chest, on base, 3"..**$150.00**
Figurine, boy skier, 7" **$225.00**
Figurine, Collie dog, W, G, I, hand painted, TW-602, 7½" **$65.00**
Figurine, deer, recumbent, dated 1940-1943, 3x5" **$75.00**
Figurine, deer, standing, #208, dated 1940-1943, 6"....**$75.00**
Figurine, elf in stump, 3"..**$60.00**
Figurine, elf on turtle, 5" **$75.00**
Figurine, football player & girl, no base, 5x6" **$275.00**
Figurine, Mickey the Sorcerer, 8" **$150.00**
Figurine, Quick Draw McGraw, made for Idea Inc, 7"..**$75.00**
Figurine, rabbit, lg smile, dated 1940-1943, 6" **$45.00**
Figurine, shaggy dog, W, G, I, hand painted, TW-604, 8"..**$65.00**
Figurine, squirrel holding stomach, 2¼x4" **$30.00**
Figurine, squirrel w/arms extended, 2½"...................**$25.00**
Lamp, monkey, W, TW-259, 13"...........................**$175.00**
Lamp, raccoon, W, TW-253, 12"...........................**$175.00**
Lamp, squirrel, TW-255, W, 12"...........................**$175.00**
Mug, Bamboo Line, 6"..**$20.00**
Mug, coffee; Burgie, cartoon-like face, 5½" **$40.00**
Mug, elephant, W, I, G, A, P, O, R, 3¼" **$85.00**
Mug, lamb, W, I, G, A, P, O, R, TW-502, 3¼" **$85.00**
Napkin holder, bear, W, I, G, A, P, O, R, 9x4" **$75.00**
Napkin holder, cow, W, I, G, A, P, O, R, TW-479, 6x7"..**$85.00**
Napkin holder, elephant, W, I, G, A, P, O, R, TW-486, 7x5" **$75.00**
Planter, Bambi, W, TW-325, 8"...........................**$50.00**
Planter, bear beside stump, W, TW-324, 8" **$50.00**
Planter, fisherman's creel, 6" **$60.00**
Planter, rabbit crouching beside basket eating carrot, 5x8" **$85.00**
Planter, rabbit w/cart, 7x10"...........................**$85.00**
Plate, dinner; Wood Grain Line, 10"...........................**$40.00**
Salt & pepper shakers, apple, W, I, G, A, P, O, R, pr.**$75.00**
Salt & pepper shakers, barn, W, I, G, A, P, O, R, pr ..**$40.00**
Salt & pepper shakers, bear, W, I, G, A, P, O, R, pr...**$40.00**
Salt & pepper shakers, Bronco Group, saddles, B207, 3", pr..**$50.00**
Salt & pepper shakers, cable car, W, I, G, A, P, O, R, pr..**$50.00**
Salt & pepper shakers, cart, W, I, G, A, P, O, R, pr....**$50.00**
Salt & pepper shakers, cookie pot, W, I, G, A, P, O, R, pr...**$30.00**
Salt & pepper shakers, cop, W, I, G, A, P, O, R, pr....**$40.00**
Salt & pepper shakers, Dutch girl, W, I, G, A, P, O, R, pr **$35.00**
Salt & pepper shakers, elf, W, I, G, A, P, O, R, pr......**$40.00**
Salt & pepper shakers, goose, W, I, G, A, P, O, R, pr ..**$45.00**
Salt & pepper shakers, Hotei, W, I, G, A, P, O, R, pr.**$30.00**

Salt & pepper shakers, kitten, W, I, G, A, P, O, R, pr $40.00

Salt & pepper shakers, lion, W, I, G, A, P, O, R, pr..$45.00

Salt & pepper shakers, nut, W, I, G, A, P, O, R, pr $75.00

Salt & pepper shakers, owl, W, I, G, A, P, O, R, pr....$30.00

Salt & pepper shakers, poodle, W, I, G, A, P, O, R, pr....$50.00

Salt & pepper shakers, raccoon, W, I, G, A, P, O, R, pr ..$45.00

Salt & pepper shakers, snail, W, I, G, A, P, O, R, pr...$125.00

Salt & pepper shakers, squirrels, 2½", pr $50.00

Salt & pepper shakers, teddy bear, W, I, G, A, P, O, R, pr..$50.00

Spoon rest, bear, W, I, G, A, P, O, R, WT-12, 5x10" ...$40.00

Spoon rest, cow, W, I, G, A, P, O, R, TW-23, 5x10" ...$40.00

Spoon rest, elf, W, I, G, A, P, O, R, TW-17, 5x10" $40.00

Talking picture, bear, Keep the Home Fires Burning, W, I, G, A, P, O, R, 11x7" $110.00

Talking picture, elephant, W, I, G, A, P, O, R, TW-436, 11x7" $110.00

Tumbler, Wood Grain Line, 4" $20.00

Wall planter, bear's head, W, TW-304, 5½" $100.00

Wall planter, lamb's head, W, TW-301, 5½" $100.00

Hillbilly Line

Ice buckets: Bottoms Up, $250.00; Bathing, $450.00. (Photo courtesy Joyce and Fred Roerig)

Men of the Mountains, bank, Mountain Dew Loot, 7"..$75.00

Men of the Mountains, bowl, hillbilly bather at side, 6x6"..$80.00

Men of the Mountains, cigarette box, outhouse, #H-109, 7" $75.00

Men of the Mountains, mug, #H-102, 5".....................$30.00

Men of the Mountains, napkin holder, hillbilly, 1969 ...$150.00

Men of the Mountain, pitcher, #H-101, 7½" $85.00

Men of the Mountains, pouring spout, man's head, #H-104, 6½"..$30.00

Men of the Mountains, punch cup, #H-111, 3" $15.00

Men of the Mountains, salt & pepper shakers, man & woman's heads on barrels, 4", pr......................$40.00

Men of the Mountains, stein, figural hillbilly handle, 8" ..$40.00

Universal Dinnerware

This pottery incorporated in Cambridge, Ohio, in 1934, the outgrowth of several smaller companies in the area. They produced many lines of dinnerware and kitchenware items, most of which were marked. They're best known for their Ballerina dinnerware (simple modern shapes in a variety of solid colors) and Cat-Tail (see Cat-Tail Dinnerware). The company closed in 1960.

Baby's Breath, bowl, soup/cereal; lug handled, 6⅞"..$15.00

Baby's Breath, plate, bread & butter...........................$12.00

Baby's Breath, plate, dinner.......................................$19.00

Baby's Breath, sugar bowl, w/lid................................$30.00

Ballerina (Burgundy), bowl, fruit/dessert.....................$7.00

Ballerina (Burgundy), plate, bread & butter.................$3.00

Ballerina (Burgundy), saucer $2.00

Ballerina (Dove Grey), bowl, vegetable; open, round..$12.00

Ballerina (Dove Grey), cup...$5.00

Ballerina (Dove Grey), plate, dinner...........................$6.00

Ballerina (Forest Green), bowl, fruit/dessert $5.00

Ballerina (Forest Green), cup & saucer $12.00

Ballerina (Forest Green), plate, bread & butter.............$8.00

Ballerina (Forest Green), plate, dinner; from $6 to $10.00

Ballerina (Mist), bowl, soup......................................$16.00

Ballerina (Mist), bowl, vegetable; round, from $25 to ..$30.00

Ballerina (Mist), chop plate, tab handles $25.00

Ballerina (Mist), creamer $25.00

Ballerina (Mist), cup & saucer $15.00

Ballerina (Mist), plate, bread & butter; from $6 to......$10.00

Ballerina (Mist), plate, dinner; from $15 to $18.00

Ballerina (Mist), plate, salad.....................................$12.00

Ballerina (Mist), platter, round..................................$25.00

Ballerina (Mist), salt & pepper shakers, pr.................$20.00

Ballerina (Mist), saucer $4.00

Ballerina (Mist), sugar bowl, w/lid.............................$35.00

Ballerina (White), bowl, cream soup; handled..............$4.00

Ballerina (White), platter, lug handles, 13" $12.00

Bittersweet, bowl, mixing; lg.....................................$20.00

Bittersweet, bowl, mixing; sm....................................$30.00

Bittersweet, bowl, vegetable; open, round..................$45.00

Bittersweet, bowl, vegetable; w/lid............................$20.00

Bittersweet, salt crock, flat back, 6x4" $30.00

Calico Fruit, bowl, serving; tab handles......................$12.00

Calico Fruit, bowl, 4¼"..$25.00

Calico Fruit, pitcher, 6¼"...$50.00

Calico Fruit, plate, 9" $8.00

Camwood, plate, dinner; 9⅛" $7.00

Camwood, saucer...$3.00

Cattail, batter jug, metal lid, part of set.......................$80.00

Cattail, jug, canteen; angle handle $30.00

Cattail, plate, luncheon..$11.00

Cattail, plate, Old Holland, Wheeling, 6"....................$6.00

Cattail, saucer, Old Holland, Wheelock.......................$6.00

Circus, teapot, white over blue, w/lid $32.00

Harvest, cup & saucer, from $16 to............................$18.00

Harvest, custard $12.00

Harvest, plate, dinner $18.00
Harvest, plate, sq, 7¼", from $15 to.............................$20.00
Harvest, salt & pepper shakers, 3", pr $17.50
Highland, bowl, cereal; from $10 to $12.50
Highland, bowl, fruit/dessert; from $7 to $10.00
Highland, creamer, from $10 to.....................................$15.00
Highland, cup & saucer, from $10 to.............................$12.00
Highland, gravy boat, no underplate $35.00
Highland, plate, bread & butter; from $5 to.................$8.00
Highland, plate, dinner $12.00
Highland, plate, salad; from $7 to $10.00
Highland, saucer, from $3 to $4.00
Highland, sugar bowl, w/lid...$20.00
Iris, jug, canteen; refrigerator.......................................$18.00
Iris, pitcher, cream; 5½x6"..$25.00
Iris, water server $35.00
Rambler Rose, plate, 9" $6.00
Windmill, bowl, utility; w/lid $8.00
Woodvine, bowl, berry; 5¼" $7.50
Woodvine, bowl, vegetable..$15.00
Woodvine, casserole, w/lid, 10¼" $32.50
Woodvine, cup & saucer...$9.00
Woodvine, gravy boat, from $15 to................................$20.00
Woodvine, pitcher, 1-qt, 7"..$27.50
Woodvine, plate, bread & butter; 6"...............................$8.00
Woodvine, plate, dinner; 9"...$15.00
Woodvine, platter, 11¾"...$25.00
Woodvine, sugar bowl, w/lid..$35.00
Woodvine, tray, utility; tab handles, from $15 to........$20.00
Woodvine, utility jar, 26-oz $20.00

Valentines

As public awareness of valentine collecting grows, so does the demand for more categorization (ethnic, comic character, advertising, transportation, pedigree dogs and cats, artist signed, etc.). Valentine cards tend to be ephemeral in nature, but to the valentine elitist that carefully preserves each valuable example, this is not true. Collectors study their subject thoroughly, from the workings of the lithography process to the history of the manufacturing companies that made these tokens of love. Valentines are slowly making their way into more and more diversified collections as extensions of each collector's original interest.

It is now time to address valentine values 'after the Internet.' As is true with all collectibles, values are changing constantly. Valentines are not any different. Some have sky-rocketed, while other have gone down in value due to the infiltration of cards coming out of attics, basements, etc., and going directly onto the Internet. Fear not! After several years the novelty of the Internet auctions will subside, and values will begin to balance out again. Look at this as an opportunity to expand your collecting knowledge and perhaps venture into other categories of valentine collecting. No matter how the Internet changes our collecting values, 'what to look for' when purchasing valentines still remains the same: age,

condition, size, manufacturer, artist signature, category, and scarcity. For more information we recommend *Valentines With Values; Valentines for the Eclectic Collector;* and *100 Years of Valentines,* all by Katherine Kreider (available from the author).

Because space in our description lines is limited, HCPP has been used to abbreviate honeycomb paper puff, and PIG indicates 'Printed in Germany.'

Advisor: Katherine Kreider (See Directory, Valentines)

Newsletter: *National Valentine Collectors Bulletin*
Evalene Pulati
P.O. Box 1404
Santa Ana, CA 92702; 714-547-1355

Dimensional, big-eyed child in front of castle, PIG, 1920s, 5½x4x2¾", EX...$20.00
Dimensional, cherub fishing, HCPP base, PIG, early 1900s, 5x4x4", EX...$15.00
Dimensional, cowboy/cowgirl on pony, unsigned Drayton, 1930s, 9x6x3", EX..$40.00
Dimensional, dirigible w/jumping horse, PIG, ca 1940s, 6x4x1½, EX..$25.00
Dimensional, garden w/child, PIG, early 1900s, 4x6x4½", EX...$20.00
Dimensional, gazebo w/Dutch children, PIG, early 1900s, 9x4x4", EX...$40.00
Dimensional, girl w/spinning wheel, PIG, 1920s, 3¾x1½x3", EX...$10.00
Dimensional, pansies & child, PIG, early 1900s, 4x3½x¾", EX $10.00
Dimensional, train, American Greetings, 1950s, 6x7x5", EX...$10.00
Dimensional, train, PIG, early 1900s, 5¾x6x3", EX $20.00
Flat, African American chef, 1930s, Norcross, 7x4½", EX $10.00
Flat, Army man w/bullet, 1940s, 3½x2½", EX...............$3.00
Flat, Art Deco lady w/Scottie dog, Carrington Co, 1920s, 9½x5", EX...$5.00
Flat, boy playing accordion, 1950s, 2¾x4", EX $1.00
Flat, Bull Mastiff w/Dachsund, 1940s, 6x3", EX............$3.00
Flat, children playing checkers, 1940s, 3x2¾", EX........$1.00
Flat, crossword puzzle, 1950s, USA, 6¾x2½", EX.........$2.00
Flat, girl troll, 1960s, 4x3½", EX....................................$3.00
Flat, girl w/basket of flowers, Gibson, unsigned Scott, 4x2½", EX...$2.00
Flat, letter P w/child, 1940s, series, 4½x3", EX $2.00
Flat, Scarecrow (Wizard of Oz), creased bottom for standing, American Colortype, 1940, 5x3", EX+ $85.00
Flat, Tin Man/Wizard of Oz, 1960s, 3½x2½", EX..........$2.00
Flat, Tom & Jerry, 1960s, 3½x5", EX $3.00
Flat, Yogi Bear, 1960s, 3½x5", EX..................................$3.00
Folded-flat, Army man typing, 1940s, 3½x4", EX..........$2.00
Folded-flat, girl w/ruler, 1940s, 5x2½", EX $1.00
Greeting card, Fun 'n Laffs, Gibson, 1950s, 6x4½", EX...$3.00
Greeting card, girl roller skating, series, 1940s, 4½x3", EX...$1.00

Greeting card, Jimmy Durante caricature, 1940s, 4½x4½", EX...**$5.00**

Greeting card, Mary Jane paper doll, Hallmark, 1960s, 6½x4¼", EX..**$5.00**

Greeting card, oversized jar of honey, series, 1940s, 5x5", EX...**$2.00**

Greeting card, pig in top hat, series, 1940s, 4½x3", EX..**$1.00**

Greeting card, real photo children w/pedal car, 1940s, 4x4", EX...**$5.00**

HCPP, big-eyed child having tea party, PIG, 1920s, 7½x6x3", EX..**$20.00**

HCPP, cherub sitting on flowerette, PIG, early 1900s, 5x3x3", EX...**$10.00**

HCPP, lamp, PIG, 1920s, 8x5x2¾", EX.....................**$20.00**

HCPP, pedestal w/clown, 1920s, 5x5", EX...................**$2.00**

Mechanical-flat, Army men in woods, USA, 9½x7½", EX...**$10.00**

Mechanical-flat, Art Deco airplane, Carrington Co, 1940s, 3½x5½", EX...**$5.00**

Mechanical-flat, children reading books, USA, Katz, 1920s, 6¾x6¾", EX...**$5.00**

Mechanical-flat, girl getting manicure, Twelvetrees, PIG, 1940s, 4x3", EX...**$3.00**

Mechanical-flat, girl standing on dresser, Twelvetrees, PIG, 1940s, 6¾x6¾", EX...**$5.00**

Mechanical-flat, scissors, 1930s, USA, 4x4", EX.............**$3.00**

Mechanical-flat, St Bernard, PIG, 1920s, 5x4", EX........**$3.00**

Mechanical-flat, tennis player, PIG, 1920s, 7½x3½", EX..**$5.00**

Novelty, Advertising, Fuller Brush Sparkling Gold, tennis player, 1950s, 5x2", EX...**$20.00**

Novelty, candy container w/dimensional top, Philadelphia, 1925,½x2", EX...**$20.00**

Novelty, gift giving, pup w/hankie, original box, 1940s, 8x5½", EX...**$20.00**

Novelty, HCPP basket, USA, Beistle, 1920s, 4x4", EX...**$3.00**

Novelty, HCPP basket, USA, Beistle, 1920s, 8½x8", EX **$25.00**

Novelty, suitcase, USA, 3½" x 4", EX, $2.00. (Photo courtesy Katherine Kreider)

Penny Dreadful, Bar Fly, 1940s, USA, 10½x7½", EX....**$2.00**

Penny Dreadful, Big Business, USA, 1932, 5x6", EX.....**$3.00**

Penny Dreadful, Conceited, signed Hugh Chenoweth, 1934, USA, 11x8", EX...**$10.00**

Penny Dreadful, Lawyer, USA, 1930s, 9½x6", EX..........**$8.00**

Penny Dreadful, Slow Suicide, 14½x9½", EX.............**$15.00**

Vallona Starr

Triangle Studios opened in the 1930s, primarily as a gift shop that sold the work of various California potteries and artists such as Brad Keeler, Beth Barton, Cleminson, Josef Originals, and many others. As the business grew, Leona and Valeria, talented artists in their own right, began developing their own ceramic designs. In 1939 the company became known as Vallona Starr, a derivation of the three partners' names — (Val)eria Dopyera de Marsa, and Le(ona) and Everett (Starr) Frost. They made several popular ceramic lines including Winkies, Corn Design, Up Family, Flower Fairies, and the Fairy Tale Characters salt and pepper shakers. There were many others. Vallona Starr made only three cookie jars: Winkie (beware of any jars made in colors other than pink or yellow); Peter, Peter, Pumpkin Eater (used as a TV prize-show giveaway); and Squirrel on Stump (from the Woodland line). For more information we recommend *Vallona Starr Ceramics* by Bernice Stamper.

See also Cookie Jars.

Advisor: Bernice Stamper (See Directory, Vallona Starr)

Ashtray, stump w/2 squirrels along side, shadow gray & green, 8" dia, from $25 to...................................**$30.00**

Bowl, Humpty Dumpty..**$75.00**

Bowl, Indian decor, brown tones, minimum value....**$25.00**

Butter dish, corn design, natural green & yellow, from $35 to...**$40.00**

Cake plate, Cosmos, pink & green, 10", minimum value...**$25.00**

Candy dish, Cosmos, various color combinations, ea...**$20.00**

Creamer, blue, hand-painted floral.........................**$20.00**

Figurines, snowbirds w/gold trim, pr, from $15 to.....**$20.00**

Honey jar, Cosmos, bee on lid, blue or yellow, ea....**$20.00**

Honey pot, off-white flower form w/gold trim, bee finial, 1950s-60s, 4x3½"..**$22.50**

Jam jar, corn design, natural green & yellow, 10", from $25 to...**$30.00**

Planter, heart shape w/wild roses at base...................**$16.50**

Relish dish, 4-leaf clover, natural green.........................**$5.00**

Salt & pepper shakers, Aladdin & lamp, he: 4⅞", pr.**$69.00**

Salt & pepper shakers, daisies, gold trim, pr, from $25 to.**$30.00**

Salt & pepper shakers, Drip & Drop, pr, from $25 to..**$30.00**

Salt & pepper shakers, ears of corn, #49, 5½", pr......**$17.50**

Salt & pepper shakers, goose & golden egg, 1950s, goose: 5¾", pr...**$40.00**

Salt & pepper shakers, Indian & corn, pr, from $35 to .**$40.00**

Salt & pepper shakers, kittens, white w/painted details, pr from $25 to...**$30.00**

Salt & pepper shakers, Little Miss Muffet & tuffet, pr, from $40 to...**$50.00**

Salt & pepper shakers, man in doghouse & lady w/rolling pin, lady: 3½", pr...**$125.00**

Salt & pepper shakers, tortoise & hare, 3", 3½", pr....**$55.00**

Salt & pepper shakers, vegetable heads, gold trim, pr, from $40 to...**$50.00**

Shelf sitter, Sunbeam Fairy, seated, yellow iridescent wings, from $30 to...**$35.00**

Spoon rest, corn design $25.00
Sugar bowl & creamer, corn design, natural green & yellow, 4½" $40.00
Vase, heart shape, white iridescent w/gold trim, from $25 to $30.00
Vase, red-headed woodpecker on side, medium........$35.00
Wall pocket, squirrel in tree knothole, shadow gray & green, from $55 to...$60.00

Vandor

For more than thirty-five years, Vandor has operated out of Salt Lake City, Utah. They're not actually manufacturers but distributors of novelty ceramic items made overseas. Some pieces will be marked 'Made in Korea,' while others are marked 'Sri Lanka,' 'Taiwan,' or 'Japan.' Many of their best things have been made in the last few years, and already collectors are finding them appealing — anyone would. They have a line of kitchenware designed around 'Cowmen Mooranda' (an obvious take off on Carmen), another called 'Crocagator' (a darling crocodile modeled as a teapot, a bank, salt and pepper shakers, etc.), character-related items (Betty Boop and Howdy Doody, among others), and some really wonderful cookie jars reminiscent of '50s radios and jukeboxes.

For more information, we recommend *The Collector's Encyclopedia of Cookie Jars, Vol II,* by Joyce and Fred Roerig (Collector Books).

Advisor: Lois Wildman (See Directory, Vandor)

All Star, bank, batter on top of lg baseball, c 1991 Pelzman designs (for Vandor), 7", MIB $48.00
Beatles, clock, Yellow Submarine, features numbers from the Sea of Time scene of movie, 1999, M...................$30.00
Beatles, cookie jar, Sgt Pepper's drum, 1998, MIB......$50.00
Beatles, lamp, Yellow Submarine base w/multicolored shade, MIB $35.00
Beatles, lava lamp, Yellow Submarine, 19½", MIB $80.00
Beatles, tea set, Yellow Submarine, submarine teapot, character head mugs (2), & tray, MIB.........................$35.00

Betty Boop, bank, paper label: Vandor Made in Japan c 1986 KFS, 4", $50.00. (Photo courtesy Beverly and Jim Mangus)

Betty Boop, bookends, Betty on 1 and Pudgy on other, ea stand beside half of juke box, 6¾x5¾", pr........$150.00
Betty Boop, bookends, celestial style, 7x5¼x6¾", MIB..$45.00
Betty Boop, clock, Betty in cowboy attire beside covered wagon w/dog sticking out in back, 1985, EX $60.00
Betty Boop, clock, Betty on 1 side w/quarter moon on other, battery-operated, 1985, EX....................................$30.00
Betty Boop, music box, Betty plays piano as 2 dogs sit on top & spin, EX $75.00
Betty Boop, picture frame, Betty in long pink gown stands beside black frame, 1991, M..................................$25.00
Betty Boop, string holder, c KFS 1985 Vandor, 5¾x6"..$275.00
Betty Boop, toothbrush holder, C 1983 KFS, 5"..........$95.00
Betty Boop, vase, embossed Betty & purple roses on gray background, 1990, M...$30.00
Cowman Mooranda, salt & pepper shakers, 5", pr.....$42.00
Curious George, cookie jar, MIB $70.00
Curious George, mug, monkey sits on handle of yellow mug, w/Curious George in red & 'a good little monkey' in black, EX $36.00
Curious George, shadow box, book shape w/George riding a bike at a circus, 10x6x2", MIB...........................$30.00
Elvis, jewelry box, musical, plays Heartbreak Hotel, 6x4x3", MIB $35.00
I Love Lucy, mug, Lucy & Ethel in 3-D on side, Forever Friends, 1996, 4", MIB $28.00
I Love Lucy, salt & papper shakers, Lucy bust before tray w/2 chocolate shakers, 1996, 5½", 3-pc set $36.00
I Love Lucy, snow globe, musical, 4x4x5¼", MIB $40.00
I Love Lucy, teapot, Lucy climbs out of TV, 1996, EX..$45.00
Jetsons, mugs, 1 ea of ea family member's face, 1990, EX.$60.00
Juke Box, bank, 5x5"...$38.00
Mona Lisa, bank, c 1992 Pelzman Designs, 7¾" $36.00
Pig & Guitar, salt & pepper shakers, 4¼", 3½", pr, MIB..$28.00
Pink Panther salt & pepper shakers, playing bongos (shakers), 5½x4¼", MIB..$22.00
Poodle, salt & pepper shakers, 1992, 3½", pr............$28.00
Poodle, wall sconce, pink w/sunglasses, 1987, 5x4½"..$42.00
Popeye, bank, sits on pile of rope, 7¾", VG+ $70.00
Popeye, box, w/pipe in mouth & mug in hand he sits on spinach box, 5", MIB $35.00
Popeye & Olive, salt & pepper shakers, King Features Syndicate Vandor Imports, 7½", pr $125.00
Popeye & Olive Oyl, salt & pepper shakers, 7¼", M, pr..$45.00
Roy Rogers, salt & pepper shakers, 1991, 5x4", pr.....$35.00
Shadows of Yesterday, shadow box, Toys in the Cupboard series, metal train w/picture of boy playing w/train, M........$35.00
Socks (Presidential Cat) w/lg saxophone, salt & pepper shakers, 4", 3", pr $36.00
Sweet Pea (Popeye), bank, sitting in yellow pajamas, 1980, 6", EX...$125.00

Vernon Kilns

Founded in Vernon, California, in 1930, this company produced many lines of dinnerware, souvenir plates, decorative pottery, and figurines. They employed several well-known artists whose designs no doubt contributed substantially to their success. Among them were Rockwell Kent, Royal Hickman, and Don Blanding, all of whom were responsible for creating several of the lines most popular with collectors today.

In 1940 they signed a contract with Walt Disney to produce a line of figurines, vases, bowls, and several dinnerware patterns that were inspired by Disney's film *Fantasia*. The Disney items were made for a short time only and are now expensive.

The company closed in 1958, but Metlox purchased some of the molds and continued to produce some of their bestselling dinnerware lines through a specially established 'Vernonware' division.

Most of the ware is marked in some form or another with the company name and in some cases the name of the dinnerware pattern.

If you'd like to learn more, we recommend *The Collector's Encyclopedia of California Pottery, Second Edition,* by Jack Chipman; and *Collectible Vernon Kilns,* (now out of print) by Maxine Feek Nelson. (Both are published by Collector Books.)

Advisor: Maxine Nelson (See Directory, Vernon Kilns)

Newsletter: *Vernon Views*
P.O. Box 24234
Tempe, AZ 85285; Published quarterly beginning with the spring issue

Anytime Shape

Patterns you will find on this shape include Tickled Pink, Heavenly Days, Anytime, Imperial, Sherwood, Frolic, Young in Heart, Rose-A-Day, and Dis 'N Dot.

Bowl, chowder; 6", from $8 to	**$10.00**
Bowl, vegetable; divided, 9", from $15 to	**$20.00**
Butter tray, w/lid, from $25 to	**$35.00**
Coffeepot, w/lid, 8-cup, from $30 to	**$45.00**
Cup & saucer, tea; from $8 to	**$12.00**
Mug, 12-oz, from $12 to	**$20.00**
Plate, bread & butter; 6", from $4 to	**$6.00**
Plate, snack; indented for tumbler, 12x8", from $35 to	**$40.00**
Platter, 11", from $12 to	**$18.00**
Relish, ring handle, oval, 6", from $35 to	**$45.00**
Tumbler, 14-oz, from $12 to	**$22.00**

Chatelaine Shape

This designer pattern by Sharon Merrill was made in four color combinations: Topaz, Bronze, Platinum, and Jade.

Bowl, chowder; decorated Platinum & Jade, 6", from $18 to	**$25.00**
Cup, coffee; flat base, Topaz & Bronze, from $15 to	**$20.00**
Plate, chop; Topaz & Bronze, 14", from $45 to	**$50.00**

Plate, salad; decorated Platinum & Jade, 7½", from $15 to	**$20.00**
Teapot, decorated Platinum & Jade, w/lid, from $250 to minimum of	**$300.00**

Lotus and Pan American Lei Shape

Patterns on this shape include Lotus, Chinling, and Vintage. Pan American Lei was a variation with flatware from the San Marino line. To evaluate Lotus, use the low end of our range as the minimum value; the high end of values apply to Pan American Lei.

Bowl, chowder; 6", from $10 to	**$18.00**
Bowl, mixing; Pan American Lei only, 9"	**$50.00**
Bowl, mixing; Pan American only, 6"	**$35.00**
Bowl, salad; Lotus only, from $35 to	**$45.00**
Butter tray, oblong, w/lid, from $35 to	**$60.00**
Coffeepot, w/lid, 8-cup, from $35 to	**$80.00**
Mug, 9-oz, from $15 to	**$35.00**
Plate, coupe; Pan American Lei only, 10"	**$25.00**
Plate, offset; Lotus only, 6½", from $6 to	**$8.00**
Platter, Pan American only, 13½"	**$50.00**
Salt shaker, from $7 to	**$20.00**
Sugar bowl, w/lid, from $15 to	**$35.00**

Melinda Shape

Patterns found on this shape are: Arcadia, Beverly, Blossom Time, Chintz, Cosmos, Dolores, Fruitdale, Hawaii (Lei Lani on Melinda is priced at two times base value), May Flower, Monterey, Native California, Philodendron. The more elaborate the pattern, the higher the value.

Bowl, fruit; 5½", from $5 to	**$10.00**
Bowl, salad; footed base, 12", from $45 to	**$75.00**
Bowl, serving; oval, 9", from $15 to	**$25.00**
Casserole, w/lid, individual, 4¾" dia, from $25 to	**$35.00**
Cup & saucer, AD; from $15 to	**$27.00**
Jam jar, w/lid, from $55 to	**$65.00**
Plate, bread & butter; 6½", from $5 to	**$8.00**
Plate, luncheon; 9½", from $9 to	**$18.00**
Platter, 14", from $20 to	**$45.00**
Relish, leaf shape, 4-part, 14", from $45 to	**$85.00**
Sauce boat, from $20 to	**$30.00**
Tidbit server, 2-tiered, wooden fixture, from $20 to	**$30.00**

Montecito Shape (and Coronado)

This was one of the company's more utilized shapes — well over two hundred patterns have been documented. Among the most popular are the solid colors, plaids, the florals, westernware, and the Bird and Turnbull series. Bird, Turnbull, and Winchester 73 (Frontier Days) are two to four times base values. Disney hollow ware is seven to eight times base values. Plaids (except Tweed and Calico), solid colors, and Brown-eyed Susan are represented by the lower range.

Ashtray, 5½" dia, from $12 to.......................................**$15.00**

Bowl, chowder; angular, open, w/applied pierced handles, 6", from $15 to **$25.00**

Bowl, fruit; 5½", from $6 to.................................**$8.00**

Bowl, mixing; 6", from $19 to **$25.00**

Bowl, rim soup; 8½", from $12 to....................**$18.00**

Bowl, salad; 13" dia, from $45 to **$75.00**

Bowl, serving; w/out ridge, 9" dia, from $15 to **$25.00**

Bowl, serving; 8½" dia, from $15 to **$20.00**

Buffet server, trio; scarce, from $50 to.............**$75.00**

Candle holder, teacup style, pr from $65 to.............**$95.00**

Casserole, chicken pie; stick handle, w/lid, 4", from $18 to..**$25.00**

Coaster, ridged, 3¾" dia, from $18 to **$22.00**

Compote, footed, early, scarce, 9½" dia, from $45 to...**$65.00**

Cup, custard; scarce, 3", from $20 to **$25.00**

Flowerpot, 3", from $23 to.................................**$28.00**

Jam jar, notched lid, 5", from $55 to **$65.00**

Lemon server, center brass handle, 6", from $20 to....**$25.00**

Muffin tray, tab handles, dome lid, 9", from $50 to....**$75.00**

Mug, straight sides, later style, 9-oz, 3½", from $16 to...**$30.00**

Pepper mill, metal fitting, lg, from $30 to **$45.00**

Pitcher, jug; bulbous bottom, 1-pt, from $25 to **$35.00**

Pitcher, streamlined, ¼-pt, 4", from $20 to **$30.00**

Pitcher, tankard; 1½-qt, from $50 to **$65.00**

Plate, bread & butter; 6½", from $5 to.............**$8.00**

Plate, chop; 14", from $20 to **$50.00**

Plate, dinner; 10½", from $12 to.......................**$18.00**

Platter, 10½", from $15 to **$20.00**

Platter, 16", from $35 to....................................**$60.00**

Salt shaker, wood encased, 4½", from $30 to **$40.00**

Sugar bowl, angular or round, open, from $10 to......**$15.00**

Tidbit server, 3-tiered, wooden fixture, from $25 to...**$40.00**

Tumbler, bulbous bottom, #3, 3¾", from $18 to........**$25.00**

San Fernando Shape

Known patterns for this shape are Desert Bloom, Early Days, Hibiscus, R.F.D, Vernon's 1860, and Vernon Rose.

Bowl, chowder; 6", from $12 to.........................**$15.00**

Bowl, fruit; 5½", from $6 to................................**$10.00**

Bowl, mixing; RFD only, 5", from $15 to **$19.00**

Bowl, mixing; RFD only, 8", from $25 to **$30.00**

Bowl, serving; 9 dia, from $18 to.......................**$25.00**

Coaster, ridged, RFD only, 3¾", from $18 to.............**$22.00**

Cup & saucer, AD; from $16 to **$26.00**

Lamp, kerosene; converted teapot, scarce, from $100 to...**$125.00**

Plate, bread & butter; 6½", from $5 to............**$8.00**

Plate, dinner; 10½", from $12 to........................**$18.00**

Platter, 16", from $30 to....................................**$60.00**

Soup tureen, notched lid, w/15" plate stand, 13", from $250 to...**$350.00**

Tidbit, 3-tiered, wooden fixture, from $25 to.............**$40.00**

Tumbler, style #5, RFD only, 14-oz, from $20 to **$25.00**

San Marino Shape

Known patterns for this shape are Barkwood, Bel Air, California Originals, Casual California, Gayety, Hawaiian Coral, Heyday, Lei Lani (two to three times base values), Mexicana, Pan American Lei (two to three times base values), Raffia, Shadow Leaf, Shantung, Sun Garden, and Trade Winds.

Lei Lani, chop plate, 14", $125.00; tumbler, $75.00. (Photo courtesy Maxine Nelson)

Bowl, fruit; 5½", from $4 to...........................**$7.00**

Bowl, mixing; 6", from $15 to **$22.00**

Bowl, mixing; 9", from $28 to **$35.00**

Bowl, serving; divided, 10", from $15 to **$20.00**

Bowl, serving; 7½" dia, from $10 to **$14.00**

Casserole, w/lid, 8" (inside dia), from $25 to.............**$35.00**

Coaster, ridged, 3¾", from $10 to......................**$15.00**

Coffer server, w/stopper, 10-cup, from $25 to **$30.00**

Creamer, regular, from $7 to **$12.00**

Cup, colossal; from $125 to **$150.00**

Flowerpot, w/saucer, 4", from $30 to......................**$35.00**

Flowerpot, 3", from $15 to.............................**$22.00**

Mug, 9-oz, from $15 to......................................**$20.00**

Pitcher, syrup; drip-cut lid, from $40 to......................**$45.00**

Pitcher, 1-pt, from $18 to **$22.00**

Plate, chop; 13", from $15 to **$30.00**

Plate, salad; 7½", from $5 to.........................**$10.00**

Platter, 11", from $11 to....................................**$16.00**

Salt & pepper shakers, gourd shape, pr, from $15 to.**$20.00**

Spoon holder, from $20 to **$25.00**

Ultra Shape

More than fifty patterns were issued on this shape. Nearly all the artist-designed lines (Rockwell Kent, Don Blanding, and Disney) utilized Ultra. The shape was developed by Gale Turnbull, and many of the elaborate flower and fruit patterns can be credited to him as well; use the high end of our range as a minimum value for his work. For Frederick Lunning, use the mid range. For other artist patterns, use these formulas based on the high end: Blanding — 2X (Aquarium 3X); Disney, 7 – 8X; Kent — Moby Dick, and Our America, 2½X, Salamina, 5 – 7X.

Bowl, chowder; 6", from $12 to $20.00
Bowl, coupe soup; 7½", from $15 to...........................$20.00
Bowl, mixing; 7", from $25 to $30.00
Bowl, serving; 9" dia, from $15 to..............................$30.00
Butter tray, oblong, w/lid, from $35 to......................$50.00
Coffepot, regular, 6-cup, from $45 to.........................$80.00
Creamer, regular, open, short or tall, from $12 to $18.00
Cup, jumbo; from $35 to...$40.00
Jam jar, notched lid, from $55 to................................$65.00
Pickle, tab handle, 6" dia, from $20 to.......................$30.00
Pitcher, w/lid, 2-qt, from $50 to $75.00
Plate, chop; 14", from $35 to $75.00
Plate, luncheon; 8½", from $10 to...............................$15.00
Salt & pepper shakers, pr, from $15 to.......................$25.00
Teapot, 6-cup, from $40 to $75.00

Year 'Round Shape

Patterns on this shape include Blueberry Hill, Country Cousin, and Lollipop Tree.

Bowl, fruit; 5½", from $4 to...$6.00
Buffet server, trio; from $35 to $75.00
Butter tray, w/lid, from $25 to.....................................$35.00
Creamer, from $7 to...$12.00
Mug, 12-oz, from $12 to..$20.00
Plate, salad; 7½", from $5 to...$8.00

Viet Nam War Collectibles

In 1949 the French had military control over Viet Nam. This was true until they suffered a sound defeat at Dienbienphu in 1954. This action resulted in the formation of the Geneva Peace Conference which allowed the French to make peace and withdraw but left Viet Nam divided into North Vietnam and South Vietnam. The agreement was to reunite the country in 1956 when the general elections took place. But this didn't happen because of South Vietnam's political objections. The strife continued and slowly America was drawn into the conflict from the time of the Eisenhower administration until the Paris Peace Agreement in 1973. The war itself lingered on until 1975 when communist forces invaded Saigon and crushed the South Vietnamese government there.

Items relating to this conflict from the 1960s and early 1970s are becoming collectible. Most reflect the unpopularity of this war. College marches and political unrest headlined the newspapers of those years. Posters, pin-back buttons, political cartoons, and many books from that period reflect the anti-war philosophy of the day and are reminders of turbulent times and political policies that cost the lives of many brave young men.

Beret, black, US Naval Forces flash, Mai-Anh manufacture, M $165.00
Blood chart, US Air Force, 14-language, published by Aeronautical Chart & Info Center, St Louis MO, April 1961, EX...$40.00

Book, From Trust to Tragedy, Fredrick Nolting (Ambassador to Vietnam), Prager Publishers, paperback, 1988, EX...$32.50
Book, Special Forces of the United States Army, 1952-1982, Ian D W Sutherland, 1990 printing, M................$200.00
Cigarette lighter, From President Nguyen Van Thieu Republic of Vietnam on lid, Zippo, EX.......................$195.00
Cigarette lighter, map on 1 side, Danang & poem on other, Zippo Pat 2517191 (1950), EX..............................$75.00
Cigarette lighter, Saigon Vietnam, Yea Though I Walk... on 1 side, nude woman on other, Zenith, VG.............$35.00
Cigarette lighter, Special Forces insignia on front, From Surgeon's Office, 5th Special Forces Group on back, G $45.00
Hat, boonie; tiger-stripe camo, 1960s-early 70s, M $80.00
License plate, Vietnam Veteran, medals & ribbons, helicoptor on white, NM $35.00
Medal, Silver Star, w/lapel pin & ribbon bar, marked HLP-GI, 1960s, MIB..$40.00
Patch, F-4 Phantom II, 390 TFS, boar's head, embroidery on twill, 4⅜", NM $70.00
Patch, Vietnam 300 Missions B-52D, red, white & blue cloth shield, NM $200.00
Pin-back button, Build Not Burn, Students for a Democratic Society, 1¼", EX...$47.50
Pin-back button, Confront the Warmakers Oct 21 Washington DC Mobilization #2, green & white, EX...............$85.00
Pin-back button, Don't Think, Follow! Don't Talk, Shoot! It's the American Way, SPU (Students Peace Union), 1¼", NM $50.00
Pin-back button, man's face before mushrooming nuclear cloud, What Me Worry??, red, white & blue, EX ..$145.00
Pin-back button, March Nov 6 - Out Now, National Peace Action Coalition, yellow, blue & white, 1½", EX $25.00
Pin-back button, military crosses, green & white, 2¼", M...$20.00
Pin-back button, Negotiate Vietnam, blue & white, 1¼", VG $15.00
Pin-back button, 1971 Spring Offensive To End the War, April 24 to May 5, black lettering & white dove on blue, 2", EX+ $65.00
Plate, Friends of the Vietnam Veterans Memorial, Dave Froutman, Franklin Mint, M $35.00
Poster, October 14 March & Rally Against the War, Delores Park, 21½x14", EX $85.00
Poster, This Vacation Visit Beautiful Vietnam, war scene, black, red & white, 1960s, 34x23", EX.................$37.50
Shirt, fatigue; tiger-stripe camo, long sleeves, 2-pocket front, EX $120.00
Yearbook, 101st Airborn-Vietnam 1968, 145 pages, EX $85.00

View-Master Reels and Packets

William Gruber was the inventor who introduced the View-Master to the public at the New York World's Fair and the Golden Gate Exposition held in California in 1939. Thousands of reels and packets have been made since that time on every aspect of animal life, places of interest, and entertainment.

Over the years the company has changed ownership five times. It was originally Sawyer's View-Master, G.A.F (in the mid-sixties), View-Master International (1981), Ideal Toy and, most recently, Tyco Toy Company. The latter three companies produced them strictly as toys and issued only cartoons, making the earlier non-cartoon reels and the three-reel packets very collectible.

Sawyer made two cameras so that the public could take their own photo reels in 3-D. They made a projector as well, so that the homemade reels could be viewed on a large screen. 'Personal' or 'Mark II' cameras with their cases usually range in value from $100.00 to $200.00; rare viewers such as the blue 'Model B' start at about $100.00, and the 'Stereo-Matic 500' projector is worth $175.00 to $200.00. Most single reels range from $1.00 to $5.00, but some early Sawyer's and G.A.F's may bring as much as $35.00 each, character-related reels sometimes even more.

Club: View-Master Reel Collector
Roger Nazeley
4921 Castor Ave.
Philadelphia, PA 19124
215-743-8999; e-mail: vmreelguy2@aol.com

A Team, #446, 1983, single reel, MIP	**$15.00**
Archies, B-574, MIP	**$38.00**
Big Blue Marble, B-587, MIP	**$26.00**
Black Hole, K-35, MIP	**$28.00**
Casper viewer & reels, 1995, MIB	**$12.00**
Children's Zoo, B6176, MIP	**$18.00**
Dennis the Menace, B-539, MIP	**$22.00**
KISS, #001305, single reel	**$8.00**
Little Red Riding Hood, B-310, MIP	**$22.00**

Magazine ad showing 'Personal' camera, from $100.00 to $200.00 with case; and 'Stereo-Matic 500' projector, from $175.00 to $200.00.

Million Dollar Duck, B-506, MIP	**$30.00**

Return From Witch Mountain, J-25, MIP	**$20.00**
Robin Hood, B-342, MIP	**$25.00**
Roy Rogers — The Holdup, #946, single reel	**$5.00**
Search — NBC TV Series, B-591, MIP	**$33.00**
Snoopy & the Red Baron, B-544, MIP	**$20.00**
Talking Viewmaster (viewer only), EX	**$26.00**
Tarzan Rescues Cheetah, #975, single reel w/book	**$7.00**
Winnie the Pooh & the Blustery Day, K-37, MIP	**$22.00**

Viking Glass

Located in the famous glassmaking area of West Virginia, this company has been in business since the 1950s; they're most famous for their glass animals and birds. Their Epic Line (circa 1950s and 1960s) was innovative in design and vibrant in color. Rich tomato-red, amberina, brilliant blues, strong greens, black, amber, and deep amethyst were among the rainbow hues in production at that time. During the 1980s the company's ownership changed hands, and the firm became known as Dalzell-Viking. Viking closed their doors in 1998.

Some of the Epic Line animals were reissued in crystal, crystal frosted, and black.

Advisor: Mary Lou Bohl (See Directory, Viking)

Ashtray, amber, spherical w/slanted rim, 5"	**$50.00**
Ashtray, ruby, round w/scalloped rim & center rest, 6½" dia	**$60.00**
Ashtray & lighter, transparent ruby, Eames style, EX	**$55.00**
Bell, frosted w/flower decor, original sticker, 5½"	**$15.00**
Bookends, lion heads, clear w/brown manes, 5½x5¼", pr	**$42.00**
Bowl, blue, Epic Line, 5" tall	**$14.00**
Bowl, centerpiece; green, lg scalloped rim, 5¾x9⅜"	**$15.00**
Candy dish, blue, lg bird w/tail up on lid, round bottom, 12x6" dia	**$40.00**
Candy jar, ruby, lg ribs on sides, footed, w/lid, 7½"	**$20.00**
Compote, orange, scalloped rim, footed, 6½x8" dia	**$15.00**
Fairy lamp, Diamond Quilt, green, 6½"	**$20.00**
Fairy lamp, Diamond Quilt, pink, 5¼"	**$20.00**
Fairy lamp, Diamond Quilt, ultramarine, 7"	**$20.00**
Fairy lamp, owl shape, ruby, 7", w/original box	**$50.00**
Figurine, angelfish, crystal, #1303, minimum value	**$55.00**
Figurine, bird, dark amber, long tail, 9¾"	**$35.00**
Figurine, bird w/tail up, orchid, red or ginger, 11", ea	**$150.00**
Figurine, bunny, black, 1980s, 2½"	**$20.00**
Figurine, cat, amber, seated, 8"	**$55.00**
Figurine, cat, ruby, seated, 8"	**$75.00**
Figurine, duck, amber, on round base, 5"	**$12.00**
Figurine, duck, red or blue, long neck, looking up, 14"	**$60.00**
Figurine, duck, ruby, 9½"	**$60.00**
Figurine, duckling, ruby, floating, 2½"	**$35.00**
Figurine, egret, dark medium blue, 9½x12"	**$50.00**
Figurine, fish, green, Epic Line, 10"	**$35.00**
Figurine, lop-eared dog, crystal, 8"	**$60.00**
Figurine, Madonna bust, crystal, 5½x6½"	**$65.00**

Figurine, owl, black, 1980s, 2½" $20.00
Figurine, owl, ruby, 5½" $30.00
Figurine, penguin, amber, on round base, Epic Line, 5¾" .. $30.00
Figurine, pig, frosted w/clear clothes, eyes & nose, 4¼" $20.00
Figurine, rabbit, sitting, pink, 6½" $25.00
Jewelry tree, honey amber, 8" $80.00
Paperweight, apple, ruby w/green stem, hollow, 4" .. $35.00
Paperweight, Jesus bent over rock, clear, 4¾x5¾" $40.00
Paperweight, lion, frosted, 5x5½" $35.00
Paperweight, mushroom shape, green, 3x3½" dia at top... $15.00
Paperweight, polar bear, crystal, 3x5¼" $18.00
Paperweight, rabbit, crystal, 2¼x4¼" $25.00
Paperweight, Sea Captain, clear, 6" $35.00
Paperweight, tiger, frosted, 5¾x½" $35.00
Platter, orange, free-form shape, 12¼x18" $28.00
Stem, cordial; ruby, 5¼", 8 for................................... $40.00
Vase, cornucopia; turquoise, 12x9" dia $60.00
Vase, green, 3-footed w/flower frog insert, 3½x4½" dia.. $30.00
Vase, irregular scalloped rim, 21½" at highest point, 7½"
  W $30.00
Vase, ruby, ribbed sides, irregular rim, 25"................. $40.00
Vase, yellow frost w/boy in straw hat playing w/butterflies,
  6½" $40.00

Wade Porcelain

If you've attended many flea markets, you're already very familiar with the tiny Wade figures, most of which are 2" and under. Wade made several lines of these miniatures, but the most common were made as premiums for the Red Rose Tea Company. Most of these sell for $3.50 to $7.00 or so, with a few exceptions such as the Gingerbread man. Wade also made a great number of larger figurines as well as tableware and advertising items.

The Wade Potteries began life in 1867 as Wade and Myatt when George Wade and a partner named Myatt opened a pottery in Burslem — the center for potteries in England. In 1882 George Wade bought out his partner, and the name of the Pottery was changed to Wade and Sons. In 1919 the pottery underwent yet another change in name to George Wade & Son Ltd. In 1891 another Wade Pottery was established — J & W Wade & Co., which in turn changed its name to A.J. Wade & Co. in 1927. At this time (1927) Wade Heath & Co. Ltd. was also formed.

These three potteries plus a new Irish pottery named Wade (Ireland) Ltd. were incorporated into one company in 1958 and given the name The Wade Group of Potteries. In 1990 the group was taken over by Beauford plc. and given the name Wade Ceramics Ltd., remaining so until the present time. In early 1999, Wade Ceramics Ltd. was bought out from Beauford plc. by the Wade management.

If you'd like to learn more, we recommend *The World of Wade, The World of Wade Book 2,* and *Wade Price Trends — First Edition* by Ian Warner and Mike Posgay.

Advisor: Ian Warner (See Directory, Wade)

Newsletters: *The Wade Watch, Ltd.*
8199 Pierson Ct.
Arvada, CO 80005; 303-421-9655 or 303-424-4401 or fax: 303-421-0317; e-mail: idwarnet@home.com

Club: The Official International Wade Collector's Club
The Official Wade Club Magazine
Wade Ceramics Ltd.
Royal Works, Westport Rd., Burslem, Stoke-on-Trent, Staffordshire, ST6 4AP, England, UK; e-mail: club@wade.co.uk; www.wade.co.uk/wade

British Character, Fish Porter $240.00
British Character, Pearly Queen, ca 1959, 3⅞".......... $200.00
Cat & Puppy Dishes, Yorkshire Terrier Puppy, 1974-81 .. $40.00
Character Jug, Toby Jim Jug $140.00
Disney, Chief (Lady & the Tramp), 1981-87, 1⅞" $32.00
Disney, Copper (Fox & Hound), 1980s, 1⅝".............. $35.00
Dogs & Puppies Series, Alsatian (adult), 1969-82, 2½"..$25.00
Dogs & Puppies Series, Corgi (Adult), 2¼" $40.00
Farmyard Set, Goose, 1982-83, Tom Smith & Co, 1⅜" . $8.00
Hanna-Barbera Cartoon Character, Yogi Bear, 1959-60,
  2½" $140.00
Happy Families, Owl (Parent), 1¾" $18.00
Happy Families Series, Kitten, 1978-86, 1⅜" $24.00
Novelty Animal Figure, Bernie & Poo $220.00
Nursery Favorite, Blynkin, without flowers, 2" $195.00

Nursery Favorites, Old King Cole, 2½", $55.00.

Nursery Favorite, Queen of Hearts, 2⅞"..................... $55.00
Nursery Favorite, Willie Winkie, 1972-81, 1¾" $32.00
Red Rose Tea (Canada), Kitten $8.00
Red Rose Tea (USA), Clown w/Pie $5.00
Safari Set, Polar Bear, 1⅛".. $32.00
TV Pet Series, Droopy Jr, 2¼" $95.00
Whappas, Elephant, 1976-81, 2⅛" $28.00
Whappas, Otter, 1¼" $45.00
Whimsie, Crocodile, 1953-59, ¾x1⅝" $70.00
Whimsie, Duck, 1972, 1¼x1½" $10.00
Whimsie, Horse, 1953, 1½" $48.00

Wildlife Set, partridge, 1980-81, 1⅛" **$18.00**

Wall Pockets

A few years ago there was only a handful of avid wall pocket collectors, but today many are finding them intriguing. They were popular well before the turn of the century. Roseville and Weller included at least one and sometimes several in many of their successful lines of art pottery, and other American potteries made them as well. Many were imported from Germany, Czechoslovakia, China, and Japan. By the 1950s, they were passè.

Some of the most popular today are the figurals. Look for the more imaginative and buy the ones you especially like. If you're buying to resell, look for those designed as animals, large exotic birds, children, luscious fruits, or those that are particularly eye catching. Appeal is everything. Examples with a potter's mark are usually more pricey (for instance Roseville, McCoy, Hull, etc.), because of the crossover interest in collecting their products. For more information refer to *Made in Japan Ceramics* (there are three in the series) by Carole Bess White; or *Collector's Guide to Wall Pockets, Affordable and Others,* by Marvin and Joy Gibson.

Advisor: Carole Bess White (See Directory, Japan Ceramics)

Balcony scene, man seated on window ledge above railing, multicolored on white w/black trim, Made in Japan, 8¼" **$20.00**
Basket vase w/embossed flowers, short handles at rim, footed, multicolored, Made in Japan, 6" **$15.00**
Basket w/band of fruit & flowers, multicolored band on yellow w/brown bottom, bamboo handle & rim, Japan, 8" **$15.00**
Boy or girl applied to openwork plate, white w/multicolored detail, gold trim, 7" dia, ea **$25.00**
Clown head, head cocked w/open smile, white w/painted detail, gold-trimmed ruffled collar, 6¾" **$28.00**
Conical form w/embossed butterflies, blue & orange on black & gold mottled incised leaf background, 6⅛" **$18.00**
Conical form w/embossed hunt scene, decorative embossed trim, brown wash on black sky, black trim, 8½".**$25.00**
Conical form w/moriage Oriental scene, multicolored w/lustre, Made in Japan, 8⅜" **$35.00**
Conical form w/painted bird & flower motif, multicolors outlined in black on white w/gray lustre band around rim, 7⅜" **$15.00**
Conical form w/painted windmill scene & trees, lustre finish, Made in Japan, 6¼" **$40.00**
Cornucopia, upright w/flared leafy rim, scrolled tail, green w/touches of brown **$10.00**
Cornucopia w/boy, porcelain, boy applied to white cornucopia w/ruffles, scrolls & roses, gold trim, Japan, 5½" **$14.00**
Cornucopia w/fruit, basketweave w/band of colorful fruit around upright rim, 5½" **$15.00**

Cup & saucer, chartreuse w/sponged trim, 4½" **$12.00**
Dancing Spanish girl, bent backward from side holding up skirt showing pointed toe, floral decor on base & shoulder, 6" **$20.00**
Duckling, yellow w/brown air-brushing, on green tree-trunk shelf, California Pottery Co **$15.00**
Dust pan w/painted floral trim, white w/green, 8x8".**$15.00**
Dutch girl w/basket & goose against brick wall, multicolored, Made in Japan, 6" **$18.00**
Flower & leaves on stem, lg white blossom & bud w/mottled green leaves & brown stem, 7¾" **$25.00**
Flower House, hut w/3 pouch-type openings, pink & blue, 6⅝" **$12.00**
Flowerpot w/pansy, yellow on dark green, 2½" **$10.00**
Galleon, multicolored w/lustre trim, Made in Japan, 7¼" ..**$25.00**
Girl's head in bonnet w/neck bow, eyes closed, black ponytail & bangs, flowers on hat, gold trim, 4½" **$22.00**
Grapes, purple grapes w/dark green leaves on light green stalk w/yellow leaf, Made in Japan, 6⅝" **$14.00**
Hungry as a Bear, sq picture-frame shape w/painted bear scene on white w/gold trim, Japan, 3¾" **$12.00**
Iris conical form, lg blossom w/formed leaves, blue on white w/brown trim, Made in Occupied Japan, 4½" **$25.00**
Iron, 2 openings, white w/painted floral motif, brown trim, UCAGO China, 5½" **$15.00**
Masks (Comedy & Tragedy) on diagonal wire frames, black, 9¼" frames, ea **$15.00**
Mexican man w/basket on back on cactus base, blues, yellow & green, Japan, 5¾" **$14.00**
Oil Lamp, white w/floral decoration around bottom, gold trim, Elynor China, 6¾" **$15.00**
Pitcher in washbowl, white w/allover yellow & green floral & leaf motif, 7" **$15.00**
Pitcher w/embossed cherry branch, white w/painted motif, green rim & base, 4½" **$12.00**
Plate w/applied lambs (2), airbrushing on lambs & sky w/painted grass, 6" dia **$20.00**
Plate w/embossed peach on branch, white w/painted detail, 5¾" dia **$12.00**
Pot w/painted Mexican desert scene, scalloped wall mount, chartreuse w/painted detail, white trim, 5½" **$20.00**
Pot w/ram's head handles, ruffled rim, applied flower w/3 leaves on front, multicolored, Made in Japan, 7x4¾" **$25.00**
Rolling pin, 2 openings, white w/green decoration, 11½"..**$15.00**
Scoop w/embossed flower & leaves, light blue, 9" **$12.00**
Shamrock, light blue, 4½" **$10.00**
Simitar, white w/blue airbrushing, gold-trimmed handle, 7½" **$15.00**
Slipper w/painted pine cone motif, brown stenciled-look pine cones w/green needles on white, gold trim, 8½" **$15.00**
Squirrel nibbling on nut, side view, glossy dark brown-black wash, 4⅜" **$12.00**
Straw hat w/bird, yellow w/brown airbrushing & brown bird, marked Stewart B McCulloch, 6½" **$12.00**
Teapot w/applied cherries & leaves, red cherries w/green leaves on white w/black 'drizzled' design, 3¾" ...**$12.00**

Telephone (early wall type), brown woodgrain w/gold detail, Made in Japan label, 5⅛"................**$18.00**

Toucan & leaves embossed on basketweave conical form, airbrushed colors on white, Japan, 5"................**$15.00**

Turkey facing forward, multicolored high gloss, Made in Japan, 6⅛"................**$20.00**

Watering can w/painted rooster motif, blue, pink & black on white, Made in Japan, 5⅛"................**$12.00**

Well w/bucket, round base w/embossed stones, pitched roof, glossy light gray wash finish, 7¾"................**$20.00**

Wallace China

This company operated in California from 1931 until 1964, producing many lines of dinnerware, the most popular of which today are those included in their Westward Ho assortment, Boots and Saddles, Rodeo, and Pioneer Trails. All of these lines were designed by artist Till Goodan, whose signature appears in the design. All are very heavy, their backgrounds are tan, and the designs are done in dark brown. The Rodeo pattern has accents of rust, green, and yellow. When dinnerware with a western theme became so popular a few years ago, Rodeo was reproduced, but the new trademark includes neither 'California' or 'Wallace China.'

Advisor: Marv Fogleman (See Directory, Dinnerware)

Cup and saucer, Rodeo, $100.00.

Ashtray, Boots & Saddle, 5½", from $45 to................**$50.00**
Ashtray, Lewis & Clark, blue on white, 5½"................**$90.00**
Bowl, cereal; Boots & Saddle, from $55 to................**$65.00**
Bowl, chili; Rodeo................**$55.00**
Bowl, chili; Westward Ho (brands only), 5¾"................**$55.00**
Bowl, El Rancho, 5"................**$45.00**
Bowl, Hibiscus, 2x5"................**$45.00**
Bowl, mixing; Rodeo, 10¼"................**$415.00**
Bowl, mixing; Westward Ho, 10"................**$495.00**
Bowl, salad; Banana Leaf................**$35.00**
Bowl, soup; Rodeo, 14-oz................**$22.50**
Bowl, vegetable; Boots & Saddle, oval, 12"................**$200.00**
Bowl, vegetable; El Rancho, oval, 12"................**$160.00**
Bowl, vegetable; Rodeo, oval, 12"................**$225.00**
Butter pat, Chuck Wagon................**$50.00**
Creamer, El Rancho................**$105.00**

Creamer & sugar bowl, Rodeo, individual................**$140.00**
Cup, Shadowleaf................**$30.00**
Cup & saucer, demitasse; Westward Ho (brands only)..**$125.00**
Cup & saucer, El Rancho................**$65.00**
Cup & saucer, pink flamingo, 3", 5¼"................**$45.00**
Mug, Chuck Wagon................**$85.00**
Napkin ring, Westward Ho, brands only................**$75.00**
Pitcher, water; Boots & Saddle................**$350.00**
Pitcher, water; Rodeo, 72-oz................**$425.00**
Pitcher, water; Shadow Banana Palm, 7½"................**$415.00**
Plate, Boots & Saddle, 7"................**$40.00**
Plate, Boots & Saddle, 10½"................**$80.00**
Plate, child's; Little Buckaroo, from $100 to................**$125.00**
Plate, Chuck Wagon, 7"................**$27.50**
Plate, Dahlia, blue, 9"................**$45.00**
Plate, El Rancho, 7¼"................**$65.00**
Plate, grill; El Rancho................**$65.00**
Plate, grill; Magnolia, 9½", from $35 to................**$45.00**
Plate, Poppy, Restaurantware, 7"................**$22.50**
Plate, Rodeo, 11"................**$80.00**
Plate, Shadowleaf, 7"................**$15.00**
Plate, Shadowleaf, 9"................**$27.00**
Platter, El Rancho, 11½"................**$95.00**
Platter, Longhorn, oval, 15¼"................**$180.00**
Platter, Pioneer Trails, Till Goodan, 15¼"................**$200.00**
Salt & pepper shakers, Rodeo, pr................**$125.00**
Sugar bowl, Rodeo, w/lid................**$125.00**

Watt Pottery

The Watt Pottery Company operated in Crooksville, Ohio, from 1922 until sometime in 1935. It appeals to collectors of country antiques, since the body is yellow ware and its decoration rather quaint.

Several patterns were made: Apple, Autumn Foliage, Cherry, Dutch Tulip, Morning-Glory, Pansy, Rooster, Tear Drop, Starflower, and Tulip among them. All were executed in bold brush strokes of primary colors. Some items you'll find will also carry a stenciled advertising message, made for retail companies as premiums for their customers.

For further study, we recommend *Watt Pottery, An Identification and Price Guide,* by Sue and Dave Morris, published by Collector Books.

Advisor: Sue Morris (See Directory, Watt Pottery)

Club/Newsletter:
Watt's News
Watt Collectors Association
c/o Marty Evans
P.O. Box 30561
Winston-Salem, NC 27104
Subscription: $12 per year

Apple, bottle, oil & vinegar; #126, w/lids, 7", pr...**$1,800.00**
Apple, bowl, #067, w/lid, 6½x8½" dia................**$125.00**

Apple, bowl, #106, 3½x10¾" dia $350.00

Apple, bowl, cereal/salad; #23, apple on inside only, 1½x5¾" dia $75.00

Apple, bowl, cereal/salad; #52, 2¼x6½" dia $50.00

Apple, bowl, mixing; #65, 5¾x8½" dia....................$90.00

Apple, bowl, mixing; ribbed, #9, 5x9" dia..................$85.00

Apple, bowl, spaghetti; #44, 1½x8" dia $400.00

Apple, canister, #72, lg, 9½x7" dia..........................$500.00

Apple, casserole, #18, French handled, 4x8"............$225.00

Apple, casserole, #18, tab handled, 4x5" dia............$225.00

Apple, casserole warmer, electric, 2x7" $1,000.00

Apple, cheese crock, #80, 8x8½" dia....................$1,500.00

Apple, cookie jar, #503, 8¼" $450.00

Apple, fondue, w/out lid, 3x9"..............................$900.00

Apple, mug, #61, 3" $500.00

Apple, pitcher, #17, no ice lip, 8" $300.00

Apple, plate, dinner; 9½"......................................$450.00

Apple, plate, divided; lg shaded leaves, 10½" $2,000.00

Apple, teapot, #112, 6x9"..................................$1,500.00

Apple, tumbler, #56, 4½"...................................$1,000.00

Autumn Foliage, baker, w/lid, #98, marked Watt Oven Ware USA, 5¾x8½", dia..................$90.00

Autumn Foliage, bowl, #106, marked Watt Orchard Ware, 3½x10¾" dia $85.00

Autumn Foliage, bowl, cereal; #94, marked Watt Oven Ware USA, 1¾x6" dia $30.00

Autumn Foliage, ice bucket, w/lid, no bottom mark, 7¼x7½" dia $200.00

Autumn Foliage, mug, #121, marked Watt USA, 3¾x3" dia $200.00

Autumn Foliage, salt & pepper shakers, hourglass shape, raised letters (S or P) in front, 4½x2½" dia, pr..$190.00

Autumn Foliage, sugar bowl, w/lid, #98, marked USA, 4½" $300.00

Banded (Blue & White), bowl, mixing; 2¾x5"............$25.00

Banded (Green), bowl, #7, 7" dia $25.00

Banded (White), pitcher, 7" $85.00

Brown Banded, coffeepot, w/lid, #115, marked Watt Orchard Ware USA, 9¾"..................$850.00

Brown Banded, mug, #121, marked Watt USA, 3¾"..$125.00

Butterfly, ice bicket, w/lid, no bottom mark, very rare, 7¼x7½" dia $800.00

Cherry, bowl, cereal/salad; cherry on inside, #23, 1½x5¾" dia $50.00

Cherry, bowl, spaghetti; #39, 3x13" dia $150.00

Cherry, pitcher, w/advertising, #15, 5½"..................$175.00

Cherry, salt shaker, barrel shape, no bottom mark, 4" ..$90.00

Cut-Leaf Pansy, bowl, spaghetti; 3x13" dia..................$80.00

Cut-Leaf Pansy, plate, bull's-eye pattern, 7½" dia.......$55.00

Cut-Leaf Pansy, plate, pie; 9" dia $150.00

Cut-Leaf Pansy, platter, 15" dia..............................$110.00

Cut-Leaf Pansy, saucer, bull's-eye pattern w/red swirls, 6½" dia $20.00

Dogwood, bowl, serving; marked Watt Oven Ware USA, 3x15"..................$110.00

Double Apple, bowl, #73, 4x9" dia..........................$125.00

Double Apple, bowl, mixing; #8, 4½x8" dia.............$175.00

Double Apple, creamer, #62, 4¼x4½" $400.00

Dutch Tulip, bean pot, handles, #76, 6½x7½" dia ...$350.00

Dutch Tulip, bowl, #6, 3½x6" dia..........................$100.00

Dutch Tulip, pitcher, refrigerator; sq, #69, 8"..........$600.00

Eagle, bowl, mixing; #12, marked Oven Ware USA, 6x12"..$145.00

Eagle, pitcher, w/ice lip, no bottom mark, rare, 8" ..$450.00

Goodies, jar, #76, marked Watt Oven Ware USA, 6½x7½"..................$275.00

Kla Ham'rd, pie plate, #43-13, marked Oven Ware Kla Ham'rd Made in USA, 1½x9" dia..................$45.00

Morning Glory, cookie jar, #95, marked Watt Oven Ware USA, 10¾x7½" dia..................$400.00

Morning Glory (Yellow), bowl, mixing; #6, marked Watt Oven Ware USA, 3½x6"..................$75.00

Old Pansy, casserole, #3/19, 5x9" dia..................$75.00

Old Pansy, pitcher, crosshatch pattern, 7x7¾"..........$275.00

Old Pansy, platter, #49, 12" dia $85.00

Old Pansy, platter, crosshatch pattern, 15" dia..........$175.00

Raised Pansy, casserole, French-handled, individual, 3¾x7½"..................$90.00

Rooster, bowl, #67, marked 67 USA, no lid, 3½x8¼"..$90.00

Rooster, bowl, spaghetti; 3x13" $375.00

Rooster, bowl, w/lid, #05, 4x5" dia..........................$190.00

Rooster, casserole, French handled, individual, #18, 4"..$245.00

Rooster, ice bucket, w/lid, 7¼x7½" dia..................$275.00

Rooster, pitcher, #15, 5½" $145.00

Rooster, pitcher, #16, $165.00.

Starflower, bowl, #39, 3x13" $110.00

Starflower, bowl, berry; 1½x5¾" dia..........................$35.00

Starflower, casserole, #54, 6x8½" dia......................$125.00

Starflower, cookie jar, w/lid, #21, 7½" $185.00

Starflower, grease jar, #47, 5x4½"..........................$250.00

Starflower, ice bucket, 7¼x7½" dia..........................$185.00

Starflower, mug, #121, 3"....................................$275.00

Starflower, pitcher, refrigerator; #69, sq shape, 8" $700.00

Starflower, platter, #31, 15" dia..............................$110.00

Starflower, salt & pepper shakers, red & green bands, barrel shape, 4", pr..................$375.00

Starflower (Green-on-Brown), bowl, spaghetti; #39, 3x13" dia..................$90.00

Starflower (Green-on-Brown), cookie jar, w/lid, #21, 7½"..**$125.00**

Starflower (Green-on-Brown), platter, #31, 15" dia.....**$90.00**

Starflower (Pink-on-Black), casserole, w/lid, 4½x8¾" dia...**$125.00**

Starflower (Pink-on-Green), plate, dinner; 10" dia ...**$100.00**

Starflower (White-on-Blue), bowl, spaghetti; #39, very rare, 3x13"...**$250.00**

Starflower (White-on-Green), bowl, 3x13" dia..........**$125.00**

Starflower (White-on-Red), mug, #121, rare, 3¾x3" .**$400.00**

Tear Drop, bowl, #66, 3x7"..**$45.00**

Tear Drop, bowl, #73, 4x9½"......................................**$130.00**

Tear Drop, casserole, w/lid, no bottom mark, 6x8" .**$850.00**

Tear Drop, cheese crock, w/lid, #80, 8x8¼" dia.......**$375.00**

Tear Drop, pitcher, refrigerator; sq, #69, 8".............**$500.00**

Tulip, bowl, #73, 4x9½" dia.......................................**$150.00**

Tulip, creamer, #62, 4¼"..**$225.00**

Tulip, pitcher, #15, 5½"...**$550.00**

White Daisy, pitcher, marked Eve-N-Bake Watt Ware Oven Ware USA, 7"..**$165.00**

Woodgrain, bowl, w/lid, #608 W, marked Oven Ware, 7½x9"...**$65.00**

Woodgrain, cookie barrel, #617W, marked Oven Ware 617W, 11x8" dia...**$90.00**

Woodgrain, pitcher, #615W, marked Oven Ware, 9".**$100.00**

Weeping Gold

In the mid- to late 1950s, many American pottery companies produced lines of 'Weeping Gold.' Such items have a distinctive appearance; most appear to be covered with irregular droplets of lustrous gold, sometimes heavy, sometimes fine. On others the gold is in random swirls, or there may be a definite pattern developed on the surface. In fact, real gold was used; however, there is no known successful way of separating the gold from the pottery. You'll see similar pottery covered in 'Weeping Silver.' Very often, ceramic whiskey decanters made for Beam, McCormick, etc., will be trimmed in 'Weeping Gold.' Among the marks you'll find on these wares are 'McCoy,' 'Kingwood Ceramics,' and 'USA,' but most items are simply stamped '22k (or 24k) gold.'

Basket, woven look, sm open handles, Holley Ross 22k Gold, 3½x4" **$27.50**

Bell, w/original clapper, 5¾" **$20.00**

Bowl, incurvate scalloped rim, marked Hand Decorated Weeping Gold Brite Gold USA, 4x6" dia **$15.00**

Candy dish, leaf shape, marked Hand Decorated Weeping Brite Gold USA Holley Ross, 10x6¼"....................**$22.00**

Candy dish/compote, unmarked, 3¾x5⅝" **$22.00**

Creamer & sugar bowl, w/lid, on 7¾x4¾" tray, all marked Hand Decorated Weeping Bright Gold **$38.00**

Figurine, elephant, 8¾x10x3½" **$40.00**

Novelty, Victorian shoe, Distinguished China 22k Gold, 2½x5½" **$25.00**

Pitcher, ewer form w/slender foot, bulb center, 8¾x3½" **$32.50**

Planters, swan mother (5x8"), 2 babies (2½x2¼"), marked Hand Decorated 22k Gold USA Weeping Brite Gold..**$20.00**

Salt & pepper shakers, 22k gold, 3½", pr...................**$25.00**

Teapot, angle handle, Hand Painted 22k Gold USA Weeping Bright Gold, 7"..**$55.00**

Tray, advertising; Weeping Gold in script in center, 4¾x7¾"..**$25.00**

Vase, cornucopia form on base, 3½", pr **$35.00**

Vase, marked Bel-Terr China 22k, 7" **$18.00**

Vase, pillow form w/embossed flower, sm foot, 6x4".....**$20.00**

Vase, Savoy China Hand Decorated 24k gold, 12", from $35.00 to $40.00.

Vase, slim waisted form w/embossed floral decor, slightly scalloped rim, 12" **$40.00**

Vase, tulip; marked Hand Decorated 22k Gold USA Weeping Brite Gold, 7" **$18.00**

Wall pocket, swan form, 5¾x5"...................................**$25.00**

Weil Ware

Though the Weil company made dinnerware and some kitchenware, their figural pieces are attracting the most collector interest. They were in business from the 1940s until the mid-1950s, another of the small but very successful California companies whose work has become so popular today. They dressed their 'girls' in beautiful gowns of vivid rose, light dusty pink, turquoise blue, and other lovely colors enhanced with enameled 'lace work' and flowers, sgraffito, sometimes even with tiny applied blossoms. Both paper labels and ink stamps were used to mark them, but as you study their features, you'll soon learn to recognize even those that have lost their labels over the years. Four-number codes and decorators' initials are usually written on their bases.

If you want to learn more, we recommend *The Collector's Encyclopedia of California Pottery, Second Edition,* by Jack Chipman.

Ashtray, Malay Bambu, 6x4" **$15.00**

Bowl, Malay Blossom, rectangular, 9x7x3" **$25.00**

Bowl, Malay Blossom, 2¼x8½" sq $20.00

Bowl, rose inside, green outside, scalloped edge, #735, 6¼"
    sq $20.00

Bowl, serving; Malay Bambu, 11½" $30.00

Bowl, vegetable; Malay Blossom, w/lid, 9x5½x4" $40.00

Candle holder/shelf sitter, Oriental lady in yellow dress &
    yellow flowers in hair sits w/holder on ea side...$25.00

Cigarette box, Malay Bambu...............................$25.00

Cup & saucer, Malay Blossom $12.00

Dish, serving; Malay Blossoms, 4-part, 10½" sq.........$40.00

Figurine, boy in blue shirt w/pink details holds flowers,
    stands before cream wall, #4033, 10¾"................$55.00

Figurine, lady in purple dress w/blue floral design, gown
    drops off 1 shoulder, 11".....................................$55.00

Figurine, Oriental girl in yellow shirt w/rose-colored details,
    rose-colored pants, holding black scarf, #3056, 8½".$30.00

Flower holder, lady in blue dress w/black details sits on front
    of white receptacle, 9½" $60.00

Flower holder, lady in blue dress w/floral design, purple scarf
    & belt, stands in between 2 pillars, #4027, 11".......$70.00

Flower holder, lady in blue dress w/flower decor & yellow
    scarf sits between 2 sm white vases, 7½x7".........$62.00

Flower holder, lady in pink dress w/flower decor stands
    before cornucopia vase, #4026, 11"......................$70.00

Flower holder, lady in yellow dress w/pink & blue floral
    design, stands beside blue vase, 10" $45.00

Flower holder, young lady in pale blue dress w/sailboat design
    sits on white base w/sailboat design, 10¼" $50.00

Gravy boat, Malay Blossom, from $18 to $22.00

Pitcher, Rose, 6-cup, 6½" $55.00

Pitcher, syrup/milk; Malay Blossom, sq, 4½" $18.00

Planter, Ming Tree, 3x5" sq.....................................$25.00

Plate, Climbing Rose, 8" sq......................................$10.00

Plate, dinner; Malay Blossom, 9¾", set of 4, from $50 to...$60.00

Plate, Malay Blossom, 5½" sq...................................$10.00

Plate, relish; Malay Blossom, 3 sections, 9¼x6"..........$20.00

Platter, Malay Bambu, 13x9", from $30 to $35.00

Platter, Malay Blossom, rectangular, 11x7"...................$22.50

Platter, snack; Birchwood, 4-part, 11½" sq $35.00

Salt cellar, flower shape, turquoise, 3" dia...................$6.00

Saucer, Malay Bambu, 6" dia $7.00

Snack set, Malay Bambu, sq cup on 9¼x5½" tray......$25.00

Sugar bowl, Malay Bambu, w/lid, 4½" $20.00

Tidbit, Malay Blossom, 1-tier, metal handle, 9½".......$20.00

Tidbit, Malay Blossom, 3-tier, metal handle, 15".........$35.00

Vase, Ming Tree, sq top w/round bottom, 8" $20.00

Vase, Ming Tree, 6" sq...$28.00

Wall pocket, Oriental lady in ruby red sitting on bench
    w/decorated vase on ea side, #4045.....................$28.00

Weller

Though the Weller Pottery has been closed since 1948,
they were so prolific that you'll be sure to see several pieces
anytime you're 'antiquing.' They were one of the largest of
the art pottery giants that located in the Zanesville, Ohio,
area, using locally dug clays to produce their wares. In the
early years, they made hand-decorated vases, jardinieres,
lamps, and other useful and decorative items for the home,
many of which were signed by notable artists such as
Fredrick Rhead, John Lessell, Virginia Adams, Anthony
Dunlavy, Dorothy England, Albert Haubrich, Hester
Pillsbury, E.L. Pickens, and Jacques Sicard, to name only a
few. Some of their early lines were First and Second Dickens,
Eocean, Sicardo, Etna, Louwelsa, Turada, and Aurelian.
Portraits of Indians, animals of all types, lady golfers, nudes,
and scenes of Dickens stories were popular themes, and
some items were overlaid with silver filigree. These lines are
rather hard to find at this point in time, and prices are generally high; but there's plenty of their later production still
around, and some pieces are relatively inexpensive.

If you'd like to learn more, we recommend *The Collector's
Encyclopedia of Weller Pottery* by Sharon and Bob Huxford.

Arcadia, covered dish, embossed leaf decor w/leaf finial on
    lid, #A-8, from $55 to $65.00

Arcadia, vase, jar shape w/allover embossed berries & leaves,
    upright rim, flat bottom, #A-6, from $75 to.............$85.00

Atlas, bowl, 5-point star-shaped opening, #C-3, 4", from $85
    to $95.00

Atlas, dish, 5-point star shape, #C-2, 2", from $45 to .$50.00

Atlas, vase, upright 6-point star shape, #C-10, 13", from $175
    to $225.00

Barcelona, ewer, ribbed bulbous form w/slim neck, painted
    floral medallion, 9½", from $225 to $275.00

Barcelona, vase, ribbed tumbler form, painted decor, 7", from
    $175 to $200.00

Blossom, cylindrical w/scalloped rim, flared scalloped base,
    fancy handles, embossed flowers, 9½", from $60 to..$70.00

Blossom, double cornucopia, embossed flower decor, 6½",
    from $50 to...$60.00

Blossom, ewer, squat/bulbous form w/slim neck, ruffled rim,
    fancy handle, embossed flowers, 7", from $75 to..$85.00

Blossom, vase, bulbous w/trumpet neck, scalloped rim, fancy
    handles, embossed flowers, 9½", from $85 to........$95.00

Blue Drapery, jardiniere, tapered pot w/lipped rim, embossed
    roses on drapery-type ground, 5", from $100 to......$125.00

Blue Drapery, wall pocket, conical form w/embossed roses
    on drapery-type ground, 9", from $200 to.........$250.00

Bonito, candle holder, footed bowl w/high looped handles,
    painted swags, 3½", from $100 to......................$125.00

Bonito, vase, heart shape w/upturned scrolled handles, foot-
    ed, painted ferns, 5", from $100 to $145.00

Bonito, vase, tapered urn w/scrolled tab handles, painted floral
    bouquet tied w/blue bow, 10½", from $350 to......$450.00

Bouquet, console bowl, scrolled tab handles, embossed
    flowers, #B-12, 5x12½", from $50 to.....................$60.00

Bouquet, pillow vase, tulip-shaped rim, footed, embossed
    flowers, #B-5, 5½", from $45 to...........................$50.00

Bouquet, pitcher, cylindrical w/slightly flared rim, round
    base, embossed jonquils, #B-17, from $75 to.......$85.00

Bouquet, pitcher, embossed jonquils, #B-18, 9½", from $125
    to..$175.00

Bouquet, vase, long cylindrical neck w/bulbous body, fluted rim, embossed jonquils, 15", from $150 to **$200.00**

Cactus, camel planter, glossy tan, 4", from $100 to ..**$125.00**

Cactus, Chanticleer Rooster, 7", from $500 to **$600.00**

Cactus, horse planter, glossy tan, from $100 to **$125.00**

Cameo, basket, 4-footed ball shape w/ornate scrolled handle, white embossed flowers on pastel, 7½", from $75 to **$85.00**

Cameo, ewer, bulbous w/single ring around neck, fancy handle, white embossed flowers on pastel, 10", from $65 to **$75.00**

Cameo, vase, trumpet form on pedestal base w/scrolled handles, white embossed flowers on pastel, 7", from $45 to **$50.00**

Chengtu, covered jar, upturned handles, footed, Chinese Red, 8", from $200 to **$250.00**

Chengtu, vase, paneled cylinder tapering to flat bottom, lipped rim, Chinese Red, 11", from $150 to **$175.00**

Classic, fan vase, cut-out scallops w/embossed flowers form rim, 5", from $75 to **$85.00**

Classic, plate, cut-out scallops & embossed flowers form rim, 11½", from $60 to **$70.00**

Coppertone, ashtray, textured bowl w/frog on rim, 6½", from $175 to **$225.00**

Coppertone, basket, fan shape w/embossed floral motif, branch handle, 8½", from $175 to **$225.00**

Coppertone, candle holder, w/figural turtle & flower bud, 3", from $225 to **$275.00**

Coppertone, fan vase, 8", from $700.00 to $800.00; tray, 15", from $900.00 to $1,000.00; bowl, 10½" long, from $500.00 to $600.00.

Coppertone, flowerpot w/saucer, textured green finish, 5", from $175 to **$250.00**

Cornish, bowl, squatty w/embossed berry & leaf design on ribbed band, sm scrolled handles, 7½", from $50 to **$60.00**

Cornish, vase, cylindrical w/flared & angled bottom, tiny scrolled tab handles, berry & leaf design, 10", from $95 to..**$120.00**

Creamware, candle holder, sq column w/sq handles, cameo decor, 11", from $115 to **$140.00**

Creamware, compote, open design around rim of bowl w/sm angled handles, pedestal foot, 6", from $150 to..**$200.00**

Creamware, Decorated; teapot, decaled floral decor, 5½", from $100 to..**$125.00**

Creamware, Decorated; vase, lg painted flower, 11½", from $300 to..**$400.00**

Darsie, flowerpot, flared scalloped rim, flat bottom, embossed tasseled rope swag design, 5½", from $50 to **$60.00**

Darsie, vase, tapered bowl w/deeply scalloped rim, embossed tasseled rope swag design, 5½", from $60 to **$70.00**

Delsa, ewer, squat/bulbous body w/upright spout, embossed pansies on textured ground, #10, 7", from $55 to..**$65.00**

Delsa, vase, bulbous w/flared scalloped rim, branch handles, ribbed pedestal base, blossom branch, 6", from $45 to..**$55.00**

Delsa, vase, bulbous w/thick trumpet neck, scalloped rim, footed, embossed blossom branch, 7", from $40 to........**$45.00**

Elberta, bowl, 3-part irregular form, shaded greens & browns, 3½", from $75 to **$85.00**

Elberta, candle holder, canoe shape w/open handles, shaded greens & browns, 3", from $75 to....................**$85.00**

Elberta, console bowl, canoe shape w/open handles, shaded greens & browns, 6x11½", from $90 to.............**$115.00**

Fleron, bowl, ribbed w/everted scalloped rim, #J-6, 3", from $75 to..**$100.00**

Fleron, vase, ribbed bulbous form w/fluted rim, tab handles, 8", from $125 to..**$175.00**

Fleron, vase, ribbed urn w/flared rim, ear-shaped handles, 19½", from $500 to..**$750.00**

Florenzo, basket, fluted flared shape w/embossed flowers on handle, 5½", from $115 to **$140.00**

Florenzo, double bud vase, fluted vessels w/connecting handle, 2 embossed flowers & leaves at base, 5½", from $60 to..**$75.00**

Florenzo, vase, 4-footed & ribbed w/slightly flared scalloped rim, embossed fruit & flower decor, 7", from $90 to.......**$100.00**

Florenzo, vase, 4-footed pot w/frog cover, ribbed & scalloped w/bud finial, 7", from $125 to **$150.00**

Forest, hanging basket, woodland scene, 8", from $200 to..**$250.00**

Forest, teapot, woodland scene, 4½", from $250 to.**$300.00**

Forest, window box, oblong w/woodland scene, 5½x14½", from $400 to..**$500.00**

Gloria, vase, ornate fan shape w/open handles & scrolled base, scalloped, embossed floral, #G-14, 6½", from $50 to..**$60.00**

Gloria, vase, 4-footed swirled pot w/fluted rim, embossed butterfly & flower design, #G-13, from $100 to .**$125.00**

Gloria, vase, 4-footed treen trunk form w/irregular rim, embossed iris & leaf decor, 12½", from $100 to ..**$125.00**

Goldenglow, bud vase, cylindrical w/embossed leaf design, 3-footed, 8½", from $100 to **$125.00**

Goldenglow, console bowl, 4-footed oblong form w/ribbon tab handles, embossed leaf design, 3½x16", from $100 to..**$125.00**

Goldenglow, vase, high/low handles on footed cylindrical form w/slightly flared rim, ribbed base, 8½", from $150 to...**$175.00**

Goldenglow, vase, 3-footed conical form w/embossed leaf design, 6", from $100 to......................................**$125.00**

Greenbriar, high/low handles on jar w/angled base, flat bottom, drip glaze on smooth surface, 7½", from $150 to...**$175.00**

Greenbriar, vase, ribbed bulbous form w/irregular handles from rim, drip glaze, 9½", from $225 to............**$275.00**

Greora, flower frog, stepped form, mottled & shaded brown texture, 4½", from $110 to.................................**$135.00**

Greora, strawberry pot, mottled & shaded brown texture, 8½", from $225 to...**$275.00**

Greora, vase, cylindrical w/slightly flared rim & base, mottled & shaded brown texture, 11½", from $225 to....**$275.00**

Hudson, vase, signed McLaughlin, 8", from $1,500.00 to $1,600.00; White and Decorated, vase, 9½", from $1,100.00 to $1,200.00.

Lido, basket, swirled pot w/3 corners forming handle at ruffled rim, 8½", from $85 to.....................................**$95.00**

Lido, cornucopia, scrolled tail meeting deeply fluted rim, scalloped base, 5", from $35 to **$45.00**

Lido, vase, cylindrical 3-petal floral shape w/ring around flared leaves forming base, 12", from $80 to........**$85.00**

Lorbeek, flower frog, leaping gazell, 7", from $175 to...**$225.00**

Loru, bowl, scalloped rim, footed, embossed leaves, 4", from $45 to...**$50.00**

Loru, vase, cylindrical w/slightly flared scalloped rim & base, embossed leafy branch decor, 8½", from $70 to..**$80.00**

Loru, vase, vertical panels w/flared scalloped rim, footed, embossed leaves aound bottom, 11½", from $95 to...**$110.00**

Malverne, boat bowl, embossed bud & leaf decor on textured ground w/integral branch handles, 5½x11", from $110 to..**$135.00**

Malverne, pillow vase, embossed bud & leaf decor on textured ground, 8½", from $125 to.........................**$175.00**

Manhattan, pitcher, cylindrical w/ear-shaped handle at plain rim, embossed flower stems & leaves, 10", from $100 to .**$125.00**

Manhattan, urn w/ribbed band near rim, ear-shaped handles, embossed leaves & flowers in random pattern, 8", from $80 to..**$85.00**

Melrose, vase, bowl w/deeply fluted rim, branch handles, rose branch decor, 5x7", from $100 to...............**$125.00**

Melrose, vase, urn w/comma-shaped indents, fluted rim, branch handles, rose branch decor, 5", from $85 to..............**$95.00**

Mi-Flo, vase, bulbous w/fancy angled handles, trumpet neck, round base, stemmed flowers, #M-12, 9½", from $150 to...**$175.00**

Noval, bowl, tapered, black-trimmed panels on white w/applied apple & berry decor, 3½x9½", from $85 to...**$95.00**

Noval, compote, bowl on tall pedestal base, black trim on white w/applied apple & berry decor, 5½", from $90 to...**$115.00**

Novelty Line, ashtray, 3 pigs, 4", from $125 to........**$150.00**

Novelty Line, tray, seal, 3x5½", from $100 to..........**$125.00**

Oak Leaf, basket, 4-corners come together to form handle w/acorn finial, embossed oak leaves, 9½", from $100 to...**$125.00**

Oak Leaf, vase, flat-sided pitcher form (handleless), embossed oak leaf decor, 8½", from $75 to........**$85.00**

Oak Leaf, wall pocket, conical form, embossed decor, 8½", from $125 to...**$150.00**

Panella, cornucopia, scalloped rim, embossed pansy decor, 5½", from $45 to...**$55.00**

Panella, vase, bulbous w/long neck, fancy angled handles, pedestal foot, embossed pansy decor, 9", from $60 to.................**$70.00**

Panella, wall pocket, ruffled & flared rim, embossed pansy decor, 8", from $125 to...**$150.00**

Paragon, bowl vase, incised allover flower & leaf decor, 4½", from $150 to...**$175.00**

Paragon, vase, bulbous urn w/straight-sided rim, incised allover flower & leaf decor, 6½", from $275 to..**$325.00**

Pastel, circle vase, flat-sided w/embossed fan-type decor, 6", from $45 to...**$50.00**

Pastel, footed swirled boat form, #P-5, 4x8", from $35 to..**$40.00**

Pastel, pitcher, embossed fan-like decor makes up part of rim, 10", from $60 to **$70.00**

Patra, basket, textured w/embossed floral handle, footed, 5½", from $175 to...**$225.00**

Patra, jardiniere, bowl w/embossed floral motif within V shape at scalloped rim, textured ground, 6", from $225 to...**$250.00**

Patricia, bowl, figural ducks form lid, 7", from $150 to ..**$200.00**

Patricia, pelican planter, 5", from $95 to...................**$110.00**

Pearl, basket, 4-footed, embossed pearl & rose swags, 6½", from $200 to...**$250.00**

Pearl, bud vase, cylindrical w/embossed pearl & rose swags, 7", from $100 to **$125.00**

Pierre, cookie jar, embossed basketweave pattern, 10", from $100 to...**$150.00**

Pierre, creamer, embossed basketweave pattern, 2", from $100 to...**$15.00**

Pierre, pitcher, embossed basketweave pattern, 5", from $40 to...**$45.00**

Raydance, vase, bulbous w/trumpet neck, scalloped rim, scrolled handles, ribbed base, embossed leaf design, 8".........**$50.00**

Roba, cornucopia, ruffled rim, scrolled base, embossed blossom branch decor, 5½", from $5 to **$50.00**

Roba, ewer, bulbous w/ruffled rim, ear-shaped handle, round base, embossed blossom branch decor, 11", from $125 to...**$175.00**

Roba, planter, flared scalloped rim, footed, embossed blossom branch decor, 4½", from $80 to **$90.00**

Rosemont, jardiniere, slightly tapered pot w/apple branch decor on black & white lattice background, 5", from $125 to...**$150.00**

Rosemont, jardiniere, slightly tapered pot w/bluebird on blossom branch on cream, integral handles, 7", from $300 to...**$350.00**

Rudlor, vase, bulbous w/beaded handles, embossed flowers & leaves, 6", from $50 to.......................................**$60.00**

Rudlor, vase, cylindrical w/handles, embossed flowers, 6½", from $45 to...**$50.00**

Rudlor, vase, cylindrical w/slight tapering at rim, angled handles, round base, embossed flower branch, 8", from $30 to...**$35.00**

Sabrinian, basket, double shell bowl w/handle, 7", from $250 to...**$300.00**

Sabrinian, bowl, irregular shape w/embossed sea motif interior, 2½x9", from $150 to.....................................**$190.00**

Scenic, pillow vase, embossed lake scene, #S-11, 7½", from $85 to...**$95.00**

Scenic, vase, shaped like money bag w/embossed scene on flat side, fluted rim, open handles, footed, #S-14, from $150 to...**$175.00**

Scenic, vase, 3-footed bulbous style w/ruffled rim, embossed palm tree decor, #S-4, from $65 to........................**$75.00**

Softone, cornucopia, 8½", from $30 to **$35.00**

Softone, ewer, embossed swag design, loop handle at rim, 9½", from $50 to...**$60.00**

Softone, hanging basket, 10", from $100 to...............**$125.00**

Stellar, vase, star motif on urn w/upright rim, 5½", from $400 to...**$500.00**

Sydonia, double candle holder, flower-shaped cups on scrolled base, 2-tone mottled texture, 7", from $100 to...**$125.00**

Sydonia, planter, fluted fan shape on round base, 2-tone mottled texture, 3½", from $35 to **$45.00**

Sydonia, triple bud vase, 3 cone shapes on round base, 2-tone mottled texture, 8½", from $95 to **$120.00**

Turkis, bowl vase, upturned handles, drip glaze over dark plum, 4", from $55 to **$65.00**

Turkis, vase, bulbous w/embossed detail, slightly tapered neck, flat bottom, drip glaze over dark plum, 5", from $75 to...**$85.00**

Turkis, vase, w/handles, drip glaze on dark plum, 7½", from $125 to...**$150.00**

Tutone, basket, canoe shape w/embossed flower & leaf decor, leaf handle, 7½", from $125 to **$150.00**

Tutone, candle holders, 3-footed triangular form, 2½", pr, from $100 to...**$125.00**

Tutone, vase, sq w/rounded corners & irregular rim, pancake base, 12½", from $200 to **$250.00**

Tutone, vase, 3-sided w/embossed flower & leaf decor, triangular base, 6", from $75 to............................**$85.00**

Utility Ware, covered jar, crosshatched color bands, 4½", from $30 to...**$40.00**

Utility Ware, teapot, pumpkin form w/handle, stem finial, 8", from $125 to...**$150.00**

Utility Ware, water bottle, upright gourd shape on underplate, 11", from $75 to...**$100.00**

Velva, console bowl, lipped rim, upturned tab handles, footed, paneled flower & leaf design, 3½x12½", from $85 to...**$95.00**

Velva, shouldered w/upright rim, upturned tab handles, footed, single panel w/leaf & flower decor, 9½", from $95 to...**$115.00**

Warwick, basket, wood-textured w/branch handle, folded-over ruffled rim, 9", from $175 to **$225.00**

Warwick, jardiniere, embossed bud & branch decor on textured wood-look ground, 7", from $125 to **$150.00**

Wild Rose, basket, ball shape, 5½", from $50 to **$60.00**

Wild Rose, vase, cylindrical w/closed handles, lg embossed rose on branch decor, 6½", from $30 to...............**$35.00**

Wild Rose, vase, 4-footed trumpet shape w/closed handles, lg embossed rose on branch decor, 7½", from $40 to...**$45.00**

Woodcraft, bowl, 4-footed, scalloped rim, embossed woodland scene w/squirrel, 3½", from $100 to **$125.00**

Woodcraft, fan vase, embossed fruit tree decor, 8", from $100 to...**$125.00**

Woodcraft, mug, tree-trunk form w/embossed fox family, 6", from $250 to...**$300.00**

Woodrose, jardiniere, wooden bucket form w/embossed rose motif, handled, 7", from $125 to **$175.00**

Woodrose, vase, wooden bucket form w/embosed rose motif, no handles, 7", from $75 to **$85.00**

Zona, bowl, painted embossed rabbit & bird on tapered sides, 5½", from $95 to **$110.00**

Zona, compot lg flowers w/leaves on textured bowl w/thick pedestal foot, 5½", from $100 to.........................**$125.00**

Zona, pickle dish, cream oval dish w/brown branch handle, 11", from $85 to...**$95.00**

Zona, vase, apple branch on cream, sm brown branch handles, brown rolled rim, 9", from $150 to............**$175.00**

West Coast Pottery

This was a small company operating in the '40s and '50s in Burbank, California. The founders were Lee and Bonnie Wollard; they produced decorative pottery such as is listed here. For more information on this company as well as many others, we recommend *The Collector's Encyclopedia of California Pottery, Second Edition,* by Jack Chipman (Collector Books).

Bowl, flowing flared rim, #610, 3¼x12" dia **$15.00**

Candle holders, bow-tie shape, creamy white, 2½x5" dia, pr...$18.00

Dish, dark green, 2 lg oval handles, cornucopia finial on lid, oval, #29, 3¾x8"..$15.00

Figurine, 2 horses, #461, 3x8½"....................$22.50

Planter, rose over gray, #217, 13x5"..............$35.00

Planter, snail form, creamy white, #206, 5x6"..........$15.00

Vase, embossed leaves, white, 7x5½x3½"............$25.00

Vase, mauve & green, scalloped rim, curved panel sides, #222, 5½x7¼" (at top).....................$25.00

Vase, peacock form, #440, 11"......................$25.00

Vase, rose & green, paneled sides, #469, 9"............$18.00

Vase, sea shell shape, rose, #201, 5½"............$15.00

Vase, stylized basket form, turquoise to mauve, #209, 9x6x3"...$20.00

Vase, yellow, #472, 13"...............................$15.00

Wall pocket, bow, mauve & turquoise, #451, 8x6½", pr..$45.00

Wall pocket, exotic bird w/peacock-like tail down, white, paper label, 14½"................................$32.00

Wall pocket, plume, white, #305, 8½x6¼".........$25.00

Wall pocket, springtime hat, white w/multicolored flowers, 8¼"...$30.00

Western Collectibles

Although the Wild West era ended over one hundred years ago, today cowboy gear is a hot area of collecting. These historic collectibles are not just found out West. Some of the most exceptional pieces have come from the East Coast states and the Midwest. But that should come as no surprise when you consider that the largest manufacturer of bits and spurs was the August Buemann Co. of Newark, New Jersey (1868 – 1926).

For more information refer to *Old West Cowboy Collectibles Auction Update & Price Guide*, which lists auction-realized prices of more than 650 lots, with complete descriptions and numerous photos. You can obtain a copy from our advisor, Dan Hutchins.

Advisor: Dan Hutchins (See Directory, Western Collectibles)

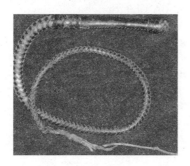

Bull whip, short, from $175.00 to $250.00. (Photo courtesy David L. Wilson)

Bit, basic port-mouth, from $40 to.................$65.00

Bit, jointed mouth w/twist, from $15 to...........$20.00

Branding iron, wrought iron, 2 initials, 1940s, 70x45", EX...$100.00

Branding iron, wrought iron, 3 in circle...........$85.00

Bridle, hand-tooled leather w/bit & reins, ca 1940, 25x6x72"..$75.00

Bridle, leather w/brass tacks, old curb bit, ca 1920s, 27x6"...$70.00

Bronze, long-horn steer, recumbent, on marble base, signed CMR, 5½x7½".......................................$75.00

Bull whip, braided leather w/wooden handle, ca 1900, 60", EX...$120.00

Chaps, leather, batwing type w/conchos, ca 1935, 37" L, EX...$175.00

Collar tips, engraved sterling, marked EH Bohlin, 1940s...$385.00

Hat, black Stetson, 1930s, MIB......................$295.00

Hat, Winchester original Stetson 3X, beaver skin w/leather band, EX..$80.00

Hat rack, buffalo horns...............................$125.00

Holster, hand-tooled leather, marked Meier & Frank Portland Oregon, ca 1920, 9x4".............................$65.00

Reins, braided leather, ornate silver ferrules, fancy, 1930s...$495.00

Saddle, child's, hand-tooled leather w/padded 15" seat, ca 1950, EX...$225.00

Saddle, lady's side; leather, from $375 to.........$550.00

Saddle, youth's, tooled/decor in German silver, EX original...$225.00

Spurs, brass, lady's, rowels, ca 1900, 6½x3", EX......$150.00

Spurs, floral silver inlay, lg rowels, Mexican, 1900s, pr, EX...$200.00

Spurs, nickel-plated w/floral pattern, Crockett, 1950s, pr..$275.00

Spurs, silver & copper lady's leg style w/rowels, ca 1920, 9½x3½"...$300.00

Spurs, silver mounted w/heart, spade, diamond & club design, ca 1920, 11x3¼", EX.....................$450.00

Spurs, silver-mounted star, drop shank, Buermann, pr..$375.00

Spurs, spoke rowels, Mexican, pr from $175 to......$375.00

Stirrups, carved wood, pr, from $45 to.............$75.00

Westmoreland Glass

The Westmoreland Specialty Company was founded in 1889 in Grapeville, Pennsylvania. Their mainstay was a line of opalware (later called milk glass) which included such pieces as cream and sugar sets, novel tea jars (i.e., Teddy Roosevelt Bear Jar, Oriental Tea Jars, and Dutch Tea Jar), as well as a number of covered animal dishes such as hens and roosters on nests. All of these pieces were made as condiment containers and originally held baking soda and Westmoreland's own mustard recipe. By 1900 they had introduced a large variety of pressed tablewares in clear glass and opal, although their condiment containers were still very popular. By 1910 they were making a large line of opal souvenir novelties with hand-painted decorations of palm trees, Dutch scenes, etc. They also made a variety of decorative vases painted in the fashion of Rookwood Pottery, plus sprayed finishes with decorations of flowers, fruits, animals, and Indians. Westmoreland gained great popularity with their line of painted, hand-decorated wares. They also made many fancy-cut items.

These lines continued in production until 1939, when the Brainard family became full owners of the factory. The Brainards discontinued the majority of patterns made previously under the West management and introduced dinnerware lines, made primarily of milk glass, with limited production of black glass and blue milk glass. Colored glass was not put back into full production until 1964 when Westmoreland introduced Golden Sunset, Avocado, Brandywine Blue, and Ruby.

The company made only limited quantities of carnival glass in the early 1900s and then re-introduced it in 1972 when most of their carnival glass was made in limited editions for the Levay Distributing Company. J.H. Brainard, president of Westmoreland, sold the factory to Dave Grossman in 1981, and he, in turn, closed the factory in 1984. Westmoreland first used the stamped W over G logo in 1949 and continued using it until Dave Grossman bought the factory. Mr. Grossman changed the logo to a W with the word Westmoreland forming a circle around the W.

Milk glass was always Westmoreland's main line of production. In the 1950s they became famous for their milk glass tableware in the #1881 'Paneled Grape' pattern. It was designed by Jess Billups, the company's mold maker. The first piece he made was the water goblet. Items were gradually added until a complete dinner service was available. It became their most successful dinnerware line, and today it is highly collectible, primarily because of the excellence of the milk glass itself. No other company has been able to match Westmoreland's milk glass in color, texture, quality, or execution of design and pattern.

For more information see *Westmoreland Glass* by Charles West Wilson (Collector Books).

Advisor: Cheryl Schafer (See Directory, Westmoreland)

Covered Animal Dishes

Duck on wavy base, purple marbled carnival, Levey, 8", $150.00.

Camel, emerald green or turquoise carnival, ea **$175.00**
Cat on rectangular lacy base, Antique Blue **$160.00**

Cat on rectangular lacy base, caramel, green, or purple marbled, ea..**$250.00**
Cat on rectangular lacy base, milk glass....................**$125.00**
Cat on vertical rib base, black carnival or ruby marbled, 5½", ea **$150.00**
Cat on vertical rib base, purple marbled, 5½" **$75.00**
Dove & hand on rectangular lacy base, milk glass ..**$175.00**
Duck on wavy base, Almond, Almond Mist, Antique Blue or Antique Blue Mist, 8x6", ea..................................**$85.00**
Duck on wavy base, caramel, 8x6", ea **$125.00**
Duck on wavy base, crystal, Dark or Light Blue Mist, 8x6", ea **$50.00**
Fox on diamond or lacy base, chocolate or Electric Blue carnival, ea..**$200.00**
Fox on diamond or lacy base, milk glass w/hand-painted realistic fur, ea..**$300.00**
Fox on diamond or lacy base, purple marbled, purple marbled carnival, ruby or green marbled, ea **$275.00**
Fox on lacy base, milk glass......................................**$255.00**
Hen on basketweave base, Antique Blue, Golden Sunset or any mists, 3½", ea..**$30.00**
Hen on basketweave base, milk glass, 3½" **$20.00**
Hen on basketweave base, milk glass w/hand-painted accents, 3½" **$25.00**
Hen on basketweave base, Mint Green w/hand-painted accents, 3½" **$30.00**
Hen on diamond base, Antique Blue, Bermuda Blue or Brandywine Blue, 5½", ea **$60.00**
Hen on diamond base, chocolate, 7½"....................**$195.00**
Hen on diamond base, milk glass, 7½" **$40.00**
Hen on diamond base, purple, green or ruby marbled, 7½", ea **$200.00**
Hen on diamond base, ruby or purple marbled (noniridized), 5½", ea...**$85.00**
Hen on diamond base, ruby or purple marbled carnival, 5½", ea **$100.00**
Hen on lacy base, milk glass, 7½" **$60.00**
Lamb on picket fence base, Antique Blue, 5½".........**$60.00**
Lamb on picket fence base, caramel or purple slag carnival, 5½", ea **$125.00**
Lamb on picket fence base, milk glass, 5½" **$40.00**
Lion on diamond base, Electric Blue carnival (500 made), turquoise or emerald green carnival, 8", ea **$225.00**
Lion on diamond base, milk glass, 8"........................**$150.00**
Lion on diamond base, purple marbled, 8"..............**$200.00**
Lion on lacy base, milk glass, 8" **$175.00**
Lion on picket fence base, milk glass w/blue head, 5½" **$125.00**
Lovebirds on base, black or pink carnival, 6½", ea .**$100.00**
Lovebirds on base, Butterscotch carnival or vaseline (400 made), 6½", ea...**$125.00**
Lovebirds on base, Crystal Mist, Moss Green or olive green, 6½", ea...**$45.00**
Lovebirds on base, dark or light blue, green, pink or Yellow Mist, 6½", ea...**$55.00**
Lovebirds on base, Golden Sunset, Bermuda Blue or Brandywine Blue, 6½", ea **$55.00**

Lovebirds on base, milk glass or milk glass carnival, 6½", ea $50.00

Mother eagle & babies on basketweave, milk glass, 8", ...$130.00

Mother eagle & babies on basketweave base, Crystal Mist top on Brown Mist base, 8" $65.00

Mother eagle & babies on basketweave base, purple marbled carnival (160 made), 8" $250.00

Mother eagle & babies on basketweave base, purple or ruby marbled, 8", ca $200.00

Mother eagle & babies on basketweave base, turquoise carnival (limited edition) or chocolate, 8", ea $225.00

Mother eagle & babies on lacy base, milk glass, 8" .$180.00

Rabbit (mule-earred) on picket-fence base, caramel or purple marbled, 5½", ea...................................$100.00

Rabbit (mulc-earred) on picket-fence base, hand-painted milk glass or pink opaque top, on milk glass base, 5½", ea $60.00

Rabbit (mule-eared) on picket-fence base, white carnival (1,500 made) or caramel marbled carnival, 5½", ea..........$130.00

Rabbit w/eggs on diamond or lacy base, blue opaque, 8", ea $175.00

Rabbit w/eggs on diamond or lacy base, chocolate, ruby or purple marbled, 8", ea...................................$200.00

Rabbit w/eggs on diamond or lacy base, milk glass, 8", ca...$150.00

Rabbit w/eggs on diamond or lacy base, purple slag carnival (150 made), 8", ea $250.00

Rabbit w/eggs on diamond or lacy base, white carnival (1,500 made) or Electric Blue carnival (500 made), 8", ea $200.00

Robin on twig nest base, any mist color, 6¼"............$60.00

Robin on twig nest base, caramel, vaseline, purple marbled or turquoise carnival, 6¼", ea...................$150.00

Robin on twig nest base, milk glass, 6¼"...................$50.00

Robin on twig nest base, pink (160 made), black carnival (experimental) or ruby (2,000 made), 6¼", ea $150.00

Rooster on diamond base, crystal (1,500 made), turquoise carnival (1980) or Electric Blue carnival, 7½", ea $175.00

Rooster on diamond base, milk glass, 7½".................$70.00

Rooster on diamond base, milk glass w/Minorca decoration (hand-painted realistic feathers), 7½" $125.00

Rooster on diamond base, ruby, purple marbled or purple marbled carnival, 7½", ea $200.00

Rooster on ribbed base, milk glass, 5½".................$35.00

Rooster on ribbed base, purple marbled, 5½" $85.00

Rooster on ribbed base, ruby, caramel or marbled carnival, made for Levay, 1978, limited edition, 5½", ea..$100.00

Rooster standing, Antique Blue, 8½" $85.00

Rooster standing, milk glass, 8½"...........................$35.00

Rooster standing, milk glass w/Minorca decoration, hand-painted, 8½"...$75.00

Rooster standing, purple marbled or Almond w/hand-painted accents, 8½", ea..................................$125.00

Swan (closed neck) on diamond base, milk glass or blue opaque, ea...$95.00

Swan (raised wing) on lacy base, black milk glass, 6x9½"...$275.00

Swan (raised wing) on lacy base, emerald green, purple marbled, pink or cobalt carnival, 6x9½", ea.............$225.00

Swan (raised wing) on lacy base, Ice Blue or turquoise carnival, 6x9½", ea...$200.00

Swan (raised wing) on lacy base, milk glass, milk glass Mother of Pearl, light blue or Pink Mist, 6x9½", ea..........$175.00

Toy chick on basketweave base, Brandywine Blue, Dark Blue Mist or Moss Green, 2", ea............................$20.00

Toy Chick on basketweave base, milk glass or milk glass w/red accents, 2", ea...$15.00

Toy chick on basketweave base, milk glass w/any fired-on color, 2", ea...$20.00

Figurals and Novelties

Bird, ashtray or pipe holder, green marbled $35.00

Bulldog, Crystal Mist, painted collar, rhinestone eyes, 2½"...$35.00

Butterfly, Almond, Mint Green, Mint Green Mist or milk glass, 2½", ea...$25.00

Butterfly, Almond, Mint Green, vaseline or Antique Blue, lg, ea...$40.00

Butterfly, any mist colors, lg, ea.................................$40.00

Butterfly, Green Mist, 2½".................................$25.00

Butterfly, mist colors other than Mint Green Mist, 2½", ea $20.00

Butterfly, pink opaque or purple carnival, 2½", ea $30.00

Butterfly, purple, caramel or green marbled, lg, ea....$50.00

Butterfly, purple carnival, 1977 limited edition, lg, ea..$55.00

Cardinal, crystal, solid $20.00

Cardinal, purple marbled, solid $35.00

Cardinal, ruby carnival, solid $30.00

Cardinal, ruby or any mist colors, solid, ea.................$25.00

Cat in boot, green, dark blue or Yellow Mist, hollow, ea...$35.00

Duck, salt cellar, crystal carnival (1,500 made)...........$35.00

Duck, salt cellar, milk glass, Apricot or Green Mist, ea..$25.00

Egg, trinket box, any color w/beaded bouquet, w/lid.$35.00

Egg, trinket box, any Crystal Mist w/decal, w/lid.......$25.00

Egg, trinket box, ruby w/Mary Gregory style or cameo, w/lid, ea $40.00

Egg on gold stand, Almond w/any decal or Crystal Mist w/floral spray, blown, hollow, ea $50.00

Egg on gold stand, Almond w/any hand-painted decor, blown, hollow, ea...$60.00

Egg on gold stand, black glass (plain), blown, hollow .$40.00

Egg on gold stand, black glass w/Oriental Poppy, blown, hollow...$60.00

Grandma's slipper, Antique Blue, Antique Blue Mist, Almond, Mint Green, dark blue or Green Mist, ea.............$30.00

Grandma's slipper, any Mist color, ea $25.00

Grandma's slipper, any mist color w/hand painting...$30.00

Grandma's slipper, black glass or milk glass Mother of Pearl, ea $35.00

Grandma's slipper, Honey, Ice Blue carnival or cobalt blue carnival, ea...$40.00

Mantel clock, candy container, Brandywine Blue, hollow, no markings **$35.00**

Mantel clock, candy container, milk glass w/hand-painted clock face, hollow, no markings **$45.00**

Mantel clock, milk glass or Moss Green, hollow, no markings, ea **$30.00**

Napkin ring, brown, light blue or Pink Mist w/flower, 6-sided, ea **$35.00**

Napkin ring, milk glass w/holly decor, 6-sided **$50.00**

Napkin ring, milk glass w/pink flower, 6-sided.............**$35.00**

Owl on 2 stacked books, Almond, Mint Green, Antique Blue or black glass, 3½", ea **$30.00**

Owl on 2 stacked books, any mist color, 3½", ea **$25.00**

Owl on 2 stacked books, blue, pink, yellow opaque or Brandywine Blue, 3½", ea **$25.00**

Owl on 2 stacked books, milk glass, 3½" **$20.00**

Owl on 2 stacked books, purple marbled, 3½" **$40.00**

Owl standing on tree stump, Almond Mist, Antique Blue or Antique Blue Mist, not marked, 5½", ea **$40.00**

Owl standing on tree stump, crystal, dark blue or Yellow Mist, not marked, 5½", ea **$35.00**

Owl standing on tree stump, crystal carnival, ruby or milk glass w/22k gold rubbed feathers, 5½", ea **$45.00**

Owl standing on tree stump, milk glass or milk glass Mother of Pearl, not marked, 5½", ea...............................**$30.00**

Owl standing on tree stump, purple marbled or ruby carnival, 5½", ea..**$55.00**

Owl toothpick holder, aqua, milk glass, Moss Green or pink, 3", ea **$20.00**

Owl toothpick holder, crystal, 3" **$15.00**

Owl toothpick holder, green, ruby or purple marbled, 3", ea **$30.00**

Penguin on ice floe, blue or Blue Mist, ea...............**$100.00**

Penguin on ice floe, Crystal Mist or milk glass, ea **$80.00**

Porky pig, cobalt carnival, 3"......................................**$40.00**

Porky pig, Crystal Mist w/hand-painted decor, yellow opaque, milk glass, crystal, Dark Blue Mist or Mint Green, 3", ea........**$30.00**

Porky pig, milk glass or Mint Green w/hand-painted decor, 3", ea **$35.00**

Pouter pigeon, Apricot, dark or light blue, green or Pink Mist, ea **$35.00**

Pouter pigeon, Lilac Mist...**$40.00**

Revolver, black glass or crystal w/black hand-painted grips, solid, ea **$90.00**

Revolver, crystal, solid..**$70.00**

Robin, Almond, Antique Blue, Antique Blue Mist or ruby, solid, 3¼", ea **$30.00**

Robin, crystal, solid, 3¼"..**$20.00**

Robin, crystal, solid, 5¼"..**$20.00**

Robin, dark blue, green or Pink Mist, solid, 3¼", ea..**$25.00**

Robin, ruby or any mist colors, solid, 5¼", ea............**$25.00**

Robin, Smoke, 5⅛"...**$24.00**

Swallow, Almond, Antique Blue or Mint Green, solid, ea **$30.00**

Swallow, green or Yellow Mist, solid..........................**$25.00**

Turtle, ashtray or pipe holder, green, Pink Mist, dark or light blue, ea **$25.00**

Turtle, paperweight, dark blue, green or Lilac Mist, no holes, ea **$50.00**

Turtle, paperweight, milk glass, no holes...................**$75.00**

Wren, Almond, Almond Mist or any opaque color, solid .**$35.00**

Wren, milk glass or any other color mist, solid, ea **$30.00**

Wren, pink, 2½"..**$20.00**

Wren, Smoke, 2½" **$20.00**

Wren on sq-base perch, any color combination, solid, ea ..**$55.00**

Lamps

Boudoir, English Hobnail/#555, milk glass, stick type w/flat base **$45.00**

Candle, Almond, Mint Green or ruby w/hand-painted decor, w/shade, mini, ea **$45.00**

Candle, any mist color w/out decal, w/shade, mini ...**$27.50**

Candle, Crystal Mist w/any decal, w/shade, mini **$30.00**

Candle, Crystal Mist w/child's decal, w/shade, mini...**$65.00**

Candle, Crystal Mist w/roses & bows, w/shade, mini...**$75.00**

Candle, milk glass w/child's decal, w/shade, mini ...**$125.00**

Candle, milk glass w/roses & bows, w/shade, mini.**$135.00**

Electric, any child's decor, w/shade, mini **$80.00**

Electric, any color w/Mary Gregory-style decor, w/shade, mini..**$100.00**

Electric, any color w/roses & bows, w/shade, mini .**$125.00**

Electric, Colonial; any color or decor, brass base w/scroll work, glass shade, ea **$125.00**

Electric, Crystal Mist w/decal, w/shade, mini.............**$35.00**

Electric, Dolphin; crystal **$125.00**

Electric, Dolphin; green or pink, ea..........................**$175.00**

Electric, ruby w/ruby & floral, w/shade, mini..........**$100.00**

Fairy, Almond w/hand-painted flowers, footed, 2-pc.**$65.00**

Fairy, Brandywine Blue carnival, footed, 2-pc **$75.00**

Fairy, Waterford, clear w/ruby stain, 2-pc **$40.00**

Modern Giftware

Ashtray, Beaded Grape/#1884, Brandywine Blue, 6½x6½" **$30.00**

Ashtray, Colonial, purple slag....................................**$30.00**

Basket, English Hobnail/#555, Light Blue or Pink Mist & Blue or Pink Pastel, 9" ea **$45.00**

Basket, Paneled Grape/#1881, milk glass, Brandywine Blue or Golden Sunset, 8", ea **$150.00**

Basket, Paneled Grape/#1881, red carnival, limited edition of 500, 8"..**$200.00**

Basket, Pansy/#757, purple or green slag, split handle, ea.**$35.00**

Bell, Cameo/#754, w/Beaded Bouquet trim, any color, ea.**$35.00**

Bell, Cameo/#754, w/HP Cameo, any color, ea..........**$30.00**

Bonbon, Waterford/#1932, ruby on crystal, metal w/handle **$38.00**

Bottle, toilet, Paneled Grape/#1881, milk glass, 5-oz .**$65.00**

Bowl, centerpiece; Colonial/#1776, Bermuda Blue, w/2 candle holders, 3-pc set...**$125.00**

Bowl, console; Paneled Grape/#1881, milk glass, round, on epergne base, 12" **$125.00**

Bowl, Lotus/#1821, black, round, lg **$50.00**

Bowl, Lotus/#1921, milk glass, oval $30.00

Bowl, purple or green slag, leaf form, #300, ea $45.00

Bowl, Rose Trellis/#1967, milk glass w/hand-painted decor, 10" $75.00

Bowl, Striped/#1814, Apricot Mist, round, footed, lg .$35.00

Bowl, wedding; ruby on crystal, #1874, 8" $50.00

Bowl, wedding; ruby on crystal, #1874, 10" $65.00

Bowl (Grandfather), Sawtooth/#556, Brandywine Blue or Golden Sunset $80.00

Box, trinket; any mist color, 4-footed, sq, #1902 ....$20.00

Box, trinket; Crystal Mist w/Roses & Bows, 4-footed, sq..$35.00

Box, trinket; Purple Mist, 4-footed, sq, #1902 ....$27.50

Candle holders, ruby on crystal, Waterford, 6", pr......$65.00

Candy dish, Beaded Bouquet/#1700, Colonial pattern, milk glass $35.00

Candy dish, Beaded Grape/#1884, Brandywine Blue, 3½", w/lid $35.00

Candy dish, Beaded Grape/#1884, milk glass w/Roses & Bows, low footed, w/lid, 5" $47.50

Candy dish, Paneled Grape/#1881, Almond, Almond Mist or Antique Blue, open ruffled edge, 3-toed, ea $30.00

Candy dish, Paneled Grape/#1881, Dark Blue Mist, crimped, 3-footed, 7½" $35.00

Compote, Brandywine Blue Opalescent, crimped & ruffled, footed, 6½" $45.00

Dresser set, yellow or Green Mist, w/Daisy design, 4-pc set $50.00

Flowerpot, purple, Beaded Bouquet trim, #1707........$45.00

Grandma's slipper, hand-painted Christmas decor, #1900 ..$40.00

Grandma's slipper, no painting...................................$20.00

Pin tray, Heart/#1820, Blue Mist.................................$30.00

Pitcher set, child's, Paneled Grape/#1881, lg creamer w/6 toothpicks as tumblers, purple carnival, 500 made $250.00

Soap dish, Paneled Grape/#1881, milk glass............$110.00

Urn, ruby on crystal, footed, #1943, w/lid...................$95.00

Plates

Beaded Edge/#22, milk glass w/birds, florals, or poultry, 7", ea $20.00

Beaded Edge/#22, milk glass w/painted fruit & Zodiac back, 14½" $80.00

Bicentennial decoration, Paneled Grape/#1881, limited edition, 14½" $225.00

Forget-me-not/#2, black, Mary Gregory style, 8" $55.00

Forget-me-not/#2, blue or Brown Mist, Mary Gregory style, 8", ea $60.00

Hearts, heart shape/#HP-1, Almond or Mint Green w/dogwood decal, 8", ea $30.00

Hearts, heart shape/#HP-1, any color w/daisy decal, 8", ea..$25.00

Lattice Edge/#1890, black milk glass or milk glass w/any hand-painted decor, 11", ea $95.00

Lattice Edge/#1890, Dark Blue Mist, Mary Gregory style, 11" $65.00

Luncheon, Paneled Grape/#1881, milk glass w/hand-painted decor, 8½" $40.00

Plain, dinner/#PL-8; black glass w/Christmas nativity decor, 8½" $80.00

Tableware

Bowl, banana; Old Quilt/#500, milk glass, footed, 11"..$150.00

Bowl, banana; Paneled Grape/#1881, Electric Blue carnival, footed, 12" $175.00

Bowl, banana; Paneled Grape/#1881, milk glass, 12" $150.00

Bowl, Old Quilt/#500, milk glass, round, 10¼" $120.00

Bowl, Paneled Grape/#1881, milk glass, belled or lipped, footed, oval, 11", ea..$75.00

Bowl, Paneled Grape/#1881, milk glass, cupped, 8" ..$45.00

Bowl, Paneled Grape/#1881, milk glass, round, 10½"..$120.00

Bowl, Paneled Grape/#1881, milk glass, shallow, skirted foot, 6x9" $60.00

Bowl, relish; Old Quilt/#500, milk glass, round, 3-part ..$35.00

Box, chocolate; Paneled Grape/#1881, milk glass, w/lid, 6½" dia $45.00

Butter dish, Paneled Grape/#1881, ¼-lb, milk glass, w/lid $25.00

Butter/cheese dish, Old Quilt/#500, milk glass, w/lid, round $45.00

Butter/cheese dish, Old Quilt/#500, purple marbled, w/lid, round $125.00

Butter/cheese dish, Old Quilt/#500, purple marbled carnival, w/lid, round $125.00

Butter/cheese dish, Paneled Grape/#1881, milk glass, w/lid, round, 7"..$125.00

Butter/cheese dish, Paneled Grape/#1881, purple marbled, w/lid, round, 7"..$75.00

Cake plate, Irish Waterford/#1932, ruby on crystal, low footed, 12" $95.00

Cake salver, Beaded Grape/#1884, milk glass, sq, footed, 11" $95.00

Cake salver, Old Quilt/#500, milk glass, skirted, bell footed, 12" $125.00

Cake salver, Paneled Grape/#1881, milk glass, skirted, 11" $65.00

Canape set, Paneled Grape/#1881, milk glass, 3-pc, 12½" tray, 3½" cocktail & ladle..$120.00

Candelabra, Lotus/#1921, any mist color, 3-light, pr...$70.00

Candelabra, Lotus/#1921, milk glass, 3-light, pr..........$60.00

Candelabra, Paneled Grape/#1881, milk glass, 3-light, pr $400.00

Candle holder, Paneled Grape/#1881, milk glass, arc shape, 2-light, 8", ea..$45.00

Canister, Paneled Grape/#1881, green or purple marbled, footed, w/lid, 7½x4½", ea $150.00

Canister, Paneled Grape/#1881, green or purple marbled, footed, w/lid, 10x5¾", ea...$175.00

Canister, Paneled Grape/#1881, green or purple marbled, footed, w/lid, 11½x6¾", ea $200.00

Canister, Paneled Grape/#1881, milk glass, footed, w/lid, 10x5¾" $500.00

Canister, Paneled Grape/#1881, milk glass, footed, w/lid, 11½x6¾" $400.00

Canister, Paneled Grape/#1881, milk glass, footed, w/lid, 7½x4½" $300.00

Compote, Paneled Grape/#1881, milk glass, lipped or crimped, 9", ea $65.00

Cup & saucer, Paneled Grape/#1881, milk glass $21.00

Decanter, Paneled Grape/#1881, Lime Green carnival, w/stopper $175.00

Decanter, Paneled Grape/#1881, milk glass, w/stopper ..$150.00

Egg tray, Paneled Grape/#1881, milk glass, w/center handle, 10" $75.00

Egg tray, Paneled Grape/#1881, milk glass, w/center handle, 12" $90.00

Epergne, Paneled Grape/#1881, Almond or Mint Green, flared, 3-pc set, 14", ea $300.00

Epergne, Paneled Grape/#1881, milk glass, flared, 3-pc set, 14" $250.00

Epergne, Paneled Grape/#1881, milk glass, lipped, 2-pc set (no base), 9" $150.00

Epergne, Paneled Grape/#1881, milk glass, lipped, 3-pc set, 12" $250.00

Goblet, water; Old Quilt/#500, Brandwine Blue, Golden Sunset or milk glass, footed, 8-oz, ea $15.00

Goblet, water; Paneled Grape/#1881, milk glass, footed, 8-oz $15.00

Goblet, wine; Paneled Grape/#1881, milk glass, footed, 2-oz $22.00

Pitcher, syrup; Old Quilt/#500, milk glass, 3-oz, 3½" .$40.00

Plate, dinner; Paneled Grape/#1881, milk glass, 10½"..$45.00

Plate, dinner; Paneled Grape/#1881, Mint Green, 10½" .$60.00

Plate, Old Quilt/#500, milk glass, 10½" $70.00

Plate, salad; Della Robbia, crystal $15.00

Plate, salad; Old Quilt/#500, milk glass, 8½" $35.00

Plate, salad; Paneled Grape/#1881, milk glass, 8½"....$22.00

Plate, Waterford, clear w/ruby stain, 10" $65.00

Punch bowl set, Fruits, Honey or Ice Blue Carnival, 15-pc, ea $450.00

Punch bowl set, Fruits, Lilac Opalescent, 15-pc $500.00

Punch bowl set, Fruits, purple or turquoise carnival, 15-pc, ea $500.00

Punch bowl set, Old Quilt/#500, milk glass, bowl, base, ladle & 12 cups $960.00

Punch bowl set, Paneled Grape/#1881, milk glass, bowl, base, ladle & 12 cups $575.00

Toothpick, Paneled Grape/#1881, milk glass $30.00

Tray, tidbit; Beaded Grape/#1884, milk glass, 2-tier...$95.00

Tray, tidbit; Paneled Grape/#1881, milk glass, w/Christmas decor, 1-tier, 10½" $85.00

Tray, tidbit; Paneled Grape/#1881, milk glass, 1-tier, 10½" $50.00

Tray, tidbit; Paneled Grape/#1881, milk glass, 2-tier, 8½" & 10½" plates $80.00

Tray, tidbit; Paneled Grape/#1881, milk glass, 2-tier, 8½" & 10½" plates w/poinsettia decor $100.00

Tray, tidbit; Paneled Grape/#1881, w/daisy design, any mist color, ea $35.00

Tumbler, iced tea; Paneled Grape/#1881, milk glass, 12-oz $22.50

Tumbler, iced tea; Waterford, clear w/ruby stain, 12-oz ..$25.00

Tumbler, juice; Old Quilt/#500, milk glass, flat, 5-oz .$25.00

Tumbler, old-fashioned; Paneled Grape/#1881, milk glass, flat, 6-oz $35.00

Tumbler, water; Old Quilt/#500, milk glass, flat, 9-oz ..$12.00

Water set, Old Quilt/#500, purple slag or carnival, 3-pt pitcher & 6 9-oz tumblers $280.00

Water set, Paneled Grape/#1881, Lime Green carnival, 1-qt pitcher & 6 8-oz tumblers $290.00

Water set, Swirl & Ball, purple carnival, 3-pt pitcher & 6 8-oz tumblers $265.00

Wexford

Wexford is a diverse line of glassware that Anchor Hocking has made since 1967. At one time, it was quite extensive, and a few pieces remain in production yet today. It's very likely you'll see it at any flea market you visit, and it's common to see a piece now and then on your garage sale rounds. It's not only very attractive but serviceable — nothing fragile about this heavy-gauge glassware! Right now, it's not only plentiful but inexpensive, so if you like its looks, now's a good time to begin your collection. Gene Florence lists seventy-seven pieces in his book *Anchor Hocking's Fire-King and More* and says others will no doubt be reported as collectors become more familiar with the market.

Bowl, centerpiece; footed, 8" $12.00

Bowl, fruit; footed, 10" $12.00

Bowl, salad; 5¼" $3.50

Bowl, trifle; plain top $10.00

Cake stand & dome $21.00

Candle holders, 5", pr $35.00

Candy dish, footed, w/lid, 7¼" $12.00

Goblet, cordial; 3½-oz $2.50

Goblet, water; 9-oz $3.00

Ice bucket, w/lid $15.00

Jar, storage; 17-oz $3.00

Pitcher, 64-oz $8.00

Platter, 12" dia $4.00

Punch bowl, 11-qt $10.00

Relish, 3-part, 8½" $4.00

Salt & pepper shakers, 2-oz, pr $3.00

Sugar bowl, w/lid $7.00

Tidbit tray, 2-tier (6" & 11" plates) $10.00

Tray, relish, 11" $4.00

Tumbler, wine/juice; 6-oz $2.00

Wheaton

The Wheaton Company of Millville, New Jersey, has produced several series of bottles and flasks which are very collectible today. One of the most popular features portraits of our country's presidents. There was also a series of twenty-one Christmas bottles produced from 1971 through 1991, and because fewer were produced during the last few years, the newer ones can be hard to find and often bring good prices. Apollo bottles, those that feature movie stars, ink bottles, and bitters bottles are among the other interesting examples. Many colors of glass have been used, including iridescents.

Apollo II Moon Landing, cobalt, 8¼" **$15.00**
Ball & Claw Bitters, World's Best, green, 9⅛" **$15.00**
Benjamin Franklin, milk glass, 8" **$12.50**
Berring's Bitters, amber, sq, 10" **$12.50**
Betsy Ross, ruby red, 8", MIB **$11.00**
Carter's Ink, red, 8-sided, 2⅝" **$16.00**
Christmas Holly 1973, ruby, round, 6x8¼" **$15.00**
Col Sam Johnson, Richmond VA 1852, cobalt, 3½x8"...**$14.00**
Dr Fisch's Bitters, fish shape, milk glass, 7½" **$30.00**
Dr Martin Luther King, amber carnival, MIB **$18.00**
EC Booz's, cabin shape, amber, 3x3½x8" **$12.00**
Frank's Safe Kidney & Liver Cure, Big Safe on front, blue, 9¼" **$13.00**
George Washington, Father of His Country, amber **$11.00**
Jenny Lind, Swedish Nightingale on back, blue carnival, 3¾" **$12.50**
John F Kennedy, blue carnival, round, 7¼" **$12.00**
Mark Twain, Samuel L Clemens, amethyst carnival, 1972, 8".**$11.00**
McGiver's American Army, smoky gray, 7" **$13.50**
Pocahontas, cobalt, 5¼" **$15.00**
Poison, skull & crossbones, coffin shape, amber, 3" ..**$25.00**
Poison, skull & crossbones on 1 side, RIP on other, amber, 3¾" **$45.00**
Rogers Bros 1850 Salem NJ, blue, 9¼" **$17.50**
Thomas Jefferson, ruby red, round, 1970, 7¾" **$14.00**
Tuckahoe Country School 1891, dark blue, 2½" **$22.00**
WC Fields, carnival glass, star shape, 6x8½" **$15.00**

Will-George

This is a California-based company that began operations in the 1930. It was headed by two brothers, William and George Climes, both of whom had extensive training in pottery science. They're most famous today for their lovely figurines of animals and birds, though they produced many human figures as well. For more information on this company as well as many others, we recommend *The Collector's Encyclopedia of California Pottery* by Jack Chipman (Collector Books).

Figurine, Baltimore Oriole **$155.00**
Figurine, bluebird, on base, 3¼" **$45.00**
Figurine, cardinal on branch, 10" **$100.00**
Figurine, dachshund, sitting, 6½x8" **$200.00**
Figurine, eagle on rock, white & brown, 10" **$150.00**
Figurine, female pheasant **$110.00**
Figurine, flamingo, head down, 6" **$110.00**
Figurine, flamingo, looking backwards, 8" **$150.00**
Figurine, flamingo, preening, 10¼" **$200.00**
Figurine, flamingo, wings up, 7½" **$275.00**
Figurine, monk, brown bisque, 5½" **$75.00**

Figurine, robin, seated, 3" **$45.00**
Figurine, young Pan, w/attendant forest creatures, 7" ..**$95.00**
Figurines, giraffes, 1 standing, 14½", 1 reclining, 11⅛", pr **$275.00**
Pitcher, chicken figural, mc, 7" **$135.00**
Wine glass, chicken figural, mc, 5" **$55.00**

Winfield

The Winfield pottery first began operations in the late 1920s in Pasadena, California. In 1946 their entire line of artware and giftware items was licensed to the American Ceramic Products Company, who continued to mark their semiporcelain dinnerware with the Winfield name. The original Winfield company changed their trademark to 'Gabriel.' Both companies closed during the early 1960s. For more information, see *The Collector's Encyclopedia of California Pottery* by Jack Chipman (Collector Books).

Bowl, cereal; Bamboo, blue, 2x5¾" dia **$12.50**
Bowl, dark purple outside w/pink inside, angular sides, 4½x10½" dia **$65.00**
Bowl, serving; Bamboo, blue, 2⅞x9¼" dia **$40.00**
Bowl, serving; Bamboo, green, 3x9¼" **$28.00**
Bowl, serving; Bamboo, green, 4¾x10½" dia **$35.00**
Card holder, blue w/embossed flower, #163, 2x3" **$25.00**
Casserole, Bamboo, blue, w/lid, 5½x9" dia **$25.00**
Dish, divided; Desert Dawn, 13" **$25.00**
Egg cup, Dragon Flower, white on pink & brown, 3¼" **$23.00**
Ewer, Primitive Pony, prancing horse, marked Gabriel, 1⅞".**$20.00**
Gravy boat, Bamboo, blue, stick handle, 2½x3½x8¾" ..**$45.00**
Mug, coffee; Dragon Flower, 5¼" **$15.00**
Plate, modern abstract Christmas tree, 10½" dia **$30.00**
Platter, Bird of Paradise, 8x12" **$30.00**
Platter, Desert Dawn, 8x12" **$30.00**
Salt & pepper shakers, rose buds on base, 1 pink & 1 blue, 2⅜", pr **$22.50**
Sugar bowl, turquoise outside w/yellow inside, flat lid w/fruit finial, #272, 3½" **$30.00**
Tea set, green w/brown trim, teapot, creamer & sugar bowl, teapot & sugar bowl lids have fruit finials, EX.....**$60.00**
Teapot, Desert Dawn, w/2 matching mugs, EX **$70.00**
Teapot, yellow w/green leaves & bell-shaped brown flowers, 7½" **$35.00**
Tray, Bamboo, blue, oblong, 4⅞x9¼" **$60.00**
Tray, blue w/yellow flower & green leaves, 12x8" **$30.00**

World's Fairs and Expositions

Souvenir items have been issued since the mid-1800s for every world's fair and exposition. Few fairgoers have left the grounds without purchasing at least one. Some of the older items were often manufactured right on the fairgrounds by glass or pottery companies who erected working kilns and furnaces just for the duration of the fair. Of course, the older items are usually more valuable, but even souvenirs from the past fifty years are worth hanging on to.

Advisor: Herbert Rolfes (See Directory, World's Fairs and Expositions)

Newsletter: *Fair News*
World's Fair Collectors' Society, Inc.
Michael R. Pender, Editor
P.O. Box 20806
Sarasota, FL 34276; 941-923-2590; Dues: $20 (6 issues) per year in USA; $25 in Canada; $30 for overseas members

Chicago, 1933

Bank, Fort Deerborn, cast iron, copper colored, EX ..**$80.00**

Bible, miniature; The Four Gospels...Lord & Savior Jesus Christ, gilted cover, C&S Sales, 237 pages, 1¼x1⅛", NM **$35.00**

Brush, dog's-head handle, leather strap in back w/ring for hanging, marked Century of Progress Chicago 1933, 7" L, EX **$100.00**

Bus, Greyhound Lines, Arcade, A Century of Progress 1933 on back, minor paint loss, 14" L, VG+...............**$360.00**

Candlesticks, Hall of Science on 1 side, Federal Building on back, N Shure Co Importers, Made in Japan, 4", EX, pr **$40.00**

Cane, beer keg on top w/goblet underneath, marked w/fair logo, wooden, 4" L, EX **$85.00**

Cigarette case, green metal w/fair emblem on front, push-button lid, 3x2½x¾", NM...................................**$50.00**

Coaster set, Electrical Group Building, Fort Deerborn, Administration Building, Golden Pavillion of Jehol, EX.**$65.00**

Compact, green enamel w/Chicago skyline on top, solid green on bottom, 2 compartments & mirror inside, 2½x1½", EX...**$36.00**

Cuff bracelet, brass w/black enameled logo in center, 1" W, EX...**$50.00**

Desk thermometer, 8-sided metal frame in green leather case, Rochester Mfg, 3x3", EX.......................................**$50.00**

Glass, clear w/Century of Progress in red, 1833-1933 in white, Chicago World's Fair in blue, 5⅛", EX **$32.00**

Globe, tilted on axis in embossed metal base, 4½" H, M ..**$65.00**

Hat, Administration Building, Fort Deerborn & Science Building, felt, 4x11", EX **$35.00**

Jewelry box, wood w/Hall of Science under glass, 3 compartments, all original, 9x7x3¼" H, NM................**$55.00**

Mug, coffee; Stewarts Private Blend, Stewart & Ashby Co, made by Bauscher China, 3½", EX **$95.00**

Paperweight, bulldog w/shield on back, cast iron, 1⅝", EX..**$80.00**

Paperweight, 3-D of fair logo, heavy metal, round, EX **$33.00**

Picture, fair scene in gold & brown tones, attached to glass, wooden frame, 5¾x4¼", EX **$50.00**

Pillow, American Indian Chief in center, needlecraft, 13x13", EX..**$42.00**

Pillowcase, multicolored fair scenes on front, 16" sq, NM **$55.00**

Pin, 1933 Zeppelin Day, enameled brass, 1⅜x2", EX...**$70.00**

Puzzle, Enchanted Island by Tom Saw, Century Novelty Co, 225+ pcs, EX (VG box) **$45.00**

Puzzle, jigsaw; Fort Deerborn Building, Tom Saw, 8½x10", EX (EX Art Deco box)..**$40.00**

Ring, fair logo center w/1933 on sides, sterling silver, Robbins Co, EX..**$40.00**

Spoon, fair logo on handle, bowl has cutouts of tulips & swirls, sterling silver, 9", EX..............................**$40.00**

Tapestry, multicolored scene from fair, 19½x56¾" L, EX+ **$100.00**

Thermometer, key shape, various fair buildings, 10" L, EX ...**$45.00**

Tip tray, Towers of the Federal Building in center, A Century...Chicago 1933 on rim, 4" dia, EX **$38.00**

New York, 1939

Book, See the New York World's Fair in Pictures, Rogers-Kellogg-Stillson Inc, 56 pages, 9⅝x6½", EX.........**$33.00**

Booklet, New Hampshire Troubadour, Maxfield Parrish cover of Cornish landscape, 96 pages, EX+................**$100.00**

Bracelet, charms spell out NY Worlds Fair 1939, w/fair logo in center, NMIB...**$33.00**

Cap, blue w/New York World's Fair & logo in gold, NM **$55.00**

Charm bracelet, 6 charms of different fair buildings, 7½" L, EX...**$40.00**

Cigarette tin, blue & gold w/fair logo, slide top, 3x2¼x1", EX **$60.00**

Compact, wood & embroidery (New York 1939 World's Fair) w/Communications Building in background, 2¾" dia, EX **$80.00**

Diary, black faux leather w/Trylon & Perisphere in silver, 5-year, NM (VG box) **$35.00**

Elongated coin, 1928 Lincoln cent, rope border w/Jell-O Everybody World's Fair Greetings 1939 From Jack Benny, EX **$60.00**

Film, silent; from officials arriving to fireworks, Official Motion Picture Producers, Communication Building, 16mm, EX **$115.00**

Kan-O-Seat, wooden, use as cane or fold out for seat, fair logo in center of seat, EX **$75.00**

License plate, New York & World's Fair in orange w/Trylon & Perisphere in center w/blue background, NG Slater Corp, EX...**$75.00**

Locket, gold-colored metal bird w/sq locket below, enameled Trylon & Perisphere, holds 2 pictures, EX ...**$35.00**

Magazine, New York Times, George Washington w/Trylon & Perisphere in background, March 5, 1939, EX **$35.00**

Napkin ring, Trylon & Perisphere, navy blue Bakelite, EX **$150.00**

Pencil, bullet; Trylon & Perisphere label, EX **$45.00**

Pin, Trylon & Perisphere w/flag above stating The Dawn of a New Day, blue w/orange border, 1¾" dia, EX **$35.00**

Plaque, Trylon & Perisphere in white relief on wood-tone leaf plate, Syroco Wood, 9" dia, EX **$35.00**

Plate, George Washington looking over Trylon & Perisphere, blue transferware, Lamberton Scammell, 11", NM..**$95.00**

Plate, Trylon & Perisphere center w/blue & orange ring border w/gold inner ring, Atlas China #A-1247, 8", EX **$60.00**

Plate, Trylon & Perisphere in center, fair scenes on border, gold embossed plate on back, Homer Laughlin, 10" dia, EX.**$235.00**

Poster, Best Routes to the Fair/Ask Shell, paper, features Trylon & Perisphere landscape, 53½x39¼", EX.**$700.00**

Scarf, fair buildings & main attractions, silk, 19" sq, EX ...**$35.00**

Tablecloth, Flags of the World border, linen, 52x51", EX .**$80.00**

Tumbler, earthenware, blue & tan w/Trylon & Perisphere, Made in Japan, 4", EX **$33.00**

Walking stick, blue w/New York World's Fair in orange, logo, ceramic baseball on top, 34" L, EX **$55.00**

Walnut, holes drilled for tag strings, NY World's Fair in a Nutshell, Goldfarb Novelty Corp, VG...................**$30.00**

Seattle, 1962

Bottle opener, Space Needle shape, 5", EX.................**$22.00**

Charm bracelet, Space Needle, Coliseum 21, Century 21 Expo, Monorail, US Science Pavilion & totem pole charms, EX **$20.00**

Cups, Bolero; yellow & white w/Space Needle scene in black, set of 8, EX..**$20.00**

Decanter, Space Needle shape, Beam, Regal China, NM..**$25.00**

Glass, Herfy's 20th Anniversary Commemorating Seattle World's Fair 1962, clear w/blue & yellow decor, M................**$20.00**

Glass set, frosted w/colored fair scene, 3 different colors/scenes, EX..**$20.00**

Handkerchief, Seattle World's Fair 1962 in center, fair buildings on ea corner, rayon & silk, 17x18", EX.........**$35.00**

Match book, Alweg Monorail, Space Needle & other fair attractions, 12½" L, EX..**$5.00**

Mug, clear w/blue Space Needle on 1 side & fair emblem & Century 21 Exposition on other, w/handle, 5¼", EX...**$35.00**

Patch, Service Scouts, gold, red, white & blue, M **$30.00**

Plate, shows 5 attractions, floral border, gold trim, Japan, Century Souvenir Co, 10¼" dia, EX **$25.00**

Plate, 10 different scenes & logo, gold trim on edge, Viletta's Art Studio Roseburg Oregon, 10½" dia, EX..........**$33.00**

Puzzle, frame-tray, multicolored fair scene, Ad-ventures, M (original mailing envelope).....................................**$20.00**

Stamp sheet, Space Needle, Scott 1196, M **$15.00**

Tray, Science Pavilion, porcelain w/gold trim, scalloped edge, 4x3", EX...**$15.00**

New York, 1964

Bank, Unisphere shape, hard plastic, 6", NMIB **$30.00**

Book, Official Guide New York World's Fair, published by Time Inc, 312 pages, 8x5", EX...............................**$25.00**

Booklet, General Motors From the World's Fair, 38 pages, 4x9", EX **$28.00**

Booklet, NY WF, A Disney Retrospective, 12 pages, sepia ink on tan paper, given to Disney Employees only, 8½x11", EX...**$30.00**

Coin purse, multicolored fair scene on white, tan & white strap & sides, vinyl, Bearse Mfg Co, 5" sq, 2" thick, EX......**$32.00**

Game, WF Panorama Game, NM (G envelope)..........**$25.00**

Glass set, frosted w/colored scenes, 6 different scenes, 6½", EX..**$35.00**

Glasses, New York Central System, clear w/black & gold lettering, train circles bottom, set of 4, 4½x2¾" dia, M.....**$25.00**

Matchbooks, gray & black w/Unisphere, US Steel, 25 packs in original box, NM **$27.00**

Medal, gold metal, Unisphere on front, Anniversary of the Founding of the City of NY on back, M (velvet-lined case)...........**$20.00**

Playing cards, World's Fair scenes on back, Stancroft Bridge Model #2400, MIB (w/plastic case) **$50.00**

Puzzle, jigsaw; Astral Fountain, Milton Bradley, 750+ pcs, 19x20½", w/brochure of fair facts, M (EX box) ...**$25.00**

Snowdome, Vatican Pavilion, 2x3", EX...................**$23.00**

Tray, Bell Systems Building, info below picture, 4¾x6¾"..**$25.00**

Viewmaster reel set, Industrial Area, #A675, 3 reels, EX..**$35.00**

Yona

Yona Lippin was a California ceramist who worked for Hedi Schoop in the early 1940s and later opened her own studio. Much of her work is similar to Schoop's. She signed her work with her first name. You'll also find items marked Yona that carry a 'Shafford, Made in Japan' label, suggesting a later affiliation with that importing company. For more information, see *The Collector's Encyclopedia of California Pottery* by Jack Chipman (Collector Books).

Ashes pot, Country Club, cold-painted red stripes, 4¾", +handle..**$50.00**

Bean pot, Country Club, cold-painted red stripes, 4½", +ladle, NM..**$135.00**

Christmas tree ornament, choir boy, 4½" **$9.00**

Decanter, clown figural, cold-painted, 13"...................**$65.00**

Figurine, angel carrying dog in her arms, gold trim, 5"..**$30.00**

Figurine, Oriental lady in kimono holding fan, hand-painted orchid & green designs, 8¾x4¼", NM **$35.00**

Figurines, exotic dancers, green w/gold headpiece, bra & hip drape, 1 swaying, 1 down on knee, tallest: 8", pr.**$110.00**

Figurines, Oriental man & lady, #15/#16, 9", pr..........**$50.00**

Flower holder, girl w/2 openings in basket held before her, #47, 7¼"...**$45.00**

Ice bucket, Country Club, cold-painted red stripes, w/lid & handle, 6", NM...**$100.00**

Napkin holder, Country Club, cold-painted red stripes, chef standing behind, #8751 ....**$90.00**

Pill jar, plump lady, hair is lid, Shafford label, c 1960 ..**$45.00**

Pretzel jar, Country Club, cold-painted red stripes, #8741..**$150.00**

Salt & pepper shakers, clowns (Salty & Peppy), 1957, MIB, pr..**$40.00**

Tumbler, Country Club, cold-painted red stripes, 5", NM...**$20.00**

Wall plaques, Egyptian faces, black & gold, 11", pr ...**$55.00**

Wall pocket, clown pulling cart, multicolored, c 1957, marked Shafford, 6" **$75.00**

Auction Houses

Many of the auction galleries we've listed here have appraisal services. Some, though not all, are free of charge. We suggest you contact them first by phone to discuss fees and requirements.

American Social History and Social
Movements
P.O. Box 203
Tucker, GA 30085
678-937-1835 or fax: 678-937-1837
www.asham.com

Aston Macek Auctions
2825 Country Club Rd.
Endwell, NY 13760-3349
Phone or fax: 607-785-6598
Specializing in and appraisers of Americana, folk art, other primitives, furniture, fine glassware, and china

Bill Bertoia Auctions
1881 Spring Rd.
Vineland, NJ 08361
856-692-1881 or fax: 856-692-8697
e-mail: bill@bertoiaauctions.com
www: Bertoiaauctions.com
Online auctions: Bertoiaonline.com
Specializing in antique toys and collectibles

Cincinnati Art Gallery
225 E. Sixth St.
Cincinnati, OH 45202
513-381-2128
www.cincinnatiartgalleries.com
Specializing in American art pottery, American and European fine paintings, watercolors

Collectors Auction Services
RD 2, Box 431
Oil City, PA 16301
814-677-6070
Specializing in advertising, oil and gas, toys, rare museum and investment-quality antiques

David Rago
Auction hall: 333 N. Main St.
Lambertville, NJ 08530

609-397-7330
Gallery: 17 S Main St.
Lambertville, NJ 08530
Specializing in American art pottery and Arts & Crafts

Dynamite Auctions
Franklin Antique Mall & Auction
    Gallery
1280 Franklin Ave.
Franklin, PA 16323
814-432-8577 or 814-786-9211

Early Auction Co.
123 Main St.
Milford, OH 45150
www.EarlyAuction.com

Flying Deuce
1224 Yellowstone
Pocatello, ID 83201
208-237-2002; fax: 208-237-4544
e-mail: flying2@nicoh.com
Specializing in vintage denim apparel; catalogs $10.00 for upcoming auctions; contact for details on consigning items

Garth's Auctions, Inc.
2690 Stratford Rd.
Box 369, Delaware, OH 43015
740-362-4771
www.garth's.com

Jackson's Auctioneers & Appraisers
    of Fine Art & Antiques
2229 Lincoln Street
Cedar Falls, IA 50613
www.jacksons@jacksonsauction.com
Specializing in American and European art pottery and art glass, American and European paintings, decorative arts, toys, and jewelry

James D. Julia
P.O. Box 830, Rt. 201

Showhegan Rd.
Fairfield, ME 04937
207-453-7125
www.juliaauctions.com

Kerry and Judy's Toys
1414 S. Twelfth St.
Murray, KY 42071
502-759-3456; e-mail: kjtoys@apex.com
Specializing in 1920s through 1960s toys; consignments always welcomed

L.R. 'Les' Docks
Box 691035
San Antonio, TX 78269-1035
Providing occasional mail-order record auctions, rarely consigned (the only consignments considered are exceptionally scarce and unusual records)

Lloyd Ralston Toys
447 Stratford Rd.
Fairfield, CT 06432

Manion's International Auction House,
    Inc.
P.O. Box 12214
Kansas City, KS 66112
913-299-6692; fax: 913-299-6792
e-mail: manions@qni.com
www.manions.com

Michael John Verlangieri
Calpots.com
PO Box 844, Cambria, CA 93428; 805-927-4428. Specializing in fine California pottery; cataloged auctions (video tapes available); www.calpots.com

Monson & Baer, Annual Perfume Bottle
    Auction
Monsen, Randall; and Baer, Rod
Box 529, Vienna, VA 22183; 703-938-2129
or fax: 703-242-1357. Cataloged auctions of perfume bottles; will purchase, sell,

and accept consignments; specializing in commercial, Czechoslovakian, Lalique, Baccarat, Victorian, crown top, factices, miniatures

Noel Barrett Antiques & Auctions
P.O. Box 1001
Carversville, PA 18913
215-297-5109; fax: 215-297-0457

Richard Opfer Auctioneering, Inc.
1919 Greenspring Dr.
Timonium, MD 21093
410-252-5035

Smith House
P.O. Box 336
Eliot, ME, 03903
207-439-4614; fax: 207-439-8554
e-mail: smithtoys@aol.com
Specializing in toys

Toy Scouts Inc.
137 Casterton Ave.
Akron, OH 44303
330-836-0668; fax: 330-869-8668
e-mail: toyscouts@toyscouts.com
www.toyscouts.com.
Specializing in baby-boom era collectibles

Treadway Gallery Inc.
2029 Madison Rd.
Cincinnati, OH 45208
513-321-6742; fax: 513-871-7722
www.treadwaygallery.com
Member: National Antique Dealers Association, American Art Pottery Association, International Society of Appraisers, and American Ceramic Arts Society

Clubs and Newsletters

There are hundreds of clubs and newsletters mentioned throughout this book in their respective categories. There are many more available to collectors today; some are generalized and cover the entire realm of antiques and collectibles, while others are devoted to a specific interest such as toys, coin-operated machines, character collectibles, or railroadiana. We've listed several below. You can obtain a copy of most newsletters simply by requesting one. If you'd like to try placing a 'for sale' ad or a mail bid in one of them, see the introduction for suggestions on how your ad should be composed.

Akro Agate Collectors Club., Inc.
Clarksburg Crow (The Crow)
newsletter
Roger and Claudia Hardy
10 Bailey Street, Clarksburg, WV 26301-2524
Dues: $25.00; Canadian or foreign, $35.00. US checks or money orders only

America's Most Wanted To Buy
P.O. Box 171707, CB
Little Rock, AR 72222
800-994-9268
Subscription $12.95 per year for 6 issues; up to date information about what collectors big and small are buying *now*

American Matchcover Collecting
    Club (AMCC)
P.O. Box 18481

Asheville, NC 28814
828-254-4487; fax: 828-254-1066
www.matchcovers.com
e-mail: bill@matchcovers.com
Dues $25 yearly + $3 registration fee for first year, includes *Front Striker Bulletin*. Also available: *Matchcover Collector's Price Guide*, 2nd edition, $25.20+$3.25 shipping and handling

Antique Advertising Association of
    America (AAAA)
P.O. Box 1121
Morton Grove, IL 60053
708-446-0904
Also *Past Times* newsletter for collectors of popular and antique advertising. Subscription: $35 per year

*Antique and Collectors
    Reproduction News*

Mark Chervenka, Circulation Dept.
P.O. Box 12130
Des Moines, IA 50312-9403
800-227-5531
Monthly newsletter showing differences between old originals and new reproductions. Subscription: $32 per year

Antique Journal
Michael F. Shores, Publisher
Jeffery Hill Editor/General Manager
2329 Santa Clara Ave. #207
Alameda, CA 94501

The Antique Trader Weekly
P.O. Box 1050 CB
Dubuque, IA 52004-1050
800-334-7165
Subscription: $37 (52 issues) per year

Antique Week

P.O. Box 90
Knightstown, IN 46148
Weekly newspaper for auctions, antique shows, antiques, collectibles, and flea markets. Write for subscription information.

The Bicycle Trader Newsletter
510 Frederick
San Francisco, CA 94117
415-876-1999 or 415-564-2304
fax: 415-876-4507
e-mail: info@bicycletrader.com
www.bicycletrader.com/

Bobbing Head Doll Newsletter
Tim Hunter
4301 W. Hidden Valley Dr.
Reno, NV 89502
e-mail: thunter885@aol.com

The Carnival Pump
International Carnival Glass Assoc., Inc.
Lee Markley
Box 306
Mentone, IN 46539
Dues: $20 per family per year US and Canada payable each July 1st

Cast Iron Marketplace
P.O. Box 16466
St. Paul, MN 55116
Subscription $30 per year, includes free ads up to 200 words per issue

Coin-Op Newsletter
Ken Durham, Publisher
909 26th St., NW; Suite 502
Washington, DC 20037
www.GameRoom.Antiques.com
Subscription (10 issues): $15; Sample: $5

Compact Collectors Club
Roselyn Gerson
PO Box 40, Lynbrook, NY 11563
516-593-8746 or fax 516-593-0610
e-mail: compactlady@aol.com. Publishes *Powder Puff* Newsletter, which contains articles covering all aspects of compact collecting, restoration, vintage ads, patents, history, and articles by members and prominent guest writers; seeker and sellers column offered free to members

Dorothy Kamm's Porcelain Collector's Companion
P.O. Box 7460
Port St. Lucie, FL 34985-7460
561-465-4008

Dragonware Club
c/o Suzi Hibbard
849 Vintage Ave.
Fairfield, CA 94585
Information requires long SASE

Early Typewriter Collectors Association
ETCetera Newsletter
Chuck Dilts/Rich Cincotta
PO Box 286
Southboro, MA 01772
etcetera@writeme.com
http://typewriter.rydia.net/etcetera.htm

Grandpa's Depot
John Grandpa White
1616 17th St., Suite 267

Denver, CO 80202
303-628-5590; fax: 303-628-5547
Publishes catalogs on railroad-related collectibles

International Golliwog Collector Club
Beth Savino
PO Box 798
Holland, OH 43528
1-800-862-TOYS; fax: 419-473-3947

International Ivory Society
11109 Nicholas Dr.
Wheaton, MD 20902
301-649-4002
Membership: $10 per year; includes 4 newsletters and roster

International Match Safe Association
PO Box 791
Malaga, NJ 08328
856-694-4167;
email: IMSAoc@aol.com;
www.matchsafe.org
Quarterly newsletter and annual convention

National Bicycle History Archive
Box 28242
Santa Ana, CA 92799
714-647-1949
e-mail: Oldbicycle@aol.com
www.members.aol.com/oldbicycle
Resource for vintage and classic cycles from 1920 to 1970; collection of over 1,000 classic bicycles; over 30,000 original catalogs, books, photos; also over 100 original old bicycle films 1930s – 70s; restoration and purchase

Newspaper Collectors Society of America
517-887-1255
e-mail: info@historybuff.com
Publishes booklet with current values and pertinent information

Nutcracker Collectors' Club
Susan Otto, Editor
11204 Fox Run Dr.
Chesterland, OH 44026;
$15.00 annual dues, quarterly newsletters sent to members, free classifieds

Old Stuff
Donna and Ron Miller, Publishers
336 N Davis
P.O. Box 1084
McMinnville, OR 97128
Published 6 times annually; Copies by mail: $3.50 each; Annual subscription: $18 ($32 in Canada)

Paper Collectors' Marketplace
470 Main St.
P.O. Box 128
Scandinavia, WI 54977-0128
715-467-2379; fax: 715-467-2243
Subscription: $19.95 (12 issues) per year in USA; Canada and Mexico add $15 per year

Paperweight Collectors Association, Inc.
P.O. Box 1263
Barker, TX 77413

The Trick or Treat Trader
P.O. Box 499, Winchester, NH 03470
4 issues: $15 (USA) or $20 (International)

Paper Pile Quarterly
P.O. Box 337
San Anselmo, CA 94979-0337
415-454-5552
Subscription: $20 per year in USA and Canada

Pen Fancier's Club
1169 Overcash Dr.
Dunedin, FL 34698

Southern Oregon Antiques and Collectibles Club
P.O. Box 508
Talent, OR 97540
541-535-1231
Meets 1st Wednesday of the month; Promotes 2 shows a year in Medford, OR

Stanley Tool Collector News
c/o The Old Tool Shop
208 Front St.
Marietta, OH 45750
Features articles of interest, auction results, price trends, classified ads, etc.;
Subscription: $20 per year; Sample: $6.95

Statue of Liberty Collectors' Club
Iris November

P.O. Box 535
Chautauqua, NY 14722
216-831-2646

Table Toppers
1340 West Irving Park Rd.
P.O. Box 161
Chicago, IL 60614
312-769-3184
Membership $19 (single) per year, includes *Table Topic*, a bimonthly newsletter for those interested in table-top collectibles

Thimble Collectors International
6411 Montego Rd.
Louisville, KY 40228

Three Rivers Depression Era Glass Society
Meetings held 1st Monday of each month at DeMartino's Restaurant, Carnegie, PA
For more information call:
Edith A. Putanko
John's Antiques & Edie's Glassware
Rte. 88 & Broughton Rd.
Bethel Park, PA 15102
412-831-2702

Tiffin Glass Collectors
P.O. Box 554
Tiffin, OH 44883
Meetings at Seneca Cty. Museum on 2nd Tuesday of each month

The Wheelmen
Wheelmen Magazine
63 Stonebridge Road
Allen Park, NJ 07042-1631
609-587-6487
e-mail: hochne@aol.com
www.thewheelmen.org
A club with about 800 members dedicated to the enjoyment and preservation of our bicycle heritage

The '50s Flea
April and Larry Tvorak
P.O. Box 94
Warren Center, PA 18851
570-395-3775
e-mail: april@epix.net
Published once a year, $4 postpaid; free classified up to 30 words

Special Interests

In this section of the book we have listed hundreds of dealers/collectors who specialize in many of the fields this price guide covers. Many of them have sent information, photographs, or advised us concerning current values and trends. This is a courtesy listing, and they are under no obligation to field questions from our readers, though some may be willing to do so. If you do write to any of them, don't expect a response unless you include an SASE (stamped self-addressed envelope) with your letter. If you have items to offer them for sale or are seeking information, describe the piece in question thoroughly and mention any marks. You can sometimes do a pencil rubbing to duplicate the mark exactly. Photographs are still worth a 'thousand words,' and photocopies are especially good for paper goods, patterned dinnerware, or even smaller three-dimensional items.

It's a good idea to include your phone number if you write, since many people would rather respond with a call than a letter. And suggesting that they call back collect might very well be the courtesy that results in a successful transaction. If you're trying to reach someone by phone, always stop to consider the local time on the other end of your call. Even the most cordial person when dragged out of bed in the middle of the night will very likely *not* be receptive to you.

With the exception of the Advertising, Books, Bottles, Character Collectibles, and Toys sections which we've alphabetized by character or type, buyers are listed alphabetically under bold topics. A line in italics indicates only the specialized interests of the particular buyer whose name immediately follows it. Recommended reference guides not available from Collector Books may be purchased directly from the authors whose addresses are given in this section.

Advertising
Aunt Jemima
Fee charged for appraisal
Judy Posner
P.O. Box 2194 SC
Englewood, FL 34295

941-475-1725
www.judyposner.com
e mail: judyandjef@aol.com

Big Boy
Steve Soelberg

29126 Laro Dr.
Agoura Hills, CA 91301
818-889-9909

Campbell's Soup
Author of book

Dave Young
414 Country Ln. Ct.
Wauconda, IL 60084
847-487-4917

Cereal boxes and premiums
Dan Goodsell
P.O. Box 48021
Los Angeles, CA 90048
323-930-0763

Green Giant
Edits newsletter
Lil West
2343 10000 Rd.
Oswego, KS 67356
Also other related Pillsbury memorabilia

Jewel Tea products and tins
Bill and Judy Vroman
739 Eastern Ave.
Fostoria, OH 44830
419-435-5443

Mr. Peanut
Judith and Robert Walthall
P.O. Box 4465
Huntsville, AL 35815
256-881-9198

Old Crow
Geneva D. Addy
116 E. Grade
Winterset, IA 50273
Also Moss Rose (contemporary) and
Old Crow advertising

Poppin' Fresh (Pillsbury Doughboy)
Editor of newsletter: The Lovin'
Connection
Lil West
2343 10000 Road
Oswego, KS 67356
Also other related Pillsbury memorabilia

Reddy Kilowatt and Borden's Elsie
Lee Garmon
1529 Whittier St.
Springfield, IL 62704

Smokey Bear
Glen Brady
1134 Quines Creek Rd.
Azalea, OR 97410
541-837-3462

Tins
Author of book
Linda McPherson
P.O. Box 381532
Germantown, TN 38183
e-mail: tinlady@prodigy.net

Watches
Editor of newsletter: The Premium
Watch Watch
Sharon Iranpour
24 San Rafel Dr.
Rochester, NY 14618-3702
716-381-9467; fax: 716-383-9248
e-mail: watcher1@rochester.rr.com

Airline Memorabilia
Richard Wallin
P.O. Box 1784
Springfield, IL 62705
217-498-9279
e-mail: RRWALLIN@aol.com

Akro Agate
Author of book
Claudia and Roger Hardy
10 Bailey St.
Clarksburg, WV 26301-2524
(Home, evenings) 304-624-4523;
(days) 304-622-1500

Order from the authors: *Complete Line of*
Akro Agate (with prices), 1992; Pictures all
pieces, $20.00 plus $3.50 priority mail;
Akro Agate Price Guide, revised 2nd edition, price updates 1998 (corresponds with
first book), $10.00 plus $3.50 priority, or
both books $30.00 plus $3.95 priority mail

Aluminum
Author of book
Everett Grist
P.O. Box 91375
Chattanooga, TN 37412-3955

Author of book
Dannie Woodard
P.O. Box 1346
Weatherford, TX 76086

Animal Dishes
Author of book
Everett Grist
P.O. Box 91375
Chattanooga, TN 37412-3955
423-510-8052
Has authored books on aluminum, adver-
tising playing cards, letter openers, and
marbles

Appliances
Jim Barker
Toaster Master General
P.O. Box 746
Allentown, PA 18105

Ashtrays
Author of book
Nancy Wanvig
Nancy's Collectibles
P.O. Box 12
Thiensville, WI 53092

Autographs
Don and Anne Kier
2022 Marengo St.
Toledo, OH 43614
419-385-8211
e-mail: d.a.k.@worldnet.att.net

Automobilia
Leonard Needham
118 Warwick Dr. #48
Benicia, CA 94510
707-748-4286
www.tias.com/stores/macadams

Tire ashtrays
Author of book ($12.95 postpaid)
Jeff McVey
1810 W State St., #427
Boise, ID 83702

Autumn Leaf
Gwynneth Harrison
P.O. Box 1
Mira Loma, CA 91752-0001
909-685-5434
e-mail: morgan99@pe.net

Avon Collectibles
Author of book
Bud Hastin
P.O. Box 11530
Ft. Lauderdale, FL 33339

Banks
Modern mechanical banks
Dan Iannotti
212 W Hickory Grove Rd.
Bloomfield Hills, MI 48302-1127S
248-335-5042

e-mail: modernbanks@ameritech.net
Character Banks
Robin Stine
P.O. Box 140502
Toledo, OH 43614
419-385-7387

Barware
Especially cocktail shakers
Arlene Lederman Antiques
150 Main St.
Nyack, NY 10960

Specializing in vintage cocktail shakers
Author of book
Stephen Visakay
P.O. Box 1517
W Caldwell, NJ 07707-1517

Beanie Babies
Amy Hopper
PO Box 3009
Paducah, KY 42002-3009

Beatnik and Hippie Collectibles
Richard M. Synchef
208 Summit Dr.
Corte Madera, CA 94925
415-927-8844
Also Peter Max

Beatrix Potter
Nicki Budin
679 High St.
Worthington, OH 43085
614-885-1986
Also Royal Doulton

Bells
Unusual; no cow or school
Author of books
Dorothy J. Anthony
2401 S Horton St.
Ft. Scott, KS 66701-2790

Bicycles and Tricycles
Consultant, collector, dealer
Lorne Shields
Box 211
Chagrin Falls, OH 44022-0211
440-247-5632; fax: 905-886-7748
e-mail: vintage@globalserve.net
Alternate address: P.O. Box 87588
300 John St. Post Office
Thornhill, Ontario, Canada L3T 7R3

Black Americana
Buy, sell, and trade; fee charged for
appraisal
Judy Posner
R.R. 1, Box 273
Effort, PA 18330
www.tias.com/stores/jpc
e-mail: judyandjef@aol.com
Also toys, Disney, salt and pepper
shakers, general line

Black Glass
Author of book
Marlena Toohey
703 S Pratt Pky.
Longmont, CO 80501
303-678-9726

Blue Danube
Lori Simnionie
Auburn Main St. Antiques
124 E. Main St.
Auburn, WA 98002
253-927-3866 or 253-804-8041

Bobbin' Heads by Hartland
Author of guide; newsletter
Tim Hunter
4301 W. Hidden Valley Dr.
Reno, NV 89502
702-626-5029

Bookends
Author of book
Louis Kuritzky
4510 NW 17th Pl.
Gainesville, FL 32605
352-377-3193

Books
Big Little Books
Ron and Donna Donnelly
6302 Championship Dr.
Tuscaloosa, AL 35405

Little Golden Books, Wonder, and Elf
Author of book on Little Golden Books
Steve Santi
19626 Ricardo Ave.
Hayward, CA 94541

Bottle Openers
Charlie Reynolds
2836 Monroe St.
Falls Church, VA 22042
703-533-1322
e-mail: reynoldstoys@erols.com

Bottles
Bitters, figurals, inks, barber, etc.
Steve Ketcham
P.O. Box 24114
Minneapolis, MN 55424
612-920-4205
Also advertising signs, trays, calendars, etc.

Dairy and Milk
John Shaw
2201 Scenic Ridge Court
Mt. Flora, FL 32757 (Nov – May)
352-735-3831
43 Ridgecrest Dr.
Wilton, ME 04294 (June – Oct)
207-645-2442

Boyd
Joyce M. Pringle
Antiques and Moore
3708 W Pioneer Pky.
Arlington, TX 76013
Chipdale@flash.net
Also Summit and Mosser

Breyer
Felicia Browell
123 Hooks Lane
Cannonsburg, PA 15317
e-mail: fbrowell@nauticom.net

British Royal Commemoratives
Author of book
Audrey Zeder
1320 SW 10th St
North Bend, WA 98045
Specializing in British Royalty Com-
memoratives from Queen Victoria's
reign through current royalty events

Brush-McCoy Pottery
Authors of book
Steve and Martha Sanford
230 Harrison Ave.
Campbell, CA 95008
408-978-8408

Bubble Bath Containers
Matt and Lisa Adams
PO Box 441014
Jacksonville, FL 32222-1014
904-389-9534
e-mail: mattradams@earthlink.net

Cake Toppers
Jeannie Greenfield
310 Parker Rd.
Stoneboro, PA 16153-2810
724-376-2584

Calculators
Author of book
Guy Ball
14561 Livingston St.
Tustin, CA 92780
www.mrcalc@usa.net

California Perfume Company
*Not common; especially items
marked Goetting Co.*
Dick Pardini
3107 N El Dorado St., Dept. G
Stockton, CA 95204-3412
Also Savoi Et Cie, Hinze Ambrosia,
Gertrude Recordon, Marvel Electric
Silver Cleaner, and Easy Day Automatic
Clothes Washer

*Specializing in California pottery
and porcelain; Orientalia*
Marty Webster
6943 Suncrest Drive
Saline, Michigan 48176
313-944-1188

*Editor of newsletter: The California
Pottery Trader*
Michael John Verlangieri Gallery
Calpots.com
P.O. Box 844
W Cambria, CA 93428-0844
805-927-4428. Specializing in fine California
pottery; cataloged auctions (video tapes
available); www.calpots.com

Camark
Tony Freyaldenhoven
P.O. Box 1295
Conway, AR 72033

Cameras
Classic, collectible and usable
C.E. Cataldo
Gene's Cameras
4726 Panorama Dr. SE
Huntsville, Alabama 35801
256-536-6893
e-mail: mtsand@aol.com

Wooden, detective and stereo
John A. Hess
P.O. Box 3062
Andover, MA 01810
Also old brass lenses

Candy Containers
Glass
Jeff Bradfield
90 Main St.
Dayton, VA 22821
540-879-9961
Also advertising, cast-iron and tin
toys, postcards, and Coca-Cola

Author of book
Doug Dezso
864 Paterson Ave.
Maywood, NJ 07607

Other interests: Tonka Toys, Shafford
black cats, German bisque comic character nodders, Royal Bayreuth creamers, and Pep pins

Cape Cod by Avon
Debbie and Randy Coe
Coes Mercantile
Lafayette School House Mall #2
748 3rd (Hwy. 99W)
Lafayette, OR 97127
Also Elegant and Depression glass, art
pottery, Golden Foliage by Libbey Glass
Company, and Liberty Blue dinnerware

Carnival Chalkware
Author of book
Thomas G. Morris
P.O. Box 8307
Medford, OR 97504-0307
e-mail: chalkman@cdsnet.net
Also Ginger Rogers memorabilia

Cast Iron
*Door knockers, sprinklers, figural
paperweights, and marked cookware*
Craig Dinner
P.O. Box 4399
Sunnyside, NY 11104
718-729-3850
e-mail: ferrouswheel123@aol.com

Cat Collectibles
Karen Shanks
PO Box 150784
Nashville, TN 37215
615-297-7403 or
www.catcollectors.com
e-mail: musiccitykitty@yahoo.com

Ceramic Arts Studio
BA Wellman
P.O. Box 673
Westminster, MA 01473
e-mail: ba@dishinitout.com
Also most areas of American clay
products

Character and Personality Collectibles
Author of books
*Dealers, publishers, and appraisers
of collectible memorabilia from
the '50s through today*
Bill Bruegman
Toy Scouts, Inc.
137 Casterton Ave.
Akron, OH 44303
330-836-0668; fax: 330-869-8668
e-mail: toyscouts@toyscouts.com
www.toyscouts.com

Any and all
Terri Ivers
Terri's Toys
114 Whitworth Ave.
Ponca City, OK 74601
580-762-8697 or 580-762-5174
e-mail: toylady@cableone.net

Batman, Gumby, and Marilyn Monroe
Colleen Garmon Barnes
114 E Locust
Chatham, IL 62629

Beatles
Bojo
Bob Gottuso
P.O. Box 1403
Cranberry Twp., PA 16066-0403
Phone or fax: 724-776-0621

www.bojoonline.com
Beatles sale catalog available 4X a
year, send $3 for copy

California Raisins
Ken Clee
Box 11412
Philadelphia, PA 1911
215-722-1979

California Raisins
Larry De Angelo
516 King Arthur Dr.
Virginia Beach, VA 23464
757-424-1691

Dick Tracy
Larry Doucet
2351 Sultana Dr.
Yorktown Hts., NY 10598
314-245-1320
e-mail: LDoucetDM@aol.com

*Disney, Western heroes, Gone With the
Wind, character watches ca 1930s
to mid-1950s, premiums, and games*
Ron and Donna Donnelly
6302 Championship Dr.
Tuscaloosa, AL 35405

Disney
*Buy, sell and trade; lists available;
fee charged for appraisal*
Judy Posner
R.R. 1, Box 273
Effort, PA 18330
www.tias.com/stores/jpc
e-mail: judyandjef@aol.com

Elvis Presley
Author of book
Rosalind Cranor
P.O. Box 859
Blacksburg, VA 24063

Elvis Presley
Lee Garmon
1529 Whittier St.
Springfield, IL 62704

Roy Rogers and Dale Evans
*Author of books; biographer for
Golden Boots Awards*
Robert W. Phillips
1703 N Aster Pl.
Broken Arrow, OK 74012-1308
918-254-8205; fax: 918-252-9362
e-mail: rawhidebob@aol.com
One of the most widely-published writers in
the field of cowboy memorabila and author
of *Roy Rogers, Singing Cowboy Stars, Silver
Screen Cowboys, Hollywood Cowboy Heroes,*
and *Western Comics: A Comprehensive
Reference;* research consultant for TV docu-
mentary *Roy Rogers, King of the Cowboys*
(AMC-TV/Republic Pictures/Galen Films)

Shirley Temple
Gen Jones
294 Park St.
Medford, MA 02155

Smokey Bear
Glen Brady
1134 Quines Creek Rd.
Azalea, OR 97410
541-837-3462

Wizard of Oz
Bill Stillman
Scarfone & Stillman Vintage Oz

P.O. Box 167
Hummelstown, PA 17036
717-566-5538

Character and Promotional Drinking Glasses
*Authors of book; editors of Collector
Glass News*
Mark Chase and Michael Kelly
P.O. Box 308
Slippery Rock, PA 16057
412-946-2838; fax: 724-946-9012
e-mail: cgn@glassnews.com
www.glassnews.com

Character and Clocks and Watches
Bill Campbell
1221 Littlebrook Ln.
Birmingham, AL 35235
205-853-8227; fax: 405-658-6986
Also Character Collectibles, Advertising Premiums

Character Nodders
Matt and Lisa Adams
PO Box 441014
Jacksonville, FL 32222-1014
904-389-9534
e-mail: mattradams@earthlink.net

Chintz
Mary Jane Hastings
310 West 1st South
Mt. Olive, IL 62069
Phone or fax: 217-999-1222

Author of book
Joan Welsh
7015 Partridge Pl.
Hyattsville, MD 20782
301-779-6181

Christmas Collectibles
*Especially from before 1920 and
decorations made in Germany*
J.W. 'Bill' and Treva Courter
3935 Kelley Rd.
Kevil, KY 42053
Phone: 270-488-2116; fax: 270-488-2055

Clocks
All types
Bruce A. Austin
1 Hardwood Hill Rd.
Pittsford, NY 14534
716-387-9820

Clothes Sprinkler Bottles
Ellen Bercovici
5118 Hampden Ln.
Bethesda, MD 20814
301-652-1140

Clothing and Accessories
Ken Weber
11744 Coral Hills Place
Dallas TX 75229
e-mail: cecilimose@aol.com;
www.vintagemartini.com

Author of book
Sue Langley
101 Ramsey Ave.
Syracuse, NY 13224-1719
315-445-0113
e-mail: langshats@aol.com

Flying Deuce
1224 Yellowstone
Pocatello, ID 83201
208-237-2002; fax: 208-237-4544
e-mail: flying2@nicoh.com

Coca-Cola
Also Pepsi-Cola and other brands of soda
Craig Stifter
218 S. Adams St.
Hinsdale, IL 50421
630-789-5780
e-mail: cocacola@enteract.com

Coin-Operated Vending Machines
Ken and Jackie Durham
909 26th St., NW
Washington, D.C. 20037

Compacts
Unusual shapes, also vanities and accessories
Author of book
Roselyn Gerson
P.O. Box 40
Lynbrook, NY 11563

Cookbooks
Author of book
Bob Allen
P.O. Box 56
St. James, MO 65559
Also advertising leaflets

Cookie Cutters
Author of book and newsletter
Rosemary Henry
9610 Greenview Ln.
Manassas, VA 20109-3320

Cookie Jars
Joe Devine
1411 3rd St.
Council Bluffs, IA 51503
712-323-5233 or 712-328-7305
Also Black Americana, salt and pepper shakers

Buy, sell, and trade; lists available; fee charged for appraisal
Judy Posner
R.R. 1, Box 273
Effort, PA 18330
www.tias.com/stores/jpc
e-mail: judyandjef@aol.com

Corkscrews
Author of books
Donald A. Bull
PO Box 596
Wirtz, VA 24184
540-721-1128
www.corkscrewmuseum.com
e-mail: corkscrew@bullworks.net

Cow Creamers
Shirley Green
1550 E. Kamm Ave. #116
Kingsburg, CA 93631
209-897-7125
e-mail: granas@psnw.com

Cracker Jack Items
Phil Helley
Old Kilbourn Antiques
629 Indiana Ave.
Wisconsin Dells, WI 53965
Also banks, radio premiums, and wind-up toys

Wes Johnson, Sr.
106 Bauer Ave.
Louisville, KY 40207

Author of books
Larry White

108 Central St.
Rowley, MA 01969-1317
978-948-8187
e-mail: larrydw@erols.com

Crackle Glass
Authors of book
Stan and Arlene Weitman
101 Cypress St.
Massapequa Park, NY 11758
516-799-2619; fax: 516-797-3039
Also specializing in Overshot

Cuff Links
National Cuff Link Society
Eugene R. Klompus
P.O. Box 5700
Vernon Hills, IL 60061
Phone or fax: 847-816-0035;
e-mail: genek@cufflink.com
Also related items

Cups and Saucers
Authors of books
Jim and Susan Harran
208 Hemlock Dr.
Neptune, NJ 07753
www.tias.com/stores/amit

Dakins
Jim Rash
135 Alder Ave.
Egg Harbor Township, NJ 08234

Decanters
Homestead Collectibles
Art and Judy Turner
R.D. 2, Rte. 150
P.O. Box 173
Mill Hall, PA 17751
570-726-3597; fax: 717-726-4488

deLee
Authors of book
Joanne and Ralph Schaefer
3182 Williams Rd.
Oroville, CA 95965-8300
530-893-2902 or 530-894-6263

Dinnerware
Blue Ridge
Author of several books; columnist for The Depression Glass Daze
Bill and Betty Newbound
2206 Nob Hill Dr.
Sanford, NC 27330
Also milk glass, wall pockets, figural planters, collectible china, and glass.

Blue Willow
Mary Gaston
Box 342
Bryan, TX 77806

Cat-Tail
Ken and Barbara Brooks
4121 Gladstone Ln.
Charlotte, NC 28205

Currier & Ives Dinnerware
Author of book
Eldon R. Bud Aupperle
29470 Saxon Road
Toulon, IL 61483
309-896-3331; fax: 309-856-6005

Fiesta, Franciscan, Lu Ray, Metlox, and Homer Laughlin
Fiesta Plus
Mick and Lorna Chase
380 Hawkins Crawford Rd.

Cookeville, TN 38501
931-372-8333
e-mail: fiestaplus@yahoo.com
www.fiestaplus.com

Homer Laughlin China
Author of book
Darlene Nossaman
5419 Lake Charles
Waco, TX 76710

Johnson Brothers
Author of book
Mary Finegan, Marfine Antiques
P.O. Box 3618
Boone, NC 28607
828-262-3441

Liberty Blue
Gary Beegle
92 River St.
Montgomery, NY 12549
914-457-3623
Also most lines of collectible modern American dinnerware as well as character glasses

Restaurant China
Author of books (Volume 1 and Volume 2)
Barbara J. Conroy
P.O. Box 2369
Santa Clara, CA 95055-2369
e-mail: restaurantchina@home.com
http://members.home.net/restaurantchina/homepage.htm

Royal China
BA Wellman
P.O. Box 673
Westminster, MA 01473-0673
e-mail: ba@dishinitout.com
Also Ceramic Arts Studio

Russel Wright, Eva Zeisel, Homer Laughlin
Charles Alexander
221 E 34th St.
Indianapolis, IN 46205
317-924-9665

Wallace China
Marv Fogleman
Marv's Memories
73 Waterman
Irvine, CA 92602
Specializing in American, English, and Western dinnerware

Dollhouse Furniture and Accessories
Renwal, Ideal, Marx, etc.
Judith A. Mosholder
186 Pine Springs Camp Rd.
Boswell, PA 15531
814-629-9277
e-mail: jlytwins@floodcity.net

Dolls
Annalee Mobilitee Dolls
Jane's Collectibles
Jane Holt
P.O. Box 115
Derry, NH 03038

Betsy McCall and friends
Marci Van Ausdall, Editor
P.O. Box 946
Quincy, CA 95971-0946
530-283-2770

Chatty Cathy and Mattel talkers
Authors of books
Don and Kathy Lewis
Whirlwind Unlimited
187 N Marcello Ave.
Thousand Oaks, CA 91360
805-499-8101
e-mail: chatty@ix.netcom.com

Dolls from the 1960s – 70s, including Liddle Kiddles, Barbie, Tammy, Tressy, etc.
Co-author of book on Tammy, author of Collector's Guide to Dolls of the 1960s & 1970s
Cindy Sabulis
P.O. Box 642
Shelton, CT 06484
203-926-0176

Dolls from the 1960s – 70s, including Liddle Kiddles, Dolly Darlings, Petal People, Tiny Teens, etc.
Author of book on Liddle Kiddles; must send SASE for info
Paris Langford
415 Dodge Ave.
Jefferson, LA 70121
504-733-0676

Editor of newsletter: The Holly Hobbie Collectors Gazette
Donna Stultz
1455 Otterdale Mill Rd.
Taneytown, MD 21787-3032
410-775-2570
e-mail:hhgazette@netscape.net

Ideal
Author of book; available from author or Collector Books
Judith Izen
P.O. Box 623
Lexington, MA 02420
781-862-2994; e-mail:
jizenres@aol.com

Liddle Kiddles and other small dolls from the late '60s and early '70s
Dawn Diaz
20460 Samual Drive
Saugus, CA 91530-3812
661-263-TOYS

Strawberry Shortcake
Geneva D. Addy
116 E. Grade
Winterset, IA 50273
Also Moss Rose (contemporary) and Old Crow advertising

Vogue Dolls, Inc.
Co-author of book; available from author or Collector Books
Judith Izen
P.O. Box 623
Lexington, MA 02173-5914
781-862-2994
e-mail: jizenres@aol.com

Vogue Dolls, Inc.
Co-author of Book; available from author or Collector Books
Carol J. Stover
81 E Van Buren St.
Chicago, IL 60605

Door Knockers
Craig Dinner
Box 4399
Sunnyside, NY 11104
718-729-3850

Egg Beaters
Author of Beat This: The Egg Beater
Chronicles
Don Thornton
Off Beat Books
1345 Poplar Ave.
Sunnyvale, CA 94087

Egg Cups
Author of book
Brenda Blake
Box 555
York Harbor, ME 03911
207-363-6566

Egg Timers
Ellen Bercovici
5118 Hampden Ln.
Bethesda, MD 20814
301-652-1140

Jeannie Greenfield
310 Parker Rd.
Stoneboro, PA 16153-2810
724-376-2584

Roselle Schleifman
16 Vincent Rd.
Spring Valley, NY 10977

Erich Stauffer Figurines
Joan Oates
685 S Washington
Constantine, MI 49042
616-435-8353
e-mail: koates120@earthlink.net
Also Phoenix Bird china

Ertl Banks
Homestead Collectibles
P.O. Box 173
Mill Hall, PA 17751
Also decanters

Eyewinker
Sophia Talbert
921 Union St.
Covington, IN 47932
765-793-3256

Fast-Food Collectibles
Author of book
Ken Clee
Box 1142
Philadelphia, PA 19111
215-722-1979

Authors of several books
Joyce and Terry Losonsky
7506 Summer Leave Lane
Columbia, MD 21046-2455
McDonald's® Collector's Guide to Happy
Meal® Boxes, Premiums and Promotions
($9 plus $2 postage), *McDonald's®*
Happy Meal® Toys in the USA and
McDonald's® Happy Meal® Toys
Around the World (both full color, $24.95
each plus $3 postage), and *Illustrated*
Collector's Guide to McDonald's®
McCAPS® ($4 plus $2) are available from
the authors

Bill and Pat Poe
220 Dominica Cir. E.
Niceville, FL 32578-4085
850-897-4163; fax: 850-897-2606
e-mail: McPoes@aol.com
Also older McDonald's collectibles,
Pez, Smurfs and California Raisins,
and M&M items

Fenton Glass
Ferill J. Rice
302 Pheasant Run
Kaukauna, WI 54130

Figural Ceramics
Especially Kitchen Prayer Lady
April and Larry Tvorak
PO Box 493401
Leesburg, FL 34749-3401
Also interested in Pyrex

Fisher-Price
Author of book
Brad Cassity
2391 Hunters Trail
Myrtle Beach, SC 29579
843-236-8697

Fishing Collectibles
Publishes fixed-price catalog
Dave Hoover
1023 Skyview Dr.
New Albany, IN 47150
Also miniature boats and motors

Flashlights
Editor of newsletter
Bill Utley
P.O. Box 4095
Tustin, CA 92781
714-730-1252; fax: 714-505-4067

Florence Ceramics
Author of book
Doug Foland
2014 SE Ankeny St.
Portland, OR 97214-1622

Authors of book; autographed copies
available from the authors
Jerry and Barbara Kline
Florence Showcase
PO Box 937
Kodak, TN 37764
865-933-9060
e-mail: floshow@msn.com
Book contains many details previous not
know; all known figures shown (600
photos), values included; $29.95 or
$36.00 including postage and shipping

John and Peggy Scott
4640 S Leroy
Springfield, MO 65810

Flower Frogs
Author of book
Bonnie Bull
Flower Frog Gazette Online
www.flowerfrog.com

Frankoma
Authors of book
Phyllis and Tom Bess
14535 E 13th St.
Tulsa, OK 74108

Fruit Jars
Especially old, odd, or colored jars
John Hathaway
3 Mills Rd.
Bryant Pond, ME 04219
Also old jar lids and closures

Games
Paul Fink's Fun and Games
P.O. Box 488
59 S Kent Rd.
Kent, CT 06757
203-927-4001

Gas Station Collectibles
Scott Benjamin
Oil Co. Collectibles Inc.
Petroleum Collectibles Monthly Magazine
PO Box 556
LaGrange, OH 44050-0556
440-355-6608
Specializing in gas globes, signs, and
magazines

Gay Fad Glassware
Donna S. McGrady
P.O. Box 14, 301 E. Walnut St.
Waynetown, IN 47990
765-234-2187

Geisha Girl China
Author of book
Elyce Litts
P.O. Box 394
Morris Plains, NJ 07950
e-mail: happymemories@worldnet.att.net
Also ladies' compacts

Glass Animals
Author of book
Lee Garmon
1529 Whittier St.
Springfield, IL 62704

Glass Knives
Michele A. Rosewitz
3165 McKinley Avenue
San Bernardino, CA 92404
909-862-8534
e-mail: rosetree@sprintmail.com

Glass Shoes
Author of book
The Shoe Lady
Libby Yalom
P.O. Box 7146
Adelphi, MD 20783

Granite Ware
Author of books
Helen Greguire
864-457-7340
Also carnival glass and toasters

Griswold
Grant Windsor
P.O. Box 72606
Richmond, VA 23235-8017
804-320-0386

Guardian Service Cookware
Dennis S. McAdams
3110 E. Lancaster Rd.
Hayden Lake, ID 83835
e-mail: HAYDENMAC4@aol.com

Guardian Service Cookware
2110 Harmony Woods Road
Owings Mills, MD 21117-1649
410-560-0777;
http://members.aol.com/vettelvr93/

Hagen-Renaker
Gayle Roller
PO Box 222
San Marcos, CA 92079-0222

Hallmark
The Baggage Car
3100 Justin Dr., Ste. B
Des Moines, IA 50322
515 270 9080

Halloween
Author of books; autographed
copies available from the author
Pamela E. Apkarian-Russell
Chris Russell & The Halloween
Queen Antiques
P.O. Box 499
Winchester, NH 03470
e-mail: halloweenqueen@cheshire.net
http://adam.cheshire.net/~halloween
queen/home.html
Also other holidays, postcards, and Joe
Camel

Hartland Plastics, Inc.
Author of book
Gail Fitch
1733 N Cambridge Ave. #109
Milwaukee, WI 53202

Specializing in Western Hartlands
Buy and sell; hold consignment auc-
tions specializing in vintage toys
Kerry and Judy Irvin
Kerry and Judy's Toys
1414 S. Twelfth St.
Murray, KY 42071
270-759-3456; e-mail: kjtoys@apex.net

Specializing in sports figures
James Watson
25 Gilmore St.
Whitehall, NY 12887

Homer Laughlin
Author of book
Darlene Nossaman
5419 Lake Charles
Waco, TX 76710

Horton Ceramics
Darlene Nossaman
5419 Lake Charles
Waco, TX 76710

Hull
Author of several books on Hull
Brenda Roberts
906 S. Ann Dr.
Marshall, MO 65340

Imperial Glass
Joan Cimini
67183 Stein Rd.
Belmont, OH 43718-9715
740-782-1327
e-mail: upperiglady@1st.net
Also has Candlewick matching service

Imperial Porcelain
Geneva D. Addy
P.O. Box 124
Winterset, IA 50273

Indiana Glass
Donna Adler
502 E. Birch St.
Shelton, WA 98584
360-426-5303
Donna's Place on the web:
http://dr54eagle.rubylane.com
Also Wedgwood, Mosser, Depression,
and more

Indy 500 Memorabilia
Eric Jungnickel
P.O. Box 4674
Naperville, IL 60567-4674
630-983-8339

Insulators
Jacqueline Linscott
3557 Nicklaus Dr.
Tutusville, FL 32780

Japan Ceramics
Author of books
Carole Bess White
PO Box 819
Portland, OR 97207

Jewel Tea
Products or boxes only; no dishes
Bill and Judy Vroman
739 Eastern Ave.
Fostoria, OH 44830
419-435-5443

Jewelry
Author of books
Marcia Brown (Sparkles)
P.O. Box 2314
White City, OR 97503
541-826-3039; fax: 541-830-5385
Author of *Unsigned Beauties of Costume Jewelry* and *Signed Beauties of Costume Jewelry*; co-author and host of seven *Hidden Treasure* book-on-tape videos

Men's accessories and cuff links only; edits newsletter
The National Cuff Link Society
Eugene R. Klompus
PO Box 5700
Vernon Hills, IL 60061
Phone or fax: 847-816-0035

Josef Originals
Authors of books
Jim and Kaye Whitaker
Eclectic Antiques
P.O. Box 475, Dept. GS
Lynnwood, WA 98046

Kay Finch
Co-authors of book, available from authors
Mike Nickel and Cynthia Horvath
P.O. Box 456
Portland, MI 48875
517-647-7646
Also fine Ohio art pottery

Kentucky Derby and Horse Racing
B.L. Hornback
707 Sunrise Ln.
Elizabethtown, KY 42701
e-mail: bettysantiques@KVNET.org
Inquiries require a SASE with fee expected for appraisals and/or identification of glasses. Booklet picturing Kentucky Derby, Preakness, Belmont, and other racing glasses available for $15 ppd.

Kreiss; Psycho Ceramics
Authors of book
Michelle and Mike King
P.O. Box 3519
Alliance, OH 44601
330-829-5946; www.quest-for-toys.com
Exclusive source for Kreiss book; International mail-order vintage toy company specializing in toys and memorabilia from 1960s to 1980s; collect novelty and character ceramics, vintage Barbies, ad characters, Arts & Crafts home furnishings

Kitchen Prayer Ladies
Issues price guide ($6.96 plus $1 postage and handling)
April and Larry Tvorak

P.O. Box 493401
Leesburg, FL 34749-3401
Also interested in Enesco, Pyrex, and figural ceramics

Lamps
Aladdin
Author of books
J.W. Courter
3935 Kelley Rd.
Kevil, KY 42053
502-488-2116

Motion lamps
Eclectic Antiques
Jim and Kaye Whitaker
P.O. Box 475, Dept. GS
Lynwood, WA 98046

Authors of book
Sam and Anna Samuelian
P.O. Box 504
Edgemont, PA 19028-0504
610-566-7248
Also motion clocks, transistor and novelty radios

Lefton
Author of books
Loretta DeLozier
PO Box 50201
Knoxville, TN 37950-0201

Letter Openers
Author of book
Everett Grist
P.O. Box 91375
Chattanooga, TN 37412-3955
423-510-8052

License Plates
Richard Diehl
5965 W Colgate Pl.
Denver, CO 80227

Longaberger Baskets
The *only* reference tool for consultants, collectors, and enthusiasts of Longaberger Baskets®
Jill S. Rindfuss
The Bentley Collection Guide®
5870 Zarley Street, Suite C
New Albany, OH 43054
Monday through Friday, 9:00 a.m. – 5:00 p.m. (EST)
1-800-837-4394
www.bentleyguide.com
e-mail: info@bentlyguide.com
The most accurate and reliable reference tool available for evaluating Longaberger Products®. Full color with individual photographs of most baskets and products produced since 1979; Published once a year in June with a free six-month update being sent in January to keep the guide current for the entire year

Holds exclusive auctions
Greg Michael
Craft & Michael Auction/Realty Inc.
PO Box 7
Camden, IN 46917
219-686-2615 or 219-967-4442
Fax: 219-686-9100
e-mail: gpmmgtco@netusal1.net.

Lunch Boxes
Norman's Ole and New Store
Philip Norman
126 W Main St.

Washington, NC 27889-4944
252-946-3448

Terri's Toys and Nostalgia
Terri Ivers
206 E. Grand
Ponca City, OK 74601
580-762-8697 or 580-762-5174
Fax: 405-765-2657
e-mail: toylady@poncacity.net

Magazines
Issues price guides to illustrators, pin ups, and old magazines of all kinds
Denis C. Jackson
Illustrator Collector's News
P.O. Box 1958
Sequim, WA 98382
e-mail: ticn@olypen.com

Pre-1950 movie magazines, especially with Ginger Rogers covers
Tom Morris
P.O. Box 8307
Medford, OR 97504
e-mail: chalkman@cdsnet.net

National Geographic
Author of guide
Don Smith's National Geographic Magazines
3930 Rankin St.
Louisville, KY 40214
502-366-7504

Marbles
Author of books
Everett Grist
P.O. Box 91375
Chattanooga, TN 37412-3955
423-510-8052

Block's Box is the longest continuously running absentee marble auction service in the country; catalogs issued
Stanley A. & Robert S. Block
P.O. Box 51
Trumbull, CT 06611
203-261-3223 or 203-926-8448
e-mail:bblock@well.com
pages.prodigy.com/marbles/mcc.ht ml
Prodigy: BWVR62A

Match Safes
George Sparacio
P.O. Box 791
Malaga, NJ 08328
856-694-4167; fax: 856-694-4536
e-mail: mrvesta@aol.com

Matchcovers
Author of books
Bill Retskin
P.O. Box 18481
Asheville, NC 22814
704-254-4487; fax: 704-254-1066
e-mail: bill@matchcovers.com
www.matchcovers.com

McCoy Pottery
Author of books
Robert Hanson
16517 121 Ave. NE
Bothell, WA 98011

Melmac Dinnerware
Co-author of book
Gregg Zimmer
4017 16th Ave. S
Minneapolis, MN 55407

Metlox
Author of book; available from author
Carl Gibbs, Jr.
P.O. Box 131584
Houston, TX 77219-1584
713-521-9661
www.ccdinnerware.com

Milk Bottles
John Shaw
2201 Scenic Ridge Court (Nov – May)
Mt. Flora, FL 32757
352-735-3831
43 Ridgecrest Dr. (June – Oct)
Wilton, ME 04294
207-645-2442

Miller Studios
Paul and Heather August
7510 West Wells St.
Wauwatosa, WI 53213
414-475-0753
e-mail: packrats@execpc.com

Mood Indigo
David and Debbie Crouse
2140 Capitol Ave.
Des Moines, Iowa 50317
515-265-4880
Watch for website listing Mood Indigo with numbers and pictures:
www.crouse.ws/inarco

Morton Pottery
Authors of books
Doris and Burdell Hall
B&B Antiques
210 W Sassafras Dr.
Morton, IL 61550-1245

Motion Clocks
Electric; buy, sell, trade, and restore
Sam and Anna Samuelian
P.O. Box 504
Edgemont, PA 19028-0504
610-566-7248
Also motion lamps, transistor and novelty radios

Motorcycles and Motorcycle Memorabilia
Bob 'Sprocket' Eckardt
P.O. Box 172
Saratoga Springs, NY 12866
518-584-2405
e-mail: sprocketbe@aol.com

Buying and Trading
Bruce Kiper
Ancient Age Motors
2205 Sunset Ln.
Lutz, FL 33549
813-949-9660
Also related items and clothing

Movie Posters
Movie Poster Service
Cleophas and Lou Ann Wooley
Box 517
Canton, OK 73724-0517
580-886-2248; fax: 580-886-2249
e-mail: mpsposters@pldi.net
In business full time since 1972; own/operate mail-order firm with world's largest movie poster inventory

Napkin Dolls
Co-Author of book
Bobbie Zucker Bryson
1 St. Eleanoras Ln.

Tuckahoe, NY 10707
914-779-1405
e-mail: napkindoll@aol.com
www.reamers.org
To order a copy of the second edition of
Collectibles for the Kitchen, Bath & Beyond
(featuring napkin dolls, egg timers, string
holders, children's whistle cups and baby
feeder dishes, razor blade banks, pie
birds, laundry sprinkler bottles, and other
unique collectibles from the same era),
contact Krause Publications, 700 E. State
St., Iola, WI, 54990-4612; 800-258-0929.

Orientalia and Dragonware
Suzi Hibbard
849 Vintage Ave.
Fairfield, CA 94585

Paper Dolls
Author of books
Mary Young
P.O. Box 9244
Wright Bros. Branch
Dayton, OH 45409

Pencil Sharpeners
Phil Helley
629 Indiana Ave.
Wisconsin Dells, WI 53965
608-254-8659

Advertising and figural
Martha Hughes
4128 Ingalls St.
San Diego, CA 92103
619-296-1866

Pennsbury
Joe Devine
1411 3rd St.
Council Bluffs, IA 51503
712-323-5322 or 712-328-7305

Shirley Graff
4515 Graff Rd.
Brunswick, OH 44212

Pepsi-Cola
Craig Stifter
218 S. Adams St.
Hinsdale, IL 60521
630-389-5780
e-mail: cocacola@enteract.com
Other soda-pop memorablia as well

Perfume Bottles
*Especially commercial, Czechoslovakian,
Lalique, Baccarat, Victorian, crown
top, factices, miniatures*
*Buy, sell, and accept consignments
for auctions*
Monsen and Baer
Box 529
Vienna, VA 22183
703-938-2129

Pez
Richard Belyski
P.O. Box 124
Sea Cliff, NY 11579
516-676-1183
e-mail: peznews@juno.com

Pie Birds
Linda Fields
158 Bagsby Hill Lane
Dover, TN 37058
931-232-5099
e-mail: Fpiebird@compu.net
Organizer of Piebird Collector's Convention and

author of *Four & Twenty Blackbirds*; Specializing
in pie birds, pie funnels, and pie vents

Pin-Back Buttons
Michael and Polly McQuillen
McQuillen's Collectibles
P.O. Box 50022
Indianapolis, IN 46250
317-845-1721
e-mail: michael@politicalparade.com
www.politicalparade.com

Pinup Art
*Issues price guides to pinups, illus-
trations, and old magazines*
Denis C. Jackson
Illustrator Collector's News
P.O. Box 1958
Sequim, WA 98382
360-452-3810; fax: 360-683-9807
e-mail: ticn@olypen.com

Pocket Calculators
Author of book
International Assn. of Calculator Collectors
Guy D. Ball
P.O. Box 345
Tustin, CA 92781-0345
Phone or fax: 714-730-6140
e-mail: mrcalc@usa.net

Political
Michael and Polly McQuillen
McQuillen's Collectibles
P.O. Box 50022
Indianapolis, IN 46250
317-845-1721
e-mail: mmcquillen@political
parade.com
www.politicalparade.com

Before 1960
Michael Engel
29 Groveland St.
Easthampton, MA 01027

Pins, banners, ribbons, etc.
Paul Longo Americana
Box 5510
Magnolia, MA 01930
978-525-2290

Poodle Collectibles
Author of book
Elaine Butler
233 S Kingston Ave.
Rockwood, TN 37854

Porcelier
Jim Barker
Toaster Master General
P.O. Box 746
Allentown, PA 10106

Author of book
Susan Grindberg
1412 Pathfinder Rd.
Henderson, NV 89014
702-898-7535
e-mail: porcelier@anv.net or
sue@porcelierconnection.com
www.porcelierconnection.com

Postcards
Pamela E. Apkarian-Russell
Chris Russell and the Halloween
Queen Antiques
P.O. Box 499
Winchester, NH 03470
Also Halloween and other holidays
Sharon Thoerner

15549 Ryon Ave.
Bellflower, CA 90706
562-866-1555
e-mail: rthoerner@juno.com
Also slag glass

Purinton Pottery
Author of book
Susan Morris
PO Box 158
Manchester, WA 98353
360-871-7376

Puzzles
*Wooden jigsaw type from before
1950*
Bob Armstrong
15 Monadnock Rd.
Worcester, MA 01609

Radio Premiums
Bill Campbell
1221 Littlebrook Ln.
Birmingham, AL 35235
205-853-8227; fax: 405-658-6986

Radios
*Authors of several books on antique,
novelty and transistor radios*
Sue and Marty Bunis
R.R. 1, Box 36
Bradford, NH 03221-9102

Author of book
Harry Poster
P.O. Box 1883
S Hackensack, NJ 07606
201-410-7525
Also televisions, related advertising
items, old tubes, cameras, 3-D viewers
and projectors, View-Master and Tru-
View reels, and accessories

Railroadiana
*Also steamship and other
transportation memorabilia*
Lila Shrader
Shrader Antiques
2025 Hwy. 199
Crescent City, CA 95531
707-458-3525
Also Buffalo, Shelley, Niloak, and Hummels

*Any item; especially china and silver
Catalogs available*
John White, 'Grandpa'
Grandpa's Depot
1616 17th St., Ste. 267
Denver, CO 80202
303-628-5590; fax: 303-628-5547
Also related items

Razor Blade Banks
Debbie Gillham
47 Midline Ct.
Gaithersburg, MD 20878
301-977-5727

Reamers
*Co-author of book, ordering info
under Napkin Dolls*
Bobbie Zucker Bryson
1 St. Eleanoras Ln.
Tuckahoe, NY 10707
914-779-1405
e-mail: napkindoll@aol.com
www.reamers.org

Picture and 78 rpm kiddie records
Peter Muldavin
173 W 78th St. Apt 5-F

New York, NY 10024
212-362-9606
e-mail: kiddie78s@aol.com

Especially 78 rpms, author of book
L.R. 'Les' Docks
Box 691035
San Antonio, TX 78269-1035
Write for want list

Red Wing
Authors of books
B.L. and R.L. Dollen
Dollen Books & Antiques
P.O. Box 386
Aboca, IA 51521-0386
Collector Book authors specializing in
Red Wing art pottery and dinnerware

Red Wing Artware
Hold cataloged auctions
Wendy and Leo Frese
Three Rivers Collectibles
P.O. Box 551542
Dallas, TX 75355
214-341-5165
e-mail: rumrill@ix.netcom.com

Rooster and Roses
Jacki Elliott
9790 Twin Cities Rd.
Galt, CA 95632
209-745-3860

Rosemeade
NDSU research specialist
Bryce Farnsworth
1334 14½ St. S
Fargo, ND 58103
701-237-3597

Roseville
Mike Nickel
PO Box 456
Portland, MI, 48875
517-647-7646
Also Kay Finch, other Ohio art pottery

Royal Bayreuth
Don and Anne Kier
2022 Marengo St.
Toledo, OH 43614
419-385-8211
e-mail: d.a.k@worldnet.att.net

Royal Copley
Author of books
Joe Devine
1411 3rd St.
Council Bluffs, IA 51503
712-323-5233 or 712-328-7305
Buy, sell, or trade; Also pie birds

Royal Haeger
Author of book
David D. Dilley
Indianapolis, IN
317-251-0575
e-mail: glazebears@aol.com or
bearpots@aol.com

RumRill
Hold cataloged auctions
Wendy and Leo Frese
Three Rivers Collectibles
P.O. Box 551542
Dallas, TX 75355
214-341-5165;
e-mail: rumrill@ix.netcom.com

Ruby Glass
Author of book
Naomi L. Over
8909 Sharon Ln.
Arvada, CO 80002
303-424-5922

Salt and Pepper Shakers
Figural or novelty
Buy, sell, and trade; lists available; fee charged for appraisal
Judy Posner
R.R. 1, Box 273
Effort, PA 18330
717-629-6583
www.tias.com/stores/jpc
e-mail: judyandjef@aol.com

Scouting Collectibles
Author of book: A Guide to Scouting Collectibles With Values; available by sending $30.95 (includes postage)
R.J. Sayers
P.O. Box 629
Brevard, NC 28712

Sebastians
Jim Waite
112 N Main St.
Farmer City, IL 61842
800-842-2593

Sewing Machines
Toy only
Authors of book
Darryl and Roxana Matter
P.O. Box 65
Portis, KS 67474-0065

Shawnee
Van Tellingen, Bendel, Old MacDonald's Farm
Rick Spencer
Salt Lake City, UT
801-973-0805

Shot Glasses
Author of book
Mark Pickvet
Shot Glass Club of America
5071 Watson Dr.
Flint, MI 48506

Silhouette Pictures (20th Century)
Author of book
Shirley Mace
Shadow Enterprises
P.O. Box 1602
Mesilla Park, NM 88047
505-524-6717; fax: 505-523-0940
e-mail: shadow-ent@zianet.com
www.geocities.com/MadisonAvenue/Boardroom/1631/

Silverplated and Sterling Flatware
Rick Spencer
Salt Lake City, UT
801-973-0805
Will do appraisals

Skookum Indian Dolls
Jo Ann Palmieri
27 Pepper Rd.
Towaco, NJ 07082-1357

Snow Domes
Author of book and newsletter editor
Nancy McMichael
P.O. Box 53262
Washington, DC 20009

Soda Fountain Collectibles
Harold and Joyce Screen
2804 Munster Rd.
Baltimore, MD 21234
410-661-6765
e-mail: hscreen@home.com

Soda-Pop Memorabilia
Craig Stifter
217 S. Adams St.
Hinsdale, IL 60521
630-789-5789
e-mail: cocacola@enteract.com

Sports Collectibles
Sporting goods
Kevin R. Bowman
P.O. Box 4500
Joplin, MO 64803
417-781-6418 (Mon through Fri after 5 pm CST, Sat and Sun after 10 am CST)
e-mail: showmequail@joplin.com

Equipment and player-used items
Don and Anne Kier
2022 Marengo St.
Toledo, OH 43614
419-385-8211
e-mail: d.a.k.@worldnet.att.net

Bobbin' head sports figures
Tim Hunter
4301 W Hidden Valley Dr.
Reno, NV 89502
702-856-4357; fax: 702-856-4354
e-mail: thunter885@aol.com

Golf collectibles
Pat Romano
32 Sterling Dr.
Lake Grove, NY 11202-0017

St. Clair Glass
Ted Pruitt
3350 W 700 N
Anderson, IN 46011
Book available ($15)

Stangl
Birds, dinnerware, artware
Popkorn Antiques
Bob and Nancy Perzel
P.O. Box 1057
Flemington, NJ 08822
908-782-9631
e-mail: popcorn@blast.net

Statue of Liberty
Mike Brooks
7335 Skyline
Oakland, CA 94611

String Holders
Ellen Bercovici
5118 Hampden Ln.
Bethesda, MD 20814
301-652-1140

Swanky Swigs
Joyce Jackson
900 Jenkins Rd.
Aledo, TX 76008-2410
817-441-8864
e-mail: jjpick3@earthlink.net

Teapots and Tea-Related Items
Author of book
Tina Carter
882 S Mollison
El Cajon, CA 92020

Tiara Exclusives
Author of Books
Mandi Birkinbine
P.O. Box 121
Meridian, ID 83680-0121
www.shop4antiques.com
e-mail: tiara@shop4antiques.com
Collecting Tiara Amber Sandwich Glass, $15.95; *Collecting Tiara Bicentennial Blue Sandwich Glass*, $12.95; and *Collecting Tiara Chantilly Green Sandwich Glass*, $15.95, are all available from author at above address. Please allow four to six weeks for delivery; Postage not included

Tire Ashtrays
Author of book ($12.95 postpaid)
Jeff McVey
1810 W State St., #427
Boise, ID 83702-3955

Toothbrush Holders
Author of book
Marilyn Cooper
8408 Lofland Dr.
Houston, TX 77055-4811

Toys
Any and all
June Moon
1486 Miner Street
Des Plaines, IL 60016
847-294-0018
e-mail: junmoonstr@aol.com
www.junemooncollectibles.com

Aurora model kits, and especially toys from 1948 – 1972
Author of books; dealers, publishers and appraisers of collectible memorabilia from the '50s through today
Bill Bruegman
137 Casterton Dr.
Akron, OH 44303
330-836-0668; fax: 330-869-8668
e-mail: toyscout@salamander.net

Diecast vehicles
Mark Giles
P.O. Box 821
Ogallala, NE 69153-0821
308-284-4360

Fisher-Price pull toys and playsets up to 1986
Author of book; available from the author
Brad Cassity
2391 Hunters Trail
Myrtle Beach, SC 29579
843-236-8697

Hot Wheels
D.W. (Steve) Stephenson
11117 NE 164th Pl.
Bothell, WA 98011-4003

Model kits other than Aurora
Gordy Dutt
Box 201
Sharon Center, OH 42274-0201

Puppets and marionettes
Steven Meltzer
1255 2nd St.
Santa Monica, CA 90401
310-656-0483

Rings, character, celebrity, and souvenir

Bruce and Jan Thalberg
23 Mountain View Dr.
Weston, CT 06883-1317
203-227-8175

Sand toys
Authors of book
Carole and Richard Smyth
Carole Smyth Antiques
P.O. Box 2068
Huntington, NY 11743

Slot race cars from 1960s – 70s
Gary T. Pollastro
5047 84th Ave. SE
Mercer Island, WA 98040

Tin litho, paper on wood, comic character, penny toys, and Schoenhut
Wes Johnson, Sr.
3606 Glenview Ave.
Glenville, KY 40025

Tops and spinning toys
Bruce Middleton
5 Lloyd Rd.
Newburgh, NY 12550
914-564-2556

Toy soldiers, figures, and playsets
The Phoenix Toy Soldier Co.
Bob Wilson
8912 E. Pinnacle Peak Rd.
PMB 552
Scotsdale, AZ 85225
480-699-5005 or toll free: 1-877-269-6074
Fax: 480-699-7628
e-mail: bob@phoenixtoysoldier.com
www.phoenixtoysoldier.com

Transformers and robots
David Kolodny-Nagy
Toy Hell
PO Box 75271
Los Angeles, CA 90075
e-mail: toyhell@yahoo.com
www.angelfire.com/ca2/redpear

Walkers, ramp-walkers, and windups
Randy Welch
Raven'tiques
27965 Peach Orchard Rd.
Easton, MD 21601-8203
410-822-5441

Trolls
Author of book
Pat Peterson
1105 6th Ave. SE
Hampton, IA 50441-2657
SASE for information

TV Guides
Giant illustrated 1948 – 1999 TV Guide Catalog, $3.00; 2000+ catalog, $2.00
TV Guide Specialists
Jeff Kadet
P.O. Box 20
Macomb, IL 61455

Twin Winton
Author of book; available from the author or through Collector Books
Mike Ellis
266 Rose Ln.
Costa Mesa, CA 92627
949-646-7112; fax: 949-645-4919
e-mail: TwinWinton.com

Valentines

Author of books, available from author; fee charged for appraisal
Katherine Kreider
Kingsbury Antiques
P.O. Box 7957
Lancaster, PA 17604-7957
717-892-3001
e-mail: Kingsbry@aol.com

Vallona Starr

Author of book
Bernice Stamper
7516 Eloy Ave.
Bakersfield, CA 93308-7701
805-393-2900

Vandor

Lois Wildman
177 E Chick Rd.
Camano Island, WA 98282

Vernon Kilns

Author of Collectible Vernon Kilns (out of print)
Maxine Nelson

7657 E. Hazelwood St.
Scottsdale, AZ 85251

Viking

Mary Lou Bohl
1156 Apple Blossom Dr.
Neenah, WI 54956

Wade

Author of book
Ian Warner
P.O. Box 93022
Brampton, Ontario
Canada L6Y 4V8
e-mail: idwarner@home.com

Watt Pottery

Author of book
Susan Morris
P.O. Box 1519
Merlin, OR 97532
541-955-8590
e-mail: sue@wattpottery.com
www.wattpottery.com
www.applebarrel.com

Western Collectibles

Author of book
Warren R. Anderson
American West Archives
P.O. Box 100
Cedar City, UT 84721
435-586-9497
Also documents, autographs, stocks
and bonds, and other ephemera

Author of books
Dan Hutchins
Hutchins Publishing Co.
P.O. Box 25040
Colorado Springs, CO 80936
719-572-1331
Also interested in cowboy collectibles,
carriages, wagons, sleighs, etc.

Western Heroes

*Author of books, ardent researcher
and guest columnist*
Robert W. Phillips
Phillips Archives of Western Memorabilia
1703 N Aster Pl.

Broken Arrow, OK 74012-1308
918 254 8205; fax: 918-252-9363

Westmoreland

Cheryl Schafer
RR 2, Box 37
Lancaster, MO 63548
660-457-3510
e-mail: cschafer@atlantic.net
Winter address (November 1 – May 1)
PO Box 1443
Webster, FL 33597
352-568-7383

World's Fairs and Expositions

Herbert Rolfes
Yesterday's World
P.O. Box 398
Mount Dora, FL 32756
352-735-3947
e-mail: NY1939@aol.com

Index

Abingdon 13,161
Action Figures 459
Adams, Matthew 14
Advertising ..42,46-47,135,158-159,161-162,174,185,320,414-415
Advertising Character Collectibles .14-30
Advertising Tins 30-32
Advertising Watches 32-34
Airline Memorabilia.................34
Akro Agate 34-36
Aladdin Lamps 314-315
Alice in Wonderland 198
Alka-Seltzer.......................29
Alps 461,467
Aluminum 36-38,414
American Art Potteries 348
American Bisque 162
Anchor Hocking.................38-40
Angels 40-41
Animal Dishes, See Covered Dishes
Annalee Dolls 207-208
Anodized Aluminum 38
Apple Peelers 310
Appliances 309-310
Art Deco 42
Ashtrays 41-43;14,35,86,88,143,237,251,286,291,313,345,387,403-404,410-411,452,473
Aunt Jemima 14-15
Aurora 342
Autographs 43-45
Automobilia 46-47
Autumn Leaf Dinnerware 47-49
Avon 49
Badges 387
Bakelite..........................362
Bambi 198
Banana Splits 123
Bandai 461-462
Banks ..17,19,119-120,286,318,336,343-344,473
Barbie Doll and Her Friends.......49-51
Barware..........................53-54
Baseballs, Bats, and Gloves 440-441
Basketballs........................441
Baskets 233-234,317
Batman 120,123-124
Battery-Operated Toys...........461-462
Bauer Pottery......................55
Beam Decanters 186-187
Beanie Babies...................55-64
Beanie Buddies 61-63
Beaters 309
Beatles Collectibles 64-65,477
Beatnik Collecibles...........65-66,313
Beatrix Potter....................66-67
Beer Cans........................67-68
Bellaire, Marc 68-69
Bells 69-70,114,234,401
Best of the West..................459
Betsy McCall 208-209
Betty Boop..................124,477
Big Boy 15-16
Big Jim 459
Big Little Books 79
Black Americana............70-71,226,416
Black Americana, See Also Aunt Jemima
Black Cats......................71-73
Blair Dinnerware...................73
Blenders 309
Blotters..........................373
Blue Danube 73-75
Blue Garland 75
Blue Ridge Dinnerware 75-77
Blue Willow Dinnerware 77-78,407
Bluegrass Stakes Glasses 307
Book of Knowledge Banks 343-344
Bookends 78,317,452

Books.............78-84;65,70,295,376,428
Bottle Carriers....................363
Bottle Openers 84
Boxes (Ammunition).................439
Boy Scouts, See Scouting Collectibles
Boyd Crystal Art Glass.............84-85
Boyds Bears and Friends.............85
Bozo the Clown 124
Bracelets 228,301
Brady Bunch 124
Brass 69,320
Brastoff, Sascha 85-87,162
Brayton Laguna 87-88
Bread Boxes 310
Breeders Cup Glasses 307
Breweriana........................88-90
Breyer Horses 90-92
British Royal Commemoratives ...92-93
Brock of California................93-94
Brooches 301-302
Brown Drip Dinnerware.........337-338
Bruce Springsteen 398
Brush 162-163
Bubble Bath Containers...........94-95
Bugs Bunny 120,124-125
Bumper Stickers 376
Buttons 387
Cake Toppers 95-96
Calculators 96-97
Calendars 46,143,374,387
California Originals............163,353
California Raisins................97-99
Camark Pottery................99-101
Cambridge Glassware 101-103
Cameras 103-105
Campbell Kids 16-18
Can Openers...........309,310-311
Candle Holders 283,291,318-319,393
Candlewick Glassware............105-106
Candy Containers 106-107,132
Canisters 311,312,324,495-496
Cap'n Crunch.......................18
Cape Cod by Avon 107-108
Captain Action 459
Captain America 125
Captain Kangaroo 125
Cardinal China Company..108-109;163
Carnival Chalkware 109-110
Carnival Glass 234,293-294
Carryalls 150-151
Cast Iron, See Griswold Cast Iron
Cat Collectibles 110-113,226,235
Cat in the Hat..................111-112
Cat-Tail Dinnerware.............113-114
Catalogs 46,440
Celebrity Dolls 209-210
Ceramic Arts Studio 114-116
Character and Promotional Drinking Glasses 116-119
Character Banks.............119-120;17,19
Character Clocks and Watches....120-123
Character Collectibles...123-131;43-45,83-84,94-95,145-147,184-185,254-256,328-330,360-361,362,366-367,383-384,416-417
Charlie McCarthy 125
Charlie's Angels 125
Charlie Tuna 18-19,33
Chatty Cathy and Other Mattel Talkers...................210-212
Cherished Teddies.................131
Chessie 112
Chicago World's Fair..............498
Children's Books 79-81
Children's Dishes..................36
CHiPs 125
Choppers 311
Christie 51

Christmas Collectibles 131-134,252,268,271,274-275,283-284,417
Christmas Psycho Ceramics 313
Christmas Tree Pins 134-135
Cigar Cutters 456
Cigarette Lighters 135-136;14,72,387
Cinderella 198
Clay Art 164
Cleminson Pottery 136-137,388-389
Cliftwood Art Potteries...........347
Clocks 46,121,143,256,311,335
Clothes Sprinkler Bottles...137-138,312
Clothing and Accessories...........138-142
Coca-Cola Collectibles 142-145
Cocktail Shakers 54,258
Coffeepots 237,264
Collins, Enid 382
Colonel Sanders 19
Coloring and Activity Books ...145-147
Comic Books 147-150
Compacts and Purse Accessories..150-153
Condiment Sets 153-154
Cookbooks and Recipe Leaflets....154-159,335
Cookie Cutters 159-160
Cookie Jars.................160-171,324
Coor Rosebud Dinnerware.......171-172
Coppercraft Guild 172
Corgi............................466
Corkscrews 172-173
Corn Ware 424
Costumes 276
Cottage Ware 173
Covered Dishes.......317,321-322,492-493
Cow Creamers 173-174
Cowboy Character Collectibles....175-178
Cracker Jack Toys 178-179
Crackle Glass 179-180
Creek Chub 243
Crown Dinnerware..................454
Cuff Links 180-181
Cup and Saucer Sets 181-182
Currier & Ives China 408
Czechoslovakian Glass and Ceramics 182-184
Dakin 184-185
Dale Evans 175
Daniel Boone 175
Davy Crockett.................175-176
Dawn Dolls by Topper..............212
Decanters....185-188;72,80,228-229,285
DeForest of California 164,188
Degenhart 188-190
deLee Art Pottery 190-191
Denim (Vintage)...................142
Depression Glass 191-198
Dick Tracy 117,125
Disney 198-201;83-84,112,117-118,150,340
Dog Collectibles 202-205
Dollhouse Furniture ...205-206;52,217
Dolls 206-221,229,359,428
Dolls, See Also Advertising Character Collectibles, GI Joe Action Figures
Donald Duck 199
Door Knockers 221-222
Doorstops ....222=223
Doranne of California 164-165
Dr Dolittle 125
Dr. Pepper 436
Dresses 139-140
Dumbo 199
Duncan and Miller Glassware .223-224
Dur-X Glass Knives................263
Early American Prescut 39
Earrings 3021
Easter Collectibles 225,268

Eastman Kodak 104
Egg Beaters.......................311
Egg Cups 225-226,319
Egg Timers 226-227
Elegant Heirs 313
Elsie the Cow and Family.....19-20,117
Elvgren 373-374
Elvis Presley Memorabilia 227-229
Enesco 229-230;165
ET 126
Eye Winker 230-231
Ezra Brooks Decanters 187
Farberware 37
Fast-Food Collectibles 231-233
Felix the Cat 112
Fenton Glass 233-236
Festival Glasses 307
Fiesta 236-240
Figaro the Cat 112
Figural Lamps 315
Figurals and Novelties......234-235,282,317-318,493-494
Finch, Kay 240
Fire-King 38-40,296-297
Fire-King, See Also Jade-ite; Kitchen Collectibles
Fishbowl Ornaments...............240-241
Fisher-Price 241-242;205
Fishing Lures 242-244
Fitz & Floyd 244-245;165
Fleetwood Mac 399
Flintstones 120,126
Flipper...........................126
Florence Ceramics..............245-246
Flower Frogs 246-247
Flowerpots 35
Fostoria 247-249
Francie 51
Franciscan Dinnerware 249-251
Frankoma 251-252
Freeman-McFarlin.............252-253
Furniture 253-254
Game Calls 440
Games 254-256,276,441
Garfield 112
Gas Station Collectibles 256-258
Gay Fad Glassware 258-259
Geisha Girl China.............259-261
Georgene Novelties................216
Gene Autry 83,176
Gerber Baby 20-21
GI Joe 261-262
Gift Sets (Barbie).................53
Gilner 262-263
Ginny Dolls 220
Girl Scouts, See Scouting Collectibles
Glass Knives 263
Globes 256
Goebel 165,227
Golden Foliage 263-264
Goofy 199
Gourmet Royale 368-369
Graniteware 264-265
Grapette 436-437
Green Giant 21-22
Green Hornet 126
Gremlins 126
Griddles 266
Griswold Cast-Iron Cooking Ware ..265-266
Guardian Ware 266-267
Guns (Toy) 462-463
Gurley Candle Company 267-268
Haddon Clocks 349
Hadley, M.A. 268-269
Hagen-Renaker 269-270
Hall China Company.............270-274
Hallmark 274-275;165-166

Halloween....275-276,268
Happy Days....117,126-127
Hardy Boys....127
Harker Pottery....277
Hartland Plastics, Inc. 277-278
Hats....140
Head Vases....278-280;115,356
Heisey Glass....280-282
Hillbilly Line....474
Hippie Collectibles....282-284
Hires....437
Hobnail....235-236
Holly Hobbie....212-213;212-213
Holt Howard....283-286
Homer Laughlin China Co....286-287
Honey Boxes....454
Hopalong Cassidy....117,122,176
Horton Ceramics....287-288
Hot Wheels....466
Howdy Doody....127
Hubley....463
Huckleberry Hound....127
Hull....288-290;166,324
Humidors....456
I Love Lucy....477
Ice Buckets....54
Ice Picks....311
Ideal Dolls....213
Imperial Glass....290-292
Incredible Hulk....127
Indiana Glass....292-294
Indianapolis 500 Racing Collectibles....294-295
Italian Glass....295-296
Jack Daniels Decanters....187
Jack-o-Lanterns....276
Jackets....142
Jade-ite Glassware....296-297
Japan Ceramics....297-299;153-154,166,174,226-227
Jeans....142
Jell-O....158
Jem Dolls....213-214
Jewel Tea Company....299-300
Jewelry....300-303
Jewelry, See Also Christmas Tree Pins
Jim Beam Stakes Glasses....307-308
Joe Camel....22-23
Johnson Bros....303-304
Josef Originals....304-305;41
Jungle Book....117-118
Juvenile Series Books....81-82
Kanawha....305
Kaye of Hollywood....305
Keeler, Brad....305-306
Kellogg's Pep Pins....372-373
Ken Dolls....51
Kentucky Derby Glasses....306-308
Kindell, Dorothy....308
King's Crown, Thumbprint....308-309
KISS....399
Kitchen Collectibles....309-312;296-297
Kitchen Prayer Ladies....312
Kitty Cucumber....112-113
Kliban....113
Knickerbocker....216
Knowles....413
Kozy Kitten....284
Kreiss & Co....313,353
L.E. Smith....316-318
L.G. Wright....321-322
Lady & the Tramp....199-200
Lamps...314-316;236,318,322,336,346,494
Led Zeppelin....399
Lefton China....318-320;40-41
Leiber, Judith....382
Leslie-Henry....463
Letter Openers....320-321
Levi's Denim....142
Liberty Blue....322-323
License Plates....323-324
Liddle Kiddles....214-215
Light Bulbs....132
Lighters, See Cigarette Lighters
Linemar....462,468
Lionstone Decanters....187
Lipsticks....151-152
Little Chap Family....215
Little Golden Books....82-83
Little Hostess....206
Little Mermaid....200
Little Red Riding Hood....324
Little Tikes....324-325
Lladro Porcelains....325
Lobster Ware....424
Lone Ranger....176-177,460
Longaberger Baskets....325-327
LP Albums....392-393
Lu Ray Pastels....327
Lunch Boxes....327-330
Lunch Pails....456-457
M&M Candy Men....23
Maddux of California....330;166
Madonna....399
Magazines....330-333;65,387,429
Male Action Figures, See GI Joe, Star Trek, Star Wars
Maps....387
Marbles....333-334;36
Marvel Super Heroes....460
Marx....206,463,468
Mastercrafters Clocks....349
Match Safes....334-335
Matchbox....467
Mattel....206,210-212,463
Max, Peter....335
McCormick Decanters....187,228-229
McCoy Pottery....335-338;166-168
McDonald's....118,232-233
McDonald's Happy Meal Teenie Beanie Babies....63
Measuring Cups and Pitchers....311
Melmac Dinnerware....338-339
Men of the Mountain....474
Menus....388
Metlox Pottery....339-340;168
Michael Jackson....399-400
Michelin Man (Bibendum or Mr. Bib)....23-24
Mickey Mouse....118,122,149,200-201
Midwest Potteries, Inc....347-348
Milk Bottles....340-341
Miller Studio....341-342
Milton Bradley, See Games
Minolta....104
Mirror Almond and Mirror Brown.290
Mirrors....152
Mixers....309-310
Model Kits....342-343
Modern Mechanical Banks....343-344
Molds....264-265
Monkees....83,400
Monogram....343
Mood Indigo by Inarco....344
Moon and Star....344-346
Moon Beings....313
Moran....373-374
Mortens Studios....346-347
Morton Pottery....347-348
Moss Rose....348-349
Motion Clocks (Electric)....349-350
Motion Lamps....315-316
Motorcycle Collectibles....350-351
Movie and TV Tie-Ins (Books)...83-84
Movie Posters and Lobby Cards...351-353
Moxie....437
Mr. Peanut....24-25
Muppets....128
Music Boxes....230
Nancy Ann Storybook Dolls....215-216
Napco....41
Napkin Dolls....353-354
NASCAR Collectibles....354
National Geographic Magazine....332
New Kids on the Block....400
New Martinsille....355
New York World's Fair....498-499
Nichols, Betty Lou....355-356
Nightmare on Elm Street....128
Niloak Pottery....356-357
Noisemakers....276
Norcrest....41
Novelty Radios....357-358
Novelty Telephones....358
NuGrape....437
Occupied Japan Collectibles....358-360,362
Oil Cans....257
Old Commonwealth Decanters....187
Old Crow....25-26
Old MacDonald's Farm....360
Orange-Crush....437
Ornaments....132-134
Paper Dolls....360-361
Paperback Books....283
Paperweights....295,318,442,482
Peanuts Characters....118,128-129
Pencil Sharpeners....361-362
Pennants....441
Pennsbury Pottery....362-363
Pepsi-Cola....363-364
Percolators....310
Perfume Bottles....364-366;184,236
Peter Rabbit and Related Character Figurines....66-67
Pez Candy Containers....366-367
Pfaltzgraff Pottery....367-369
Pie Birds....369-370
Pierce, Howard....370-371
Pillsbury Doughboy, see Poppin' Fresh
Pin-Back Buttons.371-373;317,441-442
Pinocchio....201
Pins, See Brooches
Pinup Art....373-374
Pipes....457
Pixie Ware....284-285
Planters....13,36,191,252,263,305,319,337,357,359,394,404,409-410-411
Planters Peanuts, See Mr. Peanut
Plasco....206
Plastic....320,329,382-383,413-414
Playboy Magazine....332
Playing Cards....374-376
Pocket Tins....457
Pocket Watches....121-122
Polaroid....104
Political Memorabilia....376-377
Ponytail Princess....285
Poodle Collectibles....203-204;477
Popcorn Poppers....310
Popeye....122,129,146-147
Poppets....340
Poppin' Fresh and Family....26-27
Porcelier China....377-378
Porky Pig....122
Postcards....20,388
Posters....229,257,283,351,354,377
Potato Mashers....311
Powder Jars....378-379
Precious Moments....379-380
Prints....374
Programs....442
Psycho Ceramics....313-314
Pulp Magazines....332-333
Purinton Pottery....380-382
Purses....382-383
Puzzles....383-384
Pyrex....384-385
Quick Draw McGraw....129
Radios....469-470
Raggedy Ann and Andy.129-130,216-217
Railroadiana....385-388
Ramp Walkers....463-464
Razor Blade Banks....388-389
Reamers....389-390
Records....391-393;66,283
Red Wing....393-395;169
Reddy Kilowatt....27-28
Reels....440
Regal China....395;169,360
Restaurant China....395-398
Revell....343
Reynolds Banks....343-344
Rin Tin Tin....177
Ring Holders....442
Rings....303
Rings (Toy)....464
Robinson-Ransbottom....169
Robotech....460
Robots and Space Toys....464-465
Rock 'n Roll Memorabilia....398-400
Rolling Pins....311
Rolling Stones....400
Rookwood....400-401
Rooster and Roses....401-403
Rooster Pattern....285
Roselane Sparklers....403
Rosemeade....403-404
Roseville Pottery....404-407
Roy Rogers....83,177
Royal China....407-409
Royal Copley....409-410
Royal Crown Cola....437
Royal Haeger....410-411
Rozart....411-412
RumRill....412-413
Russel Wright Designs....413-414
Salt Shakers...414-420;17,19,20,27,72,116,244,252,284,286,292,311-312,324,349,402,404,423,473-474,476
Sandwich Pattern....454-455
Schoop, Hedi....420-421
Scottie Collectibles....204-205
Scouting Collectibles....421-422
Seattle World's Fair....499
Sebastians....422
Seven-Up....438
Shawnee Pottery....422-424;169-170
Sheet Music....424-427
Shelf Sitters....116
Shell Pink Glassware....427-428
Shirley Temple....428-429
Shoes....141
Shot Glasses....429;308
Sierra Vista....170
Sifters....312
Sigma....170
Signs....46-47,71,89-90,144-145,354,364,457
Silhouette Pictures....429-431
Silverplate....386-387
Silverplated and Sterling Flatware..431-433
Simmons, Robert....433-434
Simpsons....121,130
Ski Country Decanters....187-188
Skillets....266
Skipper....51
Skookum Indian Dolls....434
Slot Car Racers....465
Smiley Face....434-435
Smokey Bear....28
Snap!, Crackle!, and Pop!....28-29
Snoopy....120-129
Snow Domes....435-436
Snow White & the Seven Dwarfs.201-202
Soda Bottles With Painted Labels.438-439
Soda-Pop Memorabilia....436-439;363-364
Solid Perfumes....152-153
Spartus Clocks....350
Spatulas....312
Special Edition Teenie Beanies and International Bears....63-64
Spider-Man....130

Sporting Goods 439-440
Sports Collectibles.........................440
Sports Figures 278
Sports Illustrated Magazine............332
Squirt..438
St. Clair Glass 442-443
Stanford Corn 443
Stangl Birds.................................443
Stangl Dinnerware...................444-445
Star Wars 445-447
Starburst 251
Stauffer, Erich 447
Steiff Animals........................447-449
Steins...90
Sterling (Dinnerware) 414
Stonex Glass Knives.....................263
Strawberry Shortcake and Friends .217
String Holders.......................449;312
Strombecker.................................206
Super Powers 460-461
Superman......................................130
Swanky Swigs.........................449-451
Swizzle Sticks 388
Syroco 451-453
Tammy and Friends 217-218
Tap Knobs 90
Tarzan 149
Taylor, Smith, and Taylor........453-454
Teapots...............................49,73,77,
111,239,244245,265,274,299,319,424
Thanksgiving Collectibles...............268
Thermometers......................47,145,
257-258,364,452,458
Thermoses 329-330
Tiara Exclusives.....................454-455
Timers 312
Timetables...................................388
Tire Ashtrays.........................455-456
TN.......................................462,468
Toasters.......................................310
Tobacco Collectibles................456-458
Tom Mix 177
Tony the Tiger 29
Toothbrush Holders 458
Toothpick Holders 443
Tootsietoys...................................206
Toys.............................458-470;145
Transistor Radios.....................469-470
Trays...364
Tressy 218-219
Trivets 252
Trolls 470-471
TV Guides.............................471-472
TV Lamps.............................316,330
Twin Winton.............472-474;170-171
Uneeda Doll Co., Inc....................219
Uneeda Wishnik............................471
Unique Art 468
United Clocks 350
Universal Dinnerware 474-475
U2..400
Valencia 424
Valentines 475-476
Vallona Starr...........................476-477
Van Tellingen Shakers 395
Vandor...................................477;171
Vehicles (Toy) 465-467
Vernon Kilns..........................477-480
Viet Nam War Collectibles.............480
View-Master Reels and Packets...480-481
Viking Glass...........................481-482
Village Pattern (Pflatzgraff)............369
Virginia Rose 287
Vistosa...454
Vogue Dolls, Inc. 219-221
Voigtlander 105
Wade Porcelain 482-483
Waffle Irons 266
Wall Pockets...................383-384;
13,137,183,263,337
Wallace China...............................484
WAMZ Radio Kentucky Bar Glasses..308
Warner Bros.........................119,171
Watt Pottery.........................484-486
Weeping Gold...............................486
Weil Ware...............................486-487
Weller.....................................487-490
Wells Art Glaze 287
West Coast Pottery..................490-491
Western Characters 277-278
Western Collectibles......................491
Westmoreland Glass 491-496
Wexford.......................................496
Wheaton.................................496-497
Whisks...312
Whistle..438
Whitman...........83-84,360-361,383-384
Wild Turkey Decanters..................188
Will-George 497
Willow, See Blue Willow
Wind-Ups...............................467-469
Winfield.......................................497
Winnie the Pooh 202
Wizard of Oz................................461
Wolverine 468-469
Wonder Woman............................131
Woody Woodpecker......................131
World's Fairs and Expositions .497-499
Yearbooks.....................................442
Yellowstone..................................287
Yogi Bear.....................................131
Yona..499
Young Decorator...........................206
Zorro...178